Frommer's®

Ireland

FROM $60 A DAY

19th Edition

TELEPHONE TIPS

To call Ireland from another country: Dial the international access code (011 in the U.S., 00 in the U.K. and New Zealand, 0011 in Australia), plus the country code (353 for the Republic of Ireland, 44 for the North), and then the local number, minus the initial 0.

To make a direct international call from the Republic of Ireland: Dial the international access code (00) plus the country code (U.S. and Canada 1, the U.K. 44, Australia 61, New Zealand 64), the area or city code, and the local number.

To charge international calls to the U.S.: Dial **AT&T Direct** 1-800/550-000, **Sprint** 1-800/552-001, **MCI Worldcom** 1-800/551-001.

To make local calls: Dial the local number, with the initial 0.

Directory assistance: Dial 1190 within Ireland. From the United States, the toll number to call is 00353-91-770220.

For further information, see Fast Facts in chapter 2. For important information concerning phone numbers in Northern Ireland, see chapter 15.

METRIC CONVERSIONS

Temperature

To convert F to C, subtract 32 and multiply by $\frac{5}{9}$ (.555)

To convert C to F, multiply by 1.8 and add 32

32° F = 0° C

110° F	
100° F	40° C
90° F	
80° F	30° C
70° F	20° C
60° F	
50° F	10° C
40° F	
32° F	0° C
20° F	
10° F	−10° C
0° F	−18° C
−10° F	
−20° F	−30° C

Distance

To convert	multiply by
inches to centimeters	2.54
centimeters to inches	.39
feet to meters	.30
meters to feet	3.28
yards to meters	.91
meters to yards	1.09
miles to kilometers	1.61
kilometers to miles	.62
1 mi = 1.6 km	1 km = .62 mi
1 ft = .30 m	1 m = 3.3 ft

Liquid Volume

To convert	multiply by
U.S. gallons to liters	3.8
Liters to U.S. gallons	.26
U.S. gallons to imperial gallons	.83
Imperial gallons to U.S. gallons	1.20
Imperial gallons to liters	4.55
Liters to imperial gallons	.22
1 liter = .26 U.S. gal	
1 U.S. gal = 3.8 liter	

Weight

To convert	multiply by
Ounces to grams	28.35
Grams to ounces	.035
Pounds to kilograms	.45
Kilograms to pounds	2.20
1 ounce = 28 gr	1 gr = .04 ounce
1 lb = .4555 kg	1 kg = 2.2 lb

A New Star-Rating System & Other Exciting News from Frommer's!

In our continuing effort to publish the savviest, most up-to-date, and most appealing travel guides available, we've added some great new features.

Frommer's guides now include a new **star-rating system.** Every hotel, restaurant, and attraction is rated from 0 to 3 stars to help you set priorities and organize your time.

We've also added **seven brand-new features** that point you to the great deals, in-the-know advice, and unique experiences that separate travelers from tourists. Throughout the guide look for:

Finds	Special finds—those places only insiders know about
Fun Fact	Fun facts—details that make travelers more informed and their trips more fun
Kids	Best bets for kids—advice for the whole family
Moments	Special moments—those experiences that memories are made of
Overrated	Places or experiences not worth your time or money
Tips	Insider tips—some great ways to save time and money
Value	Great values—where to get the best deals

We've also added a **"What's New"** section in every guide—a timely crash course in what's hot and what's not in every destination we cover.

Other Great Guides for Your Trip:

Frommer's Ireland

Frommer's Europe from $70 a Day

Frommer's England from $75 a Day

Frommer's London from $85 a Day

Frommer's Scotland

Frommer's Great Britain

Frommer's Best Loved Driving Tours in Ireland

Frommer's®

Ireland
from $60 a Day

19th Edition

by Mark Meagher

Here's what the critics say about Frommer's:

"Amazingly easy to use. Very portable, very complete."

—Booklist

"The only mainstream guide to list specific prices. The Walter Cronkite of guidebooks—with all that implies."

—Travel & Leisure

"Complete, concise, and filled with useful information."

—New York Daily News

"Hotel information is close to encyclopedic."

—Des Moines Sunday Register

"Detailed, accurate, and easy-to-read information for all price ranges."

—Glamour Magazine

Wiley Publishing, Inc.

About the Author

Mark Meagher has long been fascinated with the Irish landscape. During his frequent sojourns in Ireland, Mark has catalogued castles, mapped rocks, traced the footsteps of Irish writers and combed the countryside in search of the best B&Bs. He is currently pursuing graduate studies in architecture at Harvard University.

WILEY PUBLISHING, INC.

909 Third Avenue
New York, NY 10022
www.frommers.com

ISBN 0-7645-6547-8
ISSN 0276-9026

Editor: Naomi P. Kraus
Production Editor: Bethany André
Cartographer: John Decamillis
Photo Editor: Richard Fox
Production by Wiley Indianapolis Composition Services

For information on our other products and services or to obtain technical support, please contact our Customer Care Department within the U.S. at 800-762-2974, outside the U.S. at 317-572-3993 or fax 317-572-4002.

Wiley also publishes its books in a variety of electronic formats. Some content that appears in print may not be available in electronic formats.

Manufactured in the United States of America

5   4   3   2

Contents

List of Maps

An Invitation to the Reader

In researching this book, we discovered many wonderful places—hotels, restaurants, shops, and more. We're sure you'll find others. Please tell us about them, so we can share the information with your fellow travelers in upcoming editions. If you were disappointed with a recommendation, we'd love to know that, too. Please write to:

Frommer's Ireland from $60 a Day, 19th Edition
Wiley Publishing, Inc. • 909 Third Ave. • New York, NY 10022

An Additional Note

Please be advised that travel information is subject to change at any time—and this is especially true of prices. We therefore suggest that you write or call ahead for confirmation when making your travel plans. The authors, editors, and publisher cannot be held responsible for the experiences of readers while traveling. Your safety is important to us, however, so we encourage you to stay alert and be aware of your surroundings. Keep a close eye on cameras, purses, and wallets, all favorite targets of thieves and pickpockets.

New! Frommer's Star Ratings & Icons

Every hotel, restaurant and attraction listing in this guide has been ranked for quality, value, service, amenities, and special features using a star-rating scale. In country, state, and regional guides, we also rate towns and regions to help you narrow down your choices and budget your time accordingly. Hotels and restaurants are rated on a scale of zero (recommended) to two stars (very highly recommended); exceptional "worth a splurge" options may get three stars. Attractions, towns, and regions are rated according to the following scale: zero stars (recommended), one star (highly recommended), two stars (very highly recommended), and three stars (must-see).

In addition to the rating system, we also use seven icons to highlight insider information, useful tips, special bargains, hidden gems, memorable experiences, kid-friendly venues, places to avoid, and other useful information:

Finds	Fun Fact	Kids	Moments	Overrated	Tips	Value

The following abbreviations are used for credit cards:

AE	American Express	DISC	Discover	V	Visa
DC	Diners Club	MC	MasterCard		

FROMMERS.COM

Now that you have the guidebook to a great trip, visit our website at **www.frommers.com** for travel information on nearly 2,000 destinations. With features updated regularly, we give you instant access to the most current trip-planning information available. At Frommers.com, you'll also find the best prices on airfares, accommodations, and car rentals—and you can even book travel online through our travel booking partners. At Frommers.com, you'll also find the following:

• Daily Newsletter highlighting the best travel deals
• Hot Spot of the Month/Vacation Sweepstakes & Travel Photo Contest
• More than 200 Travel Message Boards
• Outspoken Newsletters and Feature Articles on travel bargains, vacation ideas, tips & resources, and more!

What's New in Ireland

If you're looking for somewhere new—in search of the Great Irish Destination for 2002—point your compass north. Should you be the outdoorsy type and crave unspoiled wilderness and pubs that feature excellent traditional music, head to the **Inishowen Peninsula,** in County Donegal (see chapter 13, "The Northwest"); if you're yearning for a healthy dose of culture, head to the historic walls of **Derry City,** County Derry, in Northern Ireland (see chapter 15, "Northern Ireland"). Both are destined to be huge tourist haunts, so go now, before the word gets out.

Of course, Ireland's major tourist destinations—Dublin, Cork, Connemara, the Ring of Kerry, etc.—deserve your attention as well. And, though its hospitality remains constant, Ireland is always in a constant state of flux. Here are some of the more notable developments for the year.

PLANNING AN AFFORDABLE TRIP No doubt the biggest practical change returning travelers to Ireland will notice in 2002 is the introduction of the **euro** as the country's national currency. The official currency of the Republic of Ireland since January 1, 1999, the first euro coins and notes debuted on January 1, 2002. As of February 9, 2002 all transactions in Ireland and much of the European Union take place exclusively in euros. To make matters confusing, the United Kingdom has decided to sit out this first round of the European Monetary Union, so for the time being everyone in the six counties of Northern Ireland will continue to use Pounds Sterling.

The transition to the euro in Ireland has been the subject of ongoing debate. There's no doubt that it's going to be a nightmare for retailers, but consumers are also worried about uniform increases in the cost of goods when the price in punts gets converted to euros. Everyone is affected by the change, and everyone seems to have a reason for concern—the Catholic Church has even sent a message to all parishes requesting that parishioners avoid substituting a 1 euro coin for the weightier (and more valuable) punt coin in the collection box. For tourists in Ireland the euro won't present much of an obstacle; although those who have stockpiled quantities of punts from previous trips should be aware that after February 9, 2002, retailers will no longer be obliged to accept this currency. You can get the latest information on the Irish conversion to the euro at **www.euro.ie**.

The Irish Tourist Board has closed its **Toronto office,** leaving New York as the only walk-in ITB office in North America. There is a toll-free information number for the U.S. and Canada (© **800/223-6470**) linked directly to helpful Tourist Board operators in Ireland.

For more information on planning an affordable trip to Ireland, see Chapter 2, "Planning an Affordable Trip to Ireland."

OUTDOOR PURSUITS The year 2001 was a dismal one for Ireland's tourist industry. Though spared the foot-and-mouth epidemic that afflicted Britain and other European countries, hotel and restaurant owners were hit hard as thousands of fearful travelers cancelled trips to Ireland. The fact that you're reading this book suggests that you plan to travel to Ireland in the near future, and you can rest assured that **Ireland is foot-and-mouth free.**

The **Delphi Adventure Centre** (www.delphiadventureholidays.ie) in Leenane, County Galway, arguably the best outdoor activity center in Ireland, has expanded its facilities to include a health spa and upscale accommodations. For more information on outdoor activities in Ireland, see chapter 3.

DUBLIN Dublin now has a **New Zealand consulate,** located at 46 Mount St. Upper, Dublin 2 (✆ **01/ 660-4233**), located just off Merrion Square.

Orientation The district known as "The Liberties" was for many years a quiet corner of the city, full of local character and rich in history but somewhat depressed economically. Like so much of Dublin, this neighborhood is changing fast, and with the opening of **Media Lab Europe** (**www.medialabeurope.org**) in collaboration with MIT's Media Lab in Massachusetts, it has been designated as the city's new "Digital Hub." Another sign of change in The Liberties is the closing of **Mother Red Caps Market**—the building that housed this Dublin institution for many years and the adjoining Mother Red Caps Tavern are currently up for sale.

Getting Around **AirCoach** is an excellent new private coach service from Dublin airport to Dublin's south side, servicing the city's major hotels and shopping districts. For more information call ✆ **01/844-7118** or visit **www.aircoach.ie**.

The Irish have one of the highest rates of cellular phone use in Europe, so it's not surprising that Dublin may soon be the first city in the world where you can hail a cab by sending a text message (SMS) from your phone. **City Cabs** (✆ **01/473-1333**) of Dublin is piloting a service that will automatically locate the closest driver, send the driver the caller's exact location, and return a text message to the caller with the driver's current location and estimated time of arrival. If all goes well, the service will be up and running some time in 2002.

Seeing the Sights The completion of the 44,000-square foot **Millennium Wing at the National Gallery** was postponed once again and it's expected to open in the Spring of 2002. The architects of the new wing, Benson & Forsyth, are known for their recent renovation of the Museum of Scotland in Edinburgh.

If you're seeking an overview of the Dublin skyline, two new attractions should fit the bill. The 185-feet brick **Jameson Chimney,** part of the Old Jameson Distillery in the recently restored Smithfield Village on Dublin's northside, has been converted into an observation tower and now provides unparalleled views of the city—you can find images of the chimney at **www.smithfieldvillage.com**. The newly opened **Guinness Storehouse** (**www.guinnessstorehouse.com**) also offers a fantastic panorama from its "Gravity Bar," on the top floor of the new visitor center. You'll also find abundant exhibits here presenting Guinness lore as well as a large shop, restaurant, and conference center.

Dublin Nights Dublin's Temple Bar district continues to reign as the city's cultural hub; for the latest information on events visit **www. temple-bar.ie**. Students with an International Student Identity Card (ISIC) can take advantage of the **Temple Bar Culture Club Stamp,** which offers discounts on the abundant events staged here. Discounted items include film tickets, concerts, plays, and merchandise. You can get the stamp at the **Union of Students in Ireland/Irish Student Travel Service (USIT),** 19 Aston Quay, Dublin 2 (© **01/ 677-8117**).

For more information on Dublin, see chapter 4, "Dublin."

COUNTIES MEATH & WICK-LOW **Trim Castle,** the largest and most impressive Norman Castle in Ireland, has been re-opened to the public after several years of closure following its occupation by movie crews during the filming of *Braveheart*. It's a great castle to explore, and is nothing short of spectacular now that the central keep has been restored.

A new visitor center at **Glendalough** (© **0404/45325** or 0404/ 45352), County Wicklow's most famous set of ruins, features exhibits on the archaeology, history, folklore, and wildlife of the area. Other attractions in the two counties can be found in chapter 5, "Out from Dublin."

COUNTIES WEXFORD & TIP-PERARY The **Westgate Heritage Tower** in Wexford, which until recently housed exhibits describing the town's medieval and recent history, has closed for an indefinite period of time. Also in Wexford, the **hedge maze** at Dunbrody Abbey continues to grow, having reached a respectable five plus feet (1.5m). Restoration work is complete on **Cormac's Chapel,** the masterpiece of Irish Romanesque architecture at the Rock of Cashel in Tipperary: The sandstone of the exterior walls has been cleaned, and the remarkable frescoes on the chapel's interior walls have been restored.

Tipperary is great country for pony trekking and trail riding, especially in the Galtee Mountains and the Glen of Aherlow. Con Marnane of Bansha House has decided to close his excellent equestrian program and focus on raising and selling horses; visitors to the area can still arrange trail riding through **Bansha House,** or at the nearby **Hillcrest Riding Centre.**

For more information on things to see and do in the southeastern counties of Ireland, see chapter 6, "The Southeast."

KINSALE & WEST CORK Alas, **Scilly House,** one of our favorite places to stay in Kinsale, has been sold and is no longer operating as a guesthouse.

Mizen Head, at the tip of the Mizen peninsula in West Cork, is one of the county's most ruggedly beautiful outposts, and now there's also a visitor center (**www.mizenvision.com**) with a teashop and exhibits on the theme of safety at sea. While you're there, take the time to stroll across Barleycove Cove or north along the cliff-face.

Jim Kennedy of **Atlantic Sea Kayaking** (**www.atlanticseakayaking.com**) continues to expand his excellent kayaking program, based at Maria's Schoolhouse in Union Hall. Don't miss his moonlight kayak trips on Lough Ine, a salt-water lake known for its phosphorescence.

Check out all your travel options in Kinsale and West Cork in chapter 8, "Out from Cork."

COUNTY KERRY The last year-round inhabitants of the Blasket Islands moved to the mainland in 1954, and these remote outposts have come to represent in the Irish imagination a way of life that's gone forever. Ferries departing from Dunquin connect the islands to the mainland, and a new tour departing from Dingle circumnavigates the islands and provides commentary describing the geology, wildlife and history of the islands; for more information about the **Blasket Islands Cruise** contact **Dingle Marine Ecotours** (**www.dinglemarine.com**).

Two of our favorite restaurants in the Southwest have closed their doors: **Greene's** in Killarney and **Larkin's** in Tralee.

A selection of our favorite affordable restaurants in southwestern Ireland an be found in chapter 9, "The Southwest: County Kerry."

COUNTIES CLARE & COUNTY MAYO Scattery Island in the Shannon Estuary is the site of 6th century monastic settlement, still thought of as a holy place. Starting in 2002, the Scattery Island Information Centre (© **065/905-2144**) on the mainland, in Kilkee, is planning to start guided tours of the island—call ahead to ask if the tours have started.

In September of 2001, the **Museum of Ireland** opened a new branch in County Mayo, it's first location outside Dublin. **The Museum of Country Life** is in Turlough, just outside Castlebar, set on the grounds of a grand 19th century manor house. The exhibits present a story of rural life in Ireland told through everyday objects; admission to the museum is free.

Check out other things to see and do in both counties in chapter 10, "The West."

THE ARAN ISLANDS & COUNTY GALWAY Perched on a cliff high above the Atlantic breakers, the Dun Aengus stone fort on the island of Inishmore is one of Ireland's most impressive monuments. A new interpretive center at the foot of the hill includes a gift shop and coffee shop; it's also a good place to get out of the rain.

The Benedictine Nuns of **Kylemore Abbey** have been working on the restoration of their walled garden since 1995, and opened it to the public for the first time in 2001. The garden is bisected by a stream, with a flower garden to one side and a kitchen garden on the other. There is a separate admission charge for the garden, which is only open during the summer months.

See chapter 12, "Out from Galway," for the lowdown on accommodations, dining, and the best sights in the Aran Islands and County Galway.

COUNTIES SLIGO & COUNTY DONEGAL The **Sligo Arts Festival** was cancelled in 2000 and 2001, and its future remains uncertain; call North West Tourism (© **071/61201**) to ask if it will be staged in 2002.

The Corncrake Restaurant in Carndonagh, County Donegal, one of our favorite restaurants in all of Ireland, has moved to new quarters not far from its original home, and there are plans to add on to the building in the near future.

A list of other attractions, dining, and lodging recommendations for the region can be found in chapter 13, "The Northwest."

COUNTY DERRY Derry has opened a massive new theater and conference center within the confines of the old walled city: the **Millennium Forum** (**www.millenniumforum.co.uk**) is now the city's principal venue for opera, theater, ballet, musicals and pantomime. For information call © **028/7126-4426.**

See chapter 15, "Northern Ireland," for more information on all the counties of Northern Ireland.

1

The Best of Ireland from $60 a Day

The Irish landscape remains breathtaking, its natural beauty intact, its rivers and lakes more or less pollution-free, and its people disarmingly gracious. These are the essential components of Irish tourism, and they're what bring 3.6 million visitors to Ireland each year, an ever-growing number that currently equals Ireland's population. Irish hospitality, in particular, is legendary, and deservedly so.

But beyond those seemingly timeless qualities, much of the country is changing rapidly. Twenty years ago, life in Ireland's rural west resembled the 19th century more than the 20th. Small farms were still the norm, and some remote areas had yet to receive electricity and running water. These days tourism and foreign investment have brought a new prosperity, and the country is changing fast. Computer firms employ the children of farmers, and the traditional cottage is being replaced in most places by modern bungalows. New restaurants and places to stay sprout from the fields like mushrooms, and yesterday's quiet seaside retreat is today's bustling resort town. The whole country is lunging into the 21st century at a pace that leaves most visitors—and many natives—feeling a little bewildered.

There's so much happening in Ireland these days that it can be hard to get your bearings. Within this exciting, shifting land, we've worked to find some constants—some things you can count on. So consider this a starting point, a springboard for your explorations and a base from which to build your own list of Irish favorites.

1 The Best Picture-Postcard Irish Towns

- **Dalkey** (County Dublin): This charming south-coast suburb of Dublin enjoys easy access to the city and freedom from its snarls and frenzy. It has a hilltop castle, an island, and a few parks, all in ample miniature. With all the fine and simple restaurants, pubs, and shops anyone needs for a brief visit or a long stay, Dalkey is a tempting town to settle into. See chapter 4, "Dublin."
- **Kilkenny** (County Kilkenny): Kilkenny offers the best Irish example of a medieval town. Its walls and splendidly restored castle—with a renowned design center housed in its stables—draw visitors from both Ireland and abroad. Kilkenny, however, is no museum and is regarded by many as perhaps the most attractive large town in Ireland. See chapter 6, "The Southeast."
- **Kinsale** (County Cork): Kinsale's narrow streets, dropping steeply from the hills that rim beautiful Kinsale Harbor, all lead to the sea. This is undoubtedly one of Ireland's most picturesque and picture-perfect towns, and the myriad visitors who crowd the streets every summer attest to the fact that the secret is out. The

Ireland

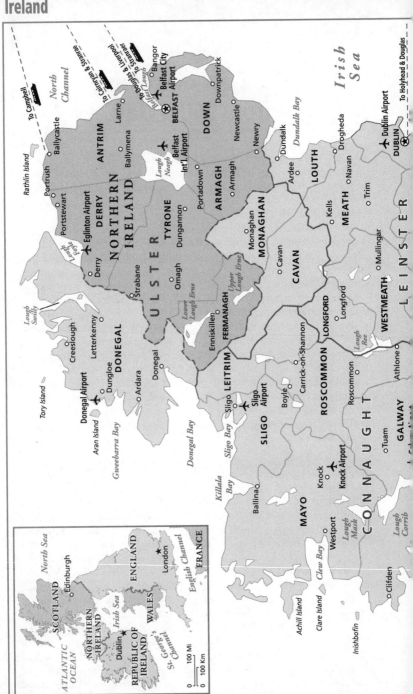

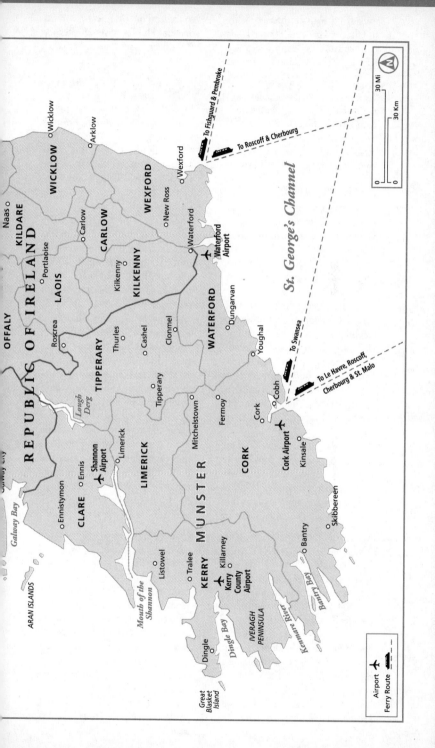

walk from Kinsale through Scilly to Charles Fort and Frower Point is breathtaking. Another plus: Kinsale has Ireland's greatest concentration of fine restaurants outside Dublin. See chapter 8, "Out from Cork.

2 The Best Tiny Seaside Villages

- **Ardmore** (County Waterford): Ardmore is best known for its complex of medieval ruins, including a beautiful round tower and a chapel with a remarkable set of carvings on its gable. The town itself is clustered around a sandy bay between craggy headlands. See chapter 6, "The Southeast."

- **Glandore and Union Hall** (County Cork): These two stunning port towns, which face each other across the waters of beautiful Glandore Harbour, are connected by an intimidating one-lane bridge. Glandore consists of streets stepping steeply to the sea, and on the port, a hotel, and a locally renowned gourmet restaurant. Union Hall's busy main street is filled with humbler establishments, including a few memorable pubs. See chapter 8, "Out from Cork."

- **Brandon** (County Kerry): This town is so small, you could easily miss it if you didn't know it was here. Grab a seat at Murphy's Pub on the pier and enjoy a pint while you watch the fishermen come in from the bay. Brandon sits in the shadow of Mt. Brandon, Ireland's second highest mountain, and just down the road from the great ocean views at Brandon Point. See chapter 9, "The Southwest: County Kerry."

- **Dunfanaghy** (County Donegal): There are outstanding beaches and coastal scenery within walking distance of this resort town on Ireland's northern coast. Don't miss the Horn Head Drive, or the traditional music that bursts into spontaneous life most nights in Dunfanaghy or nearby Falcarragh. See chapter 13, "The Northwest."

- **Glencolumbkille** (County Donegal): Modern conveniences, such as electricity, came only recently to this village on a tiny cove among the mountains of southwest Donegal, and there's still a sense of stepping back in time when you enter some of the local pubs and shops. Don't miss the Folk Museum, which preserves the past in a reconstructed village of thatched cottages. See chapter 13, "The Northwest."

3 The Best Free Attractions & Open Sites

- **National Museum of Ireland** (Dublin): This is where most of the nation's archaeological treasures are kept—the Ardagh Chalice, the Tara Brooch, the Cross of Cong. There's no better place to get in touch with Dublin's past, from the first Viking settlement to the Easter Rising of 1916. On the same block are the (also free) National Gallery and Natural History Museum. See p. 138.

- **Trinity College** (Dublin): Although you do have to pay to enter the Old Library, where the renowned Book of Kells is displayed, the rest of this historic campus is free and open for you to explore. As soon as you pass through the gates, you leave the noises of the city behind and enter another world. Watch a cricket match in the College Park, and stroll through the college's cobbled squares. See p. 139.

- **Kells** (County Kilkenny): This priory and fortified town is one of Ireland's most spectacular medieval ruins. Because there's no visitor center, you're on your own to explore and to interpret what you see; a small book available at the town post office offers assistance with the interpretation. See chapter 6, "The Southeast."

- **Athassel Priory** (County Tipperary): The largest medieval priory in Ireland, Athassel is spread in ruins over 4 acres. Although it's not as well preserved as Kells, there's still a lot here to explore, and the picturesque stones are sure to excite your imagination. Rarely visited, it's in the middle of a field, on a quiet back road near Cashel. See p. 240.

- **Black Fort** (County Galway): The dramatic 220-foot (67m) long wall of this promontory fort cuts off access to a small peninsula on Inishmore. Its site is spectacular and the defensive field of sharp stones that makes up its front yard is well worth negotiating. See p. 418.

- **Carrowkeel** (County Sligo): Eerily isolated atop several steep hills, and connected by sight with nearby Maeve's Tomb atop Knocknarea and the Neolithic tombs of Carrowmore, this collection of passage tombs is among the earliest surviving records of Ireland's prehistoric peoples. A visit here is an experience not to be missed. See p. 438.

4 The Best Festivals & Special Events

- **Fleadh Cheoil na hEireann** (location varies; the 2002 festival will be in Listowel, County Kerry): This is an all-Ireland traditional music competition, which also attracts performers from around the world. Usually taking place over 2 days in August, it's well worth a detour. For information on this and the many other *Fleadh* (traditional music festivals) that take place throughout Ireland, contact **Comhaltas Ceoltóirí Éireann,** 32 Belgrave Sq., Monkstown, County Dublin (*C* **01/2800295**). See p. 42.

- **Bloomsday** (Dublin): From June 12 through 17 of each year, Dubliners meet to celebrate their city and its greatest writer, James Joyce, whose novel *Ulysses* takes place on this day. Events include tours retracing the steps of Leopold Bloom and other characters, reenactments of scenes from the novel, lectures, and spontaneous gatherings at many of the pubs in *Ulysses. See* p. 152.

- **Dublin Theatre Festival** (Dublin): This October festival offers visitors the chance to see the best in current Irish drama, as well as an assortment of international productions. Several famous Irish plays, such as Brian Friel's *Philadelphia Here I Come,* have premiered here and gone on to performances throughout the world. See p. 153.

- **Wexford Festival Opera** (Wexford): During the last 2 weeks of October, the otherwise quiet streets of Wexford are filled with an international crowd that flocks here to enjoy this curious event: first-rate performances of little-known operas in a small Irish town. That's Ireland for you—full of delightful experiences in the most unlikely places. See p. 211.

- **Galway Arts Festival** (Galway): The largest festival of its kind in Ireland, this raucous event fills Galway for 12 days in mid-July. The schedule of happenings is diverse, with films, musical concerts, and theatrical performances taking place simultaneously in the many city-center venues. See p. 408.

5 The Best Active Vacations

- **Sailing Ireland's West Coast:** Spectacular coastal scenery, interesting harbor towns, and an abundance of islands make the West Coast a delight for cruising sailors. Yacht charter is available in Kilrush, County Clare. See "Sailing Resources," in chapter 3, "Ireland Outdoors."

- **Horseback Riding in the Galtee Mountains:** The gentle contours of Tipperary's Galtees offer the perfect scenic backdrop for trail riding. You'll be provided with all you need for a horse-riding holiday at Bansha House, a commodious B&B with an excellent equestrian program. See chapter 6, "The Southeast."

- **Sea Kayaking in West Cork:** The many bays, headlands, and islands of this wild, rocky coast provide innumerable opportunities for kayak exploration. A great base is Maria's Schoolhouse, where you'll find comfortable and friendly accommodations and an outstanding sea-kayaking program run by Jim Kennedy. See chapter 8, "Out from Cork."

- **Bicycling in the Southwest:** The peninsulas and islands of Cork and Kerry are perfect for cycling, with low traffic and an abundance of beautiful places to visit. Roycroft's Stores in Skibbereen, County Cork, rent bikes that are a notch above the usual rental equipment. See chapters 8, "Out from Cork," and 9, "The Southwest: County Kerry."

- **Walking the Donegal Coast:** The cliff-rimmed headlands of Donegal are the most spectacular in Ireland, and the best way to explore them is on foot. Among the finest walks are Slieve League, Glen Head, and Horn Head. See chapter 13, "The Northwest."

6 The Best Beaches

- **Raven Point** (County Wexford): The Raven Nature Reserve, just north of Wexford Harbour, is a place of forested dunes and uncrowded beaches. During the winter and spring a large population of migratory wildfowl makes this their temporary home. See p. 220.

- **Barleycove** (County Cork): Barleycove is an inlet at the tip of Mizen Head, a place of great rugged beauty. Despite some development in the form of a hotel and trailer park, the beach doesn't get too crowded, and is a great place to walk or swim. See p. 300.

- **Kilcummin** (County Kerry): Brandon Bay on the north side of the Dingle Peninsula offers many kilometers of pristine sand; the beach at Kilcummin, near Stradbally, is especially scenic and good for walking or windsurfing, though it's often a bit rough for swimming. See p. 348.

- **Portacloy** (County Mayo): With a curving crescent of white sand, a tranquil bay, and a fleet of diving cormorants, this beach is a gem that (surprisingly) doesn't draw large crowds. It is strikingly rural and shimmers a silky aquamarine amidst sheep fields and a cluster of farm cottages. Come here for a spectacular cliffside walk as well as a refreshing dip. See p. 386.

- **Trabane** (County Donegal): Donegal has some of the most beautiful stretches of unpopulated beach in Ireland, and Trabane Strand near Dunfanaghy is a prime example. You have to be willing to walk, as there isn't road access, but on a fine day a stroll on this glorious expanse of sea sand, with the cliffs of Horn Head on the horizon, will amply reward the effort. As for swimming in these chilly northern waters, it's best to leave that to the seals and the truly courageous. See p. 463.

- **Culdaff** (County Donegal): This long, golden beach is one of the best beaches in Donegal, a county with much more than its share of glorious sea sand. Culdaff is also well sheltered from Atlantic turbulence. See p. 474.

7 The Best Bird-Watching

- **Shannon Callows** (Counties Galway, Tipperary, and Offaly): The low-lying meadows along the Shannon and Little Brosna River flood in the winter, creating a massive temporary lake that is the wintering grounds for many species of wildfowl. In the summer, the meadows are home to one of the few remaining corncrake populations in Ireland. See "Bird-watching" in chapter 3, "Ireland Outdoors."
- **Great Saltee** (County Wexford): A barren and seemingly lifeless rock during much of the year, this island becomes an avian paradise during the summer months, when it fills to overflowing with nesting seabirds. See chapter 6, "The Southeast."
- **North Slob** (County Wexford): The north side of Wexford Harbor is the site of the Wexford Wildfowl Reserve, home to thousands of geese from October to April each year. Its interpretive center is open year-round and has exhibits on the geese, other avian visitors to the Slob, and nearby areas of ornithological interest. See chapter 6, "The Southeast."
- **Cape Clear** (County Cork): This island at the southernmost extremity of Ireland has a bird observatory and resident warden. Many important discoveries regarding patterns of migration have been made here. Boat tours for birders are available from North Harbor. See chapter 8, "Out from Cork."
- **Loop Head** (County Clare): Remote Loop Head and the nearby Bridges of Ross are known as great seabird-watching sites from late summer to early fall. See chapter 10, "The West."
- **Strangford Lough** (County Down): The shores of Strangford Lough mark one of the premier bird-watching sites in the world. Although best known for the thousands of pale-bellied Brent geese that can be seen there every fall, the area offers wonders year-round, and hosts the family-friendly wildlife reserve, Castle Espie. See chapter 15, "Northern Ireland."

8 The Best Natural Wonders

- **MacGillycuddy's Reeks** (County Kerry): One of several mountain ranges on the Iveragh Peninsula, MacGillycuddy's Reeks boasts Carrantuohill, at 3,404 feet (1,037m) the highest mountain in Ireland. Whether gazed at from afar or explored up close on foot, the Reeks are among Ireland's greatest spectacles. See chapter 9, "The Southwest: County Kerry."
- **The Burren** (County Clare): The Burren—from the Irish *Boireann,* meaning "a rocky place"—is one of the strangest landscapes you're ever likely to see: a vast limestone grassland, spread with a quilt of wildflowers. Its inhabitants

include the pine marten and nearly every species of butterfly found in Ireland. See chapter 10, "The West."

- **The Cliffs of Moher** (County Clare): Rising from Hag's Head to the south, these magnificent sea cliffs reach their full height of 760 feet (232m) just north of O'Brien's Tower. The views of the open sea, of the distant Aran Islands, and of the Twelve Bens of Connemara are spectacular. A walk south along the cliff edge at sunset makes a perfect end to any day. See chapter 10, "The West."

- **Croagh Patrick** (County Mayo): Rising steeply 2,500 feet (762m) above the Mayo coast, Croagh Patrick is Ireland's holiest mountain, where Patrick is said to have retreated in penance. The place is biblically imposing. The view from above can be breathtaking or nonexistent, as the summit is often wrapped in clouds, adding to its mystery. See chapter 10, "The West."

- **The Twelve Bens** (County Galway): Amidst Connemara's central mountains, bogs, and lakes rises a rugged range known as the Twelve Bens, crowning a landscape that is among the most spectacular in Ireland. Among the peaks themselves, some are bare and rocky while others are clothed in peat. The loftiest of the Bens, Benbaun, reaches a height of 2,395 feet (730m) and lies inside the Connemara National Park. See chapter 12, "Out from Galway."

- **Slieve League** (County Donegal): The Slieve League peninsula stretches for 30 miles (48km) into the Atlantic and is 12 miles (19km) across at its widest point. Its wonderfully pigmented cliffs are the highest sea cliffs in Europe, and can either be gazed at from Carrigan Head or walked along, if you dare. From below or from above, Slieve League serves up some of the most dazzling sights in Ireland. See chapter 13, "The Northwest."

- **The Slieve Bloom Mountains** (County Laois): Slieve Bloom, Ireland's largest and most unspoiled blanket bog, has been described as a "scenic bulge" rising gently above the midland's peat fields. Its beauty—comprised of gentle slopes, glens, rivers, waterfalls, and bog lands—is subtle rather than dramatic, but it's comparatively untouched and you can have it more or less to yourself—apart from its deer, foxes, badgers, and an occasional marten or otter, that is. See chapter 14, "Along the River Shannon's Shores."

- **The Giant's Causeway** (County Antrim): In case you lose count, there are roughly 40,000 tightly packed and mostly hexagonal basalt columns said to comprise the giant Finn McCool's path from the Antrim headland into the sea toward the Scottish island of Staffa. This volcanic wonder, formed 60 million years ago, can either be marveled at from a distance or negotiated cautiously on foot. See chapter 15, "Northern Ireland."

9 The Best Castles

- **Cahir Castle** (County Tipperary): One of the largest of Ireland's castles, Cahir is in an extraordinary state of preservation. Tours explain some fascinating features of the castle's military architecture, and you're free to roam through a maze of tiny chambers, spiral staircases, and vertiginous battlements. See p. 240.

- **Kilkenny Castle** (County Kilkenny): Although parts of the castle date back to the 13th century, the existing structure has the feel of an 18th-century palace. There have been many modifications since medieval times, including the addition of beautiful landscaping on the grounds. See p. 251.

- **Blarney Castle** (County Cork): Despite the mobs of visitors that besiege the castle daily, this majestic tower house is worth a visit. While you're here, check out the Badger Cave and dungeons at the tower's base, as well as the serpentine paths that wind through the castle gardens, set in a picturesque rocky glen. Need we mention the Stone? You sidle in under the upper wall with your head hanging over a 10-story drop, and there it is. You kiss it. It's a thing people do. See p. 278.

- **Charles Fort** (County Cork): Located on a promontory in stunning Kinsale Harbor, the fort's massive walls enclose a complex array of buildings in varying states of repair. At the entrance you're handed a map and then left on your own to explore, discover, and almost certainly get lost in the maze of courtyards, passages, walls, and barracks. See p. 286.

- **Parke's Castle** (County Leitrim): Once an important citadel in this part of the country, the now masterfully restored castle commands great views over Lough Gill. Exhibits demonstrate the life and activities of castle inhabitants, and the tea shop serves up some admirable pastries. See p. 442.

- **Carrickfergus Castle** (County Antrim): This fortress on the bank of Belfast Lough is the best-preserved Norman castle in Ireland. It consists of an imposing tower house and high wall punctuated by corner towers. See p. 516.

- **Dunluce Castle** (County Antrim): The castle ruins stand atop a razor-sharp promontory jutting into the sea. This was no doubt a highly defensible setting, and the castle wasn't abandoned until a large section collapsed and fell into the breakers one day in 1639. See p. 524.

10 The Best of Ancient Ireland

- **Newgrange** (County Meath): Poised atop a low hill north of the River Boyne, Newgrange is the centerpiece of a dramatic megalithic cemetery dating from more than 5,000 years ago. Archaeological speculation is that this massive, heart-shaped mound and passage tomb was constructed as a communal vault to house the cremated remains of the dead. The tomb's narrow passage is so perfectly aligned with the equinoctial sunrise that the central chamber, deep within the mound, is marvelously illuminated at each year's winter solstice. See p. 200.

- **Loughcrew** (County Meath): At this little-known site, not far from Newgrange, a series of cruciform passage tombs crown two hills. On the east hill, a guide unlocks the door to one of the domed tombs, answering your questions with an individuality not possible at the larger, more populous sites. More rewarding however, is a hike up the west hill to a second, more solitary series of tombs where the connections to be made between ruin and imaginative reconstruction are your own. See p. 200.

- **Tara** (County Meath): Of ritual significance from the Stone Age to the Christian period, Tara has seen it all and kept it all a secret. This was the traditional center and seat of Ireland's high kings, who could look out from here and survey their realm. Although it's only 512 feet (156m) above sea level, from the Tara hill you can see each of

Ireland's four Celtic provinces on a clear day. The site is mostly unexcavated and tells its story in whispers. It's a place to be walked slowly, with an imagination steeped in Ireland's past. See p. 200.

- **Lough Gur** (County Limerick): This lakefront site will convince you that the Neolithic farmers of Ireland had an estimable sense of real estate. Inhabited for more than 4,000 years, this ancient farming settlement offers a number of prehistoric remains, the most impressive of which is the largest surviving stone circle in Ireland, consisting of 113 stones. See p. 363.

- **Dun Aengus** (County Galway): No one knows who built this massive stone fort, or when. The eminent archaeologist George Petrie called Dun Aengus "the most magnificent barbaric monument in Europe." Facing the sea, where its three stone rings meet steep 200-foot (61m) cliffs, Dun Aengus stands guard today over the southern coast of the island of Inishmore, the largest of the Arans. See p. 418.

- **Carrowmore and Carrowkeel** (County Sligo): Located on the Coolera Peninsula, these two megalithic cities of the dead may have once contained well over 200 passage tombs. The two together, Carrowmore in a valley and Carrowkeel atop a nearby mountain, convey an unequaled sense of the scale and wonder of the ancient megalithic peoples' reverence for the dead. Carrowmore is well presented and interpreted, while Carrowkeel is left to itself and to those who seek it out. See p. 438.

11 Remnants of the Golden Age: The Best Early Christian Ruins

- **Glendalough** (County Wicklow): Nestled in "the glen of the two lakes," this important monastic settlement was founded in the 6th century by St. Kevin. Its setting is disarmingly scenic—exactly the opposite of the harsh environment you'd expect ascetic medieval monks to have sought out. Although quite remote, Glendalough suffered numerous assaults by the Vikings and the English, and it eventually dwindled into insignificance. Today its picturesque ruins collude with the countryside to create one of the loveliest spots in Ireland. See p. 182.

- **The Rock of Cashel** (County Tipperary): In both appearance and name (*cashel* or *caiseal* means "fortress" in Irish), "the Rock" suggests a citadel, a place more familiar with power than prayer. Physically, it is a huge outcropping—or rather *upcropping*—of limestone topped with some of the most spectacular ruins in Ireland, including what was once the country's finest Romanesque chapel. Socially, the place was in former times the seat of clerics and kings, a center to rival Tara. Now, however, the two sites vie only for tourists. See p. 241.

- **Jerpoint Abbey** (County Kilkenny): Jerpoint is perhaps the finest representative of the many Cistercian abbeys whose ruins dot the Irish landscape. Visitors are drawn to Jerpoint's splendid cloister, the most richly carved in Ireland, and its impressive tomb sculptures. The abbey's tower is the tallest of its kind in Ireland. See p. 255.

- **Skellig Michael** (County Kerry): This stunning crag of rock, dedicated to the Archangel Michael, stands 8 miles (13km) offshore of the Iveragh Peninsula and rises sharply 714 feet (218m) out of the Atlantic. Early Irish monks in pursuit of self-imposed hardship and exile chose this spot to build their austere hermitage. Today, the journey to Skellig across choppy seas and the arduous climb to its summit are challenging and unforgettable. See p. 314.

- **Inishmurray** (County Sligo): This uninhabited island nearly 4 miles (6.5km) off the Sligo coast is home to a striking monastic complex, surrounded by what appear to be the walls of an even more ancient stone fort. Despite its remoteness, this outpost of peace-seeking monks was sought out for destruction by the Vikings in AD 802. Today its circular ruins and the surrounding sea present a

stunning sight, well worth the effort required to reach it. See p. 438.

- **Clonmacnois** (County Offaly): This was once one of Ireland's most important religious, artistic, and literary centers, a place of pilgrimage and high culture. Founded in the mid-5th century at the axis of the Shannon River and the medieval east–west thoroughfare known as the Eiscir Riada, Clonmacnois thrived for centuries until its prime riverfront location nearly proved its undoing. In the 830s, Vikings sailed up the Shannon from Limerick and brought a havoc that returned many times in the ensuing centuries. Today, even in ruins, Clonmacnois remains a place of peculiar beauty and serenity. See p. 486.

12 The Best Literary Spots

- **Newman House** (Dublin): Cardinal John Henry Newman was the first rector of the Catholic University in Dublin, housed in two buildings on St. Stephen's Green in the center of the city's south side, and worked in this capacity from 1852 to his retirement in 1859. The Catholic University later became University College Dublin, and it is to this institution that Gerard Manley Hopkins was sent in 1884, as a professor of Greek; after 5 years of teaching here, Hopkins died at the age of 44. James Joyce studied here from 1899 to 1902. See p. 145.

- **Glasnevin Cemetery** (Dublin): Besides being the setting for part of the sixth episode of *Ulysses,* this is the resting place of Joyce's parents and several other members of his family. The English-born poet Gerard Manley Hopkins is also buried here, in the Jesuit plot. Maud Gonne, the Irish nationalist

and longtime Dublin resident who is said to have inspired Yeats's play *Cathleen ní Houlihan,* is buried in the Republican plot. See p. 144.

- **North Dublin:** The streets north of the Liffey are home to many of the characters in James Joyce's stories and novels; this is a part of Dublin in which Joyce himself lived and for which he had a special affinity. Much has changed since Joyce's time, and Bloom's house at 7 Eccles Street has been replaced by a new wing of the Mater Private Hospital, but there are still many mementos of the city as it was in 1904. Tours of the area begin from the James Joyce Center. See p. 145.

- **St. Patrick's Cathedral** (Dublin): Jonathan Swift was born in Dublin in 1667, and entered Trinity College in his 15th year. He later became dean of St. Patrick's Cathedral, and is buried alongside

Hester Johnson (Stella) in the Cathedral's south aisle. See p. 154.

- **County Sligo:** It seems at times that every hill, house, and lake in the county is signposted to note its relation to the poet W. B. Yeats, whose writing was informed by the landscape, mythology, and people of this region. Many of the natural and historic monuments of Sligo appear in Yeats's poetry, including Lough Gill, Glencar Lake, Benbulben Mountain, and Maeve's tomb atop Knocknarea Mountain. There are also several museums housing first editions, photographs, and other memorabilia, and of course Yeats's grave in Drumcliff. See "Sligo and Yeats Country," in chapter 13, "The Northwest."

- **The Aran Islands:** John Millington Synge set his play *Riders to the Sea* on Inishmaan, and wrote an account of life on the islands, titled simply *The Aran Islands.* Native islander Liam O'Flaherty, known for his novel *Famine,* is from the island of Inishmore. See "The Aran Islands" in chapter 12, "Out from Galway."

13 The Best Gardens

- **Powerscourt** (County Wicklow): This is one of the most grandiose of Irish gardens, set amidst the natural splendor of the northern Wicklow Hills, yet it's only 12 miles (19km) from Dublin. The gardens and nearby waterfall make a great day's outing and a welcome respite from the noise and congestion of the city. See p. 186.

- **Kilruddery** (County Wicklow): A grandiose formal garden whose initial plan was laid out in the 17th century, Killruddery's appeal lies in places like the beech hedge pond and the ornamental dairy. The house is also full of curious treasures. See p. 186.

- **Butterstream** (County Meath): Butterstream is renowned for its splendor, spring and summer. It is a series of delightful garden compartments whose variety attest to the skill of its designer, Jim Reynolds. His manipulation of floral color and texture yields spectacular results, from an austere white garden to the floral fireworks of brilliant herbaceous borders. See p. 199.

- **Altamont** (County Carlow): Altamount is a sumptuous garden. Lush plantings set up a sequence leading from a formal garden to a rugged forest, rock-walled glen, and riverbank walk. See chapter 6, "The Southeast."

- **Creagh** (County Cork): Meandering paths lead the visitor past a sequence of exquisite vistas, with many hidden corners to explore. The garden is situated on a beautiful estuary. See p. 297.

- **Ilnacullin** (County Cork): A ferry conveys visitors from a lovely, rhododendron-rimmed bay in the town of Glangarriff to **Garinish Island,** the unlikely site of a fine Italianate garden. The formal garden, with the Casita at its center, is linked to a "wild garden" that showcases a collection of rhododendrons, azaleas, and rare trees. See p. 297.

- **Heywood** (County Laois): Heywood is one of just four gardens in Ireland designed by English architect Edward Lutyens. Its rows of lime trees, tall iron fountain, and walled garden create a tranquil enclave in a countryside that is already calm, green, and soft. The house for which Heywood was built has burnt down; nevertheless, the garden recalls its elegance. See p. 489.

- **Mount Stewart** (County Down): Built upon an elaborate plan, Mount Stewart comprises several small gardens of distinctive character. A touch of whimsy is reflected in the statuary, topiary, and planting designs. See p. 518.

14 The Best Attractions for the Whole Family

- **The Ark: A Cultural Centre for Children** (County Dublin): A unique chance for kids to have a hands-on learning experience of art, music, and theater in workshop sessions with artists. There are also excellent theater productions for families. See p. 150.
- **Dublin's Viking Adventure** (County Dublin): This is a fun learning experience where kids can travel back in time and be part of Viking life with "real Vikings," while working and interacting in a model Norse town on the actual site where the Vikings made their home in Dublin. See p. 150.
- **Dublin Zoo in Phoenix Park** (County Dublin): Kids love this 30-acre zoo with its array of creatures, animal-petting corner, and train ride. The surrounding park has room to run, picnic, and explore for hours (or days!). See p. 150.

- **The Irish National Heritage Park** (County Wexford): Nearly 9,000 years of Irish history come alive here in ways that will fascinate visitors of every age. The whole family will be captivated by the story of ancient Ireland, from its first inhabitants to its Norman conquerors. See p. 212.
- **Muckross House & Gardens** (County Kerry): This stunning Victorian mansion with exquisite gardens is also home to skilled artisans at their work. Nearby is a series of reconstructed traditional farms, complete with animals and docents, providing a gateway to rural Ireland as it was for centuries. See p. 325.
- **Marble Arch Caves** (County Fermanagh): Adventurous families are guided by boat through well-lit underground waterways to explore caves and view amazing stone formations. See p. 552.

15 The Best Pubs

- **Abbey Tavern** (County Dublin): A short outing from Dublin center, the Abbey Tavern is the perfect place to recover and refuel after exploring Howth Head, Ireland's Eye, and the attractive fishing and yachting village of Howth on the northern tip of Dublin Bay. The Abbey is known far and wide for its ballads as well as its brew. See p. 171.
- **The Brazen Head** (County Dublin): Nearly qualifying as one of Ireland's ancient sites, the Brazen Head, commissioned by Charles II, is more than 300 years old, and its stout is as fresh as it comes. Among its illustrious

alums are Wolfe Tone, Daniel O'Connell, and Robert Emmet, who planned the Dublin rising of 1803 under the Head's low timbers. In fact, he was hanged not far from here when everything went wrong. See p. 168.
- **An Bodhran** (County Cork): A hangout for UCC (University College Cork) students serious about their traditional music and stout, An Bodhran has a lot of old-style character, which recent renovations have only enhanced. See p. 281.
- **The Blue Haven** (County Cork): Everything the Blue Haven offers is first rate: food, drink, lodging,

and a cozy bar with an open fire. This particular haven is also in the center of one of Ireland's most appealing seaside towns, Kinsale. You'll soon measure everyone else's traditional Irish lamb stew by what you found here. See p. 289.

- **O'Connor's Pub** (County Clare): Doolin, a dot of a town on the Clare Coast, is a hot spot for traditional Irish music, and Gus O'Connor's has been at the center of the action here for more than 150 years. Great music and distinguished seafood make this otherwise ordinary pub worth a major detour. See p. 375.

- **Moran's Oyster Cottage** (County Galway): Famed for its seafood, this centuries-old thatched-cottage pub on the weir also draws a perfect pint. This may well be the oyster capitol of Ireland. It's 12 miles (19km) out of Galway and well worth the drive—or the walk, for that matter. See p. 415.

- **Smugglers Creek** (County Donegal): This place would be worth a stop if only for its spectacular cliff-top views of Donegal Bay. Stonewalls, beamed ceilings, open fires, excellent fare, and the brew that's true are among the charms proprietor Conor Britton has on tap. See p. 457.

- **Hargadon's** (County Sligo): This is the epitome of the Irish pub. Conversation and the gentle sipping of Guinness reign supreme here: no televisions, radios, or stereos disrupt an atmosphere of quiet enjoyment honed over more than a hundred years of pulling pints. See p. 446.

- **Crown Liquor Saloon** (County Antrim): This National Trust pub, across from the Grand Opera House in Belfast, is a Victorian gem. Your mouth will drop open at its antique publican splendor even before you lift your first pint. See p. 513.

16 The Best of Irish Baking

- **Ballinatona Farm** (County Cork): Few bakers can top the Irish soda bread, scones, and pan bread of Jytte Storm, who uses traditional Irish recipes. Guests at Ballinatona wake up to the comforting smell of baking bread, better than coffee to get you going in the morning. See p. 303.

- **Goya's** (County Galway): Goya's is a Galway institution, a place to sip tea and gossip. Emer Murray ensures that its selection of bread,

scones, and pastries is fresh every day and you will want to ensure that you arrive in time to taste a tart or two. See p. 403.

- **Country Choice** (County Tipperary): This is a cornucopia of Irish specialties. Counters are heaped with warm, crisp loaves of round bread. The scent alone is irresistible, the texture homely and satisfying, and the taste beyond description. See p. 483.

17 The Best Restaurants You Can Afford

- **Chameleon** (County Dublin): Step into this small restaurant on a side street of Temple Bar and you'll be rewarded with an Indonesian feast. Shrimp crackers and hot red curry paste are at every table to begin and from

there it only gets spicier. A good budget bet are the early-bird dishes—huge, well-seasoned bowls of noodles or rice with a choice of seafood, chicken, beef, or vegetables. See p. 125.

- **Steps of Rome** (County Dublin): The perfect antidote to rain-induced hunger lies within the walls of this small cafe off Dublin's Grafton Street: a thick, satisfying slab of potato and rosemary pizza. See p. 131.

- **Adele's** (County Cork): This unassuming eatery on Main Street in Schull is a bakery during the day, serving great sandwiches of herbed Italian bread and delicious local cheese. The real revelation comes in the evening, when you can come here for meals that are simple and astonishingly good. See p. 307.

- **Da Tang Noodle House** (County Galway): Spicy. spicy. spicy. This is where the locals slip in if they want a quick bite in Galway. Steaming bowls of noodles are spiked with cilantro and chili, and you won't want to put down your chopsticks until you've slurped up every bit. See p. 403.

- **Moran's Oyster Cottage** (County Galway): A short drive from Galway center, this seafood mecca is worth a drive from Dublin. For six generations, the Morans have focused on what they know and do best, and have a menu—the *same* menu, all day and every day, featuring seafood and nothing but—that brings the point home. You may not find better oysters and salmon anywhere, and surely not at these prices. See p. 415.

18 Where to Forget Your Budget: The Best Places to Eat

- **L'Ecrivain** (Dublin): Everything at L'Ecrivain is accomplished with art and precision, from the service and presentation to the food itself. Vegetarian and lunch menus are an especially good value. L'Ecrivain continues to quietly assert itself as one of the very best Irish restaurants. See p. 131.

- **The Motte** (County Kilkenny): Slow delectation is the requirement at the Motte. Everything demands it—from the dimly glowing dining room to the thoughtful staff and the exquisitely prepared food. Chef Alan Walton's concoctions of cream and fresh herbs and rich dark chocolate desserts defy speed, making a delicious, lingering evening the only real possibility. See p. 260.

- **Arbutus Lodge** (County Cork): Formerly the home of the lord Mayor of Cork, Arbutus Lodge House is king of the hill in more ways than one, with commanding views of the River Lee and the surrounding hills. The restaurant, however, is what puts it on the map. The chef's eight-course tasting menu and a fine wine from the lodge's extensive list will leave a lasting impression. See p. 274.

- **Lettercollum House** (County Cork): The emphasis here is on fresh, local, and organic ingredients; a walled garden provides the vegetables, and pigs are raised on the premises. With these fine materials, chef Con McLoughlin concocts dishes of pure delight, simple yet surprising. There's always a vegetarian entree, too. See p. 309.

- **Beginish Restaurant** (County Kerry): A relaxed atmosphere pervades this small restaurant on one of Dingle's narrow side streets. The seafood is as fresh as it gets, and is always presented in its unadorned majesty—these people really know how to let seafood speak for itself. See p. 346.

- **Corncrake Restaurant** (County Donegal): Such a judicious blend of fresh ingredients and culinary imagination is a rare treat. The nettle soup, roast lamb, and desserts of Noreen Lynch and Brid McCartney warrant a detour to the town of Carndonagh where the living room of a small row house has been transformed into an extraordinary restaurant. See p. 476.

19 The Best Offbeat Activities

- **Illauntannig Island Cottage** (County Kerry): This small island off the Dingle Peninsula promises absolute solitude. For a very reasonable sum, you can rent the only house on the island, your only company a herd of cows and flocks of seabirds. The only way over is via fishing boat and curragh. See "The Northern Dingle Peninsula" in chapter 9, "The Southwest: County Kerry."
- **Croagh Patrick Pilgrimage** (County Mayo): On the final Sunday of July, join the more than 60,000 pilgrims who ascend the 2,513-foot summit of Croagh Patrick at night—some in bare feet. There is a 4am mass before the descent. The date of this strenuous climb coincides with that of Lughnasa, the Celtic festival. Another ancient pilgrimage route commences at Ballintubber Abbey— the walk predates Christianity and many people still undertake the 22-mile journey, which ends at the base of Croagh Patrick. The route is punctuated by several mass rocks; groups sometimes travel with a priest, and mass is said at these markers. See "Country Mayo" in chapter 10, "The West."
- **Bog Tours** (County Offaly): You shouldn't visit Ireland without stepping in a peat bog, without smelling its distinctive smoke from cottage chimneys, without seeing its rich brown blocks heaped at the side of the road. The Irish Peat Board gives railway tours of the Blackwater bog—you can even try your hand at digging the turf. See p. 486.
- **Cattle Market or Horse Sale.** A good way to recapture the essence of rural Ireland is to attend local livestock auctions, which take place throughout the country. One good cattle market is held on Tuesday mornings in Nenagh, County Tipperary. If you find yourself in Dublin, there's an urban horse market on the first Sunday of each month in the Smithfield district; for more information contact Dublin Tourism (© **066/979-2082**). See the "Lower Shannon: The Lough Derg Drive" in chapter 14.

20 The Best B&Bs

- **Lennoxbrook   Countryhouse** (County Meath): Lennoxbrook is a thoughtful, well-crafted place. The rooms are beautiful, with bay windows overlooking a tangled forest and a magnificent beech tree. Guests are invited to pull up a chair in the Mullan family sitting room. See p. 202.
- **Ballinatona Farm** (County Cork): Set in a quiet and underrated corner of West Cork, this modern farmhouse commands astonishing views of the surrounding hills. Jytte Storm and Tim Lane, the energetic and outgoing hosts, will direct you to the Coomeenatrush Waterfall and other beautiful spots within walking distance of the house. See p. 303.
- **Lettercollum House** (County Cork): Lettercollum is a well-worn manor house with fine stained glass and elegant common

rooms, but despite its elegance, it's a laid-back retreat and a great place for families. No guest should depart without sampling the excellent afternoon and evening meals served in a former chapel. See p. 304.

- **Ross Castle** (County Cavan): A tower room in a haunted (and centrally heated) castle awaits you here, and it won't take too big a bite out of your wallet, either. This may not be elegance, but it's unquestionably memorable. Ross Castle and nearby Ross House are warm, comfortable, and a great place to relax beside Lough Sheelin, a noteworthy source of trout and pike. See p. 496.

- **The Saddler's House and Old Rectory** (County Derry): Compared to the Old Rectory, the Saddler's house is modest. Its rooms are clean and spare, decorated with the simplicity that its merchant origins seem to demand. The Rectory rooms are more lavish—high ceilings and plaster roses evoke its elegant Georgian origins. Both houses, run by the inimitable Joan Pyne, are a brief stroll from the center of Derry. See p. 543.

21 Where to Forget Your Budget: The Best Places to Stay

- **Delphi Lodge** (County Galway): This was once the country hideaway for the marquis of Sligo, and now it can be yours, too. Inside, the emphasis is on clean, bright simplicity in perfect taste, while outside the grounds and environs are among the most beautiful in Ireland. Tranquility, comfort, and fishing are the operative words here. By renting one of the cottages for a week or more, you can make this indulgence more affordable. See p. 431.

- **Temple House** (County Sligo): The house is set on the shores of Temple House Lake, on an estate of some 1,000 acres, with a gorgeous walled garden and elaborate coach houses. Sandy Percival's family has lived in Temple House for more than 300 years, and Sandy has many a story to tell of their exploits. The evening meal, prepared by Deborah Percival, is a memorable experience. The atmosphere of casual elegance and affable unpretentiousness is truly seductive, and chances are you'll want to spend more than one night. See p. 445.

- **Castle Leslie** (County Monaghan): A stay here is one of Ireland's unique surprises, an experience well worth any detour required. The 1,000-acre estate, with its three lakes (famous for pike) and ancient hardwood forests, casts its own relaxing spell, and the great house—27,000 square feet of history—is as comfortable as an old slipper. Expect the unexpected, and enjoy. See p. 355.

2

Planning an Affordable Trip to Ireland

Budget travel in Ireland is not only possible, it's the best way to get to know the country and its people. It's an irony of travel that the more money you spend, the more you're able to isolate yourself from the places and people you've journeyed so far to visit. Bottom line: Don't lament that you can't afford a night in that luxurious hotel; you may not find the Ireland you're looking for there, anyway.

So, what do we mean by "from $60 a day"? Basically, we assume that you're traveling as a couple, with at least $60 each to spend per day on a double room and meals. The figure would have to be somewhat higher for a single traveler, because B&Bs either add a "single supplement" or simply charge the same amount whether the room is occupied by one person or two. The average B&B in this book is about 30€ ($27) per person for a double room with breakfast, which leaves you about 36€ ($33) for lunch and dinner. Although eating out can be expensive in Ireland, this is plenty for two decent, filling meals or one extravagant splurge of a meal, especially if you can get used to eating your main meal at lunch. Of course, we all have our own preferences regarding where to skimp and where to splurge; I often prefer to sleep cheap at one of Ireland's fine hostels and use the pounds saved on a really good meal.

Transportation costs aren't included in our "$60 a day" premise, and how you choose to get around could be the biggest factor in determining the total expense of your trip. Public transportation is the best option in Dublin, where driving is usually more of a hassle than it's worth. Bus and train access to rural Ireland can be quite limited, though we've tried to highlight public transportation options wherever they're available. For the most part, when it comes to rural Ireland, we've assumed that you're traveling either by car or, if you're the intrepid type, by bicycle. If you think that cycling might be an option for you, check out "Bicycling" in chapter 3, "Ireland Outdoors"; if you decide to rent a car, though, be prepared to pay some hefty prices for gasoline (more than three times what you'd pay in the United States).

In this chapter, we've collected the information you need to anticipate where you want to count your pennies and where you might want to forget your budget in the pure enjoyment of the moment.

1 Fifty Money-Saving Tips

GETTING TO IRELAND

1. Budgeting for transportation begins with your flight over—be sure to take advantage of **discounted airfares** that require advance booking.

2. There are numerous free **Internet services** that can help you find the cheapest regular fare. For more information, see "Planning Your Trip Online," later in this chapter.

3. Students and teachers are eligible for substantially reduced tickets through **Council Travel;** contact the national office (© **888/ COUNCIL;** www.counciltravel. com) where they can make your reservations or refer you to the Council Travel office nearest you. In Canada, Council's counterpart is **Travel CUTS,** 200 Ronson St., Ste. 320, Toronto, ONT M9W 5Z9 (© **800/667-2887** within Canada, or 416/614-2887; www. travelcuts.com). **Campus Travel,** 52 Grosvenor Gardens, London SW1W 0AG (© **0870/240-1010** or 020/7730-7285; www.campus travel.co.uk), opposite Victoria Station, is Britain's leading specialist in student and youth travel. In Australia, try **STA Travel,** 855 George Street, Sydney 2007 (© **02/9212-1255**).

4. **Charter flights** to Ireland are often available at bargain-basement rates, but be prepared for service that may not be up to the same standards as the big airlines. See "Getting There," later in this chapter.

5. **Consider traveling off-season,** when airfares (as well as the price of accommodations) drop substantially. Peak-season fares generally extend from June to late October; prices are low in November, then rise again from mid-December to mid-January; late winter and early spring fares are predictably low. But be advised that winter in Ireland can be truly miserable. May is often the most beautiful month of the year, with lots of sun, warm temperatures, and cheap airfares.

6. Check with travel agents for **air/drive package** deals—double transportation savings. **Sceptre Tours** regularly offers combined airfare, car rental, and/or accommodation packages at very reasonable rates (© **800/221-0924;** www.sceptretours.com).

GETTING AROUND

7. Car rental and gasoline could be your biggest single expense. **Public transportation** is an option for major towns and cities—look up the places you'd like to go in this book to see if they're accessible by bus or train.

8. Travel by rail or bus becomes even cheaper with the **Irish Explorer Pass,** good for unlimited travel for 5 or 8 days throughout the Republic. In Northern Ireland, the **Freedom of Northern Ireland** pass is a recommended money-saver. For itineraries that encompass both the Republic and Northern Ireland, there's the umbrella **Emerald Card,** good on both sides of the border. These may be purchased from **CIE Tours International (www. cietours.com);** tickets must be purchased 3 weeks in advance of the first day of travel. The Emerald Card can also be purchased from any Irish Rail ticket office.

9. Be sure to ask about Bus Eireann (the main Irish bus company) and Irish Rail **promotional midweek, weekend, and excursion fares** when you're buying your ticket.

10. You can save on both transportation and accommodations by booking Bus Eireann **Breakaway** holiday packages. See "Getting Around," later in this chapter.

11. Bus Eireann's **regional day trips** cost far less than driving, and visit a tremendous number of places. Information on these trips is available from local Bus Eireann stations.

12. In Dublin, ask bus drivers or at the Dublin Bus Office or Tourist Office about **city bus discounts** during certain hours of the day.

13. Holders of an International Student Identity Card travel at a 50% discount on trains throughout the Republic with a **Travelsave**

Stamp, obtained from the USIT Office, 19 Aston Quay, Dublin 2. The stamp also provides a 15% discount on bus fares outside Dublin, and substantially reduced weekly transit passes in Dublin.

14. **Regional bus companies** are often cheaper and more direct than Bus Eireann; so, ask at the bus station ticket office to find the cheapest and fastest service to your destination.

15. Always **book your rental car before you arrive in Ireland,** as last-minute rentals can often cost you an arm and a leg. Auto-Europe often has the lowest rates for economy cars. Shop around.

16. If you'll be spending some time in Dublin, try to schedule your car rental so you *don't have a car* during your stay in the city. If, say, you're spending the last week of your trip in Dublin, drop off the car a week early and use public transportation for all your Dublin sightseeing—you'll save a week's rental charges, and spare yourself the worry and hassle of having a car in the city.

17. Some credit cards provide **full collision and theft insurance** for rentals paid with the card. This can save you up to $30 a day, but be sure to be clear with your credit card company about the exact circumstances of the rental, because you don't want to find out the hard way that you aren't covered. *Important note:* Visa discontinued its insurance waiver policy for the Republic of Ireland in 1999, so be certain to verify before departure that your card offers this service *in the Republic of Ireland,* as well as Northern Ireland if you will be traveling there.

18. Consider renting a car with **standard transmission.** With most Irish rental companies automatic transmission isn't available on economy models.

ACCOMMODATIONS

19. **Don't travel alone.** Single rates can cost 10€ to 20€ ($9 to $18) more than what you'd pay for a shared room. During peak season and special events, many B&Bs will charge the full double rate even if there's only one person in the room. Single rooms, when available, are often tiny and substandard.

20. **Hostels** are Ireland's best budget option, and they're as diverse as the people who run them. Many have private rooms at about half the rate you'd pay in the average B&B. All have self-catering kitchens where you can save by preparing your own meals, and an increasing number have their own reasonably priced restaurants. Hostels aren't just for students; although most hostelers are young, you'll also meet families and travelers of all ages.

21. When booking at a B&B consider **forgoing that private bathroom**—this sacrifice can save you 2€ to 6€ ($1.80 to $5.45) on each night's cost.

22. **Renting a self-catering cottage** can be a great budget option, especially for groups and families—the per-person rates are often cheaper than those of B&Bs, especially if you count the money you save by cooking some of your own meals. Rentals are usually weekly, although weekend rentals are sometimes offered.

23. Consider carrying a tent and some basic camping equipment. Ireland has many fine **campgrounds,** with rates averaging about 14€ ($13) for a campsite. Use of a kitchen and showers is usually included in this rate. You can buy a cheap tent once you arrive in Ireland, and campgrounds

sometimes have used equipment for sale.

24. The only instance in which **hotels** become a real budget option is in the case of a few chains, such as Jurys and Forte, which charge *by the room,* not per person. For families or groups willing to share space, these rooms can be cheaper than a B&B, and often offer a great center-city location. Also, if you want to book accommodations for your first night in Ireland but don't want to shell out the bucks for an expensive international call, Jurys has a toll-free number from the United States (© **800/44-UTELL**).

25. Most B&Bs, farmhouses, and guesthouses offer **reductions from 20% all the way up to 50% for children** under the age of 12 sharing a bedroom with their parents. Be sure to confirm the discount when booking. More and more of these accommodations are providing at least one family-size room.

26. Most hostels and B&Bs offer a **discounted weekly rate,** especially during the off-season, and some will even offer a discount for a stay of 2 or 3 nights. You'll benefit by saving the time and hassle of packing and unpacking each day, and you'll also get to know a town in a way you never would as a 1-day visitor.

27. Similarly, many hotels and guesthouses offer 2- and/or 3-day **midweek discounts** that bring the per-person rates down considerably.

28. The tourist board publishes the illustrated booklet *Discover Ireland Holiday Breaks,* which catalogs discount packages that sometimes offer substantial savings. Some apply to low-season months only, and all require stays of more than 1 day.

29. **Bus Eireann and Irish Rail package holidays** also offer substantial discounts on accommodations. See "Getting Around," later in this chapter.

30. As you read through this book, look for the "Ask about possible **discounts to our readers**" in accommodation listings. Reductions can range from 5% to 15%.

DINING

31. **Prepare your own meals** in the kitchen of your hostel or self-catering cottage. Also, consider bringing along **picnic meals** while you're on the road, instead of stopping at a restaurant for lunch.

32. There's an increasing number of **hostel restaurants** that offer good food at budget prices. A few of the better ones are **Mainistir House** (p. 419) on Inishmore (one of the Aran Islands), **Maria's Schoolhouse** (p. 304) in West Cork, and **The Old Monastery** (p. 430) in Letterfrack, County Galway.

33. **Eat your main meal at lunch.** The lunch menu is often affordable at restaurants where dinner would be out of the question.

34. Have your evening meal early to take advantage of **early bird specials** offered by many restaurants between 5:30 and 7pm.

35. Moderately priced **hotel coffee shops** will feed you well at prices far below more expensive hotel dining rooms.

36. Choose **high tea** instead of a dinner menu. Typically, high tea is a "mini-dinner" of only two courses—meat (often in a salad plate) and vegetables, but no soup or dessert. Nowadays, however, high tea is a rather ambiguous term. I've had a high tea that offered more nourishment than I could comfortably handle. On the other hand, I've had a high tea that consisted of one or two skimpy sandwiches and maybe a

sweet. If your B&B or a local restaurant offers high tea, ask what it consists of. Having high tea rather than dinner can save you as much as 50%.

37. Take advantage of the **half-board rate** in B&Bs, guesthouses, and farmhouses, which includes bed, breakfast, and dinner each night at a reduced price.

SIGHTSEEING

38. A **Heritage Card** entitles you to unlimited admission into the more than 50 attractions all over Ireland operated by the Office of Public Works (also known as *Duchas*). These include castles, stately homes, historic monuments, national parks, and more. The card costs 20€ ($18) for adults, 13€ ($12) for seniors, 8€ ($7.25) for children/students, and 47€ ($43) for families. It's available at all Duchas sites, on **www.heritageireland.ie**, or by calling ⓒ **1850/600601** (within Ireland) or 01/647-2461. If you plan to see many of these sights, this is a wise purchase. It's far more pleasant to pick up one of these cards the first time you visit a Heritage site than to realize a week later how much you would have saved if you had.

39. *Ireland at a Glance,* a guide to 100 major Irish attractions, North and South—museums, zoos, castles, historical parks—also contains discount vouchers to each listed site, usually in the form of "buy one, get one free" adult admissions. The current cost of the booklet is 16.45€ ($14.95) ($19.95 in Canada). Contact Britnell Books (ⓒ **800/387-1417;** fax 416-362-9177) to order.

40. Most sightseeing attractions have **family discounts** for parents traveling with two or more children. If they are not posted at the entrance, be sure to ask. Do the math before buying a family ticket, though, because it can be cheaper to buy the individual tickets if you have a small family.

41. **Student discounts** can cut admission prices by as much as 50%— bring a valid student ID. In addition, if you're in the 55-and-older age bracket, never pay an admission fee without asking for the **senior discount** granted by almost all sightseeing highlights.

42. Look for **combination tickets** to closely associated sightseeing attractions. In Dublin, for instance, you can get a combination ticket to the Joyce Tower, the Writer's Museum, and the Shaw Birthplace. (Other combination discounts are noted throughout this book.)

43. Focus your attention on Ireland's **free attractions.** Ireland has far more historic sites than it can afford to develop for tourism, and many of the country's most interesting archaeological remains are there for you to discover. Look out for the many "open sites" mentioned in this guide, and get ready for some great adventures!

SHOPPING

44. **Dunnes' Stores,** located in most major cities and many of the larger towns, is a good chain to look for if you are in need of an extra shirt, skirt, trousers, etc. They carry a good line of clothing at excellent prices.

45. **Seasonal sales** can be real money savers. Large department stores in Dublin, Cork, and Limerick run spring and fall sales with reductions of up to 50%. Sale items often include Waterford glass, Royal Tara china, and the like.

46. Whenever possible, **use credit cards or debit cards.** The exchange rate given by these cards

is often better than that offered in Irish banks, and you don't have to pay a commission (try to choose a bank in your home country that doesn't charge for each use of the debit card).

GENERAL ADVICE

47. Take advantage of **pub meals** at lunch. We've highlighted the best of Ireland's pub grub—it's hard to top a fine bowl of Irish stew served with freshly baked brown bread and pint of stout.

48. Always cash your traveler's checks at a **bank,** or even better, get cash from an ATM. Bureaux de change at airports and elsewhere often charge high commissions and may inflate rates, so avoid them if possible.

49. Instead of using your calling card, use phone cards, sold at most newsstands, for **short international calls.** The advantage of the phone card is that you don't pay anything for the connection, while most calling cards charge $4 to $5 for the first minute. Because the per minute rate is often a bit lower on the calling card than the phone card, especially for daytime calls, it may be cheaper to use a calling card for calls longer than 20 to 30 minutes.

50. Buy all the **film** you're likely to need before you leave home. It'll almost definitely be cheaper, and in the rural areas of Ireland slide film or any film with speeds other than ASA 400 can be hard to come by.

2 The Regions in Brief

The division of Ireland into four provinces dates from the island's earliest recorded history, and is still in use. Broadly speaking, the provinces correspond to the points of the compass: To the north is Ulster, to the east Leinster, to the south Munster, and to the west Connaught. The mythical center of Ireland is the Hill of Uisneach in County Westmeath, from which you can see 20 of the 32 counties. The hill continues to possess resonance for the Irish; James Joyce had his character Stephen Dedalus visit it in the novel *Stephen Hero.*

The island's newest division is that between North and South, a line drawn when Ireland became an independent nation in 1921. The six counties of Northern Ireland remained part of Britain, creating a jagged national border that's been the source of bitter conflict ever since. What was a boundary between counties has become a border between two countries, with the usual practical considerations for the visitor.

Each province is divided into counties: 32 in total, with 26 in the Republic of Ireland and 6 in Northern Ireland. Each county has its own character, sports teams, and strong sense of pride, a fact you're sure to become aware of as you travel from one county to another. The breakdown of counties by province is as follows:

In Ulster to the north: Cavan, Donegal, and Monaghan in the Republic; Antrim, Armagh, Derry, Down, Fermanagh, and Tyrone in Northern Ireland.

In Munster to the south: Clare, Cork, Kerry, Limerick, Tipperary, and Waterford.

In Leinster to the east: Dublin, Carlow, Kildare, Kilkenny, Laois, Longford, Louth, Meath, Offaly, Westmeath, Wexford, and Wicklow.

In Connacht to the west: Sligo, Mayo, Galway, Roscommon, and Leitrim.

In organizing the chapters of this book, we've chosen to define regions that correspond more to the needs of the visitor than to county and provincial boundaries. These regions are the Southeast, the Southwest, the West, the Northwest, the Midlands, and Northern Ireland. Round this off with Ireland's principal cities—Dublin, Cork, and Galway—and you have the principal areas of interest to the visitor.

DUBLIN & ENVIRONS Dublin is ground zero for the profound, high-speed changes transforming Ireland into a prosperous, venturesome European country. What was old and venerable in the city remains so, though it now shares space with an all-out 20- and 30-something Irish renaissance. There's something here for everyone. Within an hour or slightly more north and south of Dublin, either by car or by public transport, lie a handful of engaging coastal towns, the barren beauty of the Dublin Mountains, some of the most important prehistoric and early Christian ruins of Europe, Kildare thoroughbred country, the beaches and lush gardens of County Wicklow, and Wicklow Mountains National Park.

THE SOUTHEAST Boasting the best—read: warmest and least wet—weather in Ireland, the southeast coast is on most days one alternative to a pub for getting out of the rain (but don't expect Hawaii). Besides its weather, the southeast offers sandy beaches, Waterford's city walls and crystal works, Kilkenny and Cahir castles, the Rock of Cashel, the Irish National Heritage Park at Ferrycarig, and Ireland's largest bird sanctuary on the Saltee Islands. The inland Comeragh and Galtee Mountains are gentle hills, hiding some of the country's most beautiful valleys in their folds.

CORK & ENVIRONS Cork, Ireland's second-largest city, is Dublin's rival in sport and stout but little else. All the same, Cork provides a congenial gateway to the south and west of Ireland, which many consider Ireland's Oz—the ultimate destination. Within arm's reach of Cork is the truly impressive Blarney Castle with its less impressive stone, the culinary and scenic delights of Kinsale, the Dromberg Stone Circle, Dursey and Cape Clear Islands, Mizen Head, and the spectacular expanses of West Cork, one of my very favorite landscapes.

THE SOUTHWEST The mountains and seascapes of the southwest, the wettest corner of Ireland, make the same point as Seattle and southeast Alaska: There are more important things in life than staying dry. The once-remote splendors of County Kerry are no longer a secret, so at least during high season, visitors must be prepared to share the view. Some highlights of this region are the Dingle Peninsula, the Skellig and the Blaskett Islands, Staigue Fort, Tralee and its annual international and folk festivals, and dazzling views of sea, shore, and mountains—a new one, it seems, at every bend in the road. Killarney is a world-class destination not for itself but for what lies nearby: its famed lakes, mountain peaks (the tallest in Ireland), and the ever-present sea. The "Ring of Kerry" is a 110-mile (177km) circuit of the Iveragh Peninsula; it's less glamorously known as N70 and N71. Next to the Book of Kells, it is the most visited attraction in Ireland, which is both a recommendation and a warning. Nearby, Killarney National Park—25,000 acres of mountains, woodlands, waterfalls, and wildlife—provides a carless and dramatic haven from tour buses and the din and clatter of massed camera shutters clicking away.

THE WEST The west of Ireland, once a land of last resort, today offers a first and hardly disappointing taste of Ireland's beauty and diversity for those who fly into Shannon Airport. County Clare's natural offerings, including the 700-foot (213m) Cliffs of Moher and the limestone grasslands of the Burren, are unforgettable. Counties Limerick and Clare also contain a number of historic sites, from the Stone Age center at Lough Gur to an array of impressive castles, including Knappogue, Bunratty, King John's, Ashrod, and Dunguaire (which is actually just over the county line in Galway). Farther to the north of Galway lies Mayo, whose most charming attraction may be the town of Westport on Clew Bay. Nearby, though 2,500 feet (762m) up, stands Croagh Patrick, a place of pilgrimage for centuries. Another, more recent pilgrimage site is the shrine of Knock with its massive basilica. Also nearby, off the Connemara and southern Mayo coasts, are a string of islands—Inishbofin, Inishturk, and Clare—that are well worth the crossing. Achill Island, Ireland's largest, is a favored holiday spot and is accessible by car.

GALWAY & ENVIRONS Located on the threshold of Connemara, one of the more desolate inhabitable landscapes in the world, Galway is like an exile's last fling—that is, it defies what lies just around the corner. It's a prospering port and university city, sought out by foreign tourists and Irish youth. There's nothing sleepy about Galway. Just beyond the city stretches Connemara, which boasts (besides the greatest number of rocks you'll ever see in one place) the Twelve Bens, Kylemore Abbey, a nearly 4,000-acre national park, and its charming "capital," the town of Clifden. Meanwhile, offshore, lie the legendary Aran Islands—Inishmore, Inishmaan, and Inisheer—further studies in irresistible desolation.

THE NORTHWEST If bleak is beautiful—and one becomes convinced of this in Ireland—then the northwest surely matches the rest of the country in beauty. This is especially true of Donegal, with its 200 miles (320km) of drenched, jagged coastline that, for the cold-blooded, offers some of the finest surfing in the world. Inland, the Deeryveagh Mountains and Glenveagh National Park offer as much wilderness as can be found anywhere in Ireland. County Sligo, for its part, contains the greatest concentration of megalithic sites in Ireland: the stone circles, passage tombs, dolmens, and cairns of, most notably, Carrowmore, Knocknarea, and Carrowkeel. Also among Sligo's timeless monuments is the poetry of Yeats, a Sligo native. Nearby Leitrim's unspoiled lakes are a favorite retreat, particularly for people carrying fishing poles.

THE MIDLANDS & THE SHANNON The thought of midlands, *any* midlands, is likely to bring yawns, until you get there. The lush center of Ireland, bisected by the mighty but lazy Shannon, is no exception. This is a land of pastures, rivers, lakes, woods, and gentle mountain slopes, an antidote to the barren beauty of Connemara and a retreat, in high season, from the throngs of tourists who crowd the coasts. The midlands have no cities, and their towns are not their attractions; the shores and waters of the Shannon and Lough Derg and of their many lesser cousins provide much of the lure. Outdoor activities—cycling, boating, fishing, trekking, hunting—are at the heart of the matter here, as well as visits to some remarkable sites, such as Birr Castle and its splendid gardens or Clonmacnois, the stunning ruins of a famous Irish monastic center.

NORTHERN IRELAND Northern Ireland's six counties, located across the border, in a corner of both Ireland and the United Kingdom, are well worth an excursion or a stay. The stunning Antrim coast (particularly between Ballycastle and Cushendum), the 37,000 black basalt columns of the Giant's Causeway, and the nine Glens of Antrim are perhaps the greatest draw for sightseers. Written in a minor key is the loveliness of the Fermanagh Lake District to the south, while County Down with its Mourne Mountains marks the sunniest and driest spot in the North. The city walls of Derry, Carrickfergus Castle, Belfast's "Golden Mile," and Navan Fort (or Emain Macha, the royal center of Ulster for 800 years), are only some of the sites and sights, ancient and current, that the North has to offer.

3 Visitor Information & Entry Requirements

SOURCES OF INFORMATION

To get your planning underway, contact the following offices of the Irish Tourist Board and/or the Northern Ireland Tourist Board. They're anxious to answer your questions, and they've got oodles of genuinely helpful information, mostly free of charge. After you've looked at the brochures, take a quick surf through the Web to scoop up even more info.

In addition, the Irish Tourist Board operates an **All-Ireland Accommodations Reservation** number: from the U.S. toll free © **011 800/6686-6866** (within Ireland omit the 011); you can also use © **066/979-2082.**

IN THE UNITED STATES

- **Irish Tourist Board,** 345 Park Ave., New York, NY 10154 (© **800/223-6470** or 212/418-0800; fax 212/371-9052; info@irishtouristboard.com).
- **Northern Ireland Tourist Board,** 551 Fifth Ave., Ste. 701, New York, NY 10176 (© **800/326-0036** or 212/922-0101; fax 212/922-0099; www.discover northernireland.com).

IN CANADA

- There are no walk-in Irish Tourist Board offices in Canada, but it is possible to call the information line in Ireland toll-free on © **800/223-6470.**
- **Northern Ireland Tourist Board,** 2 Bloor Street West, Suite 1501, Toronto, ON, M4W 3–2 (© **416/925-6368;** fax 416/925-6033).

IN THE UNITED KINGDOM

- **Irish Tourist Board/Bord Failte,** 150 New Bond St., London W15 ZAQ (© **0800/039-7000;** fax 020/7493-9065; info@irishtourist board.co.uk).
- **Northern Ireland Tourist Board/All Ireland Desk,** 24 Haymarket, London SW1 Y4DG (© **020/7766-9920**).

IN AUSTRALIA

- **All Ireland Tourism,** 36 Carrington St., 5th Level, Sydney, NSW 2000 (© **02/9299-6177;** fax 02/9299-6323).

IN IRELAND

- The **Irish Tourist Board/Bord Failte** (www.ireland.travel.ie) operates numerous information centers throughout the country. For general information by phone, call © **1850/230330** from within Ireland (a local call from anywhere in the country), or © **066/979-2083;** for accommodations reservations, call © **011 800/6686-6866** (when calling within Ireland omit the 011). **Dublin Tourism** has its headquarters at St. Andrew's Church, Suffolk Street, Dublin 2 (© **066/979-2083;** www.visitdublin.com).
- **Northern Ireland Tourist Board,** 16 Nassau St., Dublin 2 (© **01/679-1977;** fax 01/679-1863; infodublin@nitb.com).

IN NORTHERN IRELAND

- **Irish Tourist Board,** 53 Castle St., Belfast BT1 1GH (© **028/**

9032-7888; fax 028/9024-0201; info@irishtouristboardni.com).

- **Northern Ireland Tourist Board,** St. Anne's Court, 59 North St., Belfast BT1 1NB (© **028/ 9023-1221;** fax 028/9024-0960; VisitorServices@nitb.com).

ENTRY REQUIREMENTS

For citizens of the United States, Canada, Australia, and New Zealand entering the Republic of Ireland for a stay of up to 3 months, no visas are necessary, but a valid passport is required.

Citizens of the United Kingdom, when traveling on flights originating in Britain, do not need to show documentation to enter Ireland. Nationals of the United Kingdom and colonies who were not born in Great Britain or Northern Ireland must have a valid passport or national identity document.

If you're a British citizen born in Great Britain or Northern Ireland, you can travel freely in Ireland without a passport, but I'd strongly advise bringing it along if you have one because on some occasions it may be the only acceptable form of identification (for picking up money orders sent from abroad, etc.). If you're a citizen of any other country, be sure to check with the Irish embassy in your nation to ascertain what (if any) additional documents you may need; you can find information on embassies and consulates at **www.irlgov.ie/iveagh**.

For entry into Northern Ireland, the same conditions apply.

FOR RESIDENTS OF THE UNITED STATES

If you're applying for a first-time passport, you need to do it in person at a U.S. passport office; a federal, state, or probate court; or a major post office (though not all post offices accept applications; call the number below to find the ones that do). You need to present a certified birth certificate as proof of citizenship, and it's wise to bring along your driver's license, state or military ID, and social security card as well. You also need two identical passport-sized photos (2 in. by 2 in.), taken at any corner photo shop (not one of the strip photos, however, from a photo-vending machine).

For people over 15, a passport is valid for 10 years and costs $60; for those 15 and under, it's valid for 5 years and costs $40. If you're over 15 and have a valid passport that was issued within the past 12 years, you can renew it by mail for $40. Allow plenty of time before your trip to apply; processing normally takes 3 weeks but can take longer during busy periods (especially spring). For general information, call the **National Passport Agency** (© 202/647-0518). To find your regional passport office, either check the U.S. State Department website (http://travel.state.gov) or call the **National Passport Information Center** (© 900/225-5674); the fee is 35¢ per minute for automated information and $1.05 per minute for operator-assisted calls.

American Passport Express (© 800/841-6778; www.american passport.com) will process your passport for you in a week for $50, plus the cost of the passport itself ($75 for a renewal; $95 for a first-time or lost passport). If you need the passport in 3 to 4 days, the cost is $100, and for $150 you can receive your passport in 24 hours.

FOR RESIDENTS OF CANADA

Canadian passports are valid for 5 years and cost $60. Children under 16 may be included on a parent's passport but need their own to travel unaccompanied by the parent. Applications, which must be accompanied by two identical passport-sized photographs

Ireland on the Web

Here are some useful and interesting websites relating to Ireland:

- **Go Ireland.** www.goireland.com
- **Interactive Ireland.** www.iol.ie/~discover/
- **The Irish Times Online.** www.ireland.com
- **Irelandseye.com.** www.irelandseye.com
- **Irish Tourist Board (Bord Failte).** www.ireland.travel.ie
- **Island Ireland.** http://islandireland.com/

In addition to these general listings, a number of cities, provinces, and regions have sites of their own on the Internet, providing up-to-date local information. Here are a few of the best of these:

- **Life@Belfast.** www.belfastcity.cjb.net
- **Cork-Guide.** www.cork-guide.ie/corkcity.htm
- **Galway.net homepage.** www.galway.net
- **Web Guide to Sligo.** www.sligo.ie
- **Derry Visitor and Convention Bureau.** www.derryvisitor.com
- **Clare Ireland.** www.clareireland.com/

And some additional sites for Dublin:

- **The Event Guide.** www.eventguide.ie
- **Dublin Tourism.** www.visitdublin.com
- **Sonaco City Guide to Dublin.** www.sonaco.com/cityguide/Dublin/
- **National Concert Hall.** www.nch.ie/home.htm
- **The Ark Centre for Children.** www.ark.ie

and proof of Canadian citizenship, are available at passport offices throughout Canada, post offices, or from the central **Passport Office, Department of Foreign Affairs and International Trade,** Ottawa, Ont. K1A 0G3 (© 800/567-6868; www.dfait-maeci.gc.ca/passport). Processing takes 5 to 10 days if you apply in person, or about 3 weeks by mail.

FOR RESIDENTS OF THE UNITED KINGDOM

As a member of the European Union, you need only an identity card, not a passport, to travel to other EU countries. However, if you already possess a passport, it's always useful to carry it. To pick up an application for a regular 10-year passport (the Visitor's Passport has been abolished), visit your nearest passport office, major post office, or travel agency. You can also contact the **United Kingdom Passport Service** at © 0870/571-0410 or search its website at www.ukpa.gov.uk. Passports are £30 for adults and £16 for children under 16.

FOR RESIDENTS OF IRELAND

You can apply for a 10-year passport, costing 57€ at the **Passport Office,** Setanta Centre, Molesworth Street, Dublin 2 (© 01/671-1633; www.irlgov.ie/iveagh). Those under age 18 and over 65 must apply for a 3-year passport, costing 12€. You can also apply at 1A South Mall, Cork (© 021/272-525) or over the counter at most main post offices.

FOR RESIDENTS OF AUSTRALIA

Apply at your local post office or passport office or search the government website at **www.passports.gov.au**. Passports cost A$136 for adults and A$68 for those under 18. The **Australia State Passport Office** can be reached at © **131232;** travelers must schedule an interview to submit their passport application materials.

FOR RESIDENTS OF NEW ZEALAND

You can pick up a passport application at any travel agency or Link Centre. For more info, contact the **Passport Office,** Dept. of Internal Affairs, P.O. Box 10-526, Wellington (© **0800/ 225-050;** www.passports.govt.nz). Passports are NZ$80 for adults and NZ$40 for those under 16.

4 Money

Currency Ireland, as of January 1, 1999, has adopted the single European currency known as the "euro." First appearing as hard currency on January 1, 2002, it is the actual medium of exchange in the Republic. As of February 9th of 2002, the former unit of currency, the punt, was out of circulation. For abundant information about the changeover visit **www.euro.ie**. The Euro is divided into 100 cents, with coins in denominations of 1, 2, 5, 10, 20, and 50 cents; and 1 and 2 Euros. Notes will be issued in denominations of 5, 10, 20, 50, 100, 200, and 500 Euros.

Remember that the six counties of Northern Ireland, as part of Great Britain, use the British pound, not the Euro. The British currency has notes in denominations of £5, £10, £20,

£50, and £100; coins are issued to the value of 1p, 2p, 5p, 10p, 20p, 50p, £1, and £2. The conversion value for the British pound can be found in chapter 15, "Northern Ireland."

Note: The values of both the Euro and the British pound fluctuate daily, so it's best to begin checking the exchange rates well in advance of your visit so as to gain a sense of their recent range. Once in the country, it's always a gamble when and where to convert and how much. Shop around and avoid exchanging in airports and train stations. ATM's are best, and they're completely ubiquitous in both the Republic of Ireland and the North. Purchases made with a debit card or credit card also offer an exchange rate somewhat more favorable than the banks. In any case, don't convert small

Euro & U.S. Dollar Equivalents

At press time, 1€ equals approximately US$0.91 (or US$1 = 1.10€), and that is the rate of exchange used in calculating the dollar values cited in this book.

€	U.S.$
0.50	.46
1.00	0.91
5.00	4.53
10.00	9.06
50.00	45.30
100.00	90.60

Tips Small Change

When you change money, ask for some small bills or loose change. Petty cash will come in handy for tipping and public transportation. Consider keeping the change separate from your larger bills, so it's readily accessible and you'll be less of a target for theft.

---

amounts daily, as if you were shopping for bread. The fees alone will impoverish you. Rates of exchange are, of course, available daily in most newspapers, and on the Web you can consult **www.x-rates.com**.

ATMs   As an alternative to exchanging currency, you can simply use one of the automated teller machines (ATMs) that are available throughout Ireland. Anyone with a debit or credit card can withdraw currency in Irish pounds. All Bank of Ireland and most Allied Irish Bank (AIB) branches have ATMs that accept Cirrus network cards, as well as MasterCard and Visa; the **PLUS** (✆ **800/843-7587**; www.visa.com) network is supported by many machines but is somewhat less common. Exchange rates are updated daily.

If you plan to use an ATM, be sure you know your four-digit PIN before you leave home and be sure to find out your daily withdrawal limit before you depart. You can also get cash advances on your credit card at an ATM. Keep in mind that credit card companies try to protect themselves from theft by limiting the funds someone can withdraw away from home. It's therefore best to call your credit card company before you leave and let them know where you're going and how much you plan to spend. You'll likely get a favorable exchange rate if you withdraw money from an ATM, but keep in mind that many banks impose a fee every time a card is used at an ATM in a different city or bank. On top of this, the bank from which you withdraw cash may charge its own fee.

CREDIT CARDS   Leading international credit cards such as American Express, MasterCard, and Visa are readily accepted throughout all 32 counties. Other cards, including Carte Blanche and Diners Club, are accepted by the larger hotels and some restaurants. Keep in mind that your credit card company will likely charge a commission (1% or 2%) on every foreign purchase you make. *Important note:* Many small restaurants, B&Bs, and shops operate on a cash-only basis.

TRAVELER'S CHECKS   Traveler's checks are readily accepted in the Republic of Ireland and Northern Ireland, and they bring a better exchange rate than does cash. Hotels, restaurants, and stores also accept traveler's checks, though often at a less-than-favorable rate. *Note:* Personal checks, even when presented with your passport, are not usually accepted by banks or places of business.

You can get traveler's checks at almost any bank. **American Express** offers denominations of $20, $50, $100, $500, and (for cardholders only) $1,000. You'll pay a service charge ranging from 1% to 4%. You can also get American Express traveler's checks over the phone by calling ✆ **800/221-7282;** Amex gold and platinum cardholders who use this number are exempt from the 1% fee. AAA members can obtain checks without a fee at most AAA offices.

Visa offers traveler's checks at Citibank locations nationwide, as well as at several other banks. The service charge ranges between 1.5% and 2%; checks come in denominations of

What Things Cost in Dublin	€	U.S.$
Taxi from the airport to the city center	22.00	20.00
Express bus from airport to city center		4.10
Flat-rate bus fare	1.00	.90
Tram (DART) and bus discount day ticket inside the city		4.60
Local telephone call	.40	.35
Double room at Fitzwilliam Guesthouse (moderate)	121.00	110.00
Double room at Jurys Christchurch (inexpensive)	88.00	80.00
Double room at Kinlay House (budget)	57.00	52.00
Lunch for one at L'Ecrivain (deluxe)	22.00	20.00
Lunch for one at Fitzers (moderate)	15.00	14.00
Lunch for one at Govinda's (inexpensive)	8.00	7.25
Breakfast for one at Bewley's (budget)	5.00	4.55
Dinner for one at Il Primo (moderate)	30.00	27.00
Dinner for one at The Steps of Rome (inexpensive)	15.00	14.00
Pint of Guinness		3.20
Coca-Cola in a cafe		1.35
Cup of coffee		1.15
Roll of Kodacolor film, ASA 400, 36 exposures		7.75
Admission to see the Book of Kells at Trinity College	6.00	5.45
Admission to the National Museum	Free	
Movie ticket	9.00	8.20
Ticket to the Abbey Theatre	18.00	16.00

$20, $50, $100, $500, and $1,000. Call ✆ **800/732-1322** for information. **MasterCard** also offers traveler's checks. Call ✆ **800/223-9920** for a location near you.

5 Health & Insurance

HEALTH   As a general rule, there are no health documents required to enter Ireland or Northern Ireland from the United States, Canada, the United Kingdom, Australia, New Zealand, or most other countries. If in the last 14 days a traveler has visited areas where a contagious disease is prevalent, however, proof of immunization for such disease may be required.

If you worry about getting sick away from home, consider purchasing **medical travel insurance** and carry your ID card in your purse or wallet. In most cases, your existing health

What Things Cost in Galway	€	U.S. $
Flat-rate bus fare	1.00	.90
Local telephone call		.35
Double room at Jurys Inn (moderate)	95.00	86.45
Double room at Roncalli House (inexpensive)	51.00	46.40
Lunch for one at Da Tang Noodle House (inexpensive)	11.00	10.00
Lunch for one at Goya's (budget)		5.90
Dinner for one at Tulsi (moderate)	25.00	22.75
Dinner for one at the River God Café (inexpensive)	17.00	15.45
Pint of Guinness		2.80
Glass of wine		4.05
Coca-Cola in a cafe		1.15
Cup of coffee		1.05
Admission to the Dunguaire Castle		3.45
Admission to Galway Museum		1.15
Cruise on Lough Corrib	8.00	7.25
Round-trip boat to Aran Islands	16.00	15.00
Ticket to the Druid Theatre	16.00	14.55

plan will provide the coverage you need. See the section on insurance earlier in this chapter for more information.

If you suffer from a chronic illness, consult your doctor before your departure. For conditions like epilepsy, diabetes, or heart problems, wear a **Medic Alert Identification Tag** (© 800/ 825-3785; www.medicalert.org), which will immediately alert doctors to your condition and give them access to your records through Medic Alert's 24-hour hotline.

Pack **prescription medications** in your carry-on luggage, and carry prescription medications in their original containers. Also bring along copies of your prescriptions in case you lose your pills or run out. Carry the generic name of prescription medicines, in case a local pharmacist is unfamiliar with the brand name.

And don't forget sunglasses and an extra pair of contact lenses or prescription glasses.

Contact the **International Association for Medical Assistance to Travelers (IAMAT)** (© 716/754-4883 or 416/652-0137; www.sentex. net/~iamat) for tips on travel and health concerns in the countries you're visiting, and lists of local, English-speaking doctors. The United States **Centers for Disease Control and Prevention** (© 800/311-3435; www.cdc.gov) provides up-to-date information on necessary vaccines and health hazards by region or country (Their booklet, *Health Information for International Travel,* is $25 by mail; on the Internet, it's free). Any foreign consulate can provide a list of area doctors who speak English. If you require the services of a physician, dentist, or other health professional during your stay in Ireland, your accommodations host may be in the best position to recommend someone local.

TRAVEL INSURANCE AT A GLANCE

Check your existing insurance policies before you buy travel insurance to cover trip cancellation, lost luggage, medical expenses, or car rental insurance. You're likely to have partial or complete coverage. But if you need some, ask your travel agent about a comprehensive package. The cost of travel insurance varies widely, depending on the cost and length of your trip, your age and overall health, and the type of trip you're taking. Insurance for extreme sports or adventure travel, for example, will cost more than coverage for a cruise. Some insurers provide packages for specialty vacations, such as skiing or backpacking. More dangerous activities may be excluded from basic policies.

For information, contact one of the following popular insurers:

- **Access America** (℗ 800/284-8300); www.accessamerica.com/)
- **Travel Guard International** (℗ 800/826-1300; www.travelguard.com)
- **Travel Insured International** (℗ 800/243-3174; www.travelinsured.com)
- **Travelex Insurance Services** (℗ 800/228-9792; www.travelex-insurance.com)

TRIP-CANCELLATION INSURANCE (TCI)

There are three major types of trip-cancellation insurance—one, in the event that you pre-pay a cruise or tour that gets cancelled, and you can't get your money back; a second when you or someone in your family sets sick or dies, and you can't travel (but be aware that you may not be covered for a pre-existing condition); and a third,

when bad weather makes travel impossible. Some insurers provide coverage for events like jury duty; natural disasters close to home, like floods or fire; even the loss of a job. A few have added provisions for cancellations due to terrorist activities. Always check the fine print before signing on, and don't buy trip-cancellation insurance from the tour operator that may be responsible for the cancellation; buy it only from a reputable travel insurance agency. Don't overbuy. You won't be reimbursed for more than the cost of your trip.

MEDICAL INSURANCE

Most health insurance policies cover you if you get sick away from home—but check, particularly if you're insured by an HMO. With the exception of certain HMOs and Medicare/Medicaid, your medical insurance should cover medical treatment—even hospital care—overseas. However, most out-of-country hospitals make you pay your bills up front, and send you a refund after you've returned home and filed the necessary paperwork. Members of **Blue Cross/Blue Shield** can now use their cards at select hospitals in most major cities worldwide (℗ **800/810-BLUE** or www.bluecares.com/blue/bluecard/wwn for a list of hospitals).

Some credit cards (American Express and certain gold and platinum Visa and MasterCards, for example) offer automatic flight insurance against death or dismemberment in case of an airplane crash if you charged the cost of your ticket.

If you require additional insurance, try one of the following companies:

- **MEDEX International**, (℗ 888/MEDEX-00 or 410/453-6300; fax 410/453-6301; www.medexassist.com; 9515 Deereco Rd., Timonium, MD 21093-5375)

Planning an Irish Wedding

For those with Irish roots, getting married on the auld sod has become an extremely popular, romantic way to kick off your new life together. The basic requirements for getting married in Ireland can be found on the Dublin info page on the U.S. Embassy website at **http://www. usembassy.ie/consulate/marriage.html**. For help finding the perfect church, reception hall, florist, and band, visit **www.anirishwedding.ie**, **www.wedding-ireland.com**, or **www.weddingsonline.ie**.

- **Travel Assistance International** (© **800/821-2828;** www.travel assistance.com), 9200 Keystone Crossing, Suite 300, Indianapolis, IN 46240 (for general information on services, call the company's Worldwide Assistance Services, Inc., at © **800/777-8710**).

The cost of travel medical insurance varies widely. Check your existing policies before you buy additional coverage. Also, check to see if your medical insurance covers you for emergency medical evacuation: If you have to buy a one-way same-day ticket home and forfeit your nonrefundable roundtrip ticket, you may be out big bucks.

LOST-LUGGAGE INSURANCE

On international flights (including US portions of international trips), baggage is limited to approximately $9.07 per pound, up to approximately $635 per checked bag. If you plan to check items more valuable than the standard liability, you may purchase "excess valuation" coverage from the airline, up to $5,000. Be sure to take any valuables or irreplaceable items with you in your carry-on luggage. If you file a lost luggage claim, be

prepared to answer detailed questions about the contents of your baggage, and be sure to file a claim immediately, as most airlines enforce a 21-day deadline. Before you leave home, compile an inventory of all packed items and a rough estimate of the total value to ensure you're properly compensated if your luggage is lost. You will only be reimbursed for what you lost, no more. Once you've filed a complaint, persist in securing your reimbursement; there are no laws governing the length of time it takes for a carrier to reimburse you. If you arrive at a destination without your bags, ask the airline to forward them to your hotel or to your next destination; they will usually comply. If your bag is delayed or lost, the airline may reimburse you for reasonable expenses, such as a toothbrush or a set of clothes, but the airline is under no legal obligation to do so.

Lost luggage may also be covered by your homeowner's or renter's policy. Many platinum and gold credit cards cover you as well. If you choose to purchase additional lost-luggage insurance, be sure not to buy more than you need. Buy in advance from the insurer or a trusted agent (prices will be much higher at the airport).

6 When to Go

THE CLIMATE The Atlantic brings along with it the Gulf Stream's warming currents to create a climate that deals in moderation rather than extremes—temperatures are seldom more than 65°F in July or August (occasionally "soaring" to 70°F) or less than 40°F in January or February.

Ireland is notoriously wet, and you should always be prepared for a

Average Monthly Temperatures in Dublin

	Jan	Feb	Mar	Apr	May	June	July	Aug	Sept	Oct	Nov	Dec
Temp (°F)	36–46	37–48	37–49	38–52	42–57	46–62	51–66	50–65	48–62	44–56	39–49	38–47
Temp (°C)	2–8	3–9	3–9	3–11	6–14	8–17	11–19	10–18	9–17	7–13	4–9	3–8

shower. The saving grace of Ireland's weather is that nothing lasts for long—most days bring a rapidly changing succession of conditions, and it's a rare day when you don't see the sun at least once.

Despite this changeability, though, there are some patterns. March, April, and May tend to be the driest months, while December and January have the most rain. The western side of the country also gets more rain and wind than the east, because the western hills force rain-laden clouds to rise and discharge their moisture.

When packing, remember that even the summers can be chilly, and that dampness tends to accentuate the cold. Wool and Polartec (or similar materials) are good, versatile choices, and a trusty raincoat/windbreaker is a must.

For a complete guide to Irish weather on the Web, including year-round averages and daily updates, consult **www.iol.ie/~discover/meteo1.htm**.

HOLIDAYS In the Republic, the whole country shuts down for these national holidays: January 1 (New Year's Day); March 17 (St. Patrick's Day); Good Friday and Easter Monday; May Day (the first Monday in May); the first Monday in June and August (summer bank holidays); the last Monday in October (autumn bank holiday); December 25 (Christmas Day); and December 26 (St. Stephen's Day). In the North, the schedule of holidays is the same as in the Republic, with a few exceptions: the North's bank holidays fall on the last Mondays of May and August; the Battle of the Boyne is celebrated on Orangeman's Day (July 12); and Boxing Day (December 27), not St. Stephen's Day, follows Christmas.

Also, some towns observe an "early closing day," with shops closing at 1pm; because the day of the week varies from community to community, be sure to inquire if you have shopping to do.

IRELAND CALENDAR OF EVENTS

Most of the exact dates for events in the years 2002 and 2003 had not yet been set at press time, so where those dates were not available, I used the dates from 2001. The actual dates may change by a few days each year; consult the calendars available from the tourist boards of Ireland and of Northern Ireland before you leave home.

For a calendar of events in Dublin, see p. 44.

January

Easter Walking Festival. The Connemara Walking Centre hosts several "walking festivals" throughout the year: these are 4 to 5 day programs of classic day hikes, mostly in mountainous country or sites of archaeological significance. Contact Michael Gibbons, Connemara Walking Centre (© **095/21379;** fax 095/21845; www.walkingireland.com). The first festival of 2002 will take place over the Easter weekend (last weekend of March).

Coca-Cola International Cross-Country. The International Amateur Athletics Federation world competition race is 5 miles (8km) long. Usually, there is an open race that is run simultaneously and is open to any athlete. Barnett's Park, Belfast. Call © **028/9060-2707;** fax 028/9030-9939. January 19.

February

All Ireland Dancing Championships. Traditional Irish ceili dancing. West County Hotel, Ennis,

County Clare. Contact Irish Dancing Commission (© **01/475-2220;** fax 01/475-1053). First or second week in February.

21st Cavan International Song Festival. An international competition for original (popular) songs. Hotel Kilmore, Cavan, County Cavan. Contact Maire Maloney (© **049/433-1604;** fax 049/32237). February 20 to 21.

March

Belfast Musical Festival. Held every year since 1911, this is a youth competition in speech, music, and drama categories. Balmoral, Belfast. Contact Desmond Shaw (© **028/ 9066-8944**). March 1 to 13.

Celtic Spring Festival. A cultural feast whose menu includes a drama festival and a celebration of the Irish language. Derry City. Contact Nuala McGee (© **028/7136- 5151**). March 7 to 24.

St. Patrick's Day. Traditionally a quiet religious holiday in Ireland, St. Patrick's Day has come to be a major public event, largely in imitation of spectacles such as the New York and Boston parades. All over Ireland, North and South. March 17.

Inishowen Traditional Singers Circle—13th Annual International Folk Song and Ballad Seminar. Ballyliffen and Clonmany, County Donegal. The theme for 2002 is "Rural Songs and Urban Ballads." Contact Jimmy MacBride, 66 The Woods, Buncrana (© **077/ 61210;** jimmymcb@iol.ie; http:// sites.netscape.net/milnerconroy/inis howenseminar). March 22 to 25.

World Irish Dancing Championships. Location varies. The premier international competition in Irish Dancing, with contenders from as far as New Zealand. Contact Irish Dancing Commission (© **01/475-2220;** fax 01/475- 1053). Late March or early April.

April

AA Circuit of Ireland Rally. An international cycling race starting from Bangor, County Down, and finishing in Tallaght, County Dublin. Contact Mrs. Hilary Maginnis (© **028/9042-6262**). April 2 to 5.

Tour of the North. Cyclists from Britain, Ireland, and continental Europe compete in this race beginning in Ballyclare. Contact Bobbie Currie (© **028/2564-7205**). April 2 to 6.

Irish National Surfing Championships—Main Event. Surf's up and Ireland's finest are here. Castlegregory, County Kerry. Contact Zoe Lally (© **096/49428;** fax 096/ 49020). April 3 and 4.

Samhlaíocht Chiarrai/Kerry Arts Festival. A spring festival of music, drama, dance, film, literature, craft, and visual art. Contact Maurice Galway (© **066/712-9934;** fax 066/ 712-0934; samhlaiochtchiarrai@ eircom.net). First or second week in April.

North-West Storytelling Festival. A spellbinding celebration of stories from the spinners of Ireland's tallest tales. Derry City. Contact Jenny Ross (© **028/7126-6946**). April 27 to May 1.

Cork International Choral Festival. Ireland's premier choral event, featuring competitive and noncompetitive performances by adult choirs of international standing, as well as performances by Irish and foreign dance groups. Multiple venues in Cork. Contact John Fitzpatrick (© **021/430-8308;** fax 021/430-8309; chorfest@iol.ie). April 29 to May 2.

May

Belfast City Marathon. An epic race with 6,000 runners participating. Start and finish at Maysfield, Belfast. Call © **028/9027-0345**

or visit **www.belfastcity.gov.uk/ marathon**. First week in May.

County Wicklow Gardens Festival. Heritage properties and gardens, as well as many private properties, open their gates to visitors on selected dates. Throughout County Wicklow and surrounding areas. Contact Wicklow County Tourism (✆ **0404/66058;** fax 0404/66057). May 14 to July 11.

Sligo Arts Festival. A burst of music, street events, and exhibitions spread across 30 sites in renascent Sligo town. Contact Danny Kirrane (✆ **0471/69802**). May 27 to June 7.

June

Edenderry Three-Day Canal Angling Festival. A festival organized by the Edenderry Coarse Angling Club to promote angling in the area. Tourists are welcome to take part, provided they book in advance. Canals around Edenderry, County Offaly. Contact Pauric Kelly (✆ **0405/32071** or 087/245-8275). First or second week in June.

AIB Music Festival in Great Irish Houses. A series of classical music concerts in great houses throughout Ireland. Contact Crawford Tipping, Blackrock Post Office, County Dublin (✆ **01/278-1528;** fax 01/278-1529). June 10 to 20.

Feis na nGleann. A festival of traditional Irish music, dance, poetry, crafts, and sports. A chance to see a number of traditional Gaelic games. Ballycastle, County Antrim. Contact Paddy J. Clerkin Sr., 61 Coast Rd., Cushendall (✆ **028/ 2177-1349**). Mid- to late June.

Sense of Cork Arts Festival. A celebration of music, theater, literature, and visual art throughout Ireland's second city. Contact Hilary O'Malley (✆ **021/310597;** fax 021/314033). June 23 to July 4.

Budweiser Irish Derby. One of the richest races in Europe and widely accepted as the definitive European middle-distance classic, this race is Ireland's version of the Kentucky Derby or Royal Ascot. It's a fashionable gathering of racing fans from all over Ireland and abroad. Curragh, County Kildare. For full information, contact the Curragh Racecourse Office, the Curragh, County Kildare (✆ **045/441205;** fax 054/441442). *Note:* An Irish Racing Calendar for each calendar year is also available from the Irish Tourist Board. June 27.

Murphy's Irish Open Golf Championship. This is Ireland's premier international golf event, televised to over 90 countries and featuring the world's top players. Venue changes annually. For details, contact the Golfing Union of Ireland (✆ **01/ 269-4111;** fax 01/269-5368; www. gui.ie). Last week of June or first week of July.

July

Battle of the Boyne Commemoration. This annual event, sometimes called Orangeman's Day, recalls the historic battle between two 17th-century kings and is a national day of parades and celebration all over Northern Ireland. Belfast and 18 other centers. Contact the House of Orange, 65 Dublin Rd., Belfast BT2 7HE (✆ **028/9032-2801**). July 12.

Galway Arts Festival and Races. A 2-week feast in the streets of Galway, featuring international theater, big-top concerts, literary evenings, street shows, arts, parades, music, and more, followed by 5 days of racing and more merriment, music, and song. Galway City and Racecourse. Contact Elizabeth McDonagh (✆ **091/509700;** fax 091/562655; www.galwayartsfestival.ie). Mid- to late-July.

Lughnasa Fair. A spectacular revival set in a 12th-century Norman castle. Costumed magicians, entertainment, and crafts. Carrickfergus Castle, County Antrim. Contact Gerard Treacy (℃ **028/ 9335-1273**). July 24.

August

International Maiden of the Mournes Festival. With the Mountains of Mourne as its setting, this festival includes concerts, music, dance, cabaret, banquets, and the crowning of the Maiden of the Mournes. Warrenpoint, County Down. Contact Liz Boyle (℃ **028/ 4177-3556**). August 1 to 15.

Puck Fair. Each year the residents of this tiny Ring of Kerry town carry on an ancient tradition by capturing a wild goat and enthroning it as "king" over 2 days of unrestricted merrymaking. Killorglin, County Kerry. Contact Brid Moriarty (℃ **066/976-2366**; fax 066/976-2059). August 10 to 12.

Kilkenny Arts Festival. This 1-week festival features a broad spectrum of the arts, from classical and traditional music to plays, one-person shows, readings, films, poetry, and visual arts exhibitions. Kilkenny. Contact Maureen Kennelly (℃ **056/63663**; fax 056/ 51704). August 13 to 22.

Rose of Tralee International Festival. A carnival-like atmosphere prevails at this 5-day event, with a full program of concerts, street entertainment, horse races, and a beauty/talent pageant leading up to the selection of the "Rose of Tralee." Tralee, County Kerry. Contact Eileen Kenny or Eleanor Carrick, Rose of Tralee Festival Office, Ashe Memorial Hall, Denny Street, Tralee, County Kerry (℃ **066/712-1322**; fax 066/712-2654). Late August.

Fleadh Cheoil na hÉireann 2002. This is Ireland's major summer festival of traditional music, with competitions to select the all-Ireland champions in all categories of instruments and singing. The venue changes each year. The 2002 Fleadh Cheoil na hÉireann will take place in Listowel, County Kerry. Contact Comhaltas Ceoltoiri Éireann (℃ **01/280-0295**; fax 01/ 280-3759). Late August.

Lisdoonvarna Matchmaking Festival. Come and see how the pros do it. Lisdoonvarna, County Clare. Contact James or Marcus White (℃ **065/707-4005**; fax 065/707-4406; www.matchmakerireland. com). August 27 to October 3.

Oul' Lammas Fair. Chartered in 1606, this is Ireland's oldest continuous fair, featuring horse and sheep sales and hundreds of street stalls. Ballycastle, County Antrim. Contact Ballycastle Tourist Information (℃ **028/2076-2024**). August 30 and 31.

September

Cape Clear Island International Storytelling Festival. Performances and workshops on a magically beautiful island that inspires stories of its own. Cape Clear Island, County Cork. Contact Chuck Kruger (℃/fax **028/39157**). September 3 to 5.

Searching for the Elusive Irish Ancestor. An annual conference based in Belfast and focused on family history and on practical research in the main genealogical archives in Ireland. Includes lectures, tours, and entertainment. For information, check out **www. uhf.org.uk**. Late September.

Galway International Oyster Festival. First held in 1954, this event attracts oyster aficionados from all over the globe. Highlights include the World Oyster-Opening Championship, golf tournament, yacht race, art exhibition, gala banquet, traditional music and song, and lots of oyster eating. Galway and environs. Ann Flanagan (℡ **091/522066;** fax 091/527282; oysters@indigo.ie). September 23 to 26.

October

Derry City Two Cathedrals Festival. Derry City. 2002 marks the eleventh year of this extraordinary celebration of harmony and counterpoint between Derry's Catholic and Protestant Cathedrals. The combined-cathedrals Festival Chorus is joined by international musical luminaries in a 2-week world-class concert series. Contact Dermot Carlin (℡ **028/7126-8335**). October 9 to 23.

Cork International Film Festival. Hosted by theatrical venues across the city, this world-renowned film festival offers screenings of features, documentaries, short films, and special programs. Contact Georgia Hopkins (℡ **021/271711;** fax 021/275945). October 10 to 17.

Wexford International Festival Opera. For fifty years, the Wexford Festival has presented three major productions of operatic rarities along with popular opera, recitals, and lunchtime concerts, all part of a festival described by critics as "one of the most remarkable in the world." Held every October/November; for precise dates contact Wexford Festival Opera (℡ **053/22144;** fax 053/47438; www.wexfordopera.com).

Guinness Cork Jazz Festival. Ireland's No. 2 city hosts a first-rate festival of jazz. (Meanwhile, not to be outdone, nearby Kinsale hosts its own fringe jazz festival.) Cork City (and Kinsale). Contact Ray

Fitzgerald (℡ **021/278979;** fax 021/270463). October 22 to 25.

Banks of the Foyle Halloween Festival. A colorful riverside carnival of clowns, buskers, and street theater, with a spectacular fireworks display on the 31st. Derry City. Contact Nuala McGee, Derry City Council (℡ **028/7136-1515**). October 27 to November 6.

Belfast Festival at Queens. Ulster's best-known arts festival, this annual 19-day event attracts a huge following to enjoy drama, opera, music, and film events in and around Queens University, Belfast. Contact Rosie Turner, Festival House, 25 College Gardens, Belfast BT9 6BS (℡ **028/9066-7687;** fax 028/9066-5577). October 29 to November 14.

November

Foyle Film Festival. Derry, County Derry. Northern Ireland's largest film festival features screenings of works by local, national, and international film makers. Venues change annually. For information contact **The Nerve Centre** (℡ **028/7126-7432;** fax: 028/7137-1738) or visit the festival web site at **www.foylefilmfestival.com.** Ten days in mid-November.

December

Cinemagic International Film Festival for Young People. Ten-day festival of short and feature-length films for children and teenagers. Various venues throughout the North. Contact Frances Cassidy, 4th Floor, 38 Dublin Rd., Belfast BT2 7HN (℡ **028/9031-1900**). Early December.

Woodford Mummers Feile. A festival of traditional music, song, dance, and mime performed by mummers in traditional costume. Woodford, County Galway. Contact Marie McMahon (℡ **0509/49248**). December 26 to 27.

DUBLIN CALENDAR OF EVENTS

January

Dublin International Theatre Symposium. Samuel Beckett Centre, Trinity College, Dublin 2. Contact Mary O'Donovan (℗ 01/280-0544; fax 01/239-0918; pan pan@iol.ie). Early January.

February

Rugby International, Five Nations Tournament. In this prestigious international rugby tournament, Ireland plays either France and England or Wales and Scotland at home. If you can't get tickets, join the rowdy crowd watching the matches at the local pub. Landsdowne Road, Ballsbridge. Contact Irish Rugby Football Union, 62 Lansdowne Rd., Dublin 4 (℗ 01/668-4601; fax 01/660-5640). February through April.

March

The National St. Patrick's Day Festival. Street theater, fireworks, music, and other festivities culminating in Ireland's grandest parade, with marching bands, drill teams, floats, and delegations from around the world. Dublin. Contact Veronica Taylor, Festival Office, St. Stephen's Green House, Earlsfort Terrace, Dublin 2 (℗ 01/676-3205; fax 01/676-3208; www.stpatricksday.ie). March 15 to 18.

Dublin Film Festival. The best in Irish and international cinema. More than 100 films are featured, with screenings of the best of Irish and world cinema, plus seminars and lectures on filmmaking. Cinemas throughout Dublin. Contact: **www.iol.ie/dff/**. April.

June

AIB Music Festival in Great Irish Houses. This is a continuous 10-day festival of classical music performed by leading Irish and international artists in some of the Dublin area's great Georgian buildings and mansions. Various venues throughout Dublin and neighboring Counties Wicklow and Kildare. Contact Crawford Tipping, Blackrock Post Office, County Dublin (℗ 01/278-1528; fax 01/278-1529). June 10 to 20.

Bloomsday. Dublin's unique day of festivity commemorates 24 hours in the life of Leopold Bloom, the central character of James Joyce's *Ulysses*. Every aspect of the city, including the menus at restaurants and pubs, seeks to duplicate the aromas, sights, sounds, and tastes of Dublin on June 16, 1904. Special ceremonies are held at the James Joyce Tower and Museum, and there are guided walks of Joycean sights. The streets of Dublin and various venues. Contact the James Joyce Centre, 35 N. Great George's St., Dublin 1 (℗ 01/878-8547; fax 01/878-8488; www.jamesjoyce.ie). June 12 to 17.

July

Summer Schools. Study sessions meeting in Dublin include the Irish Theatre Summer School in conjunction with the Gaiety School of Acting at Trinity College, the Synge Summer School in County Wicklow, the James Joyce Summer School at Newman House, and the International Summer Schools in Irish Studies at Trinity College and the National University of Ireland. Contact the Irish Tourist Board. July and August.

Dun Laoghaire Festival. A week-long celebration in the seafront suburb of Dun Laoghaire, 7 miles (11km) south of Dublin, with arts and crafts, concerts, band recitals, sports events, and talent competitions. Mid-July.

Guinness Blues Festival. Dublin's "West Bank" plays host to bands from England, Ireland, and the United States, offering more than 200 hours of blues performances, films, and workshops, including a free open-air concert at College Green and a "blues trail" of free live blues in 18 different pubs. Streets and pubs, Temple Bar area. Contact Lisa Tinley (℡ **01/497-0381;** fax 01/491-0631). July 23 to 25.

August

Kerrygold Horse Show. This is the principal sporting and social event on the Irish national calendar, attracting visitors from all parts of the world. More than 2,000 horses, the cream of Irish bloodstock, are entered for this show, with dressage, jumping competitions each day, and more. Highlights include a fashionable ladies' day (don't forget your hat!), formal hunt balls each evening, the Kerrygold Nation's Cup competition, and the awarding of the Aga Khan Trophy by the president of Ireland. RDS Showgrounds, Ballsbridge. Contact Niamh Kelly, RDS, Merrion Road, Ballsbridge, Dublin 4 (℡ **01/668-0866;** fax 01/660-4014; www.rds.ie). Second week of August.

Summer Music Festival. St. Stephen's Green is the setting for this series of free lunchtime band concerts of popular and Irish traditional music, as well as afternoon open-air performances of Shakespearean plays, sponsored by the Office of Public Works. Last 2 weeks of August.

September

All-Ireland Hurling and Football Final. Tickets must be obtained months in advance for these two national amateur sporting events, the equivalent of Super Bowls for Irish national sports. Croke Park, Dublin 3. Contact the Gaelic Athletic Association (℡ **01/836-3222;** fax

01/836-6420). Two weekends in September; dates vary from year to year.

Irish Antique Dealers' Fair. Annual show sponsored jointly by the RDS and the Irish Antique Dealers' Association. This is Ireland's premier annual antiques fair. RDS Showgrounds, Ballsbridge. Contact Louis O'Sullivan (℡ **01/ 285-9294**). September 29 to October 3.

October

Dublin Theatre Festival. A world-class theater festival showcasing new plays by Irish authors and presenting a range of productions from abroad. Theaters throughout Dublin. Contact Tony O Dálaigh, director, 47 Nassau St., Dublin 2 (℡ **01/677-8439;** fax 01/679-7709). October 4 to 16.

Dublin City Marathon. More than 3,000 runners from both sides of the Atlantic and the Irish Sea participate in this popular run through the streets of Dublin. Dublin city center. For entry forms and information, contact the Irish Tourist Board (℡ **01/602-4000;** fax 01/475-8046). October 25.

December

Dublin Grand Opera. This is the second half of Dublin's twice-yearly operatic fling, with great works presented by the Dublin Grand Opera Society at the Gaiety Theatre. Gaiety Theatre, S. King Street, Dublin 2 (℡ **01/677-1717**). Early December.

National Crafts Fair of Ireland. Retail crafts fair, displaying the work of Ireland's finest craftworkers. RDS Showgrounds, Ballsbridge, Dublin. Contact Patrick O'Sullivan (℡ **01/867-1517;** fax 01/878-6276). December 15 to 19.

Christmas Horse Racing Festival. Three days of winter racing for thoroughbreds. Leopardstown Race track. December 26 to 29.

7 Tips for Travelers with Special Needs

TRAVELERS WITH DISABILITIES

The best source of information on accessible accommodation in Ireland is the **Irish Tourist Board.** All Irish Tourist Board accommodation brochures indicate whether the rooms and facilities at each property are wheelchair accessible. The information in *Be Our Guest,* their guide to hotels and guesthouses, is particularly complete and up-to-date; this information is also available online at **www.beourguest.ie,** which is a particularly handy, searchable site. Unfortunately, not all of the tourist board's publications are as reliable, because many of them are based on information from 2000, the last year that a comprehensive survey of accessible accommodation was completed. Also, at present, there does not exist a complete list of accessible accommodation in Ireland; hopefully this gap will soon be filled by the Tourist Board.

The **Irish Wheelchair Association,** 24 Blackheath Dr., Clontarf, Dublin 3 (© **01/833-8241**), loans free wheelchairs to travelers in Ireland. A donation is appreciated. Branch offices are at Parnell Street, Kilkenny (© **056/ 62775**); White Street, Cork (© **021/ 966354**); Henry Street, Limerick (© **061/313691**); and Dominick Street, Galway (© **091/771550**), as well as in a range of smaller towns.

If you plan to travel by rail in Ireland be sure to check out Irish Rail's website at **www.irishrail.ie**, which provides information on how to order a service guide for mobility impaired travelers.

For advice on travel to Northern Ireland, contact **Disability Action,** 189 Airport Rd West., Belfast BT3 9€D (© **028/9029-7880;** www. disabilityaction.org). The Northern Ireland Tourist Board also publishes a helpful annual *Information Guide to Accessible Accommodation,* available from any of its offices worldwide.

There are also plenty of sources of help and information in the United States.

AGENCIES/OPERATORS

- **Flying Wheels Travel** (© **800/ 535-6790;** www.flyingwheels travel.com) offers escorted tours and cruises that emphasize sports and private tours in minivans with lifts.
- **Access Adventures** (© **716/889-9096**), a Rochester, New York–based agency, offers customized itineraries for a variety of travelers with disabilities.
- **Accessible Journeys** (© **800/ TINGLES** or 610/521-0339; www.disabilitytravel.com) caters specifically to slow walkers and wheelchair travelers and their families and friends.

ORGANIZATIONS

- **The Moss Rehab Hospital** (© **215/456-9603,** www.moss resourcenet.org) provides friendly, helpful phone assistance through its **Travel Information Service**.
- **The Society for Accessible Travel and Hospitality** (© **212/447-7284,** fax 212-725-8253; www. sath.org) offers a wealth of travel resources for all types of disabilities and informed recommendations on destinations, access guides, travel agents, tour operators, vehicle rentals, and companion services. Annual membership costs $45 for adults; $30 for seniors and students.
- **The American Foundation for the Blind** (© **800/232-5463;** www.afb.org) provides information on traveling with Seeing Eye dogs.

PUBLICATIONS

- **Mobility International USA** (© 541/343-1284; www.miusa. org) publishes *A World of Options*, a 658-page book of resources, covering everything from biking trips to scuba outfitters, and a biannual newsletter, *Over the Rainbow*. Annual membership is $35.
- **Twin Peaks Press** (© 360/694-2462) publishes travel-related books for travelers with special needs.
- ***Open World for Disability and Mature Travel*** magazine, published by the Society for Accessible Travel and Hospitality (see above), is full of good resources and information. A year's subscription is $13 ($21 outside the U.S.).

SENIORS

Seniors, known in Ireland and Northern Ireland as old-age pensioners (OAPs), enjoy a variety of discounts and privileges. Native OAPs ride the public transport system free of charge, but this privilege does not extend to tourists. Visiting seniors can avail themselves of other discounts, particularly on admission to attractions and theaters. Always ask about a senior discount if special rates are not posted; the discount is usually 10%.

The Irish Tourist Board publishes a list of reduced-rate hotel packages for seniors, ***Golden Holidays/For the Over 55s.*** The brochure listing these packages is currently available only from tourist board offices within Ireland.

Members of **AARP** (formerly known as the American Association of Retired Persons), 601 E St. NW, Washington, DC 20049 (© **800/424-3410** or 202/434-2277; www. aarp.org), get discounts on hotels, airfares, and car rentals. AARP offers members a wide range of benefits, including *Modern Maturity* magazine and a monthly newsletter. Anyone over 50 can join.

AGENCIES/OPERATORS

Some tour operators in the United States give notable senior discounts. **CIE Tours International** (© **800/243-8687** or 973/292-3438; www. cietours.com), which specializes in Ireland and Northern Ireland, gives a $75 discount to travelers age 55 and up who book early on selected departures of regular tour programs. Other options include:

- **Grand Circle Travel** (© **800/221-2610** or 617/350-7500; www.gct.com) offers package deals for the 50-plus market, mostly of the tour-bus variety, with free trips thrown in for those who organize groups of 10 or more.
- **SAGA Holidays** (© **800/343-0273;** www.sagaholidays.com) offers inclusive tours and cruises for those 50 and older. SAGA also offers a number of single-traveler tours and sponsors the "Road Scholar Tours" (© **800/621-2151;** e-mail: sales info@saga holidays.com), vacations with an educational bent. Order a free brochure from the website.
- **Elderhostel** (© **877/426-8056;** www.elderhostel.org) arranges study programs for those aged 55 and over (and a spouse or companion of any age) in the U.S. and in more than 80 countries around the world. Most courses last 5 to 7 days in the U.S. (2 to 4 weeks abroad), and many include airfare, accommodations in university dormitories or modest inns, meals, and tuition.
- **Interhostel** (© **800/733-9753;** www.learn.unh.edu/interhostel), organized by the University of New Hampshire, also offers educational travel for senior citizens. On these escorted tours, the days are packed with seminars, lectures, and field trips, with sightseeing led by academic

experts. **Interhostel** takes travelers 50 and over (with companions over 40), and offers one- and two-week trips, mostly international.

PUBLICATIONS

- *The Book of Deals* is a collection of more than 1,000 senior discounts on airlines, lodging, tours, and attractions around the country; it's available for $9.95 by calling ℂ **800/460-6676**.
- *101 Tips for the Mature Traveler* is available from Grand Circle Travel (ℂ **800/221-2610** or 617/350-7500; fax 617/346-6700).
- *The 50+ Traveler's Guidebook* (St. Martin's Press).
- *Unbelievably Good Deals and Great Adventures That You Absolutely Can't Get Unless You're Over 50* (Contemporary Publishing Co.).

STUDENTS, TEACHERS & YOUTH

With almost half of its population under age 25, Ireland is well geared to students, whether you're planning to study there or are just passing through.

The country has a distinguished and vital academic tradition. Dublin alone is home to three universities—Trinity College Dublin, University College Dublin, and Dublin University—and to many other fine schools and institutes. Campuses of the National University of Ireland are located in Cork, Limerick, Galway, and Maynooth. In Northern Ireland, the leading universities are Queen's University in Belfast, and Ulster University, with branches in Belfast, Coleraine, and Derry.

An excellent source book that will help you explore the opportunities for study in Ireland is *The Transitions Abroad Alternative Travel Directory,* published by Transitions Abroad (**www.transitionsabroad.com**).

Another good book is *Work, Study, Travel Abroad: The Whole World Handbook,* compiled by CIEE, the Council on International Educational Exchange. Both are available in bookstores.

U.S. firms offering educational programs to Ireland include **Academic Travel Abroad,** 1920 N St. NW, Suite 200, Washington, DC 20036 (ℂ **800/556-7896** or 202/785-9000); **Cultural Heritage Alliance,** 107–115 S. Second St., Philadelphia, PA 19106 (ℂ **800/323-4466** or 215/923-7060; www.cha-tours.com); and **Irish American Cultural Institute,** 1 Lackawanna Place, Morristown, NJ 07960 (ℂ **800/232-3746** or 973/605-1991; www.iaci-usa.org).

Ireland in general is extremely student-friendly. Most attractions have a reduced student-rate admission charge, with the presentation of a valid student ID card. A range of travel discounts are available to students, teachers (at any grade level, kindergarten through university), and youths (age 12–25). For further information on international student, teacher, and youth ID cards and fares, call **Council Travel** (ℂ **800/226-8624;** www.counciltravel.com), which operates more than 40 offices in the United States and works through a network of world affiliates.

In Canada, **Travel CUTS** (ℂ **800/667-2887** or 416/614-2887; www.travelcuts.com), offers similar services. In London, **Campus Travel** (ℂ **0171/730-3402;** www.campustravel.co.uk), opposite Victoria Station, is Britain's leading specialist in student and youth travel.

In Ireland, Council Travel's affiliate is **USIT, the Irish Student Travel Service,** 19 Aston Quay, Dublin 2 (ℂ **01/602-1600;** fax 01/679-2124; www.usitnow.ie). In Northern Ireland, contact USIT in the Sountain Centre, College Street, Belfast BT1 6€T (ℂ **028/9032-4073**), or at Queens

University Travel, Student Union Bldg., University Road, Belfast BT7 1PE (✆ **028/9024-1830**). In the United States, USIT is located at 895 Amsterdam Ave., New York, NY 10025 (✆ **212/663-5435**).

One of USIT's most valuable services for students is the **TravelSave Stamp,** which when affixed to your International Student Identity Card entitles you to such benefits as a 50% discount on rail travel throughout the country, a 15% discount on most bus fares outside Dublin, and substantially reduced weekly transit passes in Dublin. The stamp can be purchased for 10€ ($9) at all USIT offices. In Dublin, your ISIC and TravelSave stamp will bring big discounts on city bus and rail weekly passes, available at **Dublin Bus,** 59 Upper O'Connell St. (✆ **01/873-4222**); the student weekly bus pass is 13€ ($12) for local and 14€ ($13) for all-zone travel.

PUBLICATIONS

The Hanging Out Guides (www.frommers.com/hangingout/), published by Frommer's, is the top student travel series for today's students, covering everything from adrenaline sports to the hottest club and music scenes.

FAMILIES

Roughly 27% of the Irish population is under 15 years of age, so it's no wonder that Ireland is so youth and family oriented. A love of children (*lots* of them) is one of the hallmarks of the Irish-Catholic tradition, and of the country in general, so you'll always find people quick to be helpful and to suggest places to go and things to do with children.

Instead of hotels or B&Bs, families might well consider a farm stay or a vacation rental home, where kids are likely to have the opportunity to meet and to make friends with local children. The information provided below regarding farmhouse accommodation

and self-catering will be helpful in pursuing such options. To sort the wheat from the chaff, the most helpful website is **www.beourguest.ie**, for its no-nonsense "search by suitability" facility. Just check the options that are important to you: Kids' meals? Pool? Outdoor playground? Babysitting service? Supervised playroom? The site churns out a list of hotels and guesthouses that have exactly what you need.

En route, airlines, if given 24-hour advance notice, will arrange for a special children's menu, and will warm any baby food you bring with you. On arrival, car rental companies will have children's car seats on hand, provided a request has been made ahead of time. Throughout the island, entrance fees and tickets on public transportation are often reduced by at least half for children, and inclusive family rates for parents with more than two children may be available. Many hotels and restaurants offer children's menus, and there's also that all-too-familiar fast-food fare. Babysitting is provided in some hotels, guesthouses, and B&Bs, and can be arranged in others. See the "Fast Facts" feature later in this chapter for each major city for listings of pharmacies and other crucial health information.

AGENCIES/OPERATORS

Familyhostel (✆ **800/733-9753;** www.learn.unh.edu/familyhostel) takes the whole family on moderately priced domestic and international learning vacations. All trip details are handled by the program staff, and lectures, fields trips, and sightseeing are guided by a team of academics. For kids ages 8 to 15 accompanied by their parents and/or grandparents.

PUBLICATIONS

Some helpful family travel resources include the following: **Wilderness Press,** 1200 5th St., Berkeley, CA 94710 (✆ **800/443-7227**), offers the guide *Backpacking with Babies and Small Children.* An especially helpful general source for planning an overseas family trip is *Take Your Kids To Europe* (3rd Edition) published by Globe Pequot Press, available at bookstores.

WEBSITES

- **Family Travel Network** (www.familytravelnetwork.com) offers travel tips and reviews of family-friendly destinations, vacation deals, and thoughtful features such as "What to Do When Your Kids Are Afraid to Travel" and "Kid-Style Camping."
- **Travel with Your Children** (www.travelwithyourkids.com) is a comprehensive site offering sound advice for traveling with children.
- **The Busy Person's Guide to Travel with Children** (http://wz.com/travel/TravelingWithChildren.html) offers a "45-second newsletter" where experts weigh in on the best websites and resources for tips for traveling with children.

GAY & LESBIAN TRAVELERS

Gay Ireland has rapidly come out of the closet since homosexuality became legal in the North in 1982 and in the Republic in July 1993, though much of Ireland on the whole (particularly the rural areas) continues to discourage its gay population. In cities such as Dublin, Cork, and Galway, gay and lesbian visitors will find more formal support and an open, if small, gay community.

Two essential publications for the gay or lesbian visitor to Ireland are the *Gay Community News* and *In Dublin* magazine. *Gay Community News* is a free newspaper of comprehensive gay-related information published the last Friday of each month. You can pick up a copy in Dublin at the Temple Bar Information Centre at 18 Eustace St.; Books Upstairs at 36 College Green, across from Trinity College; Waterstone's on Dawson Street, also near Trinity; The Well Fed Café on Crow Street in Temple Bar; The George on South Greater St. George's Street off Dame Street; and other progressive haunts. *In Dublin,* which comes out twice a month and is for sale at news agents and bookstores throughout the city, has a page of gay events, current club information, AIDS and health information resources, accommodation options, and helpful organizations.

The following help lines are staffed by knowledgeable and friendly people:

- **Gay Switchboard Dublin** at Carmichael House, North Brunswick Street, Dublin 7 (© 01/872-1055; fax 01/873-5737; www.gayswitchboard.ie), Sunday to Friday 8 to 10pm and Saturday 3:30 to 6pm.
- **Lesbian Line Dublin** (© 01/872-9911), Thursday 7 to 9pm.
- **AIDS Helpline Dublin** (© 01/872-4277), Monday to Friday, 7 to 9pm and Saturday 3 to 5pm, offering assistance with HIV/AIDS prevention, testing, and treatment.

The International Gay & Lesbian Travel Association (IGLTA) (© 800/448-8550 or 954/776-2626; fax 954/776-3303; www.iglta.org) links travelers up with gay-friendly hoteliers, tour operators, and airline and cruise-line representatives. It offers monthly newsletters, marketing mailings, and a membership directory that's updated once a year. Membership is $150 yearly, plus a $100 administration fee for new members.

Also, **Council Travel** (© 888/COUNCIL for an office near you) can supply a free pamphlet—*AIDS and International Travel*—that includes information on hotlines, HIV testing, blood transfusions, and traveling with AIDS overseas.

AGENCIES/OPERATORS

- **Above and Beyond Tours** (© 800/397-2681; www.above beyondtours.com) offers gay and lesbian tours worldwide and is the exclusive gay and lesbian tour operator for United Airlines.
- **Now, Voyager** (© 800/255-6951; www.nowvoyager.com) is a San Francisco–based gay-owned and operated travel service.
- **Olivia Cruises & Resorts** (© 800-631-6277 or 510/655-0364; http://oliviatravel.com) charters entire resorts and ships for exclusive lesbian vacations all over the world.

PUBLICATIONS

- *Frommer's Gay & Lesbian Europe* is an excellent travel resource.
- *Out and About* (© 800/929-2268 or 415-644-8044; www.outandabout.com) offers guidebooks and a newsletter 10 times a year packed with solid information on the global gay and lesbian scene.
- *Spartacus International Gay Guide* and *Odysseus* are good, annual English-language guidebook focused on gay men, with some information for lesbians. You can get them from most gay and lesbian bookstores, or order them from **Giovanni's Room** bookstore, 1145 Pine St., Philadelphia, PA 19107 (© 215/923-2960; www.giovannisroom.com).
- *Gay Travel A to Z: The World of Gay & Lesbian Travel Options at Your Fingertips,* by Marianne Ferrari (Ferrari Publications; www.ferrariguides.com), is a very good gay and lesbian guidebook series.

WEBSITES

Ferrariguides.com (www.ferrariguides.com) is a comprehensive gay travel website that grew out of the Ferrari Guides, one of the world's oldest gay publishing companies. Buy books, find planning and booking information on a variety of tours, and learn of upcoming gay events.

SINGLE TRAVELERS

Many people prefer traveling alone. Unfortunately, the solo traveler is often forced to pay a punishing "single supplement" charged by many resorts, cruise lines, and tours for the privilege of sleeping alone.

Many reputable tour companies offer single-only trips. **Experience Plus!** (© 800/685-4565; fax 970-493-0377; www.xplus.com) offers a number of singles-only hiking and biking trips. **Backroads** (© 800/462-2848; www.backroads.com) offers more than 260 active trips to some 60 destinations worldwide, including Ireland.

OPERATORS/ROOMMATE FINDERS

- **Travel Companion Exchange (TCE)** (© 631/454-0880; www.travelcompanions.com) is one of the nation's oldest roommate finders for single travelers. Register with them and find a travel mate who will split the cost of the room with you and be around as little, or as often, as you like during the day.
- **Travel Buddies Singles Travel Club** (© 800/998-9099; www.travelbuddiesworldwide.com) runs small, intimate, single-friendly group trips and will match you with a roommate free of charge and save you the cost of single supplements.
- **TravelChums** (© 212/799-6464; www.travelchums.com) is an Internet-only travel-companion matching service hosted by respected New York–based Shaw Guides travel service.
- **The Single Gourmet Club** (© 212/980-8788; fax 212/980-3138; www.singlegourmetny.com),

is the charter club of an international social, dining, and travel club for singles of all ages, with offices in 21 cities in the USA and Canada. Membership costs $75 for the first year; $40 to renew.

PUBLICATIONS

- *Traveling Solo: Advice and Ideas for More Than 250 Great Vacations,* by Eleanor Berman (Globe Pequot), gives advice on traveling alone, whether on your own or on a group tour.
- *Outdoor Singles Network* (P.O. Box 781, Haines, AK 99827; http://kcd.com/ci/osn) is a quarterly newsletter for outdoor-loving singles, ages 19 to 90. The network will help you find a travel companion, pen pal, or soulmate. Subscriptions are $55, and your own personal ad is printed free in the next issue. Current issues are $15.

8 Getting There

BY PLANE

About half of all visitors from North America arrive in Ireland via direct transatlantic flights to Dublin Airport, Shannon Airport (in the west), or Belfast Airport. The other half fly first into Britain or Continental Europe and then backtrack into Ireland by air or sea. In Ireland, there are seven smaller regional airports, each of which receives some European traffic: Cork, Donegal, Galway, Kerry, Knock, Sligo, and Waterford. As services and schedules are always subject to change, be sure to consult your preferred airline or travel agent as soon as you begin to sketch your itinerary. The routes and carriers listed below are provided to suggest the range of possibilities for air travel to Ireland.

FLYING FOR LESS: TIPS FOR GETTING THE BEST AIRFARE

The expression "You get what you pay for" has dubious relevance to airfares. We all know that the fellow in the seat next to us, the silent fellow with the grin, may be paying a lot less than we are. Passengers who book their ticket long in advance, who stay over Saturday night, or who are willing to travel on a Tuesday, Wednesday, or Thursday after 7pm, pay a fraction of the full fare. On many flights, even the shortest hops, the full fare is close to $1,000 or more, while a 7- or 14-day advance purchase ticket may cost less than half that amount. Budget fares are not always loudly hawked. Like newts, they sometimes hide under rocks. But a little looking around can often uncover them.

Avoiding high season, which generally falls between late May and mid-October, is the first and most effective step anyone can take in reducing the cost of travel, lodging, car rental, and so on. The next step is to plan far enough ahead to be able to meet advance-purchase restrictions, which mostly vary from a week to a month.

Here are a few other easy ways to save.

- Airlines periodically lower prices on their most popular routes. Check the travel section of your Sunday newspaper for advertised discounts or call the airlines directly and ask if any **promotional rates** or special fares are available. You'll almost never see a sale during the peak summer vacation months of July and August, or during the Thanksgiving or Christmas seasons; but in periods of low-volume travel, you should pay no more than $400 for a domestic cross-country flight. If your schedule is flexible, say so, and ask if you can secure a cheaper fare by staying an extra day, by flying midweek, or by flying at less-trafficked hours. If you already

Tips All About E-Ticketing

Only yesterday **electronic tickets (E-tickets)** were the fast and easy ticket-free alternative to paper tickets. E-tickets allowed passengers to avoid long lines at airport check-in, all the while saving the airlines money on postage and labor. With the increased security measures in airports, however, an E-ticket no longer guarantees an accelerated check-in. You often can't go straight to the boarding gate, even if you have no bags to check. You'll probably need to show your printed E-ticket receipt or confirmation of purchase, as well as a photo I.D., and sometimes even the credit card with which you purchased your E-ticket. That said, buying an E-ticket is still a fast, convenient way to book a flight; instead of having to wait for a paper ticket to come through the mail, you can book your fare by phone or on the computer, and the airline will immediately confirm by fax or e-mail. In addition, airlines often offer frequent flier miles as incentive for electronic bookings.

hold a ticket when a sale breaks, it may even pay to exchange your ticket, which usually incurs a $100 to $150 charge.   *Note:* The lowest-priced fares are often nonrefundable, require advance purchase of 1 to 3 weeks and a certain length of stay, and carry penalties for changing dates of travel.

- **Consolidators**, also known as bucket shops, are a good place to find low fares. Consolidators buy seats in bulk from the airlines and then sell them back to the public at prices usually below even the airlines' discounted rates. Their small ads usually run in Sunday newspaper travel sections. And before you pay, request a confirmation number from the consolidator and then call the airline to confirm your seat. Be aware that bucket shop tickets are usually nonrefundable or rigged with stiff cancellation penalties, often as high as 50% to 75% of the ticket price. Protect yourself by paying with a credit card rather than cash. Keep in mind that if there's an airline sale going on, or if it's high

season, you can often get the same or better rates by contacting the airlines directly, so do some comparison shopping before you buy. Also check out the name of the airline; you may not want to fly on some obscure Third World airline, even if you're saving $10. And check whether you're flying on a charter or a scheduled airline; the latter is more expensive but more reliable.

Council Travel (✆ 800/226-8624; www.counciltravel.com) and **STA Travel** (✆ 800/781-4040; www.sta.travel.com) cater especially to young travelers, but their bargain-basement prices are available to people of all ages. **The TravelHub** (✆ 888/AIR-FARE; www.travelhub.com) represents nearly 1,000 travel agencies, many of whom offer consolidator and discount fares. Other reliable consolidators include **1-800-FLY-CHEAP** (www.1800flycheap.com); **TFI Tours International** (✆ 800-745-8000 or 212/736-1140; www.lowestprice.com), which serves as a clearinghouse for unused seats; or "rebators" such as **Travel Avenue** (✆ **800/333-3335;** www.travelavenue.com) and the **Smart Traveller** (✆ **800/448-3338** in the U.S. or 305/448-3338), which rebate part of their commissions to you.

- Search **the Internet** for cheap fares. Great last-minute deals are available through free weekly e-mail services provided directly by the airlines. See "Planning Your Trip Online," below, for more information.
- Book a seat on a **charter flight**. Discounted fares have pared the number available, but they can still be found. Most charter operators advertise and sell their seats through travel agents, thus making these local professionals your best source of information for available flights. Before deciding to take a charter flight, however, check the restrictions on the ticket: You may be asked to purchase a tour package, to pay in advance, to be amenable if the day of departure is changed, to pay a service charge, to fly on an airline you're not familiar with (this usually is not the case), and to pay harsh penalties if you cancel—but be understanding if the charter doesn't fill up and is canceled up to 10 days before departure. Summer charters fill up more quickly than others and are almost sure to fly, but if you decide on a charter flight, seriously consider buying cancellation and baggage insurance. Also be prepared for late departure hours and long airport delays, as charters usually do not have priority.

  The largest and most reliable charter program to Ireland from the United States is operated by **Sceptre Charters** (✆ **800/221-0924** or 516/255-9800). This operator flies to Dublin and

Shannon from New York, Boston, Philadelphia, Chicago, and Los Angeles.

Several companies in Canada operate summer charter flights from Toronto to Ireland, including **Signature Vacations** (✆ **416/967-1112;** www.signaturevacations.com); and **World of Vacations** (✆ **800/263-8776;** www.worldofvacations.com).

- Look into **courier flights**—though they are usually not available on domestic flights. These companies hire couriers to hand-deliver packages or mail, and use your luggage allowance for themselves; in return, you get a deeply discounted ticket—for example, $300 round-trip to Europe in winter. Flights often become available at the last minute, so check in often. **Halbart Express** has offices in New York (✆ **718-656-8189**), Los Angeles (✆ **310-417-9790**), and Miami (✆ **305-593-0260**). **Jupiter Air** (www.jupiterair.com) has offices in New York (✆ **718-656-6050**), Los Angeles (✆ **310-670-5123**), and San Francisco (✆ **650-697-1773**).
- Join a travel club such as **Moment's Notice** (✆ **718/234-6295;** www.moments-notice.com) or **Sears Discount Travel Club** (✆ **800/433-9383,** or 800/255-1487 to join; www.travelersadvantage.com), which supply unsold tickets at discounted prices. You pay an annual membership fee to get the club's hotline number. Of course, you're limited to what's available, so you have to be flexible.
- Join **frequent-flier clubs.** It's best to accrue miles on one program, so you can rack up free flights and achieve elite status faster. But it makes sense to open as many accounts as possible, no matter how seldom you fly a particular

airline. It's free, and you'll get the best choice of seats, faster response to phone inquiries, and prompter service if your luggage is stolen, your flight is canceled or delayed, or if you want to change your seat.

SCHEDULED SERVICE
FROM THE UNITED STATES
The Irish national "air fleet" or **Aer Lingus** (© 800/474-7424; www.aerlingus.ie) is the traditional leader in providing transatlantic flights to Ireland. Aer Lingus offers scheduled flights from Boston, Chicago, Los Angeles, Newark, and New York to Dublin, Shannon, and Belfast International Airports, with connecting flights to Ireland's regional airports. Connections are available from more than 100 U.S. cities via American, TWA, or U.S. Airways.

Note: Aer Lingus offers educational discounts to full-time students, which can be booked through CIEE/Council Travel (listed under "Students, Teachers & Youth," above), and an attractively priced Eurosaver Green Pass for those who wish to combine an Aer Lingus round-trip transatlantic flight to Ireland with a side-trip to Britain or the Continent, or with a domestic flight within Ireland, including the North.

Excellent transatlantic service is also provided by **Delta Airlines** (© 800/241-4141; www.delta.com), which offers scheduled daily flights from Atlanta and New York to both Dublin and Shannon, with feed-in connections from Delta's network of gateways throughout the United States.

Continental Airlines (© 800/231-0856; www.continental.com) offers non-stop service to Dublin and Shannon from their Newark hub. **American Trans Air** (© 800/435-9282; www.ata.ie) offers chartered flights from New York (JFK) and Boston to Dublin and Shannon. And finally, **Royal Jordanian Airlines** (© 800/223-0474 or 212/949/0050; www.rja.com.jo) flies directly from Chicago to Shannon.

FROM CANADA   Because there are no direct flights to Ireland from Canada, the best option is to fly via New York or via London. **Air Canada** (© 800/268-7240 in Canada, or 800/776-3000 in the U.S.) offers direct service to New York from Montreal, Toronto, Ottawa, and Halifax; other airlines flying direct between Canada and New York include **Canadian Airlines** (© 800/665-1177 in Canada, or 800/426-7000 in the U.S.), **Delta Airlines** (© 800/241-4141), and **American Airlines** (© 800/433-7300). **Air Canada** flies direct to London from Vancouver, Calgary, Montreal, Toronto, Halifax, St. John's, and Ottawa.

FROM AUSTRALIA & NEW ZEALAND   There's no direct service from Australia or New Zealand to

---

⌒Tips **Backtracking to Ireland**

Your favorite airline doesn't fly to Ireland? Many travelers opt to fly to Britain and backtrack into Ireland (see "From Britain," below). Carriers serving Britain from the United States include **American Airlines** (© 800/433-7300; www.aa.com), **British Airways** (© 800/247-9297; www.british-airways.com), **Continental Airlines** (© 800/231-0856; www.continental.com), **Delta Airlines** (© 800/241-4141; www.delta.com), **Northwest Airlines** (© 800/447-4747; www.nwa.com), **TWA** (© 800/892-4141; www.im.aa.com), **United Airlines** (© 800/241-6522; www.ual.com), and **Virgin Atlantic Airways** (© 800/862-8621; www.fly.virgin.com).

Ireland, so you'll have to choose from among the multitude of possible routes. **Qantas** (© **13-13-13** in Australia, or 800/227-4500 in the U.S. and Canada) has direct flights to London from Sydney, Melbourne, and Brisbane. **Air New Zealand** (© **0800/ 737-000** in New Zealand, 800/ 063-385 in Australia, or 800/262-1234 in the U.S.) flies to London via Los Angeles from Auckland and Sydney. **Japan Airlines** (© **0292/721-111** in Australia, or 800/525-3663 in the U.S.) offers service to London via Tokyo, with an overnight stop in Tokyo. **British Airways** (© **800/247-9297;** www.british-airways.com) flies to London from Sydney, Perth, and Melbourne. Flying time for all these routes is about 24 hours.

FROM BRITAIN   Air service from Britain into Dublin is operated by **Aer Lingus** (© **800/474-7424** from the U.S., or 081/899-4747 in Britain) from Birmingham, Bristol, Edinburgh, Glasgow, Leeds/Bradford, London/ Heathrow, Manchester, and Newcastle; **British Midland** (© **800/788-0555** from the U.S., or 01345/ 554554 in Britain; www.iflybritish midland.com) from London/ Heathrow; **Jersey European** (© **01232/676676** in Belfast) from Belfast, Derry, Exeter, and Jersey; **British Airways Express** (© **0345/ 222111** in Britain) from Cardiff, Isle of Man, and Jersey; and **Ryanair** (© **800/365-5563** from the U.S., or 0541/569569 in Britain; www.ryanair. com) from Birmingham, Bristol, Glasgow, Liverpool, London/Gatwick, London/Heathrow, London/Stansted, Luton, and Manchester. There is also regular service from Britain into Ireland's regional airports.

Direct flights into **Belfast International Airport** (www.bial.co.uk) include flights by **British Airways** (© **0345/222111**) from Birmingham, Edinburgh, and London/

Heathrow; and by **Virgin Express** (© **800/891199**) from London/ Heathrow. In addition, there is service into **Belfast City Airport** (© **01232/ 457745;** www.belfastcityairport.com) by a range of carriers, including **British Airways** flights from Edinburgh, Glasgow, Leeds, Liverpool, and Manchester and by **Jersey European** (© **0990/676676**) from Birmingham, Bristol, Exeter, London Stansted, and London Gatwick. Service to **Derry City Eglinton Airport** is provided by **British Airways** from Glasgow and Manchester, and by **Ryanair** (© **0541/569569** in Britain) from London Stansted.

FROM THE CONTINENT   Major direct flights into Dublin from the continent include service from Amsterdam on **KLM** (© **800/374-7747** from the U.S.; www.klm.com); Madrid and Barcelona on **Iberia** (© **800/772-4642** in the U.S.; www.iberia.com); Brussels on **Sabena** (© **800/952-2000** in the U.S.; www.sabena.com); Copenhagen on **Aer Lingus** and **SAS** (© **800/221-2350** in the U.S.; www.scandinavian. net); Frankfurt on **Aer Lingus** and **Lufthansa** (© **800/645-3880** in the U.S.; www.lufthansa.com); Paris on **Aer Lingus** and **Air France** (© **800/ 237-2747** in the U.S.; www.airfrance. com); Prague on **CSA Czech Airlines** (© **212/765-6588** in the U.S.; www. csa.cz); and Rome on **Aer Lingus.**

Quite recently, **Cork Airport** (www.cork-airport.com) passed Shannon to become the second-ranked airport in Ireland, though it offers no nonstop transatlantic service. **Aer Lingus, British Airways, KLM,** and **Ryanair** are among the airlines flying into Cork from Great Britain and the Continent (see above for their contact info). Direct service to Shannon from the Continent includes **Aer Lingus** from Düsseldorf, Frankfurt, Paris, and Zurich; **Aeroflot** from Moscow; and **Virgin Express** from Brussels.

Tips   What You Can Carry On—And What You Can't

The Federal Aviation Administration (FAA) has devised new restrictions on carry-on baggage, not only to expedite the screening process but to prevent potential weapons from passing through airport security. Passengers are now limited to bringing just one carry-on bag and one personal item onto the aircraft (previous regulations allowed two carry-on bags and one personal item, like a briefcase or a purse). For more information, go to the FAA's website www.faa.gov. The agency has released a new list of items passengers are not allowed to carry onto an aircraft:

Not permitted: Knives and box cutters, corkscrews, straight razors, metal scissors, metal nail files, golf clubs, baseball bats, pool cues, hockey sticks, ski poles, ice picks.

Permitted: Nail clippers, tweezers, eyelash curlers, safety razors (including disposable razors), syringes (with documented proof of medical need), walking canes and umbrellas (must be inspected first).

The airline you fly may have **additional restrictions** on items you can and cannot carry on board. Call ahead to avoid problems..

NEW AIR TRAVEL SECURITY MEASURES

In the wake of the terrorist attacks of September 11, 2001, the airline industry began implementing sweeping security measures in airports. Expect a lengthy check-in process and extensive delays. Although regulations vary from airline to airline, you can expedite the process by taking the following steps:

- **Arrive early.** Arrive at the airport at least 2 hours before your scheduled flight.
- **Try not to drive your car to the airport.** Parking and curbside access to the terminal may be limited. Call ahead and check.
- **Don't count on curbside check-in.** Some airlines and airports have stopped curbside check-in altogether, whereas others offer it on a limited basis. For up-to-date information on specific regulations and implementations, check with the individual airline.

- **Be sure to carry plenty of documentation.** A government-issued photo ID (federal, state, or local) is now required. You may need to show this at various checkpoints. With an E-ticket, you may be required to have with you printed confirmation of purchase, and perhaps even the credit card with which you bought your ticket (see "All about E-Ticketing," above). This varies from airline to airline, so call ahead to make sure you have the proper documentation. And be sure that your ID is **up-to-date:** an expired driver's license, for example, may keep you from boarding the plane altogether.
- **Know what you can carry on— and what you can't.** Travelers in the United States are now limited to one carry-on bag, plus one personal bag (such as a purse or a briefcase). The FAA has also issued a list of newly restricted carry-on items; see the box "What You Can Carry On—and What You Can't."

- **Prepare to be searched.** Expect spot-checks. Electronic items, such as a laptop or cellphone, should be readied for additional screening. Limit the metal items you wear on your person.

- **It's no joke.** When a check-in agent asks if someone other than you packed your bag, don't decide that this is the time to be funny. The agents will not hesitate to call an alarm.

- **No ticket, no gate access.** Only ticketed passengers will be allowed beyond the screener checkpoints, except for those people with specific medical or parental needs.

BY FERRY

If you're traveling to Ireland from Britain or the Continent, ferries can be a good way to go, especially if you want to bring your car. The Irish Sea is very choppy, however, so it's always a good idea to consider an over-the-counter pill or patch to guard against seasickness.

Several car/passenger ferries offer reasonably comfortable furnishings, cabin berths (for the longer crossings), restaurants, duty-free shopping, and lounges. Prices fluctuate seasonally and further depend on your route, time of travel, and whether you are on foot or in a car. It's best to check with your travel agent for up-to-date details.

FROM BRITAIN Irish Ferries (www.irishferries.ie) operates from Holyhead, Wales, to Dublin, and from Pembroke, Wales, to Rosslare, County Wexford. For reservations, call **Scots-American Travel** (© 561/ 563-2856 in the U.S.; info@scots american.com) or **Irish Ferries** (© 08705/171717 in the U.K.; 01/638-3333 in Ireland). **Stena Line** (© 888/274-8724 in the U.S. or 01233/647022 in Britain; www2. stenaline.com) sails from Holyhead to Dun Laoghaire, 8 miles (13km) south

of Dublin; from Fishguard, Wales, to Rosslare; and from Stranraer, Scotland, to Belfast, Northern Ireland. **Swansea/Cork Ferries** (© 011792/ 456116 in Britain; www.swansea-cork.ie) links Swansea, Wales, to Ringaskiddy, just outside Cork City, County Cork. **P&O European Ferries** operates from Liverpool to Dublin and from Cairnryan, Scotland, to Larne, County Antrim, Northern Ireland. For reservations, call Scots-American Travel (© 561/ 563-2856 in the U.S., or 01/638-3333 in Ireland; www.poferries.com). **Norse Merchant Ferries** (© 0870/ 6004321 in Britain; 01/819-2999 in Ireland; www.norsemerchant.com) sails from Liverpool to both Dublin and Belfast. **Seacat Scotland Ltd.** (© 800/551743 in Britain or 01/ 874-1231 in Ireland; www.seacat. co.uk) operates ferries from Liverpool to Dublin; and from Heysham and Troon, both in Scotland, to Belfast.

FROM CONTINENTAL EUROPE
Irish Ferries sails from Roscoff and Cherbourg, France, to Rosslare. For reservations, call Scots-American Travel (© 561/563-2856 in the U.S.; info@scotsamerican.com) or **Irish Ferries** (© 08705/171717 in the U.K.; 01/638-3333 in Ireland). **P&O European Ferries** operates from Cherbourg, France, to Rosslare. For reservations, call Scots-American Travel (© 561/563-2856 in the U.S., or 01/638-3333 in Ireland; www. poferries.com). **Brittany Ferries** (© 021/427-7801 in Cork; www. brittany-ferries.com) connects Roscoff, France, to Cork.

Note to Eurail Pass holders: Because Irish Ferries is a member of the Eurail system, you can travel free between Rosslare and Roscoff or Cherbourg.

BY BUS & RAIL FROM BRITAIN

Even without an Irish Chunnel, bus and rail service links Dublin with

London and other major cities in Britain, using the B&I or Stena ferry trips as part of the ride. Bus routes are operated jointly by Ireland's Bus Eireann and Britain's National Express (the system is called **Supabus**) and run daily. One-way fares between Dublin and London start at 24€ ($22); round-trip fares start at 46€ ($41), making this connection a true bargain. From Dublin, this same express coach service from London extends to a number of Irish cities. For full details on the Supabus routes, contact **Bus Eireann** (© **01/703-2426**). For information on rail/ferry service from Britain, contact **BritRail** (© **800/677-8585** from the United States; www.raileurope.com).

PACKAGE TOURS

Dedicated budget watchers have long known that when it comes to travel, some of the best bargains going are package tours (escorted or unescorted). Once upon a time that meant you were herded around with a group of other tourists, with little opportunity to break out on your own. But this is no longer true: You can now realize enormous savings on airfare and accommodations and still enjoy the freedom of an independent traveler.

It's wise to prepay for a vacation package in U.S. dollars soon after you make reservations, as many tour operators guarantee no increase in the land costs of a tour package as soon as the deposit is paid. So, even if the dollar weakens, your price is locked in at the original rate.

The leading firms offering package tours of Ireland and Northern Ireland include the following:

- **Aer Lingus** offers "Discover Ireland" Vacations (© **800/223-6537**), which feature an array of options, including Dublin City packages, golf tours, cycling holidays, and self-drive vacations designed for individual travelers. One of the most attractive choices for budgeteers is the "Discover Ireland B&B" packages, which offer a discount on accommodation and car rental.

- **CIE Tours International** (© **800/CIE-TOUR**), Ireland's national tour company, offers Dublin-based packages, self-drive vacations, and Ireland/Britain combination trips. It's the leading Irish package tour company. CIE also offers rail/bus touring arrangements within Ireland for individuals and for groups.

- Other tour operators include: **Brendan Tours** (© 800/421-8446; www.brendantours.com); **Brian Moore International Tours** (© 800/982-2299; www.bmit.com); **Lismore Tours** (© 800/547-6673; www.lismoretours.com); **Lynott Tours** (© 800/221-2474; www.lynotttours.com); and **Owenoak-Castle Tours** (© 800/426-4498; www.owenoak.com).

9 Planning Your Trip Online

Researching and booking your trip online can save time and money. Then again, it may not. It is simply not true that you always get the best deal online. Most booking engines do not include schedules and prices for budget airlines, and from time to time you'll get a better last-minute price by calling the airline directly, so it's best to call the airline to see if you can do better before booking online.

On the plus side, Internet users today can tap into the same travel-planning databases that were once accessible only to travel agents—and do it at the same speed. Sites such as **Frommers.com**, **Travelocity.com**, **Expedia.com**, and **Orbitz.com** allow consumers to comparison shop for airfares, access special bargains, book flights, and reserve hotel rooms and rental cars.

But don't fire your travel agent just yet. Although online booking sites offer tips and hard data to help you bargain shop, they cannot endow you with the hard-earned experience that makes a seasoned, reliable travel agent an invaluable resource, even in the Internet age. And for consumers with a complex itinerary, a trusty travel agent is still the best way to arrange the most direct flights to and from the best airports.

Still, there's no denying the Internet's emergence as a powerful tool in researching and plotting travel time. The benefits of researching your trip online can be well worth the effort.

Last-minute specials, such as weekend deals or Internet-only fares, are offered by airlines to fill empty seats. Most of these are announced on Tuesday or Wednesday and must be purchased online. They are only valid for travel that weekend, but some can be booked weeks or months in advance. Sign up for weekly e-mail alerts at airline websites or check mega-sites that compile comprehensive lists of last-minute specials, such as **Smarter Living** (smarterliving.com) or **WebFlyer** (www.webflyer.com).

Some sites, such as Expedia.com, will send you **e-mail notification** when a cheap fare becomes available to your favorite destination. Some will also tell you when fares to a particular destination are lowest.

TRAVEL PLANNING & BOOKING SITES

Keep in mind that because several airlines are no longer willing to pay commissions on tickets sold by online travel agencies, these agencies may either add a $10 surcharge to your bill if you book on that carrier—or neglect to offer those carriers' schedules.

The list of sites below is selective, not comprehensive. Some sites will have evolved or disappeared by the time you read this.

- **Travelocity** (www.travelocity.com or www.frommers.travelocity.com) and **Expedia** (www.expedia.com) are among the most popular sites, each offering an excellent range of options. Travelers search by destination, dates and cost.

- **Orbitz** (www.orbitz.com) is a popular site launched by United, Delta, Northwest, American, and Continental airlines. (Stay tuned: At press time, travel-agency associations were waging an antitrust battle against this site.)

- **Qixo** (www.qixo.com) is another powerful search engine that allows you to search for flights and accommodations from some 20 airline and travel-planning sites

---

Frommers.com: The Complete Travel Resource

For an excellent travel planning resource, we highly recommend **Arthur Frommer's Budget Travel Online** (www.frommers.com). We're a little biased, of course, but we think you'll find the travel tips, reviews, monthly vacation giveaways, and online-booking capabilities indispensable. Among the special features are **Arthur Frommer's Daily Newsletter**, for the latest travel bargains and insider travel secrets; the electronic version of Frommer's travel guides, including expert travel tips, hotel and dining recommendations, and recommended sights in more than 2000 destinations worldwide; and guidebook updates. Once your research is done, the **Online Reservation System** (www.frommers.com/booktravelnow) takes you to Frommer's favorite sites for booking your vacation at affordable prices.

(such as Travelocity) at once. Qixo sorts results by price.

- **Priceline** (www.priceline.com) lets you "name your price" for airline tickets, hotel rooms, and rental cars. For airline tickets, you can't say what time you want to fly—you have to accept any flight between 6am and 10pm on the dates you've selected, and you may have to make one or more stopovers. Tickets are nonrefundable, and no frequent-flyer miles are awarded.

SMART E-SHOPPING

The savvy traveler is armed with insider information. Here are a few tips to help you navigate the Internet successfully and safely.

- **Know when sales start.** Last-minute deals may vanish in minutes. If you have a favorite booking site or airline, find out when last-minute deals are released to the public. (For example, Southwest's specials are posted every Tuesday at 12:01 am central time.)
- **Shop around.** If you're looking for bargains, compare prices on different sites and airlines—and against a travel agent's best fare. Try a range of times and alternative airports before you make a purchase.
- **Stay secure.** Book only through secure sites (some airline sites are not secure). Look for a key icon (Netscape) or a padlock (Internet Explorer) at the bottom of your web browser before you enter credit card information or other personal data.
- **Avoid online auctions.** Sites that auction airline tickets and frequent-flier miles are the number-one perpetrators of Internet fraud, according to the National Consumers League.
- **Maintain a paper trail.** If you book an E-ticket, print out a confirmation, or write down your confirmation number, and keep it safe and accessible—or your trip could be a virtual one!

ONLINE TRAVELER'S TOOLBOX

Veteran travelers usually carry some essential items to make their trips easier. Following is a selection of online tools to bookmark and use.

- **Visa ATM Locator** (www.visa.com), for locations of Plus ATMs worldwide, or **MasterCard ATM Locator** (www.mastercard.com), for locations of Cirrus ATMs worldwide.
- **Foreign Languages for Travelers** (www.travlang.com). Learn basic terms in more than 70 languages and click on any underlined phrase to hear what it sounds like. *Note:* Free audio software and speakers are required.
- **Intellicast** (www.intellicast.com) and **Weather.com** (www.weather.com). Gives weather forecasts for all 50 states and for cities around the world.
- **Mapquest** (www.mapquest.com). This best of the mapping sites lets you choose a specific address or destination, and in seconds, it will return a map and detailed directions.
- **Cybercafes.com** (www.cybercafes.com) or **Net Café Guide** (www.netcafeguide.com/map index.htm). Locate Internet cafes at hundreds of locations around the globe. Catch up on your e-mail and log onto the web for a few dollars per hour.
- **Universal Currency Converter** (www.xe.net/currency). See what your dollar or pound is worth in more than 100 other countries.
- **U.S. State Department Travel Warnings** (www.travel.state.gov/travel_warnings.html). Reports on places where health concerns or unrest might threaten U.S. travelers. It also lists the locations of U.S. embassies around the world.

Tips   Easy Internet Access Away from Home

There are a number of ways to get your e-mail on the web, using any computer.

- Your **Internet Service Provider (ISP)** may have a web-based interface that lets you access your e-mail on computers other than your own. Just find out how it works before you leave home. The major ISPs maintain local access numbers around the world so that you can go online by placing a local call. Check your ISP's website or call its toll-free number and ask how you can use your current account away from home, and how much it will cost. Also ask about the cost of the service before you leave home. If you're traveling outside the reach of your ISP, you may have to check the yellow pages in your destination to find a local ISP.
- You can open an account on a free, web-based **e-mail provider** before you leave home, such as Microsoft's **Hotmail** (hotmail.com) or **Yahoo! Mail** (mail.yahoo.com). Your home ISP may be able to forward your home e-mail to the web-based account automatically.
- Check out **www.mail2web.com**. This amazing free service allows you to type in your regular e-mail address and password and retrieve your e-mail from any web browser, anywhere, so long as your home ISP hasn't blocked it with a firewall.
- Call your hotel in advance to see whether Internet connection is possible from your room.

10 Getting Around

BY PLANE

Because Ireland is such a small country, it's unlikely you'll be flying from place to place. If you do require an air transfer, however, **Aer Lingus** (© 01/705-3333; www.aerlingus.com) operates daily scheduled flights linking Dublin with Cork, Galway, Kerry, Knock, Shannon, Sligo, and Belfast.

BY TRAIN

Iarnrod Eireann/Irish Rail Travel Centre, 35 Lower Abbey St., Dublin 1 (© 01/703-1839; www.irishrail.ie), operates a network of train services throughout Ireland. With the exception of flying, train travel is the fastest way to get around the country. Most lines radiate from Dublin to other principal cities and towns. From Dublin, the journey time to Cork is 3 hours; to Belfast, 2 hours; to Galway,

3 hours; to Limerick, 2¼ hours; to Killarney, 4 hours; to Sligo, 3¼ hours; and to Waterford, 2¾ hours. For train departure times and fares, call (in Dublin) © 01/836-6222 Monday through Saturday 9am to 6pm, and Sunday 10am to 6pm. Outside of regular business hours, call © 01/703-1842/1843. For rail inquiries anywhere in Ireland, you can call toll-free: © 1850/366222. If you're Web savvy, Iarnrod Eireann has an award-winning interactive site at **www.irishrail.ie**, where you can map out and schedule all your comings and goings in Ireland. You'll find updated timetables for DART, Intercity, and Suburban lines, as well as useful links to other travel services.

Irish Rail also operates many special trains: day-trips in the summer, pilgrimage trains, and special excursions

Irish Rail Routes

to sporting and entertainment events, many offering discounts to groups and families. **Rail Breaks holiday packages** vary from luxury weekends in Cork, Dublin, Killarney, and Galway to 3-day family breaks in several locations, with hotel or self-catering accommodation. For full details and current prices, contact any local station or the **Iarnrod Eireann/Irish Rail Travel Centre** (see above). In addition to the Irish Rail service between Dublin and Belfast, **Northern Ireland Railways** (© 888/ BRITRAIL or 028/9089-9411; www. nirailways.co.uk) operates routes from Belfast that include Coleraine and Derry; and suburban routes from Belfast to Portadown, Bangor, and Larne.

BY BUS

Bus Eireann, with its hub at Busaras/Central Bus Station, Dublin 1 (© 01/836-6111; www.buseireann.ie), operates an extensive system of express bus service on routes such as Dublin to Donegal (4¼ hours), Killarney to Limerick (2½ hours), Limerick to Galway (2 hours), and Limerick to Cork (2 hours), as well as local service to nearly every town in Ireland. The company's website provides the latest timetables and fares for bus service throughout Ireland. Timetables and other travel information are also available at bus stations, bus-ticket offices, and train depots around the country. Round-trip fares are only marginally more than one-way fares; children under 15 go for half fare. Also, Bus Eireann constantly offers special fares (weekends, midweek). Whenever you travel, be sure to ask about the cheapest fare available at the time. One of Bus Eireann's most popular offerings is its **Breakaways program,** whose rates include round-trip coach fare to your destination and lodging at a hotel, B&B, or hostel—a real bargain. Senior citizen discounts are offered.

Regional bus companies are often cheaper or more direct than Bus Eireann, so ask around about **alternative service providers** before purchasing your ticket. For obvious reasons, the Bus Eireann ticket counter may not be the best place to ask—often local bus companies operate a small ticket office in the bus station, so keep an eye out for these. In Northern Ireland contact **Ulsterbus,** Europa Buscentre, 10 Glengall St., Belfast (© **028/9032-0011;** www.ulsterbus.co.uk), which serves all six counties and offers money-saving travel passes as well as periodic special promotional fares.

BY CAR

Although Ireland offers an extensive network of public transportation, the advantages of having your own car for your travels are obvious. The disadvantages begin with the cost of rental and continue with each refueling. In high season, weekly rental rates on a compact vehicle begin at around $300 (if you've shopped around) and ascend steeply from there—but it's at the pump that you're likely to go into shock. Irish gas prices can easily be triple what you pay in the United States. The consolation here is that Ireland is comparatively small, so distances are comparatively short. Another fact of life on the road in Ireland is that space is limited. The majority of Irish roads and highways are surprisingly narrow, made to order for what many Americans would regard as miniature cars, just the kind you'll wish you had rented once you're underway. So think small when you pick out your rental car. The choice is yours—between room in the car and room on the road.

Unless your stay in Ireland extends beyond 6 months, your own valid U.S. or Canadian driver's license (provided you've had it for at least 6 months) is all you need to drive in Ireland. Rules and restrictions for car

Irish Bus Routes

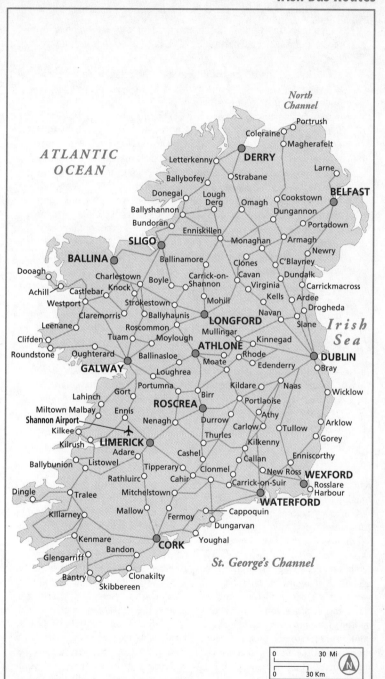

(Value) Money-Saving Rail & Bus Passes

For extensive travel by public transport, you can save money by purchasing a rail/bus pass or a rail-only pass. The options include the following:

- **Eurailpass:** Of the dozens of different Eurailpasses available, some are valid for unlimited rail travel in 17 European countries—but none include Britain or Northern Ireland. Other passes let you save money by selecting fewer countries. In the Irish Republic, the Eurailpass is good for travel on trains, Expressway coaches, and the Irish Continental Lines ferries between France and Ireland. For passes that let you travel throughout continental Europe and the Republic of Ireland, 1st class passes begin at 609€ ($554) for 15 consecutive days of travel; youth passes (passengers must be under 26 years old) begin at 426€ ($388) for 15 consecutive days of travel in second class. The pass must be purchased 21 days before departure for Europe by a non–European Union resident. For further details or for purchase, call **Rail Pass Express** (© 800/722-7151; www.eurail.com). It's also available from **Council Travel** (© 800/2COUNCIL; www.counciltravel.com) and other travel agents.

- **BritRail Pass +Ireland:** Includes all rail travel throughout the UK and Ireland, including a round-trip ferry crossing on Stena Line. A pass good for any 5 days unlimited travel within a 30-day period costs 581€ ($529) 1st class, 438€ ($399) 2nd class; 10 days unlimited travel within a 30-day period costs 823€ ($749) 1st class, 625€ ($569) 2nd class. It must be purchased before departure for Ireland or the UK. Available from **BritRail** (© 800/BRITRAIL, or 800/555-2748 in Canada; www.raileurope.com) or from **CIE Tours International,** 100 Hanover Ave., P.O. Box 501, Cedar Knolls, NJ 07927-0501 (© **800/243-8687** or 973/292-3438 from the U.S., 800/387-2667 in Canada; www.cietours.com).

rental vary slightly and correspond roughly to those in the United States.

Car-rental rates as quoted by many companies do not include the inevitable 12.5% government tax (VAT), nor do they include CDW (collision damage waiver) or insurance against theft of the rental vehicle. If you have a credit card that provides free collision protection on rental cars and/or theft protection, be sure to call your card's customer service line to make certain there are no silent, invisible restrictions on that coverage. It is best to tell them exactly where you are going and for how long, and let them assure you that all is well. One common hitch is that the complimentary CDW may be invalid beyond 30 consecutive days, which means you must return the car within 30 days and then take out a second rental to extend the coverage beyond the 30-day limit. In 1999, Visa eliminated all coverage on rental cars in Ireland and MasterCard limited their coverage; be certain that your information is current. In fact, it is advisable to confirm the details of your coverage at the very same time you charge your car rental to your credit card; and in all this, make certain that the distinction between

- **Emerald Card:** Valid for second-class rail and bus service throughout Ireland and Northern Ireland, this pass is priced at 272€ ($246) adult, 136€ ($123) child for 15 days of travel within a 30-day period; and 158€ ($143) adult, 79€ ($72) child for 8 days of travel within a 15-day period. It's available from **Iarnrod Eireann/Irish Rail,** Travel Centre, 35 Lower Abbey St., Dublin 1 (☎ **01/703-1839; www. irishrail.ie);** from **Busaras/Central Bus Station,** Dublin 1 (☎ **01/836-6111;** www.buseireann.ie), as well as all major bus and train stations. You must purchase a voucher 21 days before departure for Ireland, available from **CIE Tours International.** Once in Ireland, you then exchange the voucher for your pass.

- **Irish Explorer:** For use in the Republic of Ireland, this pass gives 8 days of combined rail and bus services in a 15-day period for 136€ ($123) adult, 68€ ($62) child. It's available from **Iarnrod Eireann/Irish Rail Travel Centre,** 35 Lower Abbey St., Dublin 1 (☎ **01/703-1839; www. irishrail.ie);** from **Busaras/Central Bus Station,** Dublin 1 (☎ **01/ 836-6111;** www.buseireann.ie); and at all major bus and train stations.

- **Irish Rover:** For use both in the Republic of Ireland and in the North, this pass entitles you to 5 days of rail travel in a 15-day period for 114€ ($103) adult, 57€ ($52) child. It's available from **Iarnrod Eireann/Irish Rail Travel Centre,** 35 Lower Abbey St., Dublin 1 (☎ **01/703-1839),** and at all major train stations.

- **Freedom of Northern Ireland:** Seven days of unlimited travel on bus and train in the North for £40 ($58) adult, £16.50 ($24) child; or 1 day for £11 ($16) adult, £5 ($7.25) child. This pass is available from **Northern Ireland Railways,** Central Station, East Bridge Street, Belfast (☎ **028/9089-9400;** www.nirailways.co.uk); from **Ulsterbus,** Europa Buscentre, 10 Glengall St., Belfast (☎ **028/9032-0011;** www.ulsterbus. co.uk); and at all major bus and train stations in Northern Ireland.

Ireland and Northern Ireland is clear both to you and to those with whom you are negotiating.

If you are renting a car in the Republic and taking it into the North (or vice versa), be sure to ask the car rental firm if the rental insurance they provide covers cross-border transport. If not, you may be required to purchase extra insurance. If you rent a car in the Republic, it is best to return it to the Republic, and if you rent it in the North, return it in the North (some firms charge extra for cross-border drop-offs).

DRIVING LAWS & TIPS   A common concern for would-be motorists from North America is the fact that the Irish, in both the North and South, **drive on the left.** The thought of this whitens some knuckles even before they touch the wheel. But it really isn't a matter for dread. Most drivers get used to the idea quickly—the sight of oncoming vehicles in their accustomed lane immediately hammers the point home. Those traffic circles known as "roundabouts" (what some of us call "rotaries") admittedly take a little getting used to. Just remember always to turn left into a roundabout and to yield to vehicles on the right. If you're going to slip up and forget momentarily where you belong, it's more likely to happen after you return home, when your guard is down and before you realize you've formed a strange habit overseas. Seriously, be careful in the first days and weeks after you return home, especially when making sharp left turns.

One signal that could be particularly misleading to U.S. drivers is a flashing yellow light at a pedestrian traffic light. This means drivers should yield to pedestrians and proceed only if the crossing is clear.

There are few major **highways** (labeled "M") in the Republic. Almost all roads are national (labeled "N"), regional (labeled "R"), or rural and unclassified roads. N50 and higher are primary roads; numbers lower than 50 indicate secondary roads. Regional roads are usually given a name, not a number. In the north, there are two **Major Motorways** (labeled "M"), equivalent to interstates, as well as a network of lesser A- and B-level roads. Speed limits are posted. In general, the limit for urban areas is 30 mph (48kmph); for open but undivided highways 60 mph (97kmph); and for major motorways 70 mph (113kmph).

The enforcement of **speed limits** is becoming increasingly stringent, and Irish roads have some built-in enforcers. Roads are often slick, with many bends and rises, any one of which can present a sheep or other four-legged pedestrian on very short notice. Also, many roads in the country have only one lane, which often means that if a car is coming the other way, you have to pull over to the shoulder to let it by. The low density of traffic on some of Ireland's roads can promote the deadly fantasy that you have the road to yourself. Don't wait to be contradicted.

Both the North and the South have appropriately severe laws on the books against **drunk driving,** and they will gladly throw them at you. Irish hospitality has its limits. Both also enforce the mandatory use of seat belts in the front seat, and the North extends that to rear-seated passengers. Additionally, it is against the law in the Republic for any child under 12 to sit in the front seat.

It is regrettably necessary to attach here a strong note of caution. Highway safety, or the lack thereof, has reached the level of a national crisis in Ireland during the last several years. The number of fatalities on Ireland's highways is shocking; Ireland is ranked the second most dangerous country in Europe in which to drive (Greece wins the prize) and is twice as dangerous as its next "competitor." In the light of Ireland's unfortunate highway statistics, every possible precaution is in order. Try to avoid driving late at night, after dark and as the pubs close; get off the road when driving conditions are compromised by rain, fog, or excessive holiday traffic; and don't drive alone. Getting used to left-side driving, stick shift (almost all rental cars have standard transmissions), and a new landscape are enough for the driver to manage, without having to find his or her way as well. Every novice driver in Ireland needs a hawk-eyed navigator alongside. With this in mind, I strongly recommend driving only an hour or two on the day of arrival, just far enough to get to a nearby hotel or bed-and-breakfast. Finally, it goes without saying that driving either intoxicated or exhausted or both (which is often the state of visitors disembarking from an overnight transatlantic flight) is only asking for notice in the next day's *Irish Times.*

CAR RENTALS Major international car-rental firms are represented at airports and cities throughout

Ireland and Northern Ireland. They include **Alamo-Treaty** (© 800/522-9696 from the U.S.; www.goalamo.com), **Auto-Europe** (© 800/223-5555 from the U.S.; www.autoeurope.com), **Avis** (© 800/331-1084 from the U.S.; www.avis.com), **Budget** (© 800/472-3325 from the U.S.; www.budgetrentacar.com), **Hertz** (© 800/838-0826 from the U.S.; www.hertz.com), **Murrays Europcar** (© 800/800-6000 from the U.S.; www.europcar.ie), **National** (© 800/227-7368 from the U.S.; www.nationalcar.com), and **Payless/Bunratty** (© 800/729-5377 from the U.S.; www.paylesscarrental.com). It's best to shop around, because it is impossible to know who'll be offering the best rate for your travel needs, although Budget and Hertz seem consistently quite competitive.

I definitely urge you to make any car-rental arrangements long in advance of departure. Leaving such arrangements to the last minute—or worse, leaving them until your arrival in Ireland—can mean that you will wind up either walking or wishing you were. Ireland is a small country, and in high season it can completely run out of rental cars—but before it does, it will run out of *affordable* rental cars. Discounts are common in the off-season, of course, but it's also possible to negotiate a decent deal for July and August, if you put in enough time and effort.

Auto Europe (© 800/223-5555; fax 207/828-1177; www.autoeurope.com) offers superior rates and service on overseas rentals and long-term leases. Their agreements are clear, straightforward, and all-inclusive. Better yet, they can beat any bona fide offer from another company; ask for the "Beat Rate Desk."

If you plan to rent or lease a car in Britain or Europe and then bring it by ferry to Ireland (which will entail a modest additional surcharge), I recommend a long-term rental or lease from **Europe by Car** (© 800/223-1516), a company whose rates and service are hard to beat on the Continent.

In addition, there are a variety of Irish-based companies, with desks at the major airports and/or full-service offices in city or town locations. The leader among the Irish-based firms is **Dan Dooley Rent-a-Car** (© 800/331-9301 in the U.S.).

PARKING When arriving in cities, be sure to observe local rules, including where to park. Some small cities and most towns have free street parking, but larger cities confine parking to metered spaces or parking garages and lots. "Disc-parking" is also in effect in many places, requiring you to purchase a paper disc and display it for the time you are parked in a certain area. Single discs in Dublin cost 1.25€ ($1.15), a five-pack of discs currently costs 6.35€ ($5.75); each disc has a maximum of 3 hours of parking and they're sold in most shops, hotels, and tourist offices. Some towns also follow the "pay and display" system, which is very similar to the disc system: You buy a parking voucher (in Dublin prices range from 0.65€–1.90€ [60¢–$1.75] per hour) from a machine at the site and display the voucher for the time you are parked. Dublin, in particular, has recently taken the gloves off in an effort to crack down on parking violations—so be extra vigilant.

In Belfast and other large cities in the North, certain security measures are in place. Signs stating CONTROL ZONE indicate that no unattended vehicle can be left there at any time. That means if you are a single traveler, you cannot leave your car; if you are a traveling twosome, one person must remain in the car while it's parked. Also, unlocked cars anywhere in the North are subject to a fine, for security reasons.

BY FERRY

The coast of Ireland is not so razor-straight as, say, the borders of Kansas. A number of passenger and car ferries cut across the wider bays, shaving hours off land-only driving times. Ferries operate between Tarbert, County Kerry, and Killimer, County Clare; Passage East, County Waterford, and Ballyhack, County Wexford; and Glenbrook, east of Cork City, and Carrigaloe, outside of Cobh. For details, see chapter 10, "The West" (particularly the section on County Clare); chapter 6, "The Southeast"; and chapter 7, "Cork City."

Additionally, because Ireland includes a number of must-see islands, getting around includes getting on a boat now and then. Some boats, including all major ferries, have official licenses and offer regular scheduled service. Sometimes, however, making a crossing is a matter of staring out across a body of water to where you want to be and asking someone with a boat to take you there. Both methods work. To supplement the boat listings in this guide, you might want to request a copy of Information Sheet 50C—*Island Boat/Air Services*—from the Irish Tourist Board.

11 Suggested Itineraries

To make the rounds of Ireland, north and south, you'll need at least 2 or, better, 3 weeks. With even a week, however, you can convince yourself and others you've been there.

Here are a few recommended itineraries, with the number of days suggested for each city or touring center indicated in parentheses. Each tour starts or finishes near Shannon or Dublin, the two main arrival/departure points. You can ask your travel agent to design a trip based on your interests or on the amount of time you can spend. Although these itineraries assume that you have a car, distances are so small in Ireland that with a little adjustment these could also be used by two-wheeled travelers; see "Bicycling" in chapter 3, "Ireland Outdoors," for some routing recommendations specific to cyclists.

One Week—Southern Coast Shannon area (1), Kerry (2), Cork (2), Wexford (1), Dublin (1).

One   Week—Main   Highlights Shannon area (1), Kerry (1), Cork (1), Waterford (1), Dublin (2), Galway (1).

One Week—East Coast Dublin (3), Dundalk (1), Kilkenny (1), Waterford (1), Wexford (1).

One Week—West Coast Kerry (2), Galway and Connemara (2), Sligo (2), Shannon area (1).

One Week—The Northwest Shannon area (1), Sligo (2), Donegal (3), Shannon (1).

One Week—The North Newcastle (1), Belfast (2), Antrim Coast (2), Derry (1), Enniskillen (1).

Two Weeks—The Coastal Circuit Shannon (1), Kerry (2), Cork (1), Dublin (2), Belfast (2), Sligo (1), Donegal (2), Galway, Mayo, and Connemara (2), Shannon (1).

Three Weeks—The Complete Tour Shannon (1), Kerry (2), Cork (1), Kilkenny (1), Waterford or Wexford (1), Dublin (3), Belfast (2), Portrush (1), Derry or Enniskillen (2), Sligo (1), Donegal (2), Mayo (1), Galway and Connemara (2), Shannon (1).

All of the above itineraries describe circles, which are not for everyone. When time is scarce, some people, like myself, prefer to settle into one place for a week and to reach out and down from there. This is the "hub" plan, surely a viable alternative to the 7-day dash. If it's your first time in Ireland, Dublin, and Galway make great choices for hubs. Whether you decide to tour or to stay put may depend on whether you're primarily in search of sights or stories. You'll see more sights moving around, but you'll likely hear more stories if you plant yourself somewhere and become available to them.

12 Finding an Affordable Place to Stay

Accommodations will be one of the biggest expenses of your stay in Ireland, so it pays to consider before leaving what you really need and what you can do without. If you're on a very tight budget, but you still need more privacy than a bunk at a hostel offers, consider taking a private room in a hostel—they're usually austere but they put a roof over your head for about half the price of a B&B. Or, if you prefer to stay in B&Bs, consider forgoing the private bathroom, which will save you a few dollars a night. By saving a dollar here and there, you'll be able to splurge at that delightful country manor house or Norman castle you've been dreaming of.

As with most aspects of budgeting, planning ahead is an essential element of finding affordable places to stay. I always prefer the spontaneity that comes with being able to decide from night to night where I'll lay my head, but in some cases this just isn't a luxury I can afford. As a rule, weekends in Dublin from June to September are booked weeks or even months in advance, and the places with the best deals are always the first to go. During festival times in Dublin and throughout the country this will also be the case, so consult the calendar of events in this chapter or the more complete calendar available from the Irish Tourist Board to determine where you'll need advance bookings. Unfortunately, some proprietors aren't above taking advantage of increased demand, and will jack up their rates when they know people are desperate, so plan ahead to avoid paying through the nose.

Single travelers will find it harder to sleep on a budget, because most B&Bs charge a single supplement of 10€ to 20€ ($9–$18) in addition to the per person rate when a double room is occupied by one person. Sometimes single rooms are available for a charge closer to the per-person rate, but these rooms are usually tiny and of a much lower quality than double rooms in the same B&B. Hostels are probably the best bet, because most will charge the per-person rate without supplement for a double room occupied by one person. (The exception would be periods of high demand, when they'll charge the full two-person rate for single occupancy.) An increasing number of B&Bs in Ireland have eliminated their single rates entirely, charging the same rate regardless of whether the room is occupied by one or two people.

The Irish Tourist Board operates an approval system for all accommodations in Ireland. There are certain standards of cleanliness and services offered corresponding to each type of place to stay—just look for the shamrock emblem. The *Irish Accommodation Guide* is a helpful publication that lists all approved premises with the maximum prices they're allowed to charge and other useful information. Look for it in most tourist information offices. Non-approved premises tend to be cheaper—they can afford to be, because the tourist board listing is rather costly—and they're often quite good. I'd recommend being more wary of non-approved hostels, though. Some of them are simply *scary.*

ACCOMMODATIONS TERMINOLOGY When we refer to a *double room* we mean any room that will sleep two people; but in Irish parlance, *double room* usually refers to a room with a double bed, and a *twin-bedded room* means a room with two twin beds. When we say that a B&B has "3 units, two with bathroom," that means that two of the three bedrooms has *a bathroom with shower and bathtub* in the room; if there's a shower but no bathtub, we indicate the number of rooms with shower only. In Ireland, the term for a room with private bathroom is an *en-suite room*. When we say that there's a reduction for children, that means a reduction for *children under 12 sharing a room with an adult*, unless specified otherwise.

Also, please note that most budget accommodations in Ireland *do not offer telephones in the guest rooms*. If a property does offer phones, we note it in the listing data for the hotel.

CAMPING   If you have a car (or a strong back), carrying a tent and sleeping bag is an easy way to cut your costs and expand your accommodation options—B&Bs, hostels, and hotels when you find a place you really like, and sleeping under the stars when you don't. All the campgrounds in Ireland are private; unfortunately, camping isn't allowed in any of the national parks. Most of the private campgrounds cater primarily to mobile homes, with space for tents on the edges or in between. Rural hostels will often permit camping, and offer campers use of their self-catering kitchen and showers, all for a fee substantially lower than that of a hostel bed.

The tourist board publishes *Caravan and Camping Ireland*, a booklet that lists all the approved campsites and trailer parks and outlines their amenities. It's common for campgrounds to offer showers and a place to do your cooking (sometimes with stoves and utensils provided, sometimes not). Some have clothes-washing facilities, rec rooms, even restaurants and swimming pools. Most campgrounds are closed between November and March, although there are a few that remain open year-round.

HOSTELS   The hostels of Ireland offer a surprising range of services in an incredible diversity of settings, and prices that are hard to beat. Although they're sometimes called Youth Hostels, the clientele generally spans all ages and includes quite a few families. It's true that there are some hostels that tend to be the exclusive retreat of rowdy college kids on holiday, but these are the exception. All the hostels you'll find in this book have been chosen because they're places that appeal to a broad range of people—places where you're as likely to meet an older couple, a young family, or an elementary class on school vacation. Hostelers are a sociable and outgoing lot, and you're guaranteed to meet many interesting people over a meal or a pint. Prices range from 9€ to 22€ ($8.15–$20) for a dorm bed and 10€ to 28€ ($9.10–$25) per person for a private room.

At every hostel, you can expect to find a self-catering kitchen with all utensils and dishes provided; a dining room; a sitting room, or some other kind of common space; dorm rooms that sleep 4 to 20 people, usually in bunk beds; and bathrooms with showers. Private rooms with either a double bed or two twin beds are usually the first rooms to go, so consider booking in advance. Many hostels close their doors between 11am and 5pm for cleaning and maintenance, and some lock up at midnight (you can usually ask for a key if you want to stay out later).

An Óige, the Irish affiliate of Hostelling International, is a nonprofit organization with 37 hostels throughout Ireland. Membership in Hostelling International is supposedly required at all *An Óige* hostels, but this rule is not widely enforced. I recommend waiting to buy membership until you actually need it, because every *An Óige* hostel can sell you a temporary membership. You can check out their hostels and make bookings on their website (**www.irelandyha.org**) or by contacting the head office at 61 Mountjoy St., Dublin 7 (*©* **01/830-4555;** fax 01/830/5808; anoige@iol.ie). The center city hostels in Dublin, Cork, Limerick, and Galway are all huge and institutional—okay if you just want a bed and a central location, but low on character. Most of *An Óige's* hostels are in the rural areas of Ireland, often in incredibly remote and beautiful settings—you'll need your own transportation, because few of these hostels are on bus lines. The facilities here are severely spartan, cleanliness is variable, and accommodation is exclusively in dorms. In Northern Ireland, the Hostelling International affiliate is the **Youth Hostel Association of Northern Ireland (YHANI),** also known as HINI (Hostelling International Northern Ireland), 56 Bradbury Place, Belfast, BT7 1RU (*©* **028/9032-4733;** www.hini.org.uk), which operates eight hostels.

The other hosteling organization you should know about is **Independent Holiday Hostels (IHH),** a marketing group that includes about 150 hostels approved by the tourist board. The group publishes a list of member hostels with prices and other stats; you can pick one up in any tourist office or request one from the IHH office, 57 Lower Gardiner St., Dublin 1 (*©* **01/836-4700;** fax 01/836-4710; www.hostels-ireland.com). No membership is required, and there are no curfews or lockouts. Quality does vary, but the standards are generally quite high.

BED & BREAKFAST HOMES

Throughout Ireland, in cities and countryside, a huge number of private homes are open to lodgers, by the night or longer. A warm bed and a substantial Irish breakfast can be expected, and other meals are negotiable. While most B&Bs are regulated and inspected by Tourism Quality Services (look for the shamrock seal of approval), approximately 12,000 premises are under no external supervision. Regulated or not, they are all different, as are your hosts. (*Note:* Establishments without governmental supervision or approval are not necessarily inferior to those stamped with the green shamrock. Approval involves an annual fee, as well as specific restrictions that some proprietors prefer not to embrace.)

For a modest fee, the Irish Tourist Board will send you a detailed listing of roughly 2,000 approved B&Bs, complete with a color photo of each. Or, you can follow the recommendations in this book. Needless to say, you receive the personal touch when you stay in someone's home, and more often than not, this is a real bonus. For anyone on a budget who is touring the country and spending only a night or two in each location, B&Bs are often hard to beat.

In high season, it's a good idea to make your reservation at least 24 hours in advance; your room will ordinarily be held until 6pm. The cost for a room with private bath is roughly 28€ to 44€ ($25–$40) per person, per night. *Note:* Many B&Bs still do not accept credit cards.

In the North, the Northern Ireland Tourist Board inspects each of its recommended bed-and-breakfasts annually. Its *Information Guide to Bed & Breakfast* is available free from the NITB. The NITB also sells a useful comprehensive annual listing titled *Where to Stay in Northern Ireland.*

FARMHOUSES The vast majority of Irish farms—170,000 in all—are relatively small and remain family owned and operated. In recent years, many of these farms have opened their doors to visitors and provide attractive alternatives to hotels, guesthouses, and more standard bed-and-breakfast homes, particularly for families. The **Irish Farm Holidays Association (www.irishfarmholidays.com)** produces an annual book of listings of farmhouse accommodations throughout the country. It is available from the Irish Tourist Board (see "Visitor Information & Entry Requirements," earlier in this chapter). The **Irish Organic Farmers and Growers Association** (IOGFA), 56 Blessington St., Dublin 7 (© **01/830-7996;** http://homepage.eircom.net/~iofga), provides a list of Irish guesthouses with organic kitchen gardens' on their website. In the North, the **Northern Ireland Farm and Country Holidays Association** offers a similar list, available as a booklet from the Northern Ireland Tourist Board (see "Visitor Information & Entry Requirements," earlier in this chapter).

Farm holidays can take various forms, from one-night-at-a-time B&Bs to extended self-catering rentals. In addition to breakfast, many of the farmhouse accommodations offer high tea and/or a full dinner. Some of these farms are everything you could dream of—full working family farms in untouched, often spectacular surroundings—while others stretch the definition of *farm* to include country houses with a garden and a dog nearby, or guesthouses that are more "lodging with greenery" than "farm with lodging."

One of the newest developments on the Irish tourism scene is **Irish Country Holidays,** a program that invites visitors to share everyday life with the Irish in communities that are usually off the tourist track. Visitors are put up in homes, farms, self-catering cottages, or hotels, and they're given the opportunity to take part in turf cutting, bread baking, cheese making, butter churning, salmon smoking, wood turning, and pottery making. Leisure activities such as fishing, canoeing, rock climbing, hill walking, cycling, and horse riding are also part of the holiday. At night there's traditional Irish music, song, dance, and amateur drama productions. Each holiday package is custom-planned. For more information, contact Dervla O'Neill, Irish Country Holidays, 5 Lord Edward Ct., Bride Street, Dublin 8 (© **01/676-5790;** fax 01/676-5793).

GUESTHOUSES   Irish guesthouses are something like the traditional small inn—a combination of the services you expect in hotels (most, for instance, have telephones, TVs, and hair dryers) with the personalized service and informality of a B&B. Some have been built for this specific purpose, others are in period residences, and others started as a popular B&B and just expanded to meet demand.

Even though you'll be paying a higher rate than in the B&Bs, there are several advantages to staying in a guesthouse. For example, many have a restaurant right on the premises, which can be a real convenience. And they are also allowed to sell wine (but not spirits) to guests. Most have single rooms. In the disadvantage column, all guesthouse rates are subject to a small value-added tax (VAT) for accommodation, food, drink, and other services.

Depending on facilities, location, and season, guesthouse rates range from 30€ to 65€ ($27–$59) per person sharing. The Irish Tourist Board includes all approved guesthouses in its *Ireland Accommodation Guide,* available at all tourist offices. Its *Be Our Guest* booklet includes pictures, and is also online at **www.beourguest.ie**, which is a particularly handy, searchable site. A new marketing group called Premier Guesthouses publishes a booklet listing its more than 50 members; it's available from the tourist office, or you can contact the **Premier Guesthouses** office (© **01/4751813;** fax 01/4755321; www.premier-guesthouses.ie).

SELF-CATERING One of the most effective money-saving plans for families and groups traveling together is to rent your own "home" and eat in when it suits you. Most self-catering rentals have one-week minimums, but that doesn't necessarily mean that your travels are restricted; Ireland is small enough that you could comfortably see the whole country by making short day trips from three or four different bases. There are many advantages to having a home base: You don't have to pack every day, and you have more privacy and autonomy than either hostels or B&Bs can offer. Kitchens are usually stocked with the basic utensils but little more, so plan to stop by the nearest Dunnes Stores or some other inexpensive department store to pick up the cooking supplies you can't do without. Laundry machines are sometimes provided, as are dishwashers and televisions.

Self-catering accommodations come in all guises, from inner-city town houses and apartments to freestanding houses in small towns, country and seaside bungalows, thatched cottages, and chalets. In off-season months, it's possible in some locations to rent for a few midweek days or weekends only, but most rental periods run from Saturday (beginning at 4pm) to the following Saturday (ending before noon). There are generally three price periods: April, May, June, and September (midrange prices); July and August (peak prices); and October through March (lowest price). Rates can range from about 250€ to 1,200€ ($226–$1,087) in the peak season for a two or three bedroom cottage. Rates drop sharply in low season. If you're traveling with a gaggle of children or friends, your per-person costs can be comparable to those of hostelling or the cheapest B&Bs.

Make sure to ask about additional charges—most rentals do not include heat or electricity, and many cottages have additional per-person, cleaning, and other charges.

Contact **Family Homes of Ireland** or the Irish Tourist Board for a copy of the *All Ireland Self-Catering Accommodation Guide;* the address is Family Homes of Ireland, Fough West Business Park, Oughterard, County Galway (© **091/552000;** fax 091/552666; www.family-homes.ie;). Information can also be requested from **Irish Cottage Holiday Homes,** Central Reservations Office, 4 Whitefriars, Aungier Street, Dublin 2 (© **01/475-1932;** fax 01/475-5321; www.ichh.ie); or from **Rent an Irish Cottage plc.,** 85 O'Connell St., Limerick, County Limerick (© **061/411109;** fax 061/314821; www.rentacottage.ie).

Finally, for self-catering in any of the areas of outstanding natural beauty in the North, there is one sureshot recommendation: Contact **Rural Cottage Holidays Ltd.,** St. Anne's Court, 59 North St., Belfast BT1 1NB (© **028/9024-1100;** fax 028/9024-1198; www.ruralcottageholidays.com). Founded in 1994 by the Northern Irish Tourist Board, Rural Cottage Holidays has restored and refurbished over 30 traditional homes of character and charm, and done so with remarkable care and style. Each of these gems is set in an area of special beauty and interest and is hosted by a nearby local family.

RESERVATIONS Many hotels can be booked through toll-free 800 numbers in the United States. For those properties that do not have a U.S. reservation number, the fastest way to reserve is by telephone or fax. Fax is preferable because you'll have a printed confirmation. You can follow up by sending a deposit check (usually the equivalent of 1 night's room rate) or by giving your credit card number.

If you arrive in Ireland without a reservation, the staff members at the tourist offices throughout the Republic and Northern Ireland will gladly find you a room via a computerized reservation service known as Gulliver. You can also call the **Gulliver** line directly yourself by dialing ✆ **0800/668-668-66.** This is a nationwide and cross-border "freephone" facility for credit-card bookings, operated daily 8am to 11pm. Gulliver is now accessible as well from the United States by dialing ✆ **011800/668-668-66.**

QUALITY & VALUE Despite the various systems of approval, regulation, and rating, guest accommodations in Ireland are quite uneven in quality and cost. A budget hostel may be cleaner and more accommodating than a guesthouse or hotel and be only a third as costly. Tourism in Ireland is a boom industry and there's a general rush to be a part of it, and as with all rushes, it takes a while for standards and practices to shake themselves out. It's always well to consult a fellow traveler or a reliable guidebook in booking your lodgings—which, of course, is what you're doing as you read this.

If possible, ask to see your room before committing yourself to a stay. In any given lodging, the size and quality of the rooms can vary considerably, often without any corresponding variation in cost. This is particularly true of single rooms, which even in a semi-luxurious hotel can approach boardinghouse standards. Don't be discouraged by this, but be alert so you're not disappointed.

Note: Many hotels, guesthouses, and so forth close for a few days or more on and around Christmas, even when they announce that they are open year-round. Consequently, if you plan to visit Ireland during the Christmas holidays, double-check that the hotels, restaurants, and attractions you are counting on will, in fact, be open. Furthermore, in this guide, what is true of Sundays is nearly always true for bank holidays.

13 Finding the Best Shopping Bargains

ARAN SWEATERS At the top of most visitors' shopping lists is one of Ireland's famed Aran knit sweaters. As much a part of the Irish landscape as stone walls and green fields, they're perfect to buy early in your trip to wear during chilly weather. They've been made in Ireland as far back as the 9th century, and originated with fishermen along the west coast (especially in the Aran Islands, hence the name) who valued their water resistance as well as their warmth. Today, most of the heavy natural oil has been removed from the wool and they're much softer than they used to be.

Designs, however, haven't changed at all, and for good reason. Long ago, each stitch depicted a different part of Irish life: The cable stitch stood for the fisherman's strong rope (it's also supposed to bring good luck), and the trellis stitch represented stone walls. Using a combination of many such symbolic stitches, fishing villages designed patterns unique to each community, making it possible to return any drowned fisherman to his hometown for burial. Interestingly, in the beginning, the sweaters were knit by men—women were relegated to the spinning of the wool.

A word of caution is in order about these sweaters (called *jerseys* in Ireland), because not all the creamy, off-white, cable-stitched sweaters you see are handmade. More and more machine knits are appearing in shops, and if a lower price is your primary consideration or if you prefer a lighter-weight garment, you may be just as happy with one of these. They will not, however, have anything like the longevity of the real thing.

Hand-knits wear like iron, and I have one that I'm sure will be passed on for several generations. You should be able to tell the difference by the sheer weight of a hand-knit, but if you have any doubt, be sure to ask the salesperson. **Standun's**, in Galway, and **Macken of Ireland,** in Killarney, both have good stocks and prices.

WOOLENS & TWEEDS   For centuries, Donegal homes came complete with looms from which poured the lovely tweeds and other woolens that are known all over the world. It's rare, however, to find a home loom today; most of the weaving is done in small factories concentrated in Donegal and in a few other spots around the country. You can watch a weaver at work if you call on **Magee's of Donegal** in Donegal Town, or **Avoca Handweavers** in County Wicklow. All department stores carry woolens sold by the yard or made up into coats, suits, capes, and skirts, but some of the best selections are to be found at **Magee's of Donegal** and at **Padraic O Maille's** in Galway. The **House of Ireland,** in Dublin, has a stylish selection of woolen garments.

WATERFORD GLASS   Waterford "glass" is actually crystal, because it contains 33% lead oxide in addition to basic ingredients of silica sand and potash (crystal must contain no less than 22%, no more than 33.5%). Waterford is both beautiful and expensive.

You can tour the factory in Waterford (see chapter 6, "The Southeast") and browse through its shop. Waterford crystal is, of course, found in many shops and department stores around Ireland. **Shannon Duty-Free Shops** carry a pretty good selection, and you'll find extensive stocks and good prices at **Joyce's** in Wexford, **Joseph Knox Ltd.** in Waterford, and the **House of Ireland** in Dublin.

BOOKS   What better memento to carry home from Ireland than a book!

After all, words have been pouring from Irish minds to the printed page in a veritable flood since the beginning of history. Any book lover is quite likely to go a bit mad at the sight of such a wealth of bookshops, and the bargain hunter will happily spend hours sifting through used-book stalls and bookstore basements with their tables of reduced-price volumes.

Dublin has lost a few of its oldest, most revered bookshops, which fell victim to increased taxes and rental costs. **Greene's Bookshop** on Clare Street is one of the city's best second-hand bookshops; **Cathach Books** on Duke Street is good for first editions and rare books; and **Fred Hanna's** on Nassau Street has the best selection of new books. In Galway, **Kenny's Bookshop** is a national treasure, and a treat not to be missed.

SHOPPING IRELAND'S MARKETS   Markets have a venerable tradition in Ireland, and are an important part of the country's social life. When the English penal code was in effect, and most trade was forbidden among the Irish, covert markets in caves and other out-of-the-way places did a flourishing business. These days you can find markets throughout the country—from famous ones in the big cities to popular country markets, usually held on Saturday or Sunday—that are often cleared out within minutes of opening.

Cork has a couple of renowned markets that you shouldn't miss. The **Coal Quay** on Cornmarket Street is a treasure trove of secondhand clothes, old china, and used books. A Cork tradition since 1610, the stalls of the **English Market** overflow with meats, fish, vegetables, and fruit. In Dublin, you can visit the **Moore Street Market** for fruit, flowers, fruit and vegetables.

VAT TAX REFUNDS
All goods and services in Ireland are subject to a 17.36% tax, known as the

VAT (value-added tax). For non-European visitors to Ireland it's relatively easy to arrange a **refund** of all VAT tax paid on goods (the tax paid on services is nonrefundable).

The first thing you should know is that VAT is a "hidden tax"—it's already added into the purchase price of any items you see in shops. (The two notable exceptions: no VAT on books and no VAT on children's clothing and footwear). There are two ways to get your money back.

Global Refund (© 800/566-9828; www.globalrefund.ie) is the world's largest private company offering VAT refunds, with over 5,000 stores in Ireland displaying "Tax Free for Tourists" stickers in their front windows. Unlike all other EU countries, Ireland requires no minimum purchase in a single store. The system works like this:

> **Step 1:** Collect refund cheques at every store where you make a purchase.
>
> **Step 2:** Fill in the blanks (name, address, passport number, etc.) on the cheques, noting whether you'd like your refund in cash or credit card.
>
> **Step 3:** Hand in your completed cheques to the VAT-refund desk at the airport just before departing Ireland. The VAT desk is in the departures hall at Dublin airport and in the arrivals hall at Shannon airport. If you're running late at the airport, you can have the cheques stamped by customs and post them to Global Refund in an international prepaid envelope. Finally, if you forget to get your cheques stamped at customs, all is not lost. Just get them stamped by either a notary public, justice of the peace, or a police officer (with a badge number) in your home country, and mail them back.

What if the shop isn't part of the Global Refund network? For a **store refund,** get a full receipt at the time of purchase that shows the shop's name, address, and VAT paid. (Customs does not accept generic cash-register tally slips.) Save your receipts until you're ready to depart Ireland; go to the Customs Office at the airport or ferry port to have your receipts stamped and your goods inspected. A passport and other forms of identification (a driver's license, for example) may be required. Then send your stamped receipts back to the store where you made the purchase, which will then issue a VAT refund check to you by mail to your home address. Most stores deduct a small handling fee for this service.

AVOIDING THE VAT HASSLE

Don't want to fill out those forms? Hate the thought of lining up at the airport refund desk? There are three ways to pay no VAT from the beginning.

- **Mail your purchases home.** Arrange for the store to ship your purchases home, and the VAT will be subtracted at the point of sale. You save having to fill out those forms, and you don't have to lug around your stuff. But you still have to pay shipping costs, which may outweigh any hassle you save.
- **Buy at the airport.** When returning home from Ireland, non-EU citizens are entitled to shop in the Duty-Free Shops at Shannon and Dublin Airports. If you're flying on Aer Lingus, you can also shop onboard at the airline's "Duty-Free Sky Shop." These shops offer prices that are free of duty or tax. There are no forms to fill out and no lines to reclaim money. The main drawback is the very limited variety of goods compared to the shops around Ireland.
- **Support a good cause.** Ireland's non-profit organizations that sell

goods operate as charitable trusts and are not subject to VAT, so all their prices are VAT-free. Check out **Oxfam** shops (www.oxfam ireland.org) for pottery and other trendy housewares.

CUSTOMS   Upon returning home, you may have to report your purchases in Ireland to customs officials, but only if they exceed certain limitations.

Citizens of the U.K. & Other EU Countries   The Republic of Ireland and Northern Ireland are both members of the European Union. If you're a citizen of the European Union returning home from Ireland, you'll go through a separate Customs Exit (called the "Blue Exit") especially for EU travelers. In essence, there is no limit on what you can bring back from an EU country, as long as the items are for personal use (this includes gifts), and you have already paid the necessary duty and tax. However, customs law sets out guidance levels. If you bring in more than these levels, you may be asked to prove that the goods are for your own use. Guidance levels on goods bought in the EU for your own use are 800 cigarettes, 200 cigars, 1 kilogram smoking tobacco, 10 liters of spirits, 90 liters of wine (of this not more than 60 liters can be sparkling wine), and 110 liters of beer. For more information, contact **HM Customs & Excise, Passenger Enquiry Point,** 2nd Floor Wayfarer House, Great South West Road, Feltham, Middlesex, TW14 8NP (② **0181/910-3744;** from outside the U.K. 44/181-910-3744), or consult its website **at www. hmce.gov.uk**.

U.S. Citizens   Returning U.S. citizens are allowed to bring back, once every 30 days, $400 worth of merchandise duty-free. You'll be charged a flat rate of 10% duty on the next $1,000 worth of purchases. Be sure to have your receipts handy. You cannot bring fresh foodstuffs into the United States; tinned foods, however, are allowed. You can also mail gifts back to people in the U.S. duty-free if the value of the entire gift package does not exceed $100 (be sure to write on the wrapping of the package its dollar value and that it's a gift). For more information, contact the **U.S. Customs Service,** 1301 Constitution Ave. (P.O. Box 7407), Washington, DC 20044 (② **202/927-6724**) and request the free pamphlet "Know Before You Go," which is also available on the Web at **www.customs. gov/travel/travel.htm**.

Canadian Citizens   For a clear summary of Canadian rules, write for the booklet "I Declare," issued by **Revenue Canada,** 2265 St. Laurent Blvd., Ottawa K1G 4KE (② **613/ 993-0534**). Canada allows its citizens a $500 duty-free exemption, which includes 200 cigarettes, 2.2 pounds of tobacco, 40 imperial ounces of liquor, and 50 cigars. In addition, you're allowed to mail gifts to Canada from abroad at the rate of Can$60 a day, provided they're unsolicited and don't contain alcohol or tobacco (write on the package "Unsolicited gift, under $60 value"). *Note:* The $500 exemption can only be used once a year and only after an absence of 7 days.

Australian Citizens   The duty-free allowance in Australia is $400 or, for those under 18, $200. Citizens can bring in 250 cigarettes or 250 grams of loose tobacco, and 1,125 milliliters of alcohol. A helpful brochure, available from Australian consulates or customs offices, is "Know Before You Go." For more information, contact **Australian Customs Services,** GPO Box 8, Sydney, NSW 2001 (② **02/ 9213-2000**).

New Zealand Citizens   The duty-free allowance for New Zealand is $700. Citizens over 17 can bring in 200 cigarettes, or 50 cigars, or 250 grams of tobacco (or a mixture of all three if their combined weight doesn't exceed 250 grams); plus 4.5 liters of wine and beer, or 1.125 liters of liquor. Most questions are answered in a free pamphlet, available at New Zealand consulates and customs offices, called "New Zealand Customs Guide for Travellers, Notice no. 4." For more information, contact **New Zealand Customs,** 50 Anzac Ave., P.O. Box 29, Auckland (✆ **09/359-6655**).

14 Tracing Your Irish Roots

If you're one of the countless millions of Americans, Canadians, and Australians whose forebears came from Ireland, it's a good bet you'll want to investigate your family history while you're visiting. Tracking down your Irish roots may not prove to be a simple matter. To find a particular branch of your family tree, you'll want to know all you possibly can about your family history before leaving home. Search any and all records (letters, Bibles, relatives' memories, and so on). Try to get the names of the towns, villages, or counties where your kinfolk lived and the year they emigrated. The more you know about what they did, whom they married, and the like, the easier it will be to find your ancestral home or maybe even a distant cousin once you arrive.

You can hire the services of a commercial agency to trace your ancestors. One of the best firms to contact is **Hibernian Research Co.,** 24 Bainagowan, Palmerstown Park, Dublin 6 (✆ **01/496-6522;** fax 01/497-3011). Its researchers, all trained by the Chief Herald of Ireland, have a combined total of over 100 years' professional experience in working on all aspects of family histories. Among the cases that Hibernian Research has handled in the past were U.S. President Ronald Reagan, Canadian Prime Minister Brian Mulrooney, and Ireland's own President Mary Robinson. If your ancestors were from the North, a similar service is operated by the **Irish Heritage Association,** A. 215–217, Portview, 310 Newtownards Rd., Belfast BT4 1HE (✆ **028/9045-5325**). Minimum search fees average 70€ ($63).

Interested in doing the research yourself? Dublin is the location for all the Republic of Ireland's centralized genealogical records, and Belfast is the place to go for ancestral searches in the North. You can receive a special consultation on how to trace your ancestry at **The Genealogical Office,** 2 Kildare St., Dublin (✆ **01/6618811**), which is the office of the Chief Herald. It operates a specialist consultation service on how to trace your ancestry. Minimum personal consultation fee is 30€ ($27).

The Office of the Registrar General, Joyce House, 8/11 Lombard St. East, Dublin 2 (✆ **01/671-1000**), is the central repository for records relating to births, deaths, and marriages in the Republic (Catholic marriages from January 1, 1864; all other marriages from April 1, 1845). This office does not engage in genealogical research. Full birth, death, or marriage certificates each cost 7.50€ ($6.80). General searches cost 17€ ($15). The office is open weekdays from 9:30am to 12:30pm and 2:15 to 4:30pm.

The Manuscripts Reading Room in the **National Library,** Kildare Street, Dublin 2 (✆ **01/603-0200;** fax 01/676-6690; www.nli.ie) has an extensive collection of pre-1880 Catholic records of baptisms, births, and marriages. Its other genealogical material includes trade directories, journals of historical and archaeological societies, local histories, and most newspapers. In addition, the library has a comprehensive indexing system that enables you to identify the material you need to consult.

As mentioned above, **The National Archives,** Bishop Street, Dublin 8 (*C* **01/407-2300;** fax 01/407-2333; www.nationalarchives.ie) is a key resource. Until 1988, it was known as the Public Record Office. A fire severely damaged this facility in the early 1920s, and many valuable source documents were lost. However, numerous records rich in genealogical interest are still available. They include *Griffith's Primary Valuation of Ireland, 1848–63,* which records the names of all those owning or occupying land or property in Ireland at the time; the complete national census of 1901 to 1911; and tithe listings, indexes to wills, administrations, licenses, and marriage bonds. In addition, there is also an ever-expanding collection of Church of Ireland Parish Registers on microfilm. You'll also find partial surviving census returns for the 19th century, reports and records relating to the period of the 1798 rebellion, crime and convict records, and details of those sentenced to transportation to Australia.

There is no fee for conducting personal searches for family history and genealogy in the archives, and an instruction booklet is provided to get you started. There is a fee for photocopies. The National Archives reading room is open Monday to Friday, 10am to 5pm.

The Registry of Deeds, Kings Inns, Henrietta Street, Dublin 1 (*C* **01/670-7500;** fax 01/804-8406; www.irlgov.ie/landreg), has records that date from 1708 and relate to all the usual transactions affecting property—notably leases, mortgages, and settlements—and some wills. A fee of 14€ ($13) per day is charged, which includes instructions on how to handle the indexes.

North of the border, **The Public Record Office of Northern Ireland,** 66 Balmoral Ave., Belfast BT9 6NY (*C* **028/9025-1318;** fax 028/ 9025-5999; http://proni.nics.gov.uk), has most of the surviving official records of Northern Ireland. They include tithe and valuation records from the 1820s and 1830s, copies of wills from 1858 for Ulster, the records of many landed estates in Ulster, and copies of most pre-1900 registers of baptisms, marriages, and burial papers for all denominations in Ulster. The office is open weekdays 9:15am to 4:45pm (until 8:45pm on Thurs, closed for 2 weeks in late Nov). The website has a useful section entitled "How to Trace Your Family Tree," accessible through the Frequently Asked Questions rubric.

For post-1900 birth, marriage, and death certificates, contact the **General Register Office Northern Ireland,** Oxford House, 49–55 Chichester St., Belfast BT1 4HC (*C* **028/1232-251318**). No matter how you plan to go about your search, my best and strongest advice is to subscribe to *Inside Ireland,* P.O. Box 1886, Dublin 16 (*C* **01/493-1906;** fax 01/ 493-4538), and receive their **genealogical supplement** with your very first issue.

Once you have the basic data, it's off to the locality of your ancestors, where **parochial registers** often hold exactly what you're looking for. (You can also consult the various local genealogical centers and libraries throughout the Republic and Northern Ireland.) A talk with the parish priest may well send you off to shake the hand of a distant cousin or two still living in the neighborhood. Or you can begin your search by visiting the home of Irish genealogy on the Web: **www.genealogy.ie**. You can also consult **www.familysearch.com**.

15 Recommended Books & Films

BOOKS

Published in 1984, *The Course of Irish History* remains an excellent, accessible introduction to the full sweep of Irish history and prehistory, written by a collection of Irish scholars and edited by T. W. Moody and F. X. Martin, of Trinity College Dublin and University College Dublin, respectively (Cork: Mercier, 1987). Another Irish scholar, Peter Harbison, has produced a number of fine books on Ireland's history, art, and architecture, any of which, read in advance, would enhance your visit to Ireland. His most recent, written with Jacqueline O'Brien, is *Ancient Ireland* (London: Weidenfeld and Nicolson, 1996), a coffee-table book with dazzling photographs of ancient sites and generous, illuminating text. He has also written a *Guide to the National and Historic Monuments of Ireland,* an indispensable companion for anyone interested in Ireland's architectural and archaeological heritage. Next, a recent bestseller, Thomas Cahill's *How the Irish Saved Civilization,* presents a compelling and extremely readable glimpse into Ireland's golden age.

With the framework of Irish history in place, you may want to read some of Ireland's oldest texts—in translation, of course. Thomas Kinsella's translation of *The Tain* (New York: Oxford University Press, 1970) provides a stunning version of this epic, which recounts the invasion of Ulster and the feats of Cuchulainn, a Bronze-age superhero. John J. O'Meara's translation of *The Voyage of St. Brendan,* available from The Humanities Press, and Tim Severin's *The Brendan Voyage* (New York: McGraw Hill, 1978) make a fascinating double-feature for anyone intrigued by the claim that Irish monks discovered America in the 6th century. Next,

Seamus Heaney's version of the medieval classic *Buile Suibhne* (Sweeney Astray) retells the adventures of Sweeney, a king who went mad in battle, was cursed by a saint, and finally turned poet (New York: Noonday, 1995). Lastly, Marie Heaney, wife of the Nobel laureate, has provided a marvelous compendium of Irish stories, from the oldest myths to the lives of the Irish saints, in *Over Nine Waves: A Book of Irish Legends* (Boston: Faber and Faber, 1994).

Let's face it: Celts are really in at the moment, and so it may be helpful to recommend several titles for Celts or Celtic wannabes eager to explore their roots. Peter Beresford Ellis, made an official Cornish bard in 1987, has written two books of special interest: *The Celtic Empire: The First Millennium of Celtic History* (Durham, N.C.: Carolina Academic Press, 1990) and *The Druids* (Grand Rapids, Mich.: Eerdmans, 1994). Two other related and intriguing books are Nigel Pennick's *Celtic Sacred Landscapes* (New York: Thames and Hudson, 1996) and Miranda Green's *Celtic Goddesses: Warriors, Virgins and Mothers* (New York: George Braziller, 1996).

Finally, there's about a zillion books by and about Irish immigration, but a recent standout is New York educator and author Frank McCourt's best-selling memoir *Angela's Ashes,* which recounts the author's boyhood in County Limerick and eventual emigration as a young man (New York: Simon and Schuster, 1996). The sequel, *'Tis* (New York: Simon and Schuster, 1999), tells the story of McCourt's life as an Irish immigrant in New York City.

For general information about Ireland, one volume, available from the Irish Department of Foreign

Affairs, is nearly indispensable. Its understated title, *Facts About Ireland,* might well be altered to read *Everything You Ever Wanted to Know about Ireland but Didn't Know Who to Ask.* Copies may be requested from your nearest Irish consulate.

FILMS

Throughout film history, Ireland and the Irish have been focal movie subjects, and everyone has his or her favorites—*The Quiet Man,* various Bing Crosby films, Barry Fitzgerald as the Irish curmudgeon or the Irish drunk. What many of these films have partly created and unquestionably preserved is an impression of Irish life that may be endearing at a distance but can be demeaning at close range. Sentimentality, superstition, and stout form the core of that impression— malarkey, in a word. As an antidote, I'd suggest a handful of films that are more realistic in their depiction of contemporary Irish life. The following describe the Ireland visitors are more likely to encounter on the ground: Noel Pierson and Jim Sheridan's *My Left Foot;* Alan Parker's *The Commitments; A Man of No Importance,* starring Albert Finney; and *In the Name of the Father,* filmed partly in Dublin's Kilmainham Jail. Two additional films for the whole family, deeply magical without bursting into sentimentality, are *Into the West* and *The Secret of Roan Innish.* Lastly, for a highly affecting look at the war of independence and the civil war, check Neil Jordan's *Michael Collins.*

 FAST FACTS: **Ireland**

American Express   The American Express office is located opposite Trinity College, just off College Green, at 41 Nassau St., Dublin 2 (✆ **01/ 679-9000**), and is open Monday to Friday 9am to 5pm. American Express also has a currency exchange desk at the Dublin Tourism Office on Suffolk Street. In an emergency, traveler's checks can be reported lost or stolen by dialing collect ✆ **1-44-1-273-571-600.** The only other American Express offices in Ireland are in Galway and Killarney. There are no longer any American Express offices in the North.

Business Hours   As a rule, Irish banks are open for service 10am to 12:30pm and 1:30 to 3pm, Monday through Friday, with one late-closing day (Thursdays in Dublin), when they close at 5pm. In larger cities many banks remain open through the lunch hour as well. Airport banks are open 7:30am to 11pm every day of the year, with the exception of Christmas.

Most business offices are open from 9am to 5pm, Monday through Friday. Stores and shops are open from 9am to 5:30pm Monday through Saturday. In cities such as Dublin, Belfast, Cork, and Galway, stores remain open until 8pm or 9pm on Thursday or Friday. In some country towns, there is an early closing day when shops close at 1pm. Many tourist-oriented shops also open on Sunday from 11am or noon until 5pm or later. For exact shopping hours, see each individual chapter.

Currency Exchange   A currency exchange service in Ireland is signposted as a bureau de change. There are bureaux de change at all banks and at many post office branches. In addition, many hotels and travel agencies offer bureau de change services, although the best rate of exchange is usually given at banks.

Doctor In an emergency, most hotels and guesthouses will contact a house doctor for you. You can also call either the Eastern Health Board Headquarters, Dr. Steevens Hospital, Dublin 8 (✆ **01/679-0700**); or the Irish Medical Council, (✆ **01/496-5588**). See also "Doctors—Medical" in the Golden Pages of the telephone book.

Drugstores Drugstores are usually called "chemist shops" or "pharmacies." Look under "Chemists—Pharmaceutical" in the Golden Pages of the Irish telephone book or "Chemists—Dispensing" in the Yellow Pages of the Northern Ireland telephone book.

Electricity The standard electrical current is 220 volts AC in the Republic of Ireland and 240 volts in Northern Ireland. Most hotels have 110-volt shaver points for use in bathrooms, but other 110-volt equipment (such as hair dryers) will not work without a transformer and a plug adapter. Computers and sensitive electronic equipment may require more than the standard over-the-counter voltage converter. Some laptops, on the other hand, have built-in converters. Consult the manufacturer of your computer for specifics. In any event, you will always need a plug adapter.

Embassies/Consulates The **American Embassy** is located at 42 Elgin Rd., Ballsbridge, Dublin 4 (✆ **01/668-8777**); the **Canadian Embassy** at 65/68 St. Stephen's Green, Dublin 2 (✆ **01/678-1988**); the **British Embassy** at 33 Merrion Rd., Dublin 4 (✆ **01/205-3700**); the **Australian Embassy** at Fitzwilton House, Wilton Terrace, Dublin 2 (✆ **01/676-1517**); and the **New Zealand consulate,** opened in 2000, is located at 46 Upper Mount St., Dublin 2 (✆ **01/660-4233**). In addition, there is an **American Consulate** at 14 Queen St., Belfast BT1 6EQ (✆ **0232/328239**).

Emergencies For police, fire, or other emergencies, dial ✆ **999.**

Fare Terminology Transport fares—air, ferry, train—are either "single" (one-way) or "return" (round-trip).

Hospitals See listings in the individual destination chapters.

Liquor Laws Individuals must be age 18 or over to be served alcoholic beverages in Ireland. In the Republic closing time for pubs is 12:30am Thursday, Friday and Saturday; 11:30pm Monday, Tuesday, and Wednesday; and 11pm Sunday. In the North pubs are open year-round from 11:30am to 11pm Monday through Saturday, and from 12:30 to 2pm and 7 to 10pm on Sunday. Restaurants with liquor licenses are permitted to serve alcohol during the hours meals are served. Hotels and guesthouses with licenses can serve during normal hours to the general public; overnight guests, referred to as residents, can be served after closing hours. Alcoholic beverages by the bottle can be purchased at liquor stores, at pubs displaying "off-license" signs, and at some supermarkets.

Ireland has very strict laws and penalties regarding driving while intoxicated.

Mail In Ireland, mailboxes are painted green with the word Post on top. In Northern Ireland, they are painted red with a royal coat of arms symbol. From the Republic, an airmail letter or postcard to the United States or Canada, not exceeding 25 grams, costs .57€ (55¢) and takes from 5 to 7 days to arrive. Pre-stamped aerogrammes or air-letters are also .57€

(55¢) individually and 2.80€ ($2.55) for five. From Northern Ireland to the United States or Canada, airmail letters and postcards both cost .64€ (58¢). Delivery also takes about 5 days to a week.

The best way to receive mail while in Ireland is to have it sent care of your hotel or guesthouse. Otherwise, you can have mail sent to the GPO (general post office). This service is called *Poste Restante*. To use it, mail should be addressed to your name, in care of the post office in the city where you will be staying. *Poste Restante* mail is ordinarily held for a maximum of 3 months. If unclaimed during that period, it is returned to the sender. There is no charge for this service. Mail can be picked up at the Dublin GPO Monday through Saturday, 8am to 8pm and Sunday 10:30am to 6:30pm. Generally, other post offices in Dublin and the larger cities and towns are open Monday through Saturday, 9am to 6pm; in the smaller villages the hours are generally weekdays from 9am to 5:30pm (closing for lunch from 1 to 2:15pm) and Saturdays 9am to 1pm.

Newspapers/Magazines The national daily newspapers in the Republic of Ireland are *Irish Times, Irish Independent, The Examiner, The Herald, Cork Examiner,* and *Evening Echo.* The national Sunday editions are *Sunday Independent, Sunday Press, Sunday Tribune, Sunday World,* and Irish-language *Anola.* Prime dailies in the North are the *Belfast Newsletter* and the *Belfast Telegraph.* For useful and up-to-date listings of events throughout Ireland, *The Event Guide* is published biweekly and is available free of cost practically wherever you look for it.

Police In the Republic of Ireland, a law enforcement officer is called a *Garda,* a member of the *Garda Siochana* (guardian of the peace); in the plural, it's *Gardai* (pronounced *gar*-dee) or simply "the Guards." Dial ℂ **999** to reach the Gardai in an emergency. Except for special detachments, Irish police are unarmed and wear dark blue uniforms. In Northern Ireland, the police can also be reached by dialing ℂ 999.

Radio/TV In the Republic of Ireland, RTÉ (Radio Telefis Éireann) is the national broadcasting authority with two nationwide TV channels, RTÉ 1 and Network 2; a new Irish language channel, Teilifís na Gaelige; and three nationwide VHF radio networks, Radio 1, 2FM, and Radió na Gaeltachta (in both Irish and English). Additionally, FM3 offers classical music programming. Other, smaller local stations, like Cork Local Radio, serve specific regions. In North America, RTÉ radio is available via the Galaxy 5 satellite and on the World Wide Web at **www.rte.ie.** RTÉ, jointly with Telecom Éireann, owns and operates Cablelink Ltd., providing a range of cable and satellite channels from Britain and further abroad.

The latest addition to the Irish airwaves is TV3, Ireland's first independent and wholly commercial station.

In the North, there is Ulster Television, BBC-TV (British Broadcasting Corporation), and ITN-TV (Independent), plus BBC Radio 1, 2, and 3. Satellite programs via CNN, SKY News, and other international operators are also received.

Restrooms Public restrooms are usually simply called "toilets," or are marked with international symbols. In the Republic of Ireland, some of the older ones still carry the Gaelic words *Fir* (Men) and *Mna* (Women).

The newest and best-kept restrooms are found at shopping complexes and at multistory car parks—some cost .40€ (35¢) to enter. Free use of restrooms is available to customers of sightseeing attractions, museums, hotels, restaurants, pubs, shops, theaters, and department stores. It is not ordinary for gas stations to have public toilets.

Safety The Republic of Ireland has enjoyed a traditionally low crime rate, particularly when it comes to violent crimes. Those days are not entirely over, but they do regrettably seem to be passing, especially in the cities. By U.S. standards, Ireland is still very safe, but not so safe as to warrant carelessness. Travelers should take normal precautions to protect their belongings from theft and themselves from harm.

In recent years, the larger cities have been prey to pickpockets, purse snatchers, car thieves, and drug traffickers. To alert visitors to potential dangers, the Garda Siochana publishes a small leaflet, *A Short Guide to Tourist Security,* available at tourist offices and other public places. The booklet advises you not to carry large amounts of money or important documents like your passport or airline tickets when strolling around (leave them in a safety deposit box at your hotel). Do not leave cars unlocked or cameras, binoculars, or other expensive equipment unattended. Be alert and aware of your surroundings, and do not wander in lonely areas alone at night. It is now appropriate to ask which areas are safe and which are not, and when.

In the north of Ireland, safety is a somewhat greater concern because of the political unrest that has prevailed there for the past 30 years. Before traveling to Northern Ireland, visitors are advised to contact the U.S. State Department and the Northern Ireland Tourist Board to obtain the latest safety recommendations. The **U.S. Department of State 24-hour hotline** provides travel warnings and security recommendations, as well as emergency assistance. Call © **202/647-5225.**

Taxes As in many European countries, sales tax is called value-added tax (VAT) and is often included in the price quoted to you. In the Republic, VAT rates vary—for hotels, restaurants, and car rentals, it's 12.5%; for souvenirs and gifts, it is 17.36%. In Northern Ireland, the VAT is 17.5% across the board. VAT charged on services such as hotel stays, meals, car rentals, and entertainment cannot be refunded to visitors, but the VAT charged on products such as souvenirs is refundable. For full details on VAT refunds for purchases, see "VAT Tax Refunds," earlier in this chapter.

Telephone In the Republic, the telephone system is known as Telecom Éireann; in Northern Ireland, it's British Telecom.

To telephone Ireland, dial the international access code (**011** from the United States), then the country code—**353** for the Republic, **44** for the North—and finally the number, remembering to omit the initial 0, which is for use only within Ireland. For example, to call the County Kerry number 066/00000 from the United States, you'd dial 011/353-66/00000. For direct-dial calls to the United States from Ireland, dial the international access code (**00** from Ireland), then the country code (1), followed by the area code and number. To place a collect call to the United States from Ireland, dial © **1-800/550-000** for USA Direct service.

Phone numbers both in Ireland and in Northern Ireland are currently in flux, as digits are added to accommodate expanded service. Every effort has been made to ensure that the numbers and information in this guide are accurate at the time of writing. If you have difficulty reaching a party, the Irish toll-free number for directory assistance is ✆ **1190.** From the United States, the (toll) number to call is ✆ **00353-91-770220.**

Local calls from a phone booth cost .40€ (35¢) within the Republic of Ireland, and 20p (33¢) in the North for the first minute. The most efficient way to make calls from public phones is to use a Callcard in the Republic and a Phonecard in the North. Both are prepaid computerized cards you insert into the phone in lieu of coins. They can be purchased in a range of denominations at phone company offices, post offices, and many retail outlets (such as newsstands).

Overseas calls from Ireland can be quite costly, whether you use a local Phonecard or your own calling card. If you think you will be wanting to call home regularly while in Ireland, you may want to open an account with **Swiftcall** (✆ **800-BE-SWIFT;** www.swiftcall.com), whose rates represent a considerable savings, not only from Ireland to the United States but vice versa (handy for planning your trip as well as keeping in touch afterward). **Premiere WORLDLINK** (✆ **800-432-6169**) offers an array of additional services for overseas travelers, such as toll-free voicemail boxes, fax mail, news services, and so on, all of which can be crucial for keeping in touch when you don't know where or when you can be reached from one day to the next.

Time Ireland is normally five time zones ahead of the eastern United States (that is, when it's noon in New York, it's 5pm in Ireland), and 8 hours ahead of the western United States (when it's noon in Los Angeles, it's 8pm in Ireland). Clocks are turned back the last Sunday in October and advanced the last Sunday in March. This is somewhat different from the U.S., where clocks are changed the last Sunday in October and the first Sunday in April.

Ireland's latitude makes for longer days and shorter nights in the summer, and the reverse in the winter. In mid-June, there is bright sun until 10pm, but in December, it is truly dark at 4pm.

Tipping Most hotels and guesthouses add a service charge to the bill, usually 12.5% to 15%, although some smaller places add only 10% or nothing at all. Always check to see what amount, if any, has been added to your bill. If it is 12.5% to 15%, and you feel this is sufficient, then there is no need for further gratuities. However, if a lesser amount has been added or if staff members have provided exceptional service, then it is appropriate to give additional cash gratuities. For taxi drivers, hairdressers, and other providers of service, tip as you would at home, an average of 10% to 15%.

For restaurants, the policy is usually printed on the menu—either a gratuity of 10% to 15% is added to your bill or, in some cases, no service charge is added, leaving it up to you. Always ask if you are in doubt. As a rule, bar staff do not expect a tip, except when table service is provided.

Water Tap water throughout the island of Ireland is generally safe to drink, though contamination of ground water and private wells is an increasing problem. If you prefer bottled water, it is readily available at all hotels, guesthouses, restaurants, and pubs.

Yellow Pages The classified section of telephone books in the Republic of Ireland is called the Golden Pages. In the North, it's the Yellow Pages.

3

Ireland Outdoors

To many a prospective visitor, "Ireland Outdoors" might prompt only images of rain and more rain. Well, I'm not going to deny that it rains a lot in Ireland. What's missing in that picture is what people *do* in the rain. I wouldn't be able to count the number of times I've been told, "if we waited for the sun to blaze, we'd never do anything." And the Irish do plenty.

The truth is that the Irish climate doesn't stop the Irish from doing anything they want, when they want to do it, from golfing to hiking to windsurfing to cycling. And the same is becoming true of their visitors. The days are long gone when the most aerobic thing tourists did in Ireland was to trace their roots. Practically every corner of Ireland is packed with opportunities for outdoor activities, and even when it absolutely pours or when the sun sets—both equally inevitable—there's always the health and leisure clubs offered at hundreds of hotels from Mizen Head to the North Antrim coast. There may not be much wilderness in Ireland, but there are some of the clearest streams and most unspoiled landscapes in all of Europe.

For some, the Irish weather invigorates, and even for the rest of us, mist, cold rain, and incessant dampness can be conquered if not avoided. The rosy cheeks of Irish campers, cyclists, and windsurfers can be yours; just be sure to bring high-quality rain gear. Finally, remember that not even the Irish go hiking in the fog and that even the best cyclists falter in blinding rain with wet brakes. Most of the time, a little rain won't hurt you—but sometimes, that Guinness in front of a crackling fire really is the best choice.

1 Bicycling

If you don't mind the occasional shower, cycling is an excellent way to see the Irish landscape in its many forms, from barren bog land to crashing surf and inland lakes. The distances are manageable, and, with a week or two on a bike, you can travel through several of the regions described in this guide, or explore one in greater detail. Accommodations in the form of hostels, B&Bs, and hotels is abundantly available for touring cyclists who don't want to deal with the extra weight of a tent and sleeping bag. For those on more conventional (read: motorized) tours, day trips on a bike are a great way to stretch your legs after spending too much time in the car. Rentals are available in most towns that cater in any way to tourists.

Cycling in Ireland is not without its **perils,** however. Back roads are often dangerously narrow, and cars are perilously fast—and there's always the weather. Be sure to carry good rain gear, ride a bike with good fenders, and plan your route carefully.

Roads in Ireland are categorized as either **M** (Motorway), **N** (National), or **R** (Regional), with some still bearing the older **T** (Trunk) and **L** (Link) designations. For reasons of scenery as well as safety, you'll probably want to avoid the busier roads; the "R" and "L" roads are always suitable for cycling, and the "N" roads are as well in outlying areas where there isn't too much traffic. The disadvantage of the smallest roads in remote areas is that they are rarely signposted, so you'll want a good map and compass to be sure of your way. In some areas of the west and northwest, *only* the "N" roads are consistently signposted.

Any serious cyclist planning a tour will want to bring his or her own bicycle—the ones available for rent are, with few exceptions, impossibly heavy and fitted with unreliable components. If you must rent a bike, there are a few small items you'll want to bring. Helmets are only sporadically available, and your chances of finding one that fits are poor, so bring one if you care about your head. The panniers (saddlebags) offered for rental are often unbelievably flimsy, and may begin to fall apart shortly after departure, so bring your own unless you want to leave a trail of your stuff as you go. If you have cycling shoes and good pedals, you can easily attach them to the rental bike; this will make your trip immeasurably more enjoyable. With advance notice, most rental shops can outfit a bike with such handy extras as toe clips, bar ends, and water bottle cages; an advance booking will also improve your chances of reserving the right-size bike. Many rental outfits can also arrange a one-way rental over a short distance—up to 100 miles (160km) or so—and the national companies such as Irish Cycle Hire or Raleigh Rent-A-Bike are set up for one-way rentals throughout the country. (See "Bicycling Resources," below, for information.)

Anyone cycling in Ireland should be prepared for two inevitable obstacles to forward progress: **wind** and **hills.** Outside of the midlands, there are hills just about anywhere you go, and those on the back roads can have outrageously steep grades: Road engineering is primitive, and instead of using switchbacks on a steep slope, a road will often climb by the most direct route. The prevailing winds on Ireland's west coast blow from south to north, so by traveling in the same direction you can save yourself a lot of effort over the course of a long tour.

The **coastal roads** of the southwest, west, and northwest have long been favored by cyclists. The quiet roads and rugged scenery of the **Beara Peninsula** (see chapter 8, "Out from Cork") make it perfect for a cycling tour, along with the nearby **Dingle Peninsula** (see chapter 9, "The Southwest: County Kerry"). **Donegal** (see chapter 13, "The Northwest") is one of the hilliest regions, but it rewards the energetic cyclist with some of the most spectacular coastal and mountain scenery in Ireland.

Also ideal for cycling are Ireland's many **islands:** You can bring your bike on all the passenger ferries, often for no extra charge, and discover roads with little or no traffic. Some of the best islands with accommodations are **Cape Clear,** County Cork (see chapter 8, "Out from Cork); **Great Blasket Island,** County Kerry (see chapter 9, "The Southwest: County Kerry"); and the **Aran Islands,** County Galway (chapter 12, "Out from Galway").

If you want your cycling trip in Ireland to be orchestrated and outfitted by affable experts on the ground, you may wish to consult or sign on with **Irish Cycling Safaris,** run by Eamon Ryan and family, who offer trips to practically every part of Ireland suitable for two wheels. They're found at Belfield House, UCD, Dublin 4 (*©* **01/260-0749;** fax 01/706-1168; www.cyclingsafaris.com).

A Few Helpful Addresses

The following organizations provide useful resources, including maps and accommodations information, of use to anyone investigating Ireland's outdoors.

- **An Óige** (Irish Youth Hostel Association), the Irish Youth Hostel Association, 61 Mountjoy St., Dublin (© **01/830-4555**; www. irelandyha.org).
- The **Mountaineering Council of Ireland** (© **01/450-7376**; fax 01/450-2805; www.mountaineering.ie) is the national governing body for mountaineering (hillwalking and rockclimbing) in Ireland, north and south. You can contact them at House of Sport, Longmile Road, Dublin 12.
- **YHANI**, also known as **HINI** (Hostelling International Northern Ireland), Northern Ireland's Youth Hostel Association, 56 Bradbury Place, Belfast, BT7 1RU (© **028/9032-4733**; www.hini.org.uk).

BICYCLING RESOURCES

There are several rental agencies with depots nationwide that permit one-way rental, including **Irish Cycle Hire,** Unit 6, Enterprise Centre, Ardee, County Louth (© **041/685-3772;** fax 041/685-3809; www.irishcyclehire.com); and **Raleigh Rent-a-Bike** (Ireland's largest), Raleigh House, Kylemore Road, Dublin 10 (© **01/626-1333;** fax 01/626-1770; http://ireland.iol.ie/raleigh/). Bike rental rates average 15€ ($14) per day or 70€ ($63) per week, with a one-way drop-off fee of about 20€ ($18), where available.

2 Walking

In recent years, much work has been done to promote walking in Ireland, a notable example being the creation of a network of long-distance trails. The first of these to open was the **Wicklow Way** (see chapter 5, "Out from Dublin"), which begins just outside Dublin and proceeds through rugged hills and serene pastures on its 82-mile (132km) course. Others include the **Beara trail** (see chapter 8, "Out from Cork"), the **Kerry Way** (see chapter 9, "The Southwest: County Kerry"), and the **Dingle Way** (see chapter 9, "The Southwest: County Kerry"). Most trails are routed so that meals and accommodations are never more than 1 day's walk away, whether in B&Bs, hostels, or hotels.

These long-distance routes are the best-marked trails in Ireland, although the standards for signposting will seem surprisingly inadequate to those familiar with similar trails in America. It is generally assumed in Ireland that walkers possess a map and compass and know how to use them. Markers are frequently kilometers apart, and often seem to be lacking at crucial crossroads. Because visibility is rarely impeded by trees on Irish hillsides, the way between two peaks is usually indicated by a post or cairn on the summit of each peak, with the expectation that the walker can find his or her own way in between. A compass becomes absolutely crucial when a fog blows in, as all landmarks quickly disappear. *Be warned:* This can happen quite unexpectedly, and the safest strategy when you can't see your way is to stay exactly where you are until the fog clears.

The walks listed in this guide are on clearly marked trails whenever possible, and if sections are without markings, this is indicated. We can't give you all the information you'll need for the walks, of course, so you should consult the appropriate sources before setting out. Guides with maps published for most of the long-distance trails in Ireland are available from bookstores, shops, and tourist offices in the local area. For those wanting to plan ahead, many of the relevant guides can be obtained from **An Óige,** the Irish Youth Hostel Association, 61 Mountjoy St., Dublin (© **01/830-4555;** www.irelandyha.org), or in the North from **YHANI,** Northern Ireland's Youth Hostel Association, 56 Bradbury Place, Belfast, BT7 1RU (© **028/9032-4733;** www.hini.org.uk). Ordnance survey maps are available in several scales; the most helpful to the walker is the 1:50,000 or 1.25-inches-to-1-mile scale. This series is currently available for all of Northern Ireland and a limited number of locations in the Republic. The half-inch-to-one-mile series covers the whole country in 25 maps, and local maps are available in most shops. These indicate roads, major trails, and historic monuments in some detail, and although they are on too small a scale for walkers, they are all that is available in many areas. For ordnance survey maps, contact **Ordnance Survey Service,** Phoenix Park, Dublin 8 (© **01/802-5345;** www.irlgov.ie/osi); or **Ordnance Survey of Northern Ireland,** Colby House, Stranmillis Court, Belfast BT9 5BJ (© **028/9025-5755;** www.osni.gov.uk). The Irish Tourist Board's booklet *Walking Ireland* and the Northern Ireland Tourist Board's *An Information Guide to Walking* are both very helpful. Other excellent resources include *Best Irish Walks,* edited by Joss Lynam, Passport Books, 1995; or *Irish Long Distance Walks: A Guide to the Waymarked Trails,* by Michael Fewer, Gill and Macmillan, 1993.

For inland hill walking try the **Wicklow Hills** (see chapter 5, "Out from Dublin"), the **Galtees** (see chapter 6, "The Southeast"), or **Glenveagh National Park** (see chapter 13, "The Northwest"). For coastal walks, try the **Beara Peninsula** (see chapter 8, "Out from Cork"), the **Iveragh Peninsula** (see chapter 9, "The Southwest: County Kerry"), the **Dingle Peninsula** (see chapter 9, "The Southwest: County Kerry"), the **Maumturks in Connemara** (see chapter 12, "Out from Galway"), and the **Donegal Coast** (see chapter 13, "The Northwest").

 Outdoor Equipment Retailers

You forgot the dehydrated pineapple and the camp stove, didn't you? Now what are you going to do? Don't sweat it: Ireland has a number of outlets for outdoors gear. Here are a few of them:

Great Outdoors, Chatham Street, Dublin 2 (© **01/679-4293**).

The Mountain Man, Strand Street, Dingle, County Kerry (© **066/ 51868**).

Outside World, 7 Parnell Place, Cork (© **021/278833**).

Radar Stores, 7 Fox's Bow, Limerick (© **061/417262**).

River Deep Mountain High, Middle Street, Galway (© **091/562269**).

Great Outdoors, Eglinton Street, Galway (© **091/562869**).

WALKING RESOURCES

The Ballyknocken House B&B, Ashford, County Wicklow (© **0404/44614;** fax 0404/44627; www.ballyknocken.com) offers 2- to 7-day walking tours of the Wicklow Mountains for individuals or groups. In the west of Ireland, a wide selection of guided walks in the Burren, from 1 day to a week or more, are offered by **Burren Walking Holidays,** with the Carrigann Hotel, Lisdoonvarna (© **065/707-4036;** fax 065/707-4567; carrigannhotel@eircom.net). In the southwest, contact **SouthWest Walks Ireland,** 40 Ashe St., Tralee, County Kerry (© **066/712-8733;** fax 066/712-8762; swwi@iol.ie); or, for a full walking holiday package to County Kerry, consult **BCT Scenic Walking,** 6183 Paseo Del Norte, Suite 270, Carlsbad, CA 92009 (© **800/473-1210;** fax 760/431-7782; www.bctwalk.com).

The Northern Ireland Tourist Board's official website (**www.discovernorth ernireland.com**) has a walking and hiking page listing self-guided tours, basic information on way-marked paths, and names and addresses of organizations offering guided walks throughout the North. For package walking holidays in Northern Ireland contact **Walk Ulster,** The Bleach Centre, Lurgan Road, Banbridge BT32 4LU (© **028/4066-2126;** info@wrightlanes.co.uk).

3 Bird-Watching

Because of its small size, Ireland cannot offer a tremendous diversity of habitats to its avian residents and, partially for this reason, has only two-thirds as many recorded nesting species as Great Britain. Nevertheless, the country has remained a place of great interest to birders primarily because of its position on the migration routes of many passerines and seabirds, which find the isle a convenient stopping point on their Atlantic journeys. Most of the important seabird nesting colonies are on the west coast; exceptions to this rule are Lambey Island, near Dublin, and Great Saltee in County Wexford. Sandy beaches and tidal flats on the east and west coasts are nesting grounds for large populations of winter waders and smaller, isolated tern colonies.

The lakes and wetlands of Ireland serve as a wintering ground for great numbers of wildfowl. Every year as many as 10,000 **Greenland white-fronted geese** winter on the north shores of Wexford Harbor, making this a mecca for birders. In the winter, flooded fields (or *callows*) provide a habitat for **wigeons, whooping swans,** and **plover;** the callows of the Shannon and the Blackwater are especially popular with birders. Another spectacular avian event is the annual fall migration of **Brent geese.** On the shores of Strangford Lough in County Down—Europe's premier Brent-watching site—you might see as many as 3,000 on a single day.

Until recently, rural Ireland was home to large numbers of a small bird known as the **corncrake** (*Crex crex*), whose unusual cry during breeding season was a common feature of the Irish early summer night. Sadly, the introduction of heavy machinery for cutting silage has destroyed the protective high-grass environment in which the mother corncrake lays her eggs and raises her chicks. (The period for cutting silage coincides with the corncrake breeding period.) There are now only a few areas where the corncrake still breeds in Ireland, one of these being the Shannon Callows, where their cry can often be heard after night's quiet replaces the noises of the day.

One of the best resources for finding information about birding in Ireland is the **Wexford Wildfowl Reserve,** North Slob, Wexford (© **053/23129;** fax 053/24785; cjwilson@iol.ie), which has a visitor center with information on local bird-watching sites and a full-time warden, Chris Wilson, who can direct you to other places corresponding to your particular areas of interest. Clive Hutchinson's book *Where to Watch Birds in Ireland* (Gill and Macmillan) is a great help in choosing sites to visit. You can also get information from **Bird Watch Ireland,** Ruttledge House, 8 Longford Place, Monkstown, County Dublin (© **01/280-4322;** www.birdwatchireland.ie), an organization devoted to bird conservation in the Republic of Ireland. An equivalent organization in Northern Ireland is the **Royal Society for the Protection of Birds,** Belvoir Park Forest, Belfast BT8 4QT (© **028/9049-1547;** www.rspb.org.uk). The umbrella organization for birding in the North is called **Birdwatch Northern Ireland,** 12 Belvoir Close, Belfast BT8 7PL (© **028/9069-3232;** fax 028/9064-4681; www.birdwatch-ni.co.uk).

Some of Ireland's best bird-watching sites are **Great Saltee** in early summer (see chapter 6, ""The Southeast"), the **Wexford Waterfowl Reserve** from October to April (see chapter 6, "The Southeast"), **Cape Clear Island** in the summer and fall (see chapter 8, "Out from Cork"), the **Skellig Islands** during the summer (see chapter 9, "The Southwest: County Kerry"), and **Loop Head** in the summer and fall (see chapter 10, "The West").

BIRD-WATCHING RESOURCES

Birdwatch Ireland (www.birdwatchireland.ie) is a conservation organization dedicated to the protection of endangered birds and their habitats. The website links you to information on birding events, sites, and news.

On **Cape Clear Island,** there is a bird observatory at the North Harbour, with a warden in residence from March to November and accommodations for bird-watchers. To arrange a stay, write **Kieran Grace,** 84 Dorney Ct., Shankhill, County Dublin. **Ciarán O'Driscoll,** (© **028/39153;** fax 028/39164; codriscoll@eircom.net), who operates a B&B on the island, also runs boat trips for bird-watchers around the island and has a keen eye for vagrants and rarities.

In Northern Ireland, two first-class nature centers for bird enthusiasts, both ideal for families, are **Castle Espie,** Ballydrain Road, Comber, County Down BT23 6A (© **028/9187-4146**), home to Ireland's largest collection of ducks, geese, and swans; and the **Lough Neagh Discovery Centre,** Craigavon, County Armagh (© **028/3832-2205**), located within the outstanding Oxford Island National Nature Reserve. For all-inclusive bird-watching packages in the North, contact **Murphy's Wildlife Tours,** 12 Belvoir Close, Belfast BT8 4PL (© **028/ 9069-3232;** fax 028/9064-4681).

4 Golf

With nearly 300 championship courses and myriad others of lesser repute, Ireland has devoted a greater percentage of her soil to the game of golf than has any other country in the world. The Irish landscape and climate, like those of Scotland, seem to have been custom-designed to provide some of the fairest fairways, the greenest greens, and the most dramatic traps you'll ever encounter. In short, Ireland is for the golfer a place of pilgrimage.

GOLF RESOURCES

Apart from the tourist boards, who are glad to supply brochures on golfing holidays, the principal organizations you may want to contact for detailed information on golf in Ireland are the **Golfing Union of Ireland (GUI),** Glencar House, 81 Englington Rd., Donnybrook, Dublin 4 (© **01/269-4111;** fax 01/269-5368; www.gui.ie), and the **Irish Ladies Golf Union (ILGU),** 1 Clonskeagh Sq., Clonskeagh Road, Dublin 14 (© **01/269-6244;** fax 01/283-8670; www.ilgu.ie).

   Golfing Ireland, c/o Gulliver InfoRes Services Ltd., Killorglin, County Kerry (© **1800/201515** or 066/979-2022; fax 066/979-2035; www.golfing-ireland. com), will book your tee times and arrange your itinerary for 27 clubs located throughout Ireland. **Jerry Quinlan's Celtic Golf,** 1129 Route 9 South, Cape May Court House, NJ 08210 (© **800/535-6148** or 609/465-0600; fax 609/465-0670; www.jqcelticgolf.com), offers package tours of the championship courses, British Open and Ryder Cup Tours, an Annual Father & Son Tournament, and deluxe chauffeured Golf Vacations. **Owenoak International** (© **800/426-4498** or 203/854-9000; fax 203/854-1606; www.owenoak.com), offers a variety of tours, including competition in handicap tournaments. Other organizations to contact include **AtlanticGolf,** 237 Post Road West, Westport, CT 06880 (© **800/542-6224** or 203/454-1086; fax 203/454-8840; www. atlanticgolf.com); **Golf International,** 14 East 38th St., New York, NY 10016 (© **800/833-1389** or 212/986-9176; www.golfinternational.com); and **Wide World of Golf,** P.O. Box 5217, Carmel, CA 93921, (© **800/214-4653** or 831/626-2400; fax 831/625-9671; www.wideworldofgolf.com).

5 Horseback Riding

Ireland is a horse-loving country, and there are few areas where you cannot find a stable offering trail rides and instruction. **AIRE,** the Association of Irish Riding Establishments (**www.equine-net.com/AIRE/index1.htm**), is the regulatory body that accredits riding stables, ensuring adequate safety standards and instructor competence. A list of accredited stables throughout the country is available from the Irish Tourist Board.

   A great variety of riding options can be found to suit different interests and levels of experience. Pony trekking excursions into the countryside cater primarily to beginners, and usually no experience is needed. Trail riding over longer distances requires the ability to trot for extended periods, and can be quite exhausting for the novice. Riding establishments also commonly offer such advanced options as jumping and dressage, and some have enclosed arenas, an attractive option on rainy days. There are a number of establishments that have on-site accommodations and offer packages that include meals, lodging, and riding. Post-to-post trail riding allows a rider to stay at different lodgings each night, riding on trails all day. Not all stables are able to accommodate young children, although some make a point of being open to riders of all ages.

   The Irish National Stud and **The Curragh** in County Kildare are the center of a region famous for horse racing, and there are many fine stables nearby (see chapter 5, "Out from Dublin"). The **Wicklow Hills** (see chapter 5, "Out from Dublin") have a number of fine riding establishments, as do Counties **Wexford** and **Tipperary** (see chapter 6, "The Southeast"). A number of riding stables and equestrian centers provide horse-riding holiday packages. These include **Horetown House,** Foulksmills, County Wexford (© 051/565771); **Dingle Horse Riding,** Ballinaboula House, Dingle (© **066/915-2199**); **Glen Valley Stables,** Glencroff, Leenane, County Galway (© 095/42269); and **Beech Cottage,** Dromahair, County Leitrim (© **071/64808;** fax 071/64110).

6 Fishing

With a coastline of more than 3,472 miles (5,590km), a plethora of lakes and ponds, and countless creeks, rills, streams, and rivers, Ireland offers an abundance of prime fish habitats, and the sport of catching those fish—referred to by the Irish as angling—is a cherished tradition. Many festivals and competitions are held during the summer to celebrate the various forms of this sport.

The seasons are as follows: **salmon,** January 1 to September 30; **brown trout,** February 15 to October 12; **sea trout,** June 1 to September 30; and **coarse fishing** and **sea angling,** January to December. A license is required for salmon and sea trout angling; the cost is 3.80€ ($3.45) for 1 day, 13€ ($12) for 21 days, and 32€ ($29) annually. For all private salmon and sea trout fisheries, a permit is required in addition to the license; prices vary greatly, from 6€ to 200€ ($5.45–$181) per rod per day, although most permits run 25€ to 35€ ($23–$32). There is no license required for trout fishing on most large lakes. A helpful brochure titled *Angling in Ireland,* which details what fish can be caught where, is available from the **Central Fisheries Board,** Balnagowan House, Mobhi Boreen, Glasnevin, Dublin 9 (✆ **01/837-9206;** fax 01/836-0060; www.cfb.ie). Another helpful resource, *The Angler's Guide,* is published by the Irish Tourist Board. Permits, licenses, and specific information can be obtained from local outfitters or the Central Fisheries Board.

In Northern Ireland, you have to get a rod license from the **Fisheries Conservancy Board,** 1 Mahon Rd., Portadown, County Armagh BT62 3E (✆ **028/3833-4666;** fax 028/3833-8912; www.fcbni.com), or in the Derry area from the **Foyle Fisheries Commission,** 8 Victoria Rd., Derry BT47 2AB (✆ **028/7134-2100**). A permit may be required in addition; information can be obtained from local outfitters or the **Department of Agriculture, Fisheries Division,** Stormont, Belfast BT4 3PW (✆ **028/9052-3434**). A license for game fishing costs £10.50 ($15.75) for 8 days. You can find a wealth of information and contacts in *An Information Guide to Game Fishing,* available from any office of the Northern Ireland Tourist Board.

Some B&Bs and hotels possess exclusive access to lakes and ponds, and provide boats, angling gear, and ghillies (fishing guides) for hire by their patrons. Examples include **Enniscoe House** in County Mayo (see chapter 10, "The West"), **Ballynahinch Castle Hotel** in County Galway (see chapter 12, "Out from Galway"), and **Delphi Lodge** in County Galway (see chapter 12, "Out from Galway").

Most of Ireland's angling festivals and competitions take place between March and September; for dates and locations, contact the Irish Tourist Board. Advance notice must be given for participation in most of the competitions. Among the festivals are **Killybegs International Fishing Festival** in July, the **Baltimore Angling Festival** in July, and the **Cobh Sea Angling Festival** in September.

In the northwest, **Killybegs** (see chapter 13, "The Northwest") is a center for sea angling, while in the west, **Loughs Corrib, Conn, and Mask** (see chapters 10, "The West," and 13, "The Northwest") offer much to entice the freshwater angler. The **Killarney** area (see chapter 9, "The Southwest: County Kerry") is a popular angling destination, as is **Kinsale** (see chapter 8, "Out from Cork"). Also, be sure to consider the **River Shannon** and its lakes, especially **Lough Derg** (see chapter 14, "Along the River Shannon's Shores").

7 Kayaking

Known as canoeing in Ireland, this sport enjoys considerable popularity. The season for **white water** is the winter, when frequent rains fill the rivers sufficiently for good paddling. By early summer, most white-water streams are reduced to a trickle, the one exception being the Liffey, which is dam-controlled and has some minor rapids upstream from Dublin that are sometimes passable during the summer months.

Sea kayaking is much better suited to the Irish landscape and climate, as it can be done year-round and permits access to one of the isle's greatest treasures: its remote sea coast. In a sea kayak, the myriad wonders of the Irish coast can be investigated at close hand. You'll find caves and tiny inlets, and out-of-the-way cliffs and reefs inhabited by abundant sea birds, colorful crustaceans, seals, and the occasional dolphin. Many islands are within easy reach of the mainland, and with experience and good conditions, a sea kayaker can reach any of Ireland's innumerable island outposts.

A number of adventure centers offer kayaking lessons, and a few schools are devoted to kayaking. Some of these will rent equipment as long as you can demonstrate adequate proficiency; call ahead to make arrangements if this is what you plan to do. For those new to the sport or unfamiliar with the Irish coast, a guided excursion is the best option.

The deeply indented coast of **West Cork** (see chapter 8, "Out from Cork") is a sea kayaker's paradise, with clear water, cliffs rising to dizzying heights, and rocky shorelines so full of caves in some places that they seem hollow.

KAYAKING RESOURCES

Atlantic Sea Kayaking, Union Hall, West Cork (℃ **028/33002;** www. atlanticseakayaking.com) is run by Jim Kennedy, a former world champion in kayak marathon racing, who offers instruction and guided excursions along the spectacularly beautiful West Cork coast, (see chapter 8, "Out from Cork). Kayaking vacations are also available at **Delphi Adventure Center,** Leenane, County Galway (℃ **095/42307;** fax 095/42303; www.delphiadventureholidays.ie), (see chapter 12, "Out from Galway"); and the **National Adventure Centre,** Tiglin, Ashford, County Wicklow (℃ **0404/40169;** fax 0404/40701; www.iol.ie/~tiglin), (see chapter 5, "Out from Dublin).

8 Sailing

There are many regions of Ireland that can best be experienced from the water. The elaborately indented coastline offers a plethora of safe havens for overnight stops—there are more than 140 between Cork Harbor and the Dingle Peninsula alone. This region of West Cork and Kerry is the most popular coastline for cruising, and has several companies offering yacht charters.

The country's sailing schools hold courses for sailors at all levels of experience and sometimes offer day sailing as well. Ireland also has over 120 yacht and sailing clubs along the coast and lakes. The best sources for information are the **Irish Tourist Board;** and the **Irish Sailing Association,** 3 Park Rd., Dun Laoghaire, County Dublin (℃ **01/280-0239;** fax 01/280-7558; www.sailing.ie).

Some of the harbors in the southwest that are most popular with sailors include **Cork, Kinsale, Glandore, Baltimore,** and **Bantry.** On the west coast, **Killary Harbour, Westport,** and **Sligo** have sailing clubs and are in areas of great beauty. There are also a number of sailing clubs and yacht charter companies in the **Dublin** area.

SAILING RESOURCES

The Glenans Irish Sailing Club, 5 Lower Mount St., Dublin 2 (© **01/ 661-1481;** fax 01/676-4249; www.glenans-ireland.com), has locations in West Cork and Mayo, and offers classes at all levels; day sailing is available during the summer at the Baltimore location. Yacht charters are available from **Sail Ireland Charters,** Trident Hotel Marina, Kinsale, County Cork (© **021/477-2927;** fax 021/477-4170; www.sailireland.com) and **Shannon Sailing Ltd.,** The Marina, Dromineer, Nenagh, County Tipperary (© **067/24499;** fax 067/33488; www.shannonsailing.com). Hobie Cat sailing can be arranged at the **Killary Adventure County,** Leenane, County Galway (© **095/43411;** fax 095/42359; www.killary.com/Adventure.htm).

9 Diving

With visibility averaging 50 feet (15.2m) and occasionally reaching 100 feet (30.5m), and many wrecks to explore, the west coast of Ireland is a great place for divers—in fact, it offers some of the best scuba diving in Europe.

The Irish dive season generally starts in March and ends sometime in October, though, of course, these dates are entirely dependent on your comfort zone—outside of these months weather and ocean conditions may make jumping into the sea unappealing for some. The PADI open water diver certification is the minimum requirement for all dives; introductory dives for novices are also offered at most schools.

The rocky coast of West Cork and Kerry is great for diving, with centers in **Baltimore** (see chapter 8, "Out from Cork") and **Dingle** (see chapter 9, "The Southwest: County Kerry"). On the west coast there are many great locations, one of which is the deep and sheltered **Killary Harbour** (see chapter 12, "Out from Galway"). Northern Ireland also offers many interesting dives, with over 400 named wrecks located off the coast, many in the **Irish Sea** and in **Belfast Lough.**

DIVING RESOURCES

The **Irish Underwater Council** (CFT, or Comhairle Fo-Thuinn), 78A Patrick St., Dun Laoghaire, County Dublin (© **01/284-4601;** fax 01/284-4602; www. scubaireland.com) is an association of more than 70 Irish diving clubs, operating under the aegis of the CMAS (Confederation Mondiale des Activites Subaquatiques), the world federation for diving. Its website lists information on diving, dive centers, and dive hotels (no pun intended) throughout the Republic, and publishes the *CFT Guide to Dive Sites* and other information on exploring the Emerald Isle's emerald waters. Another excellent site is **Dive Ireland** (www.tempoweb.com/diveireland), which offers an abundance of information on the best places to dive. The **UK Diving** website (www.ukdiving.co.uk/) features information on diving in the North, including a wreck database you can access either through a conventional listing or by pinpointing on a map.

Irish dive centers and schools include **Kinsale Dive Centre,** Castlepark Marina Centre, Kinsale, County Cork (© **021/477-4959;** fax 021/477-4958; www.activeireland.com); **Baltimore Diving & Watersports Centre** in Baltimore, County Cork (© **028/20300;** fax 028/20300; http:// divingfoundmark.com); **Dingle Marina Dive Centre,** on the marina, Dingle (© **066/915-2422;** fax 066/915-2425; www.divedingle.com); and **Scubadive West,** Renvyle, County Galway (© **095/43922;** fax 095/43923; www. scubadivewest.com).

10 Windsurfing

Windsurfing has become a popular sport in Ireland, and some spots are host to vast flotillas of colorful sails and wet-suited windsurfers when the conditions are good. Many of the best locations, though, are in remote areas of the west coast, and these spots are rarely crowded. Windsurfing schools with board rentals can be found in most regions of the country, with the greatest concentration on the southeast and southwest coast.

In Dublin, the most popular spot is **Dollymount Beach;** another good choice is **Salthill,** behind Dun Laoghaire Harbour. In the southeast, try **Brittas Bay** (County Wicklow), **Cahore** (County Wexford), and **Rosslare** (County Wexford); **Dunmore East** (County Waterford), **Dungarvan** (County Waterford), and **Cobh** (County Cork) are good in the south. The most challenging waves and winds are to be found in the west: **Brandon Bay** on the Dingle Peninsula, **Roundstone** in Galway, **Achill Island** in Mayo, and **Magheroarty** and **Rossnowlagh** in Donegal.

WINDSURFING RESOURCES

Equipment rental and lessons are widely available on Ireland's coasts and lakes and, specifically, at the following centers: the **Dunmore East Adventure Centre,** Dunmore East, County Waterford (© **051/383783;** fax 051/383786; www.dunmoreadventure.com); **The Oysterhaven Centre,** Oysterhaven, Kinsale, County Cork (© **021/477-0738;** fax 021/477-0776; www.oysterhaven. com/activity.html); **Jamie Knox Watersports,** Maharees, Castlegregory, County Kerry (© **066/713-9411;** www.jamieknox.com); and, in the North, the **Ardclinis Activity Center,** High Street, Cushendall, County Antrim (©/fax **028/2177-1340;** Ardclinis@aol.com).

4

Dublin

Dublin lies on the shore of a sheltered crescent bay, bisected by the dark waters of the River Liffey. It's a small city, easily traversed on foot, built on a scale that's comfortable rather than magnificent. The hills and rocky headlands rimming it are lovely in the gentle, unassuming way typical of Ireland's east coast.

Dublin has changed remarkably in the past 20 years. European Union membership has brought capital for countless building projects and a cosmopolitan atmosphere to Dublin's once sleepy streets. With nearly 40% of its population under 25, Dublin has a youthful vigor that comes as a surprise to many, and in some parts of the city you might feel over the hill if you're past 30. Just what the new Dublin will look like is hard to say: It's already an eclectic mix of visions for the future, like Sam Stephenson's bulky concrete Wood Quay towers and the meticulously planned **Temple Bar,** an area that is as good an index of change in Dublin as you'll find.

When I first visited this cluster of narrow streets just south of the Liffey, across from the main entrance to Trinity College, it was 1980 and Dublin's air was still suffused on winter days with a suffocating fog reeking of coal smoke and fermenting hops. Temple Bar's dingy streets were dark and quiet. Like adjacent Trinity College, with its walled seclusion, Temple Bar offered a respite from the noise and bustle of Westmoreland Street. But a major renovation of the district within the past 10 years has resulted in a complete metamorphosis, transforming the seedy back-alleys into a trendy neighborhood filled with restaurants, pubs, and galleries. The reconstruction was carefully planned, and there's some stunning new architecture that integrates well with the older buildings.

Still, the city's transformation has been piecemeal, and a stroll across any of the numerous bridges spanning the Liffey will reveal that the prosperity hasn't been shared equally. The south side of the Liffey has seen the bulk of restoration: Layers of soot have been sandblasted from buildings, expensive shops and restaurants abound, and continental cafes vie with traditional pubs. In contrast, many of the neighborhoods in North Dublin, known by its postal code Dublin 1, preserve the language and character that James Joyce recorded, a Dublin of pubs whose pedigree can be measured by the thickness of the creosote left on its walls by generations of heavy smokers.

1 Orientation

ARRIVING

BY PLANE Dublin Airport is 8 miles (13km) north of the city center, in Collinstown. Should you land without a place to stay, help is available at the Tourist Information Desk located in the Arrivals Terminal (no phone). It's open daily in the summer from 8am to 10:30pm and the rest of the year from 8am until 10pm, and there's an automated information service at the office that you can use to track down a reservation when the office is closed.

Getting into Town   **AirCoach** is a new private coach service from Dublin airport to the city center, operating 60 trips a day at 15-minute intervals between 5:30am and 11:30pm seven days a week, servicing the city's major south side hotels and shopping districts. The one-way fare is 5.10€ ($4.60). For more information, call © **01/844-7118** or visit **www.aircoach.ie**. Also reliable are the express Airlink buses run by Dublin Bus (© **01/873-4222**) between Dublin Airport and the **Busáras Central Bus Station,** Store Street (© **01/836-6111**) for 4.50€ ($4.10) adult, 2.60€ ($2.35) child, which will get you into town in under 30 minutes; bus no. 41, which can take as long as an hour, costs only 1.50€ ($1.35; note that you must have exact change for this bus). A taxi into town will cost 20€ to 25€ ($18–$23)—see note on taxis under "By Taxi," on p. 108.

BY FERRY   Passenger/car ferries from Britain arrive at the **Dublin Ferryport** (© **01/855-2222**), on the eastern end of the North Docks and at the **Dun Laoghaire Ferryport** (© **01/661-0511**). Call for Irish ferry bookings and information. There's bus and taxi service from both ports.

BY TRAIN   **Irish Rail** (© **1850/366222;** www.irishrail.com) operates daily train service into Dublin from Belfast in Northern Ireland and all major cities in the Irish Republic, including Cork, Galway, Limerick, Killarney, Sligo, Wexford, and Waterford. Trains from the south, west, and southwest arrive at **Heuston Station,** Kingsbridge, off St. John's Road; from the north and northwest at **Connolly Station,** Amiens Street; and from the southeast at **Pearse Station,** Westland Row, Tara Street.

BY BUS   **Bus Eireann** (© **01/836-6111;** www.buseireann.ie) operates daily express coach and local bus service from all major cities and towns in Ireland into Dublin's central bus station, **Busaras,** Store Street.

BY CAR   If you are arriving by car from other parts of Ireland or via car ferry from Britain, all main roads lead into the heart of Dublin and are well signposted to An Lar (or "City Centre"). To bypass the city center en route to points due south of Dublin, follow signs to the East Link Toll Bridge; from here you can connect up to N11 and continue south to Wicklow and Wexford. For points northwest, west, and southwest of Dublin follow signs for M50, a divided highway that skirts the city on three sides, and provides access to a number of Ireland's major roads. Traffic tends to back up before exits, and at the West Link Toll Bridge, just south of the N3 exit.

VISITOR INFORMATION

Dublin Tourism operates six walk-in visitor centers in greater Dublin that are open every day except Christmas. The principal center is on Suffolk Street, Dublin 2, open from June to August Monday to Saturday from 9am to 8:30pm, Sunday and Bank Holidays 10:30am to 2:30pm, and the rest of the year Monday to Saturday 9am to 5:30pm, Sunday and Bank Holidays 10:30am to 3:00pm. The Suffolk Street office includes a currency exchange counter, a car-rental counter, an accommodation reservations service, bus and rail information desks, a gift shop, and a cafe. For accommodation reservations throughout Ireland by credit card, contact Dublin Tourism at © **01/605-7700;** www.visitdublin.com).

Dublin Orientation

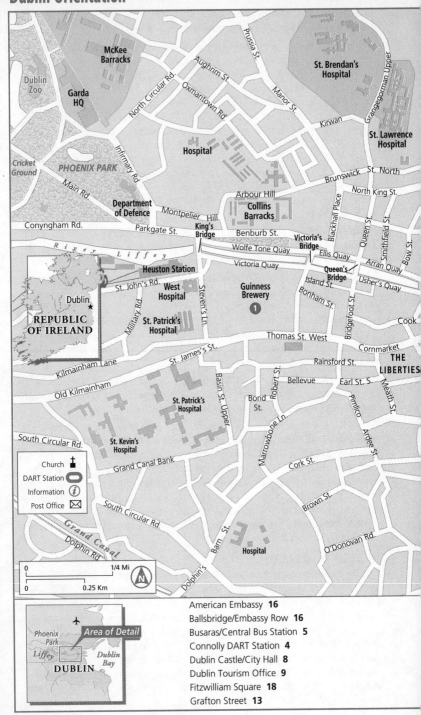

American Embassy **16**
Ballsbridge/Embassy Row **16**
Busaras/Central Bus Station **5**
Connolly DART Station **4**
Dublin Castle/City Hall **8**
Dublin Tourism Office **9**
Fitzwilliam Square **18**
Grafton Street **13**

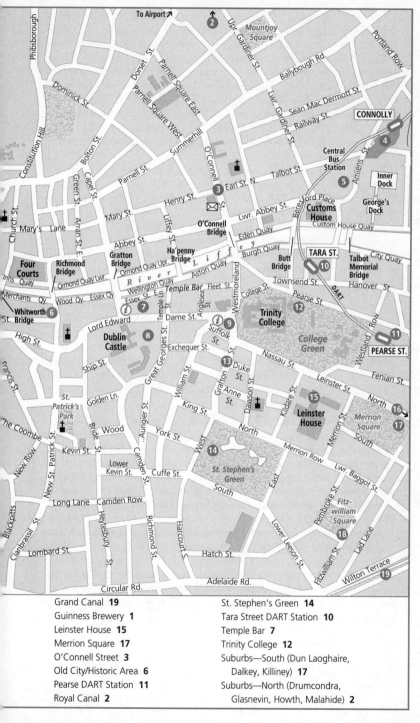

For other information, call **Bord Failte** information at © **1850/230330** from within Ireland (a local call from anywhere in the country) or © **066/ 979-2083;** you can also send e-mail queries to **information@dublintourism.ie**.

The **O'Connell Street** tourist information center, closed since 1995, has reopened and offers accommodation reservations, a Dublin bus information desk, and a limited selection of books and gifts. The other four centers are at the Arrivals Hall of **Dublin Airport;** the new ferry terminal, **Dun Laoghaire;** the **Baggot Street Bridge,** Dublin 2; and **The Square,** Tallaght, Dublin 24 (all telephone inquiries should be directed to the numbers listed above). All centers are open year-round with at least the following hours: Monday to Friday 9am to 5:30pm and Saturday 9am to 1pm.

In addition, an independent center offers details on concerts, exhibits, and other arts events in the **Temple Bar** section at 18 Eustace St., Temple Bar, Dublin 2 (© **01/671-5717**), open year-round Monday to Friday 9:30am to 5:30pm, and Saturday 10am to 5:30pm.

At any of these centers you can pick up the free *Tourism News;* or the free *Event Guide,* a biweekly entertainment guide, online at **www.eventguide.ie**. *In Dublin,* a biweekly arts-and-entertainment magazine selling for 2.50€ ($2.45) is available at most newsstands.

CITY LAYOUT

Compared with other European capitals, Dublin is relatively small and easily traversed. The city center, identified in Irish on bus destination signs as "An Lar," is bisected by the west-to-east flow of the River Liffey and ringed by the Royal Canal to the north and the Grand Canal to the south. To the north of the Royal Canal are the north-side suburbs, such as Drumcondra, Glasnevin, Howth, Clontarf, and Malahide; to the south of the Grand Canal are the south-side suburbs of Ballsbridge, Blackrock, Dun Laoghaire, Dalkey, Killiney, Rathgar, and Rathmines, among others.

MAIN ARTERIES, STREETS & SQUARES   Today, as in the past, Dublin is divided by the none-too-pristine waters of the Liffey, which flow beneath some 14 bridges en route east to Dublin Bay. Of these, O'Connell Bridge is probably the most important one for travelers, because it connects those sections of the mile-long city center north of the Liffey and south of the Liffey. Keep that geography firmly in mind, because Dubliners locate everything by its relation to the river—"north of" and "south of" are a part of the city's vocabulary you'll soon adopt as your own.

The main thoroughfare north of the river is **O'Connell Street,** which extends from the bridge to Parnell Square at its northern end. This is where you'll find the historic General Post Office and statues of Parnell, Father Matthew, and Daniel O'Connell. At the base of O'Connell's statue, look for the heroic "Victories," representing Fidelity, Eloquence, Courage, and Patriotism. On O'Connell Street, you'll also find several good hotels, one large department store, and a jumble of fast-food options.

Impressions

I am afraid I am more interested, Mr. Connolly, in the Dublin street names than in the riddle of the universe.

—James Joyce (1882–1941)

To the south of O'Connell Bridge, the 1-block-long **Westmoreland Street** gives onto the wide, statue-filled intersection known as **College Green,** which sprawls before the entrance to Trinity College. College Green, in turn, funnels into Dublin's most fashionable shopping thoroughfare, **Grafton Street,** which is blocked off for pedestrian traffic only. If you've walked that city-center mile to the southern end of Grafton, you'll sigh with gratitude for the restful, beautifully landscaped refuge of **St. Stephen's Green.**

Nassau Street, which starts at the north end of Grafton Street and rims the south side of Trinity College, is noted not only for its fine shops but also because it leads to **Merrion Square,** another fashionable Georgian park noted for the historic brick-front town houses that surround it. Adjacent to the park you'll find the National Gallery, the National Museum, and Leinster House, home of the Irish Parliament.

In the older section of the city, **High Street** is the gateway to much of medieval and Viking Dublin, from the city's two medieval cathedrals to the old city walls and nearby Dublin Castle. The other street of note in the older part of the city is **Francis Street,** which serves as Dublin's antiques row.

NEIGHBORHOODS IN BRIEF
See the "Dublin Orientation" map on p. 102.

O'Connell Street (North of the Liffey) A wide and sweeping thoroughfare, O'Connell Street was once a fashionable and historic focal point in Dublin, but it's lost much of its charm and importance in recent years. Lining its sidewalks you'll find shops, fast-food restaurants, movie theaters, and a few great landmarks like the General Post Office and the Gresham Hotel. Within walking distance are four theaters plus the Catholic Pro-Cathedral, the Moore Street open markets, the all-pedestrian shopping area of Henry Street, the new Financial Services Centre, the ILAC Centre, and the Central Bus Station. Regrettably, it is wise to be cautious after hours and especially after dark in this section of the city. Most of this area lies in the Dublin 1 postal code.

Trinity College Area On the south side of the River Liffey, the Trinity College complex is a 42-acre center of academia in the heart of the city, surrounded by fine bookstores and shops. This area lies in the Dublin 2 postal code.

Temple Bar Wedged between Trinity College and the Old City, this section has recently been spruced up to become the cultural and entertainment hub of Dublin. As Dublin's self-proclaimed Left Bank, Temple Bar is the place to see and to be seen. It offers a vibrant array of unique shops, art galleries, recording studios, theaters, trendy restaurants, and atmospheric pubs. Largely the preserve of the young, it is easy to feel over the hill here if you're past 30. This area lies in the Dublin 2 postal code.

Old City/Historic Area Dating from Viking and medieval times, this cobblestone enclave includes Dublin Castle, the remnants of the city's original walls, and the city's two main cathedrals, Christ Church and St. Patrick's. The adjacent Liberties section, just west of High Street, takes its name from the fact that the people who lived here long ago were exempt from the local jurisdiction within the city walls. Although it prospered in its early days, the Liberties fell on hard times in the 17th and

18th centuries and is only now feeling a touch of urban renewal. Highlights here range from the Guinness Brewery and Royal Hospital to the original Cornmarket area. Most of this area lies in the Dublin 8 postal code.

St. Stephen's Green/Grafton Street Area A focal point for visitors to Dublin, this district is home to some of the city's finest hotels, restaurants, and shops. There are some residential town houses near the Green, but this area is primarily a business neighborhood. It is part of the Dublin 2 postal code.

Fitzwilliam Square & Merrion Square These two little square parks are surrounded by beautiful brick-faced Georgian town houses,

each with its own distinctive and colorful doorway. Some of Dublin's most famous citizens once resided here, although today many of the houses have been turned into offices for doctors, lawyers, and other professionals. This area is part of the Dublin 2 postal code.

Ballsbridge/Embassy Row Situated south of the Grand Canal, Ballsbridge is Dublin's most prestigious suburb, yet it is within walking distance of downtown. Although primarily a residential area, it is also home to some of the city's leading hotels and restaurants as well as many embassies, including that of the United States. This area is part of the Dublin 4 postal code.

2 Getting Around

BY DART The **Dublin Area Rapid Transit** (DART) is a light rail line connecting Dublin with the suburbs along the coast north and south of the city. It's the best way to explore the sights in Howth, Sandycove, Dalkey, Killiney, Bray, and Greystones, and tends to be quicker and easier to figure out than the bus system. Admirably punctual, service operates roughly every 10 to 20 minutes Monday to Saturday from 7am to midnight and Sunday from 9:30am to 11pm. Times of operation vary, of course, from station to station: Schedules are available at all stations during operating hours. Depending on the time of day and the particular station, you can generally expect that the time between trains will be 10 to 20 minutes. Fares vary with the distance you travel, with the minimum single-journey fare 0.90€ (80¢) and the maximum 2.20€ ($2). An individual 1-day Rambler ticket for unlimited DART travel is available for 5.10€ ($4.60) and a family ticket (any two adults with up to two children) for 9€ ($8). For further information, contact **DART,** Pearse Station, Dublin 2 (© **1850/366222** in Ireland or 01/836-6222; www.irishrail.ie).

BY BUS Dublin Bus operates a fleet of double-decker buses, high-frequency single-deck buses, and minibuses throughout the city and its suburbs. Because of the traffic congestion in the center of Dublin, public buses can be agonizingly slow, but they're still the best way to reach places that are too distant for walking and not on a DART line. Destinations and bus numbers are posted above the front windows; buses destined for the city center are marked with the Gaelic words *an lar.*

Bus service runs daily throughout the city, starting around 6am (10am on Sun) and ending with the last bus at 11:30pm on most routes; the Nitelink service from city center to the suburbs extends bus hours to 2 or 3am Monday to Wednesday, and 3:30 or 4:30am on Thursday, Friday, and Saturday. Frequency ranges from every 10 to 20 minutes for most runs; schedules are posted on

Dublin Area Rapid Transit (DART) Routes

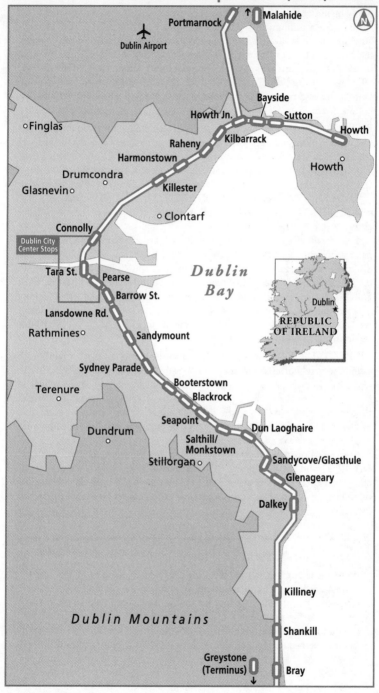

revolving notice boards at each stop. Fares depend on the distance you travel and fall between a minimum of 0.80€ (70¢) and a maximum of 1.65€ ($1.50). Nitelink fare is 3.80€ ($3.45). Tickets should be purchased from a ticket machine as you enter the bus; note that exact change is now required on most buses, and only coins are accepted. For more information, contact **Dublin Bus,** 59 Upper O'Connell St., Dublin 1 (© **01/873-4222;** www.dublinbus.ie); Dublin Bus also operates an information desk at the central Tourist Office on Suffolk Street.

BY TAXI　Dublin taxis do not cruise the streets looking for fares; instead, they line up at ranks. Ranks are located outside all of the leading hotels, at bus and train stations, and on prime thoroughfares such as Upper O'Connell Street, College Green, and the north side of St. Stephen's Green. You can also phone for a taxi. Some of the companies that operate a 24-hour radio-call service are **Co-Op** (© **01/677-7777**); **National** (© **01/677-2222**); and **VIP Taxis** (© **01/ 478-3333**). If you need a wake-up call, VIP offers that service, along with especially courteous dependability.

Taxi rates are fixed by law and posted in each taxi. The minimum fare for one passenger within a 10-mile radius of O'Connell Street is 2.50€ ($2.25) for any distance not exceeding ½ mile (1km) or 3 minutes and 20 seconds; after that, it's 0.15€ (15¢) for each additional tenth of a mile or 40 seconds. At peak times in Dublin's backed-up traffic, it's often the minutes and not the miles that add up. The per-journey additional charge for each suitcase is 0.50€ (45¢). The most costly add-ons are 1.50€ ($1.35) for dispatched pick-up and 1.65€ ($1.50) for service from Dublin airport.

BY RENTAL CAR　Unless you're going to be doing a lot of driving from Dublin to neighboring counties, it's not logistically or economically advisable to rent a car. In fact, the city is aggressively discouraging the car as the vehicle of choice for commuters, much less for tourists. If you must drive in Dublin, though, remember to keep to the *left-hand side of the road* and do not drive in bus lanes. The speed limit within the city is 30 mph and seat belts must be worn at all times by driver and passengers.

Murray's Europcar, Baggot Street Bridge, Baggot Street, Dublin 4 (© **01/ 668-1777**) and at the airport (© **01/614-2888**), is reliable and one of the cheapest. Expect to pay between 35€ ($32) and 60€ ($54) per day (depending on the length of rental and time of year), for the smallest car including tax and insurance.

⟨Tips　Rider Beware!

When taking a taxi, be on the lookout for typical tricks of the trade. Always ask for a fare estimate before getting in the car, and if the driver refuses to give one start looking for another taxi. If you see that the meter isn't on, let the driver know that you've noticed this. Drivers sometimes charge for *every* item of luggage including purses, handbags and cameras, despite the regulation stating that bags must be at least 2 feet (0.5m) in length to be charged as luggage. In addition, some hotel, guest house or B&B staff when asked to call for a taxi will arrange for the driver to tack on as much as 5€ ($4.55) as their commission, although this practice violates city taxi regulations.

⌒Value **Getting Around Dublin (Cheap)**

Here are a few ways to keep your in-Dublin transportation budget under control:

- Bus discounts are offered during certain hours on certain lines. One of the most useful is the shopping fare offered between 10am and 4:30pm. Ask about various discounts at **Dublin Bus,** 59 Upper O'Connell St. (✆ **01/873-4222**).

- You can get **discount passes** for travel on Dublin's extensive network of buses and commuter trains. The most useful passes: the **1-day bus/rail ticket** (6.60€/$6) valid for unlimited travel on all city services; the **1-day family pass** (9.60€/$9) allowing two adults and up to four children under 16 unlimited use of the bus and suburban rail system during off-peak hours; the three-day **Rambler Pass** offering unlimited travel on Dublin buses for 8.30€ ($8); and the **4-day Dublin Explorer Pass** (13€/$12) offering unlimited travel on Dublin bus and rail. Both the Rambler and Explorer pass can be purchased online at **www.buseireann.ie.**

- Students should consider the **TravelSave stamp,** including a 50% discount on rail travel throughout the country, a 15% discount on most bus fares outside Dublin, and substantially reduced weekly transit passes in Dublin. You can buy the stamp for 10€ ($9) at the **Union of Students in Ireland/Irish Student Travel Service (USIT),** 19 Aston Quay, Dublin 2 (✆ **01/677-8117;** www.usitnow.ie); you'll need a valid International Student Identity Card (ISIC). In Dublin, your ISIC and TravelSave stamp will bring big discounts on city bus and rail weekly passes, available at **Dublin Bus,** 59 Upper O'Connell St. (✆ **01/873-4222**); the weekly pass is 13€ ($12) for local and 14€ ($13) for all-zone travel.

International firms represented in Dublin include: **Avis/Johnson and Perrott** (www.avis.com), 1 Hanover St. E., Dublin 1 and Dublin Airport (both ✆ **01/605-7500**); **Budget** (www.budgetcarrental.ie), at Dublin Airport (✆ **01/844-5150**); **Hertz,** 149 Upper Leeson St., Dublin 4 (✆ **01/660-2255**) and at Dublin Airport (✆ **01/844-5466;** www.hertz.co.uk); **Europcar** (www.europcar.com), Baggot Street Bridge, Dublin 4 (✆ **01/614-2800**) and at Dublin Airport (✆ **01/812-0410**); and **Thrifty** (www.thrifty.com), at Dublin airport (✆ **01/840-0800**).

If you can arrange a rental before you leave home, the rate can be substantially less than the price of a last-minute rental in Dublin. One of the cheapest and most reliable companies is **Auto-Europe** (✆ **800/223-5555** in the U.S. and Canada, 00800/2235-5555 in the U.K., and 0011800/2235-5555 in Australia).

PARKING   Individual **parking meters** in the city center are currently being phased out in favor of multi-bay meters, "disc parking," and "pay-and-display" parking. In Dublin city center the most common form of on-street parking is pay-and-display, with an average hourly rate of 2€ ($1.70). Disc parking is more common in the suburbs—the cost of one disc is 0.70€ (65¢), and each disc is

A Writer's Town

Dublin is certainly a city of literary ghosts, and for many, its streets are peopled with the shades of those long dead and those who live only in the pages of Irish novels. Even if your head isn't full of passages from *Ulysses*, you can't walk far without coming across a plaque or statue commemorating some event from Joyce's great celebration of Dublin and its people. More books of poetry are sold in Ireland than in any other European nation, and this shows in their self-conscious promotion of the city as a place of literary pilgrimage.

good for 20 minutes to 2 hours depending on the location of the parking site. The most reliable and safest places to park are at surface parking lots or in multistory car parks in central locations such as Kildare Street, Lower Abbey Street, Marlborough Street, and St. Stephen's Green West. Parking lots charge 2€ to 3€ ($1.80 to $2.70) per hour and 10€ to 38€ ($9.10 to $35) for 24 hours; the highest rates are of course for the most convenient city center locations. If you locate a parking lot whose rates seem too expensive, don't hesitate to ask the staff where you can find a lot with lower rates. Abundant information on parking (with maps) is available at **www.dublincorp.ie**; for information on private parking lots visit **www.parkrite.ie**.

BY BICYCLE   The steady flow of Dublin traffic rushing down one-way streets may be a little intimidating for most cyclists, but there are many opportunities for more relaxed pedaling in residential areas and suburbs, along the seafront, and around Phoenix Park. We recommend **Dublin Bike Tours,** Harding Hotel, Fishamble Street (next to Christchurch; ⓒ **01/679-0899** or 087/284-0799; www.dublinbiketours.com), who take the anxiety out of taking to the street on two wheels. 3-hour tours of the city are offered, as well as bike rentals and self-guided tours. The cost is 19€ ($17) per person for a guided tour, offered Saturday and Sunday at 10am and 2pm; other days are by request only. Bike rentals are available daily April to October from 9:30am to 5:30pm; the rate is 13€ ($12) per day including lock, helmet, repair kit, and route advice.

ON FOOT   Small and compact, Dublin is ideal for walking, so long as you remember to look right and left (in the direction opposite your inclinations) for oncoming traffic and to obey traffic signals. Each traffic light has timed "walk/don't walk" signals for pedestrians. Pedestrians have the right of way at specially marked, zebra-striped crossings; as a warning, there are usually two flashing lights at these intersections. For some walking tour suggestions, see "City Strolls," later in this chapter.

FAST FACTS: Dublin

American Express   The American Express office is located opposite Trinity College, just off College Green, at 41 Nassau St., Dublin 2 (ⓒ **01/ 679-9000**), and is open Monday to Friday 9am to 5pm. American Express also has a desk at the **Dublin Tourism Office** on Suffolk Street (ⓒ **01/ 605-7709**). In an emergency, traveler's checks can be reported lost or stolen by dialing toll-free in Ireland ⓒ **1800/626000**.

ATMs One of the most centrally located machines is at College Green outside the Bank of Ireland, facing the gates of Trinity College; others can be found at all Bank of Ireland and most Allied Irish Bank (AIB) branches throughout the city. Cirrus network cards, as well as MasterCard and Visa, are universally accepted; the PLUS network is supported by some machines but is much less common.

Banks Two convenient banks are the **National Irish Bank,** 27 College Green (© **01/673-5555**), and the **Allied Irish Bank,** 100 Grafton St. (© **01/ 671-3011**). Most banks are open Monday to Friday 10am to 4pm (to 5pm Thurs); some also have Saturday hours.

Business Hours Most **business offices** are open Monday to Friday 9am to 5pm. Most **stores and shops** are open Monday to Wednesday and Friday and Saturday 9am to 5:30pm and Thursday 9am to 8pm. May to September, many gift and souvenir shops post Sunday hours.

Dentist For dental emergencies, contact the Eastern Health Board Headquarters, Dr. Steevens Hospital, Dublin 8 (© **01/679-0700**). See also "Dental Surgeons," in the Golden Pages (yellow pages) of the telephone book.

Doctor In an emergency, most hotels and guesthouses will contact a house doctor for you. You can also call either the Eastern Health Board Headquarters, Dr. Steevens Hospital, Dublin 8 (© **01/679-0700**), or the Irish Medical Council, (© **01/496-5588**). See also "Doctors—Medical," in the Golden Pages of the telephone book.

Drugstores Centrally located drugstores, known locally as pharmacies or chemist shops, include **Hamilton Long and Co.,** 5 Lower O'Connell St., Dublin 1 (© **01/874-8456**); and **Byrnes Late Night Pharmacy,** 4 Merrion Rd., Dublin 4 (© **01/668-3287**).

Embassies/Consulates The **United States** Embassy is located at 42 Elgin Rd., Ballsbridge, Dublin 4 (© **01/668-8777**); **Canadian** Embassy, 65/68 St. Stephen's Green, Dublin 2 (© **01/478/1988**); **British** Embassy, 29 Merrion Rd., Dublin 4 (© **01/205-3700**); **Australian** Embassy, Fitzwilton House, Wilton Terrace, Dublin 2 (© **01/676-1517**); and the **New Zealand** consulate, opened in 2000, is located at 46 Upper Mount St, Dublin 2 (© **01/660-4233**).

Emergencies For police, fire, or other emergencies, dial © **999.**

Eyeglasses For 1-hour service on glasses or contact lenses, try **Specsavers,** Unit 9, GPO Arcade, Henry Street (© **01/872-8155**), or at 112 Grafton St., Dublin 2 (© **01/677-6980**); or look in the Golden Pages of the telephone book under "Opticians—Ophthalmic."

Gay & Lesbian Resources Contact **Gay Switchboard Dublin,** Carmichael House, N. Brunswick St., Dublin 7 (© **01/872-1055**; fax 01/873-5737; www.gayswitchboard.ie); **National Lesbian and Gay Federation,** 10 Fownes Street Upper, Dublin 2 (© **01/671-0939**); or **Lesbian Line Dublin** (© **01/872-9911**), Thursday 7 to 9pm. **Ireland's Pink Pages (www. pink-pages.org)** provides abundant useful information and links about the gay scene in Dublin and throughout Ireland; and *In Dublin,* a biweekly sold at newsstands and bookstores throughout the city, has a page of gay events, current club information, AIDS and health information resources, accommodation options, and helpful organizations.

Hairdressers/Barbers The leading hairstyling names for women and men are Peter Mark and John Adam. **Peter Mark** has more than two dozen locations throughout Dublin and its suburbs, including 74 Grafton St., Dublin 2 (② **01/671-4399**), and 11A Upper O'Connell St., Dublin 1 (② **01/ 874-5589**). **John Adam** has shops at 13A Merrion Row, Dublin 2 (② **01/ 661-0354**) and 112A Baggot St., Dublin 2 (② **01/661-1952**). Also consult the Golden Pages under "Hairdressers."

Hospitals For emergency care, two of the most modern health-care facilities are **St. Vincent's Hospital,** Elm Park (② **01/269-4533**), on the south side of the city, and **Beaumont Hospital,** Beaumont Road, Dublin 9 (② **01/837-7755** or 01/809-3000), on the north side.

Hotlines In Ireland, hotlines are called "helplines." For emergencies, police, or fire, dial ② **999**; Alcoholics Anonymous (② **01/453-8998** and after hours 01/679-5967); Narcotics Anonymous (② **01/830-0944**); Rape Crisis Centre (② **1800/778-888**); and Samaritans (② **01/872-7700** and 1850/609-090).

Information For information on finding a telephone number, dial ② **1190.** For visitor information, see "Visitor Information," under "Orientation," earlier in this chapter.

Internet Access In cyber-literate Dublin public access terminals are no longer hard to find, appearing in shopping malls, hotels, hostels, and on every street corner in Temple Bar. One of the best of these is **Does Not Compute,** 2 Pudding Row, Essex St. West, Temple Bar, Dublin 8 (② **01/670-4464**; www.doesnotcompute.ie), on a back street between Kinlay House Hostel and Essex Quay. Fifteen minutes online will set you back 1.30€, $1.20); one hour is 4.80€ ($4.35) or 3.80€ ($3.45) for students. They also offer photocopying, scanning, and fax service. It's open Monday to Friday 8am to 11pm and Saturday to Sunday 10am to 11pm. **Planet Cybercafe** has two branches in city center: 23 South Great Georges St., Dublin 2 (② **01/679-0583**), or 13 St. Andrew St., Dublin 2 (② **01/670-5183**), just around the corner from the Suffolk St. office of Dublin Tourism; 30 minutes online cost 3.50€ ($3.15).

Laundry In the city center, try **Suds,** 60 Upper Grand Canal St., Dublin 2 (② **01/668-1786**). Take your dry cleaning to **Craft Cleaners,** 12 Upper Baggot St., Dublin 4 (② **01/668-8198**).

Libraries For research materials and periodicals, try the **National Library of Ireland,** Kildare Street, Dublin 2 (② **01/603-0200**), or **Dublin's Central Library,** ILAC Centre, Henry Street, Dublin 1 (② **01/873-4333**).

Lost Property Most hotels have a lost-property service, usually under the aegis of the housekeeping department. For items lost in public places, contact the **Dublin Garda Siochana (Police) Headquarters,** Phoenix Park, Dublin 8 (② **01/666-0000**).

Newspapers/Magazines The three morning Irish dailies are the *Irish Times* (except Sun), *Irish Independent,* and *The Examiner.* In the afternoon, one tabloid, *The Herald,* hits the stands. There are also two weeklies,

The Sunday World and *The Sunday Tribune.* Papers from other European cities can be purchased at **Eason and Son,** 40 Lower O'Connell St., Dublin 1 (✆ **01/873-3811**). The leading magazines for upcoming events and happenings are *In Dublin,* published every 2 weeks (2.50€/$2.25); and the *Event Guide* (**www.eventguide.ie**), also published biweekly, containing a useful and up-to-date listing of events throughout Ireland with a focus on Dublin (available free of cost practically wherever you look for it). *Where: Dublin,* published bimonthly, is aimed specifically at tourists and visitors and is a useful one-stop source for shopping, dining, and entertainment (free at most hotels). Note that the *Irish Times* has an award-winning website at **www.ireland.com** where you can keep your finger on the Irish pulse 6 days a week. One of the pages on this site is a "what's on" daily guide to cinema, theater, music, and whatever else you're up for.

Photographic Needs For photographic equipment, supplies, and repairs, visit **Dublin Camera Exchange,** 9B Trinity St., Dublin 2 (✆ **01/679-3410**), or **City Cameras,** 23A Dawson St., Dublin 2 (✆ **01/676-2891**). For fast developing, try the **Camera Centre,** 56 Grafton St., Dublin 2 (✆ **01/677-5594**). Or try **One Hour Photo,** at 5 St. Stephen's Green, Dublin 2 (✆ **01/ 671-8578**), at 110 Grafton St., Dublin 2 (✆ **01/677-4472**), at the ILAC Centre, Henry Street, Dublin 1 (✆ **01/872-8824**), and at 6 St. Stephens Green, Dublin 2 (✆ **01/671-8578**).

Police Dial **999** in an emergency. The metropolitan headquarters for the **Dublin Garda Siochana (Police)** is in the Phoenix Park, Dublin 8 (✆ **01/677-1156**).

Post Office The **General Post Office (GPO)** is located on O'Connell Street, Dublin 1 (✆ **01/705-7000;** www.anpost.ie). Hours are Monday through Saturday 8am to 8pm, Sunday and holidays 10am to 6pm. Dublin branch offices, identified by the sign OIFIG AN POST/POST OFFICE, are open Monday through Saturday only, 9am to 6pm.

Radio/TV **RTÉ (Radio Telefis Éireann)** is the national broadcasting authority and controls two TV channels—RTÉ 1 and Network 2—and three radio stations—RTÉ 1, 2FM, and Radió na Gaeltachta (all Irish-language programming). Besides RTÉ programming, there are other privately owned local stations, including Anna Livia Radio on 103.8 FM and Classic Hits Radio and Ireland Radio News on 98 FM. In addition, programs from Britain's BBC-TV (British Broadcasting Corporation) and ITN-TV (Independent) can be picked up by most receivers in the Dublin area. BBC Radio 1, 2, and 3 can also be heard.

Shoe Repairs Two reliable shops in midcity are **O'Connell's Shoe Repairs,** 3 Upper Baggot St. (✆ **01/667-2020**), and **Mister Minit,** Parnell Mall, ILAC Centre, Henry Street (✆ **01/872-3037**).

Weather Phone ✆ **1850/241-222,** or on the Web at **www.ireland.com/ weather/.**

Yellow Pages The classified section of the Dublin telephone book is called the Golden Pages.

3 Accommodations You Can Afford

The most troublesome aspect of accommodations in Dublin these days is availability; so, if you're planning to arrive between June and September, be sure to book several months in advance. The most appealing city-center accommodations are always the first to go, and the busy season for these locations now extends from the late January until sometime in November. Also, be aware of the local calendar of events, because these can cause a sudden accommodations shortage—the biggies are Easter, the Spring Show in May, the Horse Show in August, All-Ireland Finals in September, and international rugby matches.

If you arrive without a reservation, stop by one of the six **Dublin Tourism** locations (see "Visitor Information," earlier in this chapter) and make use of the room-finding service.

Self-catering apartments become a budget option when you're traveling as a group of three or more. Rates are best for stays of a week at a time, although weekend and sometimes even daily rates can be okay.

You might consider finding a room in one of the outlying **suburbs** such as Howth, Dalkey, Killiney, or Bray. Then you can spend mornings on the beach and afternoons or evenings in town. On the other hand, if you want to be able to stay out later than the last buses and train departures, you'll find it a good value to avoid the taxi fares and pay more to stay right in the city.

Safety note: Within the city center, accommodations tend to be cheapest in the area immediately north of the Liffey, but you should be aware that the crime rate is also higher in this part of town.

CITY CENTER
SOUTH OF THE LIFFEY

Avonlee House 🔆   Shelagh Moynihan's cozy 19th-century brick town house offers an abundance of simple comforts. The house was recently renovated and guest rooms are generously proportioned, with refreshingly contemporary furnishings and firm beds; windows are equipped with double-pane glass, and even the rooms facing busy Sandford Road retain a high level of tranquility. The breakfast menu includes smoked salmon and several varieties of omelet in addition to the traditional Irish breakfast. The city center is a 20-minute-walk from the house and there is also a convenient bus stop nearby.

68 Sandford Rd., Ranelagh, Dublin 6. ℭ 01/496-7822. Fax 01/491-0523. 5 units. 57€ ($56) single; 102€ ($100) double. Rates include full breakfast. MC, V. Closed Christmas to 1st week in Jan. Bus: 11, 11A, 11B, 11C, 44, 44A, 44B, 48A, 86; Aircoach. *In room:* TV, tea/coffeemaker.

Fitzwilliam Guesthouse 🔆   This guesthouse occupies a meticulously restored 18th-century town house on Fitzwilliam Street, the best-preserved Georgian thoroughfare in Dublin and a convenient location for exploring the city. The entrance parlor has a homey atmosphere, with a carved marble fireplace and antique furnishings. The bright bedrooms have high ceilings; bathrooms are small, but impeccably clean. Tea/coffeemakers are available just outside every room. A full Irish breakfast is served in the vaulted basement dining room.

41 Upper Fitzwilliam St., Dublin 2. ℭ 01/662-5155. Fax 01/676-7488. 12 units. 121€ ($109) double. Rates include full breakfast. AE, DC, MC, V. DART to Pearse Station (then a 10-min. walk southeast). Bus: 10. *In room:* TV, hair dryer, iron.

Harding Hotel   Built in 1996 by USIT, Ireland's youth travel organization, the Harding is an unexciting budget hotel with a great location at the foot of

Christ Church Cathedral. The rooms are comfortable and plain; most have a double bed and a couch with a foldout bed. The bathrooms are basic. Rooms facing west toward Christ Church offer the best views. There's a restaurant on the ground floor, but it doesn't compete with the culinary delights of neighboring Temple Bar.

Copper Alley, Fishamble St Christ Church, Dublin 2. ℂ **01/679-6500.** Fax 01/679-6504. www.iol.ie/usitaccm/. 53 units. 57€ ($52) single; 88€ ($79) double or triple. Breakfast from 5€ ($4.55). MC, V. Bus: 21A, 50, 50A, 78, 78A, or 78B. **Amenities:** Restaurant. *In room:* TV, tea/coffeemakers, hair dryer.

Jurys Christchurch Inn   Across from Christ Church Cathedral, this relatively new four-story hotel was conceived on the American model of predictability and value for money. Geared to the budget traveler, it's the first of its kind in the city's historic district, offering quality hotel lodgings at guesthouse prices. The bedrooms, decorated with contemporary furnishings, can accommodate up to three adults or two adults and two children—all for the same price. There are 38 nonsmoking rooms available, and 2 rooms that have been adapted for disabled guests. Rooms 419, 501, and 507 are especially spacious; all were refurbished in 1998. Request a fifth-floor room facing west for a memorable view of Christ Church.

Christ Church Place, Dublin 8. ℂ **800/44-UTELL** from the U.S., or 01/454-0000. Fax 01/454-0012. www.jurys.com. 182 units. 88€ ($80) double. No service charge. AE, DC, MC, V. Public car park nearby. Bus: 21A, 50, 50A, 78, 78A, or 78B. **Amenities:** Restaurant, lounge; laundry/dry cleaning service; nonsmoking rooms available. *In room:* A/C, TV, tea/coffeemaker, hair dryer.

Kilronan House ✿✿   Terry Masterson is the proprietor at this comfortable guesthouse, within five minutes' walk of St. Stephen's Green and just north of the Royal Canal. Terry is a great host, a rarity in these days of increasingly generic accommodations. The sitting room on the ground floor is small and intimate, with a fire glowing through the cold months of the year. The rooms are very well kept, and those facing the front have commodious bay windows. If you don't like stairs, request a room on the second floor, because there isn't an elevator. When you book, ask about a reduction for *Frommer's* readers.

70 Adelaide Rd., Dublin 2. ℂ **01/475-5266.** Fax 01/478-2841. www.dublinn.com. 15 units, 13 with bathroom (shower only). 90€–127€ ($82–$115) double. Children under 7 free. Rates include full breakfast. AE, MC, V. Free parking. Bus: 14, 15, 19, 20, or 46A. *In room:* TV, tea/coffeemaker, hair dryer.

Kinlay House Hostel   Open year-round and run by USIT, Kinlay House occupies a beautiful redbrick town house in one of Dublin's oldest neighborhoods, steps from Christ Church Cathedral and on the edge of trendy Temple Bar. There's a large self-catering kitchen and dining room on the ground floor and a smaller kitchen on the third floor. Other common spaces include a TV room and meeting room. The rooms are small but clean. You won't have to worry about a lockout, because there's someone at the front desk 24 hours. Though there's supposedly a nonsmoking policy, in my experience it isn't respected by staff or guests.

2–12 Lord Edward St., Dublin 2. ℂ **01/679-6644.** Fax 01/679-7437. www.iol.ie/usitaccm/. 36 units, 12 with bathroom (shower only): 13 doubles, 6 with bathroom; 23 dorms, 6 with bathroom. 22€ ($20) per person in dorm; 35€ ($32) single; 50€ ($45) double without bathroom, 57€ ($52) double with bathroom. MC, V. Rates include continental breakfast. Bus: 21A, 50, 50A, 78, 78A, or 78B. **Amenities:** TV room; self-catering kitchen.

Trinity College Accommodation   During the summer months Trinity College rents student rooms to visitors on a per night basis, offering a great base from which to explore the city. Trinity is the oldest university in Ireland, occupying a venerable campus within the heart of downtown Dublin. Most

Dublin Accommodations & Dining

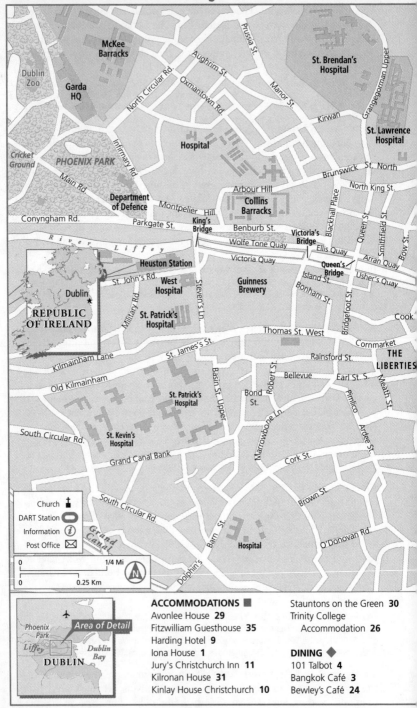

ACCOMMODATIONS ■
Avonlee House **29**
Fitzwilliam Guesthouse **35**
Harding Hotel **9**
Iona House **1**
Jury's Christchurch Inn **11**
Kilronan House **31**
Kinlay House Christchurch **10**
Stauntons on the Green **30**
Trinity College
    Accommodation **26**

DINING ◆
101 Talbot **4**
Bangkok Café **3**
Bewley's Café **24**

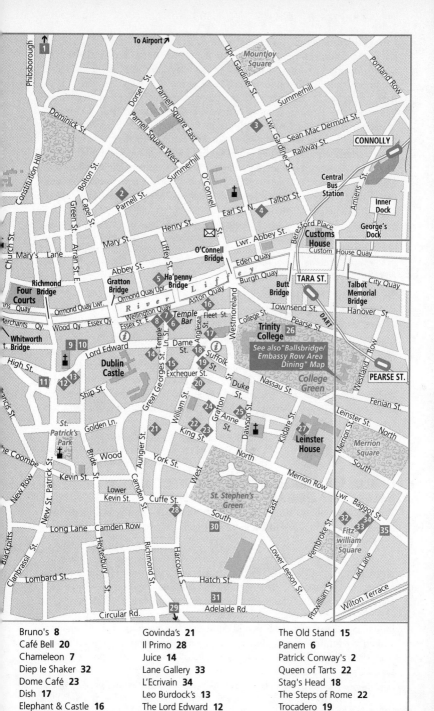

Bruno's **8**
Café Bell **20**
Chameleon **7**
Diep le Shaker **32**
Dome Café **23**
Dish **17**
Elephant & Castle **16**
Fitzers Café **25**

Govinda's **21**
Il Primo **28**
Juice **14**
Lane Gallery **33**
L'Ecrivain **34**
Leo Burdock's **13**
The Lord Edward **12**
National Museum Café **27**

The Old Stand **15**
Panem **6**
Patrick Conway's **2**
Queen of Tarts **22**
Stag's Head **18**
The Steps of Rome **22**
Trocadero **19**
Winding Stair **5**

rooms are located inside the college walls, either in 19th-century buildings typical of the historic campus or in a group of attractive dorms built in 1990 adjacent to the Beckett Theatre; the rest of the rooms are in Goldsmith Hall, a dormitory built in 1996 next to the Pearse Street DART station. Most rooms have a twin bed, a desk, plenty of built-in cupboards, a closet, and a compact bathroom with shower; rooms with double beds are also available. Other permutations include suites with two (or four) single rooms, a living room, one (or two) shared bathrooms and minimal kitchen facilities (perfect for families or friends traveling together). The rooms in the Graduate Memorial Building have the most character (high ceilings, views across the green to the Old Library), while the most spacious rooms are in Goldsmith Hall, the newest dorm on campus. The generous continental breakfast is served cafeteria-style in The Buttery, a comfortable student eatery.

Trinity College, Dublin 2. © **01/608-1177.** Fax 01/671-1267. www2.tcd.ie/Accom. 760 units, 360 with bathroom (shower only). 45€–50€ ($41–$45) single without bathroom; 56€ ($51) single with bathroom; 74€–89€ ($67–$81) double without bathroom, 99€ ($90) double with bathroom. Rates include continental breakfast. MC, V. Secure parking. Rooms available June 7–Sept 30. Bus: 21A, 50, 50A, 78, 78A, or 78B. **Amenities:** Restaurant; all rooms nonsmoking.

NORTH OF THE LIFFEY
WORTH A SPLURGE

Stauntons on the Green   Opened in 1993, this beautifully restored guesthouse occupies a four-story Georgian town house on the south side of St. Stephen's Green, next door to the Irish Department of Foreign Affairs. As befits a landmark building, there is no elevator, but there are rooms on the ground level. All rooms are decorated in traditional style, enhanced by tall windows and high ceilings; front rooms overlook the Green, and rooms at the back have views of the adjacent Iveagh Gardens. Public areas include a breakfast room and a parlor with open fireplace.

83 St. Stephen's Green, Dublin 2. © **01/478-2300.** Fax 01/478-2263. http://indigo.ie/~hotels. 30 units. 95€ ($86) single; 150€ ($136) double. Rates include full breakfast. No service charge. AE, DC, MC, V. Valet parking 6.50€ ($5.90) per night. DART: Pearse St. Bus: Any city-center bus. *In room:* TV, hair dryer.

DUBLIN SUBURBS (SOUTH OF THE LIFFEY)
BALLSBRIDGE/EMBASSY ROW AREA

Within reasonable walking distance of city center, Ballsbridge is a prestigious, largely residential suburb that also harbors many hotels, embassies, and restaurants among its streets.

Ariel House ⭐⭐   In the age of the generic, Ariel House remains a bastion of distinction and quality. For Dublin guesthouses, this one sets the standard. Michael and Maurice O'Brien are warm and consummate hosts. Guests are welcome to relax in the Victorian-style drawing room, with its Waterford glass chandeliers, open fireplace, and delicately carved cornices. The bedrooms are individually decorated, with period furniture, fine paintings and watercolors, and crisp Irish linens, as well as an array of modern extras. Facilities include a conservatory-style dining room where breakfast, morning coffee, and afternoon tea are served; and a wine bar.

50/52 Lansdowne Rd., Ballsbridge, Dublin 4. © **01/668-5512.** Fax 01/668-5845. www.ariel-house.com. 40 units. 127€–215€ ($115–$195) double (rates vary seasonally). Service charge 10%. Full Irish breakfast 11€ ($10); continental breakfast 7.60€ ($6.90). MC, V. Private car park. DART to Lansdowne Rd. Station. Bus: 7, 7A, 8, or 45. *In room:* TV, tea/coffeemaker, hair dryer, iron.

Ballsbridge/Embassy Row Area

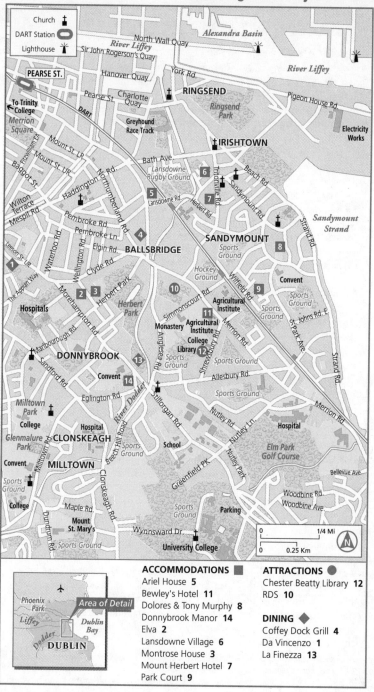

Map Legend:
- Church †
- DART Station
- Lighthouse ☀

PEARSE ST.

← To Trinity College

Merrion Square

River Liffey

Sir John Rogerson's Quay

North Wall Quay

Alexandra Basin

River Liffey

Hanover Quay

York Rd.

Pearse St

Charlotte Quay

RINGSEND

Pigeon House Rd.

Ringsend Park

Greyhound Race Track

IRISHTOWN

Electricity Works

Mount St LR

Mount St UR

Fitzwilliam St.

Baggot St.

Haddington Rd.

Northumberland Rd.

Bath Ave.

Lansdowne Rugby Ground

Beach Rd.

Tritonville Rd.

Sandymount Rd.

Wilton Terrace

Mespil Rd.

Pembroke Rd.

Pembroke Ln.

Lansdowne Rd.

Herbert Rd.

Sandymount Strand

Waterloo Rd.

Wellington Rd.

Elgin Rd.

BALLSBRIDGE

SANDYMOUNT

Leeson St. UR

The Appian Way

Clyde Rd.

Sports Ground

Convent

Morehampton Rd.

Herbert Park

Hockey Ground

Whitfield Rd.

Sports Ground

St. Johns Rd. E.

St. Park Ave.

Strand Rd.

Hospitals

Herbert Park

Simmonscourt Rd.

Agricultural Institute

Marlborough Rd.

Sandford Rd.

DONNYBROOK

Monastery

Anglesea Rd.

Agricultural Institute

College Library

Shrewsbury Rd.

Merrion Rd.

Sports Ground

Convent

Sports Ground

Ailesbury Rd.

Sports Ground

Milltown Park

Eglinton Rd.

River Dodder

Stillorgan Rd.

Nutley Rd.

Nutley Ln.

Merrion Rd.

College

Hospital

Hospital

Glenmalure Park

CLONSKEAGH

Beech Hill Road

Sports Ground

School

Nutley Park

Elm Park Golf Course

Convent

MILLTOWN

Milltown Rd.

Greenfield PK.

Bellevue Ave.

Sports Ground

Clonskeagh Rd.

Woodbine Rd.

Woodbine Ave.

College

Maple Rd.

Mount St. Mary's

Sports Ground

Parking

Dundrum Rd.

Sports Ground

Wynnsward Dr.

University College

0 ――――――― 1/4 Mi

0 ――――――― 0.25 Km

Area of Detail

Phoenix Park

Liffey

Dodder

DUBLIN

Dublin Bay

ACCOMMODATIONS ■
Ariel House **5**
Bewley's Hotel **11**
Dolores & Tony Murphy **8**
Donnybrook Manor **14**
Elva **2**
Lansdowne Village **6**
Montrose House **3**
Mount Herbert Hotel **7**
Park Court **9**

ATTRACTIONS ●
Chester Beatty Library **12**
RDS **10**

DINING ◆
Coffey Dock Grill **4**
Da Vincenzo **1**
La Finezza **13**

Value **Saving Money on Accommodations in Dublin**

Here are a few money-saving tips:

- Some Dublin guesthouses offer attractive weekend and 3- or 6-day **package rates** during the low season, with discounts for seniors, so be sure to ask when booking.
- Check with travel agents for package deals including airfare and accommodation—these are usually offered during the off-season only. Bus Eireann and Irish Rail (see "Arriving," earlier in this chapter) both offer package holidays with substantial discounts on accommodation, and **Sceptre Tours** regularly offers combined airfare, car rental, and/or accommodation packages at very reasonable rates (© **800/221-0924;** www.sceptretours.com).
- Be aware that if your stay in Dublin is a week or longer, you might save money by booking one of the many apartments available on a **self-catering** basis. Minimum rental is usually 1 week, though some are available for 3-day periods. Inquire about credit-card acceptance—many of these operators prefer to work on a cash basis. Check with Dublin Tourism (**www.visitdublin.com**) about available apartments throughout the city.
- Note that Jury's Christchurch Inn (p. 115) and Bewley's Hotel (below) in Ballsbridge charge by the room, not per person. For families or groups willing to share a room, this hotel offers a great bargain, and an ideal center-city location. For your first night in Ireland, you can save on phone calls by booking at any Jurys Hotels using their 800 number at © **800/44-UTELL** (toll-free from the U.S.).

Bewley's Hotel ★ *Kids*   The new Bewley's Hotel, located in a fashionable suburb 2 miles (3km) south of the city center, occupies an elegant 19th-century brick Masonic school building adjacent to the R.D.S. showgrounds and next to the British Embassy. A new wing harmonizes well with the old structure, and is indistinguishable on the interior. Public lounges and reception areas are spacious and thoughtfully restored, with mahogany wainscoting, marble paneling, and polished bronze creating a formal ambience. Rooms are spacious and generously furnished—all have a writing desk, armchair, and either a king bed or a double and a twin bed. Bathrooms are moderate in size. The suites include an additional room with a foldout couch, table (seats six), a tiny kitchen/bar cleverly hidden in a cabinet, and an additional bathroom (shower only). A basement restaurant (O'Connell's) is run by the Allen family of Ballymaloe fame, and offers very good food at reasonable prices; there's also an informal Bewley's tearoom. The *per room* rate makes this hotel an excellent value for families and groups; the only downside is it's location outside the city center, a small obstacle given the frequent bus and DART service.

Merrion Rd., Ballsbridge, Dublin 4. © **01/668-1111.** Fax 01/668-1999. www.bewleyshotels.com. 220 units. 88€ ($80) per room (sleeps up to 3 adults); suite 175€ ($159). AE, DC, MC, V. DART: Sandymount (5-min. walk). Bus: 7, 7A, 7X, 8, 45. **Amenities:** Restaurant, tearoom. *In room:* TV, tea/coffeemaker, trouser press.

Elva   Convenient to the American embassy, Royal Dublin Society grounds, and the National Concert Hall, Elva is a lovely Victorian home presided over by Mrs. Sheila Matthews. There's a private parking area and good transportation into the city center, and restaurants are within easy walking distance.

5 Pembroke Park, Ballsbridge, Dublin 4. ℂ **01/660-2931.** Fax 01/660-5417. 3 units. 51€ ($46) single; 64€–76€ ($58–$69) double. Rates do not include breakfast. No credit cards. Parking available. Closed Dec–Feb. DART: Lansdowne Rd. Station. Bus: 10. *In room:* TV, TEL.

Montrose House   Just off Herbert Park, not far from the American embassy, Montrose House is a two-story, redbrick house, fronted by a flower garden and run by a gracious host, Mrs. Catherine Ryan. Inside, you'll find lots of mahogany and antique furnishings. The white-walled dining room looks out onto the garden through a bay window. All three bedrooms are attractively decorated and comfortable.

16 Pembroke Park, Ballsbridge, Dublin 4. ℂ **01/668-4286.** 3 units, 1 with bathroom. 44€ ($40) single without bathroom; 76€ ($69) double without bathroom, 89€ ($81) double with bathroom. Rates include full breakfast. No credit cards. Bus: 10, 46A, or 64A.

Mount Herbert Hotel *(Kids)*   Very conveniently located near the Lansdowne Road DART Station and just over a mile from city center, this hotel offers comfortable accommodation for a reasonable price. Over 40 years ago, the Loughran family welcomed their first guests to what had once been the family home of Lord Robinson—there's little to be seen of the original house, although its former splendor can be imagined in the ornate ceiling of the entrance hall. Guest rooms are simply furnished and moderate in size; bathrooms are moderate to small. The primary disadvantage here is the view: Most rooms face the parking lot or an adjacent wing of the hotel. There are two wheelchair-friendly rooms on the ground floor. During the winter of 2001, a third of the rooms underwent a substantial renovation, including the addition of all-new furniture and ISDN dataports; the rest of the rooms should be renovated by 2003. The hotel grounds are thoughtfully planted, with a small garden and children's playground in back.

7 Herbert Rd., Ballsbridge, Dublin 4. ℂ **01/668-4321.** Fax 01/660-7077. www.mountherberthotel.ie. 180 units. 89€–126€ ($81–$114) double. Rates include full breakfast. No service charge. AE, DC, MC, V. Secure parking for 100 cars. DART to Lansdowne Rd. Station. Bus: 3, 5, 7, 7A, 8, 18, or 45. **Amenities:** Restaurant; wine bar; cafe; sauna; room service (7am–11:30pm). *In room:* TV, TEL, dataports (some rooms), tea/coffeemaker, hair dryer, garment press.

RANELAGH

Ranelagh is a walk of 15 to 20 minutes south from St. Stephens Green, just on the far side of the Grand Canal. Numerous buses connect Ranelagh with Dublin city center.

St. Dunstan's   Mrs. Bird's brick Edwardian home has been a favorite with *Frommer's* readers for several years. Set in a lovely residential area near Rathgar, the house is also within walking distance of shopping and good restaurants. The place is spotlessly clean, and the bedrooms all include sinks. It's a nonsmoking house.

25a Oakley Rd., Ranelagh, Dublin 6. ℂ **01/497-2286.** 3 units, none with bathroom. 35€ ($32) single; 52€–58€ ($47–$53) double. Rates include full breakfast. No credit cards. Bus: 11, 11A, 11B, 13B, 48A, or 62. *In room:* TV, tea/coffeemaker.

RATHFARNHAM & TEMPLEOGUE

These inland towns are about 6 miles (9.5km) south of Dublin, connected by bus with city center.

Arus Mhuire   Mrs. Colette O'Brien's modern home is 5 miles (8km) from the city center; four bus routes are nearby. There's a laundry service for guests and a locked parking lot. Her bedrooms are comfortable—and nonsmoking.

8 Old Bridge Rd., Templeogue, Dublin 16. ✆ 01/494-4281 or 01/493-7022. 9 units, 7 with bathroom (5 with shower only). 36€ ($32) single without bathroom, 38€ ($35) single with bathroom; 56€ ($51) double without bathroom, 61€ ($55) double with bathroom. Rates include full breakfast. MC, V. Parking available. Bus: 15B, 49, 65, or 65A. *In room:* TV, tea/coffeemaker, hair dryer.

Mrs. Noreen McBride   Mrs. McBride's modern suburban home is in a quiet, peaceful residential area, far removed from the inner city and a block from the bus route into town. Both Noreen and her husband, Dennis, are very helpful to guests in planning itineraries and sightseeing. Smoking isn't permitted on the premises.

3 Rossmore Grove (off Wellington Lane), Templeogue, Dublin 6. ✆ 01/490-2939. Fax 01/492-9416. denismb@iol.ie. 4 units, 2 with bathroom. 38€–40€ ($34–$36) single with bathroom; 56€–60€ ($51–$54) double without bathroom, 66€ ($60) double with bathroom. Rates include full breakfast. No credit cards. Private parking lot. Bus: 150 or 54A. Located off M50 south, junction 1; at the Spawell roundabout turn left, take the first right (Rossmore Rd.), then immediately right again (Rossmore Grove). *In room:* tea/coffeemaker, hair dryer, iron.

DUN LAOGHAIRE

The seaside suburb of Dun Laoghaire (pronounced "Dun Leary") lies some 7 miles (11km) south of Dublin; both Dun Laoghaire houses below are near the DART station, making them convenient for Dublin sightseeing.

Annesgrove *Kids*   A two-story home set in a cul-de-sac, Annesgrove is a short walk from the DART and close to the car ferry. Mrs. Anne D'Alton is the gracious hostess, and she'll provide an early breakfast for those with a morning departure. All rooms have sinks, and there's a family room with a double bed and twin beds. There's no smoking in the rooms.

28 Rosmeen Gardens, Dun Laoghaire, Co. Dublin. ✆ 01/280-9801. 4 units, 2 with bathroom (shower only). 32€ ($29) single without bathroom, 38€ ($34) single with bathroom; 51€ ($46) double without bathroom, 58€ ($53) double with bathroom. 25% reduction for children (sharing with parents). Rates include full breakfast. No credit cards. Closed mid-Dec to Jan. DART: Dun Laoghaire. Bus: 7, 7A, or 8 from O'Connell Bridge.

Rosmeen House ✦   Rosmeen House and its host, Mrs. Joan Murphy, have long been popular with *Frommer's* readers. This Mediterranean-style villa sits on its own grounds (with private parking), just minutes away from the ferry and train and bus transportation into town. Mrs. Murphy is happy to supply an early breakfast if you have an early sailing.

13 Rosmeen Gardens, Dun Laoghaire, Co. Dublin. ✆ 01/280-7613. 5 units, 2 with bathroom (showers only). 38€ ($35) single; 57€ ($52) double without bathroom, 63€ ($58) double with bathroom. 20% reduction for children. Rates include full breakfast. No credit cards. Parking available. Closed mid-Dec to mid-Jan. DART: Sandycove. Bus: 7, 7A, or 8. *In room:* Hair dryer.

DUBLIN SUBURBS (NORTH OF THE LIFFEY)
GLASNEVIN

Glasnevin, which lies some 2 miles (3km) north of Dublin, is easily reached by city bus. This residential suburb has many fine old houses and is also the site of the National Botanical Gardens and of Glasnevin Cemetery, where many of Dublin's most famous literati and political figures are buried.

Iona House   Located in a charming Victorian section, Iona House is a lovely old redbrick house built around the turn of the century. Karen and Jack Shouldice provide such extras as perked coffee and American-style bacon to make visiting Yanks feel at home. Guest rooms (which tend to be on the small side) are attractive and comfortable. There's also a lounge and a private garden. Nonsmoking bedrooms are available.

5 Iona Park, Glasnevin, Dublin 9. ✆ **01/830-6217**. Fax 01/830-6732. 10 units, all with bathroom (shower only). 89€ ($81) double. 50% reduction for children (sharing with parents). AE, MC, V. Free parking. Bus: 11, 13, 19, 19A, 34, or 34A. *In room:* TV, tea/coffeemakers, hair dryer, radio.

CLONTARF

This seaside town is only 4 miles (6.5km) from city center, and is accessible by bus or DART. A long seafront promenade fronts Dublin Bay, and the vast Bull Island Nature Reserve is also a great place for a stroll.

Aishling House ⭐ *(Kids)* A large garden, a location very near the sea, and a warm welcome from hosts Frances and Robert English make Aishling house an exceptionally pleasant base. Several *Frommer's* readers have written to praise this beautifully refurbished Victorian house for the many thoughtful though simple details that distinguish the rooms: fluffy towels and highly comfortable beds. Three of the rooms are particularly spacious, making them very suitable for families.

19/20 St. Lawrence Rd., Clontarf, Dublin 3. ✆ **01/833-9097**. Fax 01/833-8400. www.aishlinghouse.com. 9 units. 70€ ($63) single; 90€ ($82) double. Rates include full breakfast. 25%–50% discount for children (sharing with parents); children 11 months and under free. MC, V. Free parking. Bus: 130. *In room:* TV.

Mrs. Eileen Kelly Mrs. Eileen Kelly is an outstanding host who welcomes guests into the family circle around a cozy open fire in the lounge. Her large bedrooms are tastefully furnished and nonsmoking. Bus transportation to the city center is not far away.

17 Seacourt, St. Gabriel's Rd., Clontarf, Dublin 3. ✆ **01/833-2547**. 3 units, 2 with bathroom (shower only). 51€ ($46) double without bathroom; 63€ ($58) double with bathroom. Rates include full breakfast. No credit cards. Free parking. Closed Nov–Feb. Bus: 130. *In room:* Hair dryer.

Sea Breeze This 100-year-old house offers the best view on Clontarf Road; try to get Room 4 with the bay window facing Dublin Bay. Rooms are basic and rather small, and the beds are uncomfortably soft. Breakfast is of the basic "full Irish" variety. Visitors who smoke should stay elsewhere.

312 Clontarf Rd., Dublin 3. ✆ **01/833-2787**. 4 units, 3 with bathroom (shower only). 40€ ($36) single; 63€ ($58) double. 10% discount for children (sharing with parents). Rates include full breakfast. MC, V. Closed Christmas to 1st week of Jan. Bus: 130. *In room:* TV, tea/coffeemaker, hair dryer.

Springvale Moira Kavanagh is the host at this attractive home in a quiet residential area off Kincora Grove. Although none of the rooms has its own toilet, there is a tiny private shower and washbasin in every room. Nearby attractions include Clontarf Castle, Malahide Castle, Hill of Howth, golf and tennis facilities, a swimming pool, and a good beach. Bedrooms are nonsmoking.

69 Kincora Dr., Clontarf, Dublin 3. ✆/fax **01/833-3413**. www.springvaledublin.com. 4 units, none with bathroom. 35€ ($30) single; 54€ ($46) double. 20% reduction for children under 12. Rates include full breakfast. No credit cards. Closed Christmas. Bus: 29A, 31, 32, or 130. *In room:* Tea/coffeemaker, hair dryer.

SWORDS (NEAR DUBLIN AIRPORT)

Forte Travelodge *(Kids)* Located just 1½ miles (2.5km) north of Dublin airport (16 miles/26km north of the city center) in the southbound carriageway of the Swords Bypass at the Swords roundabout, this new motel-type lodging is especially appealing for families and other groups. Rooms are quite spacious, with a double bed, single sofa bed, and child's bed and/or baby cot if requested.

Each room also has its own central-heating controls. The attached restaurant specializes in snacks, drinks, and a wide variety of moderately priced meals. Both the accommodations and the restaurant have facilities for travelers with disabilities.

N1 Dublin-Belfast Rd., Swords, Co. Dublin. ✆ **800/CALL-THF** from the U.S., or 1800/709-709 in Ireland. Fax 01/840-9235. 40 units. 90€ ($82) double. No service charge. AE, DC, MC, V. Bus: 41, 43. **Amenities:** Restaurant. *In room:* TV, tea/coffeemaker.

SELF-CATERING
BALLSBRIDGE & SANDYMOUNT
Lansdowne Village   Lansdowne Village is a modest and appealing residential development on the banks of the River Dodder and directly across from Lansdowne Stadium. Within this community, Trident Holiday Homes offers fully equipped two- and three-bedroom rental units, each with an additional pullout double-bed sofa in the living room. They are bright and comfortable, and so well maintained that everything really works. The location is ideal. Not only are you a 5-minute walk from the DART and less than a half-hour's walk from St. Stephen's Green, but also, the Sandymount Strand, a favorite walking spot for Dubliners, is only 10 minutes away on foot for a pleasant after-dinner stroll. Shops and supermarkets are also nearby, so you can manage here quite well without a car, feeling apart from the city's frenzy and yet not at all cut off. The smaller units are perfect for couples, perhaps with one child; the considerably more spacious three-bedroom units are recommended for larger families or for more than one couple.

Newbridge Ave. off Lansdowne Rd., Ballsbridge, Dublin 4. ✆ **01/668-3534.** Fax 01/660-6465. 19 units (2- or 3-bedroom). 700€–900€ ($634–$815) per week, depending on size of apt and season. Shorter periods available at reduced rates Oct–Mar. MC, V. DART to Lansdowne Rd. Station. Bus: 2, 3, 5, 7, 7A, 8, 18, 45. *In room:* TV.

Park Court   Trident Holiday Homes, which runs Lansdowne Village above, also maintains these two-story town-house accommodations on private, landscaped grounds. Two- and three-bedroom units are available, and each is outfitted with a washer/dryer, linen, and towels. Cots and high chairs can be requested, and there's a babysitting service. The property is convenient to the DART station for quick transportation into city center.

Sandymount. c/o Amorey O'Connor, Trident Holiday Homes, 24 Lansdowne Rd., Ballsbridge, Dublin 4. ✆ **01/668-3534.** Fax 01/660-6465. www.thh.ie. 12 units (each sleeps 5–7 people). 700€–960€ ($634–$870) per unit per week, depending on season. Holiday weekend rates available. AE, MC, V. DART: Sandymount. Bus: 3, 5, 7, 7A, 18. *In room:* TV.

DONNYBROOK
Brookman Town Homes ⭐ *Kids*   Donnybrook Manor, a community of tasteful modern redbrick town houses with stained-glass doors, is strategically situated in Donnybrook, only a 25-minute walk from Grafton Street and College Green. Set well back from Donnybrook Road (N11) on its own parklands, the town houses are newly refurbished and equipped with virtually every appliance and convenience you could ask for. The immediate environs are thick with exceptional gourmet shops such as the Butler's Pantry, the Gallic Kitchen, Roy Fox, and Terroirs, guaranteeing the finest of provisions for home-cooked feasts. Otherwise, you can order out via "Restaurant Express" or walk to a range of fine restaurants. Each town house has its own enclosed garden, complete with table

and chairs for sitting out. Cots, cribs, high chairs, and so on are available for the asking. Naomi Kidney, your host at Donnybrook Manor, goes the extra mile to respond to your needs and to help make your stay memorable.

36 Donnybrook Manor, Donnybrook, Dublin 4. 🕐 **01/676-6784.** Fax 01/676-6868. www.brookman.ie. 20 units (2-, 3-, or 4-bedroom). 800€–1500€ ($725–$1,359) per week, depending on size of apt and season. 4-day minimum. AE, DC, MC, V. Bus: 10, 46A, or 46B. *In room:* TV, tea/coffeemaker, hair dryer, iron.

4 Great Deals on Dining

The food scene is changing in Ireland, and while Dublin may not always be at the forefront of this change, it certainly is keeping up. You'll find an increasing number of informal restaurants with small menus and big ambitions, serving food based on the best local ingredients. Plates heaped high with limp vegetables and dubious meats are definitely out—you're more likely to find the capital's culinary imagination at work on an Indian curry, a retake on a great continental dish, or a succulent spinach cannelloni.

For a taste of Dublin before you leave home visit **www.ireland.com**, where you can browse archived *Irish Times* restaurant reviews.

Note: You can find the restaurants discussed in this section on the "Dublin Accommodations & Dining" map on p. 116, and on the "Ballsbridge/Embassy Row Area" map on p. 119.

SOUTH OF THE LIFFEY

bruno's FRENCH/MEDITERRANEAN 🦊   This is a surefire spot for a flawlessly prepared, interesting lunch or dinner that won't do serious damage to your budget. The atmosphere is light and modern, with the focus on food that is consistently excellent without flourish or pretense. The spinach and goat cheese tart, salad of prawns with honey, lime, sesame seeds, and jalapeno peppers, and the bruscetta of chicken are all worthy of mention. The new Millennium Bridge makes bruno's all the more convenient, as it crosses the Liffey at Eustace Street, which is directly opposite the restaurant. You can now also find a bruno's at 21 Kildare Street, Dublin 2 (🕐 **01/662-4724**).

30 E. Essex St., Dublin 2. 🕐 **01/670-6767.** www.brunos.ie. Reservations recommended. Dinner main courses 17€–29€ ($15–$26). Service charge 10% on tables over 4. AE, DC, MC, V. Mon–Fri 12:30–3pm; Mon–Sat 6:30–10:30pm. DART to Tara St. Station. Bus: 21A, 46A, 46B, 51B, 51C, 68, 69, 86.

Caviston's SEAFOOD   Fresh, fresh fish is the hallmark of this tiny restaurant in Dun Laoghaire. It's run by the Caviston family, whose neighboring delicatessen and fish shop is legendary. There's no doubt that such expertise in scales and fins transfers to the preparation of fish in the restaurant itself. Fish dishes are simply prepared, depending on one or two well-chosen ingredients to enhance delicate flavors. Unfortunately, the pleasure of lunch here dissipates quickly under the impatient influence of wait staff who rush diners in order to accommodate three lunchtime sittings.

59 Glasthule Rd., Dun Laoghaire. 🕐 **01/280-2715.** Reservations recommended. Main courses 13€–25€ ($12–$23). DC, MC, V. Tues–Sat 3 sittings: noon, 1:30pm, 3pm. DART: Sandycove/Glasthule. Bus: 7D, 59.

Chameleon 🦊🦊 INDONESIAN   Only a dim candlelit window and an orange sign signal Chameleon, well camouflaged on a small side street off Temple Bar Square. The air is tinged with incense, and rich Indonesian batiks are sumptuous backdrops for the traditional puppets and dark woodcarvings that

Taking Afternoon Tea

As in Britain, afternoon tea is a revered tradition in Ireland, especially in the grand hotels of Dublin. Afternoon tea in its fullest form is a sit-down event and a relaxing experience, not just a quick hot beverage taken on the run.

Properly presented, afternoon tea is almost a complete meal, including a pot of freshly brewed tea accompanied by finger sandwiches, pastries, hot scones, cream-filled cakes, and other sweets arrayed on a silver tray. To enhance the ambience there is often live piano or harp music. Best of all, this sumptuous mid-afternoon pick-me-up is reasonably priced at 18€ ($16) per person in most of the city's fine hotels (the Shelburne is somewhat more expensive at 22€/$20 per person).

Afternoon tea is offered daily between 3 and 4:30pm or 5:30pm. Just off Grafton Street, the **Westbury Hotel** (© 01/679-1122) has afternoon tea in the Terrace Lounge, often with a pianist. At the **Gresham Hotel,** 23 Upper O'Connell St., 4 blocks north of O'Connell Bridge (© 01/874-6881), tea is served in the relaxing lobby. At the **Shelbourne Hotel,** St. Stephen's Green North (© 01/676-6471), an elegant lounge just off the lobby is the setting. At the **Berkeley Court Hotel,** Lansdowne Road in the Ballsbridge area (© 01/660-1711), tea is served in the comfortable lobby.

lurk in the corners of the restaurant. Chameleon offers a variety of menus featuring samplings of seven different dishes and an assortment of condiments. The staff is quick in explaining how to best complement chicken sate with roasted peanuts. *Sambal-badjak,* a red curry paste, gives the rice a robust, pleasantly spicy flavor. Finally, a small morsel of pickled vegetable is suggested as a "palate cleanser"—good advice to swallow if you want to take advantage of the abundance of delicately flavored dishes that Chameleon has to offer.

No.1 Fownes St. Lower, Temple Bar, Dublin 2. © 01/671-0362. Main courses 13€–18€ ($12–$16); set menus 21€ ($19), 24€ ($22), and 27€ ($24). Service charge 12.5%. MC, V. Tues–Sat 6–11pm; Sun 5:30–10pm. Bus: Any city-center bus.

Da Vincenzo ITALIAN Occupying a storefront location within a block of the Hotel Burlington, this informal and friendly owner-run bistro offers ground level and upstairs seating. The casual decor consists of glowing brick fireplaces, pine walls, vases and wreaths of dried flowers, modern art posters, blue and white pottery, and a busy open kitchen. Pizza, with a light, pita-style dough cooked in a wood-burning oven, is a specialty here. Other main courses range from pastas to veal and beef dishes, including an organically produced filet steak.

133 Upper Leeson St., Dublin 4 (beside the Burlington Hotel). © 01/660-9906. Reservations recommended. Fixed-price lunch 10€ ($9); dinner main courses 9€–19€ ($8.15–$17). AE, DC, MC, V. Mon–Fri 12:30–11pm; Sat 1–11pm; Sun 3–10pm. Bus: 10, 11A, 11B, 46A, or 46B.

Diep le Shaker THAI Image is important at Diep le Shaker, a new venture on a tiny side street off Pembroke Street, just five minute's walk from Stephen's Green. Very subdued lighting, crisp linens and attentive though unobtrusive service make this a good choice for a romantic outing. My meal began with the

Tom Yum soup, which manages to be very spicy and subtle at the same time, not an easy achievement. The steamed seabass with coriander and lemon is similarly satisfying, and the vegetable curries are also excellent, although vegetarians will wish for tofu or some other form of protein. Most desserts are not made on the premises and the dessert menu seems to be an afterthought.

Pembroke Lane, Dublin 2. ℭ **01/661-1829.** www.diep.net. Main courses 15€–25€ ($14–$23). MC, V. Mon–Wed 12:30–2:15pm and 6:30–10:30pm; Thurs–Fri 12:30–2:15pm and 6:30–11:30pm; Sat 6:30–11:30pm. DART: Pearse. Bus: Any city-center bus.

Dish ⚜ NOUVEAU INTERNATIONAL   Dish promises to be one of Temple Bar's finest venues. With expansive floor-to-ceiling windows, wide-beamed pine floors, light walls, and dark blue linens, it offers a relaxed, tasteful atmosphere. The menu is eclectic and enticing, with an emphasis on fresh, grilled seafood and Mediterranean flavors that are complex without being confusing. The grilled salmon with avocado, papaya, and tequila-lime dressing, the baked hake, and the chargrilled tiger prawns are particularly outstanding. The desserts we tried—caramelized lemon tart with cassis sauce and the amaretti chocolate cheesecake—were superior. And it all comes at a modest price.

2 Crow St., Dublin 2. ℭ **01/671-1248.** Reservations recommended. Main courses 13€–23€ ($12–$21). Service charge 10% on tables over 5. AE, DC, MC, V. Daily noon–11:30pm. DART to Tara St. Station. Bus: 21A, 46A, 46B, 51B, 51C, 68, 69, or 86.

Elephant and Castle *(Kids* BURGERS/STEAKS   In the heart of Temple Bar, this favorite with kids is informal and fun, with simple pinewood tables and benches. The menu is made up of salads, multi-ingredient omelets, and a selection of burgers including the house-special: the Elephant Burger with curried sour cream, bacon, scallions, cheddar, and tomatoes. Chicken wings seemed to be the most popular evening fare—nearly every table had at least two brimming baskets of spicy wings accompanied by celery and dip.

18 Temple Bar, Dublin 2. ℭ **01/679-3121.** Main courses 7.60€–22€ ($6.90–$20). AE, DC, MC, V. Sun–Thurs 11:30am–11:30pm; Fri–Sat 11:30am–midnight. Bus: Any city-center bus.

Fitzers Cafe INTERNATIONAL   In the middle of a busy shopping street, this airy Irish-style bistro has a multi-windowed storefront facade and a modern Irish decor of light woods. The contemporary cuisine is excellent, reasonably priced, and quickly served. Choices range from chicken breast with hot chili cream sauce to brochette of lamb tandoori with mild curry sauce to gratin of smoked cod.

Fitzers has two other locations, each with a different menu and character: in the Royal Dublin Society (RDS), Ballsbridge, Dublin 4 (ℭ **01/667-1302**); and in Temple Bar Square, Dublin 2 (ℭ **01/679-0440**). The Fitzers in the National Gallery will remain closed until the gallery's new Millennium Wing is opened at some point in 2002.

51 Dawson St., Dublin 2. ℭ **01/677-1155.** Reservations recommended. Lunch main courses 10€–16€ ($9–$14); dinner main courses 13€–22€ ($12–$20). AE, DC, MC, V. Daily 11:30am–11pm. DART: Pearse. Bus: 10, 11A, 11B, 13, or 20B.

Il Primo ⚜ *(Finds* MODERN ITALIAN   Word of mouth is what brought me to Il Primo—little else would have, so obscurely is it tucked away off Harcourt Street. It's certainly full of surprises. From the street all you see are several tables, a bar, an assembly of wooden stools, and a staircase, which happens to lead to some of the most distinguished, innovative Italian cuisine you'll ever meet up with outside Rome or Tuscany. Awaken your palate with a glass of sparkling

Venetian prosecco; open with a plate of Parma ham, avocado, and balsamic vinaigrette; and then go for broke with the ravioli Il Primo, an open handkerchief of pasta over chicken, Parma ham, and mushrooms in a light tarragon cream sauce. The proprietor, Dieter Bergman, will assist gladly in selecting appropriate wines, all of which he personally chooses and imports from Tuscany. Wines are served by the milliliter, not the bottle; open any bottle and you pay for only what you drink.

16 Montague St., Dublin 2 (off Harcourt St., 50 yards down from St. Stephen's Green). *C* 01/478-3373. Reservations required on weekends. Dinner main courses 13€–29€ ($12–$26). 10% service charge. AE, DC, MC, V. Mon–Fri 12:30–3pm and 6–11pm; Sat 6–11pm. DART: Pearse. Bus: Any city-center bus.

La Finezza ✦ MEDITERRANEAN One of the Dublin restaurants causing quite a buzz these days, it has garnered a number of awards, including a "restaurant of the year." La Finezza deserves its accolades. Its candlelit mirrored-gallery decor is quite tasteful and the menu is imaginative and ambitious, perhaps overly so for a purist's palate. The pan-fried lamb cutlets and the fresh pepper and black bean mousse are simply exquisite. The presentation is delightful and the service superb. The early-bird menu, available 5 to 7pm daily, is a good deal at 18€ ($16) for three courses with tea or coffee.

Over Kiely's, Donnybrook Rd. (N11), Donnybrook, Dublin 4. *C* 01/283-7166. Reservations recommended. Main courses 11€–22€ ($10–$20). No service charge. AE, MC, V. Mon–Sat 5–11pm; Sun 4–9:30pm. Bus: 10, 46A.

Panem Bakery and Restaurant ✦✦ NEW IRISH/ITALIAN Panem is about the celebration of simple delights. Unlike many of Ireland's proponents of *nouvelle cuisine,* you won't find elaborate presentation or culinary showmanship here. In fact, it's difficult to isolate the qualities that make the food so very memorable: Straightforward dishes that would be ordinary elsewhere are truly inspiring here, transformed in the kitchen of Anne Murphy and her assistants. As the name suggests, Panem began as a bakery, and the fabulous breads are an important part of any meal here; I highly recommend at least one order of the selection of Panem breads as an accompaniment. All the main courses are characterized by excellent ingredients presented simply and flawlessly; I had the Provençal crostata with goat's cheese, a heavenly concoction of bread, vegetables and melted cheese. The desserts are subtle and wholly satisfying and should not be skipped.

Panem baked goods are also available for take-out at the eponymous bakery and sandwich shop, directly across the Liffey at 21 Lower Ormond Quay, open 8:30am to 5pm Monday to Saturday.

6 Cope St., Temple Bar, Dublin 2. *C* 01/671-0132. Main courses 12€–21€ ($11–$19). MC, V. Tues–Sat 12–3pm and 6–10:30pm. DART: Tara St. Bus: Any city-center bus.

Trocadero INTERNATIONAL Located close to the Andrews Lane and other theaters, Trocadero is a favorite gathering spot for theatergoers, performers, and journalists. As might be expected, the decor is theatrical, with subdued lighting, banquet seating, close-knit tables, and photos of entertainers on the walls. Steaks are the specialty, but the menu also includes rack of lamb, daily fish specials, pastas, and such traditional dishes as Irish stew and corned beef and cabbage with parsley sauce.

3 St. Andrew St., Dublin 2. *C* 01/677-5545. Reservations recommended. 6–7:30pm early-bird menu 17€ ($16); main courses 15€–25€ ($14–$23). AE, DC, MC, V. Mon–Sat 6pm–midnight; Sun 6–11:15pm. DART to Tara St. Station. Bus: 16A, 19A, 22A, 55, 83.

Tips **Picnic, Anyone?**

The parks of Dublin offer plenty of sylvan settings for a picnic lunch; so feel free to park it on a bench, or pick a grassy patch and spread a blanket. In particular, try **St. Stephen's Green** at lunchtime (in the summer there are open-air band concerts), the **Phoenix Park**, and **Merrion Square**. You can also take a ride on the DART to the suburbs of **Dun Laoghaire, Dalkey, Killiney,** and **Bray** (to the south) or **Howth** (to the north) and picnic along a bayfront pier or promenade.

In recent years, some fine delicatessens and gourmet food shops—ideal for picnic fare—have sprung up. For the best selection of fixings, try any of the following: **Gallic Kitchen,** 49 Francis St., Dublin 8 (© **01/454-4912**), has gourmet prepared food to go, from salmon en croûte to pastries filled with meats or vegetables, patés, quiches, sausage rolls, and homemade pies, breads, and cakes. **Magills Delicatessen,** 14 Clarendon St., Dublin 2 (© **01/671-3830**), offers Asian and Continental delicacies, meats, cheeses, spices, and salads. For a fine selection of Irish cheeses, luncheon meat, and other delicacies, seek out **Sheridan's Cheesemongers,** 11 S. Anne St., Dublin 2 (© **01/ 679-3143**), perhaps the best of Dublin's cheese emporiums, or the **Big Cheese Company,** 14/15 Trinity St. (© **01/671 1399**).

SOUTHSIDE CAFES & OTHER CHEAP EATS

Bewley's Cafe TRADITIONAL/PASTRIES   This is Dublin's old reliable, a chain with a 150-year history. The interior is a subdued, mellow mix of dark wood, amber glass, and deep red velvet. Bewley's bustles with the clink of teapots and the satisfied hum of customers sated on scones, almond buns, and baked goods. Full meals are also served cafeteria-style. Grafton Street is home to the original Bewley's, where you can check out fine stained glass in the Harry Clarke Room (a self-service cafe), take in lunchtime theater in the Café Theatre (9€/$8.05 for lunch and a show), or watch the activity on Grafton Street from the Mezzanine Café (full service). Other locations can be found at 11 Westmoreland St., Dublin 2; 40 Mary St., Dublin 1 (near the ILAC shopping center north of the Liffey); shopping centers in Dundrum, Stillorgan, and Tallaght; Dublin Airport; and the Bewley's Hotel in Ballsbridge.

78 Grafton St. (between Nassau St. and St. Stephen's Green). © **01/635-5470.** www.bewleys.com. Cafeteria main courses 4€–8.50€ ($3.60–$7.70); lunch specials from 6.50€ ($5.90). AE, MC, V. Daily 7:30am–11pm (continuous service for breakfast, hot food, and snacks). Bus: Any city-center bus.

Café Bell IRISH/SELF-SERVICE   In the cobbled courtyard of early 19th-century St. Teresa's Church, this serene little place is one of a handful of dining options springing up in historic or ecclesiastical surroundings. With high ceilings and an old-world decor, Café Bell is a welcome contrast to the bustle of Grafton Street, a block away, and Powerscourt Town House Center, across the street. The menu changes daily but usually includes homemade soups, sandwiches, salads, quiches, lasagna, sausage rolls, hot scones, and other baked goods.

St. Teresa's Courtyard, Clarendon St., Dublin 2. © **01/677-7645.** All items 2.50€–6.50€ ($2.25–$5.90). No credit cards. Mon–Sat 9am–5:30pm. Bus: 16, 16A, 19, 19A, 22A, 55, or 83.

The Dome Café CAFETERIA/TEASHOP   Situated at the top of the St. Stephen's Green shopping center, this cafe is worth a visit for the view alone: a sweeping prospect over the crowds emerging from Grafton Street and toward the heart of Stephen's Green. The curious dining room is filled with potted plants, surmounted by a large glass dome, and traversed at ceiling level by yellow ventilation ducts. The pastries are excellent, but I found the savories to be bland and rather disappointing.

St. Stephen's Green Shopping Centre, Dublin 2. ℂ **01/478-1287.** Lunch main courses 5€–8€ ($4.55–$7). No credit cards. Mon–Sat 9:30am–5:30pm. Bus: Any city-center bus.

Govinda's VEGETARIAN   Govinda's serves healthy square meals on square plates for very good prices. The meals are generous, belly-warming concoctions of vegetables, cheese, rice, and pasta. Two main courses are offered cafeteria-style each day: one East Indian and the other a simple, plain-flavored staple such as lasagna or macaroni and cheese. Veggie burgers are also prepared to order. All are accompanied by a choice of two salads (and are unaccompanied by smoke, as the restaurant is nonsmoking throughout). Desserts—the rich wedge of carob cake with a dollop of cream or homemade ice cream (each 2.10€/$1.90), among others—are healthy and huge.

4 Aungier St., Dublin 2. ℂ **01/475-0309.** Main courses 7€ ($6.35); soup of the day 2.50€ ($2.25). MC, V. Mon–Sat noon–9pm. Bus: 16, 16A, 19, 22.

Juice VEGETARIAN   Juice tempts carnivorous, vegan, macrobiotic, celiac, and yeast-free diners alike, using organic produce to create delicious dressings and entrees among its largely conventional but very-well-prepared offerings. The avocado filet of blue cheese and broccoli wrapped in filo was superb, and I highly recommend the spinach and ricotta cheese cannelloni. The latter is sometimes included in the early bird menu—a great deal. Coffees, fresh-squeezed juices, organic wines, and late weekend hours add to the allure of this modern, casual eatery, frequented by mature diners who know their food.

Castle House, 73 S. Great Georges St., Dublin 2. ℂ **01/475-7856.** Reservations recommended Fri–Sat. Main courses 12€–15€ ($10–$14); early bird fixed-price dinner 13€ ($11) (Mon–Fri 5–7pm). AE, MC, V. Daily 11am–11pm. Bus: 50, 50A, 54, 56, or 77.

Leo Burdock's ⭐ FISH & CHIPS   Established in 1913, this quintessential fish-and-chips take-out shop remains a cherished Dublin institution, despite a devastating fire in 1998. Rebuilt from the ground up, Burdock's is back. For three generations, Brian Burdock's family has been serving up the country's best fish-and-chips. Cabinet ministers, university students, poets, visitors who've had the word passed by locals, and almost every other person in Ireland can be found in the queue, waiting for fish bought fresh that morning and those good Irish

---

⸜Tips Late-Night Bites

Although Dublin is keeping later and later hours, it is still nearly impossible to find anything approaching 24-hour dining. One place that comes close is the **Coffee Dock at Jurys Hotel,** Ballsbridge, Dublin 4 (ℂ **01/660-5000**). It's open Monday 7am to 4:30am, Tuesday to Saturday 6am to 4:30am, Sunday 6am to 10:30pm. **Bewley's,** 78/79 Grafton St., Dublin 2 (ℂ **01/677-6761**), is open until 1am on Friday and Saturday. **Juice,** 73–83 S. Great George's St., Dublin 2 (ℂ **01/475-7856**), serves a limited menu Friday and Saturday until 4am.

potatoes, both cooked in "drippings" (vegetarians beware). Service is take-out only—there's no seating, but you can sit on a nearby bench or stroll down to the park at St. Patrick's Cathedral. It's located across from Christ Church, around the corner from Jury's Inn.

2 Werburgh St., Dublin 8. ✆ **01/454-0306.** Main courses 3.50€–6.50€ ($3.15–$5.90). No credit cards. Mon–Sat noon–midnight; Sun 4pm–midnight. Bus: 21A, 50, 50A, 78, 78A, 78B.

National Museum Cafe ⚘ CAFETERIA/TEASHOP   The tall windows of the National Museum cafe look out toward the National Library across a cobbled yard; inside the cafe, an elaborate mosaic floor, enameled fireplace, marble tabletops and chandelier lend an element of elegance to this otherwise informal eatery. Everything is made from scratch: beef salad, chicken salad, quiche, and an abundance of pastries. The soup of the day is often vegetarian, and quite good. This is a great place to step out of the rain, warm yourself, and then wander among the nation's treasures. Admission to the museum is free, so you can visit at your own pace, as often as curiosity (and appetite) demand.

National Museum of Ireland, Kildare Street, Dublin 2. ✆ **01/662-1269.** Soup 3.20€ ($2.90); lunch main courses under 7.50€ ($6.80). MC, V. Tues–Sat 10am–5pm; Sun 2–5pm. Bus: 7, 7A, 8, 10, 11, 13.

Queen of Tarts ⚘ TEASHOP   This tea room is David to the Goliath of Irish tea rooms, Bewley's, but its diminutive physical size packs a solid pie-filled punch. Tarts of ham and spinach or cheddar cheese and chives can be followed up with the flaky sweetness of warm almond cranberry or blackberry pie. The scones here are tender and light, dusted with powdered sugar and accompanied by a little pot of fruit jam. The tarts are delicious. The dining room is small and smoke-free.

4 Corkhill, Dublin 2. ✆ **01/670-7499.** Soup and fresh bread 3€ ($2.70); sandwiches and savory tarts 4€–6.50€ ($3.60–$5.90); baked goods and cakes 0.75€–4€ (70¢–$3.60). No credit cards. Mon–Fri 7:30am–7pm; Sat 9am–6pm; Sun 10–6pm. Bus: Any city-center bus.

The Steps of Rome ⚘ ITALIAN/PIZZA   Word is out that this restaurant, just off the busy shopping thoroughfare of Grafton Street, offers some of the best simple Italian fare in Dublin. Large, succulent pizza slices available for take-out are one way to enjoy the wonders of this authentic Italian kitchen when the dining room is full—the seven tables huddled within this tiny restaurant seem to be perennially occupied. The potato, mozzarella and rosemary pizza, with a thick crust resembling focaccia, is unusual and exceptionally delicious. Although the pasta dishes are also quite good, it's that pizza that is unforgettable.

Chatham Court, off Chatham St., Dublin 2. ✆ **01/670-5630.** Main courses 7.60€–10€ ($6.90–$9); pizza slices 2.50€ ($2.25). No credit cards. Mon–Sat 10am–midnght; Sun 1–11pm. DART: Pearse. Bus: Any city-center bus.

WORTH A SPLURGE

L'Ecrivain ⚘⚘⚘ FRENCH/IRISH   This is one of Dublin's truly fine restaurants. The atmosphere is relaxed and welcoming without the bother of pretense, and there's a garden terrace for open-air dining in good weather. The menu's emphasis is on the best Irish ingredients, which are allowed to argue their own cases without having to deliberate through dense sauces. The seared sea trout with sweet potato puree and the entrecôte steak with caramelized onion are perfectly prepared, and the presentation borders on modern art (and I mean that in a good way). The desserts here are not an afterthought; they're the creations of a single-minded pastry chef and stand on their own. They may have the best crème brûlée outside of France.

109 Lower Baggot St., Dublin 2. ℭ **01/661-1919**. www.lecrivain.com. Reservations recommended. Fixed-price 2-course lunch 22€ ($20), fixed-price 3-course lunch 25€ ($23); fixed-price 3-course dinner 44€ ($40); main courses 30€–33€ ($28–$30). 10% service charge on food only. AE, MC, V. Mon–Fri 12:30–2pm and 7–11pm; Sat 7–11pm. Closed Dec 24–Jan 4. DART: Pearse. Bus: 10. Ample street parking on nearby Merrion Sq. 5-min. walk from St. Stephen's Green.

NORTH OF THE LIFFEY

Bangkok Café THAI   Located in a run-down section of town east of Parnell Square (turn right at the top of O'Connell St.), this unassuming restaurant would be very easy to miss. Nevertheless, on every night, scores of devotees pack the tiny candlelit dining room, with its loudly creaking wood floor. It's hard to say quite what makes this place so popular, and so delightful—the food is very good, though not extraordinary; the atmosphere is casual and romantic, but not unique for these qualities. The food is admirably subtle, despite the strong presence of garlic and hot chilis; the chili sauce is excellent, though it's used too universally. Service is friendly and accommodating, and highly informal. The desserts are inconsistently available, and inconsistent in quality as well—choose something that's made on the premises, though, and you won't go wrong.

106 Parnell St., Dublin 1. ℭ **01/878-6618**. Reservations recommended. Main courses 9€–11€ ($8–$10). No credit cards. Tues–Sun 5:30–10:30pm. Bus: 33, 3B, 51A, 41, 41B, 41C.

101 Talbot INTERNATIONAL/VEGETARIAN   This second-floor shop-front restaurant, convenient to the Abbey Theatre, features light and healthy foods, with a strong emphasis on vegetarian dishes, including choices for vegans. The setting is bright and casual, with contemporary Irish art on display, big windows, yellow rag-rolled walls, ash-topped tables, and newspapers to read. Entrees change on a weekly basis, and there are always a few imaginative vegetarian dishes, such as the spicy bean and sweet potato casserole with pineapple salsa and grilled polenta. Espresso and cappuccino are always available, and there's a full bar.

101 Talbot St. (near Marlborough St.), Dublin 1. ℭ **01/874-5011**. Reservations recommended. Dinner main courses 13€–17€ ($12–$16). AE, DC, MC, V. Tues–Sat 5–11pm. Closed Sun and Mon. DART: Connolly Station. Bus: 27A, 31A, 31B, 32A, 32B, 42B, 42C, 43, or 44A.

Winding Stair IRISH   Those who resist reading the texts that paper the walls of this cafe's three-story, 18th-century winding staircase will soon find themselves in a comforting enclave overlooking the Ha'penny bridge and the Liffey River. Solicitous staff members are quick to serve the bookish clientele, who like the tea, espresso, and healthy sandwiches and cakes as much as the many new and used books that line the surrounding shelves. Thick sandwiches heaped with fresh vegetables and a choice of cheeses and salamis are made to order. Salads run from the exotic to the local with both a hearty tabouli and an Irish Brie and Cranberry gracing the chalkboard menu. Banana and honey sandwiches, as well

---

Impressions

I have a total irreverence for anything connected with society except that which makes the roads safer, the beer stronger, the food cheaper, the old men and old women warmer in the winter and happier in the summer.

—Brendan Behan (1923–64)

as carrot cake and lemon poppy seed loaf, comprise the sweet menu. Soup is also offered, but go early if it's your lunch time goal as it tends to disappear quickly on rainy Dublin days. Evening events include poetry readings and recitals.

40 Lower Ormond Quay, Dublin 1. ✆ **01/873-3292**. All items 2€–6.50€ ($1.80–$5.90). MC, V. Mon–Sat 10am–6pm; Sun 1–6pm Bus: 70 or 80.

PUB GRUB

The listings below barely scratch the surface of pubs that serve decent and inexpensive meals during the lunch hours. If you've had a substantial breakfast in your B&B, this could well be your main meal of the day—and at a tiny fraction of a full restaurant meal's cost.

SOUTH OF THE LIFFEY

The Lord Edward TRADITIONAL/SEAFOOD   The Lord Edward, in the Liberties, near Christ Church Cathedral, has a genuine old-world atmosphere, complete with stone fireplaces, a beamed ceiling, and white stucco walls in the ground-floor pub. Upstairs is one of the city's better seafood restaurants, but the same high-quality food and excellent service come at modest prices in the pub during lunch hours. Choose from heaping plates of hot dishes (roasts, fish, chicken) or a selection of salad plates.

23 Christchurch Place, Dublin 8. ✆ **01/454-2420**. ledward@indigo.ie. Lunch main courses 6.50€–13€ ($5.90–$12); dinner main courses 15€–23€ ($14–$21). AE, DC, DISC, MC, V. Mon–Fri noon–3pm and 6–11:45pm; Sat 6–11:45pm. DART: Pearse or Tara St. Bus: Any city-center bus.

The Old Stand TRADITIONAL   A century and a half ago this was a forge, but today you'll find outstanding figures of the sporting world gathered to enjoy the craic and good pub grub. There's a daily special of soup, meat, vegetables, and tea or coffee, as well as omelets or salad plates, and hot platters of chicken, steak, or fish. *Note:* This is one of the only pubs that serves meals during evening hours.

37 Exchequer St. (just off Great George's St.), Dublin 2. ✆ **01/677-7220**. www.theoldstandpub.com. Lunch main courses 8€ ($7.25); dinner main courses 8€–13€ ($7.25–$12). Daily noon–9pm. MC, V. DART: Pearse or Tara St. Bus: Any city-center bus.

Stag's Head TRADITIONAL   Built in 1770, the Stag's Head had its last "modernization" in 1895. Wrought-iron chandeliers, stained-glass skylights, huge mirrors, gleaming wood, and mounted stags' heads set the mood. Choose a light lunch of soup and toasted sandwiches or heaping platters of bacon, beef, or chicken plus two vegetables. The pub is just off Exchequer Street (from Great George's St.)—look for the mosaic depicting a stag's head, embedded in the sidewalk of Dame Street, in the middle of the second block, on the left side coming from College Green, then turn onto the small lane that leads to Dame Court—a complicated journey, but worth the effort.

1 Dame Ct., Dublin 2. ✆ **01/679-3701**. Main courses 5€–10€ ($4.55–$9). No credit cards. Mon–Fri 12:30–3:30pm and 5–7pm; Sat 12:30–2:30pm. DART: Pearse or Tara St. Bus: Any city-center bus.

NORTH OF THE LIFFEY

Patrick Conway's TRADITIONAL   Dating from 1754, Patrick Conway's is just off O'Connell Street, opposite Rotunda Hospital and the Gate Theatre. You'll often find theater people bending an elbow here before and after a show in the evening. At lunchtime, there's very good pub grub to be had (the hot apple tart is a specialty).

70 Parnell St. ✆ **01/873-2474**. Pub grub 5€–8€ ($4.55–$7.25). No credit cards. Mon–Fri 12:30–2:30pm. DART: Connolly or Tara St. Bus: Any city-center bus.

5 Seeing the Sights

Dublin's face today mirrors the lines and wrinkles, blemishes and beauty spots left by a long, rich, and colorful history. The past is everywhere for you to explore; it's preserved in stone and parchment, on canvas, and in the heritage of traditional music. But Dublin isn't all about the past: Parts of the city are quickly moving into the new millennium and moving fast. Be sure to check out the new Dublin at Temple Bar or in one of the city's many hip nightclubs. See "Dublin Nights," later in this chapter.

SUGGESTED ITINERARIES

If You Have 1 Day

Start at the beginning—Dublin's medieval quarter, the area around Christ Church and St. Patrick's Cathedrals. Tour these great churches and then walk the cobblestone streets and inspect the nearby old city walls at High Street. From Old Dublin, take a turn eastward and see Dublin Castle and then Trinity College, with the famous Book of Kells. Cross over the River Liffey to O'Connell Street, Dublin's main thoroughfare. Walk up this wide street, passing the landmark General Post Office (GPO), to Parnell Square and the picturesque Garden of Remembrance. If time permits, visit the Dublin Writers' Museum, then hop on a doubledecker bus heading to the south bank of the Liffey for a relaxing stroll amid the flora of St. Stephen's Green. Cap the day with a show at the Abbey Theatre and a drink or two at a nearby pub.

If You Have 2 Days

Day 1 Spend Day 1 as above.

Day 2 In the morning, take a Dublin Bus city-sightseeing tour to give you an overview of the city— you'll see all of the local downtown landmarks, plus the major buildings along the River Liffey and some of the leading sites on the edge of the city, such as the Guinness Brewery, the Royal Hospital, the Irish Museum of Modern Art, and the Phoenix Park. In the afternoon, head for Grafton Street for some shopping. If time allows, stroll Merrion or Fitzwilliam Square for a sampling of Dublin's best Georgian architecture.

If You Have 3 Days

Days 1–2 Spend Days 1 and 2 as above.

Day 3 Make this a day for Dublin's artistic and cultural attractions. Visit some of the top museums and art galleries, from the mainstream (the National Museum and National Gallery, Natural History Museum, and Museum of Modern Art) to the more specialized (the Irish Jewish Museum, the Kilmainham Jail Museum) to the very specialized (the Irish Whiskey Corner or the Guinness Hop Store). Save time for a walk around Temple Bar, the city's Left Bank district, lined with art galleries and film studios, interesting secondhand shops, and bistros.

If You Have 4 Days or More

Days 1–3 Spend Days 1 to 3 as above.

Day 4 Take a ride aboard DART, Dublin's rapid transit system, to the suburbs, either southward to Dun Laoghaire or Dalkey or northward to Howth. The DART routes follow the rim of Dublin Bay in both directions, so you'll enjoy a scenic ride and get to spend some time in an Irish coastal village.

THE TOP ATTRACTIONS

Archaeology and History Museum ⭑⭑ This important museum, a branch of the National Museum of Ireland, reflects Ireland's heritage from 2000 B.C. to the present. It's the home of many of the country's greatest historical finds, including the Ardagh Chalice, Tara Brooch, and Cross of Cong. Other highlights range from the artifacts from the Wood Quay excavations of the Old Dublin Settlements to an extensive exhibition of Irish gold ornaments from the Bronze Age. The **museum cafeteria** ⭑ is a great place to go for a simple lunch— see description above.

Kildare St., Dublin 2. ✆ **01/677-7444**. www.museum.ie. Free admission. Tues–Sat 10am–5pm; Sun 2–5pm. DART to Pearse Station. Bus: 7, 7A, 8 (from Burgh Quay), 10, 11, or 13 (from O'Connell St.).

Christ Church Cathedral and Dublinia ⭑⭑ *Kids* Christ Church Cathedral is one of the oldest and most beautiful of Dublin's buildings. Founded by King Sitric in 1038, it was originally a wooden structure but was rebuilt in stone after the 1169 Norman invasion. There are lovely architectural details and stonework in the nave, transepts, choir, and chancel, and the crypt (the oldest section) is said to be one of the best of its kind in Europe. Note that the cathedral is in use for services daily 9:30am and 5:30pm and Sundays 11:15am and 3:15pm.

Cross the elegant bridge from the cathedral to the enter the **Dublinia** ⭑ exhibit and you walk straight into medieval Dublin as it was between 1170, when the Anglo-Normans arrived, and 1540, when its monasteries were closed. Pick up your personal audio headset and enter the Medieval Maze, where life-like exhibits depict dramatic, sometimes mystical, episodes from this period. It's great for all ages.

Christ Church Place (off Lord Edward St.), Dublin 8. ✆ **01/677-8099** (cathedral) or 01/679-4611 (Dublinia). www.dublinia.ie. Dublinia and cathedral 5.50€ ($5) adults, 4.50€ ($4.10) seniors, students, and children, 15€ ($14) families. Cathedral only 2.55€ ($2.30) adults, 1.30€ ($1.20) children. Christ Church daily 10am–5:30pm. Dublinia Apr–Sept daily 10am–5pm; Oct–Mar Mon–Sat 11am–4pm, Sun 10am–4:30pm. Bus: 21A, 50, 50A, 78, 78A, or 78B.

Collins Barracks ⭑ This is the latest venue of the National Museum, which already occupied 2 of the 4 available wings of the barracks. Even if it were empty, Collins Barracks—the oldest military barracks in Europe—would be well worth a visit; the structure itself is a splendidly restored early 18th-century masterwork by Colonel Thomas Burgh, Ireland's Chief Engineer and Surveyor General under Queen Anne. So far, the collection housed here focuses on decorative arts and weaponry—most notable is the extraordinary display of Irish silver and fur-niture. Collins Barracks also houses a cafe and gift shop.

Benburb St., Dublin 7. ✆ **01/677-7444**. www.museum.ie. Free admission. Tours at varying hours, depend-ing on groups, 1.30€ ($1.20). Tues–Sat 10am–5pm; Sun 2–5pm. Bus: 25, 25A, 66, 67 (from Middle Abbey St.), or 90 (from Aston Quay). Free parking available.

Dublin Castle ⭑ Built between 1208 and 1220, this complex represents some of the oldest surviving architecture in the city, and was the center of British power in Ireland for more than 7 centuries until it was taken over by the new Irish government in 1922. Highlights include the 13th-century Record Tower; the State Apartments, once the residence of English viceroys; and the Chapel Royal, a 19th-century Gothic building with particularly fine plaster decoration and carved oak gallery fronts and fittings. The newest developments are the Undercroft, an excavated site on the grounds where an early Viking fortress stood, and the Treasury, built between 1712 and 1715 and believed to be the

Dublin Attractions

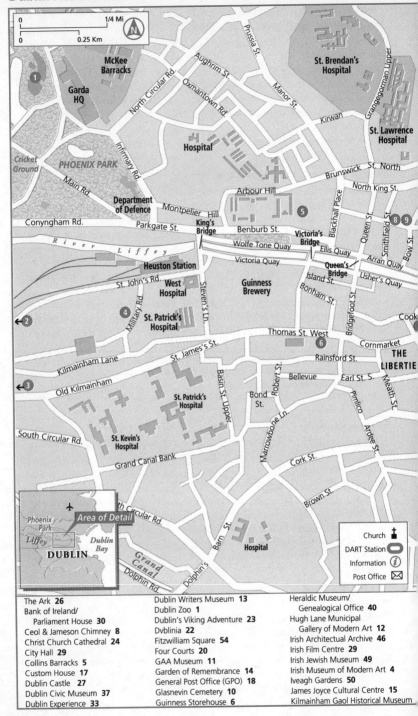

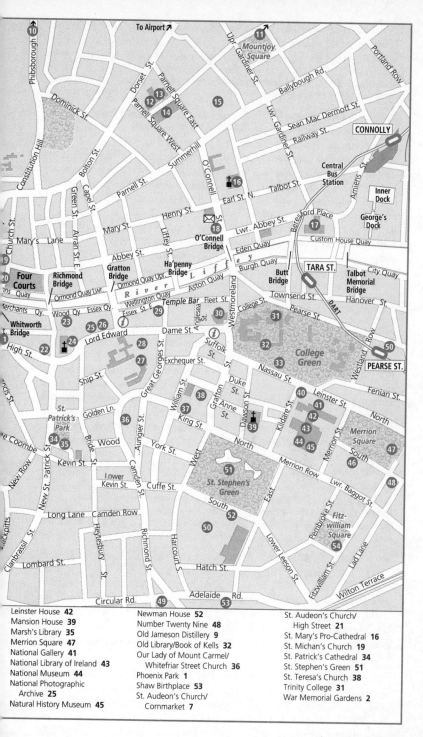

Leinster House **42**
Mansion House **39**
Marsh's Library **35**
Merrion Square **47**
National Gallery **41**
National Library of Ireland **43**
National Museum **44**
National Photographic
    Archive **25**
Natural History Museum **45**

Newman House **52**
Number Twenty Nine **48**
Old Jameson Distillery **9**
Old Library/Book of Kells **32**
Our Lady of Mount Carmel/
    Whitefriar Street Church **36**
Phoenix Park **1**
Shaw Birthplace **53**
St. Audeon's Church/
    Cornmarket **7**

St. Audeon's Church/
    High Street **21**
St. Mary's Pro-Cathedral **16**
St. Michan's Church **19**
St. Patrick's Cathedral **34**
St. Stephen's Green **51**
St. Teresa's Church **38**
Trinity College **31**
War Memorial Gardens **2**

oldest surviving office building in Ireland. At hand, as well, are a craft shop, heritage center, and restaurant.

Palace St. (off Dame St.), Dublin 2. © **01/677-7129.** Admission 4€ ($3.60) adults, 3.10€ ($2.80) seniors/students, 1.50€ ($1.35) children. Tours given every 20–25 min Mon–Fri 10am–5pm, Sat–Sun and bank holidays 2–5pm. The State Apartments are sometimes closed to the public due to official state functions. Bus: 50, 50A, 54, 56A, 77, 77A, or 77B.

Dublin Writers Museum Dublin celebrates its rich literary heritage in two splendid 18th-century Georgian mansions, each with permanent displays on George Bernard Shaw, Sean O'Casey, W. B. Yeats, James Joyce, Brendan Behan, and a host of other writers who have enriched the fabric of Dublin's past. Special-interest exhibitions are mounted on a regular basis. Contemporary writers are nurtured through the Irish Writers' Centre, which provides workrooms, offices, and meeting rooms for their use. The fully licensed restaurant, Chapter One, is much favored by Dubliners, as well as visitors (see "Great Deals on Dining," earlier in this chapter), and there's also a coffee shop. The superb bookshop, with mail-order service and specialized book lists, stocks a wide range of Irish titles and also provides an out-of-print and antiquarian book search service.

18–19 Parnell Sq. N., Dublin 1. © **01/872-2077.** Fax 01/872-2231. Admission 5.10€ ($4.60) adults, 3.80€ ($3.45) seniors/students, 2.60€ ($2.35) ages 3–11, 14€ ($13) families (2 adults and up to 4 children). AE, DC, MC, V. Mon–Sat 10am–5pm (6pm June–Aug); Sun and holidays 11am–5pm. DART to Connolly Station. Bus: 11, 13, 16, 16A, 22, or 22A.

National Gallery ⍟ Around the corner from the National Museum and a block away from the National History Museum, the National Gallery's collections include impressive works by Dutch masters as well as 10 major landscape paintings and portraits by Gainsborough and canvases by Rubens, Rembrandt, El Greco, Monet, Cézanne, and Degas. John Butler Yeats, said to be Ireland's greatest modern portrait painter, is well represented, as are leading 18th- and 19th-century Irish artists. The gallery has a branch of the reliable Fitzer's chain of restaurants, open for breakfast, lunch, and afternoon tea. A new wing, designed by architects Benson and Forsythe (known for their renovation of the Museum of Scotland in Edinburgh) is expected to be open by the time this book hits the shelves and will house a new center for the study of Irish art, a large retail store, and two additional restaurants.

Merrion Sq. West, Dublin 2. © **01/661-5133.** www.nationalgallery.ie. Free admission. Mon–Wed and Fri–Sat 9:30am–5:15pm; Thurs 9:30am–8:15pm; Sun 12–5:15pm. Free public tours Sat 3pm; Sun 2:15, 3 and 4pm. Closed Good Friday and Dec 24–26. DART: Pearse (then 5-min. walk). Bus: 5, 6, 7, 7A, 8, 10, 44, 47, 47B, 48A, or 62.

Natural History Museum A division of the National Museum of Ireland, the recently renovated Natural History Museum is considered one of the finest traditional museums in the world. In addition to presenting the zoological history of Ireland, there are examples of major animal groups from around the world, including many rare or extinct groups. The Blaschka glass models of marine animals are worth a look.

Merrion St., Dublin 2. © **01/677-7444.** www.museum.ie. Free admission. Tues–Sat 10am–5pm; Sun 2–5pm. Bus: 7, 7A, 8.

St. Patrick's Cathedral Founded in 1190, St. Patrick's has, over its varied history, been both a university (from 1320–1465) and a stable for the mounts of Cromwell's troops in the 17th century. Its best-known dean (from 1713–45) was Jonathan Swift, author of *Gulliver's Travels* and a host of other sharp-tongued attacks on the humbuggery of his times. His tomb is in the south aisle,

---

Tips **Moving Through the Museums**

The National Museum of Ireland currently comprises three separate venues and plans to add a fourth. A special **MuseumLink** shuttle bus (Rte. 172) runs daily between these museums; shuttle schedules are available at any of the three museums.

---

and his beloved "Stella" (Esther Johnson in real life) lies nearby. The cathedral had fallen into near ruin by 1860, when a member of the Guinness family financed the restoration that brought it to its present magnificence. All services are ecumenical and all weekday choral services are also open to the public. Check with the Dublin tourist board for exact days and hours. "Living Stones" is an exhibition that explores the role the cathedral has played in civic and national life. Other treasures here include the Door of Reconciliation, an 18th-century parchment awarding Jonathan Swift the Freedom of the City, and two 10th-century Christian grave slabs.

St. Patrick's Close, Dublin 8. ℂ **01/475-4817.** www.stpatrickscathedral.ie. Admission 3.50€ ($3.15) adults, 2.60€ ($2.35) seniors/students, 8.50€ ($8) families. MC, V. Year-round Mon–Fri 9am–6pm; Mar–Oct Sat 9am–6pm and Sun 9–11am, 12:45–3pm, 4:15–6pm; Nov–Feb Sat 9am–5pm and Sun 10–11am, 12:45–3pm. No admittance Sun 11am–12:45pm and 3pm–4:15pm except for worship. Bus: 50, 50A, 54, 54A, or 56A.

Trinity College and the Book of Kells 🟌🟌🟌   Trinity College was founded by Elizabeth I in 1592, but its oldest surviving buildings are the redbrick structures put up in the early 1700s. The striking West Front is especially noteworthy, as are the 1740 Printing House and the 1760 Dining Hall. However, it's the **Old Library** 🟌🟌 that you should be sure not to miss. The Colonnades Gallery, together with the lofty, vaulted Long Room (which holds over 200,000 ancient volumes) and marble busts of famous Trinity graduates combine to create an awe-inspiring atmosphere you'll not soon forget. In the gallery, you'll find a priceless link to Ireland's antiquity, the magnificently illustrated **Book of Kells** 🟌🟌🟌. The book, which consists of the four Gospels illuminated by monks, was discovered in the monastery at Kells, and has been bound in four separate volumes, two of which are displayed in glass cases. Pages are turned daily, and you may well find yourself returning for a second look. The exhibition **"Turning Darkness into Light"** 🟌 places the Book of Kells in its historical and cultural context together with other illuminated manuscripts on display.

Nearby in the Arts Building (facing Nassau St.) is the **Dublin Experience** (ℂ **01/608-1688**), an excellent multimedia introduction to the history and people of Dublin (see description below).

College Green, Dublin 2. ℂ **01/608-2320.** Free admission to the college grounds; admission to Old Library/ Book of Kells 6€ ($5.45) adults, 5€ ($4.55) students and seniors, 12€ ($11) families, free for children under 12. Dublin Experience 4.15€ ($3.75) adults, 3.50€ ($3.15) seniors/students. Combination tickets also available. AE, MC, V. Oct–May Mon–Sat 9:30am–5pm, Sun noon–4:30pm; June–Sept Sun 9:30am–4:30pm. Dublin Experience May–Sept daily 10am–5pm; closed Oct–Apr. DART: Pearse St. Station. Bus: Any city-center bus.

MORE ATTRACTIONS
MUSEUMS

Dublin Civic Museum   Located in the old City Assembly House, a fine 18th-century Georgian structure next to the Powerscourt Town House Centre, this museum focuses on the history of the Dublin area from medieval to modern times. In addition to old street signs, maps, and prints, you can see Viking artifacts, wooden water mains, coal covers, and even the head from the statue of

Lord Nelson, which stood in O'Connell Street until it was blown up in 1965. Exhibits change three or four times a year.

58 S. William St., Dublin 2. ℭ **01/679-4260.** Free admission. Tues–Sat 10am–6pm; Sun 11am–2pm. Bus: 10, 11, 13 (all from O'Connell St.).

GAA Museum On the grounds of Croke Park, principal stadium of the Gaelic Athletic Association, this museum dramatically presents the athletic heritage of Ireland. The history of the Gaelic Games extends into Ireland's mythical past, and since the founding of the GAA in 1884 the games have been contested on an annual basis between teams representing the various regions of Ireland. The museum isn't just for fans—if you've never heard of Gaelic football, hurling, or camogie, you'll find clear explanations of the sports and compelling stories of Ireland's greatest athletes. Test your skills at the interactive exhibits and peruse the extensive video archive of football finals dating back to 1931. The twelve-minute film *A Sunday in September* admirably captures the hysteria of a final match. Note that on match days the museum is open only to ticket holders seated in the "news stand" at Croke Park.

Croke Park, Dublin 3. ℭ **01/855-8176.** Admission 3.80€ ($3.75) adults, 2.55€ ($2.50) students, 1.90€ ($1.90) children, 7.60€ ($7.50) families. May–Sept daily 9:30am–4:30pm; Oct–Apr Tues–Sat 10am–4:30pm, Sun 12–4:30pm. Bus: 3, 11, 11A, 16, 16A, 51A, 123.

Irish Jewish Museum Housed in a former synagogue, this museum of Irish/Jewish documents, photographs, and memorabilia traces the history of the Jews in Ireland over the last 400 years. The museum was dedicated in 1985 by Chaim Herzog, the former president of Israel, who was born in Belfast and educated in Dublin.

3–4 Walworth Rd. (off Victoria St.), S. Circular Rd., Dublin 8. ℭ **01/676-0737.** Free admission; donations welcome. May–Sept Tues, Thurs, and Sun 11am–3:30pm; Oct–Apr Sun 10:30am–2:30pm. Bus: 15A, 15B, 16, 47, or 47B.

Irish Traditional Music Centre (Ceol) and Jameson Chimney ⍟ Ceol offers a good introduction to Irish traditional music for the uninitiated, and a few items which may be of interest to experienced listeners and performers. The center houses several interactive audiovisual displays that present the basic components of Irish traditional music—song, dance, and instruments. An impressive diversity of material is packed into the small space, the most interesting of which is an archive of songs, categorized by region and topic. Videos demonstrating set dancing are projected onto six-foot screens, and audio recordings of early Irish radio broadcasts are continuously played in a small circular chamber at the center of the museum. A thirty-minute film intersperses brief interviews with performers, clips from live sessions, and spectacular views of the Irish countryside. Adjacent to the center is the **Jameson Chimney** ⍟, a 150-foot industrial tower with a recently constructed observation deck that provides unparalleled views of the city.

Smithfield Village, off Arran Quay, Dublin 1. ℭ **01/817-3820.** www.ceol.ie. Ceol Admission (Ceol *or* the tower) 6.35€ ($5.75) adults, 5.10€ ($4.60) students, 4.50€ ($4.10) children, 19€ ($17) families. Mon–Sat 10am–6pm; Sun 12–7pm (last film 45 min. before closing). Bus: 67, 67A, 68, 69, 79, 90.

Kilmainham Gaol Historical Museum ⍟ Thanks to an excellent museum and interpretive slide presentation, the Kilmainham Gaol is a great place to get situated within the context of Irish Republican history. Many famous Dubliners have lived within these severe stone walls, from the prison's opening in 1796 until 1924, when the late President Eamon de Valera left as its final prisoner.

The tour takes you past cells occupied by Robert Emmett, James Connolly, Patrick Pearse, and others who died here for the cause of Irish independence. The claustrophobic corridors and stone-paved yard resonate with the voices of the past, a chilling reminder of Ireland's recent history.

Inchicore Rd., Kilmainham, Dublin 8. ℭ 01/453-5984. Admission 4.50€ ($4.10) adults, 3.20€ ($2.90) seniors, 2€ ($1.80) children, 10€ ($9) families. Tours given Apr–Sept daily 9:30am–4:45pm; Oct–Mar Mon–Fri 9:30am–4pm, Sun 10am–4:45pm. Bus: 21, 78, 78A, 78B, or 79 at O'Connell Bridge.

Number Twenty Nine   Situated in the heart of one of Dublin's fashionable Georgian streets, this is a unique museum—a restored four-story Georgian-style house designed to reflect the lifestyle of a Dublin middle-class family during the period from 1790 to 1820. The exhibition ranges from artifacts and artworks of the time to carpets, curtains, decorations, plasterwork, and bell pulls. The nursery includes dolls and toys of the era. An audiovisual introduction to the house and a guided tour are also available.

29 Lower Fitzwilliam St. ℭ 01/702-6165. www.esb.ie/education. Admission 3.50€ ($3.20) adults, 1.50€ ($1.40) students and seniors, children under 16 free. Tues–Sat 10am–5pm; Sun 2–5pm. DART: Pearse St. Station. Bus: 6, 7, 8, 10, or 45.

HISTORIC BUILDINGS

Bank of Ireland/Parliament House   This building was erected in 1729 to house the Irish Parliament, but it became superfluous when the British and Irish Parliaments were merged in London. Now it's a busy bank. (In fact, the Irish Parliament voted itself out of existence, becoming the only recorded parliament in history to do so.) Highlights include the windowless front portico, built to avoid distractions from the outside when Parliament was in session; and the unique House of Lords chamber, famed for its Irish oak woodwork, 18th-century tapestries, golden mace, and sparkling Irish crystal chandelier of 1,233 pieces, dating from 1765.

This is also the home of the **Bank of Ireland Arts Centre,** hosting an impressive program of art exhibitions, concerts, and poetry readings. Entry to readings, lunchtime recitals, and exhibitions is free of charge. Another denizen of the bank center is **The Story of Banking,** an interactive museum offering its own glimpse of the history of banking and of Ireland more generally over the past 2 centuries. It's open Tuesday to Friday 10am to 4pm; admission 1.90€ ($1.75) adults, 1.25€ ($1.15) students.

2 College Green, Dublin 2. ℭ 01/661-5933, ext. 2265. Free admission. Mon–Wed and Fri 10am–4pm; Thurs 10am–5pm. Guided 45-min. tours of House of Lords chamber Tues 10:30am, 11:30am, and 1:45pm (except holidays). DART: Tara St. Bus: Any city-center bus.

Four Courts   Home to the Irish law courts since 1796, this fine 18th-century building overlooks the north bank of the Liffey on Dublin's west side. It was designed by James Gandon and is distinguished by its graceful Corinthian columns, massive dome, sprawling 440-foot (134m) facade, and exterior statues of Justice, Mercy, Wisdom, and Moses (sculpted by Edward Smyth). The building was severely damaged during the Irish Civil War of 1922, but it has been artfully restored. The public is admitted only when court is in session, so it is best to phone in advance.

ℭ 01/872-5555. Free admission. Mon–Fri 11am–1pm and 2–4pm. Bus: 34, 70, or 80.

General Post Office   To touch recent Irish history, take a look around the imposing General Post Office, built in 1818. The massive granite building with its six fluted columns is where Padraic Pearse gathered his Volunteers in 1916,

Fun Fact A Monumental Kind of Humor

Dublin boasts countless public monuments, some so modest as to be easily overlooked, others boldly evident. Many of them Dubliners have honored with irreverent nicknames. Here's a sampler:

- **Anna Livia,** Joyce's mythical personification of the River Liffey, may be found cast in bronze on O'Connell Street across from the General Post Office, where she reclines in a pool of streaming water. Locals call her "the floozy in the Jacuzzi."

- **Sweet Molly Malone,** another figment of Irish imagination who's inspired poetry, song, and, most recently, sculpture, survives larger than life, complete with her flower cart, at the intersection of Nassau and Grafton across from the Trinity College Provost's house. Ms. Malone's plunging neckline must have something to do with her sobriquet: "the tart with the cart."

- Another sculpture stands on Dame Street, just around the corner from Molly: a silent frenzy of trumpeters and streaming columns of water, bearing the words "you're a nation again," but popularly transliterated as "urination again."

- Then there's Dublin's testimonial to the man who was arguably Ireland's greatest patriot, **Theobald Wolfe Tone.** Born at 44 Stafford St. in 1763 and graduated from Trinity College, Tone went on to spark a revolutionary fervor among the Irish which proved unquenchable. His timeless contribution to Ireland and the world is commemorated on the north side of St. Stephen's Green in a semicircular assemblage of rough-hewn columns that's come to be known as "Tonehenge."

- Across the Liffey, on Dublin's north side, two theaters rank among Dublin's monuments: the **Gate** and the **Abbey,** which have set the standard for Irish theater in this century. Their stature, of course, makes them not immune but prey to Irish irreverence. Because the Gate was founded by and flourished for decades under its two luminaries, the respected and openly gay couple Micháel MacLiammóir and Hilton Edwards, and because the Abbey for its part gained a reputation for Irish stage productions served up for overseas tourists, the theaters were commonly referred to as "Sodom and Begorrah."

hoisted the Irish Tricolour, and from the portico proclaimed to the Irish people and the world that Ireland would henceforth be an independent Republic. From the nearby Liffey, an English gunboat shelled the building, starting a fire that gutted its interior. In a front window position facing O'Connell Street, look for a statue of Ireland's ancient mythical warrior hero Cuchulain, who tied himself upright to a stake in order to fight a superior force to the death. The statue serves as a memorial to the men who fought here in 1916; its marble base is inscribed with the words of Pearse's Proclamation.

O'Connell St. ✆ 01/705-7000. www.anpost.ie. Free admission. Mon–Sat 8am–8pm; Sun and bank holidays 10am–6pm. DART to Connolly Station. Bus: Any city-center bus.

Leinster House   Leinster House, in the city center south of the Liffey, is the home of the Irish Parliament, comprised of the *Dáil Éireann* (Irish House of Representatives) and *Seanad Éirean* (Irish Senate). Dating back to 1745 and originally known as Kildare House, this building is said to have been the model for Irish-born architect James Hoban's design for the White House in Washington, D.C. Guided tours are conducted when the Dáil is in session (Oct–May Tues–Thurs); tickets must be arranged in advance from the Public Relations Office (*€* **01/618-3066**).

Leinster House. Kildare St. and Merrion Sq., Dublin 2. *€* **01/618-3000**. www.irlgov.ie/oireachtas. Free admission. By appointment only Oct–May Mon and Fri 10am–4:30pm. DART: Pearse. Bus: Any city-center bus.

Mansion House   Built by Joshua Dawson, this Queen Anne–style building has been the official residence of Dublin's lord mayors since 1715. It was here that the first Dail Eireann assembled, in 1919, to adopt Ireland's Declaration of Independence and ratify the Proclamation of the Irish Republic by the insurgents of 1916. You can't go inside, but the exterior is worth a look.

Dawson St., Dublin 2. *€* **01/676-1845**. www.dublincorp.ie. Not open to the public. DART: Pearse St. Station. Bus: 10, 11A, 11B, 13, or 20B.

CHURCHES & CATHEDRALS
Our Lady of Mount Carmel/Whitefriar Street Carmelite Church   This church, one of the city's largest, was built between 1825 and 1827 on the site of a pre-Reformation Carmelite priory (1539) and an earlier Carmelite abbey (13th century). This is a favorite place of pilgrimage on February 14th, because the body of St. Valentine is enshrined here, having been presented to the church by Pope Gregory XVI in 1836. The other highlight is the 15th-century black oak Madonna, Our Lady of Dublin.

56 Aungier St., Dublin 2. *€* **01/475-8821**. Free admission. Mon and Wed–Fri 8am–6:30pm; Sat 8am–7pm; Sun 8am–7:30pm; Tues 8am–9:30pm. Bus: 16, 16A, 19, 19A, 122, 155, 83.

St. Audeon's Church   Situated next to the only remaining gate of the Old City walls (dating from 1214), this church is said to be the only surviving medieval parish in Dublin. Although partly in ruins, the 13th century nave and the west doorway (dating to 1190) have survived. In addition, the 17th-century bell tower houses three bells cast in 1423, making them the oldest in Ireland. This church is a Church of Ireland property, but nearby is another St. Audeon's Church, a Catholic one that dates from 1846. It was here that Father "Flash" Kavanagh used to say the world's fastest mass so that his congregation could be out in time for the football matches. Renovations were underway in 2001, and a new visitor center may be open by 2002.

Cornmarket (off High St.), Dublin 8. Currently closed to visitors—check with tourist office (*€* **066/979-2083** or 1850/230330) for the latest information. Bus: 21A, 78A, or 78B.

St. Mary's Pro-Cathedral   Because Dublin's two main cathedrals (Christ Church and St. Patrick's) belong to the Church of Ireland, St. Mary's is the closest the Catholics get to having a cathedral of their own. Tucked into a corner of a rather unimpressive back street, it's situated in the heart of the city's north side and is considered the main Catholic parish church of the city center. Its style is Greek Revival Doric, which provides a distinct contrast to the Gothic Revival look of most other churches of the period. The exterior portico is modeled on the Temple of Theseus in Athens, with six Doric columns, while the Renaissance-style interior is patterned after the Church of St. Philip de Reule of Paris.

The church was built between 1815 and 1825. It's noted for its Palestrina Choir, which sings a Latin Mass every Sunday at 11am.

Cathedral and Marlborough sts., Dublin 1. ℂ **01/874-5441**. www.procathedral.ie. Free admission. Daily 9am–6pm. DART: Connolly. Bus: Any city-center bus.

St. Michan's Church ⚝ The square tower of St. Michan's, north of the Liffey, dates from the 1096 Danish church that stood on this site; the rest of the present structure is of 17th-century origin. Handel is said to have played the organ here (perhaps when in Dublin to conduct the first performance of his *Messiah* in 1742), but most visitors are drawn by the perfectly preserved bodies that have lain in its vaults for centuries. The Sheare brothers, executed during the 1798 rebellion, rest here, and on my last visit it was a young Crusader and a 15th-century nun whose mummified bodies could be viewed. The rector of St. Michan's attended Robert Emmet in his last hours, and the patriot is supposedly buried in the churchyard (the guide can fill you in on the story). The church is wheelchair accessible, though the vaults are not.

Church St., Dublin 7. ℂ **01/872-4154**. stmichan@iol.ie. Free admission. Guided tour of church and vaults 2.60€ ($2.40) adults, 2€ ($1.80) seniors and students, 0.65€ (60¢) children under 12. Nov–Feb Mon–Fri 12:30–3:30pm and Sat 10am–1pm; Mar–Oct Mon–Fri 10am–12:45pm and 2–4:45pm, Sat 10am–1pm. Bus: 134 (from Abbey St.).

St. Teresa's Church With its foundation stone laid in 1793, the church was opened in 1810 by the Discalced Carmelite Fathers, and was continuously enlarged until its present form was reached in 1876. This was the first post–Penal Law church to be legally and openly erected in Dublin following the Catholic Relief Act of 1793. Among the artistic highlights are John Hogan's *Dead Christ,* a sculpture displayed beneath the altar, and Phyllis Burke's seven beautiful stained-glass windows.

Clarendon St., Dublin 2. ℂ **01/671-8466**. Free admission; donations welcome. Daily 8am–8pm or longer. Bus: 16, 16A, 19, 19A, 22, 22A, 55, or 83.

FOR THE LITERARY ENTHUSIAST

Glasnevin Cemetery ⚝ *Finds* This is the Irish National Cemetery, founded in 1832 and covering over 124 acres. Literary figures buried here include the poet Gerard Manley Hopkins, whose grave can be found in the Jesuit plot; although born in England, Hopkins spent the last years of his life in Dublin, and died here at the age of 44. James Joyce's parents' grave is here, across the lane from the boulder of Wicklow granite marking Parnell's gravesite. Other writers in the cemetery include Christy Brown and Brendan Behan; also buried here are political heroes Michael Collins, Daniel O'Connell, and Roger Casement. A heritage map, on sale in many local bookshops, serves as a guide to who's buried where. Free guided tours are also offered by members of the National Graves Association on Wednesdays and Fridays, June to August, at 2:30pm. For more information, call ℂ **01/830-1133**.

Finglas Rd. (north of the city center), Dublin 11. ℂ **01/830-1133**. Fax 01/830-5194. www.glasnevin-cemetery.ie. Free admission. Daily 8am–4pm. Bus: 19, 19A, 40, 40A, 40B, or 40C.

Impressions

An author's first duty is to let down his country.

—Brendan Behan (1923–64)

James Joyce Centre ✦ Located near Parnell Square and the Dublin Writers Museum, this newly restored Georgian town house, built in 1784, gives literary enthusiasts one more reason to visit Dublin's north side. The house itself was once the home of Denis J. Maginni, a dancing instructor who appears briefly in *Ulysses*. The Ulysses Portrait Gallery on the second floor has a fascinating collection of photographs and drawings of characters from Ulysses who had a life outside the novel. The Paul Leon Exhibition Room holds the writing table used by Joyce in Paris when he was working on Finnegan's Wake as well as Joyce's beloved piano; the room is named after Paul Leon, an academic who aided Joyce in literary, business, and domestic affairs and salvaged many of Joyce's papers after Joyce and his family left Paris. Talks and audiovisual presentations are offered daily, as are pastries and teas in the coffee shop. Guided walking tours are offered through the neighboring streets of "Joyce Country" in Dublin's northern inner city.

35 N. Great George's St., Dublin 1. ✆ 01/878-8547. Fax 01/878-8488. www.jamesjoyce.ie. Admission 4€ ($3.60) adults, 2.60€ ($2.35) seniors and students, 1€ (90¢) children, 7.60€ ($6.90) families; walking tours 8.50€ ($8) adults, 6.50€ ($5.90) seniors and students, 15€ ($14) families; tour of house with Ken Monaghan 5.70€ ($5.20) adults, 5.10€ ($4.60) seniors and students. AE, MC, V. Mon–Sat 9:30am–5pm; Sun and holidays 12:30–5pm. Closed Dec 24–26. DART to Connolly Station. Bus: 1, 40A, 40B, 40C.

The Joyce Tower Museum ✦ No James Joyce fan should miss this small museum housed in the Sandycove Martello Tower where Joyce lived for a while in 1904—it's described in the first chapter of Ulysses. The museum contains exhibits on Joyce and Dublin at the time Ulysses was written. If you pick up a copy of the "Ulysses Map of Dublin," you can make this the starting point of a Joyce tour of the city. Robert Nicholson, the museum's curator, is a great source of information on all topics relating to Joyce and has published the best guide to Ulysses sites in Dublin, titled simply *The Ulysses Guide* (for sale at the museum and in bookshops throughout Dublin).

Sandycove, Co. Dublin. ✆ 01/280-9265. joycetower@dublintourism.ie. Admission 5.10€ ($4.60) adults, 3.80€ ($3.45) seniors and students, 2.60€ ($2.40) children, 14€ ($13) families. AE, MC, V. Apr–Oct Mon–Sat 10am–1pm and 2–5pm; Sun 2–6pm; open Nov–Mar by appointment only (call ✆ 01/872-2077). DART to Sandycove Station. Bus: 8.

Newman House ✦ Situated in the heart of Dublin on the south side of St. Stephen's Green, this is the historic seat of the Catholic University of Ireland. Named for Cardinal John Henry Newman, the 19th-century writer and theologian and first rector of the university, it comprises two of the finest Georgian town houses in Dublin, dating from 1740 and decorated with outstanding Palladian and Rococo plasterwork, marble tiled floors, and wainscot paneling. No. 85 has been magnificently restored to its original splendor. As a literary site, it is worthwhile noting that Gerard Manley Hopkins spent the last years of his life teaching here, between 1884 and 1889, and that James Joyce studied here between 1899 and 1902.

85–86 St. Stephen's Green, Dublin 2. ✆ 01/706-7422 or 01/475-7255. Fax 01/706-7211. Guided tours 4€ ($3.60) adults, 3€ ($2.70) seniors, students, and children under 12. June–Aug Tues–Fri noon–4pm; Sat 2–5pm; Sun 11am–2pm. Otherwise by appointment only. Bus: 10, 11, 46A.

Shaw Birthplace This simple two-story terraced house, built in 1838, was the birthplace in 1856 of George Bernard Shaw, one of Dublin's three literary Nobel Prize winners. Recently restored, it has been furnished in Victorian style to re-create the atmosphere of Shaw's early days. Rooms open for viewing are the

Walk the Streets, Find the Writers

Ireland's greatest gift to the rest of the world may well be its writers, whose keen, sharp-witted insights have prodded the hearts and minds of so many around the world. From this sparsely populated little island have sprung some of the English language's greatest wordsmiths, and of these writers, a good many were born, lived, or died in Dublin. Here are a few places where you can connect with their lives and works.

- The house at 7 Hoey's Court where **Jonathan Swift** was born is now gone. It stood very near St. Patrick's Cathedral, where Swift served as dean for 32 years, and where he was laid to rest. Listen for his footsteps, too, at Trinity College, where he was a student.
- **Thomas Moore** also studied at Trinity, and you'll find his birthplace at 12 Aungier St.
- **Oscar Wilde** began his life in Dublin in the year 1854 at 21 Westland Row.
- **W. B. Yeats** was born at 5 Sandymount Ave., and 42 Fitzwilliam Sq. was his residence from 1928 to 1932.
- **James Joyce** was born in Rathgar at 42 Brighton Sq. W. The martello tower he occupied with Oliver St. John Gogarty in 1904 is now a Joyce museum. Devoted Joyce fans can trace the Dublin meanderings of his Leopold Bloom as unerringly as if *Ulysses* was a guidebook rather than fiction. Following in Bloom's footsteps has become so popular that the tourist board offers a *Ulysses* Map of Dublin to guide you through the locales of the book's 18 episodes. If you should be in Dublin on June 16, there are scores of events commemorating "Bloomsday." The James Joyce Cultural Centre is a great resource, and their tour of North Dublin is a good way to begin your exploration of Joyce's Dublin. Other sites of interest to Joyceans are Newman House, where Joyce attended university from 1899 to 902;

kitchen, maid's room, nursery, drawing room, and a couple of bedrooms, including young Bernard's.

33 Synge St. (off S. Circular Rd.), Dublin 2. ☏ 01/475-0854. Fax 01/872-2231. shawhouse@dublintourism.ie. Admission 5.10€ ($4.60) adults, 3.80€ ($3.45) students, seniors and children 12–18 years, 2.60€ ($2.35) children under 12, 14€ ($13) family. Combination ticket with the Dublin Writers Museum available at reduced rate. Apr–Oct Mon–Sat 10am–1pm and 2–5pm; Sun 11am–1pm and 2–5pm. Bus: 16, 19, 122. 15-min. walk from Stephen's Green.

ART GALLERIES

Hugh Lane Municipal Gallery of Modern Art   Housed in a finely restored 18th-century building known as Charlemont House, this gallery is situated next to the Dublin Writers Museum. It is named after Hugh Lane, an Irish art connoisseur who was killed during the sinking of the Lusitania in 1915 and who willed his collection (including works by Courbet, Manet, Monet, and Corot) to be shared between the government of Ireland and the National Gallery of London. With the Lane collection as its nucleus, this gallery also contains paintings from the Impressionist and post-Impressionist periods, sculptures by

Glasnevin Cemetery, where Joyce's parents are buried and the site of Paddy Dignam's funeral in *Ulysses;* and the National Library of Ireland, where the ninth chapter of *Ulysses* takes place. For an entertaining and informative guide to Joyce's Dublin, buy a copy of *The Ulysses Guide,* available in most book-stores; the author, Robert Nicholson, is the curator of the James Joyce Museum in Sandycove, where you can address your queries to a true Joyce expert.

- **Sean O'Casey** was born in the Dublin slums in 1884. He became the Abbey Theatre's leading dramatist until he broke with them in 1928. His experiences are detailed in his four-volume autobiography, which is a vivid and realistic chronicle of Dublin and Ireland in the first part of the century.
- **Brendan Behan** captured the heart and soul of modern Dublin in words that his country folk sometimes agonized over but never denied. He was born in Dublin in 1921 and remained its irreverent, wayward son until the early end of his life in 1964, when the president of Ireland led a huge crowd to Glasnevin Cemetery for the interment.
- Novelist **Elizabeth Bowen** was born at 15 Herbert Place, off Lower Baggot Street, in 1899.
- **Cornelius Ryan,** author of outstanding World War II novels, first saw the light of day in 1920 at 33 Heytesburn St., off the South Circular Road.
- **Bram Stoker,** whose book *Dracula* seems to be (ahem) immortal and undying, was born at 15 Marino Crescent, Clontarf, in 1847.

Want to wet your whistle and get a little culture in the bargain? Try Dublin's Literary Pub Crawl, later in this chapter, under "Organized Tours."

Rodin, stained glass, and works by modern Irish artists. In 1998, the museum received its most important donation since its establishment in 1908: the studio of Irish painter Francis Bacon, which opened early in 2001 in a new space designed by British architect David Chipperfield. An archive contains numerous unfinished works by the artist, books, and a collection of photographs, some of which are on display. There is a separate admission charge for the studio. A bookshop is open during museum hours.

Parnell Sq. N., Dublin 1. ✆ **01/874-1903.** Fax 01/872-2182. www.hughlane.ie. Museum free admission. Francis Bacon studio admission 7.60€ ($6.90) adults, children under 18 free. Tues–Thurs 9:30am–6pm; Fri–Sat 9:30am–5pm; Sun 11am–5pm. DART to Connolly or Tara stations. Bus: 10, 11, 11A, 11B, 13, 16, 16A, 19, 19A, 22, 22A, and 36.

The Irish Museum of Modern Art *(Kids)*   One of the city's newest museums is located in its oldest classical building, the stately Kilmainham Hospital. Modeled on Les Invalides in Paris, the old hospital is a quadrangle with chapel and majestic dining hall in the north wing and a row of stables to the south, now converted to artists' studios. Situated in an expansive parkland setting, the

building has an elaborate formal garden on its north side and a long, tree-lined ceremonial entrance to the west, extending all the way to the Kilmainham Gaol. The museum occupies the east, west, and south wings of the hospital; the high entrance hall on the south side is adjoined by a fine bookshop and tea house, serving light meals under 6.50€ ($5.90). The galleries contain the work of Irish and international artists from the small but impressive permanent collection, with numerous temporary exhibitions at any given time. There's even a drawing room, where kids and parents can record their impressions of the museum with the crayons provided.

Royal Hospital, Military Rd., Kilmainham, Dublin 8. ℂ **01/612-9900.** Fax 01/612-9999. info@modernart.ie. Free admission. Tues–Sat 10am–5:30pm; Sun noon–5:30pm. DART: Feeder bus from Connolly and Tara St. stations to Heuston. Bus: 68A, 69, 78A, 79, 90, and 123. Unlimited parking.

National Photographic Archive   The newest member of the Temple Bar cultural complex, the National Photographic Archive houses the extensive photo collection of the National Library and serves as its photo exhibition space. This is a striking contemporary building sure to offer exciting programs in the years ahead.

Meeting House Sq., Temple Bar, Dublin 2. ℂ **01/603-0200.** Fax 01/677-7451. www.nli.ie. Free admission. Mon–Fri 10am–5pm; Sat 10am–2pm. DART: Tara St. Station. Bus: 21A, 46A, 46B, 51B, 51C, 68, 69, or 86.

BREWERIES & DISTILLERIES

Guinness Storehouse *Overrated*   Founded in 1759, this is one of the world's largest breweries, and it's fascinating to walk through narrow back alleys between the dark forms of giant warehouses. Part industrial icon and part shopping mall, the new visitor center (opened in 2001) is in our opinion somewhat overpriced and overrated. Exhibits presenting everything you ever wanted to know about Guinness are organized around a high atrium in the shape of a pint glass: History, the brewing process, and even the companies' advertising campaigns are on display. On the top floor, you can sample a pint in the Gravity Bar, a glass-walled room on the top floor that does offer a truly panoramic view of Dublin. The complex also includes a conference center, a restaurant, and an additional bar/lounge.

James's Gate, Dublin 8. ℂ **01/408-4800.** www.guinnessstorehouse.com. Admission 12€ ($11) adults, 7.60€ ($6.90) students over 18, 5.10€ ($4.60) seniors and students under 18, 25€ ($23) families. Apr–Sept daily 9:30am–6pm; Oct–Mar Mon–Sat 9:30am–5pm. Bus: 51B and 78A from Aston Quay, or 123 from O'Connell St.

The Old Jameson Distillery   The unique blend of barley, yeast, and water that is Irish whiskey was first (back in the 6th century) called *uisce beatha* (ish-ke ba-ha), which translates as "the water of life." When King Henry II's soldiers spread its fame to England, the name took on an anglicized sound, *fuisce*, before eventually evolving into "whiskey." From the beginning, nothing about this blend was usual, and today it's still unique, even in the spelling of its name—it's the only European whisk(e)y that's spelled with an "e."

The Old Jameson Distillery was established by the Irish Distillers Group (which includes all seven of the great whiskey houses in Ireland) to present an all-encompassing picture of the history of Irish whiskey. Facilities include an audio-visual presentation, a museum, a tasting bar, a restaurant, and a whiskey shop. In the summer, there is an evening whiskey tour, dinner, and traditional music—the Shindig. For times and prices, call the distillery.

Bow St., Smithfield, Dublin 7. ℂ **01/872-5566.** Admission 6.30€ ($5.70), 5.10€ ($4.60) seniors and students, 2.50€ ($2.30) children, 14.60€ ($13) family (2 adults, 2 children). Tours daily 9:30am and 6pm. Last tour at 5pm. Bus: 67, 67A, 68, 69, 79, or 90.

FOR THE GENEALOGY-MINDED

Heraldic Museum   This unique museum focuses on the uses of heraldry. Exhibits include shields, banners, coins, paintings, porcelain, and stamps depicting coats of arms. The office of Ireland's chief herald also offers a consultation service on the premises, so this is also an ideal place to start researching your own roots.

2 Kildare St., Dublin 2. ✆ **01/603-0200**. Fax 01/662-1062. www.nli.ie. Free admission. Mon–Wed 10am–8:30pm; Thurs–Fri 10am–4:30pm; Sat 10am–12:30pm. DART to Pearse Station. Bus: 5, 7A, 8, 9, 10, 14, 15.

FOR THE ARCHITECTURAL ENTHUSIAST

Irish Architectural Archive   While neither a museum nor an art gallery, this archive will certainly intrigue anyone interested in Ireland's past, and is the perfect place to begin an architectural tour of the city. Since its establishment in 1976, the archive has become the central source of information on architecturally and historically significant Irish buildings from 1600 to the present. In addition to more than 200,000 photographs and 50,000 architectural drawings, the reference library holds a vast number of publications such as pamphlets, press cuttings, historical manuscripts, and engravings. The archive may be moving across the square to new lodgings in 2002—if you don't find it at this address try contacting the **Royal Institute of the Architects of Ireland** (✆ **01/676-1703**), located at 8 Merrion Square.

73 Merrion Sq. ✆ **01/676-3430**. Fax 01/661-6309. iaa1@iaa.iol.ie. Free admission. Tues–Fri 10am–1pm and 2:30–5pm. Closed Aug.

A SIGHT & SOUND SHOW

Dublin Experience   An ideal orientation for first-time visitors to the Irish capital, this 45-minute multimedia sight-and-sound show traces the history of Dublin from the earliest times to the present. It's in the Arts Building, facing Nassau Street.

Trinity College, Davis Theatre, Dublin 2 (on Nassau St.). ✆ **01/608-1688**. Admission 4.15€ ($3.75) adults, 3.50€ ($3.15) seniors and students. Combination tickets with the Book of Kells/Old Library also available. May–Sept daily 10am–5pm; closed Oct–Apr. DART: Pearse St. Station. Bus: Any city-center bus.

LIBRARIES

Chester Beatty Library and Gallery of Oriental Art ✸   Sir Alfred Chester Beatty, an American mining millionaire who made his home in Dublin, bequeathed to the city his extensive collection of manuscripts, prints, icons, and miniature paintings. Highlights here are biblical papyri, Persian and Turkish paintings, Qur'ans, Japanese woodblock prints, and Chinese jade books. Also on site are a restaurant, gift shop, and roof garden. The library is wheelchair accessible.

Dublin Castle, Palace St. (off Dame St.), Dublin 2. ✆ **01/407-0750**. Fax 01/407-0760. www.cbl.ie. Free admission. May–Sept Mon–Fri 10am–5pm, Sat 11am–5pm, Sun 1–5pm; Oct–Apr Tues–Fri 10am–5pm, Sat 11am–5pm, Sun 1–5pm. Free guided tours Wed at 1pm and Sun at 3pm and 4pm. DART to Sandymount Station. Bus: 50, 50A, 54 (Burgh Quay), 56A, 77, 77A, 77B (Aston Quay).

Marsh's Library ✸   This magnificent example of a 17th-century scholar's library is Ireland's oldest public library, founded in 1701 by Narcissus Marsh, Archbishop of Dublin. It is a repository of more than 25,000 scholarly volumes, chiefly on theology, medicine, ancient history, maps, Hebrew, Syriac, Greek, Latin, and French literature. In his capacity as Dean of St. Patrick's Cathedral, Jonathan Swift was a governor of Marsh's Library. The interior of the library has remained very much the same for 3 centuries. Special exhibits are designed and mounted annually.

St. Patrick's Close, Upper Kevin St., Dublin 8. ©/fax **01/454-3511**. www.marshlibrary.ie. Admission 2.60€ ($2.40) adults, 1.30€ ($1.20) seniors and students, free for children. Mon and Wed–Fri 10am–12:45pm and 2–5pm; Sat 10:30am–12:45pm. Bus: 50, 50A, 50C, 77, 77A.

National Library of Ireland   For visitors who come to Ireland to research their roots, this library is often the first point of reference, with thousands of volumes and records yielding ancestral information. Opened at this location in 1890, this is the principal library of Irish studies and is particularly noted for its collection of first editions and the works of Irish authors. It also has an unrivaled collection of maps of Ireland. Joyce enthusiasts will be interested in visiting, as the library figures prominently in *Portrait of the Artist* and is the setting for the ninth chapter of *Ulysses*. The office of Quaker librarian William Lyster, where Stephen Dedalus expounds his Hamlet theory, was probably the first floor room to the left of the front desk, where you'll go to get your reader's card; anyone can request a card, which is necessary if you want to look at any of the library's books.

Kildare St., Dublin 2. © **01/603-0200**. Fax 01/676-6690. www.nli.ie. Free admission. Mon–Wed 10am–9pm; Thurs–Fri 10am–5pm; Sat 10am–1pm. Closed Dec 23–Jan 2. DART: Pearse St. Station. Bus: 10, 11A, 11B, 13, or 20B.

ESPECIALLY FOR KIDS

The Ark: A Cultural Centre for Children ⚹ *Kids*   The Ark is a unique new cultural center in the Temple Bar area where children are taught with respect and sensitivity by an experienced staff. The handsomely renovated building has three modern main floors housing a wonderful semicircular theater that can open out onto Meeting House Square, a gallery, and a workshop for hands-on learning sessions. This exciting center offers organized minicourse experiences (1–2 hr. long) designed around particular themes in music, visual arts, and theater. In its debut year, The Ark offered numerous activities in photography, architecture, animal making, music, and instrument making. The workshops, performances, tours, and artist/musician-in-residence program are geared toward specific age groups and the associated activities are kept small, so check the current themes and schedule of events and book accordingly. The Ark enjoys huge popularity with children, families, and teachers.

Eustace St., Temple Bar, Dublin 2. © **01/670-7788**. Fax 01/670-7758. www.ark.ie. Prices 1€–6.50€ (90¢–$5.90) depending on activity or event. Daily 10am–4pm. Closed mid-Aug to mid-Sept. DART to Tara St. Station. Bus: 51, 51B, 37, 39.

Dublin's Viking Adventure *Kids*   This popular attraction brings you on an imaginative journey through time to an era when Dublin was a bustling Norse town. A lively, authentic atmosphere is created by the "Vikings" populating the village in period houses and detailed costumes. The Viking townspeople engage in the activities of daily life in the Wood Quay area along the Liffey, while you watch and interact with them.

Temple Bar, Dublin 8 (entrance from Essex St.). © **01/679-6040**. Fax 01/679-6033. Admission 7€ ($6.35) adults, 5.50€ ($5) seniors, 3.80€ ($3.45) children, 19€ ($17) families. AE, MC, V. Mar–Oct Tues–Sat 10am–1pm and 2–4:30pm. DART to Tara St. Station and 90 bus. Bus: 78A, 79, 90.

Dublin Zoo ⚹ *Kids*   Established in 1830, this is the third-oldest zoo in the world (after London and Paris), nestled in the city's largest playground, Phoenix Park, which lies about 2 miles (3km) west of the city center. This 30-acre zoo provides a naturally landscaped habitat for more than 235 species of wild animals and tropical birds. Highlights for youngsters include the Children's Pets' Corner and a train ride around the zoo. New additions to the zoo, part of a $24-million redevelopment, includes an Arctic exhibition called "Fringes of the Arctic," the "World of Primates," the "World of Cats," the "City Farm and Pets Corner," and an "African Plains" area opened in May of 2001. Facilities include a restaurant, coffee shop, and gift shop.

The Phoenix Park, Dublin 8. ② **01/677-1425.** www.dublinzoo.ie. Admission 9.50€ ($8.65) adults, 7.25€ ($6.55) students with student ID, 6€ ($5.45) seniors and children 3–16, free for children under 3, 28€–35€ ($25–$32) families (depending on number of children). AE, DC, MC, V. Summer Mon–Sat 9:30am–6pm, Sun 10:30am–6pm; winter Mon–Sat 9:30am–4pm, Sun 10:30am–5pm. Bus: 10, 25, 26.

Lambert Puppet Theatre and Museum Founded by master ventriloquist Eugene Lambert, this 300-seat suburban theater presents puppet shows designed to delight audiences both young and young at heart. During intermission, you can browse in the puppet museum or look for a take-home puppet in the shop.

5 Clifden Lane, Monkstown, Co. Dublin. ② **01/280-0974.** No box office; book by phone daily. Admission 6.50€ ($5.90). Shows Sat–Sun 3:30pm (daily May–June). DART to Salthill Station. Bus: 7, 7A, or 8.

PARKS & GARDENS

Dublin's city center is not much known for its greenery, but there are oases at hand if you begin to crave grass and trees. Here are a few of the best spots. (For more outdoor listings, see "Outdoor Activities," later in this chapter.)

National Botanic Gardens ✪ The gardens were founded in 1795 by the Royal Dublin Society to "increase and foster taste for practical and scientific botany." They're spread over 50 acres of an estate that was once the home of the poet Thomas Tickell. In addition to exotic trees, shrubbery, and tropical plants, you'll find an economic garden (for plants of economic value, such as flax, cotton, hemp), a vegetable garden, and a lawn garden. The vast tropical greenhouses are truly magical, as is the small and fascinating orchid room. Please note that some greenhouses close for lunch between 12:45 and 2pm each day, and closing times for the greenhouses are often earlier than those for the gardens.

Botanic Rd., Glasnevin. ② **01/837-4388.** Free admission. Gardens summer Mon–Sat 9am–6pm, Sun 11am–6pm; winter Mon–Sat 10am–4:30pm, Sun 11am–4:30pm. Bus: 13, 19, 34, or 34A.

Phoenix Park (*Kids*) This is Dublin's playground—the largest enclosed urban park in Europe, with a circumference of 7 miles (11km) and a total area of 1,760 acres. It is traversed by a network of roads and quiet pedestrian walkways, and informally landscaped with ornamental gardens, nature trails, and broad expanses of grassland separated by avenues of oak, beech, pine, chestnut, and lime trees. The homes of the Irish president and the U.S. ambassador are on its grounds. Livestock graze peacefully on pasturelands, deer roam the forested areas, and horses romp on polo fields. The new Phoenix Park Visitor Centre, adjacent to Ashtown Castle, offers exhibitions and an audio-visual presentation on the history of the Phoenix Park (the park opened in 1747), and houses its own fine restaurant (② **01/677-0090**), open daily 10am to 4:30pm. There's free parking adjacent to the center.

Parkgate St., Dublin 7 (2 miles/3km west of city center). ② **01/677-0095.** Free admission. Daily 24 hr. Visitor center admission 2.60€ ($2.40) adults, 2€ ($1.80) seniors, 1.30€ ($1.20) students and children, 6.40€ ($5.80) families. Mid- to end of Mar daily 9:30am–5pm; Apr–May daily 9:30am–5:30pm; June–Sept daily 10am–6pm; Oct daily 9:30am–5pm; Nov to mid-Mar Sat–Sun 9:30am–4:30pm. Bus: 10, 37, 39.

(*Finds* The Secret Garden

While touring St. Stephen's Green, be sure to visit the **Iveagh Gardens** ⭐,
a small garden hidden behind the National Concert Hall. Largely neglected by visitors, this is something of a hidden treasure within the city
center. The main entrance is from Clonmel Street, off Harcourt Street, less
than 5 minutes from St. Stephen's Green. The hours are the same as those
for the Green.

St. Anne's Park Rose Garden   This is one of the prettiest gardens in the city
with climbers, floribunda, hybrid tea, and old garden roses in profusion. In April
and May, the daffodils are in full bloom.

Mount Prospect Ave., Clontarf. Free admission. Daily dawn–dusk. Bus: 30 or 44A.

St. Stephen's Green   St. Stephen's Green has been preserved as an open space
for Dubliners since 1690. Over the years it has evolved into the beautifully
planted park that today finds city residents and visitors alike strolling along its
paths, enjoying a lunch break picnic-style, or simply soaking up its rustic charm
as the city's traffic swirls around the edges. Formal flowerbeds, the arched stone
bridge crossing one end of the artificial lake, shaded pathways, and statuary
placed in pockets of shrubbery make this a very special place.

Grafton St. Free admission. Mon–Sat 8am–dark; Sun 10am–dark.

War Memorial Gardens ⭐ *Finds*   This is one of the finest formal gardens in
Ireland. It's located along the banks of the Liffey across from Phoenix Park, a few
minutes from Kilmainham Gaol. The designer was renowned British architect
Sir Edwin Lutyens (1869–1944), who completed a number of commissions for
houses and gardens in Ireland. The garden is fairly well maintained, and continues to present a moving testimony to Ireland's war dead.

Islandbridge. ℂ 01/677-0236. Free admission. Mon–Fri 8am–dusk; Sat 10am–dusk.

6 Special Events

There are certain days when it seems that all of Dublin enters into the spirit of
the occasion and does it proud, and if you happen to arrive in town during one
of these special times, you're in for a real treat. Check with the Irish Tourist
Board about specific dates for the year of your visit; accommodations should be
booked as far in advance as possible and will probably cost you a little more.

Bloomsday ⭐   James Joyce's novel *Ulysses* takes place during the course of a single day: June 16, 1904, a Thursday. It has long been a tradition for Joyce enthusiasts to trace on this day the meanderings through the city of the novel's principal
characters, chief among them Mr. Leopold Bloom. In recent years, Bloomsday has
become more of a festival than a ritual of scholarship, with the whole of Dublin
joining in to celebrate their home city as well as its greatest writer. The festivities
begin a good week and a half in advance, around June 7, with readings, musical
and dramatic performances, and lectures. As the big day approaches, there are
elaborate reenactments of passages from *Ulysses*. On Bloomsday itself, there are
numerous walks on both sides of the Liffey, continuous readings, and meals in
each of the pubs Bloom stopped at during the course of his day.

For up-to-date information on events contact the **James Joyce Cultural Centre**, 35 N. Great George's St.,
Dublin 1. ℂ 01/878-8547. Fax 01/878-8488. www.jamesjoyce.ie.

Eircom Dublin Theatre Festival 🎭🎭   The Dublin Theatre Festival usually takes place during the first 2 weeks of October. It's a unique theatrical celebration that incorporates all of Dublin's theaters and spreads onto the streets, university campuses, and community halls. Innovative Irish drama is offered, and major overseas theater and dance companies perform. Great Irish playwrights such as Behan, Leonard, Friel, and Murphy have been represented, and the festival has been the originator of classics such as *Da, Philadelphia Here I Come!, Translations,* and *The Morning After Optimism,* which have gone on to grace the stages of the world. The festival specializes in presenting new Irish work. Other highlights are first-class international theater and dance presentations. At Festival Club, theatergoers mingle with actors, directors, and members of the international press, as well as attend workshops, exhibitions, and an international theater conference. Tickets usually run 15€ to 25€ ($14 to $23).

44 E. Essex St., Dublin 2. ℭ **01/677-8439.** Fax 01/679-7709. www.eircomtheatrefestival.com. Admission varies with individual performances.

Kerrygold Horse Show   The undisputed highlight of Ireland's social calendar each year is the Kerrygold Dublin Horse Show, which usually takes place in August at the showgrounds of the Royal Dublin Society (the date is sometimes moved to avoid conflicts with other European horse shows). For one glorious week it draws a sophisticated international crowd, and the city dons its best duds in welcome. There's much pomp and splendor, and even more fun and frolic; many private and public parties are scheduled. As for the show itself, it features virtually nonstop jumping competitions in what are acknowledged to be some of the finest jumping enclosures in the world. The Kerrygold Nations Cup for the Aga Khan Trophy competition raises the excitement level on Friday, and the whole thing winds up with the Kerrygold International Grand Prix of Ireland on Saturday. Side events often include a fashion competition for the best-dressed woman on Ladies Day, a gorgeous floral display, and an exhibition of the prize-winning exhibits from the Royal Dublin Society's annual crafts competition. This is one of the most heavily booked weeks for Dublin accommodations, so reserve as far in advance as possible.

Royal Dublin Society, Merrion Rd., Ballsbridge, Dublin 4. ℭ **01/668-0866.** www.rds.ie. Admission 8€–30€ ($7–$27) per day.

7 City Strolls

The best way to experience most cities is from ground level, perched on your own two feet, seeing the place the way its citizens do—and Dublin is no exception. Here are a couple of walking tours to start you off on your explorations.

WALKING TOUR 1   OLD DUBLIN

Start: Capel Street Bridge.
Finish: River Liffey Quays.
Time: About 3 to 4 hours.
Best Times: Weekdays.
Worst Times: Sundays during church services or bank holidays.

Begin south of the Liffey at the Capel Street Bridge and walk east toward Dame Street. On your right is the Palace Street gate of:

❶ Dublin Castle

Representing some of the oldest surviving architecture in the city, the cathedral was the center of British power in Ireland for more than 7 centuries, until the new Irish government took it over in 1922. Film buffs might recognize the castle's courtyard as a setting in the Neil Jordan film *Michael Collins*.

Continuing east, turn right from Dame Street onto South Great George's Street, a broad and colorful shopping street. Look for the Victorian shopping arcade on the left, which has all the vigor and color of an old-time bazaar. At the end of the arcade is South William Street, where you will find the:

❷ Dublin Civic Museum

A fine 18th-century Georgian structure next to the Powerscourt Townhouse Centre, this museum focuses on the history of the Dublin area from medieval to modern times.

Continue on Aungier Street (an extension of S. Great George's St.) to Whitefriar Street, location of the:

❸ Whitefriar Street Carmelite Church

Pope Gregory XVI gave the ultimate Valentine's Day gift to this church in 1836—St. Valentine himself is enshrined here, making it a favorite place of pilgrimage, especially on February 14.

Also, note that poet and songwriter Tom Moore was born at no. 12 on this street.

Aungier Street now becomes Wexford Street. Turn right onto Lower Kevin Street and cross Heytesbury Street onto Upper Kevin Street, where you will pass the Garda barracks before coming to:

❹ Marsh's Library

Ireland's oldest public library, it is a repository of more than 25,000 scholarly volumes, and sports some exceptional 17th-century architecture.

Walk west to the intersection at The Coombe, which marks the beginning of the Liberties. Turn right into Patrick Street to reach:

❺ St. Patrick's Cathedral

The present cathedral dates from 1190, but because of a fire and 14th-century rebuilding, not much of the original foundation remains. Nevertheless, a church has stood on this spot since A.D. 450, making it the oldest Christian site in Dublin.

Continue uphill to Christchurch Place and:

❻ Christ Church Cathedral

One of Dublin's finest historic buildings, this structure's highlights include magnificent stonework and graceful pointed arches, with delicately chiseled supporting columns. The new Treasury in the crypt is now open to the public, and you can hear new bells pealing in the belfry.

Walk west from Christchurch Place to High Street, where you can see a restoration of a portion of the ancient city wall and the only surviving city gate (down and toward the river).

A short walk south on High Street brings you to:

❼ Tailor's Hall

The structure dates from 1796 and is Dublin's only surviving guild hall.

Retrace your steps to Cornmarket Square and continue on Thomas Street, which holds:

❽ St. Catherine's Church

The church will be on your left and is open to the public. This is where the patriot Robert Emmet was hanged in 1803.

The continuation of Thomas Street is James's Street, home of the:

❾ Guinness Brewery

One of the world's largest breweries, it produces the distinctive dark beer called stout, famous for its thick, creamy head. Although tours of the brewery itself are no longer allowed, visitors are welcome to explore the adjacent Guinness Hopstore, a converted 19th-century four-story building.

Walking Tour: Old Dublin

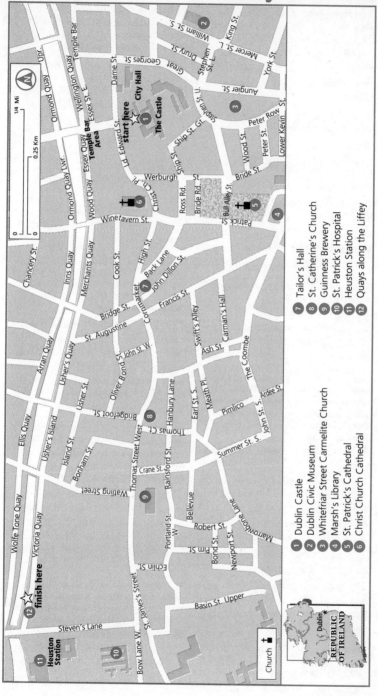

1. Dublin Castle
2. Dublin Civic Museum
3. Whitefriar Street Carmelite Church
4. Marsh's Library
5. St. Patrick's Cathedral
6. Christ Church Cathedral
7. Tailor's Hall
8. St. Catherine's Church
9. Guinness Brewery
10. St. Patrick's Hospital
11. Heuston Station
12. Quays along the Liffey

REPUBLIC OF IRELAND

Dublin

Church

James's Street forks to the right via Bow Lane to:

⑩ St. Patrick's Hospital

Founded in 1764, the hospital was funded by a bequest from Jonathan Swift and is still in use as a psychiatric center.

A sharp right turn brings you onto Steeven's Lane, heading back toward the river, where, en route to the river, you'll pass the striking Heuston Station rail depot. Keep walking until you reach the:

⑪ Quays along the Liffey

Take in the scenery along the river, then turn right to walk back to the city center along the quays; you'll have a good view of the Four Courts on the north side of the Liffey.

WALKING TOUR 2   GEORGIAN DUBLIN

Start: College Green.

Finish: Fitzwilliam Square.

Time: 2 hours.

Best Times: Daylight hours.

Worst Times: Sunday, when shops are closed.

Begin your walking tour at the foot of Westmoreland Street at:

❶ College Green

College Green is one of the city's prime thoroughfares. On your right is the Bank of Ireland, and just opposite is Trinity College.

From College Green, walk south onto Grafton Street, now a pedestrian mall lined with fashionable shops. Look for Johnson's Court, a narrow lane on your right, which leads to:

❷ Powerscourt House Shopping Centre

Housed in a restored 1774 town house, this four-story complex consists of a central skylit courtyard and more than 60 boutiques, craft shops, art galleries, snack bars, wine bars, and restaurants.

Returning to Grafton Street, walk south to:

❸ St. Stephen's Green

The north side of the Green was once known as "Beaux Walk" and now houses some of Dublin's most prestigious clubs.

Follow St. Stephen's Green North to Dawson Street, site of the:

❹ Mansion House

This is the residence of the Lord Mayor of Dublin, which is not open to the public.

Return to St. Stephen's Green North and continue to Kildare Street. On the right is:

❺ Leinster House

The home of Ireland's Parliament is flanked by the National Museum, The National Gallery, and the National Library. The building is said to have been the model for Irish-born architect James Hoban's design for the White House in Washington, D.C.

From the north end of Kildare Street, turn right onto Nassau Street, which becomes Leinster Street and then Clare Street before reaching:

❻ Merrion Square

A fashionable Georgian park surrounded by historic brick-front town houses, it's adjacent to the National Gallery of Ireland, the Natural History Museum, and the Irish Architectural Archive.

Walk south along Merrion Square West, which becomes Merrion Street, turn left into Lower Baggot Street, and continue to Fitzwilliam Street. Turn right to reach:

❼ Fitzwilliam Square

This another beautiful Dublin park surrounded by elegant Georgian mansions.

Talbot Memorial Bridge

Pearse St. Station

Fenian St.

Merrion Square

North

South

Westland Row

Fitz William Square

Pembroke Street

finish here

Fitzwilliam St.

Lad Lane

Witton Terrace

Lower Baggot Street

City Quay

Hanover Street

Tara St. Station

Townsend Street

Butt Bridge

Pearse Street

Trinity College

Leinster St.

Merrion Street

Merrion Row

Lower Leeson Street

East

Hatch Street

College St.

Westmoreland

start here

Nassau Street

Kildare St.

Molesworth St.

Dawson Street

Grafton Street

Suffolk St.

Duke St.

Anne St.

King St.

York Street

West

North

St. Stephen's Green

South

Aston Quay

Halfpenny Bridge

Wellington Quay

Temple Bar Area

Dame Street

Exchequer St.

William Street

Great Georges St.

Angier Street

Harcourt Street

Cuffe St.

Camden St.

Ormand Quay

Grattan Bridge

River Liffey

Richmond Bridge

Ormand Quay

Wood Quay

The Castle

Castle St.

Golden Lane

Bride Street

Wood

Lower

Kevin St.

Camden Row

Camden St.

St. Patrick's Park

Kevin St.

Long Lane

New St.

Patrick Street

1/4 Mi

0.25 Km

0

N

Dublin

REPUBLIC OF IRELAND

① College Green
② Powerscourt House Shopping Centre
③ St. Stephen's Green
④ Mansion House
⑤ Leinster House
⑥ Merrion Square
⑦ Fitzwilliam Square

8 Organized Tours

BUS TOURS

Dublin Bus This company operates several different tours. Seats can be booked in advance at the Dublin Bus office or at the Dublin Bus ticket desk at the Dublin Tourism office on Suffolk Street. All tours depart from the Dublin Bus office, but free pickup from many Dublin hotels is available for morning tours. For the standard see-it-all-in-under-3-hours tour, climb aboard the **Dublin Bus** open-deck sightseeing coach. The cost is 13€ ($12) adults, 6.50€ ($5.90) children under 14. Tours operate year-round at 10:15am and 2:15pm. This tour takes in most of the important sights but doesn't stop at any.

For more flexible touring, there's the **Dublin City Tour,** a continuous guided bus service connecting 10 major points: museums, art galleries, churches and cathedrals, libraries, and historic sites. For 9€ ($8) adults, 4.50€ ($4.10) children under 14, you can ride the bus for a full day, getting off and on as often as you wish. This tour operates daily from 9:30am–4:30pm.

Gray Line Tours–Ireland and Guide Friday–Ireland These companies offer a range of full-day and half-day sightseeing tours of Dublin City year-round, and tours of the surrounding area April to October. The selection includes a 90-minute hop on, hop off tour of Dublin, which provides an overview of the city's historical sights and attractions; the starting point is O'Connell Street at the Gresham Hotel. There are numerous tours radiating out from Dublin, including a tour of the Boyne Valley and Newgrange; a tour to the northern suburbs, including Malahide Castle, Portmarnock and Howth; and a day trip to Glendalough. Guide Friday and Gray Line operate an information booth at the Dublin Tourism Centre on Suffolk Street, where you can buy tickets for any of the tours; tickets for the hop on, hop off tour can also be purchased on the bus. Most of the regional tours depart from outside the Suffolk Street Tourism Centre. Prices range from 10€ to 25€ ($9 to $23) per person.

13 South Leinster St., Dublin 2. ℂ 01/605-7705. Fax 01/661-8158. dublin@guidefriday.com.

WALKING TOURS

Small and compact, Dublin lends itself to walking tours. You can grab a map and set off on your own, of course, but if you want some guidance, some historical background, and some assurance that you haven't just walked past something important, you might want to consider one of the following tours.

SELF-GUIDED WALKING TOURS

You can set out on your own with a map, but the best way to avoid any hassles or missed sights is following one of the three signposted and themed **"heritage trails":** Old City Trail for historic sights; Georgian Heritage Trail for the landmark buildings, streets, squares, terraces, and parks; and Cultural Heritage Trail for a circuit of the top literary sites, museums, galleries, theaters, and churches. Each trail is mapped out in a handy booklet, available for 3.50€ ($3.15) from any Dublin Tourism office.

Or see "City Strolls," above, for our favorite walks around the city.

Dublin Footsteps This company offers a variety of themed 2-hour tours, including a Literary Walk and an 18th-century/Georgian Walk.

Tours begin at Bewley's Cafe, Grafton St., Dublin 2, in the James Joyce Room. ℂ 01/496-0641 or 01/269-7021. Tickets 6.50€ ($5.90) per person. Rates include coffee or tea at Bewley's. June–Sept Mon, Wed, and Fri–Sat starting at 10:30am; hours vary depending on tour, so call ahead for schedule.

Historical Walking Tours of Dublin This basic 2-hour sightseeing walk takes in Dublin's historic landmarks, from medieval walls and Viking remains around Wood Quay to Christ Church, Dublin Castle, City Hall, and Trinity College. Many guides are history graduates of Trinity College, and participants are encouraged to ask questions. Tours assemble at the front gate of Trinity College; no reservations are needed. Between May and October **Trinity College Walking Tours** depart every 40 minutes (approximately) from Trinity's front gate.

Leave from Trinity College. ✆ **01/878-0227.** Tickets 8€ ($7) adults, 6€ ($5.45) seniors and students. May–Sept daily 11am, noon, and 3pm; Oct–April Fri–Sun noon only.

Jameson Literary Pub Crawl Following the footsteps of Joyce, Behan, Beckett, Shaw, Kavanagh, and other Irish literary greats, this guided tour rambles from pub to pub, with appropriate commentary between stops. The tour assembles on Duke Street and can be booked in advance by calling ✆ **01/ 454-0228.**

8€ ($7) per person. Times vary throughout the year.

James Joyce's Dublin Walking Tours Joyce fans, take note: You can walk in the footsteps of the great novelist with Joyce's nephew, Ken Monaghan, the Centre's curator, as your guide. Monaghan conducts walking tours of approximately an hour's duration through the streets of Dublin's north side. His tours are conducted by advance arrangement only. The regular city tours are more often led by local university students, well versed in Joyce literature and lore, and leave daily from the center in the afternoon.

James Joyce Cultural Centre, 35 N. Great George's St., Dublin 1. ✆ 01/878-8547. www.jamesjoyce.ie. Tickets 8.50€ ($8) adults, 6.50€ ($5.90) students, 15€ ($14) families. Center summer Mon–Sat 9:30am–5pm; Sun 12:30–5pm. Advance booking is essential.

Traditional Music Pub Crawl To explore and sample the Dublin traditional music scene, meet at the Oliver St. John Gogarty pub in Temple Bar. The tour is led by two professional musicians, who sing your way along from one famous pub to another. A songbook is included in the tour price. The tour lasts 2½ hours. The "crawl" better describes the way back to your hotel.

Leaves from Oliver St. John Gogarty pub/restaurant, corner of Fleet St. and Anglesea St., Temple Bar. ✆ 01/478-0193. www.olivergogartys.com. Tickets 8€ ($7) adults, 6.50€ ($5.90) seniors and students. MC, V. Mid-May to Oct daily 7:30pm; Nov and Feb to mid-May Fri–Sat 7:30pm. (Tickets are on sale at 7pm or in advance from the Dublin Tourist Office.)

(*Kids* **Horse-Drawn Carriage Tours**

You can tour Dublin in style in a handsomely outfitted horse-drawn carriage with a driver who will comment on the sights as you travel the city's streets and squares. To arrange a ride, consult one of the drivers stationed with carriages at the Grafton Street side of St. Stephen's Green. Rides range from a short swing around the Green to an extensive half-hour Georgian tour or an hour-long Old City tour. It's slightly touristy, but kids (and romantics) love it.

Rides are available on a first-come, first-served basis from approximately April to October (weather permitting), and will run you between 15€ and 50€ ($14 and $45) for two to five passengers, depending on duration of ride.

Trinity College Walking Tours These tours of the college include admission to the Old Library to see the Book of Kells. Tours depart every 40 minutes (approximately) from Trinity's Front Gate. Reservations aren't necessary.

(ℂ) 01/608-2308. 7.60€ ($6.90) per person. May–Oct daily 10:15am–3:30pm.

CYCLING TOURS

Dublin Bike Tours For those determined to take to the streets on wheels, Dublin Bike Tours is a good option, offering 3-hour tours of the city along mostly quieter back streets at a relaxed pace. The 3 hours are broken by frequent stops, including a break for refreshments. Bike rentals and self-guided tours are also offered.

Harding Hotel, Fishamble St. (next to Christchurch), Dublin 2. *(ℂ)* 01/679-0899 or mobile phone 087/284-0799. www.dublinbiketours.com. 19€ ($17) per person. Tours depart Sat–Sun 10am and 2pm; other days are by request only.

9 Outdoor Pursuits

Going on the theory that you can't spend your whole trip marching through museums and lifting pints in a pub, here's a rundown of your options for getting a dose of outdoors in the big city.

BEACHES The cleanliness of beaches in Dublin Bay is somewhat suspect, and we'd recommend traveling north of Howth or south of Dun Laoghaire before jumping into the water. The rocky swimming hole known as the **"Forty Foot,"** located at the base of the Joyce's Tower museum, is used as a bathing spot by hardy Sandycove residents throughout the year. For Joyce fans, a swim here has the added thrill of re-enactment because the first chapter of *Ulysses* culminates with a dip at this spot. To get to Forty Foot take the DART to Sandycove Station and follow signs for Joyce's Tower. Further south along the DART line is **Killiney,** with a long stretch of sand and cobbles that's great for swimming and sunning. North of Dublin, there are beaches at **Portmarnock** and **Malahide,** both accessible by bus (take the 32A, 102 or 230). For more ideas try inquiring at the Dublin Tourism Office.

BIRD-WATCHING The estuaries, salt marshes, sand flats, and islands in the vicinity of Dublin Bay provide varied habitat for a diversity of bird species. **Rockabill Island,** off the coast at Skerries, is home to an important colony of roseate terns; there is no public access to the island, but the birds can be seen from shore. **Rogerstown and Malahide Estuaries,** on the north side of Dublin, are wintering grounds for large numbers of Brent geese, ducks, and waders. The **North Bull** is a spit of sand just north of Dublin Harbor, accessible from Clontarf Road (take the 130 bus from Lower Abbey St.), with salt marsh and extensive intertidal flats on the side facing the mainland. It's one of the most popular spots in Dublin for bird-watching—no surprise, given that 198 species in all have been recorded here. **Sandymount Strand** on Dublin's south side has a vast intertidal zone; around dusk in July and August you can often see large numbers of terns here, including visiting roseate terns from Rockabill Island. You can reach Sandymount Strand by DART: get off at Sandymount Station.

DIVING **Oceanic Adventures** in Dun Laoghaire (*(ℂ)* 01/280-1083) offers a five-star PADI diving school and offer weekly dives every Thursday and Saturday for certified divers; they also arrange dive vacations on the west coast. Also, contact the **National Diving School** at 8 St. James Terrace, Malahide, County Dublin (*(ℂ)* 01/845-2000).

FISHING   The greater Dublin area offers a range of opportunities for fresh-water angling on local rivers, reservoirs, and fisheries. A day's catch might include perch, rudd, pike, salmon, sea trout, brown trout, or freshwater eel. The **Dublin Angling Initiative,** Balnagowan, Mobhi Boreen, Glasnevin, Dublin 9 (© **01/ 837-9209**), offers the *Dublin Freshwater Angling Guide* and the *Sea Angling Guide,* which tell you everything you'll need to know about local fishing.

GOLF   Dublin is one of the world's great golfing capitals. A quarter of Ireland's courses—including five of the top ten—lie within an hour's drive of the city. Visitors are welcome, but be sure to phone ahead and make a reservation.

The **Elm Park Golf Club,** Nutley Lane, Dublin 4 (© **01/269-3438**), is located on the south side of Dublin, within 3½ miles (5.5km) of the city center. Greens fees are a reasonable 57€ ($52) on weekdays and 70€ ($63) on weekends.

The **Portmarnock Golf Club** ☆, Portmarnock, County Dublin (© **01/ 846-2968**), is 10 miles (16km) from the city center on Dublin's north side, on a spit of land between the Irish Sea and a tidal inlet. Greens fees are 109€ ($98) on weekdays, 132€ ($120) on weekends.

The **Royal Dublin Golf Club** ☆, Bull Island, Dollymount, Dublin 3 (© **01/833-6346**), is often compared to St. Andrews in layout. Like Portmarnock, it has been rated among the top courses of the world and has also hosted several Irish Open tournaments. The home base of Ireland's legendary champion Christy O'Connor, Sr., the Royal Dublin is well known for its fine bunkers, close lies, and subtle trappings. Greens fees are 90€ ($82) on weekdays, 110€ ($100) on weekends.

St. Margaret's Golf Club, Skephubble, St. Margaret's, County Dublin (© **01/864-0400**), one of Dublin's newest championship golf venues, is a par-72 parkland course located 3 miles (5km) west of Dublin Airport. Greens fees are 66€ ($60) every day, reduced to 40€ ($36) in the winter.

HORSEBACK RIDING   There are about a dozen riding stables within easy reach of Dublin, catering to all skill levels. Prices average 20€ ($18) per hour per person for a group lesson or 40€ ($36) per hour for a private lesson, with or without instruction. Many stables offer guided trail riding as well as courses in show-jumping, dressage, prehunting, eventing, and cross-country riding. Among the riding centers nearest to downtown are **Calliaghstown Riding Centre,** Calliaghstown, Rathcoole, County Dublin (© **01/458-9236**); **Carrickmines Equestrian Centre,** Glenamuck Road, Foxrock, Dublin 18 (© **01/ 295-5990;** www.carrickminesequestrian.ie).

WALKING   The walk from **Bray to Greystones** along the rocky promontory of Bray Head is a great excursion, with beautiful views back toward Killiney Bay, Dalkey Island, and Howth. Bray, the southern terminus of the DART line, is readily accessible from Dublin. Follow the beachside promenade south through town; at the outskirts of town the promenade turns left and up, beginning the ascent of Bray Head. Shortly after the beginning of this ascent, a trail branches to the left—this is the cliff-side walk, which continues another 3½ miles (5.5km) along the coast to Greystones. From the center of Greystones, there is a train that will take you back to Bray. This is an easy walk, about 2 hours one-way. For more information on Greystones, see chapter 5.

Dalkey Hill and Killiney Hill drop steeply into the sea, and command great views of Killiney Bay, Bray Head, and Sugarloaf Mountain. To get to them, go south on Dalkey Avenue from the center of Dalkey (say, in front of the post office), a short distance from the Dalkey DART station. About half a mile (1km) from the post office you'll pass a road ascending through fields on your left—this is the entrance to the Dalkey Hill Park. From the parking lot, climb a series of steps to the top of Dalkey Hill; from here you can see the expanse of the Bay, the Wicklow Hills in the distance, and the obelisk topping nearby Killiney Hill. If you continue on to the obelisk, there's a trail leading from there down on the seaward side to Vico Road, itself a lovely place for a seaside walk. From the parking lot to Killiney Hill is another half mile.

The rocky hills and sea cliffs of **Howth** offer an excellent view of Dublin. From Howth Harbour walk east along the seafront on Balscadden Road. Continue east to the point where the paved road ends at a small parking lot and becomes the cliff walk, a well-trod path around the periphery of Howth Head. Walk south along grassy slopes, passing the Bailey lighthouse. Continue along the path to Doldrum Bay and at Red Rock Road turn right along a steep uphill path leading to Carrickbrack Road. Return to the harbor via Carrickbrack and Thormanby Lodge Roads. It's also possible to continue walking along the coast past Carrickbrack Road.

WINDSURFING, KAYAKING & SAILING   Certified level-one and level-two instruction and equipment rental for these three watersports are available at **The Surfdock Centre,** Grand Canal Dock, Ringsend, Dublin 4 (✆ 01/668-3945); fax 01/668-1215). The center has 42 acres of enclosed fresh water for its courses. It's open from June through September, and the rest of the year on demand.

10 Spectator Sports

GAELIC SPORTS   If your schedule permits, don't miss attending one of Ireland's two national games: **Gaelic football,** which vaguely resembles soccer but allows the use of the hands in punching the ball, and **hurling,** in which 30 men wielding heavy sticks rush around thrashing at a hard leather ball called a *sliotar.* These two amateur sports are played every weekend throughout the summer at various local fields, culminating in September with the All-Ireland Finals, the Irish version of the Super Bowl. For schedules and admission charges, call the **Gaelic Athletic Association,** Croke Park, Jones Road, Dublin 3 (✆ 01/836-3222).

HORSE RACING   Dublin's racing fans gather at **Leopardstown Race Course,** off the Stillorgan Road (N11), Foxrock, Dublin 18 (✆ 01/289-3607), 6 miles (9.5km) south of the city center. This is a modern facility with all-weather glass-enclosed spectator stands. Races are scheduled throughout the year, two or three times a month.

POLO   Polo is played from May to mid-September on the green fields of Phoenix Park, on Dublin's west side, with the Dublin Mountains as a backdrop. Matches often take place Saturday and Sunday afternoons and any can be attended free of charge. To confirm details contact the **All Ireland Polo Club,** Phoenix Park, Dublin 8 (✆ 01/677-6248), or check the sports pages of the newspapers.

11 Shopping

Known the world over for its handmade products and fine craftsmanship, Ireland offers many unique shopping opportunities. Dublin, as Ireland's commercial center, is a one-stop source for the country's best wares. Also, due to Ireland's wholehearted membership in the European Union, Irish shops are brimming with imported goods from the Continent.

Grafton Street, although only several blocks long, is Dublin's answer to Chicago's "Magnificent Mile," with a parade of fine boutiques, fashionable department stores, and specialty shops. Because it's limited to pedestrian traffic, Grafton Street often attracts street performers and sidewalk artists, giving it a festive atmosphere. The smaller streets radiating out from Grafton—Duke, Dawson, Nassau, and Wicklow—are also lined with fine small book, handcraft, and souvenir shops.

Nearby is **Temple Bar,** the hub of Dublin's Left Bank artsy district and the setting for art and music shops, secondhand clothing stores, and a host of other increasingly fine and interesting boutiques.

On the north side of the Liffey, the **O'Connell Street** area is the main inner-city shopping nucleus, along with its nearby offshoots—Abbey Street for crafts, Moore Street for its open-air market, and Henry Street, a pedestrian-only strip of department stores and indoor malls. Close at hand, west of O'Connell, are both the ILAC Centre and the new Jervis Shopping Centre.

Generally, Dublin shops are open from 9 to 5:30 or 6pm Monday through Saturday, Thursday until 8pm. There are exceptions, particularly during tourist season (May–Sept or Oct), when many shops also have Sunday hours, usually midmorning through 4pm or 5pm. Throughout the year, many bookshops are open on Sundays.

VALUE-ADDED TAX RETURN Be sure to request a tax refund voucher from the shop when making your purchases—part of this form must be filled out by the retailer. See "Finding the Best Shopping Bargains" in chapter 2. *Hint:* If you don't want to carry your purchases while you're traveling, take advantage of the mailing service offered by most shops for an extra charge—and remember that goods mailed directly abroad are automatically exempt from the VAT tax.

SHOPPING CENTERS & DEPARTMENT STORES
SOUTH OF THE LIFFEY

Brown Thomas and Co One of the city's most prestigious department stores, with both upmarket and moderate goods and prices. 15–20 Grafton St., Dublin 2. ✆ 01/679-5666.

Powerscourt Town House Centre ⭐ If you just can't get excited about shopping centers, wait till you see this one. It's set in a 1774 mansion built by Lord Powerscourt, and the house and courtyard have been expertly renovated to accommodate small shops, wine bars, and restaurants. The wares include all kinds of crafts, antiques, paintings, prints, ceramics, leather work, jewelry, clothing, hand-dipped chocolates, and farmhouse cheeses. Look for the sign on Grafton Street at Johnson's Court between Chatham and Wicklow Streets. Clarendon St., Dublin 2. ✆ 01/679-4144.

Royal Hibernian Way This shopping arcade on the site of the old Royal Hibernian Hotel holds some 30 shops, some of which sell high fashion, and a number of small restaurants. Dawson St., Dublin 2.

St. Stephen's Green Centre There are more than 100 stores flanking the dramatic atrium of this centrally located shopping center. Check out the Dome Café at the top level for great pastries, sweets and light meals (see description earlier in this chapter in "Great Deals on Dining"). Grafton St. and St. Stephen's Green, Dublin 2. ✆ 01/478-0888. Fax 01/478-2565.

Tips **New Kid on the Block: The Old City**

Shoppers take note: Dublin's latest "it" shopping district is **Old City,** located just west of Temple Bar and roughly comprising the area between Castle and Fishamble streets. Though still under development, there's already a good mix of hip fashion, modern interior design, crafts, and leisure shops, as well as a bakery, Internet cafe, and a hair salon. The center of the action is a cobbled, pedestrianized street called Cow's Lane, which links Lord Edward Street with Essex Street West. Granted, the name may not immediately conjure up a cool image, but it's become a destination in itself for stylemongers who like to get their retail therapy away from the crush of Grafton and Henry Streets. On Cow's Lane, don't miss **Whichcraft,** contemporary pieces for the home at **2cooldesign,** post-war home accessories from **20th Century Furniture,** and the latest looks in glasses at the swish London eyewear outlet **Kirk Originals.**

North of the Liffey, the **O'Connell Street** area is the main inner-city shopping nucleus, along with its nearby offshoots—Abbey Street for crafts, Moore Street for its open-air market, and most notably, Henry Street, a pedestrian-only strip of chain stores, department stores, and indoor malls such as the ILAC Centre and the Jervis Shopping Centre.

NORTH OF THE LIFFEY

Clerys   A Dublin tradition, Clerys is the oldest and largest department store on the north side of the river. It stocks everything from fashion, jewelry, and gifts to housewares and hardware. There are three good inexpensive restaurants on the premises. O'Connell St., Dublin 2. ✆ **01/878-6000.**

Dunne's Stores   It's crowded, busy, and lacking in charm, but Dunne's is a terrific place to pick up good buys in clothing, as well as the little necessities of life. Ilac Centre, Talbot St.

Dublin also has several clusters of shops in **multistory malls,** ideal for indoor shopping on rainy days. Among the largest of these are the **ILAC Centre,** Henry Street, Dublin 1; and the **Jervis Shopping Centre,** Mary Street, Dublin 1.

BEST BUYS & WHERE TO FIND THEM
ART

Combridge Fine Arts   In business for more than 100 years, this shop features works by modern Irish artists as well as quality reproductions of classic Irish art. 24 Suffolk St., Dublin 2. ✆ 01/677-4652. DART to Pearse Station. Bus: 15A, 15B, 15C, 55, 83.

M. Kennedy and Sons Ltd.   If you are looking for a souvenir, try this interesting shop, established more than 100 years ago. It's a treasure trove of books on Irish artists and works, and it also stocks a lovely selection of fine-arts greeting cards, postcards, and bookmarks. There are all types of artists' supplies as well, and an excellent art gallery on the upstairs level. 12 Harcourt St., Dublin 2. ✆ 01/475-1749. Bus: 62.

BOOKS

Cathach Books   This centrally located shop has a large stock of Irish literature, including numerous first editions and rare books. It also carries local history and genealogy publications, and has a collection of maps and fine prints in the basement. Ask for the catalog. 10 Duke St. ✆ **01/671-8676.** Fax 01/671-5120. www.rarebooks.ie.

Eason's Hanna's   This shop has good stocks of books of Irish interest, as well as of children's books, newly published books, and a good selection of international newspapers and magazines. Everything can be mailed overseas. 27–29 Nassau St., Dublin 2. ✆ **01/677-1255.**

Greene's Bookshop   Book lovers can browse through two floors of new and secondhand books, or the rows of trays out front on the sidewalk. The staff is friendly and helpful, and they'll hunt down scarce or out-of-print books at no charge. You can also get a free mail-order catalog. 16 Clare St., Dublin 2. ✆ **01/676-2554.** Fax 01/678-9091. greenes@iol.ie.

Waterstones Bookshop   This branch of the British chain features an extensive stock of books, as well as special reading areas, a good book-search service, and mail- and telephone-order departments. 7 Dawson St., Dublin 2. ✆ **01/679-1415.**

The Winding Stair   Retreat from the bustle of the north side's busy quays at this self-service cafe and bookshop, and enjoy a light meal while browsing through some books. There are three floors—one smoke-free, and each chock-full of used books, with a winding 18th-century staircase connecting them. (A cage-style elevator serves, on request, those who are unable or prefer not to climb the stairs.) Tall windows provide expansive views of the Halfpenny Bridge and River Liffey. The food is simple and healthy—see the review earlier in this chapter in "Great Deals on Dining." Evening events include poetry readings and recitals. 40 Lower Ormond Quay, Dublin 1. ✆ **01/873-3292.**

CRAFTS

DESIGNyard   The first thing you'll notice about DESIGNyard is its design. The building is a Victorian warehouse gorgeously converted into a chic contemporary applied-arts center; its set of four wrought-iron gates are abstracts of the city plans of Dublin, Madrid, New York, and Vienna. The ground floor Jewelry Gallery exhibits the finest contemporary Irish and European jewelry, while the first floor Crafts Council Gallery features some of the finest Irish contemporary craft, including furniture, ceramics, glass, lighting, and textiles. All pieces are for sale. You can also make an appointment here to commission an original work of Irish applied art and design. Whether you see it as a shop or a museum, DESIGNyard is well worth a visit. 12 E. Essex St., Temple Bar, Dublin 2. ✆ **01/677-8453.** DART to Tara St. Station. Bus: 21A, 46A, 46B, 51B, 51C, 68, 69, 86.

Tower Design Centre   Located along the banks of the Grand Canal, this 19th-century sugar refinery was beautifully restored in 1983 and developed into a nest of craft workshops. Watch the artisans at work and then purchase a special souvenir, from fine-art greeting cards and hand-marbled stationery to pewter, ceramics, pottery, knitwear, hand-painted silks, copper-plate etchings, all-wool wall hangings, silver and gold Celtic jewelry, and heraldic gifts. There's a restaurant and limited free parking available. Pearse St. (off Grand Canal Quay), Dublin 2. ✆ **01/677-5655.** DART to Pearse Station. Bus: 2 or 3.

FASHION/FABRICS

Blarney Woollen Mills A branch of the highly successful Cork-based enterprise of the same name, this shop is opposite the south side of Trinity College. Known for its competitive prices, it stocks a wide range of woolen knitwear made at the home base in Blarney, as well as crystal, china, pottery, and souvenirs. 21–23 Nassau St., Dublin 2. ℂ **01/671-0068.** www.blarney.ie. DART to Pearse Station. Bus: 5, 7A, 8, 15A, 15B, 46, 55, 62, 63, 83, 84.

Cleo For more than 60 years, the Joyce family has been creating designer craft clothing for men and women in a rainbow of vibrant tweed colors—elegant ponchos, capes, peasant skirts, coat-sweaters, decorative crios belts, and brimmed hats. A new line of hand-knit sweaters by Cleo incorporates four- and five-thousand-year-old designs from carved cairn stones found at Newgrange. 18 Kildare St., Dublin 2. ℂ **01/676-1421.** www.cleo-ltd.com. DART to Pearse Station. Bus: 10, 11A, 11B, 13, 20B.

Dublin Woollen Mills This Dublin institution, located at the foot of the Ha'penny Bridge, was founded by the Roche family in 1888. Four succeeding generations have carried on the high standards set in the beginning. As the name suggests, woolen goods are featured, with a wide selection of traditional and designer-style knitwear as well as shawls, scarves, blankets, and interesting craft items. James Joyce worked briefly as a sales agent for this firm in Trieste, and some of the correspondence documenting his business relations with the company is on display. The shop offers a 5% discount for students with current ISIC cards. 41–42 Lower Ormond Quay, Dublin 1. ℂ **01/677-5014** or 01/677-0301. dwm@woollen mills.ie. Bus: 70 or 80.

Jenny Vander This interesting shop stocks antique clothes, shoes, and jewelry (including a large collection antique costume jewelry) as well as Irish linen and lace sheets, curtains, tablecloths, and a collection of evening bags. Expect lots of bric-a-brac and men's clothes. Great fun, and the prices are reasonable. 20–22 Market Arcade, George's St., Dublin 2. ℂ **01/677-0406.**

Kevin and Howlin Tweed tailor-made jackets and suits for men are good value here, and last so long they're an investment rather than just a purchase. There's also a large range of ready-made men's clothing and moderately priced Donegal tweed hats and caps. 31 Nassau St. (at the bottom of Dawson St., facing Trinity College), Dublin 2. ℂ/fax **01/677-0257.**

Monaghan's Established in 1960 and operated by two generations of the Monaghan family, this store is a prime source of cashmere sweaters for men and women, with the best selection of colors, sizes, and styles anywhere in Ireland. Other items in stock include traditional Aran knits, lambswool, crochet, and Shetland wool products. Also located at 4/5 Royal Hibernian Way, off Dawson Street (ℂ **01/679-4451**). Grafton Arcade, Dublin 2. ℂ **01/677-0823.** DART: Pearse Station. Bus: 10, 11A, 11B, 13, 20B.

GIFT/SPECIALTY STORES

House of Ireland This shop is a standout for almost anything made in Ireland. You'll find Waterford crystal, fine Irish china, tweeds, cashmeres, knitcrafts, linens, Celtic jewelry, pottery, blackthorn walking sticks, and porcelain dolls dressed in traditional handcrafted clothes. The service is outstanding and the staff friendly. They'll mail or ship overseas, and orders can even be placed by e-mail. Ask for the vouchers that entitle *Frommer's* readers to a free gift equal to

10% of the total value of your purchase. 37–38 Nassau St.and Dawson St., Dublin 2. ℰ **01/671-1111**. Fax 01/679-1023. www.houseofireland.com. DART to Pearse Station. Bus: 5, 7A, 15A, 15B, 46, 55, 62, 63, 83, 84.

Peterson of Dublin   Dedicated pipe smokers will know Peterson, which has been making superior pipes in Dublin since the 1860s. The company is justly famed for its classic designs, and features such models as the Sherlock Holmes and the Mark Twain pipes. A recent addition is a walk-in cigar humidor with Cuban cigars. 117 Grafton St., Dublin 2. ℰ **01/671-4652**.

RECORDS, TAPES & COMPACT DISCS

Claddagh Records   Claddagh has one of the most comprehensive stocks of traditional Irish records, tapes, and compact discs, as well as blues, Cajun, country, Asian, European, and African music. There's a mail-order service, and the catalog includes a full listing of all Irish recordings. 2 Cecilia St., Temple Bar, Dublin 2. ℰ **01/677-0262**. Fax 01/679-3664. http://indigo.ie/~claddagh.

Waltons Musical Gallery   The best all-around music store in Dublin is at the top of O'Connell Street. The stock of Irish traditional records and sheet music here is tremendous, and there's also a complete line of musical instruments. Waltons has a branch on the south side of the Liffey as well, at 69–70 S. Great George's St., Dublin 2 (ℰ **01/475-0661**). 2–5 N. Frederick St., Dublin 1. ℰ **01/874-7805**.

MARKETS

Blackrock Market   More than 60 vendors in this indoor/outdoor market run stalls that offer everything from gourmet cheeses to vintage clothing at great prices. Open Saturday from 11am to 5:30pm and Sunday noon to 5:30pm, including public holidays. 19a Main St., Blackrock. ℰ **01/283-3522**. www.blackrockmarket.com. DART to Blackrock Station. Bus: 5, 7, 7A, 8, 17, 45, 114.

Moore Street Market   For a walk into the past, don't miss the Moore Street Market, full of streetside barrow vendors plus plenty of local color and chatter. It's the principal open-air fruit, flower, fish, and vegetable market of the city. Moore St., Dublin 1. No phone. DART to Connolly Station. Bus: 25, 34, 37, 38A, 66A, 67A.

12 Dublin Nights

To find out what's going on, pick up the biweekly *In Dublin* magazine for 3€ ($2.70), or the free biweekly *Event Guide.* In both you'll find listings for music performances, stage productions, movie theaters, museum and gallery exhibits. You can also find extensive information on Irish nightlife at **www.ireland.com** or **www.eventguide.ie**.

THE PUB SCENE

Dublin pubs are their own special kind of entertainment. It makes no difference if you wander into one known for its conversation, its music, or its pint (actually, there probably isn't a pub in Dublin that won't tell you they "pull the best pint in the city").

So if you're planning on taking one of those famous "pub crawls,"—that is, hitting several pubs in one night—you better make sure your willpower is up to it. Chances are very slim that you'll be able to walk out of the first one you enter, and very good that you'll settle in with the first pint and just enjoy the show.

With more than 1,000 pubs to choose from, every Dubliner you ask will come up with a different favorite (or list of favorites), and there probably won't be a clunker in the lot. The section below lists the ones that I've found most interesting. *Note for non-drinkers:* Irish pubs are centers of sociability, where you can chat the night away just as happily with nothing stronger than soda.

The closing time is 12:30am Thursday, Friday and Saturday; 11:30pm Monday, Tuesday and Wednesday; and 11pm Sunday. After the official closing you're usually given some time to finish the last drink.

SOUTH OF THE LIFFEY

The Brazen Head *Finds* Licensed by Charles II in 1666, this is the oldest drinking place in Ireland. It's said to have gotten its name in memory of a curious redheaded beauty who stuck her head out a window during one of Dublin's public disturbances and promptly lost it to an English sword. Be that as it may, this ancient pub sits on what used to be the only place you could cross the Liffey by bridge. It's tucked away at the back of a courtyard down an arched alleyway on the west side of Bridge Street (the entrance is easily overlooked). The low ceilings, brass lanterns, and ancient, uneven wooden floors are the same as when patriots like Wolfe Tone and Daniel O'Connell came in to drink and when Robert Emmet lodged here while plotting his ill-fated uprising (his writing desk is pointed to with pride). 20 Lower Bridge St., Dublin 8. ℭ **01/679-5186.**

The Castle Inn Situated between Dublin Castle and Christ Church Cathedral, this recently rejuvenated bi-level pub exudes an "old city" atmosphere, with stone walls, flagstone steps, suits of armor, big stone fireplaces, beamed ceilings, and lots of early Dublin memorabilia. ChristChurch Place, Dublin 8. ℭ **01/475-1122.**

Davy Byrnes James Joyce fans may want to look up the "moral pub" that was a favorite of *Ulysses* hero Leopold Bloom. The pub has been modernized into a tastefully sophisticated sort of cocktail lounge that one writer has called the closest thing Dublin has to a singles' bar. The 1890s wall murals are still here, and you can still get a very good pint, but there are now likely to be more orders for mixed drinks than Guinness. Seafood pub lunches are a specialty. 21 Duke St., Dublin 2. ℭ **01/677-5217.** www.davybyrnespub.com.

Doheny & Nesbitt *Finds* This old pub looks exactly like a Dublin pub should—a great old wooden front with polished brass proclaiming "Tea and Wine Merchant," high ceilings, mirrored partitions along the bar, iron-and-marble tables, and a snug. The place has been here for more than 130 years, and Dubliners of every age and inclination, including journalists, politicians, artists, and architects, claim it as their "local." A great place for conversation and people watching, whether in the front bar or the back room. 5 Lower Baggot St., Dublin 2. ℭ **01/676-2945.**

The Long Hall Tucked into a busy commercial street, this is one of the city's most photographed pubs, with a beautiful Victorian decor of filigree-edged mirrors, polished dark woods, and traditional snugs. The hand-carved bar is said to be the longest counter in the city. 51 S. Great George's St., Dublin 2. ℭ **01/475-1590.**

McDaids If you're a Brendan Behan devotee, you'll know about this dark, high-ceilinged pub in which he claimed a corner for himself, his pint, and his typewriter. Patrick Kavanagh and Flann O'Brien are other literary lights who drank here, and the clientele is still very much concerned with the written word and those doing the writing. 3 Harry St., Dublin 2. ℭ **01/679-4395.**

What Does "Craic" Mean?

If someone says to you, "I was at the pub last night and the crack was good," don't take it to mean that you're dealing with a dope addict. What he really said to you was *craic,* which is an Irish word that sums up conversation and the ambience of an evening into one handy-dandy five-letter package. Try it out: "Aye, the craic was good indeed." Now doesn't that sound nice?

Mulligan's *(Moments* Locals claim that this Dublin institution serves the best pint in the city—which means, according to them, that it serves the best pint in the universe. To get here, turn north on Blackhall Place from Ellis Quay, about 1 mile (1.5km) west along the Liffey from the O'Connell Street Bridge.

Since 1782, it has pulled pints for dockers, journalists, and, in recent years, scores of students from nearby Trinity. Its front bar and four rooms still retain many of their original trappings, including 19th-century gas lights. As in the past, when James Joyce and other Dublin notables were regulars, there's the ring of clubby conversation, especially around 5 in the afternoon; it settles down a bit as the evening progresses. 18 Stoney Batter, Dublin 7. ✆ **01/677-9249.**

Neary's Neary's backs up to the Gaiety Theatre's stage door, and both patrons and the craic often center around things theatrical. You'll recognize Neary's by the two black sculptured bronze arms holding light globes at its entrance. Inside, the decor is neo-Edwardian, with a pink marble bar, brass gas lamps, mirrored walls, and lots of mahogany. 1 Chatham St., Dublin 2. ✆ **01/677-7371.**

Palace Bar Just off Westmoreland Street, near Trinity College and not far from the river, the Palace is a bit of Old Dublin much loved by present-day residents. Cartoons, old prints, and paintings depict the history of the city and the bar. 21 Fleet St., Dublin 2. ✆ **01/677-9290.**

The Stag's Head *(Moments* This is one much favored by natives. Getting here is a bit complicated: Leave College Green on the left side of Dame Street and in the middle of the second block keep your eyes glued to the sidewalk, where you'll find a stag's head set in mosaic right in the pavement. It fronts a small alleyway on the left; at its end you'll find this beautiful old pub, which has been here since 1770. Coming from Great George's Street, turn onto Exchequer Street and keep your eyes peeled for Dame Court. An interesting mix of ages, occupations, and characters drink here in the evening; young executives, tourists, and others come for the excellent pub lunch (see "Great Deals on Dining," earlier in this chapter). 1 Dame Court, Dublin 2. ✆ **01/679-3701.**

Toner's This venerable pub has been around more than 150 years. The long mahogany bar is set with partitions to provide a bit of privacy. It's said that W. B. Yeats drank here. 139 Lower Baggot St., Dublin 2. ✆ **01/676-3090.**

NORTH OF THE LIFFEY

Kavanagh's This pub, which stands next to what was once the main gate to Glasnevin Cemetery, has been in existence for a century and a half and proprietor John Kavanagh is the sixth generation of his family to run it. He has an endless fund of stories, many of which concern the gravediggers who worked next door and who'd bang stones against the pub's wall signaling they needed a drink so they could get on with their work. (You can still see marks from those bangings on the wall outside.) This is, as it has always been, a workers' pub—worn wooden booths and cubbyholes, a dartboard or two, and the relaxed chatter of those who have finished an honest day's labor. 1 Prospect Sq., Glasnevin. No phone.

Patrick Conway's This pub is just across from the Gate Theatre and the Rotunda Maternity Hospital, so you'll usually find a good mix of theatergoers and obstetricians there to welcome you. The pub lunches are terrific (see "Great Deals on Dining," earlier in this chapter). Conway's claims to be Dublin's second-oldest pub, dating from 1745, and while it has been modernized for comfort, there's still much of the traditional wood, brass, and convivial atmosphere. Take note of the back bar, a marvel of carved mahogany. 70 Parnell St., Dublin 1. ℂ 01/873-2474.

Ryan's *Finds* This is one of Dublin's very special pubs. Founded in 1920, it's a traditional place, with a marvelous old oak-and-mahogany central bar fixture that holds a double-faced mechanical clock. There's a superb collection of antique wall mirrors, and four antique brass lamp fittings are mounted on the bar counter. The bar is partitioned with ornate dividers with beveled mirrors. Many heads of state and celebrities from the movie and theater worlds have passed through the pub's doors. The staff and atmosphere here are equally great, and the fine upstairs restaurant is a good place for a lunch or evening meal. 28 Parkgate St. (in the Wellington Hotel, near Phoenix Park), Dublin 7. ℂ 01/677-6097.

LIVE-MUSIC CLUBS & PUBS

Dozens of clubs and pubs all over town feature rock, folk, jazz, and traditional Irish music. This includes the so-called "late-night pubs"—pubs with an exemption allowing them to remain open past the usual closing time mandated by law. Check *In Dublin* magazine or the *Event Guide* for club schedules. One of the most popular rock clubs is **Whelan's,** 25 Wexford St., Dublin 2 (ℂ 01/478-0766); you should also visit the new **Hot Press Irish Music Hall of Fame,** 57 Middle Abbey Street, Dublin 1 (ℂ 01/878-3345), with music from Celtic to Rock most nights, and the second-oldest pub in Dublin, **Bleeding Horse,** 24–25 Camden St., Dublin 2 (ℂ 01/475-2705). Other venues, especially popular with the over-30 late crowd, include: **Break for the Border,** Lower Steven's Street, Dublin 2 (ℂ 01/478-0300); **Bad Bob's Backstage Bar,** East Essex Street, Dublin 2 (ℂ 01/677-5482); **Major Tom's,** South King Street, Dublin 2 (ℂ 01/478-3266); the **Baggot Inn,** Baggot Street, Dublin 4 (ℂ 01/676-1430); and **Sinnotts,** South King Street, Dublin 2 (ℂ 01/478-4698). All are open daily, with live music most nights. Where there is a cover charge, it's usually 4€ to 10€ ($3.60 to $9).

PUBS WITH MUSIC

Many pubs host live music at night, usually beginning around 9pm and continuing to 11pm. This is as likely to be country western as the traditional Irish music most visitors prefer to hear, so ask around or walk the streets listening for the sound of the fiddle or uilleann pipes—you're sure to find what you're seeking. Here are a few of our favorites:

O'Donoghue's O'Donoghue's is seldom without music of one sort or another, provided on a spontaneous basis by the instrument-wielding horde who crowd in here to play traditional Irish music or even bluegrass and country-and-western—on guitars, uilleann pipes, bones, and spoons. It's a lively, fun-filled gathering spot if you don't mind the crush. 15 Merrion Row, Dublin 2. ℂ 01/661-4303. No cover for music.

Oliver St. John Gogarty   Situated in the heart of Temple Bar and named for one of Ireland's literary greats, this pub has an inviting old-world atmosphere, with shelves of empty bottles, stacks of dusty books, a horseshoe-shaped bar, and old barrels for seats. There are traditional music sessions every night from 9 to 11pm and also earlier on Saturday (3:30–7pm) and Sunday (12:30–3pm). 57/58 Fleet St., Dublin 2. ✆ 01/671-1779. www.olvergogartys.com. No cover for music.

The Purty Kitchen   Housed in a building that dates from 1728, this old pub has a homey atmosphere with open brick fireplaces, cozy alcoves, a large fish mural, and pub poster art on the walls. There's often free Irish traditional music in the main bar area (usually Thurs–Sun, but the schedule varies, so call ahead). Dance music with a DJ is on tap upstairs in Coast, a late-night night open Thursday though Sunday night. Old Dunleary Rd., Dun Laoghaire, County Dublin. ✆ 01/284-3576. No cover charge for traditional music; 6.50€–9€ ($5.90–$8) cover for music upstairs.

Slatterys   Slatterys features traditional Irish music nightly during the summer and on Sunday year-round from 12:30 to 2pm. It's a session that's been going on for 25 years, and one of the city's best. Capel St. (north of the Liffey), Dublin 1. ✆ 01/872-7971. No cover for music in the bar; 5.05€–7€ ($4.50–$6) cover for upstairs music lounge.

DINNER AND A SONG

There are several venues in Dublin where you can have dinner and listen to traditional music. At the **Abbey Tavern,** Abbey Road, Howth, County Dublin. (✆ **01/839 0307**), dinner is accompanied by authentic Irish ballad music, with its blend of fiddles, pipes, tin whistles, and spoons. The cover is usually 6€ ($5.45). Traditional music is performed daily March through October; from November through February it's best to call ahead to find out on which nights music will be offered.

CABARETS & TRADITIONAL IRISH ENTERTAINMENT

Most of these shows are aimed at tourists, although they're attended and enjoyed by locals as well.

Culturlann Na hEireann *(Moments*   This is the home of Comhaltas Ceoltoiri Eireann, an Irish cultural organization that has been the prime mover in encouraging the renewal of Irish traditional music. An authentic fully costumed show featuring traditional music, song, and dance is staged mid-June through early September, Monday to Thursday at 9pm. No reservations are necessary. Year-round, ceili dances are performed Friday 9pm to midnight; informal music sessions are held Wednesdays, Fridays and Saturdays at 9pm. 32 Belgrave Sq., Monkstown. ✆ 01/280-0295. www.comhaltas.com. Tickets Ceilis 8€ ($7); informal music sessions 3€ ($2.70) Fri–Sat, free Wed; stage shows 8€ ($7).

Doyle's Irish Cabaret   Staged in the ballroom of the Hotel Burlington, this colorful dinner/show features some of Ireland's top performers in a program of Irish music, dancing, ballad singing, and storytelling. Burlington Hotel, Upper Leeson St., Dublin 4. ✆ 01/664-3186. Fax 01/660-5297. May–Oct Mon–Sat dinner 7pm, show 8pm. Dinner and show 55€ ($50); show with 2 drinks 38€ ($34).

Jury's Irish Cabaret   Ireland's longest-running show (over 30 years) offers a mix of traditional Irish music and Broadway classics, set dancing, humorous monologues, and audience participation. Shows take place May through October, Tuesday to Sunday with dinner at 7:15pm and the show at 8pm. Pembroke Rd., Ballsbridge. ✆ 01/660-5000. Dinner and show 55€ ($50); show with two drinks 38€ ($34).

THE CLUB & MUSIC SCENE

The club and music scene in Dublin is confoundingly complex and malleable. Jazz, blues, folk, country, traditional, rock, and comedy move from venue to venue, night by night. The same club could be a gay fetish scene one night and a traditional music hotspot the next, so you have to stay on your toes to find what you want. The first rule is to get the very latest listings and see what's on and where. Keeping all this in mind, a few low-risk generalizations might prove helpful to give you a sense of what to expect.

The night scene in Dublin is definitively young, with the exception of some hotel venues outside the city center. Many of the trendiest, most sizzling spots in Dublin have a "strict" or "unfriendly" door policy, admitting only those who look and feel right for the scene within—you may find yourself excluded unless you can present the appropriate image, a composite of outfit, hair, attitude, and natural endowment.

But don't be put off by this daunting assessment; many of Dublin's clubs have friendly door policies. We've organized the listings by friendliness, but be aware that door policies are as changeable as the clubs themselves. Cover charges tend to fluctuate not only from place to place, but from night to night and from person to person (some people can't buy their way in, while others glide in gratis). Cover charges range from nominal to 15€ ($14), with the highest rates on weekends.

HIPPER THAN THOU

The Kitchen Housed in the basement of the Clarence Hotel in the heart of the Temple Bar district, this is one of Dublin's hottest, hippest nightclubs, partly owned by the rock group U2. Open nightly 11pm to 2:30am. 6/8 Wellington Quay, Dublin 2. ℭ **01/677-6635.**

Lillie's Bordello This is a private three-story nightclub, with two bars open to members and nonmembers 7 nights a week. The place has a stylish and self-consciously decadent ambience, with a mix of music every night. Open nightly 10pm to 1am or later. 45 Nassau St., Dublin 2. ℭ **01/679-9204.**

POD *POD*, by the way, stands for "Place of Dance." Operated by John Reynolds (nephew of the former prime minister of Ireland, Albert Reynolds), the POD, a "European nightclub of the year," has also won a European design award for its colorful Barcelona-inspired decor and is as loud as it is dazzling to behold. The Chocolate bar opens between 5:30pm and 8pm each night, and the admission fee is usually significantly discounted if you enter through the bar. Nightclub is open Wednesday to Saturday 11pm to 2am or later. Harcourt St., Dublin 2. ℭ **01/478-0166.** www.pod.ie.

Ré-Rá Though trendy, Ré-Rá has a more friendly door policy than most of its competition, so this may be the place to try first. Open nightly 11:30pm to 4am or later. 1 Exchequer St., Dublin 2. ℭ **01/677-4835.**

KINDER & GENTLER CLUBS

Another set of established clubs, these nightspots attract young singles and couples, but have friendly door policies and are places where people of most any age and ilk are likely to feel comfortable.

Annabel's Located in the Burlington Hotel just south of the Lower Leeson Street nightclub strip, this club is one of the longest lasting in town. It welcomes a mix of tourists and locals of all ages to a disco party atmosphere. Wednesday is currently "student night"; call ahead for other themed events. Open Wednesday to Saturday 11pm to 2:30am. Burlington Hotel, Leeson St., Upper, Dublin 4. ℭ 01/660-5222. www.clubanabel.com.

Club M   Housed in the basement of Blooms Hotel in the Temple Bar district, and close to Trinity College, this club boasts Ireland's largest laser lighting system and offers either DJ-driven dance or live music, for the over-23 bracket. Open Friday and Saturday 10pm to 2:30am, and Sunday to Thursday 11pm to 2:30am. Anglesea St., Dublin 2. ℭ 01/671-5622.

COMEDY CLUBS

The Irish comedy circuit is relatively new and quite popular. The timing, wit, and twist of mind required for comedy seems to me so native to the Irish that I find it difficult to draw a sharp line between those who practice comedy as a living and those who practice it as a way of life. You'll find both in the flourishing Dublin comedy clubs. Again, this is a mobile scene, so check the latest listings for details. Admission prices range from 6€ to 20€ ($5.45 to $18).

Comedy Improv/Comedy Cellar   This is a very small, packed venue, full of enthusiastic exchange. It's all up-close, in-your-face improv, with nowhere to hide, so stake out your turf early. Comedy Improv is open Monday 9pm to 11pm; Comedy Cellar is open Wednesday 9pm to 11pm. International Bar, 23 Wicklow St., Dublin 2. ℭ 01/677-9250.

Ha'Penny Bridge Inn   This is home to the Ha'Penny Laugh Improv Comedy Club and the Battle of the Axe, the former playing host to some of Ireland's funniest people, many of whom are on stage. The latter is a weekly show in which comedians, singers, songwriters, musicians, actors, and whoever storms the open mike in pursuit of the Lucky Duck Award. Beside Merchant's Arch, Wellington Quay, Dublin 2. ℭ 01/677-0616.

Murphy's Laughter Lounge   This new 400-seat comedy venue is the current prime-time king of the Irish comedy circuit, attracting the most popular stand-ups on the Irish scene—the O'Seinfelds, as it were—as well as international acts. Doors open Thursday to Saturday at 8pm, with the first act at 9pm. O'Connell Bridge, Dublin 1. ℭ 1/800-COMEDY.

THE GAY & LESBIAN SCENE

New gay and lesbian bars, clubs, and venues appear monthly, it seems, and many clubs and organizations such as the Irish Film Centre have special gay events or evenings, so it's best to check the *Gay Community News* and *In Dublin* for the latest listings. (See "For Gay & Lesbian Travelers," in chapter 2, for details on where to pick up these publications.) Cover charges range from 5€ to 15€ ($4.55 to $14), with discounts for students and seniors. The social scene ranges from quiet pub conversation and dancing to fetish nights and hilarious contests. Folks on the help lines through **Lesbian Line Dublin** (ℭ 01/872-9911) and **Gay Switchboard Dublin** (ℭ 01/872-1055; gsd@iol.ie) are also extremely helpful in directing you to activities of particular interest. (See p. 111 for their hours of operation.) See *In Dublin, The Event Guide,* or "Dublin's Pink Pages" (**www.pink-pages.org**) for complete current listings. All that said, here are some good bars and clubs to start with:

The George Bar and Night Club   The George was the first gay bar established in Dublin. It now houses two bars—one quiet and the other trendy, with dance music—and an after-hours nightclub called The Block upstairs. This is a comfortable, mixed-age venue. Open Monday and Tuesday 12:30pm to 11pm and Wednesday to Sunday 12:30pm to 2:30am. 89 S. Great George's St., Dublin 2. ℭ **01/478-2983**. DART to Tara St. Station. Bus: 22A.

Out on the Liffey   This relaxed, friendly pub caters to a balance of men and women and serves up pub food with good conversation. In 1998, "Out" expanded to include a new and happening late-night venue called Oscar's, where you can dance (or drink) until you drop. 27 Upper Ormond Quay, Dublin 1. ℭ **01/872-2480**. DART to Tara St. Station and walk up the Liffey; cross at Parliament Bridge. Bus: 34, 70, 80.

Stonewallz   Music from the '60s to the '90s keeps feet moving at this women-only late-night venue. There are pool tables, plus a video screen and games for when your feet get tired. Open Friday 9pm to 2am. Molloy's Bar, High St., Christchurch, Dublin 8. ℭ **01/872-7770**. www.clubi.ie./stonewallz/. Cover 4.95€ ($4.50) 9–11pm; 8.25€ ($7.50) 11pm–2am. No credit cards. Bus: 19, 19A, 22.

THE PERFORMING ARTS
THEATER
Dublin has a venerable and vital theatrical tradition, in which imagination and talent have always outstripped funding. Production budgets and ticket prices are modest, even minuscule, compared to those in New York or any major U.S. city, but most theaters mount shows only as they find the funds and opportunity to do so. That said, there are a few venerable (or at least well-established) theaters that offer a dependable and more-or-less uninterrupted stream of productions.

Abbey Theatre   For more than 90 years, the Abbey has been the national theater of Ireland. The original theater, destroyed by fire in 1951, was replaced in 1966 by the current quite functional, although uninspired, 600-seat house. The Abbey's artistic reputation in Ireland has risen and fallen many times and is at present reasonably strong. Lower Abbey St., Dublin 1. ℭ **01/878-7222**. www.abbeythe atre.ie. Box office Mon–Sat 10:30am–7pm; shows Mon–Sat 8pm and Sat matinees at 2:30pm. Tickets 10€–23€ ($9–$21) with Mon–Thurs evening and Sat matinee reductions for seniors, students, and children.

Andrews Lane Theatre   This relatively new venue has an ascending reputation for fine theater. It consists of a 220-seat main theater where contemporary work from home and abroad is presented, and a 76-seat studio geared to experimental productions. 12/16 Andrews Lane, Dublin 2. ℭ **01/679-5720**. Box office Mon–Sat 10:30am–7pm. Tickets 10€–20€ ($9–$18).

The Gate   Situated just north of O'Connell Street off Parnell Square, this recently restored 370-seat theater was founded in 1928 by Hilton Edwards and Michael MacLiammoir to provide a venue for a broad range of plays. This policy prevails today, with a program that includes a blend of modern works and the classics. Although not as well known by visitors, the Gate is easily as distinguished as the Abbey. Discounted student tickets are often available at 7pm the night of the performance. 1 Cavendish Row, Dublin 1. ℭ **01/874-4368**. Box office Mon–Sat 10am–7pm; shows Mon–Sat 8pm. Tickets 17€–20€ ($15–$17), 13€ ($12) for previews. AE, DC, MC, V.

Peacock   In the same building as the Abbey, this small, 150-seat theater features contemporary plays and experimental works, including poetry readings and one-person shows, as well as plays in the Irish language. Lower Abbey St., Dublin 1. ℭ **01/878-7222**. www.abbeytheatre.ie. Box office Mon–Sat 10:30am–7pm; shows Mon–Sat at 8:15pm and Sat matinee at 2:45pm. Tickets 10€–15€ ($9–$14).

Other theatrical venues presenting fewer shows (though they're often quite impressive), as well as music and dance performances, include the **Focus Theatre,** 6 Pembroke Place, off Pembroke Street, Dublin 2 (© **01/676-3071**); the **Gaiety Theatre,** South King Street, Dublin 2 (© **01/677-1717**); the **Olympia,** 72 Dame St., Dublin 2 (© **01/677-7744**); the **Players,** Trinity College, Dublin 2 (© **01/677-3370,** ext. 1239); the **Project@The Mint,** Henry Place, off Henry Street, Dublin 1 (© **1850-260027**); and the **Tivoli,** 135–8 Francis St., opposite Iveagh Market, Dublin 8 (© **01/454-4472**).

CONCERT HALLS & BIG PRODUCTIONS

National Concert Hall *(Moments* This is a splendid auditorium that features first-rate musical events. The hall stays busy with performances several nights a week for much of the year; it's home to the Irish National Symphony Orchestra, and also hosts international orchestras and soloists. Lunchtime concerts are also offered once each week during the summer and cost only 5.50€ ($5). Check with the concert hall or the tourist office to see what's on during your visit. The Commons Café is a new restaurant on the premises, open Monday to Friday 8am to 10:30pm and Saturday to Sunday 6 to 10:30pm.Earlsfort Terrace, Dublin 2. Main office © **01/417-0077;** box office © **01/417-0000.** Fax 01/417-0078. www.nch.ie. Box office Mon–Sat 10am–7pm; Sun 2 hr. before concert. Tickets 8†–45† ($7–$41). Bus: 10, 11, 13, 14, 14A, 15, 15A, 15B, 44, 46A, 47, 47A, 47B, 48A or 86.

The Point With a seating capacity of 3,000, this is Ireland's newest large theater and concert venue, attracting top Broadway-caliber shows and international stars.East Link Bridge, North Wall Quay, Dublin 1. © **01/836-3633.** Box office Mon–Sat 10am–6pm; matinees at 2:30pm and evening shows at 8pm. Most tickets 25†–65† ($23–$59).

13 Easy Excursions from Dublin

The county of Dublin is blessed with a coastline sometimes gentle and sandy, sometimes steep and craggy. The majestic crescent of Dublin Bay curves from Howth on its rocky perch in the north to Dalkey and its island at the southern tip. The scenic seashore towns south of the bay make great day trips, with some lovely seaside walks in the vicinity of Killiney, Dalkey, and Bray; all of these places are easily accessible on the DART. For information on walks in these places, as well as in Howth, see "Outdoor Activities," earlier in this chapter.

A TRIP FROM DUBLIN

One of the best excursions from the city is to **Glendalough,** one of Ireland's most beautiful lakes and the site of a medieval monastic settlement. See chapter 5.

DUBLIN'S SOUTHERN SUBURBS
SEEING THE SIGHTS

The Ferryman Young Aidan Fennel heads the third generation of Fennels to ferry visitors to nearby Dalkey Island, whose only current inhabitants are a small herd of wild Irish goats and the occasional seal. Aidan is a boat builder and his brightly painted fleet is mostly from his hand. The island, settled about 6,000 B.C., offers three modest ruins: a church over 1,000 years old, ramparts dating from the 15th century, and a martello tower constructed in 1804 to make Napoleon think twice. Now the island is little more than a lovely picnic spot. If you want to build up an appetite and delight your children or sweetheart, row out there yourself in one of Aidan's handmade boats.

Coliemore Rd. (at stone wharf). © **01/283-4298.** Island ferry round-trip 5.10€ ($4.60) adults, 2.60€ ($2.40) children. June–Aug weather permitting.

GREAT DEALS ON DINING

Escape VEGETARIAN/VEGAN   Conveniently located on the Bray seafront, this tiny restaurant tucked away inside a gift shop offers surprisingly innovative and satisfying meals, at a great price. Lunch is an especially good deal, and though the options are somewhat ordinary—jacket potatoes, an assortment of quiches—they're prepared with a flair for spicing, which ensures that each is a delightful and unpredictable experience. Dinner main courses might include a Sicilian crepe filled with an assortment of cheese and roasted vegetables, a vegetable lasagna, or perhaps a broccoli potato pie; the menu changes daily, and the evening's offerings are usually posted at 6pm. The decor is odd; it varies from spartan simplicity to outbursts of unrestrained bric-a-brac. Among the customers you're likely to find families on holiday, tough Bray teens, and kayakers or windsurfers coming in from a day on the water. The only downside here is the smoke—there isn't a genuine nonsmoking section and ventilation within the cavelike space can be rather poor.

1 Albert Walk, Bray, Co. Wicklow. ℂ **01/286-6755.** Main courses 14€–15€ ($13–$14). MC, V. Mon–Fri 4–10:30pm; Sat–Sun noon–10:30pm.

P. D.'s Woodhouse BARBECUE BISTRO   This restaurant is brought to you by Hurricane Charlie, the worst tropical storm to hit Ireland in recent memory. The first and only oak-wood barbecue bistro in Ireland, P. D.'s Woodhouse depends daily on the oaks ripped up by Charlie and now stored in Wicklow. Like the storm itself, this bistro's wild Irish salmon in caper and herb butter is devastating, as is the white sole. Whatever you do, don't launch any meal here without trying the Halumi cheese kabobs—a conversation-stopping grilled Greek goat cheese appetizer. The nut kabobs, on the other hand, one of several vegetarian entrees, are unnecessarily austere.

1 Coliemore Rd. (Dalkey center, several blocks from DART station). ℂ **01/284-9399.** www.dalkeyhome page.ie Reservations recommended. Main courses 13€–22€ ($12–$20). 10% service charge. AE, DC, MC, V. Tues–Sat 6–11pm; Sun 4–9pm.

The Queens Bar PUB GRUB   One of Ireland's oldest inns, the historic Queens Pub in the center of Dalkey has won a pocketful of awards, including Dublin's best pub in 1992. It has great atmosphere and food to match. In addition to pub grub, there are two restaurants on the premises.

12 Castle St., Dalkey, Co. Dublin. ℂ **01/285-4569.** No reservations. Bar menu 5€–15€ ($4.55–$14). AE, DC, MC, V. Bar open Sun–Thurs noon–midnight, Fri–Sat noon–1:30am; bar food daily noon–5pm, Mon–Fri 6–8pm. DART to Dalkey Station. Bus: 8.

A Good Pub

P. McCormack and Sons   If you rent a car and head toward the city's southern seaside suburbs, this is a great pub to stop in for refreshment. Park in McCormack's lot and step into the atmosphere of your choice. The main section has an old-world feeling, with globe lamps, stained-glass windows, books and jugs on the shelves, and lots of nooks and crannies for a quiet drink. For a change of pace, there's a skylit and plant-filled conservatory area where classical music fills the air, and outdoors you'll find a festive courtyard beer garden. The pub grub here is top notch, with a varied buffet table of lunchtime salads and meats.

67 Lower Mounttown Rd. (off York Rd.), Dun Laoghaire. ℂ **01/284-2634.** cormak@iol.ie.

Easy Excursions from Dublin

Balbriggan

Bernagearagh Bay

R127

Skerries

St. Patrick's Island

Shenick's Island

N1

R127

R128

R108

Lambay Island

R126

Donabate

Irish Sea

Swords

R106

Malahide

R122

N1

R106

Dublin Airport ✈

M1

Portmarnock

R104

R107

Ireland's Eye

Sutton **Howth**

Drumcondra

Belfield

▲ Ben of Howth

R103

Raheny

N2

R105

N3

Clontarf

North Bull Island

★ **DUBLIN**

Dublin Bay

Liffey

N7

R119

Royal Canal

Ranelagh

Rathfarnam

R112

Dun Laoghaire

Templeogue

Sandycove

Dalkey Island

N11

R117

Dalkey

R113

Mount Merrion

Dalkey Hill ▲

Killiney Hill ▲

To Shankill & Bray ↓

Killiney

0   2 1/2 Mi

0   2.5 Km

Dublin ★

REPUBLIC OF IRELAND

ATTRACTIONS ●
Ardgillan Castle **1**
Casino at Marino **11**
The Ferryman **23**
Fry Model Railway Museum **5**
Glasnevin Cemetery **9**
Howth Castle Gardens **12**
James Joyce Museum **17**
Malahide Castle **6**
National Botanic Gardens **10**
Newbridge House
 & Park **2**

ACCOMMODATIONS ■
Aishling House **13**
Annesgrove **16**
Arus Mhuire **15**
Mrs. Margaret Farrely **4**
Fitzpatrick's Castle Hotel **19**
Forte Travelodge **3**
Iona House **8**
Mrs. Eileen Kelly **13**
Mrs. Noreen McBride **15**
Rosmeen House **16**
Sea Breeze **13**
Springvale **13**
St. Dunstan's **14**
Mrs. Marie Tonkin **7**

DINING ◆
Dee Gee's **13**
P.D.'s Woodhouse **18**
The Queens Bar &
 Restaurant **18**

DUBLIN'S NORTHERN SUBURBS

Dublin's northern suburbs are best known as the home of Dublin International Airport, but there is also a delightful assortment of castles, historic buildings, and gardens to draw visitors. In addition, the residential suburbs of Drumcondra and Glasnevin offer many good lodgings en route to and from the airport.

Further north, the picturesque suburb of Howth is synonymous with panoramic views of Dublin Bay, beautiful hillside gardens, and many fine seafood restaurants. Best of all, it is easily reached via DART.

SEEING THE SIGHTS

Ardgillan Castle and Park   Located between Balbriggan and Skerries, north of Malahide, this recently restored 18th-century castellated country house sits right on the Irish coastline. The house, home of the Taylour family until 1962, was built in 1738, and has some fine period furnishings and antiques. But the real draw here is the setting, right on the edge of the Irish Sea, with miles of walking paths and coastal views as well as a rose garden and herb garden. The tearooms close half an hour before the rest of the house.

Balbriggan, Co. Dublin. ⓒ **01/849-2212.** Admission to House 3.80€ ($3.45) adults, 2.60€ ($2.40) students and seniors, 8.25€ ($7.50) families. House Apr–Sept Tues–Sun 11am–6pm; Oct–Dec 22 and Feb–Mar Wed and Sun 11am–4:30pm. Closed Dec 23–31. Park Nov–Mar 10am–5pm; Apr and Oct 10am–7pm; May and Sept 10am–8pm; June–Aug 10am–9pm. Free parking year-round. Bus: 33.

Casino at Marino ⚡   This 18th-century building is considered to be one of the finest garden temples in Europe. It was designed in the Franco-Roman style of neoclassicism by Scottish architect Sir William Chambers, and constructed in the garden of Lord Charlemont's house by the English sculptor Simon Vierpyl. Work commenced in 1762 and was completed 15 years later. The building is particularly noteworthy for its elaborate stone carvings and compact structure, which makes it appear to be a single story from the outside when it's actually two stories tall.

Malahide Rd., Marino (3 miles/5km north of the center), Dublin 3. ⓒ **01/833-1618.** www.heritageireland.ie. Admission 2.60€ ($2.40) adults, 2€ ($1.80) seniors, 1.25€ ($1.15) students and children. Feb–Mar and Nov Sun and Thurs noon–4pm; April noon–5pm; May and Oct daily 10am–5pm; June–Sept daily 10am–6pm. Last guided tour 45 min. before closing. Bus: 20A, 20B, 27, 27A, 27B, 42, or 42C, 123.

The Fry Model Railway Museum 𝘒𝘪𝘥𝘴   This is an exhibit of rare handmade models of more than 300 Irish trains. The trains were built in the 1920s and 1930s by Cyril Fry, a railway engineer and draftsman. The complex includes items of Irish railway history dating from 1834, and models of stations, bridges, trams, buses, barges, boats, the River Liffey, and the Hill of Howth.

Malahide (on the grounds of Malahide Castle), Co. Dublin. ⓒ **01/846-3779.** Fax 01/846-3723. fryrail way@dublintourism.ie. Admission 5.10€ ($4.60) adults, 3.80€ ($3.45) students and seniors, 2.55€ ($2.30) children, 14€ ($13) families. AE, MC, V. Apr–Sept Mon–Fri 10am–5pm (closed Fri Apr–May), Sat 10am–5pm, Sun 2–6pm; Oct–Mar Sat–Sun 2–5pm. DART + Suburban rail: Malahide Station. Bus: 42.

Howth Castle Rhododendron Gardens   Set on a steep slope about 8 miles (13km) north of downtown, this 30-acre garden was first planted in 1875 and is best known for its 2,000 varieties of rhododendron. Peak bloom time is mid April to the end of June. *Note:* The castle and its private gardens are not open to the public.

Howth, Co. Dublin. ⓒ **01/832-2624.** Free admission. Apr–June daily 8am–sunset. DART to Howth Station. Bus: 31.

The Howth Cliff Walk

The rocky hills and sea cliffs of *Howth* make for an excellent walk. From Howth Harbour, go east along the seafront on Balscadden Road. Continue east to the point where the paved road ends and becomes the cliff walk, a well-trod path around the periphery of Howth Head. (You might even see seals frolicking in the water below.) Then walk south along grassy slopes, passing the Bailey lighthouse. Continue along the path to Doldrum Bay, and at Red Rock Road turn right along a steep uphill path leading to Carrickbrack Road. Return to the harbor via Carrickbrack and Thormanby Lodge Roads. It's also possible to continue walking along the coast past Carrickbrack Road.

Malahide Castle *Kids* Malahide is one of Ireland's most historic castles, founded in the 12th century by Richard Talbot and occupied by his descendants until 1973. Fully restored, the interior of the building is the setting for a comprehensive collection of Irish furniture, dating from the 17th through the 19th centuries, and the walls are lined with one-of-a-kind Irish historical portraits and tableaux on loan from the National Gallery. The furnishings and art reflect life in and near the house over the past 8 centuries. After touring the house, you can explore the 250-acre estate, which includes 20 acres of prize gardens with more than 5,000 species of plants and flowers. The Malahide grounds also contain the **Fry Model Railway Museum** (see above), and **Tara's Palace,** an antique dollhouse and toy collection.

Malahide (8 miles/13km north of the Dublin center), Co. Dublin. ℭ **01/846-2184.** Fax 01/846-2537. malahidecastle@dublintourism.ie. Admission 5.10€ ($4.60) adults, 3.80€ ($3.45) students and seniors, 2.60€ ($2.40) children under 12, 14€ ($13) families; gardens free. AE, MC, V. Combination tickets available with Fry Model Railway and Newbridge House. Apr–Oct Mon–Sat 10am–5pm, Sun 11am–6pm; Nov–Mar Mon–Sat 10am–12:45pm and 2–5pm; gardens May–Sept daily 2–5pm. Bus: 42.

Newbridge House and Park *Kids* This country mansion dates back to 1740 and was once the home of Dr. Charles Cobbe, an archbishop of Dublin. Occupied by the Cobbe family until 1984, the house is a showcase of family memorabilia such as hand-carved furniture, portraits, daybooks, and dolls, as well as a museum of objects collected on world travels. The Great Drawing Room, in its original state, is considered one of the finest Georgian interiors in Ireland. The house sits on 350 acres, laid out with picnic areas and walking trails. There's also a 20-acre working Victorian farm stocked with farmyard animals.

Donabate (12 miles/16km north of Dublin center), Co. Dublin. ℭ **01/843-6534.** Admission to the house 5.50€ ($5) adults, 5€ ($4.55) students and seniors, 3€ ($2.70) children, 15€ ($14) family; admission to the farm 1.25€ ($1.15) adults, 1€ (90¢) seniors and students, 2.60€ ($2.40) families. Apr–Sept Tues–Sat 10am–1pm and 2–5pm, Sun 2–6pm; Oct–March Sat–Sun 2–5pm. Allow yourself at least 1 hr. before lunchtime or evening closing time. Bus: 33B.

ACCOMMODATIONS YOU CAN AFFORD
Mrs. Margaret Farrelly This comfortable, attractive house is only 10 minutes from Dublin Airport and your hostess, Mrs. Farrelly is a gracious host and most helpful to guests. There's a lovely lounge for guests' use. And your dining

options are plentiful, as there are good moderately priced restaurants in nearby Malahide village.

Lynfar, Kinsealy Lane (beside Malahide Castle), Kinsealy, Malahide, Co. Dublin. ✆ **01/846-3897.** 4 units, 3 with bathroom (shower only). 32€ ($29) single without bathroom; 63€ ($58) double. 25% reduction for children sharing with parents. Rates include full breakfast. No credit cards. Closed Dec–Jan. Bus: 42, 32A, or 102 from the Howth DART station. *In room:* TV, tea/coffeemaker, hair dryer.

Mrs. Marie Tonkin Mrs. Tonkin has won accolades from many of our readers. Her warm, comfortable, and attractive home is convenient to nearby sightseeing, and is also a good base for exploring the Eastern Region north of Dublin. Dublin Airport is only 15 minutes away.

29 Martello Court, Portmarnock, Co. Dublin. ✆ **01/846-1500.** 3 units, 2 with bathroom (shower only). 56€ ($51) double. Rates include full breakfast. No credit cards. Closed Nov to mid-Jan. Bus: 32, 32A, or 102 from the DART station.

GREAT DEALS ON DINING

Dee Gee's IRISH If you plan a day's outing at Howth, don't miss Dee Gee's. Located opposite the local DART station and overlooking Dublin Bay across from the harbor, this informal seaside spot is ideal for a cup of coffee, a snack, or a full meal. It's a self-service snackery by day and a more formal table-service restaurant at night. You can sit either indoors or outside, under umbrella-shaded tables. The entrees at dinner range from steaks and burgers to shrimp scampi, pork à la crème, breast of chicken with mushroom sauce, and vegetable lasagna. At lunchtime, soups, salads, and sandwiches are featured. Here's your chance to sit, relax, and watch all the activities of Howth from a front-row seat.

Harbour Rd., Howth, Co. Dublin. ✆ **01/839-2641.** Main courses 6.50€–8€ ($5.90–$7.25). MC, V. Daily 8am–7pm. DART: Howth Station. Bus: 31.

5

Out from Dublin

The scope of this chapter is more or less defined by what the distinguished Trinity geographer J. H. Andrews has labeled "the eastern triangle," a wedge of Ireland's east coast extending north to south from County Wicklow to County Louth and west to County Westmeath. Like a stage, compact and prominent, this relatively small space has witnessed more of the Irish drama than any other comparable part of Ireland.

The stretch of level coast from Dundalk to the Wicklows marks the greatest breach in Ireland's natural defenses, made worse—or better, depending on your perspective—by the inviting estuaries of the Liffey and the Boyne. These "opportunities" were not lost on explorers, settlers, and invaders across the millennia. Once taken, whether by Celts, Danes, Normans, or English, this area's strategic importance was soon recognized as the most likely command and control center for the whole of Ireland. Here lay Tara, the hill of kings; Dublin, the greatest of the Viking city-states in the area; and the Pale, the English colonial fist holding the rest of Ireland in its grip. Here, too, are Newgrange and Knowth, two of the most profound prehistoric sites in the world; Kells, where Ireland's greatest treasure was fished from a bog; Mellifont, where the Irish Cistercian movement made its beginning; and the Valley of the Boyne, where the Irish finally lost their country to the English.

Rimmed by the Irish Sea, this eastern triangle, every point of which is an easy distance from Dublin city, has less rain, less bog, and more history than any other region of comparable concentration on the island. To the south, County Wicklow presents a verdant and varied panorama of gardens, lakes, mountains, and seascapes; to the east sit the flat plains of County Kildare, Ireland's prime horse country; and in the north are the counties of Meath and Louth, packed with historic sites. Pair all of this with the region's central location vis-à-vis the rest of the country, and you have an area that is both a great hub from which to explore and a historical and geographic microcosm for those who don't have time to hit the four corners of the land.

1 County Wicklow: The Garden of Ireland

Co. Wicklow extends from Bray, 13 miles (20km) S of Dublin, to Arklow, 40 miles (64km) S of Dublin

Within the borders of County Wicklow lies some of Ireland's best rural scenery and **Glendalough,** one of its finest monastic sites. If you're based in Dublin, you can easily spend a day or afternoon in Wicklow and still return to Dublin in time for dinner and the theater, but you'll probably want to linger overnight at one of the many fine country inns.

One quite accessible and charming gateway to County Wicklow is the small harbor town of **Greystones** ★★, which I hesitate to mention because it's almost a secret. It is hands down one of the most unspoiled and attractive harbor towns on Ireland's east coast, with no special attractions except itself, and that's enough.

Wicklow's most stunning scenery and most interesting towns and attractions are to be found inland, between Enniskerry and Glendalough. The best way to see the **Wicklow Hills** is on foot, following the Wicklow Way past mountain tarns and secluded glens. In this region, don't miss the picturesque villages of **Roundwood, Laragh,** and **Aughrim.**

In the southernmost corner of Wicklow, the mountains become hills and share with the villages they shelter an unassuming beauty and a sleepy tranquility that can be a welcome respite from the bustle of Wicklow's main tourist attractions. In the vicinity of **Shillelagh** village are lovely forests, great hill walking, and the curious edifice of Huntington Castle.

GETTING THERE Irish Rail (© **01/836-6222;** www.irishrail.ie) provides daily train service between Dublin and Bray and Wicklow.

By Bus Bus Eireann (© **01/836-6111**) operates daily express bus service to Arklow, Bray, and Wicklow towns. **St. Kevin's Bus Company** (© **01/281-8119**) runs a bus direct from Dublin to Glendalough, departing daily from St. Stephens Green West at 11:30am. Round-trip fare is 13€ ($12). Both Bus Eireann and **Gray Line Tours** (© **01/605-7705;** fax 01/661-8158; dublin@guidefriday.com) offer seasonal (May–Sept) sightseeing tours to Glendalough, Wicklow, and Powerscourt Gardens.

By Car Take N11 south from Dublin City and follow turnoff signs for major attractions.

VISITOR INFORMATION For information about County Wicklow, contact the **Wicklow Tourist Office,** Fitzwilliam Square, Wicklow Town, County Wicklow (© **0404/69117**), open Monday to Friday year-round and Saturday during peak season. For additional Wicklow information, pay an online visit to **www.wicklow.ie.**

GLENDALOUGH 🐾🐾

Glendalough's name is derived from the Irish phrase *Gleann Da Locha,* meaning "The Glen of the Two Lakes." This idyllically secluded setting was chosen in the 6th century by St. Kevin for a monastery. Over the centuries, it became a leading center of learning, with thousands of students from Ireland, Britain, and all over Europe. In the 12th century, St. Lawrence O'Toole was among the many abbots to follow Kevin and spread the influence of Glendalough. But, like so many early Irish religious sites, the glories of Glendalough came to an end by the 15th century at the hands of the plundering Anglo-Norman invaders.

Today, visitors can stroll from the upper lake to the lower lake and walk through the remains of the monastery complex, long since converted to a burial place. Although much of the monastic city is in ruins, the remains do include a nearly perfect round tower, 103 feet (31m) high and 52 feet (16m) around the base, as well as hundreds of timeworn Celtic crosses and a variety of churches. One of these is St. Kevin's chapel, often called St. Kevin's Kitchen, a fine specimen of an early Irish barrel-vaulted oratory with its own miniature round belfry rising from a stone roof.

The main entrance to the monastic complex has been spoiled by a sprawling hotel and hawkers of various sorts; so, you may want to cross the river at the visitor center and walk along the banks, crossing back again at the monastic site and thus bypassing the trappings of commerce that St. Kevin himself once fled.

The East Coast

Counties Louth & Meath

Hill of Tara **8**
Holy Trinity Heritage
 Centre **1**
Knowth **5**
Loughcrew **7**
Mellifont Abbey **3**
Millmount Museum **4**
Monasterboice **2**
Newgrange / Bru Na Boinne
 Visitor Centre **5**
Newgrange Farm **5**
St. Colmcille's House **6**
Trim Castle **9**

County Kildare

Castletown House **10**
The Curragh **13**
Irish National Stud **12**
Irish Pewtermill **20**
Japanese Gardens **12**
Moone High Cross **26**
Newbridge Cutlery **14**
Steam Museum **11**

0 _____ 5 Mi
0 _____ 5 Km

Irish Sea

Area of Detail

Dublin

REPUBLIC OF IRELAND

County Wicklow

Avoca Handweavers **22**
Avondale House **21**
Glendalough **20**
Huntington Castle **25**
Kilruddery House & Gardens **16**
Mount Usher Gardens **18**
Noritake Arklow Pottery **24**

Powerscourt Gardens **17**
Russborough House **15**
Tiglin Adventure Centre **19**
Vale of Avoca **23**
Wicklow Mountains National Park **20**

183

There are many trails in the area; see "Outdoor Pursuits," below, for some of my favorite walks. For information on bus service from Dublin to Glendalough, see "Getting There," above.

Glendalough Visitor Center　A striking new visitor center at the entrance to the site provides helpful orientation, with an audiovisual presentation and exhibits on the archaeology, history, folklore, and wildlife of the area. The fee charged is just for the visitor center and its exhibits; there is no charge for exploring the Glendalough monastic site and its surroundings.

18 miles (30km) south of Dublin. ℂ **0404/45325.** 3€ ($2.70) adults, 2€ ($1.80) seniors, 1.50€ ($1.40) children and students. Mid-Oct to mid-Mar daily 9:30am–5pm; mid-Mar to May daily 9:30am–6pm; June–Aug daily 9am–6:30pm; Sept to mid-Oct daily 9:30am–6pm.

Wicklow Mountains National Park Information Center　A large area of County Wicklow has been designated as a national park, and enjoys protection from further exploitation and development. The core of the park is centered on Glendalough, and an information center is found at the base of the Upper Lake. Information is available here on hiking in the Glendalough Valley and surrounding hills, including maps and descriptions of routes. Free guided nature walks depart from the center on Tuesdays (departing 11am and returning 1:30pm) and Thursdays (departing 3pm and returning 4pm). The closest parking is at Upper Lake, where you'll pay 2€ ($1.80) per car; my advice is to walk up from the Glendalough Visitor Center, where the parking is free.

Glendalough, Co. Wicklow. ℂ **0404/45425.** Late Apr–late Aug daily 10am–6pm; Sept–Nov Sat–Sun 10am–6pm.

OTHER SIGHTS IN COUNTY WICKLOW

Avondale House and Forest Park　This house in a fertile valley between Glendalough and the Vale of Avoca is the former home of Charles Stewart Parnell (1846–91), one of Ireland's great political leaders. Built in 1779, the house is now a museum to his memory. Set in the surrounding 523-acre estate and boasting signposted nature trails alongside the Avondale River, Avondale Forest Park is considered the cradle of modern Irish forestry. The house contains a Parnell museum, including a room commemorating the American side of the Parnell family—Parnell's mother was American, and his grandfather was Admiral Charles Stewart of the USS *Constitution.* Teas and light lunches are available in the coffee shop, which offers homemade breads and pastries.

Rathdrum, Co. Wicklow. ℂ/fax **0404/46111.** www.coillte.ie. Admission Forest Park 3.80€ ($3.45) per car; house 4.15€ ($3.75) adults, 3.80€ ($3.45) seniors and students, 11€ ($10) family ticket (2 adults and 2 children), 1.90€ ($1.75) additional children under 16. Mar–Oct daily 11am–6pm; Nov–Feb by appointment only. Last admission 1 hr before closing. Closed Christmas.

Huntington Castle *(Finds*　Located at the confluence of the rivers Derry and Slaney, this castle was of great strategic importance from the time it was built in the early 17th century to the early 20th century, when it was briefly used as a headquarters by the IRA. Huntington is unlike most castles you might visit in that it has a lived-in feel, a magnificent decrepitude evoked by the sometimes overwhelming assortment of detritus left by previous generations—an assortment in which some real treasures lurk. The house has many stories to tell, but don't forget to visit the garden, which hides a lovely yew walk and one of the first hydroelectric facilities in Ireland among its waist-high weeds. The castle's

The Irish Round Tower

Just as the stark geometry of the pyramids instantly evoke Egypt, the round tower evokes Ireland. Its distinct, primal form—a tall cylinder capped with a conical roof—has been used as an Irish icon since its first appearance between the 9th and 12th centuries. Round towers marked the sites of Celtic Christian monasteries throughout Ireland, and 73 still exist today.

What were these solitary buildings? First and foremost, they were bell towers. At the same time, the towers marked the end of a journey for pilgrims: They could be seen and heard from great distances and were orientation points as well as destinations.

But round towers were not only devotional. In some towers, the door is positioned 6½ to 13 feet (2m–4m) above the ground. At one time, historians thought that the monks themselves would escape marauding Vikings by climbing up into the tower with a ladder and then pulling it up behind them. These days, however, it is thought that the elevated door served to protect the monks' treasures—especially illuminated manuscripts, similar to the Book of Kells—from dampness, vermin, and theft. Windows appear sporadically in the towers and mark the position of the treasuries, where works of ornamental metal would hang suspended in leather sacks.

Today, most round towers are completely hollow, so visitors can no longer ascend them. The five to eight wooden floors and ladders that once would have partitioned the interior have long since disintegrated. Nevertheless, many towers are situated in the most beautiful and historic parts of Ireland's landscape and are well worth visiting. Two well-known towers are at **Glendalough,** County Wicklow, and **Cashel,** County Tipperary. Other exceptional round tower sites include:

- **Inis Cealtra,** County Clare: This slightly ruined tower is located on a spectacular site within a monastic settlement on the isle of Lough Derg. See chapter 13, "The Northwest."
- **Devenish Island,** County Fermanagh: The best preserved of all the round towers, it has complete floors and ladders to the top, effectively and unusually re-creating the ancient interior. See chapter 15, "Northern Ireland."
- **Ardmore,** County Waterford: The last known tower to be constructed, Ardmore crowns a hill overlooking Ardmore Bay. See chapter 6, "The Southeast."
- **Killala and Rosserk Abbey,** County Mayo: A complete round tower stands in the middle of Killala, and its form is duplicated in a small carving in Rosserk Abbey. See chapter 10, "The West."

A thorough inventory and study, *The Irish Round Tower: Origins and Architecture Explored* (Cork: Collins Press, 1999) by Brian Lalor, is well worth consulting.

basement is now home to a temple of the Fellowship of Isis, a religion founded here in 1976.

Clonegal, Co. Carlow (off N80, 4 miles/6.5km from Bunclody). ℂ **054/77552.** Fax 054/77160. Admission 1.90€ ($1.75) adults, 3.80€ ($3.45) children. June–Aug daily 2–6pm; Sept Sun 2–6pm; other times by appointment.

Kilruddery House and Gardens

Both this grand house and its garden have seen better times, but visitors will still find many intriguing details and beautiful scenes. Among the most interesting features are two fascinating clocks designed by the 13th earl of Meath: One is powered by a continual jet of water, and the other is constructed out of various household implements, including a bicycle chain, a bed warmer, and the lid of a cooking pot. The plasterwork on the domed ceiling of the stair hall is said to have been designed by Inigo Jones; whether or not this is true, the plasterwork is quite impressive. The two long reflecting pools south of the house, which survive from the 17th century, are separated from the parkland beyond by a *ha-ha,* a ditch that would have created a barrier between fields and gardens while remaining invisible from the house. The beech hedge pond, a later addition, is one of the most beautiful places here, with views to the interior fountain revealed from various points within the gardens.

Off the main Dublin-Wicklow Rd. (N11), Bray, Co. Wicklow. ℂ **01/286-2777.** Admission house and garden 5.70€ ($5.20) adults, 3.80€ ($3.45) seniors and students, 1.25€ ($1.15) children under 12; garden only 3.80€ ($3.45) adults, 2.55€ ($2.30) seniors and students, 0.65€ (60¢) children under 12. House May–June and Sept daily 1–5pm; gardens Apr–Sept daily 1–5pm. Other times by appointment.

Mount Usher Gardens

Encompassing 20 acres along the River Vartry, this sylvan site—once home to an ancient lake and more recently laid out in the "Robinsonian" style—offers more than 5,000 tree and plant species from all parts of the world. You'll find spindle trees from China, North American swamp cypress, Burmese juniper trees, fiery rhododendrons, fragrant eucalyptus trees, giant Tibetan lilies, and snowy camellias. These gardens have an almost untended feel to them, without pretense yet with considerable charm. A spacious tearoom overlooks the river and gardens. The courtyard at the entrance to the gardens contains an interesting assortment of shops, open year-round. A tearoom overlooking the gardens serves light meals (soup and sandwiches) that cost under 13€ ($12).

On the main Dublin-Wicklow Rd. (N11), Ashford, Co. Wicklow. ℂ **0404/40205** or 0404/40116. www.mount usher-gardens.com. Admission 4.45€ ($4.05) adults, 3.20€ ($2.90) seniors, students, and children ages 5–12. Guided tours may be booked in advance for 25€ ($23). Mid-Mar to Oct daily 10:30am–6pm.

Powerscourt Estate & Gardens ✪

On a 1,000-acre estate less than 12 miles (19km) south of Dublin city sits one of the finest gardens in Ireland, designed and laid out by Daniel Robertson between 1745 and 1767. It's filled with splendid Greek- and Italian-inspired statuary, decorative ironwork, a petrified-moss grotto, lovely herbaceous borders, a Japanese garden, a circular pond and fountain with statues of winged horses, and the occasional herd of deer. Stories have it that Robertson, afflicted with gout, was pushed around the grounds in a wheelbarrow to oversee the work. This service is no longer offered, but I doubt you'll mind walking. An 18th-century manor house designed by Richard Cassels, the architect of nearby Russborough House and the man credited with the design of Dublin's Parliament House, stood proudly on the site until it was gutted by fire in 1974. The house has been structurally restored and now hosts a variety of high-quality gift shops and an exhibit, complete with video presentation, on the history of Powerscourt. The additional entrance fee to "the house" is actually for entrance to this exhibit, primarily the video, which is mediocre.

The Powerscourt cafeteria is pleasant and serves delicious lunches at a reasonable price and with a view not to be believed. The adjacent garden center is staffed with highly knowledgeable green thumbs who can answer all the questions you've collected while exploring the magnificent gardens. Meanwhile, the children's park and playscapes are close by if you have the youngsters along. In my opinion, the waterfall is too little too far away and a little too expensive. (After all, if you want to see water pouring down in Ireland, most days you can just look up.) For those arriving on public transport from Dublin, you can arrange to be picked up at the Bray DART station (1.60€/$1.45 one-way) or in Enniskerry (1.25€/$1.15 one-way) by Alpine Coaches (✆ 01/286-2547).

Off the main Dublin-Wicklow Rd. (N11), Enniskerry, Co. Wicklow. ✆ **01/204-6000.** Fax 01/204-6900. www.powerscourt.ie. Admission to Gardens 5.10€ ($4.60) adults, 4.45€ ($4.05) students, 2.55€ ($2.30) children ages 5–16, free for children under 5; exhibition additional 1.90€ ($1.75) adults, 1.65€ ($1.50) students, 1.25€ ($1.15) children ages 5–16, free for children under 5; waterfall additional 2.55€ ($2.30) adults, 1.90€ ($1.75) students, 1.25€ ($1.15) children ages 5–16, free for children under 5. AE, MC, V. Gardens and exhibition Mar–Oct daily 9:30am–5:30pm, Nov–Feb 9:30am–dusk; waterfall summer daily 9:30am–7pm, winter 10:30am–dusk. Closed 2 weeks prior to Christmas.

Russsborough House   Ensconced in this 18th-century Palladian house is the Beit Art Collection, with paintings by Vernet, Guardi, Bellotto, Gainsborough, Rubens, and Reynolds. Richard Cassels was one of the most prominent architects in Georgian Ireland, and designed many of the most remarkable buildings of this period; in addition to Russborough House he was also responsible for the Parliament House in Dublin and Powerscourt House in nearby Enniskerry. Russborough is furnished with European pieces and decorated with bronzes, tapestries, and some fine Francini plasterwork. The maze and rhododendron garden may be viewed by prior appointment. Facilities include a restaurant, shop, and children's playground.

25 miles (40km) southwest of Dublin, off N81, Blessington, Co. Wicklow. ✆ **045/865239.** Admission to main rooms 5.10€ ($4.60) adults, 3.80€ ($3.45) seniors and students, 2.60€ ($2.40) children under 12. Apr and Oct Sun 10:30am–5:30pm or by appointment; June–Aug daily 10:30am–5:30pm; May and Sept Mon–Sat 10:30am–2:30pm, Sun 10:30am–5:30pm.

Vale of Avoca   This peaceful riverbank was immortalized in the writings of 19th-century poet Thomas Moore. It's here, at the "Meeting of the Waters," that the Avonmore and Avonbeg rivers join to form the Avoca River. It's said that the poet sat under "Tom Moore's Tree," looking for inspiration, and penned the lines "There is not in the wide world a valley so sweet, / as the vale in whose bosom the bright waters meet . . ." The tree is a sorry sight now, as it's been picked almost bare by souvenir hunters, but the place is worth a visit.

Rte. 755, Avoca, Co. Wicklow. Free admission.

OUTDOOR PURSUITS

ADVENTURE CENTRE   Less than an hour's drive from Dublin center (it's signposted on N81), the **Blessington Adventure Centre,** Blessington, County Wicklow (✆ **045/865024**), offers a range of outdoor activity options for both adults and children. Canoeing, kayaking, sailing, and windsurfing lessons and rentals are available on the Blessington lakes; on land, there's archery, orienteering, tennis, pony trekking, and riding lessons for all levels. Some representative prices per hour for adults are 6.90€ ($7.62) for canoeing and kayaking, 13€ ($12) for sailing and windsurfing, and 15€ ($14) for pony trekking. Full- and half-day multi-activity prices are also available.

CANOEING & KAYAKING The **National Mountain & Whitewater Centre,** The Devil's Glen Forest, Ashford, County Wicklow (℅ **0404/40169;** www.tiglin.com), is an innovative state-funded facility that offers weekend courses in whitewater kayaking, mountaineering, and rock climbing in locations around Ireland. Basic equipment is provided; fees for 1- to 5-day courses range from 51€ to 340€, ($46–$310). The center attracts a young clientele, and lodging is in hostels unless you arrange otherwise.

FISHING During brown trout season (Mar 15–Sept 30), you'll find lots of angling opportunities on the Aughrim River (contact Dudley Byrne in Woodenbridge, ℅ **0402/36161**) and on the Avonmore River (contact Peter Driver in Rathdrum, ℅ **0404/46304**). The Dargle River flows from Enniskerry to the sea at Bray and offers great sea trout fishing in season from February 1 to October 12 (contact Hugh Duff in Enniskerry, ℅ **01/286-8652**). Unfortunately, the Avoca River south of the Meeting of the Waters is polluted due to old copper mines and unsuitable for fishing. Shore angling is hugely popular from beaches along the coast; contact the **Irish Federation of Sea Anglers** (℅ **01/280-6873**) for information on how to obtain permits. Note that there are currently no opportunities in Wicklow to hire boats or fishing equipment.

GOLF County Wicklow's verdant hills and dales offer numerous opportunities for golfing. Among the 18-hole courses welcoming visitors are the new **Rathsallagh Golf Club,** an 18-hole, par-72 championship course at Dunlavin, County Wicklow (℅ **045/403112**), with greens fees of 55€ ($50) Monday through Thursday, and 70€ ($63) Fridays and weekends; the seaside **European Club,** Brittas Bay, Co. Wicklow (℅ **0404/47415**), a championship links with greens fees of 102€ ($92) any day year-round; the parkland **Glenmalure Golf Club,** Greenane, Rathdrumm, County Wicklow (℅ **0404/46679**), with greens fees from 19€ ($17) weekdays and 23€ ($21) weekends; and the **Arklow Golf Club** (℅ **0402/32492**), a seaside par-68 course with year-round greens fees of 38€ ($35).

HORSEBACK RIDING With its valleys and glens and its secluded paths and nature trails, County Wicklow is perfect for horseback riding. More than a dozen stables and equestrian centers offer horses for hire and instructional programs. Rates for horse hire average 15€ to 25€ ($14–$23) per hour. Among the leading venues are **Broomfield Riding School,** Broomfield, Tinahely, County Wicklow (℅ **0402/38117**); **Calliaghstown Riding Centre,** Rathcoole, County Dublin (℅ **01/458-9236;** calliagh@iol.ie); and **Brennanstown Riding School,** Hollybrook, Kilmacanogue, County Wicklow (℅ **01/286-3778;** janeken@gofree.indigo.ie). At the **Paulbeg Riding School,** Shillelagh, County Wicklow (℅ **055/29100**), experienced riders can explore the beautiful surrounding hills, and beginners can partake of expert instruction from Sally Duffy, a friendly woman who gives an enthusiastic introduction to the sport.

Devil's Glen Holiday and Equestrian Village, Ashford, County Wicklow (℅ **0404/40637;** www.devilsglen.ie), situated at the edge of Devil's Glen, offers a full range of equestrian opportunities, from lessons to jumping to trekking to cross-country. Accommodation is offered in spotless, spacious, fully equipped self-catering two-bedroom apartments, two-bedroom bungalows, and three-bedroom cottages. This makes a great base from which to explore the Wicklow

Mountains and coastline, whether or not you ever climb into a saddle. Weekly rates run from 330€ to 394€ ($299–$357), depending on season and size of unit. Weekend (Fri–Sun) and mid-week (Mon–Thurs) rates are also available. Most lessons and rides cost 19€ ($17) per hour for adults and 15€ ($14) per hour for children under 12. Both the equestrian center and the self-catering village are open year-round.

WALKING   The **Wicklow Way** is a signposted walking path that follows forest trails, sheep paths, and country roads from the hills south of Dublin to the trail's terminus in Clonegal. To walk the whole of the Way takes about 5 to 7 days, with overnight stops at B&Bs and hostels along the route. Most people choose to walk sections as day trips, and for this reason I've highlighted some of my favorites below.

Information and maps can be obtained at the **Wicklow National Park** center in Glendalough (*(C)* **0404/45425**), at any local tourist office, or on the website **www.irishwaymarkedways.ie/TheWicklowWayE8.htm**. Information on less strenuous walks can be found in the *Wicklow Trail Sheets,* which provide a map and route description for several short walks and are available at tourist offices. The Ballyknocken House B&B (see "Walking" in chapter 3, "Ireland Outdoors") also publishes a list of walks beginning and ending at the house for their guests.

- The steep, satisfying walk up **Lugnaquilla,** which takes about 6 hours in total, passes through boggy sheep fields and alongside waterfalls on its way to the barren ridge of Lugnaquilla's peak. Here, a worn bronze plaque provides an index to a stunning panorama of surrounding mountain ranges. When the mist lifts, you can see the Blackstairs in Wexford and Brandon Hill in County Kilkenny. Lugnaquilla is the highest peak in the Wicklow mountains and its ascent is well worth the effort. The trail, however, is not an easy one: It is unmarked; its upper portion skirts the boundary of an artillery range; and there are two sections of precipitous cliffs, though they're easily avoided with a good map. The best map for the walk is the 1:50,000 ordnance survey map for the area. The walk starts in a gravel parking lot at the head of the Glenmalure valley. To get there, follow R755 for 1.2 miles (2km) outside of Laragh, going upwards towards Glenmalure. After you've driven about 4.5 miles (7km) to Drumgoff, turn right and continue 3 miles (5km) up the road to the lot. The walk begins by heading up an old forestry road and loops over the ridge of Lugnaquilla to descend through a farm; it concludes with a mile walk along the same road that you drove in on. The walk is described in greater detail in Joss Lynam's *Best Irish Walks* (see p. 92), which also outlines alternative routes.
- You won't want to miss the **southern section of the Wicklow Way** *★★*, through Tinahely, Shillelagh, and Clonegal. Although not as rugged as the terrain in central Wicklow, the hills here are voluptuously round, with delightful woods and glens hidden in their folds. Through much of this section, the path follows country roads that have been well chosen for their lack of traffic.
- On summer weekends, and some weekdays, too, the foreign tourist crowd at **Glendalough** is joined by throngs of Dubliners out for a walk in the country; the result can be a very tight squeeze. So, once you've seen the monastic sites, which truly aren't to be missed, I strongly recommend leaving the crowds behind and taking to the high country. For more

information on walks in the Glendalough area, stop by the Wicklow Mountains National Park information center (see above).

- One walk that doesn't require much time or effort is the stroll along the shores of the Upper Lake to the **Mining Village,** located at the far end of the lake. There are two paths that will take you there: a small rocky path that follows the water's edge and a wide forest road that parallels the lakeshore about 30 feet (9m) up the hillside. Once you reach the pile of tailings and the ruins of the mine buildings, continue past to the zigzag trail that ascends alongside the Glenealo River; the cascades here can be thunderous after a good rain. At the top of the cascades are some more mine buildings and a great view back toward the monastic buildings. From here, the intrepid walker can continue north to the summit of Camaderry Mountain, or south to Lugduff. Ask at the National Forest Information Center for details on these walks, which require a good map and a compass.

- One of my favorite walks, which remains on forest paths for its entirety, is the **circuit of Lugduff Valley** ⟨＊⟩. Start at the Wicklow Mountains National Park information center and follow the Wicklow Way (signposted with the symbol of a yellow walking man) uphill past the Poulanass Waterfall, a spectacular torrent of falls after a good rain. Just after the path levels off, beyond the top of the falls, there's a four-way intersection; the Wicklow Way turns left, and you want to turn right. From here, you continue on a wide logging road, the scenery marred in places by clear-cutting of the forests on either side. You will pass two major forks, and will want to veer right at each of these; numerous minor paths branch off, but these can be ignored. The second fork is just past a lovely series of moss-covered ledges at the head of the valley, known as Prizen Rock. Shortly after this second fork, you reach the Wicklow Way, here a wide gravel road; turn left. From here back to the starting point the views are fabulous: Lugduff, Camaderry and its reservoir, the upper lake, and the monastic buildings all come into view at one time or another. Total distance is 6 miles (9.5km); allow yourself 3 hours.

- One great walk that's a favorite with Dubliners out for a weekend stroll is **Great Sugarloaf,** that massive cone of granite on the north Wicklow skyline. The most popular route begins at Calary parking lot on the mountain's southern flank: This path is the most direct, but will be mobbed with people on any sunny summer weekend. If you prefer to avoid the crowds, ask in Kilmacanoge about a route that begins in the town; this path is longer and harder to find, but worth the effort if you're looking for a quiet stroll rather than a social event. To get to the parking lot, take N11 to Kilmacanoge, a small town 2 miles (3km) south of Bray. Drive straight through the town, and after 1mile (2km) turn left at a fork in the road. After another 2.5miles (4km), turn left on a small side road; continue 0.4 miles (0.5km) on this road, and the parking lot will be on your left, surrounded by a caravan settlement. The trail to the summit is well worn, so there's no question of getting lost; give yourself 2 hours for a leisurely walk to the summit and back. The view on a clear day takes in Dublin Bay, the Wicklow and Wexford coast, and the Wicklow and Blackstairs mountains.

SHOPPING

Avoca Handweavers ⟨*Finds*⟩ Be sure to save some time to stop by the little town of Avoca, not far from the junction of the Avonmore and Avonbeg Rivers, where you'll find the oldest hand-weaving mill in Ireland. Second- and third-generation weavers staff the mill, which actually sits across a little bridge from the sales shop. The patterns and weaves from this mill are marketed all over the world, and in the shop you'll find marvelous buys in bedspreads, cloaks, scarves, and a wide variety of other items, many fashioned by home workers from all over the country. A second outlet/shop is on the main N11 road at Kilmacanogue, Bray, County Wicklow (© **01/286-7466**). Avoca, Co. Wicklow. © **0402/35105.** Weaving shed open daily May–Oct 9am–4:30pm.

Bergin Clarke Studio   Stop into this little workshop and see Brian Clarke hand-fashioning silver jewelry and giftware or Yvonne Bergin knitting stylish and colorful apparel using yarns from County Wicklow. The Old Schoolhouse, Ballinaclash, Rathdrum, Co. Wicklow. © **0404/46385.**

Fisher's of Newtownmountkennedy   This shop, located in a converted schoolhouse, stocks a wide array of men's and women's sporting clothes—quilted jackets, raincoats, footwear, blazers, and accessories. There's also a new tearoom, Fisher's Buttery. The Old Schoolhouse, Newtownmountkennedy, Co. Wicklow. © **01/281-9404.** Fax 01/281-0632. www.fishers.ie.

Noritake Arklow Pottery   Beautifully situated overlooking the sea, Arklow is a seaside resort town, a fishing village, and home to these makers of fine earthenware, porcelain and bone-china tableware, tea sets, dinner sets, combination sets, and giftware. The designs are both modern and traditional. The retail shop attached to the factory carries a great selection of shapes and patterns. S. Quay, Arklow. © **0402/32401.** Call to book a guided factory tour mid-June to Aug to watch the craftspeople at their trade.

ACCOMMODATIONS YOU CAN AFFORD

Abhainn Mor House   This attractive Georgian-style house on the Rathdrum-Avoca road is run by Mr. Gerry Fulham and is convenient to Glendalough and a forest park. There is a garden for guests' use.

Corballis, Rathdrum, Co. Wicklow. © **0404/46330.** Fax 0404/43150. http://homepage.eircom.net/~wicklowbandb/. 6 units. 36€ ($32) single; 53€ ($48) double. 33% reduction for children under 10 sharing with an adult. Rates include full breakfast. MC, V. Open year-round Private parking. *In room:* Tea/coffeemaker.

Ashdene Country Home   This modern, tastefully appointed house sits in a beautiful setting near the Avoca Handweavers, not far from Glendalough. Mrs. Jackie Burns has elicited many letters of praise from readers—and won several well-deserved awards—for her friendly and thoughtful manner with guests. The rooms are attractive as well as comfortable, and there's even a grass tennis court. All bedrooms are nonsmoking.

Knockanree Lower, Avoca, Co. Wicklow. ©/fax **0402/35327.** http://homepage.eircom.net/~ashdene/. 5 units, 4 with bathroom (shower only). 30€ ($28) single; 51€ ($46) double. 25% reduction for children under 12 sharing with an adult. Reduction for 3 nights or more. Rates include full breakfast. MC, V. Free parking. Closed Nov–Easter. **Amenities:** Lounge; tennis court.

Escombe   Mrs. Maura Byrne is the charming hostess of this modern bungalow overlooking Blessington lakes (ask for directions when booking). Dinner is available by prior arrangement. The six bedrooms all have sinks, and all are nonsmoking.

Lockstown, Valleymount, Blessington, Co. Wicklow. © **045/867157.** Fax 045/867450. escombe@indigo.ie. 6 units, all with bathroom (shower only). 61€ ($57) double. Rates include full breakfast. MC, V. *In room:* TV, tea/coffeemaker.

Glendalough Youth Hostel The Glendalough Hostel received a major face-lift a few years ago—you'll find the rustic old lodge which once offered spartan lodgings embedded in a vast addition, still recognizable but definitely transformed. It's still in a fabulous location, though, just a 5-minute walk from either the monastic site or Lower Lake. Rooms are spacious enough, with large windows and standard bunk beds; the small bathrooms each have a single shower and toilet. Facilities include a game room, self-service laundry, bicycle rental, and a cafe offering cheap, decent, reliably filling meals at breakfast and dinner. The hostel desk is staffed 8am to 11pm, and there's 24-hour access to the hostel for guests through a secure back entrance. The renovation is undoubtedly an improvement over the former hostel in terms of comfort and facilities, but some of the character has been lost. The entire place is nonsmoking.

Glendalough, Co. Wicklow. © **0404/45342.** Fax 0404/45690. anoige@iol.ie. 26 units, all with bathroom (shower only): 2 8-bed units, 8 6-bed units, 14 4-bed units, 2 2-bed units. 15€ ($14) per person sharing a dorm (4–8 beds); 43€ ($39) double; 58€ ($53) triple. MC, V. On the Upper Lake road. **Amenities:** Restaurant; bicycle rental; game room; coin-operated laundry.

The Old Rectory Country House Linda and Paul Saunders welcome guests to their lovely 1870s Greek Revival–style rectory with a complimentary coffee tray with chocolates, tourist information, fresh flowers, and a welcome card. Set in landscaped grounds and 1 mile off N11 on the Dublin side of Wicklow town, the Old Rectory features Victorian wood paneling, high ceilings, log fires in marble fireplaces, and individually decorated guest rooms, most with king-size beds. Your full breakfast can be of the Irish, Scottish, or Swiss variety, and is accompanied by the *Irish Times*—you can even have breakfast served in bed if you really feel like pampering yourself. Dublin is only an hour's drive away, and County Wicklow's many sightseeing attractions and outdoor activities are right at hand, including horseback riding and golf.

Wicklow, Co. Wicklow. © **800/223-6510** from the U.S., or 0404/67048. Fax 0404/69181. 8 units. 125€ ($113) double. Rates include full breakfast. AE, MC, V. Private parking. Closed Jan–Feb. *In room:* TV, TEL, tea/coffeemaker, hair dryer.

Silver Sands Mrs. Lyla Doyle's lovely bungalow looks out on the Irish Sea and the Sugarloaf Mountains, with magnificent views and bracing cliff walks. There are sandy beaches, fishing, and golf nearby. Mrs. Doyle is very helpful to all her guests and extends a warm welcome to our readers. To get here from Wicklow town, take the Coast Road; the house is on the right about 500 meters from the monument. All bedrooms are nonsmoking.

Dunbar Rd., Wicklow, Co. Wicklow. © 0404/68243. lyladoyle@eircom.net. 5 units, 4 with bathroom (shower only). 51€ ($46) double without bathroom, 56€ ($51) double with bathroom. 50% reduction for children sharing with an adult. Ask about a discount for Frommer's readers. Rates include full breakfast. No credit cards. Private parking lot. *In room:* Tea/coffeemaker, hair dryer.

Slievemore *Finds* This mid–19th-century harbor house offers white-glove cleanliness, spacious comfort, and—if you book early and request a seafront room—a commanding view of Greystones Harbor, Bray Head, and the Irish Sea. Proprietor Pippins Parkinson says that "people stumble on Greystones, find it by accident." Whether you're accident-prone or not, stay here and reserve a table for dinner at Coopers, just paces away, and you won't forget the day you stumbled on Greystones.

The Harbour, Greystones, Co. Wicklow. © **01/287-4724.** 8 units. 64€ ($58) double. Rates include full Irish breakfast. No credit cards. Open year-round. Bus: 84 Signposted on N11. . *In room:* TV.

Thomond House   Mrs. Helen Gorman is the charming owner of Thomond House, which has splendid views of both the sea and the Wicklow Mountains. The house is conveniently located 30 minutes from Glendalough and 45 minutes from Dublin, and Wicklow Town is just half a mile (a km) away (St. Patrick's Road is just off the main street, about half a mile past the Catholic church). Mrs. Gorman is very knowledgeable when it comes to exploring the area. She will also meet you at the bus or train station if you call ahead. All bedrooms are nonsmoking.

St. Patrick's Rd. Upper, Wicklow, Co. Wicklow. ℂ/fax **0404/67940.** 5 units, 2 with bathroom. 32€ ($29) single; 48€ ($44) double without bathroom, 53€ ($48) double with bathroom. 20% reduction for children sharing with an adult. Rates include full breakfast. No credit cards. Private parking lot. Closed Nov–Mar.

Tudor Lodge *Value*   The whitewashed walls of Tudor Lodge are fresh and inviting, recalling the rusticity of a country cottage. Bedrooms are spacious, and each has a number of amenities, including a small desk, as well as both double and twin beds. The dining room and living room are equally hospitable; in both, large windows open to views of green meadows and the slopes of the Wicklow mountains. A generous stone terrace lies outside. Hosts Des and Liz Kennedy offer guests an appetizing array of breakfast choices and will also prepare dinner for larger groups; otherwise, the restaurants and pubs of Laragh are a short and scenic walk away. Tudor Lodge is a completely nonsmoking establishment.

Laragh, Co. Wicklow. ℂ/fax **0404/45554.** tudorlodgeireland@eircom.net. 6 units. 38€ ($35) single; 64€ ($58) double. MC, V. *In room:* TV, TEL, tea/coffeemaker, hair dryer, iron.

SELF-CATERING

Fortgranite Estate   Fortgranite is and has been for centuries a working farm in the rolling foothills of the Wicklow Mountains. Its meadows and stately trees create a sublime retreat. One by one, Fortgranite's unique stone cottages, formerly occupied by the estate's workers, are being restored and refurbished with appreciable care and charm by M. P. Dennis. Currently, three cottages are available year-round for rental periods of a week or longer. Two are gate lodges— Doyle's Lodge and Lennon's Lodge—each with one double bedroom that sleeps two and is fully equipped with all essentials; both of these are listed as Irish Heritage Buildings. The third, Stewards's cottage, sleeps four and is furnished with lovely antiques. All have open fireplaces, and each has its own grounds and garden, affording all the privacy and peace anyone deserves. Tranquility, charm, and warmth are the operative concepts at Fortgranite. Those in search of something grand and luxurious will be disappointed. Think "cottage" and "character" and you'll be delighted. Also, it's best to think "ahead," as the word is out about Fortgranite, and availability is at a premium. Golf, fishing, hill walking, horse racing and riding, and clay pigeon shooting are all to be found nearby.

Baltinglass, Co. Wicklow. ℂ **0508/81396.** Fax 0508/73510. 3 self-catering cottages. 330€–575€ ($299–$521) per week. 3 miles (5km) SE of Baltinglass on R747. *In room:* TV, kitchen.

Tynte House (B&B and Self-Catering) *Kids*   Dunlavin, despite a turbulent history, is now a drowsy one-dog, three-pub town in western Wicklow, guaranteed not to keep its guests up at night. And it's as convenient as it is peaceful, providing easy access to Kildare horse country; the gardens, lakes, and mountains of Wicklow; and the scenic boglands and hills of the midlands. Tynte House, a lovingly preserved 19th-century family farm complex in Dunlavin center, offers an attractive array of options for both overnight and longer-term guests. With the recent addition of Tynte House apartments, these options have been enhanced even further. The driving force behind all this hospitality is Mrs. Caroline Lawler, "brought up in the business" of divining visitors' needs and of surpassing their expectations.

The guest rooms are warm and comfortable, while the newly created self-catering mews houses and apartments (ranging from two to four bedrooms) are brilliantly designed and furnished with one eye on casual efficiency and the other on truly good taste. Bold, bright color schemes, light pine furniture (including some lovely, antique pine country pieces), spacious tiled baths, and bright open kitchens fully equipped with microwave, dishwasher, and washer-dryer combinations begin to describe what Mrs. Lawler has thought of. The no. 3 mews house and the open-plan apartment are my favorites, but none will disappoint. While all of the mattresses are new, some are more firm than others; so, it would be well to request an especially firm mattress if your back, like mine, looks for excuses to complain. This is a great base for families, with a safe grassy play area, a tennis court, and a game room with Ping-Pong and pool tables.

30 miles (48km) southwest of Dublin in Dunlavin Center, Co. Wicklow. © **045/401561.** Fax 045/401586. www.tyntehouse.com. 7 B&B rooms 58€ ($54) double. 4 self-catering mews holiday homes (1, 2, or 3 bedrooms) and 4 self-catering apts (1 or 2 bedrooms) 127€–457€ ($115–$414) per week, depending on size and season. Stays of less than a week may be negotiated off-season, as well as special weekend rates on request. Evening dinner 18€ ($16). AE, MC, V. *In room:* TV, TEL, kitchen (in self-catering apartment), tea/coffeemaker, microwave, dishwasher, washer/dryer.

GREAT DEALS ON DINING

Avoca Handweavers Tea Shop TRADITIONAL/VEGETARIAN   This innovative cafeteria is worth a visit for lunch, even if you're not interested in woolens. The place prepares wholesome meals that are often surprisingly imaginative for cafeteria fare. I had a delicate pea and mint soup, prepared with vegetable stock, accompanied by a deliciously hearty spinach tart. Other dishes might include sesame-glazed chicken or locally smoked Wicklow trout; the menu changes often, and the chefs give free reign to their sometimes-whimsical fancy. The teashop has a regular local clientele in addition to the busloads of visitors attracted by the woolens.

Avoca, Co. Wicklow. © **0402/35105.** Lunch 4€–8€ ($3.65–$7.25). AE, DC, MC, V. Daily all year 9:30am–5pm.

Chester Beatty's TRADITIONAL/IRISH   This cozy bar/restaurant just north of Wicklow on N11 (the main Dublin road), in what was once a wayside inn, dishes up hearty meals in the traditional Irish vein. The Irish stew is particularly good. The decor is consistent with the old-country-inn motif, featuring open fires, etched glass, and beamed ceilings. Plates come to the table heaped with huge portions, and homemade scones arrive hot and with plenty of butter. The staff is cheerful and friendly.

Ashford, Co. Wicklow. © **0404/40206.** Dinner main courses 15€–23€ ($14–$21); fixed-price 3-course dinner 30€ ($12); bar food 7.50€–13€ ($6.80–$12). MC, V. Daily 6–9:45pm in the restaurant and 5–9:45pm in the bar.

Poppies Country Cooking IRISH HOMESTYLE   Located a short walk from either bus or train and with the warm, familiar feel of a neighbor's kitchen, this is a hangout for locals who see no point in cooking for themselves. From fist-sized whole grain scones to vegetarian nut roast, the portions are generous and savory. Its menu outsizes this modest 10-table place, which overflows into a lovely flowered tea garden out back, if and when the sun appears.

Note: Waistline watchers beware! The Poppies' desserts are diet-breakers, so try not to even look unless you're prepared to fall. And for those who don't know when or how to stop, homemade jams, preserves, salad dressing, and even local artworks are sold here.

Trafalgar Rd., Greystones, Co. Wicklow. ✆ **01/287-4228.** Reservations not required. All items 2.50€–7.50€ ($2.30–$6.80). No credit cards. Mon–Sat 10am–6pm; Sun 11:30am–7pm.

PUBS

Cartoon Inn   With walls displaying the work of many famous cartoonists, this cottagelike pub claims to be Ireland's only cartoon-themed pub. Main St., Rathdrum, Co. Wicklow. ✆ **0404/46774.**

The Coach House   This Tudor-style inn, which dates back to 1790, sits in the mountains in the heart of Ireland's highest village. It's full of local memorabilia, from old photos and agricultural posters to antique jugs and plates. The exterior is adorned with lots of colorful hanging flowerpots. The place is well worth a visit, whether to learn about the area or to get some light refreshment. Main St., Roundwood, Co. Wicklow. ✆ **01/281-8157.**

The Meetings   This Tudor-style country-cottage pub stands idyllically at the "Meeting of the Waters" associated with poet Thomas Moore. An 1889 edition of Moore's book of poems is on display. Avoca, Co. Wicklow. ✆ **0402/35226.**

2 County Kildare: Ireland's Horse Country

15 to 30 miles (24 to 48km) W of Dublin

County Kildare and horse racing go hand in hand—or should we say neck and neck? This country is the home of the Curragh racetrack, where the Irish Derby is held each June, and other smaller tracks at Naas and Punchestown. It's also the heartland of Ireland's flourishing bloodstock industry. In this panorama of open grasslands and limestone-enriched soil, you'll find many of Ireland's 300 stud farms.

Kildare is also famed as the birthplace of Brigid, Ireland's second patron saint. Brigid was a bit ahead of her time as an early exponent for women's equality— she founded a co-ed monastery in Kildare in the 5th or 6th century.

GETTING THERE   **Irish Rail** (✆ **01/836-3333;** www.irishrail.ie) provides daily train service to Kildare. **Bus Eireann** (✆ **01/836-6111;** www. buseireann.ie) operates daily express bus service to Kildare.

By car, take the main Dublin–Limerick Road (N7) west of Dublin from Kildare, or the main Dublin–Galway Road (N4) to Celbridge, turning off on local road R403.

VISITOR INFORMATION   For information about County Kildare, contact the **Wicklow Tourist Office,** Wicklow Town (✆ **0404/69117**), open year-round Monday to Friday, and Saturdays during peak season. Seasonal information offices are located at Athy, County Kildare (✆ **0507/31859**), and in Kildare Town, County Kildare (✆ **045/22696**), both open June to mid-September.

SEEING THE SIGHTS

For a relaxing break from holiday rushing around, try a barge trip along the Grand Canal. Contact **Robertstown Barge Tours,** Robertstown Canal Hotel, Robertstown, County Kildare (✆ **045/870005**), for schedules between May and September.

Castletown ✸   Although a little removed from the heart of Kildare horse country, this great house, one of Ireland's architectural gems, deserves a detour. Closed for many years, the house has undergone extensive renovation; although the house was opened again to the public in 1999, the work of restoration continues. Castletown is a 1722 Palladian-style mansion designed by Italian architect Alessandro Galilei for William Connolly, then Speaker of the Irish House of Commons. The house is decorated with Georgian furniture and paintings, and is known for its long gallery laid out in the Pompeian manner and hung with Venetian chandeliers, its main hall and staircase with elaborate Italian plasterwork, and its 18th-century print room. A cafe in the basement serves teas and light meals.

R403, off main Dublin-Galway Rd., Celbridge, Co. Kildare. ℰ **01/628-8252.** Fax 01/627-1811. www. heritageireland.ie. Admission 3.80€ ($3.45) adults, 2.55€ ($2.30) seniors, 1.60€ ($1.45) children and students, 9.50€ ($8.65) family. Apr–Sept Mon–Fri 10am–6pm, Sat–Sun 1–6pm; Oct Mon–Fri 10am–5pm, Sun 1–5pm; Nov Sun 1–5pm.

The Curragh ✸✸   Often referred to as the Churchill Downs of Ireland, this is the country's best-known racetrack, majestically placed at the edge of Ireland's central plain. It's home to the Irish Derby, held each year in late June and early July. Horses race here at least one Saturday a month from March to October. The main stand has been extensively renovated, and new bars, a food hall, and a betting hall have been added.

30 miles (48km) west of Dublin on Dublin-Limerick Rd. (N7), Curragh, Co. Kildare. ℰ **045/441205.** www. urragh.ie. Admission 10€–15€ ($9–$14) for most races; 20€–45€ ($18–$41) for Derby. AE, DC, MC, V. Hours vary; first race usually 2pm. Rail links with all major towns. Dublin-Curragh round-trip "Racing by Rail" package for 20€ ($18), including courtesy coach to main entrance.

Irish National Stud & Japanese Gardens ✸   Some of Ireland's most famous horses have been bred and raised on the grounds of this government-sponsored stud farm. A prototype for other horse farms throughout Ireland, it has 288 stalls to accommodate the mares, stallions, and foals. Visitors are welcome to walk around the 958-acre grounds and see the noble steeds being exercised and groomed. A converted groom's house has exhibits on racing, steeplechasing, hunting, and show jumping, plus the skeleton of Arkle, one of Ireland's most famous horses.

The Japanese garden, which was laid out between 1906 and 1910, is considered to be among the finest in Europe. Its design symbolizes the journey of the soul from oblivion to eternity. The Japanese-style visitor center has a restaurant and craft shop. The garden of St. Fiachra, set within a natural setting of woods, wetlands, lakes, and islands, was built to celebrate the Millennium.

Off the Dublin-Limerick Rd. (N7), Tully, Kildare, Co. Kildare. ℰ **045/521617.** www.irish-national-stud.ie. Admission 8.50€ ($7.70) adults, 6.50€ ($5.90) seniors and students, 4.50€ ($4.10) children under 12, 18€ ($16) family. MC, V. Feb 12–Nov 12 daily 9am–6pm. Bus: Eireann stop; from Dublin each morning, returning each evening.

The Irish Pewtermill *(Finds*   Ireland's oldest pewter mill is a real find. It's ensconced in an ancient mill constructed in the 11th century for the nunnery of St. Moling, after whom the village of Timolin ("House of Moling") is named. Traditional Irish silver-bright pewter is cast here in 300-year-old molds by six skilled craftspeople. Casting takes place most days, usually in the morning. A wide selection of high-quality hand-cast pewter gifts, from bowls to brooches, is on display and for sale in the showroom. Prices are very reasonable. Custom-made gifts, such as tankards, engraved with family crests, may be commissioned.

An additional attraction here is a set of excellent reproductions of the principal panels from Moone High Cross, with explanatory plaques, all very helpful in further understanding and appreciating this nearby treasure. If he's about, be sure to meet Sean Cleary, a veritable font of information regarding pewter casting, local history, and all things Irish, and a formidable storyteller besides.

Timolin-Moone, Co. Kildare. ℰ/fax **0507/24164.** Free admission. Mon–Fri 9:30am–4:30pm; summer Sat–Sun 11am–4pm. Signposted off N9 in Moone.

Moone High Cross   This renowned high cross, recently restored on site, stands in the ruins of Moone Abbey, the southernmost monastic settlement established by St. Columba in the 6th century. The ruins and grounds are actually enhanced by the formula of neglect and care they currently receive—the overgrown path to the site, for instance, is lined with bright annuals. The high cross, nearly 1,200 years old, is quite magnificent, a splendid example of Celtic stone carving, containing finely crafted Celtic designs as well as numerous scenes and figures from the Bible, such as the temptation of Adam and Eve, the sacrifice of Isaac, and Daniel in the lions' den. The cross also contains a number of surprises, such as a dolphin. Don't miss this sight if you're nearby.

Moone, Co. Kildare. Open site. Signposted off N9 on southern edge of Moone village.

Newbridge Cutlery   Look closely at the silverware when you sit down to eat at one of Ireland's fine hotels or restaurants—there's a good chance it'll be made by Newbridge, which for the past 60 years has been one of Ireland's leading manufacturers of fine silverware. In the visitor center, you can see a display of silver place settings, bowls, candelabras, trays, frames, and one-of-a-kind items. A video on silver making is also shown. Silver pieces are sold here, including "sale" items.

Off Dublin-Limerick Rd. (N7), Newbridge, Co. Kildare. ℰ **045/431301.** Free admission. Mon–Sat 9am–5pm; Sun 11am–5pm.

Steam Museum   Housed in a converted church, this museum is a must for steam-engine buffs. It contains two collections: The Richard Guinness Hall has more than 20 prototypical locomotive engines dating from the 18th century, and the Power Hall has rare industrial stationary engines. The steam and garden shop stocks a variety of recent books and videos on the Irish Railway and serves as the sole outlet for National Trust Enterprises gifts, which can offer excellent values. The walled garden is of 18th-century origin and features several garden rooms extending to a delightful rose garden. Call ahead for information on when the engines will be in operation.

Off Dublin-Limerick Rd. (N7), Straffan, Co. Kildare. ℰ **01/627-3155.** www.steam-museum.ie. Museum 3.80€ ($3.45) adults, 2.60€ ($2.40) seniors, children, and students, 13€ ($12) family. Garden 3.80€ ($3.45). V. Museum Apr–May Sun 2:30–5:30pm; June–Aug Tues–Sun 2–6pm; Sept Sun 2:30–5:30pm. Walled garden June–July Tues–Sun 2–6pm; Aug Tues–Fri 2:30–5:30pm. Signposted off N7 at Kill Village.

OUTDOOR PURSUITS

GOLF   The par-70 **Kilkea Castle Hotel & Golf Club,** Castledermot, County Kildare (ℰ **0503/45555;** www.kilkeacastlehotelgolf.com), charges 38€ ($35) weekdays and 44€ ($40) weekends. At the par-72 championship course of **Curragh Golf Club,** Curragh, County Kildare (ℰ **045/441714**), greens fees are 25€ ($23) weekdays and 32€ ($29) on weekends.

HORSEBACK RIDING   Visitors who want to go horseback riding can expect to pay an average of 15€ to 25€ ($14–$23) per hour for trekking or trail riding in the Kildare countryside. To arrange a ride, contact the **Punchestown National Centre for Equestrian and Field Sports** (© **045/876800;** www. punchestown.com); the **Donacomper Riding School,** Celbridge, County Kildare (© **01/628-8221**); or the **Kill International Equestrian Centre,** Kill, County Kildare (© **045/877208**).

WALKING   One of Ireland's marked long-distance trails, the **Grand Canal Way** cuts through part of Kildare and is ideal for beginners because it is flat. The canal passes through many towns, such as Sallins, Robertstown and Edenderry, where you can find accommodations and stock up on provisions. For more information, contact the tourist office or see the **Irish Waymarked Ways** web-site at **www.irishwaymarkedways.ie/TheGrandCanalWay.htm**.

GREAT DEALS ON DINING

Manor Inn (Kids) FISH/STEAKS/PASTA/GRILLS   This pub-style eatery in the center of Naas is a convenient stop for those visiting the Curragh Race-course. Along with fish and steaks, there's a good selection of pastas, a vegetar-ian filo pastry bake, and grills. House specials range from Galway Bay Mussels to chicken cordon bleu to rack of lamb. There's also a children's menu and a lunchtime snack menu.

Main St., Naas, Co. Kildare. © **045/897471.** Lunch main courses 7.50€–14€ ($6.80–$13); dinner main courses 15€–22€ ($14–$20). AE, DC, MC, V. Daily noon–midnight.

WORTH A SPLURGE

Tonlegee House & Restaurant INTERNATIONAL   The restaurant in this lovely old country house has garnered a number of accolades. The relaxing din-ing room, with its chocolate-colored walls, chintz curtains, and soft lighting, is the perfect setting for the gourmet cuisine prepared by the owner Mark Molloy, who accumulated broad experience as a chef in London and in one of Dublin's most prestigious restaurants. The roast rack of lamb with a crépinette of vegeta-bles and a shallot sauce is particularly noteworthy, as are the escalope of salmon with mussels and tarragon sauce and the breast of Barbarie duck with a bran-dade of duck leg. Menus change regularly according to what's available. Desserts include thin apple tart with cinnamon cream, and chocolate-and-almond Mar-jolaine (a creamy blend of chocolate, cream, and almonds).

13 miles (21km) southwest of Naas on N78 in Athy, Co. Kildare. © **0507/31473.** www.tonlegeehouse.com. Reservations recommended. Dinner main courses 18€–22€ ($16–$20). AE, MC, V. Tues–Sat 7–9pm. Closed Chirstmas and New Year's.

3 County Meath: The County of Kings

30 to 50 miles (48 to 80km) N and W of Dublin

The **River Boyne** runs north of Dublin, along Ireland's east coast, surrounded by the rich and fertile countryside of Counties Meath and Louth. This mean-dering body of water has been at the center of Irish history.

The banks of the Boyne are lined with reminders from almost every phase of Ireland's past, from the prehistoric passage tombs of Newgrange to the storied Hill of Tara, seat of the High Kings, to early Christian sites. This land was also the setting for the infamous **Battle of the Boyne,** where, on July 1, 1690 (the 12th of July by modern calendars), King William III defeated the exiled King James II for the crown of England.

The southern portion of the Boyne belongs to **County Meath.** This area consists almost entirely of a rich limestone plain, with verdant pasturelands and occasional low hills. Once a separate province that included neighboring County Westmeath, Meath was usually referred to as the Royal County Meath, because it was ruled by the kings of pagan and early Christian Ireland, from the Hill of Tara near Navan.

Though the chief town of County Meath is Navan, nearby **Kells** is better known to the traveler because of its association with the famous Book of Kells, the illuminated gospel manuscript on display at Trinity College in Dublin. The town of Kells, known as *Ceanannus Mor* in Gaelic (meaning "Great Residence"), was originally the site of an important 6th-century monastic settlement founded by St. Colmcille and occupied for a time by monks driven from Iona in the 9th century by the Vikings. These monks may have brought with them at least an incomplete Book of Kells. The book was stolen in 1007, only to be recovered months later from a bog. The monastery was dissolved in 1551, and today only ruins and a number of crosses survive.

No one visiting Ireland should pass up an opportunity to visit **Newgrange,** one of the country's most remarkable historic monuments. The mysterious decorations and meticulous construction speak a language we can no longer comprehend, referring to rituals long since abandoned. Despite this obscurity, I think most visitors will find that the stones do speak, that they appeal to our imaginations at a very basic level. The same can be said of **Loughcrew,** where one has to do without the convenience of extensive restoration. At both sites, one is left in wonder at the abilities of people who were able to create such articulate monuments using only cold stone.

GETTING THERE   **Irish Rail** (© 01/836-6222; www.irishrail.ie) provides daily train service between Dublin and Drogheda.

Bus Eireann (© 01/836-6111) operates daily express bus service to Slane and Navan in County Meath. Both Bus Eireann and **Gray Line Tours** (© 01/661-9666) offer seasonal sightseeing tours to Newgrange and/or the Boyne Valley.

If you're traveling by car, take N1 north from Dublin City to Drogheda and then N51 west to Boyne Valley; N2 northwest to Slane and east on N51 to Boyne Valley; or N3 northwest via Hill of Tara to Navan, and then east on N51 to Boyne Valley.

VISITOR INFORMATION   For year-round information about Counties Meath and Louth, contact the **Dundalk Tourist Office,** Jocelyn Street, County Louth (© 042/933-5484). A seasonal information office is also open at Newgrange (© 041/982-4274) from Easter to October.

SEEING THE SIGHTS

Butterstream Gardens *Finds*   Butterstream is an idyllic orchestration of garden rooms, each holding the delights of spring and summer. Garden designer Jim Reynolds and his sole assistant meld the brilliant reds and yellow of a garden of hot colors with the gentle green foliage flanking a pond and the pale scepter of a white garden. Architectural notes resound throughout the garden— the vegetation is sometimes marked by a Doric folly or reshaped into topiary pyramids.

Trim, Co. Meath. © 046/36017. Admission 5.10€ ($4.60) adults, 2.60€ ($2.40) students and children. Apr–Sep daily 11am–6pm.

Hill of Tara ✦ This glorious hill is best remembered as the royal seat of the high kings in the early centuries after Christ. Every 3 years a *feis* (a banquet reaching the proportions of a great national assembly) was held. It's said that more than 1,000 people—princes, poets, athletes, priests, druids, musicians, and jesters—celebrated for a week in a single immense hall. A *feis* wasn't all fun and games, though: Laws were passed, tribal disputes settled, and matters of peace and defense decided.

The last *feis* was held in A.D. 560, and thereafter Tara went into a decline associated with the rise of Christianity. If you rally to Tara's halls today, you won't see any turrets or towers, nor moats and crown jewels; in fact, you won't even see any halls. All that remain of Tara's former glories are grassy mounds and some ancient pillar stones—the wooden halls rotted long ago, so you'll have to rely on your imagination to fill in the glories. Nevertheless, this is still a magnificent spot, with the hill rising 300 feet (91m) above the surrounding countryside, and the views surely as awesome as they were 1,500 years ago.

A visitor center, with exhibits and a stirring audiovisual presentation, is in the old church beside the entrance to the archaeological area. There's no picnicking, but there is a coffee shop/tearoom.

6 miles (9.5km) south of Navan, off N3. ℂ 046/25903. www.heritageireland.ie. 1.90€ ($1.75) adults, 1.25€ ($1.15) seniors, .75€ (70¢) students and children, 5.10€ ($4.60) family. May to mid-June and mid-Sept to Oct daily 10am–5pm; mid-June to mid-Sept daily 9:30am–6:30pm. Bus: 20, 40, or 43 from Dublin or Navan.

Loughcrew *Finds* The 30 passage tombs of Loughcrew, also known as *Slieve na Calliaghe* or "the hill of the witch," crown three hilltops in western Meath. The views of the plains of Meath and of the lakelands of Cavan are spectacular on a clear day. Two of the cairns—ornamented with Neolithic carvings—can be entered with a key. Guided tours of the eastern cairn are offered from mid-June to mid-September, and the key is available at the office for the western tomb (the more interesting of the two). A 32€ ($30) deposit is required for the key. From October to May, the keys to both cairns can be picked up from Mrs. Basil Balfe (ℂ 049/41256), whose home is the first house on your right after turning into the Loughcrew drive.

Outside Oldcastle, Co. Meath. ℂ 049/854-2009. www.heritageireland.ie. Admission 1.25€ ($1.15) adults, .90€ (80¢) seniors, .50€ (45¢) children and students, 3.80€ ($3.45) family. Mid-June to mid-Sept daily 10am–6pm. Other times: key is available (see above). From N3, take R195 through Oldcastle toward Mullingar, and look for a signposted left turn 1½ miles (2.5km) out of Oldcastle. The next left turn into Loughcrew is also signposted.

Newgrange, Knowth and Brugh na Boinne Visitor Centre ✦✦✦ The recently completed Brugh na Boinne Visitor Centre is now the required starting point for all visits to Newgrange and Knowth, both of which can only be visited by guided tour. The center has various exhibits describing the monuments of the Boyne Valley, but the real interest lies, of course, in the monuments themselves. Known in Irish as *Brugh na Boinne* (the Palace of the Boyne), Newgrange is Ireland's best-known prehistoric monument and one of the archaeological wonders of western Europe. It was built as a burial mound more than 5,000 years ago—long before the Great Pyramids and Stonehenge—and today sits atop a hill near the Boyne. The massive and impressive mound—36 feet (11m) tall and approximately 260 feet (79m) in diameter—consists of 200,000 tons of stone, a 6-ton capstone, and other stones weighing up to 16 tons each, many of which were hauled from as far away as County Wicklow and the Mountains of Mourne. Carved into the stones are myriad spirals, diamonds, and concentric circles.

Inside, a passage, 60 feet (18.3m) long, leads to a central burial chamber with a 19-foot (5.75m) ceiling. Curiosity about Newgrange reaches a peak each winter solstice, when, at 8:58am, as the sun rises to the southeast, sunlight pierces the inner chamber with an orange-toned glow for about 17 minutes. This occurrence is so remarkable that, as of this writing, the waiting list for viewing extends through the year 2005.

Still under excavation, the great mound at Knowth is believed to have been a burial site for the high kings of Ireland. Archaeological evidence points to occupation from 3000 B.C. to A.D. 1200. Knowth is more complex than Newgrange, with two passage tombs surrounded by another 17 smaller satellite tombs. The site also has the greatest collection of passage tomb art ever uncovered in Western Europe, although there is no access to the interior of the tombs at this time.

Note: Because of the great numbers of visitors to Newgrange, especially in the summer, delays are to be expected, and access is not guaranteed. Also, keep in mind that the last tour departs 1½ hours before the center's closing time.

Off N51, Slane, Co. Meath. ✆ 041/988-0300. Admission to Newgrange and Brugh na Boinne Centre 5.10€ ($4.60) adults, 3.80€ ($3.45) seniors, 2.55€ ($2.30) students and children over 6, 13€ ($12) family. Admission to Knowth and Brugh na Boinne Centre 3.80€ ($3.45) adults, 2.55€ ($2.30) seniors, 1.60€ ($1.45) students and children over 6, 9.55€ ($8.65) family. Combination tickets for Newgrange, Knowth, and the visitor center are also available. MC, V. Open daily Nov–Feb 9:30am–5pm; Mar–Apr 9:30am–5:30pm; May 9am–6:30pm; June to mid-Sept 9am–7pm; mid- to end Sept 9am–6:30pm; Oct 9:30am–5:30pm. Knowth is closed to visitors Nov–Apr.

Newgrange Farm *Kids*   Farmer William Redhouse and his family invite visitors on a 1½-hour tour of their farm, which grows wheat, oats, barley, oil seed rape, corn, and linseed (flax). You can throw feed to the ducks, groom a calf, or bottle-feed the baby lambs or kid goats. Children can hold a newborn chick, pet a pony, or play with the pigs. In the aviaries are pheasants and rare birds. In the fields romp horses, donkeys, and rare Jacob sheep. Demonstrations of sheepdog working, threshing, and horse shoeing are given as well. The Redhouses also spin and dye their own wool and have put together an exhibit of the fibers produced and the natural dyes used to color them. At the herb garden, visitors receive a lesson on picking edible plants and herbs. Many of the farm buildings date back to the 17th century. You'll find a coffee shop (see "Great Deals on Dining," below) and indoor and outdoor picnic areas on the grounds.

The high point of the week occurs at roughly 3pm every Sunday, when the sheep take to the track with Teddy Bear jockeys for the weekly Derby. This is especially engaging for children, who are given "part-owner" badges for the sheep of their choice so that they can shout their own ball of wool to victory. There is also a new Go-Karting and toy tractor play area for children.

2 miles (3km) east of Slane, signposted off N51 and directly west of Newgrange, Co. Meath. ✆ 041/982-4119. www.newgrangefarm.com. Admission 4.50€ ($4.10), 14€ ($13) family (2 adults and 2 children). Easter–Aug daily 10am–5pm.

St Colmcille's House   St. Colmcille's Oratory, whose oldest parts date from the 9th century, sits in ancient glory amidst a row of modern terraced housing. The carefully placed stones of its curving roof and unusual two-story structure are enigmatic and prompt an immediate trip down the street for the key to unlock at least some of its secrets. Once an ancient church holding relics of St. Colmcille, the first floor room still contains the traces of an ancient fireplace and entryway. But this isn't all: A narrow metal stair ascends 15 feet (4.5m) to a dark vault just under the roof. The small two-chambered space has both a structural and mythical dimension. It is thought to help reinforce the stone arch of the oratory roof and—though this is more conjectural—is also said to be the place where the Book of Kells was completed.

Church Lane, Kells, Co. Meath. Free admission. About 200 yds NW of St Columba's Church. Ask for key from caretaker Mrs. B. Carpenter on Church Lane.

ACCOMMODATIONS YOU CAN AFFORD

Lennoxbrook Country House ⊛ A dense arch of ancient rhododendron marks the entry to Lennoxbrook, the Mullan family home for five generations. Pauline Mullan and her three daughters are warm and informative hosts to those lucky enough to pull into the driveway. Tea is offered in the family's own kitchen or in the cozy sitting room. The house itself has been maintained and restored with thought and care. Guest rooms are uncluttered and beautifully furnished— antique chairs are positioned beside bay windows, and high old-fashioned beds have firm, new mattresses. The bathrooms within guest rooms have been recently redone—they're bright, pine paneled, and quite large. For those who prefer character over convenience, the rooms without their own bathrooms are particularly charming, and one of the two common bathrooms holds an enormous, intriguing old bathtub. The Mullans are refreshingly willing to go the extra mile: For example, laundry is done for a reasonable fee, and Pauline and her daughters will spend extra time at breakfast in helping guests plan the day's itinerary. Many gardens and historical sites are nearby. For those who want a longer stay, one of the upstairs rooms can be used as a self-catering apartment, with its own kitchen and sitting room on the ground floor.

Kells, Co. Meath. ⓒ/fax 046/45902. 4 units, 2 with bathroom (shower only). 32€ ($29) single without bathroom, 41€ ($37) single with bathroom; 46€ ($41) double without bathroom, 63€ ($58) double with bathroom. 20% reduction for children. V. **Amenities:** Laundry service.

GREAT DEALS ON DINING

Hudson's Bistro NOUVELLE INTERNATIONAL This snappy little bistro, decked out in sunny colors and bright pottery, is a treat for travelers en route through the Navan area, especially for couples or small groups of friends who enjoy quiet talk, wine, and terrific food. Try the tender Greek lamb kabobs with saffron rice, ratatouille chutney, and truly crisp salad, or the authentic and delicious spicy Thai curry with vegetables. The saffron fettuccine with prawns is perfectly cooked, though the sauce is a bit obscure for my taste. Daily soup and entree specials are also offered. Not to be missed are the desserts, such as "the Symphony," a house best that lives up to its name. The staff is friendly and the chefs gladly accommodate vegetarian requests and food allergies.

30 Railway St., Navan, Co. Meath. ⓒ 046/29231. Reservations required Fri–Sat. Main courses 11€–22€ ($10–$20). 10% service charge. AE, DC, MC, V. Tues–Sun 5:30–11pm.

Newgrange Farm Coffee Shop CAFETERIA Located on the premises of a working farm (see Newgrange Farm, above), this family-run restaurant is housed in a converted cow shed, now whitewashed and skylit. It has an open fireplace and local art on the walls. Ann Redhouse and her family oversee the baking and food preparation each day, using many ingredients grown on the farm or locally. The ever-changing blackboard menu ranges from homemade soups and hot scones or biscuits to sandwiches and tempting desserts, such as apple tart and cream, carrot cake, and fruit pies. Food can also be enjoyed in an outdoor picnic area. There's often live traditional music in the summer months.

Off N51, Slane, Co. Meath. ⓒ 041/982-4119. All items 2.60€–9€ ($2.40–$8.15). No credit cards. Easter–Aug daily 10am–5pm.

Wellington Court Hotel *Kids* TRADITIONAL/IRISH   In this small, charming hotel dining room, the menu, which includes such dishes as roast lamb and pork en croute, is excellent. Traditional Irish dishes, such as Irish stew or boiled ham, are also a good bet. Portions are huge, but if you can save room, try the apple tart. Children are welcomed here—good news for harried parents.

Trim, Co. Meath. © 046/31516. Main courses 11€–25€ ($10–$23); bar lunch under 10€ ($9.10). AE, DC, MC, V. Daily 12:30–3pm and 6:30–9:30pm. Closed Good Friday and Christmas Day.

4 County Louth: Where Cuchulainn Walked

County Louth, north and east of Meath, may be the smallest of Ireland's counties but it possesses a diversity of historic treasures and early Christian landmarks. **Carlingford,** one of Ireland's heritage towns, is set on a spur of the Cooley Mountains, overlooking Carlingford Lough and the Irish Sea. Established by the Vikings, it is still very much a medieval town, dominated by a massive 13th-century castle. Legend has it that long before the Vikings came, Carlingford was part of the hunting grounds of warriors. On the heights above the town, folk hero Cuchulainn is said to have single-handedly defeated the armies of Ulster in an epic battle.

Louth is not a place of outstanding scenic beauty, and most visitors will choose to move on after exploring a few sites of historic interest.

GETTING THERE   Irish Rail (© **01/836-3333**) provides daily train service between Dublin and Drogheda. **Bus Eireann** (© **01/836-6111**) operates daily express bus service to Collon and Drogheda in County Louth. If you're traveling by car, take N1 north from Dublin City to Drogheda.

VISITOR INFORMATION   For year-round information about Counties Meath and Louth, contact the **Dundalk Tourist Office,** Jocelyn Street, County Louth (© **042/933-5484**). **A seasonal information office** is also open in Drogheda (© **041/983-7070**) from June through August.

SEEING THE SIGHTS

Nestled between Carlingford Lough and Dundalk Bay, the picturesque **Cooley Peninsula** is the scenic setting for many of Ireland's myths and legends. Well known to Cuchulainn, Queen Maeve, and the great giant Finn MacCool, its mountains, rivers, and woodlands cast a spell on today's visitors as potent as in those long-ago days. This area of County Louth is well worth a little time poking around. Wander through the little medieval town of **Carlingford,** with its narrow streets and the brooding castle ruins overlooking the water from its lofty perch.

In **Dundalk,** before heading off on foot, go by the Heritage Centre on Jocelyn Street and pick up information on **St. Patrick's Cathedral,** the striking **Church of the Redeemer,** and the **Harp Lager Brewery.** Then rest your weary feet with a soul-restoring stop at the old-world-style **Windsor Pub** on Dublin Street (where you can also get a terrific pub lunch).

Townley Hall (Halla de Túinlé) is a forested area that encompasses the site of the Battle of the Boyne. There are forest walks, nature trails, and picnic sites. To get there, drive 3½ miles (5.25km) northwest of Drogheda on N51 (T26) and turn right at the signpost, continuing for 1 mile (1.6km).

It was near the ancient town of **Ardee,** on the banks of the River Dee, that Cuchulainn and Ferdiad are said to have fought hand-to-hand for 4 days in the Cattle Raid of Cooley, subject of one of Ireland's best-known epics. Look for the main street's two medieval castles, **Kings Castle** and **Hatch Castle,** as well as the majestically rebuilt (in 1693) **St. Mary's Abbey,** which was burned in 1315 by Edward Bruce while sheltering the men, women, and children of the town.

Holy Trinity Heritage Centre ⭐ This center, located in a beautifully restored medieval church, has exhibits that detail the town's history from its Norman origins. If you book ahead, a visit here includes a guided walking tour of the town and a look at King John's Castle, the Mint, The Tholsel (the sole surviving, though altered, gate to the old medieval town), and a Dominican friary. The center overlooks the south shore of Carlingford Lough at the foot of Sliabh Foy, the highest peak of the Cooley Mountains.

Carlingford, Co. Louth. ✆ **042/937-3454.** Fax 042/937-3882. Admission 1.25€ ($1.50) adults, .65€ (60¢) for children under 16. Sept–May Sat–Sun noon–5pm; June–Aug daily 1–7pm. Hours are variable, so call ahead to confirm.

Mellifont Abbey "Old Mellifont"—as distinct from "New Mellifont," a Cistercian monastery several miles away—was established in 1142 by St. Malachy of Armagh. Although little more than foundations survive here, this tranquil spot is worth a visit for a few moments of quiet. Remnants of a 14th-century chapter house, an octagonal lavabo dating from around 1200, and several Romanesque arches remain. A new visitor center contains sculpted stones from the excavations. The abbey is on the banks of the Mattock River, 6 miles (9.5km) west of Drogheda.

Off N2, Collon, Co. Louth. ✆ **041/26459.** Fax 041/982-4798. www.heritageireland.ie. Admission 1.90€ ($1.75) adults, 1.25€ ($1.15) seniors, 0.75€ (70¢) students and children under 12, 5.10€ ($4.60) family. May–Oct daily 10am–6pm.

Millmount Museum and Martello Tower This museum in the courtyard of 18th-century Millmount Fort offers exhibits on the history of Drogheda and the Boyne Valley area. A Bronze Age oracle, medieval tiles, and a collection of 18th-century guild banners are on display. Also showcased are domestic items such as spinning, weaving, and brewing equipment; antique gramophones; mousetraps; and hot-water jars. A geological exhibit contains specimens of stone from every county in Ireland, every country in Europe, and beyond. After a restoration that cost several million Euros, the tower was opened to the public in summer 2000 and houses an exhibition on the military history of Drogheda.

Duleek St., off the main Dublin Rd. (N1), Drogheda, Co. Louth. ✆ **041/983-3097.** Admission 3.15€ ($2.90) adults, 2.60€ ($2.40) students, 1.90€ ($1.75) children under 12, 7.60€ ($6.90) family. Tues–Sat 10am–5:30pm; Sun 2:30–5:30pm.

Monasterboice Once a great monastery and now little more than a peaceful cemetery, this site is dominated by Muiredeach's High Cross, which is 17 feet (5m) tall. The cross dates from the year 922 and is one of the most perfect crosses in Ireland. It's ornamented with sculptured panels of scenes from the Old and New Testaments. On the monastery grounds are the remains of a round tower, two churches, two early grave slabs, and a sundial. It's located 6 miles (9.5km) northwest of Drogheda.

Off the main Dublin Rd. (N1), near Collon, Co. Louth. Free admission. Daylight hours.

ACCOMMODATIONS YOU CAN AFFORD

Carraig Mor The guest rooms in Mrs. Sheila Magennis's attractive modern bungalow have large, multipaned windows that overlook fields and gardens. The dining room is especially light and airy. The B&B is conveniently located for those touring County Louth; there are numerous pubs, shops, and a golf course only a mile away. Mrs. Magennis is not only charming, but is especially helpful to guests who are touring the area.

Blakestown, Ardee (1 mile/1km from Ardee on N2, the Dublin-Donegal-Derry road), Co. Louth. ©/fax **041/685-3513.** www.carraigmor.com. 5 units, 4 with bathroom (shower only). 30€ ($35) single; 46€ ($41) double without bathroom, 51€ ($48) double with bathroom. 50% reduction for children sharing with an adult. Rates include full breakfast. No credit cards. Free parking. Closed Christmas. *In room:* TV, hair dryer.

Delamare House   Mrs. Eileen McGeown is your amiable hostess at this modern bungalow overlooking Carlingford Lough and the Mourne Mountains. The house is set in beautiful surroundings and is very peaceful, and Mrs. McGeown warmly welcomes singles, a blessing for those who travel on their own. The house is 3 miles (5km) from Carlingford and 0.5 miles (1km) from Omeath on the Carlingford-Omeath Road, opposite Calvary Shrine.

Ballyoonan, Omeath, Co. Louth. © 042/937-5101. eileenmcgeown@eircom.net. 3 units, 2 with bathroom. 45€ ($40) double without bathroom, 51€ ($46) double with bathroom. 50% reduction for children under 10 sharing with an adult. Rates include full breakfast. No credit cards. Private parking lot. Closed Nov–Mar. *In room:* TV, tea/coffeemaker, hair dryer.

Harbour Villa   This Victorian harbormaster's house, surrounded by gardens, is situated on the River Boyne, convenient to many of the area's prime attractions. Mrs. Eileen Valla, who has been involved in tourism for the past 30 years, purchased the house a few years back and has made great improvements. The beach is 1½ miles (2.5km) away, and the house has its own tennis court; also nearby are golf courses, horse stables, and fishing. Breakfast brings freshly baked bread or scones, and such alternatives to the full Irish fry as scrambled eggs with salmon, fruit salad, or a plate of local cheese; herbal teas are also offered. This is a great base for visiting Newgrange, Tara, Kells, Monasterboice, and other historic sites.

Mornington Rd., Drogheda (1 mile/1km from town off the main Dublin Rd.), Co. Louth. © 041/983-7441. 4 units, 2 with bathroom (shower only). 28€ ($25) single without bathroom; 51€ ($46) double without bathroom, 56€ ($51) double with bathroom. Rates include full breakfast. No credit cards. Private parking. **Amenities:** Golf courses; tennis court; stables; fishing areas.

Lynolan   If you have a problem with stairs, you'll be glad to know that Mrs. Evelyn Carolan's lovely two-story house has two guest rooms on the ground floor. Set back from the road, with a stone fountain and terrace out front, the house looks out onto surrounding green fields. Flower beds border a large back garden. The peaceful rural setting is a bonus for travelers, yet Dundalk is only 2 miles (3km) away.

On the Dublin-Belfast Rd (N1), Mullaharlin Rd., Heynestown, Dundalk, Co. Louth. ©/fax **042/933-6553.** 6 units, 5 with bathroom. 32€ ($29) single; 51€ ($46) double. 50% reduction for children sharing with an adult. Rates include full breakfast. 15€ ($14) dinner. MC, V. Free parking. Closed Christmas. **Amenities:** Babysitting (by arrangement only).

Rosemont   Maisie and John Meehan are the gracious hosts in this modern house on the outskirts of town. Maisie is the very soul of Irish hospitality, and John is a fount of information on this part of Ireland. The pleasant guest rooms are attractively furnished, and the breakfast room looks out onto a back garden. There's a golf course nearby.

Dublin Rd., Dundalk, Co. Louth. ©/fax 042/933-5878. 9 units. 36€ ($32) single; 56€ ($51) double. 50% reduction for children under 12 sharing with an adult. Rates include full breakfast. No credit cards. Free parking. *In room:* TV, TEL, tea/coffeemaker, hair dryer, iron.

GREAT DEALS ON DINING

The Brake SEAFOOD/STEAKS/SANDWICHES This appealing, rustic restaurant, directly on the seafront, has been run by the Smyth family for nearly 25 years. Its stone-walled interior is a delightful blend of old prints, lamps, jugs, old posters, and other "artifacts." Service is as warm as the glowing, open fireplace, and the menu offers something for all tastes and budgets. The specialties are seafood (crab claws, prawns, lobster in summer) and steaks, as well as porc à la crème and home-cured ham on the bone.

Main St. on Seafront, Blackrock, Co. Louth. ✆ **042/932-1393**. Main courses 9€–20€ ($8.15–$18). MC, V. Mon–Sat 6:30–10:30pm; Sun 6–9:30pm.

The Gables House and Restaurant SEAFOOD/GAME/TRADITIONAL The Gables is a fully licensed restaurant much beloved in these parts, so you'll find plenty of locals dining here. There's a friendly, relaxed air about the place, and the menu features only the freshest ingredients, whether it be fish from nearby waters or game in season. Soups and desserts are outstanding, and portions are more than ample.

Dundalk Rd. (north of Drogheda, just off N2), Ardee, Co. Louth. ✆ **041/53789**. Fixed-price dinner 28€ ($25). AE, MC, V. Mon–Sat 7–10pm; Sun 12:30–9:30pm.

McKevitt's Village Hotel SEAFOOD/TRADITIONAL Oysters and other shellfish star on the menu of this bright, cheerful eatery—the oysters in Guinness are especially popular. Other locally produced ingredients assure the freshness of all the menu items. The service is both friendly and efficient, and there's a nonsmoking dining room.

Market Sq., Darlingford, Co. Louth. ✆ **042/937-3116**. Lunch 7€–18€ ($6.35–$16); fixed-price dinner 28€ ($25). MC, V. Daily 12:30–2:15pm and 5:30–9pm.

6

The Southeast

The "Sunny Southeast," they call it—there are said to be more sunny days along this part of Ireland's coast than anywhere else in the country. Whether or not this epithet proves accurate during your visit, the Southeast is an underrated region with a lot to offer—great beaches, seascapes, wild mountain country, and abundant fishing in its rivers and coastal waters.

Note: A good source of information about the entire region, the website for all Southeast Tourism is **www.southeastireland.travel.ie.**

1 Wexford Town & County Wexford

Wexford town is 88 miles (142km) S of Dublin, 39 miles (63km) E of Waterford, 56 miles (90km) S of Wicklow, 116 miles (187km) E of Cork, 133 miles (214km) SE of Shannon Airport

County Wexford is most remarkable for the long stretches of pristine beach that line its coast and for the evocative historic monuments to be found in **Wexford town** and on the **Hook Peninsula.** The Blackstairs Mountains dominate the western border of the county, and provide excellent hill walking. Bird-watchers will find an abundance of great sites, including Wexford Wildfowl Reserve and Great Saltee Island.

Holding a strategic position on Ireland's coast, Wexford has a colorful and often bloody history. Father Murphy, famed in legend and song, led a valiant band of rebels to Vinegar Hill near Enniscorthy in 1798, and for nearly a month, the ill-fed and ill-armed patriots held out there against the English king's forces. For Americans, there is a strong tie to their own history in the **John F. Kennedy Arboretum** out by New Ross, not far from the birthplace of the Kennedy ancestors. Down on the Hook Peninsula, a light to guide sailing ships has burned continuously for more than 1,500 years, winking across the water to Crook Castle on the Waterford side and giving rise to Cromwell's declaration that he would sail up the river "by Hook or by Crook." Today's invaders are tourists, who find the now-peaceful countryside a haven for sightseeing, sailing, fishing, and swimming.

Either **Wexford town** or **Waterford** (see "Waterford Town & County Waterford," later in this chapter), a mere 40 miles (64km) apart, will serve as a base from which to explore this part of the southeast region in easy day trips. Your decision may well rest on whether you prefer Wexford's small-town informality or Waterford's slightly more sophisticated ambience (and I mean *slightly*).

GETTING THERE   Irish Rail provides daily train service to Wexford and Rosslare Pier. It serves **O'Hanrahan Station,** Redmond Place, Wexford (© **053/22522;** www.irishrail.ie).

Bus Eireann operates daily bus service to Wexford and Rosslare, into O'Hanrahan Station, Redmond Place, Wexford (© **053/22522;** www.buseireann.ie).

If you're driving from Dublin and points north, take the N11 or N80 to Wexford; if you're coming from the west, take the N25 or N8. Two bridges lead into

The Southeast

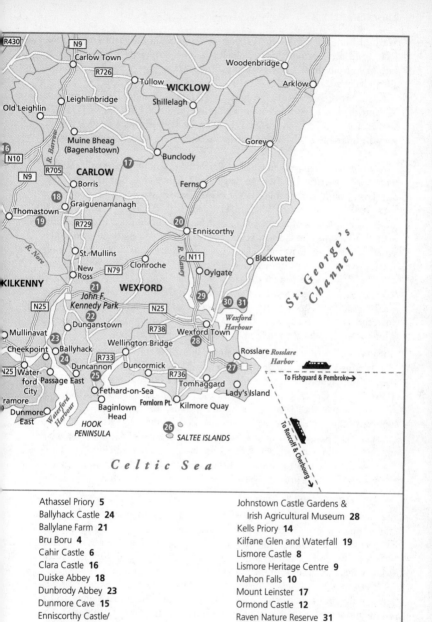

Wexford from the north—the Ferrycarrig Bridge from the main Dublin road (N11) and the Wexford Bridge from R741. The Ferrycarrig Bridge takes you into town from the west. The Wexford Bridge leads right to the heart of town along the quays.

Ferry service from Britain to Rosslare Harbour, 12 miles (19km) south of Wexford Town, is operated from Fishguard by Stena Line (© **053/33115;** www.stenaline.co.uk), and from Pembroke by Irish Ferries (© **053/33158;** www.irishferries.ie), which also provides service from Roscoff and Cherbourg, France.

If you're traveling between County Wexford and County Waterford, there's a waterborne shortcut. The **Passage East Ferry County Ltd.,** Barrack Street, Passage East, County Waterford (© **051/382488;** www.passageferry.com), operates a car ferry service across Waterford Harbour. It links Passage East, about 10 miles (16km) east of Waterford, with Ballyhack, about 20 miles (32km) southwest of Wexford. The shortcut saves about an hour's driving time between the cities. Crossing time averages 10 minutes. It's continuous drive-on, drive-off service, with no reservations required. Fares are 5.70€ ($5.20) one-way and 8.25€ ($7.50) round-trip for car and passengers 1.90€ ($1.75) round-trip and 1.25€ ($1.15) single trip for foot passengers, 2.55€ ($2.30) one-way and 3.20€ ($2.90) round-trip for cyclists. It operates April to September, Monday to Saturday 7am to 10pm, and Sunday 9:30am to 10pm; October to March, Monday to Saturday 7am to 8pm, and Sunday 9:30am to 8pm.

VISITOR INFORMATION   Year-round information services are provided by the **Wexford Tourist Office,** Crescent Quay, Wexford (© **053/23111**); the **Gorey Tourist Office,** Town Centre (© **055/21248**); and the **Rosslare Harbour Tourist Office,** Ferry Terminal, Rosslare Harbour (© **053/33622**). The Wexford town office is open year-round Monday through Saturday, 9am to 6pm; the Gorey office is open year-round Monday through Saturday 10am to 5:30pm. The Rosslare Harbour office opens daily between May and September to coincide with ferry arrivals. Other seasonal offices are maintained at **Enniscorthy,** Town Centre (© **054/34699**), open May through September; and at **New Ross,** Town Centre (© **051/421857**), open June through August.

WEXFORD TOWN

The modern English name of Wexford evolved from *Waesfjord,* which is what the Viking sea-rovers called the place when they settled here in the 9th century. The word literally means "the harbor of the mudflats." Like the rest of Ireland, Wexford was under Norman control by the 12th century, and there still remain some reminders in stone of their dominance in this region.

Wexford is a small town, somewhat dreary when the weather turns wet (yes, even in the sunny southeast!). This said, the town has preserved many fascinating reminders of its past, like **Selskar Abbey** and the **West Gate Tower.** The **Wexford Wildfowl Reserve** is a necessary stop for birders, who can gather information here on places to watch birds throughout Ireland.

There's an interesting story to be told about John Barry, a local man commemorated by a statue on Crescent Quay. Born at Ballysampson, Tacumshane, 10 miles (16km) southeast of Wexford town, Barry emigrated to the American colonies while still in his teens and volunteered for the cause of the Revolution. One of the U.S. Navy's first commissioned officers, he became captain of the *Lexington.* In 1797, George Washington appointed him commander-in-chief of the U.S. Navy.

Homely Wexford becomes quite the cosmopolitan center in October when the world-renowned **Opera Festival** is in town. Known for its promotion of little-known works, this festival is truly first-rate.

TOWN LAYOUT   Rimmed by the River Slaney, Wexford is a small and compact town. Four quays (Custom House, Commercial, Paul, and the semicircular Crescent) run beside the water, with Crescent Quay marking the center of town. One block inland is Main Street, a long, narrow thoroughfare that can be easily walked. Wexford's shops and businesses are on either North or South Main Street or on one of the many smaller streets that fan out from it.

GETTING AROUND   By Public Transportation   Because Wexford is small and compact, with narrow streets, there is no local bus transport. **Bus Eireann** (© 053/22522; www.buseireann.ie) operates daily service between Wexford and Rosslare Harbour. Other local services operate on certain days only to Kilmore Quay, Carne, and Gorey.

By Car   To see Wexford Town, walk. Park your car along the Quays; parking is operated according to the disc system, at .70€ (65¢) per hour. Discs are on sale at the tourist office or many of the shops. There is free parking off Redmond Square, beside the train/bus station, and a car park at Bright St. where you'll pay 1.25€ ($1.15) for a full day. You'll need a car to reach County Wexford attractions outside of town.

If you need to rent a car, contact **Budget** at the Quay, New Ross (© 051/ 421670); **Murrays Europcar,** Wellington Place, Wexford (© 053/33634), or Rosslare Ferryport, Rosslare (© 053/33634); or **Hertz,** Ferrybank, Wexford (© 053/23511), or Rosslare Harbour, Wexford (© 053/33238).

By Taxi   If you need a cab, try **Wexford Taxi** (© 053/23123) or **Noel Ryan** (© 053/24056).

On Foot   The best way to see the town is by strolling the entire length of North and South Main Street, taking time to detour up and down the various alleys and lanes that cross the street. The tourist office can supply you with a free map.

(C) *FAST FACTS:* Wexford

Area Codes   The telephone area code for Wexford Town is **053;** the surrounding areas use **051, 053, 054,** and **055.**

Drugstores   Try **John Fehily/The Pharmacy,** 28 S. Main St., Wexford (© 053/23163); **Sherwood Chemist,** 2 N. Main St., Wexford (© 053/ 22875); and **Fortune's Pharmacy,** 82 N. Main St., Wexford (© 053/42354).

Dry Cleaning & Laundry   Two good choices are **My Beautiful Launderette,** at St. Peter's Square, Wexford (© 053/24317); and **Marlowe Cleaners,** at 7 S. Main St., Wexford (© 053/22172).

Emergencies   Dial © **999.**

Hospital   **Wexford General Hospital** is located on Richmond Terrace, Wexford (© 053/42233).

Newspaper   The ***Wexford People*** is the weekly newspaper covering town and county events and entertainment.

Photographic Services Try **Spectra Photo,** at 6 N. Main St., Wexford (© **053/45502**).

Police The **Garda Station** is located on Roches Road, Wexford (© **053/22333**).

Post Office The **General Post Office** on Anne Street, Wexford (© **053/ 22587**), is open Monday through Saturday from 9am to 5:30pm.

SEEING THE SIGHTS IN WEXFORD TOWN

Proud of their town's ancient streets and vintage buildings, the people of Wexford spontaneously started to give tours to visitors more than 30 years ago. Today the Wexford Historical Society organizes **Walking Tours of Wexford** ⊛; the society has developed a real expertise over the years. Tours depart from West Gate Heritage Tower Monday to Saturday at 11:30am and 2:30pm, by arrangement only; for information and reservations contact Seamus Molloy (© **053/ 22663**). The cost is 3.80€ ($3.45) adults, 1.25€ ($1.15) children.

The Bull Ring   In 1798, the first declaration of an Irish Republic was made here, and a statue memorializes the Irish pikemen who fought for the cause. Earlier, in the 17th century, the town square was a venue for bull baiting, a sport introduced by the butcher's guild. Tradition has it that, after a match, the hide of the ill-fated bull was presented to the mayor and the meat used to feed the poor. Currently, the activity at the ring is much tamer—a modest weekly outdoor market, open Friday and Saturday 10am to 4:30pm.

Off N. Main St., Wexford. Open site.

Church of the Assumption & Church of the Immaculate Conception These twin Gothic structures (1851–58) were designed by architect Robert Pierce, a pupil of Augustus Pugin. Their spires rise 230 feet (70m) and dominate the skyline of Wexford. Cobbled on the main door of both churches are mosaics showing relevant names and dates.

Bride and Rowe sts., Wexford. © 053/22055. Free admission; donations welcome. Daily 8am–6pm.

Irish National Heritage Park ⊛ *(Kids)*   This 36-acre living history park on the banks of the River Slaney provides an ideal introduction for visitors of all ages to life in ancient Ireland, from the stone age to the Norman invasion. Each reconstructed glimpse into Irish history is beautifully crafted and has its own natural setting and wildlife. The 10-minute orientation video is engaging and informative, but nothing can match a guided tour by Jimmy O'Rourke, the park's head guide, who is an utter master in bringing each site to life, captivating children and intriguing adults. The park's nature trail and interpretive center, complete with gift shop and restaurant, add to its appeal. You may want to spend several hours here.

Off Dublin-Wexford road (N11), Ferrycarrig, Co. Wexford. © 053/20733. Fax 053/20911. info@inhp.com. Admission 7€ ($6.35) adults, 5.50€ ($5.00) seniors, students, and children 13–16, 3.50€ ($3.20) children 4–12, 17.50€ ($16) family. Year-round daily 9:30am–6:30pm. Last admission 5pm.

St. Iberius Church   Erected in 1660, St. Iberius was built on hallowed ground—the land had been used for previous houses of worship dating from Norse times. The church has a lovely Georgian facade and an interior known for its superb acoustics. Free guided tours are given according to demand.

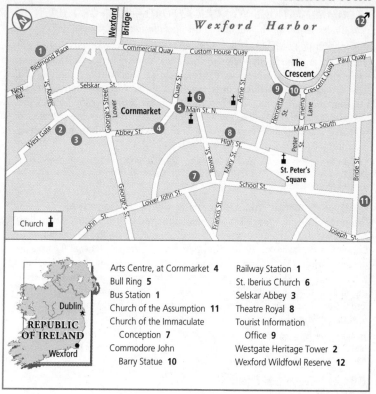

Wexford Harbor

Wexford Bridge

Commercial Quay   Custom House Quay   Paul Quay

The Crescent

Redmond Place

New Rd.   Slaney St.   Selskar St.   Crescent Quay   Henrietta St.   Cinema Lane   Main St. South

George's Street Lower

Cornmarket

Abbey St.   Quay St.   Main St. N.   Anne St.

West Gate

High St.   Rowe St.   Mary St.   Peter St.   Bride St.

St. Peter's Square

George's St.   Lower John St.   School St.   Francis St.

John St.   Joseph St.

Church ✝

Legend

REPUBLIC OF IRELAND

Dublin ★

Wexford ●

Arts Centre, at Cornmarket **4**	Railway Station **1**
Bull Ring **5**	St. Iberius Church **6**
Bus Station **1**	Selskar Abbey **3**
Church of the Assumption **11**	Theatre Royal **8**
Church of the Immaculate Conception **7**	Tourist Information Office **9**
Commodore John Barry Statue **10**	Westgate Heritage Tower **2**
	Wexford Wildfowl Reserve **12**

N. Main St. ✆ **053/43013.** Free admission; donations welcome. May–Sept daily 10am–5pm; Oct–Apr Tues–Sat 10am–3pm.

Selskar Abbey   There isn't much to see of the original abbey, said to date from the 12th century, just a few ruined arches adjacent to the Westgate Heritage Tower. The roofless church connected to the tower, with its high pointed arch windows, is of 19th-century origin. The abbey was once a place of some importance: Legend has it that the first Anglo-Irish treaty was signed here in 1169, and that Henry II spent the Lent of 1172 at the abbey doing penance for having Thomas à Becket beheaded.

Off Temperance Row at Westgate St., Wexford.

Wexford Wildfowl Reserve   This national nature reserve is part of the North Slob adjacent to Wexford Harbour, 3 miles (5km) east of Wexford town. About 10,000 Greenland white-fronted geese, more than a third of the world's population, spend the winter here, as do Brent geese, Bewick's swans, and wigeon. The area is immensely attractive to other wildfowl and birds, and more than 240 species have been seen here. The reserve has a visitor center, an audiovisual program, an exhibition hall, and an observation tower and blinds. The warden, Christopher Wilson, is highly knowledgeable and helpful regarding birding in this region and throughout Ireland.

N. Slob, Wexford. ✆ **053/23129.** Fax 053/24785. cjwilson@ealga.ie. Free admission. Mid-Apr to Sept daily 9am–6pm; Oct to mid-Apr daily 10am–5pm. Other hours by appointment.

ACCOMMODATIONS YOU CAN AFFORD—WEXFORD TOWN

Note: Prices are usually higher during the opera festival in October.

McMenamin's Townhouse ✦ Situated at the west end of town opposite the railroad station, this lovely Victorian-style town house offers up-to-date accommodations at an affordable price. Guest rooms are individually furnished with local antiques, including brass beds and caned chairs. All guest rooms are nonsmoking and have orthopedic beds. McMenamin's is operated by Seamus and Kay McMenamin, the original owners of the Bohemian Girl pub/restaurant, so your stomach is in luck: Kay puts her culinary skills to work by providing an exceptional breakfast.

3 Auburn Terrace, Redmond Rd., Wexford, Co. Wexford. ✆ 053/46442. Fax 053/46442. www.wexford-bedandbreakfast.com. 6 units. 51€ ($46) single; 89€ ($81) double. No service charge. Rates include full breakfast. MC, V. Private parking lot. *In room:* TV, tea/coffeemaker, hair dryer, iron.

Westgate House ✦ Although the decor at Westgate House recalls its Victorian origin (the place was built as a guesthouse in the 19th century), the Allens have made frequent renovations and the house is extremely comfortable. Located at the west end of town, opposite the Westgate Heritage Centre, the house is within easy walking distance of the town center and the principal historic sites. Many rooms are furnished with fine Victorian-era antiques, including mahogany four-poster beds in the spacious family rooms (numbers 7, 11, and 12 are especially impressive). Mr. and Mrs. Allen have won abundant and well-deserved praise from readers for their hospitality.

Westgate, Wexford, Co. Wexford. ✆ 053/24428. Fax 053/22167. www.wexford-online.com/westgate/index.htm. 10 units. 38€ ($35) single; 63€ ($58) double. Rates include full breakfast. MC, V. Private parking lot. *In room:* TV, tea/coffeemaker, hair dryer.

GREAT DEALS ON DINING
WEXFORD TOWN

Arts Centre Cafe IRISH/VEGETARIAN Housed in the Wexford Arts Centre, this charming eatery has a country kitchen atmosphere, with stone walls, pine furnishings, and home cooking. Selections include salads, soups, quiches, pizzas, and chili, with a particular emphasis on vegetarian items.

Cornmarket at Abbey St., Wexford. ✆ 053/23764. Reservations not accepted. All items 2€–9€ ($1.80–$8.60). No credit cards. Daily 10am–6pm.

The Wren's Nest *(Value* BAR FOOD This is one of the best places in Wexford for a good, inexpensive lunch. It's a good-looking (and award-winning) bar whose back-room lounge features an attractive stone fireplace. The menu includes a hot-plate special, salads, the house paté and brown bread (good), and sandwiches. It sits facing the harbor, a little north of the Crescent.

Custom House Quay. ✆ 053/22359. Sandwiches 2.50€–4€ ($2.30–$3.65); meals 6.50€–7.50€ ($5.90–$6.80). No credit cards. Mon–Fri noon–5pm; Sat noon–3pm.

SHOPPING IN WEXFORD TOWN

Shops in Wexford are generally open Monday to Thursday from 9am to 5:30pm, Friday and Saturday from 9am to 6pm; some shops stay open until 8pm on Friday.

Barkers Established in 1848, this has long been a mainstay in Wexford for a large selection of Waterford crystal, Belleek china, and Royal Irish Tara china, as well as Irish linens and bronze and international products such as Aynsley, Wedgwood, and Lladró. 36–40 S. Main St. ✆ 053/23159.

The Book Centre   This shop offers a wide selection of maps and books about Wexford and Ireland in general, and also carries cards, stationery, and music tapes and cassettes. There's a literary-themed coffee shop on the premises. 5 S. Main St. ℭ **053/23543.**

Wexford Silver ⟨★⟩   Pat Dolan, one of Ireland's leading silversmiths, plies his craft along with his sons at this shop, creating gold, silver, and bronze pieces by hand using traditional tools and techniques. They're members of a long line of Dolans, who trace their silversmithing connections from 1647. A second workshop is located in Kinsale. 115 N. Main St. ℭ/fax **053/21933.**

The Wool Shop   This shop in the heart of the town's main thoroughfare is Wexford's long-established best source for hand-knits, from caps and tams to sweaters and jackets, as well as tweeds, linens, mohairs, and knitting yarns. 39–41 S. Main St. ℭ **053/22247.**

THE PUB SCENE IN WEXFORD TOWN

Con Macken (The Cape)   Long a favorite with photographers, this pub is unique for the trio of services it offers, aptly described by the sign outside the door: BAR—UNDERTAKER—GROCERIES. Hardly any visitor passes by without a second look at the windows, one displaying beer and spirit bottles, the other featuring plastic funeral wreaths. An alehouse for centuries, The Cape has always been at the center of Wexford political events, and the bar walls are lined with rebel souvenirs, old weapons, and plaques. The Bull Ring, off N. Main St., Wexford. ℭ **053/22949.**

The Crown Bar   Once a stagecoach inn, this tiny pub in the center of town has been in the Kelly family since 1841. Besides its historical overtones, it is well known for its museumlike collection of antique weapons. You'll see 18th-century dueling pistols, pikes from the 1798 rebellion, powder horns, and blunderbusses, as well as vintage prints, military artifacts, and swords. Unlike most pubs, it may not always be open during the day, so it's best to save a visit for the evening hours. Monck St., Wexford. ℭ **053/21133.**

The Wren's Nest   Situated along the harbor front near the John Barry Memorial, 5 minutes from the bus and train station, this pub has redesigned its front bar to include an old-style wood floor and ceiling and attractive pine tables and chairs. The varied bar food includes Wexford mussel platters, house patés, soups, salads, and vegetarian entrees (see "Great Deals on Dining—Wexford Town," above). There is free traditional Irish music on most Tuesday and Thursday nights. Custom House Quay, Wexford. ℭ **053/22359.**

WEXFORD AFTER DARK

Some say that it was shipwrecked Cornish sailors who first brought **mumming** to Wexford. In any case, this medieval folk-dance-with-swordplay is unique in Ireland to this county. Today's mummers portray Irish patriots such as Wolfe Tone and Robert Emmet. The three or four groups are composed of Wexford natives who have inherited their place in the ritualistic performances from family members going back several generations. They don't follow a regular schedule, but the tourist office will usually be able to tell you when the next appearance is likely to occur in one of the local pubs. If you can track one down, don't miss it.

Famed for its **Opera Festival** ⟨★★⟩ each October, Wexford is a town synonymous with music and the arts. Year-round performances are given at the **Theatre Royal,** High Street, Wexford (ℭ **053/22144**), a beautiful theater dating from 1832. Booking for the opera festival opens in early May for the following October! Tickets range from 9€ to 76€ ($8.15 to $69). Visit its website at **www.wexfordopera.com**. Alternatively, there's usually something going on at the **Wexford Arts Centre,** Cornmarket, Wexford (© **053/23764;** www. wexfordartscentre.ie). Built as the market house in 1775 at the Cornmarket, this building has served as a dance venue, concert hall, and municipal office. Since 1974, it has provided a focal point for all of the arts in Wexford, and now houses three exhibition rooms and showcases a range of theatrical and artistic events. The center's staff is particularly eager to meet visiting artists in all fields, with a view toward developing ongoing links with artists worldwide. Open year-round from 10am to 6pm daily.

SEEING THE SIGHTS AROUND COUNTY WEXFORD

SALTEE ISLANDS ☆   The Great Saltee Island is one of the best places in Ireland to watch seabirds, especially during the months of May, June, and July, when the place is mobbed with nesting parents and their young. The cliffs on the island's southernmost point are packed to overflowing with raucous avian tourists, and the combined sound of their screeching, squawking, and chortling is nearly deafening at times. This is a place to get up close and personal with puffins, which nest in underground burrows, or with the graceful guillemots. Other species include cormorants, kittiwakes, gannets, and Manx shearwaters. The island is privately owned, but visitors are welcome on the condition that they do nothing to disturb the bird habitat and the island's natural beauty. Boat rides out to the island and back are provided from the town of Kilmore Quay— about 10 miles (16km) south of Wexford town—by Declan Bates (© **053/ 29684**); he charges 65€ ($59) for the boat or 15€ ($14) per adult (when there are at least four) and 7.50€ ($6.80) per child.

RING OF HOOK DRIVE   The Hook Peninsula in southwest County Wexford, a place of rocky headlands and secluded beaches, is located between Bannow Bay and Waterford Harbor, two of the most important inlets in medieval times for travelers from Britain to Ireland. The strategic significance of this area is reflected in the great abundance of archaeological remains. The end of the peninsula is popular with birders as a site for watching the spring and fall passerine migration, and is tipped with a lighthouse reputed to be one of the oldest in Europe. The route described is appropriate for bicycling or driving, and most of the places listed can be seen by walkers from the **Wexford Coastal Pathway.**

An exploration of the peninsula begins at the town of **Wellington Bridge.** Just west of town on R733 is a roadside pull-off on the left by a cemetery; from here you can look across Bannow Bay to the ruins of **Clonmines,** a Norman village established in the 13th century. This is one of the finest examples of a walled medieval settlement in Ireland, with remains of two churches, three tower houses, and an Augustinian priory. It's possible to drive to the ruins: follow R733 another mile west to a left turn posted for the Wicklow Coastal Pathway, and continue straight on this road where the Coastal Pathway turns right. The ruins are on private land, so you should ask permission at the farmhouse at the end of the road.

Continuing west on R733, turn left on R734 at the sign for the Ring of Hook, and turn right at the sign for **Tintern Abbey** ☆ (© **051/562650;** www.heritageireland.com). The abbey was founded by the monks of Tintern in South Wales in the 13th century and has been much altered since then. The abbey is open to the public mid-June to September daily from 9:30am to

6:30pm, with the last admission at 5:45pm; the admission fee is 1.90€ ($1.75) adults, 1.25€ ($1.15) seniors, .75€ (70¢) children and students, and 5.10€ ($4.60) family. The grounds are beautiful and include a restored stone bridge spanning a narrow sea inlet.

At **Baginbun Head** there's a fine beach nestled against the cliffs from where it's possible to see the outline of the Norman earthwork fortifications on the head. It's here that the Norman presence in Ireland was first established with the victory of Norman forces over the Irish at the Battle of Baginbun.

Continue out to the tip of **Hook Head,** a narrow promontory where shelves of limestone slope into the often turbulent sea. The Head has long been famous for shipwrecks, and there's been an operating lighthouse here since the 5th century. The currently standing structure was built by the Normans in the 12th century to help guide their ships safely to harbor; a fire was kept burning continuously, marking the point with smoke by day and the light of its fires by night. Then, in 1665, an enclosed lantern was added, and a coal fire replaced the Norman open bonfire. The turret surmounting the tower reached its present form in 1863. This history of continuous use and inventive re-use makes the Hook lighthouse the oldest in Europe.

The Ring of Hook road returns along the western side of the peninsula, passing the beaches at Booley Bay and Dollar Bay. On a promontory overlooking the town of **Duncannon** is a fort built in 1588 to protect Waterford Harbour from the threat of attack by the Spanish Armada. It's a star-shaped structure, with great sea views. Just north of Duncannon, along the coast, is the village of **Ballyhack,** where a ferry operates to Passage East in County Waterford, and a Knights Hospitallers castle stands on a hill over the harbor (see separate description for Ballyhack Castle, below).

A visit to the Hook Peninsula wouldn't be complete without a stop at **Dunbrody Abbey** (✆ 051/388603), about 4 miles (6.5km) north of Duncannon. Situated in a field beside the road, the abbey is a magnificent ruin. It was founded in 1210 and is one of the largest Cistercian abbeys in Ireland. Despite its grand size, it bears remarkably little ornamentation. Tours are sometimes available. Inquire at the visitor center across the road, where there is also a hedge maze (planted in 1993 and now over 5 feet/1.5m in height) and a miniature golf course that kids will love. Admission to the abbey is 1.90€ ($1.75) adults, 1.25€ ($1.15) children, 5.10€ ($4.60) family (two adults and four children); the maze and miniature golf are an additional 2.60€ ($2.40) adults, 1.25€ ($1.15) children, 6.35€ ($5.75) families. Hours are May to June and September daily from 10am to 6pm; July and August from 10am to 7pm.

Ballyhack Castle   This castle stands on a steep slope overlooking the Waterford estuary, about 20 miles (32km) west of Wexford. It's thought to have been built around 1450 by the Knights Hospitallers of St. John, one of the two great military orders founded at the beginning of the 12th century during the Crusades. Hence, the building is considered a Crusader castle. There's a heritage information center with displays on the Crusader knights, medieval monks, and Norman nobles.

Off R733, Ballyhack, Co. Wexford. ✆ 051/389468. www.heritageireland.ie. Admission 1.25€ ($1.15) adults, .90€ (80¢) seniors, .50€ (45¢) students and children, 3.80€ ($3.45) family. June–Sept daily 9:30am–6:30pm.

Ballylane Farm   This 200-acre family farm in the heart of County Wexford's verdant countryside lets visitors get a first-hand look at farm life, including such activities as tillage, sheep raising, and deer and pheasant husbandry. Guided tours, lasting about an hour, are given on a set route covering fields of crops, woodlands, boglands, ponds, and farm buildings. There's also a tearoom, shop, and picnic area.

Signposted off the New Ross–Wexford road (N25), 1¼ miles (2km) east of New Ross, Co. Wexford. ✆ 051/425666. Fax 051/422898. Admission 4.50€ ($4.10) adults, 3.20€ ($2.90) seniors, students, and children, 13.50€ ($12) family. May–Sept daily 10am–6pm.

Enniscorthy Castle/Wexford County Museum   This haphazard collection of artifacts may remind you of a yard sale more than a museum, but it makes an interesting rainy-day outing. Displays include an old Irish farm kitchen, early modes of travel, nautical memorabilia, and items connected with Wexford's role in Ireland's struggle for independence. The castle itself dates from the 13th century, and is said to have been occupied briefly by the poet Edmund Spenser.

At the eastern end of Enniscorthy is **Vinegar Hill** ☆, where the Wexford men of 1798 made their last stand. Now a scenic viewing point, it offers panoramas of Wexford from its summit.

Castle Hill, Enniscorthy, Co. Wexford. ✆ 054/35926. wexmus@iol.ie. Admission 3.80€ ($3.45) adults, 2.60€ ($2.40) seniors and students, .65€ (60¢) children, 9.50€ ($8.65) family. July–Aug Mon–Sat 10am–6pm, Sun 2–5pm; Mar–June and Sept daily 10am–5pm; Oct–Feb Sun 2–5pm.

John F. Kennedy Arboretum ☆   Dedicated to the memory of the 35th U.S. president, this 600-acre arboretum is located near a hill known as Slieve Coilte. The arboretum overlooks the simple thatched cottage that was the birthplace of John F. Kennedy's great-grandfather. Opened in 1968, the arboretum was initiated with financial help from a group of Irish Americans, though its development and maintenance are funded by the Irish government. More than 4,500 species of plants and trees from five continents grow here. Facilities include an information center and a picnic area. A hilltop observation point presents a sweeping view of County Wexford and five neighboring counties, the Saltee Islands, the Comeragh Mountains, and parts of the Rivers Suir, Nore, and Barrow.

New Ross, Co. Wexford. ✆ 051/388171. Fax 051/388172. Admission 2.55€ ($2.30) adults, 1.90€ ($1.70) seniors, 1.30€ ($1.20) students and children, 6.50€ ($5.90) family. Apr and Sept daily 10am–6:30pm; May–Aug daily 10am–8pm; Oct–Mar daily 10am–5pm. Off the Duncannon Rd. (R733), about 20 miles (32km) west of Wexford.

Johnstown Castle Gardens and Irish Agricultural Museum   The importance of farming in Wexford's history is the focus of this agricultural museum. In historic farm buildings, the museum contains exhibits relating to rural transport, planting, and the diverse activities of the farm household. There are also extensive displays on dairying, crafts, and Irish country furniture. Large-scale replicas illustrate the workshops of the blacksmith, cooper, wheelwright, harness maker, and basket maker. A 5,000-square-foot hall contains space for rotating exhibitions. The 19th-century Gothic-Revival castle on the grounds is not open to the public, but the extensive gardens are open for exploration. Paths encircle three large ornamental lakes, some of which have tower follies on their shores. Others take people through gardens that include more than 200 different kinds of trees and shrubs, a medieval tower house, hothouses, walled gardens, and a picnic area.

4 miles (6.5km) southwest of Wexford town on Bridgetown Rd., off Wexford-Rosslare Rd. (N25), Wexford. ✆ 053/42888. Fax 053/42213. Admission to museum 3.80€ ($3.45) adults, 2.60€ ($2.40) children, 13€ ($12) family; gardens 3.80€ ($3.45) per car, 1.90€ ($1.75) per pedestrian or cyclist, .65€ (60¢) per cycling student or child. No credit cards. Museum June–Aug Mon–Fri 9am–5pm, Sat–Sun 11–5pm; Apr–May and Sept–Nov 2 Mon–Fri 9am–12:30pm and 1:30–5pm, Sat–Sun 2–5pm; Nov 13 to Mar Mon–Fri 9am–12:30pm and 1:30–5pm. Gardens year-round daily 9am–5:30pm.

The New Ross Galley   Skipper Dick Fletcher conceived the idea of this cruising restaurant some 25 years ago, and now the Galley sets sail for lunches (2 hours), afternoon teas (2 hours), and dinners (2 to 3 hours). Whichever you select, you'll spend 2 to 3 relaxing hours in the comfortable, heated cruiser as you slide between the scenic banks of the Rivers Barrow, Nore, or Suir. No canned music, no commentary—just the blissful comfort of good food, drink (the *Galley* is fully licensed), and conversation, and if you're curious about the ancient stately homes, castles, abbeys, and wildlife you glimpse along the shore, read the menu pages that give details of the area. The menu is limited, but the food is fresh and the views can't be equaled. There's seating for 70, and the skipper is usually aboard in the role of gracious host. The restaurant is nonsmoking.

The Quay, New Ross. (C) 051/421723. Fax 051/421950. www.rivercruises.ie. Reservations essential. Book through Wexford or Waterford tourist offices or the above telephone. 18€ ($16) for lunch cruise, 10€ ($9) for afternoon-tea cruise, 32€–38€ ($29–$35) for dinner cruise, 7.50€–14€ ($6.80–$13) for cruise only. V. From New Ross or Waterford quays lunch Apr–Oct daily at 12:30pm; tea Apr–Oct daily at 3pm; dinner Apr–Sept usually 7pm. (Note that frequency and times vary with demand.)

Yola Farmstead Folk Park *(Kids)*   A voluntary community project, this theme park depicts a Wexford farming community as it would have been 200 years or more ago. Thatched-roof buildings have been constructed, including barns housing farm animals and a working windmill. Deer, goats, and endangered breeds of poultry wander among the houses. Bread and butter making are demonstrated, and you can trace your roots in the on-site genealogy center. There's also a restaurant on the premises. The park is located about 10 miles (16km) south of Wexford town.

Wexford-Rosslare Rd. (N25), Tagoat, Co. Wexford. (C) 053/32610. yolafst@iol.ie. Admission 4.50€ ($4.10) adults, 3.15€ ($2.90) seniors and students, 1.90€ ($1.75) children, 10€ ($9.10) family. Mar–Apr and Nov Mon–Fri 10am–4:30pm; May–Oct daily 10am–6pm.

OUTDOOR PURSUITS
COUNTY WEXFORD

BEACHES   County Wexford's beaches at Courtown, Curracloe, Duncannon, and Rosslare are ideal for walking, jogging, or swimming.

BICYCLING   Mountain bikes can be rented at **Black's Cycle Center** in Arklow, County Wicklow ((C) **0402/31898**), for 13€ ($12) per day and 63€ ($58) per week including helmet and panniers. This is a good starting point for excursions along the Wexford coastal roads, although a short section of the very busy N11 road will have to be followed before reaching the coast road—use extreme caution. There is also a Raleigh Rent-a-Bike location in Wexford town: **Hayes Cycle Shop,** 108 S. Main St. ((C) **053/22462**). From Wexford, the road north up the coast through Curracloe to Blackwater is a scenic day trip.

BIRD-WATCHING   A good starting place for bird-watching in the region is the **Wexford Wildfowl Reserve** (see description under "Seeing the Sights in Wexford Town," earlier), where warden Chris Wilson can direct you to other places of interest.

The **Saltee Islands** offer one of the best summer bird-watching sites in Ireland, especially during May, June, and July when many species come here to nest (see listing under "Seeing the Sights Around County Wexford," above). **Hook Head** is a well-known spot for watching the spring and autumn passerine migration—but the lack of sizable cliffs means that it isn't popular with summer nesting seabirds. In addition to the swallows, swifts, and warblers, look out for the less common cuckoos, turtle doves, redstarts, and blackcaps. Other places of interest are **Lady's Island Lake** near Carnsore Point, an important tern colony, and the neighboring **Tacumshin Lake.**

FISHING   One center for sea angling in Wexford is the town of Kilmore Quay, south of Wexford town on R739. There are several people here who offer boats for rent, with all the necessary equipment; Dick Hayes runs **Kilmore Quay Boat Charters** (© 053/29704 or 087/254-9111), and is skipper of the *Enterprise.* The most popular rivers for fishing are the Barrow and the Slaney, where the sea trout travel upstream from mid-June to the end of August.

GOLF   In recent years, Wexford has blossomed as a golfing venue. The newest development is an 18-hole championship seaside par-72 course at **St. Helens Bay Golf Club,** Kilrane, County Wexford (© 053/33234; www.sthelensbay.com), with greens fees of 32€ ($29) on weekdays and 36€ ($32) weekends. Tennis courts, sauna, and luxury cottages are available. Another course welcoming visitors is the **Enniscorthy Golf Club,** Knockmarshall, Enniscorthy, County Wexford (© 054/33191; engc@eircom.net), an inland par-70 course with greens fees of 25€ ($23) on weekdays and 32€ ($29) on weekends.

HORSEBACK RIDING   **Horetown House** ⭐, Foulksmills, County Wexford (© 051/565771; fax 051/565633; poloxirl@iol.ie), offers riding lessons by the hour or packages that include meals and lodging. This is one of the better residential equestrian centers in Ireland. It caters particularly to families and children, but lessons in jumping and dressage are also available for more experienced riders, as well as in a game called polocross, which combines polo and lacrosse. Training in hunting and admission to the hunt can also be arranged. A minimum level of riding experience is required for hunts. For details, call Horetown House. Riding is 18€ ($16) per hour; and bed-and-breakfast is 58€ ($52) for a double without bathroom or 68€ ($62) for a double with bathroom. The fine in-house restaurant offers a "farmhouse set dinner" for residents between 6 and 9pm, a good deal at 21€ ($19) for three courses; the set dinner for non-residents is 29€ ($26).

WALKING   The entire coastline in County Wexford is posted with brown signs indicating a man with a backpack walking on water: This is the **Wexford Coastal Path,** which theoretically allows one to walk the whole coast on beaches and country roads. In reality, the roads are often too popular with cars, so I wouldn't recommend walking the entirety of the route, especially the bypass around Wexford town. The markers are handy, however, for shorter walks along and between Wexford's clean beaches.

In the northern part of the county, the section of beach from Clogga Head (County Wicklow) to Tara Hill is especially lovely, as is the walk to the top of Tara Hill, which offers many viewpoints over sloping pastures to the sea. A good base for both of these walks is **Carrigeen B&B,** Tara Hill, Gorey, County Wexford (© 055/21732), which offers basic accommodations, a spectacular view of the sea, and a welcoming family (the Leonards) quite familiar with the local walks; double rooms with a private bathroom are 56€ ($51). Farther south, the path veers off the road and sticks to the beach from Cahore Point south to Raven Point and from Rosslare Harbour to Kilmore Quay.

There's a lovely coastal walk near the town of Wexford in the **Raven Nature Reserve** ⭐, an area of forested dunes and uncrowded beaches. To get there, take R741 north out of Wexford, turn right on R742 to Curracloe just out of town, and in the village of Curracloe turn right and continue 1 mile (1.5km) to the beach parking lot. The nature reserve is now to your right—you can get there by car, driving another half mile (1km) south, or just walk the distance along the beach. The beach extends another 3 miles (5km) to Raven Point, where at low tide you can see the remains of a shipwreck, half buried in the sand. The point is also a great place to watch migratory birds in the winter and spring—the flight of the white-fronted geese at dusk is an experience you shouldn't miss.

On the border between Counties Wexford and Carlow is a long rounded ridge of peaks known as the **Blackstairs Mountains,** which offer a number of beautiful walks in an area remarkably unspoiled by tourism. A good guide is *Walking the Blackstairs* by Joss Lynam, available at Wexford tourist offices. It includes trail descriptions and information on local plants and wildlife.

ACCOMMODATIONS YOU CAN AFFORD
AROUND COUNTY WEXFORD

Clonard House   Just a few miles out of Wexford town, Clonard House is a great base for exploring the town and the southern Wexford coast. As you pass through the imposing gates, you enter the peaceful pastoral world of this 18th-century Georgian farmhouse; Kathleen Hayes is the affable host. Breakfast is served in the high-ceilinged, chandeliered dining room, with tea in a cozy parlor complete with fireplace. The rooms are simple and elegant; those in the front of the house look out over Wexford Harbour, and six have four-poster beds. The breakfast here is especially memorable. Bedrooms, the dining room, and one lounge are nonsmoking; there's a separate smoking lounge.

Clonard Great, Wexford, Co. Wexford. ℂ/fax 053/43141. http://indigo.ie/~khayes. 9 units. 34€ ($31) single; 56€ ($51) double. 50% reduction for children. Rates include full breakfast. MC, V. Closed Nov–Mar. **Amenities:** Smoking lounge. *In room:* TV, hair dryer.

Clone House ✯   You'll receive a gracious welcome at this 300-acre working farm, the home of Tom and Betty Breen. The bedrooms are furnished with handsome antiques, as is the rest of the 250-year-old farmhouse. A courtyard opens onto an attractive garden in back, and you can walk through the fields to the bank of the River Bann. Tom prides himself on his knowledge of the local area, and of Ireland as a whole, and will be glad to assist you in making plans for touring or outdoor activities. The bedrooms, dining room, and sitting room are nonsmoking.

Ferns, Enniscorthy, Co. Wexford. ℂ/fax 054/66113. http://homepage.eircom.net/~clonehouse. 5 units. 41€ ($37) single; 70€ ($63) double. Rates include full breakfast. High tea 19€ ($17), dinner 23.5€ ($21). No credit cards. Closed Oct–Feb. **Amenities:** Dining room, sitting room. *In room:* TV in 3 units, hair dryer.

Farm House ✯ *Value*   Mrs. Joan Crosbie's homey, rambling farmhouse dates to 1640, a fact that is visible in its thick stone walls and venerable woodwork. Mrs. Crosbie has been taking guests for over 30 years, and her energy and enthusiasm for entertaining visitors has not diminished. The house has also changed little during the past few decades and bears an aura of antiquity, which is often charming but sometimes inconvenient: one bathroom is shared between three bedrooms (in the wing) or four bedrooms (in the main house). The bedrooms in the main house are considerably more comfortable and appealing in decor than those in the very spartan adjacent wing, which was converted from a stable. Despite the inconveniences, Mrs. Crosbie's house is a haven of hospitality and good value. I'm particularly fond of the high-ceilinged, spacious dining room, redolent in the morning of freshly baked scones and brown bread.

Foulksmills, Co. Wexford. ℂ 051/565616. 10 units, none with bathroom. 20€ ($18) single; 41€ ($37) double. 20% reduction for children sharing with an adult. Rates include full breakfast. No credit cards. Closed Oct–Apr.

Killarney House   Mrs. Noreen Fallon's home has two excellent features: ground-floor guest rooms (a boon for those troubled by stairs) and a breakfast menu with several selections. An added bonus is the peaceful country setting, 1¼ miles (2km) from New Ross. All three bedrooms in this modern bungalow are equipped with sinks and electric blankets, and there's a TV lounge for guests.

The Maudlins, New Ross, Co. Wexford. ✆ 051/421062. 3 units, 2 with bathroom (shower only). 46€ ($41) double without bath, 51€ ($46) double with bath. 50% reduction for children under 10 sharing with parents. Rates include full breakfast. MC, V. Free parking. Closed Oct–Mar. *In room:* Hair dryer.

Kilrane House *(Kids)*   This 19th-century house, located on the Wexford–Rosslare Harbour road (N25), half a mile (1km) from Rosslare Harbour, has an elegant lounge with fine plasterwork. Siobhan Whitehead extends a special welcome to families. She has one large family room that sleeps five, and is happy to supply cots for the little ones. Bedrooms and the dining room are nonsmoking.

Kilrane, Rosslare Harbour, Co. Wexford. ✆ 053/33135. Fax 053/33739. 6 units. Rates 33€–48€ ($30–$44) single; 53€ ($48) double. 33% reduction for children sharing with parents. MC, V. *In room:* TV, tea/coffeemaker.

O'Leary's Farm   Mrs. Kathleen O'Leary and her engaging offspring (along with a grandchild or two) make their guests feel like part of the family. Their farmhouse, 3 miles (5km) from Rosslare Harbour, prominently signposted on N25, looks out to the sea across flatlands that focus the eye on ferry comings and goings at Rosslare Harbour. The house provides large family rooms as well as the usual doubles, and features a glassed-in front porch that takes advantage of the seascape, while an open fire warms the lounge. One of the O'Learys will pick up and deliver guests to the ferry port with advance notice.

Killilane, Kilrane, Co. Wexford. ✆ 053/33134. polearyfarm@eircom.net. 10 units, 7 with bathroom (shower only). 46€ ($41) double without bathroom, 51€ ($46) double with bathroom. 25% reduction for children sharing with parents. Rates include full breakfast. No credit cards. *In room:* Tea/coffeemaker.

Riversdale House   This modern split-level home is the domain of Mrs. Ann Foley, whose hospitality is legendary. The house is set in spacious grounds overlooking the town park and the river, and its terrace is a great place to sit outside in good weather. Mrs. Foley is generous with her knowledge of the locality and her willingness to provide an early breakfast for those departing Rosslare Harbour, some 45 minutes away.

Lower William St., New Ross, Co. Wexford. ✆ 051/422515. Fax 051/422800. www.riversdalehouse.com. 4 units. 37€ ($33) single; 56€ ($51) double. 20% reduction for children. Rates include full breakfast. MC, V. *In room:* TV, tea/coffeemaker, hair dryer.

Rockcliffe   Just 2 miles (3km) from town and about ½ mile (1km) down the Johnstown Castle road (off the Wexford-Rosslare road), Mrs. Sarah Lee's modern home is set high on an acre of beautifully landscaped grounds. The Rosslare ferry is 10 miles (9.5km) away, and Mrs. Lee is happy to fix an early breakfast for departing guests. From Rosslare Harbour, take N25 and at the roundabout take the Wexford exit (route 730); Rockcliffe is signposted at the next left turn (just after Farmer's Kitchen Bar/Restaurant).

Coolballow, Wexford, Co. Wexford. ✆ 053/43130. sarahlee@ireland.com. 4 units, 3 with bathroom (shower only). 46€ ($41) double without bathroom, 51€ ($46) double with bathroom. 20% reduction for children under 10 sharing with an adult. Rates include full breakfast. No credit cards. Private parking. Closed Nov–Easter.

WORTH A SPLURGE

Ballinkeele House ✪   The cozy elegance of this house and the warmth of the Maher family make this one of the best places in the southeast to forget about your budget and live it up for a few days. This grand Irish manor house, built in 1840 and owned by the Mahers for four generations, is the perfect place to recover from the rigors of travel. You'll think you've stepped into another world as you walk into the majestic entrance hall. John and Margaret Maher are exemplary hosts and see to it that their guests feel immediately at home. Despite the grandeur of the accommodations, they create an atmosphere that's relaxed and without pretension. Dinner is served by candlelight in a chandeliered dining room, and the food is quite good—main courses range from trout with fennel to steak with whisky sauce or pheasant in a cream and brandy sauce. Vegetarian options are also available. The house is surrounded by 350 acres of fields and woodlands, with some gardens in the process of being created around a pond. Numerous options exist for a short walk.

Ballymurn, Enniscorthy, Co. Wexford. ☎ **053/38105.** Fax 053/38468. www.ballinkeele.com. 5 units. 76€–92€ ($69–$83) single; 120€–154€ ($109–$140) double. Rates include full breakfast. Dinner 35€ ($32) (book before noon). AE, MC, V. Free parking. Closed Nov–Feb. Located off N11 between Enniscorthy and Wexford: turn at Oilgate and follow signs for the house. **Amenities:** Dining room, lounge. *In room:* TV, hair dryer.

GREAT DEALS ON DINING
AROUND COUNTY WEXFORD

The Antique Tavern ✪✪ PUB GRUB   It's worth a trip to Enniscorthy to see this unique Tudor-style pub, located off the main Dublin-Wexford road (N11). This cozy, friendly place has everything you'd expect of an old Irish pub. The walls are lined with memorabilia from the Wexford area—old daggers, pikes, farming implements, lanterns, pictures, and prints. You'll also see mounted elks' heads, an antique wooden bird cage, and a glass case full of paper money from around the world.

Proprietor Vincent Heffernan is proud of the fact that the Antique Tavern has won "best pub" awards for both County Wexford and the entire Leinster province. It serves some of the best bar lunches in the area—homemade soups with homemade brown bread and a vast and varied selection of sandwiches, washed down with either tea or coffee.

Enniscorthy (on the northern outskirts of town on N11), Co. Wexford. ☎ **054/33428.** Under 10€ ($9) inclusive. MC, V. Daily 12:30–3:30pm.

THE PUB SCENE
AROUND COUNTY WEXFORD

Oak Tavern   Dating from 150 years and originally a tollhouse on the River Slaney, this pub is situated 2 miles (3km) north of town, overlooking the River Slaney and near the Ferrycarrig Bridge. Bar lunches are served during the day, with the choices being of the shepherd's-pie variety. There's a riverside patio for outside seating on fine days. Traditional music sessions are held most evenings in the front bar. Wexford-Enniscorthy Rd. (N11), Ferrycarrig, Wexford. ☎ **053/20945.**

2 Waterford Town & County Waterford

Waterford town is 40 miles (64km) W of Wexford, 33 miles (53km) W of Rosslare Harbour, 98 miles (158km) SW of Dublin, 78 miles (126km) E of Cork, and 95 miles (153km) SE of Shannon Airport

Waterford town (pop. 42,000) is the main seaport of the southeast. The town is primarily a commercial center, and is dominated by its busy port. Because the rest of County Waterford is so beautiful, most travelers don't linger for long in the somewhat dingy capital town, although the historic district around Reginald's Tower is quite attractive.

Coastal highlights south of Waterford include **Dunmore East,** a picturesque fishing village; **Dungarvan,** a major town with a fine harbor; **Ardmore,** a quiet beach resort; and **Passage East,** a tiny seaport from which you can catch a ferry across the harbor and cut your driving time from Waterford to Wexford in half. Ardmore, which in Irish means "the great height," is the setting for a 7th-century monastic settlement, founded by St. Declan, which has on its grounds a 12th-century cathedral, numerous ancient grave sites, a holy well, and a 97-foot-tall (30m) round tower, one of the most perfect of its kind in this part of Ireland. Portally Cove, near Dunmore East, is the home of Ireland's only Amish-Mennonite community.

In northwest County Waterford, the **Comeragh Mountains** provide many opportunities for beautiful walks, including the short trek to Mahon Falls. These mountains also have highly scenic roads for bicycle excursions. Further west, there's great fishing and bird-watching on the **Blackwater estuary.**

GETTING THERE   **Irish Rail** offers daily service from Dublin and other points into Plunkett Station, at Ignatius Rice Bridge, Waterford (℗ **051/ 873401;** www.irishrail.ie).

Bus Eireann operates daily service into Plunkett Station Depot, Waterford (℗ **051/879000;** www.buseireann.ie), from Dublin, Limerick, and other major cities throughout Ireland.

These major roads lead into Waterford: N25 from Cork and the south, N24 from the west, N19 from Kilkenny and points north, and N25 from Wexford.

The Passage East Ferry Co., Barrack Street, Passage East, County Waterford (℗ **051/382480** or 051/382488), operates a car ferry service across Waterford Harbour, linking Passage East, about 10 miles (16km) east of Waterford, with Ballyhack, about 20 miles (32km) southwest of Wexford. This shortcut saves about an hour's driving time between the two cities. Crossing time averages 10 minutes and service is continuous. It's a drive-on, drive-off service, with no reservations required. The fares are 5.70€ ($5.20) one-way and 8.25€ ($7.50) round-trip for car and passengers, 1.25€ ($1.15) one-way and 1.90€ ($1.75) round-trip for foot passengers, 2.60€ ($2.40) one-way and 3.15€ ($2.90) round-trip for cyclists. Ferries run April through September, Monday through Saturday, 7am until 10pm, and on Sunday 9:30am until 10pm; October through March, Monday through Saturday, 7am until 8pm, and Sunday, 9:30am until 8pm.

VISITOR INFORMATION   Year-round information services are provided by the **Waterford Tourist Office,** Granary Building, Merchant's Quay, Waterford (℗ **051/875788**). It's open April through June, Monday through Saturday, from 9am to 6pm; July and August, Monday through Saturday, from 9am to 6pm and Sunday 11am to 5pm; September, Monday through Saturday, from 9am to 6pm; October, Monday through Saturday, from 9am to 5pm; November through March, Monday through Friday, from 9am to 5pm. The year-round office on the Square in **Dungarvan** (℗ **058/41741**) has comparable hours. The seasonal Tourist Office on the Square at **Tramore** (℗ **051/381572**) is open from mid-June through August, Monday through Saturday 10am to 6pm.

Additionally, here are a couple of websites that will keep you up on Waterford goings-on: **www.waterford-online.ie** and **www.waterford-today.ie.** The website for all Southeast Tourism is **www.southeastireland.travel.ie.**

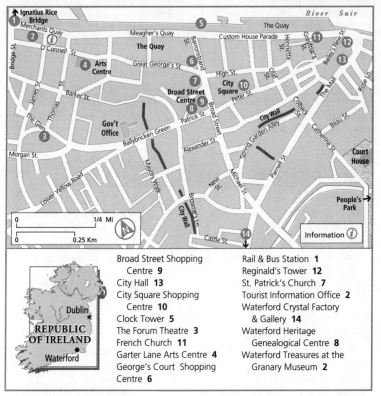

Broad Street Shopping Centre **9**	Rail & Bus Station **1**
City Hall **13**	Reginald's Tower **12**
City Square Shopping Centre **10**	St. Patrick's Church **7**
Clock Tower **5**	Tourist Information Office **2**
The Forum Theatre **3**	Waterford Crystal Factory & Gallery **14**
French Church **11**	Waterford Heritage Genealogical Centre **8**
Garter Lane Arts Centre **4**	Waterford Treasures at the Granary Museum **2**
George's Court Shopping Centre **6**	

WATERFORD TOWN

TOWN LAYOUT   Rimmed by the River Suir, Waterford is a small and compact town. The main commercial hub sits on the south bank of the river. Traffic from the north, west, and east enters from the north bank via the Ignatius Rice Bridge and onto a series of four quays (Grattan, Merchants, Meagher, and Parade), but most addresses simply say "The Quay." The majority of shops and attractions are concentrated near the quay area or on two thoroughfares that intersect with the quays—The Mall and Barronstrand Street, which change names to Broad, Michael, and John Streets.

GETTING AROUND   By Public Transportation   Bus Eireann operates daily bus service within Waterford and its environs. The flat fare is 1€ (90¢). Taxi ranks are located outside Plunkett Rail Station and along the Quay opposite the Granville Hotel. If you need to call a taxi, try **City Cabs** (② 051/852222) or **Metro Cabs** (② 051/857157).

By Car   To see most of Waterford's sights, with the exception of Waterford Glass, it's best to walk. Park your car along the Quays; the parking system is via machines at 2.50€ ($2.30) per day, or by the disc system at .50€ (45¢) per hour. Discs are on sale at the tourist office or many of the shops. You'll need a car to reach the Waterford Glass Factory and Waterford County attractions outside of town.

If you need to rent a car, you can contact **Europcar,** Sheridan Garage, Cork Road, Waterford (© **051/372891**); **Enterprise,** Westgate Business Park, Waterford (© **051/304804**); or **Euromobile,** Morgan St., Waterford (© **051/ 301222**).

On Foot   The best way to see the town is by walking along the quays and taking a right at Reginald's Tower on The Mall (which becomes Parnell Street) and then turning right onto John Street (which becomes Michael, Broad, and Barronstrand streets), which brings you back to the quays. The tourist office can supply you with a free map.

 FAST FACTS: Waterford

Drugstores   Try **Gallagher's Pharmacy,** at 29 Barronstrand St. (© 051/ 878103), and **Mulligan's Chemists,** with shops at 40–41 Barronstrand St. (© 051/875211) and at Unit 12A of City Square Shopping Centre (© 051/853247).

Dry Cleaning & Laundry   Two good spots are **Eddies Dry Cleaners,** at 82 The Quay (© 051/877677), and **Boston Cleaners,** at 6 Michael St. (© 051/874487).

Emergencies   Dial © **999.**

Gay & Lesbian Resource   Call the **Gay Line Southeast** (© 051/879907), available Wednesday 7:30 to 9:30pm.

Hospital   **Holy Ghost Hospital** is located on Cork Road (© 051/374397).

Local Newspaper & Media   The weekly newspaper covering local events and entertainment is the *Waterford News & Star.* Waterford Local Radio (WLR) broadcasts on 97.5 FM and 95.1 FM.

Photographic Supplies   Try the Camera Shop, 109 The Quay (© 051/ 75049).

Police   Phone the Garda Headquarters (© 051/874888).

Post Office   The **General Post Office** on Parade Quay (© 051/874444) is open Monday through Friday from 9am to 5:30pm and Saturday from 9am to 1pm.

SEEING THE SIGHTS IN WATERFORD TOWN

Some of Waterford's most interesting sightseeing attractions are its extensive **ruins,** relics of its long, turbulent history. Look for traces of the old Viking-built city walls at the railway station, Mayor's Walk, and Castle Street. On Greyfriars Street, the ruins of the French church are all that remain of the Franciscan foundation built in 1240 that once housed Huguenot refugees—tours of the church depart from Reginald's Tower (see description below). And all along the Quay, storefronts reflect the town's beginnings and evolution over the centuries.

City Hall   Headquarters of the local Waterford town government, this late 18th-century building houses various local memorabilia, including information on the town's charter, which was granted in 1205. In addition, a display is dedicated to Thomas Francis Meagher, a leader in an 1848 Irish insurrection. Meagher was sentenced to death but he escaped to America, where he fought in the Civil War, earned the rank of brigadier general, and eventually became acting governor of Montana. City Hall's other treasures include an 18th-century Waterford glass chandelier, a complete dinner service of priceless antique Waterford glasses, and a painting of Waterford town in 1736 by the Flemish master William Van der Hagen.

The Mall, Waterford. © 051/873501. Free admission. Mon–Fri 9am–1pm and 2–5pm.

Garter Lane Arts Centre   One of Ireland's largest arts centers, the Garter Lane occupies two buildings on O'Connell Street. No. 5 is the site of the former Waterford Library, and is now the setting for exhibition rooms and artists' studios. No. 22a, the former Friends Meeting House, now houses the Garter Lane Theatre, with an art gallery and outdoor courtyard. The gallery showcases works by contemporary and local artists. In December, a crafts fair usually takes place, with works by artists from all over Ireland.

5 and 22a O'Connell St., Waterford. © 051/855038. Fax 051/871570. lilly@garterlane.ie. Free admission to gallery; theater, music, and dance performances 2.50€–16€ ($2.30–$14). Gallery Mon–Sat 10am–6pm.

The New Ross Galley   See "Seeing the Sights Around County Wexford" in Wexford, earlier in this chapter, for details on this ship/restaurant. Reservations are essential. The *Galley* will also take passengers who are just along for the ride: Cruise-only prices from Waterford are 7.50€ to 14€ ($6.80–$13).

The Quay. © 051/421723. Lunch Apr–Oct daily at 12:30pm; tea Apr–Oct daily at 3pm. Dinner Apr–Sept usually 7pm. (Note that frequency and times vary with demand.)

Reginald's Tower   At the end of the Quay, which turns into the Mall, Reginald's Tower stands sentinel as it has for 1,000 years. When Reginald McIvor, the Danish ruler, built this stronghold, its 12-foot thick walls stood right at the river's edge, and it was constructed so that entrance could only be gained from inside the city walls. In the centuries since, the tower has proved its worth as the strongest fortification on the River Suir, having resisted attack from all sides (even Cromwell failed to conquer it, although the bitterly cold winter may have had something to do with his unsuccessful siege). And it has witnessed other events of major significance in Ireland's history, such as the marriage in 1170 of Strongbow—leader of the Norman forces that invaded Ireland in that year—to Eva, daughter of the Irish King MacMurrough, which marked the beginning of England's entanglement with Irish affairs. There are guided tours of the tower which also include French Church, the ruins of a 13th-century Franciscan Friary nearby on Greyfriars Lane, and the Undercroft, two cellars from the 13th and 15th centuries (about 4 minutes' walk from the tower).

The Quay, Waterford. ©/fax 051/304220. Admission 1.90€ ($1.75) adults, 1.25€ ($1.15) seniors, .75€ (70¢) children and students, 5.10€ ($4.60) family. Easter–Oct daily 9:30am–6pm.

Tips **Walking Your Way Through Waterford**

The very best way to begin you explorations of Waterford is to take a **Waterford City Walking Tour** ✦. Jack Burtchaell, well versed in the history, folklore, and witty anecdotes of the city, conducts an engaging hour-long tour of the old city, leaving daily from the reception area of the Granville Hotel on the Quay. Tours are offered daily at noon and 2pm from March through October and cost 5€ ($4.60) for adults, free for accompanied small children. For more information, call Waterford Tourist Services at © 051/873711.

Waterford Crystal Factory and Gallery ⊛ Founded in 1783, this glass-making enterprise thrived and Waterford became the crystal of connoisseurs. But the factory was forced to close in 1851 due to the devastating effects of the Irish famine. When the Irish government moved to revive the industry in 1947, it took 5 years to gather the necessary artisans and build a proper facility. Some 30 master glassblowers, cutters, and engravers were brought from Europe to train Irish apprentices, and in 1951 Waterford crystal was once more in production. Today, there's a staff of hundreds, turning out 90,000 finished pieces of the beautiful crystal every week, of which about 60% is shipped to the United States.

Visitors are welcome to watch a 17-minute audiovisual presentation on the glass-making process and then take a one-hour tour of the factory to see the process first-hand, from the mouth blowing and shaping of the molten glass to the delicate hand cutting. *Note:* Children under 10 are not permitted on the factory tour.

You can also stroll around the Waterford Crystal Gallery, a bilevel showroom containing the most comprehensive display of Waterford crystal in the world, from all the glassware patterns to elaborate pieces like trophies, globes, and chandeliers. Crystal is on sale in the gallery. There's also a restaurant on the premises.

Cork Rd., Waterford. ② **051/373311.** Fax 051/332716. www.waterfordvisitorcentre.com. Tour 6€ ($5.45) adults, 3.50€ ($3.20) students, free for children under 12; free admission for the audiovisual presentation and gallery. Tours Apr–Oct daily 8:30am–4pm; Nov–Mar Mon–Fri 9am–3:15pm. Showrooms Mar–Oct daily 8:30am–6pm; Nov–Apr daily 9am–5pm.

Waterford Treasures at the Granary ★ This museum on Merchants Quay was opened in May of 1999 and contains numerous items previously on display in the Waterford Heritage Museum. The Viking exhibition includes artifacts discovered during extensive excavations of Vadrafyordr, the Viking city of Waterford, paired with an audiovisual presentation. Highlights of the medieval collection include the Great Charter Roll, a 14th-century scroll depicting local events, and the Great Parchment Book, which constitutes one of the first recorded uses of the English language in Ireland. There is also an exhibition on the glass industry in Waterford. The museum complex includes a restaurant, an auditorium, and a tourist information office (② **051/875788**).

Merchants Quay, Waterford. ② **051/304500.** www.waterfordtreasures.com. Admission 7€ ($6.35) adults, 5€ ($4.55) seniors and students, 3.50€ ($3.20) children under 16, 19€ ($17) family, free for children under 5. Sept–May daily 10am–5pm; June–Aug daily 9:30am–9pm.

SIGHTSEEING TOURS

Walking Tours of Historic Waterford ★★ *(Finds)* Local Waterford residents, well versed in the history, folklore, and wit of the town, conduct 1-hour walking tours of Waterford that include two cathedrals and four national monuments. This is an exceptional tour. Tours depart from the Granville Hotel, The Quay.

Waterford Tourist Services, Jenkins Lane, Waterford. ② **051/873711.** Fax 051/850645. 5.10€ ($4.60) adults, free for small children. Mar–Oct daily 11:45am and 1:45pm.

ACCOMMODATIONS YOU CAN AFFORD
WATERFORD TOWN

Annvill House Phyllis O'Reilly is the hostess of this modern two-story home, and is happy to arrange tours and to help guests with any other holiday plans. The guest rooms are bright and comfortable, with built-in wardrobes. The house is conveniently located 100 yards off the Waterford-Cork road (N25), on the right-hand side of the roundabout, opposite the Waterford Crystal Factory entrance.

The Orchard, Kingsmeadow, Waterford, Co. Waterford. ✆ 051/373617. Fax 051/373617. 5 units, 4 with bathroom (shower only). 50€ ($45) double. 10% reduction for children. Rates include full breakfast. Dinner 19€ ($17). No credit cards. Free off-the-street parking. Bus: From the Clock Tower. *In room:* Tea/coffeemakers, hair dryer.

GREAT DEALS ON DINING
WATERFORD TOWN

Dwyer's ✿ IRISH/INTERNATIONAL   This small restaurant is situated on a quiet back street near the northern entrance to the town at Ignatius Rice Bridge. Portions are generous and the food is good without being fussy. The owners, Martin and Sile Dwyer, cook everything to order in a homey 30-seat setting. The menu changes often, and past menus have (memorably) included wild salmon in filo pastry with cucumbers and fennel, roast squab pigeon with port wine sauce, roast marinated brill with Gremolata sauce, and honey-glazed breast of duck with lemon sauce.

8 Mary St., Waterford. ✆ 051/877478 or 051/871183. www.dwyersrestaurant.com. Reservations recommended. Main courses 16€–22€ ($14–$20); early-bird (6–7pm) 4-course fixed-price dinner 22€ ($20). AE, DC, MC, V. Mon–Sat 6–10pm.

The Munster BAR FOOD/TRADITIONAL   The Munster serves a wide selection of budget-priced plates to seemingly half of Waterford's young working crowd at lunch. More than just bar food, the heaping plates of roast beef, ham, or chicken with potato and two vegetables are ample enough to be the main meal of the day. If you're not that hungry, there's soup, sandwiches, and cold salad plates, as well something called a "blaa" (lettuce, meat, onion, and tomato on a small roll), found only in Waterford. This is the "back room" of the Munster Bar on Bailey's New Street (see "The Pub Scene," below).

The Mall. ✆ 051/874656. Meals 4.50€–7€ ($4.10–$6.35); sandwiches 1.25€–2€ ($1.15–$1.80); soups 2€ ($1.80). MC, V. Mon–Fri 12:30–2:30pm.

The Olde Stand SEAFOOD/STEAKS/CARVERY/PUB GRUB   This Victorian-style pub and restaurant combines lots of mahogany (the back bar came from an old church in England), deep shades of green, and a liberal dose of charm to come up with an ambience full of character. The downstairs bar is a cozy, intimate space, and the upstairs restaurant has two pleasant, relaxing rooms, with candles on the tables and a fireplace adding a cheery glow. As for the food, the lunchtime carvery features a roast joint (beef, lamb, pork) of the day, as well as homemade soups, salad plates, and a salad bar. From teatime on, the menu lists seafood (fresh from local waters), steaks from Ireland's Golden Vale, chicken, lamb, duck, and other local specialties. An excellent Irish cheese board puts a perfect finish to your meal. As a crowning touch, the staff here is both friendly and efficient.

45 Michael St. ✆ 051/879488. Bar food 5.50€–8.50€ ($5.00–$7.70); main courses 14€–25€ ($13–$23); early-bird menu (served 5:30–7:30pm) 15€ ($14); carvery lunch under 7.50€ ($6.80). AE, MC, V. Mon–Sat 12:15–2:30pm and 3:30–11pm; Sun 12:30–10pm.

The Reginald IRISH   One of the town's original walls (ca. 850) is part of the decor at this pub/restaurant next to Reginald's Tower. In keeping with its Viking-inspired foundations, the Reginald is laid out in a pattern of caverns, alcoves, and arches. The restaurant offers innovative choices using local ingredients, such as filet steak Aoife topped with avocado, chives, tomatoes, and green peppercorn sauce; and filet of pink trout with vermouth sauce. Monday, Tuesday, and Wednesday evenings there's live traditional Irish music, and Thursday through Saturday the Reginald becomes the Excalibur "Knight Club" (named after the film and housing a number of its props) with live music and dancing. There's no cover charge before midnight. This is reputedly where the Norman leader Strongbow met Aoife. Who knows who you'll meet?

2/3 The Mall, Waterford. ℂ **051/855087.** Reservations recommended for dinner. Bar food 2.60€–13€ ($2.40–$12); early-bird dinner (served 3–7:30pm) 15€–19€ ($14–$17); dinner main courses 14€–25€ ($13–$23); fixed-price 4-course dinner 28€ ($25). AE, DC, MC, V. Mon–Sat 9:30am–10:30pm; Sun noon–10pm.

Thomas Francis Meagher Bar PUB GRUB   This attractive ground-floor bar in the Granville Hotel offers such specialties as smoked salmon and brown bread, along with several tasty hot dishes, salad plates, and snacks. It's a good place for a quick bite in a historic atmosphere.

In the Granville Hotel, The Quay. ℂ **051/305555.** www.granville-hotel.ie. 3€–9€ ($2.70–$8.15). AE, MC, V. Daily 12:30–2:30pm.

SHOPPING IN WATERFORD TOWN

Many people come to Waterford to buy Waterford crystal, but the truth is that prices for Waterford crystal in Ireland are generally the same as those in the U.S. It's still fascinating to see the crystal being made, however. Besides crystal, there are many other fine products in Waterford's shops and three multilevel enclosed shopping centers—**George's Court** off Barronstrand Street, **Broad Street Centre** on Broad Street, and **City Square** off Broad Street. Hours are usually Monday to Saturday from 9am or 9:30am to 6 or 6:30pm. Some shops are open until 9pm on Thursday and Friday, and are open Sundays during the summer months.

Aisling   Located opposite the town's Catholic cathedral, this small and interesting shop (whose name means "dream" in Gaelic) offers an assortment of unique crafts, from quilts, tartans, and kilts to floral art and miniature paintings and watercolors of Irish scenes and subjects. 61, The Quay, Waterford. ℂ **051/873262.**

The Book Centre   This huge, four-level bookstore sells all types of books, newspapers, and magazines, as well as posters, maps, and music tapes and CDs. There's a small cafe where you can relax with a book; you can also make a quick photocopy here or zap off a fax. Barronstrand St., Waterford. ℂ **051/873823.** Fax 051/870769. bookcentre@eircom.net.

Joseph Knox   For visitors to Waterford, this store has long been a focal point, offering a large selection of Waterford crystal, particularly in specialty items such as chandeliers. 4 Barronstrand St., Waterford. ℂ **051/875307.**

Kelly's   Dating from 1847, this store offers a wide selection of Waterford crystal, Aran knitwear, Belleek china, Royal Tara china, Irish linens, and other souvenirs. 75–76 The Quay, Waterford. ℂ **051/873557.**

Penrose Crystal   Established in 1786 and revived in 1978, this is Waterford's other glass company, turning out delicate handcut and engraved glassware. The craftspeople here practice the stipple engraving process, the highest art form in glass. A retail sales outlet is also located at Unit 8 of the City Square Shopping Centre. 32A John St., Waterford. ℂ **051/876537.**

Wool Craft   For more than 100 years, the Fitzpatrick family has operated this midtown shop, a reliable source for quality Irish knitwear. The focus here is on hand-loomed and hand-knit Aran sweaters, 2,000 square feet of 'em—at exceptionally low prices. 11 Michael St., Waterford. ✆ 051/74082.

WATERFORD AFTER DARK

Waterford has two main entertainment centers. Housed in one of Ireland's largest arts centers, the **Garter Lane Theatre,** 22a O'Connell St. (✆ **051/ 855038**), presents the work of local production companies, such as the Red Kettle and Waterford Youth Drama. Visiting troupes from all over Ireland also perform contemporary and traditional works at this 170-seat theater. Performances are usually Tuesday through Saturday, and tickets average 6.50€ to 13€ ($5.90 to $12) for most events. The box office is open Monday to Saturday from 10am to 6pm. It accepts MasterCard and Visa.

When big-name Irish or international groups come to Waterford, they usually perform at **The Forum Theatre at The Glen** (✆ **051/871111;** www.forumwaterford.com), a 1,000-seat house off Bridge Street. Tickets are 7.50€ to 23€ ($6.80–$21), depending on the event. Tickets can be purchased in the off-license booth next to the theatre, open Monday through Saturday, 11am to 11pm.

From May through September on Tuesdays, Thursdays, and Saturdays at 9pm the historic Waterford City Hall is home to **The Waterford Show,** a festive evening of music, storytelling, song, and dance. In high season, be sure to reserve a place in advance. Credit card bookings may be made at ✆ **051/ 358397** or after 5pm at 051/381020. Admission is 11.70€ ($10.50), which includes a pre-show drink and a complimentary glass of wine during the show.

Otherwise, Waterford's nightlife is centered in the hotel lounges and in the town's interesting assortment of pubs. Thursday through Saturday, the Reginald becomes a nightclub (see "Great Deals on Dining," above).

TRADITIONAL MUSIC SESSIONS   There's music most nights at **T&H Doolans,** 32 George's St. (✆ **051/841504**), as well as other Waterford pubs; check with the tourist office and in local papers or ask around to find out what's on during your visit.

THE PUB SCENE IN WATERFORD TOWN

Henry Downes & Co   Step into the marvelous maze of rooms that make up Downes, which dates from the 1700s, and you step back into a world long gone. The pub's spacious seating areas are made cozy by lots of old wood, and a spotlighted glass wall highlights an ancient spring-fed well. Lots of locals, good *craic,* and a superb "No. 9" Irish whiskey that Downes has produced since 1797 (ask about the origin of its name) make this one a local favorite. 10 Thomas St., Waterford. ✆ 051/874118.

Jack Meades *(Finds*   Waterford's most unusual pub is not in the town at all, but nestled beneath an old stone bridge in an area known as Halfway House, 4 miles (6.5km) south of Waterford. Dating from 1705, this old pub is widely known by the locals as Meade's Under the Bridge, or "Ireland's only fly-over pub." As a public house with a forge, it was a stopping-off point for travelers between Waterford and Passage East in the old days. The facade and interior haven't changed much in the intervening years: wooden beams, historical paintings, antiques, and open, crackling fireplaces. The grounds include an icehouse, a corn mill, lime kilns, a viaduct, and a beer garden/barbecue area. On most days in summer there are barbecues all day long. Bar food is served daily. Cheekpoint Rd., Halfway House, Ballycanavan, Co. Waterford. ✆ 051/850950.

The Munster Bar   This cozy, wood-paneled, etched-glass haven of conviviality began life as a coaching inn 200 years ago. The small room known as Peter's Bar is a gathering place for some of Waterford's liveliest conversationalists. On cool evenings, a coal fire reflects off wall sconces and chandeliers of "old" (pre-1851) Waterford glass. Peter's sons, Peter, Michael, and Tom, carry on their father's traditions of hospitality, and will see to it that you're not long a stranger. Frequently on Saturday and Sunday nights the large upstairs room rings to the strains of traditional music. What was probably the stables for the old Munster Inn has been converted into an extension. The place can be mobbed at lunchtime (see "Great Deals on Dining—Waterford Town," above), and is usually full in the evenings too. Bailey's New St., Waterford. ℭ 051/874656.

T. & H. Doolan's   You'll know T. & H. Doolan's by its Tudor-style front and frosted-glass door. Inside, there's a wonderfully eclectic collection of old farm implements, whiskey jars, stone crocks, mugs, copper jugs, and anything else the late Thomas Doolan took a fancy to hang from rough wooden beams or the whitewashed walls. He was, of course, the "T" of the proprietorship, and if anything went amiss, blame promptly fell on the "H" of that partnership—and here hangs a tale. H. Doolan, it turns out, was purely a figment of T. Doolan's imagination, and came into being when "Thomas" was too long and "T." and "Tom" too short for the establishment's sign. The spirited characters of T. & H. still linger in this 150-year-old pub that was for many years a stagecoach stop. There's an extensive bar menu (served 3 to 6pm), and an a la carte menu at dinnertime; bar food ranges from 3.80€ to 9€ ($3.45 to $8.15), and a la carte main courses from 13€ to 19€ ($12 to $17). There's also traditional music most nights throughout the year. 32 George's St., Waterford. ℭ 051/841504.

AROUND COUNTY WATERFORD
SEEING THE SIGHTS IN COUNTY WATERFORD

Besides the two attractions in Lismore (see listings below), there's much to see in County Waterford.

DUNMORE EAST   The little town of **Dunmore East** ✿ lies 9 miles (15km) from Waterford town via a picturesque stretch of R683/684. Mail ships used to put in at the town's historic harbor, as did smugglers, pirates, and a variety of other characters. You, too, may be tempted to stay and enjoy the fine beaches, sheltered coves, excellent fishing and sailing, and/or the good *craic.*

ARDMORE   Set on Ardmore Bay, with a long, sandy beach, **Ardmore** ✿ is a very appealing little seaside village, the descendant of a 7th-century settlement founded by St. Declan. It has won Ireland's Tidy Town Award seven times, and has a fine group of medieval ecclesiastical remains, including **St. Declan's Oratory,** whose west gable is adorned on the outside with a remarkable group of round-headed panels filled with sculptured figures. The **round tower** soars 97 feet (30m) into the air, with its four stories clearly delineated by rings of projecting stones. There's a beautiful **seaside walk** around nearby Ram Head, beginning behind the Cliff House Hotel and ending at St. Declan's Oratory, a distance of about 3 miles (5km).

MOUNT MELLARY   About 4½ miles (7km) east of the town of Cappoquin, in the foothills of the Knockmealdown Mountains, lies this monastic center for the Cistercian Order of the Strict Observance. It was built more than a century ago, when the monks were banished from France. There's an impressive stone church and a cluster of other large stone buildings. Rising at 2am to do all their own work and retiring at 8pm each evening, the monks have transformed a bare mountainside into productive fields and pastures. Until recently, they observed a strict rule of silence, with only the guest master permitted to speak. Visitors are welcome here, and many Irish Catholics come to stay for several days in the peaceful retreat.

BALLYDUFF   For a 6-week period between late June and early August, visitors to the area should be sure to inquire about performances—usually on a Wednesday—of **The Booley House** ✪ in St. Michael's Hall, Ballyduff, County Waterford (book through Lismore Heritage Centre, ✆ **058/54975** or 60287); admission is around 7.60€ ($6.90). Staged by talented locals, it's an authentic and delightful look into Ireland's rural past, when farm families moved cattle and sheep to the hills for summer grazing. Many of the small stone cottages you see today on high lands once served as homes for farm families during the more carefree months, and they were the scene of many a gathering of an evening for homegrown entertainment of music, song, dance, and storytelling. Tea, scones, and cake were always on hand then, and the Booley House carries on that tradition. Light-footed dancers float through the old step and set dances; the fiddles, whistles, and bodhrans swing into jigs and reels of long ago, and a storyteller brings on fits of laughter.

THE VEE   One of the most breathtaking roads in the area is that through a gap in the Knockmealdown Mountains known as the **Vee** (R668). It's signposted from the outskirts of Lismore and climbs to a height of 1,114 feet (340m), through mountainsides covered with heather to the V-shaped pass, with turnouts that overlook sweeping views of Tipperary's Golden Vale, before descending to the little town of **Clogheen** ✪, County Tipperary. Between the gap and Clogheen, keep a watch on the high side of the road for one of the most curious graves in the region, that of one **Samuel Grubb**, one-time owner of Castle Grace, who so loved his lands that he decreed he should be buried upright on the mountain slopes overlooking them. There's a small pathway leading up to the stone cairn that is his final resting place. About halfway over the Vee, you pass into South Tipperary.

Lismore Castle Gardens ★

Perched high on a cliff above the River Blackwater, this multiturreted castle has a long history, dating from 1185 when Prince John of England built a similar fortress on this site. Local lore says that Lismore Castle was once granted for 12 Irish punts ($13.75) a year to Sir Walter Raleigh, although he never occupied it. One man who did choose to live here was Richard Boyle, the first earl of Cork, who rebuilt the castle, including the thick defensive walls that still surround the garden, in 1626. Richard's son Robert, who was born at the castle in 1627, is the celebrated chemist whose name lives on in Boyle's Law. Most of the present castle was added in the mid–19th century. Today, this 8,000-acre estate of gardens, forests, and farmland is the Irish seat of the duke and duchess of Devonshire, whose primary home is at Chatsworth in England. Although the castle itself is not open for tours, the public is welcomed in the splendid walled and woodland gardens. *Note:* The castle can be rented, complete with the duke's personal staff (minimum five persons/ 4 nights), but this definitely isn't a budget option!

Lismore, Co. Waterford. ✆ **058/54424**. www.lismorecastle.com. Admission to gardens 3.80€ ($3.45) adults, 1.90€ ($1.75) children under 16; the castle is closed to the public. Apr–June and Sept daily 1:45–4:45pm; July–Aug daily 11am–4:45pm. Lismore lies 4 miles (6.5km) west of Cappoquin on N72.

Lismore Heritage Centre Where is the only Hindu Gothic bridge in Ireland located? Come here to find out. This interpretive center, housed in the town's Old Courthouse, will not only answer that question but also tell the history of Lismore, a charming town founded by St. Carthage in the year 636. The **Lismore Experience** ⟨★ is an exceptional award-winning multimedia presentation on the town's unique treasures, including the Book of Lismore, more than 1,000 years old, and the Lismore Crozier from 1116, both of which were discovered hidden in the walls of Lismore Castle in 1814. The presentation also provides an excellent introduction to the surrounding area and its attractions. There's a gift shop adjacent to the heritage center.

Lismore. ℂ 058/54975. www.lismore-ireland.com. Admission 3.80€ ($3.45) adults, 3.15€ ($2.90) seniors, 2.55€ ($2.30) children, 7.60€ ($6.90) family. Apr–Oct Mon–Sat 9:30am–5:30pm, Sun 12–5:30pm; Nov–Mar call ahead for hours.

OUTDOOR PURSUITS
COUNTY WATERFORD
BEACHES For walking, jogging, or swimming, visit one of County Waterford's wide, sandy beaches at Tramore, Ardmore, Clonea, or Dunmore East.

BICYCLING Neither of the rental venues in town offers helmets or panniers, so plan to bring your own. Bikes can be rented from 13€ ($12) daily and 76€ ($69) weekly at **Wright's Cycle Depot Ltd.,** Henrietta Street, Waterford (ℂ 051/874411), or **Altitude Cycle and Outdoor,** 22 Ballybricken, Waterford (ℂ 051/870356; altitude@indigo.ie). Altitude Cycle also offers an emergency repair service for travelers, whereby just about any repair is completed on the same day you bring the bike in; the shop also carries a large stock of hiking and camping equipment. From Waterford you can ride 8 miles (13km) to Passage East and take the ferry—it costs 3.15€ ($2.90) round-trip with a bicycle—to Wexford and the beautiful Hook Peninsula. Or, you can continue on from Passage East to Dunmore East, a picturesque seaside village with a small beach hemmed in by cliffs. The road from there on to Tramore and Dungarvan is quite scenic.

FISHING For sea fishing, picturesque **Dunmore East,** 8 miles (13km) south of Waterford, is a good bet. A boat can be chartered from **John O'Connor** (ℂ 051/383397) for reef, wreck, and shark fishing. Boat charter rates (per day) are 350€ ($317) for shark and wreck fishing; 300€ ($272) for reef fishing; single fares from 30€ to 40€ ($27 to $36), and rod and reel hire at 6€ ($5.45). The species you're likely to encounter in this area during the summer include blue shark, cod, bass, whiting, conger, and ling. At **Clonanav Fly Fishing Centre,** Nire Valley, Ballymacarbry, County Waterford (ℂ 052/36141; fax 052/36294; www.flyfishingireland.com) you'll find clinics at all levels of experience, equipment rental, guides, and permits. Accommodation is offered at Clonanav Farm Guesthouse (see description below under "Accommodations You Can Afford").

GOLF County Waterford's golf venues include three 18-hole championship courses: **Faithlegg Golf Club,** Faithlegg House, County Waterford (ℂ 051/382241), a par-72 parkland course beside the River Suir, with greens fees of 32€ ($29) weekdays and 44€ ($40) on weekends; **Dungarvan Golf Club,** Knocknagranagh, Dungarvan, County Waterford (ℂ 058/43310; www.cablesurf.com/dungarvangolf), a par-72 parkland course with greens fees of 25€ ($23) on weekdays and 32€ ($29) on weekends; and **Waterford Castle**

Finds **A Walk to Mahon Falls**

Mahon Falls is located in the Comeragh Mountains, on R676 between Carrick-on-Suir and Dungarvan. At the tiny village of Mahon Bridge, 16 miles (26km) south of Carrick-on-Suir, turn west on the road marked for Mahon Falls, then continue to follow signs for the falls and the "Comeragh Drive." In about 3 miles (4.8km), you reach a parking lot along the Mahon River (in fact, just a tiny stream). The trail, indicated by two boulders, begins across the road from the parking lot. Follow the stream along the floor of the valley to the base of the falls. From here you can see the fields of Waterford spread out below you, and the sea a glittering mirror beyond. Walking time is about 30 minutes round-trip.

Golf and Country Club, The Island, Ballinakill, Waterford (② **051/871633;** www.waterfordcastle.com), a par-72 parkland course with greens fees of 38€ ($35) Monday to Friday and 44€ ($40) Friday to Sunday. In addition, there is the 18-hole par-71 inland course at **Waterford Golf Club,** Newrath, Waterford (② **051/876748**), a mile from the center of the town, with greens fees of 32€ ($29) on weekdays and 38€ ($35) on weekends.

HORSEBACK RIDING   County Waterford is filled with trails for horseback riding, with fees averaging 32€ ($29) for a 2-hour ride. You can arrange to ride at **Melody's Riding Stables,** Ballmacarberry, County Waterford (② **052/ 36147;** nirevalleyequestrian@eircom.net), where guides Ann McCarthy and Pat Melody will see that you are seated correctly. The horses are gentle and sure-footed, and there's a choice of paths from 5 to 20 miles (8–20km), through wooded mountainsides and alongside rushing river waters and sparkling lakes. Several 3- and 4-day riding vacations are available. Especially in July and August, it's advisable to reserve ahead by phone. Also recommended is **Killoteran Equestrian Centre,** Killoteran, Waterford (② **051/384158**), where the cost of an hour ride is about 33€ ($30).

SAILING, WINDSURFING & SEA KAYAKING   Courses are offered from May to September at the Dunmore East Adventure Centre, **Dunmore East, County** Waterford (② **051/383783;** fax 051/383786; www.dunmoreadventure.com). Courses last 1 to 4 days and are priced at 50€ ($45) per day, or 25€ ($23) for a half-day (including equipment rental). Summer programs for children are also available. This is a great spot for an introductory experience, but there isn't much wave action for thrill-seeking windsurfers.

ACCOMMODATIONS YOU CAN AFFORD
AROUND COUNTY WATERFORD

Ashbourne House   Mrs. Agnes Forrest is the gracious hostess of this two-story, renovated farmhouse on 20 acres of mixed farming 2 miles (3km) northeast of Waterford just off N25, the Waterford–New Ross road (well signposted). One ground-level room has its own entrance. The scenic setting can be enjoyed from the garden, and both river and sea angling are close by, as is horseback riding.

Slieverue, Co. Waterford. ② **051/832037.** Fax 051/833783. ashbourne@gofree.indigo.ie. 7 units. 57€ ($52) double. 50% reduction for children sharing with parents. Rates include full breakfast. MC, V. Closed Dec–Mar. *In room:* TV, tea/coffeemaker, hair dryer.

Ashgrove   Mrs. Breda Battles's modern bungalow sits back off the road on a slight rise, about half a mile from Dunmore East. Guests often take evening walks along nearby clifftops to reach secluded coves or sandy beaches. Mrs. Battles is eager to share her knowledge of the area with her guests.

Coxtown, Dunmore E., Co. Waterford. ℂ **051/383195.** battlesb@gofree.indigo.ie. 4 units. 33€ ($30) single; 51€ ($46) double. 25% reduction for children sharing with parents. Rates include full breakfast. MC, V. Closed Nov–Feb. *In room:* TV, tea/coffeemaker.

Ballyguiry Farm *(Kids*   This lovely Georgian house in the foothills of the Drum Hills, 2½ miles (4km) south of Dungarvan, dates from the 1830s. Kathleen and Sean Kiely make guests feel right at home, as do their four charming children. They will even map out sightseeing itineraries on an ordinance survey map for your use on day trips. The guest rooms are exceptionally pretty, with floral wallpaper, pastel bedspreads, and electric blankets for added comfort. Three family suites with private bathrooms are suitable for parents and up to three children. There's a playground, a hard tennis court, and a pony for children to pet and ride. Dinner is prepared with farm-fresh ingredients.

Dungarvan (just off N25, the main Dungarvan-Youghal road), Co. Waterford. ℂ **058/41194.** www.water fordfarms.com/ballyguiryfarm. 5 units, 4 with bathroom. 39€ ($36) single; 63€ ($58) double. 50% reduction for children under 10 sharing with parents. Rates include full breakfast. Dinner 16€ ($14). MC, V. Closed Nov–Apr. *In room:* TV (in some rooms), tea/coffeemaker (in some rooms).

Bayside   Mrs. Sheila Norris's spacious modern home overlooks Dungarvan Bay, and is adjacent to the Gold Coast Golf and Leisure complex. The Dungarvan Golf Range is right on the premises, for duffers who want a little practice before heading off to the links; two free vouchers are provided for each guest. All guest rooms are attractive as well as comfortable; a hair dryer and trouser press are available for guests' use. The whole house is nonsmoking.

Gold Coast Rd., Dungarvan, Co. Waterford. ℂ **058/44318.** 3 units, all with bathroom (shower only). 25€–32€ ($23–$29) single; 47€–51€ ($43–$46) double. Rates include full breakfast. MC, V. Private parking. 1¼ miles (2km) south of R675. *In room:* TV, tea/coffeemaker.

Byron Lodge *(★*   More than 150 years old, Byron Lodge is a Georgian home with lovely views of Ardmore's beach and monastic ruins (it's signposted on Main Street in the town center). Guest rooms are exceptionally spacious, and the whole house is nonsmoking. The owners are knowledgeable about the area's history and sightseeing attractions, and will gladly arrange tours of the Blackwater and Youghal areas. Dinners, which must be booked in advance, feature seafood specialties. Breakfast options include two types of omelet and smoked salmon with scrambled eggs in addition to the standard fry.

Ardmore, Co. Waterford. ℂ **024/94157.** 6 units, 4 with bathroom (shower only). 30€ ($27) single with bathroom; 48€ ($44) double without bathroom, 51€ ($46) double with bathroom. 20% reduction for children under 10 sharing with parents. Rates include full breakfast. No credit cards. Closed Nov–Mar.

Cliff House Hotel *(★*   Perched above the breakers, this hotel has spectacular views of the bay at Ardmore and a long stretch of rocky coast. The guest rooms are plain and moderately spacious, and every room but one has a great view of the sea. A restaurant and pub are on the building's lower level, and a terrace permits outdoor dining. A beautiful walk around the point begins at the edge of the parking lot, taking in the Ardmore chapel and round tower as well as the majestic sea cliffs; a leaflet published by the hotel describes this and other local walks. There are also two bikes for hire at the hotel, and good cycling roads run from here along the coast.

Ardmore, Co. Waterford. © **024/94106.** Fax 024/94496. www.cliffhotelardmore.com. 13 units. 70€ ($63) single; 108€ ($98) double. No service charge. Rates include full breakfast. AE, DC, MC, V. Closed Nov–Feb. *In room:* Tea/coffeemaker.

Clonanav Farm Guest House
Eileen and Larry Ryan's farmhouse, well signposted 1½ miles (2.5km) from Ballymacarbry on the Clonmel-Dungarvan road (T27), has one of the most peaceful, scenic settings around, with landscaped gardens and beautiful Nire Valley views. The house itself has comfortable guest rooms, a cozy family room with a glowing fire, a conservatory with a free tea/coffee bar, and an electric blanket on every bed. Meals are a delight in the spacious dining room, with prime Irish meats, fish, fruit, and vegetables and herbs fresh from their garden. It's the Ryans themselves, however, who win the most accolades. All bedrooms and the dining room are nonsmoking. The Clonanav Fly Fishing Centre (on the premises) offers instruction, guides, and equipment for fishing on several local streams renowned for their wild brown trout.

Nire Valley, Ballymacarbry, Co. Waterford. © **052/36141.** www.clonanav.com. 14 units. 89€–102€ ($81–$92) double. 50% reduction for children sharing with parents. Rates include full breakfast. Dinner 13€–19€ ($12–$17). Package fly-fishing and walking, holiday rates available. AE, MC, V. *In room:* TV, hair dryer.

Copper Beech
The modern dormer bungalow, home of Liz and Kevin Hayes, is located in the heart of this lovely seaside village. The house is tastefully decorated throughout. Two rooms have views of Hook lighthouse and the sea. Smoking is allowed in all the bedrooms, but not in the lounge or dining room. The breakfast offerings include smoked kippers and baked beans on toast.

Dunmore E., Co. Waterford. © **051/383187.** copperbeech@ireland.com. 4 units. 36€ ($32) single; 56€ ($51) double. 25% reduction for children. Rates include full breakfast. MC, V. Private parking. Closed Nov–Feb. *In room:* TV, TEL, tea/coffeemaker, hair dryer, iron.

Creaden View
Mrs. Kathleen Martin's home, right in the center of Dunmore East, has fine views of nearby cliffs and the sea. Bedrooms are spacious and comfortably furnished; they're a restful retreat when the spirit begins to flag. Kathleen is always delighted to share her knowledge of this beautiful area with her guests.

Dunmore E., Co. Waterford. ©/fax **051/383339.** 6 units. 38€ ($34) single; 56€ ($51) double. 25% reduction for children under 12 sharing with parents. Rates include full breakfast. MC, V. Closed Nov–Feb. *In room:* TV, tea/coffeemaker, hair dryer.

Diamond Hill Guesthouse
This modern house is set amidst lawns and gardens that have won the National Garden Award for guesthouses no fewer than four times. Its interior is as attractive as the exterior, with beautifully decorated bedrooms. In good weather, chairs are set out in the sunny gardens for a bit of outdoor relaxation. New owner Marjorie Smith ably manages the property, and she's been refurbishing over the past year.

Slieverue, Co. Waterford. © **051/832855** or 051/832254. Fax 051/832254. 18 units. 76€ ($69) double. Rates include full breakfast. MC, V. Private parking lot. Just off the Waterford-Rosslare road (N25), signposted at Slieverue Junction, about 2 miles (3km) outside Waterford. *In room:* TV, tea/coffeemaker, hair dryer.

Flynn's River View Guesthouse *Kids*
This three-story rambling house was built by the Sisters of Mercy as an orphanage in the late 19th century and has blossomed into one of the most unusual lodgings in the region under the loving direction of Evelyn and John Flynn. The house is fascinating, with multiple

stairways and corridors, a private dining room in what was once the chapel, two lounges, and a games room with pool tables, table tennis, darts, and board games. My favorite rooms are the four on the top floor under the eaves, whose swing-out windows open onto views of the town and the Blackwater River. Outside is a play area with swings, swing balls, pitch 'n' putt, croquet, and a merry-go-round. Children are very welcome here, and the Flynn family makes certain that no River View guest, young or old, is neglected. Evelyn is always up-to-date on what's going on—where the best fishing holes are, where entertainment may be found locally—and if you're planning a day trip, she'll gladly pack a lunch. John will see that you have bait and fishing equipment if you decide on the spur of the moment to test your skill. Evening meals are good, and tea and home-made scones are a regular feature in the evening.

Cook St. (on N72 as you enter town from Dungarvan), Cappoquin, Co. Waterford. ✆ 058/54073. 21 units, 10 with bathroom (9 shower only). 51€ ($46) double. 33% reduction for children. Rates include full breakfast. Dinner 10€ ($9). No credit cards. Enclosed parking lot. *In room:* TV, hair dryer, iron, safe.

Foxmount Farm ★★ (Kids)   This is a perennial favorite with Frommer's readers. The 230-acre working farm is 4 miles (6.5km) out of Waterford town, just off the Dunmore East road (turn left on Passage East road; keep right at next junction, where it's signposted, then right at the bridge). The elegant old home, dating from 1700, sits on a slight rise overlooking a verdant lawn edged with flowering shrubs, pastures, and tilled acres. Margaret and David Kent are always eager to accommodate their guests, whether by booking a glass-factory tour, explaining the history of the region, or simply showing them around the farm. Children enjoy riding Tiny, the resident donkey; there's also a horse and pony in the farmyard. Other amenities include table tennis and a tennis court. The house is furnished with lovely antiques, and evening tea around a glowing fire in the drawing room is a special event. Meals are superb, featuring all fresh ingredients and home baking, and you're welcome to bring your own wine. Let Margaret know by noon if you want the evening meal.

Passage E. Rd., Waterford, Co. Waterford. ✆ 051/874308. Fax 051/854906. www.tipp.ie/foxmount.htm. 5 units. 89€ ($81) double. Special 3-, 5-, or 7-day rates. 25% reduction for children. Rates include full breakfast. Dinner 25€ ($23). No credit cards. Free parking. Closed Nov–Feb. *In room:* TV, hair dryer.

Seaview Lodge   Frances Darcy has won high praise from our readers, with comments such as, she "gives that little extra effort to guests that separates the great from the merely good." Her spacious bungalow, with its private parking lot, has a beautiful sea view. There's also a breakfast menu, just in case you want a change from the traditional fare. Mrs. Darcy is one of Ireland's most obliging hostesses, always ready to help with itinerary plans and local sightseeing. A conservatory offers a great view of the surrounding seascape. The whole house is nonsmoking.

Seaview Park, Tramore, Co. Waterford. ✆/fax 051/381122. www.seaviewlodge.com. 6 units. Rates 41€ ($37) single; 58€ ($53) double. Dinner 15€ ($14) extra. MC, V. Free parking. *In room:* Tea/coffeemaker, hair dryer.

GREAT DEALS ON DINING
AROUND COUNTY WATERFORD

An Bialann   BREAKFAST/TRADITIONAL/SALADS/SANDWICHES This cozy restaurant has an attractive traditional front and high-backed booths inside. Everything on the menu is fresh and home-cooked. Selections range from soup and sandwiches to salad plates, hot savories (try the curried chicken and savory rice), spaghetti Bolognese, pizza, quiche, and five-course complete meals. There's a children's menu, as well as a full a la carte menu, and beer, wine, and specialty coffees. Because service is continuous, this is a handy, relaxing stop any time of day.

31 Grattan Sq., Dungarvan, Co. Waterford. ℂ **058/42825.** Snacks, salads, savories, and hot dinners 4.50€–15€ ($3.75–$15). AE, MC, V. Oct–Easter Mon–Sat 9:30am–7pm; Easter–Sept Mon–Sat 9:30am–7pm, Sun 11am–5pm.

Eamonn's Place 🐾 *(Finds)* PUB GRUB You'll be missing some of the best home cooking in the region if you don't stop in here at least once. This attractive little pub is a cozy place, with a corner fireplace and three-legged iron pot for turf and wood. Try Eamonn Walsh's chicken-liver paté on Joan's homemade brown bread—scrumptious! And if local Blackwater salmon is available I guarantee you'll get portions so ample you'll be hard-pressed to finish the plate. There's a fixed-price meal that varies from roast beef to bacon and cabbage.

Main St., Lismore, Co. Waterford. ℂ **058/54025.** Lunch 6€–9€ ($5.45–$8.15); dinner 11€–20€ ($10–$18). No credit cards. Mon–Fri 12:30–3pm and 6–9pm; Sat 6–9pm (open Sat June–Oct only).

The Shamrock Restaurant *(Value)* TRADITIONAL The Shamrock serves all three daily meals at bargain prices. The extensive menu includes a T-bone steak with salad or vegetable, buttered trout with two vegetables, burgers, quiche Lorraine, and a variety of light meals. There's a full wine license, and the continuous service makes this a good place for an afternoon snack.

O'Connell St. (past the square on the Cappoquin road), Dungarvan, Co. Waterford. ℂ **058/42242.** Complete dinners 6.50€–13€ ($5.90–$12); light meals 3.80€–6.50€ ($3.45–$5.90); dessert and tea 3.15€ ($2.90). MC, V. Mon–Sat 9am–9pm.

3 Easy Excursions into South Tipperary

South Tipperary is one of Ireland's best-kept secrets. Here, far from lines of tour buses and the din of camera shutters, you may just find the Ireland everyone is looking for: lush, welcoming, unspoiled, and splendidly beautiful. **Clonmel,** the capital of Tipperary and the largest inland town in Ireland, is the region's unassuming gateway. A working town, poised on the banks of the Suir, it's as yet unspoiled by massive tourism. Clonmel has everything you'll need to establish a strategic and pleasant base of operations in the southeast.

North of Clonmel and deep into the Tipperary countryside, **Cashel** is not to be missed. Because it's right on the main N8 road, most people pass through en route from Dublin to Cork, but this major attraction is worth a side trip no matter what.

VISITOR INFORMATION The **Clonmel Tourist Office** is on Sarsfield Street, Clonmel (ℂ **052/22960**). **Seasonal offices,** open June to August, are at Castle Street, Cahir (ℂ **052/41453**), and at the Town Hall, Cashel (ℂ **062/61333**). The website for all Southeast Tourism is **www.southeastireland.travel.ie**. To get the latest on news, listings, and events in Clonmel and the surrounding area, buy a copy of the local *Nationalist,* which hits the stands every Saturday. Among other things, it will tell you what's on at the Regal Theatre or the White Memorial Theatre, Clonmel's principal venues for the arts.

SCENIC DRIVES Whether you're staying in Clonmel or moving on, several marvelously scenic drives converge and present themselves here: the Comeragh or **Nire Valley Drive** deep into the Comeragh Mountains, which rise from the south banks of the Suir; the **Suir Scenic Drive;** and the **Knockmealdown**

Drive, which passes through the historic village of Ardfinnan and on through the **Vee.** These are all signposted from Clonmel.

The Vee, in particular, is one of the most dramatic drives in the southeast. Its high point is at the Tipperary/Waterford border where the two slopes of the pass converge to frame the patchwork fields of the Galtee Valley far below. At this point, numerous walking trails lead to the nearby peaks as well as down to the mountain lake of Petticoat Loose, which was named after a, shall we say, less than exemplary lady.

I also recommend the following route. At Cahir, embark in a northerly direction through the **Galtee Mountains,** Ireland's highest inland mountain range, to the Glen of Aherlow. Often called Ireland's Greenest Valley, the 7-mile (11km) **Glen of Aherlow** is a secluded and scenic area that was an important pass between the plains of Counties Tipperary and Limerick.

SEEING THE SIGHTS

Athassel Priory 🐾 *Finds* This is the largest medieval priory in Ireland, spread out over 4 acres. Although it is in ruins, many delightful details from the original structure remain, and its many pinnacles offer a strikingly picturesque scene. This was an Augustinian priory, founded in the late 12th century; the remaining structures date from that time until the mid–15th century. The main approach is over a low stone bridge and through a gatehouse that was the focal point of the outer fortifications. The church is entered through a beautifully carved doorway at its west end. To the south of the church is the cloister, whose graceful arches have been largely eroded away by time. Don't miss the carved face protruding from the southwest corner of the chapel tower, about 30 feet (9m) above ground level.

Open site. Take the signposted road about 2 miles (3km) south from the town of Golden, located between Tipperary and Cashel on N74; the priory is in a field just east of the road.

Brú Ború This modern complex adds a musical element to the historic Cashel area. Operated by Comhaltas Ceoltoiri Eireann, Ireland's foremost traditional music organization, Brú Ború presents daily performances of authentic Irish traditional music at an indoor theater, and on many summer evenings concerts are given at an open-air amphitheater. A heritage center, gift shop, restaurant, and self-service snack shop are also on hand.

Rock Lane (at the foot of the Rock of Cashel), Cashel, Co. Tipperary. ✆ **062/61122.** Fax 062/62700. www.comhaltas.com. Free admission to center; 11€ ($10) per person for music performances, 34€ ($31) banquet and performance; parking 1.25 ($1.15). June–Sept Mon–Sat 9am–11pm, Sun 10am–5pm; Oct–May Mon–Fri 9am–5pm. Evening music shows June–Sept Tues–Sat at 9pm.

Cahir Castle 🐾🐾 *Kids* This magnificent castle stands on a rocky islet in the River Suir that has been the natural site of fortifications since the 3rd century. Brian Boru maintained a residence here as high king of Ireland. The castle you see today on this ancient site was built by the Norman de Bermingham in the 13th century, and was held by the Anglo-Norman Butlers until 1599, when the earl of Essex captured it after a short siege. In 1650, it was surrendered to Cromwell without a single shot, and within its walls the articles ending the long Cromwellian wars were signed in 1652. Butler descendants held the castle title until the last of them died in 1961. Now restored to near-original condition, the castle today brings alive the life and times of all its centuries-old history. Guided tours are conducted upon request during summer months, when there's a resident tourist office; in winter, there's an informative caretaker on hand. Be sure to explore the many staircases and passageways that riddle the walls and towers of the castle, which aren't included on the tour; you are freer to explore on your own here than in most restored Irish castles.

Cahir, Co. Tipperary. ⓒ 052/41011. cahircastle@ealga.ie. Admission 2.60€ ($2.40) adults, 1.90€ ($1.75) seniors, 1.25€ ($1.15) children and students, 6.40€ ($5.80) family. Mid-Mar to mid-June and mid-Sept to mid-Oct daily 9:30am–5:30pm; mid-June to mid-Sept daily 9am–7:30pm; mid-Oct to mid-Mar daily 9:30am–4:30pm.

GPA–Bolton Library　In this library you'll see the smallest book in the world as well as other rare, antiquarian, and unusual books and maps dating from as early as the 12th century. Ensconced here are works by Dante, Swift, Calvin, Newton, Erasmus, and Machiavelli. Outside the hours mentioned above, the library can sometimes be visited by appointment; call the Dean of Cashel (ⓒ **062/61232**) to inquire.

John St. (on the grounds of St. John the Baptist Cathedral), Cashel. ⓒ/fax 062/61944. Admission 1.90€ ($1.75) adults, 1.25€ ($1.15) seniors and students, 0.65€ (60¢) children. June–Aug Tues–Sun 10am–6pm; Sept–May Mon–Fri 9:30am–5:30pm.

Ormond Castle　The mid–15th-century castle built by Sir Edward MacRichard Butler on this strategic bend of the river Suir has lain in ruins for centuries. What still stands attached to the ancient battlements is the last surviving Tudor manor house in Ireland. Trusting that "if he built it she would come," Thomas Butler ("Black Tom") constructed an extensive manor in honor of his most successful relation, Queen Elizabeth I, whose mother, Anne Boleyn, is rumored to have been born in Ormond Castle. In fact, she never came, but many others have, especially since the Office of Public Works partially restored this impressive piece of Irish history. Current restoration plans include an elaborate furnishing of the "Earl's Room" to period. The manor's plasterwork, carvings, period furniture, and startling collection of original 17th- and 18th-century royal charters will make you glad you bothered to visit and wonder why Queen Elizabeth didn't.

Carrick-on-Suir, Co. Tipperary. ⓒ **051/640787**. www.heritageireland.ie. Admission 2.60€ ($2.40) adults, 1.90€ ($1.75) seniors, 1.25€ ($1.15) students and children, 6.35€ ($5.75) family. Mid-June to Sept daily 9:30am–6:30pm. Signposted from the center of Carrick-on-Suir.

Rock of Cashel ★★★　High above the South Tipperary town of Cashel (Caiseal, or "Stone Fort") is Ireland's most majestic historical landmark, the lofty Rock of Cashel. It stands perched on an outcrop of limestone 300 feet (90m) above the surrounding plains. This stunning cluster of ruins tells the tale of 16 centuries: It was the seat of the kings of Munster as far back as A.D. 360, and remained a royal fortress until 1101, when King Murtagh O'Brien granted it to the church. Since then, the Rock has been the scene of numerous conflicts, and has been handed back and forth several times between the Catholic and Protestant Churches.

The visitor today will find a cluster of church and castle ruins within the 2-acre enclosure formed by the outer walls. The apse of Cormac's Chapel, a Romanesque gem built in the 12th century, contains a number of fine mural paintings. You can also explore the 13th-century cathedral, which holds a complex network of passageways within its thick walls. The visitor center is housed in the "Hall of the Vicars Choral," the only building in the complex to have been fully restored; inside there are various carved stones from Cashel and nearby sites on display. For a great view of the Rock from a distance, head to Hore Abbey (see "More Sights & Attractions," below).

Cashel, Co. Tipperary. ✆ **062/61437.** www.heritageireland.ie. Admission 4.45€ ($4.05) adults, 3.15€ ($2.90) seniors, 1.90€ ($1.75) students and children, 10€ ($9) family; 1.90€ ($1.75) parking fee. Mid-Sept to mid-Mar daily 9am–4:30pm; mid-Mar to mid-June daily 9am–5:30pm; mid-June to mid-Sept daily 9am–7:30pm. Last admission 45 min. before closing.

Swiss Cottage   Odd to find a Swiss cottage in Ireland? Maybe nowadays, but back in the early 1800s, Irish romantics held the notion that this picturesque rustic style was just right for hunting and fishing lodges. Designed by the famous Regency architect John Nash and built on the estate of the Earls of Glengall, the two-story thatched cottage is fairly broken out with timberwork. Rustic it may be, but no expense was spared—some of the wallpaper was even produced in Paris. Access is by guided tour only; the tour lasts approximately 40 minutes.

Off Dublin-Cork Rd. (N8), Cahir. ✆ **052/41144.** Admission 2.55€ ($2.30) adults, 1.90€ ($1.75) seniors, 1.25€ ($1.15) students and children, 6.35€ ($5.75) family. Mid-Mar to end of Mar Tues–Sun 10am–1pm and 2–4:30pm; Apr Tues–Sun 10am–1pm and 2–5pm; May–Sept daily 10am–6pm; Oct–Nov Tues–Sun 10am–1pm and 2–4:30pm.

Tipperary Crystal   If you're nearby, don't miss this crystal factory, laid out in the style of traditional Irish cottages complete with a thatched roof. Visitors are welcome to watch master craftspeople as they mouth-blow and hand-cut crystal. Unlike at other crystal factories, there are no restrictions on photographs and video recorders here. The facility includes a showroom and restaurant.

Waterford-Limerick road (N24), Ballynoran, Carrick-on-Suir, Co. Tipperary. ✆ **051/641188.** www.tipperary-crystal.com. Free admission. Mon–Fri 9am–5:30pm; Sat–Sun 11am–5pm. Guided tours mid-Mar to Sept Mon–Fri 10am–3:30pm.

MORE SIGHTS & ATTRACTIONS

The ruins of **Hore Abbey** sit in the shadow of the Rock of Cashel, and are less spectacular and less visited than their famous neighbor. Still, it's worth a brief side trip to wander through the remains of this Cistercian abbey, founded in 1272, and take in the view of "The Rock" from inside its vaulted chambers and crumbling archways. To get there, follow the Dundrum Road from Cashel about a half-mile, and turn left at the O'Brien Farmhouse Hostel—you'll see the ruins on your left. Some fine details of stone carving survive, particularly in the windows and the column capitals; it's assumed that many of the same masons who worked on the Rock of Cashel also crafted the details of this abbey.

Holycross Abbey is 4 miles (6.5km) south of Thurles (pronounced "*Thur*-less" or, native style, "*Tur*-less") on the west bank of the River Suir, some 13 miles (21km) north of Cashel on R660. It was founded in 1168 and was a revered place of pilgrimage because it held a particle of the True Cross, preserved in a golden shrine set with precious stones that had been presented to King Murtagh O'Brien, grandson of Brian Boru, in 1110. The shrine is now in the Ursuline Convent in Blackrock, Cork, but the abbey still contains many interesting and religiously significant ruins, and Sunday pilgrimages still take place from May to September.

From Cashel, take R688 southeast, then turn onto R692 for a 20-minute drive to the little village of **Fethard,** where you'll find the **Fethard Folk, Farm and Transport Museum,** Cashel Road, Fethard, County Tipperary (✆ **052/31516**). It's in the Old Railway Goods Store and holds a collection of rural antiques relating to farming, family life, and transport. The proprietors, Christopher and Margaret Mullins, live on the site and will open it at any time for groups by request, but regular hours are year-round Sunday from 12:30 to 5pm, coinciding with a collector's flea market held nearby. Admission on Sunday is 1.25€ ($1.15) adult, .65€ (60¢) child; the admission by appointment is 2.60€ ($2.40) adult, 1.25€ ($1.15) child.

Clonmel is a South Tipperary country town (in Irish, Cluain Meala, "Meadow of Honey") on the banks of the River Suir. Its rich history reaches back to the 1100s, and its town walls and fortifications withstood a 3-week siege by Cromwell in 1650. In later years, it was a garrison town and the home of Charles Bianconi, a poor Italian who founded the first public transport system in Ireland with a coaching service based here. Today a thriving market town, Clonmel retains traces of the original town walls (you can't miss the impressive West Gate in the very center of the town), as well as several impressive public buildings. The Old St. Mary's Church of Ireland was built in the 13th century and is dedicated to Our Lady of Clonmel. Other buildings of note are the Town Hall, the Court House, and the Franciscan Friary.

OUTDOOR PURSUITS

BIRD-WATCHING   As many as 15 species of Irish waterbirds, including mute swans, coots, wigeons, gadwalls, teals, gray herons, and moorhens, may be seen at the **Marlfield Lake Wildfowl Refuge,** several miles west of Clonmel in Marlfield. On your way, you will likely pass signposts for **St. Patrick's Well,** less than a mile away, a tranquil spot with an effervescent pool of reputedly healing crystalline water. In the middle of the pool rises a seriously ancient Celtic cross. The legend that Patrick visited here seems more solidly rooted than most such claims—even saints get thirsty, after all.

FISHING   The **River Suir,** from Carrick-on-Suir to Thurles, was once one of the finest salmon rivers in Europe, but recent excessive trawling at its mouth has threatened its stock. But it's still a decent salmon river, especially in the February run and from June through September. Trout (brown and rainbow) are in abundance here in the summer months. A State Permit is required for fishing anywhere in the country: the fee is 3.80€ ($3.45) for 1 day or 13€ ($12) for 21 days. You'll also need a ticket for fishing on the River Suir: a single weekday permits runs 20€ ($18) for salmon and 6.50€ ($5.90) for trout. There's fly-fishing for brown trout on several local stretches of the River Suir between March 1 and September 1. Permits are available from **Kavanagh Sports,** West Gate, Clonmel, County Tipperary (℗/fax **052/21279**). Additionally, the River Nore and the nearby River Barrow are known for good salmon and trout fishing.

HORSEBACK RIDING   **Hillcrest Riding Centre,** Glenbally, Tipperary (℗ **062/37915**) is a registered riding stable based in the Galtee Mountains. It offers trail rides, a cross-country course, and instruction in show jumping. Trail rides range from 18€ ($16) an hour to 63€ ($58) for a full day's ride with picnic lunch. Hillcrest is a keen hunting stable, and for those anxious for the chase, horses and participation in local and neighboring hunts can be arranged. Hillcrest also offers longer trekking holidays, up to a week in duration.

SWIMMING   If you're staying in the Clonmel area, you're welcome to swim at the Clonmel civic swimming pool (℗ **052/21972**) near the Market Place. It's open intermittently Monday through Friday from 10am to 9:45pm and Saturday and Sunday from 10am to 8pm; call ahead for exact times.

WALKING   R668 between Clogheen and Lismore is one of the most scenic stretches of road in the southeast, and there are some great walks beginning at the Vee, a dramatic notch in the Knockmealdown Mountains. About 1½ miles (2.5km) north of R669 and R668, you reach the highest point in the gap; there is a parking lot here, and a dirt road continuing down to a lake nestled into the hillslope below. This is Bay Lough, and the dirt road used to be the main thoroughfare over the gap; it now offers a fine walk to the shores of the lake, with outstanding views of the valley to the north. For a truly panoramic perspective of the region, start walking due east from the gap parking lot to the summit of **Sugarloaf Hill;** the hike is extremely steep, but well worth the effort, as the views from the ridge are superb.

In the **Clonmel** area, there are a number of excellent river and hill walks, some more challenging than others, the most spectacular being the ascent of famed **Slievenamon,** a mountain rich in myth and lore. Detailed trail maps for at least a half a dozen walks are available for .81€ (75¢) at the Clonmel Tourist Office on Sarsfield Street, Clonmel. Also available is a free leaflet guide to the birds, butterflies, and flora of nearby **Wilderness Gorge.**

The **Galtee Mountains,** located just northwest of the Knockmealdowns, offer some great long and short walks. One beautiful walk on a well-defined trail is the circuit of **Lake Muskry,** on the north side of the range. To get there, take R663 west out of Bansha, and follow signs for the town of Rossadrehid. To get to the trail, ask for directions in Rossadrehid; there are several turns to be made, and the landmarks change frequently due to logging in the region. The trail leads you up a glaciated valley to the base of a ring of cliffs, where lie the crystalline waters of Lake Muskry; from here you can walk around the lake, take in the tremendous views of the valley, and return the way you came. Walking time to the lake and back is 3 hours. Another option on this walk is to continue on up past the lake to the top of the ridge, and from there along the ridgetop to Galtymore, a prominent dome-shaped peak about 3 miles (5km) west of Lake Muskry; this is a beautiful but extremely demanding walk, about 6 hours to Galtymore and back. There are many other extraordinary walks in the Glen of Aherlow. Trail maps and all the information and assistance you could think of asking for are available at the **Glen of Aherlow Failte Centre,** Coach Road, Newtown (© **062/56331**), ably directed by Helen Morrissey. It's open year-round, Monday to Friday 10am to 4pm, and daily June to September 9am to 6pm. Guided 2-hour walks are best booked in advance. Or drop in, and one may just be leaving shortly. As you're leaving the centre, take a brief detour on a narrow paved road to the **Christ the King statue** ⍟, perched high above the valley with a fantastic view of the region—it's a great way to get oriented in the Glen of Aherlow. The statue is 1 mile (1.6km) straight up the hill from the Glen of Aherlow Failte Centre.

ACCOMMODATIONS YOU CAN AFFORD

Ballyowen House ⍟   This is a secluded retreat from which to explore Cashel, Cahir, and the immediate area. The rather imposing manor house, dating from 1750, is both elegant and charmingly antiquated. Surrounding the house are vast fields dotted with sheep and beautiful old trees. The rooms are extravagantly large and furnished with handsome antiques. Tea is available upon arrival, breakfast is served in the spacious dining room, and dinner is also offered—Aoife McCann is a Ballymaloe-trained chef. The McCan family offers a warm welcome and knowledgeable advice on walks and nearby sightseeing.

Dualla, Cashel, Co. Tipperary. ℂ 062/61265. www.ballyowenhouse.com. 3 units, 2 with bathroom (1 with shower only). 64€ ($58) double. Rates include full breakfast. Dinner 19€–28€ ($17–$25). AE, MC, V. Free parking. Closed Oct–Apr. *In room:* Hair dryer.

Bansha House   The Marnanes have won many well-deserved awards during the 25 years they've offered accommodations in their comfortable Georgian farmhouse. Mary Marnane is a host who doesn't rest upon ceremony, and you'll quickly feel at ease, drinking tea and talking in the comfortable sitting room or in the Marnanes' kitchen. There is an atmosphere of comfortable informality to the place; guests who enjoy horses will likely find themselves involved in the elaborate daily operations of the thoroughbred stable, expertly run by Con Marnane. The equestrian program at Bansha is excellent, with half-board and riding packages available. The town of Bansha sits at the base of the magnificent Galtee Mountains, which dominate the skyline on a clear day and make this house a great base for walking and bicycling or just taking in the beautiful scenery. Mary and John Marnane can also direct you to walks, bike rides, and drives in the area.

Bansha, Co. Tipperary. ℂ 062/54194. Fax 062/54215. www.tipp.ie/banshahs.htm. 8 units, 5 with bathroom (shower only). 39€ ($35) single without bath, 43€ ($39) single with bath; 64€ ($58) double without bath, 72€ ($65) double with bath. 25% reduction for children sharing with parents. Rates include full breakfast. Dinner 22€ ($20); reserve by 4pm. MC, V. Free parking. Closed Dec 20–Jan 1. **Amenities:** Sitting room. *In room:* Hair dryer.

Carrigeen Castle   This 17th-century castle on the edge of town has a colorful past, having twice been used as a prison for rebellious Irish, but since 1919 it has taken back its function as family home. Bedrooms have been fashioned from the original upstairs rooms—this is one of the few B&Bs in Ireland in which you enter your bedroom through a centuries-old stone doorway. Peig is a thoughtful hostess, always ready with the extra cup of tea as well as good advice about sightseeing in the area. Her son, David, takes a special interest in greeting and assisting guests. The house is centrally heated, and there's a fire in the lounge on cool evenings.

Cork Rd., Cahir, Co. Tipperary. ℂ 052/41370. www.iol.ie/tipp/butlerca.htm. 7 units, 3 with bathroom (shower only). 46€ ($41) double without bathroom, 56€ ($51) double with bathroom. Rates include full breakfast. MC, V. *In room:* TV, hair dryer.

The Chestnuts   Phyllis and John O'Halloran's modern bungalow is set amidst mature gardens and 100 acres of farmland in a beautiful rural landscape. Just 2½ miles (4km) from Cashel, the Chestnuts is an ideal touring base. It has a "relaxation room" with TV and an open fire. Meals feature home baking. Traditional music is usually on tap in the village just down the road.

Dualla-Kilkenny road (R691), Cashel, Co. Tipperary. ℂ/fax 062/61469. www.thechestnuts.com. 5 units, 4 with bathroom (shower only). 28€ ($25) single without bathroom, 34€ ($31) single with bathroom; 46€ ($42) double without bathroom, 52€–55€ ($47–$50) double with bathroom. 20% reduction for children. Rates include full breakfast. Dinner 17€ ($15). MC, V. Free parking.

Dualla House ⭐   The farmhouse now inhabited by the Power family was built on a grand scale, and is an elegant and comfortable base for exploring the region. It's perched on a hill overlooking the Knockmealdown and Comeragh Mountains and offers great views from the two front rooms. The bedrooms are large and tastefully furnished. An elegant sitting room with a fireplace is a good place to relax in the evening. The extensive breakfast menu here includes much local produce in season (farmhouse cheese, honey, apple juice, free-range eggs), and delicious homemade items (soda bread, preserves, marmalade). *Note:* When you're visiting the Rock of Cashel, look for the prominent crypt of the Scully family, eminent landlords in the area, who built this house in 1790.

Dualla-Kilkenny Rd. (R691), Cashel, Co. Tipperary. ©/fax 062/61487. www.tipp.ie/dualla-house.htm. 5 units, 4 with bathroom (3 shower only). 32€–44€ ($29–$40) single; 57€–69€ ($52–$63) double. 50% reduction for children under 12 sharing with parents. MC, V. *In room:* TV, tea/coffeemaker, hair dryer.

Mr. Bumbles *Value*　If you crave a night off from the social rituals of the standard B&B and want an excellent breakfast, this is the place. These four bright and simple rooms are located above Mr. Bumble's restaurant (see "Great Deals on Dining," below), although they have their own exterior staircase. They're meticulously clean and have firm beds. Furthermore, it's possible to negotiate a B&B/dinner combination, which all but guarantees sweet dreams.

Richmond House, Kickham St., Clonmel, Co. Tipperary. © 052/29380. Fax 052/29007. 4 units. 32€ ($29) single; 64€ ($58) double; 76€ ($69) family room, sleeps 3. No service charge. Includes full breakfast. MC, V. At top of Clonmel Market Place. **Amenities:** Restaurant. *In room:* TV, tea/coffeemaker.

O'Brien's Holiday Lodge *Value*　Tom and Brid O'Brien have renovated this 200-year-old stone coach house at the base of the Rock of Cashel into a hostel with lots of rustic charm. Two of the private rooms are small, and the sloped ceilings make them seem a bit smaller, but all are bright, with wood floors and whitewashed walls. The self-catering kitchen facilities are minimal, adequate for the most elementary meals. The location, however, is great—in the shadow of the Rock and just across a field from the impressive ruins of Hore Abbey. To get here, take the road signposted for Dundrum out of Cashel, and look for the hostel on the left as soon as you leave town. You can also stay in one of the six-bed dorm rooms for 13€ ($12) per person.

Dundrum Rd., Cashel, Co. Tipperary. © 062/61003. Fax 062/62797. obriensholidayhostel@eircom.net. 3 units. 40€ ($36) double. No credit cards.

Rahard Lodge　Mrs. Moira Foley runs this modern farmhouse overlooking the Rock of Cashel and only a short walk to the center of town. The small gardens are one of the main attractions here: These lovingly maintained lawns and ornamental beds are a great place to relax and plan your next day's excursions. There are electric blankets on every bed in the comfortable guest rooms. Dinner can be arranged with advance notice. Mrs. Foley has been in the B&B accommodation business longer than almost anyone else in town, and has many stories to tell of Cashel past and present.

Dualla-Kilkenny Rd. (R691), Cashel, Co. Tipperary. © 062/61052. 6 units. 58€ ($53) double. 25% reduction for children sharing with parents. Rates include full breakfast. V. Closed Dec–Jan. *In room:* Tea/coffeemaker, hair dryer.

SELF-CATERING

Coopers Cottage　Stella and Eamonn Long have lovingly restored and renovated this 19th-century cooper's cottage, once Eamonn's family home, into an extraordinarily comfortable and tasteful country hideaway. While retaining the cozy proportions and traditional lines of the original dwelling, the Longs have created a house full of light, with generous skylights and windows opening to spectacular views of the Galtee Mountains. The furnishings have a bright, contemporary feel. The house comes with absolutely everything, including a barbecue and a lovely, modest, fenced-in garden, with a patio area for sunny days. This is an ideal base for exploring the beautiful southeastern counties of Tipperary, Waterford, and Kilkenny. The town of Bansha is 2 miles (3km) down the lane.

Raheen (1 mile off N24), Bansha, Co. Tipperary. ✆/fax **062/54027.** www.dirl.com/tipperary/coopers.htm. 3-bedroom self-catering cottage (sleeps 6). 254€–444€ ($230–$403) per week, depending on season. No credit cards. Free parking. **Amenities:** Patio. *In room:* TV, kitchen, fridge, microwave, tea/coffeemaker, hair dryer, iron.

WORTH A SPLURGE

Lismacue House ✦ This spacious country house on a low hill with fine views of the Galtee Mountains combines elements of a rustic retreat with those of an elegant estate. A long, straight drive lined with antiquated lime trees announces the house, which looks imposing with its crenellated roofline and carved limestone porch. Jim and Kate Nicholson are the hosts here, and they've succeeded in creating the relaxed atmosphere of a comfortable summer lodge without underplaying the grandeur of the place. Jim presides over the dinner table—he's a great storyteller—and Kate prepares memorable meals with the best of ingredients from home and abroad—seafood from West Cork; local lamb, beef, and vegetables; free-range eggs; and wines personally collected in France. The guest rooms are all located in a grand 19th-century addition, now the main house, where ceilings are lofty and large windows look out over fields and hills. The bedrooms are simply furnished, always in accord with the languorous elegance of the house; bathrooms are adequately spacious.

Bansha, Co. Tipperary. ✆ 062/54106. Fax 062/54126. www.lismacue.com. 5 units, 3 with bathroom (bathtub and shower). 75€ ($68) single without bathroom, 90€ ($82) single with bathroom; 130€ ($118) double without bathroom; 150€ ($136) double with bathroom. Rates include full breakfast. Dinner from 38€ ($34). AE, MC, V. Closed Nov–Jan.

GREAT DEALS ON DINING

Angela's Wholefood Restaurant *(Value)* INTERNATIONAL Angela's Wholefood Restaurant offers scrumptious and substantial fare at remarkable prices. The breakfast menu includes croissants, homemade sausage rolls, and fruit salad; at lunchtime there's spicy Moroccan lamb stew or savory tomato-and-spinach flan Provençal, homemade soups, sandwiches-to-order, and an array of delicious salads to accompany your selection. The food is vibrant and fresh, and appreciated by the bustling clientele—from barristers (in garb) to baby-sitters—who line up with trays in hand.

14 Abbey St., Clonmel, Co. Tipperary. ✆ 052/26899. Breakfast menu 1.50€–4€ ($1.40–$3.65); lunch menu sandwiches 3.80€–6€ ($3.45–$5.45); lunch main courses 5€–8€ ($4.55–$7.25). No service charge. No credit cards. Mon–Fri 9am–5:30pm; Sat 9–5pm.

Mr. Bumbles INTERNATIONAL For a newcomer to Clonmel, Mr. Bumbles has already created quite a buzz. With its natural woods, bright colors, and bistro feel, you almost expect a waterfront view—instead, there's a parking lot. But no matter, Mr. Bumbles is very inviting and the food is simply first-rate. Many dishes are grilled or pan-seared with a Mediterranean slant on the spicing, all brilliantly fresh. Wild sea trout, Tipperary sirloin, and Mediterranean vegetables are representative entrees. The presentation is gorgeous and the portions are generous. The French house wines are quite fine; they're augmented by a considered international wine list whose French and Australian entries are particularly strong.

Richmond House, Kickham St., Clonmel, Co. Tipperary. ✆ 052/29188. Reservations recommended. Fixed-price 4-course dinner 32€ ($29); main courses 15€–22€ ($14–$20). No service charge. MC, V. Mon–Sat 12:30–2:30pm and 6–10pm; Sun 12:30–3pm and 6–9:30pm.

The Spearman Restaurant *(Value)* IRISH/INTERNATIONAL   Once a grocery store, this attractive restaurant offers an excellent, sophisticated menu at a very reasonable price. By combining the freshest local produce and some culinary imagination, it has gained a fine reputation. The menu includes such entrees as baked chicken with Gruyère cheese and Dijon mustard, poached salmon in a creamy tarragon sauce, and steak with red pepper and mushroom sauce.

97 Main St. (behind the tourist office), Cashel, Co. Tipperary. ✆ **062/61143.** Reservations recommended. Dinner main courses 13€–22€ ($12–$20). AE, MC, V. May–Sept daily 12:30–3pm and 6–9:30pm; Oct–Apr Tues–Sat 12:30–3pm and 6–9:30, Sun 12:30–3pm. Closed Nov and on holidays.

THE PUB SCENE

Gerry Chawkes   Chawke's is a Clonmel landmark, a shrine not so much to stout as to sport. A fanatic fan of hurling and racing (dogs and horses), Gerry Chawke has made his pub a cult place, lined with fascinating memorabilia. Sports teams and clubs from throughout Ireland make a point of stopping here, as do local politicians in recovery from council meetings. You too will be quickly at home here. Gerry will see to that. 3 Gladstone St. Upper, Clonmel, Co. Tipperary. ✆ 052/21149.

Railway Bar *(Finds)*   You'll need on-the-ground directions to find Kitty's, which is how this pub is known to locals. Roughly, it's in a cul-de-sac behind the train station, but the best way to find it is to ask a local. Any effort you make to find your way here will not be wasted, especially on weekends, when a traditional music session is likely to break out anytime. This is the mother of all Irish music pubs in Clonmel. No one is paid or even invited to play here; they just do it. Often, there are so many musicians and so many wanting to hear them that Kitty's bursts its own banks and the music spills outside, down the lane. No frills, just the best Irish music around, and a pub out of the who-knows-when past. Clonmel, Co. Tipperary. No phone.

4 Kilkenny Town & Environs

Kilkenny town is 30 miles (48km) N of Waterford, 50 miles (80km) NW of Wexford, 75 miles (121km) SW of Dublin, 85 miles (137km) SE of Shannon Airport, 92 miles (148km) NE of Cork, and 38 miles (61km) NE of Cashel

Kilkenny town, the centerpiece of County Kilkenny and the southeast's prime inland town, is considered the medieval capital of Ireland because of its remarkable collection of well-preserved medieval castles, churches, public buildings, streets, and lanes. Situated along the banks of the River Nore, Kilkenny (population 11,000) takes its name from a church founded in the 6th century by St. Canice. In the Irish language, *Cill Choinnigh* means "Canice's Church."

Like most Irish towns, Kilkenny had fallen into Norman hands by the 12th century. Thanks to its central location, it became a prosperous walled medieval city and served as the venue for many parliaments during the 14th century. Fortunately, much of Kilkenny's great medieval architecture has been preserved and restored, and the basic town plan has not changed with the passing of the centuries. It's still a very walkable community of narrow streets and arched lanes.

Primarily a farming area, the surrounding County Kilkenny countryside is dotted with rich river valleys, rolling pasturelands, gentle mountains, and picture-postcard towns. Don't miss **Jerpoint Abbey,** on the River Nore and just southwest of Thomaston on N9, one of the finest of Ireland's Cistercian ruins.

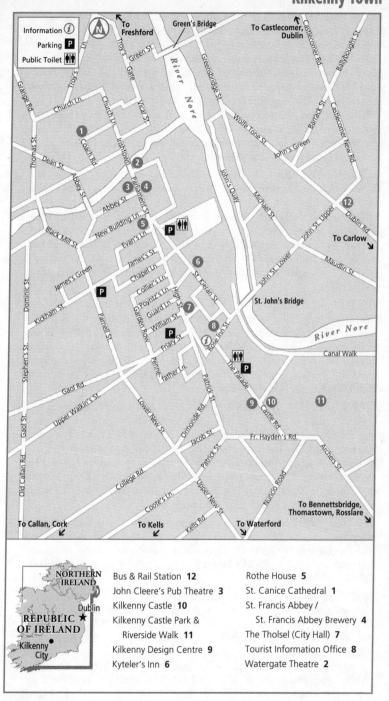

Also on the Nore is the village of **Inistioge,** about 15 miles (24km) southeast of Kilkenny town. Inistioge has an attractive tree-lined square and an 18th-century bridge of nine arches spanning the river.

The town of **Graiguenamanagh** (its name means "village of the monks") is home to Duiske Abbey. Surrounded by vistas of Brandon Hill and the Blackstairs Mountains, Graiguenamanagh is situated at a bend of the River Barrow, about 20 miles (32km) to the southeast of Kilkenny town.

Kells ⋆⋆, about 6 miles (9.5km) south of Kilkenny town, is the only completely walled medieval town in Ireland, and one of Ireland's most spectacular historic monuments. The extensive curtain walls, seven towers, and some of the monastic buildings have been well preserved.

GETTING THERE   **Irish Rail** provides daily service from Dublin into the Irish Rail McDonagh Station, Dublin Road, Kilkenny (© **056/22024;** www.irishrail.ie).

Bus Eireann, McDonagh Station, Dublin Road, Kilkenny (© **056/64933;** www.buseireann.ie), operates daily service from Dublin and all parts of Ireland.

Many roads pass through Kilkenny, including the N9/N10 from Waterford and Wexford, the N8 and N76 from Cork and the southwest, the N7 and N77 from Limerick and the west, and the N9 and N78 from Dublin and points north and east.

VISITOR INFORMATION   For year-round information, maps, and brochures about Kilkenny and the surrounding area, contact the **Kilkenny Tourist Office,** Shee Alms House, Rose Inn Street, Kilkenny (© **056/51500;** www.southeastireland.travel.ie). It's open May through September, Monday through Saturday from 9am to 6pm and Sunday from 11am to 5pm; April and October, Monday through Saturday from 9am to 6pm; and November to March, Mon through Saturday from 9am to 5pm.

TOWN LAYOUT   The main business district of Kilkenny sits on the west banks of the River Nore. A mile-long north-south thoroughfare, High Street, runs the entire length of the town, although it changes its name to Parliament Street at midpoint. The street starts at The Parade, on the south end near Kilkenny Castle, and continues through the town to St. Canice's Cathedral at the northern end. Most of the town's attractions are to be found along this route or on offshoot streets such as Patrick, Rose Inn, Kieran, and John. The tourist office can supply you with a good street map.

GETTING AROUND   There is no downtown bus service in Kilkenny. Local buses run to nearby towns on a limited basis, departing from the Parade. Check with **Bus Eireann** (© **056/64933;** www.buseireann.ie) for details.

If you need a taxi, call **Nicky Power Taxi** (© **056/63000**), or **Billy Delaney Cabs** (© **056/22457**).

By Car   Don't attempt to drive—Kilkenny's narrow medieval streets make for extremely slow-moving traffic, and you'll almost certainly get stuck. If you have a car, park it at one of the designated parking areas at The Parade, the rail station, or one of the shopping centers. On-street parking is .80€ (70¢) per hour with a maximum of 3 hours in most places; parking is on the disc system, and you can buy discs with the tourist office or in most shops. There are also several parking lots in town; the average fee for these is also .80€ (70¢) per hour. If you need to rent a car to see the surrounding countryside, check with **Michael Lyng,** Hebron Road, Kilkenny (© **056/70700;** sales@lingmotors.ie) or **Barry Pender Motors,** Dublin Road, Kilkenny (© **056/65777**).

On Foot   The best way to see Kilkenny town is on foot. Plot your own route or join one of the guided Kilkenny walking tours (see "Sightseeing Tours," below).

FAST FACTS: Kilkenny

Drugstores Try **John Street Pharmacy,** at 47 John St., Kilkenny (© 056/65971); **John O'Connell,** at 4 Rose Inn St., Kilkenny (© 056/21033); or **Whites,** 5 High St., Kilkenny (© 056/21328).

Dry Cleaning & Laundry **Ormonde Cleaners,** at 29 High St., Kilkenny (© 056/21949); and **Bretts Launderette,** Michael Street, Kilkenny (© 056/63200), are two good spots.

Emergencies Dial © **999.**

Library There's a **Carnegie Library** in town, at John's Quay, Kilkenny (© 056/22021). It's open Tuesday to Wednesday from 10:30am to 1pm, 2 to 5pm, and 7 to 9pm; Thursday to Friday 10:30am to 1pm and 2 to 5pm; and Saturday 10:30am to 1:30pm.

Newspapers & Local Media The *Kilkenny People* is the weekly newspaper covering local events and entertainment. **Radio Kilkenny** broadcasts on 96.6 FM and 96 FM.

Photographic Services Try **White's One-Hour Photo,** at 5 High St., Kilkenny (© 056/21328).

Police The local **Garda Station** is on Dominic Street, Kilkenny (© 056/22222).

Post Office The **Kilkenny District Post Office,** at 73 High St., Kilkenny (© 056/21813), is open Monday through Friday from 9:30am to 5:30pm, Saturday from 9:30am to 1pm.

SEEING THE SIGHTS IN KILKENNY TOWN

The oldest house in town is purported to be **Kyteler's Inn** on St. Kieran Street. It was once the home of Dame Alice Kyteler, a lady of great wealth who was accused of witchcraft in 1324. She escaped and forever disappeared, but her maid, Petronilla, was burned at the stake. Now restored, the inn is currently used as a pub/restaurant, but it retains an eerie air, with appropriately placed effigies of witches and other memorabilia and decorations.

One building that really stands out on the Kilkenny streetscape is the **Tholsel** on High Street, with its curious clock tower and front arcade. It was erected in 1761 and served originally as the tollhouse or exchange. Milk and sugar candy were sold at the Tholsel, and dances, bazaars, and political meetings were held here, too. Today the building houses the town's municipal archives.

Kilkenny Castle ✪   Majestically standing beside the River Nore on the south side of the town, this landmark castle remained in the hands of the Butler family, the dukes of Ormonde, from 1391 until 1967, when it was given to the Irish government to be reconstructed and restored to period splendor as an enduring national monument. The work on all but the west wing has been completed with great success. From its sturdy corner towers (three of which are original and date from the 13th century) to its battlements, Kilkenny Castle retains the lines

---

Fun Fact **Did You Know?**

Kilkenny is often referred to as the Marble City. Fine black marble used to be quarried on the outskirts of town. Up until 1929, some of the town streets also had marble pavements.

---

of an authentic medieval fortress and duly sets the tone for the entire town. The exquisitely restored interior includes a fine collection of Butler family portraits, some dating from the 14th century. The 50-acre grounds include a riverside walk, extensive gardens and parkland, and a well-equipped children's play area (see Kilkenny Castle Park and Riverside Walk listing below). Access to the main body of the castle is by guided tour only, prefaced by an informative video introduction to the rise, demise, and restoration of this splendid structure. The most recent phase of renovation included the construction of a conference center in the west wing (not open to the public), and the opening of a sally port at the entrance to the castle.

The Parade. ℭ **056/21450.** Fax 056/63488. www.heritageireland.ie. Admission 4.50€ ($4.10) adults, 3.15€ ($2.90) seniors, 1.90€ ($1.75) students and children, 10€ ($9.10) family. Apr–May daily 10:30am–5pm; June–Sept daily 10am–7pm; Oct–Mar Tues–Sun 10:30am–12:45pm and 2–5pm.

Kilkenny Castle Park and Riverside Walk   Admission to the lawns and wooded paths known as the Castle Park is included in the admission fee to the castle; you can also enter the park for free from one of several entrances along the path that follows the south bank of the River Nore. This path is a great place to get away from the bustle of the town and go for a run, stroll, or picnic. To get here, head toward the river on Rose Inn Street (the tourist office is on this street) and turn right on a gravel path just before crossing John's Bridge. If you feel like having a picnic, you can get a great selection of sandwiches, salads, and baked goods at **Shortis Wong Delicatessen** (see listing under "Great Deals on Dining," later in this chapter).

Free admission. Park hours are the same as those for Kilkenny Castle (see above).

Rothe House   This home of a prosperous Tudor merchant, built in 1594 and now a museum and library, has been meticulously restored. You'll come away keenly aware of life in medieval Ireland's merchant class. Take time to examine the old pikes and other relics of local historical and cultural significance. A genealogical service for County Kilkenny is also available here.

Parliament St., Kilkenny. ℭ **056/22893.** Admission 2.60€ ($2.40) adults, 1.90€ ($1.75) seniors and students, 1.25€ ($1.15) children. Apr–Oct Mon–Sat 10:30am–5pm, Sun 3–5pm; Nov–Mar Mon–Sat 1–5pm, Sun 3–5pm.

St. Canice Cathedral   This is the church that gave Kilkenny its name. The St. Canice's Cathedral that stands today is actually a relative newcomer, built in the 13th century on the site of the 6th-century church of St. Canice. The structure, which has benefited from much restoration work in recent years, is noteworthy for its interior timber and stone carvings, its colorful glasswork, and its roof, which dates from 1863. The round tower in the churchyard is believed to be a leftover from the ancient church, although its original conical top has been replaced by a slightly domed roof. Unlike most round towers in Ireland, you can sometimes climb to the top of this one—the tower is occasionally open to visitors. During the Kilkenny Arts Festival in August, the cathedral is the venue for a series of concerts.

At the northern end of the town, Coach Rd., Irishtown, Kilkenny. Ⓒ **056/64971.** Free admission; requested donations of 1.90€ ($1.75) adults, 1.25€ ($1.15) students. Easter–Sept Mon–Sat 9am–1pm and 2–6pm, Sun 2–6pm; Oct–Easter Mon–Sat 10am–1pm and 2–4pm, Sun 2–4pm; closed Wed 10–11:15am.

St. Francis Abbey Brewery   Established in 1710 by John Smithwick, this brewery occupies a site that originally belonged to the 12th-century Abbey of St. Francis. A beer called Smithwick's (pronounced *Smith*-icks) is produced here, as are Budweiser and Land Kilkenny Irish Beer. A video presentation and free samples are offered in the summer months.

Parliament St., Kilkenny. Ⓒ **056/21014.** Free admission. June–Aug Mon–Fri visits at 3pm.

SIGHTS IN NEARBY COUNTY KILKENNY

Clara Castle   This is one of the finest ruined tower houses of Ireland. Although it hasn't been restored, many of the original features are still there, so it's a great place to reconstruct in imagination the life of the castle in medieval times. Even some of the floor timbers remain. The timber roof is also in good repair. Other interesting castle features include the secret room on the fourth floor, to the right of the stairs, now revealed by a hole in the wall but once accessible only through the bedroom. The top floor was probably a kitchen, and has three "cupboards" recessed in the walls. The third and fourth floors were most likely sleeping chambers—a conclusion indicated by the windows, which are larger than those below, making these rooms somewhat more pleasant to inhabit. To get to the castle, take N10 east from Kilkenny, and turn left 3½ miles (5.5km) out of town—there's a small sign for the castle at this turn. Continue to follow signs to the castle for another 2 miles (3km). The key can be requested from the Murphys, in the first house past the castle on the right.

Open site. Located 6 miles (9.5km) east of Kilkenny.

Duiske Abbey and Visitor's Centre   The Duiske Abbey (1207) has a long and colorful history. It was suppressed in 1536, but its monks continued to occupy the site for many years. In 1774, the tower of the ruined abbey church collapsed. Things took a turn for the better in 1813, when the missing roof was replaced and religious services returned to the church, but the abbey didn't approach its former glory until the 1970s, when a group of local people pooled their time and talents to mount a major reconstruction effort. The roof has been restored using Irish oak beams and medieval construction methods (for instance, wedges and dowels are used in place of nails)—an awesome accomplishment on the part of the local craftsmen. Not everything about the restoration was faithful to the past, however; the architect in charge of the project worked with the parish priest to create a plan that would provide for modern liturgical needs as well. There are two early high crosses in the churchyard, both of which have elaborate decorations. A visitor center across the street from the abbey contains a gift shop and exhibits describing the process of restoration. Classical music concerts are occasionally held in the abbey—inquire at the visitor center for details.

Graiguenamanagh, Co. Kilkenny. Ⓒ **0505/24238.** Free admission; donations welcome. Abbey daily 7:30am–7:30pm. Visitor center Mon–Fri 10am–1pm and 2–5pm; July–Aug only Sat–Sun 2–5pm.

Dunmore Cave   This cave isn't worth a big detour, but the sight of the cave's gaping mouth should be irresistible to all closet spelunkers, claustrophiliacs, and lovers of the mysterious. Known as one of the darkest places in Ireland, the cave's chambers took shape over millions of years, and contain some fine calcite

Reading Ireland's Castles

During your stay in Ireland it's likely that you'll visit a few castles, or perhaps even stay in one of the country's castle hostels, hotels, or B&Bs. Spend enough time around castles and you'll find that the stones speak eloquently of the people who lived there. Like the whorled shell that retains an imprint of its maker long after the snail is dead and gone, the castle reflects the daily actions and needs of those who occupied it centuries ago. As you'll soon discover, there's nothing about castles that wasn't done for a purpose.

When you're visiting a castle, first take a look at where it's situated in the landscape. Whenever possible, castles were built on rock to prevent invaders from digging tunnels under the walls, causing them to collapse. Often, castles were built in strategic positions—commanding a harbor mouth, a pass, or a river, for example. The location of other castles—for instance, the *crannogs* built on tiny islands in the centers of lakes—seems to suggest that their dwellers were more interested in hiding than in domination.

The first thing to look for inside a ruined castle is signs of the wooden features which have long since rotted away. A pair of vertical slots opposite each other in the entrance corridor of the castle often indicates that a portcullis, or heavy sliding barricade, was used as part of the entrance fortifications. Doors often rested on donut-shaped rings carved from stone; if you can find these rings you'll know where the doors were and which way they opened. The wooden floor timbers rested on stone corbel blocks that protruded at regular intervals from the walls—imagine the floor at a level 1 or 2 feet (0.5m) above the corbels. Wooden partitions dividing rooms are sometimes indicated by slots or a row of holes in a stone floor.

The windows of the castle can also tell an interesting story. In the central tower or keep, considerations of defense usually dictated that the walls of the lower floors be pierced only with arrow loops, making these lower rooms intolerably dark and stuffy. The most important rooms for the life of the castle dwellers were on the upper floors, where windows could be somewhat larger, allowing light and air to enter the room. The brightest room of the castle, on the top floor, was often the kitchen and dining area, the center of social life. Signs of a former kitchen might be an especially large fireplace or a slop-stone, a drain of sorts that passes through the outer wall at floor level.

Of course, most of Ireland's castles are records of the lives not only of their original inhabitants, but of everyone who has lived in them, shaped them, and reshaped them during centuries of inhabitation. Ireland has a great legacy of creatively integrating the past into the present, and its castles are no exception.

formations. The cave may have been the site of a Viking massacre in A.D. 928. Exhibits at the visitor center describe geological formations and archaeological finds. The cave is about 6 miles (9.5km) north of Kilkenny town.

Off Castlecomer road (N78), Ballyfoyle, Co. Kilkenny. ℂ **056/67726.** www.heritageireland.ie. Admission 3.30€ ($3) adults, 2.50€ ($2.25) seniors, 1.70€ ($1.50) students and children, 8.50€ ($7.50) family. Mid-Mar to mid-June daily 10am–5pm; mid-June to mid-Sept daily 10am–7pm; mid-Sept to Oct daily 10am–5pm; winter Sat–Sun and holidays 10am–4:30pm.

Jerpoint Abbey ⊛   The impressive ruins of this 12th-century Benedictine (and later Cistercian) monastery, preserved in a peaceful country setting, offer a splendid array of artifacts from medieval times—from unique stone carvings on walls and tombs to a 14th- or 15th-century tower and cloister, as well as Irish Romanesque details of a late 12th-century Abbey church. A tasteful interpretive center with an adjoining picnic garden make this a perfect midday stop. Ms. Sheila Walsh in the interpretive center is quite knowledgeable and articulate concerning the abbey and its art and history.

11 miles (18km) southeast of Kilkenny in Thomastown, Co. Kilkenny. ℂ 056/24623. jerpointabbey@ealga.ie. Admission 2.60€ ($2.40) adults, 1.90€ ($1.70) seniors, 1.30€ ($1.20) students and children, 6.40€ ($5.80) family. Mar–May and mid-Sept to Oct Wed–Mon 10am–5pm; June to mid-Sept daily 9:30am–6:30pm; Nov 10am–4pm. Closed Dec–Feb. On Waterford road (N9), 1½miles (2.5km) south of Thomastown.

Kells Priory ⊛⊛⊛ _(Finds)_   The first time I set eyes on the Kells Priory, I couldn't believe that no one had mentioned it to me. With its encompassing fortification walls and towers, as well as complex monastic ruins, all enfolded into the sloping south bank of the Kings River in unspoiled countryside, Kells is one of the most spectacular ruins in Ireland, a must for anyone entranced or intrigued with the medieval world. It's my favorite kind of paradox: an intact ruin, a feast for the eyes and the imagination. It seems almost alive. In 1193, Baron Geoffrey FitzRobert founded the priory and established a Norman-style town beside it. The current ruins date from the 13th to the 15th centuries. Because you have to be your own guide here, you may want to stop by the post office in town and shell out 5€ ($4.55) for a copy of _The Augustinian Priory of Kells, Co. Kilkenny_ by Daniel Tietzsch-Tyler, an excellent guidebook with maps and descriptions of the many fascinating architectural details you can seek out. Also, before you leave Kells, drop a mile down the road to Kilree Abbey, whose small church and virtually intact round tower are well worth a slight detour.

Kells, Co. Kilkenny. Open site. Off N76 or N10. From N76 south of Kilkenny, follow signs for R699/Callan and stay on R699 until you see signs for Kells. The priory is less than ½ mile (1km) from the village of Kells.

Kilfane Glen and Waterfall   The main place of interest in this small garden is the glen, created in true picturesque style, with an artificial waterfall and rustic cottage. The paths have been strategically placed to enhance one's sense of the grandeur of this place: views of cottage and waterfall have been carefully composed, and the sound of water is used as counterpoint to the visual delights of the garden. An installation by the American artist James Turrell, "Air Mass," is open to visitors, although the time of day when it was intended to be seen (dusk) unfortunately doesn't correspond with the garden's hours in summer.

Thomastown, Co. Kilkenny. ℂ **056/24558.** www.nicholasmosse.com. Admission 5.10€ ($4.60) adults, 3.80€ ($3.45) seniors, 3.15€ ($2.90) students and children, 13€ ($12) families. Open Apr–June and Sept Sun 2–6pm; July–Aug daily 11am–6pm.

SIGHTSEEING TOURS

Tynan's Walking Tours   With these tours, you can spend an hour walking the streets and lanes of medieval Kilkenny, accompanied by a local guide who will regale you with information on everything from the town's history to regional architecture. Tours depart from the tourist office on Rose Inn Street.

10 Maple Dr., Kilkenny. ⓒ 087/265-1745. Fax 056/65929. www.tynantours.com. 4.50€ ($4.10) adults, 4€ ($3.65) seniors and students, 2€ ($1.80) children. Apr–Oct Mon–Sat 9:15am, 10:30am, 12:15, 1:30, 3, 4:30pm; Sun 11am, 12:15, 2, 3pm. Nov–Mar Tues–Sat 10:30am, 12:15, 3pm.

OUTDOOR PURSUITS

BICYCLING   Consider renting a bike to ride around the outskirts of Kilkenny, especially along the shores of the River Nore. For rentals, consult the Kilkenny Tourist Office; or contact **J. J. Wall,** 88 Maudlin St., Kilkenny (ⓒ **056/21236**). Rates average 10€ ($9.10) per day.

FISHING   The River Nore, southeast of Kilkenny, is known for its salmon and trout. For advice, permits, and supplies, visit the **Sports Shop,** 82 High St., Kilkenny (ⓒ **056/21517**). A day permit for salmon fishing is about 25€ ($23).

GOLF   The annual Irish Open Golf Tournament, the pinnacle of the Irish golfing year, took place 2 years in a row (1993/1994) at the **Mount Juliet Golf and Country Club,** Thomastown, County Kilkenny (ⓒ **056/24725;** www.mountjuliet.com), situated 10 miles (16km) south of Kilkenny town. You too can play a round on this 18-hole par-72 championship course designed by Jack Nicklaus, for greens fees of 108€ ($98) Monday to Thursday and 127€ ($115) Friday to Sunday. Alternatively, try the 18-hole championship course at the **Kilkenny Golf Club,** Glendine, County Kilkenny (ⓒ **056/65400**), an inland par-71 layout 1 mile from the town. Greens fees are 30€ ($28) on weekdays and 38€ ($35) on weekends. If you're in the area you should try the course at the **County Tipperary Golf and Country Club,** Dundrum, County Tipperary (ⓒ **062/71717;** www.dundrumhousehotel.com), designed by Philip Walton. Greens fees are 36€ ($32) midweek and 38€ ($35) weekends.

ACCOMMODATIONS YOU CAN AFFORD
KILKENNY TOWN

Ashleigh   Ashleigh is set amidst award-winning gardens on the Waterford road, half a mile (1km) from the town center. This house is the domain of Mrs. Pauline Flannery, who is helpful and well up on all that's going on in the area. Her home is beautifully appointed, and nonsmoking rooms are available.

Waterford Rd. (N10), Kilkenny, Co. Kilkenny. ⓒ 056/22809. 3 units, 2 with bathroom. 33€ ($30) single; 48€ ($44) double without bathroom; 53€ ($48) double with bathroom. 25% reduction for children. Rates include full breakfast. AE, MC, V. Free parking.

Danville House   The Stallard family farmhouse is just on the edge of town, within easy walking distance of Kilkenny Castle, but feels like a rural retreat. A walled vegetable garden opens onto the back of the house, and some of its produce will surely find its way to your breakfast plate. You should request the bedroom with a half-canopy bed, which is particularly spacious and stately, yet doesn't cost more than the other rooms. Kitty and Edwin Stallard are very welcoming hosts.

New Ross Rd., Kilkenny, Co. Kilkenny. ⓒ/fax 056/21512. 4 units. 38€ ($35) single; 53€ ($48) double. 10% reduction for children under 12 sharing with parents. Rates include full breakfast. MC, V. Free parking.

Hillgrove   Mrs. Margaret Drennan is the delightful hostess of this country home, which is furnished with antiques and has an attractive garden that guests are free to use. Margaret has won regional and national awards for her breakfasts. There's a TV and tea/coffeemaking facilities in the Victorian lounge. Bedrooms are tastefully decorated and beds have comfortable orthopedic mattresses. Close at hand are fishing, golf, and horseback riding. Hillgrove is 2 miles (3km) from Kilkenny town on the New Ross–Rosslare road (T20). This is a nonsmoking house.

Warrington, Bennetsbridge Rd., Kilkenny, Co. Kilkenny. ℂ **056/22890** or 056/51453. Fax 056/51453. http://homepage.eircom.net/~hillgrove. 5 units. 32€ ($29) single; 53 ($48) double. 50% reduction for children sharing with parents. Rates include full breakfast. V. Closed Dec–Jan. *In room:* Tea/coffeemaker (only in some rooms), hair dryer.

WORTH A SPLURGE

Blanchville House ✿   Tim and Monica Phelan's warm hospitality has won raves from our readers, as has this elegant Georgian-style home, just a 10-minute drive from Kilkenny town. The early 19th-century home is the heart of a working farm and retains many of its original features (such as the drawing room), with many original furnishings and an open fire. Bedrooms are tastefully furnished and meals feature homegrown produce translated into traditional dishes (dinner must be booked before noon). Three self-catering apartments (two- and three-bedroom) in a handsome stone gabled century coach house (built in 1840 and recently renovated) can be rented by the week or for a 3-day period (during July and August only bookings of a week or longer are accepted).

Dunbell, Maddoxtown, Co. Kilkenny. ℂ **056/27197.** Fax 056/27636. www.blanchville.ie. 6 units. 63€ ($58) single; 102€ ($92) double. Coach house 444€ ($403) per week or 108€ ($98) per day. Rates include full breakfast. Dinner 32€ ($29). AE, MC, V. House closed Nov–Mar; coach house open year-round. *In room:* TV, tea/coffeemaker, hair dryer, iron.

ACCOMMODATIONS YOU CAN AFFORD—NEARBY COUNTY KILKENNY

Abbey House   The setting of this attractive period residence alongside the Little Arrigle River is quite appealing. The front garden with sitting area is a perfect spot to relax at any hour, and the house's spacious living room, complete with piano and stacks of books, caters well to either a quiet read or a round of songs. Mrs. Helen Blanchfield has done a fine job of maintaining the period character of her home. The six rooms, while they vary in size, are all comfortable and pleasant. The extensive breakfast menu includes many alternatives to the full Irish breakfast—French toast, pan-fried rainbow trout, and Irish cheese plate are among the varied offerings; a new breakfast room overlooking the stream is a recent addition. Tea and scones are offered to guests on arrival.

Thomastown, Co. Kilkenny. ℂ **056/24166.** Fax 056/24192. 6 units, 4 with bathroom (shower only). 44€ ($40) single; 89€ ($81) double. Rates include full breakfast. MC, V. Free parking. On Waterford Rd. (N9), 1 mile (2.5km) south of Thomastown, directly across from Jerpoint Abbey. **Amenities:** Sitting room. *In room:* TV on request, tea/coffeemaker, hair dryer.

Brandon View House   Martin McCabe and his son Michael are the hosts at this 18th-century farmhouse on the gentle slopes of Mount Brandon. With the low ceilings, small windows, and meter-thick walls, the house itself is characterized by rustic simplicity. This was one of the first B&Bs in the area, and it offers present-day guests the same comforts enjoyed by visitors in the '60s. The decor doesn't seem to have been altered much, including the mattresses, which are a bit soft. It's the expansive hospitality of Martin McCabe—he's a great storyteller—that makes this place so appealing. It's also a great location: a pond across the road is home to a family of swans, there's little traffic along the narrow country road, and as the name suggests, the view is splendid.

Ballyogan, Graiguenamanagh, Co. Kilkenny. ℂ **0503/24191.** Fax 0503/24451. 3 units. 32€ ($29) single; 48€ ($44) double. 20% reduction for children under 12 sharing with an adult. Rates include full breakfast. No credit cards. Private parking. Closed Nov–Dec.

Cullintra House ⚘ Atmosphere is of primary importance at this quaint country farmhouse, presided over by the energetic Mrs. Cantlon and her several cats. Dinner begins late, announced by the sound of a gong, and guests linger long over their meals in the candlelit dining room. A lovely conservatory has tea-making facilities and a piano; food is set out here for the neighborhood foxes in the evening. Morning brings a relaxed breakfast schedule (served between 9 and noon), and perhaps a walk to Mount Brandon or a nearby prehistoric burial mound—the trail departs from the back gate. Ms. Cantlon is an enthusiastic host, and clearly enjoys entertaining her guests and making them feel at home. If you enjoy candles, cats, and good food, this place is for you.

The Rower, Inistioge, Co. Kilkenny. ℂ 051/423614. http://indigo.ie/~cullhse. 6 units, 3 with bathroom. 58€–76€ ($53–$69) double. 10% reduction for children. Rates include full breakfast. Dinner 23€ ($21). No credit cards. **Amenities:** Conservatory. *In room:* Hair dryer.

Foulksrath Castle Hostel Not only is this hostel situated in a beautiful 15th-century tower house, but the grounds comprise a veritable medieval complex of walls, courtyards, and outbuildings—a real treat for anyone who has ever fantasized about living in a castle. You won't find any luxuries here; little has been done to diminish the severity of the building, and you still climb a spiral stair to your stone-floored dorm. Common rooms have massive exposed beams and a carved stone window. The kitchen is in a 19th-century addition to the castle, and is quite spacious. Extensive renovations are still underway—in 1999, underfloor heating was installed in the 16th-century dining room, and in 2000 the original roof was rebuilt. Dorms have 10 to 12 beds, and some are a bit cramped, but the common rooms are spacious. A shuttle bus travels between the hostel and the gates of Kilkenny Castle. The charge is 2€ ($1.80), and the last bus leaves town at 5:30pm; call the hostel office for the current schedule.

Jenkinstown, Co. Kilkenny. ℂ/fax 056/67144 or 056/67674. www.irelandyha.org. 3 units (dormitories). 9.50€ ($8.65) per person. MC, V accepted for advance reservations. Free parking. 8 miles (13km) north of Kilkenny on N77.

Grove Farm House Grove Farm House was built 200 years ago high on a hill above the sheep-spotted fields of Kilkenny. The upper rooms command excellent views. Room Four is especially appealing: it has views of both distant agricultural fields and a colorful garden, tended by hostess Nellie Cassin. Other rooms are pleasantly, if pinkly, furnished. Electric blankets are provided as a counter to rain-induced chills. Hothouse tomatoes from the garden greenhouse make an appearance at breakfast.

Ballycocksuist, Inistioge, Co. Kilkenny. ℂ 056/58467. grovefarmhouse@unison.ie. 4 units, 3 with bathroom (shower only). 43€ ($39) double without bathroom, 48€ ($44) double with bathroom. MC, V. Free parking.

Norebridge House Norebridge's gabled roof recalls old Irish schoolhouses, and its interior, though new, also takes its cue from the past. Antique wardrobes, dressing tables, and homemade patchwork quilts inhabit each bedroom. The house shares a grassy slope above Inistioge with sheep fields, and the modestly sized ground-floor rooms overlook either the Nore River valley and village or a distant tower. Unfortunately, they also overlook the driveway and car park, which runs a little too close to the house's front. Frank Storie is especially proud of the state-of-the-art hot-water system in the house—high-pressure steaming showers are guaranteed. Once a pub owner, Frank is a genial, gregarious host who will quickly fill you in on who pulls the best Guinness locally.

Inistioge, Co. Kilkenny. ℂ 056/58158 or 056/58117. www.norebridgehouse.com. 4 units. 38€ ($35) single; 63€ ($58) double. V. Free parking. *In room:* TV, tea/coffeemaker.

WORTH A SPLURGE

Berryhill 𝄡   The ivy-clad gables of this eccentric country house overlook the River Nore, just outside the picturesque village of Inistioge. George and Belinda Dyer have created a uniquely pleasant retreat of this rambling house, built by the Dyer family in 1780. Each of the three spacious bedrooms (all nonsmoking) is attached to a private sitting room, and each is decorated with a particular, unmistakable animal theme. In the Elephant Room, for example, the distinctive feature is a cozy bathroom with a red bathtub, a small sofa, and fireplace, where you can bathe before a blazing fire while watching elephants cavort along the walls; the disadvantage here is the ground-floor location, adjacent to the car park. There are walks to be had on the hill behind the house, and a path provides a short walking route to Inistioge village. Breakfast here is a memorable occasion; options include fresh trout from the river.

Inistioge, Co. Kilkenny. ⓒ/fax **056/58434.** www.berryhillhouse.com. 3 units. 70€ ($63) single; 114€ ($104) double. Rates include full breakfast. MC, V. Free parking. Closed Nov–Apr. *In room:* TV, tea/coffeemaker, hair dryer, iron.

GREAT DEALS ON DINING
IN KILKENNY TOWN

The Italian Connection ITALIAN/INTERNATIONAL   Located just half a block from the Watergate Theatre, this small storefront restaurant is popular for pre- and post-theater dining. The decor is appealing, with dark woods, wine casks, and crisp pink linens, and the menu is noted for pasta and pizza dishes prepared on the premises. In addition, there are steaks, five variations of veal, seafood, and curries.

38 Parliament St., Kilkenny. ⓒ **056/64225.** Reservations recommended. Dinner main courses 7€–14€ ($6.35–$13). MC, V. Daily noon–11pm.

Kilkenny Design Centre Restaurant TRADITIONAL/SNACKS   Over-looking Kilkenny Castle's cobbled courtyard, this attractive self-service restaurant features a wide range of hot dishes, along with a large selection of salads based on seasonal produce, quiches, soups, and paté. The layered terrines and fresh salmon are outstanding, as are fruit pies served with cream. The Irish cheese board is excellent.

Castle Yard. ⓒ **056/22118.** Average meal under 18€ ($16); snacks 8.5€–14.75€ ($7.50–$13). AE, MC, V. Mon–Sat 9am–6pm; Sun 10am–5pm.

Kyteler's Inn IRISH/TRADITIONAL   Kyteler's Inn is a sightseeing attraction as well as a pleasant bar-come-restaurant (see "Seeing the Sights in Kilkenny Town," earlier in this chapter). The menu features dishes based on local meats and vegetables, with a selection for seafood and meat lovers, as well as vegetarian dishes prepared from fresh local produce.

Kieran St. ⓒ **056/21064.** kytelers@indigo.ie. Main courses 7.50€–15€ ($6.80–$14); fixed-priced Sun lunch 15€ ($14); bar food under 9€ ($8.15). MC, V. Mon–Sat 10:30am–11:30pm; Sun 12:30–11:30pm. Closed Good Friday and Christmas.

Langton House Restaurant and Bar *Value* PUB GRUB   It's no wonder that this bar has won numerous national awards—not only is the food good, but it's also a great value for the money. There are a few offerings for vegetarians, and all the traditional choices are here as well. The old-world ambience is delightful, so even if you don't plan to eat a meal here, at least nip in for a pint—it's worth the trip.

69 John St. ⓒ **056/65133** or 056/21728. Pub grub under 9€ ($7.50); lunch main courses 7.60€–10€ ($6.90–$9.10); dinner main courses 11€–18€ ($10–$16); fixed-price dinner 25€ ($23). AE, DC, MC, V.

Restaurant Mon–Sat 7:30am–11am, 12:30–2:30pm, and 6:30–10pm; bar daily 10:30am–7:30pm. Closed Good Friday and Dec 25–26.

Shortis Wong Delicatessen SNACKS/SANDWICHES/VEGETARIAN
This eclectic delicatessen serves a variety of sandwiches and baked goods, perfect for a picnic along the River Nore or in the grounds of Kilkenny Castle. In addition to the standard deli fare, they have great spicy vegetable sandwiches, samosas, and spring rolls. The offerings change often, so prepare to be surprised. There's no seating in the shop—it's strictly take-out.

74 John St. ℭ **056/61305.** Most items under 5€ ($4.55). Mon–Sat 9am–7pm.

NEARBY COUNTY KILKENNY

The Maltings IRISH/CONTINENTAL Overlooking the River Nore about 10 miles (16km) southeast of Kilkenny town, this venerable restaurant offers simple, well-prepared food in an idyllic and romantic county-house setting. The menu includes Chicken Kiev, roast half duck, filet steak, and grilled salmon. No provisions are made for nonsmokers other than prohibiting pipes and cigars.

Bridge House, Inistioge, Co. Kilkenny. ℭ **056/58484.** Reservations required. Soup with scone 3.20€ ($2.90); lunch main courses 5€–9€ ($4.55–8.15); dinner main courses 9€–18€ ($8.15–$16). MC, V. Daily 10am–10pm.

The Water Garden TEA/SNACKS Just outside Thomastown on the road to Kilkenny, you'll find this cafe and small garden operated by a local Camphill community for children and adults with special needs. The cafe is open for lunch, tea, and baked goods; meals are prepared Monday through Friday with organic vegetables and meats raised on the community farm. Lunches include sandwiches made with home-baked bread, soups, and a vegetable or meat paté. The garden (admission is 1.7€, $1.50) runs along a small stream, with numerous aquatic plants on display; there's also a garden shop.

Ladywell St., Thomastown, Co. Kilkenny. ℭ **056/24690.** Lunch 3.50€–5€ ($3.20–$4.55). Tues–Fri 10am–5pm and Sun noon–5pm (Sun tea and cakes only).

WORTH A SPLURGE

The Motte ☆☆ NEW IRISH In both cuisine and ambience, The Motte is fresh and exuberant. Guests are welcomed with a menu that takes advantage of locally available ingredients, and each table is crowned with a fantastic bouquet of Irish field flowers. The Motte dining room glows dimly with traces of gilt and candlelight; its space is intimate and the hosts expansive. For starters, the creamy broccoli and cilantro soup is vigorously seasoned. Equally good but more daring were profiteroles filled with Cashel Blue and laced with chile chocolate sauce. Main courses range from sirloin in burgundy butter sauce to a selection of fish. Tantalizing filets of plaice are combined with a delicately flavored lemon butter. Sorbet preceded an excellent choice of rich desserts. Final orders are taken at 9:30pm, although diners often remain until late in the evening. Just book a table well in advance and surrender your evening to conversation and good food.

Plas Newydd Lodge, Inistioge, Co. Kilkenny. ℭ **056/58655.** atmotte@gofree.indigo.ie. Reservations recommended. 3-course fixed-price menu 29€ ($26). MC, V. Tues–Sat 7–9:30pm.

SHOPPING

Shops are generally open from 9am to 6pm Monday to Saturday, and many post Sunday hours between May and August.

The Book Centre This shop offers a fine selection of books about Kilkenny and its surroundings, as well as books of Irish interest. Current bestsellers, maps, stationery, cards, and posters are also sold. You can grab a quick daytime snack at the Pennefeather Cafe upstairs. 10 High St., Kilkenny. © 056/62117. www.kilkenny bookcentre.com.

Jerpoint Glass Studio   Keith and Kathleen Leadbetter sell factory seconds at reduced prices. Glassmaking takes place Monday to Thursday 9am to 5pm and Friday 9am to 2pm. Stoneyford, Co. Kilkenny. © 056/24350. enquiries@jerpointglass.com.

Kilkenny Crystal *Finds*   This is the retail shop for Kilkenny's own handcut crystal enterprise, specializing in footed vases, rose bowls, bells, ring holders, wine glasses, carafes, and decanters. The factory is on Callan Road (© **056/25132**), 10 miles (16km) outside of town, and also welcomes visitors. 19 Rose Inn St. © 056/21090. www.kilkennycrystal.com.

Kilkenny Design Centre *Finds*   The 18th-century stables of Kilkenny Castle have been converted in recent years into an assembly of shops and workshops for craftspeople from all over Ireland. The Kilkenny Design Centre, located in the original coach house with an arched gateway and topped by a copper-domed clock tower, as well as the other smaller shops nearby, provide a showcase for many of the country's top handcrafted products—jewelry, glassware, pottery, clothing, candles, linens, books, leatherwork, and furniture. An excellent coffee shop/restaurant is on the upstairs level of the Design Centre (see "Great Deals on Dining," above). Castle Yard, The Parade, Kilkenny. © 056/22118. Fax 056/65905. www.kilkennydesign.com.

Nicholas Mosse Pottery   This enterprise, located in a former flour mill on the banks of the River Nore, is the brainchild of Nicholas Mosse, a potter since age 7. Using hydropower from the river to fire the kilns, he produces colorful earthenware from Irish clay, including jugs, mugs, bowls, and plates. All are hand-slipped and hand-turned, then decorated by hand with cut sponges and brushes. An on-site museum displays antique Irish earthenware made with this process. The shop was expanded greatly in 1999 to include tasteful housewares. Bennettsbridge, Co. Kilkenny. © 056/27505. www.NicholasMosse.com.

KILKENNY AFTER DARK

Kilkenny is home to the **Watergate Theatre,** Parliament Street (© **056/61674;** www.watergatekilkenny.com). This modern, 328-seat showplace presents both local talent and visiting professional troupes performing a variety of classic and contemporary plays, concerts, opera, ballet, one-person shows, and choral evenings. Ticket prices average 10€ to 20€ ($9.10–$18), depending on the event. Most evening shows start at 8pm.

Across the street is **John Cleere's,** 28 Parliament St. (© **056/62573**), a small pub theater presenting a variety of local productions, including the "Cat Laughs" comedy fest from May to July. It is also a venue for the Kilkenny Arts Week. Tickets average 10€ to 15€ ($9.10–$14), and most shows start at 8:15 or 9:30pm.

THE PUB SCENE IN KILKENNY TOWN

Note that the pubs listed here aren't likely to have traditional music; contact the tourist office for an up-to-date schedule of music in pubs.

Caislean Ui Cuain (The Castle Inn)   A striking facade with a mural of Old Kilkenny welcomes guests to this pub, founded in 1734 as a stagecoach inn. The interior decor is equally inviting, with dark wood furnishings, globe-style lights, a paneled ceiling, and local memorabilia. Irish is spoken by the patrons and staff. Castle St., Kilkenny. © 056/65406.

Kyteler's Inn If you're in a medieval mood, try this stone-walled tavern in the center of town. An inn since 1324, it was once the home of Dame Alice Kyteler, a colorful character who was accused of being a witch. The decor suggests caverns and arches, and the art and memorabilia have a witchcraft theme. St. Kieran St., Kilkenny. 𝄢 **056/21064.**

Langton House Restaurant and Bar *(Moments)* This place is a frequent "Pub of the Year" winner. Pub enthusiasts delight in Langton's rich wood tones, etched mirrors, stained-glass windows, brass globe lamps, and green velour banquettes. On cool evenings, the hand-carved limestone fireplace is warming, and for summer days, there's a conservatory/garden area backed by the old city walls. Pub meals are a specialty here (see "Great Deals on Dining," above). 69 John St., Kilkenny. 𝄢 **056/65133.**

Marble City Bar One of the best storefront facades in Ireland belongs to this pub in the middle of the town. Its exterior is a showcase of carved wood, wrought iron, polished brass, and globe lamps, with flower boxes overhead— and the interior is equally inviting. Even if you don't stop for a drink here, you'll certainly want to take a picture. 66 High St., Kilkenny. 𝄢 **056/62091.**

Tynan's Bridge House *(Finds)* The Tynan family cheerfully welcomes all comers to this award-winning 225-year-old pub, situated along the River Nore next to St. John's Bridge, on a street that was once used as an exercise run for horses. The interior is fitted with a horseshoe-shaped marble bar, gas lamps, shiny brass fixtures, and silver tankards. Side drawers marked "mace," "citron," and "sago" are not filled with exotic cocktail ingredients, but remain from the years when the pub also served as a grocery and pharmacy. Shelves display 17th-century weighing scales, shaving mugs, and teapots; there is even a tattered copy of Chaucer's *Canterbury Tales* for rainy days. 2 Horseleap Slip, Kilkenny. 𝄢 **056/21291.**

NEARBY IN CARLOW TOWN

There isn't much of interest to visitors in this unassuming town, which is more functional than exceptional. The town's main appeal is its proximity to several places of interest. It's a good base for visiting nearby Kilkenny, Wicklow, and Wexford.

SEEING THE SIGHTS

Near the Barrow bridge, on the grounds of Corcoran's Mineral Water Factory, you'll find the ruins of **Carlow Castle.** This was one of Cromwell's victims in 1650, but it survived to be returned to the earls of Thomond in the 1800s. The castle's final demise came about when a local doctor, who wanted to use it as a lunatic asylum, tried to thin its walls with explosives, rendering it so unsafe that it finally had to be demolished. All that remains today is a single wall.

The 1833 cruciform Gothic-style **Cathedral of the Assumption,** off Tullow Street, holds a marble monument by the celebrated Irish sculptor Hogan, dedicated to one Bishop Doyle, who wrote extensively about 19th-century politics, using a pen name to stay out of trouble. The cathedral's lantern tower is some 151 feet (46m) high, and there are magnificent stained-glass windows designed by **Harry Clarke.** It's open daily from 10am to 6pm, with no admission fee.

Two miles (3km) east of Carlow on L7, **Browne's Hill** demesne holds an impressive dolmen—its capstone weighs 100 tons, the largest in Europe.

Cyclists can explore the lovely Barrow and Nore valleys, and the vicinity of Kilkenny town, on a 7- or 14-day tour available through **Celtic Cycling,** Lorum Old Rectory, Bagenalstown, County Carlow (𝄢 **0503/75282;** fax 0503/75455;

www.celticcycling.com). Included are bike rental, safety equipment, rain gear, daily route maps and itineraries, insurance, B&B accommodations, and a 24-hour backup service. The suggested itineraries can be modified to fit your level of skill and stamina.

NEARBY ATTRACTIONS IN COUNTY CARLOW

Altamount Gardens ⚘ *Finds*　The lush, colorful extravagance of Altamont is the result of 55 years of nurturing by the late Mrs. Corona North. A shadowy avenue of venerable beech trees leads to bright lawns and the splash of flowers growing beneath ancient yew trees. Gravelled walks weave around a large lake, constructed as a famine relief project; the delights of this garden lie not only in its aesthetic and botanical diversity but also in the many birds that find sanctuary here. In early June, spectacular drifts of blue bells fill the forest floor on slopes overlooking the River Slaney. The moss-green depths of the Ice Age Glen, a rock-strewn cleft leading to the river, are currently closed to the public, but the walk through the Glen can sometimes be made with a guide, by request: It's a beautiful walk, concluding with an ascent up 100 hand-cut granite steps through the bluebell wood, and past a small temple with fine views of the southern Wicklow Hills.

Tullow, Co. Carlow. Call Carlow Tourist Information ⓒ 0503/31554 or the garden office ⓒ 0503/59444 for hours. Admission 2.60€ ($2.40) adults, 1.90€ ($1.75) seniors, 1.25€ ($1.15) students and children, 6.35€ ($5.75) families.

ACCOMMODATIONS YOU CAN AFFORD

Meeltrane House　Meeltrane House is located in the Brownshill section of Carlow town, 1¼ miles (2km) from the town center. Mrs. Mary Ruane's modern, two-story home features spacious guest rooms, and Mrs. Ruane is a helpful and accommodating hostess.

Link Rd., Brownshill, Carlow, Co. Carlow. ⓒ 0503/42473. 3 units, 2 with bathroom (shower only). 51€ ($46). Rates include full breakfast. No credit cards. Free parking. Closed Oct–Feb.

Sherwood Park House ⚘ *Kids*　An 18th-century Georgian country house and working farm, Sherwood Park is a place of green fields, distant mountains, hot tea, and real sheep to count from the warmth of a canopy bed piled high with pillows. Rooms are comfortably large; the two on the second floor even have smaller, adjoining rooms with twin beds that are perfect for children. Guests are invited to use the sitting room, where peat fills the fireplace and an old piano sits in the corner. Patrick and Maureen Owens are the genial hosts, and they help to create a festive occasion of even the rainiest evening. Maureen prepares a delightful, conversation-filled dinner, served to all in a high-ceilinged dining room with a long wood table.

Kilbride, Ballon, Co. Carlow. ⓒ 0503/59117. Fax 0503/59355. www.sherwoodparkhouse.ie. 4 units. 50€ ($45) single; 80€ ($73) double. 25% reduction for children. Dinner 35€ ($32). AE, MC, V. Free parking. Off N80, 1¾ miles (3km) south of Ballon. *In room:* Hair dryer.

WORTH A SPLURGE

Kilgraney Country House ⚘⚘　Kilgrany House harbors the unexpected. Once you pass through its late-Georgian front door, the eclectic taste of the proprietors, Martin Marley and Bryan Leech, takes over. High ceilings and richly colored walls complement the bold lines of 20th-century drawings and hammered metal furniture of Asian influence. Rooms are soothing and simple and demonstrate a careful consideration of the tactile as well as the visual, but even here the unexpected slips in: Perhaps the light pull is a horn-headed cane, or a

Thai puppet waves from a bedside table. Dinner, served on a long table of Kilkenny black marble, is also a fusion of old and new, of the exotic and the traditionally Irish—wild salmon is wrapped with a band of Japanese seaweed, and a creamy potato soup is laced with curry. The ritual of dinner and the conversation it inspires means that a meal can last well into the night. Breakfast is also excellent.

Bagenalstown, Co. Carlow. ⓒ/fax 0503/75283. kilgrany@indigo.ie. 6 units. 65€ ($59) single; 90€–140€ ($82–$127) double. Dinner 40€ ($36). MC, V. Free parking. Closed Nov–Feb. Just off R705 (L18), 3½ miles (5.5km) from Bagenalstown on the Borris road.

Lorum Old Rectory ⚹ Bobbie and Don Smith's 150-year-old stone farmhouse is located in the midst of County Carlow's rich countryside, at the foot of the Blackstairs Mountains, a mere 15 miles (24km) from Kilkenny and midway between Bagenalstown and Borris on R704/L18. It's a good base for local sightseeing or crafts shopping. Croquet, tennis, and lawn games will help while away your leisure hours, and golf, swimming, tennis, and horse racing are nearby. Furnishings include many antiques, and homegrown fruits and vegetables grace the table. This is also the home of Celtic Cycling, (see "Seeing the Sights," above) offering custom bicycle tours with manor house accommodation.

Bagenalstown, Co. Carlow. ⓒ 0503/75282. Fax 0503/75455. www.lorum.com. 5 units. 67€–70€ ($60–$63) single; 95€–102€ ($86–$92) double. 20% reduction for children sharing with an adult. Rates include full breakfast. Dinner 35€ ($32). AE, MC, V. Free parking. Closed Christmas. *In room:* TEL, tea/coffeemaker, hair dryer.

GREAT DEALS ON DINING

Lord Bagenal Inn CONTINENTAL/SEAFOOD The Lord Bagenal, set on the banks of the River Barrow, has a warm, inviting, old-world air. Locally grown vegetables and meats are used, and shellfish are kept in a tank to ensure freshness with each order. Roast duck, tournedos steak, escalopes of pork, and a wide variety of seafood are menu stars in the restaurant; the bar serves meals from noon to 10pm, including a carvery lunch, pasta dishes, fried fish, and various steaks.

Leighlinbridge (signposted off the Dublin-Carlow-Kilkenny road), Co. Carlow. ⓒ 0503/21668. www. lordbagenal.com. Bar main courses 9€–22€ ($8.15–$20); restaurant main courses 16€–22€ ($14–$20). DC, MC, V. Mon–Sat 8am–10pm; Sun 8am–9pm. Closed Christmas.

7

Cork City

Cork, Ireland's second-largest city, is stuck in the middle, neither as cosmopolitan as Dublin nor as scenic and historic as the countryside in nearby West Cork. It's nevertheless the sporting, brewing, and university center of the southwest, and thus, definitely worth a visit.

Its ancient Irish name is Corcaigh, or "Marshy Place." Druids once held their religious rites in the dense woods of the nearby southern hills. Celtic tribes built forts and fought battles over territorial rights in the hills to the north. And in the 7th century, St. Finbarre came to establish a monastery on a small island in the swamp, asserting that there would be "an abundance of wisdom continually in Cork."

Attracted by the religious foundation's riches, the Vikings arrived in the 9th century to plunder, and then to settle in. Normans took over in the 12th century, fortified the city, and proceeded to build great churches and abbeys. But it was the arrival of Oliver Cromwell, who captured Cork in December 1649, that finally settled the hash of the native Irish in the district.

Unlike the Danes and Normans, who had assimilated happily with the resident populace, those who came after Cromwell held in contempt everything that was Irish. No doubt it is from the strangling repression of this period that present-day Corkmen date their fierce sense of independence and abhorrence of injustice. Nor did being on the losing side ever lessen their fighting spirit. For a few centuries, in fact, they consistently allied themselves with defeat, standing behind Charles I, James II, and Perkin Warbeck, the servant of a Breton silk merchant who claimed he was the Duke of York and tried to usurp the English crown.

Today, Cork (pop. 136,000) is a busy commercial hub for the south of Ireland. Be warned that the traffic moves fast and the people talk even faster. Don't leave without tasting the local stouts, **Beamish** and **Murphy's,** and if you care for tea, ask for **Barry's,** blended in Cork since 1901.

Oh, and by the way, nearby is Blarney, where they keep the **Blarney Stone,** the rock that launched a thousand kisses (and a helluva lot of tourist revenue). To kiss or not is a deeply personal decision that no guidebook could hope to help with.

1 Orientation

Cork is 160 miles (258km) SW of Dublin, 128 miles (206km) SE of Galway, 63 miles (101km) S of Limerick, 76 miles (122km) S of Shannon Airport, 78 miles (126km) W of Waterford, and 54 miles (87km) E of Killarney

GETTING THERE   By Plane   Aer Lingus (© 021/432-7155; www. aerlingus.ie) flights from Dublin regularly serve Cork Airport, Kinsale Road (© 021/313131; www.cork-airport.com), 8 miles (13km) south of the city. In addition, there are direct flights from Amsterdam, Bristol, Exeter, Glasgow, Guernsey, Isle of Mann, London, Manchester, Paris, Plymouth, and Rennes. Cork Airport is in the process of dramatically expanding its services, and it may eventually handle transatlantic flights. **Shannon Airport** is 76 miles (126km) away.

By Rail Iarnrod Eireann/Irish Rail (© 1850/366222 [toll-free] or 01/836-6222; www.irishrail.ie) operates the train services in Ireland. Trains from Dublin, Limerick, and other parts of Ireland arrive at **Kent Station,** Lower Glanmire Road, Cork (© 021/450-4777), on the city's eastern edge.

By Bus Bus Eireann (© 021/450-8188; www.buseireann.ie) provides bus service from the airport to **Parnell Place Bus Station,** Cork (© 021/450-8188), in the city center; the fare is 3.15€ ($2.90) one-way, 4.60€ ($4.20) round-trip.

By Ferry Car ferry routes into Cork from Britain include service from Swansea via **Swansea/Cork Ferries** (© 021/427-1166; www.swansea-cork.ie); and from Roscoff via **Brittany Ferries** (© 021/437-8401; www.brittany-ferries.com). All ferries arrive at Cork's Ringaskiddy Ferryport.

When driving from the east, be sure to take the Carrigaloe–Glenbrook ferry, operated by **Cross River Ferries Ltd.,** from 6:45am to 11:45pm. The fare for a car is 3.20€ ($2.90) one-way, 4.45€ ($4.05) round-trip. For cyclists/pedestrians, the fare is .80€ (70¢) one-way, 1.30€ ($1.15) round-trip. This ferry will save you at least an hour's driving time between the east and west sides of Cork Harbour, avoiding Cork city traffic. The trip lasts less than 5 minutes. For more information, contact Cross River Ferries, Ltd., Atlantic Quay, Cobh (© 021/481-1485).

By Car If you're driving, many main national roads lead into Cork, including N8 from Dublin, N25 from Waterford, N20 from Limerick, N22 from Killarney, and N71 from West Cork.

GETTING AROUND **By Public Transportation** Bus Eireann operates frequent bus service from Parnell Place Bus Station (© 021/450-8188) to all parts of the city and its suburbs, including Blarney and Kinsale. The flat fare is 1€ (90¢). Buses run from 7am to 11pm Monday through Saturday, and for slightly shorter hours on Sunday.

By Taxi Taxis are readily available throughout Cork. The chief taxi ranks are located along St. Patrick's Street, along the South Mall, and outside major hotels. To call for a taxi, try **ABC Cabs** (© 021/496-1961), **Shandon Cabs** (© 021/450-2255), or **Tele-Cabs** (© 021/450-5050).

By Car Most hotels have parking lots or garages for guests' use, so if you drive into Cork, it's best to take advantage of this and explore the city on foot or by public transport. If you end up having to park your car in public areas, it will cost 1.25€ to 2.25€ ($1.15–$2.05) per hour, whether you park in one of the city's two multistory parking lots, at Lavitt's Quay and Merchant's Quay, or on the street, where the disc system is in use. Parking discs are sold singly or in books of 10 for 6€ ($5.45) and are available at many shops and newsstands. There are also at least a dozen ground-level parking lots throughout the city.

Many international car-rental firms maintain rental desks at Cork Airport, including **Avis/Johnson and Perrott** (© 021/432-7460), **Budget** (© 021/431-4000), **Hertz** (© 021/496-5849), and **Europcar** (© 021/491-7300). **Avis/Johnson and Perrott** also has a large depot in Cork city at Emmet Place (© 021/428-1100).

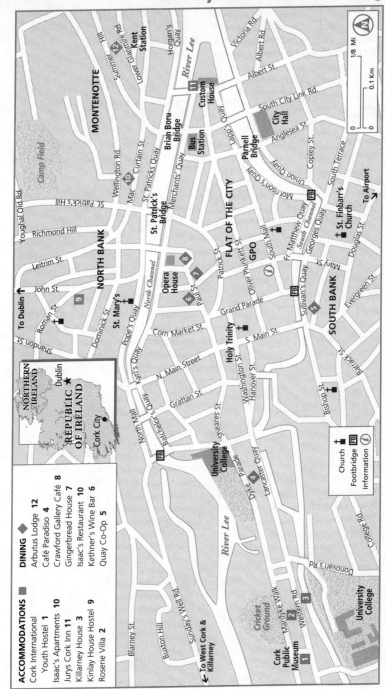

ACCOMMODATIONS

Cork International
Youth Hostel **1**
Isaac's Apartments **10**
Jurys Cork Inn **11**
Killarney House **3**
Kinlay House Hostel **9**
Roserie Villa **2**

DINING ◆

Arbutus Lodge **12**
Café Paradiso **4**
Crawford Gallery Café **8**
Gingerbread House **7**
Isaac's Restaurant **10**
Kethner's Wine Bar **6**
Quay Co-Op **5**

Church ✝
Footbridge 🅵🅱
Information ⓘ

NORTHERN IRELAND
REPUBLIC OF IRELAND
Dublin ★
Cork City ●

1/8 Mi
0.1 Km

MONTENOTTE
NORTH BANK
FLAT OF THE CITY
SOUTH BANK

Camp Field
River Lee
Cricket Ground

Summer Hill
Kent Station
Lower Glanmire Rd.
Horgan's Quay
Victoria Rd.
Albert Rd.
Albert St.
Custom House
South City Link Rd.
City Hall
Anglesea St.
Copley St.
South Terrace
To Airport
St. Finbarr's Church
Douglas St.
Evergreen St.
Barrack St.
Bishop St.
S. Main St.
Hanover St.
Washington St.
Holy Trinity
Grand Parade
Corn Market St.
N. Main Street
Grattan St.
Sullivan's Quay
Georges Quay
Man St.
Fr. Matthew Quay
South Mall
GPO
Oliver Plunkett St.
Patrick St.
Opera House
St. Paul's
St. Mary's
Pope's Quay
Domnick St.
North Channel
Roman St.
Shandon St.
John St.
Leitrim St.
Richmond Hill
Youghal Old Rd.
St. Patrick's Hill
Wellington Rd.
Mac Curtain St.
St. Patricks Quay
Merchants' Quay
St. Patrick's Bridge
Brian Boru Bridge
Bus Station
Parnell Bridge
Lapp's Quay
Union Quay
Morrison's Quay
South Channel
Sullivan's Quay
St. Patrick's Bridge
North Mall
Batchelor's Quay
Kyrl's Quay
University College
Dyke Parade
Lancaster Quay
Sheares St.
Blarney St.
Buxton Hill
Sunday's Well Rd.
To West Cork & Killarney
Cork Public Museum
Mardyke Walk
Western Rd.
Donovan's Rd.
College Rd.
University College
River Lee
To Dublin ←

On Foot   As I said, the best way to see Cork is on foot, but don't try to do it all in one day. The South Bank and the central part, or flat, of the city can easily take a day to explore; save the Cork Hills and the North Bank for another day. You might want to follow the signposted **Tourist Trail** to guide you to all the major sights.

VISITOR INFORMATION   For brochures, maps, and other information, visit the **Cork Tourist Office,** Tourist House, 42 Grand Parade, Cork (℡ **021/ 427-3251**). Its hours are October to May, Monday to Saturday 9:15am to 1pm and 2:15 to 5:30pm; June and September, Monday to Saturday 9am to 6pm; July and August, Monday to Saturday 9am to 7pm and Sunday 10am to 5pm. For online information, consult the **Cork Guide** (www.cork-guide.ie).

CITY LAYOUT

There are lots of bridges in Cork, which can be quite confusing. Before you start thinking you're going around in circles, realize that central Cork is actually on an island that lies between two limbs of the River Lee. The city is divided into three sections:

SOUTH BANK   Running south of the River Lee, South Bank encompasses the grounds of St. Finbarre's Cathedral, the site of St. Finbarre's 6th-century monastery, and also includes 17th-century city walls, the remains of Elizabeth Fort, and the City Hall, Cork's chief administrative center.

FLAT OF THE CITY   This is the downtown core of Cork, surrounded on both north and south sides by channels of the River Lee. The area includes the South Mall, a wide tree-lined street with mostly Georgian architecture and a row of banks, insurance companies, and legal offices; the Grand Parade, a spacious thoroughfare that blends 18th-century bow-fronted houses and the remains of the old city walls with modern offices and shops; and a welcome patch of greenery, the Bishop Lucey Park.

Extending from the northern tip of the Grand Parade is the city's main thoroughfare, **St. Patrick Street.** Referred to simply as Patrick Street by Corkonians, this broad avenue was formed in 1789 by covering in an open channel in the river. It is primarily a street for shopping, but it is also a place for the Cork folks to stroll and be seen and to greet friends. Patrick Street is also the site of one of the city's best-known meeting places: the statue of 19th-century priest Fr. Theobald Matthew, a crusader against drink who is fondly called the apostle of temperance. The statue—or "the stacha," as the locals call it—stands at the point where Patrick Street reaches St. Patrick's Bridge and is the city's most central point of reference.

NORTH BANK   St. Patrick's Bridge (or Patrick's Bridge), opened in 1859, leads over the river to the north side of the city, a hilly and terraced section where the continuation of Patrick Street is called St. Patrick's Hill. And is it ever a hill, with a San Francisco-style incline. If you climb the stepped sidewalks of St. Patrick's Hill, you will be rewarded with a sweeping view of the Cork skyline.

To the east of St. Patrick's Hill is MacCurtain Street, a busy commercial thoroughfare that goes one-way in an easterly direction, leading to Summerhill Road and up into the Cork hills to the residential districts of St. Luke's and Montenotte. To the west of St. Patrick's Hill is one of the city's oldest neighborhoods, home of St. Ann's Shandon Church and the city's original Butter Market building.

FAST FACTS: Cork City

Drugstores Try **Duffy's Dispensing Chemists,** 96 Patrick St. (℡ **021/ 427-2566**); **Hayes Conyngham and Robinson,** Wilton Shopping Centre (℡ **021/454-6500**); or **Murphy's Pharmacy,** 48 N. Main St. (℡ **021/ 427-4121**).

Emergencies For emergencies, dial ℡ **999.**

Gay & Lesbian Resources For information and aid, call the **Lesbian and Gay Resource Group and Community Centre,** 8 S. Main St. (℡ **021/ 427-8470**).

Hospitals Try **Cork University Hospital,** Wilton Road (℡ **021/454-6400**); **Bon Secours Hospital,** College Road (℡ **021/454-2807**); or **City General Hospital,** Infirmary Road (℡ **021/431-1656**).

Information See "Visitor Information," under "Orientation," above.

Library **Cork Central Library,** 57 Grand Parade (℡ **021/427-7110**), is the best-stocked public library in Cork.

Police The local Garda Headquarters is on Barrack Street (℡ **021/431-6020**).

Post Office The **General Post Office,** on Oliver Plunkett Street (℡ **021/ 427-2000**), is open Monday to Saturday 9am to 5:30pm.

2 Accommodations You Can Afford

Note: Prices in Cork are often higher during holiday and special-events periods.

CITY CENTER

Jurys Inn Cork *Value*   This five-story hotel is situated in the busy heart of the city overlooking the River Lee, next to the bus station and 3 blocks from Patrick Street. The brick facade, with a mansard-style roof, blends in with Cork's older architecture, yet the interior is bright and modern, with contemporary light wood furnishings. Because the flat-rate room price covers one or two adults and two children, it offers amazingly good value for a city-center hotel.

Anderson's Quay, Cork, Co. Cork. ℡ **800/44-UTELL** from the U.S., or 021/427-6444. Fax 021/427-6144. www.jurys.com. 133 units. 75€ ($68) per room. AE, DC, MC, V. **Amenities:** Restaurant, pub, dry cleaning/laundry. *In room:* TV, tea/coffeemaker, hair dryer.

Kinlay House Hostel   Operated by the Irish Student Travel Service (USIT), Kinlay House is a renovated town house located in the old city neighborhood of Shandon, just behind St. Ann's Church. Facilities include self-catering kitchens, a TV/video lounge, a launderette, internet access, a BBQ area, security lockers, and luggage storage facilities.

Bob and Joan Walk, Shandon, Cork, Co. Cork. ℡ **021/450-8966.** Fax 021/450-6927. www.kinlayhouse.ie. 58 units, 9 with bathroom (shower only): 8 single rooms, 8 double rooms (with double bed), 30 4-bed rooms, 2 family rooms (double bed and 3 twin beds), 5 5-bed rooms, 5 8-bed rooms. 13€ ($12) per person in dorm; 23€ ($21) single without bathroom; 38€ ($35) double without bathroom, 46€ ($41) double with bathroom. Rates include continental breakfast. AE, MC, V. **Amenities:** Self-catering kitchen, lounge, laundry.

SELF-CATERING

Isaac's Apartments *Kids*   These well-equipped apartments, located in the same building as the new Isaac's Hotel, can be a great budget option for families or groups. Because each bedroom has a double and a twin bed, and the rooms are all quite spacious, the apartments can comfortably house two or three people per bedroom. Each apartment has a kitchen/dining room and a comfortable sitting room. Although they're located in one of Cork's historic structures, the interiors and furniture were all installed in 1997. The lack of on-site parking is an unfortunate drawback; there is parking available, however, about 5 minutes from the apartments on foot.

48 MacCurtain St., Cork, Co. Cork. ℂ 021/450-0111. Fax 021/450-6355. www.isaacs.ie. 11 apts, 2- and 3-bed units. 2-bedroom apts from 100€ ($91) per night, 510€ ($462) per week; 3-bedroom apts from 130€ ($118) per night, 570€ ($516) per week. AE, MC, V. Open year-round. *In room:* TV, kitchen, hair dryer, iron.

WESTERN ROAD AREA (INCLUDING UNIVERSITY AREA)

This area lies west of the city center. University College Cork is located here, and some parts of the area are also called Wilton. There's heavy truck traffic along this road, but the accommodations listed below are either on quiet side streets or are set back from the road in their own grounds. The Western Road area is within walking distance of the city center (though it's a rather long walk), and there's frequent bus service.

Cork International Youth Hostel The hostel is housed in a grand brick mansion near the University College, and was extensively renovated in 1997. For couples or families who want more privacy than the dorm rooms offer, two- and four-bed rooms are available; be sure to book well in advance, as these rooms are quite popular. In addition to the excellent sleeping accommodations and showers, there's a common room with TV and a bureau de change.

½ Redclyffe, Western Rd., Cork, Co. Cork. ℂ 021/454-3289. Fax 021/434-3715. www.irelandyha.org. 20 units, all with bathroom (shower only): 3 doubles, 5 4-bed rooms, 11 6-bed rooms, 1 10-bed room. 14€ ($13) per person in dorm; 37€ ($33) double. Breakfast 3€–6€ ($2.70–$5.45). MC, V. Bus: 8. **Amenities:** Coin-op laundry service.

Killarney Guest House Mrs. Margaret O'Leary, a nurse for many years, now devotes her time and energies to the comfort of her guests. Home cooking is a specialty. Coffee and biscuits appear every evening, and she'll also furnish sandwiches upon request. She can even organize Irish language courses, or answer any burning questions you might have about the language. Nonsmoking bedrooms are available—you should request one when you book the room.

Western Rd., Cork, Co. Cork. ℂ 021/427-0179. Fax 021/427-1010. www.killarneyguesthouse.com. 19 units. 89€ ($81) double. Rates include full breakfast. AE, MC, V. Parking available. Bus: 8. *In room:* TV, TEL, tea/coffeemaker, hair dryer, iron.

Mrs. Rita O'Herlihy This modern two-story home is located just off Killarney road, near the university. It has a warm, welcoming air, as well as a garden for relaxing. The whole house is nonsmoking.

55 Wilton Gardens, Wilton, Cork, Co. Cork. ℂ 021/541705. 3 units, 2 with bathroom (shower only). 46€ ($41) double without bathroom, 51€ ($46) double with bathroom. Rates include full breakfast. No credit cards. Free parking. Bus: 5 or 8. *In room:* Hair dryer.

Roserie Villa Mrs. Nora Murray is the hostess at this converted schoolhouse, and her guest rooms are both attractive and comfortable. The villa is opposite the university, only a short stretch of the legs into the city center, and away from the Western Road traffic.

Mardyke Walk, Cork, Co. Cork. ℂ 021/427-2958. Fax 021/427-4087. www.roserievilla.com. 16 units. 32€–51€ ($29–$46) single; 51€–76€ ($46–$60) double. Rates include full breakfast. AE, MC, V. Free parking. Bus: 5 or 8. *In room:* TV, tea/coffeemaker, hair dryer, iron.

DOUGLAS AREA

Douglas is located a far distance southwest of the city center, but there's good bus service into town. The area is clearly signposted from the South Ring road as you leave the city.

Fatima House *(Kids)* Fatima House is 2½ miles (4km) from the city center and convenient to the airport and Ringaskiddy ferry (signposted on the Airport-Kinsale road, R600). The owner, Mrs. Elizabeth O'Shea, is especially fond of children and is quite willing to provide babysitting. Her bedrooms are all attractively furnished. Nearby, you'll find many good restaurants and a local pub that offers live music on weekends.

Grange Rd., Douglas, Cork, Co. Cork. ℰ/fax **021/436-2536**. fatimabandb@eircom.net. 4 units. 67€ ($60) double. 40% reduction for children. Rates include full breakfast. MC, V. Free parking. Bus: 6 or 7. *In room:* TV, tea/coffeemaker, hair dryer, iron.

KINSALE ROAD (AIRPORT)

You'll need a car for this area, which is about 5 miles (8km) out from the city center. It's a nice rural area, though, close to the airport and a good base for exploring nearby **Kinsale**, as well as Cork city itself.

Forte Travelodge *(Kids)* This motel-type lodge between Cork city and the airport is ideal for families on a budget. Rooms are quite spacious, with a double bed, single sofa bed, and a child's bed and/or baby cot if requested. Each unit has its own heating controls. The adjacent Little Chef restaurant specializes in snacks, drinks, and a wide variety of moderately priced meals. Both the accommodations and the restaurant have facilities for travelers with limited mobility.

Kinsale Rd. Roundabout, Airport Rd., Cork, Co. Cork. ℰ **800/709709** or 021/431-0722. Fax 021/431-0723. 40 units. 63€ ($58) per room (sleeps up to 3 adults or 2 adults, 1 child, and an infant). AE, MC, V. *In room:* TV, tea/coffeemaker, hair dryer, iron.

BLARNEY

Blarney, some 4 miles (6.5km) northwest of Cork city, makes a good touring base if you don't mind the hordes of tourists that descend on the town and castle every summer. The Cork-Blarney road (N617) is well signposted from Cork city at the Patrick Street Bridge.

Ashlee Lodge Mr. and Mrs. O'Leary run this outstanding guesthouse, located about 2½ miles (4km) from the City Center on the Blarney-Killarney road (R617). It's beautifully decorated and immaculate, and every convenience is thoughtfully anticipated and provided. Extensive renovations are planned for the spring of 2002: Several suites with whirlpool baths are being added, as well as a sauna and hot tub. Guests can enjoy the lovely gardens in fine weather. This is a nonsmoking house.

Tower, Blarney, Co. Cork. ℰ 021/385346. Fax 021/385726. www.ashleelodge.com. 8 units. 102€ ($92) double; 165€ ($150) master suite. Rates include full breakfast. MC, V. Private parking lot. Closed Nov–Mar. *In room:* A/C, TV (with CD player), tea/coffeemaker.

Birch Hill Farmhouse Birch Hill Farmhouse is a longtime favorite with readers. This century-old Victorian home sits on a wooded bluff, part of a 105-acre farm half a mile (1km) off N20, 4 miles (6.5km) from Blarney (signposted from Blarney town center). Mrs. Dawson is the hostess of this plant-filled and nonsmoking home. Some of the guest rooms are quite large, and all come with sinks. There are wood fires downstairs and electric heaters in the rooms.

Grenagh, Blarney, Co. Cork. ℰ 021/488-6106. 6 units, 1 with bathroom (shower only). 51€ ($46) double. 25% reduction for children. Rates include full breakfast. High tea 10€ ($9.10); dinner 13€ ($12). MC, V. Free parking. Closed Nov–April.

The Gables   Anne Lynch will make you feel right at home in this lovely period house set in its own grounds, 1½ miles (2.5km) from Blarney. The house was once given to the parish priest by the owners of Blarney Castle. Guest rooms are attractive as well as comfortable, and home baking is a specialty here. Anne will also help plan touring itineraries. Nonsmoking house.

Stoneview, Blarney, Co. Cork. ⓒ **021/438-5330.** www.gablesblarney.com. 3 units. 40€ ($36) single; 55€ ($50) double. 25% reduction for children under 12 sharing with an adult. Rates include full breakfast. No credit cards. Free parking. Closed Dec–Feb. *In room:* hair dryer.

Maranatha Country House ⚘   Olwen Venn is the energetic host at this 19th-century manor house, situated on 27 acres of fine woodland. Olwen's keen aesthetic sense is evident throughout the house, and she has gone to extraordinary lengths to make each room a unique experience. If the lacy frills and elaborate velvet constructions in one bedroom aren't to your taste, you can be assured that the next room will offer another experience altogether. In all the rooms, it is clear that conventions of decoration have been discarded in favor of thoughtful (and often whimsical) effusiveness. The most luxurious is the ground floor suite, which contains a canopy bed and a large Jacuzzi within its ample space. The breakfast conservatory houses an abundance of fresh blossoms, and the breakfast itself is both plentiful and delicious. The entire house is nonsmoking.

Tower, Blarney, Co. Cork. ⓒ/fax 021/385102. www.corkguide.ie/blarney/maranatha/welcome.html. 6 units. 38€–95€ ($35–$86) single; 63€–127€ ($58–$115) double. 50% reduction for children under 12 sharing with an adult. Rates include full breakfast. MC, V. Free parking. Closed mid-Nov to Mar. *In room:* TV, tea/coffeemaker, hair dryer, iron.

Phelan's Woodview House   Catherine and Billy Phelan operate this guest house on the outskirts of Blarney on the main Cork-Blarney road (N617), and as one reader wrote to us, "Both are charming, intelligent, and provide the utmost of excellent company and conversation." Rooms are tastefully decorated, and there's a bright, sunny lounge overlooking peaceful fields. A big bonus here is the restaurant run by the Phelans in their dining room, which offers reduced dinner prices to residents.

Tweedmount, Blarney, Co. Cork. ⓒ/fax 021/438-5197. 8 units, 7 with bathroom (shower only). 25€ ($23) single without bathroom, 32€ ($29) single with bathroom; 51€ ($46) double. 20% reduction for children sharing with an adult. Rates include full breakfast. Dinner 22€ ($20). MC, V. Free parking. Closed Dec–Feb. *In room:* TV, tea/coffeemaker, hair dryer.

SOUTHEAST OF THE CITY

On the southern side of Cork Harbour, the coastal village of Myrtlesville—about 12 miles (19km) from Cork city, 8 miles (13km) from the airport, and 7 miles (11km) from Ringaskiddy—makes an idyllic sightseeing base. Follow the signs for the ferry port of Ringaskiddy, then the signs on R613 and R612.

Bellevue ⚘ *Finds*   Gaby and Benny Neff, both of whom have worked for many years in the travel business, have put their combined knowledge into the task of creating a truly great B&B. They started with a fabulous location on a hill overlooking the sea in a quiet coastal town, just a short drive from downtown Cork. The house is extraordinary, with a conservatory that lets you enjoy the sea view in the shade of a 100-year-old grape vine, and an inconspicuous second floor addition that provides spacious, modern, en-suite rooms. Breakfast options include French toast and homemade jams. Both the Neffs have lived abroad (Gaby is from Switzerland), and between the two of them command some five European languages. The house is completely nonsmoking.

Myrtleville, Co. Cork. ☎ 021/483-1640. Fax 021/483-1138. www.bellevuebb.com. 5 units. 40€ ($36) single; 60€–70€ ($54–$63) double. 50% discount for children under 12. MC, V. Free parking. *In room:* TV, hair dryer.

3 Great Deals on Dining

For a map of the city's restaurants, see p. 267.

Café Paradiso ✦✦ VEGETARIAN   The dining experience here lives up to the restaurant's name, and this may be the best vegetarian restaurant in Ireland. Everything here is prepared with freshness and flavor in mind, and the result is usually heavenly. Moroccan spiced vegetables fill almond spring rolls, and crepes harbor baked Stilton and chard. Unusual, savory twists on the familiar, such as gingered sweet potato wontons or the butterscotch and walnut cheesecake offered for dessert, testify to the inventiveness of chef Denis Cotter, one of Ireland's most notable culinary personalities. The well-selected wine list offers a number of choices by the glass or half-bottle. Cotter and his partner, Bridget Healy, have spilled their secrets in their very popular *Café Paradiso Cookbook,* on sale here and in bookstores for 25€ ($23). The cafe's small size means that the nominal nonsmoking section is of negligible value.

16 Lancaster Quay, Western Rd., Cork, Co. Cork. ☎ 021/427-7939. Reservations recommended. Lunch main courses 10€–12.20€ ($9–$11); dinner main courses 16.70€–22.20€ ($15–$20). MC, V. Tues–Sat 12:30–3pm and 6:30–10:30pm. Teas, coffees, and cakes from 10:30am. Closed last 2 weeks of Aug and Easter week. Located across from the Jurys Hotel.

Crawford Cafe IRISH   Ensconced amid oil paintings and statuary in a ground-floor room at the Crawford Art Gallery, this restaurant is widely known as a westward extension of Ballymaloe, County Cork's most renowned cooking school and restaurant. The menu, which covers breakfast, lunch, and afternoon tea, holds few surprises—it includes such traditional dishes as lamb braised with vegetables and rosemary and served with champ (a traditional dish of buttery mashed potatoes with chopped green onions), and more contemporary open-faced sandwiches such as a wonderful smoked salmon, cheese, and pickle combination. All fish are brought in fresh daily from Ballycotton Bay, and breads and baked goods are from Ballymaloe kitchens.

Emmet Place. ☎ 021/427-4415. www.ballymaloe.com. Reservations suggested for parties of 6 or more. Set lunch 17€ ($15); main courses 11€ ($10). MC, V. Mon–Sat 10am–4:30pm.

Gingerbread House SELF-SERVICE/SNACKS   Conveniently located between Patrick and Paul Streets in the main shopping area, this patisserie and casual restaurant is popular with locals for its wide array of delicious baked goods, freshly roasted coffees and teas, soups, sandwiches, and pizzas. You can choose from their wine list or bring your own wine for a small corkage fee. Breakfast is also served daily.

Paul St. Plaza. ☎ 021/427-6411. All items 1.25€–9€ ($1.15–$8.15). AE, MC, V. Mon–Sat 8:15am–9pm; Sun 10am–9pm.

Isaac's Restaurant INTERNATIONAL   This restaurant on the city's north side is housed in a vintage warehouse-style building, with stone arches, brick walls, big globe lights, high ceilings supported by columns, and modern art. It can be noisy when full, but the din never disturbs the enthusiastic patrons who come for the trendy food. Chef Canice Sharkey's signature is modern, understated cuisine, with absolutely no showing off. Think simple, fresh pasta dishes

---

Impressions

An Irishman is just a machine for turning Guinness into urine, which as any Murphy's drinker will tell you is a superfluous exercise.

—Niall Tóibín (1929–)

---

and hearty stews, mouthwatering grilled meats, and interesting salads. Every dish is perfectly prepared, be it a classic Caesar salad, a char-grilled burger, or the prawn tempura with soy and ginger dip. Daily blackboard specials add to the variety. The best-value deal is at lunchtime, when you can easily get out of here for 10.16€ ($9.20) a head.

48 MacCurtain St. ✆ **021/450-3805.** Reservations advised for dinner. Lunch main courses 5€–10€ ($4.55–$9.10); dinner main courses 7.50€–18€ ($6.80–$16). AE, MC, V. Mon–Sat 10am–10:15pm; Sun 6:30–9pm.

Kethners Wine Bar MEDITERRANEAN/GRILLS   This is an attractive eatery, with exposed brick walls, lace curtains, and traditional decor. Everything is based on the freshest of ingredients—try the seafood pancake in a cheese-and-mustard sauce and the chicken Kiev, highly flavored with garlic. Service is friendly and efficient, and there's a good wine list.

9 Paul St. ✆ **021/427-0287.** Lunch main courses 7.50€–9€ ($6.80–$8.15); dinner main courses 8€–20€ ($7.25–$18). MC, V. Mon–Sat noon–11:30pm; Sun 4–10pm.

Quay Co-op VEGETARIAN/VEGAN   The ground floor of this insider establishment is a whole-foods store that also sells delicious breads and cakes. The main attraction, however, is on the second floor. Reached by a narrow, steep, winding staircase, the restaurant far surpasses its rather inauspicious first impression. An array of delicious hot and cold dishes spreads out before you, including spinach and sun-dried tomato roulade, spanakopita, and lentil and coconut soup. Homemade breads and cakes are especially good here. Although some vegan offerings may seem bland if you're not used to this diet, don't let that deter you; they make up a small proportion of the menu. The clientele includes much of Cork's countercultural community, both young and old.

24 Sullivan's Quay. ✆ **021/431-7026.** www.quaycoop.com. Lunch main courses 5.30€–8€ ($4.80–$7.20); dinner main courses 6.50€–10€ ($5.90–$9.10). Daily 9am–9pm. AE, MC, V.

The Wilton Pub & Restaurant PUB GRUB/TRADITIONAL   No need to drive into town for a meal if you're staying in the Wilton area—this large pub, with traditional decor, offers an extensive menu that can meet just about any need, be it for a snack, a light lunch, or an excellent full hot meal. Portions are more than ample, and there's a friendly, convivial air about the place.

Wilton Shopping Centre. ✆ **021/434-4454.** Carvery lunch (in the bar) 8.90€ ($8.05); dinner main courses (restaurant) 11€–19€ ($10–$17). MC, V. Bar Mon–Sat 12–6pm, Sun 12:30–6pm; restaurant Mon–Sat 6–10:30pm, Sun 6–9:30pm.

WORTH A SPLURGE

Arbutus Lodge Hotel ⚓ INTERNATIONAL   Overlooking the city skyline from a hilltop, this lovely Georgian town-house restaurant has long been synonymous with gourmet cuisine in Cork—and, for that matter, in Ireland. It has long ranked among a handful of restaurants setting the standard toward which everyone else strives; and now, with a new chef, it, too, must strive to maintain its place. To even a jaded palate, a meal here can be startling. On many evenings, the chef prepares an eight-course tasting menu, which is an excellent way to discover the full scope of his talent. The wine list has won more decorations than Patton and offers a more delicate finish. It provides marvelous reading, even before a cork is lifted. The skilled, gracious service staff adds to the rare pleasure of a dinner at Arbutus Lodge. In addition to the dining room, there is food served all day in the Galley Bar.

St. Luke's Hill, Montenotte, Cork. ✆ **021/450-1237**. www.arbutuslodge.net. Reservations required. Fixed-price lunch 20€ ($18), fixed-price dinner 35€ ($32); dinner main courses 20€–24€ ($18–$22). AE, DC, DISC, MC, V. Mon–Sat 1–2:30pm and 7–9:30pm; Galley bar daily 7am–10pm.

4 Seeing the Sights

ATTRACTIONS IN TOWN

Coal Quay Market This is Cork's open-air flea market—a treasure trove of secondhand clothes, old china, used books, and memorabilia. It all happens on a street, now a little ragged, that was once Cork's original outdoor market. You won't find the place listed anywhere under "Coal Quay"—the signs say "Corn Market Street"—but no one in town will know what you're asking for unless you say "Coal Quay." Thursday is the best day to visit the market.

Cornmarket St. Free admission. Mon–Sat 9am–5pm.

Cork City Gaol This restored prison was infamous in the 19th century, housing many of Ireland's great patriots. Sound effects and lifelike characters inhabiting the cells re-create the social history of Cork. The place also presents the "Radio Museum Experience," an exhibition drawn from the RTE Museum Collection, an "unforgettable journey down the wavelengths of time" or, more simply, a restored 6CK Radio Studio and an array of antique radio equipment and memorabilia.

Convent Ave. (a mile west of the city center), Sunday's Well, Cork. ✆ **021/430-5022**. Admission to gaol: 5€ ($4.55) adult, 4€ ($3.65) seniors and students, 3€ ($2.70) children under 16, 14€ ($13) family. Exhibition if purchased with gaol tickets an additional 2.50€ ($2.30) adult, 2€ ($1.80) seniors and students, 1.50€ ($1.40) children under 16, 7€ ($6.35) family. Mar–Oct daily 9:30am–6pm; Nov–Feb daily 10am–5pm.

Cork Heritage Park This new park is set in a 19th-century courtyard on lovely grounds beside an estuary of Cork Harbour. The site was originally part of the estate of the Pike family, Quakers who were prominent in banking and shipping in Cork in the 1800s. The center's exhibits trace the maritime and shipping routes of Cork, as well as the history of the Pike family, in a series of colorful tableaux. There is also an environmental center, an archaeology room, a small museum dedicated to the history of Cork fire fighting from 1450 to 1945, and stables that house models of a saddler and blacksmith.

Bessboro Rd., Blackrock, Cork. ✆ **021/435-8854**. Fax 021/435-9395. Admission 4.50€ ($4.10) adults, 3.15€ ($2.90) seniors and students, 1.90€ ($1.75) children, 9.50€ ($8.65) family. May–Sept daily 10:30am–5:30pm; Apr Sat–Sun 12–5:30pm. 2 miles (3km) south of the city center.

Cork Museum This museum is located in a magnificent Georgian building set in a park on the western edge of the city. Its exhibits include models depicting early medieval times; artifacts recovered from excavations within the city, some dating back as far as 4,000 years; a working model of an early flour mill with an unusual horizontal water wheel; and an archive of photographs and documents relating to Cork-born Irish patriots Michael Collins, Terence McSwiney, and Thomas MacCurtain. Antique Cork silver, glass, and lace are also displayed.

Fitzgerald Park. ✆ **021/427-0679**. Free admission except Sun 1.25€ ($1.15) per person, 2.60€ ($2.40) family. Mon–Fri 11am–1pm and 2:15–5pm; Sun 3–5pm. July–Aug closes at 6pm. Bus: 8.

Crawford Municipal Art Gallery   Works by well-known Irish painters Jack Yeats, Nathaniel Grogan, William Orpen, John Lavery, James Barry, and Daniel Maclise are the focal point of this gallery in Cork's 18th-century former customhouse. Also on display are sculptures and handcrafted silver and glass pieces. There's a fine restaurant (see "Great Deals on Dining" above) and bookstore on the premises. In 2000, the Gallery received a dramatic facelift, with a major futuristic extension.

Emmet Place (next to the Opera House). © 021/427-3377. www.synergy.ie/crawford/. Free admission. Mon–Sat 10am–5pm.

Lavitts Quay Gallery   This gallery, operated by the Cork Arts Society, promotes the contemporary visual arts of the Cork area. It's in an early 18th-century Georgian house that overlooks the River Lee. The ground floor presents a variety of work by established artists, and the upper floor showcases up-and-coming talent.

5 Father Matthew St., Cork. © 021/427-7749. Free admission. Mon–Sat 10am–6pm.

Old English Market/City Market ⭐   Ireland's best food market dates to a Charter of James 1 in 1610. The present building, finished in 1786, was damaged by fire in 1980 and was refurbished by Cork Corporation to an award-winning design by T.F. MacNamara, the City Architect. Foodstuffs peculiar to Cork may be purchased here. Stands brim with meats, fish, vegetables, and fruit, and you'll also see such traditional Cork foods as hot buttered eggs, *tripe* (animal stomach), *crubeens* (pigs' feet), and *drisheens* (local blood sausage). The market's name is a holdover from the days of English rule.

Grand Parade, Cork. Free admission. Mon–Sat 9am–5:30pm. Enter from Patrick St., Grand Parade, Oliver Plunkett St., or Princes St.

St. Anne's Shandon Church ⭐   This is Cork's prime landmark, famous for its giant pepper-pot steeple and eight melodious bells. No matter where you stand in the downtown area, you can usually see the 1722 church's stone tower, crowned with a gilt ball and a fish weathervane. Visitors are often encouraged to climb to the belfry and play a tune, so you might hear the bells of Shandon ringing at all times of the day. There's also a great view from the summit of the church tower. Short talks on the church are given for visitors twice daily, at noon and 3pm.

Church St. © 021/450-5906. www.shandonsteeple.com. Admission to church, tower, and bells 4.50€ ($4.10) adult, 3.80€ ($3.45) seniors and students. Open year-round 10am–5pm.

St. Finbarre's Cathedral   This Church of Ireland cathedral sits on the spot St. Finbarre chose in A.D. 600 for his church and school. The current building dates back to 1880 and is a fine example of early French Gothic style; its three giant spires dominate the skyline, and the interior is highly ornamented with unique mosaic work. The bells were inherited from the 1735 church previously on this site.

Bishop St. © 021/496-3387. http://cathedral.cork.anglican.org. Admission 3€ ($2.70) donation requested. Mon–Sat 10am–12:45pm and 2–5:30pm.

University College—Cork (UCC)   This center of learning is housed in a quadrangle of Gothic Revival–style buildings. Lovely gardens and wooded grounds grace the campus. Tours take you to the Crawford Observatory, the Harry Clarke stained glass windows in the Honan Chapel, and the Stone Corridor, a collection of stones inscribed with the ancient Irish Ogham writing.

Western Rd. © 021/490-3000. Tours are conducted by arrangement: call © 021/490-3098. www.ucc.ie.

Cork City Attractions

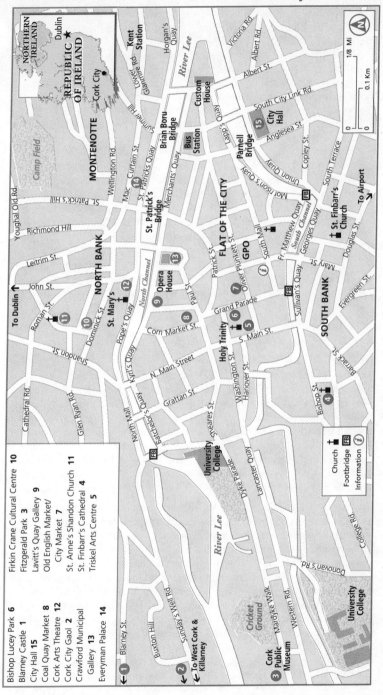

Bishop Lucey Park **6**
Blarney Castle **1**
City Hall **15**
Coal Quay Market **8**
Cork Arts Theatre **12**
Cork City Gaol **2**
Crawford Municipal
Gallery **13**
Everyman Palace **14**

Firkin Crane Cultural Centre **10**
Fitzgerald Park **3**
Lavitt's Quay Gallery **9**
Old English Market/
City Market **7**
St. Anne's Shandon Church **11**
St. Finbarr's Cathedral **4**
Triskel Arts Centre **5**

Tips Touring Cork

One of Cork's chief charms is that it's so easily walkable, allowing you to capture its real flavor and mingle easily with the people who give it life. You can take to the streets on your own, of course, but if you want to get a little of the local history there are a number of regular walking tours you can hook into.

Free evening **guided walking tours** depart from the Tourist Office 2 or 3 days a week during July and August. Inquire when you're there to see if they're on.

If your dogs get tired, **Bus Eireann,** Parnell Place Bus Station (© 021/ 450-8188), offers 3-hour open-top bus tours of Cork city during July and August for a flat fare of 7.60€ ($6.90). Hop-on, hop-off tour buses depart from the tourist office, 42 Grand Parade (© 021/427-3251) five times daily; the charge is 11€ ($10) adult, 9.50€ ($8.65) student, 3.15€ ($2.90) child under 14, and 25€ ($22) family. Buses start at 10:20am, and the last bus leaves at 4:10pm; the travel time for the loop is 70 minutes.

During the summer months, there are regular 4-hour **harbor cruises** down the Lee, departing from nearby Cobh. Schedules vary, and they don't always run the same days every week, so call directly (© 021/ 481-1485) or check with the tourist office (© 021/427-3251).

NEARBY ATTRACTIONS

Ballincollig Gunpowder Mills   This industrial complex beside the River Lee was a hub for the manufacture of gunpowder from 1794 to 1903, a time of wars between Britain and France. In its heyday as Cork's prime industry, it employed about 500 men as coopers, millwrights, and carpenters. You can tour the restored buildings, and there are exhibits and an audiovisual presentation that tell the story of gunpowder production in the Cork area.

Ballincollig, Co. Cork. © 021/487-4430. Fax 021/487-4836. http://indigo.ie/~ballinco. Admission 3.80€ ($3.45) adults, 3.15€ ($2.90) seniors and students, 2.30€ ($2.05) children, 10€ ($9.10) family. Apr–Oct daily 10am–5pm. About 5 miles (8km) west of Cork city on the main Cork-Killarney Rd. (N22).

Blarney Castle and Stone *(Overrated*   Blarney Castle is an impressive ruin, but in our opinion, it's not worth the crowds and the hype. What remains of the castle today is a massive square tower, with a parapet rising 83 feet (25.3m). Admittedly, it's one of the finest castle ruins in Ireland, with many hidden corners, passages, and chambers to explore. The famous Blarney Stone is wedged far enough underneath the battlements to make it uncomfortable to reach, but not far enough that countless tourists don't abandon all concern for health to kiss it.

After bypassing the stone, take a stroll through the gardens and a nearby dell beside Blarney Lake. The Badger Cave and adjacent dungeons, penetrating the rock at the base of the castle, can be explored by all but the claustrophobic with the aid of a flashlight.

Blarney, Co. Cork. © 021/438-5252. www.blarneycastle.ie. Castle 4.50€ ($4) adults, 3.20€ ($2.90) seniors and students, 1.30€ ($1.15) children aged 8–14, 9.55€ ($8.65) family. Open May and Sept Mon–Sat 9am–6:30pm, Sun 9:30am–5:30pm; June–Aug Mon–Sat 9am–7pm, Sun 9:30am–5:30pm; Oct–Apr Mon–Sat 9am–sundown, Sun 9:30am–sundown. Bus: 154 from bus station on Parnell Place, Cork city. 5 miles (8km) northwest of Cork city on R617.

5 Special Events

If you doubt that Cork is a party-loving town, just take a look at the festivals they put on every year. A festival in Cork is a gala affair, with the entire city involved in the activities, and if you hit town in the middle of one, you're in for a treat.

One of the best events is the **Guinness Cork Jazz Festival** ⍟, usually in October (on the last bank holiday of the year). Some of the world's finest musicians show up for concerts held all around town, as well as impromptu jam sessions that break out in pubs, B&B drawing rooms, and wherever two or more musicians happen to meet. It's a joyous, free-spirited time. Contact the Festival Office (℗/fax **021/427-0463;** www.corkjazzfestival.com).

In April or May, the **Cork International Choral and Folk Dance Festival** (℗ **021/430-8308;** fax 021/430-8309) attracts top performers from America, Great Britain, and the Continent.

The **Murphy's Cork Film Festival** has enjoyed a worldwide reputation for years as a showcase for independent filmmakers. You can contact the box office in early October at ℗ **021/427-1711.** The festival has occasionally been canceled in past years, so contact the tourist office for current information before getting your hopes up.

6 Spectator Sports & the Great Outdoors

LET THE GAMES BEGIN—SPECTATOR SPORTS

GAELIC GAMES   Hurling and Gaelic football are both played on summer Sunday afternoons at Cork's **Pairc Ui Chaoimh Stadium,** Marina Walk (℗ **021/496-3311**). Check the local newspapers for details.

GREYHOUND RACING   Go to the dogs, as they say in Cork, at **Cork Greyhound Track,** Western Road, Cork (℗ **021/454-3013**), on Wednesday, Thursday, and Saturday at 8pm. Admission is 6.50€ ($5.90).

HORSE RACING   The nearest racetrack is **Mallow Race Track,** Killarney Road, Mallow (℗ **022/50207**), approximately 20 miles (32km) north of Cork. Races are scheduled in mid-May, early August, and early October.

OUTDOOR PURSUITS

FISHING   The River Lee, which runs through Cork, the nearby Blackwater River, and the many lakes in the area present fine opportunities for fishing. Salmon licenses and lake fishing permits, as well as tackle and equipment, can be obtained from **T. W. Murray,** 87 Patrick St., Cork (℗ **021/427-1089**), and **The Tackle Shop,** Lavitt's Quay, Cork (℗ **021/427-2842**).

GOLF   The following local clubs allow visitors to play on their 18-hole courses, all within a 5-mile (8km) radius of the city: **Cork Golf Club,** Little Island, Cork (℗ **021/435-3451**), 5 miles (8km) east of Cork, with greens fees of 63€ ($58) weekdays and 70€ ($63) weekends; **Douglas Golf Club,** Maryboro Hill, Douglas (℗ **021/489-5297;** www.douglasgolfclub.ie), 3 miles (5km) south of Cork, with greens fees of 44€ ($40) weekdays and 53€ ($48) weekends; and **Harbour Point,** Little Island (℗ **021/435-3094**), 4 miles (6.5km) east of Cork, with greens fees of 29€ ($26) weekdays and 33€ ($30) weekends.

WALKING   The **Old Railway Line** is a dismantled train route running from Cork to the old maritime town of Passage West. It is from here that Captain

Roberts set out and crossed the Atlantic in the first passenger steamship, *The Sirius*. Following along the rails, a scenic walk affords the visitor excellent views of the inner harbor.

7 Shopping

Cork city is a major shopping center. The **City Market** 🌟, sometimes called the Old English Market, is a block-long covered space between Patrick Street, Prince's Street, and Grand Parade. Its origins stretch from the 1610 Charter of James I. It's a lively marketplace, with Cork homemakers busily stall-hopping for the best buys on vegetables, fruits, meats, flowers, and occasionally secondhand clothes. (See "Seeing the Sights," earlier in this chapter.)

Patrick Street is the main shopping thoroughfare, and many stores are scattered throughout the city on side streets and in lanes. In general, shops are open Monday to Saturday 9:30am to 6pm, unless indicated otherwise. In the summer, many shops remain open until 9:30pm on Thursday and Friday, and some are open on Sunday.

The city's antiques row is **Paul's Lane,** an offshoot of Paul Street, which sits between Patrick Street and the Quays in the Huguenot Quarter. There are three shops along this lane, each brimming with old Cork memorabilia and furnishings: **Anne McCarthy,** 2 Paul's Lane (✆ **021/427-3755**); **Mills,** 3 Paul's Lane (✆ **021/427-3528**); and **O'Regan's,** 4 Paul's Lane (✆ **021/427-2902**). All three are open Monday to Saturday from 10am to 6pm.

The main mall is **Merchant's Quay Shopping Centre,** Merchant's Quay and Patrick Street. This enclosed complex houses large department stores, such as **Marks and Spencer** (✆ **021/427-5555**), as well as small specialty shops, such as **Laura Ashley** (✆ **021/427-4070**).

Cork's legendary department store is **Cashs,** 18–21 St. Patrick St. (✆ **021/427-6771**), which dates back to 1830. It offers three floors of wares and gift items, including Waterford crystal, Irish linen, and all types of knitwear and tweeds.

Blarney Woollen Mills   About 6 miles (9.5km) northwest of Cork City, on the same grounds as the famous castle of the same name, this huge store is housed in an 1824 mill. It's a one-stop source for Irish products, from cashmeres to crystal glassware, hats to heraldry, and tweeds to T-shirts, as well as the distinctive Kelly green Blarney Castle–design wool sweaters, made on the premises. Best of all, it's open until 10pm every night in summer. Blarney, Co. Cork. ✆ **021/438-5280.** www.blarney.ie.

Crafts of Ireland   Turn left at Cash's department store to reach Cork's only "All Irish" shop, which stocks a wide and wonderful range of Irish crafts, including weavings, wrought iron, batik hangings, candles, glass, graphics, leather work, pottery, toys, Irish wildlife mobiles, and Irish floral stationery. It's opposite the GPO. 11 Winthrop St., Cork, Co. Cork. ✆ **021/427-5864.**

Eason's & Son Ltd   Eason's stocks books of Irish interest, as well as a full line of current and classic fiction, and carries an extensive range of stationery, CD's, CD-ROM's, videos, magazines, and international newspapers. There's also a new coffee shop. 113–115 Patrick St., Cork, Co. Cork. ✆ **021/427-0477.** easoncrk@iol.ie.

House of Donegal   "Tailoring to please" is the theme of this showroom and workshop. You can buy ready-made or specially tailored raincoats, classic trench coats, jackets, suits, and sportswear for men and women. The handsome rainwear, with Donegal tweed linings, is a special souvenir to bring home from Ireland. 6 Paul St. (off the Grand Parade), Cork, Co. Cork. ✆ **021/427-2447.**

Kelly's Music Shop   There's not much in the way of Irish music that you won't find at Kelly's, which stocks records, tapes, books, and musical instruments. 15 Grand Parade, Cork, Co. Cork. ✆ 021/427-2355. kelmus@iol.ie.

The Living Tradition *(Finds)*   This small shop on the North Bank specializes in Irish folk and traditional music—CDs, cassettes, books, videos, sheet music, and songbooks—as well as instruments such as *bodhrans* (Irish frame drums) and tin whistles. Here's where to buy the real thing, the kind of music you actually hear in Ireland at a pub session or a Fleadh Ceoil (Irish music festival). In addition, it stocks a good selection of recordings of musicians from around the world, along with handcrafted goods. 40 MacCurtain St., Cork, Co. Cork. ✆ 021/450-2040. www.ossian.ie.

Mercier Press and Bookshop   Long a part of Cork's literary tradition, this shop stocks a variety of books, including those published by Cork-based Mercier Press, founded in 1944 and now Ireland's oldest independent publishing house. It has an extensive Irish-interest section, including volumes on history, literature, folklore, music, art, humor, drama, politics, current affairs, law, and religion. 5 French Church St., Cork, Co. Cork. ✆ 021/427-5040. www.mercier.ie.

Shandon Craft Centre   Inside the Old Butter Exchange (see "Seeing the Sights," earlier in this chapter), this enclosed emporium showcases the workshops of artisans, who practice a range of traditional trades and display their wares for sale. The crafts include porcelain dolls, jewelry, clothing, crystal, pottery, and handmade violins, cellos, and violas. From June to August, folk, traditional, jazz, and classical musicians offer free concerts from 1 to 2pm. Cork Butter Exchange, John Redmond St., Cork, Co. Cork. ✆ 021/450-8881.

Waterstone's Booksellers   With entrances on two streets, this large branch of the British-owned chain is always busy. It has a good selection of books about Cork and of Irish interest, as well as sections on art, antiques, biography, religion, and travel. 69 Patrick St. and 12 Paul St., Cork, Co. Cork. ✆ 021/427-6522. www. waterstones.co.uk.

8 Cork After Dark

THE PUB SCENE

According to some experts, Cork has a pub for every 200 residents—and in a city populated by some 129,000 souls, that's a helluva lot of pubs. The pubs of Cork come in all sizes, styles, and decor, and I have no doubt you'll find your own "local" during your stay. Don't pass up the chance to sample Beamish and Murphy's close to the source. Many pubs host traditional music sessions from time to time.

An Bodhran   This is a small, cozy place with brick walls, dim lights, low ceiling, lots of timbered beams, and a lively clientele. It's a student hangout, but you'll usually find a mix of older types as well. The traditional music sessions here are very informal. You'll often find the ballads going Wednesday to Saturday nights, but you might drop in other nights as well to see what's going on. 42 Oliver Plunkett St., Cork, Co. Cork. ✆ 021/427-4544. Fax 021/427-5531.

An Phoenix   An Phoenix dates from the early 1700s, when it set up shop in the premises of an old mill. Its walls are of old brick and there are pitch-pine verticals, exposed rafters, and redwood-and-pine seating. There's usually traditional music on Thursday, beginning at 8pm. Union Sq. (alongside City Hall), Cork, Co. Cork. ✆ 021/496-4275.

An Spailpin Fanac (The Migrant Worker)   Located opposite the Beamish Brewery, this is another of the city's choice spots for traditional Irish music, Sunday to Friday starting at 9:30pm. It dates back to 1779, making it one of Cork's oldest pubs. It is a lovely, soothing place—as all the best pubs are—with low ceilings, exposed brick walls, flagstone floors, open fireplaces, a simple wooden bar, and woven rush seats. Oh, and there's a darling, authentic snug. 28–29 S. Main St., Cork, Co. Cork. ✆ 021/427-7949.

Mutton Lane Inn   Old Cork is alive and well at this tiny pub down an alley that was first trod as a pathway for sheep going to market. It was opened in 1787 as a public house by the Ring family, who used to make their own moonshine whiskey. It's now the domain of Maeve and Vincent McLoughlin, who have preserved the old-world aura, which incorporates lantern lights, dark wood-paneled walls, exposed-beam ceilings, a noteworthy old pewter collection, and an antique cash register. 3 Mutton Lane, off Patrick St., Cork, Co. Cork. ✆ 021/427-3471.

THE BAR SCENE

Half Moon   After the main stage empties, this bar at the Opera House swings into action. The ever-changing program of contemporary music ranges from blues and ragtime to pop and rock, with comedy gigs on occasion. Cork Opera House, Emmet Place. ✆ 021/427-1168. Cover 7.50€–11€ ($6.80–$10). Thurs–Sun 11:30pm–3am.

The Lobby Bar   This bar opposite City Hall presents a variety of musical entertainment, from folk, traditional, bluegrass, and blues to jazz, gypsy, rock, classical, and New Age. 1 Union Quay (opposite City Hall). ✆ 021/431-1113. www.lobby.ie. Cover 6.50€–10€ ($5.90–$9.10), depending on the act. Nightly, with music starting at 9pm for most performances.

THEATERS

Cork Arts Theatre   This busy theater presents a wide variety of contemporary dramas, comedies, and musical comedies. A multistory parking lot and the city center main street are a 10-minute walk away. Knapp's Sq. (across the river from the Opera House), Cork, Co. Cork. ✆ 021/450-8398. Tickets 6.50€–9.50€ ($5.90–$8.60) adults, reduction for seniors and students. Shows Tues–Sat at 8pm. Box office open 10am–6pm (until 8pm on show nights).

Everyman Palace   The Old Palace Theatre, built in 1897 beside the Metropole Hotel, was first used as a music hall and later as a cinema, and now is well known as a showcase for new plays, both Irish and international. The building is so revered that its gilt-and-gingerbread decor is protected by a preservation order. Resident company productions of outstanding quality are presented regularly, and leading companies from Dublin, Belfast, Derry, Galway, Limerick, Great Britain, and America play here as well, as does the Irish National Ballet. A nice feature is the intermission coffee service. You can often hobnob with the actors after productions by dropping in at the Theatre Bar. 17 MacCurtain St., Cork, Co. Cork. ✆ 021/450-1673. Tickets 14€–22€ ($13–$20). Box office Mon–Fri 9am–9pm; Sat–Sun 10am–9pm. Curtain at 8pm.

PERFORMING ARTS CENTERS

Cork Opera House   This is the major venue in southwest Ireland for opera, drama, musicals, comedies, dance, concerts, and variety nights. Renovations of the front of the house and main auditorium were recently completed. Emmet Place (just off Lavitt's Quay along the River Lee). ✆ 021/427-0022. Tickets 13€–32€ ($12–$29); 1.25€ ($1.15) fee for telephone bookings. Box office Mon–Sat 9am–6pm; curtain usually 8pm; matinee times 1:30 or 3pm.

Institute for Choreography and Dance   Dating from the 1840s, this unique rotunda was part of Cork's original Butter Market (the building's name is derived from Danish words pertaining to measures of butter). Although destroyed by fire in 1980, the place was completely rebuilt and opened as a cultural center in 1992. It's now a venue for Irish and international dance performances, community dance projects, and workshops—call or check the website for a current program of events. John Redmond St., Shandon, Cork, Co. Cork. ⓒ **021/450-7487.** Fax 021/450-1124. www.instchordance.com. Tickets 10€–13€ ($9.10–$12). Box office hours Mon–Fri 9am–5pm.

Triskel Arts Centre   Located next to City Park, Triskel is host to a wide variety of talented artists and performers, many of them in the early stages of their careers. Contemporary film, literary readings, theatrical productions, and music sessions take place here. There is also a full curriculum of daytime art workshops and gallery talks. One of the recent ventures is a Fusion club Tuesday evening from 10pm. There's also an intimate little cafe, the Yumi Yuki Club, that serves homemade food all day. Tobin St., off S. Main St., Cork, Co. Cork. ⓒ **021/427-2022.** triskel@iol.ie. Tickets from 7.50€ ($6.80). Box office Mon–Sat 9:30am–9pm; performances Tues–Sun 8pm, Sat–Sun matinees 1:15 or 1:30pm.

8

Out from Cork

The countryside of County Cork presents two faces. On the eastern side of the county, the Cork coast is gentle and refined. The port town of **Kinsale** is a true gem, even if it has overdone its self-promotion as a destination for the well-heeled. The recently opened Old Head of Kinsale golf course may turn out to be one of Ireland's finest golf venues, and several of the county's best restaurants are to be found nearby.

But as you travel west along the Cork coast, the hills move in toward the sea and form a series of craggy promontories, like the talons of a splayed claw. This is **West Cork,** once the haunt of outlaws and still adamantly unconventional and countercultural. Lush subtropical vegetation, cave-riddled sea cliffs, and rugged islands are features of this untamed landscape. Of all the peninsulas of West Cork, the **Sheep's Head** is the most untouched by tourism, and the **Beara Peninsula** the most wild and beautiful.

1 Kinsale

18 miles (29km) S of Cork, 54 miles (87km) SE of Killarney, 97 miles (156km) SE of Shannon Airport, 177 miles (285km) SW of Dublin, and 20 miles (32km) E of Clonakilty

Kinsale fits the picture-postcard image of a charming Irish seaport—narrow, winding streets, well-kept 18th-century houses, imaginatively painted shop fronts, window boxes and street stanchions brimming with colorful flowers, and a harbor full of sailboats. Consequently, the place has become a tourist mecca, so add traffic jams and tour buses to the list of the town's sights.

Although Kinsale has dubbed itself the "Gourmet Capital of Ireland," there are several towns in County Cork that better deserve the title. So, before blowing your allowance for culinary splurges in Kinsale, take a look at some of the excellent restaurants listed in the East Cork and West Cork sections, below.

Scilly, just across the Bay from Kinsale, is a great place to base yourself. Near Scilly is Charles Fort, one of Ireland's best preserved and most beautifully situated military edifices. The walk past the fort to Frower Point is a memorable one, with many small coves that invite a quick swim; this walk is also a good way to escape the summer crowds.

GETTING THERE   **Bus Eireann** (© 021/450-8188; www.buseireann.ie) operates regular daily service from Cork City to Kinsale. The arrival and departure point is the Esso gas station on Pier Road, opposite the tourist office.

Kinsale is 18 miles (29km) south of Cork city via the Airport Road; from the west, take N71. From East Cork, the Cross River Ferries provide regular service via Cork Harbour (see chapter 7).

GETTING AROUND   Kinsale's streets are so narrow that walking is the best way to get around. There is no local transport, but if you need a taxi to take you to outlying areas call **Cabs 3000** (© 021/477-3000) or **Allied Cabs** (© 021/477-3600).

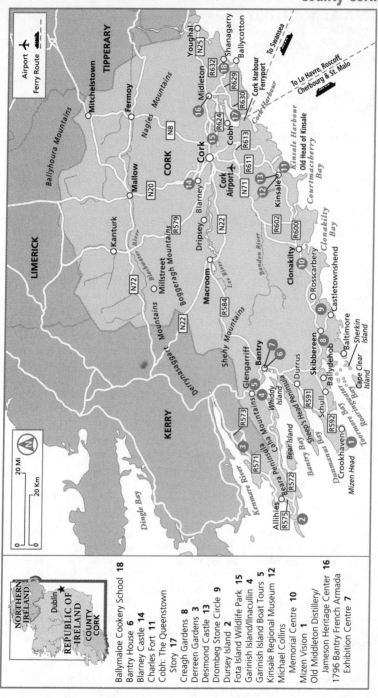

County Cork

Ballymaloe Cookery School **18**
Bantry House **6**
Blarney Castle **14**
Charles Fort **11**
Cobh: The Queenstown
  Story **17**
Creagh Gardens **8**
Derreen Gardens **3**
Desmond Castle **13**
Drombeg Stone Circle **9**
Dursey Island **2**
Fota Island Wildlife Park **15**
Garinish Island/Ilnacullin **4**
Garinish Island Boat Tours **5**
Kinsale Regional Museum **12**
Michael Collins
  Memorial Centre **10**
Mizen Vision **1**
Old Middleton Distillery/
  Jameson Heritage Center **16**
1796 Bantry French Armada
  Exhibition Centre **7**

VISITOR INFORMATION The Kinsale Tourist Office, Pier Road, Kinsale (© 021/477-2234), is open March through November Monday to Saturday 9:30am to 5:30pm, and Sundays July to September 9:30am to 5:30pm. The Kinsale Chamber of Tourism website (www.kinsale.ie) is packed with useful information.

SEEING THE SIGHTS

Charles Fort ✦ This coastal landmark at the head of the harbor dates from the late 17th century. A classic star-shaped fort, it was constructed to prevent foreign naval forces from approaching Kinsale, then an important trading town. Additions and improvements were made throughout the 18th and 19th centuries, and the fort remained garrisoned until 1921. It's a delight to explore, with innumerable towers, parapets, and passageways. Across the river is James Fort (1602). The complex includes an exhibition center and cafe.

Off the Scilly road, southeast of Kinsale, Co. Cork. © 021/477-2263. Fax 021/477-4347. Admission 3.20€ ($2.90) adults, 2.20€ ($2.00) seniors, 1.30 ($1.15) students, 7.60€ ($6.90) family. Tours available. Nov to mid-Mar Sat–Sun 10am–5pm, weekdays by appt.; mid-Mar to Nov daily 10am–6pm. Last admission 45 mins. before closing.

Desmond Castle This tower house has a colorful history. It was built as a customhouse by the earl of Desmond around 1500. In 1601, the Spanish occupied the castle and later used it as a prison for captured American sailors during the American Revolution. Locally, it's known as "French Prison," because 54 French seamen prisoners died here in a 1747 fire. During the years of the Great Famine, the castle became a poorhouse for the starving populace. At various times, its vaults have also been used as a wine storage depot. The structure has recently undergone considerable restoration and now houses the International Museum of Wine, celebrating the viticultural contributions of the Irish diaspora.

Cork St., Kinsale, Co. Cork. © 021/477-4855. www.heritageireland.ie. Admission 2.60€ ($2.40) adults, 1.90€ ($1.75) seniors and students, 1.25€ ($1.15) children, 6.35€ ($5.75) family. Mid-June to mid-Oct daily 10am–6pm; mid-Apr to mid-June Tues–Sun 10am–6pm; last admission 45 min. before closing.

Kinsale Crystal Started in 1991 by a former Waterford Crystal mastercraftsman, this small workshop produces a traditional full-lead, mouth-blown and hand-cut crystal, with personalized engraving. Visitors are welcome to watch the entire fascinating process and admire the sparkling results.

Market St., Kinsale, Co. Cork. © 021/477-4493. www.kinsalecrystal.ie. Free admission. Mon–Sat 9:15am–1pm and 2–6pm.

Kinsale Regional Museum This museum tells the town's story from its earliest days, with exhibits, photos, and memorabilia, highlighting such events as the Battle of Kinsale in 1601 and the sinking of the *Lusitania* in 1915, and featuring extensive traditional craft exhibits. It's in the Market House (1600), which gained an arched facade in 1706. An extensive renovation and extension, doubling its exhibition space, was completed in July 2000.

Market Sq. © 021/477-7930. Admission 2.60€ ($2.40) adults; 1.25€ ($1.15) students, seniors and children; 6.35€ ($5.75) family. May–Sept daily 10:30am–5:30pm, Sunday 2–5:30pm; Oct–Mar call ahead for opening times.

Kinsale Silver Silversmithing is a craft that traces its origins back more than 300 years. This local silversmithing workshop is run by the Dolan family (see listing for Wexford Silver under "Shopping in Wexford Town," in chapter 6, "The Southeast"). Visitors can watch as each piece is wrought and forged by hand. In the summer, the shop is open until 7:30pm.

Sceilig House Mrs. Mary Hurley is the warm, friendly hostess here, and her charming husband is a fount of information on County Cork in particular, and on Ireland in general. Guest rooms have magnificent sea views. One room comes with its own private patio, a perfect spot to sit and watch the harbor lights come on at sunset; another has a private sunroom. When you book, ask about a reduction for Frommer's readers.

Ard-Brack, Kinsale, Co. Cork. ℰ 021/772832. hurleyfamily@eircom.net. 3 units, all with bathroom (2 with shower only). 38€–64€ ($35–$58) single; 44€–64€ ($40–$58) double. 35% reduction for children sharing with an adult. Rates include full breakfast. MC, V. Free parking. ½ mile (1km) from Kinsale town center. *In room:* TV, hair dryer, iron.

Walyunga This strikingly designed modern home is perched on a hill with panoramic views of the Atlantic Ocean and quiet green valleys. It's surrounded by landscaped gardens, and sandy beaches, and scenic coastal walks are close by. Mrs. Myrtle Levis presides over the bright, spacious house, and our readers have lauded her breakfasts and coffee. Floor-to-ceiling windows in the lounge and dining room open onto the magnificent views, and guest rooms look out to the ocean, countryside, or garden. Smokers will need to look elsewhere.

Sandycove, Kinsale, Co. Cork. ℰ/fax 021/477-4126. www.walyunga.com. 5 units, 4 with bathroom (2 with shower only). 51€–61€ ($46–$55) double. 20% reduction for children sharing with an adult. Rates include full breakfast. MC, V. Free parking. Closed Nov to mid-Mar. 2 miles (3km) west of Kinsale. *In room:* Tea/coffeemaker, hair dryer.

FARMHOUSE ACCOMMODATIONS

Ballymountain House This solid, Georgian-style farmhouse lets you enjoy the bustle of the town and still have a rural retreat to come home to at the end of the day. Visitors will be greeted by convivial hosts Sheila and Tim Cummins. The welcome and the beds are warm, and there are numerous walks to be had in the nearby fields, including some interesting old ruins to explore.

Innishannon (20-min. drive from Kinsale), Co. Cork. ℰ/fax 021/477-5366. ballymountain@eircom.net. 6 units, 5 with bathroom (shower only). 38€ ($35) single; 51€ ($46) double without bathroom, 58€ ($53) double with bathroom. 50% discount for children under 12 sharing with an adult. 5-course dinner 19€ ($17). MC, V. Free parking. *In room:* tea/coffeemaker.

GREAT DEALS ON DINING

The Blue Haven SEAFOOD/IRISH Of all the restaurants in Kinsale, this has the hugest following because there's something to suit every budget and appetite. There are really two places to eat: the atmospheric bar for first-rate pub grub or the lovely, skylit restaurant for a full a la carte menu. The bar menu tends toward smoked seafood quiches, seafood pancakes, oak-smoked salmon, steaks, pastas, and a lamb stew that's to die for. The restaurant offers a wide array of fresh seafood, including a house special of salmon slowly cooked over oak chips. Other specialties include brill and scallop bake, farmyard duck with sage-and-onion stuffing, and local venison (in season). The wines have Irish connections—they come from many of the French wineries that were started by Irish exiles—the Chateaux Dillon, McCarthy, Barton, Kirwan, Lynch, and Phelan. The wines are also on sale in the Blue Haven's wine and cheese shop.

3 Pearse St., Kinsale. ℰ 021/477-2209. www.bluehavenkinsale.com. Reservations recommended. Bar, dinner main courses 11€–18€ ($10–$16); restaurant, 3-course dinner from 29€ ($26); dinner main courses 19€–23€ ($17–$21). AE, MC, V. Bar 12:15–3pm and 5:30–9:30pm; restaurant 7–9:30pm.

Jim Edwards SEAFOOD A classy nautical theme dominates the decor of this pub/restaurant, with colored-glass windows, ship's wheels, sailing-ship art, plush red cushioned seating, and a clock over the door that tells time by letters instead of numbers. It is known for its good food, including such dishes as boneless duck with cassis and red-currant sauce, rack of lamb, king prawns in light basil cream sauce, medallions of monkfish with fresh herbs, a variety of steaks, and a range of vegetarian dishes.

Market Quay, off Emmet Place (between the Methodist Church and the Temperance Hall), Kinsale. © 021/477-2541. Reservations recommended for dinner. Dinner main courses 13€–25€ ($12–$23). AE, MC, V. Bar daily 10:30am–11pm; restaurant daily 12:30–3pm and 6–10:30pm.

Man Friday SEAFOOD/INTERNATIONAL   Overlooking the harbor on the outskirts of town, Man Friday is the sort of cozy place that invites relaxation from your first step inside. Among the outstanding dishes are grilled black sole with a seafood stuffing, roast stuffed loin of lamb with mint-and-rosemary sauce, and Chinese beef, but anything you select will come to the table at its very best, a fact attested to by the many awards Man Friday has received over the past few years.

Scilly, Kinsale, Co. Cork. © 021/477-2260. Reservations recommended. Main courses 17€–25€ ($15–$23). MC, V. Mon–Sat 7–10:30pm. Closed 2 weeks in Jan.

Max's Wine Bar ✦ SEAFOOD/INTERNATIONAL   A must for Kinsale visitors (and a host of regulars) for more than 20 years, Max's is now owned by Anne Marie Galvin and Olivier Queva—the chef. It's a charming place, with a light, airy conservatory adjoining the dining room (there's no smoking in this part of the restaurant, which only seats 10). The menu is a delight. Seafood devotees will gravitate to the just-out-of-the-water catch of the day or baked oysters with a smoked salmon sauce, while landlubbers are in for a treat with rack of lamb with lavender sauce or steak with cashel blue and walnuts. I recommend the pan-fried goat cheese as a starter, and the great bread-and-butter pudding for dessert.

Main St., Kinsale. © 021/772443. Reservations recommended. Main courses 15€–22€ ($14–$20); fixed-price lunch and early-bird dinner 17€ ($16). AE, MC, V. Daily 12:30–3pm and 6:30–10:30pm; early-bird 6:30–7:30pm.

WORTH A SPLURGE

The Vintage ✦ IRISH/CONTINENTAL   In an elegant 200-year-old house in the heart of Kinsale, this landmark restaurant offers truly wonderful food in a charming setting. With its open fire, and original masts from sailing ships that once came into Kinsale, the dining room's atmosphere is both cozy and very romantic. Meals are traditional country recipes prepared in an international way. Under the direction of Swiss-born owner Raoul de Gendre, a crew of Irish, Swiss, and French chefs uses only fresh produce and meats, with oysters and other seafood from neighboring waters. The *soupiere atlantique,* a wonderful soup of fresh Atlantic fish, is superb. In addition to innovative seafood main courses, there's a marvelous oven-roasted Barberry duck en maigret and confit with a seed mustard sauce, as well as rack of Bandon lamb with thyme seasoning and "vegetarian paradise"—vegetables in phyllo pastry with a spicy tomato sauce. The wine list is outstanding.

Main St., Kinsale. © 021/477-2502. www.vintage-kinsale.com. Reservations advised. Main courses 22€–30€ ($20–$28); 4-course fixed-price tasting menu 49€–54€ ($44–$49). AE, DC, MC, V. May to mid-Oct daily 6:30–10pm; closed Jan; call for hours Mar–Apr, Nov–Dec.

SHOPPING

Granny's Bottom Drawer   Ireland's traditional linens and lace are the focus of this small shop, which is well stocked with tablecloths, pillowcases, and hand-crocheted place mats. 53 Main St., Kinsale, Co. Cork. © 021/477-4839. www.dragnet-systems.ie/dira/granny.htm.

The Irish Print Shop Amidst the flourishing fine arts scene in Kinsale, the London *Times* has named this spacious shop one of the area's two stand-out galleries. It was as a chef that Oliver Sears, the proprietor, first came to Ireland from London, and though I can't say anything about his palate, I'll vouch for his eye. He's assembled the largest selection of original Irish prints in the country. Why Irish art? Oliver's response is that "Irish art today still keeps its unique, Irish identity; its pure, searching, and dramatic expression is distinct and passionate." If you can't find something you love here, you might as well stop looking. Open daily from 10am to 1pm, 2 to 5:30pm, and many summer evenings. Closed for a month sometime in January or February. 20–21 Main St., Kinsale, Co. Cork. © 087/261-9154 or 021/477-2565.

KINSALE AFTER DARK
THE PUB SCENE

The Dock This pub on the outskirts of town overlooks the inner harbor. Its walls are lined with fishing-theme posters and equipment, and its windows give views of the water. If the weather is nice, you can step out onto the front deck with its row of inviting tables and chairs. Castlepark, Kinsale, Co. Cork. © 021/477-2522.

The Greyhound Photographers are enchanted with the exterior of this pub, with its neat flower boxes, rows of stout barrels, and handmade signs depicting its namesake. The interior rooms are cozy. The place is known for hearty pub grub, such as farmhouse soups, seafood pancakes, shepherd's pie, and Irish stew. Market Sq., Kinsale, Co. Cork. © 021/477-2889.

Lord Kingsale A touch of elegance prevails at this handsome pub, decorated with lots of polished horse brass and black-and-white Tudor-style trappings. It takes its name (and ancient spelling) from the first Anglo-Norman baron who took charge of this Irish port in 1223. You'll often find evening singalongs here, and the soup-and-sandwich pub grub is very good. Live entertainment nightly in summer. Main St. and Market Quay, Kinsale, Co. Cork. © 021/477-2371. www.dragnet-systems.ie/dira/kingsale.

The Spaniard This old pub, full of local seafaring memorabilia, is named for Don Juan de Aguila, who rallied his fleet with the Irish in a historic but unsuccessful attempt to defeat the British in 1601. The place has a much-photographed facade, a great location in the hills overlooking Kinsale, and tables outside for sunny-day snacks. It draws large crowds for traditional music on Wednesday, and there's often music on other nights—call ahead for details. Scilly, Kinsale, Co. Cork. © 021/477-2436. www.dragnet-systems.ie/dira/spaniard.

The White House With its Georgian facade and distinctive name over the front entrance, this is one pub that tempts most American visitors to take a photograph. Inside, you'll find a popular new bistro, the Antibes Room, with bright decor and a comfortable bar. End of Pearse St., Kinsale, Co. Cork. © 021/477-2125. www.whitehouse-kinsale.ie.

2 East Cork

The east end of County Cork is notably more tame than the west, but what the region lacks in rugged splendor it makes up for in sophisticated (if expensive) amenities: the restaurants here are among the finest in the country, and Crosshaven holds one of the most venerable yacht clubs in the world.

Lying 15 miles (24km) east from Cork city is the harbor town of **Cobh** (pronounced *cove* and meaning "haven" in the Irish language). In the days before airline travel, Cobh was Ireland's chief port of entry, with about three or four transatlantic liners calling here each week. For thousands of Irish emigrants, particularly during the famine years and in the early part of this century, Cobh was the last sight of Ireland they'd ever see. It's still an important, heavily industrialized port. The new visitor attraction "Cobh: The Queenstown Story" tells the city's history, which includes the construction of a magnificent Gothic-Revival cathedral, completed in 1915.

The county's major coastal town is **Youghal** (pronounced *yawh*), 30 miles (48km) to the east of Cork city, near the Waterford border. A leading beach resort and fishing port, Youghal is loosely associated with Sir Walter Raleigh, who was once the town mayor and is said to have planted Ireland's first potatoes here. From a tourist's-eye view, present-day Youghal is a moderately attractive, congested town with a grand stretch of beach just beyond the town center.

GETTING TO EAST CORK If you're driving from Cork City, take the main Waterford road (N25) east. Exit at R624 for Fota and Cobh, or R632 for Shana-garry and Ballycotton. Midleton and Youghal have their own signposted exits. If you're coming from West Cork and want to bypass Cork City (a good idea during rush hour), take the car ferry operated by **Cross River Ferries Ltd.,** Atlantic Quay, Cobh (© **021/481-1485**). It links Carrigaloe, near Cobh, with Glen-brook, south of Cork City. Ferries run daily from 7:15am to 12:45am; average crossing time is 5 minutes. No reservations are necessary. The fares, payable on the ferry, are 3.20€ ($2.90) one-way, 4.45€ ($4.05) round-trip.

Irish Rail (© **021/450-64777**; www.irishrail.ie) operates daily train service between Cork City and Cobh via Fota Island; the fare is 3.05€ ($2.75) one-way or 4.05€ ($3.70) round-trip. **Bus Eireann** (© **021/450-8188;** www.bus eireann.ie) also provides daily service from Cork City to Cobh and other points in East Cork.

VISITOR INFORMATION A year-round **tourist office** is open Monday to Friday 9:30am to 5:30pm (June to August Saturday and Sunday 11:30am to 5pm) at the Old Yacht Club in the lower harbor at Cobh (© **021/481-3301**). **Seasonal tourist offices** operate at 4 Main St., Midleton (© **021/461-3702**), and Market Square, Youghal (© **024/92390**), from May or June through September.

SEEING THE SIGHTS

Some 10 miles (16km) east of Cork city on N25, look for signposts pointing to **Barryscourt Castle** (© **021/488-2218**; www.heritageireland.ie) in the small town of Carrigtwohill. This place is well worth a stop. From the 12th to the 17th centuries, the castle was the principal residence of the lords of Barrymore. The present castle houses an exhibition on the history of the Barrys and the castle, and there are guided tours. Admission to the castle is 1.90€ ($1.75) adults, 1.25€ ($1.15) seniors, .75€ (70¢) children and students, and 5.10€ ($4.60) families. The castle is open daily from June to September 10am to 5:45pm; and Friday to Wednesday October through May from 11am to 5pm.

If your itinerary takes you directly from Cork to Killarney, you can join the scenic **Blackwater Valley Drive** by traveling N20 north to **Mallow** (a popular 18th-century spa resort whose riotous social activities are commemorated in the ballad "The Rakes of Mallow"), then N72 to Killarney. In the tourist office in either Cork or Youghal, pick up a copy of the *Blackwater Valley Drive* map and chart that will give details of the many historic relics along that route.

A few miles north of Mallow, on the main Cork-Limerick road (N20), there are interesting and well-preserved ruins of 13th-century **Ballybeg Abbey** ✦ just outside the village of Buttevant on the Cork side. Buttevant itself was the model for "Mole" in Spenser's *Faerie Queene*. It was also the scene of the first-ever steeplechase (from the steeple of Buttevant Church of Ireland to that of Doneraile, a distance of about 4 miles/6.5km).

Ballymaloe Cookery School ✦✦   Come to Ireland and learn to cook? Yes, if you head to this mecca of fine food, offering more than 35 different courses a year. Professional and amateur cooks from all over the world flock here to learn from Darina Allen, the Irish Julia Child. The success of the Ballymaloe House restaurant (see "Dining," below) under Darina's mother, Myrtle, led to the founding of this cooking school more than a dozen years ago. Courses, which range from 1 day to 12 weeks, appeal to all types of amateur and professional chefs, with topics such as bread making, modern entertaining, seafood, vegetarian cuisine, family food, barbecue, mushroom hunts, and Christmas cooking. Some courses are for absolute beginners; others cover new trends in cooking; and others offer chef certificates. There are beautiful and extensive gardens that visitors can enjoy from April to September. Admission to the gardens is 5€ ($4.60) adults, family discounts available. The Garden Café, open Wednesday to Sunday 11am to 6pm, serves memorable morning coffee, light lunches, and afternoon tea.

Shanagarry. ✆ 021/464-6785. www.cookingisfun.ie. 1- to 5-day courses 171€–660€ ($155–$598); 12-week certificate courses 6,063€ ($5,492). New half-day gardening courses are available. Accommodations are 20€–25€ ($18–$22) per person per night extra. Year-round; schedule varies.

Cobh: The Queenstown Story ✦   This new heritage center commemorates the days when Cobh (then known as Queenstown) was a vital link in transatlantic liner traffic, particularly in the years of high emigration. Because more than 2½ million people from all over Ireland departed from Cobh for new lives in the United States, Canada, and Australia, the city became synonymous with emigration. In a beautifully restored Victorian railway station, the center tells the story of the city, its harbor, and the Irish exodus in a series of displays, with an audiovisual presentation and exhibits that re-create the sinkings of the *Titanic* and the *Lusitania*. The center also has a restaurant, a shop, and a new genealogical referral service.

Cobh Railway Station, Cobh, Co. Cork. ✆ 021/481-3591. Fax 021/481-3595. www.cobhheritage.com. Admission 5€ ($4.55) adults, 4€ ($3.65) students, 2.60€ ($2.40) children. Daily 10am–6pm.

Fota Island Wildlife Park & Arboretum ✦ *(Kids)*   This wildlife park is located 10 miles (16km) east of Cork on the Cobh road. It's home to rare and endangered types of giraffe, zebra, ostrich, antelope, cheetah, flamingo, penguin, and peafowl. The animals and birds roam in natural wildlife settings, with no obvious barriers. Monkeys swing through the trees, and kangaroos, macaws, and lemurs have the complete run of the 40 acres of grasslands. Only the cheetahs are bounded by conventional fencing. The admission fee includes entrance to the adjacent Fota Arboretum, first planted in the 1820s. It contains trees and shrubs from the temperate and subtropical regions of the world, from China to South America and the Himalayas. A coffee shop, a small amusement park for young children, a tour train, picnic tables, and a gift shop are on the grounds.

Fota Island, Carrigtwohill. ② **021/481-2678.** Fax 021/481-2744. www.fotawildlife.ie. Admission 6.60€ ($6.00) adults; 3.95€ ($3.60) students, seniors and children; 25€ ($23) family. Mar–Oct Mon–Sat 10am–5pm, Sun 11am–5pm; Nov–Feb Sat 10am–3pm, Sun 11am–3pm. Accessible by rail via the Cork-Cobh line from Cork city to Fota station.

Old Midleton Distillery   If you've always wanted to know what makes Irish whiskey different from Scotch, you've come to the right place. At the production center for Jameson Whiskey and other leading Irish brands, you find the largest pot still in the world (with a capacity of more than 30,000 gallons) and many of the original 1825 structures, which have been meticulously preserved. They include the mill building, maltings, corn stores, still houses, warehouses, kilns, water wheel, and last copper stills manufactured in Ireland. The modern distillery uses high-tech methods, but the production areas are closed to visitors. The center offers an audiovisual presentation, photographs, working models, and a demonstration, followed by a tasting after the tour. The restaurant at the center serves country Irish fare for lunch only.

Distillery Rd., off Main St., Midleton. ② **021/461-3594.** Fax 021/461-3642. Admission 5.70€ ($5.20) adults, 2.50€ ($2.30) children. Mar–Oct, daily 10am–6pm. Last tour at 4:30pm. Nov–Feb call for hours.

ACCOMMODATIONS YOU CAN AFFORD

Avonmore House   Eileen and Jack Gaine open their Georgian home (built in 1752) to guests. The rooms are nicely decorated and the meals superb. Avonmore is conveniently located at the harbor entrance, and is only a short walk from the beach and town center.

S. Abbey, Youghal, Co. Cork. ② **024/92617.** 6 units. 32€–38€ ($29–$34) single; 51€–64€ ($46–$58) double. Rates include full breakfast. MC, V. Free parking. *In room:* TV, tea/coffeemaker, hair dryer.

Bromley House   The friendly Mrs. Eileen Fogarty gives a warm welcome to every new arrival at this modern bungalow 3 miles (5km) west of Youghal on N25. There's a TV lounge and open fires for cool evenings. The house is within walking distance of many fine pubs.

Killeagh, Youghal, Co. Cork. ② **024/95235.** 5 units. 32€ ($29) single; 51€ ($46) double. Dinner 15€ ($14). 20% reduction for children sharing with an adult. Rates include full breakfast. V. Free private parking. Closed Nov–Feb. *In room:* Tea/coffeemaker, hair dryer.

Cedarville   Breda Hayes takes a keen interest in all her guests, and her husband Dennis is a keen gardener. The house itself is spotless, and the four bedrooms are decorated in soft pastels, all with sinks as well as wide windows that look out on the garden in front and green pastures in back. Meals here are superb, reflecting Breda's College of Catering training. Sightseeing attractions such as Fota House and Midleton Heritage Centre are nearby.

Carrigtwohill, Co. Cork. ② **021/488-3246.** 4 units, 2 with bathroom (shower only). 48€ ($44) double. 50% reduction for children sharing with an adult. Rates include full breakfast. No credit cards. Free private parking. Closed Nov–Apr. 9 miles (15km) east of Cork city, 2 miles (3km) to Midleton, signposted on N25. *In room:* Tea/coffeemaker, hair dryer.

Lotamore House ✦✦   This Georgian manor is one of the county's best guest houses. Set on 4 acres of wooded grounds and gardens 2 miles (3km) east of Cork city, it overlooks the River Lee. Owned by two doctors, Leonard and Mareaid Harty, it's an exceptionally well-run facility, furnished with antiques, crystal chandeliers, and a fireplace dating back to 1791. Extra comforts such as orthopedic beds, and garment presses are provided in the guest rooms. Breakfast is the only meal served, but it is exceptional, with freshly squeezed juices and fruits on the menu every day.

Dublin-Waterford road (N8/N25), Tivoli, Cork, Co. Cork © 021/822344. Fax 021/822219. lotamore@iol.ie.
20 units. 81€ ($74) double. No service charge. Rates include full breakfast. AE, MC, V. Free parking. *In room:*
TV, hair dryer.

DINING

East Cork boasts some of Ireland's best—and most expensive—restaurants. The
region is a must stop on all gastronomic tours of the country, but if you're looking for good food at a price you can afford, I'd recommend continuing on to
West Cork.

Aherne's Seafood Restaurant ⋆ SEAFOOD/TRADITIONAL   Aherne's
serves bar food of such quality that it has won the National Bar Food award for
several years. But pub grub is not its only distinction: John and David
Fitzgibbon have also installed an outstanding full restaurant and enhanced its
decor with paintings, wood paneling, and soft lighting. Seafood dishes, such as
mussels in garlic butter, take star billing, but beef, lamb, and chicken dishes are
equally well prepared. Bar food is the only budget option, however. Elegant
luxury guest rooms are also available.

163 N. Main St., Youghal, Co. Cork. © 024/92424. Reservations recommended, especially for dinner. Main
courses 24€–29€ ($22–$26); fixed-price dinner 38€ ($35); bar food 4€–18€ ($3.65–$16). AE, DC, MC, V.
Bar daily noon–10pm; restaurant daily 6:30–9:30pm. Closed Good Friday and 4 days at Christmas.

WORTH A SPLURGE

Ballymaloe House ⋆⋆ IRISH/SEAFOOD/FRENCH   The excellence of
Myrtle Allen's internationally famous Ballymaloe House is based largely on its use
of local products—the simplest dishes on the small menu have flavor you'd never
expect to find outside the little auberges of rural France. There's no predicting
exactly what will be on the menu the evening you dine here, but every meal offers
a choice of three soups, three or four fish dishes, six main courses, and at least
four desserts, all prepared with the flair of traditional Irish recipes. You can only
hope that Mrs. Allen's superb paté is offered, followed perhaps by watercress soup,
escalopes of stuffed baby beef, and the savarin au rhum as a topper.

Shanagarry, Midleton, Co. Cork. © 021/465-2531. Fax 021/465-2021. www.ballymaloe.com. Reservations
required. Fixed-price dinner 48€ ($43). AE, DC, MC, V. Daily 6:30–10pm. Closed 3 days at Christmas.

Presidents' Restaurant ⋆⋆ TRADITIONAL/SEAFOOD   This restaurant
is one of the best in the country. If you have room in your budget, phone ahead
to book a meal here. The stately Georgian dining room has an ornate plaster
ceiling. In fine weather, the Victorian conservatory, with its massed greenery,
white ironwork, and glorious views of the garden, is open to diners as well. As
for the food, it's won just about every award and international recognition
going. Chef William O'Callaghan oversees the preparation of gourmet
selections that use produce grown in the Longueville fields, local lamb, and
fish fresh from waters that flow through the estate. Mallard and venison are
featured in season, and the wine list includes wines produced from Michael's
own vineyards (among the first in Ireland). Although the restaurant is closed
between November and March, it will open by request for parties of 30 or
more.

Longueville House, Mallow, Co. Cork. © 022/47156. Fax 022/47459. www.longuevillehouse.ie. Reservations
required. Bar lunch under 13€ ($12); fixed-price dinner 46€–61€ ($41–$55). AE, DC, MC, V. Daily
12:30–5pm and 7–9pm. Closed mid-Nov to mid-Mar. 3 miles (5km) west of Mallow on the Mallow-Killarney
road (N72).

3 West Cork

For many, West Cork is the ultimate destination in Ireland, less crowded than Kerry yet just as alluring, with the same craggy topography and jagged coastline that combine to create many hidden corners and seldom-explored byways. The amenities here may not be the finest, but those willing to rough it a little will be amply rewarded.

Some of the most beautiful coastal scenery (and severe weather) is to be found on the islands, several of which have frequent ferry service. **Cape Clear** is home to a bird-watching observatory, and is a well-known *gaeltacht* (Irish-speaking community): Many schoolchildren come here to work on their Gaelic each summer. **Dursey Island,** off the tip of the Beara Peninsula, is accessible by means of a rickety cable car. **Garinish Island** in Glengarriff is the site of Ilnacullin, an elaborate Italianate garden.

West Cork is also known for its enticing towns. **Ballydehob** has an artistic flair thanks to a cluster of artists in residence—at the local butcher, colorful drawings of cattle, pigs, and chickens indicate what meats are available, and a mural on the outside wall of a pub depicts a traditional music session. Other notable enclaves include **Schull,** an old-world yachting town, and **Barleycove,** a remote windswept resort that's the last stop before Mizen Head and the sheer cliffs at the southernmost tip of Ireland. **Glandore** and **Union Hall** are a breathtakingly scenic pair of towns, connected by an alarmingly long one-lane bridge.

West Cork's most and least favorite son was **Michael Collins,** who was both born and murdered here. A hero to some and a traitor to others, the "Big Fella's" greatness is questioned by no one. The memory of Collins, widely hailed as "the man who made Ireland," is preserved, in particular, at the Michael Collins Memorial Centre at Woodfield and at the ambush site near Macroom.

GETTING THERE N71 is the main road into West Cork from north and south; from Cork and points east, N22 also leads to West Cork.

Bus Eireann (© 021/450-8188; www.buseireann.ie) provides daily bus service to the principal towns in West Cork.

VISITOR INFORMATION Contact the **Skibbereen Tourist Office,** North Street, Skibbereen, County Cork (© 028/21766). It is open year-round Monday to Friday 9:15am to 5:30pm (closed 1–2:15pm for lunch), and on Saturday from 9am to 1pm, with expanded hours in the summer, according to demand. There are **seasonal tourist offices** in the Square, Bantry (© 027/50229); Rossa Street, Clonakilty (© 023/33226); and Main Street, Glengarriff (© 027/ 63084), operating from May or June through August or September.

SEEING THE SIGHTS

Bantry House 🎇 This house on the edge of town was built around 1750 for the earls of Bantry. It has a mostly Georgian facade with Victorian additions. Open to the public since 1946, it contains many items of furniture and objets d'art from all over Europe, including four Aubusson and Gobelin tapestries said to have been made for Marie Antoinette. Today, Bantry House is the home of Mr. and Mrs. Egerton Shelswell-White, descendants of the third earl of Bantry. The gardens, with original statuary, are beautifully kept and well worth a stroll. Climb the steps behind the house for a panoramic view of the house, gardens, and Bantry Bay.

Bantry, Co. Cork. © 027/50047. www.cork-guide.ie/bnry_hse.htm. Admission 7.60€ ($6.90) adults, 5.70€ ($5.20) seniors and students, 5.10€ ($4.60) children 12–16 (under 12 free). Admission includes gardens. Mar–Oct daily 9am–6pm.

Creagh Gardens ✿   This is one of the most beautifully situated gardens in Ireland, hemmed in by colorful meadows and the waters of an exquisitely picturesque estuary. Serpentine paths wind among magnificent old oaks, maples, and beeches, with occasional prospects through meadow and wood to the weathered facade of Creagh House. In the early summer the garden is loud with the drone of bees and the blazing colors of the massive rhododendrons, fuchsia, and hydrangeas. A walled garden encloses a greenhouse, vegetable garden, and collection of domestic fowl. Despite its modest size (somewhat over 20 acres) this garden contains many surprises and hidden corners, and really shouldn't be missed. A tearoom offers light lunches that feature produce from the walled organic garden.

Creagh, Skibbereen, Co. Cork. ✆ **028/22121.** Admission 3.80€ ($3.45) adults, 2.60€ ($2.40) children. Mar–Oct daily 10am–6pm. On R595, 3½ mi (5.5km) south of Skibbereen.

Derreen Gardens   This informal subtropical garden is located on a site of great natural beauty, a hilly promontory on the breathtaking north coast of the Beara Peninsula. In the late 19th century the garden was planted with American species of conifer, many of which have become venerable giants during the intervening years. One garden path follows the sweep of the shoreline through tunnels of rhododendron, while others wind through the dense foliage of the promontory, opening occasionally to a view of the mountains or an entrancing rocky glen. The garden is also home to several rarities, most notably the New Zealand tree ferns that flourish in a small glade, among giant blue gum and bamboo. The best months for a visit are April, May, and June.

Lauragh, Co. Kerry. ✆ **064/83588.** Admission 3.80€ ($3.75). Apr–Sept daily 10am–6pm. Signposted: 1¼ miles (2km) off R571 in Lauragh.

Drombeg Stone Circle   This ring of 17 standing stones is the finest example of a stone circle in County Cork. From the site the hills slope gently toward the sea, a short distance away—the builders could hardly have chosen a more picturesque spot. The circle has been dated to sometime between 153 B.C. and A.D. 127, but little is known about its ritual purpose. Just west of the circle are the remains of two huts and a cooking place; it's thought that heated stones were placed in a water trough that can be seen adjacent to the huts, the hot water then being used for cooking. The cooking place dates from between A.D. 368 and 608.

Open site. Off R597 between Rosscarbery and Glandore.

Glengarriff Woods Nature Reserve ✿   If you're road-weary and in need of a sublime respite from the tourist trail, you will count your blessings here under the magical canopy of one Ireland's most ancient forests, preserved and maintained by the Heritage Service. The reserve's woodlands are mostly made up of sessile oak, once sacred to the druids and still evoking instant reverence, interspersed with birch and rowan. This is home to all sorts of Celtic "critters," from the long-eared owl to the Bank Vole. The local otter is especially hard to spot, though be assured it sees you well enough. This is a simply marvelous place to stop for a snooze or a picnic or a walk on one of the many marked trails. The river walk and the climb to Lady Bantry's View are not to be missed.

Admission free. Open year-round during daylight.

Ilnacullin (Garinish Island) ✿   A visit to this island is a magical experience. You wait for the ferry by a deep pool, surrounded by lush rhododendrons (there are some great walking paths beginning at the dock). Then the boat arrives and brings you out into the waters of Glengarriff Harbour, which is filled with tiny islands, mostly barren and uninhabited. It's a most unlikely and enchanting place to find an elaborately planted Italianate garden. Officially known as Ilnacullin, but usually referred to as "Garinish," this balmy island was once barren. In 1919, it was transformed into a garden with classical pavilions and a myriad of unusual plants and flowers from many continents. It's said that George Bernard Shaw wrote parts of *St. Joan* under the shade of the palm trees here.

The island is reached by covered ferry operated by **Blue Pool Ferry,** The Blue Pool, Glengariff (② **027/63333**), or **Glengarrif Garinish Ferries** (② **027/ 63116**). Boats operate every 30 minutes during the island's visiting hours.

Glengarriff, Co. Cork. ② **027/63040.** Fax 027/63149. www.heritageireland.ie. Admission to island, 3.15€ ($2.90) adults, 2.20€ ($2.00) seniors, 1.25€ ($1.15) children and students, 7.60€ ($6.90) family; boat trips, 7.50€ ($6.80) per person. Island, Mar and Oct, Mon–Sat 10am–4:30pm, Sun 1–5pm; Apr–June and Sept, Mon–Sat 10am–6:30pm, Sun 11am–6:30pm; July–Aug, Mon–Sat 9:30am–6:30pm, Sun 11am–6:30pm. Last landings 1 hr. before closing.

Mizen Vision 🇦🇦 At the tip of the Mizen Head Peninsula, the land falls precipitously into the Atlantic breakers in a line of spectacular sea cliffs. A suspension bridge permits access to the lighthouse on a small rock promontory; from here there are fabulous views of the surrounding cliffs and nearby Three Castle Head. A visitor center houses several exhibits on the theme of safety at sea, as well as a teashop. Even if the bridge and visitor center aren't open, Mizen Head is worth a visit—for a cliffside walk from the suspension bridge parking lot see "Walking" under the "Outdoor Pursuits" section, below. On the way out to Mizen Head, you'll also pass Barleycove Beach, one of the most beautiful beaches in southwest Ireland and a great place to explore.

Mizen Head. ② **028/35591** (March–Nov call 028/35115). Fax 028/35603. www.mizenvision.com. Admission 4.50€ ($4.10) adults, 3.50€ ($2.65) seniors and students, 2.55€ ($2.30) children under 12 (under 5 free), 14€ ($13) family. Mid-Mar to May and Oct daily 10:30am–5pm; June–Sept daily 10am–6pm; Nov to mid-Mar Sat–Sun 11am–4pm. Take R591 to Goleen, and follow the signs for Mizen Head.

1796 Bantry French Armada Exhibition Centre This center commemorates Bantry Bay's role in the battle of 1796, when a formidable French Armada—inspired by Theobold Wolfe Tone and the United Irishmen—sailed from France in an attempt to expel the British. Almost 50 warships carried nearly 15,000 soldiers to this corner of southwest Ireland. Thwarted by storms and a breakdown in communications, the invasion never came to pass and ten ships were lost. Too storm-damaged to return to France, the frigate *Surveillante* was scuttled off Whiddy Island to lay undisturbed for almost 200 years. The centerpiece of this exhibition is a giant scale (1:6) model of the ship in cross section, illustrating life in the French Navy 200 years ago and various activities as they happened on board.

East Stables, Bantry House, Bantry, Co. Cork. ② **027/51796.** Fax 027/50795. www.cork-guide.ie/ bnry_hse.htm. Admission 4.50€ ($4.10) adults, 2.60€ ($2.40) seniors and students, 1.25€ ($1.15) children (free under 14). Apr–Oct daily 10am–6pm.

VISITING CAPE CLEAR ISLAND 🇦🇦🇦

Located 8 miles (13km) off the mainland, this is the southernmost inhabited point in Ireland. The islands of Ireland are a part of its last frontier, the last bits of rugged, untamed splendor. Cape Clear is struggling to preserve the balance of beauty and livelihood that allows remote settlements to remain both remote and settled. This place can be bleak, with a craggy coastline and no trees to break the rush of sea wind, but it will appeal to many for its stark beauty, rough and irregular but not without grace. In early summer the landscape is brightened by wildflowers, and in October the air is filled with passerine migrants, some on their way from North America and Siberia; seabirds are present in abundance during the nesting season, especially from July to September. At any time, Cape Clear is unforgettable.

The first step to enjoying the island is reaching it. The *Naomh Ciarán II* offers **ferry service** (no cars, passengers only) year-round, leaving the harbor at Baltimore daily in July and August at 11am (noon on Sundays), 2:15, 5, and 7pm, and leaving Cape Clear Monday to Saturday at 9am, noon, and 6pm (Sundays 11am, 1, 4, and 6pm). Service is always subject to the seas and is somewhat more limited off-season. The passage takes 45 minutes, and costs 13€ ($12) round-trip.

Once you've arrived on Cape Clear, there are a number of things to see, including birds galore, seals, dolphins, the occasional whale, ancient "marriage stones," and a goat farm offering courses on everything you ever wanted to know about goats—and don't miss the hauntingly spectacular **castle ruins** on the island's western shore. There's also a lot to do. Apart from trekking and gazing, **Cleire Lasmuigh, Cape Clear Island Activity Center** (© 028/39198; fax 028/39144; http://homepage.eircom.net/~lasmuigh), offers an array of outdoor programs, from snorkeling and sea kayaking to hill walking and orienteering. Instruction or accompanied sessions are by the hour, day, or week. For example, a 3-day long weekend sea-kayaking package (inclusive of housing, instruction, and equipment rental) is available for 102€ ($92). **Coastal cruises** for sea angling, scuba diving, or bird-watching are the specialty of Ciarán O'Driscoll (©/fax **028/39153**). There are no plans for a shopping mall, but you will enjoy the local art and crafts and books in Harpercraft and The Back Room in Cotter's Yard, in the village of North Harbour, as well as the nearby pottery shop. While you're at it, pick up a copy of Chuck Kruger's *Cape Clear Island Magic.* There's no better introduction to the wonder of this place.

Modest hostel, B&B, and self-catering accommodations are available by the day, week, or month. The island's **An Óige Youth Hostel** (© 028/39198) is open March through November. Most B&Bs are open year-round, and include **Fáilte** (contact Eleanór Uí Drisceoil at © **028/39135**); and **Ard na Gaoith** (contact Eileen Leonard at © 028/39160). For self-catering holiday cottages by the day or week, contact **Ciarán O'Driscoll** (© **028/39135**). To drop anchor, **The Southernmost House** (see "Self-Catering," later in this chapter) is without parallel. You can't miss the town's three pubs and two restaurants, which will keep you well fortified. The home-baked fruit scones at Cistin Chléire on North Harbour are the best I've had anywhere.

Cape Clear has an extensive website, which I would recommend exploring on your own: **www.oilean-chleire.ie**.

VISITING DURSEY ISLAND

This barren promontory extending into the sea at the tip of the Beara Peninsula offers no amenities for the tourist, but the adventuresome will find great seaside walks and a memorable passage from the mainland on Ireland's only operating cable car. To get here, take R571 past Cahermore to its terminus. As you sway wildly in the rickety wooden cable car, reading the text of Psalm 91, which has kindly been posted to comfort the nervous, you may wonder whether a ferry might not have been a wiser option. It wouldn't be. Apparently the channel between island and mainland is often too treacherous to permit regular crossing by boat. There is no accommodation on the island, so don't miss the last cable car. The cable car runs year-round continuously between 9 and 10:45am, and

Michael Collins Sites Around County Cork

A foreigner might think that if a man is important enough to merit a Hollywood movie about his life, he's important enough for his country to erect a good, sturdy monument or two on his own stomping grounds. That foreigner, though, wouldn't have taken into account the turbulence of Ireland's struggles, or their painful and polarizing effects. As he was when alive, Michael Collins remains today a figure revered as a hero by some and vilified as a traitor by others, and in that kind of environment, statues are perhaps best left unerected.

That said, the following are a few resources for those interested in tracing the life of Collins, a hero of the War for Independence and one of Ireland's most influential leaders.

There's very little to see at the **Michael Collins Memorial Centre,** unless you bring along your own images of Collins and his childhood, gleaned from biographies such as those by Frank O'Connor or Tim Pat Coogan. The stone farmhouse in which Collins and all his siblings were born was later turned into outbuildings, and it survives as such. The adjacent new and larger farmhouse into which his family moved when Michael was 10 was burned to the ground in 1921 by the Black and Tans to punish Britain's public enemy no. 1. Only the foundation remains, and it functions more as a shrine than an attraction. The Memorial Centre is located in Woodfield, County Cork, and is signposted off N71, 3½ miles (5.5km) west of Clonakilty.

The **ambush site** at Béal na mBláth near Macroom, where Collins was murdered on August 22, 1922, also has the air of reverence about it, and the small **town museum** on Western Road in Clonakilty centre will be of some interest to anyone tracing local history and the struggle for Irish independence. It's hours are irregular, so consider the following as a general guideline: May through October, Monday to Saturday from 10:30am to 5pm and Sunday from 2:30 to 5:30pm. Admission is 1.25€ ($1.15).

from 2:30 to 4:30pm. The trip takes 7 minutes each way. For more information, call ✆ **027/73017.**

OUTDOOR PURSUITS

BEACHES **Barleycove Beach** offers vast expanses of pristine sand and a fine view out toward the Mizen Head cliffs; despite the trailer park and holiday homes on the far side of the dunes, large parts of the beach never seem to get crowded. Take the R591 to Goleen, and follow signs for Mizen Head. There's a public parking lot at the Barleycove Hotel.

BICYCLING The Mizen Head, Sheep's Head, and Beara Peninsulas offer fine roads for cycling, with great scenery and few cars. Of these, the Beara Peninsula is the most spectacular, whereas the other two are less likely to be crowded with tourists during peak season. The loop around Mizen Head, starting in Skibbereen, is a good 2- to 3-day trip, and a loop around the Beara Peninsula from Bantry, Glengarriff, or Kenmare is at least 3 days at a casual pace. In

Skibbereen, bicycles (18 and 21 speed) can be rented from **Roycroft's Stores** (© **028/21235;** roycroft@iol.ie) from 60€ ($54) per week, including lock, pump, and repair kit; high-quality panniers are an extra 10€ ($9.10) per week. If you call ahead, toe clips can be arranged at no extra cost. The lightweight aluminum mountain bikes rented here offer a significant advantage over the leaden, battleship-like bicycles rented at most shops. One-way riding from Skibbereen to Killarney or Kenmare can be arranged from 20€ ($18) per bike.

BIRD-WATCHING Cape Clear Island is the prime birding spot in West Cork, and one of the best places in Europe to watch seabirds and passerine migrants. The best time for seabirds is July to September, and October is the busiest month for passerines (and also for bird-watchers, who flock to the island in droves during this month). There is a bird observatory at the North Harbour, with a warden in residence from March to November, and accommodations for bird-watchers; to arrange a stay, write **Kieran Grace,** 84 Dorney Court, Shankhill, County Dublin. **Ciarán O'Driscoll** (© **028/39153**), who operates a B&B on the island, also runs boat trips for bird-watchers around the island, and has a keen eye for vagrants and rarities.

DIVING The **Baltimore Diving & Watersports Centre** in Baltimore, County Cork (© **028/20300;** fax 028/20300; www.baltimorediving.com), provides equipment and boats to certified divers for exploring the many shipwrecks, reefs, and caves in this region (from 35€/$32 per dive with equipment). A range of 2-hour to 15-day certified PADI courses are available for all levels of experience; for example, beginners can take a 2- to 3-hour snorkeling course for 20€ ($18) or a scuba diving course for 35€ ($32); experienced divers can take the 2-week PADI instructor course. The center has recently added its own restaurant and hostel accommodation.

FISHING The West Cork Coast is known for its many shipwrecks, which are quickly taken over by all manner of marine life after they hit the ocean floor. Wreck fishing is popular all along the Irish coast, and this is one of the best places for it. **Mark and Patricia Gannon** of Woodpoint House, Courtmacsherry (© **023/46427;** www.sea-anglingireland.com), offer packages including bed-and-breakfast in their idyllic stone farmhouse together with a day's sea angling aboard one of their two new Aquastar purpose-built fishing boats. A day's fishing costs 44€ ($40) per person. Boats holding up to 12 people can be chartered with a qualified skipper included for 356€ ($322) per day.

KAYAKING With all its inviting islands, inlets, and sea caves, the coast of West Cork is a sea kayaker's paradise. Lough Ine offers warm, still waters for beginners, a tidal rapid for the more intrepid, and access to a nearby headland riddled with caves demanding exploration. Day trips are offered throughout the year by Jim Kennedy of **Atlantic Sea Kayaking** (© **028/33002** or 086/606-5973; www.atlanticseakayaking.com). Jim is a top competitor in flat-water racing and an expert sea kayaker. With his knowledgeable and friendly instruction, even children and rank beginners soon feel at ease in a sea kayak. He operates from Maria's Schoolhouse Hostel (see listing under "Accommodations," below) near the seaside village of Union Hall—the Schoolhouse is a fabulous base from which to explore the nearby coast by sea kayak. A two-hour kayak trip is 26€ ($24), and a full-day trip is 51€ ($46). Night time/full moon trips as well as two day, three day, and five day tours are also available; there's a minimum of four people for these trips, so be sure to call ahead.

SAILING   The **Glenans Sailing Club** (www.glenans-ireland.com) was founded in France and has two centers in Ireland, one of which is in **Baltimore Harbor** (© 028/20154; fax 028/20312). The centers provide weeklong courses at all levels, using either dinghies, cruisers, catamarans, or windsurfers; prices are 430€ to 480€ ($390 to $435). The living facilities are spartan, with dorm-style accommodations, and you cook for yourself. The clientele is mostly middle-aged and younger, from Ireland and the Continent. Day sailing is available in Baltimore on Saturdays in June, July, and August for 50€ ($45) per person, and sailing weekends (starting at 140€/$127 per person) are also offered. Call © **028/20154** or fax 028/20312 to make an advance booking.

WALKING   One of the most beautiful coastal walks in West Cork begins along the banks of **Lough Ine** ★★, the largest saltwater lake in Europe. Connected to the sea by a narrow isthmus, the lake is situated in a lush valley of exceptional beauty. To get there, follow signs for Lough Ine along R595 between Skibbereen and Baltimore; there is a parking lot at the northwest corner of the lake. The wide trail proceeds gradually upward from the parking lot through the woods on the west slope of the valley, with several viewpoints toward the lake and the sea beyond. Once you reach the hilltop, there is a sweeping view of the coast from Mizen Head to Galley Head. Walking time to the top and back is about 1½ hours.

At the mesmerizingly high cliffs of **Mizen Head,** it's possible to follow the sheep paths that skirt the rim of the precipice—only for the strong of will, though, and only on clear, dry days. Start at the parking lot for the suspension bridge at Mizen Head, and instead of entering the gate leading to the bridge and lighthouse, cut up the hill heading toward two high electrical towers. Continue to climb the hill past the towers, keeping to the left of the old lighthouse, a small abandoned stone structure on a small hill overlooking the sea. From here, continue along the cliffs, keeping a safe distance from the edge. From the parking lot to the old lighthouse is a 15-minute walk, and from there you can continue on another 30 minutes to the end of the headland, returning the way you came.

An easy seaside walk on the **Beara Peninsula** begins at Dunboy Castle, about 1¼ miles (2km) west of Castletownbere on R572; this stretch of trail is part of the O'Sullivan Beara trail, which may eventually extend from Castletownbere to Leitrim. You can park your car along the road, by the castellated gatehouse. The castle itself is a ruined 19th-century manor house overlooking the bay, with some graceful marble arches spanning the grand central hall. Just down the road are the sparse ruins of a medieval fortress, and beyond this the trail continues to the tip of Fair Head through overarching rhododendrons, with fine views across to Bere Island. From the gatehouse parking lot to the tip of Fair Head and back is about 2 hours.

The **Sheep's Head Way** makes a loop of 55 miles (89km), and numerous day-long loops can also be made. I recommend buying the *Guide to the Sheep's Head Way,* available in most local stores and tourist offices, which combines history, poetry, and topography in a fantastic introduction to the region. In the 17th century the Sheep's Head Peninsula was described as "being all rocky and frequented only by eagles and birds—never to be inhabited by reason of the rough incommodities." It still is a rough place, and you won't find many tourists in its more remote reaches. There are treasures to be found here, but you may have to work a little harder to unearth them than in regions long since "discovered."

One of Ireland's most beautiful spots, **Gougane Barra** ★★ (which means "St. Finbar's Cleft") is a still, dark, romantic lake a little northeast of the Pass of

Keimaneigh 15 miles (24km) northeast of Bantry off T64 (also well signposted on the Macroom-Glengarriff road). The River Lee rises in these deeply wooded mountains, and St. Finbar founded a monastery here, supposedly on the small island connected by a causeway to the mainland. The island now holds a tiny chapel (nothing remains of the saint's 6th-century community) and eight small circular cells dating from the early 1700s, as well as a modern chapel. Today Gougane Barra is a national forest park, and there are signposted walks and drives through the wooded hills. There's a small admission charge per car to enter the park.

WINDSURFING   Equipment rental is available during the summer on the beach at **Courtmacsherry;** rates are about 15€ ($14) per hour. This is a sheltered beach, a good place for beginners to get started.

ACCOMMODATIONS YOU CAN AFFORD

Atlantic Sunset   Mrs. Mary Holland's modern country home has a beautiful view of the Atlantic, and there's a lovely sandy beach about half a mile from the house. Golf, horseback riding, and sea fishing can be arranged at nearby facilities.

Butlerstown, Bandon, Co. Cork. ✆ **023/40115.** 4 units, 2 with bathroom (shower only). 51€ ($46) double without bathroom, 56€–64€ ($51–$58) double with bathroom. 20% reduction for children. Rates include full breakfast. No credit cards. Free parking. *In room:* Hair dryer.

Ballinatona Farm ★★ *(Finds*   Like the region in which it's situated, this place is a little-known treasure, just far enough off the beaten track to be spared the crowds of the southwest. True, the landscape here isn't wild and rugged like that of the West Cork coast; its beauty is gentler, and requires time to be discovered. Your energetic hosts, Jytte Storm and Tim Lane, know the region well; their love for this land and enthusiasm for its hidden delights are truly infectious. Even if you've chosen this as a base for exploring points further west, you'll probably find yourself spending more time than expected within walking distance of the house. Jytte and Tim, themselves avid walkers, are especially accommodating of trekkers and full of good route suggestions. The house itself is tucked into the hillside, high above the valley floor, and offers magnificent views from all but one of the rooms. Request the second floor front room, which is reached by a spiral staircase, and offers a truly breathtaking view with glass walls on three sides. Breakfast here is an unqualified delight—Jytte prepares scones and breads, all from traditional recipes and all delicious. The scrambled eggs are great, and the milk is from the farm's own cows.

Millstreet, Co. Cork. ✆ **029/70213.** Fax 029/70940. 6 units. 34.50€ ($31) single; 50€ ($45) double. 25% discount for children under 12 sharing with an adult. Rates include full breakfast. MC, V. Free parking. 3 miles (5km) out of Millstreet on the Macroom Rd. *In room:* TV, tea/coffeemaker, hair dryer.

Findus House   Findus House is the working farm of Mary O'Sullivan and her lively family, and a one-time winner of the coveted Farmhouse of the Year award. Guest rooms are pleasant. The food here is a major draw; Mary has won much praise for her dinners—salmon dishes are her specialty. Wine and Irish coffee are available at a small extra charge. A delightful base for exploring this part of West Cork, Findus Farm is 30 miles (48km) west of Cork city, 24 miles (39km) south of Killarney, 3 miles (5km) south of the main Cork-Killarney road (N22), and 19 miles (31km) northeast of Gougane Barra.

Ballyvoige, Kilnamartyra, Macroom, Co. Cork. ✆ **026/40023.** Fax 026/40023. findushouse@eircom.net. 6 units. 31€ ($28) single; 56€ ($51) double. 50% reduction for children (sharing with parents). Rates include full breakfast. Dinner 23€ ($21). AE, MC, V. Free parking. Closed Nov–Apr.

Glebe Country House   Glebe Country House was built in 1690 as a rectory and is currently the gracious home of Jill Good. The charming bedrooms, each unique and comfortable, enjoy views of the rose and herb gardens that wreath the house; a fireplace and piano accent the peaceful living room; and the spacious dining room provides a lovely setting for candlelight five-course dinners (25€, $23) partly drawn from the house's garden. You will, however, need to bring your own wine. Many enticing breakfast possibilities await you in the morning, such as waffles, scrambled eggs with rosemary shortbread, or "cheesy French toast," a Glebe House first.

The Coach House apartments behind the main house offer comfortable self-catering accommodations. The ground-floor, two-bedroom garden apartment sleeps five, with a double and single bed in one room and twin beds in the other. Equipped with all the essentials, it has an open living-dining-kitchen area decorated in simple country-cottage style. The ideal choice for families is the one-bedroom loft apartment that sleeps five, with a double and single bed in one room and a pullout sofa in the living room. A compact kitchen is equipped with all you need to prepare substantial meals. Both apartments have linens, and each has a private patio-garden. A chalet in the garden, Beech Lodge, is available for up to six guests.

Balinadee, Bandon, Co. Cork. Hotel ℂ **021/477-8294.** Fax 021/477-8456. http://indigo.ie/~glebehse/. 4 units. 64€–90€ ($58–$82) double. Includes full Irish breakfast. 2 self-catering units. 280€–510€ ($254–$462) per week depending on season. MC, V. Free parking. Located off Balinadee center. *In room:* tea/coffeemaker, hair dryer, iron.

Lettercollum House ⭐⭐   A meal and overnight stop here is, in my opinion, one of the most delightful experiences to be had in this region. Until recently a hostel—albeit one of the most luxurious hostels in Ireland—this Victorian manor house has now undergone yet another transformation, and offers comfortable en-suite accommodation. Some of the atmosphere of informality still lingers from the hostel days, however, and this continues to be one of the friendliest, most laid-back retreats in an area known for these qualities. The two front bedrooms are palatial in dimension, and make fabulous family rooms. Shrubbery has been cleared on the south side of the house, revealing a beautiful view that can be enjoyed from all the rooms. A walled garden provides vegetables for the superlative restaurant that inhabits a former chapel at the front of the house (see "Worth a Splurge" under "Great Deals on Dining," later in this chapter). Cooking courses are also held here; check the website for details. The surroundings are pastoral and the pervading atmosphere is one of tranquillity.

Timoleague, Co. Cork. ℂ **023/46251.** Fax 023/46270. www.lettercollum.ie. 7 units. 51€–76€ ($47–$70) double. Rates include full breakfast. AE, DC, MC, V. Free parking. 1 mile (1.5km) outside Timoleague on the Skibbereen Rd.

Maria's Schoolhouse Hostel ⭐   The austere and handsome fieldstone exterior of this renovated schoolhouse gives way inside to nontraditional decor in bright purple and pink. The private rooms are very comfortable, and each has its own unique character. A sunny and spacious hall is the scene of innovative dinners served from Wednesday to Saturday in the summer. They focus on ethnic and vegetarian cuisine. Breakfasts are similarly basic and healthy. Every other Saturday there's an acoustic music concert in conjunction with dinner—these events feature top musicians and are well worth attending. Maria Hoare is an amiable and outgoing host, as is Jim Kennedy, who runs his excellent sea-kayaking program from here. Bedrooms are nonsmoking, but smoking is permitted in the lounge. The self-catering kitchen is very small, so don't plan to do any elaborate cooking while you're here.

Cahergal, Union Hall, Co. Cork. ⓒ/fax **028/33002**. www.geocities.com/mariasschoolhouse. 8 units. 38€–46€ ($35–$41) double; 57€–63€ ($52–$58) family room; 10€ ($9.10) per person in a dorm. Dinner 10€–18€ ($9.10–$16); breakfast 4.50€–6.50€ ($4.10–$5.90). MC, V. Free parking. Closed Jan–Mar. **Amenities:** Self-catering kitchen.

Palm Grove   Mrs. Eileen O'Driscoll's B&B is housed in a modern bungalow set in open countryside overlooking the Ilen River. Guest rooms look out on peaceful rural scenes and offers a decent lot of amenities, including orthopedic beds. The guest lounge is a good place to have a spot of tea and the gardens are both lovely and relaxing. The B&B is close to a host of activities and sightseeing, and Mrs. O'Driscoll is wonderfully hospitable and always eager to help with sightseeing plans.

Coolnagurrane, Bantry Rd., Skibbereen, Co. Cork. ⓒ/fax **028/21703**. www.palmgrovebb.com. 4 units, 2 with bathroom (shower only). 32€–34€ ($29–$31) single; 43€–48€ ($39–$44) double. 20% reduction for children sharing with an adult. Dinner 15€ ($14). MC, V. Private parking lot. Closed Dec–Feb. 1 mile (1.5km) from Skibbereen. **Amenities:** Lounge. *In room:* TV, hair dryer.

Realt-Na-Mara   This attractive modern home run by Mrs. Mary Donovan perches on the high side of the main road into Castletownbere, with a stone terrace overlooking Bantry Bay. Guest rooms are spacious; some have views of the bay, others overlook the mountainside; there are two family rooms. Mrs. Donovan is a gracious hostess and keeps a spotless home.

Castletownbere, Co. Cork. ⓒ **027/70101**. 5 units, 4 with bathroom. 48€ ($44) double. Rates include full breakfast. No credit cards. Free parking. *In room:* Tea/coffeemaker.

Rolf's Holiday Hostel   Rolf's is a long-established, award-winning, family-run hostel beautifully situated on Baltimore Hill overlooking the harbor and the Mizen peninsula. This appealing cut-stone complex of buildings—somehow alpine, with steep lofts and wide beams—offers an array of lodging and dining options. All guests have access to the open self-catering kitchen, which is unlikely to compete with Rolf's Cafe Art and Restaurant. The art here refers to the rotating exhibits of contemporary Irish painting and sculpture selected by Frederika Haffner, Rolf's daughter, a fine sculptor. Both cafe and restaurant are open daily 8am to 9:30pm, providing excellent value across their impressive menus and wine lists. Johannes Haffner, Rolf's son, grew up here and takes great pride in offering the finest in hostel hospitality. Note that breakfast is not included in accommodation costs; a continental breakfast is 3.80€ ($3.45) and an Irish breakfast is 6.35€ ($5.75).

Baltimore, Co. Cork. ⓒ/fax **028/20289**. rolfsholidayhostel@eircom.net. 34€ ($31) double; 47€ ($43) family room (sleeps four); 11€–13€ ($10–$12) per person in a dorm; 4.50€ ($4.05) per person camping. MC, V. Free parking. ⅓ mi (.5km) off R595, signposted just outside of Baltimore centre. **Amenities:** Restaurant (International), bicycle hire. *In room:* Full kitchen, washing machine.

MIZEN HEAD PENINSULA

Fortview House   This former winner of the Irish Agritourism Award for "best B&B in the South" boasts pristine country-style rooms, with antique pine furniture, wood floors, iron and brass beds, and crisp Irish linens. Beamed ceilings and a warm color palette add to the comfortable feeling, and the spacious, inviting sitting room, equipped with tea and coffee facilities and an honor-system bar, completes the welcome. Violet Connell's copious breakfasts are legendary, with seven varieties of fresh-squeezed juices jostling for space on a menu that includes hot potato cakes, pancakes, kippers, smoked salmon, and eggs prepared any-which-way.

If you prefer self-catering, there is also a 3-bedroom cottage (sleeps 6) on the Fortview grounds that rents for 318€ ($288) per week in low season and 572€ ($518) per week in the summer.

Gurtyowen, Toormore, Goleen. ⓒ 028/35324. 5 units. 76€ ($69) double. Rates include full breakfast. No credit cards. Free parking. Closed Nov–Feb. On R591 from Durrus towards Goleen. **Amenities:** Sitting room. *In room:* TV, hair dryer.

Rock Cottage ⭐ This B&B offers a wonderfully secluded and relaxing retreat in what was once the hunting lodge of Lord Bandon. The tastefully restored Georgian lodge contains three spacious guest rooms, combining ample shares of elegance and comfort. Best of all, your host here, Barbara Klötzer, used to be the head chef at Blair's Cove and is now able to focus her culinary wizardry on a mere handful of lucky guests.

Barnatonicane, Schull. ⓒ 028/35538. www.mizen.net/rockcottage. 3 units. 63€–76€ ($57–$69) double. Rates include full breakfast. Dinner from 28€ ($25). MC, V. Free parking. Open year-round. 7 miles (11km) from Durrus on R591. *In room:* TV, hair dryer.

SHEEP'S HEAD PENINSULA

Hillside Farm ⭐ The Sheep's Head Peninsula is a little-known scenic wonder, and Hillside Farm is the best base for exploring this beautiful region. The Sheep's Head Way, a walking trail that circles the peninsula, passes through the grounds of the farmhouse: In one direction the beach is only a 5-minute walk away, and in the other the trail climbs toward the summits of a few local hills. The house was renovated in 1990, when an extension was built connecting two old stone farm buildings. Bedrooms look out across the bay toward Durrus and Mt. Gabriel. There are two family rooms that sleep up to four, one of which is on the ground floor and has its own entrance. Agnes Hegarty is an enthusiastic proponent of this region and can offer many suggestions of interesting places to visit on the peninsula.

Ahakista, Durrus, Bantry, Co. Cork. ⓒ 027/67045. agneshegarty@oceanfree.net. 4 units, 3 with bathroom (2 with shower only). 46€ ($41) double without bathroom, 51€ ($46) double with bathroom. Rates include full breakfast. No credit cards. Free parking. Closed Nov–Mar. 6 miles (9.5km) from Durrus.

BEARA PENINSULA

Bayview Farmhouse *Kids* This bright, cheerful home overlooking Bantry Bay is 9 miles (15km) from Glengarriff, and 2 miles (3km) from the foot of Healy Pass. The proprietor is Mrs. Sheila O'Sullivan. Rooms are spacious and well appointed, and there's a pony, a donkey, and a trap (riding cart) for use by guests at no charge.

Faha, Adrigole, Beara (Bantry), Co. Cork. ⓒ 027/60026. 5 units, none with bathroom. 24€ ($22) single; 46€ ($41) double. 25% reduction for children sharing with an adult. Rates include full breakfast. Dinner 15€ ($14). No credit cards. Free parking. Closed Oct–Apr.

SELF-CATERING

Baltimore Holiday Homes *Kids* These well-established holiday cottages form an attractive cluster safely set back from the road and overlooking a lovely inlet near Baltimore, a charming harbor town. They are best suited to families wanting to settle in for a week's self-contained seaside and island-hopping holiday. Tennis courts and pitch-and-putt (miniature golf) are offered, and the new leisure center of the nearby Baltimore Harbour Hotel is accessible for a fee. The cottages are bright and inviting, with white walls and pine furniture, and each has an open fireplace and three bedrooms. They are fully equipped, including washer, dryer, and microwave. Baltimore's two small food shops are minutes away on foot, and there is regular bus service to Skibbereen.

Baltimore, Co. Cork. For info/reservations, contact Home From Home Holidays, 26/27 Rossa St., Clonakilty, Co. Cork. ℂ 023/33110. Fax 023/333131. www.homefromhome.ie. 3-bedroom self-catering cottages. 560€–635€ ($506–$575) per week. In low and midseason, 2-day rates are available. MC, V. Free parking. Off R595 just before Baltimore center. *In room:* TV, kitchen, microwave, washer/dryer.

Casino Cottage   Casino Cottage, run by the nearby Casino House restaurant (see below), is a snug getaway for two set alongside a rural road amidst a rolling country landscape only a 15-minute walk from the ocean shore. The same light, simple, stylish decor of the restaurant rules here, with white walls, high ceilings, and open stone fireplace (in the living room) combining to provide both space and coziness.

Coulmain Bay, Kilbrittain, Co. Cork. ℂ 023/49944. Fax 023/49945. 1 self-catering 2-room cottage, with shower only. 330€ ($299) per week depending on season; 63€ ($57) per night. MC, V. Free parking. 10 miles (15km) from Kinsale on the coast road (R600). *In room:* Kitchen, fridge, iron.

The Southernmost House 🏠🏠   This exquisitely situated cottage is the southernmost dwelling on the southernmost inhabited Irish island, Cape Clear. Quite simply, it redefines the word *getaway.* Five years were devoted to the restoration of this centuries-old traditional island cottage, and everything was done to perfection. The exposed stone walls, pine ceilings and floors, multiple skylights, and simple, tasteful furnishings make it a most pleasing and comfortable nook, and the views from virtually every window are stunning. If Cape Clear had a king, this is where he would live. Instead, Irish folk balladeer Christy Moore, among others, has made a point of dropping anchor here. It's cozy enough for a love nest, and spacious enough for a family of six (it has three bedrooms). If it rains—and this has been known to happen on the "Cape"—the massive stone fireplace is the perfect antidote. The one down side: This place is so very popular that you'll need to book up to 9 months in advance.

Glen W., Cape Clear, Co. Cork. ℂ/fax 028/39157. http://indigo.ie/~ckstory/. 3 bedrooms. 255€–575€ ($231–$521) per week, depending on season. *In room:* TV, kitchen, tea/coffeemaker, hair dryer, iron, washing machine.

GREAT DEALS ON DINING

Adele's 🏠🏠 (Value) SEAFOOD/PASTA   Adele's is one of the very few good restaurants in Cork that won't take a big bite out of your budget. During the day this tiny establishment on Schull's Main Street serves delicious baked goods, teas, and sandwiches, the work of Adele Connor's prolific culinary imagination. Sandwiches include ciabatta with tomato and slabs of the local Gubbeen cheese, a real treat. The magic truly begins in the evening, however, when a dining room upstairs is opened and Adele's son prepares delightful, creative meals from basic local ingredients. The menu changes daily; examples include fresh mussels with angel-hair pasta and leeks, monkfish in a saffron butter sauce, or tagliatelle with rosemary and parsley pesto. The panzanella—a marinated salad with red peppers, capers, and soaked bread crumbs—is a delicious summer appetizer. The atmosphere is casual, and families are welcome. B&B lodging is also available at budget rates—a double room is 46€ ($41).

Main St., Schull, Co. Cork. ℂ 028/28459. Dinner reservations recommended. Lunch and baked goods under 8€ ($7.25). Dinner main courses 13€–25€ ($12–$23). MC, V. April–June and Sept–Oct Wed–Sun 9:30am–10:30pm; July–Aug daily 9:30am–10:30pm. Also open Christmas/New Year's season.

The Altar IRISH/SEAFOOD Situated deep in the West Cork countryside, this rustic cottage seems to appear out of nowhere on the horizon. It has all the trappings of a country retreat inside, including the requisite open, glowing fireplace and stone walls. The menu, which changes daily, emphasizes local seafood, with choices such as seafood chowder, crab salad, oysters, and seafood plates. On Sundays, a traditional Irish lunch is served, and there's Irish music on Wednesday nights. The Altar will also make up and deliver picnic baskets.

Toormore, Goleen (near Schull), Co. Cork. ✆ **028/35254.** Reservations recommended. Bar food items 2.50€–10€ ($2.30–$9.10); fixed-price traditional lunch 14€ ($13); fixed-price dinner 32€ ($29). AE, MC, V. Easter to Sept Tues–Sat 11:30am–2:30pm and 6–10pm; Oct to Easter by reservation only.

An Sugan PUB/SEAFOOD This homey, old-style pub and restaurant southwest of Cork city on N71 features a fascinating collection of bits and pieces of Irish life. It makes an ideal stop for bar food that's filling enough to serve as a main meal. Upstairs, the restaurant has a lobster tank and serves lunch and dinner at somewhat higher prices.

41 Strand Rd., Clonakilty, Co. Cork. ✆ **023/33498.** Lunch bar food 7€–20€ ($6.35–$18); dinner bar food 10€–28€ ($9.10–$25). MC, V. Daily 12:30–2:30pm and 6–10pm; bar food daily 12:30–9:30pm. Closed Good Friday, Christmas Day.

Casey's of Baltimore Hotel SEAFOOD/IRISH This nautical pub/restaurant overlooking Church Strand Bay offers lovely views of the water. The cottagelike interior has open peat fires and there's also a beer garden. The food is good and specialties feature simple fare such as fresh local seafood and steaks.

Baltimore, Co. Cork. ✆ **028/20197.** www.caseysofbaltimore.com. Reservations recommended for dinner. Bar snacks under 8€ ($7.25); lunch main courses 7.60€–19€ ($6.90–$17); dinner main courses 10€–39€ ($9.10–$36); table d'hôte menu 32€ ($29). AE, DC, MC, V. Daily 12:30–2:30pm and 6–9:30pm. Bar snacks Mon–Sat noon–9:30pm.

Casino House INTERNATIONAL Why drive out of Kinsale, the "gourmet capital of Ireland" in search of a meal? Kerrin and Michael Relja's Casino House is one good answer. The views of Courtmacsherry Bay will make you gasp, and the decor—somewhere between Nantucket and Provence—will promote both calm and appetite. Stylish without pretense, Casino House has been selected as one of the 100 best restaurants in Ireland, an honor it well deserves. You can do no better in Kinsale, although you can easily pay a lot more. The menu, which changes every week, is invariably inventive, with such choices as pan-seared asparagus tips with mixed greens and Parmesan shavings, terrine of quail with pistachio nuts and shiitake mushrooms, and filet steak with mushrooms and onion ragout and potato pancakes. An exceptional selection of German wines highlights an excellent wine list. The house wines from Italy are well selected for value and quality.

Coolmain Bay, Kilbrittain, Co. Cork. ✆ **023/49944.** Fax 023/49945. Reservations recommended. Main courses 15€–20€ ($14–$18); lunch menu 10€–15€ ($9.10–$14). MC, V. Easter–Oct 7–9pm Thursday–Tuesday; also open Sun 1-3pm. 10 miles (16km) from Kinsale on coast road (R600).

O'Connor's Seafood Restaurant SEAFOOD/TRADITIONAL/BAR FOOD Matt and Ann O'Connor run this cozy pub and restaurant. Their seafood dishes are truly special (try the mussels cordon bleu), and there's even a live lobster and oyster tank. If seafood isn't to your taste, you can order good local lamb and steak. Salads, sandwiches, shepherd's pie, and the like are on tap in the bar. O'Connor's has a separate section for nonsmokers and prohibits strong tobacco, cigars, and pipes.

The Square, Bantry, Co. Cork. ✆ **027/50221.** Dinner main courses 18€–32€ ($16–$29); bar food 6€–15€ ($5.45–$14). MC, V. Bar food daily noon–6pm; dinner daily 6–10pm. Closed Nov–Mar Sun; Apr–Oct Sun lunch.

Wine Vaults INTERNATIONAL   This restaurant in the heart of a busy market town is a handy place for lunch or a light meal in transit. The menu includes soups, sandwiches on pita bread, and pizzas, including a house-special pizza topped with mushrooms, peppers, onions, ham, and salami. There's live traditional music or jazz and blues offered nightly.

73 Bridge St., Skibbereen, Co. Cork. ✆ **028/22743.** Reservations not required. All items 4€–12€ ($3.65–$11). No credit cards. Year-round, daily noon–8pm for food; open until 11:30pm for music and drinks.

WORTH A SPLURGE

Blair's Cove ✿ INTERNATIONAL   About 8 miles (13km) south of Bantry on Mizen Head Peninsula, Blair's Cove is the loving creation of Phillippe and Sabine De Mey, who have converted the stone stables of a 250-year-old mansion overlooking Dunmanus Bay in West Cork into a casually elegant restaurant, and one of the better dining experiences in Southwest Ireland. In summer, meals are served on the covered terrace overlooking the courtyard. Don't look for cutting-edge, break-the-mold fusion; this place is all about classic dishes done in a familiar way, only better than you've likely had them elsewhere. Specialties are fresh seafood, lamb, and beef grilled over a big oak-log fire in the dining room, and there's an exceptionally good wine list. Candlelight and soft piano music complete the romantic setting. Excellent self-catering accommodation and bed-and-breakfast suites are also available.

Barley Cove Rd., Durrus, Co. Cork. ✆ **027/61127.** Fax 027/61487. blairscove@eircom.net. Reservations required. Dinner with starter buffet and dessert 44€ ($45); buffet and dessert only, 33€ ($33). MC, V. Apr–June and Sept–Oct Tues–Sat 7:30–9:30pm; July–Aug Mon–Sat 7:15–9:30pm.

Lettercollum House ✿✿ IRISH COUNTRY HOUSE   Con McLoughlin and Karen Austin create simple and original dishes based on organic produce from the adjacent walled garden, pigs raised on the premises, and locally caught fish. The menu changes daily, and there is always at least one vegetarian entree. Your choices may include grilled wild salmon with sorrel sauce, canneloni of sea spinach and brie with tomato butter sauce, or organic lamb tajine. The dining room was once a chapel, and the stained glass windows remain. The service is rather informal, but the food is so good that you won't care. After a lingering, leisurely dinner, I recommend staying in one of the simple and elegant rooms upstairs, and continuing the gastronomic delights with breakfast (see "Accommodations You Can Afford," earlier in this chapter).

Timoleague, Co. Cork. ✆ **023/46251.** www.lettercollum.ie. Main courses 15€–25€ ($14–$23). AE, DC, MC, V. June–Sept daily 7:30–9pm, Sun 1–3pm; Oct–May reservation only.

SHOPPING

The Bandon Pottery Factory Shop   Two miles (3km) out of Bandon on the Dunmanway Road, at this factory shop you can watch the pottery being made and look for bargains among the "seconds." Bandon Pottery produces a colorful line of hand-thrown tableware, vases, bowls, and other accessories. Lauragh Industrial Estate, Lauragh, Bandon, Co. Cork. ✆ 023/41360. www.bandonpottery.ie.

Courtmacsherry Ceramics   Overlooking the sea, this studio/shop offers an array of porcelain animals, birds, butterflies, and tableware, all inspired by the flora and fauna of West Cork. Visitors are welcome to watch potter Peter

Wolstenholme at work on new creations. *Note:* From October to mid-March it's open by appointment only. Main St., Courtmacsherry, Co. Cork. © **023/46239.**

Mannings Emporium *(Finds* If you want to taste Ireland, rather than just travel through it, the best place to stop is a small shop on the Bantry-Glengarriff road. Wicker baskets heaped with local produce mark the entry, and the gold and white sheen of Irish farmhouse cheeses are among the treasures in the dim interior. Owner Val Manning, one of the first promoters of Irish food, stocks his store with the best local products, such as savory organic biscuits, handmade chocolate, and dense, nutty, oatmeal. Equally impressive is the reasonably priced stock of both imported and local wines. One of the nicest things about Mannings is that it draws both those in search of a loaf of bread or quart of milk and those who come from further afield to find a round of blue cheese or a good selection of olives. Sandwiches are made to your specifications on thick slices of freshly baked bread. Ballylickey, Co. Cork (on N71). © **027/50456.**

Prince August Prince August is Ireland's only toy soldier factory. The shop also produces and displays a huge collection of metal miniatures based on J. R. R. Tolkien's classic works *The Hobbit* and *The Lord of the Rings.* The shop is located off the main N22 road, northwest of Kinsale. Kilnamartyra, Macroom, Co. Cork. © **026/40222.** Fax 026/40004. www.princeaugust.ie.

Raymond Klee's Studio *(Finds* Between Bantry and Glengarriff, on the edge of the little town of Ballylickey, you'll see an unpretentious sign in a curve of the road reading artist's studio, paintings of Irish scenes. That modest sign, however, gives little indication of the fine paintings you'll find inside. The Welsh-born artist has lived and worked all over the world and has won coveted awards from the French Salon and the Britain's Fine Arts Guild. His landscape canvases are remarkable in the way they capture the elusive colors and sweeping majesty of the Irish landscape. Ballylickey, Bantry, Co. Cork. © **027/50157.**

9

The Southwest: County Kerry

Kerry is a place of disorienting contrasts, where the tackiest tourist attractions coexist with some of Ireland's most spectacular scenic wonders. It's a rugged place for the most part, some of it so rugged that it's seldom visited and remains quite pristine; Ireland's two highest mountains, Carrantuohill and Mount Brandon, are examples of such places. You could be driving along—say, on the famous and popular Ring of Kerry, which traces the shores of the Iveragh Peninsula—make one little detour from the main road, and be in wild and unfrequented territory. The transition can be startling.

Thanks to its remoteness, County Kerry has always been an outpost of Gaelic culture. Poetry and music are intrinsic to Kerry lifestyle, as is a love of the outdoors and sports. Gaelic football is an obsession in this county, and Kerry wins most of the national championships. You'll also find some of Ireland's best golf courses here, and the fishing for salmon and trout is equally hard to resist.

1 The Iveragh Peninsula

The Iveragh Peninsula's star attraction is the **Ring of Kerry** ⊛, undoubtedly Ireland's most popular scenic drive, a 110-mile (177km) panorama of seacoast, mountain, and lakeland vistas. Bicyclists usually avoid this route, because the scores of tour buses that thunder through here every day in the summer aren't always generous about sharing the road. For the most part, the Ring follows N70 and circles the peninsula; it starts and finishes at **Killarney,** but you can also use **Kenmare** as a base. The drive can be undertaken in either direction, but we recommend a counterclockwise route.

Although it's possible to circle the peninsula in as little as 4 hours, the only way to get a feel for the area and the people is to leave the main road, get out of your car, and explore some of the inland and coastal towns. **Portmagee** is a lovely seaside town, connected by a bridge to Valencia Island, which houses the informative Skellig Heritage Centre. In **Caherdaniel** there is a museum devoted to Daniel O'Connell, one of Ireland's great historical figures.

GETTING THERE   **Bus Eireann** (© **064/34777;** www.buseireann.ie) provides limited daily service from Killarney to Caherciveen, Waterville, Kenmare, and other towns on the Ring of Kerry. The best way to get to the Ring is by car, on N70 and N71.

From Killarney, **Dero's Tours,** 22 Main St., Killarney, County Kerry (© **064/ 31251** or 064/31567; fax 064/34077; www.derostours.com), runs tours of the Ring of Kerry daily from Easter to October. The tour leaves daily from Dero's office on Main St. in Killarney at 10:30am; the cost is 19€ ($17) per person. When booking a tour, ask about possible discounts for holders of this book.

Impressions of Kenmare

As I leave behind Neidin it's like purple splashed on green
My soul is strangely fed through the winding hills ahead
She plays a melody on wind and streams for me
Won't you remember, won't you remember, won't you remember me?
And we wind and climb and fall like the greatest waltz of all
Float across the floor, her sweet breath outside the door
And it's time that I was gone across the silver tear
Won't you remember, won't you remember, won't you remember me?
—Jimmy MacCarthy, Irish songwriter

Barry O'Connor, of **O'Connor's Auto Tours,** Andross, Ross Road, Killarney, County Kerry (**©** **064/31052;** oconnorautotours@eircom.net), operates coach tours year-round.

The most popular base for touring the peninsula is Killarney. For information on getting to that town, see "Killarney & Its Lakes," later in this chapter.

VISITOR INFORMATION Stop in at the **Killarney Tourist Office,** Aras Fáilte, at the Town Centre Car Park, Beech Road, Killarney (**©** **064/31633**), before you explore the area. For hours, see section 2, "Killarney & Its Lakes," later in this chapter. The **Kenmare Tourist Office,** Market Square, Kenmare (**©** **064/41233**), is open daily Easter through September, 9:15am to 5:30pm, with extended hours in July and August. The rest of the year (Oct–Easter), it's open Monday to Saturday.

TOURING THE RING OF KERRY

The usual place to start a drive on the Ring of Kerry is **Killarney.** From there, follow the signs for **Killorglin.** When you reach this little town, you're on the N70 road. You may wish to stop and walk around Killorglin, which is known far and wide for its annual mid-August horse, sheep, and cattle fair. It's officially called the **Puck Fair,** because the local residents capture a wild goat (symbolizing the *puka* or *puki*—a mischievous sprite) from the mountains and enthrone it in the center of town as a sign of unrestricted merrymaking.

Continue on the N70 road and soon vistas of Dingle Bay appear on your right. **Carrantuohill,** Ireland's tallest mountain, at 3,414 feet (1,040m), is to your left. The open bogland constantly comes into view. From it, the local residents dig pieces of peat, or turf, to burn in their fireplaces for warmth. Formed thousands of years ago, these boglands are mainly composed of decayed trees. They tend to be bumpy if you attempt to drive over them too speedily, so do be cautious.

The Ring winds around cliffs and the edges of mountains, with nothing but the sea below—another reason that you will probably average only 30 miles (50km) an hour, at best. As you go along, you'll notice the remains of many **abandoned cottages.** These date from the famine years, in the mid-1840s, when the Irish potato crop failed and millions of people starved to death or were forced to emigrate. This peninsula is thought to have lost three-fourths of its population.

The next town on the Ring is **Glenbeigh,** a palm tree–lined fishing resort with a lovely, duney beach called Rossbeigh Strand. From Glenbeigh, continue along the southern coastline of Dingle Bay to **Kells Bay,** a lovely sandy cove.

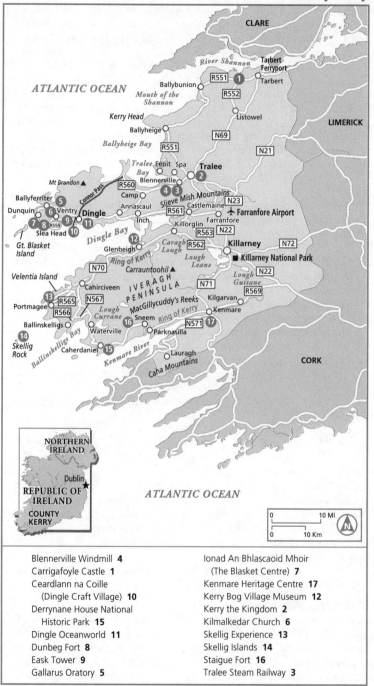

County Kerry

CLARE

River Shannon

Tarbert Ferryport

1

Tarbert

ATLANTIC OCEAN

Ballybunion

Mouth of the Shannon

R551

R552

Listowel

LIMERICK

Kerry Head

Ballyheige

N69

Ballyheige Bay

R551

N21

Tralee Bay Fenit Spa **Tralee**

Mt Brandon ▲

R560

Blennerville

2

Connor Pass

Camp

4 3

Slieve Mish Mountains

N23

Ballyferriter **5**

Annascaul

Castlemaine

✈ **Farranfore Airport**

Dunquin **6** Ventry **Dingle**

R561

7 **8** R559 **9**

Inch

Farranfore

10 **11**

Killorglin

R563 N22

Slea Head

12

Caragh Lough

R562

Killarney

N72

Gt. Blasket Island

Dingle Bay

Glenbeigh

Lough Leane

■ **Killarney National Park**

Ring of Kerry

N70

Carrauntoohil ▲

N22

Velentia Island

I V E R A G H

P E N I N S U L A

N71

Lough Guitane

R569

Cahirciveen

N567

MacGillycuddy's Reeks

Kilgarvan

13 R565

Lough Currane

Sneem

Kenmare

17

Portmagee

R566

16

Ring of Kerry

N571

Ballinskelligs

Waterville

Parknasilla

14

Ballinskelligs Bay

Caherdaniel **15**

Kenmare River

Skellig Rock

Lauragh

CORK

Caha Mountains

ATLANTIC OCEAN

NORTHERN IRELAND

Dublin ★

REPUBLIC OF IRELAND

COUNTY KERRY

0 ——— 10 Mi

0 ——— 10 Km

Blennerville Windmill **4**	Ionad An Bhlascaoid Mhoir (The Blasket Centre) **7**
Carrigafoyle Castle **1**	
Ceardlann na Coille (Dingle Craft Village) **10**	Kenmare Heritage Centre **17**
	Kerry Bog Village Museum **12**
Derrynane House National Historic Park **15**	Kerry the Kingdom **2**
	Kilmalkedar Church **6**
Dingle Oceanworld **11**	Skellig Experience **13**
Dunbeg Fort **8**	Skellig Islands **14**
Eask Tower **9**	Staigue Fort **16**
Gallarus Oratory **5**	Tralee Steam Railway **3**

You can make a slight detour to see **Valentia,** an offshore island 7 miles (11.5km) long and one of the most westerly points of Europe. Then, travel via R565 to **Valentia Island** ✲, reached from the mainland by a causeway. Although its name would seem to imply a Spanish origin, it's from a romanticized pronunciation of the Irish *Beal Inse* ("Harbor at the Mouth of the Island") that "Valentia" evolved. Connected to the mainland by a bridge at Portmagee, this was the site from which the first telegraph cable was laid across the Atlantic in 1866. In the 18th century, the Valentia harbor was famous as a refuge for smugglers and privateers; it's said that John Paul Jones, the Scottish-born American naval officer in the American Revolution, also anchored here quite often.

Head next for **Waterville,** an idyllic spot wedged between Lough Currane and Ballinskelligs Bay off the Atlantic. For years, it was known as the favorite retreat of Charlie Chaplin, but today it's the home of the only Irish branch of Club Med.

If you follow the sea road north of town out to the Irish-speaking village of **Ballinskelligs,** at the mouth of the bay, you can also catch a glimpse of the two Skellig Rocks. Continuing on the N70 route, the next point of interest is Derrynane at Caherdaniel, the home of Daniel O'Connell, remembered as "the Liberator" who freed Irish Catholics from the last of the English penal laws in 1829. Derrynane is now a national monument and park, and a major center of Gaelic culture.

Watch for signs to **Staigue Fort,** about 2 miles (3km) off the main road. One of the best preserved of all ancient Irish structures, this circular fort is constructed of rough stones without mortar of any kind. The walls are 13 feet (4m) thick at its base, and the diameter is about 90 feet (27.5m). Not much is known of its history, but experts think it probably dates from around 1000 B.C.

Sneem, the next village on the circuit, is a colorful little hamlet with twin small parks. Its houses are painted in vibrant shades of blue, pink, yellow, purple, and orange, like a little touch of the Mediterranean or Caribbean plunked down in Ireland.

As you continue on the Ring, the foliage becomes more lush, thanks to the warming waters and winds of the Gulf Stream. When you begin to see lots of palm trees and other subtropical vegetation, you'll know you're in **Parknasilla,** once a favorite haunt of George Bernard Shaw.

The final town on the Ring of Kerry route, **Kenmare,** is by far the most enchanting. Originally called Neidin, which in the Irish language means "Little Nest," Kenmare is indeed a little nest of verdant foliage nestled between the River Roughty and Kenmare Bay. Well laid out and immaculately maintained by its proud residents (pop. 1,200), Kenmare rivals Killarney for the title of best base for County Kerry sightseeing.

On the return to Killarney, the final lap of the Ring road takes you through a scenic mountain stretch known as **Moll's Gap.**

THE SKELLIG ISLANDS ✲✲✲

A visit to the Skellig Islands, which rise precipitously from the sea, about 10 miles (16km) off the coast of the Iveragh Peninsula, is sure to be a memorable experience. Seen from the mainland, the islands have a fantastic aspect, seeming impossibly steep and sharp-angled. And yet it is on the highest pinnacle of the larger island, **Skellig Michael** ✲✲✲, that a community of monks chose to build a monastery in the 6th or 7th century, carving steps out of the rock to provide access from the stormy waters below. The monastery survived for 6 centuries before being abandoned in the 12th or 13th century. The modern-day visitor

> **Finds Don't Miss It!**
>
> The most memorable and magical site to visit on the Iveragh Peninsula is **Skellig Michael,** a rocky pinnacle towering over the sea, where medieval monks built their monastery in ascetic isolation. The crossing to the island can be rough, so you'll want to choose as clear and calm a day for your trip as possible. Seabirds nest here in abundance, and more than 20,000 pairs of gannets inhabit neighboring Little Skellig during the summer nesting season.

first makes a 45-minute boat passage from the mainland, and then upon embarking, begins a long ascent of the island using the same steps trodden by the monks. The monastic enclosure consists of six beehive-shaped huts of mortarless stone construction, two oratories, and a church; there is also a collection of carved stones that have been found on the island. The smaller of the Skellig Islands has no space for human habitation, but is home during nesting season to over 20,000 pairs of gannets. Ferries leave daily May to September from Ballinskelligs, usually between 9am and noon; call Joe Roddy (✆ **066/ 947-4268**) or Sean Feehan (✆ **066/947-9182**) to make a reservation. Ferries departing from Portmagee are run by Murphy's (✆ **066/947-7156**). Depending on the boat the cost ranges from 32€ to 44€ ($29 to $40) per person. Reservations should be made two days in advance to assure a place, and to confirm weather conditions: boats are frequently unable to sail due to rough seas.

SIGHTS ON THE IVERAGH PENINSULA

Derrynane House National Historic Park This 320-acre site along the Ring of Kerry coast (between Waterville and Caherdaniel) is where one of Ireland's most renowned political figures lived for most of his life. The house of Daniel O'Connell (popularly known as "the Liberator" because of his advocacy for Irish Catholics under British rule) is maintained as a museum by Ireland's Office of Public Works. It's filled with all kinds of documents, illustrations, and memorabilia related to O'Connell's life. Visitors can also watch a 25-minute audiovisual about the great leader entitled *Be You Perfectly Peaceable.*

Caherdaniel, Co. Kerry. ✆ **066/947-5113.** Fax 066/947-5432. Admission 2.60€ ($2.40) adults, 1.90€ ($1.75) seniors, 1.25€ ($1.15) students and children, 6.50€ ($5.90) family. May–Sept Mon–Sat 9am–5:15pm, Sun 11am–6:15pm; Nov–Mar Sat–Sun 1–4:15pm; Apr and Oct Tues–Sun 1–4:15pm.

Kenmare Heritage Centre To learn more about the delightful town of Kenmare step inside this new visitor center, where exhibits recount Kenmare's history as a planned estate town that grew up around the mine works founded in 1670 by Sir William Petty, ancestor of the Landsdownes, the local landlords. The center also displays locally made Kenmare lace, and tells the story of the woman who originated the craft. A free map is provided for a walking trail around the town; an audio guide with headset is also available for the tour. Walking time is about 40 minutes.

The Square, Kenmare, Co. Kerry. ✆ **064/41233.** Admission 2.60€ ($2.40) adults, 1.90€ ($1.75) students and seniors, 1.25€ ($1.15) children, 6.50€ ($5.90) family. Mon–Sat 9:15am–6:30pm; Sun 10am–1pm and 2:15–5:30pm. Closed Oct–Mar.

Kerry Bog Village Museum This little cluster of thatched-roof cottages shows what life was like in Kerry in the early 1800s. This museum village has a

---

Impressions

I walked up this morning along the slope from the east to the top of Sybil Head, where one comes out suddenly on the brow of a cliff with a straight fall of many hundreds of feet into the sea. It is a place of indescribable grandeur, where one can see Carrantuohill and the Skelligs and Loop Head and the full sweep of the Atlantic, and over all, the wonderfully tender and searching light that is seen only in Kerry. One wonders in these places why there is anyone left in Dublin, or London, or Paris, when it would be better, one would think, to live in a tent or hut with this magnificent sea and sky, and to breathe this wonderful air, which is like wine in one's teeth.

—John Millington Synge (1871–1909), Irish playwright

---

blacksmith's forge and house, a turf cutter's house, a laborer's cottage, a thatcher's dwelling, a tradesman's house, and a stable and dairy house. Stacks of newly cut turf sit piled high beside the road. There's also a football pitch and other recreational facilities. The interiors are furnished with authentic pieces gathered from all parts of Kerry.

Ring of Kerry road (N71), Ballycleave, Glenbeigh, Co. Kerry. © 066/976-9184. Fax 066/976-9477. Admission 3.80€ ($3.45) adults, 3.15€ ($2.90) students and seniors. Mar–Oct daily 8:30am–6pm.

The Skellig Experience   Situated 7 miles (11km) off the mainland Ring of Kerry route (via R765) on Valentia Island, this new attraction blends right in with the terrain, with a stark stone facade framed by grassy mounds. Inside, through a series of displays and audiovisuals, the center presents the story of Skellig Michael and Little Skellig, along with a detailed look at birds and plant life of the Valentia area. A cafeteria offers light meals. A sea cruise circuiting the Skellig Islands is also offered, but you should note that this cruise does not allow you to visit Skellig Michael's monastic ruins.

Valentia Island, Co. Kerry. © 066/947-6306. Fax 066/947-6351. www.skelligexperience.com Exhibition and audiovisual 4.50€ ($4.10) adults, 3.80€ ($3.45) students and seniors, 2.20€ ($2) children under 12, 10€ ($9) family (2 adults and up to 4 children); exhibition, audiovisual, and sea cruise 22€ ($20) adults, 19€ ($18) students and seniors, 11€ ($10) children, 57€ ($52) family. AE, MC, V. Apr–Sept daily 10am–7pm; Oct to mid-Nov Sun–Thurs 10am–5:30pm.

A SIGHTSEEING CRUISE

Seafari Scenic & Wildlife Cruises   See the sights of Kenmare Bay on board this 50-foot (15m) covered boat. The 2-hour cruises cover 10 miles (16km) and are narrated by well-versed guides who provide information on local history, geography, and geology. The guides often point out sea otters, gray seals, herons, oyster catchers, and kingfishers. Boats depart from the pier next to the Kenmare suspension bridge. Reservations are recommended.

Kenmare Pier, Kenmare, Co. Kerry. ©/fax 064/83171. 13€ ($12) adults, 10€ ($9.10) students and seniors, 6.50€ ($5.90) children, 32€ ($29) family. May–Sept daily every 2 hr. between sunrise and sunset.

OUTDOOR PURSUITS

WALKING   Ireland's longest low-level, long-distance path, the **Kerry Way,** traverses the Ring of Kerry. The first stage from Killarney National Park to Glenbeigh is inland through wide and scenic countryside, while the second stage provides a circuit of the Iveragh Peninsula, linking Cahirciveen, Waterville, Caherdaniel, Sneem, and Kenmare. A third inland stage along the old Kenmare

Road back to Killarney makes a total of 125 miles (201km). The route consists primarily of paths and "green" (unsurfaced) roads, such as old driving paths, butter roads, and routes between early Christian settlements. A leaflet outlining the route is available from the Killarney or Kenmare tourist office.

GOLF   The Iveragh Peninsula's most renowned course, **Waterville Golf Links,** Waterville (© **064/947-4102;** www.watgervillegolf.com), is hardly a budget option with its 130€ ($118) greens fees. Some of the region's other 18-hole courses are more reasonable, such as **Dooks Golf Club,** Glenbeigh (© **066/976-8205;** www.dooks.com), a seaside par-70 course on the Ring of Kerry road, with greens fees of 40€ ($36); and the newly expanded **Kenmare Golf Club,** Kenmare (© **064/41291;** kenmaregolfclub@eircom.net), a parkland par-71 course with greens fees from 25€ ($23) weekdays, 32€ ($29) Saturdays, and 38€ ($35) Sundays.

ACCOMMODATIONS YOU CAN AFFORD
GLENBEIGH
Ocean Wave   This attractive modern home sits on beautifully landscaped grounds on the high side of the Ring of Kerry road, with sweeping views out over Dingle Bay. Noreen O'Toole has won much praise for her breakfast menu as well as for her warm, friendly interest in her guests. One of the six rooms is a triple. If you prefer a sea view, ask for a front room—the view from those in back is one of mountains and green fields. A spacious upstairs lounge has wide windows that take full advantage of the gorgeous Dingle Bay view, and there's an 18-hole golf course just across the road.

Ring of Kerry road (N70), Glenbeigh, Co. Kerry. © **066/976-8249.** Fax 066/976-8412. oceanwave@iol.ie. 6 units. 40€ ($36) single; 64€ ($58) double. Rates include full breakfast. MC, V. Closed Nov–Feb. *In room:* TV.

KILLORGLIN
Hillcrest *Value*   The slightest of jogs off the Ring of Kerry road will land you at this quite comfortable haven, set well back from the road. The rooms of this Georgian-style bungalow are spacious and cheerful, with pastel walls offset by bright contemporary floral fabrics, painted white furniture, and dark-stained window frames. All rooms have firm beds; the front rooms enjoy views of the nearby hills. This is a clean, quiet, pleasant bargain that won't disappoint.

Killarney Road, Killorglin, Co. Kerry. © **066/976-1552.** Fax 066/976-1996. 5 units. 46€ ($41) double. Rates include full breakfast and service charge. MC, V. Closed Jan–Mar. ½ mi (1km) outside of Killorglin town. *In room:* TV, TEL, tea/coffeemaker, hair dryer.

WATERVILLE
Klondyke House   Cirean Morris is the hospitable proprietor of this attractive home overlooking Waterville's famous championship golf course on the outskirts of the village. The decor throughout is bright and cheerful and the beds in the clean and comfortable guest rooms have orthopedic mattresses. There's a spacious TV lounge and a drying room for guests, and golfing and fishing trips can be arranged.

New Line Rd., Waterville, Co. Kerry. © **066/947-4119.** Fax 066/947-4666. http://homepage.eircom. net/~klondykehouse. 6 units, 5 with bathroom (shower only). 32€ ($29) single; 48€ ($43) double. Rates include full breakfast. MC, V. Closed Nov–Mar. *In room:* TV, TEL, tea/coffeemaker; hair dryer.

SNEEM
Avonlea House   Mrs. Maura Hussey's two-story home is located just on the outskirts of town (signposted in town). The food is excellent, and there's a turf fire blazing in the residents' lounge most nights.

Sportsfield Rd., Sneem, Co. Kerry. ✆ 064/45221. avonleahouse@eircom.net. 5 units. 46€ ($42) double. Rates include full breakfast. Dinner 20€ ($18). No credit cards. Closed Dec–Feb. *In room:* Hair dryer, iron.

Bank House   Margaret and Noel Harrington welcome guests with a warmth that's exceptional, even for the Irish. Guest rooms are light and airy. Margaret excels in home baking and serves delicious snacks. And the location, in the village of Sneem, is good browsing and shopping territory.

North Sq., Sneem, Co. Kerry. ✆ 064/45226. 6 units, 5 with bathroom. 31€ ($28) single; 51€ ($46) double. AE, MC, V. Closed Dec–Feb.

KENMARE

Ardmore House *(Kids)*   A modern one-story bungalow, framed by a colorful rose garden, is located on the outskirts of Kenmare, in a quiet cul-de-sac just off the main Kenmare–Ring of Kerry road. Rooms in the front look out onto the roses, and the back view is of peaceful green pastures and mountains. There's one four-bed family room available. The house is about a 5-minute walk to the town center.

Killarney Rd., Kenmare, Co. Kerry. ✆/fax **064/41406**. 6 units. 36€ ($32) single; 56€ ($51) double. 50% reduction for children. Rates include full breakfast. MC, V. Closed Dec–Feb. *In room:* TV, tea/coffeemaker, hair dryer.

Marino House   Marino House occupies a scenic site 2 miles (3km) from the town center on a small, wooded finger of land extending out into Kenmare Bay. There's an old-fashioned air about the place, yet total modern comfort inside— an irresistible combination. Run by Mrs. Edna O'Sullivan and her family, Marino House features comfortable guest rooms and excellent meals, which are served in a dining room overlooking the green lawn. Much patronized by regulars, this place gets booked quickly from year to year, so it's best to reserve as far in advance as possible.

Reen, Kenmare, Co. Kerry. ✆ **064/41154**. Fax 064/41501. 6 units, 1 with bathroom (shower only). 24€ ($22) single; 43€ ($39) double without bathroom, 48€ ($44) double with bathroom. 20% reduction for children. Rates include full breakfast. V. Closed Oct–Apr. *In room:* Tea/coffeemaker.

KILGARVAN

Sillerdane Lodge *(Value)*   Sillerdane Lodge offers a most unusual feature for an Irish B&B: a heated outdoor swimming pool! This pretty bungalow, set in a beautiful valley, has more than just that to offer, however. Perhaps its most appealing feature is the gracious Mrs. Joan McCarthy. This lovely lady takes a personal interest in all her guests, and her home reflects her concern for their comfort. The bright dining room has huge windows to take advantage of gorgeous views, and bedrooms are beautifully decorated and spotless.

Coolnoohill, Kilgarvan, Co. Kerry. ✆ **064/85359**. 5 units, 4 with bathroom (shower only). 25€ ($23) single without bathroom, 31€ ($28) single with bathroom; 43€ ($39) double without bathroom, 51€ ($46) double with bathroom. 25% reduction for children. Rates include full breakfast. Dinner 19€ ($17). No credit cards. Closed Oct–Easter. 13 miles (21km) east of Kenmare via R569. **Amenities:** Heated pool. *In room:* Tea/coffeemaker.

GREAT DEALS ON DINING
VALENTIA ISLAND

The Ring Lyne BAR FOOD/SEAFOOD   The bar food here is good and often features local seafood, but it's in the Sceilig Room that the food really excels—scallops, scampi, plaice, and salmon are prepared in the traditional manner, with few frills to obscure the fresh, subtle flavor of each. Steak, lamb, and chicken dishes are also excellent, as are the homemade desserts (don't miss the apple pie and thick cream). There's also an attached guesthouse providing both B&B and hostel accommodations for 51€ ($46) double at the B&B and 13€ ($12) per person in the hostel.

Chapeltown, Valentia Island, Co. Kerry. ℂ 066/947-6103. Bar food under 10€ ($9); fixed-price lunch 9€ ($8); fixed-price dinner 22€ ($20). No credit cards. Daily 12:30–9pm.

WATERVILLE

The Huntsman ⊛ SEAFOOD/INTERNATIONAL It's worth a trip to Waterville just to dine at this contemporary restaurant on the shores of Ballinskelligs Bay. Owner-chef Raymond Hunt takes the time to circulate and chat with diners, offering suggestions on the extensive menu, which uses only the freshest local catch and produce. Skellig lobster fresh from the tank and Kenmare Bay scampi are among the seafood dishes; meat dishes include rack of lamb, seasonal pheasant, rabbit, venison, and Irish stew.

The Strand, Waterville, Co. Kerry. ℂ 066/947-4124. Reservations recommended. Lunch/bar food items from 5.10€ ($4.60); dinner main courses 18€–28€ ($16–$25); fixed-price dinner 33€ ($30). AE, DC, MC, V. Mar–Nov daily 10am–10pm; Nov–Feb call for opening times.

Red Fox Inn IRISH Situated adjacent to the Kerry Bog Museum, this restaurant has an old Kerry cottage atmosphere, with open turf fireplaces, family heirloom pictures on the walls, and local memorabilia. There are picnic tables outside for good-weather dining. The menu includes hearty traditional dishes such as Irish stew, seafood pie, chicken and ham, leg of lamb, and steaks. In the summer (May–Sept), there is Irish ceili band entertainment on Saturday from 9:30 to 11:30pm (and sometimes other days as well). Snacks are served all day in the bar.

Ring of Kerry road (N71), Ballycleave, Glenbeigh, Co. Kerry. ℂ 066/976-9184. Reservations recommended for dinner. Soups 3.15€ ($2.90); main courses 7.60€–19€ ($6.90–$19). AE, DC, MC, V. Daily noon–9:30pm. Closed Sept–Apr.

The Smugglers Inn ⊛ *Finds* SEAFOOD This waterside restaurant is widely known for its seafood creations; there's even a tank from which lobster and crayfish are taken alive. Although there are lovely non-fish dishes on the menu, most diners opt for seafood, and with filet of plaice Provençal, monkfish sauté with garlic butter, grilled Waterville Lake salmon with béarnaise sauce, and a score of other delicacies, who could blame them? Even the snack menu here is outstanding and includes many of the specialties from the a la carte menu. A vegetarian entree is always available for dinner.

Cliff Rd., Waterville. ℂ 066/947-4330. Snacks 2.50€–17€ ($2.25–$15); main courses 15€–24€ ($14–$22); fixed-price lunch 20€ ($18); fixed-price dinner 35€ ($32); fixed-price vegetarian dinner 20€ ($18). AE, DC, MC, V. Daily 8:30am–10pm. Closed Nov–Mar.

KENMARE

Packie's ⊛ IRISH If you're looking for a stylish place to have a great meal that won't break the bank, this little place is it. With window boxes full of colorful seasonal plantings, this informal, bistro-style restaurant in the middle of town exudes a welcoming atmosphere. The interior has a slate floor, stone walls, and dark oak tables and chairs. On the walls is a collection of wonderful contemporary Irish art, and on the menu are tried-and-true favorites: Irish stew and rack of lamb. Also offered are creative combinations, such as gratin of crab and prawns, beef braised in Guinness with mushrooms, and blackboard fish specials. Chef-owner Maura Foley uses herbs from her own garden to enhance each dish.

Henry St., Kenmare, County Kerry. ℂ 064/41508. Reservations recommended. Main courses 11€–25€ ($10–$23). MC, V. Tues–Sat 5:30–10pm. Closed mid-Nov to Easter.

The Purple Heather ⭐ *Finds* IRISH   This spot is *the* place to lunch in Kenmare. Excellent bistro food is served in a setting best described as eccentric. The walls and ceiling are decorated with objects of wood and copper, with hanging wine bottles and an assortment of other items. Lunch specialties include excellent omelets as well as salads and smoked salmon and mackerel, the latter two served with fresh brown bread, and wonderful crab or prawn open sandwiches. The O'Connell family has been running the place since 1964.

Henry St., Kenmare, Co. Kerry. ℂ 064/41016. Cold and hot plates 4€–17€ ($3.60–$15). No credit cards. Mon–Sat 10:45am–7pm.

SHOPPING

Many good craft and souvenir shops are found along the Ring of Kerry, but those in **Kenmare** offer the most in terms of variety and quality. Kenmare shops are open year-round, usually Monday to Saturday from 9am to 6pm. From May to September many shops remain open until 9pm or 10pm, and some open on Sunday from noon to 5 or 6pm.

Avoca Handweavers at Moll's Gap   Located in one of the most scenic of settings, this shop is on a high mountain pass (960 ft./293m above sea level) between Killarney and Kenmare. It's a branch of the famous tweed makers of Avoca, County Wicklow, dating from 1723. The wares range from colorful handwoven capes, jackets, throws, and knitwear to pottery and jewelry. There's an excellent coffee shop on the premises, staffed by chefs trained at the Ballymaloe Cookery School. Open mid-March to October daily from 9am to 6pm.

Ring of Kerry road (N71), Moll's Gap, Co. Kerry. ℂ 064/34720. www.avoca.ie.

Cleo   A branch of the long-established Dublin store of the same name, this trendy clothing shop is known for its colorful tweed and linen fashions, as well as specialty items like Kinsale cloaks. You'll find old reliables such as Donegal Tweed, as well as the work of current Irish designers in materials like baby alpaca, silk, cashmere, and merino. The shop is currently extending its floor space, promising an expansion of its already extensive stock. 2 Shelbourne Rd., Kenmare. ℂ 064/41410.

Kenmare Book Shop   This shop specializes in Irish-themed books, particularly Irish biographies and books by Irish writers, as well as guides and maps about the local area. Shelbourne St., Kenmare, Co. Kerry. ℂ 064/41578.

Nostalgia   In a town known for its lace, it's a natural to stop into this shop and view the new and antique lace, table and bed linens, traditional teddy bears, and accessories. Closed January to mid-March. 27 Henry St., Kenmare, Co. Kerry. ℂ 064/41389. nostalgia@eircom.net.

Quills Woollen Market   This is a branch of the store of the same name in Killarney, known for Aran hand knits, Donegal tweed jackets, Irish linen, Celtic jewelry, and colorful hand-loomed knitwear. Market Sq. and Main St., Kenmare, Co. Kerry. ℂ 064/41078.

2 Killarney & Its Lakes

Killarney is 84 miles (135km) SW of Shannon, 192 miles (309km) SW of Dublin, 54 miles (87km) W of Cork, 69 miles (111km) SW of Limerick, and 120 miles (193km) SW of Galway

Killarney is the Grand Central Station of tourism in the southwest. If you've never seen a traffic jam of battling tour buses or been besieged by a bevy of pushy horse-drawn-car drivers, this is the place to seek out such curious spectacles. If

Killarney

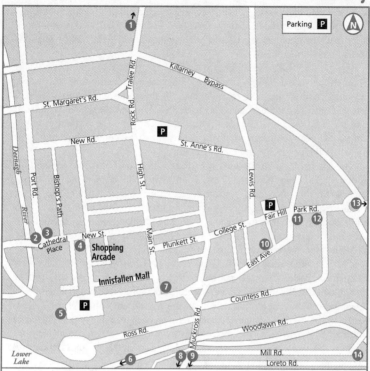

Bus Station **11**

Crag Cave **1**

Kennedy's Animal,
   Bird and Pet Farm **13**

Killarney Manor **14**

Killarney National Park **8**

Knockreer Estate **2**

Muckross Friary **9**

Muckross House, Gardens
   and Farms **9**

Museum of IrishTransport **10**

Post Office **4**

Railway Station **12**

Ross Castle **6**

St. Mary's Cathedral **3**

St. Mary's Church **7**

Tourist Office **5**

that's not your bag, however, it's easy enough to resist Killarney's gravitational pull and explore instead the incredibly scenic hinterlands that border the town on all sides, perhaps sneaking into town at some point to sample the best of what this tourist megalopolis has to offer.

The lakes are Killarney's main attraction. The first of these, the Lower Lake, is sometimes called "Lough Leane" or "Lough Lein," which means "the lake of learning." It's the largest, more than 4 miles (6.5km) long, and is dotted with 30 small islands. The second lake is aptly called the Middle Lake or Muckross Lake, and the third simply Upper Lake. The last, which is also the smallest, is full of storybook islands covered with a variety of trees—evergreens, cedars of Lebanon, juniper, holly, and mountain ash.

The lakes and the surrounding woodlands are all part of the 25-square-mile (64km^2) **Killarney National Park.** Found within its borders are two major estates, the Muckross and Knockreer demesnes, and the remains of major medieval abbeys and castles. Blossoming in season is a profusion of foliage such as rhododendrons, azaleas, magnolias, camellias, hydrangeas, and tropical ferns. At almost every turn, you'll see Killarney's own botanical wonder, the arbutus, or strawberry tree, plus eucalyptus, redwoods, and native oak.

The most noteworthy of Killarney's islands is **Innisfallen,** which sits peacefully in the Lower Lake and can be reached by rowboat, available for rental at Ross Castle. St. Fallen founded a monastery here in the 7th century, and it flourished for 1,000 years. It's said that Brian Boru, the great Irish chieftain, and St. Brendan the Navigator were educated here. From 950 to 1320, the "Annals of Innisfallen," a chronicle of early Irish history, was written at the monastery; it's now in the Bodlein Library at Oxford University. Traces of an 11th-century church and a 12th-century priory can still be seen today.

GETTING THERE **Aer Arann** (© **890/462726** within Ireland, or **01/814-1058**) offers daily direct flights from Dublin into Kerry County Airport, Farranfore, County Kerry (© **066/976-4644**), about 10 miles (16km) north of Killarney. **Aer Lingus** offers flights from Dublin into Kerry County Airport, Farranfore, County Kerry (© **066/976-4644**), about 10 miles (16km) north of Killarney. **Ryanair** flies direct from London (Stansted) to Kerry, and Manx Airlines flies to Kerry from Luton and Manchester.

Irish Rail trains from Dublin, Limerick, Cork, and Galway arrive daily at the **Killarney Railway Station** (© **064/31067;** www.irishrail.ie), Railway Road, off East Avenue Road.

Bus Eireann operates regularly scheduled service into Killarney from all parts of Ireland. The bus depot (© **064/34777;** www.buseireann.ie) is adjacent to the train station at Railway Road, off East Avenue Road.

Kerry folk like to say that all roads lead to Killarney, and at least a half dozen major national roads do. They include N21 and N23 from Limerick, N22 from Tralee, N22 from Cork, N72 from Mallow, and N70 from the Ring of Kerry and West Cork.

VISITOR INFORMATION The **Killarney Tourist Office,** Aras Fáilte, is located at the Town Centre Car Park, Beech Road, Killarney (© **064/31633**). It's open January to April, Monday to Saturday 9:15am to 1pm and 2:15 to 5:30pm; May, Monday to Saturday 9:15am to 5:30pm; June, Monday to Saturday 9am to 6pm, Sunday 10am to 1pm and 2:15 to 6pm; July to August, Monday to Saturday 9am to 8pm, Sunday 10am to 1pm and 2:15 to 6pm; September, Monday to Saturday 9am to 6pm, Sunday 10am to 1pm and 2:15 to 6pm; October to December, Monday to Saturday 9:15am to 1pm and 2:15

Tips Get Outta Town!

It's important to remember that the reason Killarney draws millions of visitors a year has nothing to do with Killarney town. Rather, it's all about the lakes and mountains of enchanting beauty just beyond the town's reach; and it's ever so easy to approach these wonders. Just walk from the town car park toward the cathedral and turn left into the National Park. In a matter of minutes, you'll see for yourself why there's all the fuss. During the summer, the evenings are long, the light is often indescribable, and you needn't share the lanes with jaunting carts. Apart from deer and locals, the park is all yours until dark.

---

to 5:30pm. It offers many helpful booklets, including the *Tourist Trail* walking-tour guide and the *Killarney Area Guide,* with maps.

Useful local publications include *Where: Killarney* (www.wherekillarney.com) a quarterly magazine distributed free at hotels and guesthouses. It is packed with current information on tours, activities, events, and entertainment.

TOWN LAYOUT   Killarney is small, with a year-round population of approximately 7,000. The town is built around one central thoroughfare, Main Street, which changes its name to High Street at midpoint. The principal offshoots of Main Street are Plunkett Street, which becomes College Street, and New Street, which, as its name implies, is still growing. The Deenagh River edges the western side of town, and East Avenue Road rims the eastern side. It's all very walkable in an hour or two.

The busiest section of town is at the southern tip of Main Street, where it meets East Avenue Road. Here the road curves and heads southward out to the Muckross road and the entrance to the Killarney National Park.

GETTING AROUND   Killarney town is so small and compact that there is no local bus service; the best way to get around is on foot.

By Taxi   Taxicabs line up at the rank on **College Square** (© 064/31331). You can also phone for a taxi from **Eurotaxis** (© 064/43255), **Dero's Taxi Service** (© 064/31251), **Eddie Williams** (© 064/36395), or **Con Moynihan** (© 064/43255).

By Car   In Killarney town, it's best to park your car and walk. Most hotels and guesthouses offer free parking to their guests. If you must park on the street for any reason, you need to buy a parking disc and display it on your car; parking costs .65€ (60¢) per hour and discs can be purchased at hotels or shops. A car is necessary to drive from town on the Muckross and Kenmare road (N71) to get to Killarney National Park.

If you need to rent a car in Killarney, contact **Avis,** Kerry County Airport, Farranfore (© **066/976-4499;** www.avis.com); **Budget,** c/o International Hotel (© **064/34341;** www.budget.com); **Hertz,** 28 Plunkett St. (© **064/34126;** www.hertz.com).

By Jaunting Car   Horse-drawn jaunting cars (a light, two-wheeled vehicle) line up at Kenmare Place in Killarney town, offering rides to Killarney National Park sites and other scenic areas. Depending on the time and distance required prices range from 15€ to 41€ ($14–$37) per ride per person, based on four passengers participating. (For more details, see "Sightseeing Tours," later in this chapter.)

FAST FACTS: **Killarney**

Drugstores Try **O'Sullivans Pharmacy,** at 81 New St., Killarney (℗ **064/ 35866**), or **Donal Sheahan,** at 34 Main St., Killarney (℗ **064/31113**).

Emergencies Dial ℗ **999.**

Hospital **Killarney District Hospital** is located on St. Margaret's Road, Killarney (℗ **064/31076**).

Internet Access Internet access (via super fast ISDN lines) along with tea, coffee, and pastries, are available at **Café Internet,** 18 Lower New St., Killarney (℗ **064/36741;** www.cafe-internet.net). Facilities include scanners, color printers, and quik-cams. Internet fees run 3.80€ ($3.45) for 30 minutes and 6.50€ ($5.90) per hour. Open daily 9:30am to 11pm.

Laundry & Dry Cleaning Head to **Gleeson Launderette,** Brewery Lane, off College Square, Killarney (℗ **064/33877**).

Library The **Killarney Public Library** is located on Rock Road, Killarney (℗ **064/32972**).

Local Publications & Radio Local weekly newspapers include *The Kerryman* and *The Killarney Advertiser. Where: Killarney,* a quarterly magazine, is chockful of helpful, up-to-date information for visitors; it is distributed free at hotels and guesthouses. The local radio station is Radio Kerry, 97 FM.

Photographic Needs Try **Eugene Ferris Photography,** at 105 New St., Killarney (℗ **064/36118**), or **Killarney Photographic Centre,** 69 New St., Killarney (℗ **064/31225**).

Police The **Killarney Garda Station** is on New Road, Killarney (℗ **064/ 31222**).

Post Office The **Killarney Post Office,** New Street, Killarney (℗ **064/31051**), is open Monday through Saturday from 9am to 5:30pm, and Tuesday from 9:30am to 5:30pm.

Shoe Repairs Try **The Cobbler,** Innisfallen Shopping Mall, Killarney (no phone), or **M.K. O'Sullivan,** St. Anne's Road, Killarney (℗ **064/31825**).

SEEING THE SIGHTS

To see the best of Killarney Town, follow the signposted "Tourist Trail," encompassing the highlights of the main streets and attractions. It takes about 2 hours to complete the walk. A booklet outlining the trail is available at the tourist office.

Killarney National Park ★★★ This is Killarney's centerpiece: a 25,000-acre area of natural beauty including three storied lakes, myriad waterfalls, rivers, islands, valleys, mountains, bogs, and woodlands, and lush foliage and trees. Add in the large variety of wildlife, including a rare herd of red deer, and you have the total Killarney outdoor experience. No automobiles are allowed within the park, so touring is best done on foot, on bicycle, or by horse-drawn jaunting car. The park offers four signposted walking and nature trails along the lakeshore. Access is available from several points along the Kenmare road (N71), with the main entrance at Muckross House, home to a new visitor center featuring background exhibits on the park.

Kenmare road (N71), Killarney. ℗ **064/31440.** Fax 064/33926. Free admission. Year-round daylight hours.

Knockreer Estate   Lovely views of the Lower Lake can be enjoyed in this setting, a part of the National Park grounds most recently opened to the public (1986). Once the home of Lord Kenmare, the estate has a turn-of-the-century house, a pathway along the River Deenagh, and gardens mixing 200-year-old trees with flowering cherries, magnolias, and azaleas. The house, not open to the public, is now a field study center for the National Park. Main access to Knockreer is via Deenagh Lodge Gate, opposite the cathedral, in town.

Cathedral Place, off New St., Killarney. © 064/31440. Free admission to gardens. Daily daylight hours.

Muckross Friary   This gem of a ruin near the banks of Lough Leane is a delight to explore and a good place to get away from the crowds at Muckross House (see below), a short walk away. Numerous spiral staircases lead to the upper levels, where the adventuresome can walk the ramparts or survey some great views of the lakes. The exquisite cloisters are a peaceful retreat, shaded by the massive form of an ancient tree whose branches soar out over the friary roof. The Friary was the last resting place for Kerry's four great Gaelic poets: Piaras Feirtéar (Pierce Ferriter, 1616–53) is buried in the churchyard, and inside the Abbey are the remains of Geoffrey O'Donoghue (1620–90), Aodhgan O'Rahilly (1670–1726), and Eoghan Ruadh O'Sullivan (1748–84). The tomb of The McCarthy Mór, king of Munster, is in the chancel.

Kenmare road (N71), Killarney. Free admission. Year-round daylight hours.

Muckross House & Gardens 🐾🐾   The focal point of the Middle Lake is the Muckross Estate, often called "the jewel of Killarney." It consists of a gracious ivy-covered Victorian mansion and its elegant surrounding gardens. Dating back to 1843, the 20-room Muckross House has been converted into a museum of County Kerry folklife, showcasing locally carved furniture, prints, maps, paintings, and needlework. Imported treasures such as Oriental screens, Venetian mirrors, Chippendale chairs, Turkish carpets, and curtains woven in Brussels are also displayed. The house's cellars have been converted into craft shops where local artisans demonstrate traditional trades such as bookbinding, weaving, and pottery. The adjacent gardens, known for their fine rhododendrons and azaleas, are also worth exploring.

Kenmare road (N71), Killarney. © 061/31440. www.muckross-house.ie. Admission 5€ ($4.55) adults, 3.80€ ($3.45) seniors, 2€ ($1.80) students and children, 12.70€ ($12) family. Combination ticket covering both Muckross Traditional Farms and Muckross House also available. Daily mid-Mar to June and Sept–Oct 9am–5:30pm; July–Aug 9am–6pm; Nov to mid-Mar 9am–5:30pm. Closed during Christmas holidays.

Muckross Traditional Farms 🐾 *Kids*   This 70-acre park near the Muckross House estate is home to authentically detailed displays of traditional farm life and artisans' shops. The animals and household environments are equally fascinating for children and adults, making for a great family exploration. Visitors can watch sowing and harvesting or potato picking and hay making, depending on the season. Farmhands work in the fields and tend the animals, while the blacksmith, carpenter, and wheelwright ply their trades in the old manner. Women draw water from the wells and cook meals in traditional kitchens with authentic utensils, crockery, and household items. *Note:* The combination ticket allows you to visit Muckross House for less than 2.50€ ($2.45) extra per person.

Kenmare road (N71), Killarney. © 064/31440. www.muckross-house.ie. Admission 5€ ($4.55) adults, 3.80€ ($3.45) seniors, 2€ ($1.80) students and children, 12.70€ ($12) family. Combination ticket covering both Muckross Traditional Farms and Muckross House 7.50€ ($6.80) adults, 5.50€ ($5.00) seniors, 3€ ($2.70) students and children, 19€ ($17) family. May daily 1–6pm; June–Sept daily 10am–7pm; mid-Mar to Apr and Oct Sat–Sun 1–6pm.

Ross Castle   This 15th-century fortress sits on the edge of the Lower Lake, about 1½ miles (2.5km) outside of Killarney town; the walk from town along the lake is highly recommended. Built by the O'Donoghue chieftains, this castle distinguished itself in 1652 as the last stronghold in Munster to surrender to Cromwell's forces. All that remains today is a tower house, surrounded by a fortified bawn with rounded turrets. The tower has been furnished in the style of the late 16th and early 17th centuries and offers a magnificent view of the lakes and islands from its top. Access is by guided tour only.

Ross Rd., off Kenmare road (N71), Killarney. ℂ 064/35851. Admission 3.80€ ($3.45) adults, 2.50€ ($2.30) seniors, 1.60€ ($1.45) students and children, 9.50€ ($8.60) family. Apr daily 10am–5pm; May daily 10am–6pm; June–Aug daily 9am–6:30pm; Sept daily 10am–6pm; Oct Tues–Sun 10am–5pm. Last admission 45 min. before closing.

THE GAP OF DUNLOE ⭐

In an area renowned for its scenic wonders, this is one of the most remarkable places for rugged beauty. The Gap is a narrow defile between high ridges, whose craggy slopes rise abruptly from the valley floor. Groves of trees and a series of lakes lining the valley soften the barrenness of the landscape. More road than path, the route through the Gap is paved much of the way, and well traveled by walkers, cyclists, and droves of horse-drawn carts. The usual starting point for a visit to the Gap is its northern end; the access road is signposted just west of Fossa on N72, about 5 miles (8km) out of Killarney. An excellent way to go is by bicycle: the 25- or 40-mile (40- or 64km) loop from Killarney through the Gap is a beautiful ride, which can be shortened with a boat trip to 15 miles (24km) or so (see "Outdoor Pursuits," below). If you want to walk I recommend driving to the southern end of the Gap, a little harder to find but much less crowded, and the drive in is as scenic as the Gap itself; you can also take a tour that drops you off at Kate Kearney's cottage and brings you back to Killarney by boat from the southern end of the gap (about 19€/$17), offered by **Gap of Dunloe Tours** (ℂ 064/30200). Horse fanciers may want to take one of the horseback excursions offered by **Gap of Dunloe Tours,** 7 High St. (ℂ 064/30200); **Corcoran's Tours,** Kilcummin (ℂ 064/36666; www.kerry-insight.com/corcorans); and **Dero's Tours,** 22 Main St. (ℂ 064/31251 or 064/31567; www.derostours.com). A tour on horseback, including coach to the gap and return by boat on the lake costs about 44€ ($40). If you'd rather have someone else handle the horse, consider taking a 7-mile jaunting car tour (see "Jaunting-Car Tours," below) from Kate Kearney's cottage through the Gap of Dunloe to Lord Brandon's Cottage and back—the cost for this tour is about 35€ ($32) per person, including the bus to Kate Kearney's cottage and a boat trip from the southern end of the Gap to Ross Castle.

MORE SIGHTS TO SEE

Crag Cave   Believed to be more than a million years old, these limestone caves were discovered and first explored in 1983. Guides accompany you 12,510 feet (4km) into the passage on a well-lit tour, revealing some of the largest stalactites in Europe. Exhibits, a crafts shop, and a restaurant are on the premises.

Off Limerick road (N21), Castleisland, Co. Kerry. ℂ 066/41244. www.cragcave.com. Admission 5€ ($4.55) adults, 3.80€ ($3.45) students and seniors, 3.15€ ($2.90) children over 6, 15€ ($14) family. Mar–Oct daily 10am–5:30pm (6pm July–Aug). 15 miles (24km) north of Killarney.

Kennedy's Animal, Bird and Pet Farm *Kids*   At this 75-acre dairy and sheep farm surrounded by mountain vistas, you'll see cows being milked, piglets being fed, and peacocks strutting their stuff. Horse-drawn machinery is also on display. For those who can't pull themselves away, five three-bedroom holiday homes and town houses have been added, for 340€ to 724€ ($300 to $638) per week, depending on the season.

Brewsterfield, Glenflesk, Killarney. ℂ 064/54054. www.kennedys.rural-bixnet.com. Admission 5€ ($4.55). Daily 10am–7pm. Closed Dec–Jan. 6 miles (9.5km) east of Killarney, off the main Cork road (N22).

Museum of Irish Transport   This museum presents a unique collection of vintage and classic cars, motorcycles, bicycles, carriages, and fire engines, including an 1825 hobby horse bicycle; a 1907 Silver Stream (the only model ever built); a 1904 Germain, one of four remaining in the world; a 1910 Wolseley Siddeley, once driven by the poet William Butler Yeats (the museum has the world's largest collection of Wolseleys); and an example of the ill-fated DeLorean, a futuristic, stainless-steel car that was manufactured over its short life at a plant in Ireland. Lining the walls are early motoring and cycling periodicals and license plates from all over the world.

College St., Killarney. ℂ 064/32638. Admission 3.80€ ($3.45) adults, 2.60€ ($2.40) students and seniors, 1.25€ ($1.15) children, 10€.($9.10) family. Apr–Oct daily 10am–6pm; other times by appointment.

St. Mary's Cathedral   Officially known as the Catholic Church of St. Mary of the Assumption, this limestone cathedral is the town's most impressive building. Designed in the Gothic Revival style by Augustus Pugin, it's cruciform in shape. Construction began in 1842, was interrupted by the famine years, and concluded in 1855. The magnificent central spire was added in 1912. The entire edifice was extensively renovated from 1972 to 1973. It's at the edge of town, on the far end of New Street.

Cathedral Place, off Port Rd., Killarney. ℂ 064/31014. Free admission; donations welcome. Daily 10:30am–6pm.

St. Mary's Church   It's commonly believed that St. Mary's, an 1870 neo-Gothic church, stands on the site of the original "Church of the Sloe Woods" (in Irish called *Cill Airne*—which was anglicized to "Killarney"). It's located in the heart of town, across from the tourist office.

Church Place, Killarney. ℂ 064/31832. Free admission; donations welcome. Year-round 9:30am–5pm.

SIGHTSEEING TOURS
BUS TOURS
In addition to the tours below, which concentrate on Killarney's main sights, some bus tours also venture into the two prime scenic areas nearby, the Ring of Kerry and Dingle Peninsula. In the May-to-September period, tours are offered daily; prices average 22€ ($20) per person. Check the following companies if that's the kind of tour for you: **Bus Eireann,** Bus Depot, Railway Road, off East Avenue Road (ℂ 064/34777); **Gap of Dunloe Tours,** 7 High St. (ℂ 064/ 30200;** www.castlelough-tours.com); **Corcoran's Tours,** 10 College St. (ℂ 064/36666); and **Dero's Tours,** 22 Main St. (ℂ 064/31251 or 064/31567; www.derostours.com).

Killarney Highlights   Besides showing off Killarney's Lakes from the best vantage points, this 3-hour tour takes you to Aghadoe, the Gap of Dunloe, Ross Castle, Muckross House and Gardens, and Torc Waterfall. Frommer's readers should inquire about discounts when booking directly with the Deros office.

Dero's Tours, 22 Main St., Killarney. ℂ 064/31251 or 064/31567. www.derostours.com. 11€ ($10). May–Sept daily 10:30am, but schedules vary, so check in advance.

Gap of Dunloe   This tour includes a bus trip to Kate Kearney's cottage at the northern end of the Gap, and a boat trip from the southern end to Ross Castle.

The trip through the Gap is up to you—jaunting cars can be arranged for about 16€ ($14) per person, or you can choose to walk.

Gap of Dunloe Tours, 7 High St., Killarney. 🕜 **064/30200.** Fax 064/30201. 19€ ($17) bus and boat. May–Sept call for current hours and bookings.

JAUNTING-CAR TOURS

If you prefer walking or bicycling, just say no to the numerous drivers who will inevitably offer their services as you make your way around the Killarney lakes. But these quaint horse-driven buggies are one of the main features of the landscape here, and if at some point you decide to give them a try, keep in mind that jaunting-car rates are set and carefully monitored by the Killarney Urban District Council. Current rates, all based on four persons to a jaunting car, run roughly from 6.50€ to 15€ ($5.90 to $14) per person round-trip, depending on destinations, which include Ross Castle, Muckross House and Gardens, Torc Waterfall, Muckross Abbey, Dinis Island, and Kate Kearney's Cottage, gateway to the Gap of Dunloe. To arrange a tour in advance, contact **Tagney Tours,** Kinvara House, Muckross Road, Killarney (🕜 **064/33358**).

BOAT TOURS

There's nothing quite like seeing the sights from a boat on the Lakes of Killarney. Two companies operate regular boating excursions, with full commentary:

M.V. Lily of Killarney Tours   Also departing from the pier at Ross Castle, this enclosed water bus cruises the lakes for just over an hour. Again, make reservations.

3 High St., Killarney. 🕜 **064/31068.** 8€ ($7.25) adults, 4€ ($3.65) children, 20€ ($18) family. May–Sept daily 10:30am, noon, 2pm, 3:15pm, and 4:30pm.

M.V. Pride of the Lakes Tours   This enclosed boat offers daily sailings from the pier at Ross Castle. The trip lasts just over an hour, and reservations are suggested.

Scotts Gardens, Killarney. 🕜 **064/32638.** 7.50€ ($6.80) adults, 4.50€ ($4.10) students, 3.80€ ($3.45) children. Apr–Oct 11am, 12:30pm, 2:30pm, 4pm, and 5:15pm.

OUTDOOR PURSUITS
SPECTATOR SPORTS

GAELIC GAMES   The people of Killarney are passionately devoted to the national sports of hurling and Gaelic football. Games are played almost every Sunday afternoon during the summer at **Fitzgerald Stadium,** Lewis Road, Killarney (🕜 **064/31700**). For complete details, consult the local *Kerryman* newspaper or the Killarney tourist office.

HORSE RACING   Killarney has two annual horse-racing events in early May and mid-July. Each event lasts for 3 or 4 days and is very heavily attended. For more information, contact the **Killarney Racecourse,** Ross Road, Killarney (🕜 **064/31125**) or the Killarney tourist office.

THE GREAT OUTDOORS

BICYCLING   The **Killarney National Park,** with its many lakeside and forest pathways, trails, and byways, is a paradise for bikers. Various types of bikes are available for rent, from 21-speed touring bikes and mountain bikes to tandems. Rental charges average 9€ ($8) per day or 44€ ($40) per week. Bicycles can be rented from **Killarney Rent-a-Bike,** High Street (🕜 **064/32578**); **O'Neills Cycle Shop,** 6 Plunkett St., Killarney (🕜 **064/31970**); and D. O'Sullivan's **The Bike Shop,** High Street, Killarney (🕜 **064/31282**). Most shops are open year-round from 9am to 6pm daily, with extended hours until 7 or 8pm in the summer months.

One great ride beginning in Killarney takes you through the Gap of Dunloe along a dirt forest road, where you'll see some of the best mountain scenery in the area; it can be made into a 35-mile (56km) loop if you return on N71. You can also shorten this ride by returning from the south end of Gap by boat to Ross Castle, a service offered by **Gap of Dunloe Tours** (*© 064/30200); it's called the "bike and boat tour," and the charge is 10€ ($9.10), not including bike rental.

FISHING Fishing for salmon and brown trout in Killarney's unpolluted lakes and rivers is a big attraction. Brown trout fishing is free on the lakes, but a permit is necessary for the Rivers Flesk and Laune. A trout permit costs 3.80€ to 13€ ($3.45–$12) per day.

Salmon fishing anywhere in Ireland requires a license; the cost is 3.80€ ($3.45) per day or 13€ ($12) for 21 days. In addition, some rivers also require a salmon permit, which costs 10€ to 13€ ($9 to $12) per day. Permits and licenses can be obtained at the Fishery Office at the **Knockreer Estate Office,** New Street, Killarney (*© 064/31246*).

For fishing tackle, bait, rod rental, and other fishing gear, as well as permits and licenses, try **O'Neill's,** 6 Plunkett St., Killarney (*© 064/31970*). This shop also arranges the hire of boats and ghillies (fishing guides) on the Killarney Lakes, leaving from Ross Castle.

GOLF Visitors are always welcome at the twin 18-hole championship courses of the **Killarney Golf & Fishing Club,** Killorglin Road, Fossa, Killarney (*© 064/31034*; www.killarney-golf.com) located 3 miles (5km) west of the town center. These courses, known as "Killeen" and "Mahony's Point," are surrounded by lake and mountain vistas and are widely praised as two of the most beautiful in the world. Greens fees are 64€ ($58) on either course.

HORSEBACK RIDING Many trails in the Killarney area are suitable for horseback riding. The cost of hiring a horse ranges from 13€ to 19€ ($12 to $17) per hour at the following establishments: **Killarney Riding Stables,** R562, Ballydowney, Killarney (*© 064/31686*); **O'Donovan's Farm,** Mangerton Road, Muckross, Killarney (*© 064/32238*; muckross_stables_bandb75@yahoo.ie); and **Rocklands Stables,** Rockfield, Tralee Road, Killarney (*© 064/32592*). Lessons and weeklong trail rides can also be arranged. For horseback tours of the Gap of Dunloe see "Seeing the Sights," above.

WALKING Killarney is ideal for walking enthusiasts. The **Killarney National Park** offers four signposted nature trails. The **Mossy Woods Nature Trail** starts near Muckross House near Muckross Lake and rambles 1½ miles (2.5km) through yew woods along low cliffs. **Old Boat House Nature Trail** begins at the 19th-century boathouse below Muckross Gardens and leads ½ mile (1km) around a small peninsula by Muckross Lake. **Arthur Young's Walk,** 3 miles (5km), starts on the road to Dinis, traverses natural yew woods, and then follows a 200-year-old road on the Muckross Peninsula. The **Blue Pool Nature Trail** goes from Muckross village through woodlands and past a small lake known as the Blue Pool (1½ miles/2.5km). Leaflets with maps of these four trails are available at the park visitor center.

Rising steeply from the south shore of Muckross Lake, **Torc Mountain** provides spectacular views of the Killarney Lakes and nearby **MacGillycuddy's Reeks.** Start at the Torc Waterfall parking lot, about 4 miles (6.5km) south of

Killarney, and follow the trail to the top of the falls. At a "T" intersection, turn left toward the top parking lot, and almost immediately turn right on the Old Kenmare Road, which follows a small stream along the south slopes of Torc Mountain. After leaving the woods, you'll see Torc Mountain on your right. Look for a crescent-shaped gouge in the side of the road, about 30 feet (9m) across, with a small cairn at its far edge—this is the beginning of the path to the ridgetop, marked somewhat erratically by cairns along the way. Return the way you came; the whole trip is 6 miles (9.5km), takes about 4 hours, and is moderate in difficulty.

In addition to walking independently, visitors to the Killarney area can use a range of guided walks varying in grade and duration (from 1 day to a weekend to a full week). These walks and full guided walking holidays are offered by **SouthWest Walks Ireland Ltd.,** 40 Ashe St., Tralee, County Kerry (© **066/ 712-8733;** swwi@iol.ie). Or you can arrange in advance to meet up with the **Wayfarers,** an international organization of passionate pedestrians, who schedule 5-week-long footloose circuits of the Ring of Kerry each spring, summer, and fall. To receive a schedule and reserve your place, contact the **Wayfarers,** 172 Bellevue Ave., Newport, RI 02840 (© **800/249-4620;** www.thewayfarers.com).

For long-distance walkers, there's the 125-mile (201km) **Kerry Way,** a signposted walking route that extends from Killarney around the Ring of Kerry (see "Touring the Ring of Kerry," earlier in this chapter).

ACCOMMODATIONS YOU CAN AFFORD
IN TOWN

Gleann Fia Country House ★ *(Kids)* Although it's just a mile from town, this modern guesthouse feels pleasantly secluded, tucked away in 26 acres of lawns and woodlands. Jerry and Nora Galvin are thoughtful hosts whose presence makes it a highly personable place. The house has an airy conservatory with tea-making facilities, a guest lounge, and an unusually extensive breakfast menu. Although the entire house is modern, it has been thoughtfully and tastefully constructed, and definitely isn't your average purpose-built guesthouse. There is a nature walk along the stream by one side of the house. Bicycles can be rented on the premises.

The rooms in the most recent addition are slightly larger and more elegantly furnished than those in the main house, and are correspondingly pricier. All bedrooms are nonsmoking. There's also a spacious family room on the ground floor of the main house with a double bed, single bed, and couch.

Deerpark, Killarney, Co. Kerry. © 064/35035. Fax 064/35000. www.gleannfia.com. 19 units. 64€–76€ ($58–$69) single; 102€–114€ ($92–$103) double. No service charge. Rates include full breakfast. AE, DC, MC, V. Closed Dec 22–27. *In room:* TEL, hair dryer.

Knockcullen Located on a quiet, tree-lined street, Knockcullen is the sparkling-clean two-story home of Marie and Sean O'Brien. The four guest rooms are all attractively furnished, and Marie's table is laden with fresh and healthy fare, including a fruit salad and yogurt breakfast option. The town center is a short walk away, and the railway station and Killarney National Park are nearby as well.

New Rd., Killarney, Co. Kerry. © 064/33915. 4 units. 24€ ($22) single; 41€ ($37) double. Rates include full breakfast. No credit cards. Closed Nov–Feb.

Mystical Rose On a residential road less than a mile out of town to the south, this was one of the first B&B's in Killarney and it's still a good base for exploring the town and the National Park. Host Noreen O'Mahony's green thumb and whimsical humor are apparent in the small but beautiful rose garden in front, complete with pink bicycle (to match the breakfast room). Noreen will arrange tours for guests who want them. Two of the guest rooms on the upper floor have views of the mountains.

Woodlawn Rd., Killarney, Co. Kerry. © 064/31453. mysticalr@eircom.net. 6 units. 41€ ($37) single; 62€ ($56) double. 33⅓% reduction for children. Rates include full breakfast. No credit cards. Closed Nov–Feb. *In room:* TV, hair dryer.

Neptune's Killarney Town Hostel   Neptune's is a well-maintained hostel right in the heart of town, tucked away in an alley and surprisingly quiet. The facilities include social (games/TV) rooms, a spacious self-catering kitchen and dining room, laundry/drying room, a safe for valuables, and an internet access terminal. Most of the hostel is wheelchair accessible, and all the bedrooms are nonsmoking. Neptune's will also store your luggage at no cost, as well as furnish babysitters.

New St., Killarney, Co. Kerry. © 064/35255. Fax 064/36399. www.neptune_hostel.com. 22 units, 14 with bathroom (shower only). 10€ ($9) per person in dorm; 11€ ($10) per person in 4-bed dorm; 23€–28€ ($21–$25) double. MC, V. **Amenities:** Self-catering kitchen; babysitting.

St. Anthony's Villa   Mrs. Mary Connell is the friendly host of this modern bungalow, about a mile east of town on the Cork Road. There are no views, but the house is exceptionally well cared for and the bedrooms are spacious and immaculate. A new sun porch in the back makes a great breakfast room.

Cork Rd., Killarney, Co. Kerry. © 064/31534. 4 units. 28€ ($25) single; 47€ ($43) double. 50% reduction for children sharing with an adult. Rates include full breakfast. V. Closed Nov–Feb. *In room:* TV, tea/coffeemaker, hair dryer, iron.

OUTSIDE KILLARNEY

Beauty's Home   Mrs. Catherine Spillane is the lively and gracious hostess in this modern bungalow about a 5-minute drive from the town center. All guest rooms have satellite TV (with CNN), a rarity in the budget category. Mrs. Spillane will be happy to meet guests at the bus or railway station if requested. Ask about possible discounts for holders of this book.

Cleeney, Killarney, Co. Kerry. © 064/31567. Fax 064/34077. www.beautyshome.com 6 units, 3 with bathroom (shower only). 32€–38€ ($29–$35) single; 48€ ($44) double without bathroom, 57€ ($52) double with bathroom. 20% reduction for children. Rates include full breakfast. MC, V. Free private parking. *In room:* TV, tea/coffeemaker.

Coffey's Loch Lein House *Value*   Just 3 miles (5km) from Killarney, this modern, one-story guesthouse is set in green lawns sloping down to the Lower Lake, and is approached by a country lane that's signposted on the main Ring of Kerry road (R562) just past the golf course (on your left as you approach from Killarney). The L-shaped guesthouse contains exceptionally large and well-furnished guest rooms. There's a TV lounge with a fireplace and a bright, window-walled dining room. The Coffee family has been in this area for generations, so Eithne Coffee and her son Sean can serve up a treasure trove of local legends. Several bedrooms, the dining room, and a lounge are reserved as nonsmoking areas.

Fossa, Killarney, Co. Kerry. © 064/31260. Fax 064/36151. www.lochlein.com. 12 units. 44€–57€ ($40–$52) single; 76€–102€ ($69–$92) double. 50% reduction for children. Rates include full breakfast. MC, V. Closed Nov–Feb. **Amenities:** Lounge. *In room:* TV, dataport, hair dryer, safe.

Killarney International Youth Hostel   This impressive 200-year-old brick mansion, set in 75 wooded acres, is located about 2 miles (3km) from the town center (signposted on R562, the main Ring of Kerry road), with a courtesy bus from the railway station (phone the warden when you arrive or notify the hostel in advance). There's a TV room, a self-catering kitchen and dining room, free hot showers, laundry facilities, rental bikes, and a small store. Try to book in advance during July and August. The wardens can arrange discounted tours of the Ring of Kerry, as well as the lakes and several other areas, and there's an excellent activities program. Breakfast and dinner are served in the cafe; all meals are under 10€ ($9). There is a midnight curfew.

Aghadoe House, Killarney, Co. Kerry. ✆ **064/31240.** Fax 064/34300. www.irelandyha.org. 26 units, none with bathroom: 3 double rms, 23 dorm rooms (4–16 beds). 12€ ($11) per person in dorm; 38€ ($35) double. V. **Amenities:** Self-catering kitchen; laundry.

Marian House   Marian House sits just off the main Muckross road, atop a small hill—guest rooms at the front of the house have a good view of the mountains. Simplicity is the key word here, and bedrooms are refreshingly spare without sacrificing comfort (the beds are admirably firm). Bathrooms are quite small, and very clean. Mrs. Eileen Lucey, the hostess, is always helpful to guests in planning their Killarney stay. The house is a 10-minute walk from the town center.

Woodlawn Rd., Killarney, Co. Kerry. ✆/fax **064/31275.** 6 units. 51€ ($46) double. 50% reduction for children. Rates include full breakfast. No credit cards.

Osprey   Nature lovers will enjoy this well-kept B&B. Osprey's scenic location overlooks the lakes and mountains, less than a mile from Killarney National Park. Hosts Maureen and Genie Fogarty are keen walkers and can advise on easy or difficult walks in the vicinity. And if you decide to try your luck fishing on the lakes, Genie is just the man to send you off to the best spots. Maureen's home baking is a decided bonus. The property is entirely nonsmoking.

Lough Guitane Rd., Muckross, Killarney, Co. Kerry. ✆ **064/33213.** osprey3@indigo.ie. 3 units, 2 with bathroom (shower only). 34€ ($31) single; 51€ ($46) double. Rates include full breakfast. MC, V. Closed Oct–Apr. **Amenities:** Lounge. *In room:* Hair dryer.

Peacock Farm Hostel ⊛   If the summer crowds in Killarney are getting to you, this is the perfect place to retreat to at the end of the day. High on a mountain slope overlooking Lough Guitane, Peacock Farm Hostel is an idyllic refuge and a great base for exploring Killarney and the surrounding hills. Owen and Rose Barnes are the most generous and friendly hosts you could hope for, and the hostel they've created is delightfully unique. Peacocks strut through the yard, occasionally surprising visitors by peering down at them through the translucent kitchen roof. The kitchen/dining room is in a long, bright room that overlooks the adjacent mountains and lake; walls inside and out are brightly painted with fanciful scenes. Private rooms are small and comfortable, with bunk beds. The hostel is 7 miles (11km) from Killarney, and a shuttle brings residents to and from the town twice a day; call for departure times and places. The whole hostel is nonsmoking.

Gortdromakiery, Muckross, Killarney, Co. Kerry. ✆ **064/33557.** 6 units, none with bathroom: 2 doubles, 1 family room (5 beds), 1 4-bed dorm, 2 8-bed dorms. 10€ ($9) per person dorm room; 48€ ($43) per room family room; 28€ ($25) per room double. 3.15€ ($2.90) continental breakfast. No credit cards. Closed Oct–Apr. **Amenities:** Self-catering kitchen.

FARMHOUSES

Carriglea House 〈Value〉   This beautiful 200-year-old country home sits 1¼ miles (2km) from the town center on a rise overlooking the lakes. From the sweeping front lawn, approached by a tree-lined curving avenue, the view takes in the Lower Lake and Purple, Torc, and Mangerton Mountains. Marie and John Beazley own this working dairy farm and take great pleasure in helping guests plan their holiday time in Killarney. The house has spacious rooms furnished with many antiques and tastefully decorated in restful colors. Particularly noteworthy is the dining room chandelier of gold, blue, and pink porcelain. There are several additional guest rooms in the adjoining coach house. One large coach-house room has a bay window overlooking the front lawn.

Muckross Rd., Killarney, Co. Kerry. © 064/31116. Fax 064/37693. carriglea@oceanfree.net. 9 units. 56€ ($51) double. Rates include full breakfast. MC, V. Closed Nov–Mar. *In room:* TV.

Gap View Farm   Mrs. Kearney is the hostess of this large 18th-century farmhouse 8 miles (13km) from Killarney, off the Farranfore road (N22) with its fine views of the Gap of Dunloe and the Kerry mountains. The house has turf fires, and fresh farm foods are served at every meal. There is a garden that guests can use, and six lovely bedrooms, all with good views. Killarney Golf Course is just 5 miles (8km) away. Both the dining room and the sun lounge are nonsmoking.

Firies, Killarney, Co. Kerry. © 066/976-4378. 6 units. 51€ ($46) double. 33% reduction for children. Rates include full breakfast. No credit cards. Closed Nov–Apr. **Amenities:** Restaurant.

GREAT DEALS ON DINING
IN KILLARNEY

Bricín ✷ TRADITIONAL IRISH   Old-time Kerry boxty dishes (potato pancakes with various fillings, such as chicken, seafood, curried lamb, or vegetables) are the trademark of this restaurant above a very good craft and bookshop. The menu also offers a variety of fresh seafood, pastas, Irish stew, and specials. Housed in one of Killarney's oldest buildings, Bricín sports original stone walls, pine furniture, turf fireplaces, and—very rare in Ireland—a completely nonsmoking room that seats 40. Snacks and light fare are served during the day. In addition to the shop downstairs, the building houses the Bricín Art Gallery, which displays oils and watercolors by local artists.

26 High St., Killarney. © 064/34902. www.bricin.com Reservations recommended for dinner. Main courses 11€–19€ ($10–$17); snacks 2.50€–6.50€ ($2.25–$5.90). AE, DC, DISC, MC, V. Year-round Tues–Sat 10am–4:30pm; Easter–Oct Mon–Sat 6–9:30pm.

The Cooperage Café and Restaurant ✷✷ IRISH/CONTINENTAL Open just a couple of years, this creation of "Martin and Mo," two of Ireland's most touted restaurateurs, has created quite a buzz among both locals and tourists. Coopers has clearly broken the mold here in Killarney, with its chic, urban, nightclub decor, making the most of glass, stone, aluminum, and sharp black/white contrasts. Overhead, the many-tendrilled wire-sculpture chandeliers with flower-cup lights cast a magical fairylike illumination. The total effect is as captivating as the inventive and varied menu, which focuses on local Irish seafood and wild game. Menu options include wild pheasant cooked in Irish cream liqueur, escalope of venison, filet of wild pigeon, grilled swordfish and salmon, wild filet of sea trout, and baked cod Provençale. For vegetarians, the warm goat-cheese salad with two pestos is but one tasty selection. The alluring array of desserts includes crumbles, tarts, homemade ice creams, meringues, and crème brûlées, although it requires rare strength of character to get past the duo of dark chocolate and pistachio mousse.

Old Market Lane, off High St. (where New St. intersects High), Killarney. © 064/37716. Reservations recommended. Dinner main courses 14.75€–24€ ($13–$21). MC, V. Mon–Sat 12:30–2:30pm and 6–9:30pm; Sun 4–9:30pm.

Dingles Restaurant IRISH/TRADITIONAL   Gerry and Marion Cunningham have created an eatery traditional in both decor and menu. This is a low-ceilinged, flagstone place, with an open fire on cool evenings and a rustic look. The very freshest, most wholesome ingredients are used, and there's usually at least one vegetarian dish on the menu. Specialties include mussels in a sauce of wine and cream; smoked wild Killarney salmon; tender spring lamb chops; steak in a piquant sauce of green peppercorns, white wine, cream, and whiskey; and old-fashioned Irish stew.

40 New St. ℂ 064/31079. dingles@eircom.net. Reservations recommended. Main courses 14€–32€ ($13–$32). AE, DC, MC, V. Wed–Mon 6–10:30pm. Closed Nov–Mar.

Foley's Seafood & Steak Restaurant SEAFOOD/BAR FOOD   Foley's was a coaching inn many years ago and there's an old-style air about the front bar lounge, where a fireplace with turf fires adds to the coziness. The two pretty back dining rooms are more formal, decorated in soft shades of rose and green. Carol and Denis Hartnett are the family team responsible for turning out the meals. Seafood, Kerry mountain lamb, and steaks are the specialties. Carol (who does the cooking) uses only the freshest produce. Denis cuts all their steaks and buys Kerry mountain lamb, using nothing but centerline cuts.

23 High St. ℂ 064/31217. Reservations recommended. Lunch main courses 12€–15€ ($11–$14); dinner main courses 13€–23€ ($12–$21). AE, MC, V. Daily noon–11pm.

The Laurels Pub BAR FOOD   There's good pub grub at the Laurels in old-style surroundings of low, beamed ceilings and rustic wooden tables. The food is good, the company congenial, and the *craic* stimulating. In addition to soup, sandwiches, and salad plates, there are hot specialties such as Irish lamb stew, Guinness beef stew, and stuffed roast pork. On summer evenings there's often musical entertainment for a cover of 5€ ($4.55).

Main St. ℂ 064/31149. Bar food lunch main courses 6.50€ ($5.90); dinner main courses 13€–17€ ($12–$15). MC, V. Mon–Sat 12–3pm and 6–9pm.

Linden House ⚘ TRADITIONAL EUROPEAN   One of the best places in town for a delicious, home-cooked evening meal is this small hotel run by owners Ann and Peter Knoblauch, who have created a Bavarian-type dining room of exposed brick and wooden booths. It's a cozy place, very popular with locals, and the menu is good, solid family fare. Peter supervises the spotless kitchen and insists on the freshest ingredients. In July and August, it's a good idea to book ahead; other months you'll usually have only a few minutes' wait at the most. There's also an a la carte menu available.

New Rd. ℂ 064/31379. Fixed-price dinner 28€ ($25). MC, V. Daily 6:30–9pm. Closed Nov–Jan and Mon in off-season.

IN KILLORGLIN

Some 14 miles (23km) west of Killarney is the village of Killorglin, with two restaurants worthy of mention.

The Bianconi BAR FOOD   Rick and Ray Sheehan have created one of Killorglin's most popular dining spots in this large bar/restaurant. Lots of dark wood, leather seats, and cozy booths create a traditional setting, and the kitchen serves up excellent home-cooked meals, seafood dishes, and salads made from fresh local ingredients.

Annadale Rd., Killorglin, Co. Kerry. ℂ 066/976-1146. Bar food under 13€ ($12) salads or 17€ ($16) hot meals; dinner main courses 16€–21€ ($14–$19). AE, MC, V. Mon–Sat bar food 10:30am–9pm, restaurant 7–9pm; Sun bar food only 12:30–2pm and 5:30–9pm.

Nick's Restaurant STEAKS/SEAFOOD   Nick and Ann Foley have converted what was once a butcher shop into a multilevel steak-and-seafood restaurant with exposed stone walls, lots of dark wood, open fires, and comfortable seating. Nick himself is a master butcher, so you'll only be served the best meats. Prime beef comes in enormous steaks that really do melt in your mouth (I swear). Lobsters, crayfish, and oysters reside in the restaurant's fish tank, and other fish dishes feature same-day catches. The soups are thick and hearty, tasting unmistakably homemade. If you have a yen for a special dish not listed— and if the makings are available—the Foleys are happy to prepare it for you. There's also an extensive wine list, with all the varieties imported directly from France, and traditional music some nights. This popular place can get very busy after about 7:30pm, so my advice is to arrive early.

Lower Bridge St., Killorglin, Co. Kerry. ⓒ 066/976-1219. Main courses 15€–23€ ($14–$21). AE, MC, V. Daily 6–10pm. Closed Nov.

SHOPPING

During the summer many Killarney shops stay open until 10pm, and most are open on Sunday.

Brian de Staic   Goldsmith Brian de Staic, whose home base is Dingle town, now offers his distinctive jewelry in this shop, with an attractive traditional storefront. In addition to the Ogham nameplate pendants for which he is best known, there are also gold and enamel items, all at reasonable prices. There is an additional shop in the new shopping mall on Park Road. 18 High St., Killarney, Co. Kerry. ⓒ/fax 064/33822.

Bricín   This attractive, stone-walled shop specializes in pottery and other Irish crafts, handmade pine furniture, and Irish books. Upstairs, there's a moderately priced cafe serving traditional Irish dishes (see "Great Deals on Dining," above). 26 High St., Killarney, Co. Kerry. ⓒ 064/34902.

Frank Lewis Gallery   This gallery shows and sells a variety of contemporary and traditional paintings, sculptures, and photographic work—much of it with a Kerry theme—by some of Ireland's most acclaimed emerging artists. It's on one of Killarney's enchanting lanes, in a restored artisan's dwelling near the post office. 6 Bridewell Lane, Killarney, Co. Kerry. ⓒ 064/31108. Fax 064/31570. www.franklewisgallery.com.

John J. Murphy, Weaver   This store, approximately 10 miles (16km) from Killarney on the Tralee road (N22), sells a lovely range of woolen shawls; scarves in wool, lamb's wool, mohair, alpaca, and linen/cotton; and place mats in wool and linen/cotton. The small retail shop is an extension of John Murphy's larger workshop and is just off the main road (clearly signposted). Currow Rd., Farranfore, Co. Kerry. ⓒ 066/976-4659. Fax 066/976-4993.

Killarney Bookshop   Along with a good selection of Irish-interest books, this shop also stocks best-sellers and a comprehensive range of general publications. 32 Main St., Killarney, Co. Kerry. ⓒ 064/34108. www.killarneybookshop.ie.

Macken of Ireland *(Finds)*   A short, 3-mile (5km) drive from the town center on the main Ring of Killarney road, this shop has shelves brimming with what must be Killarney's largest stock of Aran knits. There's also a wide range of tweed, cashmere, and mohair jackets, and a large selection of jewelry in Celtic motifs. A coffee shop with terrace in back offers pleasant fine-weather dining. Fossa, Co. Kerry. ⓒ 064/34766. Fax 064/34761.

Quill's Woollen Market There's an enormous selection of designer hand-knits and woolen goods in this large store, along with a good selection of other Irish-made goods and souvenirs. Market Sq., Main St., Killarney, Co. Kerry. ✆ 064/32277.

KILLARNEY AFTER DARK

At the **Killarney Manor Banquet,** Loreto Road, Killarney (✆ **064/31551;** www.killarneymanor.com), you can have a five-course dinner in 19th-century style with a complete program of songs, ballads, and dance. The banquet is held in a stately 1840s stone-faced mansion set on a hillside 2 miles (3km) south of town overlooking the Killarney panorama. It's staged from April through October nightly (except Sun), starting at 7:30pm. The price is 40€ ($36) per person. It's also possible to attend the entertainment segment only for 17.75€ ($16) from 9pm to 10:30pm. Reservations are required (major credit cards accepted).

THE PUB SCENE

Dunloe Lodge This simple pub in the heart of town has a friendly and comfortable atmosphere. Don't be surprised if some of its local patrons spontaneously pull out a harmonica, an accordion, a banjo, or a fiddle and start to play. You'll hear anything from Irish ballads to folk or rock music. Plunkett St., Killarney, Co. Kerry. ✆ 064/33503.

Kate Kearney's Cottage Almost everyone who ventures through the famous Gap first visits this former coaching inn, which is named for a woman who was believed to be a witch. Today this outpost, 9¼ miles (15km) west of town, is a somewhat touristy refreshment stop at the start of the Gap, with souvenirs on sale. From May to September, very good traditional music is performed on Sunday, Tuesday, and Wednesday from 9 to 11:30pm. Gap of Dunloe, Co. Kerry. ✆ 064/44146.

Kit Flaherty's Pub at Whitegates Hotel Kit Flaherty's, part of the large, modern, purpose-built Whitegates Hotel, hosts traditional music sessions on a regular basis—call ahead to ask when the next one will be held. Unexceptional bar food is served as well. Muckross Rd., Killarney, Co. Kerry. ✆ 064/31164.

The Laurels One of the more popular "sing song" pubs in town, this place rings to the rafters with the lilt of Irish ditties. Ballad singers are booked nightly from April through October, starting at 9pm. The cover is usually 5€ ($4.55). Main St., Killarney, Co. Kerry. ✆ 064/31149.

Molly Darcy's Across from Muckross House, this is one of Killarney's best traditional pubs, with a thatched roof, stone walls, an oak-beamed ceiling, open fireplaces, alcoves, snugs, public phones in what were confession boxes salvaged from a monastery, and lots of Killarney memorabilia. There's dancing on Sunday evenings. Muckross Park Hotel, Muckross Rd., Killarney, Co. Kerry. ✆ 064/34973.

Scotts Bar and Beer Garden On a warm summer's night, this is the place to enjoy an outdoor drink. Music ranges from ballads to piano or jazz. Scott's Hotel, College St. ✆ 064/31060.

3 The Western Dingle Peninsula

Dingle town is 30 miles (48km) W of Tralee and 50 miles (81km) NW of Killarney

Like the Iveragh Peninsula, Dingle has a spectacularly scenic peripheral road, along which there has blossomed over time a substantial tacky tourist trade. As soon as you veer off the main roads, however, or penetrate to such far hinterlands of the peninsula as the Blasket Islands or Brandon Head, you'll discover extraordinary, desolate beauty seemingly worlds away from the tour buses and shamrock-filled shops. The Dingle Peninsula is also known for a remarkable abundance of archaeological remains—to date, no fewer than 2,000 sites have been identified here. In addition, Dingle is home to many native Gaelic speakers.

GETTING THERE   Bus Eireann (© 066/712-3566; www.buseireann.ie) provides daily coach service to Dingle from all parts of Ireland. The boarding and drop-off point is on Upper Main Street.

By car, the most direct route to Dingle is along N86 west from Tralee. Alternately, you can take the scenic route through the Connor Pass by taking N86 to T68, which follows the north coast of the peninsula, turning left at Kilcummin on the Connor Pass Road.

GETTING AROUND   By Public Transportation   Dingle town has no local bus service. **Bus Eireann** (© 066/712-3566) provides service from Dingle to other towns on the peninsula. For local taxi or minibus service, contact **John Sheehy** (© 066/915-1301).

On Foot   The best way to get around Dingle town, with its narrow, winding, and hilly streets, is to walk. The town is small and compact and easy to get to know.

By Car   To see the sights beyond the town, you'll need to drive westward along R559 or take one of the sightseeing tours suggested below.

VISITOR INFORMATION   The **Dingle Tourist Office** is located on Main Street, Dingle (© 066/915-1188). It's open seasonally, usually April to June, Monday through Saturday from 9:15am to 5:30pm and Sunday from 11am to 5pm; July and August, Monday through Saturday from 9:15am to 7pm and Sunday from 10am 1, 2:15 to 5pm; September and October, Monday through Saturday from 9:30am to 5:15pm; closed 1pm to 2:15pm.

For extensive, detailed tourist information on the Dingle Peninsula, see **www.dingle-peninsula.ie**, **www.kerrygems.ie**, and **www.kerry.tourguide.ie**.

 FAST FACTS: Dingle

Hospital **The Dingle Hospital** is on Upper Main Street, Dingle (© **066/915-1455** or 066/915-1172).

Library The **Dingle District Library** is on Green Street, Dingle (© **066/915-1499**).

Local Publications **In & About Dingle Peninsula** is a newspaper-style publication distributed free at hotels, restaurants, shops, and the tourist office. It lists events, attractions, activities, and more.

Police The **Garda Station** is at Holy Ground, Dingle (© **066/915-1522**).

SEEING THE SIGHTS

Don't miss **Slea Head,** at the southwestern extremity of the Dingle peninsula, a place of pristine beaches, great walks, and fascinating archaeological remains. **Dunbeg Fort** sits on a rocky promontory just south of Slea Head, its walls rising from the cliff edge. Although much of the fort has fallen into the sea since it was built, the place is well worth a visit. There is a small charge for admission.

The village of **Dunquin** is stunningly situated just north of Slea Head, and is home to the **Blasket Centre.** Offshore from Dunquin are the seven Blasket Islands; a ferry (© **066/915-6455** or 066/915-6422) connects Great Blasket with the mainland when the weather permits. The islands were abandoned by the last permanent residents in 1953, and now are only inhabited by a few summer visitors who share the place with the seals and seabirds. There's a magnificent 8-mile (13km) walk to the west end of Great Blasket and back, passing sea cliffs and ivory beaches; you can stop along the way at the only cafe on the island, which serves lunch and dinner.

Continuing north and east of Dunquin, in the center of Ballyferriter, stop at the old school that houses the **Oidhreacht Chorca Dhuibhne** (the Corca Dhuibhne Regional Museum; © **066/915-6100**) for an overview of the peninsula's history, from its geological beginnings through its rich archaeological heritage right through to modern-day topics. Curator Isabel Bennett is usually on hand to answer questions and advise on how to visit the spectacular archaeological sites of the region, some famous and others less well known. The museum is open May to September daily from 9am to 5pm, and the admission fee is 2.50€ ($2.30) per person. In summer months, those interested in learning or improving their knowledge of Irish can arrange language courses with stays in Irish-speaking homes and many social activities based on traditional music and dance; contact the curator for information.

East of Ballyferriter is **Gallarus Oratory** ⚜, one of the best-preserved early Christian church buildings in Ireland. It's constructed of unmortared stone, yet is still completely watertight after more than 1,000 years—an assertion that you'll probably be able to test personally given the peninsula's frequent showers. The Oratory's shape is often compared with that of an overturned boat, which is lucky for us: The reason that few of the early Christian oratories have survived is that the typical square plan with corbelled roof was inherently unstable, and rarely lasted long. Much more stable are the round corbel-roofed structures, like the beehive huts on Skellig Michael. You can see the roof at Gallarus sagging on one side, the only sign that this structure is beginning to give way to gravity. There is a charge of 1.90€ ($1.75) per person for admission.

Just a few kilometers north of Gallarus, in the town of Tiduff, is another early Christian church at **Kilmalkedar.** This is a 12th-century Romanesque structure, with carved human and animal heads over the doorway. The graveyard has several ancient carved stones, including an Ogham stone, and inside the church is the Alphabet Stone, a pillar inscribed with the Roman and Ogham alphabets. Just up the access road for church and cemetery is the medieval structure known as **St. Brendan's House,** which was probably used as a priest's residence.

North of Kilmalkedar, at nearby **Brandon Creek** (the legendary starting point of St. Brendan's voyage to the New World), stop in at **An Bother** ⚜ (© **066/915-5342**)—it means "the road," and the pub sits right at the roadside. This is a place to relax by the fire in the lounge or sit at the bar in the small front room, with the constant flow of conversation lulling you into a sense of timelessness. You'll meet mostly locals here, and they welcome visitors warmly.

Ceardlann Na Coille   Just west of the Dingle Marina, this cluster of traditional cottages is a circular craft village, set on a hillside above the town and harbor. A local craft worker who produces and sells his or her craft staffs each workshop. Handmade felts, fun jewelry and mosaics, and traditional Irish musical instruments are offered, as well as silver jewelry and ceramic pictures. A cafe on the premises serves excellent homemade soups, salads, and hot dishes.

Saving the Land

The story of the **West Kerry Co-op,** located in Ballyferriter, is an inspiring one. It begins in 1968, when young people were leaving in droves and there was great concern that the unique culture and heritage of this Gaelic-speaking region would wither and die. Much of the land on the peninsula had been untillable, but by banding together, 800 members of the farming community were able to import a special deep-plowing machine to break up the layer of iron that lay just inches beneath the surface of the land, to turn it into productive acres. The co-op has now reclaimed more than 12,000 acres. Incidentally, the co-op sells an excellent illustrated guidebook, which outlines a driving tour. Its office in Ballyferriter is open Monday to Friday from 9am to 5:30pm.

The Wood (just west of the Dingle Marina), Dingle, Co. Kerry. ⓒ **066/915-1778.** Free admission. Daily 10am–6pm; hours of individual workshops variable.

Dingle Oceanworld ⭐ *Kids* This is Ireland's best aquarium—light years ahead of the National Sealife Centre in Bray, County Wicklow—and a main attraction for families, local and from afar. Dedicated to the exploration and understanding of the ocean's depths, it's also committed to excitement and fun. Along with the sea critters behind glass in the aquarium's 29 tanks, young docents carry around live lobsters, crabs, starfish, and other "inner space" creatures, and introduce them up-close to visitors. During feeding time at 2, 3, and 4pm, children are allowed to hand out the grub. This is a compact, hands-on, interactive place of wonder and learning. It has plenty of special features, like the walk-through tunnel tank, the creepy creatures tank, and the nursery (for deep-sea babes born at Oceanworld). All but the sharks in the new shark tank are indigenous to local waters; this is your chance to view live the entrees at Dingle's great seafood restaurants, or to all but rub noses with some of the most exotic of Dingle's offshore inhabitants. In addition, there are exhibits on Brendan the Navigator and the Spanish Armada, a cafe, and a gift shop.

Dingle Harbour, Dingle. ⓒ **066/915-2111.** www.dingleoceanworld.ie. Admission 6.35€ ($5.75) adults, 5.10€ ($4.60) students and seniors, 3.80€ ($3.45) children, 15€ ($14) family. May–June and Sept daily 9:30am–6pm; July–Aug daily 9:30am–8:30pm; Oct–Apr daily 9:30am–5pm.

Eask Tower Eask Tower was a famine-relief project, built in 1847 as a signal for Dingle Harbour. It's a remarkable edifice, a 40-foot (12m) tall tower built of solid stone, some 15 feet (4.5m) thick, with a wooden arrow pointing to the mouth of the harbor. The main reason, however, for making the 1-mile (1.5km) climb to the summit of Carhoo Hill is not to visit the tower but to take in the incredible panoramic views of Dingle Harbour, Connor Pass, Slea Head and, on the far side of Dingle Bay, the high peaks of the Iveragh Peninsula. This is a great place to get your bearings in the region, as you can see most of the southern part of the Dingle Peninsula from here.

Carhoo Hill, Dingle, Co. Kerry. No phone. Admission 3.15€ ($2.90). 4 miles (6.5km) out of Dingle, on the Slea Head Rd. From Dingle, follow Slea Head Rd. 2 miles (3km), turn left at road signposted for Coláiste Ide, and continue another 2 miles (3km).

Ionad An Bhlascaoid Mhoir/The Blasket Centre ⭐⭐ A thin line stretched along the stark Dunquin seafront, this innovative building commands stunning views and is a powerful testament to a way of life that is gone forever, the life of the Blasket Islanders. The Great Blasket was once an outpost of Irish civilization and nurturing ground for a small group of great Irish-language writers, but its inhabitants abandoned the island in 1953. Through a series of displays, exhibits, and a video presentation, this center celebrates the cultural and literary traditions of the Blaskets. Visitors from Massachusetts may be interested to see an exhibit on Springfield, a town where several of the islanders have chosen to settle. This center also has a research room, a bookshop specializing in local literature, and a wide-windowed restaurant with views of the Blaskets. Among the many interpretive centers that have recently been built in Ireland, this is one of the best.

Dunquin, Co. Kerry. ② **066/915-6371.** Admission 3.15€ ($2.90) adults, 2.20€ ($2.00) seniors, 1.25€ ($1.15) students and children, 7.60€ ($6.90) family. Apr–June and Sept–Oct daily 10am–6pm; July–Aug daily 10am–7pm.

SIGHTSEEING TOURS

Sciuird Archaeological Tours   These archaeological tours, lasting 2 to 3 hours, are led by a local expert. They involve a short bus journey and some easy walking. Four or five monuments from the Stone Age to medieval times are visited. All tours start from the tourist office in Dingle town, or you can arrange for a pick-up at your accommodation. Reservations are required.

Holy Ground, Dingle. ② **066/915-1606.** collinskarrary@eircom.net. Tickets 13€ ($12). May–Sept daily 10:30am; afternoon tour offered if there is sufficient demand.

Blasket Islands Cruise   Departing from Dingle Harbour, this new guided tour offers information on the recent history, archaeology, geology, and wildlife of the Blasket Islands. This cruise circumnavigates the islands but does not stop at any of them—those interested in seeing the islands up close should find out if the ferry from Dunquin is operating. Reservations are necessary.

Dingle Marine Ecotours, The Pier, Dingle. ② **086/285-8802.** www.dinglemarine.com. 19€ ($17) adults, 6.35€ ($5.75) children 10–14, 3.80€ ($3.45) children under 10. Apr–Oct daily; call for departure time.

Fungie the Dolphin Tours *(Kids)*   Forget Flipper. In Dingle, the name to know is Fungie the Dolphin. In 1984, Fungie, an adult male bottlenose dolphin, swam solo into the waters of Dingle harbor. Since then, a whole industry has grown up around him. **The Dingle Boatmen's Association** (② **066/915-1163**) will ferry you out to find him (if there's no sighting, you don't pay). Fungie happily swims alongside the boats, although his enthusiasm has abated slightly in recent years. More adventurous visitors can swim with him on a dolphin encounter—see "Outdoor Pursuits" below for a full description.

The Pier, Dingle, Co. Kerry. ② **066/915-1163.** 1-hr. boat trip 8.90€ ($8) adults, 3.80€ ($3.45) children under 12.

OUTDOOR PURSUITS

BICYCLING   Rentals average 7.60€ ($6.90) per day or 38€ ($34) per week. Contact **Foxy John's Hardware Store,** Main Street (② **066/915-1316**) for

---

Fun Fact **Don't Call Me Dingle**

The English named the town "Dingle" (in Irish, *An Daingean*, "the fortress") because it's the largest town on the Dingle peninsula. Its ancient Irish name, however, which is still in wide use, is *Corca Dhuibhne*, which means the seeds of Duibhne, a local goddess.

St. Brendan Sails to America

Saint Brendan, known as "the Navigator Saint," is said to have been born near Tralee in County Kerry toward the end of the 5th century A.D. This was a time of great asceticism in the monasteries of Ireland, and the monks practiced many severe penances, the most extreme of which was considered to be voluntary exile from one's homeland, a path taken by many of Ireland's saints. So Brendan was not doing anything unusual when he set off on the Atlantic in a small curragh, accompanied by 17 monks from his monastery at Clonfert in County Galway, but as they rowed away from the shores of Ireland, they left history behind and entered legend.

What shores did Brendan and his monks reach in their curragh? This question has been a matter of contention ever since, and the only fact that seems certain is that they were gone much longer than expected. The first written account of the voyage describes in delightful detail the islands reached by the travelers—the island of the birds, where there was a tree so densely covered with white birds that one could not see its leaves or branches; the island of grapes, where the grapes grew to the size of apples; and Jasconius, actually a whale who allowed the monks to celebrate Mass on his back. The last island they reached, after 7 years at sea, was the Promised Land of the Saints; it was surrounded by a great blinding fog through which Brendan had to sail before reaching the object of his journey.

Although this account is clearly more allegory than history, many have attempted to interpret the topographic detail and give real place names to the points on Brendan's itinerary. Since the 16th century, the idea that Brendan reached the New World has intrigued scholars and sailors, and the accounts of his travels were used by the English to defend their claim to North America. Some have identified the island of the birds as the Faroes, the island of grapes as Jamaica, and the region of fog as Newfoundland. Others have contrarily claimed that all the places described are to be found in Galway Bay, with the Promised Land of the Saints a few kilometers off the Irish coast. Be this as it may, the story of Brendan's voyage has captured the imaginations of many since the 5th century, including navigator and explorer Tim Severin, who in 1976 built a replica of Brendan's tiny curragh and with a small crew sailed from Brandon Creek on the Dingle Peninsula to the coast of Newfoundland.

mountain bikes or touring bikes. Mountain bikes with rear panniers can also be rented at **The Mountain Man,** Strand Street, Dingle (© **066/915-2400** or 066/915-1868): Mike Shea knows the area well, and can suggest a number of 1-day or overnight touring options on the Dingle Peninsula.

BIRD-WATCHING   Great Blasket Island is of some interest for the fall passerine migration, and in summer there's a great abundance of nesting seabirds on the small, uninhabited islands surrounding Great Blasket, including over 20,000 pairs of storm petrels. From Clogher Head north of Dunquin at the western extremity of the Dingle Peninsula, rare autumn migrants can sometimes be seen. Inch Peninsula, extending into Castlemaine Harbour south of Inch town, is a wintering ground for Brent geese, which arrive here in late August and move on in April; there is also a large wigeon population during the fall.

DIVING The **Dingle Dive Centre,** on the marina, Dingle (© 066/915-2422; fax 066/915-2425; www.divedingle.com) offers a wide range of PADI lessons and certification courses for beginners and experienced divers, as well as day-trip dives. A day trip to the Blaskett Islands including two dives and all gear hire is 63€ ($58).

GOLF Head 10 miles (16km) west of Dingle town, to the western edge of the Dingle Peninsula, and you'll find the **Dingle Golf Club** (Ceann Sibéal), Bally-ferriter (© 066/915-6255), which welcomes visitors to play its 18-hole, par-72 course overlooking the waters of the Atlantic. Greens fees are 44€ ($40) week-days, 51€ ($46) weekends, and 32€ ($29) if you start before 8:30am.

HORSEBACK RIDING At **Dingle Horse Riding,** Ballinaboula House, Dingle (© 066/915-2018; http://homepage.tinet.ie/~irishart/horseriding/) rides are available along nearby beaches or through the mountains; the cost is 19€ ($17) for a 1-hour ride. Half-day, full-day, and 3- to 5-day packages includ-ing accommodations, meals, and riding can be arranged.

SAILING The **Dingle Sailing Club,** c/o Brenda Farrell, The Marina, Dingle Town (© 066/915-1984; lfarrell@eircom.net) offers an array of sailing courses taught by experienced, certified instructors. To charter a yacht, contact **Dingle Sea Ventures,** Dingle (© 066/915-2244; www.charterireland.com). Yachts sleeping from 6 to 10 persons are available, ranging in price from 1,156€ to 2,794€ ($1,047 to $2,531) per week, depending on boat and season. Skipper's fees are 63€ ($57) per day.

SEA ANGLING For sea angling packages and day trips, contact Nicholas O'Connor at **Angler's Rest,** Ventry (© 066/915-9947; avalon@iol.ie); or Seán O'Conchúir (© 066/915-5429), representing the **Kerry Angling Association.**

SWIMMING WITH A DOLPHIN *(Moments* A unique watersport in Dingle Bay is to swim with Fungie, the resident dolphin. Although Fungie can swim about 25 mph (40kph), he enjoys human company and is usually willing to slow down so as to swim along with his new acquaintances. To arrange a dolphin encounter, contact Bridgit Flannery at © 066/915-1967 or 066/915-1163, any day from 8am to 8pm. The procedure is to book a swim the day before, when you rent your gear (semi-dry suit, mask, snorkel, boots, and fins—all in one duffel). The full overnight outfitting cost is 18€ ($16) per person. Then, you show up in your gear early the next morning to be brought out by boat to your aquatic rendezvous. The 2-hour escorted swim costs an additional 13€ ($12). If you prefer, you can use your rented outfit and swim out on your own—Fungie welcomes drop-ins. This outing is for teenagers on up, although smaller children will certainly enjoy watching.

WALKING The **Dingle Way** begins in Tralee and circles the peninsula, cov-ering 95 miles (153km) of gorgeous mountain and coastal landscape. The most rugged section is along Brandon Head, where the trail passes between Mount Brandon and the ocean; the views are tremendous, but the walk is long (about 15 miles/24km, averaging 9 hr.) and strenuous, and should only be attempted when the sky is clear. The section between Dunquin and Ballyferriter (also 15 miles/24km) follows an especially lovely stretch of coast. For more information, see *The Dingle Way Map Guide,* available in local tourist offices and shops.

The **Inch Peninsula** offers miles of walking along the east-side beach or through the dunes; there's a parking lot off R561 just west of Inch town.

ACCOMMODATIONS YOU CAN AFFORD
DINGLE TOWN

Ballintaggart House Hostel Ballintaggart House is a large stone manor, built in 1703 as a hunting lodge and recently restored as a bustling hostel and equestrian center. The front rooms are quite elegant, with high ceilings and large fireplaces—they make great sitting rooms, and are well used. Other imposing rooms in the main house have been made into gargantuan dormitories, packed with bunk beds. I'd recommend avoiding these cramped dorms, and spending a few extra pounds for one of the cozy private or 4-bed rooms that line the handsome stone-flagged courtyard. There's a restaurant off the courtyard that serves breakfast for 4€ to 6.50€ ($3.65 to $5.90). The courtyard rooms adjoin the stables, a fact you won't be oblivious to for long—the air is full of the whinny and whiff of horses. A shuttle connects the hostel with Dingle town, making several runs during the day and one at night to the pubs; call for times and places of pickup.

Dingle, Co. Kerry. ℂ 066/915-1454. Fax 066/915-2207. www.dingleaccommodation.com. 29 units, 21 with bathroom (shower only): 10 doubles, all with bathroom; 2 family units, both with bathroom; 10 4-bed dorms, 5 with bathroom; 7 8–10 bed dorms, 4 with bathroom. 38€ ($35) double; 63€ ($58) family room (4 beds); 15€ ($13) per person 4-bed dorm with bathroom; 13€ ($12) per person 4-bed dorm without bathroom; 12€ ($11) per person 8-bed dorm with bathroom. MC, V. Head east from Dingle for 1¼ miles (2km) on R86; the hostel is signposted on the left. **Amenities:** Restaurant.

Dúinin House This modern bungalow, fronted by a green lawn bordered by colorful flowers, is the home of the charming Mrs. Anne Neligan. Her husband, who teaches history in the local secondary school, plays and teaches traditional music, a real bonus for guests. In addition to the attractive guest rooms, there's a lounge and TV room for guests and tea/coffee-making facilities in the conservatory. The breakfast menu is extensive—pancakes, omelets, fruit salad, and porridge with Bailey's are among the varied options.

Conor Pass Rd., Dingle, Co. Kerry. ℂ/fax 066/915-1335. 5 units. 53€ ($48) double. Rates include full breakfast. MC, V. Closed Dec–Feb. ½ mile (1km) from Dingle. **Amenities:** Lounge. *In room:* TV, hair dryer.

Marian House Mrs. Ann Cahillane's attractive town house is in a quiet cul-de-sac in Dingle town, with pubs and restaurants an easy walk away. Mrs. Cahillane is the soul of Irish hospitality, always happy to help with touring plans.

Marian Park, Dingle, Co. Kerry. ℂ 066/915-1773. 5 units. 46€ ($42) double. 13€ ($12) extra for children under 10. Rates include full breakfast. No credit cards. Closed Nov–May. *In room:* TV, hair dryer.

AROUND THE PENINSULA

Cleevaun Sean and Charlotte Cluskey's aptly named modern bungalow (*Cliabhan* in Irish means "cradle") is only about a 10-minute walk from Dingle town. From the pleasant lounge and dining room there are views of green pastures dotted with grazing sheep and a panorama that takes in Dingle Bay and Mount Brandon. There's an ancient Ogham stone in the field out back and a ring fort down in the pasture. The lounge and breakfast room decor makes use of pine and yellow walls, and guest rooms have an old-country pine theme and orthopedic beds. On arrival, you'll be offered coffee or tea and homemade porter cake. The award-winning breakfast menu not only includes the traditional Irish breakfast, but adds choices of pancakes, cheese, and fruit. The entire house is nonsmoking.

Lady's Cross, Miltown, Dingle, Co. Kerry. ℂ **066/915-1108.** Fax 066/915-2228. www.cleevaun.com. 9 units. 83€–100€ ($75–$90) double. 25% reduction for children. Rates include full breakfast. MC, V. Closed Dec–Feb. *In room:* TV, tea/coffeemaker.

Drom House Rita and Gerald Brosnan, of Drom House (it means "hilly"), are both Dingle Peninsula natives. Rita was born in a house just up the road, and Gerald is manager of the West Kerry Co-op that has resurrected farming as a viable occupation hereabouts. Their hillside home sits amid sweeping mountain vistas 3 miles (5km) from Dingle town.

Coumgaugh, Dingle, Co. Kerry. ℂ **066/915-1134.** 3 units. 48€–51€ ($44–$46) double. 50% reduction for children sharing with an adult. Rates include full breakfast. No credit cards. *In room:* TV, tea/coffeemaker, hair dryer.

Gorman's Clifftop Guesthouse Sile and Vincent O'Gormin run this charming B&B/restaurant in one of the peninsula's most scenic locations near the small fishing village of Ballydavid (a great place to watch the glorious sunsets in this region). Rooms are both attractive and comfortable, and meals in the restaurant are good (see "Great Deals on Dining," below). The O'Gormans also have a bike-rental service, and can arrange guided cycle tours.

Glaise Bheag, Ballydavid, Dingle, Co. Kerry. ℂ/fax **066/915-5162.** www.gormans-clifftophouse.com. 3 units. 90€–102€ ($82–$92) double. Rates include full breakfast. MC, V. **Amenities:** Restaurant. *In room:* TV, TEL, hair dryer.

Slea Head Farm ✿ The waters of the Atlantic wash the rocks immediately below this cozy stone farmhouse, which has private access to the glorious Couminole Strand. The Firtear family are your thoughtful hosts. All the rooms have great sea views, looking out over Dunmore Head and the Blasket Islands; the two in the older part of the house are small, but have more character than the newer rooms. The house is on the Dingle Way, a day's walk from Dingle town, and is often used as a base by hikers. The Blasket Island Ferry is 1½ miles (2.5km) away. The house is situated in the midst of one of the most beautiful and unspoiled stretches of seacoast in Ireland, a fact that more than compensates for its slight austerity. This is an Irish-speaking household.

Couminole, Dunquin, Ventry, Co. Kerry. ℂ **066/915-6120.** www.sleaheadfarm.com. 5 units, 4 with bathroom (2 with shower only). 35€ single; 53€–58€ ($48–$53) double. Rates include full breakfast. MC, V. Closed Oct–Mar. On R559 from Dingle, about 0.62miles (1km) past Slea Head (first house on left). *In room:* Hair dryer.

Worth a Splurge

Greenmount House ✿✿ This outstanding accommodation, with its beautifully landscaped garden, is set on a secluded site with panoramic views of Dingle town and harbor. The owners, John and Mary Curran, have a deep knowledge of the peninsula, coming as they do from families rooted in this area for many generations. Their interest in helping guests makes staying here much like having your own personal guide. All bedrooms have orthopedic beds with electric blankets. The Currans' award-winning breakfasts are served in a plant-filled conservatory looking out to Dingle Bay. To find them, turn right at the roundabout on the eastern edge of town, then right again at the next junction, and drive to the top of the hill, where you'll see Greenmount on your left.

Gortanora, Dingle, Co. Kerry. ℂ **066/915-1414.** Fax 066/915-1974. www.greenmounthouse.com 12 units. 63€–114€ ($57–$103) double depending on season. Rates include full breakfast. MC, V. Closed Dec 20–26. *In room:* TV, TEL, tea/coffeemaker, hair dryer, radio.

Milltown House ✿   You couldn't wish for a more picturesque Dingle setting than this bayside haven. A narrow road leads to it and, once inside, you'll see why much of their business is repeat. The property incorporates the amenities of a hotel with the informal warmth of a B&B. The spacious guest rooms—each uniquely designed—have sitting areas and firm, orthopedic beds. Half have sea views and nearly all have patios. The non-smoking sitting room—all easy chairs and open fires—is elegant and comfortable, while the conservatory breakfast room (where you'll enjoy a lavish breakfast menu) looks out on Dingle Bay. Film buffs might want to request Room 2, where Robert Mitchum stayed while filming *Ryan's Daughter.*

Dingle, County Kerry. ✆ **066/915-1372.** Fax 066/915-1095. http://indigo.ie/~milltown. 10 units. 84€–120€ ($76–$109) double. Rates include full breakfast. AE, MC, V. *In room:* TV, TEL, tea/coffeemaker, hair dryer, trouser press.

SELF-CATERING

Beginish Apartments   These apartments are in the ultimate convenient location, in the heart of Dingle town, just two doors up from the Beginish Restaurant (see below). They're decorated and furnished to a high standard, complete with dishwasher, microwave, washing machine and dryer. The ground-floor apartment has a patio garden and one bedroom suitable for two people. The two first-floor apartments have two bedrooms that will accommodate three.

Green St., Dingle, Co. Kerry. ✆ **066/915-1588.** Fax 066/915-1591. johnpmoore@eircom.net. 3 units: 1 1-bedroom, 2 2-bedroom. 222€–419€ ($201–$380) per week depending on season. No credit cards. *In room:* TV (satellite), coffeemaker, washer and dryer, microwave, dishwasher.

Ventry Holiday Cottages   These charming cottages overlook the pictur-esque little village of Ventry and its harbor. They're traditional in design, yet equipped with fully stocked kitchens and other conveniences. Each features a large lounge/dining area, and has a stove for cool days and nights. The three carpeted bedrooms will sleep six adults.

℅ O'Shea's Property Management, 6 High St., Tralee, Co. Kerry. ✆ **066/718-1222.** Fax 066/718-1223. 8 cottages. 165€–700€ ($149–$634) per week depending on season. 4½ miles (7km) from Dingle town on the coast road to Slea Head. **Amenities:** Full kitchen.

GREAT DEALS ON DINING
IN DINGLE TOWN

An Cafe Liteartha CAFE/TEA ROOM   "The Literary Cafe" is a self-service tea room and a fabulous bookstore with books and maps of Irish interest, and a focus on life in this corner of County Kerry. The cafe section features soups, salads, seafood, and freshly baked scones and cakes, as well as traditional dishes such as Irish stew. It's an ideal spot to browse and to enjoy a quick lunch or snack in the middle of town.

Dykegate St., Dingle. ✆ **066/915-2204.** Reservations not necessary. All items under 4€ ($3.65). No credit cards. Mon–Fri 10am–6pm; Sat–Sun 11am–6pm.

Dingle Skellig Hotel *Value* SEAFOOD/TRADITIONAL IRISH   Budget watchers can dine in style in the bar of this waterfront hotel, which has one of the best bar menus around. Seafood is featured, along with the usual pub fare of sandwiches, soup, hot plates, and salads. The pricier Coastguard Restaurant overlooks Dingle Bay. While I find it almost impossible to bypass fresh seafood here, the menu also includes Kerry mountain lamb, filet of Irish beef on a cracked pepper and brandy cream sauce, pork, chicken, and duck. Vegetarian dishes, when available, are imaginative as well as healthy—try the vegetarian Stroganoff, served with a paprika and brandy sauce on a bed of pasta.

Dingle, Co. Kerry. ℭ **066/915-1144**. www.dingleskellig.com. Bar food 6.50€–18€ ($5.90–$16); fixed-price dinner 41€ ($37); dinner main courses 27€ ($24). AE, DC, MC, V. Daily bar food 12:30–9pm; dinner 7–9:30pm.

Doyle's Seafood Bar SEAFOOD   This cozy old pub has rock walls, a flagstone floor, and a blackboard menu showing a selection of seafood from local fishing boats' same-day catch. The owners even smoke their own salmon. Specialties include baked filet of lemon sole with prawn sauce, salmon filet in puff pastry with sorrel sauce, rack of lamb, and a signature platter of seafood (sole, salmon, lobster, oysters, and crab claws). There's also good homemade soup. If you haven't booked in advance you can expect a wait for a seat in this small dining room. There's a separate nonsmoking room.

John St., Dingle, Co. Kerry. ℭ **066/915-1174**. Reservations recommended. Main courses 15€–32€ ($14–$29). 10% service charge. DC, MC, V. Mid-Feb to Dec Mon–Sat 5:30–9:30pm.

Fenton's INTERNATIONAL   This restaurant in the heart of town combines a country cottage interior of pine furniture and stone walls with a bright and airy garden courtyard setting that seats 12 people for alfresco dining. The diverse menu includes dishes like hot buttered lobster, mussels in garlic with white wine sauce, and medallions of filet steak on a garlic croûte topped with Cashel Bleu cheese. Between 6 and 7pm the price of the fixed-price dinner is reduced to 24€ ($22).

Green St., Dingle. ℭ **066/915-2172**. Reservations recommended. Lunch main courses 4€–9€ ($3.60–$8); fixed-price dinner 28€ ($25). AE, V. Tues–Sun noon–2:30pm and 6–9:30pm. Closed Nov–Mar.

Worth a Splurge

Beginish Restaurant ✦✦ SEAFOOD   If you're after the best seafood in Dingle, look no further. Mrs. Pat Moore runs this delightful small restaurant, and she's managed to achieve an atmosphere of quiet elegance, unassuming and comfortable. There's a lovely conservatory overlooking the garden in back, with room for outdoor tables in summer. Although there are lamb and beef dishes and a vegetarian special each night, the emphasis is on fish—the cooking is simple, traditional, and always delightful. Among the starters, the smoked salmon with shallots, capers, and horseradish cream is exquisite—nothing fancy, just excellent ingredients combined in the perfect proportions. Also delicious is the tomato and goat cheese mousse with fennel. You can't go wrong with any of the fish main courses, such as the monkfish with Provençal sauce or cod on thyme-scented potatoes and sweet red peppers.

Green St., Dingle, Co. Kerry. ℭ **066/915-1588**. Reservations recommended. Lunch 8.90€–20€ ($8–$18); dinner main courses 17€–28€ ($15–$25). AE, DC, MC, V. Tues–Sun 12:30–2:15pm and 6–10pm.

AROUND THE PENINSULA

Gorman's Clifftop Restaurant SEAFOOD/IRISH   This charming restaurant and B&B (see "Accommodations You Can Afford," earlier in this chapter) offers wide windows that take advantage of the surrounding scenery. The place specializes in fresh local produce and seafood just out of the local waters. There's also a wide variety of beef, lamb, and chicken dishes, as well as a vegetarian dish of the day. The Irish stew is especially good here. Light meals are served from noon to 6pm, and dinner from 6pm to 9pm.

Ballydavid, Dingle, Co. Kerry. ℭ **066/915-5162**. Lunch main courses 7€–19€ ($6.35–$17); dinner main courses 15€–25€ ($14–$23). MC, V. Daily noon–9pm. Closed Nov–Feb.

SHOPPING

Most shops in Dingle are open daily 9am to 7pm or 8pm in summer (June–Sept), with reduced hours during the rest of the year.

Brian De Staic   Considered by many to be Ireland's leading goldsmith, Brian de Staic plies his trade in his workshop, located just west of the Dingle Pier. He specializes in unusual Irish jewelry, hand-crafted and engraved with the letters of the Ogham alphabet, an ancient Irish form of writing dating from the 3rd century. His collection includes pendants, bracelets, earrings, cuff links, brooches, and tie clips. There are two other retail shops as well: Green Street, Dingle (© Kerry. © **066/915-1298**. www.brian-de-staic.ie.

Dunquin Pottery   Operated by local people—Maureen, Eiblin, Helena, and Sean Daly, who worked for founder Jean Oldfield for many years—this place turns out hand-thrown, oven-proof stoneware in shades of sand and browns and blues. The prices are reasonable. The small cafe on the premises serves Rambouts coffee, Irish porter cake, and other snacks. On the road between Slea Head and Dunquin, Co. Kerry.© **066/915-6194**.

Greenlane Gallery   This gallery/shop offers a wide selection of contemporary Irish paintings, watercolors, sculpture, and ceramics. Works by leading Irish artists are always available, and private viewings can be arranged. Images are available by e-mail on request. Green St., Dingle. © **066/915-2018**. www.greenlanegallery.com.

Holden Dingle *(Finds* Jackie and Conor Holden offer beautiful handcrafted suede and silk-lined leather handbags, suede and leather pouches, and duffel and travel bags, as well as briefcases, belts, wallets, and key cases. Their workshop is in a converted schoolhouse, signposted 3 miles (5km) west of Dingle town on the Ventry road (R559), off Slea Head Drive. The Old School House, Burnham, Dingle. © **066/915-1796**. holdenj@iol.ie.

Irish Wildflowers Ltd. *(Finds* Marianne Begley, a transplanted American, lost her heart to the wildflowers of Ireland and set up what has become a thriving business, with annual, perennial, and biennial wildflower seed packets on sale in gift and craft shops around the country. She also stocks a variety of other fine floral gifts here and welcomes mail order. Prices run all the way from 1€ to 250€ (90¢ to $226). The new Fisherman's Old Stone Cottage Gallery features the work of local artists. 132 The Wood, Dingle, Co. Kerry. © **066/915-2200**. Fax 066/915-2201.

Lisbeth Mulcahy/The Weavers' Shop *(Finds* One of Ireland's leading weavers, Lisbeth creates fabrics and tapestries inspired by seasonal changes in the Irish landscape and seascape. She uses pure wool, Irish linen/cotton, and alpaca in the weaving of scarves, shawls, knee rugs, wall hangings, tapestries, tablemats, and napkins. A range of Irish goods is also sold here, including leather and glass. Green St., Dingle, Co. Kerry. © **066/915-1688**.

Louis Mulcahy Pottery   This is a large working pottery studio, producing a range of pottery made from local clay and glazes devised at the shop. The finished products include giant vases, teapots, platters, and huge lamps. Furniture and hand-decorated silk and cotton lampshades are available, as well as a selection of Lisbeth Mulcahy's tapestries and weavings. Clogher, Ballyferriter, Co. Kerry. © **066/915-6429** or 066/915-6484.

McKenna's   For good buys in Waterford crystal, Aran sweaters, and other Irish goods, McKenna's is hard to beat. The shop offers a discount for payment in cash. Dykegate St., Dingle, Co. Kerry. © **066/915-1198**.

Sheehy's Pottery Penny Sheehy specializes in unique ceramic Celtic murals and explanation plaques of old Celtic myths. She also has a range of unusual small kitchen utensils, ashtrays, and personalized mugs with your name in the Gaelic style. The old timber-ceilinged building that was once a ballroom is almost a sightseeing attraction in itself, and light meals of home-cooked food are served as well. Mrs. Sheehy has another shop at Holy Ground in Dingle town. Ventry, Co. Kerry. ℰ **066/915-9962.**

DINGLE AFTER DARK
THE PUB SCENE
An Droichead Beag/The Small Bridge With its old-Dingle decor and a friendly atmosphere, this pub, right in the heart of town, draws crowds each night throughout the year for its sessions of traditional Irish music, usually starting at 9:30pm. Be sure to arrive early if you want even standing room! Lower Main St., Dingle, Co. Kerry. ℰ **066/915-1723.**

Dick Mack's Although Richard "Dick" Mack died years ago, his family keeps on the traditions of this unique pub where Dick handcrafted leather boots, belts, and other items in between his pub chores. The small leather shop is still on the left, opposite a tiny bar. The walls are lined with old pictures, books, and mugs, all part of the Dick Mack legend. It's a favorite among locals, as it has been for celebrities such as Robert Mitchum, Timothy Dalton, and Paul Simon, whose names are commemorated with stars on the sidewalk just outside. Green St., Dingle, Co. Kerry. ℰ **066/915-1070.**

O'Flaherty's *Finds* For a night of traditional music and song that comes from true family tradition, look for the red-and-white pub on Bridge Street with the name *UaFlaibeartaig*, which translates to "O'Flaherty's." The late father of the present O'Flaherty clan was recognized as one of the country's best traditional musicians, and now son Fergus and daughter Maire raise instruments and voice each night surrounded by locals and visitors who've come to hear the best. It's a warm, informal gathering in a setting that's as traditional as the music. Bridge St., Dingle, Co. Kerry. ℰ **066/915-1983.**

4 The Northern Dingle Peninsula

The northern side of the Dingle Peninsula, especially along the west shore of **Brandon Bay,** is a treasure waiting to be discovered. Tiny port towns, beautiful clean beaches, rugged mountain walks, and little-known archaeological sites are the main appeal of this extraordinary region. To reach the town of Castlegregory and the northern shores of the peninsula from Dingle town, take the **Conor Pass** road north from Dingle, turning left just past Stradbally on the R560. There are great views and fine walks from the summit of Conor Pass, so leave yourself some time to park the car or bicycle and explore some of this high country.

EXPLORING THE AREA

A good place to base yourself is **Castlegregory,** a charming town between Brandon Bay and Tralee Bay. Head first to the **Visitor Information** center (ℰ **066/713-9422**), located on the main street. While you're there, stop in for a cup of tea and a scone at **The Milesian Cafe** (no phone), located in a rustic cottage, where you can have your tea sitting in front of the peat fire or among the rafters in a cozy loft. Frank Fitzgerald is the friendly proprietor, whose eclectic interests are reflected in the books that fill every nook. The cafe is open from

11am to 9:30pm, and meals are served from 6:30 to 9:30pm; main courses are 9€ to 13€ ($8.15–$12).

A few kilometers north of Castlegregory you'll find the tiny port towns of **Fahamore** and **Kilshannig,** both popular with divers and windsurfers. **Spillane's Bar** (© 066/713-9125) in Fahamore is a local institution, and a great place for a pint and a simple meal selected from the day's catch (for better or worse, most of the fish here is fried).

West of Castlegregory lies Brandon Bay, which is lined with many kilometers of glorious beaches, and generally has bigger waves than the calmer (and safer) Tralee Bay. **Cloghane** and **Brandon** , two of the loveliest towns in the region, are on the west side of the Bay, on the lower slopes of Mount Brandon. There's an **information center** (© 066/713-8142) in Cloghane village, open daily June to Sept 10am to 1pm and 2pm to 5pm; it's also open holiday weekends throughout the year. Hours can be irregular. The center offers extensive information on the Cloghane/Brandon region and a selection of local crafts.

The path to **Mount Brandon** from the Cloghane side is clearly marked, unlike most high-country walks in Ireland (for more details, see "Outdoor Pursuits," below). The walk to the summit of Ireland's second-highest mountain is most enjoyable and safest when the peaks are free of clouds, but unfortunately that doesn't happen very often. The summit is marked by the remains of an ancient building known as St. Brendan's Oratory, and it's said that the navigator saint spent some time here before setting out on his epic sea journey from Brandon Creek, on the mountain's west side. The oratory is the site of a pilgrimage on the last Sunday in June, when Mass is celebrated on the mountaintop, sometimes with hundreds in attendance.

OUTDOOR PURSUITS

DIVING **Harbour House,** The Maharees, Castlegregory, County Kerry (© **066/713-9292;** fax 066/712-5032; www.waterworld.ie), is a diving center that offers packages including diving, room, and board at remarkable rates. The house is yards from the Scraggane Pier, and a 5- to 15-minute boat ride from most of the diving sites. All members of the Fitzgibbon family are active divers, and they offer a great vacation for people who share their passion for this sport. Classes for beginners are also available. A leisure center with pool, gym, and sauna was added in 2000. A week's diving, including accommodation and meals, is about 445€ ($403), and a single dive is 25€ ($23).

WALKING The best walk in the region, and one of the best in Ireland, is the ascent to **Brandon's summit** . The approach from the west is a more gradual climb, but the walk from the Cloghane (eastern) side is far more interesting and includes the beautiful Paternoster Lakes.

The road to the trailhead is signposted just past Cloghane on the road to Brandon town; drive about 3 miles (5km) on this road to a small parking lot and the Lopsided Tea House. Be sure to bring plenty of water and food, gear for wind and rain, and a good map, preferably the ordnance survey map, available in most local stores. The trail climbs through fields, past an elaborate grotto, and along the slope of an open hillside where flashy red and white poles mark the way. As you round the corner of the high, open hillside, the Paternoster Lakes and Brandon itself come into view—the walk through this glacial valley toward the base of the mountain is the most beautiful part of the trail, and when the weather's bad you won't have wasted your time if you turn around before reaching the summit. The only seriously strenuous leg of the journey is the climb out of this valley to the ridge top, a short but intense scramble over boulders and around ledges. Once you reach the ridge top, turn left and follow the trail another third of a mile or so to the summit.

You can return the way you came or continue south along the ridge, returning to Cloghane via the Pilgrim's Route, an old track that circumnavigates the Dingle Peninsula. Although this is a short walk (about 4 hr. to the summit and back) and very well marked, it shouldn't be taken too lightly—bring all necessary supplies and let someone know when you expect to return. Information on climbing routes and weather conditions is available at the Cloghane visitor center (see above).

Brandon Point is the headland at the end of the road connecting Cloghane and Brandon town, and has superb views across the Bay and toward the open Atlantic. You can also walk along the headland toward Sauce Creek, a large inlet about 2 miles (3km) to the west. There isn't any trail here, but so long as the visibility is good navigation should be easy.

The section of the **Dingle Way** along Brandon Head, between Brandon Point and Brandon Creek, is particularly rugged and remote, and should only be undertaken when visibility is good.

WINDSURFING   The beaches around Castlegregory offer a variety of conditions for windsurfing, with the beaches on the eastern side of the peninsula generally calmer than those to the west. Equipment can be rented from **Jamie Knox Adventure Watersports,** Maharees, Castlegregory, County Kerry (© **066/ 713-9411;** www.jamieknox.com), located on the road between Castlegregory and Fahamore. Kayaks are also available.

ACCOMMODATIONS YOU CAN AFFORD

Benagh ⭐   Benagh is on the west side of Brandon Bay, where Mount Brandon gently slopes away into the sea. The area is breathtakingly beautiful, and the view from the house across the Bay toward the Magharee Islands and the inland mountains is one you won't soon forget. The guest rooms have been built on as a second-floor addition, and each has a window facing the bay and decor that's refreshingly simple, with wooden floors and white walls. The McMorran family is actively involved in local tourism, and will give you expert guidance in seeking out local walks and archaeological sites. The bedrooms are all nonsmoking.

Cloghane, Co. Kerry. © **066/713-8142.** 4 units. 41€–46€ ($37–$41) double. Rates include full breakfast. Dinner 18€ ($16); reservations for dinner must be made before noon. No credit cards.

The Shores ⭐   The Shores is a modern house on the south side of Brandon Bay, commanding good views of the bay and Mount Brandon. Proprietor Annette O'Mahoney has decorated so thoughtfully and tastefully that each room has a unique ambience. Furnishings are lavish, with a canopy bed in one of the upstairs rooms and writing desks in three of the rooms. The downstairs room has a private entrance and a fireplace. Breakfast options are particularly extensive, with smoked salmon and waffles given as alternatives to the standard fry, and dinner or packed lunches are also available if you arrange in advance.

Cappatigue, Castlegregory, Co. Kerry. ©/fax **066/713-9196.** http://shores.main-page.com. 6 units. 40€–50€ ($36–$45) single; 55€–66€ ($50–$60) double. Rates include full breakfast. Dinner 23€ ($21). MC, V. Closed Dec–Feb. ½ mi (1km) west of Stradbally on the Conor Pass road. *In room:* TV.

SELF-CATERING

Illauntannig Island Cottage ⭐⭐ *(Finds)*   For those who really want to get away from it all in a stunningly beautiful place, this cottage presents a unique opportunity: having an Irish island all to yourself for a week. Illauntannig is one of the seven Maharees Islands, located about 1 mile (1.5km) offshore from Scraggane Bay, on the north shore of the Dingle Peninsula. The island covers an area of about 36 acres, and has been inhabited since at least the 6th century, when St. Seanach founded a monastery here. The remains of this monastic site, now a national monument, are a short walk from the house; perched on the water's edge are several beehive huts, an oratory, some beautiful stone crosses, and an enclosing wall.

The self-catering cottage is the only one on the island. It's a small stone structure with four bedrooms, a sitting room with fireplace, and a sunny kitchen with dining alcove. You're definitely roughing it out here, with oil lamps substituting for electric ones, and precious drinking water brought over from the mainland. Still, the basic necessities are all provided for, with gas-powered refrigeration, a hot water heater, and a toilet with shower. Your only companions for the week will be the seabirds (many species nest on the island) and the cows, the island's only year-round residents. Bob Goodwin, a venerable seaman with a wealth of knowledge on local bird life and history, will check in on you every day via two-way radio, and can take you to the mainland as often as necessary for supplies. Although some might balk at the isolation or the austerity of the accommodation, for the right person this place is a dream come true.

Contact Bob Goodwin, Maharees, Castlegregory, Co. Kerry. ℂ/fax **066/713-9443**. 4 bedrooms, none with bathroom (sleeps up to 8). Apr–May and Sept–Oct 380€ ($345) per week; June–Aug 445€ ($403) per week. Rates include transport to and from the island, bedding, and all utilities. No credit cards.

Kerry Cottages ⊛ *Kids* These traditional style cottages are sited off a quiet back road, just a few minutes on foot to the beach and another 20 minutes or so to Castlegregory village. Three of the cottages have three bedrooms and semi-private back yards. The smallest cottage is a cozy two-bedroom retreat with a small private garden; the largest is a palatial construction with five bedrooms, each with a private bathroom. Two others have four and five bedrooms. Second-story bedrooms in the larger cottages have great sea views. Each place is equipped with washer/dryer and dishwasher, and the kitchens are well stocked. There's a fireplace in the front room, and an electric heating system with outlets throughout the house. A small playground area for kids with swing set and slide is part of the complex. Special rates are available for couples.

Castlegregory, Dingle Peninsula, Co. Kerry. ℂ **066/713-9240**. Fax 066/713-9392. Book through Ray, Christine, and Jasmine Marshall, Kerry Cottages, 3 Royal Terrace West, Dun Laoghaire, Co. Dublin. ℂ 01/284-4000. Fax 01/284-4333. www.kerrycottages.com. 6 cottages; 2, 3, 4, and 5 bedrooms. Weekly rates 2- and 3-bedroom cottages Jan–Apr and Sept–Dec 261€–510€ ($236–$462), May–June 342€–680€ ($310–$616), July–Aug 797€–1015€ ($722–$919); 4-bedroom cottage supplement 500€–1225€ ($453–$1,110) weekly year-round; 5-bedroom cottage 785€–1915€ ($711–$1734) weekly year-round. MC, V. 1 mile (1.5km) from Castlegregory. **Amenities:** TV, full kitchen, washer and dryer, microwave, dishwasher.

GREAT DEALS ON DINING

Thomasin's Bar PUB GRUB You can't miss this bright yellow bar and restaurant on the edge of Stradbally village. The bar is housed in a traditional-style two-story house, and there's an adjacent craft shop that stocks gift items, many of them made locally. In the small courtyard, umbrella tables afford outside eating. Seafood is the specialty here, but homemade soups, sandwiches, and other traditional pub grub are available.

Stradbally, Castlegregory, Co. Kerry. ℂ **066/713-9179**. Bar food under 13€ ($12); average dinner 20€ ($18). MC, V. Daily noon–3pm and 6–9pm.

5 Tralee & North Kerry

20 miles (32km) NW of Killarney

North Kerry is a vibrant mixture of busy county capital Tralee (its Irish name is *Traighli*, "the Strand of the River Lee"), sandy beaches quite safe for swimming, sites of medieval settlements, and bogs imbued with their own haunting beauty.

Tralee is the commercial center of County Kerry. With its population of 22,000, it's three times the size of Killarney. Tralee is more a functioning town than a tourist center, and locals outnumber visitors except perhaps during the ever-popular "Rose of Tralee" festival in August. This famous event is an international beauty contest for unmarried women of Irish ancestry. The contest is accompanied by street entertainment, music, dance, and other elements of general merrymaking, taking place in and around Tralee.

While there are several tourist attractions here, the town is not known for its scenic beauty, and most visitors just stop by briefly on their way to Dingle or County Clare. Tralee's greatest claim to fame is the National Folk Theatre of Ireland, Siamsa Tire, open year-round but most active during July and August.

The harbor of Tralee is located 4 miles (6.5km) northwest of the town, at **Fenit.** A major sailing center, Fenit is the spot where St. Brendan the Navigator is said to have been born in 484 (see box on p. 341).

GETTING THERE **Aer Lingus** operates daily nonstop flights from Dublin into **Kerry County Airport,** Farranfore, County Kerry (© **066/976-4644**), about 15 miles (24km) south of Tralee.

Buses from all parts of Ireland arrive daily at the **Bus Eireann Depot,** John Joe Sheehy Road (© **066/712-3566;** www.buseireann.ie).

Trains from major cities arrive at the **Irish Rail Station,** John Joe Sheehy Road (© **066/712-3522;** www.irishrail.ie).

Four major national roads converge on Tralee: N69 and N21 from Limerick and the north, N70 from the Ring of Kerry and points south, and N22 from Killarney, Cork, and the east.

VISITOR INFORMATION The **Tralee Tourist Office,** Ashe Memorial Hall, Denny Street (© **066/712-1288**), offers information on Tralee and the Dingle Peninsula. It is open weekdays 9am to 1pm and 2 to 5pm, with weekend and extended hours in the spring and summer. There is also a first-rate cafe on the premises. For Tralee tourist information on the Web, explore **www.tralee-insight.com**.

SEEING THE SIGHTS

In the little village of **Ardfert,** some 5 miles (8km) north of Tralee, a ruined medieval cathedral sits fully excavated and partially restored. The Romanesque doorway is one of the oldest parts of the existing structure, and probably dates back to the 12th century. In the northwest corner of the church is a niche containing the effigy of a bishop, dating from the 15th century. Nearby are the ruins of a 13th-century Franciscan friary. Both churches are thought to owe their existence to a local cult of St. Brendan, who is traditionally thought to have been born in nearby Fenit.

Over the years, **Listowel,** 17 miles (27km) northeast of Tralee, has produced a host of important Irish writers, including John B. Keane and Bryan MacMahon, and there's an interesting display of the town's literary activity in the library. (Incidentally, John B. Keane's pub is on William St.) **Writer's Week** *©*, in June or July, is an event not to miss if you're in the area—a solid week when serious-minded

Tips **A Shortcut to County Clare**

County Clare can be reached directly from North Kerry, bypassing Limerick, via the **Tarbert-Killimer Car Ferry,** which crosses the Shannon River from Tarbert, County Kerry, to Killimer, County Clare. Crossing time is 20 minutes, via a drive-on/drive-off service; no reservations are needed. Ferries operate April through September, Monday through Saturday from 7 or 7:30am until 9 or 9:30pm, and Sunday from 9 or 9:30am until 9 or 9:30pm; and October through March, Monday through Saturday from 7 or 7:30am to 7 or 7:30pm, and Sunday from 10 or 10:30am to 7 or 7:30pm. Crossings from Tarbert are on the half-hour, and from Killimer, on the hour. The summer fares for cars with passengers are 13€ ($12) one-way and 19€ ($17) round-trip. For more information, contact **Shannon Ferry Ltd.,** Killimer/Kilrush, County Clare (② **065/905-3124;** www.shannonferries.com). The Killimer Ferry terminal has a gift shop and restaurant, open daily from 9am to 9pm.

workshops and lectures rule the daytime and unrestrained revelry breaks loose in the pubs at night. In the town square, look for the **St. John's Arts & Heritage Centre** (② **068/22566**), which features work and performances by Irish and international artists. In September, the **Listowel Races** draw huge crowds of equestrian fans from around the country.

A short drive northeast of Listowel brings you to **Ballybunion,** 21 miles (34km) from Tralee, a popular seaside resort famous for its golf course and dramatic seascape of soaring cliffs and sandy cove beaches. There are some 14 Celtic promontory forts in this area. If time permits, walk at least a portion of the celebrated Cliff Walk (out the Doon road; turn left after the convent).

Carrigafoyle Castle , 8 miles (13km) west of Tarbert along the shores of the Shannon Estuary, is unique in that it's situated between the high and low tide marks and originally held a dock for ships within its walls. The tower commands great views of the Shannon estuary, and the battlements are accessible by a spiral stair in the northeast corner of the castle. Built in the 16th century, the tower was originally surrounded by two enclosing walls; little remains of the outer walls, and half the tower was leveled in 1580 during a siege. This demolition offers a rare treat for visitors—the opportunity to see the layout of the castle in cross section, including the secret chambers in the thickness of the vault. Look for the impression left in the underside of the vault by the wickerwork that was used as a support during the construction of the castle. To get to the castle from Tarbert, take the Ballybunion road and follow the signs.

Blennerville Windmill   Located just 3 miles (5km) west of Tralee and reaching 65 feet (20m) high, this landmark mill is the largest working windmill in Ireland or Britain. It was built in 1800 by Sir Rowland Blennerhasset and flourished until 1850. After decades of neglect, the mill was restored in the early 1990s and is now fully operational, producing 5 tons of ground whole-meal flour per week. The visitor complex has an emigration exhibition center, an audiovisual theater, craft workshops, and a cafe.

R559, Blennerville, Co. Kerry. ② **066/712-1064.** Admission 3.50€ ($3.15) adults, 2.90€ ($2.65) students and seniors, 1.90€ ($1.70) children over 5, 8.90€ ($8) family. Mar–Oct daily 10am–6pm.

Kerry the Kingdom One of Ireland's largest indoor heritage centers, the Kingdom offers three separate attractions that give an in-depth look at 7,000 years of life in County Kerry. A 10-minute video, *Kerry in Colour,* presents the seascapes and landscapes of Kerry; the Kerry County Museum chronologically examines the county's music, history, legends, and archaeology through interactive and hands-on exhibits; and there's an exhibit on Gaelic football. Many items of local origin that were previously on view at the National Museum in Dublin are now here. Complete with lighting effects and aromas, a theme park–style ride, "Geraldine Tralee," takes you through a re-creation of Tralee's streets and houses during the Middle Ages. The gift shop was recently expanded to include many unique items.

Ashe Memorial Hall, Denny St., Tralee, Co. Kerry. (✆) **066/712-7777.** Admission 7€ ($6.35) adults, 6€ ($5.45) students, 3.80€ ($3.45) children, 22€ ($20) family. Mid-Mar to July and Sept–Oct daily 10am–6pm; Aug daily 10am–7pm; Nov–Dec daily noon–5pm.

Tralee Steam Railway ✇ This restored steam train, Europe's most westerly railway, offers narrated, scenic, 2-mile (3km) trips from Tralee's Ballyard Station to Blennerville (and back again). The train uses equipment that was once part of the Tralee & Dingle Light Railway (1891–1953), one of the world's most famous narrow-gauge railways. Trains run hourly on the hour from Ballyard Station, starting at 11am; and hourly on the half-hour from Blennerville starting at 10:30am.

Ballyard, Tralee. (✆) **066/712-8888.** 3.50€ ($3.45) adults, 2.90€ ($2.80) students and seniors, 1.90€ ($1.90) children, 8.90€ ($8.75) family. May–Sept daily noon–5:30pm; June–Aug daily 11am–5:30pm. Closed 2nd Mon and Tues each month for maintenance.

OUTDOOR PURSUITS

GOLF Like its neighbor Killarney, Tralee is great golfing turf, particularly at the **Tralee Golf Club,** Fenit/Churchill Road, West Barrow, Ardfert (✆ **066/ 713-6379;** www.traleegolfclub.com), which overlooks the Atlantic 8 miles (13km) northwest of town. This was the first Arnold Palmer–designed golf course in Europe. One of Ireland's newer courses, it's expected in time to rank among the great courses of the world. Greens fees are 95€ ($86). A 9-hole course at the Ballybeggan Park racecourse opened in 1997 (✆ **068/712-6188**), with greens fees of 19€ ($17).

About 25 miles (40km) north of Tralee in the northwest corner of County Kerry is the famous **Ballybunion Golf Club,** Ballybunion, County Kerry (✆ **068/27146;** www.ballybuniongolfclub.ie). This facility offers visitors a new clubhouse and the chance to play on two challenging 18-hole seaside links, both on the cliffs overlooking the Shannon River estuary and the Atlantic. Tom Watson has rated the "old" course one of the finest in the world; the "new" one was designed by Robert Trent Jones. Greens fees are 95€ ($86) on the old course.

HORSE RACING Horse racing takes place twice a year (in early June and late Aug) at **Tralee Racecourse,** Ballybeggan Park, Tralee (✆ **066/712-6188**). Post time is usually 2:30pm. Admission is 13€ ($12) adults, 6.50€ ($5.90) students and seniors, and .65€ (60¢) for children under 14.

ACCOMMODATIONS YOU CAN AFFORD
TRALEE

Brianville This pretty modern bungalow is the home of Joan Smith. The house is fronted by green lawns and has wide floor-to-ceiling windows that give the interior a light, airy ambience and afford striking views of the nearby mountains. Guest rooms are attractive as well as comfortable.

Clogherbrien, Fenit Rd., Tralee, Co. Kerry. © 066/712-6645. 5 units, 4 with bathroom (shower only). 63€ ($58) double. 50% reduction for children sharing with an adult. No credit cards. 1 mile (1.5km) from Tralee. *In room:* TV, tea/coffeemaker, hair dryer.

Collis-Sandes House Hostel. This hostel is fortuitously situated in one of the most spectacular manor houses in the region, built by Morris Fitzgerald Sandes upon his return from India in 1857. The front portion of the house is used as a language school—if it's open, you should make a point of visiting the entrance hall, one of the finest of its kind in Ireland. There are two self-catering kitchens, and the one in the old stable yard is especially appealing with its exposed stone walls and rustic decor. The rooms in the old coach house are small and have ultrathin walls, so you should request a room in the back wing of the house, where rooms are more spacious and better constructed. Like most hostels, accommodations are spartan here, but reliably clean and comfortable.

Tralee, Co. Kerry. ©/fax 066/712-8658. www.colsands.com. 16 units, 2 with bathroom. 19€ ($17) single; 33€ ($30) double; 14€ ($13) per person triple; 13€ ($12) per person 4- to 6-bed dorm; 10€ ($9.10) per person 8-bed dorm. MC, V. **Amenities:** Self-catering kitchen; coin-op laundry.

Curraheen House   Mrs. Bridget Keane's traditional farmhouse is on the Tralee-Dingle road (R559), 4 miles (6.5km) from Tralee, overlooking Tralee Bay, with mountain views in the distance. The very embodiment of Irish hospitality, Mrs. Keane is known for her delicious high tea and dinner, often featuring salmon and fish fresh from local waters, as well as a lovely mixed grill. In fact, she has opened Keanes Bar and Restaurant, adjacent to the house (see "Great Deals on Dining," below). Those fantastic Dingle Peninsula sandy beaches are only 2 miles (3km) away, and golfing, pony trekking, and sea fishing are all available locally.

Curraheen, Tralee, Co. Kerry. © 066/712-1717. 4 units. 48€ ($44) double. 25% reduction for children sharing with an adult. Rates include full breakfast. MC, V. Closed Nov–Feb. *In room:* Tea/coffeemaker.

Mountain View   Eileen Curley is the gracious host at Mountain View, set on its own landscaped grounds just outside Tralee. Her lively interest in guests' welfare adds immeasurably to their stay, because she knows the area well. Guest rooms are exceptionally well decorated. Three bedrooms and the dining room are designated as nonsmoking.

Ballinorig West, Tralee, Co. Kerry. © 066/712-2226. 6 units, 4 with bathroom (shower only). 36€ ($33) single without bathroom, 38.50€ ($35) single with bathroom; 46€ ($42) double without bathroom, 51€ ($46) double with bathroom. 25% reduction for children under 12 sharing with an adult. No credit cards. Closed Christmas. Approaching Tralee on the N21, turn right just before the roundabout. *In room:* TV, tea/coffemaker, hair dryer.

NORTH KERRY

Ashgrove House   Tim and Nancy O'Neill offer a warm welcome. Their four guest rooms are on the ground floor (a boon for those with limited mobility), and the dining room overlooks the garden, where there's a pleasant patio. Out front, tea and scones are often served on the glassed-in sun porch. The bedrooms, dining room, and sun porch are nonsmoking; there's a separate smoking lounge.

Ballybunion Rd., Listowel, Co. Kerry. © 068/23668 or 068/21268. Fax 068/21268. ashgrovehouse@ hotmail.com. 4 units. 40€ ($36) single; 52€ ($47) double. 25% reduction for children. Rates include full breakfast. MC, V. Closed Oct–Mar. ½ mile (1km) out of town on the Ballybunion road (R553). *In room:* TV, hair dryer, tea/coffeemaker.

Burntwood House   Mrs. Josephine Groarke is the pleasant hostess of this Georgian-style house set in very scenic countryside ½ mile (1km) from town.

The house is comfortable and modernized, and the food is delicious—homemade brown bread is a specialty. All six guest rooms are attractive and offer views of the country landscape.

Listowel, Co. Kerry. © 068/21516 or 068/21724. 6 units, 4 with bathroom (shower only). 58€ ($53) double. 20% reduction for children sharing with an adult. Rates include full breakfast. No credit cards. Closed Nov–Mar. *In room:* Tea/coffeemaker.

Ceol Na hAbhann ★★ *(Finds)*   Our readers have been profuse in their praise of this beautiful two-story, thatch-roofed home on a riverbank near a lovely wooded area about ½ mile (1km) outside Listowel. Mrs. Kathleen Stack takes great pride in her beautifully furnished home, one of the few thatch-roofed homes open to guests in Ireland. One room (the largest) has a double and twin bed, and a balcony overlooking the river. Mrs. Stack offers tea and scones upon arrival, and breakfasts are served in the Georgian dining room with fine linen, china, and silver. The famous Ballybunion golf course and beach are only 9 miles (14.5km) away. In case you were wondering, the name means "music of the river."

Tralee Rd., Ballygrennan, Listowel, Co. Kerry. ©/fax **068/21345.** knstack@eircom.net. 4 units. 51€–63€ ($46–$58) double; slight increase during events and holidays. Rates include full breakfast. MC, V. Free parking. Closed Nov–Mar. **Amenities:** Nonsmoking rooms available.

GREAT DEALS ON DINING

Keanes Bar and Restaurant BAR FOOD   Keanes is located 4 miles (6.5km) from Tralee on the main Tralee-Dingle road. The place serves bar food all through the day. Its restaurant menu features fresh local ingredients, with specialties such as pork filet with mushrooms and brandy cream or trout papillote. Desserts are noteworthy, especially the brandy, honey, and almond trifle.

Curraheen, Tralee, Co. Kerry. © **066/712-8054.** Lunch soup and sandwiches 2.50€–5€ ($2.30–$4.55); dinner main courses 7.50€–25€ ($6.80–$23). MC, V. Bar Mon–Sat 10:30am–11:30pm, Sun 12:30–2:30pm and 4–11pm; restaurant daily 6–9pm.

The Skillet *(Value)* BAR FOOD/SEAFOOD   Located in one of Tralee's historic narrow lanes, The Skillet has earned a local reputation for good food at good prices. Seafood here is outstanding, but its old-world ambience also makes the restaurant a pleasant place just to drop in for a morning or afternoon cup of tea or coffee. In addition to succulent steaks, there are curries, pizzas, and salads.

Barrack Lane, Tralee, Co. Kerry. © **066/712-4561.** Bar food under 10€ ($9.10); dinner main courses 10€–23€ ($9.10–$21). V. Mon–Sat 10am–10pm; Sun 6–10pm.

The Tankard SEAFOOD/IRISH   This restaurant, located 6 miles (9.5km) northwest of Tralee, is one of the few that capitalizes on sweeping views of Tralee Bay. Situated right on the water's edge, it's outfitted with wide picture windows and a sleek contemporary decor. The straightforward menu primarily features local shellfish and seafood such as lobster, scallops, prawns, and black sole, but also includes rack of lamb, duck, quail, and a variety of steaks. Bar food is available all day, but this restaurant is at its best in the early evening, especially at sunset.

Kilfenora, Fenit. © **066/713-6164.** Reservations recommended. Main courses 13€–23€ ($12–$21). AE, DC, MC, V. Bar daily noon–10pm; restaurant daily 6–10pm.

TRALEE AFTER DARK

Siamsa Tire *(Moments)*   At the top of the list for nighttime entertainment in Tralee is this National Folk Theatre troupe that performs in its own Siamsa Tire ("*Sheem*-sa *Tee*-ra") Theatre in the center of town. "Merrymaking" is the English translation of the Gaelic *siamsa,* and this is as merry a show as you'll come across. It depicts Irish country life of the past through music, song, dance, and mime. So professional is the performance that it will come as a surprise that the troupe operates on a very limited budget, with just a handful of full-time performers, and that most of those skilled musicians, actors, singers, and dancers give hours and hours of their time to perfect the show and travel with it on a strictly voluntary basis. National Folk Theatre, Town Park, Tralee. (C) 066/712-3055 or 066/712-3049 (for credit cards). Fax 066/712-7276. www.siamsatire.com. Admission 16€ ($15) adults. AE, MC, V. Box office open May to mid-Oct Mon–Sat 9am–10pm.

THE PUB SCENE

An Blascaod (The Blasket Inn)   This pub has a lovely modern facade and interior using a stark red-and-black color scheme. The inside includes a two-story atrium with an open fireplace, plus shelves lined with old books and plates. Castle St., Tralee. (C) 066/712-3313.

Harty's Lounge Bar   This pub is celebrated as the original meetinghouse where the Rose of Tralee festival was born. It is also known for its traditional pub grub such as steak and kidney pie, shepherd's pie, and Irish stew. Castle St., Tralee. (C) 066/712-5385.

Kirby's Olde Brogue Inn   This pub has a barnlike layout, with an interior that incorporates agricultural instruments, farming memorabilia, and rush-work tables and chairs. There's excellent pub grub, specializing in steaks, as well as traditional music and folk ballads when the right people show up. Rock St., Tralee. (C) 066/712-3357.

Oyster Tavern   The nicest location of any pub in the Tralee area belongs to this tavern, just 3 miles (5km) west of downtown, overlooking Tralee Bay. The pub grub available includes seafood soups and platters. Fenit Rd., Spa, Tralee. (C) 066/713-6102.

The West

In the west of Ireland, between lush Kerry and the rugged austerity of the Northwest, lie four counties: Limerick, Clare, Galway, and Mayo. Limerick, Clare, and Mayo—unlike Galway (the county and the town)—are not principal tourist destinations, though they have much to offer—but neither are they well-kept secrets. Westport, in County Mayo, for instance, is justifiably one of the most popular resort towns in Ireland, and the Burren in County Clare is well-known as a unique spectacle, though there's seldom a tour bus in sight.

County Galway, home to Ireland's most vibrant city and some of the country's best-known tourist attractions, needs to be dealt with on its own; we'll do so in chapters 11, "Galway City," and 12, "Out from Galway." For now, this chapter focuses on Galway's less-traveled yet surprisingly beautiful western neighbors.

1 Limerick City & Environs

Limerick is 15 miles (24km) E of Shannon Airport, 123 miles (198km) SW of Dublin, 65 miles (105km) N of Cork, 69 miles (111km) NE of Killarney, and 65 miles (105km) S of Galway

Limerick is the third-largest city in the Republic, with a population approaching 80,000. As a port on the River Shannon, Limerick has long been a city of strategic and commercial importance, and during the years that transatlantic flights were required to land at Shannon Airport, the city profited mightily from its proximity.

Very little of Limerick's ancient past strikes the eye of the visitor, apart from its 12th-century cathedral, its 13th-century castle, the restored Customs House, and remnants of Norman fortifications. What does strike the eye is a sprawling, struggling, hardworking city with limited resources and yet some residual energy to expend on polishing and preening itself for visitors. Limerick doesn't have the highest reputation at the moment—Frank McCourt's best-selling *Angela's Ashes* didn't help—but the town is working hard to re-create its image. Its recently developed riverside cultural and historic area, the **Heritage Precinct,** has considerable appeal and is well worth a day's visit. This may mark the beginning of an emergent renaissance for this proud city, which has had such a turbulent past.

The countryside around Limerick has a number of interesting sites to offer. Southwest of Limerick, the village of **Adare** is worth a visit, as are **Glin Castle, Lough Gur,** and **Rathkeale.** In addition to the attractions described below, see "Sights & Attractions Just Outside Limerick City," later in this chapter, for more suggestions about sightseeing when based in Limerick city.

GETTING THERE From the United States, Aer Lingus, Continental, and Delta Airlines operate regularly scheduled flights into **Shannon Airport,** off the Limerick-Ennis road (N18), County Clare (© **061/471444;** www.shannon airport.com), 15 miles (24km) west of Limerick. Domestic flights from Dublin

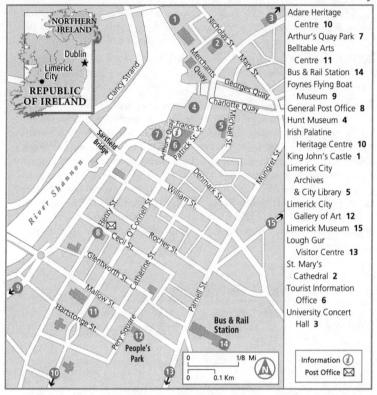

Adare Heritage
  Centre **10**
Arthur's Quay Park **7**
Belltable Arts
  Centre **11**
Bus & Rail Station **14**
Foynes Flying Boat
  Museum **9**
General Post Office **8**
Hunt Museum **4**
Irish Palatine
  Heritage Centre **10**
King John's Castle **1**
Limerick City
  Archives
  & City Library **5**
Limerick City
  Gallery of Art **12**
Limerick Museum **15**
Lough Gur
  Visitor Centre **13**
St. Mary's
  Cathedral **2**
Tourist Information
  Office **6**
University Concert
  Hall **3**

Information ⓘ
Post Office ✉

and overseas flights from Britain and the Continent are available from a range of carriers.

Bus Eireann (ⓒ **061/313333;** www.buseireann.ie) provides bus service from Shannon Airport to Limerick's Railway Station. The fare is 4.70€ ($4.25). A taxi costs about 25€ ($23).

Irish Rail operates direct trains from Dublin, Cork, and Killarney, with connections from other parts of Ireland. They arrive at Limerick's Colbert Station, Parnell Street (ⓒ **061/315555;** www.irishrail.ie).

If you're driving, Limerick city can be reached via N7 from the east and north; N20, N21, N24, and N69 from the south; and N18 from the west and north.

VISITOR INFORMATION The **Limerick Tourism Centre** is located on Arthur's Quay, Limerick (ⓒ **061/317522**). It's open year-round Monday through Friday from 9:30am to 5:30pm and Saturday 9:30am to 1pm; the center is sometimes closed for lunch between 1 and 2pm, particularly during the off season. From July to August the hours are 9am to 6pm daily. Ask for a free copy of the *Shannon Region Visitors Guide,* which is packed with helpful information about activities and events in Limerick and the surrounding areas.

A seasonal tourist office is open March to November in the **Adare Heritage Centre,** Main Street, Adare (ⓒ **061/396255**).

For good all-around visitor information on the Web, see **Visit Limerick** (www.visitlimerick.com).

GETTING AROUND By Public Transportation Bus Eireann (℃ 061/ 313333) operates local bus service around Limerick and its environs; the flat fare is 1€ (90¢). Buses depart from Colbert Station, Parnell Street.

By Taxi Taxis line up outside Colbert Station, at hotels, and along Thomas and Cecil Streets, off O'Connell Street. To call a taxi contact **Economy Taxis (℃ 061/ 411422), Express Taxis (℃ 061/417777),** or **Top Cabs (℃ 061/417417).**

By Car Driving around Limerick can be confusing because of the profusion of one-way streets. It's best to park your car and walk to see the sights, although you might want to drive to King's Island for King John's Castle and the other historic sights (there's a free parking lot opposite the castle). If you must park downtown, head for the multistory parking lot at **Arthur's Quay,** very convenient to all sight-seeing and shopping and well signposted. Parking is from 1.25€ ($1.15) per hour.

If you need to rent a car in Limerick, there are two car rental companies on the Ennis road: **Sixt-Irish Car Rental (℃ 061/206088)** and **O'Meara Freeway Car Hire (℃ 061/451611).** In addition, most major international car-rental firms maintain desks at Shannon Airport (see the "County Clare" section, later in this chapter).

FAST FACTS: Limerick City

Drugstores Try **Hogan's Pharmacy,** at 45 Upper William St., Limerick (℃ **061/415195).** After-hours service available by calling ℃ **088/526800.**

Emergencies Dial ℃ **999.**

Gay & Lesbian Resource Call the Gay and Lesbian Switchboard, Limerick (℃ 061/310101).

Hospital **St. John's Hospital** is located on St. John's Square, Limerick (℃ **061/415822).**

Laundry & Dry Cleaning Try Gaeltacht Cleaners, 58 Thomas St. (℃ 061/ 415124), or Speediwash Laundrette & Dry Cleaners, 11 St. Gerard St., Limerick (℃ 061/319380).

Library **Limerick County Library** is located at 58 O'Connell St., Limerick (℃ **061/318477).**

Local Publications & Radio Local papers include The *Limerick Leader,* published four times a week, and the *Limerick Chronicle,* a weekly. The weekly *Clare Champion,* published in Ennis, is also widely read in Limerick. The *Limerick Events Guide,* issued free every 2 weeks, gives news of entertainment. Radio Limerick broadcasts on 95 FM.

Parks Limerick's **People's Park** is located on Pery Square off Upper Mallow Street, 1 block east of O'Connell Street. Other smaller parks include Arthur's Quay Park and the Custom House Park.

Photographic Needs Try **Whelans Cameras,** 30 O'Connell St. (℃ **061/415246),** or **Photo World,** 3 William St. (℃ **061/417515),** for all your shutterbug needs.

Police The local **Garda Headquarters** is located on Henry Street (℃ **061/ 414222).**

Post Office The **General Post Office** is on Post Office Lane, off Lower Cecil Street, Limerick (℃ **061/314636).** There is a branch of the post office at Arthur's Quay Shopping Centre, Patrick Street (℃ **061/415261).**

SEEING THE SIGHTS

Follow the signposted **Tourist Trail** to see most of the city's main attractions; a booklet outlining the trail is available at the tourist office or in bookshops. Guided bus tours are also available.

Hunt Museum ⭑   The Hunt Museum is now happily ensconced in its new permanent home, the tastefully restored Old Custom House, the finest 18th-century building in Limerick, whose facade is a reduced copy of the Petit Trianon's at Versailles. The museum's collection of ancient, medieval, and modern treasures—reputed to be the finest in Ireland outside of Dublin's National Museum—includes antiquities and art objects from Europe and Ireland, ancient Irish metalwork, and medieval bronzes, ivories, and enamels. The museum also offers a shop and a most attractive restaurant, serving both snacks and full meals.

The Custom House, Rutland St., Limerick. ✆ 061/312833. www.ul.ie/~hunt/. Admission 5.35€ ($4.85) adults, 4.05€ ($3.70) students and seniors, 2.60€ ($2.40) children, 13€ ($12) family. Mon–Sat 10am–5pm; Sun 2–5pm.

King John's Castle ⭑   This royal fortress, strategically built on the banks of the Shannon River, is the centerpiece of Limerick's historic area. It is said to date from 1210, when King John of England visited and was so taken with the site that he ordered a "strong castle" to be built here. The castle survives today as one of the oldest examples of medieval architecture in Ireland, with rounded gate towers and curtain walls. Thanks to a recent $7 million restoration, the interior includes an authentic on-site archaeological excavation dating back to Hiberno/Norse times, as well as gallery displays and an audiovisual presentation portraying Limerick's 800 years of history. On the outside, the impressive facade has battlement walkways along the castle's walls and towers, offering sweeping views of the city. It is floodlit at night.

Nicholas St., Limerick. ✆ 061/411201. Admission 6.50 ($5.90) adults, 5€ ($4.55) seniors and students, 4€ ($3.65) children, 16€ ($14) family. Mar–Oct daily 10:30am–5:30pm (last admission 4:30pm).

Limerick City Gallery of Art   This gallery is situated in the neo-Romanesque Carnegie Building (built in 1903) in the People's Park, on the corner of Mallow Street. It houses a permanent collection of 18th-, 19th-, and 20th-century art, and also plays host to a wide range of traveling contemporary art exhibitions, including touring exhibitions from the Irish Museum of Modern Art.

Pery Sq., Limerick. ✆ 061/310633. Fax 061/415266. www.iol.ie/eva. Free admission. Mon–Wed and Fri 10am–6pm; Thurs 10am–7pm; Sat 10am–1pm.

Limerick Museum   Housed in two stone town houses dating from 1751, this museum provides an insight into the history of Limerick. It contains displays on Limerick's archaeology, natural history, civic treasures, and traditional crafts of lace, silver, furniture, and printing, plus historical paintings, maps, prints, and photographs. Of particular interest are the city's original charters from Cromwell and King Charles II, and the civic sword presented by Queen Elizabeth I.

Castle Lane, Nicholas St., Limerick. ✆ 061/417826. Free admission. Tues–Sat 10am–1pm and 2:15–5pm.

St. Mary's Cathedral ⭑   Founded in the 12th century on a hill on King's Island, this site originally held a palace belonging to one of the kings of Munster, Donal Mor O'Brien. In 1172, he donated it for use as a church. Currently undergoing restoration, the building contains many fine antiquities including a Romanesque doorway, a stone altar, and a huge stone coffin lid said to be that of Donal Mor O'Brien himself. Features added in later years include 15th-century *misericords* (supports for standing worshippers) with carvings in black oak, and a *reredos* (ornamental partition) on the high altar carved by the father of Irish patriot Patrick Pearse.

Bridge St., Limerick. ℂ **061/416238**. Donation 1.25€ ($1.15). June–Sept Mon–Sat 9am–5pm; Oct–May Mon–Sat 9am–1pm.

SIGHTS & ATTRACTIONS JUST OUTSIDE LIMERICK CITY

Dotted about the County Limerick countryside within a 25-mile (40km) radius of Limerick city are many historic and cultural attractions. Some of County Limerick's most scenic and historic attractions lie southwest of the city on the **Shannon Estuary Drive** ☆ (N69), a pleasant day's outing from the city.

At **Askeaton,** 16 miles (26km) west of Limerick, you'll pass virtually in the shadow of the ruined 15th-century **Desmond Castle** on a rocky islet in the River Deel just beside the road. There are also extensive remains of a **Franciscan friary** on the river bank. Farther west is the village of Glin, with its ruined castle (see listing), destroyed in 1600, and lofty 19th-century castellated Hamilton's Tower overlooking the pier.

The little town of **Drumcollogher,** 25 miles (40km) southwest of Limerick city (turn off N21 at Newcastle West onto R522), is where you can visit the **Irish Dresden Ltd.** factory and shop (ℂ **063/83030**), open Monday to Friday from 9am to 1pm and 2 to 5pm. Watch exquisite Dresden figurines being made, then browse through their showroom. Note that factory and shop are closed the last week in August.

Although **Adare** is unquestionably charming, I find it overdeveloped, its appeal obscured by the rampant tourist trade. There are good reasons for the town having become as popular as it is, but be prepared for rather unrestrained consumerism. To get to Adare, take N20 southwest from Limerick, turn right on N21 just past Patrickswell, and continue for 2½ miles (4km).

Adare Heritage Centre   For those who want to linger and learn more about Adare's history, the heritage center offers a walk-through display, along with a model of the town as it looked in medieval times. There's also a 20-minute audio-visual presentation illustrating the many facets of Adare today. The center, which is housed in a stone building with a traditional courtyard, operates an on-premises cafe, craft shop, knitwear shop, and library with books on the local area.

Main St., Adare, Co. Limerick. ℂ **061/396666**. Fax 061/396932. Admission 4€ ($3.65) adults, 2.60€ ($2.40) seniors and students, 8.25€ ($7.50) family. May–June and Sept–Oct daily 9am–5:30pm; July–Aug daily 9am–6pm.

Foynes Flying Boat Museum   For aviation buffs, this museum is a must. This is the first Shannon Airport, the predecessor to the modern Shannon Airport in County Clare. It has now been restored and reopened as a visitor attraction, to commemorate an era begun on July 9, 1939, when Pan Am's luxury flying boat *Yankee Clipper* landed at Foynes, marking the first commercial passenger flight on the direct route between the United States and Europe. A few years later, on June 22, 1942, Foynes was the departure point for the first nonstop commercial flight from Europe to New York. This was also the airport where Irish coffee was invented in 1942 by bartender Joe Sheridan. The complex includes a 1940s-style cinema and cafe, the original terminal building, and the radio and weather rooms with original transmitters, receivers, and Morse code equipment.

Foynes, Co. Limerick. ℂ **069/65416**. Admission 4.50€ ($4.10) adults, 3.80€ ($3.45) seniors, 2.60€ ($2.40) children, 11€ ($10) family. MC, V. Apr–Oct daily 10am–6pm (last admission at 5pm). Located 23 miles (37km) east of Limerick via N69.

Glin Castle 🐸🐸   Lillies of the valley and ivy-covered ash, oak, and beech trees line the driveway leading to this gleaming-white castle, home to the knights of Glin for the past 700 years. On the south bank of the Shannon Estuary, the sprawling estate contains 400 acres of gardens, farmlands, and forests. Although there were earlier residences on the site, the present home was built in 1785. It is more of a Georgian house than a castle, with added crenellations and gothic details. The current (29th) knight of Glin, Desmond FitzGerald, a noted historian and preservationist, maintains a fine collection of 18th-century Irish furniture and memorabilia. The house features elaborate plasterwork, Corinthian columns, and a unique double-ramp flying staircase. It's protected by three sets of toy fort lodges, one of which houses a craft shop and cafe.

Limerick-Tarbert Rd. (N69), County Limerick. ✆ 068/34173. Admission (for nonguests) to house and gardens 3.80€ ($3.45) adults, 1.25€ ($1.15) students. May–June daily 10am–noon, 2–4pm, and by appointment. Approximately 25 miles (40km) east of Limerick City.

Irish Palatine Heritage Centre   Ireland's unique links with southwestern Germany are the focus of this museum, located 18 miles (29km) south of Limerick off the main road. The extensive display of artifacts, photographs, and graphics illustrates the history of the several hundred Palatine families who emigrated from Germany and settled in this part of Ireland in 1709. In addition, the museum seeks to illustrate the Palatines' innovative contributions to Irish farming life and their formative role in the development of world Methodism.

Limerick-Killarney Rd. (N21), Rathkeale, Co. Limerick. ✆ 069/64397. Admission 2.60€ ($2.40) adults, 1.25€ ($1.15) children, 6.50€ ($5.90) family. May–Sept Mon–Sat 10am–1pm and 2–5pm, Sun 2–6pm; other times by appointment.

Lough Gur Visitor Centre   Lough Gur is one of Ireland's principal archaeological sites. The area was occupied continuously from the Neolithic period to late medieval times, and the site includes the foundations of a small farmstead built circa A.D. 900, a lake island dwelling built between A.D. 500 and 1000, a wedge-shaped tomb that was a communal grave around 2500 B.C., and the Grange Stone Circle, the largest and finest of its kind in Ireland. There's free access to its lake and shores, which make a great place to explore and have a picnic.

The museum and audiovisual program, however, are worth neither the time nor the fee. It's better to explore on your own and use your imagination.

Lough Gur, Co. Limerick. ✆ 061/360788 or 061/361511. Museum and audiovisual presentation 4€ ($3.65) adults, 3.30€ ($3.00) seniors and students, 2€ ($1.80) children, 8€ ($7.25) family. Mid-May to Sept daily 9:30am–5:30pm. Situated 7 miles (11km) southeast of Limerick city via R512.

OUTDOOR PURSUITS

FISHING   Visitors are welcome to cast a line in the River Shannon for trout and other freshwater fish. For information and equipment sales contact **Steve's Fishing and Shooting Store,** 7 Denmark St., Limerick (✆ **061/413484**).

GOLF   The Limerick area has three 18-hole golf courses, including a championship par-72 parkland layout at the **Limerick County Golf & Country Club,** Ballyneety (✆ **061/351881**), 5 miles (8km) east of Limerick, with greens fees of 34€ ($30) weekdays and 43€ ($38) weekends. In addition, there is the par-72 inland course at the **Limerick Golf Club,** Ballyclough (✆ **061/415146; www.limerickcounty.com**), 3 miles (5km) south of Limerick, charging greens fees of 25€ ($23) weekdays and 38€ ($35) weekends; and the par-69 inland course at **Castletroy Golf Club,** Castletroy, County Limerick (✆ **061/335753; cgc@iol.ie**), 3 miles (5km) east of Limerick, with greens fees of 32€ ($29) weekdays and 38€ ($35) weekends.

HORSEBACK RIDING   County Limerick's fertile fields provide good turf for horseback riding and pony trekking, at rates starting at about 23€ ($21) per hour. The **Clonshire Equestrian Centre,** Adare, County Limerick (*©* **061/ 396770;** www.clonshire.com), offers riding for all levels of ability, horsemanship classes, and instruction for cross-country riding, dressage, and jumping. Riding and board packages are available.

HORSE RACING   The **Tipperary Race Course,** Limerick Junction (*©* **062/ 51357**), is about 20 miles (32km) southeast of Limerick near Tipperary. There is racing throughout the year; check the local newspapers for exact fixtures and times. Admission is 13€ ($12) adults and 6.50€ ($5.90) students and seniors for most events.

ACCOMMODATIONS YOU CAN AFFORD
IN LIMERICK CITY

Glen Eagles   Carole O'Toole is the sort of caring hostess who will pack a lunch for you to take along on a day trip. She's active in all kinds of city activities and an invaluable source of information about local goings-on. Husband Paddy is retired from many years in the tour business and puts together personally conducted driving tours for visitors. Their two-story house is in a quiet cul-de-sac signposted on Ennis Road (just before you reach Jurys Hotel if you're coming from the airport). There's a TV lounge and a pretty garden.

12 Vereker Gardens, Ennis Rd., Limerick, Co. Limerick. *©*/fax 061/455521. 3 units. 51€ ($46) double. Rates include full breakfast. No credit cards. Free off-street parking. Closed Nov–Feb. **Amenities:** Lounge. *In room:* Tea/coffeemaker, hair dryer.

Jurys Inn Limerick *★ ⊘alue*   The budget arm of the Jurys chain has a knack for providing centrally situated, attractive, affordable accommodation in Ireland's major cities. This property's riverfront location is particularly appealing. The river-facing rooms, especially on the upper floors, have splendid views of the Shannon and the city's historic area. If you can get a corner room, you'll feel positively spoiled. Rooms are tastefully contemporary and eminently functional, with firm beds, large bathtubs, desks, and ample shelf and wardrobe space— everything you need, and very little you don't. All rooms accommodate up to 3 adults or 2 adults and 2 children. Nonsmoking rooms are available on request. Facilities include a moderately priced and more than moderately good restaurant, The Arches, and the Inn Pub. Parking is available at the adjoining multistory car park at reduced rates.

Dock St., Limerick. *©* **800/843-3311** from the U.S., or 061/207000. Fax 061/400966. www.jurys.com. 151 units. 70€ ($63) double, triple, or family room. No service charge. AE, DC, MC, V. **Amenities:** Restaurant (International), bar; laundry service; nonsmoking rooms. *In room:* TV, dataport, tea/coffeemaker, hair dryer.

St. Anthony's   This two-story house is the family home of Mary and Kathleen Collins. It's neat as a pin and has a warm, homey atmosphere. Meals are served in a dining room overlooking a garden, and breakfast comes with homemade apricot and other fruit jams. Guests also enjoy a lovely afternoon tea with home baking. The rooms are comfortably furnished and have sinks and built-in wardrobes.

8 Coolraine Terrace, Limerick, Co. Limerick. *©* 061/452607. 3 units, 1 with bathroom (shower only). 47€ ($43) double. Rates include full breakfast. No credit cards.

IN NEARBY COUNTY LIMERICK

Abbey Villa   Mrs. May Haskett owns a modern bungalow in a scenic setting. Like the best of hostesses, she invites guests to sit and chat while working out the best travel routes, but she also recognizes that they sometimes want somewhat less attention. All rooms are tastefully decorated and have electric blankets. There are also laundry facilities and private parking.

Kildimo Rd., Adare, Co. Limerick. (ⓒ 061/396113. Fax 061/396969. abbeyvilla@esatclear.ie. 6 units. 45€ ($41) single; 65€ ($59) double. 33% reduction for children. Rates include full breakfast. MC, V. *In room:* TV (satellite), hair dryer.

Ballyteigue House ★★ A stay at Ballyteigue is a celebration of Margaret Johnston's skill in welcoming guests, and a symphony of burnished wood, freshly baked bread, and lovely gardens. The large bedrooms overlook an old stone wall and garden or a stretch of fields that ends on the horizon with the Ballyhoura Mountains. Rooms have hardwood floors, bright yellow or gold walls, fine antiques, and admirably firm beds; all but one of the bathrooms are rather small. Ballyteigue is a tranquil house, a place for savoring the comforts of a thoughtfully furnished old house, the beauty of its surroundings, and the company of fellow guests.

Rockhill, Bruree, Co. Limerick (1½ miles/2km off N20, 7 miles/11km south of Croom). (ⓒ/fax 063/90575. ballyteigue@eircom.net. 5 units, 4 with bathroom (3 with shower only). 32€ ($29) single; 63€ ($58) double. MC, V. *In room:* Tea/coffemaker, hair dryer, trouser press.

Hillcrest Country House Jennie and Michael Power's home sits amid peaceful, bucolic beauty, some 3 miles (5km) outside Adare off the main Limerick-Killarney road (N21) and convenient to many of the region's attractions. The Powers are warm, hospitable hosts who take a keen interest in their visitors. With advance notice, Jennie will prepare an excellent dinner. Travel itineraries, especially for anglers, can be arranged by request.

Ballinvera, Croagh, Adare, Co. Limerick. (ⓒ/fax 061/396534. www.dirl.com/limerick/hillcrest.htm. 4 units, 3 with bathroom. 38.50€ ($35) single; 53€ ($48) double. 25% reduction for children. Rates include full breakfast. 27€ ($24) dinner. MC, V. **Amenities:** Lounge.

GREAT DEALS ON DINING
IN LIMERICK CITY

Pub grub, including Irish specialties, salad plates, hot dishes, sandwiches, and soup, is served at the following Limerick pubs between the hours of 12:30 and 2:30pm at a cost of 4€ to 6.50€ ($3.65–$5.90) per item (most also serve soup and sandwiches throughout the day): **Flannery's,** 20 Catherine St., Limerick (ⓒ **061/414450**), at the corner of Cecil Street; **W.J. South's** 🐾 on the Crescent (ⓒ **061/318850**); **Nancy Blake's,** 19 Denmark St. (ⓒ **061/416443**); and the **Jockey Club** in Hotel Greenhills (ⓒ **061/453033**).

Moll Darby's Pizzeria & Bistro PIZZA Tree-lined George's Quay is the setting for this cozy old-style bistro. Loaded with charm, and blessed with a friendly and efficient staff, it has also gained wide popularity with locals for its extensive array of moderately priced meals. The pizza is special, and the fish, meat, and poultry dishes are prepared with care.

7–8 George's Quay, Limerick. (ⓒ **061/411511**. Pizza 9€–12€ ($8.15–$11); main courses 13€–19€ ($12–$17). MC, V. Daily 6–10pm.

Patrick Punch's IRISH/INTERNATIONAL This popular pub-restaurant is on the main road on the southern edge of town, surrounded by gardens, ancient trees, and lots of parking. It offers a variety of settings in which to dine, ranging from a three-tier lounge area and a glass-enclosed conservatory overlooking the gardens to a clubby main room with an eclectic decor of Tiffany-style lamps, dark woods, an open turf fireplace, and old photos of movie stars. The menu is equally varied, and changes often; choices often include filet of beef Wellington, chicken Cleopatra with lemon and prawn sauce, and vegetable lasagna.

O'Connell Ave. (N20), Punches Cross, Limerick. ✆ 061/229588. Reservations suggested for dinner. Main courses 13€–20€ ($12–$18). MC, V. Daily 10:30am–11pm.

SHOPPING

Shopping hours in Limerick are Monday through Saturday from 9:30am to 5:30pm. Many stores also stay open until 9pm on Thursday and Friday nights.

Arthur's Quay Centre   With a striking four-story brick facade, this shopping complex overlooks Arthur's Quay Park and the Shannon River. It houses more than 36 shops and services, ranging from Irish handcrafts to fashions, casual wear, shoes, music recordings, and books. Arthur's Quay, Limerick, Co. Limerick. ✆ 061/419888.

Cruises Street Shopping Centre   This is the centerpiece of Limerick's retail downtown shopping district, situated just off Patrick Street. The developers took the original street and spent almost 31 million€ ($27 million) to turn it into an old-world, village-style pedestrian shopping mall, with a total of 55 retail outlets and 20 residential apartments and offices. Cruises St., Limerick, Co. Limerick.

Heirlooms   Long established in downtown Limerick, this shop moved to the new Cruises Street Shopping Centre for more space to show off its vast stock of local collectibles, which includes old books and maps, dolls and puppets, and biscuit tins, as well as frames, wood carvings, pottery, clocks, sculptures, jewelry, and candles. Cruises St., Limerick, Co. Limerick. ✆ 061/419111.

Irish Handcrafts   This family-run business, more than 100 years old, specializes in products made by people from the Limerick area, with particular emphasis on women's hand-knit and hand-loomed sweaters of all types, colors, and styles. There are also linen and lace garments. 26 Patrick St., Limerick, Co. Limerick. ✆ 061/415504.

Leonards   This long-established shop is a good source of men's tweed jackets, hats, caps, ties, and cravats, as well as silk ties and cashmere and lamb's wool knitwear. 23 O'Connell St., Limerick, Co. Limerick. ✆ 061/415721.

Todd's   For more than 100 years, this has been Limerick's leading department store, selling a wide array of Waterford crystal, Aran knitwear, Donegal tweeds, and ready-to-wear clothing of all types. O'Connell St., Limerick, Co. Limerick. ✆ 061/417222.

White and Gold   Irish Dresden figurines, the delicate porcelain pieces made at nearby Drumcollogher, are the special attraction of this chic gift shop. Other wares include fanciful European Christmas ornaments, intricate wind chimes, and Hummels. 34 O'Connell St. at Roches St., Limerick, Co. Limerick. ✆ 061/419977.

LIMERICK AFTER DARK
THE PUB SCENE

Sadly, a good many of the city's finest pubs have been modernized right out of their character, but **W.J. South's** ✰ (✆ 061/318850), on the Crescent (where Daniel O'Connell's statue commands the center of O'Connell Street), holds firmly to the trappings of age. There's a long white-marble bar up front, divided by wood and etched-glass partitions. Faded tapestries line the wall, and behind the bar is an elaborate mahogany structure, its arched niches framing old bottles and backed by mirrors speckled with age. Just back of the small front bar, a larger room has walls devoted to a display of rugby photos (the Garyowen rugby team consider South's their "local"). The best pint in Limerick is said to be pulled here, and you'll hear a lot about sports. An attractive lounge bar has been added to the old pub; morning coffee is also served, as well as good, traditional Irish food at pub-grub prices (see "Great Deals on Dining," above).

The aged look at **Flannery's,** 20 Catherine St., at the corner of Cecil Street (© **061/414450**), comes from woodwork that once graced an old distillery, and according to Jerry Flannery, "there's still plenty of whiskey salted in it." The place itself is only a little more than 50 years old, but it has the comfortable atmosphere of a country pub, with a small snug at one end and a core of regulars every evening. Flannery's also serves good pub grub at lunch.

A bit out from the city center, but easily reached via either a longish walk or a short bus ride, is **Matt Fennessy's Pub** ⚡, New Street, Punches Cross (© **061/229038**), the epitome of a neighborhood local. Inside, there's an old-fashioned bar, a lounge, and a snug affectionately dubbed "The Senate" by regulars. While there's no scheduled music at Fennessy's, spontaneous song often breaks out on weekend nights. The clientele is nearly all local, and they make visitors very welcome. The pub is located where New Street turns off O'Connell, at the intersection with Dan Ryan's Garage on one corner and Punches Pub on the opposite.

Nancy Blake's, 19 Upper Denmark St. (© **061/416443**), is a cozy, old-style pub popular for pub lunches and traditional music (see below) and for its summer barbecues in the courtyard out back.

TRADITIONAL MUSIC

Limerick has many atmospheric pubs that host traditional music evenings. In addition, several pubs are now bringing in other types of music, including blues, jazz, country/western, and rock. Those listed below are likely to have music of one genre or another during your visit—a telephone call before you go (and maybe a quick chat with your B&B or hotel host) should help you find what you're looking for.

Nancy Blake's, 19 Denmark St. (© **061/416443**), has traditional music most summer nights in the old-style front rooms, made cozy with glowing fireplaces, as well as blues and jazz in the large, stone-walled lounge and bar out back. You can also try **The Locke Bar,** George's Quay (© **061/413733**).

THE PERFORMING ARTS

Belltable Arts Centre   Dramas, musicals, and concerts are staged year-round at this mid-city theater and entertainment center. The summer program includes a season of professional Irish theater. By day, the building is also open for gallery exhibits, showing the works of modern Irish artists as well as local crafts. 69 O'Connell St., Limerick. © 061/319866. Tickets 6.50€–15€ ($5.90–$14). Mon–Sat 8pm for most shows; check in advance. 5-min. walk from bus and train station.

University Concert Hall   This hall on the grounds of the University of Limerick presents a broad program of national and international solo stars, variety shows, and ballet, as well as the Irish Chamber Orchestra, RTÉ Concert Orchestra, University of Limerick Chamber Orchestra, the Limerick Singers, and the European Community Orchestra. It publishes a monthly list of events, available from the tourist office. University of Limerick, Plassey, Co. Limerick. © 061/331549. www.uch.ie. Box office: Mon–Fri 9:30am–5:30pm; Sat 11am–3pm. Most performances start at 8pm.

2 County Clare

Among the counties of Ireland, Clare is not a major celebrity, like its neighbors, Kerry and Galway. But this underappreciated county boasts some dazzling sites. The dramatic Cliffs of Moher; the strange, lunar landscape of the Burren; the silent prehistoric dolmens; and the county's reputation for the finest traditional music in Ireland all contribute to Clare's appeal.

GETTING THERE   From the United States, Aer Lingus, Aeroflot, Continental, and Delta Airlines operate regularly scheduled flights into **Shannon Airport,** off the Limerick-Ennis road (N18), County Clare (© **061/471444;** www.shannonairport.com), 15 miles (24km) west of Limerick. Domestic flights from Dublin and overseas flights from Britain and the Continent are available from a range of carriers.

Irish Rail provides service to **Ennis Rail Station,** Station Road (© **065/ 684-0444;** www.irishrail.ie), and Limerick's **Colbert Station,** Parnell Street (© **061/315555**), 15 miles (24km) from Shannon.

Bus Eireann provides bus services from all parts of Ireland into **Ennis Bus Station,** Station Road (© **065/682-4177;** www.buseireann.ie), and other towns in County Clare.

If you're arriving by car, County Clare can be reached via N18. At Shannon Airport, cars can be rented from the following international firms: **Alamo** (© **061/472633;** www.alamo.com), **Avis Johnson & Perrott** (© **061/715600;** www.avis.com), and **Hertz** (© **061/471369;** www.hertz.ie). Several local firms also maintain desks at the airport; among the most reliable is **Dan Dooley Rent A Car** (© **061/471098;** www.dan-dooley.ie).

From points south, County Clare can be reached directly, bypassing Limerick, via the **Tarbert-Killimer car ferry,** crossing the River Shannon from Tarbert, County Kerry, to Killimer, County Clare—for schedule information see "Tralee & North Kerry," chapter 9, "The Southeast: County Kerry."

VISITOR INFORMATION   As soon as you land in Ireland, you will find a **tourist office** in the Arrivals Hall of Shannon Airport (© **061/471664**). It's open daily year-round: October to March from 7:30am to 5:30pm and April to September from 6:30am to 6pm.

The **Ennis Tourist Office,** Clare Road, Ennis, County Clare (© **065/ 682-8366**), is about 1 mile (1.5km) south of town on the main N18 road. Open year-round Monday to Friday 9:30am to 5:15pm, with weekend and extended hours April to October.

Seasonal tourist offices in County Clare are at the Cliffs of Moher (© **065/ 708-1171**); O'Connell Street, Kilkee (© **065/905-6112**); and Town Hall, Kilrush (© **065/905-1577**). These offices are usually open May or June to early September (the Cliffs of Moher office remains open until late October).

You can also find visitor information at **www.county-clare.com**.

FROM SHANNON AIRPORT TO ENNIS

For many years all planes entering Ireland were required to make a stop at Shannon, and most American visitors spent their first night in the country within a small radius of the airport (visitors from the continent more often arrive on the ferry in Rosslare or one of the other eastern ports). This policy was devised as a way to boost tourism in the west of Ireland, which was a depressed region sorely in need of revenue. The ploy succeeded, and a horde of hotels and B&Bs sprang

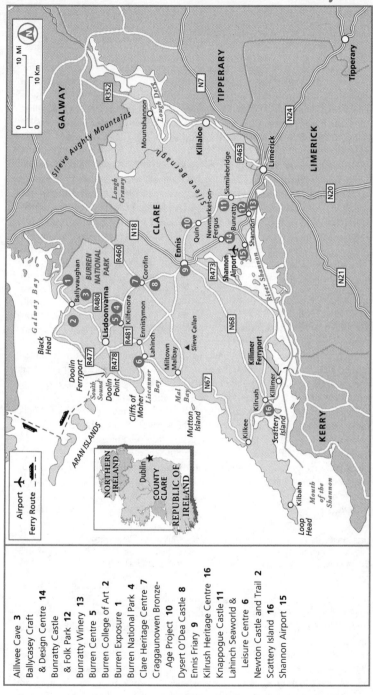

Airport ✈

Ferry Route - - - -

up along with an accompaniment of tourist attractions. Even though the ban on transatlantic flights to Dublin was lifted in 1994, many still choose to enter the country at Shannon, which offers better access to Ireland's more scenic western side.

The downside of the region immediately surrounding the airport is that it has more than its share of kitsch and tourist traps. **Bunratty** is a fine castle, but on the average summer's day it's besieged by tourist legions larger than the most fearful medieval horde, and the **Craggaunowen Bronze-Age Project** fails to live up to the hype it receives in the tourist offices. I'd recommend passing quickly through this area, en route to the more appealing Clare Coast and Burren regions.

From the airport, you can turn right or left on the N18 road. To the right and about 5 miles (8km) down is the village of Bunratty and its famous 15th-century medieval castle and theme park. To the left, you pass through the charming river town of Newmarket-on-Fergus, home of **Dromoland Castle,** before eventually hitting Ennis, the main town of County Clare. **Ennis** (population 6,000) is a compact enclave of winding, narrow streets on the banks of the River Fergus. The original site was an island on the river—hence the name "Ennis," an Anglicized form of the Gaelic word *Inis,* meaning "island." Easily explored on foot, Ennis offers a walking trail developed by the Ennis Urban District Council. A leaflet outlining the route is available free throughout the town.

SEEING THE SIGHTS

Bunratty Castle and Folk Park   Nestled beside the O'Garney River, Bunratty Castle (1425) is Ireland's most complete medieval castle. The ancient stronghold has been carefully restored, with authentic furniture, armorial stained glass, tapestries, and works of art. By day, the building's inner chambers and grounds are open for public tours; at night, the castle's Great Hall serves as a candlelit setting for medieval banquets and entertainment.

Bunratty Castle is the focal point of a 20-acre theme park, Bunratty Folk Park. Don't just write it off as a giant cliché, because it's all done very well. The re-creation of a typical 19th-century Irish village includes thatched cottages, farmhouses, and an entire village street, with school, post office, pub, grocery store, print shop, and hotel—all open for browsing and shopping. Fresh scones are baked in the cottages, and craftspeople ply such trades as knitting, weaving, candle making, pottery, and photography.

Note: Be prepared for the crowds; seemingly thousands of visitors storm the castle daily in summer.

Limerick-Ennis Rd. (N18), Bunratty, Co. Clare. ✆ **061/360788.** www.shannonheritagetrade.com. Castle and Folk Park admission 8.25€ ($7.50) adults, 4€ ($3.60) children, 23€ ($21) family. Sept–May daily 9:30am–5:30pm; June–Aug daily 9:30am–6:30pm (last admission 5:30pm).

Bunratty Winery   Housed in a coachhouse dating from 1816, this winery produces mead, a medieval drink made from honey, fermented grape juice, water, matured spirits, and a selection of herbs. In days long ago, it was served by the jugful at regal gatherings and at weddings. In fact, custom required that a bride and groom continue to drink mead for one full moon in order to increase the probability of a happy marriage. (Some speculate that this is where the term "honeymoon" came from.) Today, the Bunratty Winery produces mead primarily for consumption at Bunratty Castle's medieval-style banquets. Visitors are welcome to stop by, watch the production in progress, and taste the brew. Also available is traditional Irish poteen (pronounced *potcheen),* the first of this heady moonshine to be legally made and bottled in Ireland since it was banned in 1661.

Bunratty, Co. Clare. ℂ 061/362222. Free admission. Mon–Sat 9:30am–5:30pm.

Craggaunowen Bronze-Age Project *Overrated* Making use of an actual castle, *crannóg* (fortified island), and ring fort, the Craggaunowen Project has attempted to reconstruct and present glimpses of Ireland's ancient past, from the Neolithic period to the Christian Middle Ages. A special glass house has been created to exhibit Tim Severin's sea-proven replica of the curragh in which Brendan and his brother monks may have sailed to America in the 5th century. This project must have been launched with great vision and enthusiasm, but much of the original wind seems to have left its sails. As a "living history" project, it is currently on life support. The possibilities here are exciting, but the reality is disappointing.

Quin, Co. Clare. ℂ 061/367178. www.shannonheritage.com. Admission 7.15€ ($6.30) adults, 5.60€ ($4.95) seniors, 4.40€ ($3.90) children. AE, DC, MC, V. Open weekends mid-Mar to Easter 10am–6pm; daily Easter–May 10am–6pm, June–Oct 9am–6pm (last admission 5pm). About 10 miles (16km) east of Ennis, signposted off R469.

Ennis Friary This Franciscan abbey, founded in 1241 and a famous seat of learning in medieval times, made Ennis a focal point of western Europe for many years. Records show that in 1375 it buzzed with the activity of no fewer than 350 friars and 600 students. Although it was finally forced to close in 1692 and thereafter fell into ruin, the abbey still contains many interesting sculpted tombs, decorative fragments, and carvings, including the famous McMahon tomb. The nave and chancel are the oldest parts of the friary, but other structures, such as the 15th-century tower, transept, and sacristy, are also rich in architectural detail.

Abbey St., Ennis, Co. Clare. ℂ 065/682-9100. www.heritageireland.ie. Admission 1.25€ ($1.15) adults, .90€ (80¢) seniors, .50€ (45¢) children and students, 3.80€ ($3.45) family. June–Oct daily 9:30am–6:30pm.

Knappogue Castle This castle, built in 1467, was the home of the McNamara clan, who dominated the area for more than 1,000 years. The original Norman structure includes elaborate late-Georgian and Regency wings that were added in the mid–19th century. Now fully restored, it is furnished with authentic 15th-century pieces and, like Bunratty Castle, serves as a venue for nightly medieval banquets in the summer season.

Quin, Co. Clare. ℂ 061/360788. www.shannonheritage.com. Admission 3.80€ ($3.45) adults, 2.60€ ($2.40) seniors and students, 2.15€ ($1.95) children, 9.50€ ($8.65) family. Apr–Oct daily 9:30am–5:30pm (last admission 4:30pm). Located midway between Bunratty and Ennis.

ACCOMMODATIONS YOU CAN AFFORD
Near the Airport
Bunratty Lodge Along the road between Bunratty Castle and Durty Nelly's (see "Great Deals on Dining," below), about 3 miles (5km) from Shannon Airport, you'll come to Mary Browne's lovely modern two-story home. It's beautifully decorated and furnished. All guest rooms have orthopedic mattresses and heated towel racks.

Bunratty, Co. Clare. ℂ 061/369402. Fax 061/369363. www.bunrattylodge.com. 6 units. 57€ ($52) single; 63€ ($58) double. 20% reduction for children. Rates include full breakfast. MC, V. Closed Nov to mid-Mar. Nonsmoking house. *In room:* TV (satellite), tea/coffemaker, hair dryer.

Bunratty Country House ⭐ *Value* A 10-minute walk from Bunratty Folk Park and only 6 miles (9.5km) from Shannon Airport, Bunratty Woods is an ideal spot to spend your first or last night in Ireland, or both. Just beyond the tourist thicket, you'll enjoy both convenience and tranquillity in this especially tasteful guesthouse, furnished in antique pine, with bare wood floors, handmade patchwork quilts, and firm beds. Most rooms have lovely views of the rolling Clare countryside. Smoking is permitted in the guest rooms, but not in the lounge or breakfast room. Be sure to ask the delightful hostess, Maureen O'Donovan, about local lore—she has some startling stories ready for the sharing. You really won't go wrong here, which is precisely what you don't want to do as you inaugurate or conclude your visit to Ireland.

Low Road, Bunratty, Co. Clare. ℰ **061/369689.** Fax 061/369454. http://www.iol.ie/~bunratty. 15 units. 57€–70€ ($60–$68) double; 76€–89€ ($68–$90) minisuite. No service charge. Rates include full breakfast. MC, V. Open year-round. **Amenities:** Lounge. *In room:* TV, tea/coffeemaker, hair dryer.

Gallow's View   Donal and Mary McKenna offer a special brand of hospitality at this modern two-story bungalow that's reached by a scenic country road that runs between Bunratty Castle and Durty Nelly's, 1¼ miles (2km) from the castle. One family room and a double are on the ground floor, a blessing for those who have trouble with stairs. Several of Mary's interesting antique pieces are scattered throughout the house, and there's an inviting air to the lounge and dining room.

Bunratty East, Co. Clare. ℰ/fax **061/369125.** 5 units. www.bunratty.net/gallowsview. 38€ ($35) single; 53€ ($48) double. 20% reduction for children under 12. Rates include full breakfast. MC, V. Closed Dec–Feb. Private parking lot. **Amenities:** Lounge. *In room:* TV, tea/coffeemaker, hair dryer, iron.

Grange   You won't find a warmer welcome in these parts than the one Mrs. Mary Corcoran extends to all her guests. Her comfortable home is quite conveniently located, and she's most helpful to guests in planning their sightseeing. The bedrooms and dining room are nonsmoking areas.

Wood Rd., Cratloe, Co. Clare. ℰ/fax **061/357389.** alfie@iol.ie. 5 units, 4 with bathroom (shower only). 32€ ($29) single; 43€ ($39) double without bathroom, 48€ ($44) double with bathroom. 25% reduction for children. Rates include full breakfast. Dinner 16€ ($14). MC, V. 1 mile (1.6km) off N18 (at Limerick Inn Hotel), 4 miles (6.5km) from Limerick. *In room:* A/C, TV, hair dryer, iron.

Ennis & Vicinity

Cill Eoin House   Just off the main N18 road at the Killadysert Cross, a half mile south of Ennis, this two-story yellow guesthouse is a real find. It offers bright, comfortable rooms with hotel-quality furnishings and firm beds at a very affordable price, capped by attentive service from the McGann family. Although it's within walking distance of Ennis, the rooms offer lovely views of the countryside. The house is named after the nearby medieval Killone Abbey ("Killone" is the Anglicization of *Cill Eoin*).

Killadysert Cross, Clare Rd., Ennis, Co. Clare. ℰ/fax **065/684-1668.** www.euroka.com/cilleoin. 14 units. 58€–63€ ($53–$58) double. Rates include full breakfast. AE, MC, V. Free parking. Closed Dec 24–Jan 8. Just off the main N18 road at the Killadysert Cross, half a mile (1km) south of Ennis. *In room:* TV, tea/coffeemaker.

Cloneen   This pretty two-story home is set back from the road on an elevated site, only a short walk from the town center. Martina Brennan is a gracious, lively hostess, and her intimate knowledge of Ennis and its surroundings helps ensure that you'll get the most from your stay. Guest rooms are quite comfortable. The breakfast room overlooks colorful flower beds and a spacious lawn.

Clonroad, Ennis, Co. Clare. ℰ **065/682-9681.** 3 units, 1 with bathroom (shower only). 48€ ($44) double. 33% reduction for children sharing with an adult. No credit cards. Private parking lot and bicycle shed. Closed Nov–Mar. Nonsmoking house.

Massabielle   A small lawn bordered by colorful flower beds gives some indication of the attractive interior here. Monica O'Loughlin has made extensive use of antiques and authentic reproductions in her furnishings, and her musical children (they play piano) echo their mother's warm hospitality. Among the four bedrooms, one family room will sleep three. Outside, there's a well-maintained tennis court. Massabielle is 2 miles (3km) from Ennis off the Quin road (from Shannon Airport and Limerick turn right at the first traffic light, then right again at the roundabout; it's signposted on the Quin road). The entire house is nonsmoking.

Off Quin Rd., Ennis, Co. Clare. ℂ/fax **065/682-9363**. 4 units. 39€ ($35) single; 53€ ($48) double. 25% reduction for children. Rates include full breakfast. MC, V. Closed Oct–May.

GREAT DEALS ON DINING

Brogans Restaurant and Bar PUB GRUB/GRILLS   This old-time pub in the center of town is known for its hearty meals. Choices include Irish stew, beef stroganoff, and chicken curry. In addition, roast duck, Dover sole, and local salmon are served. The atmosphere is casual and the decor cozy, with brick walls, a copper-fluted fireplace, and ceiling fans. Brogans also serves bar food, salads, and hot or cold lunch plates and grills in the evening. Soup and sandwiches are available in the bar continuously, beginning at noon. On Tuesday and Thursday night, ballad music is usually offered.

24 O'Connell St., Ennis, Co. Clare. ℂ **065/682-9480**. Lunch main courses 6.50€–9€ ($5.90–$8.15); dinner main courses 11€–20€ ($10–$18). AE, MC, V. Daily noon–10pm.

Cloister Restaurant IRISH   Built right into the remains of a 13th-century Franciscan friary, with windows overlooking what was the friary garden, this old-world pub offers innovative cuisine. The decor is warmly elegant, with open turf fireplaces and stoves, beamed ceilings, and reproductions from the Book of Kells adorning the walls. The menu includes poached monkfish with red-pepper sauce, wild venison with juniper-and-Armagnac sauce, and suprême of chicken layered with Carrigline cheese and Irish Mist. A house specialty starter is Inagh goat cheese laced with port-wine sauce. Pub-style lunches are served in the skylit Friary Bar, adjacent to the old abbey walls.

Club Bridge, Abbey St., Ennis. ℂ **065/682-9521**. Reservations recommended. Fixed-price menu 23€ ($21). AE, DC, MC, V. Daily 6:30–9:30pm.

Durty Nelly's BAR FOOD   Established in 1620 next door to Bunratty Castle, this ramshackle, thatched-roof cottage was originally a watering hole for the castle guards. Today, Durty Nelly's draws huge crowds: Tourists you'd surely expect, but, amazingly, locals come here as well. That the place is now commercialized is no matter—it's still sheer fun. The decor—mounted elk heads and old lanterns on the walls, sawdust on the floors, and open turf fireplaces—hasn't changed much over the centuries. It's a warren of little nooks, crannies, snugs, and "courtin' corners." Pub grub includes soup, sandwiches, salads, and hot dishes featuring roasts, seafood, or chicken. There are also two attached restaurants, but they're not worth the money—bar food is the best choice here. After about 8:30pm on weekdays, things get pretty lively with music and singing, and even those drinking on the outside patio join in; on weekends, the music starts earlier—Saturday at 4pm, and Sunday at 12:30pm.

Bunratty, Co. Clare. ℂ **061/364861**. 3.80€–18€ ($3.45–$17). AE, DC, MC. Daily 10:30am–10:30pm (hot meals served 10:30am–8pm only).

Tips **They Won't Play "Freebird"**

If there's one thing County Clare has plenty of, it's traditional music and good fiddlers, tin-whistle players, bodhran players, and pipers to play it. Out at Bunratty, **Durty Nelly's** (*©* **061/364861**) rings with music—mostly staged, some spontaneous—every night. The music starts at 8pm Monday through Friday, 4pm Saturday, and 12:30pm Sunday.

Medieval Banquets

These banquets are among Ireland's most popular attractions. If you're interested, try to book before leaving home. Should you arrive without a reservation, any tourist office will try to get you a seat, or you can give the reservations manager a call to ask about an opening—sometimes there are cancellations.

Bunratty Castle MEDIEVAL BANQUET   When you walk across the drawbridge into Bunratty Castle's Great Hall and are handed your first mug of mead, the spirit of merriment takes over and Americans, Germans, Australians, Russians, Italians, and every other nationality represented become fellow conspirators in the evening's fantasy plot. Don't come for the food—it's not great. As for the show, of course it's hokey—it's meant to be. Blarney may have originated in County Cork, but there's lots of it afoot in Bunratty.

Limerick-Ennis Rd. (N18), Bunratty, Co. Clare. *©* **061/360788.** Fax 061/361020. Reservations required. Dinner and entertainment 43€ ($39). AE, DC, MC, V. Daily year-round; 2 sittings, 5:30 and 8:45pm.

Knappogue Castle MEDIEVAL BANQUET   This massive 1467 stronghold is some 19 miles (31km) from Limerick city, which means you must have a car, because it's not served by local buses. The banquet here differs from that at Bunratty in that the group is smaller and more intimate, and the entertainment tends to be somewhat less ribald, with sketches that bring to life myths and legends of Old Ireland and lots of song and dance.

Quin, Co. Clare. *©* **061/360788.** Fax 061/361020. Reservations required. Dinner and entertainment 42€ ($38). AE, DC, MC, V. May–Oct daily; 2 sittings, 5:30 and 8:45pm.

Traditional Irish Night ✶ TRADITIONAL IRISH   Irish country life of yesteryear is the focus of this "at home" evening in a thatched farmhouse cottage. You'll have a traditional meal of Irish stew, homemade bread, and apple pie and fresh cream. Then the music begins: the flute and fiddle, accordion, bodhran, and spoons—all at a spirited, foot-tapping pace.

Bunratty Folk Park, off the Limerick-Ennis Rd. (N18), Bunratty, Co. Clare. *©* **061/360788.** Reservations required. Dinner and entertainment 38€ ($40.50). AE, DC, MC, V. May–Sept daily at 7pm.

SHOPPING

Ballycasey Craft and Design Centre   This group of craft workshops, clustered around the farmyard of the 18th-century Ballycaseymore House, is signposted on the Limerick-Shannon road, and it's a must for crafts hunters. Individual workshops are home to artisans, from weaver to potter to fashion designer to silversmith. The Rowan Berry Restaurant serves fresh, appetizing light lunches, with wine available, at modest prices. Shannon, Co. Clare. *©* **061/362105.**

Belleek Shop   This 90-year-old shop in the heart of Ennis, overlooking the 16th-century Franciscan Abbey, was the first Belleek china outlet in southern Ireland. It's renowned for its extensive range of Waterford, Galway, and Tipperary crystals; fine chinas; tableware; and figurines. In recent years, it has expanded to include other Irish products such as handmade character dolls and turf crafts, pewter, jewelry, and fashionable tweeds. 36 Abbey St., Ennis, Co. Clare. © 065/ 682-9607. www.belleekshop.com.

Custy's Traditional Music Shop   If you'd like to bring back the melodious sounds of County Clare, this is the place to shop. The wares include a full range of traditional and folk music tapes and CDs as well as books, photos, paintings, and crafts pertaining to traditional music. You can also buy your own fiddle, tin whistle, banjo, concertina, accordion, or flute here. Francis St., Ennis, Co. Clare. © 065/682-1727. www.custysmusic.com.

THE CLARE COAST
KILRUSH TO DOOLIN

One of Ireland's most photographed scenes, the **Cliffs of Moher** draw busloads and carloads of visitors to Clare's remote reaches every day of the year. Rising sheer above the Atlantic Ocean to heights of over 700 feet (213m) and extending about 5 miles (8km) along the coast, these cliffs are County Clare's foremost natural wonder.

The Cliffs are only the beginning, however. Other highlights of the Clare Coast include the world-renowned golf resort at **Lahinch,** praised by ace golfers as the "St. Andrews of Ireland" and the paradigm of Irish links golf. Farther up the coast is the secluded fishing village of **Doolin,** often referred to as the unofficial capital of Irish traditional music. Doolin, like Galway to the north, is also a departure point for the short boat trip to the Aran Islands.

The Clare Coast is dotted with a variety of small towns and seaside resorts, such as Kilrush, Kilkee, Miltown Malbay, and Ennistymon, that are particularly popular with Irish families. As you drive around this craggy coastline, you'll find many other off-the-beaten-path delights, some with intriguing place names: Pink Cave, Puffing Hole, Intrinsic Bay, Chimney Hill, Elephant's Teeth, Mutton Island, Loop Head, and Lovers Leap.

The principal road in this area is N67; not all the area's attractions are on this road, but they can be reached from it.

SEEING THE SIGHTS

Doolin is a tiny coastal village that has gained international fame as a center for traditional Irish music. You'll find the bodhrans pounding most nights at 9:30pm (4pm on Sunday) in **O'Connor's Pub** (© 065/707-4168), a large, rustic place filled with musicians, singers, tellers of tales, and students who may have hitchhiked across Europe to get here. There's also excellent bar food, featuring fresh seafood, for 3.15€ to 15€ ($2.90–$14). The tiny town is packed with tourists throughout the summer, resulting in a less-than-pleasant congestion at times. Another attraction in town is the Doolin Crafts Gallery (see "Shopping," later in this chapter), renowned for its extensive stock of Irish-made goods.

The **Loop Head Peninsula** is a much-overlooked County Clare attraction. A delightful day is one spent driving to seaside **Kilkee,** with its curved bay and strand, then down to the end of the long finger that is the West Clare Peninsula, where the Loop Head lighthouse holds solitary vigil. The coastline is one of clifftops, inlets and coves, sandy beaches, and a softly wild, unspoiled landscape. Along the way there are the ruins of forts, castles, and churches, and should you stop for a pint in a country pub, there are legends to be heard, like that of Kisstiffin Bank, a shoal that lies beneath the Shannon's waters. According to local legend, it was once a part of the mainland, but was swept into the Shannon during a fierce storm in the 9th century, carrying people and their homes to a watery grave. (According to the older residents of this area, when sailing ships used to drop anchor off the Kisstiffin Bank, they'd be visited during the night by a small man from beneath the water who would climb the anchor cable and ask them to take up the anchor, for it had gone down his chimney.)

In the little Shannonside village of **Kilbaha** (Cill Bheathach, or "Birch Church"), the Church of Moheen holds a small wooden structure that is one of Ireland's most unusual testaments to the devotion of the people to their faith: a tiny three-sided chapel on wheels known as the **Little Ark of Kilbaha** ✿. During the years when English-imposed law forbade any landlord to permit a Catholic mass to be held on his land, the Ark was hidden away during the week, but pulled down to the shore of Kilbaha Bay on Sunday and placed below the high-tide mark on land that belonged to no man. There, mass was said in safety, reverence, and peace.

Cliffs of Moher ✿✿

Ireland's spectacular coastline really outdoes itself at the Cliffs of Moher, near Liscannor on R478. In Irish, they're named Ailltreacha Mothair ("The Cliffs of the Ruin"), and they stretch for 5 miles (8km), rising at places to 700 feet (213m). They're breathtaking and shouldn't be missed. After you park at the large lot, you'll have a moderate walk to O'Brien's Tower, which affords the best view of the magnificent cliffs. There are also cliff-walking trails, but you're warned (by frequent signs and by common sense) to be extremely cautious, as there's some danger that the ground may give way near the edge.

The Visitors Centre at the Cliffs of Moher has a self-service tearoom offering inexpensive soups, sandwiches, and assorted snacks. There's also a gift, literature, music, and souvenir shop, as well as exhibits on wildlife and local attractions.

R478, Co. Clare. ✆ 065/708-1171. Free admission to cliffs; 1.25€ ($1.15) adult, .75€ (70¢) child to O'Brien's Tower. Cliffs visitor center, daily 9am–7:30pm in July and August; slightly reduced hours during the rest of the year. O'Brien's Tower Mar–Sept daily 10am–6pm.

Kilrush Heritage Centre

Housed in the town's historic Market House, this center provides historic and cultural background on Kilrush—the "capital of West Clare"—and the south Clare coast. An audiovisual presentation, *Kilrush in Landlord Times,* tells of the struggles of the area's tenant farmers during the 18th and 19th centuries, particularly during the Great Famine. The museum is also the focal point of a signposted heritage walk around the town. The building, erected in 1808 by the Vandeleur family, the area's chief landlords, was burned to the ground in 1892 and rebuilt in its original style in 1931.

Town Hall, Market Sq., off Henry St., Kilrush. ✆ 065/905-1577 or 065/905-1047. www.westclare.com. Admission 2.60€ ($2.40) adults, 1.25€ ($1.15) children, 6.50€ ($5.90) family. May–Sept Mon–Fri 10am–5pm.

Lahinch Seaworld and Leisure Centre

After stretching your legs along the vast strand and exploring its countless tidepools, you can get a closer look at the denizens of the Clare Coast by visiting this compact, well-designed local aquarium. Among the sea creatures in residence here are conger eels, sharks, and rays. In the "touch pool" you can tickle a starfish or surprise an anemone, and then admire the rays' efforts at water ballet. If you or your family is then inspired to take to the water yourselves, head next door to the reasonably priced Leisure Centre. For extra savings, combined tickets for aquarium and Leisure Centre are also available.

The Promenade, Lahinch. ✆ 065/708-1900. www.iol.ie/~seaworld. Admission to aquarium 4.75€ ($4.30) adults, 3.50€ ($3.15) seniors and students, 2.85€ ($2.60) children, 14€ ($13) family. Combined ticket with Leisure Center 8.90€ ($9.05) adults, 7€ ($6.35) seniors and students, 5.40€ ($4.90) children, 24€ ($22) family. Open year-round daily 10am–9pm.

Scattery Island   Scattery, a small and unspoiled island in the Shannon Estuary near Kilrush, is the site of a group of monastic ruins dating to the 6th century. A high round tower and several churches are all that remain of a once extensive settlement, founded by St. Sennan. There are legends of a massive sea monster known by the name of Cata, which was defeated on this island by St. Sennan; it's from this fabulous beast that the island derives its name in Gaelic, *Inis Cathaig*. The island has long been respected as a holy place, and sailors are said to have carried pebbles from its beaches as a talisman against shipwreck and other misfortunes. You can visit Scattery by contacting one of the boatmen who arrange ferries—frequency depends on demand, with a minimum of six people per trip. Contact **Gerald Griffen** (℃ **065/905-1327**) or ask at the Information Center on the mainland when the next ferry departs; the round-trip fare is about 8€ ($7.25).

Note: There are plans to arrange guided tours of the island leaving from the visitor center, and these may be offered in 2002—call ahead to confirm details. The information center houses exhibits on the history and folklore of the island.

Information Center, Merchants Quay, Kilrush. ℃ 065/905-2144. www.heritageireland.ie. Free admission. Mid-June to mid-Sept daily 10am–6pm; closed 1–2pm for lunch. Just past the pier, in the village of Kilrush.

TRIPS TO THE ARAN ISLANDS

Doolin Ferry Co.   Although many people come to Doolin to see the local sights and enjoy the music, many also come to board this ferry to the Aran Islands. The three fabled islands, sitting out in the Atlantic, are just 30 minutes away, closer to Doolin than they are to Galway. Service is provided to Inisheer, Inishmore, and (less frequently) to Inishmaan. (For more information about excursions to the Aran Islands, see chapter 12, "Out from Galway.")

The Pier, Doolin, Co. Clare. ℃ 065/707-4455. Fax 065/707-4417. www.doolinferries.com. Inisheer 25€ ($23) round-trip, Inishmaan 28€ ($25) round-trip, Inishmore 32€ ($29) round-trip. Mid-Apr to mid-May, once daily to Inisheer and Inishmore, inquire at office for Inishmaan; mid-May to Aug, multiple sailings to Inisheer, twice daily to Inishmore and Inishmaan; Sept, 4 daily to Inisheer, twice daily to Inishmore, inquire at office to Inishmaan.

OUTDOOR PURSUITS

BIRD-WATCHING   The **Bridges of Ross** ✦ on the north side of Loop Head is one of the prime autumn bird-watching sites in Ireland, especially during northwest gales, when several rare species have been seen with some consistency. The lighthouse at the tip of the Head is also a popular spot for watching seabirds.

DOLPHIN-WATCHING   The Shannon Estuary is home to about 70 bottlenose dolphins, one of four such resident groups of dolphins in Europe. Dolphin-watching cruises leave daily April through September from Carrigaholt with **Dolphinwatch** (℃ **065/905-8156;** www.dolphinwatch.ie); there are several cruises every day, each two hours in duration. Advance booking is essential. The cruise fees are 17€ ($15) adults and 10€ ($9) for children under 14. Carrigaholt is 4 miles (7km) south of Kilkee on Loop Head, just off R487.

GOLF   For golfers coming to Clare's Atlantic coast, a day at **Lahinch Golf Club,** Lahinch (℃ **065/708-1003**), is not to be missed. There are two 18-hole courses, but the longer championship links course is the one that has given Lahinch its far-reaching reputation. This course's elevations, such as those at the 9th and 13th holes, reveal open vistas of sky, land, and sea; they also make the winds an integral part of the scoring. Watch out for the goats, Lahinch's legendary weather forecasters. If they huddle by the clubhouse, it means a storm is approaching. Visitors are welcome to play any day, especially on weekdays; greens fees are 76€ ($69) for the Old course and 38€ ($35) for the Castle course.

ACCOMMODATIONS YOU CAN AFFORD

Bruach-na-Coille *(Kids)* Michael and Mary Clarke's two-story home is a good landing place if you're coming from North Kerry over to County Clare via the car ferry, or for an overnight before going the other way. Mary's home-cooked meals feature superb baking. The Clarkes will also arrange babysitting if you fancy a night out. The bedrooms, dining room, and lounge are nonsmoking.

Killimer Rd., Kilrush, Co. Clare. (🕐 065/905-2250. www.clarkekilrush.com 4 units, 2 with bathroom (shower only). 56€ ($51). No credit cards. 1 mile (1.6km) from Kilrush, 4 miles (6.5km) from Tarbert ferry. **Amenities:** Lounge, babysitting. *In room:* TV, tea/coffeemaker, hair dryer.

Churchfield Maeve Fitzgerald's modern two-story home is ½ mile (1km) north of Doolin village, at the post office. Guest rooms are moderate in size and simply furnished; some have a fine view toward the sea. Maeve has been running this B&B for nearly 2 decades, and her experience shows—the house is quite well kept, the breakfast is good, and Maeve's advice on touring the area is second to none.

Doolin, Co. Clare. (🕐 065/707-4209. Fax 065/707-4622. http://homepage.eircom.net/~churchfield. 6 units, 5 with bathroom (shower only). 52€–56€ ($47–$51) double. 33% reduction for children sharing with an adult. Rates include full breakfast. MC, V. *In room:* Tea/coffeemaker, hair dryer.

Grove Guesthouse For people who like to be in town, near the pier and the pubs, this guesthouse is a good option. Rooms are bright and simply furnished, and a large sitting room opens onto the private garden and tennis court in back. Along a stream, you'll find forest paths that start at the back yard and continue inland or toward the sea. The Kiely family do their best to make you feel at home—you can even use their kitchen late at night to fix a snack or a pot of tea.

Frances St., Kilrush, Co. Clare. (🕐 065/905-1451. Fax 065/905-2815. info@groveguesthouse.net. 9 units, all with bathroom (shower only). 32€ ($29) single; 51€ ($46) double. Rates include full breakfast. MC, V. In the center of town, near the pier. **Amenities:** Tennis court, use of kitchen. *In room:* TV.

Harbour Sunset Farmhouse 🕭 *(Kids)* Charming Harbour Sunset Farmhouse is set amid green fields on an 86-acre dairy farm. Panoramic views of the nearby golf course and beach add to the beauty of the site. The 200-year-old farmhouse maintains some of its traditional aura, but it's Mrs. Bridget O'Gorman and her talented and gracious family who make the place special. Not only do the O'Gormans extend a warm welcome, but at day's end, they sometimes gather around the living room fire for a lively evening of traditional Irish music. The "pet corner" is filled with a variety of pet farm animals for hands-on visits by guests. The family also does Irish crochet work, some of which is for sale.

Cliffs of Moher Rd., Rannagh, Liscannor, Co. Clare. (🕐)/fax **065/708-1039.** harbsunfarmhse@eircom.net. 4 units, 3 with bathroom (shower only). 37€ ($34) single; 56€ ($51) double. 25% reduction for children. Rates include full breakfast. Dinner 23€ ($21). MC, V. Closed mid-Oct to mid-May. *In room:* Hair dryer.

Knockerra House 🕭🕭 *(Kids)* The Troy family house is set in the shelter of a beautiful grove of old trees, which is rare on Ireland's windswept west coast. The place defines serenity, with gardens tucked into a hillside and views of the neighboring fields. The house (built ca. 1875) has aged well, and bears the marks of time on its ivy-covered facade and the antiques that populate the spacious rooms. This is a good place for families—each room has a double and a twin bed, and the extensive grounds offer many places to explore. Fishing is free at

Knockerra Lake, a 10-minute walk from the house. Knockerra House is a perfect first or last night stay in Ireland for those traveling through Shannon, and also a good base for day trips in County Clare.

Kilrush, Co. Clare. ☎ 065/905-1054. 3 units. 63€ ($58) double. 50% discount for children under 12 sharing with an adult. Rates include full breakfast. No credit cards. Signposted on the Ennis Rd., 4 miles (6.5km) north of Kilrush.

Tullamore Farmhouse   Mrs. Eileen Carroll is the charming hostess of this large modern house, set in lovely countryside 6 miles (9.5km) from the Cliffs of Moher (signposted on the main Lahinch-Cliffs road). The sunny guest rooms are decorated in light colors and are nonsmoking. There's a TV lounge with a view overlooking the hills. The place has a very relaxed atmosphere, and the food is excellent.

Kilshanny, Ennistymon, Co. Clare. ☎ 065/707-1187. Fax 065/707-2023. www.tullamorefarm.com. 6 units, 5 with bathroom (2 with shower only). 32€ ($29) single without bathroom, 35€ ($32) single with bathroom; 46€ ($41) double without bathroom, 51€ ($46) double with bathroom. 20% reduction for children. Rates include full breakfast. MC, V. Closed Nov–Feb. **Amenities:** Lounge. *In room:* Hair dryer.

GREAT DEALS ON DINING

Bruach Na Haille SEAFOOD   Beside the bridge over the River Aille, this restaurant's name means "bridge of the River Aille." Helen and John Browne serve marvelous seafood and local dishes in a restored country house with flagstone floors and whitewashed walls. The menu features everything from soup and salads to fresh mackerel, salmon, and local shellfish, plus a limited range of international specialties, with the emphasis on local seafood. Soups, desserts, and bread are all homemade. Wine is available by the glass or the bottle.

Doolin, Co. Clare. ☎ 065/707-4120. Main courses 15.80€–22.60€ ($14–$20); early-bird menu (6–7:30pm) 17.80€–22.65€ ($15.75–$20). No credit cards. May–Oct daily 6–9:30pm; June–Sept daily 10am–4pm, 6–10pm; Oct–Mar Thurs–Sat 6–10.

The Long Dock Bar & Seafood Restaurant SEAFOOD/BAR FOOD This cozy establishment is a happy blend of open fires in the bar and gracious informality in the dining room. The menu, featuring freshly caught local seafood (as well as meat and poultry dishes), makes this a good place to stop for a snack or to indulge in one of the fine evening meals. Vegetarian dishes are also available. There's a separate nonsmoking room.

West St., Carrigaholt, Co. Clare. ☎ 065/905-8106. Bar food under 10.20€ ($9.00); main courses 13.50€–28.25€ ($12–$25). MC, V. Daily 12:30am–9pm.

Vittles Restaurant SEAFOOD   This place well deserves its reputation for reasonable food at good prices. Meals in the dining room feature seafood fresh from local waters, as well as lamb, pork, steak, and chicken main courses. The cozy bar has an old-fashioned air, with lots of dark wood. There's an open-hearth fireplace in the lounge.

Halpins Hotel. Erin St., Kilkee, Co. Clare. ☎ 065/905-6032. Fixed-price dinner 32€ ($29). AE, DC, MC, V. Daily 6:30–9:30pm. Closed Nov 15–Mar 15.

SHOPPING

Doolin Crafts Gallery   Matthew O'Connell and Mary Gray own and operate this terrific crafts shop beside the church and cemetery in Doolin. Every item is Irish made: sweaters (both wool and mohair), classic fashions, ceramics, crystal, linens, lace, sculpture, leather bags, and even Christmas ornaments. Mary is a designer of contemporary and traditional gold and silver jewelry, much of it with themes drawn from the Burren. The shop will happily mail goods anywhere in the world at cost. A restaurant/coffee shop on the premises opens during the major tourist seasons. Doolin, Co. Clare. ⓒ **065/707-4309.**

NORTHERN CLARE COAST
THE BURREN

Moving westward from Ennis into the heart of County Clare, you'll come to an amazing district of 100 square miles (260 sq. km) called **The Burren** ⭐⭐⭐. The word *burren* is derived from the Irish word *boirreann,* which means "a rocky place" and pretty accurately describes the landscape here. It's a strange, lunarlike region, roughly bordered by the towns of Corofin, Ennistymon, Lahinch, Lisdoonvarna, and Ballyvaughan. Massive sheets of rock, jagged and craggy boulders, caves, and potholes are visible for kilometers, yet amidst the barren stoniness lie little lakes and streams and an amazing assemblage of flora. There's always something in bloom, even in winter—from fern and moss to orchids, rock roses, milkworts, wild thyme, geraniums, violets, and fuchsia. The Burren is also famous for its butterflies, which thrive on the rare flora. In addition, such animals as the pine martin, stoat, and badger, rare in the rest of Ireland, are common here.

The story of the Burren began more than 300 million years ago, when layers of shells and sediment were deposited under a tropical sea, only to be thrust above this surface many millions of years later and left open to the erosive power of Irish rain and weather, producing the limestone landscape that appears today. As early as 7,000 years ago, humans began to leave their mark on this landscape in the form of Stone Age burial monuments such as the Poulnabrone Dolmen and Gleninsheen Wedge Tomb.

The Burren area also has some charming little towns. **Lisdoonvarna,** on the western edge, is known for its spa of natural mineral springs. Each summer it draws thousands of people to bathe in its therapeutic waters of sulfur, chalybeate (iron), and iodine. Lisdoon, as the natives call it, is also known worldwide for its annual matchmaking festival.

One of the most scenic Burren drives is along R480, a corkscrew-shaped road that leads from Corofin to Ballyvaughan, a delightful little village overlooking Galway Bay.

SEEING THE SIGHTS

Aillwee Cave   One of Ireland's oldest underground sites, Aillwee was formed millions of years ago but remained hidden until a local farmer discovered it less than 50 years ago. The cave has more than 3,400 feet (1,036m) of passages and hollows running straight into the heart of a mountain. Its highlights are bridged chasms, deep caverns, a frozen waterfall, and the Bear Pits—hollows scraped out by the brown bear, one of the cave's original inhabitants. Guided tours, which last approximately half an hour, are conducted continuously. The site has a cafe and a craft-rock shop; a unique farmhouse cheese-making enterprise called Burren Gold Cheese, near the cave's entrance; and an apiary where honey is produced.

Ballyvaughan, Co. Clare. ⓒ **065/707-7036.** Fax 065/707-7107. www.aillweecave.ie. Admission 7.50€ ($6.80) adults, 6€ ($5.45) seniors, 4.50€ ($4.10) children ages 4–16, 24€ ($22) family (2 adults and 4 children). 1.25€ ($1.15) per car parking fee. Mid-Mar to June 10am–5:30; July–Aug 10am–6:30pm; Sept–early Nov 10am–5:30pm; Nov–early Mar limited tours.

Burren Exposure ⭐   Before hitting the rocky surfaces of the Burren Way, take in this slick, tripartite audiovisual presentation. Stark black-and-white photographs and clear diagrams are projected on a wall to illustrate the

---

> **Tips Walking the Burren**
>
> With its unique terrain and pathways, The Burren lends itself to walking. Visitors who want to amble through the hills and turloughs, limestone pavements and terraces, shale uplands and inland lakes should follow **The Burren Way,** a 26-mile (42km) signposted route stretching from Ballyvaughan to Liscannor. An information sheet outlining the route is available from any tourist office.

---

geological formation of the Burren in the opening display. The second section of the presentation explains the genesis and location of local ancient and modern human settlements and artifacts. The rich plant life of the Burren is the subject of the final part. The presentation is clear and informative, and the images are often beautiful. The whole show lasts just over half an hour. It's very helpful in preparing you to explore this strange and beautiful landscape.

Side by side with Burren Exposure is the **Whitethorn Restaurant,** one of the most tasteful and tasty cafes in County Clare, offering excellent seaside snacks and full lunches, as well as dazzling seascapes through slanted, floor-to-ceiling glass panels. The Whitethorn's dinner schedule is a matter of current experiment, so it's best to inquire on the spot when dinner is being served. Last but not least, there's a truly fine gift shop containing an excellent selection of Irish clothing, crafts, jewelry, and books. In sum, a stop here brings rewards on several fronts.

Galway Rd. (N67), Ballyvaughn, Co. Clare. © **065/707-7277.** Fax 065/707-7278. Admission 4.50€ ($4.10) adults, 3.50€ ($3.15) senior and students, 2.50€ ($2.25) children, and 13€ ($12) family. 1 week before Easter to Oct daily 10am–6pm (last admission 5:20pm). ¼ mile (0.4km) north of town on N67.

Burren National Park ✦✦✦   Currently under development as a national park, the confines of this park encompass the entire Burren area (100 square miles/260km²), a remarkable limestone plateau dotted with ruined castles, cliffs, rivers, lakes, valleys, green road walks, barren rock mountains, and plant life that defies all of nature's conventional rules. The area is particularly rich in archaeological remains from the Neolithic through the medieval periods—dolmens and wedge tombs (approximately 120), ring forts (500), round towers, ancient churches, high crosses, monasteries, and holy wells. In recent years, there has been some local controversy with regard to the defining of the park and the placement of a permanent visitor/interpretive center along the lines of those at Connemara and Glenveagh National Parks. Until these issues are resolved, the park remains without an official entrance point, with no admission charges or access restrictions.

The Burren, Co. Clare.

Clare Heritage Centre   If you have Clare family roots, you'll be especially fascinated by this heritage museum and genealogical research center. Even if you don't, this center is worth a visit to learn about Irish history and emigration. Housed in a former Church of Ireland edifice built by a first cousin of Queen Anne in 1718, it has exhibits on Clare farming, industry, commerce, education, forestry, language, and music. All are designed to reflect life in County Clare during the past 300 years. There is also a tearoom and gift shop. The genealogical research facility is open year-round.

Corofin, Co. Clare. © **065/683-7955.** www.clareroots.com. Admission 3.80€ ($3.45) adults, 1.90€ ($1.75) children. Museum: Apr–Oct daily 10am–5:30pm. Genealogical Centre: Mon–Fri 9am–5pm.

Dysert O'Dea Castle & Archaeology Centre   Built in 1480 by Diarmaid O'Dea on a rocky outcrop of land, this castle was badly damaged during the Cromwellian years. It was restored and opened to the public in 1986 as an archaeology center and museum. Today, the castle offers exhibitions and an audiovisual show on the history of the area. It is also the starting point for a sign-posted trail that leads to 25 sites of historical and archaeological interest within a 2-mile (3km) radius. They include a church founded by St. Tola in the 8th century that contains a unique Romanesque doorway surrounded by a bor-der of 12 heads carved in stone. The O'Deas, who were chieftains of the area, are buried under the church. Also at the center are a round tower from the 10th or 12th century, a 12th-century high cross, a holy well, a 14th-century battle-field, and a stone fort believed to date to the Iron Age. The castle bakery is currently under excavation.

Corofin, Co. Clare. ⓒ 065/683-7401. Admission 4.50€ ($4.10) adults, 3.50€ ($3.15) students and seniors, 2.20€ ($2.00) children, 9.50€ ($8.65) family. May–Sept daily 10am–6pm; Oct–Apr by appointment; call ⓒ 065/ 683-7305. R476 to Corofin.

Newton Castle and Trail   Newton Castle is a restored 16th-century tower house whose four floors have been given over to a series of exhibits that include a facsimile of the Book of Kells and a record of the castle's restoration. An informative guided tour of the castle points out its distinctive features both defensive and domestic, like the gun loops and murder holes or a curious circu-lar larder. Visitors can go out onto the newly constructed roof for a fantastic view of the Burren and Galway Bay. Beginning near the castle is an educational trail about 1¼ miles (2km) in length that highlights the flora and archaeology of the Burren. In an adjacent complex is the **Burren College of Art** (ⓒ **065/ 707-7200**), founded in 1993. Although geared to 15-week semester programs and full academic year or summer programs, the school also offers a range of weekend and 1-week courses ideal for the visitor.

Ballyvaughn, Co. Clare. ⓒ **065/707-7200.** Fax 065/707-7201. www.iol.ie/~burren/. 4.50€ ($4.10) adults, 2.60€ ($2.35) children ages 4–12, reduced rates for families and for those who see just the castle or the trail. Easter to Oct 10am–6pm; Nov–Easter by appointment only.

ACCOMMODATIONS YOU CAN AFFORD

Fernhill Farmhouse   This marvelous old farmhouse, set on a hill overlooking fields and distant hills, has twice won Best Farmhouse awards. There's a large front lounge with picture windows looking out to the fields. One guest room is on the ground floor, a boon for those with limited mobility. Upstairs bedrooms have kept the character of the house, some with wooden peaked or slanted ceilings. Tess's lively personality is a bonus.

Doolin Rd., Lisdoonvarna, Co. Clare. ⓒ/fax **065/707-4040.** www.fernhillfarm.net. 6 units. 34€ ($31) single; 60€ ($54) double. 15% reduction for children. Rates include full breakfast. Dinner 19€ ($17). MC, V. Paved parking lot. Closed Nov to mid-Mar. 2 miles (3km) from Lisdoonvarna and 2 miles (3km) from Doolin. *In room:* Tea/coffeemaker, hair dryer, iron.

Lismactigue House   Lismactigue house is a 500-year-old thatched cottage, tucked within an ash and beech copse. Peat smoke from a large kitchen fireplace permeates the house, and the breakfast room, with its flagstones, thick white-washed walls, and beamed ceilings, recalls a traditional rural life that has all but disappeared in most parts of Ireland. The guest bedrooms, located in a small modern wing, are thoroughly 20th century: They're plainly furnished, with small bathrooms, and each has a single and a queen-size bed. Rooms face the limestone hills of the Burren.

Lismactigue, Ballyvaughn, Co. Clare. ℂ/fax **065/707-7040**. mike-g.keane@analog.com. 3 units. 29€ ($26) single; 44€ ($40) double; 67€ ($60) triple. No credit cards.

Sunville   Sunville is a 10-minute walk from the center of Lisdoonvarna on N67 (turn off at Kincora House). Teresa and John Petty are the friendly owners. Their guest rooms are all comfortably furnished, and beds come equipped with electric blankets. There's a TV lounge for guests, and the entire house is non-smoking. The breakfast menu includes such unexpected and welcome offerings as French toast, pancakes, grilled cheese sandwiches with tomato, herbal teas, and hot chocolate.

Off Doolin Rd. (N67), Lisdoonvarna, Co. Clare. ℂ/fax **065/707-4065**. tpetty@gofree.indigo.ie. 5 units. 38€ ($34) single; 56€ ($51) double. 33% reduction for children. Rates include full breakfast. MC, V. Free private parking. **Amenities:** Lounge. *In room:* Tea/coffeemakers.

Worth a Splurge

Ballinalacken Castle Hotel ★★   The first delight of Ballinalacken is its location: situated just below the crest of a hill overlooking the Aran Islands, all rooms but three command fine sea views. The hotel is only a few minutes' drive from the traditional music sessions in Doolin, but it's completely isolated from the town's touristic atmosphere and only a few minutes' walk away from the rocky drama of the Burren. The hotel itself, run by the O'Callaghan family for over 40 years, was built in the 1840s. Most of the guest rooms can be found in a new wing, but it's worthwhile to request a room in the old house, where you'll find high ceilings, marble fireplaces, and, in room 16, a sweeping panorama of hill and sea. All rooms are traditionally furnished and are quite spacious. Bathrooms are compact, white tiled, and modern, with strong showers (two of the rooms have showers only, no tubs). An added bonus: The exceptional ruined 15th century castle tower of the O'Brien clan just behind the hotel is open only to guests. Before you leave, be sure to climb its worn stairs to its dizzy top to scan the sea from crumbling battlements.

Doolin, Co. Clare. ℂ/fax **065/74025**. www.ballinalackencastle.com. 13 units. 101€–129€ ($90–$114) double. AE, DC, MC, V. Free parking. *In room:* TV, hair dryer.

GREAT DEALS ON DINING

Tri na Cheile IRISH   Formerly Claire's, this homey, intimate restaurant in the middle of the village is now the common venture of Adele Laffan and Barry Richards, committed to offering the freshest and finest of Irish ingredients at reasonable prices. Sirloin, mussels and linguini, whole crab, beef curry, filet of salmon, roast lamb with anchovies, garlic and rosemary, and roast chicken run the modest yet enticing gamut of current offerings. An additional vegetarian option, a vegetable curry, is also available.

Main St., Ballyvaughan, Co. Clare. ℂ **065/707-7029**. Reservations recommended. Main courses 13€–18€ ($12–$16). MC, V. May–Sept Mon–Sat 6–10:45pm, Sun 12:30–3:30pm.

Bofey Quinn's IRISH/BARFOOD   An informal atmosphere prevails at this pub/restaurant in the center of town. Dinner specialties include fresh wild salmon and cod as well as a variety of steaks, chops, and mixed grills. Pub-grub lunches are also available throughout the day. Sometimes, during the summer, dinner is accompanied by the sounds of a harp.

Main St., Corofin, Co. Clare. ℂ **065/683-7321**. Reservations not necessary. Main courses 7€–13€ ($6.35–$12). MC, V. Daily noon–9:30pm.

SHOPPING

Burren Perfumery   Ireland's oldest perfumery, this family-run business is located on a small road east of Carron village. Soap, perfumes, and aroma-therapy products are made here, distilled from plants within the shop itself (because many Burren plants are protected by law, some plant material is brought in from elsewhere). Scents include "Ilaun," made from wild orchid and Frond, which has a moss and lichen base. Particularly appealing are soft squares of handmade soap, scented with geranium. The free audiovisual presentation and photographic display offer an introduction to the Burren and its flora, and a new organic herb garden cultivates a large selection of native and exotic herb species. Carron, Co. Clare. © 065/708-9102. Fax 065/708-9200. www.burrenperfumery.com/.

3 County Mayo

Ballina is 63 miles (101km) N of Galway, 120 miles (193km) N of Shannon Airport, 153 miles (246km) NW of Dublin, and 193 miles (311km) NW of Cork

Rimmed by Clew Bay and the Atlantic Ocean, County Mayo boasts many diverse attractions, although it has been most widely identified as *The Quiet Man* country ever since the classic movie was filmed here in 1951. The exact set-ting for the film was **Cong,** a no-longer-so-quiet village wedged between Lough Mask and Lough Corrib and backed up against the County Galway border. Much of Mayo, however, has resisted the pull of Hollywood and still provides remote bogs, beaches, cliffs, and crags where quiet splendor prevails.

Among Mayo's other attractions are the 5,000-year-old farmstead settlement at **Ceide Fields,** the Marian shrine at **Knock,** and some of Europe's best fishing waters at **Lough Conn, Lough Mask,** and the **River Moy.** Ballina, Mayo's largest town, calls itself the home of the Irish salmon.

Mayo's northwestern corner remains wild and largely untouched. You won't find many amenities here, but you will discover some of the most beautiful and least-traveled of Ireland's scenic wonders.

GETTING THERE   By Air   Aer Lingus provides daily service from Dublin into **Knock International Airport,** Charlestown, County Mayo (© **094/ 67222**). Charter flights from the United States operate in the summer. From Britain, there's service to Knock on **Aer Lingus** from Birmingham, **British Regional Airlines** from Manchester, and **Ryan Air** from London's Stansted.

By Public Transportation   Irish Rail and **Bus Eireann** (© **096/21011;** www.buseireann.ie) provide daily service from Dublin and other cities into Ballina, Westport, and Castlebar, with bus connections into smaller towns. There is also express service from Galway into most Mayo towns.

By Car   From Dublin and points east, the main N5 road leads to many points in County Mayo; from Galway, take N84 or N17. From Sligo and points north, take N17 or N59. To get around County Mayo, it's best to rent a car. Two firms with outlets at Knock International Airport are **National Car Rental** (© **094/ 67252**) and **Irish Car Rentals** (© **094/67567**). Also, **Casey Auto Rentals, Ltd.** (© **094/24618**).

VISITOR INFORMATION   For year-round information, visit or contact the **Westport Tourist Office,** The Mall, Westport (© **098/25711;** http://westport. mayo-ireland.ie/). It's open all year Monday through Saturday from 9am to 5:45pm October to May; Mon to Fri 9am to 7pm June to Aug 9am to 7pm. The **Knock Airport Tourist Office** (© **094/67247**) is open June through September at times coinciding with flight arrivals.

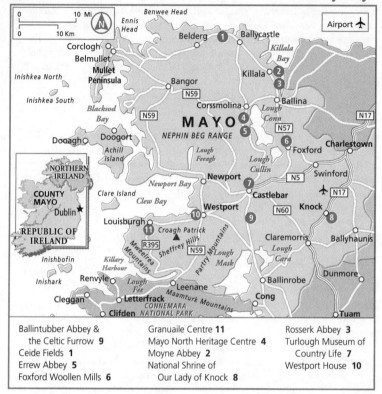

| 0 | 10 Mi |
| 0 | 10 Km |

Airport ✈

Benwee Head

Ennis Head

Corclogh
Belmullet
Mullet Peninsula

Inishkea North

Inishkea South

Belderg **1**

Ballycastle

Killala Bay

Killala **2**
3

Bangor

N59

Corrsmolina

Blacksod Bay

Lough Conn

Ballina

N17

N59

M A Y O
NEPHIN BEG RANGE

4
5

N57

Dooagh
Doogort
Achill Island

NORTHERN IRELAND

COUNTY MAYO
Dublin ★

REPUBLIC OF IRELAND

6 Foxford

Charlestown

Lough Feeagh

Lough Cullin

Swinford

Clare Island

Newport Bay

Newport **7**

N5

Knock **8**

Castlebar ✈ N17

Clew Bay

Westport **9**
10

N60

Inishbofin

Louisburgh
11

Croagh Patrick ▲

R395

Mweelrea Mountains

Sheffrey Hills

N59

Lough Mask

Partry Mountains

Claremorris

Ballyhaunis

Lough Cara

Dunmore

Inishark

Renvyle
Killary Harbour

Lough Fee

Leenane

Maamturk Mountains

Ballinrobe

Cong

Cleggan

Letterfrack
Clifden

CONNEMARA NATIONAL PARK

Tuam

Ballintubber Abbey & the Celtic Furrow **9**	Granuaile Centre **11**	Rosserk Abbey **3**
Ceide Fields **1**	Mayo North Heritage Centre **4**	Turlough Museum of Country Life **7**
Errew Abbey **5**	Moyne Abbey **2**	Westport House **10**
Foxford Woollen Mills **6**	National Shrine of Our Lady of Knock **8**	

Seasonal tourist offices, open from May/June to September/October, include the **Ballina Tourist Office,** Cathedral Road, Ballina, County Mayo (℃ 096/70848); **Castlebar Tourist Office,** Linenhall Street, Castlebar, County Mayo (℃ 094/21207); **Knock Village Tourist Office,** Knock (℃ 094/88193); **Cong Village Tourist Office** (℃ 092/46542); and **Achill Tourist Office,** Achill Sound (℃ 098/45384). There's also a community-operated tourist information center in **Newport** (℃ 098/41895).

EXPLORING THE COUNTY

Cong is a charming little village, where the waters of Lough Mask, which go underground 3 miles (5km) to the north, come rushing to the surface to surge through the center of town before they dissipate into several streams that empty into Lough Corrib. The phenomenon is known as "The Rising of the Waters." The **Royal Abbey Cong,** at the edge of town, was built by Turlough Mor O'Connor, High King of Ireland, in 1120 on the site of an earlier 7th-century St. Fechin community. It's considered one of the finest early-Christian architectural relics in the country, and is also the final resting place of Rory O'Connor, the last High King, who was buried here in 1198.

You'll find **Ashford Castle** just outside Cong on the shores of Lough Corrib. The oldest part of the castle was built by the de Burgoes, an Anglo-Norman family, in 1228. The castle's keep is now a part of the impressive, slightly eccentric Ashford Castle Hotel, which also incorporates a French-chateau-style mansion of the Oranmore and Browne families built in the early 1700s and the additions made by Sir Benjamin Guinness in the mid-1800s (undertaken as much to provide employment for famine-starved natives as to improve the property). The hotel's rates are quite high, but anyone can take a stroll through its elegant public rooms, with massive fireplaces and wall-high oil paintings, or have a drink in the **Dungeon Bar.** The gardens around the castle are also great for strolling, and connect up with other local paths for longer walks. These paths can be rather serpentine and hard to follow, so it's best to get the local 1:50,000 ordnance survey map if you plan to do much walking.

County Mayo's loveliest town, **Westport** ⍟, is nestled on the shores of Clew Bay. Once a major port, it's one of the few planned towns of Ireland, designed by Richard Castle with a splendid tree-lined mall, rows of Georgian buildings, and an octagonal central mall. A nice end to a Westport day is a drop-in at **Matt Malloy's Pub**—Matt is the flute player with the well-known Irish group The Chieftains, and you may just catch him in residence.

The road between Louisburgh and Westport (R335) touches the bay at several points, and on the other side of the road rises 2,510-foot (765m) high **Croagh Patrick,** where St. Patrick is believed to have fasted for 40 days. Modern-day pilgrims climb the stony paths in their bare feet in July for a 4am mass at its summit.

Set on the banks of the River Moy, 31 miles (50km) northeast of Westport, **Ballina** is the largest town in County Mayo. There are pleasant river walks in the town, and this is one of Ireland's best angling centers, especially noted for salmon fishing.

Eight miles (13km) north of Ballina via R314, **Killala** is home to a small harbor that was the landing place for French forces under the command of General Humbert in 1798. There's a fine round tower, and the nearby well-preserved ruins of 15th-century Moyne Abbey include a six-story square tower.

You'll find two extraordinary ruined 15th-century Franciscan friaries signposted off the R314 between Killala and Ballina—they're located about 2 miles (3km) apart, and both are dramatically situated on the shores of Killala Bay. The last friar at **Moyne Abbey** probably died in the 1800s, but processions of brown-robed monks are easily imagined in the beautiful stone cloister. **Rosserk Abbey** is particularly fascinating: Not only are its chapel windows well preserved, but visitors can climb a winding stone stair to see the domestic rooms of the friary and look out across the bay. The piscina of the church (a place for washing altar vessels) is carved with angels, and on its lower left-hand column is a delightful detail: a tiny, elegant carving of a round tower that recalls its 75-foot (23m) tall counterpart in nearby Killala.

The landscape of **Northwest Mayo** ⍟ is one of the most wild and bleak in all Ireland. There's something deeply stirring about watching the cloud shadows and sunbreaks sweep slowly across the bog land and out to sea. There's not much here in the way of established tourist attractions, though, so buy yourself a good map and choose a few areas to explore. Belmullet, 39 miles (63km) west of Ballina, is the gateway to the Mullet Peninsula, a region of mostly flat bog land and sand dunes. T. H. White, author of *The Once and Future King,* once spent some time exploring the islands off the **Mullet Peninsula,** and recorded his impressions in the book *The Godstone and the Blackymor.*

The region to the east of the Mullet peninsula, **Portacloy** ⍟ and **Benwee Head,** offers a spectacular array of sheer sea cliffs and craggy islands. The small, secluded beach at Portacloy, 8½ miles (13.5km) north of Glenamoy on R314, is

> ### *Finds* A Great Pub
>
> Pipe smokers should look for **Gaughan's Pub** on O'Rahilly Street in Ballina, a pub that has changed little in the last half century. Along with a popular public house trade, Edward Gaughan carries on a well-loved tobacco counter started by his father, Michael, and is adept at matching smokers with the appropriate pipe. The pub also serves an excellent lunch special Monday to Friday.

a good starting point for a dramatic walk. On a sunny day, its aquamarine waters and fine-grained white sand recall the Mediterranean more than the North Atlantic. At its western edge, there is a concrete quay. From here, head north up the steep green slopes of the nearest hill. But do not fall into a reverie at the fantastic view or adorable little sheep: The unassuming boggy slopes on which you are walking end precipitously at an unmarked cliff edge (the walk is not recommended for children). Exercise caution and resist the urge to try to get a better view of mysterious sea caves or to reach the outermost extents of the coast's promontories. Instead, use a farmer's fence as a guide and head west toward the striking profile of Benwee Head, about 1½ miles (2.5km) away. Return the same way to have a final swim in the chill, tranquil waters of Portacloy.

Ballintubber Abbey and The Celtic Furrow   Founded in 1216 by Cathal O'Connor, king of Connaught, Ballintubber survived early fires and other tragedies to become known as the abbey that refused to die—it's been in continuous use for almost 800 years. Even though the forces of Cromwell took off the church's roof in 1653 and attempted to suppress services, clerics persisted in discreetly conducting religious rites through the centuries. The Celtic Furrow is a visitor center presenting the festivals and rituals of pre-Christian peoples in Ireland, and the ways in which these practices were assimilated into Christianity.

Ballintubber, Co. Mayo. © 094/30934. Free admission to the abbey; admission to the Celtic Furrow 3.80€ ($3.45) adult. June–Sept daily 10am–4:30pm. Off the main Galway-Castlebar Rd. (N84), about 20 miles (32km) west of Knock.

Ceide Fields ⭐   Here, in a dramatic sea-edge setting, lies the oldest enclosed landscape in Europe, revealing a pattern of once-tilled fields as they were laid out and lived in 50 centuries ago. Preserved for millennia beneath the bog to which it had been lost, this Neolithic farming settlement, home to the builders of the nearby megalithic tombs, now shows its face again. Admittedly, it's a nearly inscrutable face, requiring all the resources of the interpretive center to make meaningful eye contact with the visitor. The visitor center offers a 20-minute video presentation and tours of the site.

Ballycastle, Co. Mayo. © 096/43325. www.heritageireland.ie. Admission 3.15€ ($2.90) adults, 2.20€ ($2.00) seniors, 1.25€ ($1.15) students and children, 7.60€ ($6.90) family. Mid-Mar to May and Oct daily 10am–5pm; June–Sept daily 9:30am–6:30pm; Nov daily 10am–4:30pm. Last tour 1 hour before closing. Situated on R314, the coastal road north of Ballina, between Ballycastle and Belderrig.

Errew Abbey (Open Site)   This ruined 13th-century Augustinian church sits on a tiny peninsula in Lough Conn and has great views of the lake. The cloister is well preserved, as is the chancel with altar and *piscina* (a basin for washing sacred vessels). An oratory with massive stone walls is in the field adjacent to the abbey—on the site of a church founded in the 6th century, and

Finds **Two Islands**

Achill ✿ is Ireland's largest island. Its 57 square miles (148km²) are connected to the mainland by a causeway that takes you into breathtakingly beautiful, unspoiled, and varied scenery. High cliffs overlook tiny villages of whitewashed cottages, golden beaches, and heathery bog lands. The signposted **Atlantic Drive** is spectacular, and will whet your appetite for exploring more of the island's well-surfaced roadways. This is a wild, and at the same time profoundly peaceful, place. In late May, the entire island is covered with such a profusion of rhododendrons that my bed-and-breakfast hostess once smilingly told me, "Every car that leaves will be loaded with those blooms, and we won't even miss them!" Achill has long been a favorite holiday spot for Irish from other parts of the country, and there are good accommodations available in most of the beach villages. If time permits, I highly recommend an overnight stay on Achill (in summer there's traditional music in many of the pubs), but even if you can only spare part of a day, this is one off-the-beaten-path place you really shouldn't miss.

Clare Island, which floats a mere 3½ miles (5.5km) off the Mayo Coast, just beyond Clew Bay, is roughly 40 square miles (105 sq km) of unspoiled splendor. Inhabited for 5,000 years and once quite populous—with 1700 pre-famine residents—Clare is now home to a scant 150 year-round islanders, plus perhaps as many sheep. Grace O'Malley's modest **castle,** and the partially restored **Cistercian Abbey** where she is buried, are among the island's few man-made attractions. The rest is a matter of remote natural beauty, in which Clare abounds. The sea cliffs on the north side of the island are truly spectacular. Two ferry services, operating out of Roonagh Harbour, offer 15-minute conveyance to and from the island for 13€ ($12) per person, round-trip: O'Malley's Ferry Service, aboard the *Ocean Star* and *Island Princess* (✆ **098/25045**); and Clare Island Ferries, aboard the *Pirate Queen* (✆ **098/28288**). Once you arrive on Clare Island, if you want the grand tour, look for Ludwig Timmerman's 1974 Land Rover. Ludwig offers cordial, informative tours from June through August. Otherwise, your transport options are either mountain bikes or your own sturdy pinions.

known locally as Templenagalliaghdoo, or "Church of the Black Nun." The site of the abbey is a remarkably tranquil place, and great for a picnic.

Signposted about 2 miles (3km) south of Crossmolina on the Castlebar Rd., then 3 miles (5km) down a side road.

Foxford Woollen Mills ✿ Founded in 1892 by a local nun, Mother Agnes Morrogh-Bernard, to provide work for a community ravaged by the effects of the Irish famine, Foxford Woollen Mills brought prosperity to the area through the worldwide sales of beautiful tweeds, rugs, and blankets. The center first tells the story of this local industry with a multimedia audiovisual presentation, and then provides an on-site tour of the working mills to see the production of the famous Foxford woolen products. Tours run every 20 minutes. A restaurant, a shop, an exhibition center, an art gallery, a heritage room, and other craft units (including a doll-making and -restoration workshop and a jewelry designer) enrich a visit.

St. Joseph's Place, Foxford, Co. Mayo. ℭ 094/56756. foxfordwoollenmills@eircom.net. Admission 4.75€ ($4.30) adults; 3.80€ ($3.45) seniors, students, and children; 15€ ($14) family. Nov–Apr Mon–Sat 10am–6pm, Sun 2–6pm; May–Oct Mon–Sat 10am–6pm and Sun noon–6pm. Off the Foxford-Ballina Rd. (N57), 10 miles (16km) south of Ballina.

Granuaile Centre   Using an audiovisual display and graphic exhibits, this center tells the story of one of Ireland's great female heroes, Granuaile (Grace) O'Malley (1530–1600). Known as the "pirate queen," Grace led battles against the English and ruled the baronies of Burrishoole and Murrisk, around Clew Bay. Her extraordinary exploits are recounted in Elizabethan state papers. The center also includes a craft shop and coffee shop.

Louisburgh, Co. Mayo. ℭ 098/66341. Admission 3.15€ ($2.90) adults, 1.90€ ($1.75) seniors and students, 1.60€ ($1.45) children. June to mid-Sept Mon–Sat 10am–6pm.

Mayo North Heritage Centre   If your ancestors came from Mayo, this center will help you trace your family tree. The data bank includes indices to church registers of all denominations (up to 1901) as well as Civil registers of births, deaths, and marriages from 1864 to 1901. Even if you have no connections in Mayo, you'll enjoy the adjacent museum, with its displays of rural household items, farm machinery, and farm implements, including the *gowl-gob*, a spade-like implement exclusive to this locality. The center also offers a new 5- to 10-day blacksmithing course. The lovely Victorian-style Enniscoe Gardens adjoin the center; combined tickets to the center and gardens are available. A new tearoom opened in 1999.

Note: If your ancestors were from the southern part of Ireland, try the **South Mayo Family Research Centre,** Town Hall, Neale Road, Ballinrobe, County Mayo (ℭ 092/41214). It's open Monday to Friday 9:30am to noon, 1:30 to 4pm.

Enniscoe, Castlehill, Ballina, Co. Mayo. ℭ 096/31809. Fax 096/31885. normayo@iol.ie. Admission to museum 3.80€ ($3.45) adults, 3.15€ ($2.90) seniors, 1.25€ ($1.15) children, 9€ ($8) families; admission to garden 5€ ($4.55) adults, 3.15€ ($2.90) seniors, 1.25€ ($1.15) children, 11€ ($10) families. Oct–April Mon–Fri 9am–4pm; May–Sept Mon–Fri 9am–6pm; June–Aug Mon–Fri 9am–6pm, Sat–Sun 2–6pm. Situated on Lough Conn, about 2 miles (3km) south of Crossmolina, off R315.

National Shrine of Our Lady of Knock   It's said that here, in 1879, local townspeople witnessed an appearance of Mary, the mother of Jesus. Considered the Lourdes or Fatima of Ireland, Knock came to the world's attention in 1979 when Pope John Paul II visited the shrine. The town's centerpiece is a huge circular basilica seating 7,000 people, it's outer columns built of stone quarried from each county in Ireland. The grounds also contain a folk museum and a religious bookshop.

Knock, Co. Mayo. ℭ 094/88100. info@knock-shrine.ie. Admission to shrine, free; museum 3.80€ ($3.45) adults, 3.15€ ($2.90) students, 2.55€ ($2.30) seniors and children over age 5. Shrine and grounds, year-round, daily 8am–6pm or later; museum, May–Oct daily 10am–6pm. On the N17 Galway Rd.

Turlough Museum of Country Life ⟨𝒦⟩   This new museum, the first branch of the National Museum outside Dublin, is dedicated to displaying and interpreting the artifacts of everyday life in rural Ireland. The museum records a simple way of life that saw little change for centuries, and then disappeared during this century completely within the span of a few decades. The only traces left behind are the objects used by Ireland's rural poor: furniture, hunting and agricultural implements, religious objects, clothing, and games. The museum is housed in a new building, incised into the terraced lawns of a large Victorian country house with extensive gardens and a fine artificial lake (*turlough*).

Turlough Park, Castlebar, Co. Mayo. © 094/31589. Fax 094/31498. tpark@museum.ie. Admission free. Tues–Sat 10am–5pm and Sun 2–5pm.

Westport House *(Kids)*   At the edge of town you can visit Westport House, a late 18th-century residence that's home of Lord Altamont, the Marquis of Sligo, who is in residence with his family. The work of Richard Cassels and James Wyatt, the house is graced with a staircase of ornate white Sicilian marble, unusual Art Nouveau glass and carvings, family heirlooms, and silver. The grandeur of the residence is admittedly compromised by the commercial enterprises in its midst, including video games and a small amusement park.

Westport, Co. Mayo. © 098/25430. Fax 098/25206. www.westporthouse.ie. Admission to house and children's zoo 13€ ($12) adults, 6€ ($5.45) seniors and students, 6.50€ ($5.90) children; admission to house only 8€ ($7.25) adults, 5.50€ ($5.00) seniors and students, 4€ ($3.65) children. Westport House only, open May Sat–Sun 2–5pm, Sept daily 2–5pm; Westport House and children's zoo open June daily 2–6pm, July–Aug Mon–Sat 11:30am–6pm and Sun 2–7pm, Sept daily 2–5pm.

OUTDOOR PURSUITS

FISHING   The County Mayo waters of the River Moy and Loughs Carrowmore and Conn offer some of the best fishing in Europe, and some of Ireland's premier sources for salmon and trout. For general information about fishing in County Mayo, contact the **North Western Regional Fisheries Board,** Ardnaree House, Abbey Street, Ballina (© **096/22788;** www.cfb.ie).

County Mayo is also home to the **Pontoon Bridge Fly Fishing School,** Pontoon, County Mayo (© **094/56120;** www.pontoonbridge.com). This school offers 1- to 4-day courses in the art of fly casting, as well as fly-tying, tackle design, and other background information necessary for successful game fishing. Fees range from 44€ to 133€ ($40–$121), depending on the duration of the course. Courses run daily from April to late September. You can hire a boat and guide for 76€ ($69) per day, and a rod for 6.50€ ($5.90) per day.

Permits and state fishing licenses can be obtained at the **North Mayo Angling Advice Centre** (Tiernan Bros.), Upper Main St., Foxford, County Mayo (© **094/56731**). Tiernan Brothers offer, as well, a wide range of services, including boat hire and ghillies (guides).

For fishing tackle, try **Jones Ltd., General Merchants,** Main Street, Foxford, County Mayo (© **094/56121**), or **Walkins Fishing Tackle,** Market Square, Ballina, County Mayo (© **096/22442**).

GOLF   County Mayo's 18-hole golf courses include a par-72 links course at **Belmullet Golf Course,** Carne, Belmullet, County Mayo (© **097/82292;** www.belmulletgolfclub.ie), with greens fees of 32€ ($29) weekdays, 38€ ($35) weekends; a par-71 inland course at **Castlebar Golf Club,** Rocklands, Castlebar, County Mayo (© **094/21649;** castlebargolf@eircom.ie), with greens fees of 25€ ($23) weekdays and 32€ ($29) weekends; and a par-73 championship course at **Westport Golf Club,** County Mayo (© **098/28262;** wpgolf@iol.ie), with greens fees of 32€ ($29) on weekdays and 38€ ($35) on weekends. Set on the shores of Clew Bay, the last course winds its way around the precipitous slopes of Croagh Patrick Mountain. It's one of western Ireland's most challenging and scenic courses.

ACCOMMODATIONS YOU CAN AFFORD
WESTPORT

Cedar Lodge   You'll be greeted with a welcome cuppa on arrival at Maureen Flynn's split-level bungalow on route N59. The house sits on beautifully landscaped, award-winning grounds, and is only a short walk from the seafront and the town center. The tastefully furnished guest rooms and quiet location offer a welcome refuge. Duffers will be quite happy with the lodge's close location to the Westport Golf Club (see above); if you prefer a game of tennis, there are a number of courts next door. The entire house is nonsmoking.

Kings Hill, Newport Rd., Westport, Co. Mayo. ℂ 098/25417. http://homepage.eircom.net/~cedarlodge westport. 4 units, 3 with bathroom (shower only). 39€–43€ ($35–$39) single; 52€–56€ ($47–$51) double. Rates include full breakfast. MC, V. Free private parking. *In room:* TV, tea/coffeemaker, hair dryer.

Dun Maeve ⭐⭐ *Value*   This beautifully restored and expanded 19th-century Georgian town house provides elegance, comfort, and extraordinary convenience—it is in the heart of Westport town, around the corner from the tourist office. It is clearly a cut above almost any B&B you'll come across. Each room is unique and eminently tasteful; the range of accommodations will meet the needs of couples, families, and single travelers. The beds are firm, the bathrooms are spacious, and the breakfast-room conservatory is a real treat.

If you want to stay in the Westport area for a week or more, hostess Maria Hughes also offers two self-catering four-bedroom holiday homes. Each sleeps seven. They come fully furnished with virtually everything you'll need, except for perfect weather. Weekly rates range from 509€ to 848€ ($450–$750) per week, depending on season.

Newport Road, Westport, Co. Mayo. ℂ 098/26529. Fax 098/28761. 6 units. 76€ ($69) double. Rates include full breakfast. MC, V. Open year-round. Located just around the corner from the tourist office. **Amenities:** Sitting room. *In room:* TV.

CONG & VICINITY
Ballykine House ⭐⭐   The older part of this house is finely crafted in limestone, and was part of the Ashford Castle estate when it was owned by the Guinness family. The house is set far back from the road, just over ½ mile (1km) from charming Clonbur village. The primary appeal of this place is the many wooded walks that depart from the house: one toward the lake, another to ruined Ballykine Castle, a third to some local caves en route to Ashford Castle and Cong. Rooms on the north side of the house have great views of Lough Corrib, at a distance of about 1 mile (1.5km). Anne Lambe knows the area well: She grew up in this house, and has many insightful tips for visitors, such as a back entrance to the Ashford Castle grounds and the best local places for hill walking.

Clonbur, Co. Galway. ℂ/fax 092/46150. 5 units, 4 with bathroom (shower only). 48€ ($44) double. Rates include full breakfast. No credit cards. Closed Nov–Mar. 2 miles (3km) west of Cong on R345. *In room:* TV, hair dryer.

Lydon's Lodge   Mrs. Carmel Lydon's large, modern house in the village is set on Lough Corrib and near Ashford Castle. The house is nicely decorated throughout, with comfortable guest rooms. Boats can be rented for use on the lake, at a cost of 43€ ($38) per day for a boat with engine, and fly-casting lessons are also available. During the summer months, there's live traditional music at the hotel at least three times weekly.

Cong, Co. Mayo. ℂ 092/46053. www.lydonslodge.freesavers.com. 10 units, all with bathroom (3 with shower only). 63€–76€ ($58–$69) double. Rates include full breakfast. 3-course dinner 23.75€ ($21). MC, V. Closed Oct–Mar. *In room:* TV, tea/coffeemaker, hair dryer.

ACHILL ISLAND
Rockmount   This modern bungalow, set at the eastern edge of Achill Sound village and convenient to a bus stop, is the home of Mrs. Frances Masterson,

who happily shares her knowledge of the island with guests. Guest rooms are all comfortably furnished, and off-street parking is available.

Achill Island, Co. Mayo. ℂ **098/45272.** 6 units, 4 with bathroom (shower only). 48€ ($44) double. 25% reduction for children sharing with an adult. Rates include full breakfast. No credit cards. *In room:* Tea/coffeemaker.

Teach Mweewillin Across the sound and 5½ miles (9km) from Achill Island, this modern bungalow sits on a hill overlooking sound and island. Mrs. Margo Cannon keeps a pony for children to ride, and gladly helps guests arrange fishing, sailing, or golf. Guest rooms are all nonsmoking.

Currane, Achill Island, Co. Mayo. ℂ **098/45134.** Fax 098/45225. scannon@anu.ie. 4 units, 3 with bathroom (shower only). 48€ ($44) double. 50% reduction for children sharing with an adult. Rates include full breakfast. Dinner 20€ ($18). No credit cards. Closed Oct–Mar.

West Coast House Mrs. Teresa McNamara's modern bungalow sits in a quiet location just off the main road, surrounded by some of Achill's most spectacular scenery. The bedrooms have gorgeous views, and each comes with orthopedic beds and electric blankets. Breakfast options include pancakes, and evening meals feature the freshest seafood. Mrs. O'Gorman also has bicycles (a great way to get around the island) for hire. The house is nonsmoking.

School Rd., Dooagh, Achill Island, Co. Mayo. ℂ/fax **098/43317.** westcoast@anu.ie. 5 units. 63€ ($58) double. 20% reduction for children sharing with an adult. Dinner 19€ ($17). No credit cards. 1¼ miles (2km) from Keel. *In room:* TV, tea/coffeemaker, hair dryer.

AROUND COUNTY MAYO

Ashfort Philip and Carol O'Gorman's two-story Tudor-style home is the perfect base for exploring this part of the West, from Connemara to Castlebar and Ballina to Knock to Sligo. Guest rooms are well appointed and beautifully decorated. The O'Gormans are the epitome of Irish hospitality and you're sure to receive a warm welcome. The entire house is nonsmoking.

Galway-Knock Rd., Charlestown, Co. Mayo. ℂ **094/54706.** ashfort@esatclear.ie. 5 units. 48€ ($44) double. 20% reduction for children sharing with an adult. No credit cards. Free parking. Closed Dec–Feb. 15 miles (24km) north of Knock on N17. **Amenities:** Lounge. *In room:* TV, hair dryer, iron (on request).

Drom Caoin ★★ *Kids* The view of Blacksod Bay is terrific from Mairin Maguire-Murphy's comfortable home, a short walk from the center of Belmullet. Two of the guest rooms have recently been renovated into self-catering apartments that can be rented by the night or by the week, with or without breakfast. It's a great concept—you can actually settle in, cook some of your own meals, and enjoy the extra space of a suite for little more money than an average B&B room. The ground-floor apartment faces a parking lot at the back of the house—not a great view, but there's plenty of room for a family with a pullout couch in the sitting room, a bedroom with a double bed, and a loft-nook which is just the right size for a small child. The other apartment is on the upper floor of the house, and is very comfortable for a couple—the kitchen adjoins a small dining room/sitting room with a sloping ceiling, and a skylight view of the bay. It's not spacious, but very comfortable. The other two bedrooms are small, with compact bathrooms. Breakfast is something to look forward to here—omelets, fresh fish, and toasted cheese are offered periodically as alternatives to the standard fry, and the fresh scones are delicious.

Belmullet, Co. Mayo. ℂ/fax **097/81195.** dromcaoin@esatlink.com. 4 units. 38.50€ ($35) single; 60€ ($54) double; 47€ ($43) apartment (without breakfast), 60€ ($54) apartment (with breakfast), 300€ ($272) apartments by the week (without breakfast). 33% reduction for children. MC, V. Free parking. *In room:* TV.

Kilcommon Lodge Hostel   This gem of a hostel is hidden in a grove of trees, with views of Sruwaddacon Bay, in what must be one of the most extraordinarily scenic corners of Ireland. Betty and Fritz Schult moved here from Germany and know the region well, so be sure to consult them when planning your excursions. Double rooms come with a double bed or two twins; the beds are a bit soft. The sitting room would be the envy of many B&Bs, and is a great place to read. Meals are prepared on request (vegetarians are catered to), or guests can buy produce from the hostel garden for their own cooking. An assortment of sculptures, a small greenhouse, and a vegetable garden adorn the eclectic and delightful yard. Unfortunately, there's no nonsmoking area in the hostel.

Bus service is available from Ballina to the hostel door for 5.70€ ($5.20) one-way—contact Mick McGrath (© **097/87842**). The bus leaves Dunnes Stores in Ballina at 6pm Monday to Saturday.

Pollatomish, Ballina, Co. Mayo. © 097/84621. www.kilcommonlodge.net. 6 units, none with bathroom: 4 double rooms, 2 dorm rooms (6–9 beds). 9.50€ ($8.65) per person in dorm; 22€ ($20) double. 4-course dinner 9.50€ ($8.65); breakfast 4.50€ ($4.10). MC, V. **Amenities:** Sitting room; guest kitchen.

Kilmurray House   You won't find luxury at the Moffatt farmhouse, but you will discover a casually inviting place that encourages visitors to make themselves at home. The front two bedrooms are especially spacious and bright, while the two single rooms are small. The farm is in a beautiful pastoral setting at the foot of Nephin Mountain. Smoking is permitted in the bedrooms and sitting room but not in the dining room. Boats and guides can be arranged for salmon fishing on the local rivers and Lough Conn.

Crossmolina, Co. Mayo. © 096/31227. 6 units, 4 with bathroom (shower only). 48€ ($44) double. 50% discount for children sharing with an adult. Rates include full breakfast. No credit cards. Closed Oct–Mar. 3½ miles (5.5km) outside Crossmolina on the Castlebar Rd.. *In room:* Tea/coffeemaker.

Lakeview House *Kids*   Mary and Joe Moran's bungalow sits on spacious grounds with a large, sloping lawn out front, 2½ miles (4km) from Castlebar on the Westport Road. Both the lounge (with fireplace) and dining room look out to green fields and rolling hills. Mary bakes her own brown bread and scones and is always happy to share the recipe with guests (a frequent request). The four guest rooms include one family-size room with two double beds. Mary offers free babysitting until midnight.

Westport Rd., Castlebar, Co. Mayo. © 094/22374. 4 units. 48€ ($44) double. 50% reduction for children sharing with an adult. Rates include full breakfast. No credit cards. **Amenities:** Lounge; babysitting. *In room:* Tea/coffeemaker, hair dryer.

Riverside   Anthony and Anne Kelly are the hosts of this attractive, century-old B&B, conveniently located northeast of Knock in Charlestown at the intersection of N5 and N17. Guest rooms are bright and quite comfortable, and the entire property is nonsmoking. The family-run restaurant offers good food in an attractive setting for very reasonable prices. The restaurant is open throughout the year, except November.

Charlestown, Co. Mayo. ©/094/54200. www.riversiderest.com. 10 units, 8 ensuite. 34€ ($31) single; 57€ ($52) double. 33% reduction for children sharing with an adult. Rates include full breakfast. Dinner 28€ ($25). MC, V. Free private parking. **Amenities:** Restaurant. *In room:* TV, iron and ironing board (on request).

San Remo   Mrs. Patricia Murphy Curham is the gracious hostess at this house, half a mile (1km) from the town center. Guest rooms are tastefully furnished, and guests are welcomed with tea and homemade brack (a hearty Irish sweet bread).

Bunree, Sligo Rd., Ballina, Co. Mayo. ©/fax 096/70162. 4 units. 56€ ($51) double. Rates include full breakfast. No credit cards.

Suantrai ☞ *Suantrai* means "lullaby," and true to its name, this is an extremely relaxing place. The rooms are spacious, bright, meticulously clean, and mercifully uncluttered, requiring only minutes to feel comfortably familiar. This modest, welcoming home sets a standard rarely met by B&Bs. It's only open in the summertime, because the Chamberses are both full-time teachers in the local school. They seem to truly love their summer job and enjoy their guests—and the feeling is mutual.

Ballycastle, Co. Mayo (on R314 at the east edge of town). ② 096/43040. suantrai@iol.ie. 3 units. 32€ ($29) single; 48€ ($44) double. Includes full Irish breakfast. No credit cards. Free parking. Open June 20–Aug 20.

WORTH A SPLURGE

Enniscoe House ☞☞ Here is a terrific place for unwinding and escaping the real world. Overlooking Lough Conn and surrounded by a wooded estate with more than 3 miles (5km) of nature walks, this two-story Georgian country inn has been described as "the last great house of North Mayo." It is owned and run by Susan Kellett, a descendant of the original family that settled on the lands in the 1660s. Enniscoe's interior is truly magnificent, with delicate plasterwork, lovely fireplaces, and the fabulous staircase. The place abounds with family portraits, antique furniture, early drawings, and pictures of the house and surrounding area. Guest rooms are individually furnished, and those at the front of the house are particularly impressive, with huge hand-carved armoires and canopied or four-poster beds with firm mattresses. All of the nonsmoking rooms have views of parkland or the lake. Meals here feature fish from local rivers, produce from the house's farm, and vegetables and herbs from the adjacent garden. Enniscoe also has its own fishery. Self-catering apartments are also available.

Castlehill, near Crossmolina, Ballina, Co. Mayo. ② 800/323-5463 from the U.S., or 096/31112. Fax 096/31773. www.enniscoe.com. 6 units. 156€–172€ ($141–$156) double. Rates include full breakfast. Dinner 30€ ($27). AE, MC, V. Free parking. Closed mid-Oct to Mar. 2 miles (3km) south of Crossmollina off R315, next to the North Mayo Heritage Centre. **Amenities:** Drawing room. *In room:* TV.

GREAT DEALS ON DINING

Burke's ☞ IRISH   The bright dining room is hidden beyond a long, dark barroom where traditional music often starts up around 10pm. The first thing you'll notice here is that everyone is so *friendly*—from the barman to the waiters, everyone seems remarkably devoted to ensuring that you enjoy your evening. Friendliness may not be a rare commodity in most pub/restaurants, but really good food is, and I was delighted to discover that this place has more than its share of both. The meal begins well, with delicious home-baked breads. Vegetables are locally grown and mostly organic, and their flavor isn't concealed by heavy sauces. Main courses include a honey-roasted duck breast with orange port sauce, or rack of lamb—nothing ostentatious, just local produce thoughtfully prepared and presented. The vegetarian special changes daily. The food here is consistently simple in its conception and presentation, and consistently satisfying.

Mount Gable House, Clonbur (just west of Cong on R345), Co. Galway. ② 092/46175. Reservations recommended. Main courses 12€–24€ ($11–$22); bar food 4€–19€ ($3.65–$17). MC, V. Restaurant Apr–Oct Mon–Sat 6–9:30pm, Sun 1–5pm; bar year-round 10:30am–6pm.

Murphy Bros. Pub and Restaurant PUB GRUB/SEAFOOD   A giant pub restaurant with a saloon-style appearance, Murphy's offers delicious food at decent prices. Seafood creations such as monkfish and prawn aioli (monkfish cubes sautéed with tiger prawns in a garlic, wine, and cream sauce) set your mouth watering, and nonfish dishes are equally appealing. Lighter offerings include salads, burgers, and a good selection of pastas. And if you want to wash your food down with something local, the pub stocks almost 60 types of whiskey.

Clare St., Ballina, Co. Mayo. ℭ 096/22702. Bar food 9€–13€ ($8.15–$12); main courses 11€–23€ ($10–$21); fixed-price dinner 32€ ($29). MC, V. Mon–Sat bar food 12:30– 8:30pm; restaurant dinners 6–9:30pm.

The Old Mill IRISH   The Old Mill is located on the grounds of the Foxford Woollen Mills (see "Exploring the County," earlier in this section). It serves a wide array of light meals and snacks in a historic setting that's bright and airy. On the menu are freshly prepared soups, salads, sandwiches, and cold meat plates, as well as quiche, lasagna, sausage rolls, scones, muffins, and desserts. There are also daily hot meal specials.

St. Joseph's Place, Foxford, Co. Mayo. ℭ 094/56756. Reservations not necessary. All items 4.60€–6.30€ ($4.15–$6.30). MC, V. Mon–Sat 10am–5:30pm; Sun 11:30am–5:30pm.

The Quay Cottage ☆ SEAFOOD/INTERNATIONAL   Overlooking Westport Harbour, Quay Cottage is done up from top-to-bottom with nautical bric-a-brac. The menu presents fresh, beautifully prepared seafood, such as lemon sole beurre blanc or wild local salmon, with an array of daily specials; a request for a plain steak can also be fulfilled. A separate nonsmoking room is available. You can take a waterside stroll after your meal.

The Quay, Westport. ℭ 098/26412. www.quaycottage.com. Reservations recommended. Dinner main courses 17€–23€ ($15–$21). AE, MC, V. Mar–Sept daily 6–10pm; Oct–Feb Tues–Sat 6–10pm. Closed Dec 24–26.

Galway City

Galway owes its existence to a tragedy: Breasail, an ancient Celtic chieftain, was so overwhelmed with grief when his daughter drowned in the River Corrib that he established a permanent camp on the riverbank, near where the river flows into Galway Bay. Located at the only point at which the river could be forded, the camp had become a small fishing village by the time the Normans arrived. The newcomers set about building a trading town utilizing the fine harbor, and, in time, a medieval town with fine houses and shops grew up, around which were built stout stone walls. Trade soon flourished between Galway, Spain, and France. Fourteen of the most prosperous merchant families became known early on as the "Tribes of Galway," and in 1984, when the city celebrated the 500th anniversary of its charter, there was a great "Gathering of the Tribes" with the descendants of the 14 families arriving from around the globe.

In recent years, Galway has grown and developed dramatically without losing its character. It is said to be the fastest-growing city in Europe, but its boom has meant only more and better of the same, not uncontrolled expansion and disfigurement. Galway is perhaps the most prosperous city in Ireland and arguably the most immediately appealing. It's managed to attract droves of outsiders, either to visit or to settle, without alienating its own long-standing population. The result is a city that feels lived in, a down-to-earth place that at the same time attracts and accommodates masses of visitors. Its university community and its well-rooted and lively arts scene contribute mightily to its vitality and appeal.

Activity in the city revolves around a pedestrian park at **Eyre** (pronounced *air*) **Square,** originally a market area known as the Fair Green. It's officially called the John F. Kennedy Park in commemoration of the president's visit here in June 1963, and a bust of Kennedy shares space in the park with a statue of a man sitting on a limestone wall—a depiction of Galway-born local hero Padraig O'Conaire, a pioneer in the Irish literary revival of the early 20th century and the epitome of a Galway Renaissance man.

1 Orientation

Galway is 57 miles (92km) N of Shannon Airport, 136 miles (219km) W of Dublin, 65 miles (105km) NW of Limerick, 130 miles (209km) NW of Cork, and 120 miles (193km) N of Killarney

GETTING THERE Aer Arann Express operates twice-daily service from Dublin into Galway Airport, Carnmore (© **091/755569** or 01/814-5240; www.aerarann.ie), about 10 miles (16km) east of the city. A taxi from the airport to the city center costs about 11€ ($10); the occasional bus, if it happens to coincide with your arrival, costs 3.80€ ($3.45).

Irish Rail trains from Dublin and other points arrive daily at **Ceannt Station** (© **091/564222;** www.irishrail.ie), off Eyre Square, Galway.

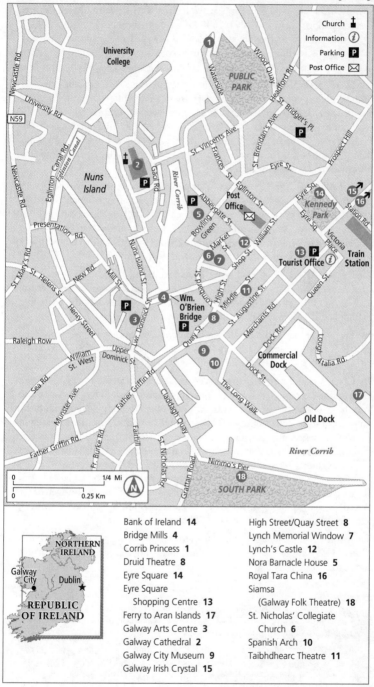

Galway City

Legend:
- Church ✝
- Information ⓘ
- Parking 🅿
- Post Office ✉

Bank of Ireland **14**
Bridge Mills **4**
Corrib Princess **1**
Druid Theatre **8**
Eyre Square **14**
Eyre Square
  Shopping Centre **13**
Ferry to Aran Islands **17**
Galway Arts Centre **3**
Galway Cathedral **2**
Galway City Museum **9**
Galway Irish Crystal **15**

High Street/Quay Street **8**
Lynch Memorial Window **7**
Lynch's Castle **12**
Nora Barnacle House **5**
Royal Tara China **16**
Siamsa
  (Galway Folk Theatre) **18**
St. Nicholas' Collegiate
  Church **6**
Spanish Arch **10**
Taibhdhearc Theatre **11**

Buses from all parts of Ireland arrive daily at **Bus Eireann Travel Centre,** Ceannt Station, Galway (© **091/562000;** www.buseireann.ie).

As the gateway to the West of Ireland, Galway is the terminus for many national roads, leading in from all parts of Ireland, including N84 and N17 from northerly points, N63 and N6 from the east, and N67 and N18 from the south.

VISITOR INFORMATION   For information about Galway and the surrounding areas, contact **Ireland West Tourism** (Aras Fáilte), Victoria Place, off Eyre Square, Galway (© **091/563081;** info@western-tourism.ie). Hours are May, June, and September daily from 9am to 5:45pm; July and August daily from 9am to 7:45pm; and the rest of the year, Monday through Friday from 9am to 5:45pm and Saturday from 9am to 12:45pm. You'll also find abundant information at **www.galway.net.**

CITY LAYOUT   The core of downtown Galway lies between Eyre Square on the east and the River Corrib on the west. To the west of Eyre Square, Galway's main thoroughfare begins—a street that changes its name four times (from William to Shop, Main Guard, and Bridge) before it crosses the River Corrib and changes again. If that sounds confusing, don't worry. The streets are all very short, well marked, and, with a map in hand, easy to follow.

GETTING AROUND   By Public Transportation   Galway has an excellent local bus service, with buses running from the **Bus Eireann Travel Centre,** Galway (© **091/562000**), just off Eyre Square, to various suburbs, including Salthill and the Galway Bay coastline. The flat fare is 1€ (90¢).

By Taxi   There are taxi ranks at Eyre Square and all the major hotels within the city. If you need to call a cab, try **Abbey Cabs** (© **091/569369**), **Cara Cabs** (© **091/563939**), or **Galway Taxis** (© **091/561112**).

By Car   A city of medieval arches, alleyways, and cobblestone lanes, Galway is at its best when explored on foot (with comfortable shoes). Once you check into your hotel or guesthouse, leave your car and tour by walking. If you must bring your car into the center of town, park it and then walk. There's free parking in front of Galway Cathedral, but the majority of street parking follows the disc parking system. It costs .65€ (60¢) for 1 hour; a book of 10 discs costs 6.35€ ($5.75). Multistory parking garages average 1.50€ ($1.40) per hour.

To rent a car, contact one of the following firms with offices in Galway: **Avis Rent-A-Car,** Headford Road (© **091/568886;** www.avis.com); **Budget Rent-A-Car,** 2 Eyre Sq. (© **091/566376;** www.budget.com); or **Murrays Europcar,** Headford Road, Galway (© **091/562222;** www.europcar.com).

On Foot   To see the highlights of the city, follow the signposts on the Tourist Trail of Old Galway. The tour is explained in a handy 32-page booklet available at the tourist office and at most bookshops.

 FAST FACTS: **Galway City**

Drugstores   Try **Flanagans Pharmacy,** at 32 Shop St., Galway (© 091/562924); **Matt O'Flaherty Chemist,** at 16 William St., Galway (© 091/561442), and 39 Eyre Sq., Galway (© 091/562927; after hours 091/525426); and **Whelan's Chemist,** Williamsgate Street, Galway (© 091/562291).

Emergencies   Dial © **999.**

Gay & Lesbian Resources Contact **Galway Gay Help Line** (© 091/566134), open Tuesday and Thursday 8 to 10pm; or the **Galway Lesbian Line** (© **091/564611,** open Wednesday 8 to 10pm). You can also visit www. pink-pages.org/galway.html.

Hospital University College Hospital is located on Newcastle Road (© 091/544544). There's also Merlin Park Regional Hospital (© 091/775775).

Laundry & Dry Cleaning **Olde Malte Launderette,** Olde Malte Arcade, off High Street, Galway (© **091/564990),** or **Heaslips Dry Cleaners,** William Street and Prospect Hill, Galway (© **091/568944),** can get your spots out for you.

Library The **Galway Library/An Leabhar,** located in the Hynes Building, Augustine Street, Galway (© **091/561666),** is open Monday 2 to 5pm, Tuesday to Thursday 11am to 8pm, Friday 11am to 5pm, and Saturday 9am to 1pm and 2 to 5pm.

Local Newspapers The weekly *Connacht Tribune,* published in Galway, is the largest newspaper covering the west of Ireland. Other weeklies include the *City Tribune* and the *Connacht Sentinel.* Free weekly publications that cover entertainment and the arts include the *Galway Advertiser, Galway Observer,* and *Entertainment Weekly.*

Photographic Needs Try **Fahyfoto Camera Shop,** 13 High St., Galway (© 091/562283; www.fahyfoto.com); **Galway Camera Shop,** 58 Dominick St., Galway (© 091/565678); or **One Hour Photo,** Eglinton Street, Galway (© 091/562682).

Police The local **Garda Station** is on Mill Street, Galway (© 091/563161).

Post Office The **Post Office,** on Eglinton Street, Galway (© **091/562051),** is open 9am to 5:30pm, Monday to Saturday.

Shoe Repairs To save your sole, consult **Mister Minit,** U4 Corbetts Ct., Williamsgate Street (© **091/565055).**

2 Accommodations You Can Afford

IN TOWN

Jurys Inn Galway   This relatively new four-story hotel opposite the Spanish Arch was designed in keeping with the area's historic character. Geared to the cost-conscious traveler, it was the first of its kind for Galway's downtown area, providing quality hotel lodgings at guesthouse prices. But the real draw here is the ideal central location, right in the heart of things, yet edged on one side by an almost lulling canal. The guest rooms look out on expansive views of the river or nearby Galway Bay; each room is simply decorated in contemporary "motel" style and is enhanced by pictures of Old Galway and Connemara. The beds are firm, and nonsmoking rooms are available on request. Facilities include a moderately priced restaurant, The Arches, and the Inn Pub. Parking is available at the adjoining multi-story car park at reduced rates.

Quay St., Galway, Co. Galway. © **800/44-UTELL** from the U.S., or 091/566444. Fax 091/568415. www. jurys.com. 128 units. 94€ ($85) double or triple. No service charge. Breakfast 6€–8.50€ ($5.45–$7.70). DC, MC, V. Discounted parking. **Amenities:** Restaurant (International), bar, laundry service. *In room:* TV, tea/coffeemaker, hair dryer.

IN SALTHILL

Salthill is a village composed primarily of modern bungalows, a little under a mile (1.5km) from Galway town center. Most of the houses listed here are within a short (15-minute-or-less) walk from town center, and from May to October there's good bus service along the Seapoint Promenade—you can catch the Salthill bus at the city bus station or at Eyre Square.

Alkenver Mrs. Rushe will welcome you warmly to her home, on a quiet side street off Fr. Griffin Road, a 10-minute walk from Galway center. Rooms are small and clean, and the beds are firm; bathrooms are quite small. All bedrooms are nonsmoking. Breakfast is limited to the standard Irish fry.

39 Whitestrand Park, Lower Salthill, Galway, Co. Galway. ℭ 091/588758. 3 units. 51€ ($46) double. 25% reduction for children sharing with an adult. Rates include full breakfast. No credit cards. Closed Sept–May.

High Tide 🐾 Location and a gracious welcome combine to make this one of the most appealing B&Bs around. Patricia Greaney's home, on a short, quiet cul-de-sac off coastal Grattan Road, faces Galway Bay and the distant hills of the Burren. Three of the rooms face the water—be sure to ask for one of these. Patricia is an energetic and efficient host, and takes good care of her guests. The guest rooms are moderate in size and simply furnished, while bathrooms are tiny (in two cases, the sink is in the bedroom). Galway city is a 10-minute walk away, and a local bus to city center stops every 30 minutes in front of the house. The excellent breakfast includes such unusual offerings as toasted cheese sandwich and filet of lemon sole in addition to the more familiar French toast, pancakes with syrup or homemade jams, and plate of Irish cheeses (these are *mature* cheeses, mind you, not processed and shrink-wrapped). All bedrooms are nonsmoking.

9 Grattan Park, Galway, Co. Galway. ℭ 091/589470. Fax 091/584324. hightide@iol.ie. 4 units. 51€ ($46) double. 20% reduction for children. Rates include full breakfast. AE, MC, V. Closed Dec–Jan. *In room:* TV, tea/coffeemaker, hair dryer.

Knockrea Guesthouse In operation since the 1960s, Knockrea is situated on a commercial street in Salthill, a 15-minute walk from Galway city center and 5 minutes from the waters of Galway Bay. Eileen and Padraic Storan purchased the place in 1995, and since then, they've completely transformed the interior, bringing this cozy guesthouse up-to-date. The guestrooms are furnished in simple pine furniture with pine floors. There are two family rooms, which offer more space and two twin beds in addition to the double bed found in most rooms. Bathrooms are about the size of your average closet. Smoking is discouraged in the bedrooms but is permitted in one of the three sitting rooms. Eileen Storan is an able and sympathetic host—she knows the area well and helps her guests make the most of their time in Galway. A small kitchen is available for guests to make tea, and perishables can be stored in the fridge.

Lower Salthill, Galway, Co. Galway. ℭ 091/520145. Fax 091/529985. www.galway.net/pages/knockrea. 6 units. 63€–76€ ($58–$69) double. 25% reduction for children. Rates include full breakfast. MC, V. Private car park. **Amenities:** 3 sitting rooms, use of kitchen. *In room:* TV, tea/coffeemaker, hair dryer.

Lawndale Lawndale is set back on a quiet street just off Grattan Road, overlooking Galway Bay, about 15 minutes from the city center on foot. Ask for one of the two front bedrooms (numbers 1 and 2), which have a fine view across the bay. All the bedrooms have a double and twin bed, and can comfortably sleep three people. Breakfast is unexceptional, with no alternative to the standard Irish fry. Smoking is discouraged in the bedrooms and breakfast room.

5 Beach Court, Salthill, Galway, Co. Galway. ✆ **091/586676.** 5 units. 51€ ($46) double. Rates include full breakfast. No credit cards. *In room:* TV, tea/coffeemaker.

Marless House ⭐ *Value*   Mary and Tom Geraghty's large, modern house sits on Threadneedle Road, just steps from the promenade along Galway Bay. The city is a 30-minute walk away, along the Seapoint Promenade. The cheery rooms are spacious, with orthopedic beds and electric blankets; bathrooms are clean and compact. The Geraghtys are generous hosts and provide good sightseeing advice for Galway city; Mary has also compiled a helpful map of the city and neighboring Salthill, which she offers to all guests. Breakfast consists of an extensive buffet in addition to the cooked breakfast—pancakes, French toast, and beans on toast are all alternatives to the standard Irish fry. This is a popular spot in summer, so you'll need to reserve well in advance. This is a nonsmoking house.

Threadneedle Rd., Salthill, Galway, Co. Galway. ✆ **091/523931.** Fax 091/529810. www.marlesshouse.com. 6 units. 50€ ($45) single; 66€ ($60) double. 25% reduction for children. Rates include full breakfast. MC, V. Closed Christmas. *In room:* TV, tea/coffeemaker, hair dryer.

Roncalli House ⭐   The O'Halloran home is an exceptionally comfortable base for your explorations in Galway. Carmel and her husband Tim have been welcoming guests to their home for many years, and they're great hosts. A glowing fireplace takes the chill off cool evenings, and in good weather guests can relax on the outdoor patio or in an enclosed sun porch at the front of the house. There are two ground-floor bedrooms and four others upstairs, all exceptionally clean and moderate to small in size, while bathrooms are quite compact. The breakfast is admirably diverse—oatmeal, French toast, and pancakes are among the plentiful options. Galway city is a 12-minute walk from the house.

24 Whitestrand Ave., Lower Salthill, Galway, Co. Galway. ✆ **091/589013** or 091/584159. Fax 091/584159. roncallihouse@eircom.net. 6 units. 40€ ($36) single; 58€ ($53) double. 20% reduction for children. Rates include full breakfast. MC, V. **Amenities:** Conservatory, sitting room. *In room:* TV, tea/coffeemaker, hair dryer.

Ross House   Mrs. Sara Davy's home is located near Galway Bay in a quiet cul-de-sac, about 13 minutes away on foot from Galway city. Though somewhat small, guest rooms are immaculate and furnished with firm beds, as well as hair dryers and tea-making facilities. The breakfast is noteworthy—Sara Davy is a good cook, and her varied menu includes French toast and a crepe filled with fruit. There are numerous thoughtful details, like the fridge in the hall where guests can store fresh juice, medications, and other perishables. The whole house is nonsmoking.

14 Whitestrand Ave., Lower Salthill, Galway, Co. Galway. ✆ **091/587431.** rosshousebb@eircom.net. 4 units. 58€ ($53) double. 20% reduction for children. Rates include full breakfast. MC, V. *In room:* TV.

Villa Maria   Frances Tiernan's home is conveniently located, within a 10-minute walk of city center and 5 minutes from the seafront. Guest rooms are

---

Value Budget Lodging

In many cities and large towns in Ireland (Dublin is a prime example), city center hostels and hotels offer better value than the B&Bs in adjacent residential neighborhoods. For reasons unknown, the B&Bs of Salthill, a neighborhood 1 mile (1.5km) from Galway center, are an exception to this rule: They adhere for the most part to a very high standard of facilities and services, making them the best budget option in town.

small but clean, and the beds are all admirably firm. The bedrooms are non-smoking. Breakfast options are limited, with no substantial alternative to the standard Irish fry. A native of Roundstone, Frances has many tips to offer for sightseeing in the Connemara region.

94 Fr. Griffin Rd., Lower Salthill, Galway. (℃) **091/589033.** 3 units. 53€ ($48) double. Rates include full breakfast. V. *In room:* TV, tea/coffeemaker.

A FEW MILES TO THE NORTH

Corrib View Farm   Corrib View Farmhouse is 7 miles (12km) north of Galway city. It's a good place from which to enjoy the urban buzz, and then retreat to a more rural setting. The farm is a few minutes' walk from Lake Corrib, which can be seen from two of the bedrooms. The house itself has the thick walls of 19th-century farmhouses, and its small bedrooms are reasonably comfortable. Host Mary Scott-Furey has a large garden, and occasionally its raspberries and strawberries make an appearance at breakfast. The farmhouse is also a 2-hour drive from Shannon Airport, and rooms can be made available for morning arrivals.

Annaghdown, Co. Galway. (℃) **091/791114.** www.corribviewfarm.com. 5 units, 3 with bathroom (shower only). 32€ ($29) single; 64€ ($58) double. No credit cards. Free private parking. Closed Oct–Mar. *In room:* tea/coffeemaker.

Cregg Castle ★ *Finds*   Casual comfort reigns at Cregg castle. It is a large, rambling edifice built in 1648, and this shows in its 5-foot (1½m)thick walls and a general air of happy fatigue. At Cregg Castle, one forgoes the antiseptic for the eccentric, the friendly, and the unceremonious. The newest object in the Great Hall seems to be a well-used CD player, but it's not only recorded music that fills the room—hosts Anne Marie and Pat Broderick, both highly accomplished musicians, often pick up a bodhran or fiddle and play a set or two. Guest rooms are generously sized and are furnished with old finds—the effect is not one of studied elegance, but rather of thoughtful improvisation. Bathrooms have been carved out of the corners of rooms without spoiling their character, and for this reason, they are a bit small. Guests are invited to come to breakfast whenever they get up. A small alcove has been given over to kettles: Tea and coffee can be made as desired throughout the day and night. The extensive and inviting woods are also free for exploration.

Corrandulla, Co. Galway. (℃)/fax **091/791434.** www.creggcastle.com. 8 units, 7 with bathroom (5 shower only). 90€ ($82) single; 120€ ($109) double. 50% reduction for children (sharing with parents). Rates include full breakfast. V. Free parking. *In room:* Hair dryer.

3 Great Deals on Dining

As one of Ireland's most popular vacation spots (for natives as well as visitors), Galway is blessed with numerous decent places to eat. Pub grub is plentiful, but there are many moderately priced restaurants as well. In addition, the surrounding area has restaurants that have gained nationwide kudos for the quality of the food, service, and ambience (see chapter 12, "Out from Galway," for listings).

Conlon & Sons SEAFOOD   If you love seafood, this is a good address to know. Conlon boasts approximately 20 varieties of fresh fish and shellfish at any given time. The house specialties are wild salmon and oysters. Entrees include grilled wild salmon, steamed Galway Bay mussels, and fishermen's platters (smoked salmon, mussels, prawns, smoked mackerel, oysters, and crab claws).

Eglinton Court, Galway. (℃) **091/562268.** Oyster bar items 4.55€–9.85€ ($4.15–$8.95); main courses 17.75€–32.25€ ($19.55–$35.50); fish-and-chips 13.20€–29.70€ ($12–$27), with most at the lower end of this range. AE, DC, MC, V. Mon–Sat 11am–11pm; Sun 5pm–10pm.

Da Tang Noodle House CHINESE   The noodles at Da Tang are superlative. Bowls of homemade soup noodles are large and result in more than a few appreciative slurps. The broth, seasoned with fresh coriander and chilies, has a pleasant bite. Vegetables abound: carrot, mushroom, bamboo shoots, and shreds of Chinese cabbage are all cooked to crunchy perfection. Go for a mid afternoon meal, when the service is admirably fast, making this a great place to nourish your noodle along with a steady stream of Galwegians looking for a quick, healthy lunch.

Middle St., Galway, Co. Galway. ✆ **091/561443.** Lunch main courses 6.50€–9.50€ ($5.90–$8.65); dinner main courses 10€–18€ ($9–$16). Mon–Fri 12:30–3pm and 5:30–10:30pm. MC, V. Mon–Thurs 6–10:30; Fri 6–11; Sat 12:30–11; Sun 6–10:30.

Goya's TEAROOM/BAKED GOODS   Goya's recently moved from its tiny spot on Quay Street to this bright, much more spacious venue. Its reputation for seductive pastries has followed, and the new cafe is every bit as crowded as the old, with Galwegians lining up for Emer Murray's pastries and desserts. The emphasis is on simplicity. You probably won't find anything unexpected, but everything is delightful. Stop in for tea and a scone, or buy a loaf of exceptional soda bread for lunch.

Kirwans Ln., Galway, Co. Galway. ✆ **091/567010.** Under 6.50€ ($5.90). Bakery Mon–Sat 9:30am–6pm; lunch 12:30–3pm.

Maxwell McNamara's Restaurant SEAFOOD/STEAK   There's a delightful old-fashioned look about this centrally located place just off Eyre Square. Renovations include dark-wood booths, lots of brass, and old prints on the walls. The extensive menu offers light selections (hamburgers, salads). The restaurant is fully licensed, with wine by the glass. Service is continuous, making it handy if hunger pangs strike outside regular meal hours.

Williamsgate St., Galway, Co. Galway. ✆ **091/565727.** Lunch under 15€ ($13); dinner main courses 7.50€–19€ ($6.80–$17). AE, DC, MC, V. Mon–Sat 9am–10pm; Sun 12:30–10pm.

McDonagh's Seafood Bar FISH & CHIPS/SEAFOOD   For seafood straight off the boats, served up in an authentic maritime atmosphere, this is Galway's best choice. The place is divided into three parts: a traditional "chipper" for fish-and-chips and takeout, a smart restaurant in the back, and a fish market where you can buy raw. The McDonaghs, fishmongers for more than four generations, buy direct from local fishermen every day—and it shows; crowds line up every night to get in. The menu includes salmon, trout, lemon or black sole (or both), turbot, and silver hake, all cooked to order. In the back restaurant, you can crack your own prawns' tails and crab claws in the shell, or tackle a whole lobster.

22 Quay St., Galway, Co. Galway. ✆ **091/565001.** Reservations not accepted. Main courses 7.50€–32€ ($6.80–$29). AE, MC, V. Mon–Sat noon–10pm; Sun 5–10pm.

Rabbitt's Bar and Restaurant PUB GRUB   This is Galway's oldest family-run pub, a place for good conversation and conviviality as well as moderately priced food. More locals than tourists come here, a sign of both authentic and good cuisine. Pub food is served between 12:30 and 2:30pm, and the regular lunch and dinner menu includes fresh seafood, Irish stew, oysters, lamb, and chicken. There's a separate nonsmoking room and an off-license shop that's open during bar hours.

23 Forster St. (just off Eyre Square), Galway, Co. Galway. ✆ **091/566490.** rabbitts@iol.ie. Bar food under 8€ ($7); lunch main courses 6.50€–13€ ($5.90–$12); dinner main courses 9€–18€ ($8–$16). MC, V. Daily 12:30–2:30pm and 6–9pm.

Finds Say Cheese!

If you're looking for picnic supplies, head to **Sheridan's Cheesemongers Ltd.**, Kirwans Lane (① **091/564829**; www.irishcheese.com). You can smell this extraordinary shop from the street: Sharp scents waft from enormous rounds of cheddar and soft triangles of Irish Farmhouse Camembert. Step inside, and you can sample a creamy morsel of goat's cheese from Clare or a shaving of herb gouda. Bread, cheese, olives from capacious clay jars, and an assortment of condiments are also available.

The River God Cafe *Value* IRISH/CONTINENTAL This is a rewarding destination for those with a hearty appetite. The byline here is rib-sticking comfort food in a rustic setting. The casserole of cod and potato Connemara style, served in a wide and deep tureen, will put the color back into any hungry face. An equally lavish portion of wild mushroom tart with paprika potatoes will similarly restore the vegetarian visitor. Other offerings include sheep cheese gouda with pesto, and loin of pork with Guinness mustard sauce. Neither the decor nor the cuisine is particularly refined or subtle, but both are satisfying to the more youthful appetite. The 7.30€ ($6.60) two-course lunch is a particularly good value.

Quay St. at Cross St. ① **091/565811**. Reservations not taken. Fixed-price 2-course dinner 13€ ($11); dinner main courses 10€–16€ ($9.15–$15). AE, DC, MC, V. Mon–Sat 12:30–10pm.

Tulsi INDIAN Galway is becoming more cosmopolitan every week, as demonstrated by new ventures such as Tulsi. It wasn't long ago that a decent Indian restaurant was impossible to find in Dublin, let alone Galway; the pace of change in Ireland is visible in the fact that this restaurant hasn't even made much of a splash in Galway's complex culinary waters. The food here isn't superlative, but the ingredients are fresh and the spicing is pleasurable. The menu doesn't offer any surprises, and old reliables, such as *saag paneer*, won't disappoint. An extensive buffet lunch is available on Sunday afternoon. There are two restaurants under the same name and ownership in Dublin.

3 Buttermilk Walk, Galway, Co. Galway. ① **091/564831**. Reservations recommended. Main courses 19€–25€ ($17–$23). MC, V. Mon–Sat noon–2:30pm and 6–11pm; Sun 1–10pm (buffet lunch served 1–4pm).

4 Seeing the Sights

You can't really miss **Eyre Square**, right in the center of town. In summer, it's a venue for impromptu street entertainment. That statue of the old Irish storyteller, hat pushed back and pipe in hand, is of Padraic O'Conaire, who traveled the countryside telling stories to children. The other statue (of a standing figure) represents patriot Liam Mellows, a prominent Galway leader during the 1916 military engagements outside Dublin. John F. Kennedy addressed the people of Galway here on his visit in 1963. Other things to look for here include the Civic Sword and Great Mace on display in the **Bank of Ireland.**

On Market Street, look for two interesting early 17th-century **"marriage stones"** set into the walls of houses there. The stones are carved with the coats of arms of two families united in marriage.

Of even more interest on Market Street is the **Lynch Memorial Window.** It was on this site that Mayor James Lynch FitzStephen carried out a harsh sentence against his own blood in 1493. The story goes that the lord mayor's 19-year-old son, Walter, was much enamored of a lovely girl named Agnes. He was also very good friends with a young Spanish lad—until Walter began suspecting the lad of courting Agnes. In a fit of rage, he murdered his friend; then, filled with remorse, he turned himself in. It was his own father who sat as magistrate and condemned Walter to death when he entered a plea of guilty. The town executioner, however, refused to perform his grisly duty, a tribute to the boy's local popularity, and the sorrowing father gave his son a last embrace and did the deed himself. From this tragic hanging, so the legend says, came the term *lynch law.*

In the center of town, at the corner of Abbeygate Street and Shop Street, is **Lynch's Castle,** dating from 1490 and renovated in the 19th century. It remains the oldest Irish medieval town house used daily for commercial purposes (it's now a branch of the Allied Irish Bank). The exterior is full of carved gargoyles, impressive coats of arms, and other decorative stonework.

At O'Brien's Bridge on Bridge Street, you'll find the **Bridge Mills,** where milling has been going on since 1558. The mill buildings had fallen into terrible disrepair but were rescued by one Frank Heneghan in 1988, when he began a renovation that brought back to life the old stonework and mill wheel. Today the building flourishes as home to the Millwheel Café and Coffee Shop, where you can sit outside in fine weather to watch swans on the river below. This is good browsing country—craft shops, clothing boutiques, jewelry shops, art galleries, and gift shops now inhabit much of the building's interior.

Walk through Galway's version of the "Left Bank," the **High Street/ Quay Street** 🟥 quarter of old buildings that retain the old fireplaces, cut stones, and arches from centuries past. Craft shops, smart boutiques, excellent restaurants, and convivial pubs are located here.

Galway Arts Centre   Originally the town house of W. B. Yeats's patron, Lady Augusta Gregory, then for many years the offices of the Galway Corporation, this arts center offers excellent concerts, readings, and exhibitions by Irish and international artists.

47 Dominick St. and 23 Nuns Island, Galway, Co. Galway. 📞 **091/565886.** Fax 091/568642. www.galway artscentre.ie. Free admission to exhibits; performances 5€–15€ ($4.55–$14). Mon–Sat 10am–6pm.

Galway Cathedral   Galway Cathedral, which dominates the city's skyline, is officially known as the "Cathedral of Our Lady Assumed into Heaven and St. Nicholas," which explains why it's just called Galway Cathedral. Mainly in the Renaissance style, it's constructed of fine-cut limestone from local quarries with Connemara marble floors. The structure was completed in 1965. Contemporary Irish artisans designed the statues, stained-glass windows, and mosaics. It's located beside the Salmon Weir Bridge on the west bank of the River Corrib.

University and Gaol roads, Galway, Co. Galway. 📞 **091/563577.** Free admission; donations welcome. Daily 8am–6pm.

Galway City Museum   This little museum offers a fine collection of local documents, photographs, city memorabilia, examples of medieval stonework, and revolving exhibits. A rooftop-viewing platform offers a fine prospect of Galway city and environs.

Off Spanish Arch, Galway, Co. Galway. 📞/fax **091/567641.** Admission 1.25€ ($1.15) adults, .65€ (60¢) students and children. Apr–Sept daily 10am–1pm and 2:15–5:15pm; Oct–Mar Wed–Fri 10am–1pm and 2:15–5:15pm.

Fun Fact **Grandpa, Where Do Claddagh Rings Come From?**

Next to the downtown area of Galway city, on the west bank of the River Corrib, is an area known as the Claddagh, its name taken from the Irish *An Cladach,* meaning "a flat, stony shore." Originally a fishing village with its own fleet, laws, and king, the Claddagh was peopled by descendants of early Gaelic families who spoke only Irish. Their streets were of stone, and haphazardly arranged, with small squares rimmed by thatched, mud-walled houses. Thus it remained until 1934, when a modern housing development was built on the site, bringing an end to the Claddagh's old-world isolation.

One Claddagh tradition survives, however: the Claddagh ring, famously decorated with heart, crown, and clasped hands and traditionally worn facing out for engagement and facing in for marriage. The earliest known Claddagh ring was made in the 17th century by a Galway goldsmith named Richard Joyce. Its clasped hands (representing friendship) are a symbol dating from Roman times, while the crown was added to represent loyalty, and the heart, naturally, to represent love. No longer widely worn as a wedding band, the Claddagh ring is now mostly a souvenir or a token of friendship or affection.

Nora Barnacle House This restored terrace house opposite St. Nicholas's Church clock tower was once the home of Nora Barnacle, the wife of James Joyce. It contains letters, photographs, and other exhibits on the lives of the Joyces and their connections with Galway. Hosts Mary and Sheila Gallagher can connect the house and Nora's life to incidents described in *Dubliners.* She also gives a short social synopsis of working-class life in Galway during the early 20th century, using the tiny kitchen and upper room of the house to illustrate her observations. On Bloomsday (June 16), there are readings of *Ulysses* here. Opening hours can vary, but the Gallaghers do their best to be accommodating to people who call ahead for an appointment. Recent additions to the collection include an original copy of Joyce's early poem "Gas from a Burner."

Bowling Green, Galway, Co. Galway. (*C*) **091/564743.** Admission 3€ ($2.70) per person. May–Sept Tues–Thur 10am–5pm (closed for lunch).

St. Nicholas' Collegiate Church (*R*) Local legend has it that Christopher Columbus prayed here before setting out to discover the New World. Established about 1320, this church has alternated between Roman Catholic and Church of Ireland (Episcopal) at least four times and is currently under the aegis of the latter. The highlight is an authentic crusader's tomb dating from the 12th or 13th century, with a rare Norman inscription on the grave slab. In addition, there's a freestanding *benitier* (a holy-water holder) that's unique in Ireland, as well as a carved front dating from the 16th or 17th century and a stone lectern with barley-sugar twist columns dating from the 15th or 16th century. The belfry contains 10 bells, some of which were cast as early as 1590. Guided tours depart from the south porch according to demand, except on Sunday mornings.

Lombard St. ℂ 091/564648. Free admission to the church, but donations are welcomed. Tours 3.80€ ($3.45) must be pre-booked. Apr–Sept Mon–Sat 9am–5:45pm and Sun 1–5:45pm; Oct–Mar Mon–Sat 10am–4pm and Sun 1–5pm.

A SIGHTSEEING CRUISE

Corrib Princess 🐟   See the sights of Galway aboard this 157-passenger two-deck boat that cruises along the River Corrib, with a commentary on all points of interest. The trip lasts 90 minutes, passing castles and other sites of historical interest, and assorted wildlife. There is full bar and snack service. You can buy tickets at the dock or at the *Corrib Princess* desk at the Tourist Office.

Woodquay, Galway. ℂ 091/592447. 8€ ($7.25) adult, 7€ ($6.35) student, 20€ ($18) family. May, June, and Sept daily 2:30 and 4:30pm; July and Aug daily 12:30, 2:30, and 4:30pm.

5 Outdoor Pursuits

BICYCLING   To rent a bike, contact **Kearneys,** Terryland Retail Park, Headford Road (ℂ **091/563356;** mkearney@indigo.ie).

FISHING   Sitting beside the River Corrib, Galway city and nearby Connemara are popular centers for salmon and sea trout fishing in the west of Ireland. For information, check with the **Western Regional Fisheries Board,** Weir Lodge, Earl's Island, Galway (ℂ **091/563118;** fax 091/566335; www. wrfb.ie). The Board also provides free consultation for overseas anglers on where to go at different times of the season for salmon or trout, where to find the best guides, and which flies and gear to use. Maps and brochures are available on request. This is an extraordinarily fisher-friendly group, and you would do well to take advantage of their services. For gear and equipment, try **Duffys Fishing,** 5 Main Guard St., Galway (ℂ **091/562367**); **Freeney Sport Shop,** 19 High St., Galway (ℂ **091/562609**); or **Great Outdoors Sports Centre,** Eglinton Street, Galway (ℂ **091/562869**).

GOLF   Less than 5 miles (8km) east of Galway is the 18-hole, par-72 championship **Galway Bay Golf & Country Club,** Renville, Oranmore, County Galway (ℂ **091/790503;** www.gbaygolf.com), with greens fees of 51€ ($46) Monday to Friday and 57€ ($52) Friday to Sunday. Less than 2 miles (3km) west of the city is the 18-hole, par-69 seaside course at **Galway Golf Club,** Blackrock, Galway (ℂ **091/522033**), with greens fees of 32€ ($29) weekdays and 38€ ($35) weekends.

HORSEBACK RIDING   Riding enthusiasts head to **Aille Cross Equitation Centre,** Aille Cross, Loughrea, County Galway (ℂ **091/841216; www. connemara-trails.com**), about 20 miles (32km) east of Galway. Run by personable Willy Leahy (who has appeared often on American television), this facility is one of the largest in Ireland, with 50 horses and 20 Connemara ponies. For about 16€ ($15) an hour, you can arrange to ride through nearby farmlands, woodlands, forest trails, and mountain lands. Week-long trail rides in the scenic Connemara region are also a specialty of this riding center, as is hunting with the Galway Blazers in the winter months; 6 days of trail riding, including accommodation and meals, is 1,960€ ($1,775) for two people sharing. For information on trail tours, in the United States call ℂ **800/757-1667,** or check out **www.connemaratrail.com**.

6 Special Events

For information on any of these events, contact **Ireland West Tourism** (Aras Failte), Victoria Place, off Eyre Square, Galway (© **091/563081**).

Arts Festival 🍀 The largest festival of its kind in Ireland, this raucous event fills the city for 12 days in mid-July. The schedule of happenings is diverse, with films, musical concerts, and theatrical performances taking place simultaneously in the many city-center venues. A justifiably notorious parade is one of the highlights of the festival. For a current schedule of events, call © **091/566577,** visit **www.galwayartsfestival.com**, or contact any Irish Tourist Board office.

The Galway Races These famous races take place during a 6-day festival called Race Week in late July or early August. The venue is the **Galway Racecourse,** Ballybrit, Galway (© **091/753870;** www.iol.ie/galway-races), less than 2 miles (3km) east of town. It sometimes seems the entire country shuts down to travel up this way for the event. There's music throughout the city, food stalls, private parties (to which strangers are often warmly welcomed), honest-to-goodness horse trading, and lots of activity at the track. Because so many Irish descend on the town during that week, best book way ahead if you'll be arriving during the festivities. Shorter race meetings are scheduled in early September and late October. For most, admission to the track is 13€ ($12), however slightly more 15€ to 19€ ($14–$17) during the festival. Students and seniors are admitted for 6.50€ ($5.90) on most days, and 7.50€ to 8.50€ ($6.80–$7.70) per day, during the festival.

September Oyster Festival In a colorful ceremony, the lord mayor of Galway gets things underway by opening and eating the first oyster of the season. After that, it's 2 or 3 solid days (usually a weekend) of eating and drinking: Oysters, salmon, prawns, and almost anything else that comes from the sea are washed down with buckets of champagne or Guinness. Oyster-openers from around the world enter competitions for opening the most oysters in the shortest period of time. The action centers around the Spanish Arch. A ticket to all the scheduled partying is costly—the current prices are 76€ to 115€ ($69–$104) per event—but because the entire town becomes a party the general gaiety spills over into the streets and pubs at no cost at all. Again, advance booking for accommodation is an absolute must. The festival usually takes place on the third or fourth weekend in September, but you should check the tourist board's calendar of events. You can contact the festival organizers at © **091/527282,** or check out their website at **www.galwayoysterfest.com**.

Blessing of the Sea To open the herring season in mid-August, there's a lovely ceremony on the waters of Galway Bay. Fishing boats form a procession to sail out of the harbor, led by an entire boatload of priests who petition heaven for a good and profitable season.

7 Shopping

The **Eyre Square Centre,** right in the heart of town, with entrances on Williamsgate Street and Eyre Square, holds more than 50 shops, as well as a multilevel parking lot.

Most shops in Galway are open Monday through Saturday from 9 or 10am to 5:30 or 6pm. In July and August, many shops stay open late, usually till 9pm on weekdays, and some also open on Sunday from noon to 5pm.

BOOKS

Kenny's Book Shop and Galleries, Ltd. *Finds* Kenny's is widely recognized as one of the best bookshops in the country. Opened in 1940, the small shop has grown into a fascinating multilevel maze of rooms filling two 15th-century buildings, lovingly restored by the Kenny family. The collection includes antiquarian maps and prints, old magazine issues, rare books on Irish subjects, and over 1500 signed photos of authors who have visited the shop over the years; there's also an extensive collection of work by contemporary Irish painters and sculptors. Ask for details of the "Irish Book Parcel" plan that keeps you in touch with current Irish writing by sending a quarterly selection of books in your areas of interest, with the right of refusal for books you don't want to keep. The Kennys' own bindery will wrap a prized edition in fine, hand-tooled covers. They also issue catalogs of Irish-interest publications. Go by to browse, and look for that special Irish book to carry home, but be warned: This is not an easy shop to leave! High St., Galway, Co. Galway. © 091/562739 or 091/561014. Fax 091/568544. www.kennys.ie.

Charlie Byrne's Bookshop Prices are good in this mostly secondhand bookshop, specializing in paperback fiction and Irish-interest books. There are also some surprising finds to be had, with a fair selection of titles in archaeology, art history, the cinema, and music. The Cornstore, Middle St., Galway, Co. Galway. © 091/561766. chabyrne@iol.ie.

CAMPING EQUIPMENT

For camping gear, clothing, and kayaking supplies, try the **Great Outdoors** on Eglinton Street (© 091/562869), or **River Deep, Mountain High** on Middle Street (© 091/563938); both offer decent selections and knowledgeable service.

CLOTHING & TWEEDS

Mac Eocagain/Galway Woollen Market This shop brims with traditional Aran hand-knits and colorful hand-loomed sweaters and capes, as well as linens, lace, sheepskins, jewelry, and woolen accessories. Each item has two prices, one including value-added tax (VAT) and one tax-free for non-European Community (EC) residents. 21 High St., Galway, Co. Galway. © 091/562491.

O'Máille (O'Malley) Established in 1938, this shop became famous in the 1950s for outfitting the entire cast of *The Quiet Man,* starring John Wayne and Maureen O'Hara, and has done a fabulous business ever since. It's synonymous with quality Irish tweeds, Irish-designed knitwear, and traditional Aran knits. There is always a good selection of sweaters, jackets, coats, suits, capes, kilts, caps, and ties. 16 High St., Galway, Co. Galway. © 091/562696. www.iol.ie/omaille/.

GIFT/SPECIALTY STORES

An Gailearai Beag Located near the Spanish Arch, Moyra Ryan's gallery exhibits oils, watercolors, and pen-and-pencil work by native artists. Many pieces are on display for the first time. Flood St., Galway, Co. Galway. © 091/591534.

Fallers Fallers began as a jewelry shop in 1879 and today is run by the fourth generation of Fallers. The store carries a huge stock of crystal, silver, china, porcelain, linen, jewelry (including a wide range of in-house-made Claddagh rings), and quality souvenirs. There's an international mail-order business, and you can write for its color catalog (with prices in U.S. dollars). Williamsgate St., Galway, Co. Galway. © 091/561226. From the U.S.: 800/229-3892. Fax 091/565548. www.fallers.com.

Galway Irish Crystal This factory on the outskirts of town sells beautiful crystal at one-third off prices you'd pay in shops. Visitors are welcome to watch the craftspeople at work—blowing, shaping, and hand-cutting the glassware— as part of a great tour through the heritage center. Demonstrations are continuous weekdays; the factory (but not the factory shop) is closed weekends. It's located east of the city on the main road (N6). Merlin Park, Galway, Co. Galway. ✆ 091/757311. www.galwaycrystal.ie.

Royal Tara China One of Galway's oldest enterprises, this company manufactures fine bone china gift- and tableware, distinguished by delicate shamrock patterns and designs inspired by the Book of Kells, the Tara brooch, the Claddagh ring, and other images from Irish history and folklore. Recent additions include hand-painted collections and exquisite "once off" pieces by resident master craftspeople. The visitor center is located in Tara Hall, a grand 17th-century house just outside the city center. You can tour the factory and watch this fine bone china being created—tours are offered Monday to Friday, with an audio-visual presentation on Saturday and Sunday. There's also a coffee shop, and five factory showrooms selling china, glass, and bronze. Look for the sign 1 mile (1.5km) east of Galway city off the main Dublin road. Dublin Rd., Galway, Co. Galway. ✆ 091/751301. Fax 091/757574. www.royal-tara.ie. Free tours Mon–Fri 9:30am to 3:30pm hourly.

8 Galway After Dark

Galway is renowned for its pubs, its music, and its craic. Many of the local pubs feature traditional music sessions. Another great after-dark option is a medieval banquet at Dunguaire Castle (see chapter 12).

THE PUB SCENE

An Pucan A block east of Eyre Square, this old-fashioned nautical-theme pub is a great place to find some of the best Irish traditional music in Galway (daily from 9pm). It's also an Irish-language pub, where most of the patrons are native Irish speakers. 11 Forster St., Galway, Co. Galway. ✆ 091/561528.

Crane Bar In the southwestern part of Galway, at the corner of an open market area called "the Small Crane," this rustic pub is known for its nightly musical entertainment. It gives special rates to fiddlers, pipers, singers, and banjo and accordion players who pass the "efficiency" test. From 9pm every night, there is country and western downstairs and traditional Irish tunes upstairs. 2 Sea Rd., Galway, Co. Galway. ✆ 091/567419.

Hole in the Wall This old-world pub, topped with a thatched roof, stands out on a busy shopping street 1 block from Eyre Square. The interior has a low beamed ceiling, open fireplaces, old sporting prints, and an old-fashioned jukebox. Cable TV screens show major sports events; this is a regular gathering spot for fans of Gaelic football and horse racing. A DJ starts playing music each night around 9:30pm. Eyre St. ✆ 091/565593.

The King's Head There's music to suit most tastes at this pub, where a different band performs each night of the week. Rock, traditional Irish, and a Sunday morning jazz session are a few of the many alternatives offered. There is usually no cover charge. Light meals are served Monday to Saturday between 10:30am and 4pm. High St., Galway, Co. Galway. ✆ 091/566630.

Rabbitt's   Dating from 1872, this pub is much the way it was a century ago. Old lanterns hang in the corners, skylights brighten the bar area, and pictures of Galway in horse-and-carriage days line the walls. Run by the fourth generation of the Rabbitt family, it's a block east of Eyre Square. 23–25 Forster St., Galway, Co. Galway. © 091/566490.

THE PERFORMING ARTS

The Druid Theatre   There is exceptionally good drama here. The resident professional company performs avant-garde plays, new Irish plays, and Anglo-Irish classics nightly year-round. There are frequent lunchtime and late-night shows; local newspapers usually publish the schedule. Tickets can be booked by telephone or at the theater, and should be reserved as far in advance as you can manage, because the Druid is extremely popular with locals as well as visitors, and it often tours internationally. Chapel Lane, Galway, Co. Galway. © 091/568660. Fax 091/563109. Tickets 13€–17€ ($12–$15).

Taibhdhearc Theatre   Since 1928, the Taibhdhearc (*Thive*-yark, Irish for "theater") Theatre has existed for the sole purpose of preserving Gaelic drama. It also plays host to many touring theater companies. This is where renowned Irish-language actress Siobhan McKenna began her career, and you'll see talent of much the same caliber on the stage today. It's very "Irish" entertainment, and good value for money as well. The popular "Spraoi sa Taibhdhearc" is a summer performance of traditional music, dance, and song. This is a small, intimate theater, and you should book as far in advance as possible through the tourist office or at the theater. Middle St., Galway, Co. Galway. © 091/563600 (bookings), 091/562024 (office). www.iol.ie/~taibh. Tickets under 18€ ($16). Box office Mon–Fri 10am–6pm; Sat 1–6pm.

Siamsa—The Galway Folk Theatre   This delightful blend of traditional Irish music, dance, and folk drama will definitely put you in the Celtic swing of things. *Riverdance* fans will love it. The theater is located just over the Wolfe Tone Bridge in Claddagh, a 10-minute walk from Jury's. N.I.H.E, University College Galway. © 091/755479. siamsa@eircom.net. Tickets under 18€ ($16). Mid-June to Aug weeknights 8:45pm. Additional weekend shows depending on demand.

12

Out from Galway

Galway is Ireland's second-largest county, located in the heart of the province of Connaught (or Connacht). "To hell or Connacht" were the limited options offered by the invading Cromwell to the Irish in the 17th century. Like a firestorm, Cromwell and his armies ravaged everything in their path and sent the native population running to **Connemara,** on the western edge of Ireland, where there was nothing much worth coveting or destroying. It was here that the displaced Irish were left to eke out a living on minute, rock-infested farms. It was also here, where it seemed people had little left to lose, that the famine of 1845–49 took its greatest toll, as masses either starved or boarded ship sailing westward, never to return. History aside, this bleak western outpost is stunningly beautiful. Today, tourism is bringing a prosperity to the area that the potato never did.

In this chapter, we'll also take you south of Galway City, to sights related to the poet **William Butler Yeats,** and over the water to the fabled **Aran Islands,** where rugged fishermen and their families perpetuate a centuries-old heritage of self-sufficiency and Irish culture. High cliffs, pre-Christian stone forts, and lowering skies over the merciless sea make the islands a must for visitors.

1 South of Galway City

If you're a dedicated fan of William Butler Yeats (and most Yeats fans *are* dedicated), you won't want to miss a visit to **Thoor Ballylee,** his County Galway home for many summers. Lady Gregory lived and entertained her literary friends at her home in Coole Demesne nearby.

To reach the picturesque little village of **Craughwell,** take R347 off N18 at Ardrahan. This is the burial place of the 19th-century poet Anthony Raftery, but it's better known locally as the location of the colorful **Galway Blazers Hunt.**

The small seaside town of **Kinvara** is renowned throughout Ireland for the traditional music that can be heard most nights in its pubs, and is a recommended stop for this reason alone. It also happens to be one of the lovelier towns in this part of the country, and makes a great base for excursions into the Burren.

SEEING THE SIGHTS

Coole Park Now a national forest and wildlife park, Coole Park was once the setting for Coole House, the stately home of Lady Gregory, one of Ireland's most influential patrons of the arts and a founder of the Abbey Theatre. Here, she entertained and encouraged illustrious literary figures such as W. B. Yeats, George Bernard Shaw, and Sean O'Casey, as well as Douglas Hyde, the first president of Ireland. The house no longer stands, its site marked only by ruined walls and stables; however, you can still see the famous "Autograph Tree," on which many of Lady Gregory's guests carved their initials. There's a great

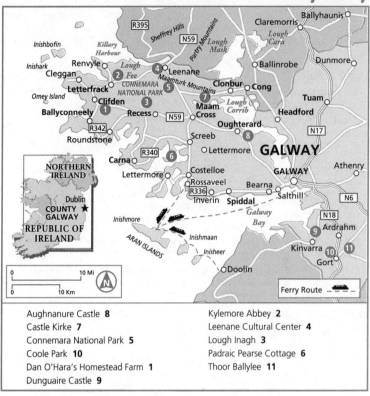

Aughnanure Castle **8**
Castle Kirke **7**
Connemara National Park **5**
Coole Park **10**
Dan O'Hara's Homestead Farm **1**
Dunguaire Castle **9**

Kylemore Abbey **2**
Leenane Cultural Center **4**
Lough Inagh **3**
Padraic Pearse Cottage **6**
Thoor Ballylee **11**

atmosphere about the place that sets the imagination to work. The visitor center has an audiovisual presentation, exhibitions, and a tea shop.

Gort, Co. Galway. 🕾 **091/631804.** Fax 091/631653. www.heritageireland.ie. Admission (visitor center) 2.60€ ($2.40) adults, 1.90€ ($1.75) seniors, 1.25€ ($1.15) children and students, 6.50€ ($5.90) family. Park year-round; visitor center Easter to mid-June Tues–Sun 10am–5pm; mid-June to Aug daily 9:30am–6:30pm; Sept daily 10am–5pm. Last admission 1 hour before closing. 2 miles (3km) north of Gort, due west of N18.

Dunguaire Castle   This castle, beautifully situated on the south shore of Galway Bay, was erected in the 16th century by the O'Hynes family at the royal seat of the 7th-century King Guaire of Connaught. Early in this century, Oliver St. John Gogarty, the Irish surgeon, author, and wit, purchased and restored it as a country retreat, though he never lived in it. The decoration you'll find in the castle today is curious and quaint and completely without pretension of historical accuracy, so you'll have to use your imagination to see the castle as it was in medieval times. There are some interesting features, such as the impression left in the ground-floor vaulted ceiling by the wicker supports used in the vault's construction. The machicolation (a protrusion from the top of the castle wall that allowed soldiers to drop projectiles onto the attacking forces below) placed at roof level above the door to the castle is also in a good state of preservation. One of the rooms is the site of medieval banquets in the evening (see below), and others house exhibits on the castle's history. The castle's best feature is the view from its battlements of the nearby Burren and Galway Bay.

Kinvara, Co. Galway. 📞 **061/360788**. www.shannonheritagetrade.com 3.80€ ($3.45) adults, 2.60€ ($2.40) seniors and students, 2.15€ ($1.95) children. May–Oct daily 9:30am–5:30pm.

Thoor Ballylee ⭐ From 1917–29, Yeats spent his summers in this square 16th-century castle keep, having bought it as a ruin for a paltry £35 and restored it to living condition. Among its chief advantages was its proximity to his dear friend Lady Gregory at Coole Demesne. On one wall is inscribed this poignant poem:

> *I, the Poet William Yeats*
> *With old millboards and seagreen slates*
> *And smith work from the Gort forge*
> *Restored this tower for my wife George,*
> *And may these characters remain*
> *When all is ruin once again.*

Fortunately, the tower has not reverted to ruins, and there's a resident staff to assist visitors as well as recorded tour cassettes that lead you through.

Gort, Co. Galway. 📞 **091/631436** or 091/563081. Admission 4.50€ ($4.10) adults, 3.80€ ($3.45) seniors and students. May–Oct Mon–Sat 10am–6pm; June–Aug Sun 10am–6pm. 4 miles (6.5km) northeast of Gort on the Loughrea Rd. (N66) or the Galway Rd. (N18).

A MEDIEVAL BANQUET

The **Medieval Banquet & Literary Evening at Dunguaire Castle** ⭐ is much more intimate than the medieval banquets at Bunratty and Knappogue. This is certainly not a budget item, but it's special enough to warrant a splurge. The castle is a small 16th-century keep, with banquet seating limited to 55. When you enter the reception hall, a young woman in medieval dress will tell you its legend while you quaff a cup of mead. In the upstairs banquet hall you'll dine by candlelight on such delicacies as smoked salmon, "chekyn supreme," and sumptuous desserts, accompanied by a plentiful supply of wine. When dinner is over, your costumed waiters and waitresses repair to the stage and bring to vivid life Ireland's literary heroes and heroines through stories, plays, and poems.

Because seating is so limited, you must reserve well in advance—through a travel agent before you leave home if possible; or by calling 📞 **061/361511.** The cost is 40€ ($36), and the banquet is presented April through October daily at 5:30 and 8:45pm (note that the number of performances per day varies based on demand).

ACCOMMODATIONS YOU CAN AFFORD

Doorus Youth Hostel In addition to the cleanliness and austerity one expects from the *An Óige* hostels, this one has a cozy sitting room with fireplace and an absolutely fabulous location. It's on a tiny peninsula that juts out into Galway Bay and offers great views across the bay and toward the hills of the Burren. The place feels utterly remote, but in fact it's less than 2 miles (3km) from the nearest shop and pub. The men's dorm is in a separate building, a stone's throw from the kitchen and women's dorm. The hostel is closed every day between 10am and 5pm.

Kinvara, Co. Galway. 📞/fax **091/637512**. 6 units, none with bathroom: 2 8-bed dorms, 4 10-bed dorms. 10€ ($9.10) per person. Follow signs from the N67, just west of Kinvara. **Amenities:** Self-catering kitchen.

GREAT DEALS ON DINING

Local oysters are a favorite in the area.

The Blazers Bar PUB GRUB The Galway Blazers Hunt members have their headquarters and kennels just behind this attractive pub, and in winter this is the meeting place before and after hunts. Run by Teresa and Donal Raftery, the pub has a reliable mixture of rural personalities, gentlemen farmers, and tourists. If you get there at tea time, you'll be served on beautiful china from a menu of seafood, soup, and sandwiches.

Main St., Craughwell, Co. Galway. © 091/846004. Hot lunches under 9€ ($8.15); bar snacks under 6.50€ ($5.90). MC, V. Bar food Mon–Fri 10am–7pm.

Moran's Oyster Cottage 😊😊 SEAFOOD If you miss the signpost for Moran's on N18, turn around and go back, because this is a place not to be missed. Presidents, prime ministers, movie stars, and locals who know their fish make a point of finding their way here. The food is simply legendary. For six generations, the Morans have been catching salmon and shucking oysters, and preparing them to perfection here on the weir. In fact, in 1960, Willie Moran caught 105 wild salmon in 1 day on the Dun Killen River in front of the family pub and went on to win the world title in oyster-opening. Two of his staff, Vincent Graham and Gerry Grealish, are also world champions. In short, they know their oysters. The wild smoked salmon is exquisite—sheer velvet. Willie Moran believes in a small menu, fresh and wild and with nothing in the way. Ambience? It's a thatched cottage with 36 swans and a blue heron outside the front door. It's rustic, but a great place to eat oysters.

The Weir, Kilcolgan, Co. Galway. © 091/796113. Reservations not required. Main courses, lunch, and dinner 10€–23€ ($9.10–$21); oysters 20€ ($18) per dozen. AE, MC, V. Daily noon–10pm. Closed Christmas Day and Good Friday.

Paddy Burkes SEAFOOD Platters of local oysters and mussels are served throughout the day at this homey tavern, with its lemon color and thatched roof, situated on the main road 10 miles (16km) south of Galway city. You can pick your favorite spot to relax amid the half-dozen rooms and alcoves with original stone walls, open fireplaces, potbelly stoves, fishing nets on the walls, and traditional sugan chairs. In good weather, there's also seating in a back garden beside a weir bridge. Lunch and other snack items range from seafood soups and chowders to sandwiches, salads, and omelets. In the evening, you can also order full meals with choices such as whole black sole, baked salmon, Atlantic plaice and crab with prawn sauce, honey roast duck with mead sauce, and medallions of beef with whiskey and mustard.

Ennis-Galway Rd. (N18), Clarinbridge, Co. Galway. © 091/796226. Reservations recommended for dinner. Lunch main courses 5.90€–20.35€ ($4.50–$18); dinner main courses 14.70€–27.15€ ($13–$24). AE, DC, MC, V. Daily noon–10pm.

2 The Aran Islands

The Aran Islands form a broken line of bare rock out where Galway Bay empties into the Atlantic. There are three inhabited islands: **Inisheer** (Inis Oirr in the Irish, meaning "eastern island"), the smallest and nearest to the mainland Doolin, County Clare, is 6 miles (9.5km) away; **Inishmaan** (or Inis Meain, meaning "middle island"), 3 miles (5km) distant from each of the other two and 3 miles (5km) long by 2 miles (3km) wide; and **Inishmore** (or Inis Mor, meaning "big island"), 7 miles (11km) from the Connemara coast, 8 miles (13km) long and 2½ miles (4km) wide, with the only safe harbor suitable for steamer docking at **Kilronan,** its main village.

Impressions

Some time ago, before the introduction of police, all the people of the islands were as innocent as the people here remain to this day. I have heard that at that time the ruling proprietor and magistrate of the north island used to give any man who had done wrong a letter to a jailer in Galway, and send him off by himself to serve a term of imprisonment.
—J. M. Synge (1871–1909), *The Aran Islands*

Don't come to the islands looking for the way of life documented by Robert Flaherty's 1934 film *Man of Aran* or books like *The Islandman;* happily for those who live here, life isn't as hard as it used to be. Much has changed on the islands during the past few decades; life has been made easier with the introduction of electricity, modern plumbing, and regular sea and air service to the mainland. Men still put out to sea in lightweight, tough little wood-and-canvas curraghs, which you'll see nestled into the many small ports, but most of the fishing is done in larger, more efficient boats. Nonetheless, much of the culture and old customs remain. People here still speak the Irish language. During the summer, Inishmore exists for tourism, so if you want to get away from the crowds, you should consider a visit to Inisheer or Inishmaan.

GETTING THERE   By Ferry   Aran Island Ferries (© 091/568903; www. aranislandferries.com), with a number of offices in Galway center, offers extensive year-round daily service to all three Aran Islands. Most boats leave from **Rossaveal** in Connemara—23 miles (37km) west of the city. Coach connection service is provided by Island Ferries from its Victoria Place office 90 minutes before sailing time. From Rossaveal, there are two daily departures from November through March and three daily departures from April through October, with additional sailings in July and August according to demand. Round-trip fares to any of the Aran Islands are 20€ ($18) adults, 16€ ($15) seniors and students, 11€ ($10) children, with family and group rates on request.

O'Brien Shipping (© 091/567676; www.doolinferries.com) operates one morning ferry daily from June to September from the Galway docks to Kilronan on Inishmore, and one ferry returning from Kilronan in the afternoon; there is also an interisland service. The cost is 16€ ($15) per person round-trip, and 7€ ($6.35) one-way interisland. Sailing time is 90 minutes. The booking office is at the Galway Tourist Office. Ask about rate reductions for seniors and children.

Doolin Ferry Co. (© 065/707-4455; www.doolinferries.com) connects Doolin in County Clare with Inisheer for 25€ ($23) round-trip, Inishmaan 28€ ($25) round-trip, and Inishmore 32€ ($29) round-trip.

By Plane   You can fly to Inishmore with **Aer Arann** in a nine-seat, twin-engine aircraft from Connemara Airport; travel time is 10 minutes. The round-trip fare is about 44€ ($40) round-trip, 23€ ($21) one-way per person. You can book through the tourist office or Aer Arann Reservations (© 091/593034 or 01/814-5240; www.aerarann.ie). Flights depart from a new airport approximately 18 miles (29km) west of Galway city; bus service between Galway city and the airport is available. From April to September flights depart four times daily, and somewhat less frequently during the rest of the year. Ask about special packages that include an overnight stay on the islands. Aer Arann can also arrange package deals with rail or bus connections to Galway from Dublin and almost any other part of the country.

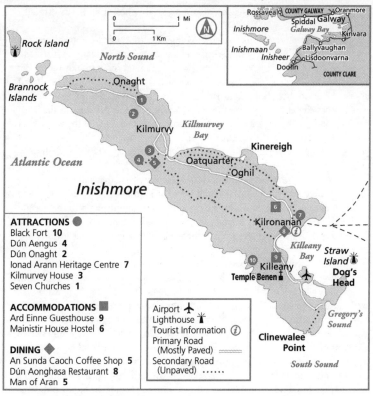

Inishmore, The Aran Islands

ATTRACTIONS ●
Black Fort **10**
Dún Aengus **4**
Dún Onaght **2**
Ionad Arann Heritage Centre **7**
Kilmurvey House **3**
Seven Churches **1**

ACCOMMODATIONS ■
Ard Einne Guesthouse **9**
Mainistir House Hostel **6**

DINING ◆
An Sunda Caoch Coffee Shop **5**
Dún Aonghasa Restaurant **8**
Man of Aran **5**

Airport ✈
Lighthouse
Tourist Information ⓘ
Primary Road
  (Mostly Paved) ════
Secondary Road
  (Unpaved) ......

VISITOR INFORMATION Detailed information on the Aran Islands is available in the tourist office in Galway (see chapter 11), where you can also book island accommodations.

SEEING THE SIGHTS

The ferry lands at Kilronan pier on Inishmore, leaving you to contend with the line of donkey-driven carts and minibuses ready and eager to sweep you away on a guided tour of the island or take you to your guesthouse. If you'd prefer to explore on your own, prepare to refuse a lift at least a dozen times before reaching the nearest bicycle rental shop, a few hundred feet along the pier. The island can also be explored on foot. There's a marked walking path called the **Inis Mor Way** that links the primary archaeological sites; maps can be purchased at the tourist office in Kilronan.

The new heritage center, **Ionad Arann,** Kilronan, Inishmore (© **099/ 61355**), explores the history and culture of these islands. Exhibits illuminate the harsh yet beautiful landscape, the Iron Age forts, and the churches of the first Christians. In addition, the 1932 film *Man of Aran,* directed by Robert Flaherty, is shown at regular intervals daily; admission is 3.15€ ($2.90). The center is open April, May, September, and October daily from 10am to 5pm, and daily May through September 10am to 7pm. Admission to the center is 3.15€ ($2.90) adults, 2.60€ ($2.40) students, 1.90€ ($1.75) seniors and children, and 7.60€ ($6.90) family. Combined center/film tickets are available at a reduced cost. A cafe is on hand serving soups, sandwiches, and pastries throughout the day.

Inishmore is renowned for its archaeological sites, and there are three you shouldn't leave without visiting. The island has several spectacular ring forts, and the most renowned of these, **Dun Aengus** ⚔, is about 4 miles (6.5km) from the Kilronan pier. It covers 11 acres and is perched on a cliff some 250 feet (76m) above the sea. Three semicircular walls ring a central enclosure, one side of which faces the cliff. The innermost wall was extensively restored in the 19th century, and much of what you see dates from that time. One of the fort's most intriguing features is the *chevaux-de-frise,* a defensive field filled with sharp stones sticking straight out of the ground, which must have been nearly impossible for invading forces to cross.

Another cliffside stone fort, just as dramatically situated as Dun Aengus and less frequented by visitors, is the **Black Fort** (or Dún Dúcathair). It's composed of a sequence of walls that cut off a narrow promontory jutting into the sea and a chevaux-de-frise on the inland side. To get there, head inland from the Kilronan pier on the Inis Mor Way; there's a short side path that leads to the fort.

There are several inland forts, thought to be built somewhat more recently than those on the cliff edge. The most spectacular of these is **Dún Onaght** (known locally as Dún Eoghanachta), which consists of a single massive wall with several small stone huts or *clochans* within its enclosure. Both wall and huts have been extensively restored. Near here, in the tiny village of Onaght, is the cluster of monastic ruins known as the **Seven Churches,** although only two of the existing structures are thought to have been used as churches. There are some ancient tombstones with beautiful carvings in the churchyard.

Like much of Ireland, these islands keep their riches concealed, and you'll have to plan to spend some time here if you want to get past the facade presented to tourists. Don't let the small size of these islands mislead you—on Inishmore alone there are significant variations in the style of wall building, and more archaeological sites than you could visit in a week. My recommendation would be to buy a copy of Tim Robinson's excellent **map of the island,** and start exploring. The map is available at Inishmore's tourist office, at the Galway tourist office, and in most local bookstores; the cost is 6.50€ ($5.90).

Inishmore's two smaller neighbors, **Inisheer** and **Inishmaan,** have been changed less by tourism and offer more of a feel for island life. Interisland ferries are operated by several companies (see "Getting There," above).

ACCOMMODATIONS YOU CAN AFFORD
INISHMORE

Ard Einne Guesthouse   Mrs. Enda Gill greets you at this modern home that sits 1¼ miles (2km) from the village on an elevated site looking out onto gorgeous views. All bedrooms have sinks, and the house is convenient to fishing, a good pub, and a lovely beach. Packed lunches are prepared on request. A minibus is available for transport to and from the port: the charge is 1.25€ ($1.15) per person.

Kilronan, Inishmore, Aran Islands, Co. Galway. ℂ **099/61126.** Fax 099/61388. www.galway.net/pages/ ardeinne. 15 units. 51€ ($46) single; 63€ ($58) double. Rates include full breakfast. Dinner 19€ ($17). MC, V. Closed Nov–Apr. *In room:* tea/coffeemaker.

Kilmurvey House ⚔   This has been the place to stay on Inishmore since Dún Aengus fell into ruin. The 18th-century stone family home of the "Ferocious

O'Flahertys" forms the core of this most hospitable and pleasant guesthouse, expanded to offer 12 diverse rooms, all quite comfortable and impeccably clean. Despite its origins, the spirit of the house could not be more gracious, thanks to Teresa Joyce's hospitality. An array of delights awaits you at breakfast, and an optional four-course dinner is served at 7pm with advance reservation. Kilmurvey House lies just below Dún Aengus, Inishmore's prime attraction. A handful of shops, cafes, and restaurants, as well as a "blue flag" (that is, pristine) white-sand beach, are within a short stroll.

Kilmurvey, Kilronan, Aran Islands, Co. Galway. ✆ 099/61218. Fax 099/61397. www.kilmurveyhouse.com. 12 units. TEL. 63€ ($58) double. Rates include full breakfast. MC, V. Open Easter–Oct. 5 miles (8km) from the ferry on the Coast Rd.

Mainistir House Hostel ✦ *Finds*   Joel D'Anjou has succeeded in creating a place that surpasses any likely expectations: It's a spartan hostel, and yet surprisingly comfortable. The private rooms are basic but offer comfortable beds and plush bathrobes for the walk to the bathroom. The dining room is highly cosmopolitan (and also popular with locals); the highlight of the day is the buffet dinner, a mostly vegetarian concoction that varies from amazing to merely filling—but the focus isn't on presentation or service so much as on the *event*, where travelers from all walks of life can meet, talk, and enjoy the simple food. The vegetables and herbs are grown on the island by Joel's neighbors. It's hard to say what combination of details makes this hostel so special, because while none of the elements are exceptional in themselves, they come together to make a place that's unique and not to be missed.

Kilronan, Inishmore, Aran Islands, Co. Galway. ✆ 099/61169. Fax 099/61351. mainistir@galway.net. 6 units, none with bathroom. 30€ ($28) double; 19€ ($17) single; 11€ ($10) dorm. Rates include continental breakfast. Dinner 11€ ($10). V. 1 mile (1.6km) from the pier. **Amenities:** Restaurant. *In room:* Bathrobes.

GREAT DEALS ON DINING
INISHMORE

At **Mainistir House Hostel** (see listing above) the 19€ ($17) mostly vegetarian evening meal is open to all.

An Sunda Caoch Coffee Shop COFFEE SHOP   Two of the best cooks on the island, Mrs. Bridget Johnston-Hernon and daughter, Treasa Hernon-Joyce (see Kilmurvey House, above), offer the perfect spot for a break in sightseeing or a light repast. Everything is homemade, and their cakes are great local favorites. The hearty soups, served with brown bread, are a meal in themselves, and there are a few light dishes to satisfy larger appetites.

Kilmurvey, Kilronan, Inishmore, Aran Islands, Co. Galway. ✆ 099/61983. Light meals under 6€ ($5.45). No credit cards. Apr–Oct daily 11am–5pm.

Man of Aran ✦ CONTINENTAL   If the Man of Aran restaurant looks familiar, it may be because you just saw it in the film at the Heritage Centre. It is in fact the traditional thatched seaside cottage constructed in 1934 for the

---

Tips **Man of Aran**

Life on the Aran Islands may have changed since the movie was made, but *Man of Aran* still makes a wonderful introduction to the islands and islanders. It's shown several times daily at the Village Hall in Kilronan, with a small admission charge.

filming of *Man of Aran.* The resemblance stops there, however, as the Man himself never for one day ate as well as you will here. After years of culinary training and experience in London, Maura Wolfe has returned to Aran with her husband, Joe, and created one of the island's great surprises, a first-class restaurant drawing upon the organic vegetables and herbs grown at great toil in their garden. Maura conjures each day's menu on the spot, inspired by what is most fresh and available from the sea and from the soil just beyond her front door. The result is perfect, simple, and without pretense. Tables are limited, especially in the separate nonsmoking room, so you must book early in the day for the restaurant's only seating at 7:30pm. If you can't stay for dinner, at least stop by for lunch. B&B accommodation is also available in case you decide to stay around for breakfast as well.

Kilmurvey, Kilronan, Aran Islands, Co. Galway. ℂ **099/61301.** Reservations required for dinner. Fixed-price dinner 22€–28€ ($20–$25). No credit cards. Mon–Sat 12:30–3pm and 1 seating for dinner at 7:30pm.

Dún Aonghasa Restaurant SEAFOOD/TRADITIONAL   If you gravitate toward traditional settings, you'll love this wood-and-stone restaurant overlooking Kileaney Bay. It specializes in the freshest of local seafood, as well as mouthwatering home baking. Inside, there's a cozy open fire.

Kilronan, Inishmore, Aran Islands, Co. Galway. ℂ **099/61104.** Reservations recommended. Lunch 12.45€–17€ ($11–$15); dinner main courses 20.35€–36.20€ ($18–$32); fixed-price dinner £18 ($27). MC, V. Daily 10am–11pm.

3 Connemara

Clifden is 40 miles (64km) W of Galway City

This westernmost point of County Galway is a wild, thinly populated, yet enchanting stretch of land between Lough Corrib and the Atlantic. The serried peaks known as the **Twelve Bens** ⊕ (or sometimes the Twelve Pins) look across a lake-filled valley at the misty peaks of the Maumturk range, and the jagged coastline is a solitary place of rocks, tiny hamlets, and stark, silent beauty. As you drive the winding little roads past blue-washed cottages, you encounter a landscape made beautiful by shifting light and shade and the starkness of rock-strewn fields and hills. This is also Gaeltacht area, populated by native speakers of the Irish language.

As in much of Ireland's western wilds, the tourism in Connemara has been focused on a few centers that are now booming and little resemble the sleepy fishing villages they were only a decade or two ago. **Clifden** is the primary tourist mecca here, although you'll also find unlikely outposts catering to travelers. You don't have to look hard, however, to find wild and remote places no matter where you are.

Roundstone, despite a recent accretion of ugly holiday homes on the surrounding hills, has retained its sleepy conviviality, and offers an assortment of excellent accommodation as well as a new summer arts festival. **Leenane** has become something of a tourist destination since the Richard Harris film, *The Field,* put it on the map, and **Killary Harbour** to the west offers one of the most beautiful stretches of rugged coastline in Ireland. Along the shores of **Lough Corrib,** the mountains become hills and the landscape is demure rather than bold; the comforting quiet of this region makes it a relaxing base for touring Connemara.

GETTING THERE & GETTING AROUND   From Galway City, **Bus Eireann** (ℂ **091/562000;** www.buseireann.ie) provides daily service to Clifden and other small towns en route. Service is also provided by private bus operators, but Bus Eireann is generally the most reliable. The best way to get around Connemara is to drive, following the N59 route from Moycullen and Oughterard.

VISITOR INFORMATION   Contact or visit the **Ireland West Tourist Office,** Aras Fáilte, Victoria Place, Galway, County Galway (© **091/563081;** www.western-ireland.ie). Open May, June, and September daily 9am to 5:45pm; July and August daily 9am to 7:45pm; October to April Monday to Friday 9am to 5:45pm, Saturday 9am to 12:45pm. The **Oughterard Tourist Office,** Main Street, Oughterard (© **091/552808**), is open year-round, Monday to Friday from 9am to 5pm with extended hours in the summer season. In addition, a **seasonal office,** open Monday to Saturday 9am to 5pm between March and October, is maintained at Clifden (© **095/21163**).

SEEING THE SIGHTS

If you drive on R336 from Galway city, you'll traverse Galway Bay coast en route to the rocky and remote scenery of Connemara. **Casla (Costelloe)** is the home of Raidio na Gaeltachta, the Irish-language radio station, and **Rosmuc** is the site of the **Padraic Pearse Cottage** (© **091/574292;** www.heritageireland.ie). This simple thatched-roof cottage served as a retreat for Dublin-based Pearse (1879–1916), who was one of the leaders of Ireland's 1916 Rising. He used his time here to improve his knowledge of the Irish language. Now a national monument, the cottage contains documents, photographs, and other Pearse memorabilia. Admission is 1.25€ ($1.15) for adults, .90€ (80¢) for seniors, .50€ (45¢) for students and children, and 3.80€ ($3.45) for a family. It's open from mid-June until mid-September daily from 10am to 6pm.

The picturesque village of **Roundstone** 🌟 is beautifully situated on Bertraghboy Bay, overlooking the Atlantic from the foot of Errisbeg Hill. Small trawlers from the village fish year-round, and in summer months there's also fishing from open lobster boats and curraghs. It's worth a stop just to walk one of the two fine white-sand beaches nearby, Goirtin and Dog's Bay. If there's time, make the easy climb up Errisbeg Hill, where your reward at the top will be spectacular views of the Aran Islands and, on a clear day, parts of Kerry. It's in Roundstone, too, that you'll find *Roundstone Musical Instruments,* one of the finest makers of the traditional bodhran in Ireland (see "Shopping," later in this chapter).

Between Ballyconneely and Kilkieran, you can sometimes watch the **seaweed harvest** (done at the full and new moons for 4 hours only in the middle of the day, usually in the spring). Little villages all along the coast hold frequent **curragh races** 🌟 in June, July and August. Finding out the when and where of the races is a matter of keeping your eyes and ears open—and of a well-placed inquiry over a pint at the local pub.

One thing you won't want to miss in **Clifden** is the spectacular **Sky Drive** 🌟, a cliff road that forms a 9-mile (14.5km) circle around a peninsula and opens up vast seascapes. It's well signposted from town. In summer evenings there's traditional music in many of Clifden's hotel bars and pubs; check with the tourist office or your accommodation host or hostess. In August, join in the fun at the **Connemara Pony Show** in Clifden (see "Special Events," later in this chapter).

North of Clifden is the village of **Cleggan,** which is the home port for small fishing trawlers and, in summer, open lobster boats and curraghs. This is an area of remarkable cliff scenery and good beaches. Cleggan is also the gateway to the offshore **Inishbofin Island** 🌟 (see description below).

Near **Maam** there's a lovely branch of Lough Corrib, rimmed by mountains on both sides. In the center of this narrow extension of the lake is a rocky islet on which the ruins of a formidable castle are perched. This is **Castle Kirke,** probably built in the early 13th century. The castle and lake present a scene of incredible romantic beauty, irresistible to anyone with a sensibility for the picturesque. You can get to the castle with the help of rowboats that can be rented from John Gavin at Leckavrea View Farmhouse (see "Accommodations You Can Afford," later in this chapter). The row out to the castle takes only 15 minutes or so.

Aughnanure Castle   You approach the castle by a path along the banks of a stream that goes underground as you enter the castle enclosure—the intrepid will want to explore some interesting caves here. When the castle was built the stream flowed under the banqueting hall, and a trap door provided for quick disposal of unwanted guests. The main tower house is in fine condition, and there are exhibits explaining the daily life of castle inhabitants on each of its floors. There's a gem of a watchtower in the courtyard, with a conical stone roof and corbelled ceiling—there isn't another tower quite like this in Ireland, making it the signature feature of the castle.

Galway Rd., Oughterard, Co. Galway. ℂ 091/552214. www.heritageireland.ie. Admission 2.60€ ($2.40) adults, 1.90€ ($1.75) seniors, 1.25€ ($1.15) students and children, 6.35€ ($5.75) family. June to mid-Sept daily 10am–6pm; mid-Sept to Oct Sat–Sun 10am–6pm. 20 miles (32km) west of Galway city off N59 (signposted).

Connemara National Park ★★★   This stunning national park incorporates nearly 5,000 acres of Connemara's mountains, bog, heaths, and grasslands. The grounds are home to herds of Connemara ponies and Irish red deer, as well as a variety of birds and smaller mammals. To orient and acquaint visitors with all of the aspects of the park, the exhibition center offers a series of displays and an informative 20-minute audiovisual presentation. There are also two guided nature trails through some beautiful woodland—each about a half-hour's walk—and unmarked trails lead into the hills. Because the emphasis here is more on conservation than exploration, there's no information given on hill walking locally. Tea, coffee, soup, sandwiches, and freshly baked goods are on hand in the tearoom; the cheesecake is excellent. During July and August, Tuesdays and Thursdays are "nature days" for children, while Mondays, Wednesdays, and Fridays feature guided walks for the whole family. Call the center for specific information on these and other special programs.

Clifden-Westport Rd. (N59), Letterfrack, Co. Galway. ℂ 095/41054. www.heritageireland.ie. Admission 2.60€ ($2.40) adults, 1.90€ ($1.75) seniors, 1.25€ ($1.15) children and students, 6.50€ ($5.90) family. Park: year-round; visitor center: daily mid-Mar to May and Sept to mid-Oct 10am–5:30pm; June 10am–6:30pm; July–Aug 9:30am–6:30pm.

Dan O'Hara's Homestead Farm   If you're wondering how Connemara farmers find soil to farm on this rocky land, head to this small farm about 4 miles (6.5km) east of Clifden off the main N59 road. As the name implies, it was once owned by Dan O'Hara, who was forced to emigrate to the United States because of the harsh conditions and high taxes of the time. Today, the newly expanded center incorporates an 8-acre pre-famine farm that reflects how life here operated in the 1840s, with local people using traditional tilling and farming methods. The land also contains a reconstructed crannog (fortified lake dwelling) and a nearby Neolithic tomb.

Lettershea, Clifden, Co. Galway. ℂ 095/21246. Fax 095/22098. www.connemaraheritage.com. Admission 5.10€ ($4.60) adults, 4.50€ ($4.10) seniors and students, 2.60€ ($2.30) children, 15€ ($14) family. Apr–Oct daily 10am–6pm.

Tips **Online in Connemara**

The **Two Dog Cafe** (© 095/22186), located on Church Hill in Clifden, offers fast Internet access. The atmosphere is techno-trendy. It costs 2€ ($1.80) for 15 minutes at the keyboard; each additional 5-minute-block is .65€ (60¢). The Two Dog is open 7 days a week (in summer) from 10:30am to 10pm; between September and May it's open Monday to Saturday 10:30am to 5pm. See description later in this chapter, in "Great Deals on Dining."

Kylemore Abbey ★★   The image of Kylemore Abbey and lake is one of the stunningly picturesque visions most visitors see in books and magazines long before their arrival in Ireland. The real wonder is that the place is almost as striking as the pictures make it out to be. Originally a private residence (ca. 1868), this castellated house overlooking Kylemore Lake is a splendid example of neo-Gothic architecture. In 1920 it was turned over to the Benedictine nuns, who have since opened the grounds and part of the house to the public.

The highlight is not the house, but the recently restored **Gothic chapel** ★★, reached by a footpath along the lake. The interior of the chapel is elaborately decorated with carvings, and the buttery warmth of the Caen sandstone blends beautifully with colorful Irish marble. Don't miss the path that ascends steeply to the statue perched on the hillside, hundreds of feet above the abbey ramparts; to get there, follow the signs for the abbey school past the entrance building, then turn left onto the trail at the school. The complex also includes a cafe, which serves produce grown on the nuns' farm; a shop with a working pottery studio; and a visitor center where a video presentation gives you an overview of life at Kylemore, both past and present. The abbey is most atmospheric when the bells are rung for midday office or for vespers at 6pm; visitors are welcome to attend these services. Admission to the Abbey is through two gates, each providing access to different attractions and facilities, and each requiring a separate fee. (It might help to think of it as a double collection.) The Abbey Gate offers access to the Abbey receptions rooms, the exhibition, the church, the lake walk, and the video; the Garden Gate opens to a Victorian walled garden, the exhibition, the tea house, the shop, and the wilderness walk.

Kylemore, Co. Galway. © 095/41146. www.kylemoreabbey.com. House, chapel and grounds: admission 5€ ($4.55) adults, 2.50€ ($2.30) seniors or students, 11€ ($10) family; garden only: admission 6.50€ ($5.90) adults, 4€ ($3.65) seniors or students, 13€ ($12) family; combined ticket 10€ ($9.10) adults, 6.50€ ($5.90) seniors or students, 20€ ($18) family. House, chapel, and grounds: Easter–Oct daily 9am–6pm; Nov–Easter daily 9am–5:30pm. Garden: Easter–Oct daily 10:30am–5:15pm, last admission 4:30; garden closed Nov–Easter. Off N59, 8 miles (13km) east of Clifden.

Leenane Cultural Center   This center, overlooking Killary Harbour, focuses on the history of wool and the 20-some breeds of sheep in Ireland, and is well worth the price of admission. The sheep are on display in a field adjacent to the center. Inside, you can peruse exhibits on the local wool industry. There are demonstrations of carding, spinning, and weaving, and visitors are invited to join in. A 13-minute audiovisual presentation provides background on local history and places of interest in the area. Demonstrations of sheep herding are given on request by a bored sheepdog that lives on the premises—ask for a demonstration and the dog will be eternally grateful. There's also a small gift shop and cafe.

Clifden-Westport Rd. (N59), Leenane, Co. Galway. © 095/42323. www.leenane-connemara.com. Admission 2.60€ ($2.40) adults, 1.25€ ($1.15) seniors, students, and children over age 8, 6.50€ ($5.90) family. Apr–Oct daily 9am–6pm.

KILLARY HARBOUR
Walking the Green Road

Killary Harbour ⓡⓡ, a fjord-like inlet rimmed by mountains on both sides, is strikingly remote and wild at its western, seaward end. The **green road,** now a sheep track for much of its length, was once the primary route from the Rinvyle Peninsula to Leenane. This area was devastated by the famine, and you'll pass an abandoned pre-famine village on the far side of the harbor, the fields rising at a devilishly steep slope from the ruined cottages clustered at the water's edge. This is a walk into Ireland's recent past, when many lived by subsistence farming and fishing, always perilously close to disaster.

The walk begins at the **Killary Harbour Youth Hostel** (see "Accommodations You Can Afford," below). Heading away from the hostel on the local access road, take a left on a grassy path just before the first house on the left. This path continues all the way to **Leenane,** a distance of about 8 miles (13km), but the most beautiful part is the first 2 miles (3km) from the youth hostel. If you prefer not to return the way you came, look for the second of two roofed but abandoned houses on the right; it's right next to the trail, and partially obscured by rhododendrons. Just past this house is a path, scarcely discernible, that heads up the slope, veering back the way you've come. If you can find this track, it's easy to

---

⎛Moments An Excursion to Inishbofin

It has been said that Ireland's last unspoiled frontiers are its islands, and Inishbofin on its own makes a strong contribution to that claim. This small emerald-green gem lies 7 miles (11km) off the northwest coast of Connemara and offers not only seclusion, but spectacular beauty, provided the skies are clear enough to deliver the not-to-be-believed views of and from its shores. Once the domain of monks, then the lair of pirate queen Grace O'Malley, later Cromwell's infamous priest-prison, and currently home to a mere 180 year-round residents, Inishbofin is both steeped in history and oozing with charm. It's well worth a day's expedition or a 1- or 2-day stay.

Numerous ferries to the island leave from and return to the sleepy port of **Cleggan,** 8 miles (13km) NW of Clifden off N59, daily April through October. The largest, newest, and fastest boat, the *Island Discovery,* is operated by **Inishbofin Island Tours,** Kings of Cleggan, Cleggan, County Galway (© **095/44642**). Tickets are available at their offices in Clifden and Cleggan, for 13€ ($12) per person, round-trip). The other, and to my mind better, option is to ride with Paddy O'Halloran (© **095/45806**) on the *Dun Aengus* the island's worn and worthy mail boat, the vessel of choice for most locals. It has both more charm and more roll than its new rival, and Skipper O'Halloran, after a half-century at the wheel, definitely knows the way. Tickets for the *Dun Aengus* cost 13€ ($12) per person round-trip and are available at the pier in Cleggan, or at the local Spar Foodstore (© **095/44750**).

follow as it climbs gradually to the ridge top, which it meets at a curious notch cut in the hillside. (Local legend attributes this groove to a time when the Devil tried to pull a local saint into hell, using a long iron chain for the purpose.) Descending on the other side of the notch, make your way down to the hostel access road, which will take you back to the starting point. Total distance for the loop is about 5 miles (8km).

SPECIAL EVENTS

The **Connemara Pony Show** ⚬ in Clifden, held in August, attracts pony buyers from around the world. The town takes on a country-fair look, with much revelry, handcraft demonstrations, and more. Sometimes there are "flapper races" in which children race ponies while families gather for a great day of eating and drinking outdoors. For information, contact the Connemara Pony Association (✆ 095/21863; fax 095/21005).

OUTDOOR PURSUITS

In terms of location, facilities, and quality of instruction, **Delphi Adventure Center** ⚬⚬, Leenane, County Galway (✆ 095/42307), is one of the best adventure centers in Ireland. It offers courses in a wide range of watersports, as well as in mountaineering, pony trekking, tennis, and archery (see full description below).

BICYCLING Bicycles can be rented year-round from **John Mannion & Son,** Bridge Street., Clifden, County Galway (✆ 095/21160). The rate for a touring bike is 9€ ($8.15) per day or 53€ ($48) per week. Mountain bikes can be rented from May through October at the **Little Killary Adventure Centre,** Salruck, Renvyle, County Galway (✆ 095/43411; www.killary.com) for a charge of 19€ ($17) per day.

DIVING You can rent equipment and receive instruction at **Scubadive West,** Lettergesh, Renvyle, County Galway (✆ 095/43922; fax 095/43923; www.scubadivewest.com).

FISHING **Lough Corrib** is renowned for brown trout and salmon fishing, with the brown trout fishing usually good from the middle of February and salmon best from the end of May. The May fly-fishing commences around the middle of May and continues up to 3 weeks. Angling on Lough Corrib is free, but a state license is required for salmon. For expert advice contact the **Cloonnabinnia Angling Centre,** Moycullen, County Galway (✆ 091/555555).

Portarra Lodge, Tullykyne, Moycullen, County Galway (✆ 091/555051; portarralodge@eircom.net), offers packages that include boats and tackle, dinners, and B&B accommodation in a modern guesthouse on the shores of Lough Corrib (known throughout Europe for its wild brown trout). Michael Canney is an avid angler and a great guide to this part of Galway. A double room is 66€ ($60) per night; weekly rates for half board are 369€ ($334) per person; and weekly rates for half board, pack lunch, boat, and ghillie are 760€ ($688).

For **sea angling,** try Connemara Sea Leisure Ltd., Derryinver, County Galway, 1½ miles (2.5km) from Letterfrack, where John Mongan (✆ 095/43473; www.oceansalive.com) runs 2-hour **fishing and sightseeing cruises** on his 31-foot (9.5m) MV *Lorraine-Marie* year-round, weather permitting. The fare is 32€ ($29) adult, 57€ ($52) family, including rod hire. Call to check on departure times and to book.

SWIMMING The Silver Strand at **Barna** and the beach at **Spiddal** are clean and sandy and ideal for swimming.

Lough Inagh and the Walk to Maum Ean Oratory

Lough Inagh, nestled between the Maumturk and The Twelve Ben Mountains in the heart of Connemara, is situated in one of the most spectacularly beautiful valleys in Ireland. The mountain slopes rise precipitously from the valley floor, and many small streams cascade into the lake in a series of sparkling waterfalls. The R344 cuts through the valley, linking Recess to the south and Kylemore Lake to the north.

The **Western Way,** a walking route that traverses the high country of Galway and Mayo, follows a quiet country road above the R344 through the Lough Inagh Valley. To reach the beginning of the walk, drive north on the R344, turning right on a side road—sign for Maum Ean—about 200m before the Lough Inagh Lodge Hotel. Continue on this side road for 4 miles (6.5km) to a large gravel parking lot on the left. Park here, and follow the well-worn trail 1¼ miles (2km) to the top of the pass, through glorious mountain scenery.

This short (2.5 mile/4km) walk follows the Western Way to the top of a mountain pass which has long been associated with St. Patrick, and which is now the site of a small oratory, a hollow in the rock known as **Patrick's Bed,** a life-size statue of the saint, and a series of cairns marking the Stations of the Cross. Together, these monuments make a striking ensemble, strangely eerie when the mists descend and conceal the far slopes in their shifting haze. On a clear day there are great views from here, with the Atlantic Ocean and Bertraghboy Bay to the southwest and another range of mountains to the northeast. The round-trip walking time is about 1 hour.

WALKING The **Connemara Walking Centre,** Island House, Market Street, Clifden, County Galway (© **095/21379;** fax 095/21845; www.walkingireland. com), offers walking tours of Connemara with expert local guides, with an emphasis on history and archaeology as well as scenery. Itineraries include the Renvyle Peninsula; Roundstone Bog; the Kylemore Valley; Maumturk Mountains; the Twelve Bens and the Sky road; and Inishbofin Island. All walks assemble at Island House in Clifden and include transportation to the walking site. Advance reservations are required. Prices are 20€ to 32€ ($18–$29), depending on the itinerary. From May to September, call ahead for departure times.

WATERSPORTS Hobie Cat sailing and sailboarding can be arranged at the **Little Killary Adventure Centre,** Salruck, Renvyle, County Galway (© **095/ 43411;** www.killary.com). The rates are 36€ ($32) for a 3-hour lesson in windsurfing or sailing; other activities at the center include kayaking, waterskiing, hill and coastal walking, and rock climbing. Hostel accommodation is available at very reasonable rates: 25€ ($23) for a double room, or 14€ ($13) for a dorm bed.

ACCOMMODATIONS YOU CAN AFFORD

The Anglers Return ⚐ This lovely 18th-century sporting lodge was originally part of the Ballynahinch Castle estate, and is situated in a grove of lush woodlands. The house feels lived in, and has many thoughtful details, such as the stove in the spacious dining room for warmth on cool mornings. The beds are memorable: One room has an ornately carved Tudor headboard while in another room the "double" bed is nearly 6 feet (2m) wide. There are two shared bathrooms available for guest use. Lynn Hill is an energetic host, and will go to unusual lengths to see your needs met. The extensive and delicious breakfast includes Lynn's homemade marmalade; vegetarians are well provided for. During the winter months (November, February, and March) advance booking is essential.

Toombeola, Roundstone, Co. Galway. ℭ/fax **095/31091.** www.anglersreturn.itgo.com. 5 units, 1 with bathroom. 66€ ($60) double. Rates include full breakfast. No credit cards. Closed Dec–Jan. 4 miles (6.5km) east of Roundstone on R341. *In room:* Hair dryer, iron.

Ardmore Country House   Mrs. Vera Feeney's Ardmore is a modern bungalow overlooking the bay and the Aran Islands; the panoramic view is framed by large windows in the lounge. The Cliffs of Moher are also visible on clear days. You can relax in the sun outside on the terrace to enjoy the landscaped gardens. The guest rooms are spacious and attractively decorated. The gracious Mrs. Feeney has thoughtfully provided washing and drying facilities. In the morning, you're offered a menu that has won the Galtee Irish Breakfast Award three times.

Greenhill, Spiddal, Co. Galway. ℭ **091/553145.** Fax 091/553596. 7 units. 45€ ($41) single; 60€ ($54) double. 20% reduction for children. Discounts for stays of 3 days or more. Rates include full breakfast. MC, V. Closed Jan–Feb. On the Galway Bay Coastal Rd. ½ mile (1km) from Spiddal. **Amenities:** Laundry facilities. *In room:* TV, hair dryer.

Ardmore House   The hosts of Ardmore House, John and Kathy Mullen, see to it that guests are well cared for. The rooms are immaculate: the most spacious are at the rear of the house and face a paved yard, while those at the front are somewhat smaller and look onto a pasture with grazing cows and sheep. The house is a short walk away from fine coastal cliffs, and John and Kathy have constructed a gravel path from the house to the sea: on the way you'll pass Connemara ponies and the chickens that supply the eggs for breakfast. The house is wheelchair accessible.

Sky Rd., Clifden, Connemara, Co. Galway. ℭ **095/21221.** Fax 095/21100. www.ardmore-house.com. 6 units. 45€ ($41) single; 60€ ($54) double. Dinner 20€ ($18). No credit cards. Closed Oct–Mar. *In room:* TV (with CNN), tea/coffeemaker, hair dryer.

Bay View   With one of the best views in this area, Mrs. Bridie Hyland's modern bungalow overlooks Streamstown Bay. Guest rooms are both attractive and comfortable, and you're likely to find a peat fire glowing in the picture-window lounge, which also has a TV. Bridie knows the area well, is always helpful in planning sightseeing for her guests, and can arrange a day's deep-sea fishing. All bedrooms, the dining room, and the sitting room are nonsmoking.

Westport Rd., Clifden, Co. Galway. ℭ **095/21286.** Fax 095/22938. 4 units. 25€ ($23) single; 51€ ($46) double. 50% reduction for children. Rates include full breakfast. MC, V. Closed Dec–Jan. *In room:* TV, tea/coffeemaker, hair dryer.

Doonmore Hotel *(Kids)*   This seasoned waterfront hotel enjoys a prime location on Inishbofin, with stunning views of the open sea and of nearby Inishshark and High Island. Small boats dot the bay and there is even a seal colony just beyond the hotel's front doors. A range of room options is available, including spacious family units with children's bunk beds. The appealing, unpretentious rooms in the newish expansion are clean, full of light, and tastefully furnished with simple pine furniture. The older rooms in the original hotel building are somewhat worn but comfortable; some enjoy the hotel's finest sea views. All rooms have firm beds. The hotel offers facilities for sea angling and scuba diving. Inishbofin is well known for both. The Doonmore is a short walk from the ferry, and provides van service to and from the main harbor on request.

Inishbofin Island, Co. Galway. ℭ 095/45814 or 095/45804. Fax 095/45804. www.doonmorehotel.com. 24 units, 19 with bathroom (15 with shower only). 88€ ($80) double with bathroom. Rates include full breakfast. AE, MC, V. Closed Nov–Mar. **Amenities:** Restaurant, bar. *In room:* TV, tea/coffeemaker, hair dryer.

Errisbeg Lodge ⟨★★⟩ Conveniently proximate to Roundstone yet blessedly ensconced between mountainside and sea, Errisbeg Lodge is a place where you may plan to spend a night and wind up lingering for days. Jackie and Shirley King's family land, reaching high onto the slopes of Errisbeg Mountain and sloping down to the sea, is a sublime haven for innumerable rare species of wildflowers and birds, and Jackie loves nothing more than sharing these wonders with his guests. The Atlantic is spread out before you, with two glorious whitesand beaches a few hundred yards away on foot. Guest rooms are rustic and serenely spare, with stucco walls, light pine furniture, and pastel floral comforters, with either mountain or ocean views. It's all about tranquillity here, and warm, gracious hospitality.

Roundstone, Co. Galway. ℭ/fax 095/35807. www.connemara.net/errisbeg-lodge. 5 units. 51€ ($46) double. Rates include full breakfast. No credit cards. Free parking. Closed Dec–Feb. Just over a mile (about 2km) outside of Roundstone on the Clifden Rd..

Glen Valley House & Stables ⟨★★⟩ Tucked away in a grove of trees at the base of a remote glaciated valley, this B&B redefines *secluded*. The entrance drive follows the base of the valley for just over a mile (about 2km) before you arrive at the house, which has great views across to the far line of hills. The O'Neills are helpful and yet unobtrusive hosts, and their home attracts people looking for a serene and restful setting. Don't miss the spectacular section of the Western Way walking trail that passes near the house and follows the hills rimming Killary Harbour, with unforgettable views of the Harbour mouth. (*Tip:* It's a great place to watch the sunset.) Connemara ponies are raised here, and there are many horses about—non–horse lovers will be glad to know the stables are far enough from the house that the sound and smell don't overwhelm.

Glencroff, Leenane, Co. Galway. ℭ 095/42269. Fax 095/42365. gvhouse@yahoo.com. 5 units, 3 with bathroom (2 with shower only). 32€ ($29) single; 50€–60€ ($51–$57) double. 20% discount for children under 12. Rates include full breakfast. No credit cards. Closed mid-Sept–Apr. 3½ miles (5.5km) west of Leenane on the Clifden Rd. (signposted).

Killary Harbour Youth Hostel If you don't mind somewhat primitive accommodations, this is the perfect base for explorations in this wild and scenic region of Ireland. When the German philosopher Ludwig Wittgenstein lived here during the summer of 1948, the house had only two rooms and no electricity or running water. He still managed to get some writing in, and maybe you too will find inspiration in the severe beauty of this landscape. The hostel is located on a pier near the mouth of Killary Harbour. This is, in my opinion, one of the most beautiful areas of Connemara. The "green road" (see listing under "Seeing the Sights," earlier in this chapter) passes the hostel on its way to Leenane and offers one of the best walks in the region; the Mweelrea Mountains are just across the harbor, looming in the mist, a challenge for the seasoned walker.

Rosroe, Renvyle, Co. Galway. ℭ 095/43417. www.irelandyha.org. 6 units: 8-bed dorms, none with bathroom. 10€ ($9.10) per person. No credit cards. Free parking. Closed Oct–Feb. Call to ask for directions—poorly signposted.

Knockferry Lodge   This lodge is set in a secluded spot on the Connemara shores of Lough Corrib, 14 miles (23km) northwest of Galway city. It was originally occupied by the author of *Galway Bay*, Dr. Arthur Colohan. There are turf fires in both of the large lounges, and there's a spacious dining room. A games room has table tennis and bar billiards. Motorboats are available for fishing or touring at 32€ ($29) per day plus fuel; there's no charge for a fishing license, except for salmon. Guest rooms are lovely, most with lake views; one large room has a double and two single beds. There's a physiotherapist on staff who can provide personalized fitness programs, massages, and sports injury treatment, for 32€ ($29) per session. The restaurant and bedrooms are nonsmoking.

Knockferry, Roscahill, Co. Galway. ℂ 091/550122. Fax 091/550328. www.knockferrylodge.com. 12 units. 63€ ($58) double. Reductions for stays of 2 nights or more; 33% reduction for children under 10. Rates include full breakfast. Dinner 22€ ($20). AE, MC, V. 13 miles (21km) from Oughterard; take N59 to Moycullen, turn left onto a small, unclassified road (the lodge is signposted) and then drive 6 miles (9.5km). **Amenities:** Restaurant. *In room:* hair dryer.

Lakeland Country Home   The lakeside home of the Faherty-Costelloe family is a relaxing haven, the size of a guesthouse but with the informality and hospitality of a good B&B. There are boats for hire at the house's dock, a few yards from the front door: Rowboats are 20€ ($18) per day, and 18-foot boats with a 4hp engine are 38€ ($38) per day—fishing rods are an additional 9€ ($8). Bedrooms are plain and comfortable, located in an addition at the back of the main house; bathrooms are small. The one "superior" bedroom faces the lake—it's somewhat larger than the others and has a spacious bathroom with Jacuzzi. There's a turf fire in the spacious sitting room, and electric blankets are supplied for cold nights.

Portacarron, Oughterard, Co. Galway. ℂ **091/552121**. Fax 091/552146. www.lakelandanglingcentre.co.uk. 9 units, 8 with bathroom (4 shower only). 38.50€ ($35) single; 58€–64€ ($53–$58) double. Rates include full breakfast. Dinner 22€ ($20). MC, V. Closed Nov–Easter. **Amenities:** Lounge.

Leckavrea View Farmhouse *(Kids*   This large farmhouse on the shores of Lough Corrib, 2½ miles (4km) from Maam Bridge and 32 miles (52km) from Galway city, is the comfortable home of John and Breege Gavin. Marvelous views of Lough Corrib include the little island just offshore crowned by Castle Kirke ("Hen's Castle"), once a stronghold of pirate queen Grace O'Malley. Fishing on the lough is free (the Gavins have boats for rent), and if Castle Kirke intrigues you, John will rent you a rowboat for a bit of exploring (see "Seeing the Sights," earlier in this chapter). For the sake of guests who've come for peace and quiet, Breege keeps the TV in a separate lounge and usually keeps a fire glowing in the main lounge. There's also a designated nonsmoking lounge. Breege will pack picnic lunches and arrange babysitting.

Maam-Cong Rd. (L101), Maam, Co. Galway. ℂ/fax 092/48040. 6 units. 51€ ($46) single; 43€ ($39) double. 25% reduction for children. Weekend rates available. Rates include full breakfast. No credit cards. Closed Christmas. **Amenities:** 2 lounges; babysitting. *In room:* TV.

O'Connor's Kilmore House *(Kids*   Josephine ("Jo") O'Connor is the hostess in this modern farmhouse 1 mile (1.5km) south of Tuam. Her warm hospitality first surfaces as she brings tea and scones to guests when they arrive. She has two family rooms, and provides a playground for children out back. Guest rooms are bright and cheerful, and Jo's substantial Irish breakfast is served in a window-walled dining room overlooking the farm and boglands beyond.

Galway Rd. (N17), Tuam, Co. Galway. ℂ/fax **093/28118** or 093/26525. 7 units. 48€ ($44) double. 20% reduction for children sharing with an adult; discounts for stays of more than 1 night. Rates include full breakfast. No credit cards. *In room:* TV.

Old Monastery Hostel   Location is a plus at this personable hostel, tucked into a beautiful old grove of trees just a stone's throw from the Connemara National Park interpretive center—the Ellis Wood nature trail passes by the hostel on its way through this fine old forest. Stephen Gannon is an outgoing host who also runs the vegetarian restaurant that serves a buffet-style dinner each night. The food may not be memorable, but it certainly is filling. The complimentary continental breakfast includes homemade scones, porridge, and organic coffee. The hostel is housed in a handsome stone building set into the steep hillside, with the restaurant on the darker bottom level and bedrooms sunnily situated above. The self-catering kitchen is small but well stocked, and there's a bright, spacious sitting room with fireplace. You can rent bikes for 8€ to 9€ ($7–$8) per day.

Letterfrack, Co. Galway. ℂ 095/41132. oldmon@indigo.ie. 8 units, none with bathroom: 2 double rooms, 6 dorm rooms. 11€–14€ ($10–$13) per person in 4-, 6-, or 8-bed dorm; 33€ ($30) double. Rates include continental breakfast. Dinner 9€ ($8). MC, V. **Amenities:** Restaurant (vegetarian); sitting room; guest kitchen.

St. Joseph's B&B   Christina and Séamus Lowry's town house sits on the high side of Roundstone's main street, and its glass-enclosed sun porch looks out over the colorful harbor. Christina's mother, often in residence, ran the guesthouse for more than 20 years, and her tradition of providing a home away from home for guests still prevails. Rooms are spacious; those in front overlook the bay. Christina is an accomplished Irish dancer and lover of traditional music and knows where it can be found locally; she hosts an evening of traditional song and dance at the Community Centre each Wednesday during July and August. The Lowrys can also arrange sea angling, as well as golf at nearby Ballyconneely.

Roundstone, Co. Galway. ℂ/fax 095/35865. christinalowry@eircom.net. 6 units. 32€ ($29) single; 43€–46€ ($39–$41) double. 25% reduction for children. Rates include full breakfast. V. *In room:* Tea/coffeemaker.

WORTH A SPLURGE
Ballynahinch Castle Hotel ★★★   Set on a 350-acre estate at the base of Ben Lettery, one of the Twelve Ben mountains, this turreted, gabled manor house overlooks the Owenmore River. Dating back to the 16th century, it has served over the years as a base for the O'Flaherty chieftains and the sea pirate Grace O'Malley. It was also the sporting residence of the Maharajah Jans Sahib Newanagar, better known as Ranjitsinhgi, the famous cricketer. The ambience can be best described as country house casual; the place feels luxurious and your every need will be satisfied by the efficient staff, yet there's absolutely no stuffiness or pretentiousness here. The guest rooms are individually decorated, and many have fireplaces and four-poster or canopy beds (all are orthopedic). The restaurant, with its impressive Connemara marble fireplace, offers sweeping views of the countryside and the lake. Most of all, this is a sportsman's lodge and is particularly renowned for top-notch sea trout and salmon fishing. Each evening, the day's catch is weighed in and recorded at the Fishermen's Bar, usually creating a cause for celebration.

Ballynahinch, Recess, Co. Galway. ℂ 095/31006. Fax 095/31085. www.commerce.ie/ballynahinch/. 40 units. 190€–380€ ($172–$344) double. 10% service charge. Breakfast 17€ ($15); dinner 42€ ($38). AE, DC, MC, V. Closed Christmas week and February. **Amenities:** Restaurant (Continental), bar; tennis courts; private fishing; limited room service; babysitting; library. *In room:* TV, hair dryer.

Delphi Adventure Holidays ★ *Kids*   Set in one of the most scenic portions of the road from Ashleagh to Louisburgh (R335), this low-slung, native stone building seems to have grown from the landscape itself. Interiors of natural woods, open fires, and flagstone floors create a warm, welcoming environment that invites lingering. Accommodation is in bright, simply furnished private or dorm-style rooms. The food in the dining room is good and plentiful, and vegetarian meals can be arranged. Residential adventure holidays for children are offered. Activities offered include watersports, mountaineering, pony trekking, tennis, and archery. A new 22-room lodge and health spa offer a more luxurious holiday option: The spa has Jacuzzi, steam room, sauna, seaweed bath, massage, and juice bar; and accommodation options in the lodge include bi-level rooms with sitting room and loft bedroom.

Leenane, Co. Galway. ℂ 095/42307. Fax 095/42303. www.delphiadventureholidays.ie. Adventure center: single, double, and dormitory rooms; self-catering cottage. Rm, full board, and activities start at 165€ ($148) for a weekend (2 nights). Spa: a 24-hour treatment including all meals and 1 night's accommodation starts at 400€ ($362). Weekend, mid-week, and public holiday special rates available. MC, V. Closed mid-Dec to Jan. **Amenities:** Restaurant; spa. *In room (only in lodge rooms):* tea/coffeemaker, hair dryer.

Delphi Lodge ★★★ *Finds*   Delphi Lodge is a dream destination, so much so that you'll pinch yourself every now and then. Built in the early 19th century as a sportsman's hideaway for the Marquis of Sligo, it sits tranquilly amidst a landscape that almost defies description: crystalline lakes and rivers, hardwood forests, unspoiled ocean beaches, and luminous velveteen mountain slopes. All that and salmon and sea trout out the front door, waiting to be caught—what more could you ask? The rooms are luxuriously simple and spacious, furnished in antique and contemporary light pine and featuring orthopedic mattresses. Fishing permits, registration, and all the equipment you'll need is available for 50€ to 120€ ($45–$109) per day; fishing is available primarily by the week, and advance booking is essential (preferably by Christmas of the preceding year). At dinner, the lodge will prepare your own personal catch of the day, or send it to you at home, smoked, after your return. Special 3-day weekend packages, including courses in fly-tying, watercolors, wine appreciation, and other diversions, are available in the off-season. All reservations must be made in writing or by fax; detailed directions are provided with your reservation confirmation.

The Delphi Estate and Fishery, Co. Galway. ℂ 095/42222. Fax 095/42296. www.delphilodge.ie. 12 units, all with bathroom; 5 cottages. 135€ ($122) standard single; 180€ ($163) standard double, 240€ ($217) lakeside double. Rates include full breakfast. 45€ ($41) fixed-price dinner daily. 700€–1000€ ($634–$905) per week 2- or 3-bedroom self-catering cottages. MC, V. Closed Christmas/New Year holidays. **Amenities:** Sitting Room. *In room:* TV.

GREAT DEALS ON DINING

Beola ★   SEAFOOD   This attractive restaurant serves perhaps the best seafood in Roundstone at near-budget prices. Beola, which belongs to the adjacent Eldon's Hotel, has an exceptionally welcoming staff to go with its fine cuisine. Smoked salmon parcels in filo pastry or hot avocado and prawns make a splendid first course. To follow, you try the roast filet of monkfish with lemon soy sauce, or grilled cod with nut dressing. For a memorable finish, it's got to be the Baileys and ginger cheesecake. The wine list offers a fine international selection at surprisingly affordable prices, and the South African house wine (Armiston Bay) is a high-quality surprise at 15€ ($14) a bottle. The only drawback here is that no significant provision is made for nonsmokers—the restaurant is a single unpartitioned space.

Roundstone Harbour, Connemara, Co. Galway. ℂ 095/35933. Reservations recommended. Dinner main courses 28€–34€ ($25–$31). AE, DC, MC, V. Easter to mid-Oct daily 7–9:30pm (last orders at 9). Bar food served 12:30–7:30pm daily.

Boluisce SEAFOOD   Seafood-lovers should head here, for scallops, prawns, lobster, smoked salmon, or the crab plate (or try the West Coast platter, which includes prawns, crab, lobster, mussels, and salmon). The house chowder is a meal in itself, brimming with salmon, prawns, monkfish, mussels, and more. Home-baked brown bread, rich and nutty, accompanies every meal.

Coast Rd., Spiddal, Co. Galway. ✆ **091/553286.** Reservations recommended for dinner. Dinner main courses 8.25€–28€ ($7.50–$25). AE, DC, DISC, MC, V. Daily 12:30pm–10pm.

The Central TRADITIONAL IRISH   This large bar/lounge is made cozy by lots of dark wood and a cheerful open fire (especially welcome on cool, dull days). The seafood chowder is especially good. Hot meals often include bacon and cabbage, lasagna, chicken curry, sandwiches, and soups. There's often traditional music in the bar, especially on summer nights.

Main St., Clifden, Co. Galway. ✆ **095/21430.** Sandwiches 3.15€–4.15€ ($2.90–$3.75). Hot plates 6€–8€ ($5.45–$7.25). AE, MC, V. Mon–Sat 12:30am–9:30pm.

Donnelly's of Barna SEAFOOD   Donnelly's, located in an old stone building that was once a stable, has created an attractive, light, and airy eatery, with stone walls, vaulted ceiling, and an open loft overlooking the main dining room. The bar menu features lots of seafood (no surprise when Galway Bay is only steps away), such as a crab bake, crab claws, salmon, and mussels. There's also a vegetarian platter and an avocado-pear dish served with smoked salmon, crab, or prawns. The back of the bar, which faces the road, is an excellent restaurant. Although steak au poivre, guinea fowl, pheasant, and vegetarian platters appear on the dinner menu, it's in the seafood department that Donnelly's really shines. Try the grilled scallops with lemon, or the Aran seafood medley Mornay, or the prawns in garlic cream. Before you make your choice, be sure to inquire about the catch of the day.

Coast Rd., Barna, Co. Galway. ✆ **091/592487.** Dinner main courses 10€–25€ ($9.10–$23). MC, V. Daily noon–10pm.

O'Grady's SEAFOOD   Since the mid-1960s, this attractive family-run restaurant has been drawing seekers of great seafood to Clifden. The owners even have their own fishing boats, so you may be sure the fish you eat has not long been out of the Atlantic waters. The menu features choices such as Clifden lobster with lemon or garlic butter, and filet of Cleggan brill. For non-fish-eaters, there's filet of beef with radish sauce, pork with peach stuffing in peppercorn cream sauce, and lamb with rosemary sauce. Lunches are served at moderate prices every day.

Market St., Clifden, Co. Galway. ✆ **095/21450.** Reservations recommended for dinner. Dinner main courses 13€–24€ ($12–$22). AE, MC, V. Apr–Sept daily 12:30–2:30pm and 6:30–10pm.

Two Dog Cafe MEDITERRANEAN   This bright, smoke-free cafe is a great place to relax and enjoy an array of homemade soups, Mediterranean sandwiches (constructed on baguettes, tortillas, and ciabatta), salads, fresh pastries, tea, and Italian coffee. The baguette with goat's cheese and grilled red peppers was particularly enticing. Wine is served by the glass or bottle.

There is also an Internet cafe on the second floor. Dell PCs and Apple iMacs, loaded with the latest browsing software, are at the ready. Discounts are given to students.

Church St., Clifden, Connemara, Co. Galway. ✆ **095/22186.** www.twodogcafe.ie. Soup 3.15€ ($2.90); sandwiches 5.50€ ($5.00); pasta 7€ ($6.35). MC, V. June–Sept daily 10:30am–10pm; Oct–May Tues–Sun 10:30am–5pm.

SHOPPING

Connemara Marble Visitor Centre   This factory store offers a tremendous stock of items made from polished marble, ranging from inexpensive souvenirs to moderately expensive items such as jewelry, bookends, clocks, and more. Prices are better here than in regular shops. Across the road, a tearoom serves tea, coffee, and cookies. Free tours of the factory are also offered. Galway-Clifden Rd. (N59), Moycullen, Co. Galway. © 091/555102. www.connemaramarble.net.

Connemara Socks   On this small industrial estate is a local business run by the Brennan family, who welcome visitors for tours of their plant. As well as spinning sock yarns for other sock knitters, they knit some 3,000 pairs of heavy socks per week on the premises. If you're a skier, fisher, hiker, hunter, or any other outdoor type, you'll surely want to take away several pairs of these moderately priced, heavy-duty socks. *Note:* There's a salmon smokery in the same industrial complex. East of Maam Bridge, near Cornamona. © 092/48254.

Mairtin Standun *(Value)*   There are very good bargains to be found in this family-run shop, located 12 miles (19km) from Galway city on R336. The selection of Aran sweaters, tweed coats and jackets, Waterford Crystal, Belleek china, souvenirs, and gifts is incredibly vast. There's also a currency-exchange service. In the rear of the shop there's a pleasant tearoom with fireplace; fresh bread and scones baked over an open turf fire are served. The shop is open February to December, Monday to Saturday from 9:30am to 6:30pm. Galway-Spiddal Rd., Spiddal. © 091/553108. standun@indigo.ie.

Millars Connemara Tweed Ltd.   Millars has long been a Clifden landmark, with shelves filled with beautifully colored pure-wool lengths produced by weavers in the locality. Their mill, one of the oldest in Ireland, uses only local mountain wool. Irish linens, glass, pottery, books of Irish interest, native food specialties, and other items complete the downstairs displays. Up the iron spiral stairs is a display of Connemara scenes as depicted by Irish painters. In a stone-walled wing of the shop, you can browse through Irish fashions in a setting that includes a turf fire on the stone hearth and furnishings such as an old spinning wheel. Patchwork quilts are beautifully executed and much sought after—and thus not always available. In short, this is a happy hunting ground for almost anything Irish-made. Main St., Clifden, Co. Galway. © 095/21038.

Roundstone Ceramics   Here you'll find high-fired stoneware and porcelain, hand-thrown by Séamus Laffan and decorated by Rose O'Toole. There is also a collection of porcelain jewelry. Each original decorative design is a reflection of the local environment, a lasting bit of Ireland to take home or give as gifts. Michael Killeen Park, Roundstone, Co. Galway. © 095/35874.

Roundstone Musical Instruments *(Finds)*   Malachy Kearns's instruments are played by many professional musicians, including those who create the sounds of the immensely popular *Riverdance* show. Malachy is a master craftsman, and one of the only full-time bodhran makers in the world. The bodhran is an ancient Irish one-sided frame drum. For the best results, it is vital to have the quality goatskin Malachy uses. While you wait, his wife, Anne, a Celtic artist, can decorate the skin with Celtic designs, initials, family crests, or any design you request in old Gaelic script. Short talks are given regularly on the history, making, and playing of the Bodhran, and drums made for *Riverdance* are on display. Malachy's workshop also makes wooden flutes (ebony), tin whistles, and Irish harps, and there's an excellent mail-order service. The workshop/craftshop,

Folk Instrument Museum, and coffee shop are open daily May to October from 9:30am to 6pm, Monday to Saturday other months. Michael Killeen Park, Roundstone, Co. Galway. ✆ 095/35875. Fax 095/35980. www.bodhran.com.

Síla Mag Aoide Designs (Shelagh Magee)   Shelagh Magee is one of Ireland's most noteworthy artisans. Although deeply inspired by ancient Celtic images and designs, her work is quite original and contemporary. In addition to a wide selection of Shelagh Magee's own handmade silver jewelry, the shop offers a range of works, including watercolor prints and art cards of Connemara scenes, baskets, handmade wooden pencils, and miniature frames. The Monastery, Michael Killeen Park, Roundstone, Co. Galway. ✆ 095/35912.

Spiddal Craft Centre   This cluster of craft shops and workshops is located on the outskirts of Spiddal, a picturesque little village. You'll find pottery, weaving, knitwear, jewelry, an art gallery, and a coffee shop for light snacks and lunch. Spiddal, Co. Galway. ✆ 091/553376.

The Northwest

Above County Mayo on the Atlantic coast, extending from the Republic like an index finger along the western border of the North, are counties Sligo, Donegal, and Leitrim.

If you're looking for a landscape of majestic wildness and splendor, **Donegal** is the place to go, though its austere beauty can become rather bleak when the weather turns gray and rainy, as it so often does. Several of Ireland's greatest natural wonders are to be found here, such as the Slieve League cliffs and Horn Head; and the most remote, pristine, and beautiful beaches in the country are tucked into the bays and inlets of Donegal's sharply indented coast.

Like Donegal, the main appeal of County **Sligo** is not in its towns but out in the countryside. The county does possess a wealth of historic sites, though, and fans of Yeats will enjoy visiting the plethora of sites associated with the poet and his writings.

There are a few sites in **Leitrim**—Glencar Waterfall, Dromahair, and Parke's Castle—that can most easily be visited from Sligo town, and for this reason we've included them in this chapter. You'll find more details on Leitrim in "Along the River Shannon's Shores," in chapter 14.

1 Sligo & Yeats Country

136 miles (219km) NE of Shannon Airport, 135 miles (217km) NW of Dublin, 47 miles (76km) NE of Knock, 37 miles (60km) NE of Ballina, 87 miles (140km) NE of Galway, 73 miles (118km) N of Athlone, and 209 miles (337km) N of Cork

Sligo town (population 18,000) is ideally located, nestled as it is in a valley between two mountains, Ben Bulben on the north and Knocknarea on the south. It's more a commercial center than a tourist attraction, however, and has little to recommend itself to the visitor. You'd be well advised to pass through here briefly, exploring instead the countryside surrounding the town. As you'll quickly discover, this is Yeats country, and every hill, rill, cottage, vale, and lake seems to bear a plaque indicating its relation to the poet or his works.

GETTING THERE **Aer Arann** (© 01/814-5240; www.aerarann.ie) operates daily flights into **Sligo Airport,** Strandhill, County Sligo (© 071/68280; www.sligoairport.com), 5 miles (8km) southwest of Sligo town.

Irish Rail, Lord Edward Street, Sligo (© 071/69888), operates daily service into Sligo from Dublin and other points.

Bus Eireann, also pulling into Lord Edward Street (© 071/60066; www.buseireann.ie), operates daily bus service to Sligo from Dublin, Galway, and other points, including Derry in Northern Ireland.

Four major roads lead to Sligo: N4 from Dublin and the east, N17 from Galway and the south, N15 from Donegal to the north, and N16 from County Fermanagh in Northern Ireland.

VISITOR INFORMATION   For information about Sligo and the surrounding area, contact the **North West Tourism Office,** Aras Reddan, Temple Street, Sligo (℃ 071/61201). It's open June to August daily 9am to 8pm; May and September Monday through Saturday from 9am to 6pm; and Monday to Friday 9am to 5pm during the rest of the year. The most comprehensive local Internet source for Sligo can be found at **www.sligo.ie.**

TOWN LAYOUT   Edged by Sligo Bay to the west, Sligo town sits beside the Garavogue River, with most of the town's commercial district on the south bank of the river. **O'Connell Street** is the main north-south artery of the downtown district. The main east-west thoroughfare is **Stephen Street,** which changes its name to Wine Street and then to Lord Edward Street. The **Tourist Office** is in the southwest corner of the town on Temple Street, 2 blocks south of O'Connell Street. Three bridges span the river, but the **Douglas Hyde Bridge,** named for Ireland's first president, is the main link between the two sides.

GETTING AROUND   **By Public Transportation**   There is no public transport in the town of Sligo, but during July and August, **Bus Eireann** (℃ 071/60066) runs from Sligo town to Strandhill and Rosses Point. The fare is 3.80€ ($3.45) round-trip.

By Taxi   Taxis line up looking for fares at the Sligo taxi rank on Quay Street. If you prefer to call a taxi, try **ACE Cabs** (℃ 071/44444), or **O'Mahony Hackney Cabs** (℃ 071/69000).

By Car   You'll need a car to see the sights outside Sligo town. If you need to hire a vehicle locally, try **Avis** at Sligo Airport, Strandhill (℃ 071/68280; www.avis.com); or **Hertz,** also at Sligo Airport (℃ 071/44068; www.hertz.com).

On Foot   The best way to see Sligo town is on foot. Follow the signposted route of the Tourist Trail. The walk takes approximately 90 minutes.

 FAST FACTS: **Sligo**

Emergencies For emergencies, dial ℃ **999.**

Hospital Try **Sligo County Hospital,** The Mall (℃ 071/71111).

Internet Access For local Internet access, try **Cygo Internet Cafe,** 19 O'Connell St. (℃ 071/40082; www.cygo.ie). This long, narrow cafe is reached via an arcade off O'Connell Street. It's open daily from 10am to 7pm, making it a convenient electronic stop. Internet access is 1.25€ ($1.15) for 10 minutes, 1.90€ ($1.75) for 15 minutes, and 3.15€ ($2.90) for half an hour. A slight reduction is offered for students.

Library **County Sligo Library** is located on Stephen Street (℃ 071/42212), and is open Tuesday through Friday from 10am to 5pm, Saturday from 10am to 1pm and 2 to 5pm.

Newspapers & Radio The weekly *Sligo Champion* and *Sligo Weekender* cover most news and entertainment of the area, and the local North West Radio broadcasts from Sligo on FM 102.5 and FM 96.3.

Police The local **Garda Station** is on Pearse Road (℃ 071/42031).

Post Office The **Sligo General Post Office,** Wine Street (℃ 071/42646), is open Monday through Saturday from 9am to 5:30pm.

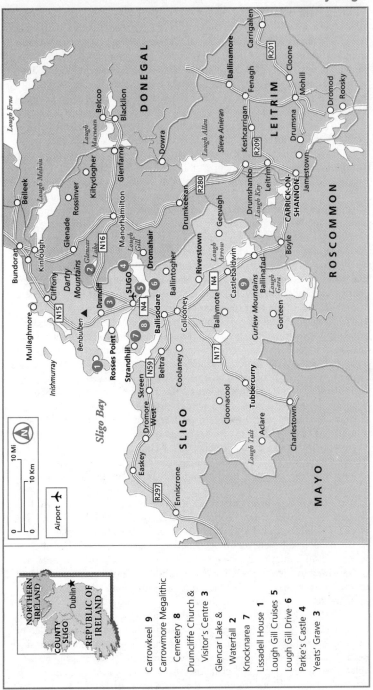

County Sligo

Carrowkeel **9**

Carrowmore Megalithic
 Cemetery **8**

Drumcliffe Church &
 Visitor's Centre **3**

Glencar Lake &
 Waterfall **2**

Knocknarea **7**

Lissadell House **1**

Lough Gill Cruises **5**

Lough Gill Drive **6**

Parke's Castle **4**

Yeats' Grave **3**

SEEING THE SIGHTS

Sligo's great antiquity can be counted in the seemingly numberless grave mounds, standing stones, ring circles, and dolmens still marking its starkly stunning landscape. In fact, County Sligo contains the greatest concentration of megalithic sites in all of Ireland. A fitting place to begin exploring ancient Sligo is at **Carrowmore** (see listing below), a vast Neolithic cemetery once containing perhaps as many as 200 passage tombs, some of which predate Newgrange by 500 years.

From Carrowmore, the Neolithic mountaintop cemetery of **Carrowkeel** is visible in the distant south. One of the best preserved Neolithic cemeteries in Ireland, Carrowkeel is little known and infrequently visited. To get there, take N4 south to Castlebaldwin, about 20 miles (32km) from Sligo town. There's a tourist information center here where you can buy maps and books describing Carrowkeel and other local archaeological remains. The turnoff for Carrowkeel is signposted in Castlebaldwin, adjacent to the information center; from here, continue another 3 miles (5km) or so, following the signs, until you reach a small parking area and the road becomes a grassy track. The tombs are widely dispersed over a series of ridges, with beautiful views of Lough Arrow and the surrounding hills. If you want to see all the tombs, you should plan to spend several hours exploring with a good map, but several are within a short walk of the parking lot. Walk straight uphill from the point where the road turns to a track, and you'll find a group of three tombs, low mounds of stone about 60 feet (18m) across. One has collapsed completely, but the other two have passageways and chambers you can explore. The configuration of the chambers is similar to that at Newgrange in County Meath: a long passage leading to a small room with chambers on either side and another in back. A visit to these tombs, eerily isolated on their high hilltop, is an experience not to be missed.

To the west of Sligo is **Knocknarea** (1,078 ft./328m), on whose summit sits a gigantic unexcavated cairn (grave mound) that's known as Miscaun Meadhbh (Maeve's Mound) even though it predates Maeve, an early Celtic warrior queen who plays a central role in the Tain Bó Cuilnge, the Celtic epic, by millennia. Legend has it that she's buried standing, in full battle gear, spear in hand, facing her Ulster enemies even in death. This extraordinary tomb is 630 feet (192m) around at its base, 80 feet (24m) high, and 100 feet (31m) in diameter, and can be seen for miles.

At the foot of Knocknarea is **Strandhill,** 5 miles (8km) from Sligo town. This delightful resort area stretches out into Sligo Bay, with a sand-duned beach and a patch of land nearby called Coney Island, which is usually credited with lending its name to the New York beach amusement area. Across the bay, about 4 miles (6.5km) north of Sligo town, is another beach resort, **Rosses Point.**

Northwest of Sligo Bay, 4 miles (6.5km) offshore, lies the uninhabited island of **Inishmurray**, containing the haunting ruins of one of Ireland's earliest monastic settlements, which was founded in the 6th century and destroyed by the Vikings in 807. The circular walls of the monastery of St. Molaise contain the remains of several churches, beehive cells, altars, and an assemblage of "cursing stones" once used to bring down ruin on those who presumably deserved it. You should note that conditions often make the crossing inadvisable—even when the day looks fair, a southwest wind or Atlantic groundswells can make for a difficult landing in the island's natural harbor. So, to avoid disappointment be sure to call well in advance, and allow for some flexibility in

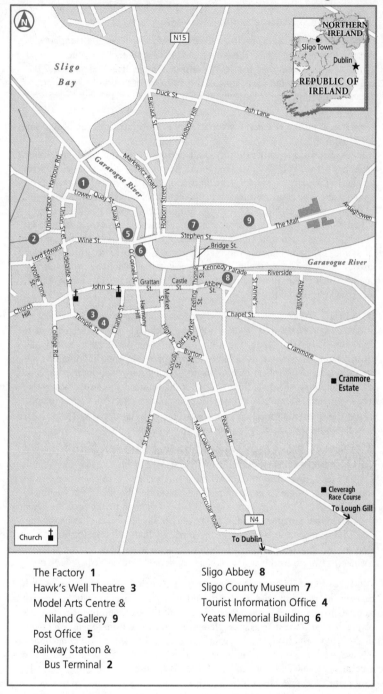

Sligo Town

Sligo Bay

N15

NORTHERN IRELAND
Sligo Town
Dublin
REPUBLIC OF IRELAND

Duck St.
Barack St.
Ash Lane
Holborn Hill
Markievicz Road
Garavogue River
Harbour Rd.
Union Place
Lower Quay St.
Union St.
Quay St.
Holborn Street
Stephen St.
The Mall
Ardaghowen
Wine St.
Bridge St.
O'Connell St.
Garavogue River
Lord Edward St.
Adelaide St.
Kennedy Parade
Riverside
Abbeyville
Wolfe Tone St.
John St.
Grattan St.
Castle St.
Thomas St.
Abbey St.
St Anne's
Church Hill
Temple St.
Charles St.
Harmony Hill
Market
Teeling St.
Chapel St.
Cranmore
College Rd.
High St.
Old Market
Burton St.
Cranmore Estate
Connolly St.
St Joseph's
Mail Coach Rd.
Pearse Rd.
Cleveragh Race Course
To Lough Gill
Circular Road
N4
To Dublin

Church †

The Factory **1**
Hawk's Well Theatre **3**
Model Arts Centre & Niland Gallery **9**
Post Office **5**
Railway Station & Bus Terminal **2**

Sligo Abbey **8**
Sligo County Museum **7**
Tourist Information Office **4**
Yeats Memorial Building **6**

Tips Tours of Sligo Town

The best way to see Sligo Town itself is on foot. Follow the signposted route of the Tourist Trail. The walk takes approximately 90 minutes. From mid-June to September, the **Tourist Office**, Temple Street, Sligo (© 071/ 61201), offers guided tours; contact the office for details and reservations.

accommodating the weather. For conveyance to the island, call **Joe McGowan** (© 071/66267).

In Sligo town, the earliest history can be traced to the ruins of **Sligo Abbey** on Abbey Street. Founded as a Dominican house in 1252 by Maurice Fitzgerald, Earl of Kildare, it was accidentally destroyed by fire in 1414, then rebuilt 2 years later. The choir features a remarkable row of tall, thin lancet windows. The abbey is well worth a visit. For more information, see the listing below.

Many of Sligo's attractions are associated in some way with the poet William Butler Yeats, as you'll note in the places described below. In addition, just over the border in County Leitrim (off N16) is lovely **Glencar Lake,** which stretches eastward for 2 miles (3km) along a verdant valley, highlighted by two waterfalls, one of which rushes downward for 50 feet (15m). Yeats's "The Stolen Child" speaks wondrously of this lake.

IN SLIGO TOWN

Model Arts Centre and Niland Gallery   Although this is a relatively new development in Sligo (opened in 1991), it carries on the Yeatsean literary and artistic traditions. Housed in an 1850 Romanesque-style stone building that was originally a school, it offers nine rooms for touring shows and local exhibits by artists, sculptors, writers, and musicians. In the summer, there are often poetry readings or arts lectures here. A cafe inside the center is open from 10am to 5pm.

The Mall, Sligo. © 071/41405. modelniland@modelart.ie. Free admission. Readings/lectures 6.50€ ($5.90). No credit cards. Tues–Sat 10am–5:30pm; evening events 8pm; dates vary.

Sligo Abbey   Founded as a Dominican house in 1252 by Maurice Fitzgerald, Earl of Kildare, this abbey was accidentally destroyed by fire in 1414, then rebuilt 2 years later. It flourished in medieval times and was the burial place of the kings and princes of Sligo. After many raids and sackings, the abbey was eventually closed in 1641. Much restoration work has been done in recent years, however, and the cloisters are now considered to be outstanding examples of stone carving. The 15th-century altar is one of the few medieval altars still intact in Ireland.

Abbey St., Sligo. © 071/46406. www.heritageireland.ie Admission 2€ ($1.80) adults, 1.25€ ($1.15) seniors, .75€ (70¢) students and children, 5.50€ ($5.00) family. No credit cards. Apr–Oct daily 10am–6pm.

Sligo County Museum ⊛   Housed in a church manse of the mid–19th century, this museum exhibits material of national and local interest dating back to pre-Christian times. One section, devoted to the Yeats family, includes a display of William Butler Yeats's complete works in first editions, poems on broadsheets, letters, and his Nobel Prize for literature (1923), as well as a collection of oils, watercolors, and drawings by Jack B. Yeats and John B. Yeats. There's also a permanent collection of general 20th-century Irish art, including works by Paul Henry and Evie Hone.

Stephen St., Sligo. © 071/714-7190. sligolib@iol.ie. Admission free. Jan–May Tues–Sat 2–4:50pm; June–Sept Tues–Sat 10am–noon and 2–4:50pm.

Yeats Memorial Building   Located in a 19th-century red-brick Victorian building, this memorial contains an extensive library with items of special interest to Yeatsean scholars. The building is also headquarters of the Sligo Art Gallery, which exhibits works by local, national, and international artists; and home to a small tourist information office. The building also houses a full cafe.

Douglas Hyde Bridge, Sligo. ☎ **071/42693** or 071/45847. www.yeats-sligo.com. Free admission. June–Aug, Mon–Fri 10am–5pm. Gallery open year-round.

AROUND COUNTIES SLIGO & LEITRIM

Carrowmore Megalithic Cemetery ★★   Here, at the dead center of the Coolera Peninsula, sits the giant's tomb, a massive passage grave that once had a stone circle of its own. Circling it, and in nearly every instance facing it, were as many as 100 to 200 passage graves, each circled in stone. Tomb 52A, excavated in August 1998, is estimated to be 7,400 years old, making it the earliest known piece of freestanding stone architecture in the world. Circles within circles within circles describe a stone-and-spirit world of the dead whose power touches every visitor who stops to see and consider it—it's one of the great sacred landscapes of the ancient world. The cemetery's interpretive center offers informative exhibits and tours.

Carrowmore Visitors Centre, Co. Sligo. ☎ **071/61534.** Admission 2€ ($1.80) adults, 1.25€ ($1.15) seniors, .75€ (70¢) students and children, 5.50€ ($5.00) family. No credit cards. May–Oct daily 9:30am–5:45pm. From Sligo, signposted on N15; from the south, signposted on N4.

Drumcliffe Church and Visitor's Centre   Five miles (8km) north of Sligo town is Drumcliffe, site of the Church of Ireland cemetery where W.B. Yeats is buried. You'll easily find the poet's grave with the simple headstone bearing the dramatic epitaph he composed: "Cast a cold eye on life, on death; Horseman, pass by." This cemetery also contains the ruins of an early Christian monastery founded by St. Columba in A.D. 745. The visitor center, opened in June 1999, has audiovisual displays explaining the history of Drumcliffe and St. Columba. The Church itself has also been restored and in the summer, classical music concerts are held there. Note that while there is an admission fee to the visitor center, access to Yeats's grave itself remains free of charge.

Drumcliffe, Co. Sligo. ☎ **071/44956.** www.drumcliffe.ie. Admission 2.60€ ($2.40) adults, 2€ ($1.80) seniors, 1.25€ ($1.15) children, 5.50€ ($5.00) family. May–Oct Mon–Sat 8:30am–6pm, Sun 1–6pm; Nov–Apr Mon–Sat 9am–5pm, Sun 1–5pm. N15 to Drumcliffe.

Lake Isle of Innisfree

I shall arise and go now, and go to Innisfree,
And a small cabin build there, of clay and wattles made;
Nine bean rows will I have there, a hive for the honey bee,
And live alone in the bee-loud glade.
And I will have some peace there, for peace comes dropping slow,
Dropping from the veils of the morning to where the cricket sings;
There midnight's all a-glimmer, and noon a purple glow,
And evening full of the linnet's wings.
I will arise and go now, for always night and day
I hear lake water lapping with low sounds by the shore;
While I stand on the roadway, or on the pavements gray,
I hear it in the deep heart's core.

—William Butler Yeats

Lissadell House   On the shores of Sligo Bay, this large neoclassical building was another of Yeats's favorite haunts. Dating from 1830, it has long been the home of the Gore-Booth family, including Yeats's friends Eva Gore-Booth, a fellow poet, and her sister Constance, who became the Countess Markievicz after marrying a Polish count. She took part in the 1916 Irish Rising and was the first woman elected to the British House of Commons and the first woman cabinet member in the Irish Dáil. The house is full of such family memorabilia as the travel diaries of Sir Robert Gore-Booth, who mortgaged the estate to help the poor during the famine. At the core of the house is a dramatic two-story hallway lined with Doric columns leading to a double staircase of Kilkenny marble.

Off the main Sligo-Donegal Rd. (N15), Drumcliffe, Co. Sligo. ✆ 071/63150. Admission 5€ ($3.45) adults. June to mid-Sept, Mon–Sat 10:30am–12:15pm and 2–4:15pm.

Parke's Castle ⭐   On the north side of the Lough Gill Drive (see below), Parke's Castle stands out as a lone outpost amid the natural tableau of lake view and woodland scenery. Named after an English family that gained possession of it during the 1620 plantation of Leitrim, this castle was originally the stronghold of the O'Rourke clan, rulers of the kingdom of Breffni. It exemplifies the 17th-century fortified manor house and has been beautifully restored using Irish oak and traditional craftsmanship. In the visitor center, informative exhibits and a truly splendid audiovisual show illustrate the history of the castle and introduce visitors to the rich and diverse sites of interest in the surrounding area, making this an ideal place from which to launch your own local explorations. As icing on the cake, the tearoom offers fresh and exceptionally enticing pastries.

Lough Gill Dr., Co. Leitrim. ✆ 071/64149. www.heritageireland.ie. Admission 2.60€ ($2.40) adults, 2€ ($1.80) seniors, 1.25€ ($1.15) students and children, 6.50€ ($5.90) family. Mid-Mar–Oct daily 10am–6pm.

THE LOUGH GILL DRIVE ⭐⭐

This 26-mile (42km) drive-yourself tour around Lough Gill is well signposted. Head 1¼ miles (2km) south of town and follow the signs for **Lough Gill,** the beautiful lake that figured so prominently in Yeats's writings. Within 2 miles (3km) you'll be on the lower edge of the shoreline. Among the sights to see are **Dooney Rock,** with its own nature trail and lakeside walk (inspiration for the poem "Fiddler of Dooney"); the **Lake Isle of Innisfree,** made famous in Yeats's poetry and in song; and the **Hazelwood Sculpture Trail,** unique to Sligo, a forest walk along the shores of Lough Gill with 13 wood sculptures en route.

You can drive the whole lakeside circuit in one sweep in less than an hour, or you can stop at the east end and visit **Dromahair,** a delightful village on the River Bonet. The road along Lough Gill's upper shore brings you back to the northern end of Sligo town. Continue north on the main road (N15) and you'll see on the right the profile of graceful and green **Ben Bulben,** 1,730 feet (527m) tall, one of the Dartry Mountains.

A SIGHTSEEING CRUISE

Lough Gill Cruises   Cruise on Lough Gill and the Garavogue River aboard the 72-passenger *Wild Rose* waterbus, as the poetry of Yeats is recited. Trips to the Lake Isle of Innisfree are also scheduled. An onboard bar is open for refreshments.

Blue Lagoon, Riverside, Sligo. ✆ 071/64266. Lough Gill cruise, 10€ ($9.10) adults, 5€ ($4.55) children over age 10. June–Sept.

OUTDOOR PURSUITS

BEACHES   For walking, jogging, or swimming, there are safe sandy beaches with promenades at **Strandhill, Rosses Point,** and **Enniscrone** on the Sligo Bay coast.

BICYCLING   With its lakes and woodlands, Yeats Country is particularly good biking territory. To rent a bike, contact **Gary's Cycles Shop,** Quay Street, Sligo (© **071/45418**); the rate is 13€ ($12) per day.

FISHING   Boats, with or without guides, are available for hire on request at **The Blue Lagoon Pub,** Riverside, Sligo. Contact Peter Henry or Peter Burns at © **071/45407** or 071/44040.

GOLF   With its seascapes, mountain valleys, and lakesides, County Sligo is known for challenging golf courses. Leading the list is **County Sligo Golf Club,** Rosses Point Road, Rosses Point (© **071/77134;** cosligo@iol.ie), overlooking Sligo Bay under the shadow of Ben Bulben mountain. It's an 18-hole, par-71 championship seaside links famed for its wild, natural terrain and constant winds; greens fees are 51€ ($46) on weekdays and 63€ ($58) on weekends.

Five miles (8km) west of Sligo town is **Strandhill Golf Club,** Strandhill (© **071/68188;** strandhillgc@eircom.net), a seaside par-69 course with greens fees of 32€ ($29) on weekdays and 38€ ($35) on weekends.

Located in the southwestern corner of the county, about 25 miles (40km) from Sligo town and overlooking Sligo Bay, the **Enniscrone Golf Club,** Enniscrone (© **096/36297;** http://homepage.eircom.net/~enniscronegolf), is a seaside par-72 course with greens fees of 38€ ($35) weekdays, 51€ ($46) weekends.

HORSEBACK RIDING   An hour's or a day's riding on the beach, in the countryside, or over mountain trails can be arranged at **Sligo Riding Centre,** Carrowmore (© **071/61353**); or at **Woodlands Equestrian Centre,** Loughill, Lavagh, Tubbercurry, County Sligo (© **071/84207**). Riding charges average 17€ ($15) per hour.

ACCOMMODATIONS YOU CAN AFFORD
IN SLIGO TOWN

Cillard   Mrs. Breid Dillon's modern farmhouse is in a scenic area just 2½ miles (4km) from Sligo, close to the Carrowmore megalithic tombs. There's a garden for guests, and meat, vegetables, and fruit fresh from the farm turn up at table. Mrs. Dillon is a warm, welcoming hostess, always eager to help with touring plans.

Carrowmore, Sligo, Co. Sligo. © 071/68201. 3 units, 2 with shower only. 51€ ($46) double. 20% discount for children sharing with an adult. Rates include full breakfast. No credit cards. Closed Nov–Apr. *In room:* Hair dryer.

Cruckawn House *(Kids)*   Readers have been full of praise for Mrs. Maeve Walsh and her modern two-story house just outside town. The recently redecorated guest rooms are fitted with built-in bookshelf/headboards, and most have good views of the Ox Mountains. There's a sun lounge, games room, and laundry facilities for guest use. Cruckawn sits on its own grounds (with a large garden) overlooking a golf course that visitors may use. Babysitting can be arranged. Meals are superb, and there's a wine license.

Ballymote-Boyle Rd., Tubbercurry, Co. Sligo. ©/fax 071/85188. www.sligotourism.com. cruckawn@ esatclear.ie. 5 units. 51€ ($46) double. 33% reduction for children sharing with an adult. Rates include full breakfast. Dinner 20€ ($18). MC, V. Paved parking lot. **Amenities:** Lounge; babysitting; laundry.

Dunfore Farmhouse   Ita Leyden, winner of two recent tourism awards, is an outgoing and energetic hostess who has done a great job of making this recently renovated farmhouse a pleasant base for exploring Sligo. Guest rooms have firm beds and fine views of the surrounding countryside (some across the bay to Rosses Point, others to Ben Bulben or the nearby Lissadell Wood). Breakfast is often enlivened by Ita's ardent recitation of her favorite Irish poetry, and you'll find literary touches throughout the house, from portraits of Irish writers to a painting by Yeats's brother Jack. When the weather is good, visitors can arrange a tour of the local coast in the Leydens' small motorboat, docked at nearby Raghly Harbor. If you'd like to rent the entire house by the week or month, inquire well in advance.

Ballinful, Co. Sligo. ✆ 071/63137. Fax 071/63574. 4 units. 40€ ($36) single; 60€ ($54) double. 25% discount for children. Rates include full breakfast. MC, V. Free parking. Closed Nov–Feb. Turn off N15 at Drumcliffe. In room: Tea/coffeemaker.

Rathnashee   Rathnashee (it means "Fort of the Fairies") is the home of Tess and Sean Haughey. This is the kind of place where guests often wind up sitting around the table for long conversations in which the Haugheys share their extensive knowledge of what to see in Sligo. They also have one of the best private libraries in town, and can arrange sightseeing tours with archaeologists. Tess serves traditional Irish food and homemade preserves. The modern bungalow has beautiful antique furnishings in the lounge and dining room, and all guest rooms are nonsmoking. When making an advance booking ask about possible discounts for holders of this book. Advance booking is requested for dinner.

Teesan, Donegal Rd. (N15), Sligo, Co. Sligo. ✆ 071/43376 or 087/220-4423 (mobile). Fax 071/42283. 3 units, 2 with bathroom. 32€ ($29) single without bathroom, 36€ ($32) single with bathroom; 46€ ($41) double without bathroom, 51€ ($46) double with bathroom. Rates include full breakfast. Dinner 18€ ($17). AE, V. 2 miles (3km) from the town center. **Amenities:** Lounge.

Renate Central House   This small, gabled B&B is surely one of the most conveniently located in Sligo town, within easy walking distance of the town center. Hosts John and Ursula Leyden offer five attractive guest rooms.

9 Upper John St., Sligo, Co. Sligo. ✆ 071/62014. 6 units, 3 with bathroom. 48€ ($44) double. Rates include full breakfast. No credit cards. Off-street parking. In room: TV, tea/coffeemaker, hair dryer.

Ross House   This farmhouse is the home of Nicholas and Oriel Hill-Wilkinson, both exceptionally voluble and generous hosts. Nicholas runs a beef farm, and can often be seen trundling in on a tractor or tinkering with a piece of machinery in his elaborate workshop. Oriel has been operating a B&B here for many years, and this experience shows in many thoughtful details—interesting books in most of the rooms, truly comfortable beds, and a tray of freshly baked scones and tea most evenings. The bedrooms in the main house are moderate in size and none have a private bathroom; two bathrooms are shared between the four rooms. Two rooms in a recent addition at the back are more spacious; both have private bathrooms and a view west across the fields.

Riverstown, Co. Sligo. ✆/fax 071/65140. 6 units, 2 with bathroom (shower only). 58€ ($53) double. Rates include full breakfast. MC, V. Turn off N4 at Drumfin, follow signs 1 mile (1.5km) past Riverstown.

Rossli House   Mrs. Noreen Donoghue's pleasant bungalow is in a peaceful location, convenient to golf, fishing, and pubs that feature Irish music. Mrs. Donoghue is active in local tourism, and has many helpful suggestions for sightseeing and activities in the region. The comfortable guest rooms sport beds with electric blankets. You can read Noreen's monthly column on www.irish poetsworldwide.com.

Doocastle, Tubbercurry, Co. Sligo. ✆/fax 071/85099 or 086/8468144. www.tubbercurrybandb.com. 4 units. 38.50€ ($35) single; 51€ ($46) double. 33% reduction for children. Dinner 19€ ($17). MC, V. 4½ miles (7km) from Tubbercurry. The turnoff to the B&B is 3½ miles (5.5km) outside Tubbercurry on the Ballymote Road (signposted on the right). **Amenities:** Lounge; laundry. In room: Tea/coffemaker, hair dryer.

Tree Tops   Mrs. Doreen MacEvilly is the hostess of this very attractive B&B, about a 5-minute walk from the town center. It's located about 100 meters off N4 (the road to Lough Gill, Inisfree, and Holy Well), making it an ideal base for touring. All five of the comfortable bedrooms are fitted with orthopedic beds. The entire house is nonsmoking.

Cleveragh Rd., Sligo, Co. Sligo. ℂ **071/60160.** Fax 071/62301. www.sligobandb.com. 5 units. 35€ ($32) single; 58€ ($53) double. 20% reduction for children. Rates include full breakfast. AE, MC, V. Nonsmoking house. *In room:* TV, TEL, hair dryer, tea/coffeemaker.

Union Farm   Union Farm is a 300-year-old farmhouse with low lintels and thick walls, evoking a time when "bed-and-breakfast" still meant a simple, comfortable room and a warm welcome. The house is situated among bucolic green hills—although the approach to the farm involves weaving through a small light industrial area, this distinctly urban setting dissipates before your arrival at the house itself. Guest rooms look out over fields that are either given over to hay or large ruminants; the rooms are modest, clean, and newly carpeted. A common bathroom has only a tub, so if a shower is a necessity, be sure to request a room with private bathroom. Breakfast takes place in a bright dining room looking out on host Tess Lang's well tended, colorful garden.

Collooney, Co. Sligo. ℂ **071/67136.** 5 units, 2 with bathroom (shower only). 32€ ($29) single; 46€ ($41) double without bathroom, 51€ ($46) double with bathroom. Rates include full breakfast. No credit cards. Closed mid-Oct to Feb.

Urlar House   Named one of Ireland's 300 best B&Bs, Mrs. Healy's large, centrally heated farmhouse sits right next to Ben Bulben mountain. There is beautiful scenery all around the 17th-century house, which is registered in Country Inns and Historical Houses of Ireland. You can rent bicycles to explore the surrounding countryside, take out a horse from the stables, or try an organized walk.

Drumcliffe, Co. Sligo. ℂ **071/63110.** urlarhouse@eircom.net. 5 units. 56€ ($51) double. 25% reduction for children sharing with an adult. Rates include full breakfast. No credit cards. Free parking. Closed Oct–Mar. Just over a mile (2km) outside Drumcliffe on N15. *In room:* TV, hair dryer.

WORTH A SPLURGE

Temple House ✦✦✦   This vast Georgian mansion is beautifully situated in 1,000 acres of woods and parkland, overlooking a lake and the ruins of a Knights Templar castle, for which the place is named. The house has seen better days and is a bit frayed at the edges, but impresses with the sheer magnitude of its spaces and the antiquity of its eclectic furnishings. The grand, sweeping staircase in the foyer is magnificent. The Percevals have lived here since 1665, and there have been many memorable events within these woods and walls since then; such tales are often recounted by Sandy Perceval, who brings life to the gallery of venerable family portraits as he tells the stories of his ancestors. Sandy and his wife, Deb, run the place with a sense of casual elegance and affable unpretentiousness. The two double rooms in the front of the house are particularly stately and have canopied beds; book them well in advance. The walled garden is a short walk from the house and supplies vegetables for the excellent evening meals.

Two caveats: The atmosphere is more intimate than you might want, much like a house party; guests meet for drinks in the drawing room and dine together at a communal table. Also, Sandy has an acute chemical sensitivity and asks guests to avoid the use of cosmetic products in the house, such as perfume, aftershave, scented lotions, or hair spray.

Ballymote, Co. Sligo. ✆ 071/83329. Fax 071/83808. www.templehouse.ie. 6 units. 80€ ($83) single; 130€ ($135) double. Rates include full breakfast. Dinner 30€ ($29). AE, MC, V. Free parking. Closed Dec to Easter. Use of cosmetic product not permitted.

GREAT DEALS ON DINING
IN & AROUND SLIGO TOWN

Beezies PUB GRUB   Even if you're not hungry, Beezies is worth a visit, if only for a drink or a look around. The turn-of-the-century marble counters, bar partitions of Tiffany glass, and lamps with tulip-shaped shades give a real 19th-century look to the place. The bar food is good and filling, with simple lunches of soup and sandwiches.

45 O'Connell St. ✆ 071/43031. Reservations not required. Lunch under 7€ ($6.35). AE, MC, V. Mon–Sat noon–3:30pm. Closed Good Friday, Christmas Day.

Hargadon's ✦ PUB GRUB   For years, Hargadon's has been a local favorite simply because, as the Irish say, they pull a good pint and the craic is mighty. Well, now they've extended the atmospheric old pub to accommodate large crowds who show up for excellent pub grub. The amazing thing about it is that the expansion has been so skillfully done that you'd swear the new rooms had been there as long as the original front pub—it's a lovely conglomeration of snugs, flagstone floors, and wooden counters. As for the food, it outshines other bar food by far, with specialties such as smoked salmon, country baked mushrooms, ratatouille, and pork Stroganoff. Be sure to sample the whiskey cake (yum).

O'Connell St. ✆ 071/70933. Bar food under 10€ ($9.10). No credit cards. Mon–Sat 9am–5pm (bar open regular bar hours).

AROUND SLIGO

Killoran's Traditional Restaurant/Lounge SEAFOOD   Service by owners Anne and Tommie Killoran is pleasant and personal in this restaurant and bar/lounge. Fresh local salmon is a specialty, along with steaks and chicken dishes. Antiques convey a traditional theme—old butter churns, lamps, and commodes grace the walls. There are quick snacks as well as full meals, and the prices are good. There are occasional music sessions, especially during the town's music festival in July.

Teeling St., Tubbercurry, Co. Sligo. ✆ 071/85111 or 071/85679. Reservations not required. Lunch 7.50€ ($6.80); dinner 13€ ($12). AE, MC, V. Apr–Oct daily 9am–9pm; Oct–Mar daily 9am–6pm.

Stanford's Inn Pub and Restaurant TRADITIONAL IRISH   Set in the pretty little village of Dromahair, just 10 miles (16km) southeast of Sligo, Stanford's is a fourth-generation family-run inn, pub, and restaurant. The atmospheric old pub has a warm, cozy feel. There are several comfortable bars with open fires, and there's a delightful blend of old stone walls, vintage pictures and posters, oil lamps, and tweed-covered furnishings. The pub food here is good. The restaurant, whose windows look out onto the lovely River Bonet, specializes in sea trout and other seafood from local waters, as well as traditional meat and poultry dishes.

Dromahair, Co. Leitrim. ✆ 071/64140. Reservations recommended for restaurant in winter months. Bar food 7.50€–13€ ($6.80–$12); fixed-price lunch 13€ ($12); fixed-price dinner 25€ ($23). MC, V. Bar daily 10:30am–10pm; restaurant daily 8am–9pm.

SHOPPING

Most Sligo shops are open Monday to Saturday from 9am to 6pm, although some may have extended hours during July and August, according to demand.

The Cat & the Moon *(Finds)*   This shop offers uniquely designed crafts from throughout Ireland, ranging from beeswax candles and baskets to modern art, metal and ceramic work, wood-turning, handweaving, Celtic jewelry, and furniture. An expanded gallery includes a large variety of paintings, limited-edition prints, and, occasionally, sculpture. There is a large jewelry workshop on the premises, and much of the jewelry on display is made in-house. The Cat and the Moon also mounts exhibitions regularly at The Factory, a local gallery and performance space—ask while you're here whether there's anything on at the moment. 4 Castle St., Sligo. *C* 071/43686. www.thecatandthemoon.com.

Innisfree Crystal   Taking its name from the Lough Gill island immortalized in Yeats's poem "The Lake Isle of Innisfree," this small crystal factory produces individually hand-cut glassware such as punch bowls, decanters, vases, and bowls. Each piece is hand-signed by one of the three craftspeople. You can watch them work or browse in the showroom. The workshop is open Saturdays from 10am to 1pm in the summer months. The Bridge, Dublin Rd. (N4), Collooney, Co. Sligo. *C* 071/67340. www.innisfreecrystal.com.

Kate's Kitchen   Step into Kate's to savor the aromas of potpourri, soaps, and natural oils, as well as Crabtree & Evelyn products. The shop also has an outstanding delicatessen section, with gourmet meats (Kate's glazed ham is a favorite), cheeses, salads, patés, and breads baked on the premises, all ideal makings for a picnic by Lough Gill. Don't miss the handmade Irish chocolates and preserves, and the locally made organic pastas. 3 Castle St., Sligo, Co. Sligo. *C* 071/43022. kateskitchen@eircom.net.

Keohanes Bookshop *(Kids)*   Keohanes is a large bookstore, part of a three-store chain (it also has branches in Galway and Ballina). Its selection of Irish history and literature is quite extensive—it's a good place to pick up a volume of Yeats, a critical review of his work, or a guide to local Yeats sites. For those with children, there is also a small alcove dedicated to storybooks. Castle St., Sligo. *C*/fax 071/42597. bookshop@iol.ie.

M. Quirke *(Finds)*   Michael Quirke started out as a butcher, but a few years ago he traded his cleaver for wood-carving tools and transformed his butcher shop into a craft studio. Step inside and watch as he transforms chunks of native timber into Ireland's heroes of mythology, from Sligo's Queen Maeve to Cu Chulainn, Oisin, and other folklore characters. The shop is open Monday to Saturday from 9:15am to 1pm and 2:30 to 6:30pm. Wine St., Sligo, Co. Sligo. *C* 071/42624.

Music Room   This small cottagelike store draws you with the sounds of Irish music. It's a great spot to purchase Irish musical instruments and accessories. A sister shop in the same building, the **Record Room** (*C* 071/43748), offers cassettes, CDs, videos, and records. Grattan St., Sligo. *C* 071/44765.

Sligo Crystal and Giftware   This workshop is noted for its personalized engraving of such items as family crests on mirrors or glassware. The craftspeople also produce hand-cut crystal candlesticks, glasses, and curio items such as crystal bells and scent bottles. Crystal pieces may be cut to a pattern of your creation or choice. You can watch the crystal being cut on a tour if you call in advance. 2 Hyde Bridge, Sligo, Co. Sligo. *C* 071/43440.

Wehrly Bros. Ltd. Established in 1875, this is one of Sligo's oldest shops, noted for a fine selection of jewelry and watches as well as cold-cast bronze sculptures of Irish figures, silverware, Claddagh rings, Waterford crystal, Belleek china, and Galway crystal. 3 O'Connell St., Sligo, Co. Sligo. ⓒ **071/42252.**

SLIGO AFTER DARK

In addition to the information below, be sure to consult *The Sligo Champion,* which carries notices of current goings-on in town and around the area.

THE PUB SCENE

Hargadon's More than a century old, this is the most atmospheric bar in the center of the downtown area. It used to be a grocery shop as well, as you'll see if you glance at the shelves on the right. The decor is a melange of dark-wood walls, mahogany counters, stone floors, colored glass, old barrels and bottles, snugs, and alcoves lined with early prints of Sligo. There's never any music in this dim, honey-brown enclave; this is a pub for conversation and for slowly sipping creamy pints of Guinness. 4 O'Connell St., Sligo, Co. Sligo. ⓒ **071/70933.**

Stanford's Village Inn If you're driving around Lough Gill from Sligo, this 160-year-old pub is a great midway stop for a drink or a snack. The decor is a delightful blend of old stone walls, vintage pictures and posters, oil lamps, and tweed-covered furnishings. Main St., Dromahair, Co. Leitrim. ⓒ **071/64140.**

The Thatch This pub, which was established in 1638 as a coaching inn, is about 5 miles (8km) south of Sligo on the main road. As its name suggests, it has a fully thatched roof and a whitewashed exterior, with a country-cottage motif inside. Irish traditional music is usually on tap from 9pm on Thursday all year and Tuesday to Friday in July and August. Dublin-Sligo road (N4), Ballisodare, Co. Sligo. ⓒ **071/67288.**

Yeats's Tavern Yeats's Tavern, located across the road from the famous churchyard where William Butler Yeats is buried, honors the poet's memory with quotations from his works as well as photos, prints, and murals. A modern tavern and restaurant with a copper-and-wood decor, it's a convenient place to stop for a snack or a full meal when touring Yeats country. Ballyshannon road (N15), Drumcliffe, Co. Sligo. ⓒ **071/63117.**

THE PERFORMING ARTS

The Factory This is home to Sligo's award-winning Blue Raincoat Theatre Company, the only professional Irish acting company, apart from the Abbey in Dublin and the Druid in Galway, to own its own theatre, which was completely renovated in 1999. During July and August, the Blue Raincoat Theatre Company often presents lunchtime performances of Yeats's plays, as well as other Sligo-related productions. Lower Quay St., Sligo. ⓒ **071/70431.** Tickets under 13€ ($12). Most shows at 8pm.

Hawk's Well Theatre The premier stage of Ireland's northwest region, this modern 350-seat theater presents a varied program of drama, comedy, ballet, opera, and concerts of modern and traditional music. It derives its name from *At the Hawk's Well,* a one-act play by Yeats. The theater occasionally produces shows, but mostly books visiting professional and local companies. Temple St., Sligo, Co. Sligo. ⓒ **071/61518.** Tickets average 9€, $8.00). Mon–Sat box office 10am–6pm; most shows 8pm.

2 Donegal Town

138 miles (222km) NW of Dublin, 176 miles (283km) NE of Shannon Airport, 41 miles (66km) NE of Sligo, 43 miles (69km) SW of Derry, 112 miles (180km) W of Belfast, 127 miles (205km) NE of Galway, 250 miles (403km) N of Cork, and 253 miles (407km) NE of Killarney

Situated on the estuary of the River Eske on Donegal Bay, Donegal town is a very walkable little metropolis (population 2,000) that's a pivotal gateway for touring the county. As recently as the 1940s, the town's central **Diamond** was used as a market for trading livestock and goods, but today the marketing is more in the form of tweeds and tourist goods. The Diamond is dominated by a 25-foot (7.5m) high obelisk erected as a memorial to the four early 17th-century Irish clerics from the local abbey who wrote *The Annals of Ireland,* the first recorded history of Gaelic Ireland.

GETTING THERE **Aer Arann** (© 01/814-5240; www.aerarann.ie) and **Aer Lingus** (© 01/886-8888; www.aerlingus.ie) operate regularly scheduled flights from Dublin to **Donegal Airport,** Carrickfinn, Kincasslagh, County Donegal (© 075/48284; www.donegalairport.ie), about 40 miles (64km) northwest of Donegal town on the Atlantic coast.

Bus Eireann (© 074/21309; www.buseireann.ie) operates daily bus service to Donegal Town to and from Dublin, Derry, Sligo, Galway, and other points. All tickets are issued on the bus. The pickup and boarding point is in front of the Abbey Hotel on The Diamond.

Additionally, **McGeehan's Coaches** (© 075/46150; www.mgbus.com) operates multiple daily buses between Donegal and Dublin, leaving from the Garda Station opposite the Donegal Tourist Office. Between Galway and Donegal (via Ballyshannon, Bundoran, and Sligo), there is at least one daily private coach operated by **Feda O'Donnell** (© 075/48114 in Donegal and © 091/761656 in Galway; www.fedaodonnell.com).

If you're driving from the south, Donegal is reached via N15 from Sligo or A46 or A47 from Northern Ireland; from the east and north, it's N15 and N56; from the west, take N56.

VISITOR INFORMATION The **Donegal Tourist Office,** Quay Street, Donegal (© 073/21148), is open year-round: June and August Monday to Saturday 9am to 8pm, Sunday 9am to 5pm; September to May Monday to Thursday 9am to 5pm and Friday 10am to 5pm. For a wealth of online tourist information, the best three websites are **www.goireland.com/donegal/,** **www.donegal.ie,** and **www.donegaltown.ie.**

TOWN LAYOUT Donegal town, which sits to the east of the River Eske, is laid out around a triangular central mall or market area called "The Diamond." **Main Street** and **Upper Main Street,** which form the prime commercial strip, extend in a northeast direction from The Diamond.

GETTING AROUND **By Public Transportation** Easily walkable, Donegal has no local bus service within the town. If you need a taxi, call **McGroary Cabs** (© 073/35240) or **Marley Taxis** (© 074/33333).

By Car If you drive into Donegal, there is free parking along the Quay beside the tourist office and off Main Street.

On Foot Follow the signposted walking tour of Donegal town; a booklet outlining the walk is available at the tourist office and most bookshops.

FAST FACTS: Donegal

Drugstores Two good local choices are **Begley's Pharmacy,** on The Diamond (© **073/21232**), and **Kelly's Pharmacy,** also on The Diamond (© **073/21031**).

Hospital **Donegal District Hospital** is located on Upper Main Street (© **073/21019**).

Library **Donegal Library,** on Mountcharles Road (© **073/21105**), is open Monday, Wednesday, and Friday from 3 to 6pm and Saturday from 11am to 1pm and 2 to 6pm.

Police The local **Garda Station** is located on Quay Street (© **073/21021**).

Post Office The **Donegal Post Office** on Tirconnail Street (© **073/21001**) is open Monday, Tuesday, and Thursday to Saturday from 9am to 5:30pm and Wednesday from 9:30am to 5:30pm.

SEEING THE SIGHTS

Lough Derg filled with many islands, lies about 10 miles (16km) east of Donegal. Legend has it that St. Patrick spent 40 days and 40 nights fasting in a cavern at this secluded spot, and since then it has been revered as a place of penance and pilgrimage. From June 1 to August 15, thousands of Irish people take turns coming to Lough Derg to do penance for 3 days at a time, remaining awake and eating nothing but tea and toast. It's considered one of the most rigorous pilgrimages in all of Christendom. To reach the lake, take R232 to Pettigo, then R233 for 5 miles (8km).

County Donegal Railway Restoration Society Heritage Centre This center houses displays dealing with County Donegal's narrow-gauge railway, which originally extended for 125 miles (201km) throughout all of County Donegal but ceased operation by 1960 (though restoration is planned; the hope is to restore a short section of the railway running from the Centre). The current displays include photographs, artifacts, posters, tickets, and equipment.

The Old Station House, Tyrconnell St., Donegal. © **073/22655**. Admission 2.60€ ($2.40) adults, 1.25€ ($1.15) children, 6.50€ ($5.90) family (2 adults, 2 children). June–Sept daily 9am–5:30pm; Oct–May Mon–Fri 9am–5pm.

Donegal Castle ✦ Built in the 15th century beside the River Eske, this magnificent castle was once the chief stronghold for the O'Donnells, a powerful Donegal clan. In the 17th century, during the Plantation period, it came into the possession of Sir Basil Brook, who added an extension with 10 gables, a large bay window, and smaller mullioned windows in Jacobean style. The standing remains of the castle were beautifully restored in 1996. Free 25-minute guided tours are available.

Castle St., Donegal. © **073/22405**. www.heritageireland.ie. Admission 4€ ($3.65) adults, 2.60€ ($2.40) seniors, 1.60€ ($1.45) students and children, 9.50€ ($8.65) family. Mid-March to Oct daily 10am–6pm.

The Friary of Donegal ✦ Often mistakenly referred to as The Abbey, this Franciscan house was founded in 1474 by the first Red Hugh O'Donnell and his wife, Nuala O'Brien of Munster. It was generously endowed by the O'Donnell family and became an important center of religion and learning. Great gatherings of clergy and lay leaders assembled here in 1539. It was from

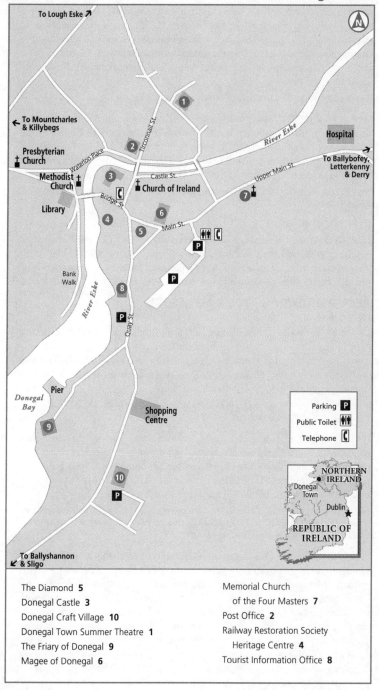

Donegal Town

To Lough Eske ↗

To Mountcharles & Killbegs ←

River Eske

Hospital

Presbyterian Church

Waterloo Place

Castle St.

Upper Main St.

To Ballybofey, Letterkenny & Derry →

Methodist Church

Church of Ireland

Library

Bridge St.

Main St.

Bank Walk

River Eske

Quay St.

Donegal Bay

Pier

Shopping Centre

To Ballyshannon & Sligo ↙

Parking **P**
Public Toilet **♟**
Telephone **C**

NORTHERN IRELAND
Donegal Town
Dublin ★
REPUBLIC OF IRELAND

this friary that some of the scholars undertook to salvage old Gaelic manuscripts and compile *The Annals of the Four Masters* (1632–36). Unfortunately, little remains now of its glory days, except some impressive ruins of a church and a cloister. The house is located on the grounds of the Franciscan Centre of Peace and Reconciliation, on an appropriately peaceful spot where the River Eske meets Donegal Bay.

The Quay, Donegal. Free admission; continual access.

Memorial Church of the Four Masters　Perched on a small hill overlooking the town, this Catholic church is officially known as St. Patrick's Church of the Four Masters. It's of fairly recent vintage, built in 1935 in an Irish Romanesque style of red granite from nearby Barnesmore. The church is dedicated to the four men who produced *The Annals of Ireland*. Its grounds are private.

Upper Main St., Donegal. ✆ **073/21026**. Free admission; donations welcome. Mon–Fri 8am–6pm; Sat–Sun 7:30am–7:30pm.

OUTDOOR PURSUITS

FISHING　For advice and equipment for fishing in Lough Eske and other local waters, contact **Doherty's Fishing Tackle,** Main Street (✆ **073/21119**). This shop stocks a wide selection of flies, reels, bait, and fishing poles. It's open year-round Monday through Saturday from 9am to 6pm; closed 1 to 2pm for lunch.

ACCOMMODATIONS YOU CAN AFFORD
IN TOWN

Castle View House　Mrs. Tessie Timoney's bright and cheerful home is a good Donegal base, just steps away from the town center, and true to its name—looking out to the castle across the river. There are two twin-bedded rooms and one family room with a double and two twin beds. There are almost always peat fires blazing in the living room and dining room.

Waterloo Place, Donegal, Co. Donegal. ✆ **073/22100**. 4 units, none with bathroom. 41€ ($37) double. Rates include full breakfast. No credit cards.

Lyndale　Lyndale is a split-level bungalow located just off the coast road (N56). Mrs. Marie Campbell, the hostess, has drawn high praise from our readers for her friendly hospitality, as well as for her home-baked soda bread and scones. Guests are served tea and/or coffee each evening. The comfortable guest rooms all have electric blankets, and there's a garden and patio for guest's use.

Doonan, Donegal, Co. Donegal. ✆ **073/21873**. www.inet-sec.com/lyndale.htm. 4 units, 3 with bathroom (2 with shower only). 43€–48€ ($39–$44) double. 20% reduction for children sharing with an adult. MC, V. Closed Nov–Mar. *In room:* TV, tea/coffeemaker, hair dryer.

Riverside House　This attractive home is just across the River Eske from Donegal Castle on a quiet residential terrace only a short walk from the center of town. Mrs. Kathleen Curristan welcomes guests here, and her comfortable guest rooms are decorated in cheerful colors. There's one large family room with a double and two twin beds. The lounge's wide front windows frame views of the river and castle, and its piano is often in use by guests or by the Curristans. Nonsmoking bedrooms are available on request.

Waterloo Place, Donegal, Co. Donegal. ✆/fax **073/21083**. kay@eircom.net. 5 units. 32€ ($29) single; 52€ ($47) double. 10% reduction for children. Rates include full breakfast. No credit cards.

IN NEARBY COUNTY DONEGAL

Ardeevin *(Value)*　This dormer bungalow sits five miles (8km) outside Donegal town, on a rise overlooking Lough Eske and the Bluestack Mountains. All the beautifully furnished guest rooms offer views of Lough Eske and the surrounding woods. Mrs. Mary McGinty is a charming hostess and offers her guests an especially warm welcome.

Lough Eske, Barnesmore, Co. Donegal. ℭ/fax **073/21790**. http://members.tripod.com/~Ardeevin/. 6 units. 40€ ($36) single; 55€–65€ ($50–$59) double. 20% reduction for children. Rates include full breakfast. No credit cards. Closed Nov–Mar. Nonsmoking house. *In room:* TV (satellite), tea/coffeemaker, hair dryer.

GREAT DEALS ON DINING

Like many towns in northwest Ireland, the best restaurants are the dining rooms in the hotels.

The Atlantic Restaurant TRADITIONAL This busy restaurant, located in the Atlantic Guest House, offers exceptionally good value. Chicken curry, plaice, salmon steaks, and lasagna are featured on the extensive menu. There's a separate nonsmoking room.

Main St., Donegal, Co. Donegal. ℭ **073/21080**. Reservations not required. Lunch and dinner 7.50€–9€ ($6.80–$8.15); children's menu 3€ ($2.75). MC, V. Daily 11am–7pm (July–Aug 10am–9:30pm).

Hyland Central Hotel TRADITIONAL A selection of no-nonsense meals is served in this small hotel. There's a lunch special (hot meat and vegetables, and ample portions) for less than 10€ ($9.10) served in the carvery/coffee shop, named Just William's. Evening meals featuring seafood and traditional Irish dishes are offered in the cream-colored dining room, which has wide windows along one wall, lots of dark-wood trim, and softly lighted gold-framed oil paintings.

The Diamond, Donegal, Co. Donegal. ℭ **073/21027**. Fax 073/22295. www.whites-hotelsireland.com. Fixed-price lunch 15€ ($14), children's menu 7€ ($6.35); dinner main courses 15€–20€ ($14–$18), fixed-price dinner 28€–30€ ($25–$28). 10% service charge. AE, MC, V. Carvery daily 9am–10pm; restaurant Mon–Sat 6–8:45pm, Sun two seatings: 12:30–1pm and 2–2:30pm.

SHOPPING

Although Donegal is not a spectacular town for shopping, it's ideal for acquiring woolens, Donegal Parian China, and other local products at competitive prices. Some shops close early on Wednesday, although this practice is disappearing.

Donegal Craft Village Just outside Donegal town on the Ballyshannon-Sligo road is a group of cottagelike buildings around a courtyard. Each is the workshop of a true artisan. You'll find pottery, hand weaving, batik, jewelry, ceramics, and crystal here. The coffee shop (summer only) is a pleasant spot for a shopping or browsing break. The craft studios are open year-round Monday to Saturday 10am to 6pm and Sunday noon to 6pm. Ballyshannon Rd., Donegal. ℭ **073/22015** or 073/22225.

Magee of Donegal Ltd. World famous for its handwoven Donegal tweed, Magee, founded in 1866, has set up a weaving demonstration right in the store during the tourist season. Woolens are handwoven in cottages, then finished at their factory in Donegal town. Tours of the factory are organized from time to time, and you can inquire at the store for specific dates and hours. The store offers a wide selection of quality clothing for men and women and a good variety of linens, knitwear, and other Irish products. The Diamond, Donegal. ℭ **073/ 22660**. www.mageeshop.com.

Wards Music Shop If you'd like to take home a harp, bodhran, bagpipe, flute, or tin whistle, this is the shop for you. It specializes in the sale of Irish musical instruments and instructional books. The stock also includes violins, mandolins, and accordions. Castle St., Donegal, Co. Donegal. ℭ **073/21313**. noelward@ eircom.net.

THE PUB SCENE

Biddy O'Barnes   It's worth a detour into the Blue Stack Mountains and the scenic Barnesmore Gap, 7 miles (11km) northeast of Donegal town, to visit this pub, which has been in the same family for four generations. Stepping inside is like entering a country cottage, with its blazing turf fires, stone floors, wooden stools and benches, and old hutches full of plates and bric-a-brac. A picture of Biddy, who once owned this house, hangs over the main fireplace. Most evenings see a session of spontaneous music in progress. Donegal-Lifford Rd. (N15), Barnesmore, Co. Donegal. ✆ **073/21402.**

The Schooner Inn   A nautical decor of model ships and seafaring memorabilia prevails at this pub. There's music on most evenings, with traditional Irish music Monday to Friday and a DJ on Saturday. *Note:* B&B accommodation is available here for 51€ ($46) double, and a simple bar menu is offered 5 to 10pm daily. Upper Main St., Donegal, Co. Donegal. ✆ **073/21671.**

3 The Donegal Bay Coast

The Donegal Bay coast extends for 50 miles (81km): from Bundoran, 20 miles (32km) S of Donegal town, to Glencolumbkille, 30 miles (48km) W of Donegal town

The Donegal Bay coast is comprised of two almost equal parts: the area from Ballyshannon north to Donegal town (Southern Donegal Bay) and the area west of Donegal town stretching to Glencolumbkille (Northern Donegal Bay). In terms of scenic beauty, however, these two parts of the coast are far from equal. The southern side tends more toward the cheesy seaside resort, with Bundoran being a case in point; **Rossnowlagh** is somewhat more appealing, and does have one of the finest beaches in the region. The northern Donegal Bay coast, on the other hand, is nothing short of spectacular. Once you travel west of Killybegs, the mountains reach right to the sea, creating the beautifully indented coastline around **Kilcar** and the incomparable **Slieve League cliffs.**

GETTING THERE & GETTING AROUND   Bus Eireann (✆ **074/21309;** www.buseireann.ie) operates daily bus service to Killybegs and Glencolumbkille, on the northern half of the bay, and to Ballyshannon and Bundoran, on the southern half of the bay.

The best way to get to and around Donegal Bay is by car. Follow the N15 route on the southern half of the bay, the N56 route on the northern half of the bay.

VISITOR INFORMATION   Contact the **North West Tourism Office,** Aras Reddan, Temple Street, Sligo (✆ **071/61201**); the **Letterkenny Tourist Office,** Derry Road, Letterkenny (✆ **074/21160**); or **Bundoran Tourist Office,** Main Street, Bundoran, County Donegal (✆ **072/41350**). The Letterkenny office is open year-round Monday to Friday 9am to 5pm, with extended summer hours; the Bundoran office is open daily April through September from 9am to 6pm, with reduced hours during the winter.

EXPLORING SOUTHERN DONEGAL BAY

To reach the southern section of Donegal Bay from Sligo, take the N15 road up the Atlantic coast, and at about 20 miles (32km) north you'll come to **Bundoran,** the southern tip of County Donegal and a major beach resort.

Continuing up the coast, you'll pass **Ballyshannon,** which dates back to the 15th century, making it one of the oldest inhabited towns in Ireland; it's another favorite with beachgoers. Evening entertainment here comes in the form of traditional music in some of the town's 21 lively pubs (inquire locally about

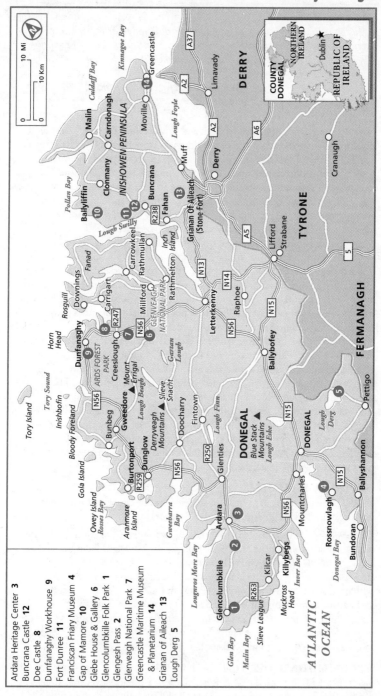

County Donegal

10 Mi
10 Km

NORTHERN IRELAND
Dublin★
COUNTY DONEGAL
REPUBLIC OF IRELAND

DERRY

A37
Limavady
A2
A2
A6
Moville
Lough Foyle
Muff
Derry
Greencastle
Carndonagh
Malin   Culdaff Bay
Kinnagoe Bay
INISHOWEN PENINSULA
Clonmany
Buncrana
Fahan
Grianan of Aileach (Stone Fort)
R238
Ballyliffin
Pollan Bay
Lough Swilly
Carrowkeel
Rathmullan
Inch Island
Rathmelton
Letterkenny
Raphoe
Lifford
Strabane
TYRONE
Cranagh
A5
N13
N14
N15
Fanad
Rosguill
Horn Head
Downings
Carrigart
Dunfanaghy
ARDS FOREST PARK
Creeslough
Millford
GLENVEAGH NATIONAL PARK
R247
N56
Tory Sound
Tory Island
Inishbofin
Bloody Foreland
Gola Island
Bunbeg
Gweedore
Mount Errigal ▲
Lough Beagh
Derryveagh Mountains ▲ Slieve Snacht ▲
Gartan Lough
Doocharry
Fintown
DONEGAL
Blue Stack Mountains ▲
Lough Eske
Ballybofey
Pettigo
Lough Derg
FERMANAGH
Owey Island
Arranmore Island
Roses Bay
Burtonport
Dunglow
R259
N56
Glenties
R250
Lough Finn
N15
Donegal
Mountcharles
N56
Ballyshannon
N15
Bundoran
Donegal Bay
Rossnowlagh
Gweebarra Bay
Loughros More Bay
Ardara
Kilcar
Killybegs
Inver Bay
Muckross Head
Glencolumbkille
R263
Slieve League
Glen Bay
Malin Bay
ATLANTIC OCEAN

Ardara Heritage Center **3**
Buncrana Castle **12**
Doe Castle **8**
Dunfanaghy Workhouse **9**
Fort Dunree **11**
Franciscan Friary Museum **4**
Gap of Mamore **10**
Glebe House & Gallery **6**
Glencolumbkille Folk Park **1**
Glengesh Pass **2**
Glenveagh National Park **7**
Greencastle Maritime Museum & Planetarium **14**
Grianan of Aileach **13**
Lough Derg **5**

455

Impressions

This light that turns Donegal into a poem for an hour, or for only a second is a terrible and disturbing thing. If any man with a sense of beauty were compelled to see it every day, it would unfit him for the practical business of life.

—H.V. Morton, English travel writer, 1892–1979

---

current venues, and check Sweenys Pub and White Horse Bar; see "Great Deals on Dining," below). In late July or early August, there's the famous **Ballyshannon Folk Festival,** when music rings through the streets day and night. Just over a mile (2km) northwest of town, the once-famous Cistercian **Assaroe Abbey,** founded in 1184, now lies in ruins, although its mill wheel has been restored and is driven by water from the Abbey River just as in ancient days. Some 50 meters away, at the edge of the Abbey River, **Catsby Cave** is a grottolike setting where a rough-hewn altar reminds you that Mass was celebrated here during the penal years, when it was prohibited by law.

At this point, leave the main road and head for the coastal resort of **Rossnowlagh,** one of the loveliest beaches in this part of Ireland. At over 2 miles (3km) long and as wide as the tides allow, it's a flat sandy stretch, shielded by flower-filled hills, and ideal for walking. You'll see horses racing on it occasionally. This spot is a splendid vantage point for watching sunsets over the churning foam-rimmed waters of the Atlantic.

Overlooking the beach from a hilltop is the **Franciscan Friary,** Rossnowlagh (© 072/51342), which houses a small museum of local Donegal history. The complex also contains beautiful gardens and walks overlooking the sea, and a shop with religious objects. It's open daily from 10am to 8pm. There's no admission charge, but donations are welcome.

From Rossnowlagh, return to the main road via the **Donegal Golf Club** at Murvagh (see "Outdoor Pursuits," below), a spectacular setting nestled on a rugged sandy peninsula of primeval duneland, surrounded by a wall of dense woodlands. From here, the road curves inland and it's less than 10 miles (16km) to Donegal town. (The northern section of Donegal Bay is covered below.)

OUTDOOR PURSUITS

BEACHES   Donegal Bay's beaches are wide, sandy, clean, and flat—ideal for walking. The best are **Rossnowlagh** and **Bundoran.**

GOLF   The Donegal Bay coast is home to two outstanding 18-hole championship seaside golf courses. **Donegal Golf Club,** Murvagh, Ballintra, County Donegal (© 073/34054; www.donegalgolfclub.ie), is 3 miles (5km) north of Rossnowlagh and 7 miles (11km) south of Donegal town. It's a par-73 course with greens fees of 38€ ($35) on weekdays and 51€ ($46) on weekends.

The **Bundoran Golf Club,** off the Sligo-Ballyshannon Road (N15), Bundoran, County Donegal (© 072/41302; www.bundorangolfclub.com), is a par-69 course designed by the great Harry Vardon. The greens fees are 25€ ($23) on weekdays and 32€ ($29) on weekends.

ACCOMMODATIONS YOU CAN AFFORD

Ardpatton Farm House   Mrs. Rose McCaffrey presides over this 200-year-old farmhouse, and she and those of her 10 children still living at home extend a traditional warm Irish farmhouse welcome to visitors. The house sits on 380 rural acres, and the large lounge and dining room overlook peaceful fields. The nicely furnished guest rooms are more spacious than most—one family room will accommodate up to six people. On cool evenings there are open fires.

Cavangarden, Ballyshannon, Co. Donegal. ℭ 072/51546. 6 units. 48€ ($44) double. 50% reduction for children sharing with an adult. Rates include full breakfast. MC, V. 3 miles (5km) north of town on the Donegal road (N15).

Bri-Ter-An   Mrs. Margaret Barrett is the gracious hostess at this modern bungalow. The house is set on the shores of Donegal Bay, and as one guest put it, "The view across the bay from the lounge is worth the price of the room." That lounge is a bright, cheerful gathering point for guests, and there's a separate TV lounge as well. Guest rooms have built-in wardrobes, and all are close to the bathroom.

Bundoran Rd., Ballyshannon, Co. Donegal. ℭ 072/51490. 3 units, 2 with bathroom (shower only). 48€ ($44) double. 20% reduction for children sharing with an adult. Rates include full breakfast. MC. Closed Nov–Mar. ½ mile (1km) from the town center. **Amenities:** 2 lounges.

Cavangarden House   This lovely old Georgian home set amidst spacious grounds dates from 1750 and is the home of Mrs. Agnes McCaffrey. Furnishings in the large three-story house include antiques, and there are turf and log fires on cool evenings, when impromptu song sometimes breaks out around the piano in the dining room. Guest rooms here are exceptionally spacious; two family rooms will accommodate up to four people each.

Cavangarden, Ballyshannon, Co. Donegal. ℭ 072/51365. cghouse@iol.ie. 6 units. 53€ ($48) double. 50% reduction for children sharing with an adult. Rates include full breakfast. Dinner 18€ ($16). AE, V. 3 miles (5km) north of town on the main Donegal road (N15).

Strand View House   Mrs. Mary Delaney and her family make you feel right at home in this centrally located two-story house on the main Sligo-Donegal road (N15). The six guest rooms include three large family rooms; all are attractive and comfortably furnished.

E. End, Bundoran, Co. Donegal. ℭ 072/41519. 6 units. 32€ ($29) single; 51€ ($46) double. 20% reduction for children sharing with an adult. Rates include full breakfast. No credit cards. Private parking lot. In room: TV.

GREAT DEALS ON DINING

Smugglers Creek ⍟ SEAFOOD   For great food and grand sunset views, head to this little gem perched on a cliff overlooking Donegal Bay. It's in an 1845 stone building that has been restored and enlarged to include a conservatory-style dining area with open fireplaces, beamed ceilings, stone walls, wooden stools, porthole windows, crab traps, and lobster pots. Seafood is the star attraction, and proprietor Conor Britton pulls his own oysters and mussels from local beds. The bar menu ranges from soups, salads, and sandwiches to buttered garlic mussels or fresh paté. Dinner entrees include Smugglers sea casserole (scallops, salmon, and prawns with Mornay sauce), deep-fried squid with Provençal sauce, tiger prawns in garlic butter, wild Irish salmon hollandaise, steaks with whiskey sauce, and vegetarian pasta or stir-fry dishes. The restaurant is nonsmoking; the bar is not. More than a dozen B&B rooms with private bathroom are available for 70€ ($63) double.

Rossnowlagh, Co. Donegal. ℭ 072/52366. Reservations required for dinner. Dinner main courses 15€–23€ ($14–$21). DC, MC, V. Two lunch sittings daily: 12:30 and 2:30pm; two dinner sittings daily at 6:30 and 8:30pm. Closed Mon–Tues Oct–Easter.

Sweenys Pub and White Horse Bar PUB GRUB   Sweenys is a delight to visit, partly because of congenial host Alan Sweeny and partly because of its warm, inviting, and atmospheric interior. The place is old—the first recorded sale of the premises is dated 1793—and the owners have managed to create a comfortable, semi-modern environment while still retaining much of the character of the old building. If you happen by on a Friday, drop in for traditional Irish music in the stone-arched Cellar Bar. Other times, excellent snacks, soup, and salads provide nourishment and a well-pulled pint provides refreshment in the casual bar/restaurant. At dinner, the menu includes a blend of traditional Irish food and some Mexican dishes.

Assaroe Rd. (N15), Ballyshannon, Co. Donegal. ℂ 072/51452. Reservations not required. Dinner main courses 11€–20€ ($10–$18). MC, V. Daily noon–3pm and 6–9:15pm.

SHOPPING

Britton and Daughters Located in a cottage opposite the Sand House Hotel, this workshop is a source of unusual artistic crafts: hand-etched mirrors or glass, Celtic carved rocks, wall hangings, and prints of Donegal, as well as posters and pottery with surfing and Irish music themes. Off the Ballyshannon-Donegal Rd., Rossnowlagh, Co. Donegal. ℂ 072/52220. www.barrybritton.com.

Celtic Weave China Owner Tommy Daly and his family learned the art of making cobweb-light woven Parian china baskets in Belleek, then opened their own factory and showroom in this little village. Each piece is individually crafted in unique designs by Tommy and his son, Adrian, and Tommy's wife, Patricia, then hand-paints each one in delicate floral shades. This is the only place in Ireland where you can buy these exquisite pieces; in the United States, Tiffany and Co. is the only outlet. The shop is 3 miles (5km) east of Ballyshannon on Belleek Road, 1¼ miles (2km) west of Belleek. Cloghore, Co. Donegal. ℂ 072/51844. www.celticweavechina.ie.

Donegal Parian China Established in 1985, this pottery works produces delicate, wafer-thin Parian china gift items and tableware in shamrock, rose, hawthorn, and other Irish floral patterns. Free guided tours, leaving every 20 minutes, enable visitors to watch as vases, bells, spoons, thimbles, wall plaques, lamps, and eggshell coffee and tea sets are shaped, decorated, fired, and polished. There's also an audiovisual room, an art gallery, a tearoom, and a showroom/shop for on-the-spot purchases. Bundoran Rd. (N15), Ballyshannon, Co. Donegal. ℂ 072/51826.

EXPLORING NORTHERN DONEGAL BAY

From Donegal town, follow the main road (N56) for a slow, scenic drive along the northern coast of Donegal Bay. You'll encounter narrow roads, sheer cliffs, craggy rocks, bog lands, and panoramic mountain and sea views. You'll also see the thatched-roof cottages that are distinctively typical of this area—they have rounded roofs, because the thatch is tied down by a network of ropes (sugans) and fastened to pins beneath the eaves, to protect it from the prevailing winds off the sea. It's only 30 miles (48km) out to **Glencolumbkille,** but plan on at least several hours' drive. Just before you come to Killybegs, the N56 road swings inland and northward. Continue on the coastal road (the R263) westward toward Killybegs and Kilcar.

Your first stop could be at **Killybegs** where, if your timing is right, you can watch the fishing boats unloading the day's catch, or at Studio Donegal in Kilcar if you'd prefer to shop for tweed. The **Kilcar coast road** is a detour you won't soon forget; the tiny road skirts craggy cliffs and gorgeous beaches on its roundabout way to Carrick, the next town to the west. Look for a turnoff to the left

---

(Finds Thirsty?

If you need a break during your driving tour of the coast—or you're just looking for good conversation and atmosphere at any time—step through the half-door at the **Piper's Rest,** Kilcar, County Donegal (② 073/38205). The thatched-roof pub has original stone walls, arches, flagged floors, an open turf fire, and a unique stained-glass window depicting a piper. As its name implies, music may erupt at any time and usually does on summer nights.

---

about 5 miles (8km) west of Killybegs on the R263, signposted for the Kilcar coast road. Along the way you won't want to miss **Muckross Head;** park the car and take a walk out to the tip of this headland, where there are great coastal views and a glimpse of the Slieve League cliffs on the western horizon. Of the several beaches you'll pass, Trá Bhán (or "The White Strand") is locally regarded as the safest for swimming.

A must-stop while in Donegal is **Slieve League** ☆☆☆, the highest sea cliffs in Europe. Unlike many of Ireland's most spectacular sea cliffs, this one has a fine road-accessible viewing point that allows anyone with a car and some courage to see this extraordinary wonder of nature. The turnoff for the Bunglas viewing point is at Carrick, just west of Kilcar. The narrow road that ascends by switchback along the cliff edge is truly scary at times, but not actually dangerous. Once at the cliffs, you must decide whether you want to merely gaze at their 1,000-foot (305m) splendor or to experience them up close and personal on the wind-buffeted walk along their ridge. This walk is for the fearless and fit. There are several short walks you can take from the viewing point, either up along the cliff edge or down toward a remarkably picturesque signal tower, to be found just over a mile (about 2km) back the way you came on the access road.

Glencolumbkille ☆ is an austere Atlantic outpost dating back 5,000 years. It's said that St. Columba established a monastery here in the 6th century and gave his name permanently to the glen. In the 1950s, this area was endangered by a 75% emigration rate, until the parish priest, James McDyer, focused the energies of the town not only on assuring the community's future but also on preserving its past. He helped accomplish both by founding the **Glencolumb-kille Folk Park** (② 073/30017). Built by the people of Glencolumbkille in the form of a tiny village, or *clachan,* this modest theme park of thatched cottages—each outfitted with period furniture and artifacts—reflects with simple clarity life in this remote corner of Ireland over the past several centuries. Two miniature playhouses are on hand for children. The tearoom, whose current specialty, Guinness cake, is to die for, will soon be serving a simple menu of traditional Irish dishes, such as stews and brútin, composed mainly of hot milk and potatoes. In the *sheebeen,* a shop of traditional products, don't dismiss the bizarre-sounding local wines—fuchsia, heather, seaweed, and tea and raisin—until you've tried them all. They're surprisingly good. The medium-dry heather wine finishes first on my list. Recent additions to the folk park include a new visitors reception hall and a new interpretive center, housing a range of engaging exhibits. Admission and tour are 3€ ($2.75) for adults and 2€ ($1.80) for seniors and children. It's open from Easter through Oct, Monday through Saturday from 10am to 6pm and Sunday from noon to 6pm.

To continue touring onward from Glencolumbkille, follow the signs for Ardara over a mountainous inland road. Soon you'll come to **Glengesh Pass,** a narrow, scenic roadway that rises to a height of 900 feet (275m) before plunging into the valley below. The road leads eventually to Ardara, known for its tweed and woolen craft centers (see "The Atlantic Highlands," below).

OUTDOOR PURSUITS

BEACHES   Glencolumbkille has two fine beaches: One is the flat, broad, sandy beach at the end of the road; the lesser-known gem is a tiny beach surrounded by a horseshoe of cliffs, accessible from a stone staircase that climbs down the cliffs from the roadside about a mile southwest of town.

BICYCLING   The north side of Donegal Bay offers great cycling roads—tremendously scenic, and very hilly. One good but arduous route from Donegal town follows the coast roads west to Glencolumbkille (day one), continuing north to Ardara and Dawros Head via Glengesh Pass (day two), then back to Donegal (day three), taking in some of the most spectacular coastal scenery in Ireland along the way. Rental bikes are available in Donegal from Pat Boyle (© **073/22515**) for roughly 10€ ($9) per day and 38€ ($35) per week.

FISHING   Surrounded by waters that hold shark, skate, pollock, conger, cod, and mackerel, **Killybegs** is one of the most active centers on the northwest coast for both commercial and sport sea-fishing. **Brian McGilloway** of Killybegs (© **073/31144**) operates full-day fishing expeditions for visitors on board two 34-foot (10.5m) boats, the M.V. *Susanne* and the *Bangor Crest,* from Blackrock Pier. Prices are 190€ to 260€ ($172–$236) to hire a boat for the day, with an additional 6.50€ ($5.90) per person for rods and tackle; one boat accommodates a party of 8 to 10 people. Reservations are required.

At **Mountcharles,** a coastal town midway between Donegal town and Killybegs, deep-sea fishing trips are organized by Michael O'Boyle, Old Road (© **073/35257**). Outings are slated daily from 11am to 5pm and cost 25€ ($23) per person. This company also offers guided boat trips and wildlife cruises on demand, priced from 25€ ($23) per person with a 2-hour minimum booking.

WALKING   The peninsula that extends westward from Killybegs possesses some of the most spectacular coastal scenery in Ireland, and much of it is accessible only from the sea or on foot. The grandeur of the **Slieve League cliffs** is not to be missed, and the best way to visit this natural monument is to hike from the Bunglass lookout point to Tramane Strand in **Malin Beg,** a few kilometers southwest of Glencolumbkille. This walk involves a crossing of the renowned "One Man's Pass," a narrow ridge with steep drops on both sides that should not be attempted by the acrophobic or anyone wearing high heels. The distance from Bunglass to Trabane Strand is 9 miles (15km), and you will have to arrange a pickup at the end. The summits of the Slieve League, rising about 1,970 feet (600m) above the sea, are often capped in cloud. You should think twice about undertaking the walk if there is danger of losing visibility along the way.

Another lesser-known walk that is just as spectacular is the coastal walk between Glencolumbkille and the town of **Maghera** (not so much a town as a small cluster of houses). Glen Head, topped by a Martello tower, overlooks Glencolumbkille to the north. This walk begins with a climb to the tower and continues along the cliff face for 15 miles (24km), passing only one remote outpost of human habitation along the way, the tiny town of Port. For isolated sea splendor, this is one of the finest walks in Ireland, but only experienced walkers with adequate provisions should undertake the walk, and only in fine weather.

ACCOMMODATIONS YOU CAN AFFORD

Bannagh House   This lovely hilltop bungalow on the outskirts of town on the coast road has sweeping views of Killybegs's harbor and fishing fleet. The house is beautifully decorated and the guest rooms are well appointed (some offer harbor views). Phyllis and Fergus Melly and their five children are as welcoming as their home.

Finta Rd., Killybegs, Co. Donegal. ℭ 073/31108. banaghhouse@eircom.net. 4 units. 38€ ($38) single; 53€ ($48) double. Rates include full breakfast. No credit cards. Private parking lot. Closed Nov–Feb. *In-room:* TV, tea/coffeemaker, hair dryer.

Castlereagh House   Castlereagh House is an early 20th-century two-story farmhouse, the family home of Elizabeth and Ernest Henry and their son, Howard. Turf and log fires are usually aglow in the dining room, and the spacious lounge has splendid views overlooking Bruckless Bay and the surrounding countryside. Guest rooms are attractive and comfortably furnished.

Castlereagh, Bruckless, Co. Donegal. ℭ/fax 073/37202. 3 units, all with bathroom (2 with shower only). Nonsmoking house. 53€ ($48) double. 20% reduction for children sharing with an adult. Rates include breakfast. MC, V. Free private parking. Closed Nov–Mar. 2½ miles (4km) east of Killybegs, 11 miles (18km) west of Donegal town on the N56 coast road. **Amenities:** Lounge. *In room:* Hair dryer.

Corner House   Mrs. John Byrne presides over this two-story home set in the peaceful valley of Glencolumbkille, 5 miles (8km) east of town on the Ardara road at a location that allows you to sink into the very special character of this remote part of Ireland. Guest rooms are quite comfortable, and sandy beaches and good fishing are within easy reach. The Glencolumbkille Folk Museum is less than 5 minutes away.

Cashel, Glencolumbkille, Co. Donegal. ℭ 073/30021. 4 units. 48€ ($44) double. 20% reduction for children sharing with an adult. Rates include full breakfast. No credit cards. Closed Oct–Mar.

Dún Ulún House ⭐ *Value*   Dún Ulún House, one of the best bargains in this part of the world, caters to a remarkably diverse clientele. First there's the B&B, in a modern, purpose-built guesthouse. The building is unremarkable, but remains in the memory long after you've left, thanks to the graciousness of the Lyons family and the extraordinary beauty of the seaside scene it overlooks. The self-catering cottage also overlooks the sea, with an open fire in the kitchen and basic, functional furnishings in the private bedrooms. The most appealing campground I've seen in Ireland is tucked into the hillside on a series of terraces that provide considerable privacy. Finally, there's an in-house band made up of five teenage girls—the Lyonses' daughter, two nieces, and two friends—who play some of the best traditional music you'll hear anywhere. They play at a local pub and also for guests at the B&B. Denis Lyons is a great source of information on the archaeology of the Kilcar region, and can direct you to many fascinating and little-known sites.

Kilcar, Co. Donegal. ℭ 073/38137. 10 units, 9 with bathroom (shower only). 46€ ($41) double; 12€ ($11) per person per night in self-catering cottage. Rates for the house include full breakfast (self-catering cottage rates do not include breakfast). MC, V. Free parking. 1¼ miles (2km) west of Kilcar on R263. **Amenities:** TV, full kitchen, washer/dryer.

Lismolin Country Home   This modern bungalow, run by the Cahill family, sits 1 mile (1.5km) from the town center, right at the edge of a beautiful forest and with views of a nearby mountain. The guest rooms are spacious and tastefully decorated. Turf and log fires are often aglow in the lounge.

Fintra Rd., Killybegs, Co. Donegal. ℭ 073/31035. Fax 073/32310. lismolincountryhome@hotmail.com. 5 units. 38.50€ ($35) single; 51€ ($46) double. 33% reduction for children. Rates include full breakfast. MC, V. **Amenities:** Lounge. *In room:* TV, tea/coffeemaker, hair dryer.

Worth a Splurge

Bruckless House ⓐ Inside and out, Bruckless House is a gem. Clive and Joan Evans have restored their mid-18th-century farmhouse with such care and taste that every room is a pleasure to enter and enjoy. Furniture and art they brought back from their years in Hong Kong add a special elegance. All the guest rooms are smoke-free, spacious, and bright. Joan's gardens have taken first prize in County Donegal's country garden competition at least twice in recent years. Inside and out, Bruckless House is a gem. Be sure to ask Clive to introduce you to his fine Connemara ponies, which he raises and treasures.

Bruckless, Co. Donegal. ⓒ 073/37071. Fax 073/37070. bruc@iol.ie. 4 units, 2 with bathroom. 76€ ($69) double without bathroom, 89€ ($81) double with bathroom. No service charge. Includes full Irish breakfast. MC, V. Free parking. Open Apr–Sept. Signposted on N56, 12 miles (19km) west of Donegal town. **Amenities:** Sitting room.

GREAT DEALS ON DINING

The Blue Haven CONTINENTAL On a broad, open sweep of Donegal Bay between Killybegs and Kilcar, this modern skylit restaurant offers 180-degree views of the bay from a semicircular bank of windows. It's an ideal stop for a meal or light refreshment while touring. The bar-food menu, available throughout the day, offers soups, sandwiches, and omelets with unusual fillings. The dinner menu includes filet of rainbow trout, T-bone and sirloin steaks, and savory mushroom pancakes. A new addition with 15 bedrooms opened in 2000, offering views of Donegal Bay and bed-and-breakfast for 64€ ($58).

Largymore, Kilcar, Co. Donegal. ⓒ 073/38090. Reservations recommended for dinner. Dinner main courses 13€–23€ ($12–$21). MC, V. May–Sept daily 11am–11pm.

Sail Inn Restaurant and Bar ⓐ TRADITIONAL IRISH This popular bar and restaurant at the western end of Main Street has loads of character in the downstairs bar, where soup, sandwiches, salads, and hot plates are all well prepared. Upstairs, the cozy restaurant seats only 26, and dinner is served by candlelight. Owners Martin McGinley and Janet Graham have made it a leading venue for traditional music in the area, with sessions nightly in the summer and each weekend throughout the year; Martin is himself an accomplished fiddle player.

Main St., Killybegs, Co. Donegal. ⓒ 073/31130. Reservations recommended for dinner. Bar food 4€–9€ ($3.65–$8.15); dinner 15€–20€ ($14–$18). MC, V. Bar menu daily 11am–9pm; June–Sept dinner daily 5:30–9pm.

SHOPPING

Studio Donegal Started in 1979, this hand-weaving enterprise is distinguished by its knobby tweed, subtly colored in tones of beige, oat, and ash. You can walk around both the craft shop and the mill and see the chunky-weave stoles, caps, jackets, and cloaks in the making. Other products fashioned of this unique tweed include tote bags, cushion covers, tablemats, tapestries, and wall hangings. Kilcar is between Killybegs and Glencolumbkille, about 20 miles (32km) west of Donegal Town. The Glebe Mill, Kilcar, Co. Donegal. ⓒ 073/38194. www. studiodonegal.ie.

4 The Atlantic Highlands

The Atlantic Highlands start at Ardara, 25 miles (40km) NW of Donegal town, 10 miles (16km) N of Killybegs

Scenery is the keynote to the Atlantic Highlands of Donegal—vast stretches of coastal and mountain scenery, beaches and bays, rocks and ruins. It's sometimes lonely but always breathtaking. Set far off the beaten track and deep amid the coastal scenery is **Mount Errigal,** the highest mountain in Donegal, at 2,466 feet (751m); it gently slopes down to one of Ireland's greatest visitor attractions, the **Glenveagh National Park.**

The best place to start a tour of Donegal's Atlantic Highlands is at **Ardara,** a small town on the coast about 25 miles (40km) northwest of Donegal town. From here, it's easy to weave your way up the rest of the Donegal coast. This drive can take 4 hours or 4 days, depending on your schedule and interests.

GETTING THERE & GETTING AROUND   Bus Eireann (© 074/21309; www.buseireann.ie) operates daily bus service to Ardara and Glenties.

Aer Arann (© 01/814-5240; www.aerarann.ie) and **Aer Lingus** (© 01/886-8888; www.aerlingus.ie) operate regularly scheduled flights from Dublin to **Donegal Airport,** Carrickfinn, Kincasslagh, County Donegal (© 075/48284; www.donegalairport.ie), about 40 miles (64km) northwest of Donegal town in the heart of the Atlantic coast.

The best way to get to and around Donegal's Atlantic Highlands is by car, following the main N56 route.

VISITOR INFORMATION   Contact the **North West Tourism Office,** Aras Reddan, Temple Street, Sligo (© 071/61201); the **Letterkenny Tourist Office,** Derry Road, Letterkenny (© 074/21160); or the **Donegal Tourist Office,** Quay Street, Donegal (© 073/21148). All three offices are open year-round.

SEEING THE SIGHTS

Ardara, known for its local tweed and sweater industries, is one of the northwest's most charming little towns. It's particularly worth a stop for shoppers (see the listings in "Shopping" later in this chapter). North of Ardara, the route travels inland near Gweebarra Bay and passes through Dungloe to an area known as the **Rosses,** extending from Gweebarra Bridge as far north as Crolly. This stretch presents a wealth of rock-strewn land, with many mountains, rivers, lakes, and beaches. Here you can visit **Burtonport** (otherwise known as *Ailt an Chorrain*), one of the country's premier fishing ports; it's said that more salmon and lobster are landed here than at any other port in Ireland or Britain.

North of the Rosses between Derrybeg and Gortahork is an area known as the **Bloody Foreland,** a stretch of land that derives its name from the fact that its rocks take on a warm ruddy color when lit by the setting sun. This is a sight that should not be missed.

By now, you'll be approaching the top rim of Donegal, which is dominated by a series of small peninsulas or fingers of land jutting out into the sea. Chief among these scenic areas are **Horn Head** ⭐ and **Ards.** The former offers one of Donegal's most extraordinary coastal walks (see "Outdoor Pursuits," below). The latter contains a forested park with a wide diversity of terrain: woodlands, a salt marsh, sand dunes, seashore, freshwater lakes, and fenland. Just west of the Head is **Trabane Strand,** one of the most beautiful, unpopulated beaches you're ever likely to see. **Dunfanaghy** is a small port town at the base of Horn Head, a great base for exploring the region.

In Tory Sound, 9 miles (15km) north of the mainland, lies **Tory Island,** treelessly desolate and seemingly uninhabitable. But the truth is that Tory Island—all of 2½ miles (4km) long and about a kilometer wide—has been settled for thousands of years, and currently boasts nearly 200 year-round inhabitants. Known for its painters and pirates, ruins and bird cliffs, Tory makes a great adventure, as does the crossing, which can be made daily, weather permitting, from either Bunbeg or Magheraroarty with **Donegal Coastal Cruises,** Magheraroarty, County Donegal (© **075/31320** or 075/31340).

Between Dunfanaghy and Creeslough, take time to visit **Ards Forest Park,** on the shores of Sheep Haven Bay. It's Ireland's most northerly forest park, and its 1,200 acres hold beautiful woodlands, salt marsh, sand dunes, seashore, fresh-water lakes, fenland, and rock faces. Legend has it that back when time began, this was the domain of Bioróg, the *bean si* (banshee) fairy woman who thwarted Balor of the Evil Eye, god of drought and plague. Be that as it may, there are traces of Ireland's earliest inhabitants in the four ring forts within the park, and nature paths are well marked. Informative literature is available at the park entrance.

After Horn Head, the next spit of land to the east is **Rosguill.** The 10-mile (16km) route around this peninsula is called the Atlantic Drive. **Downings** is a lovely town on this route, and Trá na Rosann near the tip of the peninsula a gor-geous pristine beach. The road leads you to yet another peninsula, the **Fanad,** with a 45-mile (72km) circuit between Mulroy Bay and Lough Swilly.

Just south of Creeslough, off the N56, is **Doe Castle,** one of Ireland's most enchantingly situated tower houses; it's surrounded on three sides by the waters of Sheep Haven Bay, making for a truly superb view. The castle is currently undergoing an extensive restoration, and won't be open to the public again for at least a couple more years; you can walk around it, but you can't go inside.

After driving to all these scenic peninsulas, it may come as a surprise that many of the greatest visitor attractions of the Atlantic Highlands are not along the coast at all, but inland, a few kilometers off the main N56 road near Kilmacrennan.

Ardara Heritage Centre Ardara has long been a center for weaving, and varied displays represent the history of tweed production in the region. The weaver in residence is sometimes present to demonstrate techniques. A video provides an outline of nearby places of interest. The center opened in 1995 and is building its collections and exhibits. A cafe serves inexpensive teas, soups, and simple meals.

Ardara, Co. Donegal. © **075/41262** and 075/41704. Admission free. Donations welcomed. Centre open daily 10am–6pm; historical exhibition May–Sept Mon–Fri 10am–8pm, Sat–Sun 10am–6pm. On N56 in the center of town.

Dunfanaghy Workhouse This imposing stone structure was constructed in 1844, just before the height of the famine, and it provided meals and a roof for more than 300 local people. Life in a workhouse was miserable, and they were places of last resort: families were separated, inmates were subjected to harsh physical labor on a minimal food allowance, and once you entered, you were for-bidden to leave. Still, by 1846 most of the 100,000 places in workhouses throughout Ireland were filled. The exhibits portray the life of workhouse inmates and relate local famine history. There is also an exhibit on the history of Dunfanaghy and an audiovisual presentation on the natural history of the region. Occasionally, evening music, poetry, or drama events are offered. A cozy tea and gift shop with an open fire serves baked goods.

Dunfanaghy, Co. Donegal. © **074/36540.** www.theirishfamine.com. Admission 4€ ($3.65) adults, 3.15€ ($2.90) seniors and students, 2€ ($1.80) children. Mar–Sept Mon–Sat 10am–5pm, Sun noon–5pm. Just west of Dunfanaghy on N56.

The Glebe House and Gallery ⋆ *Finds* Sitting in woodland gardens on the shores of Lough Gartan, about 4 miles (6.5km) southwest of Glenveagh, this

Tips **Gaelic Spoken Here**

The deeper you get into this countryside, the more you'll be immersed in a section known as the *Gaeltacht,* or Irish-speaking area. This should present no problems, except that most of the road signs are only in Irish. If you keep to the main road (N56), you should have no difficulties. If you follow little roads off to the seashore or down country paths, you might have a problem figuring out where you're going (unless you can read Irish). In many cases, the Irish word for a place bears no resemblance to the English equivalent (*An Clochan Liath* in Irish is *Dungloe* in English), so our best advice is to buy a map with place names in both languages or stick to the main road.

Regency-style house was built as a rectory in the 1820s. It was owned until recently by English artist Derek Hill, who donated the house and his art collection to the Irish government for public use and as an enhancement to the area he loves. The house is decorated with Donegal folk art, Japanese and Islamic art, Victoriana, and William Morris papers and textiles. The adjacent stables have been converted into an art gallery housing the 300-item Hill Collection of works by Picasso, Bonnard, Kokoschka, Yeats, Annigoni, Pasmore, and Hill himself. It's more than surprising to find this first-rate 20th-century art collection in such a remote part of the country, but then Donegal is a surprising place.

Church Hill. ✆ 074/37071. www.heritageireland.ie. Admission 3.4€ ($3) adults, 2.50€ ($2.25) seniors, 1.70€ ($1.50) students and children. Mid-May to Sept Sat–Thurs 11am–6:30pm. 11 miles (18km) northwest of Letterkenny on the Churchill Rd. (R251).

Glenveagh National Park ★★ Deep in the heart of County Donegal, far off the coastal path, this 35,000-acre estate is considered by many to be Ireland's finest national park. The core of the park is the Glenveagh Estate, originally the home of the notorious landlord John George Adair, much despised for his eviction of Irish tenant farmers in 1861. He built the castle in the 1870s. From 1937 to 1983 the estate prospered under the stewardship of Henry McIlhenny, a distinguished Philadelphia art historian (of the Tabasco Sauce family) who restored the baronial castle and planted gardens full of exotic species of flowers and shrubs. McIlhenny subsequently gave Glenveagh to the Irish nation for use as a public park, and today the fairy-tale setting includes woodlands, herds of red deer, alpine gardens, a sylvan lake, and the highest mountain in Donegal, Mount Errigal. Visitors can tour the castle and gardens and explore the park on foot. The complex includes a visitor center with a continuous audiovisual show; displays on the history, flora, and fauna of the area; and nature trails. There is a self-service restaurant in the visitor center, and a tearoom in the castle.

Churchill, Co. Donegal. ✆ 074/37090. www.heritageireland.ie. Admission 2.60€ ($2.40) adults, 1.90€ ($1.75) seniors, 1.25€ ($1.15) students and children, 6.50€ ($5.90) family; castle tour 2.60€ ($2.40) adults, 1.90€ ($1.75) seniors, 1.25€ ($1.15) students and children, 6.50€ ($5.90) family. No credit cards. Easter to first Sun in Nov daily 10am–6:30pm; July–Aug Sun 10am–7:30pm. Closed Fri Oct–Nov. Main entrance on R251.

OUTDOOR PURSUITS
BEACHES Some of the most pristine and secluded beaches in Ireland are to be found along the northern and western coasts of Donegal. There are few such

places anywhere else where you can be so alone on such magnificent expanses of sea-sand, but the trick is to find a really sunny day on which to enjoy it. Dawros Head has several popular beaches, including **Traighmore Strand** in Rossbeg and extensive beaches in Portnoo and Navan. **Magheroarty,** near Falcarragh on the northern coast, has a breathtaking beach, unspoiled by crowds or commercial development. The same goes for **Tramore** beach on the west side of Horn Head near Dunfanaghy; you have to hike a short distance to get there, but you'll be rewarded by miles of white sand and seclusion. Other secluded and sandy beaches ideal for walking and jogging include Carrigart, Downings, Marble Hill, and Port na Blagh.

BICYCLING   Raleigh mountain bikes can be rented with panniers and accessories from **Church Street Cycles,** Letterkenny, County Donegal (© **074/ 26204**), for 13€ ($12) per day and 51€ ($46) per week, with a 51€ ($46) deposit (no credit cards accepted). Letterkenny is a good starting point for exploring the coast of northern Donegal—Horn Head, Inishowen Peninsula, Tory Island, and Bloody Foreland Head are all within an easy day's ride. Cycles rented here can be left off in Sligo town, Donegal town, or Galway city for an additional fee of 19€ ($18).

BIRD-WATCHING   **Horn Head** is a nesting site for many species of seabirds, and has the largest nesting population of razorbills in Ireland. **Malin Head,** at the end of the Inishowen Peninsula (see "Seeing the Sights," under "The Inishowen Peninsula," later in this chapter), is the northernmost point on the Irish mainland, and once was the site of a bird observatory; it's a good place for watching migrants in late autumn.

FISHING   The rivers and lakes in this area produce good catches of salmon, sea trout, and brown trout, and the coastal waters yield flounder, pollock, and cod. Fishing expeditions are offered by charter boats, fishing boats, and trawlers. For details, contact the **North Western Regional Fisheries Board,** Abbey Street, Ballina, County Mayo (© **096/22623;** fax 096/70543; www.cfb.ie).

GOLF   One of Ireland's most challenging golf courses is the **Rosapenna Golf Club,** Atlantic Drive, Downings, County Donegal (© **074/55301**), an 18-hole championship seaside par-70 links course. It was laid out in 1983 by Tom Morris of St. Andrews. Greens fees are 25€ ($23) on weekdays and 32€ ($29) on weekends.

Other 18-hole courses in this part of Donegal are **Dunfanaghy Golf Club,** Dunfanaghy, County Donegal (© **074/36335;** www.golfdunfanaghy.com), a seaside par-68 course with greens fees of 22€ ($20) on weekdays and 25€ ($23) on weekends; **Narin & Portnoo Golf Club,** Narin-Portnoo, County Donegal (© **075/45107**), a par-69 seaside course with greens fees of 22€ ($20) on weekdays and 25€ ($23) on weekends; and **Portsalon Golf Club,** Portsalon, County Donegal (© **074/59459**), a seaside par-69 course with greens fees of 25€ ($23) on weekdays and 32€ ($23) on weekends.

HORSEBACK RIDING   **Dunfanaghy Stables,** Arnolds Hotel, Dunfanaghy, County Donegal (© **074/36208**), specializes in trail riding on the surrounding beaches, dunes, and mountain trails. An hour's ride averages 16€ ($14).

WALKING   A section of the **Ulster Way** passes through Donegal between the towns of Falcarragh to the north and Pettigo to the south, on the border with Fermanagh. This trail traverses some remote and wild terrain, passing Errigal Mountain and Glenveagh Park before heading south into the Blue Stack Mountains.

There are some incredible walks on **Hook Head,** signposted off N56 just west of Dunfanaghy. Follow Hook Head Drive to the concrete lookout point. From here you can walk out to a ruined castle on the headland and continue south along a line of impressive quartzite sea cliffs that glitter in the sun as though covered with a sheet of ice. This is a moderately difficult walk.

The **Ards Forest Park** is on a peninsula jutting out into Sheep Haven Bay, about 3½ miles (5.5km) south of Dunfanaghy on N56. The park is mostly forested and includes an area of dunes along the water. There are signposted nature trails, and you can buy a guidebook as you enter the park.

ACCOMMODATIONS YOU CAN AFFORD

Ardeen ★ Mrs. Anne Campbell is the delightful hostess of this beautiful country home furnished with antiques, on the outskirts of town overlooking Lough Swilly. Mrs. Campbell and her family are all helpful and friendly, and the five bedrooms here are nicely furnished. The ample breakfasts feature fresh local produce. There's a hard-surface tennis court for guests to use.

A self-catering cottage adjacent to the main house was formed from converted stables. The centrally heated structure features stone walls, lots of wood, and an open fireplace. There are three bedrooms that can sleep up to seven people, a full kitchen, a sitting room, and a dining room. It can be rented for 405€ ($368) per week in July and August, 250€ ($228) per week at other times.

Ramelton, Co. Donegal. ✆/fax 074/51243. www.ardeenhouse.com. 5 units, 4 with bathroom (shower only). 63€ ($58) double. 25% reduction for children sharing with an adult. Rates include full breakfast. MC, V. Closed Nov–Easter. **Amenities:** Tennis court.

Ardglas Breid and Paddy Kelly's spacious country home sits on extensive grounds overlooking Letterkenny and the Muckish Mountains. The entire Kelly family welcomes guests and helps with local and regional sightseeing plans. There's a large garden, much used by guests in fine weather, and a TV lounge. The entire house is nonsmoking.

Lurgybrack, Letterkenny, Co. Donegal. ✆ 074/22516. Fax 074/25140. www.ardglas.com. 6 units. 38.50€ ($35) single; 51€ ($46) double. 30% reduction for children. Rates include full breakfast. MC, V. Free parking. Closed Oct–Mar. It's 1¼ miles (2km) out from Letterkenny on the Derry road (N14), then another 1¼ miles (2km) on N13 (take the Sligo road at the Dry Arch roundabout). **Amenities:** Lounge. *In room:* TV, tea/ coffemaker, hair dryer.

Bay View Country House This house is situated on the northern edge of town on the coast road and offers magnificent views of Loughros Bay and the Owenea River. It has a spacious lounge with picture windows and turf fires and a large dining room. The Bennett Family are helpful hosts, and Marion is an active member of the local Tourism Committee and can help you plan your excursions. The bedrooms and dining room are nonsmoking. Outside, guests can enjoy the fine gardens and lawns.

Portnoo Rd., Ardara, Co. Donegal. ✆/fax 075/41145. chbennett@eircom.net. 6 units. 32€ ($29) single; 51€ ($46) double. 25% reduction for children. Rates include full breakfast. AE, MC, V. Free parking. Closed mid-Dec to Jan. **Amenities:** Lounge.

Corcreggan Mill Hostel The hostel makes imaginative use of this handsome old stone mill, fitting an airy dorm room over the main kitchen and tucking a refurbished train car under the eaves. The whimsical renovation includes several (tiny) private rooms in the train and a host of details that continue the railroad motif. There's also an appealing loft separated from the dorm room by a curtain, offering yet another unique way to sleep. A washing machine is available, with drying on the outside line. The surrounding area is great for traditional music, and a shuttle bus takes hostelers to the best music each night. The hostel is a short walk from spectacular Tramore Strand, and 4 miles (6.5km) from the sea cliffs of Horn Head.

Corgreggan, Dunfanaghy, Co. Donegal. ✆ **074/36409.** Fax 074/36902. http://homepage.eircom.net/~brendanr. 5 private units, none with bathroom. 1 dorm rm. 9€ ($8.15) per person in dorm (10 beds); 11€ ($10) per person in 4-bed rm; 28€ ($25) double. No credit cards. 2 miles (3km) west of Dunfanaghy on the N56. **Amenities:** Laundry.

Crohy Head Youth Hostel   This remote hostel is located in a former coastguard station, perched on a high bluff overlooking Aranmore Island and the open Atlantic. For untamed beauty, you can't do much better than this jagged rocky promontory jutting into the ocean west of Dungloe, a little-known treasure of this part of Donegal. The hostel facilities are the usual spartan *An Óige* fixtures: a clean institutional kitchen and a sitting room with a fireplace kept burning during the chilly nights. The building is unusually austere, a feature that is in keeping with this harsh landscape. There are numerous walks to be had on Crohy Head, along its craggy coast or inland to one of the small peaks that line the spine of the peninsula. To my mind, this is hosteling at its rugged best.

Crohy Head, Dungloe, Co. Donegal. ✆ **075/21950.** www.irelandyha.org/anoige/donegal2.html. 6 units, none with bathroom: 2 4-bed rooms, 2 6-bed rooms, 1 8-bed room, 1 10-bed room. 10€ ($9.10) per person in a dorm. No credit cards. Closed daily 10am–5pm. Closed Oct to Easter. 5 miles (8km) west of Dungloe, off N56. **Amenities:** Full kitchen; sitting room.

The Green Gate   Paul Chatenoud, a transplanted Frenchman, is the voluble and eccentric host at this beautifully situated hilltop B&B. Accommodation is in one of two stone cottages, one with a thatched roof and the other with a slate roof and exceptional views toward Maghera, Loughros Point, and the open Atlantic (the rooms with a view have the 80€ ($73) rate, while the others are 20€ ($17.50) cheaper). Rooms are small, with pleasingly austere interiors of whitewashed stone, simple furnishings, and raftered ceilings. There isn't much natural light, but the rooms do give you an experience of life in a traditional Donegal cottage. A beautiful lawn overlooks the ocean, making the best of that fabulous view, which is nothing short of breathtaking. Despite its hilltop location, this place is sheltered from the winds, and offers a cozy retreat in all seasons.

Ardvally, Ardara, Co. Donegal. ✆ **075/41546.** 4 units. 45€–55€ ($41–$50) single; 60€–80€ ($54–$73) double. Rates include full breakfast. No credit cards.

Greenhaven   Eileen and Ray Molloy are the delightful hosts at Greenhaven, at the northern edge of town on the coast road, which overlooks Loughross Bay and Slieve Tooey. There's a window-walled breakfast room that opens onto the gorgeous view and a large back garden. A modern extension holds the comfortable guest rooms, which all have lovely, puffy eiderdown quilts on the beds. The Molloys are especially helpful in pointing their guests to the things to see and do in the area (this is Ray's family territory, and he knows it well). The bedrooms and dining room are nonsmoking.

Portnoo Rd., Ardara, Co. Donegal. ✆/fax **075/41129.** 6 units. 25€ ($23) single; 51€ ($46) double. Rates include full breakfast. No credit cards. *In room:* Tea/coffeemaker.

Hill Crest House   This modern bungalow sits on a slight elevation that opens up splendid views of the River Swilly, Letterkenny, and the mountains. Four bedrooms are on the ground floor, and there are orthopedic mattresses and electric blankets in every room. In addition to the spacious no-smoking dining room, there's also a TV/video lounge, and proprietor Martin Anderson opened a new seafood restaurant here in 2001: The Crest dining rooms are open for dinner from 5:30 to 10pm.

Lurgybrack, Sligo Rd., Letterkenny, Co. Donegal. ✆/fax **074/22300**. chefma@eircom.net. 8 units, 7 with bathroom (shower only). 30.50€ ($28) single; 56€ ($51) double. 33% reduction for children sharing with an adult. Rates include full breakfast. Dinner 20€ ($18). MC, V. Free parking. 2 miles (3km) from Letterkenny on the main Ballybofey-Sligo. **Amenities:** Restaurant, lounge. *In room:* TV, tea/coffeemaker, hair dryer.

Mount Royd Country Home (Value   Not only does Mrs. Josephine Martin greet arriving guests with tea and scones, but she provides tea/coffee and biscuits in each bedroom. Her large, creeper-clad home is furnished with antiques, and sports a warm, welcoming atmosphere. Some of the spacious guest rooms have lovely views of the River Foyle, and all have comfortable beds equipped with electric blankets. Mrs. Martin's breakfasts and her home have won numerous awards—deservedly so.

Carrigans, Co. Donegal. ✆ **074/40163**. Fax 074/40400. www.mountroyd.com. 4 units. 32€ ($29) single; 51€ ($46) double. High tea 8.25€ ($7.50). 50% reduction for children. No credit cards. Free parking. *In room:* TV, tea/coffeemaker.

Sweeney's Hotel   This small, family-run hotel has been a Donegal institution for centuries; it was established in 1762. Guest rooms are quite comfortable and the food is decent, but the hotel's best features are its traditional music and warm hospitality. One reader informed me that he has returned year after year for more than 20 years, and that's a testimonial worth heeding.

Dungloe, Co. Donegal. ✆ **075/21033**. Fax 075/22487. 16 units. 72€ ($66) double. No credit cards. Closed Jan–June. *In room:* TEL, tea/coffeemaker.

Town View   May Herrity is the hostess at this two-story house perched on a hilltop on the outskirts of town. The panoramic views of Letterkenny are stunning, especially at night when the cathedral is spotlit. The guest rooms are unusually attractive, decorated, according to May, "the way I like to live myself." Those in the back of the house face peaceful green fields that resemble 18th-century landscape paintings. The lounge, where breakfast is served, has a huge fireplace and picture windows overlooking the town. Breakfast often features a selection of fresh fruits and other items, as well as the traditional full Irish menu.

Leck Rd., Letterkenny, Co. Donegal. ✆ **074/21570** or 074/25138. 6 units. 48€ ($44) double. 20% reduction for children sharing with an adult. Rates include full breakfast. MC, V. Take the Ballybofey Rd. (N56), cross the stone bridge at Dunnes Stores in Letterkenny, and keep left for one half mile. **Amenities:** Lounge. *In room:* TV, tea/coffeemaker, hair dryer.

WORTH A SPLURGE

Rathmullan Country House ✹✹✹   This is one of the most pleasurable places to stay in northern Donegal. This lovely old 19th-century house sits on the edge of town amid spacious, landscaped grounds that slope down to Lough Swilly. In the more than 30 years that Robin and Bob Wheeler have been in residence, it has become a beloved favorite with Irish from all over the Republic and nearby Northern Ireland. The mostly Georgian (ca. 1760) interior features intricate plastered ceilings, crystal chandeliers, oil paintings, white marble log-burning fireplaces, and an assortment of antiques and heirlooms. The glow of turf or log fires in the drawing room and library provides a soft light. Rooms vary in size, but all are comfortably and attractively furnished. The most expensive are luxurious, with sitting areas and views of the lake, while the least expensive are more compact with a garden view. All have orthopedic beds, and two are equipped for travelers with disabilities. The glass-enclosed Pavilion Dining Room looks out on award-winning gardens, and the cellar bar is a cozy spot for relaxed conviviality. Sumptuous dinners, for which chef Bob has earned an international reputation, are quite moderately priced and feature local seafood and other products (see "Great Deals on Dining," below). Advance reservations for both accommodations and meals in this very popular place are absolutely essential.

Rathmullan (northeast of Letterkenny), Co. Donegal. © **074/58188**. Fax 074/58200. www.rathmullanhouse. com. 24 units. 70€–80€ ($63–$72) standard double; 160€–180€ ($145–$163) superior double; 190€–200€ ($172–$181) mini suite; 12€–35€ ($11–$32) single supplement. 50% reduction for children. Half-board rates available. Rates include full breakfast. 10% service charge. AE, DC, MC, V. Free parking. Closed Jan to mid-Feb. **Amenities:** Restaurant (Modern Country), bar; indoor swimming pool; private beach; 2 tennis courts; steam room; massage treatments; drawing room; library. *In room:* TV, hair dryer.

SELF-CATERING

Donegal Thatched Cottages ★★   This cluster of cottages is on Cruit Island, an enchanting landscape of rock and sand just off the Donegal coast near Dungloe. Accessible by a small bridge, Cruit is a narrow spit of land reaching into the Atlantic, dwarfed by its nearby neighbors Aranmore and Owey Islands. The cottages are on the Atlantic side, which alternates rocky headlands with unspoiled beaches; on the lee side is a lovely quiet beach that extends for miles. The view west toward Owey Island is captivating, and sunsets are notoriously glorious. There's a great seaside walk along the western side of the island, which takes in a series of lovely half-moon beaches.

Each cottage is built according to a traditional plan, resembling many of the rural homes you're sure to have seen while exploring the region. The interiors are simple and appealing, with wooden and tiled floors, high ceilings in the living/dining rooms, and a great loft bedroom on the second floor. The kitchen comes equipped with a dishwasher and a washer and dryer for your laundry, and there's a master bedroom with its own private bathroom. Each cottage has three bedrooms, and can sleep up to seven guests. During peak season, these cottages are a budget option only if shared between several people. Although the location is somewhat remote, there are a number of pubs and restaurants within a short driving distance.

On Cruit Island, c/o Conor and Mary Ward, Rosses Point, Co. Sligo. © **071/77197**. Fax 071/77500. www.donegalthatchedcottages.com. 10 cottages, each with 3 bedrooms. 225€–840€ ($204–$761) per cottage per week, depending on season. Additional charge of 7€ ($6.35) per person per week. Special week-end rates also available. MC, V. Signposted opposite Viking House Hotel on Kincasslagh Rd., 6 miles (9.5km) north of Dungloe. **Amenities:** Full kitchen; washer/dryer.

GREAT DEALS ON DINING

Danny Minnie's Restaurant SEAFOOD   This charming traditional-style, family-run restaurant is a delight to the eye as well as to the palate. There's a warm, welcoming atmosphere very much in keeping with Irish traditions of hospitality, and the menu offers a selection of local seafood and fresh produce.

Annagry, The Rosses, Co. Donegal. © **075/48201**. Reservations recommended. Dinner main courses 13€–19€ ($12–$17). MC, V. Daily 6:30–9pm. Closed Good Friday and Christmas Day.

Nesbitt Arms Hotel TRADITIONAL IRISH   The dining room in this family-owned and -operated hotel serves meals featuring local produce, meat, and fish cooked in the traditional Irish manner. The restaurant specializes in seafood dishes, while the bistro section serves a variety of Irish dishes. The atmosphere in both is convivial, and the service is good, making the hotel a respectable choice for a hearty meal.

Ardara, Co. Donegal. ℂ 075/41103. Bistro main courses 6.50€–15€ ($5.90–$14); restaurant main courses 9.50€–19€ ($8.60–$17). MC, V. Bistro daily noon–9pm; restaurant daily 6–9:30pm. Closed Dec 24–25.

Waters Edge INTERNATIONAL   As its name implies, this restaurant is on the edge of picturesque Lough Swilly, on the south end of town. Although a glassy facade on three sides gives the 70-seat dining area a modern look, the interior is quite traditional, with beamed ceilings, an open fireplace, nautical bric-a-brac, and watercolors of Donegal landscapes. The menu blends Irish dishes with such international favorites as wild salmon in brandy-bisque sauce, chicken Kiev, prawns Provençal, and steaks. Bar food, served all day, ranges from soups and sandwiches to patés, scampi, and fish-and-chips. *Note:* Rooms with a view and breakfast are available for 51€ ($46) double.

The Ballyboe, Rathmullan, Co. Donegal. ℂ 074/58182. Reservations recommended for dinner. Dinner main courses 9€–20€ ($8.15–$18). MC, V. Bar Tues–Sat noon–4:30pm, Sun 12:30–3:30pm; restaurant Tues–Sat 6–9:30pm.

WORTH A SPLURGE

Pavilion Dining Room 🌟🌟 SEAFOOD/TRADITIONAL   This elegant glass-walled dining room inside Rathmullan Country House (see above) looks out over well-kept lawns that slope down to the shores of Lough Swilly. Its menu includes locally caught salmon; Irish beef, seafood, and lamb; and vegetables from its own garden. The breakfasts are excellent. Fresh fruits from on-premises trees go into luscious homemade pies, and if you've ever been curious about the seaweed-based Carrageen dessert, this is the place to try it. There's a very good wine list, and service is both friendly and professional.

Rathmullan Country House, Rathmullan, Co. Donegal. ℂ 074/58188. www.rathmullanhouse.com. Reservations recommended. Dinner 42.50€ ($39). 10% service charge. AE, DC, MC, V. Daily 7:30–9pm.

SHOPPING

Ardara is a hub of tweed and woolen production. Most shops here are open Monday to Saturday from 9am to 5:30pm, with extended hours in summer. These shops are all on the main street of the town (N56).

Ardara is known for its local tweed and sweater industries. Shoppers shouldn't miss the following factory shops, which also have tearooms on the premises: **John Molloy and Co.** and **Kennedy's of Ardara** (see below). No matter where you end up buying, however, prices hereabouts are likely to be the best you'll find anywhere in the country. Most shops here are open Monday to Saturday from 9am to 5:30pm, with extended hours in summer. The shops listed below are all on the main street of the town (N56).

C. Bonner & Son   This firm produces its own hand-knit and hand-loomed knitwear, including linen-cotton and colorful sheep-patterned lambswool sweaters. The shop also sells sheepskins, pottery, wildlife watercolors, wool and tweed hangings, linens, crystal, and china. Ardara, Co. Donegal. ℂ 075/41303.

John Molloy   This factory shop is well stocked with hand knits, homespun fashions, sports jackets, tweed scarves and rugs, and all types of caps, from kingfisher to ghillie styles. There's even a bargain bin. Tours of the factory itself can be arranged by calling in advance. Ardara, Co. Donegal. ℂ 075/41133.

Kennedy of Ardara   Established in 1904, this family-owned knitwear company employs about 500 home workers who hand-knit or hand-loom bainin sweaters, hats, scarves, and jackets in native Donegal patterns and colors. The shop also sells turf crafts, pottery, and dolls. Ardara, Co. Donegal. ✆ **075/41106.**

PUBS WITH TRADITIONAL IRISH MUSIC

Almost all the pubs in this Irish-speaking area provide spontaneous sessions of Irish traditional music in summer. Two places especially renowned for music are the **Lakeside Centre,** Dunlewey (✆ **075/31699**), and **Leo's Tavern,** Meenaleck, Crolly (✆ **075/48143**). The highly successful Irish group Clannad and the vocalist Enya (all part of the talented Brennan family) got their starts at Leo's.

Another good place for music and meals is **The Singing Pub,** Calontallagh, Downings (✆ **074/55176**), located on the Atlantic Drive northeast of Downings. There's music every night, although you're just as likely to find country and western as traditional Irish music.

The don't-miss pub in Ardara is **Nancy's** (✆ **075/41187**) on Front Street, which has to be one of the smallest pubs in Ireland. It's an old Victorian house with the pub in the sitting room. As the crowd pours in, other rooms open up in hospitality.

5 The Inishowen Peninsula

Buncrana, the Inishowen's chief town, is 70 miles (113km) NE of Donegal Airport, 52 miles (84km) NE of Donegal town, 12 miles (19km) NW of Derry, 90 miles (145km) NE of Sligo, 223 miles (359km) NE of Shannon, and 161 miles (259km) NW of Dublin

This long, broad finger of land stretching north to the Atlantic between Lough Swilly to the west and Lough Foyle to the east is Ireland's northernmost point. Along the shores of both loughs and the Atlantic Ocean, long stretches of sandy beaches are backed by sheer cliffs. Inland are some of Ireland's most impressive mountains, with 2,019-foot (615m) Slieve Snacht dominating the center of the peninsula. Its heritage reaches back beyond recorded history, with relics of those distant days scattered across its face.

Relatively undiscovered by most visitors to Ireland, Inishowen is a world apart, where present-day residents revere their ancient heritage, treasure the legends and antiquities of this remote region, and still observe many traditions of their ancestors. Traditional music and dance thrive here, and it's unlikely you'll face an evening when there's not a session in a nearby pub.

GETTING THERE & GETTING AROUND   The **Lough Swilly Bus Company** (✆ **074/22853;** www.sjp.clara.net/nibus/lswilly.htm) operates a regular service from Buncrana to Cardonagh and Moville, with connections to other points.

The best way to get to and around the Inishowen Peninsula is by car or bicycle, following the signposted 100-mile (160km) **Inishowen 100** route.

VISITOR INFORMATION   Contact the **North West Tourism Office,** Aras Reddan, Temple Street, Sligo (✆ **071/61201**); the **Letterkenny Tourist Office,** Derry Road, Letterkenny (✆ **074/21173**); or the **Inishowen Tourism Society,** Chapel Street, Cardonagh, County Donegal (✆ **077/74933;** www.visit inishowen). All three are open year-round, Monday to Friday 9:30am to 5:30pm, with extended summer hours.

SEEING THE SIGHTS

At the little township of Burt, 3 miles (5km) south of Bridgend and 10 miles (16km) south of Buncrana, look for signposts to the unclassified road that leads to a great circular stone cashel known as **Grianan of Aileach** ✸ ("Sun Palace of

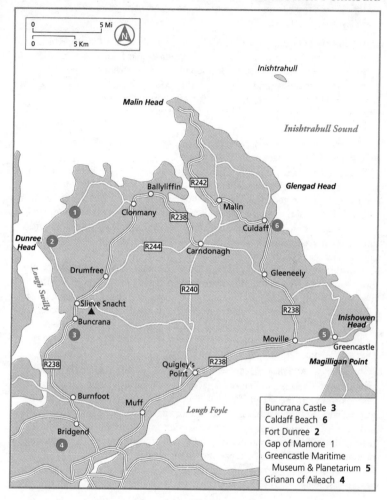

Aileach"), once the royal seat of the O'Neills and a sacred meeting place for high kings of Ireland. From its 800-foot (244m) perch atop Greenan Mountain, there are vast panoramic views of Lough Swilly, Lough Foyle, and the distant sea.

Buncrana, the principal town of Inishowen, is a pleasant seaside resort with 3 miles (5km) of sand beach. Along a pleasant walk and overlooking the Crana River are the ruins of **Buncrana Castle,** dating from the late 16th century, with extensive rebuilding in 1718. This is where Wolfe Tone was taken after his capture in 1798. Close by are the ruins of **O'Doherty's Castle.**

North of Buncrana is the stunning **Gap of Mamore,** some 820 feet (250m) above sea level, with spectacular sea views. For dedicated hill walkers, this is a good starting point for exploring the Urris Hills to the west or Mamore Hill and Raghtin to the east. Some 10 miles (16km) north of Buncrana, you encounter the village of **Clonmany,** and 2 miles (3km) east, on the face of Magheramore Hill, the huge capstone of a Bronze Age dolmen is reputed hereabouts to have

---

Tips Take a Look

As you descend from the Grianan of Aileach, look at **Burt Church,** which sits at the foot of the access road. Its circular design follows that of the fort itself. The church is being developed as a visitor center focusing on the history, legends, and folklore of the Grianan of Aileach. There's a traditional tearoom here, as well as a craft shop and a restaurant.

---

been thrown by Ireland's legendary giant hero Finn MacCool, which earns it the local name of "Finn MacCool's Finger Stone."

While **Malin Head** lacks the spectacular cliff-top heights you've seen en route, it provides marvelous panoramic views of the peninsula to the south and out to sea, and it's a good starting point for a walk to Hell's Hole, a deep cavern into which the sea thunders at high tide. On the way out to Malin Head, look for signposts to **Ballyhillion Beach,** a raised-beach system whose distinct shorelines clearly trace the sea's activities from some 15,000 years ago as the age of the great glaciers came to an end.

Your route now turns south, through the picturesque village of **Culdaff,** with lovely sandy beaches, to **Moville,** where a short detour through **Greencastle** (a fine beach resort named for the castle of Richard de Burgo, the Red Earl of Ulster) leads to **Inishowen Head,** site of a maritime disaster in 1588 when a number of Spanish Armada galleons sank in Kinnagoe Bay. One such vessel was located in near-perfect condition some years back, and artifacts recovered by the Derry Sub-Aqua Club are on display in Derry.

Fort Dunree Military Museum   Perched on a cliff overlooking Lough Swilly, Fort Dunree is a military and naval museum incorporating a Napoleonic Martello tower at the site of World War I defenses on the north Irish coast. It features a wide range of exhibitions, an audiovisual center, and a cafeteria housed in a restored forge. Even if you have no interest in military history, it's worth a trip for the view. Dunree has one of Donegal's best vantage points for observing unencumbered seascapes and broad mountain vistas.

Buncrana, Co. Donegal. (© 077/61817. Fax 074/25180. Admission 2.60€ ($2.40) per car. June–Sept Mon–Sat 10:30am–6pm, Sun 12:30–6pm. Signposted on the coast road north of Buncrana.

Greencastle Maritime Museum and Planetarium   This compact maritime museum, in the harbor home of one of the busiest fishing fleets in Ireland, is housed in the old 1857 coast-guard station. Before you go in, be sure to take in the grand views of Lough Foyle, as well as the monument to those lost in nearby waters. The museum's modest, intriguing exhibits focus on the everyday struggles as well as the historic events beyond Greencastle Harbour, from Armada wrecks to famine-period emigration to the heroism of the Irish lifeboat rescue teams. In addition, there's a Mesolithic exhibit with local 8,000-year-old finds. A small coffee, craft, and souvenir shop is also at hand. Best of all, Maire McCann's stories bring the museum's exhibits to life. The planetarium, built in 2000, has three shows daily: call ahead to confirm times.

Harbour, Greencastle. (© 077/81363. http://homepage.eircom.net/~greencastlemaritime. Admission (either museum or planetarium) 4€ ($3.65) adults; 2€ ($1.80) seniors, children, and students; 10€ ($9.10) family. Open June–Sept Mon–Sat 10am–6pm, Sun noon–6pm.

Grianan of Aileach ⭐⭐   The great circular stone cashel known as the Grianan of Aileach ("Sun Palace of Aileach") was once the royal seat of the

O'Neills and a sacred meeting place for high kings of Ireland. If you stand on its walls, which are perched 800 feet (244m) above the sea on Greenan Mountain, you'll have vast panoramic views of Lough Swilly, Lough Foyle, and the distant sea. The dry-stone fort was built around 1700 B.C. Its 76-foot (23m) diameter is enclosed by walls 13 feet (4m) thick and 17 feet (5.25m) high. Virtually dismantled stone by stone in 1101 by Murtagh O'Brien, king of Munster, it was restored in the 1870s.

Burt, Buncrana, Co. Donegal. (C) 077/68000. Fax 077/68012. Admission to the fort free; interpretive center 2.60€ ($2.40) adults, 1.90€ ($1.75) children and students, 6.50€ ($5.90) family. Apr–Sept daily 10am–5pm; Oct–Mar daily 11:30am–5pm. Signposted from Burt, 3 miles (5km) south of Bridgend and 10 miles (16km) south of Buncrana.

ACCOMMODATIONS YOU CAN AFFORD

Barraicin   Mrs. Maire Doyle will welcome you to her modern bungalow over-looking the sea, some 6½ miles (10km) north of Malin village and 3½ miles (5.5km) from Malin Head. The guest rooms are small, clean, and comfortable, all with sinks, and hair dryers and a tea kettle are available on request. Mrs. Doyle has won much praise from our readers for her warmth and graciousness, as well as for her tremendous help in steering them to highlights of the penin-sula. Bird enthusiasts will be glad to know that the corncrake can often be heard from an adjacent field—Mrs. Doyle eagerly offers information and advice regarding this rare bird species to all who are interested.

Malin Head, Co. Donegal. (C)/fax 077/70184. 3 units, 1 with bathroom (shower only). 43€ ($39) double. Rates include full breakfast. No credit cards. Closed Dec–Mar. *In room:* TV, hair dryer (on request).

Brooklyn Cottage ✦   You're not going to find a nicer lakeside B&B for this price. Only tall panes of glass separate the living room of Brooklyn Cottage from the lapping waves. This modern bungalow is right on the brink of the Inishowen peninsula, and guests eat breakfast in a conservatory that takes advantage of a spec-tacular sea view (as do the living room and two of the guest rooms). A small coastal path skirts the rocky shore in front of the house, and it's possible to follow it to the neighboring town of Moville, about 2 miles (3km) away. The guest rooms are small, but each is meticulously kept. Peter Smith, who serves as host along with his wife, Gladys, is involved with the nearby Maritime museum and shares his knowledge of the area with guests. Brooklyn Cottage is within walking distance of the center of Greencastle, yet occupies a seemingly remote site just beyond the port.

Greencastle, Inishowen, Co. Donegal. (C) 077/81087. 3 units. 48€ ($44) double. No credit cards. Free park-ing. Closed Jan–Feb. *In room:* TV, tea/coffeemaker.

Four Arches   This modern bungalow 4½ miles (7km) east of Clonmany is the perfect place to experience the splendor and spirit of the Inishowen countryside. There are panoramic views on all sides, and the property's 10 acres hold 40 sheep, 3 goats, and some chickens. This is the home of Fidelma and Michael McLaughlin and their five children, all the very essence of Irish hospitality. Fidelma's breakfasts add fruit and scrambled eggs to the traditional Irish break-fast. Guest rooms are nicely appointed, one with two double beds. Some rooms are wheelchair accessible.

Urris, Clonmany, Inishowan, Co. Donegal. (C) 077/76109 or 077/76561. 5 units. 48€ ($44) double. Rates include full breakfast. MC, V. *In room:* hair dryer.

SELF-CATERING

Ballyliffin Self Catering ✦   Ballyliffin is a tiny seaside village on the west coast of Inishowen, with two golf courses in close proximity. This group of cottages is situated along the main road through town, a 10-minute walk from the fine sand and clear waters of Pollan Bay. The six connected cottages are all built in stone and pine, with lofty vaulted ceilings in the living rooms and massive central fireplaces that the stairs circle on their way to the second floor. Each cottage has three bedrooms and two bathrooms—two of the bedrooms have a double bed and an attached bathroom, while the third bedroom has three single beds. In some cottages, second-floor bedrooms overlook the living room, where a foldout couch provides yet more sleeping space. The well-equipped kitchen includes a microwave, an electric stove, a dishwasher, and a washing machine and dryer.

Rossaor House, Ballyliffin, Co. Donegal. ©/fax **077/76498.** rossaor@gofree.indigo.ie. 6 units. Weekly rates per cottage: Oct–Mar 475€ ($430); Apr–June and Sept 540€ ($489); July–Aug 630€ ($571). Weekend rates also available. Rates include electric heat. MC, V. **Amenities:** TV, kitchen.

GREAT DEALS ON DINING

The Corncrake ★★★ *Value* CONTINENTAL   A restaurant like the Corncrake is as rare as the endangered bird from which it takes its name. The set up is "dead simple," as the Irish like to say—just one room and two talented women at the helm. The freshest of ingredients are sought out by Brid McCartney and Noreen Lynch, and then transformed using a selection of herbs grown in their own gardens in a way that is nothing short of sublime. Starters include a prawn chowder where lemon and fresh coriander bring out the flavor of locally caught fish, and a cheese soufflé whose golden crown topples to reveal a velvet textured filling of egg, cream, and sharp cheddar. Meat and fish dishes are coupled with sauces and seasonings so masterful that they seem to give lamb a new tenderness and monkfish an unanticipated delicacy. Vegetarians need to book a day in advance but will be rewarded by something downright delectable, such as goat cheese wrapped in red peppers. Desserts range from a wholesome gooseberry fool to a blissful orange and Grand Marnier *panna cotta* (an Italian dessert of reduced cream and eggs). It's only the tranquil lighting and sedate setting of the Corncrake that keeps diners from licking their plates.

Malin St, Carndonagh, Co. Donegal. © **077/74534.** Reservations recommended. Dinner main courses 13€–16€ ($12–$15). No credit cards. Easter–Sept daily 6–9pm; Sept–Dec weekends only. Closed Jan–Feb.

St John's Country House and Restaurant CONTINENTAL   On its own grounds overlooking Lough Swilly, this lovely Georgian house has two cozily elegant dining rooms. Open turf fireplaces, Waterford crystal, embroidered linens, and richly textured wallpaper add to the ambience. Importantly, the food is dependably good. The fixed-price menu offers baked Swilly salmon with lemon sauce, roast duck with port-and-orange sauce, spiced lamb en croûte with gooseberry-and-mint sauce, and John Dory with fennel. There is a significant nonsmoking area.

Fahan, Co. Donegal. © **077/60289.** Reservations recommended. Fixed-price dinner 36€ ($32). 10% service charge. DC, MC, V. Tues–Sat 7–9:30pm; Sun 12–4pm.

14

Along the River Shannon's Shores

The region covered by this chapter is defined by the path of the River Shannon, the longest waterway in Ireland or Great Britain. The Shannon makes its lazy way from County Cavan near the border with Northern Ireland through a multitude of lakes and ponds, finally reaching the waters of the Shannon estuary with its volume swollen by innumerable tributary rivers and rivulets.

The topography of Ireland is somewhat like a saucer: flat in the middle and tipped up at the edges. Most of the island's hills are clustered along the coast, and the central region or "Midlands" form an almost unbroken plain. For reasons topographic and otherwise, these central counties have a reputation as rather dull places, perhaps worth a stopover on the way to Ireland's more scenic and exciting coastal regions but not worth a lingering look. This impression is only partially correct. True, there's nothing in the Midlands to rival the grandeur of the Cliffs of Moher or the mystery of

the Giant's Causeway in Antrim, but if you step back a pace or two you'll find that this is a region characterized by subtle beauty, whose riches may take some time to discover. Take the **Slieve Bloom,** for instance, an area of hills and bogs circled by a marked walking trail; or the **Shannon Callows,** a low-lying meadowland that's home to the rare corncrake (see "Bird-Watching Resources" in chapter 3, "Ireland Outdoors"). These are a couple of good places to begin exploring.

There must be something in the faintly rolling land of Ireland's innards that nurtures literary talent. Oliver Goldsmith spent much of his life here, and the blind harpist bard O'Carolan lies buried in County Roscommon. County Longford was home to Maria Edgeworth, an 18th-century writer and angel of mercy during the famine years. Padraic Colum—poet, playwright, novelist, and essayist—was a product of County Longford, and chronicled the lives of its peasantry with an honest eye.

1 Lower Shannon: The Lough Derg Drive

Killaloe is 16 miles (26km) NE of Limerick and 25 miles (40km) E of Ennis; Portumna is 40 miles (64km) SE of Galway and 27 miles (43km) E of Gort

The Lower Shannon, stretching from Killaloe, County Clare, northward to Portumna, County Galway, encompasses one huge lake, Lough Derg. Often called an inland sea, Lough Derg was the main inland waterway trading route between Dublin and Limerick when canal and river commercial traffic was at its height in Ireland in the 18th and 19th centuries. It is the River Shannon's largest lake and widest point: 25 miles (40km) long and almost 10 miles (16km) wide, with more than 25,000 acres of water. Today, Lough Derg serves mostly as a pleasure lake, providing numerous recreational and sporting opportunities.

GETTING THERE & GETTING AROUND   The best way to get to the Lough Derg area is by car, bicycle, or boat. Although there are some limited public transportation services, you'll need a bicycle or a car to get around the lake. Major roads that lead to Lough Derg are the main Limerick-Dublin road (N7) from points east and south, N6 and N65 from Galway and the west, and N52 from northerly points. The Lough Derg Drive itself, which is well sign-posted, is a combination of R352 on the west bank of the lake and R493, R494, and R495 on the east bank.

VISITOR INFORMATION   Because Lough Derg unites three counties—Clare, Galway, and Tipperary—there are several sources of information, includ-ing the **Shannon Development Tourism Group,** Shannon, County Clare (© **061/361555;** www.Shannon-dev.ie/tourism); **Ireland West Tourism,** Vic-toria Place, Eyre Square, Galway (© **091/563081**); and **Tipperary Lake Side & Development,** The Old Church, Borrisokane, County Tipperary (© **067/ 27155**). All are open year-round. Seasonal information offices include the **Nenagh Tourist Office,** Connolly Street, Nenagh (© **067/31610** or 067/32100), open early May to early September; and the **Killaloe Tourist Office,** The Bridge, County Clare (© **061/376866**), open May through September.

THE LOUGH DERG DRIVE

The road that rims the lake for a perimeter of 95 miles (153km), the Lough Derg Drive, is one of the most scenic routes in Ireland, where panoramas of hilly farmlands, gentle mountains, bucolic forests, and glistening waters are unspoiled by condominiums, billboards, and other signs of commercialization. Most of all, the drive is a collage of colorful shoreline towns, starting with Killaloe, County Clare, and Ballina, County Tipperary, on the south banks of the lake. They're called twin towns because they're usually treated as one intertwined community—only a splendid 13-arch bridge over the Shannon separates them.

   Killaloe is home to Ireland's largest inland marina and a host of watersport centers. This lovely town has lakeside views at almost every turn and many fine restaurants/pubs offering outdoor seating on the shoreline. Of historical note here is a 9th-century oratory said to have been founded by St. Lua—hence the name Killaloe, which comes from the Irish: *Cill* (meaning "church") of Lua. (*Ballina* means "mouth of the ford.") Nearby is another oratory and cathedral, built in the 12th century and named for 6th-century St. Flannan; it boasts an exquisite Romanesque doorway. Kincora, on the highest ground at Killaloe, was the royal settlement of Brian Boru and the other O'Brien kings, but no trace of any building remains.

   Five miles (8km) inland from Lough Derg's lower southeast shores is **Nenagh,** the chief town of north Tipperary, lying in a fertile valley between the Silvermine and Arra Mountains.

   On the north shore of the lake is **Portumna,** which means "the landing place of the oak tree." A major point of traffic across the Shannon, Portumna has a lovely forest park and a remarkable castle that's currently being restored.

   The rest of the Lough Derg Drive is scattered with memorable little towns and harborside villages like Mountshannon and Dromineer. Some, like Terry-glass and Woodford, are known for atmospheric old pubs wherein spontaneous sessions of traditional Irish music are likely to occur. Others, like Puckane or Ballinderry, offer unique crafts or locally made products.

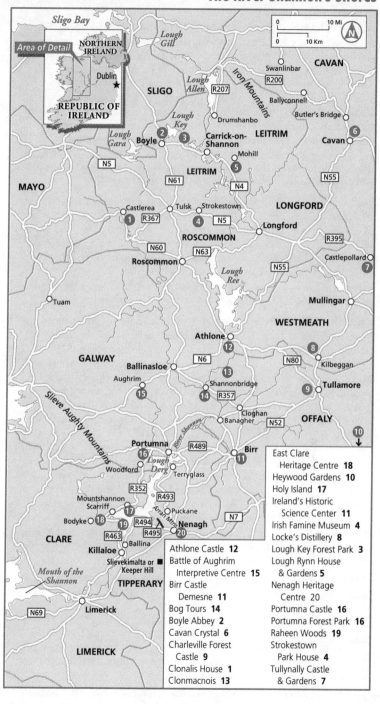

The River Shannon's Shores

0   10 Mi
0   10 Km

Sligo Bay

Area of Detail

NORTHERN IRELAND

Dublin ★

REPUBLIC OF IRELAND

Lough Gill

CAVAN

Swanlinbar

R200

Lough Allen

R207

SLIGO

Lough Key

Drumshanbo

Ballyconnell

Butler's Bridge

LEITRIM

Carrick-on-Shannon

2   3

Cavan 6

Boyle

Mohill

5

MAYO

LEITRIM

N61

N4

N55

Castlerea

R367

Tulsk

Strokestown

LONGFORD

N5

1

4

N5

Longford

ROSCOMMON

R395

N60

N63

Castlepollard 7

Roscommon

Lough Ree

N55

Tuam

Mullingar

WESTMEATH

Athlone

12

8

GALWAY

Ballinasloe

N6

N80

Kilbeggan

Aughrim

13

9

Tullamore

15

Shannonbridge

14   R357

River Shannon

Cloghan

Banagher

OFFALY

Slieve Aughty Mountains

N52

10
↓

Portumna

16

Lough Derg

R489

Birr

11

Woodford

Terryglass

East Clare
Heritage Centre **18**
Heywood Gardens **10**
Holy Island **17**
Ireland's Historic
Science Center **11**
Irish Famine Museum **4**
Locke's Distillery **8**
Lough Key Forest Park **3**
Lough Rynn House
& Gardens **5**
Nenagh Heritage
Centre **20**
Portumna Castle **16**
Portumna Forest Park **16**
Raheen Woods **19**
Strokestown
Park House **4**
Tullynally Castle
& Gardens **7**

R352

R493

Mountshannon

Scarriff

17

Puckane

N7

Bodyke 18

19

R494

Nenagh

CLARE

R463

20

Ballina

R495

Killaloe

Slievekimalta or ■
Keeper Hill

TIPPERARY

Mouth of the Shannon

N69

Limerick

LIMERICK

Athlone Castle **12**
Battle of Aughrim
Interpretive Centre **15**
Birr Castle
Demesne **11**
Bog Tours **14**
Boyle Abbey **2**
Cavan Crystal **6**
Charleville Forest
Castle **9**
Clonalis House **1**
Clonmacnois **13**

479

SEEING THE SIGHTS

East Clare Heritage Centre/Holy Island Tours ★★ The isle of Iniscealtra, also known as Holy Island, has been set apart as a sacred place since pagan times. Visitors to the island can see the remains of several churches and a high round tower, built here by Irish monastics who came to the island in the 7th century. A pier across the road from the East Clare Heritage Centre is the starting point for a 15-minute boating trip, which is followed by a 45-minute guided tour of the island. The East Clare Heritage Centre, which is housed in the restored 10th-century church of St. Cronan, explains the heritage and history of the East Clare area through a series of exhibits and an audiovisual presentation.

Tuamgraney, Co. Clare. ✆ 061/921351. www.eastclareheritage.com. Admission to Centre 2.60€ ($2.40) adults, 1.25€ ($1.15) children, 6.50€ ($5.90) family. Centre, May–Sept Mon–Sat 9am–5pm, Sun 1–5pm; Holy Island Tours, May–Sept daily, weather permitting. Off the R352 Portumna-Ennis road.

Nenagh Heritage Centre Models of the whole Lough Derg area, with its main port villages, are on display at this center, 5 miles (8km) east of the lakeshore. Located in two stone buildings dating from about 1840, this site was once a jail, then a convent and a school. Now, as a museum, it showcases collections of local arts, crafts, photography, and memorabilia. It's also the family history research center for northern Tipperary.

Off Kickham St., Nenagh, Co. Tipperary. ✆ 067/32633. Admission 2.60€ ($2.40) adults; 1.25€ ($1.15) seniors, students, and children; 5.10€ ($4.60) family. Mid-May to Sept Mon–Fri 9:30am–5pm, Sun 2–5pm.

Portumna Castle Built in 1609 by Earl Richard Burke, this castle on the northern shores of Lough Derg is said to have been one of the finest 17th-century manor houses ever built in Ireland. It was gutted by fire in 1826, but its Dutch-style decorative gables and rows of stone mullioned windows were spared. Although the castle is currently being restored, part of the first floor and the gardens are currently open to visitors, and more of the castle will be opened as restoration progresses. The garden restoration was based on a combination of archival and archaeological evidence, and is one of the more ambitious historic garden projects in Ireland. There is an interesting exhibit in the castle detailing the history of the castle's inhabitants, and describing some of the age-old techniques that have been used to restore the place. All aspects of the castle, including window panes, timber roof, and stone window mullions, have been restored using techniques similar to the ones originally used to create them. The castle and gardens are in a beautiful setting on the shore of Lough Derg, and will no doubt be an extraordinary site to visit when restoration is completed.

Off N65, Portumna, Co. Galway. ✆ 0509/41658. www.heritageireland.ie. Admission 1.90€ ($1.75) adults, 1.25€ ($1.15) seniors, .75€ (70¢) students and children, 5.10€ ($4.60) family. Open May Tues–Sun 10am–5pm; June–Oct daily 10am–6pm.

Portumna Forest Park On the shores of Lough Derg, this 1,400-acre park is east of the town, off the main road. It offers trails and signposted walks, plus viewing points and picnic areas.

Off N65, Portumna, Co. Galway. No phone. Free admission. Daily dawn–dusk.

GETTING OUT ON THE WATER

If you enjoy boating, tubing, water-skiing, windsurfing, canoeing, or other water-based sports, this is the place for you.

Whelan's Boat Hire Whelan's rents 19-foot (6m) lake boats with outboard engines for sightseeing or fishing in the waters of Lough Derg; the boat will comfortably accommodate four people. Prices include fuel, fishing gear, and rainwear.

At the Bridge, Killaloe, Co. Clare. © 061/376159. 15€ ($14) for first hr., 10€ ($9.10) each additional hr., 45€ ($41) per day. June–Aug daily 9am–9pm.

CABIN CRUISER RENTALS

The following companies rent cabin cruisers along this section of the Shannon: **Ireland Line Cruises Ltd.,** Derg Marina, Killaloe, County Clare (© **061/ 375011**); **Emerald Star Line,** The Marina, Portumna, County Galway (© **0509/41120;** www.emeraldstar.ie); **Shannon Castle Line,** The Marina, Williamstown, County Clare (© **061/927042;** www.shannoncruisers.com); **Shannon Sailing,** The Marina, Dromineer, County Tipperary (© **067/24295;** www.shannonsailing.com). The craft range from two to ten berths; rates average 150€ to 300€ ($136–$271) per person per week.

SIGHTSEEING CRUISES

R&B Marine Services Ltd.   Enjoy a cruise of Lough Derg on board the 48-seat *Derg Princess,* a covered river bus. This 1-hour cruise leaves from Killaloe marina and travels past the fort of Brian Boru and into Lough Derg.

Derg Marina, Killaloe, Co. Clare. © 061/375011. sales@irelandlinecruisers.com. 7.50€ ($6.80) adults, 3.80€ ($3.45) children, 19€ ($17) family. May–Oct.

Shannon Sailing Ltd.   This company operates a covered 53-seat water bus, the *Ku-ee-tu,* sailing from the southeastern shore of Lough Derg at Dromineer on a 1½-hour cruise with full commentary on local sights.

New Complex, Dromineer, Nenagh, Co. Tipperary. © 067/24499. www.shannonsailing.com. 6.35€ ($5.75) adults, 3.80€ ($3.45) children. May–Sept daily; schedule varies.

OUTDOOR PURSUITS

FISHING   Often called an angler's paradise, Lough Derg has good stocks of brown trout, pike, bream, and perch. Fish ranging in weight from 36 to 90 pounds have been caught in this lake. Brown trout average 1 to 6 pounds. For tackle and guidance on local fishing visit **Eddie Fahey,** Ballyminogue, Scariff, County Clare (© **061/921019**).

GOLF   Lovely parkland and woodland golfing in the Lough Derg area is offered at 18-hole clubs such as **Portumna Golf Club,** Portumna, County Galway (© **0509/41059**), with greens fees of 19€ ($17) weekdays, 23€ ($21) weekends; and **Nenagh Golf Club,** Beechwood, Nenagh (© **067/34808**), with greens fees of 19€ ($17) weekdays, 32€ ($29) weekends. In addition, the **East Clare Golf Club,** Scariff/Killaloe Road, Bodyke, County Clare (© **061/ 921322**), is expanding an 18-hole championship course. Its current greens fees are 17€ ($15) weekdays and 19€ ($17) weekends.

SWIMMING   Lough Derg is known for clear, unpolluted water that's ideal for swimming, particularly at **Castle Lough, Dromineer,** and **Portumna Bay.** Portumna Bay has changing rooms and showers.

WALKING   There are some excellent walks in **Portumna Forest Park, Raheen Woods,** and along the shoreline of **Lough Derg.** Also, for a touch of scenic wilderness, walk a portion of the **Slieve Bloom Way,** a circular 21-mile (34km) signposted trail that begins and ends in Glenbarrow, County Laois.

ACCOMMODATIONS YOU CAN AFFORD

Ashley Park House 🞧 Ashley Park has the atmosphere of a well-loved, well-used summerhouse: Fishing rods are tucked into the corners of the large front hallway and life jackets are quickly offered to guests who want to row around the house's private lake—a beautiful stretch of water, teeming with fish and wildfowl. Proprietor Sean Mounsey allows no shooting on his land, and fish that are caught must be thrown back. The house itself has been restored with a careful eye to the conservation of its character. A copper towel warmer remains in one bathroom and a curious 19th-century wooden toilet is found in another. The stair landing glows with the rich red and blue of a large stained-glass window, and the living room and dining room are furnished with dark and elaborately carved antique furniture. The two bedrooms on either end of the house are particularly large: Each has a sitting room as well as a spacious sleeping area, and bay windows facing the lake. The room at the east end has a particularly charming hexagonal sitting room. Other rooms are smaller and look out onto a stable yard where pigeons and peacocks are a spectacle for both humans and horses.

Nenagh, Co. Tipperary. ℂ/fax 067/38233. www.ashleypark.com. 6 units, 5 with bathroom (1 with shower only). 44€ ($40) single; 76€ ($69) double. No credit cards. *In room:* TV, tea/coffeemaker, hair dryer.

Clonmore Mrs. Mary Quinn's bungalow sits on its own grounds, within sight of the Galtee mountains and a 5-minute walk from town. Guest rooms are comfortable, with electric blankets. There's also a sun lounge.

Cork-Galbally Rd., Tipperary, Co. Tipperary. ℂ 062/51637. 6 units. 51€ ($46) double. 20% reduction for children sharing with an adult. Rates include full breakfast. No credit cards. Private parking. Closed Nov–Mar. *In-room:* TV, tea/coffeemaker.

The Country House This modern bungalow is the home of Joan and Matt Kennedy. It's set in rural surroundings 4 miles (6.5km) out from Nenagh on R498. The lounge has a peat-burning fireplace, and Lough Derg is only about 20 minutes away.

Thurles Rd., Kilkeary, Nenagh, Co. Tipperary. ℂ 067/31193. 6 units, 4 with bathroom (shower only). 32€ ($29) single; 51€ ($46) double. 33% reduction for children. Rates include full breakfast. No credit cards. *In room:* Tea/coffeemaker, hair dryer.

Cregganbell This is a modern bungalow on the outskirts of town via N62, with river fishing nearby. Mrs. Mae Fallon has four guest rooms, all with electric blankets.

Birr Rd., Roscrea, Co. Tipperary. ℂ 0505/21421. cregganbell@eircom.net. 4 units, 3 with bathroom (shower only). 48€ ($44) double. 25% reduction for children sharing with an adult. Rates include full breakfast. No credit cards. Free parking.

Lantern House This unpretentious guesthouse enjoys wide vistas on Lough Derg. Palm trees grow on the well-tended hilltop grounds. All the public rooms overlook the Shannon, as do some of the bedrooms. Furnishings are comfortable and homey. The cozy lounge has a fireplace, and residents can enjoy a drink at a small bar. The accompanying restaurant (see "Great Deals on Dining," below) is popular with locals. Bedrooms are nonsmoking, and the beds themselves are uneven—some are far too soft.

Ogonnelloe, Tuamgraney, Co. Clare. ℂ 061/923034. Fax 061/923139. 9 units. 56€–63€ ($51–$58) double. Rates include full breakfast. AE, DC, MC, V. Open mid-Feb to Nov. 6 miles (9.5km) north of Killaloe on the main road. **Amenities:** Restaurant, lounge, bar. *In room:* TV, TEL.

Tips Rent-a-Cottage

For an area of such amazing beauty and wide-open spaces, the Lough Derg region has surprisingly few accommodation options. Perhaps more than most other parts of Ireland, this area calls out for visitors to settle in and become part of the local way of life. And that's why the "Rent an Irish Cottage" program was pioneered here almost 30 years ago.

The Shannon Development Company came up with the idea of building small rental cottages in these rural areas where other types of satisfactory accommodations were scarce. The cottages were designed in traditional style, with exteriors of white stucco, thatched roofs, and half-doors, but aside from the turf fireplaces, all of the furnishings, plumbing, heating, and kitchen appliances inside were totally up-to-date. The cottage rental idea was an instant success with Irish people from Dublin and other large cities who wanted to get away from it all, and it's become equally popular with visitors from abroad.

The cottages, built in groups of 8 to 12, are set on picturesque sites in remote villages such as **Puckane, Terryglass,** and **Whitegate,** either overlooking or close to Lough Derg's shores. There are no restaurants or bars on site, and guests are encouraged to shop in the local grocery stores and cook their own meals and to congregate in the local pubs each evening. In other words, after a day or two, the visitors become part of the community. Rates range from 178€ to 1,524€ ($161 to $1,380) per cottage per week, depending on the size of the cottage (one to four bedrooms) and time of year. Rates include bed linen and color TV; towels and metered electricity are extra. For more information, contact **Rent an Irish Cottage plc.,** 85 O'Connell St., Limerick, County Limerick (② **061/411109;** fax 061/314821; www.rentacottage.ie).

GREAT DEALS ON DINING

Country Choice CAFE   Country Choice is just that: its shelves are brimming with the finest of Irish foodstuffs from an acclaimed local marmalade to farmhouse cheeses. Floury loaves of bread are heaped on the counter, and on the floor, baskets glisten with the clear, green orbs of local gooseberries. This is the best place to fill up on picnic fixings before heading out to the shores of Lough Derg. A cafe at the back of the shop is the place to sit with a cup of good coffee and find out what's happening locally—it's a popular gathering place for locals and visitors. There's an inexpensive lunch menu, and freshly baked goods are served in the morning.

25 Kenyon St., Nenagh, Co. Tipperary. ② **067/32596.** Lunch main courses £2.50–£5 ($3.75–$7.50). Mon–Sat 9am–6pm; lunch noon–6pm.

Lantern House CONTINENTAL   Perched high on a hillside amid palm tree-lined gardens just north of Killaloe, this country-house restaurant enjoys panoramic views of Lough Derg and the verdant hills of the surrounding countryside. Host Phil Hogan extends a warm welcome, and the candlelit dining room exudes old-world charm, with a beamed ceiling, wall lanterns, and lace tablecloths. A specialty is salmon fresh from local waters. If your taste is less finny, you can opt for pork steak with white wine or duck à l'orange.

Ogonnelloe, Co. Clare. ℂ **061/923034.** Reservations recommended. Main courses 14€–20€ ($13–$18). AE, MC, V. Mid-Mar to Oct, daily 6–9pm.

PUBS WITH TRADITIONAL MUSIC

Although there are public houses in every town around the Lough Derg route, the pubs of **Woodford,** County Galway, on the west shore, and Terryglass, County **Tipperary,** on the east shore, are particularly well known for their lively sessions of traditional music. Woodford is particularly celebrated as a mecca for Irish music of the old style. Fiddler and tin-whistle player Anthony Coen, born in Woodford of a musical family that includes six traditional musicians out of nine children, is one of the best at his instruments, and is often accompanied by his own talented daughters Dearbhla on the flute and tin whistle and Eimer on the concertina and bodhran. They can occasionally be heard at **J. Walsh's Forest Bar,** Woodford (ℂ **0509/49012**), where, if you're lucky, there'll be a traditional music session, and you can sit back and enjoy. You can also find Coen occasionally at **Moran's** (see below).

The Derg Inn   With three cozy rooms and a beer garden in the courtyard, this is one of the lake's best watering holes. It's worth a visit just to see this pub's decor of Tipperary horse pictures, old plates, books, beer posters, vintage bottles, hanging tankards, and lanterns. However, most people come for the free traditional music on Wednesday and Sunday. Terryglass, County Tipperary. ℂ **067/ 22037.**

Moran's   First let's get the pronunciation right: It's MORE-ans. Overlooking the Woodford River, this place is a curiosity—it's probably the only pub in Ireland where you'll find two clerics serving drinks at the bar during the summer. Both Carmelite Order priests, they are the owner's sons and spend their vacation time helping out in the family business—only in Ireland! Woodford, County Galway. ℂ **0509/49063.**

Paddy's Pub   From the harbor, it's a short walk up a winding lane to Paddy's—small, dark, and a jewel among Lake Derg's pubs. It is known for its fine display of antiques as well as nightly traditional music in summer. Terryglass, County Tipperary. ℂ **067/22147.**

2 Middle Shannon: From Birr to Athlone

Birr is 15 miles (24km) E of Portumna; Athlone is 60 miles (97km) E of Galway

The middle section of the River Shannon is the home of one of Ireland's greatest historic sites—the early Christian settlement of **Clonmacnois,** which has been drawing visitors since the 6th century. The area also includes vast stretches of boglands. You'll find here the inland town of **Birr,** known for its magnificent and historic gardens, and the river town of **Banagher,** with its picturesque harbor.

This stretch of the river also curves into **Athlone,** the largest town on the Shannon and a leading inland marina for mooring and hiring boats. Athlone's other claim to fame is that it produced Ireland's most famous operatic tenor, the great John McCormack.

GETTING THERE & GETTING AROUND   The best way to get to the Middle Shannon area is by car or boat. Although there's public transportation, you'll need a car to get around the riverbanks. Major roads that lead to this area are the main Galway–Dublin road (N6) from points east and west, N62 from the south, and N55 and N61 from the north.

VISITOR INFORMATION Information on this area can be obtained year-round from the **Ireland West Tourism Office,** Victoria Place, Eyre Square, Galway (𝒞 **091/563081**), and the **Midlands Tourism Office,** Clonard House, Dublin Road, Mullingar, County Westmeath (𝒞 **044/48650**). Both are open Monday through Friday from 9am to 6pm and on Saturday during peak season. Seasonal tourist information points are also operated from May or June to September at signposted sites in the following locations: **Athlone** (𝒞 **0902/94630**), and **Clonmacnois** (𝒞 **0905/74134**).

SEEING THE SIGHTS

Athlone Castle Built in 1210 for King John of England, this mighty stone fortress sits on the edge of the Shannon. It played an important part in Athlone's history, first as the seat of the presidents of Connaught and later as the headquarters of the governor of Athlone during the first Siege of Athlone in 1690 and the second in 1691. Declared a national monument in 1970, it was recently restored and adapted for use as a visitor center, museum, gallery, and tearoom. The exhibition area offers an audiovisual presentation on the Siege of Athlone, plus displays on the castle itself, the town of Athlone, the flora and fauna of the Shannon region, and John McCormack, the great Irish tenor and Athlone's most honored son. The castle's original medieval walls have been preserved, as have two large cannons dating from the reign of George II and a pair of 10-inch mortars that were cast in 1856.

Athlone, Co. Westmeath. 𝒞 **0902/92912** or 0902/72107. Admission 4.50€ ($4.10) adults, 2.60€ ($2.40) seniors and students, 1.25€ ($1.15) children to age 12, 10€ ($9.10) family. May–early Oct daily 10am–4:30pm. On the riverbank, signposted from all directions.

Battle of Aughrim Interpretative Centre Using a high-tech three-dimensional audiovisual presentation, this center invites visitors to relive July 12, 1691: the Battle of Aughrim. On that day, the army of James II of England confronted the forces of his son-in-law, William of Orange, and staged the bloodiest battle in Irish history. The confrontation involved 45,000 soldiers from eight European countries and cost 9,000 lives. The center, which also houses a bookshop, craft shop, and cafe, is in Aughrim village, adjacent to the actual Aughrim battlefield, which is now signposted for visitors. Aughrim is situated on the main Dublin-Galway road, about 12 miles (19km) west of the Shannon bridge/Clonmacnois area.

Aughrim, Co. Galway. 𝒞 **0905/73939**. Admission 3.80€ ($3.45) adults. Easter–Sept Tues–Sat 10am–6pm, Sun 2–6pm. Galway-Dublin road (N6), Aughrim, near Ballinasloe, Co. Galway.

Birr Castle Demesne and Ireland's Historic Science Centre The main attraction of this inland estate, 12 miles (19km) east of the river, is its 100-acre garden. The demesne of the Parsons family, now the earls of Rosse, the estate is laid out around a lake and along the banks of the two adjacent rivers and contains more than 1,000 species of trees and shrubs, including magnolias, cherry trees, chestnut, and weeping beech. The box hedges are featured in the *Guinness Book of Records* as the tallest in the world, and the hornbeam cloisters are a unique feature. Farther along the path you may combine a bit of stargazing with the garden stroll—the grounds also contain an astronomical exhibit, including an 1845 6-foot reflecting telescope, then the largest in the world, built by the third Earl of Rosse and recently restored to form as part of the Historic Science Centre. The telescope operates twice daily, at noon and 3pm. During the summer, you can usually find additional rotating exhibits dealing with the history of Birr Castle and its residents. The 17th-century castle and residence is not open to the public.

Birr, Co. Offaly. ✆ **0509/20336**. www.birrcastle.com. Admission 6.50€ ($5.90) adults, 4.50€ ($4.10) seniors/students 3.20€ ($2.90) children over 5. Daily 9am–6pm. 23 miles (37km) SW of Tullamore, via N52.

Bog Tours ⟨⟨ Bogland discoveries are the focus of this tour in the heart of the Irish midlands on the east bank of the Shannon. Visitors are invited to board the narrow-gauge Clonmacnois and West Offaly Railway for a 5-mile (8km) circular ride around the Blackwater bog. The commentary explains how the bogland was formed and became a vital source of fuel for Ireland. The tour includes a first-hand look at turf cutting, stacking, and drying, and close-up views of bog plants and wildlife. Participants can even take a turn at digging the turf or picking some bog cotton en route. The ride lasts approximately 45 minutes. The visitor center also offers an audiovisual story about the bog. For groups who make advance arrangements, a 2- to 4-hour nature trail and field-study tour is available.

Bord na Mona/The Irish Peat Board, Blackwater Works, Shannonbridge, Co. Offaly. ✆ **0905/74114**. www.bnm.ie. Tours 5.10€ ($4.65) adults, 4.50€ ($4.10) seniors and students, 3.45€ ($3.15) children, 15€ ($14) family. April–early Oct daily 10am–5pm. Tours on the hour. Signposted from Shannonbridge.

Clonmacnois ⟨⟨⟨ Resting silently on the east bank of the Shannon is one of Ireland's most profound ancient sites. The monastic community of Clonmacnois was founded in 548 by St. Ciaran at the crucial intersection of the Shannon and the Dublin-Galway land route and soon became one of Europe's great centers of learning and culture. For nearly 1,000 years, Clonmacnois flourished under the patronage of numerous Irish kings. The last high king, Rory O'Conor, was buried here in 1198. In the course of time, Clonmacnois was raided repeatedly by native chiefs, Danes, and Anglo-Normans, until it was finally abandoned in 1552. Today's visitor can see the remains of a cathedral, a castle, eight churches, two round towers, three sculpted high crosses, and more than 200 monumental slabs. The site includes an exemplary visitor center with a beautifully designed exhibition, a first-rate audiovisual program, and tearooms.

Shannonbridge, Co. Offaly. ✆ **0905/74195**. Admission 4.50€ ($4.10) adults, 3.15€ ($2.90) seniors, 1.90€ ($1.75) students and children, 10€ ($9.10) family. Dec to mid-Mar daily 10am–5pm; mid-Mar to mid-May daily 10am–6pm; mid-May to early Sept daily 9am–7pm; Sept–Oct daily 10am–6pm. On R357, 4 miles (6.5km) north of Shannonbridge.

Locke's Distillery Established in 1757, this 18th- and 19th-century enterprise was one of the oldest licensed pot-still whiskey distilleries in the world. After producing whiskey for almost 200 years, it closed in 1953, but in the past 15 years a local group has succeeded in restoring it as a museum. A 45-minute tour will not only tell you how whiskey was distilled using old techniques and machinery, but also inform you about the area's social history. At the end of the tour, adult visitors are given a taste of Locke's whiskey. Locke's Distillery is located east of Athlone on the main road (N6), almost midway between Dublin and Galway, making it a good stopover while you're on a cross-country journey or touring in the area. On the premises, you'll find a restaurant, coffee shop, and craft shop.

Kilbeggan, Co. Westmeath. ✆ **0506/32134**. www.lockesdistillerymuseum.com. Admission 4.15€ ($3.75) adults, 3.50€ ($3.15) seniors/students, 10€ ($9.10) family. Apr–Oct daily 9am–6pm; Nov–Mar daily 10am–4pm. On N6, east of Athlone.

GETTING OUT ON THE WATER: CRUISING THE SHANNON

The following companies rent **cabin cruisers,** usually for a minimum of 1 week, along this section of the Shannon: **Athlone Cruisers,** Jolly Mariner Marina, Athlone, County Westmeath (© **0902/72892;** fax 0902/74386; www.iol.ie/wmeathtc/acl); **Carrick Craft Cruisers,** The Marina, Carrick-on-Shannon, County Leitrim (© **078/20236;** fax 078/21336; www.carrickcraft.com); **Silverline Cruisers,** The Marina, Banagher, County Offaly (© **0509/51112;** www.silverlinecruisers.com); and **Tara Cruiser Ltd.,** Kilfaughna, Knockvicar, County Roscommon (© **079/67777;** fax 079/67888; www.taracruises.ie). Crafts range from three to eight berths; rates average 840€ to 2,720€ ($788 to $2,550) per week in high season.

SIGHTSEEING CRUISES

Athlone Cruisers Ltd. ⚓ This company operates cruises around Lough Ree on board the 60-passenger M.V. *Ross.* The average cruise time is 90 minutes, and the boat has a sun deck and a covered deck with a bar and coffee shop.

Jolly Mariner Marina, Athlone, Co. Westmeath. © **0902/72892.** www.iol.ie/wmeathtc/acl. Cruise 7.60€ ($6.90) adults, 3.80€ ($3.45) children. May–Sept, times vary.

Rosanna Cruises *Kids* This company offers cruises of the inner lakes of Lough Ree or to Clonmacnois on board the 71-passenger *Viking I.* Patrons hear live commentary on the 300-year Viking history on the Shannon and Lough Ree and refreshments. The Lough Ree trip takes 1½ hours; the 4-hour Clonmacnois trip includes a 1-hour stopover at the monastic site. The company furnishes children with Viking helmets, costumes, and plastic swords for the duration of the trip to add a touch of berserk authenticity. Buy tickets at the Strand Fishing Tackle Shop (© **0902/79277**), from where you'll also depart.

Cranagh, St. Enda's House, The Strand, Athlone, Co. Westmeath. © **0902/73383.** Fax 0902/73392. www.vikingtoursireland.com. Lough Ree trip 8€ ($7.25) adults, 6€ ($5.45) children; Clonmacnois trip 13€ ($12) adults, 8€ ($7.25) seniors, students and children. May–Sept, Lough Ree trip (1½ hrs.) daily 2:30 and 4:30pm; Clonmacnois trip (4½ hrs., including 1-hr. stopover at the monastic site) hours vary: call ahead.

Silverline Cruisers Ltd. This company operates 90-minute cruises on the *River Queen,* a 54-seat enclosed river bus. The trip starts out by passing under the seven-arched Banagher Stone Bridge, then passes Martello towers and fortresses on its way downstream to Victoria Lock, the largest lock on the Shannon system. The taped commentary covers all the historical aspects of the route. There's a bar on board.

The Marina, Banagher, Co. Offaly. © **0509/51112.** www.silverlinecruisers.com. 8€ ($7.25) adults, 4€ ($3.65) children. June–Sept, times vary.

OUTDOOR PURSUITS

GOLF **Birr Golf Club,** Birr, County Offaly (© **0509/20082**), is an 18-hole course set amid 112 acres of parkland countryside; the greens fees are 19€ ($17) on weekdays and 25€ ($23) on weekends. In the Athlone area are the 18-hole **Athlone Golf Club,** Hodson Bay, Athlone, County Roscommon (© **0902/92073**), with greens fees of 25€ ($23) on weekdays and 28€ ($25) on weekends; and the new 18-hole championship course at **Mount Temple Golf Club,** Moate, County Westmeath (© **0902/81841**), 5 miles (8km) east of Athlone, which charges greens fees of 23€ ($21) on weekdays and 30€ ($28) on weekends.

HORSE RACING Horse racing takes place in July, August, and September at the **Kilbeggan Racecourse,** Loughnagore, Kilbeggan, County Westmeath (℃ **0506/32176**), off the main Mullingar road (N52), just over a mile (2km) from town.

ACCOMMODATIONS YOU CAN AFFORD

Beechlawn Farmhouse This is a relaxing base for exploring the heart of Ireland. Mary Margaret and Sylvester Smyth's farmhouse is surrounded by landscaped lawns and colorful flower beds. The lounge, dining room, and all guest rooms are welcoming and comfortable. Mrs. Smyth's candlelight dinners are a treat, and pubs in the nearby village offer conviviality with locals in the evening.

Clyduff, Daingean, Co. Offaly. ℃ **0506/53099**. 5 units. 46€ ($41) double. 25% reduction for children sharing with an adult. Rates include full breakfast. Dinner 18€ ($16). No credit cards. Closed Nov to mid-Mar. 7 miles (11km) from Tullamore.

Hilltop Country House Dympna and Sean Casey's modern split-level home is 2 miles (3km) from town in a beautiful setting overlooking Lough Sheever. Dympna is warmly interested in seeing that all her guests are comfortable and get the most from their vacations. The bedrooms are comfortable and the breakfast is bountiful. The award-winning garden is very popular with guests.

Delvin road (N52 off N4), Rathconnell, Mullingar, Co. Westmeath. ℃ **044/48958**. Fax 044/48013. hilltop countryhouse@eircom.net. 5 units. 40€ ($36) single; 60€ ($54) double. Rates include full breakfast. MC, V. *In room:* TV, hair dryer.

The Maltings Hotel/Leisure Centre ★ *Kids* Maeve and Brendan Garry have worked wonders in these Georgian-style buildings, which date from 1820, when they were used to store malt for Guinness stout. Set on picturesque grounds on the banks of the River Camcor next to Birr Castle, the hotel offers all the modern conveniences for guests' comfort, as well as terrific views of wildlife, and the relaxing sound of water gushing over the weir outside the windows. The River Room Restaurant is set under the arch of the waterwheel.

Castle St., Birr, Co. Offaly. ℃ **0509/21345**. Fax 0509/22073. 10 units. 38€ ($34) single; 64€ ($58) double. 50% reduction for children under 16; under 4 free. Rates include full breakfast. V. Free parking. Beside Birr Castle. **Amenities:** Restaurant; gym; sauna; babysitting. *In room:* TV, TEL, tea maker, hair dryer.

Woodlands Farm *Kids* Serenity envelops you the moment you approach Mary and Willy Maxwell's home by way of a tree-lined avenue along which horses often graze. The rambling, two-story house is charming, with a 200-year-old section to which a wing was added about a century ago (it's still called the "new" addition). Parlor windows look out onto wooded grounds, and a fire is lit most evenings when a tea tray is rolled into the gracious sitting room, which is furnished with antiques. The six bedrooms include one cozy single. Breakfasts are special, featuring fresh milk from Mary and Willy's own cows and Mary's home-baked bread. Donkeys and pet sheep are an added attraction, and guests are given the run of the farmyard and grounds. To get here from Mullingar, take the Galway road, then the road to Athlone; at Streamstown, look for the sign near the school. If you get hopelessly lost, just stop and ask—the Maxwells are well known in the Streamstown area.

Streamstown (near Horseleap on N6), Co. Westmeath. ℃ **044/26414**. 6 units, 2 with bathroom (shower only). 51€ ($46) double. 30% reduction for children sharing with an adult. Rates include full breakfast. Dinner 23€ ($21). No credit cards. Closed Nov–Feb.

GREAT DEALS ON DINING

The Bridge House TRADITIONAL IRISH   The Bridge is a local institution, with something for every appetite, from its coffee shop and carvery lunch fare to full evening meals in the large, busy restaurant. Look for traditional Irish specialties such as Irish stew.

Bridge St., Tullamore, Co. Offaly. ✆ **0506/21704.** Snacks under 6€ ($5.45); carvery lunch under 11€ ($10); main courses 11€–19€ ($10–$17). MC, V. Daily 7:30–10am, 12:30–2:30pm, and 5:30–9:30pm.

Moorhill Country House IRISH/MEDITERRANEAN   This award-winning dining room is located on the outskirts of town in the converted stables of a lovely old country estate with beautifully landscaped grounds. Inside, stone walls, oak beams, and open fires add to the charm of the period country-house setting. Traditional cooking is the order of the day here, using locally grown produce and meats from nearby farms. Among the specialties is the imaginative Tullamore black pudding in puff pastry served with a port-wine sauce.

Moorhill, Clara Rd. (N80), Tullamore, Co. Offaly. ✆ **0506/21395.** Dinner main courses 13€–25€ ($12–$23). AE, DC, MC, V. Tues–Sat 7–10pm; Sun 12:30–2:30pm.

EASY EXCURSIONS INTO NEARBY COUNTY LAOIS

County Laois (pronounced *leash*) is the southern neighbor of County Offaly, and though most visitors will only pass through on their way somewhere else, this midland county is the unlikely home of a few fine, if unheralded, attractions.

Portlaoise is the principal county town, and a few kilometers southeast (via R426) is the town of **Timahoe,** where you can see a perfectly preserved 96-foot (29m) high, 12th-century round tower as well as the ruins of a castle and an abbey. Another 4 miles (6.5km) to the east, atop the 150-foot (46m) high **Rock of Dunamase,** are the ruins of a Norman castle. Built on the site of an ancient Celtic fortress, the castle was part of the dowry given to the king of Leinster's daughter when she married Strongbow, as part of the power struggle that first brought English forces to Irish soil.

Nine miles (14.5km) south of Portlaoise, a Cistercian abbey was founded by Conor O'More in 1183 at **Abbeyleix.** The de Vesci demesne, adjoining the town, holds the tomb of Malachi O'More, a Laois chieftain.

The **Slieve Bloom Mountains** ⩑ have been described as one vast environment park, and although the centuries (some 15,000 of them) have rounded the peaks into hills—the highest is just over 1,700 feet (518m)—there remain 17 major valleys, forest walks of incredible beauty and accessibility, and a blanket bog that has been named a National Nature Reserve. There are several excellent viewing points and parking lots here. If time permits, a day stolen from your cross-country travels to wander this peaceful park will do wonders for your soul.

A delightful scenic drive is to be had through the deep glen of **O Regan** in the Slieve Bloom. At Mountmellick, north of Portlaoise via N80, take the Clonaslee road and follow signposts for "The Cut." Some 7 miles (11km) south of Clonaslee, **Monick-new Woods,** with its nature trail, forest walks, viewing points, and picnic site, is an ideal spot to stop for a little spirit renewal or for a picnic lunch.

The country mansion around which English architect Edwin Lutyens designed **Heywood Garden** ⩑ (✆ **0502/33563;** www.heritageireland.ie) burned to the ground some 50 years ago, and today only its foundations remain. Two small gates mark the entry to the garden at the edge of a newly constructed school and parking lot—pass through one of these gates and you can begin to reconstruct in imagination the garden's former glory. A double avenue of pleached lime casts shadows on a series of urns ensconced in a tall granite wall, leading to the bright sparkle of fountain and pool enclosed within a round walled garden. Current plantings here and in a series of mazelike yew enclosures are only a faint shadow of the original ones by Gertrude Jekyll, but the garden is still enchanting—and unencumbered by crowds. Heywood Garden is just north of Ballinakill on the Abbeyleix Road, about 12 miles (19km) south of Portlaoise. Admission is free, and tours start daily at 3pm or by appointment.

WHERE TO STAY
Near Portlaoise

Castletown House ★ *Kids*   There's a lot to commend in this early 19th-century farmhouse at the center of a 200-acre beef and sheep farm, winner of three Agri-Tourism awards in recent years. The house itself is lovely, with taste-fully furnished guestrooms, a guest lounge, a games room for children, and a private garden. But the property's greatest asset is the gracious Moira Phelan, who displays a keen personal interest in her guests and boundless enthusiasm for rural tourism. Moira is also renowned for her home baking. The area is liberally sprinkled with historic sites, and there are the remains of an 11th-century Nor-man castle on the farm. Moira has compiled a local history book that adds much to every visitor's stay.

Donaghmore, Rathdowney, Co. Laois. ⓒ 0505/46415. Fax 0505/46788. www.castletownguesthouse.com. 4 units. 51€ ($46) double. Rates include full breakfast. MC, V. Closed Nov–Feb. **Amenities:** Lounge; babysit-ting (on request). *In room:* TV, hair dryer.

Chez Nous ★   Ms. Audrey Canavan has won raves for her warm hospitality, exceptionally good (and varied) breakfasts, and the attention to detail in the decor of her home. Antique furnishings are displayed throughout the house, and the attractive, oak-beamed TV lounge adjoins a plant-filled sunroom and out-side patio. Guest rooms have canopied beds, and all are beautifully furnished. As for breakfast, Audrey offers the traditional Irish grill or an alternative that some-times includes fish with a side salad.

Kilminchy, Portlaoise, Co. Laois. ⓒ 0502/21251. 5 units. 57€ ($52) double. Rates include full breakfast. AE, MC, V. 2 miles (3km) from town off the main Dublin road. **Amenities:** Lounge. *In room:* Tea/coffeemaker, hair dryer.

Worth a Splurge

Roundwood House ★★ *Finds*   Roundwood House offers a put-up-your-feet casual elegance equaled by few other guesthouses. Roundwood is very much lived in by the Kennans, Frank and Rosemarie and children, whose warmth and taste pervade this splendid 18th-century early Georgian Palladian country villa, set amidst 18 acres of secluded woods (beech, chestnut, and lime), pastures, and gardens. The place breathes relaxation and leisure, although more active pursuits are close at hand, most particularly the Slieve Bloom Way, a 50-kilometer hill walk through Ireland's most untrammeled range. Serious trekkers are gladly launched or fetched by the Kennans so as to be able to cover the greatest dis-tance. The six double rooms in the main house are spacious and decorated with a gifted eye for charm and simplicity. The two second-floor rooms share a large central play area ideal for families with children. The "Yellow House" across the herb garden/courtyard from the main house dates from the 17th century and has been tastefully restored to offer four additional double bedrooms, each a delight. Roundwood's soft couches, firm beds, lovely views, myriad good books, large bathtubs, and exquisite meals may not inspire an active holiday, but they go a long way toward calming the soul. Thankfully, the nearest TV is a good walk away. For the restless, croquet and boule are the house sports.

Mountrath, Co. Laois. (✆ **0502/32120.** Fax 0502/32711. roundwood@eircom.net. 10 units. 130€ ($118) double. Rates include full breakfast. Dinner 40€ ($36), to be booked by 2pm. AE, DC, MC, V. 3 miles (5km) northwest of Mountrath on R440 in the direction of the Slieve Bloom Mountains. **Amenities:** Restaurant, lounge.

GREAT DEALS ON DINING

Roundwood House ⟨★★⟩ TRADITIONAL IRISH   Rosemarie and Frank Kennan's restaurant regularly draws dinner guests from as far away as Dublin. Its small, intimate dining room seats only 26. The set menu specializes in good, solid, country-style cooking that's positively mouthwatering. You're in luck if their local roast lamb comes to table accompanied by homemade Cumberland sauce instead of the usual mint sauce. (See "Worth a Splurge," above, for description of house.)

Mountrath, Co. Laois. (✆ **0502/32120.** Reservations required: dinner must be booked before 2pm. Fixed-price dinner 40€ ($36). AE, DC, MC, V. Dinner Tues–Sat with 1 seating at 8pm only.

3 Upper Shannon: From Lough Ree to Lough Allen

Roscommon is 51 miles (82km) NE of Galway, 91 miles (147km) NW of Dublin; Longford is 80 miles (129km) NW of Dublin, 27 miles (43km) NE of Athlone; Carrick-on-Shannon is 35 miles (56km) SE of Sligo; Cavan is 65 miles (105km) NW of Dublin

The Upper River Shannon region is home to a remarkable assortment of castles, greathouses, and museums, including one of Ireland's newest and most significant collections, the **Irish Famine Museum,** at Strokestown, County Roscommon. In addition, the shores of the Upper Shannon encompass **Lough Ree,** the second largest of the Shannon's lakes. It's distinguished by long, flat vistas across the farming countryside of Counties Roscommon, Westmeath, and Longford. Above Lough Ree, the river is relatively narrow until it reaches the town of Carrick-on-Shannon, in County Leitrim, situated on one of the great ancient crossing places of the Shannon. The town is particularly known as a center for boating, with a vast marina in the middle of the town where many local companies rent cabin cruisers.

The whole county of Leitrim is uniquely affected by the Shannon's waters. It's divided into two parts, almost wholly separated from one another by **Lough Allen.** A storage reservoir for a nearby hydroelectric plant, Lough Allen is the Shannon's third-largest lake, 7 miles (11km) long and 3 miles (5km) wide. North of Lough Allen, in County Cavan, is the source of the River Shannon: the Shannon Pot, on the southern slopes of the Cuilcagh Mountain.

In the spring of 1994, the Ballinamore-Ballyconnell Canal was restored and reopened after a lapse of 125 years, allowing a clear path of water travel from the River Shannon in the Republic to Lough Erne in the North. The new passage is officially designated the **Shannon-Erne Waterway** and has become a symbol of cross-border cooperation and a touchstone in a new golden age of Irish waterways travel.

GETTING THERE & GETTING AROUND   The best way to get to the Upper Shannon area is by car or boat. Although there's public transportation, you'll need a car to get around the riverbanks and to the various attractions. Among major roads that lead to this area are the main Dublin–Sligo road (N4), the main Dublin–Cavan road (N3), N5 and N63 from Castlebar and the west, and N61 and N55 from the south.

VISITOR INFORMATION Year-round information on **County Roscommon** is available from the **Ireland West Tourism Office,** Victoria Place, Eyre Square, Galway (© **091/563081**); on **County Longford** from the **Midlands East Tourism Office,** Clonard House, Dublin Road, Mullingar, County Westmeath (© **044/48761**); and on **County Leitrim** from the **North-West Tourism Office,** Aras Reddan, Temple Street, Sligo (© **071/61201**) and from the tourist office at Carrick-on-Shannon (© **078/20170**).

Seasonal information points, operating from May or June through August or September, are signposted in the following towns: **Boyle** (© **079/62145**), **Longford** (© **043/46566**), and **Roscommon** (© **0903/26342**).

SEEING THE SIGHTS

Boyle Abbey Boyle Abbey was founded in 1161 as a daughter house of the Cistercian Abbey at Mellifont. Today it is the most impressive survivor of the early Irish Cistercian settlements of the late 12th and early 13th centuries. The Cistercian Order was founded in 11th-century France as a return to the uncompromising simplicity and tranquil austerity of the monastic calling. The abbey was to be a haven of otherworldliness, and yet the world's savagery descended on Boyle Abbey more than once. Its walls were torn down in the mid-1600s, when the English murdered the resident monks and used the monastery as a military garrison. What remains is a complex fossil clearly imprinted with both the serene and violent aspects of the abbey's history. The ruins of Boyle Abbey evoke in visitors a sense of what this place has seen, suffered, and enjoyed. The interpretive center, housed in the restored gatehouse, is informative and thoughtfully designed.

Boyle, Co. Roscommon. © 079/62604. www.heritageireland.ie. Admission 1.25€ ($1.15) adults, .90€ (80¢) seniors, .50€ (45¢) children and students, 3.80€ ($3.45) family. Apr–Oct daily 10am–6pm. On N4.

Cavan Crystal One of the country's top three crystal companies, this establishment is known for its delicate glassware, mouth-blown and hand-cut by skilled craftspeople. Visitors are invited to watch as skilled master blowers fashion the molten crystal into intricate shapes and designs, followed by the precision work of the master cutters. The glassware is sold in the extended craft and factory shop. The center also includes a restaurant. *Note:* The factory was closed to visitors in 2001 but it is likely to reopen in 2002, possibly with an admission charge. Call ahead to confirm opening hours.

Dublin road (N3), Cavan, Co. Cavan. © 049/433-1800. Fax 049/433-1198. cavancrystal@eircom.net. Free admission. Mon–Fri 9:30am–6pm; Sat 10am–5pm; Sun noon–5pm.

Clonalis House ✯ Standing on land that has belonged to the O'Conors for more than 1,500 years, this is one of Ireland's great houses. It's the ancestral home of the O'Conors, kings of Connaught, and the home of the O'Conor Don, the direct descendant of the last high king of Ireland. The house, built in

---

Fun Fact **Goldsmith Country**

This eastern bank of the Shannon in Longford is often referred to as Goldsmith country, because 18th-century dramatist, novelist, and poet Oliver Goldsmith was born here at Pallas, near Ballymahon. Although Goldsmith did much of his writing in London, it's said that he drew on many of his Irish experiences for his works, including *She Stoops to Conquer.*

1880, is a combination of Victorian, Italianate, and Queen Anne architecture, with mostly Louis XV–style furnishings, plus antique lace, horse-drawn farm machinery, and other memorabilia. It's primarily a museum of the O'Conor (O'Connor) family, with portraits, documents, and genealogical tracts dating back 2,000 years. Displays also include a rare ancient harp that's said to have belonged to Turlough O'Carolan (1670–1738), the blind Irish bard who composed tunes that are still played today. The grounds, with terraced and woodland gardens, also hold the O'Conor inauguration stone, similar to the Stone of Scone at Westminster Abbey.

Castlerea, Co. Roscommon. ℭ **0907/20014.** Admission 5.20€ ($4.75) adults, 2.60€ ($2.40) children over 7. June to mid-Sept Mon–Sat 11–5pm. Located 10 miles (16km) off the main Dublin-Longford-Castlebar road (N5).

Lough Key Forest Park ★ *Kids*   If you're driving cross-country and want to stop for a picnic and a walk, or if you're traveling with children and are in search of a perfect place to let them loose, look no further. Spanning 840 acres along the shores of Lough Key and made up of mixed woodlands, a lake, and more than a dozen islands, this is one of Ireland's foremost lakeside parks. The grounds include nature walks, ancient monuments, ring forts, a central viewing tower, picnic grounds, a cafe, and a shop. In addition to cypress groves and other diverse foliage, you'll find a unique display of bog gardens, where a wide selection of peat-loving plants and shrubs flourishes. Deer, otters, hedgehogs, birds, pheasants, and many other forms of wildlife roam the park. The lake is navigable from the Shannon on the Boyle River. Powerboats and rowboats are available to rent, and there are pony and cart rides through the park.

Boyle, Co. Roscommon. ℭ **079/62363.** Admission to park 3.80€ ($3.45) per car. Open year-round daily dawn–dusk. Park entrance located on the main Dublin-Sligo road (N4), 2 miles (3km) east of the town of Boyle.

Lough Rynn House & Gardens   Seat of the Clements, the earls of Leitrim, this estate comprises 100 acres of woodland, ornamental gardens, open pastures, and lakes. Of particular interest is the 3-acre terraced walled garden dating from 1859. It's one of the largest of its kind in the country, laid out in the manner of a Victorian pleasure garden. The arboretum contains specimens of the tulip tree, California redwood, and other exotic species, including the oldest monkey puzzle tree in Ireland. Four thousand years of history can be seen at the rear of the house in one 180-degree sweep of the eye. The Neolithic burial tomb atop Druids Hill was constructed about 2000 B.C.; Reynolds Castle, a lonely sentinel by the lakeshore, dates from the 16th century; and Lough Rynn House was built in 1832.

Mohill, Co. Leitrim. ℭ **078/31427.** Admission 4.50€ ($4.10) per car; additional 1.25€ ($1.15) adults, .65€ (60¢) children for guided tour. May–Aug daily 10am–7pm. Located south of Carrick-on-Shannon, on the outskirts of Mohill, 3½ miles (5.5km) from the main Dublin-Sligo road (N4).

Strokestown Park House, Gardens and Irish Famine Museum ★★   A Georgian Gothic arch at the end of Ireland's widest main street leads to this estate, the seat of the Pakenham–Mahon family from 1600 to 1979. The present 45-room Palladian house, designed for Thomas Mahon by German architect Richard Castle in the 1730s, incorporates parts of an earlier tower house. The center block is fully furnished as it was in earlier days, surrounded by two wings. The north wing houses Ireland's last galleried kitchen (a kitchen gallery allowed the lady of the house to observe the culinary activity without being part of it), while the south wing is an elaborate vaulted stable, often described as an equine cathedral, that now houses the Irish Famine Museum. The gardens at Stroke-stown include a 4-acre, walled pleasure garden with the longest herbaceous bor-der in Britain and Ireland as well as a newly restored fruit and vegetable garden.

One of the defining events of Ireland's history, the Great Potato Famine of the 1840s, is the focus of this museum. Housed in the stable yards of Strokestown Park House, this museum illustrates how and why the famine started, how Eng-lish colonial officials failed to prevent its spread, and how it reduced the Irish population of 8.1 million by nearly 3 million through death and mass emigra-tion. This museum is particularly interesting for Irish Americans, tens of mil-lions of whom trace their ancestry to those who left the country during and after the famine. The museum also seeks to relate the events of the Irish famine to contemporary world hunger and poverty.

Strokestown, Co. Roscommon. (C) 078/33013. www.strokestownpark.ie. Admission to house, garden, and museum are separate or in 4 combinations. Admission to all 3: 11€ ($10) adults, 10€ ($9.10) seniors and students, 5.10€ ($4.60) children, 25€ ($23) family. Admission to Famine Museum or House 4.50€ ($4.10) adults, 3.60€ ($3.30) seniors and students, 2€ ($1.80) children, 10€ ($9.10) family; admission to garden alone is slightly higher. Apr–Oct daily 11am–5:30pm. On the main Dublin-Castlebar road (N5).

Tullynally Castle and Gardens   A turreted and towered Gothic Revival manor, this house has been the home of the Pakenham family, the earls of Long-ford, since 1655. The highlights include a great hall that rises two stories, with a ceiling of plaster gothic vaulting, and a collection of family portraits, china, and furniture. There's also a collection of 19th-century gadgets. The 30-acre grounds are an attraction in themselves, with woodland walks, a linear water garden, a Victorian grotto, and an avenue of 200-year-old Irish yew trees. Tully-nally is near Lough Derravaragh, an idyllic spot featured in the legendary Irish tale *The Children of Lir.* The tearoom is open daily May to August.

Castlepollard, Co. Westmeath. (C) 044/61159. Fax 044/61856. Admission to gardens 4€ ($3.65) adults, 1.50€ ($1.40) children; castle and gardens 6.50€ ($5.90) adults, 3.50€ ($3.20) children. Castle open mid-June to July daily 2–6pm; gardens open May–Aug 2–6pm. 1½ miles (2km) from Castlepollard on the Granard road, off the main Dublin-Sligo road (N4).

OUTDOOR PURSUITS

BOATING   The following companies rent cabin cruisers along this part of the Shannon: **Athlone Cruisers,** Jolly Mariner Marina, Athlone, County West-meath (© **0902/72892;** fax 0902/74386; www.iol.ie/wmeathtc/acl); **Carrick Craft Cruisers,** The Marina, Carrick-on-Shannon, County Leitrim (© **078/ 20236;** fax 078/21336; www.carrickcraft.com); and **Star Line,** The Marina, Portumna, County Galway (© **0509/41120;** www.emeraldstar.ie).

GOLF   There are two 18-hole championship golf courses in the area that should not be missed. The **Glasson Golf and Country Club,** Glasson, County Westmeath (© **0902/85120;** www.glassongolf.ie), is situated on the shores of Lough Ree, 6 miles (9.5km) north of Athlone. Greens fees are 44€ ($40) on weekdays and 51€ ($46) on weekends. Equally new is the **Slieve Russell Hotel Golf Club,** Cranaghan, Ballyconnell, County Cavan (© **049/952-6444;** www.quinn-group.com). Greens fees for those not staying at the hotel are 46€ ($41) on weekdays and 58€ ($53) on weekends.

Two other 18-hole courses in the area are at **County Cavan Golf Club,** Arn-more House, Drumellis, County Cavan (© **049/433-1541;** www.cavangolf.ie), with greens fees of 20€ ($18) on weekdays and 23€ ($21) on weekends; and **County Longford Golf Club,** Dublin Road, Longford (© **043/46310;** colong-golf@eircom.net), with greens fees of 15€ ($14) on weekdays and 19€ ($17) on weekends.

HORSEBACK RIDING **Moorlands Equestrian & Leisure Center,** Drumshanbo, County Leitrim (© **078/41095**), offers lessons, as well as trail rides along Lough Allen and the nearby hills. Children are welcome. During the off-season, B.H.S. certification courses in equestrian science are offered. Book lessons or trail rides at least a day in advance. Mountain walking, water sports, and accommodations are also offered.

ACCOMMODATIONS YOU CAN AFFORD

Arradale House *(Kids*   Peace and serenity will descend upon you as you turn into the lane leading to Arradale House. Mrs. Christine McMahon and her family welcome guests to their rambling farmhouse on a working dairy farm set in green fields. This has been a favorite with anglers for many years, but even if you're not after fish there's still plenty to do in the vicinity: Dun-A-Ri Forest Park, with its nature trails and wishing well, is a mere 3 miles (5km) away, and nearby pubs often have live music. Guest rooms vary in size, but all are quite comfortable. There's a game room, and a friendly pony has great appeal for youngsters. Mrs. McMahon's home-cooked meals are based on farm-fresh produce and home baking.

Kingscourt Rd., Carrickmacross, Co. Monaghan. ©/fax 042/966-1941. 7 units, 4 with bathroom. 48€ ($44) double. 10% reduction for children sharing with an adult. Rates include full breakfast. AE, MC, V. Just off N2, 2½ mi (4km) south of Carrickmacross. **Amenities:** Game room. *In-room:* TV, tea/coffeemaker.

Glencarne House *(★★ (Value*   Situated on a 100-acre working farm, Glencarne is a beautifully restored and recently redecorated late Georgian house with great charm and warmth. The two front rooms (nos. 1 and 2) enjoy a sweeping view of the valley below, and an especially spacious double with an adjoining twin combine to make an elegant family suite. Rooms feature brass poster beds, antique furnishings, and fresh flowers in abundance. Dinner is the high point of life at Glencarne; the Harringtons draw from their own produce and meats and present a fresh, sumptuous fixed-price feast for 26€ ($24). Then, when there's nothing left to do but collapse, firm beds are there to catch you.

Ardcarne, Carrick-on-Shannon, Co. Leitrim (signposted on N4, between Carrick-on-Shannon and Boyle). ©/fax **079/67013**. 6 units. 64€ ($58) double. No service charge. Includes full Irish breakfast. No credit cards. Open Mar to mid-Oct.

Gortmor House   This modern farmhouse, set in quiet, scenic countryside, is the home of Imelda and Kevin McMahon, who welcome each guest as a new friend. Imelda is the Farmhouse Association representative for Counties Leitrim, Cavan, and Monaghan. This is angling country, with no less than 41 free fishing lakes, as well as the River Shannon, within a 10-mile (16km) radius, and the McMahons can help plan your assault. Rooms are quite comfortable, and there's a TV lounge for guests. All bedrooms are nonsmoking.

Lismakeegan, Carrick-on-Shannon, Co. Leitrim. © **078/20489**. Fax 078/21439. gortmorhouse@ oceanfree.net. 4 units, 3 with bathroom (shower only). 52€ ($47) double. 20% reduction for children sharing with an adult. Rates include full breakfast. High tea 15€ ($14); dinner 21€ ($19). AE, MC, V. Closed Dec–Jan. 2½ miles (4km) from Carrick-on-Shannon, 2 miles (3km) off the Dublin-Sligo road (N4), and just over 1 mile (1.5km) off the R280 road, well signposted along the way. **Amenities:** Lounge. *In room:* TV, hair dryer.

Hilltop Farm   This large modern farmhouse is about halfway between Butlersbridge and Belturbet, just off the Cavan-Belturbet road. Mrs. Philomena O'Connor is a thoughtful host, and helps guests take advantage of local fishing. Horseback riding and cruising on the Erne can also be arranged.

Kilduff, Belturbet, Co. Cavan. © 049/952-2114. 10 units. 25€ ($23) single; 46€ ($41) double. 50% reduction for children sharing with an adult. Rates include full breakfast. Dinner 15€ ($14). MC, V.

Riversdale Farmhouse   Violet and Raymond Thomas are hosts at Riversdale, a large farmhouse sitting on an 85-acre sheep farm just over 1 mile (1.6km) south of town. There are open fires on cool evenings, fishing right on the property, and a squash court, heated indoor swimming pool, and sauna.

Ballinamore, Co. Leitrim. ℂ **078/44122.** Fax 078/44813. www.riversdaleguesthouse.com. 9 units. 48€ ($44) single; 76€ ($69) double. 25% reduction for children sharing with an adult. Rates include full breakfast. Advance reservations required Nov–Feb. MC, V. Closed Christmas. **Amenities:** Heated indoor pool; sauna; squash court.

Ross Castle and House 🐾🐾 *(Finds)*   This 400-acre, family-run horse, cattle, and sheep farm on Lough Sheelin offers appealing accommodations and activities options. It's one of the most unique and affordable hideaways I've discovered in Ireland. **Ross Castle** is a 16th-century fortified tower, set on a wooded hilltop overlooking Lough Sheelin. It's said to be haunted by a lovesick bride-to-be named Sabrina, whose lover, Orwin, was drowned in Lough Sheelin en route to their elopement. They're buried together in a nearby field. Today, the place is restored, with central heating throughout (even in the tower rooms). The common rooms are especially spacious and welcoming: There's a sitting room in the tower and a large dining room with fireplace in the adjacent annex. The two tower rooms are reached by a spiral stairway, and have such intriguing features as arrow-loop windows and a bathroom built into the thickness of the wall. The annex rooms have larger windows, and open onto a terrace with views of the lake.

   Nearby **Ross House** is a spacious and comfortable manor house, the oldest portions of which date from the mid-17th century. Horseback riding, tennis courts, fishing boats with or without motors (the place is noted for its brown trout and is stocked with pike and perch), sauna, and Jacuzzi are all on hand. One of the Harkorts' daughters, a physiotherapist at the regional hospital, offers guests massages in the evening, by prior appointment. On request, four-course dinners are served for 18€ to 23€ ($16–$21), with an excellent small selection of moderately priced wines.

Mount Nugent, Co. Cavan (signposted from Mount Nugent). ℂ/fax Ross House **049/854-0218;** Ross Castle 049/854-0237. www.ross.house.com or www.ross.castle.com. 11 units. Ross Castle: 76€ ($69) double. Ross House: 63€ ($58) double. MC, V. Castle open year-round; house closed Dec–Feb. **Amenities:** Tennis court; Jacuzzi; sauna; massage treatments; babysitting; horseback riding. *In room:* (house only) TV, TEL, tea/coffeemaker.

Willow Bridge Lodge   Ann and Bill Holden extend a warm welcome in their modern country home, with the facilities of a small hotel. Ann is a superb cook and uses only the freshest ingredients. Guest rooms are tastefully furnished—some have canopy beds—with bathrobes provided. The house is set in landscaped gardens with marvelous views over the Blackwater River. Watersports enthusiasts can rent equipment and bicycles are also available.

Armagh Rd., Monaghan, Co. Monaghan. ℂ/fax **047/81054.** thelodge@eircom.net. 4 units. 76€ ($69) double. Rates include full breakfast. No credit cards. Free parking. Amenities: Water-sports equipment/rentals; bike rental. *In room:* TV (satellite and movie channels), tea/coffeemaker, hair dryer, bathrobes.

GREAT DEALS ON DINING

Andy's Restaurant TRADITIONAL   Andy's is located above an award-winning pub. The extensive menu offers a half-dozen vegetarian dishes, and also includes such interesting dishes as turkey filets rolled in crushed peppercorns and served with a Madeira sauce, and sirloin steak in a whiskey-and-beer sauce.

The chef's motto is "If you can spell it, I can cook it"; so, any dietary requirements are easily accommodated on request.

12 Market St., Monaghan. ✆ **047/82277.** Lunch under 9€ ($8.15); dinner main courses 10€–22€ ($9.10–$20); fixed-price dinner 27€ ($24). MC, V. Daily 12:30–2:30pm; Tues–Sun 6–10pm.

Dartry Bar/Braken Restaurant/Cavendish Restaurant PUB GRUB/ TRADITIONAL   The Hillgrove Hotel is home to a trio of dining choices. Good bar food is available in the convivial Dartry Bar, even during those awkward mid-afternoon hours when lunch can be hard to come by. For more substantial dining try the grills, steaks, roast beef, and so on in the informal Braken. For evening meals the Cavendish Restaurant is a good choice; try the pan-fried filet of beef, finished with cream and peppercorns; escalope of salmon filled with brill and chive mousse in a butter sauce; or one of the fine vegetarian offerings.

Hillgrove Hotel, Old Armagh Rd., Monaghan, Co. Monaghan. ✆ **047/81288.** www.quinnhotels.com. Bar food (Dartry Bar) under 6.50€ ($5.90); grills and lunches (Braken) 11€–15€ ($10–$14); evening meals (Cavendish) 15€–23€ ($14–$21). AE, MC, V. Dartry Bar daily 10am–9pm; Braken Mon–Sat 4–10:15, Sun 5–9:15pm; Cavendish daily 7–9:15pm. On south side of Monaghan town, just off main Dublin road.

Derragarra Inn BAR FOOD/IRISH   This thatched-cottage pub sits on the banks of the River Annalea and is a great place for a drink or meal. More than 200 years old, it's full of local farm implements and crafts, as well as exotic souvenirs collected by former owner John Clancy during his travels around the world. Relax by the old turf fireplace or on the garden patio. Freshwater fish, smoked salmon, and steak are among the best choices. It's 4 miles (6.5km) north of Cavan Town.

Butlersbridge, Co. Cavan. ✆ **049/433-1003.** Bar food under 7.50€ ($6.80); main courses 13€–19€ ($12–$17). MC, V. Daily 12–3pm and 7–9pm. 4 miles (6.5km) north of Cavan town.

15

Northern Ireland

Unlike the other regional titles with which we've divided the chapters of this book, "Northern Ireland" designates a political rather than a geographical destination. It is not simply a matter of longitude and latitude. Parts of "the South" (the Republic) lie farther north than "the North," whose boundaries follow historical, not topographical, contours and divisions.

To outsiders, the "Troubles"—mutually inflicted and endured by the people of Northern Ireland across several decades—are incomprehensible. Other people's prejudices and quarrels usually are. From a visitor's perspective, the violence has been remarkably contained; furthermore, foreigners, like diplomats, have enjoyed a certain immunity. Derry and Belfast at their worst have been as safe for visitors as most major American cities, and the Ulster countryside has been as idyllic and serene as Vermont. For the outsider, driving through Northern Ireland was and is no more cause for fear than driving to work. Not so for the people of Northern Ireland, whose wounds and grief run deep.

The truth is that despite its violent reputation, Northern Ireland is as welcoming and gracious as the South, and

as beautiful. It is, after all, Ireland. Long the industrial center of the island, the North has traditionally been noticeably more prosperous than the South, but that difference is less and less perceptible. The Republic's economic successes in the past 2 decades, as well as the leveling effects of participation in the European Community, continue to blur the economic and social differences.

EXPLORING THE NORTH The first thing that strikes you once you cross the border and take your bearings is how small Northern Ireland is. The next thing that strikes you is how much there is to see and do. As the Tourist Board puts it, Northern Ireland is a nation that only pretends to be small. That said, there are really only two cities in the North likely to serve as major destinations in themselves and bases for exploration: **Belfast** and **Derry**. After these, the major destinations in the North lie in its magnificent countryside, in regions officially designated as areas of outstanding natural beauty: the **Causeway Coast** and the **Glens of Antrim,** the **Mourne Mountains,** the **Sperrin Mountains,** and the **Fermanagh Lakelands.**

1 Orientation

VISITOR INFORMATION & ENTRY REQUIREMENTS
SOURCES OF INFORMATION The **Northern Ireland Tourist Board** headquarters is at 59 North St., Belfast BT1 2DS (© **028/9024-6609;** fax: 028/9031-2424; www.discovernorthernireland.com). It's open June to September Monday to Saturday 9am to 7pm, Sunday noon to 5pm; and October to May Monday to Saturday 9am to 5:30pm; please note that hours can vary. There is also an office in Dublin at 16 Nassau St., Dublin 2 (© **01/679-1977;**

> **Tips** **Money Alert! The Pound and Not the Punt**
>
> Northern Ireland uses the currency of Great Britain and not the Irish
> Republic; it will not be changing to the euro system. Note that in this
> chapter only, when we use the symbol £, we mean British Pound, and
> not the Irish Punt. As we go to press, the exchange rate against the
> American dollar is **£1 = $1.45,** and all prices quoted in these pages are
> based on that rate.
>
> Visitors coming from the Republic can change money there, before
> crossing the border, if they wish. And, of course, it's always best to
> change currency at banks rather than in department stores or hotels.
> In Belfast, the Thomas Cook office, 10 College St., Belfast (© **028/
> 9032-2455),** can also convert currency at the official rate.

fax 01/677-1587). In addition, there are over 30 Tourist Information Centers
(TICs) around the province, the majority of which are open year-round, with
helpful, friendly personnel eager to help with any problem and make sure you
see the highlights of their area. Local accommodations may be booked in any
TIC, and most offer the ability to secure reservations throughout all of Ireland
and the UK on the Web. To make your own reservations anywhere in Ireland
using a credit card, you can call the Central Accommodations Freefone number
at © **00800/6686-6866.**

ENTRY REQUIREMENTS   U.S. citizens need only a valid passport to enter
Northern Ireland. British citizens need no passport for Northern Ireland (except
as a form of identification). Canadians, Australians, and New Zealanders require
only a passport for stays of up to 3 months.

GETTING THERE

BY AIR   Aer Lingus (© 800/474-7424; www.aerlingus.ie) offers scheduled
flights from Boston and New York via Shannon to **Belfast International Airport** (© 028/94-422888; www.bial.co.uk). Other major carriers offer connecting flights from the United States and Canada via London/Heathrow, Glasgow,
or Manchester. Charter service to Shannon, Dublin, and Belfast is offered by a
range of operators, such as **Sceptre Charters** (© 800/221-0924) and **Irish
Charters** (© 888/431-6688) in the U.S., and **World of Vacations** (© 800/
263-8776; www.worldofvacations.com) in Canada.

Direct flights into **Belfast International Airport** include service by **British
Airways** (© 0845/773-3377; www.british-airways.com) from Birmingham,
Edinburgh, and London/Heathrow; by **Virgin Express** (© 800/891199;
www.virgin-atlantic.com) from London/Heathrow; and by **British European**
(© 08705/676676; www.british-european.com) from London/Stansted. In
addition, there is service into **Belfast City Airport** (© 028/9045-7745;
www.belfastcityairport.com) by a range of carriers, including **British Airways**
flights from Edinburgh, Glasgow, Leeds, Liverpool, and Manchester, and by
British European from Birmingham, Bristol, Exeter, London Stansted, and
London Gatwick. Service to **City of Derry Airport** (© 028/7181-0784;
www.derrynet.com/airport/) is provided by **British Airways** from Glasgow and
Manchester, and by **Ryanair** (© 0541/569569 in Britain; www.ryanair.com)
from London Stansted.

Northern Ireland

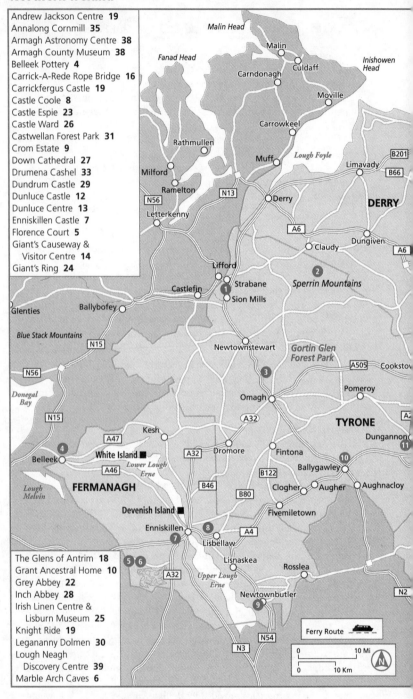

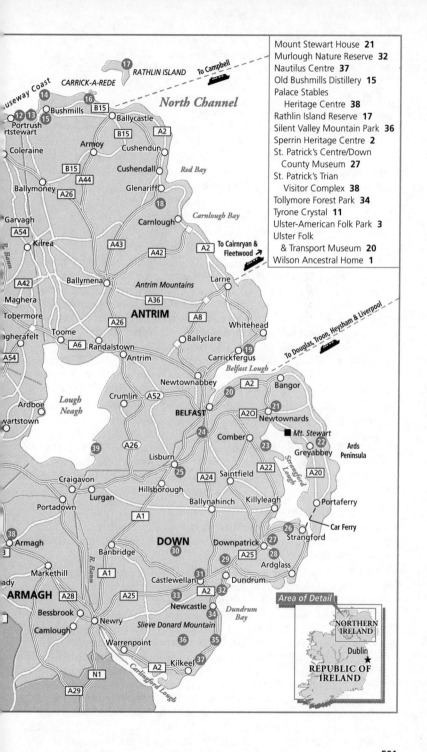

Mount Stewart House **21**
Murlough Nature Reserve **32**
Nautilus Centre **37**
Old Bushmills Distillery **15**
Palace Stables
    Heritage Centre **38**
Rathlin Island Reserve **17**
Silent Valley Mountain Park **36**
Sperrin Heritage Centre **2**
St. Patrick's Centre/Down
    County Museum **27**
St. Patrick's Trian
    Visitor Complex **38**
Tollymore Forest Park **34**
Tyrone Crystal **11**
Ulster-American Folk Park **3**
Ulster Folk
    & Transport Museum **20**
Wilson Ancestral Home **1**

Most international flights into Ireland land in Dublin, with connecting flights to Belfast. Direct service into Belfast International includes **Sabena** (© **028/ 9448-4823**) from Brussels and **Maersk Air** (© **0345/222111** in Britain) from Copenhagen.

BY TRAIN   Trains on the **Irish Rail** (© **1850/366222;** www.irishrail.ie) and **Northern Ireland Railways** (© **888/BRITRAIL** or 028/9089-9411; www.nirailways.co.uk) systems travel into Northern Ireland from Dublin's **Connolly Station** daily. They arrive at Belfast's Central Station, East Bridge Street (© **028/9089-9411**). Monday to Saturday, eight trains a day connect Dublin and Belfast; on Sunday, five. The trip takes about 2 hours.

BY BUS   Ulsterbus (© **028/9033-3000;** www.translink.co.uk) runs buses from the Republic to Belfast and virtually all bus service in and between 21 localities in Northern Ireland. To purchase or reserve a ticket, call © **028/ 9032-0011.** The express bus from Dublin to Belfast takes 3 hours and runs seven times daily Monday to Saturday, three times on Sunday.

BY FERRY   The quickest crossing from Britain to Northern Ireland is the 90-minute **SeaCat** (© **08705/523523;** www.seacat.co.uk), a catamaran service from Troon, Scotland and from Heysham. Other ferry services into Belfast include **Norse Irish Ferries** (© **0870/6004321;** www.norsemerchant.com) from Liverpool and the **Isle of Man Steam Packet Co.** (© **01624/661661;** www.steam-packet.com) from Douglas on the Isle of Man. In addition, there is **Stena Sealink** (© **028/9074-7747;** www2.stenaline.com) from Stranraer, Scotland, to Belfast. **P&O European Ferries** (© **0870/242-4777;** www. poferries.com) runs from Cairnryan, Scotland, to Larne; and, in July and August, **SeaCat** from Campbell, Scotland, to Ballycastle, County Antrim.

BY CAR   Northern Ireland is directly accessible from the Republic of Ireland via many main roads and secondary roads. It is possible, but unlikely, that you will encounter checkpoints when crossing the border. Main roads leading to Northern Ireland from the Republic include N1 from Dublin, N16 from Sligo, N15 from Donegal, and N3 from Cavan. If you are renting a car, make certain that all your insurance coverage is equally valid in the North and in the Republic. This holds for any coverage provided by your credit card.

GETTING AROUND

Northern Ireland has launched a major initiative called *Translink* to coordinate rail, bus, and auto travel in the North, which will expand and enhance transportation services in the North.

BY BUS & RAIL   Ulsterbus (© **028/9033-3000;** www.translink.co.uk) runs daily scheduled services from Belfast to major cities and towns throughout Northern Ireland. From the **Laganside Buscentre,** Oxford Street, Belfast (© **028/9032-0011**), buses leave for destinations in Counties Antrim, Down (eastern), and Derry (eastern) and Cookstown. Buses to almost every other destination in the North, including Belfast International Airport and the Larne ferries, as well as the Republic, depart from the **Europa Bus Centre,** 10 Glengall St., Belfast (© **028/9033-7011**). Bus service in the North is remarkably thorough and will get you to the most unlikely and remote destinations.

The hub of **Northern Ireland Railways** (© **028/9089-9411;** www.nirailways. co.uk) is Belfast, with two principal rail stations: **Great Victoria St. Station,** across from the Europa Bus Centre; and **Belfast Central Station,** East Bridge Street. Trains from Larne arrive at Yorkgate Station; otherwise, trains to and from all destinations depart from and arrive at Belfast Central. The three main routes in the North's rail system are north and west from Belfast to Derry via Ballymena; east to Bangor, tracing the shores of Belfast Lough; and south to Dublin via Newry.

To save money, ask about the **Freedom of Northern Ireland** bus and rail passes, valid for unlimited travel on all Ulsterbus, Citibus, and railroad services operating within Northern Ireland. A 1-day pass costs £11 ($16) adult, £5 ($7.25) child, and a 7-day pass costs £40 ($58) adult, £16.50 ($24) child. It's available from **Northern Ireland Railways,** Central Station, East Bridge Street, Belfast (© **028/9089-9411**), and **Europa Bus Centre** (© **028/9033-7011**), as well as all major bus and train stations in Northern Ireland.

Two other bus and rail passes that may be of interest—they can be used in both the Republic and Northern Ireland—are the **Irish Rover,** good for 8 days of travel within a 15-day period, at a cost of 118€ ($107) adult and 60€ ($54) child; and the **Emerald Card,** good for 8 days of travel within a 15-day period, at a cost of 157€ ($143) adult and 79€ ($71) child, or 15 days of travel within a 30-day period, at a cost of 272€ ($246) adult and 136€ ($123) child. Both passes must be purchased 21-days before departure for Ireland and are available from **CIE Tours International** (© **800/243-8687** or 973/292-3438 from the U.S., 800/387-2667 in Canada; www.cietours.com).

BY SIGHTSEEING TOUR   From June through August, **Ulsterbus** operates a wide variety of full-day and half-day coach tours from the Europa Bus Centre, Glengall Street, Belfast, to places such as the Glens of Antrim, Causeway Coast, Fermanagh Lakelands, Sperrin Mountains, the Mountains of Mourne, and Armagh. There are also tours designed to take you to specific attractions, such as the Giant's Causeway, Old Bushmills Distillery in Bushmills, Navan Centre in Armagh, Ulster-American Folk Park in Omagh, and Tyrone Crystal Factory in Dungannon. For full information on the day tours and holiday packages offered by Ulsterbus, visit or call its tourism office at the **Europa Bus Centre,** 10 Glengall St. (© **028/9033-3000**). To consider in advance the range of tours available, take a look at **www.tourulster.com** and click the "Guided Tours" link.

BY CAR   The best way to travel around the Northern Ireland countryside is by car. The roads are in extremely good condition, better than in the Republic, and are very well signposted. Distances between major cities and towns are short. If you want to rent a car, **Avis** (© 028/9024-0404; www.avis.com), **Budget** (© 028/9023-0700; www.budget.com), **Europcar** (© 028/9045-0904; www.europcar.com), and **Hertz** (© 028/9073-2451; www.hertz.com) have depots in Belfast city and/or in at least one of the Belfast airports. Or, if you rent a car in the Republic, you can drive it in the North as long as you have the proper insurance.

 FAST FACTS: Northern Ireland

Business Hours Banks are generally open Monday through Friday from 10am to 12:30pm and 1:30 to 3 or 4pm; closed Saturday, Sunday, and bank holidays. In Belfast and Derry City, the banks tend not to close for lunch. Most shops in the North are open Monday through Saturday 9:30am to 5:30pm, with one early-closing day a week, usually Wednesday or Thursday. Shops in tourist areas are likely to be open Sunday and to have extended hours, especially in the summer months.

Electricity The electrical current (220vAC) and outlets (requiring 3-pin flat, fused plugs) are the same in the North as in the Republic. Note that they are not the 2-pin round plugs standard throughout Europe (except Great Britain).

Embassies & Consulates The **U.S. Consulate General** is at Queen's House, 14 Queen's St., Belfast BT1 6€Q (ⓒ **028/9032-8239**). Other foreign offices include: the **Australian High Commission,** Australia House, Strand, London WC2 B4L (ⓒ **020/7379-4344**); **Canadian High Commission,** Macdonald House, Grosvenor Square, London W1X 0AB (ⓒ **020/7499-9000**); and **New Zealand High Commission,** New Zealand House, 80 Haymarket Sq., London SW1Y 4TQ (ⓒ **020/7930-8422**).

Emergencies Dial ⓒ **999** for fire, police, and ambulance.

Mail United Kingdom postal rates apply, and mailboxes are painted red in the North. Most post offices are open weekdays 9am to 5pm and Saturdays from 9am to 1pm.

Newspapers & Magazines The morning national newspapers are the *News Letter* and the *Irish News;* the *Belfast Telegraph* is the only evening newspaper. All are published Monday through Saturday; on Sunday most Northern Irish depend on U.K. papers, which are readily available. For listings of upcoming cultural events throughout Northern Ireland, there's the free bimonthly *Arts Link* brochure published by the Arts Council of Northern Ireland and available at any Northern Ireland Tourist Board office.

Parking Because of long-standing security concerns, parking regulations in the North are both more restrictive and more relentlessly enforced than in the Republic.

Petrol (Gas) The approximate price of 1 liter of unleaded gas is about 66p ($1.00). As there are 4 liters to the U.S. gallon, that makes the price of a gallon of unleaded gasoline about £2.64 ($4.00)!

Police The Northern Ireland police are known as the Royal Ulster Constabulary (RUC). Currently the responsibility for security in the North is still shared with the British armed forces. A thorough review of the North's security forces is presently underway.

Safety Contrary to the media image, the North has one of the lowest levels of crime in Western Europe. Historically, the high rate of serious crime, such as homicide and robbery, have been almost exclusively associated with terrorism and the "troubles." Yet common sense dictates using care to avoid pickpockets in crowded areas and to follow other basic rules of safety. It is important to follow all rules, and to cooperate with security personnel if such an occasion should arise.

Taxes You pay a VAT (Value-Added Tax) of 17.5% on almost every one of your expenses, with the exception of B&B accommodations. The percentages vary with the category of the services and purchases. Many shops offer tax-free shopping schemes, such as "Cashback," and are pleased to explain the details. The refund procedure is essentially the same as for the Republic, outlined in "VAT Tax Refunds" in Chapter 2, "Planning an Affordable Trip to Ireland." Vouchers from the North can be presented at the Dublin or Shannon airports before departure from Ireland.

Telephone To reach Northern Ireland from anywhere but the Republic of Ireland or Great Britain, dial the country code (44) and then 28 (the area code minus the initial 0) and finally the local eight-digit number. From the Republic of Ireland, omit the country code and simply dial 048 and then the local eight-digit number. From Great Britain, dial 028 and the eight-digit number. For local calls within Northern Ireland, simply dial the eight-digit local number.

Tracing Your Roots Contact the **Ulster Historical Foundation,** Balmoral Buildings, 12 College Sq. E, Belfast BTI 6DD (© **028/9033-2288;** fax 028/9023-9885; www.uhf.org.uk), for help in tracking down Irish ancestors, particularly in Belfast, County Antrim, and County Down. The office will furnish a list of helpful publications and help you get to the appropriate genealogical source. See also "Tracing Your Irish Roots," in chapter 2.

Two private organizations to contact are **Irish Genealogical Services,** 2 Lower Crescent, Belfast B17 1NR (© **028/9024-1412;** fax 028/9023-9972); and **Historical Research Associates,** Glen Cottage, Glenmachan Road, Belfast BT4 2NP (© **028/9076-1490;** contact Joan Phillipson or Jennifer Irwin) and also at 40 Carrickburn Rd., Carrickfergus BT38 7ND, County Antrim (© **028/9336-8502;** fax 028/9335-1544).

2 Belfast

Belfast is 103 miles (166km) N of Dublin, 211 miles (340km) NE of Shannon, 125 miles (201km) E of Sligo, and 262 miles (422km) NE of Cork

Belfast has a lovely setting, nestled beside the River Lagan and Belfast Lough and ringed by gentle hills. This is a very industrialized city, often referred to as the engine room that drove the whirring wheels of the industrial revolution in Ulster. Major industries range from linen production to rope-making and shipbuilding. The *Titanic* was built in Belfast port, and today the world's largest dry dock is here. Nearly half a million people, a third of Northern Ireland's population, reside within the Belfast city limits.

The city's architecture is rich in Victorian and Edwardian buildings with elaborate sculptures over the doors and windows. Stone heads of gods, poets, scientists, kings, and queens peer down from the high ledges of banks and old linen warehouses. Some of Belfast's grandest buildings are the banks of **Waring Street:** The Ulster Bank, dating from 1860, has an interior like a Venetian palace, and the Northern Bank, dating from 1769, was originally a market house.

The Queen's University, with its Tudor cloister, dominates the southern sector of the city. The original edifice was built in 1849 by Charles Lanyon, who designed more of Belfast's buildings than anyone else, and was named for Queen Victoria, who visited Belfast in that year and had just about everything named in her honor for the occasion—literally dozens of streets, a hospital, a park, an artificial island, and the harbor's deepwater channel are all named after her. Today, the university serves 12,000 students and is the setting for the annual Belfast Festival at Queen's, one of the city's major annual arts events.

Northwest of downtown is **Cave Hill,** home of the Belfast Castle estate. This 200-acre estate is a public park, ideal for walking, jogging, picnicking, and enjoying the fine views of the city.

Impressions

Ulster: where every hill has its hero and every bog its bones.
                                        —Sam Hanna Bell (b. 1909), "In Praise of Ulster"

ESSENTIALS

GETTING THERE   For details, see "Getting There," in section 1, earlier in this chapter. Belfast has two airports—Belfast International and Belfast City— and gets considerable sea traffic at Belfast Harbour and at Larne (30 min. from Belfast by train, bus, or car).

From Belfast International Airport, nearly 19 miles (31km) north of the city, your best option is the **Airbus** coach into the city center. It operates daily, leaves every half hour, and costs £5 ($7.10) per person. A taxi will run closer to £20 ($28).

From Belfast City Airport, less than 4 miles (6.5km) from the city center, there are several options. The most convenient is a taxi, which costs roughly £6 ($8.52) to get into the city. You can also take Citybus no. 21 from the airport terminal or the Sydenham Halt train from the station directly across from the airport, both for 80p ($1.14).

In Northern Ireland, all roads really do lead to Belfast. It's the point of origin for the country's principal motorways and also the rail hub of the North.

VISITOR INFORMATION   Brochures, maps, and other data about Belfast and the North are available from the **Belfast Welcome Centre,** on Royal Avenue (© **028/9024-6609;** www.discovernorthernireland.com). It's open June through September, Monday to Saturday 9am to 7pm, and Sunday noon to 5pm; October through May, Monday to Saturday 9am to 5:30pm. Another source of information is the **Northern Ireland Tourist Board** headquarters at 59 North St., Belfast BT1 2DS (© **028/9024-6609;** fax: 028/9031-2424; www.discovernorthernireland.com). It keeps the same hours as the Welcome Centre, but you should note that hours can vary.

The tourist information desk at **Belfast City Airport** (© **028/9045-7745**) is open year-round Monday to Friday 5:30am to 10pm, Saturday 5:30am to 9pm, Sunday 5:30am to 10pm. The desk at **Belfast International Airport** (© **028/9442-2888**) is open March to September daily 24 hours, October to February daily 6:30am to 11pm.

GETTING AROUND   **Citybus,** Donegall Square West, Belfast (© **028/ 9033-3000;** www.citybus.co.uk), provides local bus services within the city. Departures are from Donegall Square East, West, and North, plus Upper Queen Street, Wellington Place, Chichester Street, and Castle Street. There is an information kiosk on Donegall Square West for guidance on where to get a bus to a certain locale. Fares are determined by the number of "zones" traversed. The usual fare for city center travel is £1 ($1.45). Multitrip tickets, day tickets, and 7-day passes offer significant savings, if you anticipate extensive use of the bus services.

If you've brought a **car** into Belfast, it's best to leave it parked at your hotel and take local transport or walk around the city. If you must drive and want to park your car downtown, look for a blue P sign that shows a parking lot or a parking area. In Belfast, there are a number of control zones, indicated by a pink and yellow sign, where no parking is permitted. In general, on-street parking is limited to an area behind City Hall (south side), by St. Anne's Cathedral (north side), and around Queen's University and Ulster Museum.

Belfast

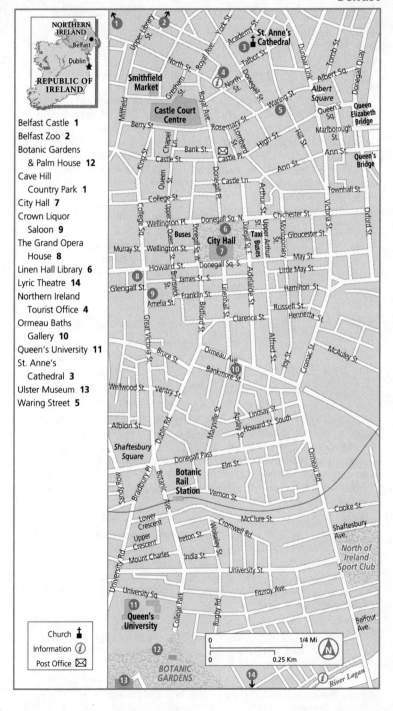

Belfast Castle **1**

Belfast Zoo **2**

Botanic Gardens & Palm House **12**

Cave Hill Country Park **1**

City Hall **7**

Crown Liquor Saloon **9**

The Grand Opera House **8**

Linen Hall Library **6**

Lyric Theatre **14**

Northern Ireland Tourist Office **4**

Ormeau Baths Gallery **10**

Queen's University **11**

St. Anne's Cathedral **3**

Ulster Museum **13**

Waring Street **5**

Church ✝

Information ⓘ

Post Office ✉

Taxis are available at all main rail stations, ports, and airports, as well as in front of City Hall. Most metered taxis are the London-type black cabs with a yellow disc on the window. Other taxis may not have meters, so you should ask the fare to your destination in advance. Belfast taxis fares run on the high side, with a £2 ($2.90) minimum and an additional £1 ($1.45) per mile. The largest cab company in Belfast is **Value Cabs** (℡ **028/9080-9080**).

Belfast is a good city for **walking.** To guide visitors on the best and safest areas for a stroll, the Belfast City Council has produced five different self-guided walking tour leaflets: city center southward to Shaftesbury Square, city center northward to the Irish News office, Shaftesbury Square southward to the university area, city center northeast to the port area, and Donegall Square south to Donegall Pass. Each walk is just over a mile (about 2km) in length and an hour in duration. Ask for a leaflet for the walk or walks that interest you at the Northern Ireland Tourist Office.

CITY ORIENTATION   The core of downtown Belfast sits beside the west bank of the River Lagan, and the city revolves around centrally located **Donegall Square,** which holds the City Hall and from which all roads radiate. Donegall Place, which extends northward from the square, leads to **Royal Avenue,** a prime shopping district. Bedford Street, which extends southward from the square, becomes Dublin Road, which, in turn, leads to the Queen's University area.

 FAST FACTS: **Belfast**

Consulates   The **U.S. consulate general** is at Queen's House, 14 Queen's St., Belfast BT1 (℡ **028/9032-8239**). For other embassies and consulates, see "Fast Facts: Northern Ireland," above.

Emergencies   Dial ℡ **999** for fire, police, and ambulance.

Gay & Lesbian Resources   The Belfast Gay and Lesbian Resource centers can be reached at **NIGRA/Northern Ireland Gay Rights Association,** Cathedral Buildings, Lower Donegall Street (℡ **028/9066-4111**). Other helpful numbers are the **Lesbian Line Belfast** (℡ **028/9023-8688**), Thursdays 7:30 to 10pm; and **Cara-Friend** (℡ **028/9032-2023**), Monday to Wednesday and Friday 7:30 to 10pm. For more information check out **www.queerspace. org.uk.**

Hospitals   On Lisburn Road you'll find **Belfast City Hospital** (℡ **028/ 9032-9241**); and, west of the city center on Grosvenor Road, the **Royal Victoria Hospital** (℡ **028/9028-0503**).

Internet Access   If you're cyber-starved you can log on at **Revelations Cafe** (℡ **028/9032-0337;** www.revelations.co.uk) on Bradbury Place just south of Donegall Road. It's open Monday to Friday 10am to 10pm, Saturday 10am to 6pm, and Sunday 11am to 7pm.

Laundry   For emergency sudsing services, seek out **Duds 'n' Suds,** 37 Botanic Ave. (℡ **028/9024-3956**), where you can have a snack while your clothes take a tumble; or **Agincourt Laundry,** 46 Agincourt Ave. (℡ **028/9033-1490**).

Post Office   The Belfast **GPO** (General Post Office) is located at Castle Place at the intersection of Royal Avenue and Donegall Place. It's open Monday through Friday from 9am to 5:30pm and Saturday 9am to 7pm.

SEEING THE SIGHTS

For an overview of the city, **Citybus Tours** (© **028/9045-8484;** www.translink.co.uk/originalbelfasttour) offers a 3½-hour **Belfast City Tour.** It departs at noon Monday and Friday from Castle Place. It costs £10 ($15) for adults, £9 ($13) students, £7 ($10) seniors and children, and £27 ($39) family. For roughly the same price, the **Black-taxi Tours** are also quite popular, and disturbing—they encompasses local sites and stories of the barely historical Troubles. To arrange **Black-taxi Tours,** call Michael at © **0800/052-3914** (toll-free) or 07860/127207 (mobile), or find all the details at **www.belfasttours.com.**

Theme-oriented **walking tours** are commonly offered during the summer months. Up-to-date information on current specialty tours is available at the office of the Northern Irish Tourist Board (see above).

Belfast Botanic Gardens & Palm House ⭐ These gardens were established by the Belfast Botanic and Horticultural Society in 1828. Ten years later a glass house was added, designed by noted Belfast architect Charles Lanyon. Now known as the Palm House, this unique building is one of the earliest examples of curvilinear cast-iron glass-house construction. It contains many rare plant specimens, including such tropical plants as sugar cane, coffee, cinnamon, banana, aloe, ivory nut, rubber, bamboo, guava, and the striking bird of paradise flower. The Tropical Ravine, also known as the fernery, provides a setting for plants to grow in a sunken glen. Take time also to stroll in the surrounding outdoor gardens of roses and herbaceous borders, established in 1927.

Stranmillis Rd. © 028/9032-4902. Free admission. Palm House and Tropical Ravine Apr–Sept Mon–Fri 10am–noon and 1–5pm, Sat–Sun 1–5pm; Oct–Mar Mon–Fri 10am–noon and 1–4pm, Sat–Sun 1–4pm; gardens 8am–sunset. Signposted from M1/M2 (Balmoral exit). Bus: 61, 71, 84, 85.

Belfast Castle Northwest of downtown and 400 feet (122m) above sea level stands Belfast Castle, whose 200-acre estate spreads down the slopes of Cave Hill. The castle, which affords panoramic views of Belfast Lough and the city, was completed in 1870. It was the family residence of the third Marquis of Donegall, and was presented to the city of Belfast in 1934 and used for private functions. After extensive restoration, the castle reopened to the public in 1988; 2 years later, its cellars were transformed into a Victorian arcade, including an antiques and craft shop, a bar, and a bistro restaurant. The extensive grounds include a public park, which is ideal for walking, jogging, picnicking, and enjoying extraordinary views of the city.

Antrim Rd. © 028/9077-6925. Free admission and parking. Castle 9am–10:30pm. Signposted off the Antrim Rd., 2½ miles (4km) north of city center.

Cave Hill Country Park ⭐ *Kids* This lovely park, which stands atop a 1,200-foot basalt cliff, is said to resemble the profile of Napoleon (Mount Rushmore without the expense!). It offers panoramic views, walking trails, and a number of interesting archaeological and historical sights. The highlights are the (Neolithic) caves that gave the hill its name, and MacArt's Fort, an ancient earthwork built (as usual) against the Vikings. It was here in this fort, in 1795, that Wolfe Tone and fellow United Irishmen planned the 1798 rebellion. On a lighter note, there's an adventure playground for the kids.

Open site. Park your car at Belfast Castle or Belfast Zoo (above). Off the Antrim Rd., 4 miles (6.5km) north of city center.

City Hall ⭐ This magnificent public building is the core of Belfast, the axis around which the whole city radiates. It was built of Portland stone after Belfast was granted the status of a city by Queen Victoria in 1888. You can't miss the place: It's large and official looking, has a big statue of Queen Victoria at the front, and dominates the main shopping area.

Donegall Sq. ℂ 028/90270456. www.belfastcity.gov.uk. Free admission. Reservations required. Guided tours available June–Sept Mon–Fri 10:30am, 11:30am, and 2:30pm, Sat 2:30pm; Oct–May Mon–Sat 2:30pm. Otherwise by arrangement.

Linen Hall Library   This is Belfast's oldest library, established in 1788 as an independent charitable institution. It's known for its collections of Irish books, local historical documents, Robert Burns's books, and books on heraldry.

17 Donegall Sq. N. ℂ 028/9032-1707. info@linenhall.com. Free admission. Mon–Fri 9:30am–5:30pm; Sat 9:30am–4pm.

Ormeau Baths Gallery ✦   The Ormeau Baths Gallery is the principal exhibition space for contemporary visual art in Belfast. It occupies the site of an old Victorian swimming bath designed by Robert Watt. This striking and versatile facility can program multiple simultaneous exhibitions in a variety of media and has become a premier showcase for the best of Northern Irish (and international) contemporary art.

18A Ormeau Ave. ℂ 028/9032-1402. Fax 028/9031-2232. www.ormeaubathsgallery.co.uk. Free admission. Tues–Sat 10am–6pm.

Ulster Museum ✦✦   Built in the grand Classical Renaissance style, with an Italian marble interior, this museum summarizes 9,000 years of Irish history with exhibits on art, furniture, ceramics, costume, industrial heritage, and a permanent display of products "Made in Belfast." One of the best-known exhibits is the collection of gold and silver jewelry recovered by divers in 1968 off the Antrim coast from the 1588 wreckage of the Armada treasure ship *Girona*. Other permanent collections focus on water wheels and steam engines, linen making, the post office, coins and medals, early Ireland, flora and fauna, and the living sea.

Stranmillis Rd. ℂ 028/9038-3000. www.ulstermuseum.org.uk. Free admission, except to major special exhibitions. Mon–Fri 10am–5pm; Sat 1–5pm; Sun 2–5pm. Signposted from M1/M2 (Balmoral exit); next to the Botanic Gardens. Bus: 61, 71, 84, 85.

OUTDOOR PURSUITS

FISHING   The 5½-mile (9km) stretch of the Lagan River from Stranmillis weir to Shaw's Bridge offers some decent coarse fishing, especially on summer evenings. Lough Neagh, from May to July, has good shore and boat fishing. Contact Paddy Prunty at the **Kinnego Marina,** Oxford Island, Craigavon (ℂ 028/3832-7573). For info, tackle, and bait, try the **Village Tackle Shop,** 55a Newtownbreda Rd., Belfast (ℂ 028/9049-1916), or **Shankill Fishing Tackle,** 366 Shankill Rd., Belfast (ℂ 028/9033-0949).

GOLF   The Belfast area offers four parkland 18-hole courses. Three miles (5km) southwest of the city, there's the **Balmoral Golf Club,** 518 Lisburn Rd., Belfast (ℂ 028/9066-7747; fax 028/9066-6759), with greens fees of £20 ($29) weekdays (except Wed) and £30 ($44) weekends; 4 miles (6.5km) southwest of the city center, there's the **Dunmurry Golf Club,** 91 Dunmurry Lane, Dunmurry, Belfast (ℂ 028/9061-0834; 028/9060-2540), £16 ($23) weekdays and £25 ($36) weekends; 3 miles (5km) south of the city center lies the **Belvoir Park Golf Club,** 73 Church Rd., Newtownbreda, Belfast (ℂ 028/9049-1693; 028/9064-6113), £33 ($48) weekdays and £38 ($55) weekends; and 3 miles

(5km) north is the **Fortwilliam Golf Club,** Downview Ave., Belfast (© **028/ 9037-0770;** 028/9078-1891), £22 ($32) weekdays and £29 ($42) weekends. Weekdays are usually better for visitors, but be sure to phone ahead. Club professionals offer lessons, usually for about £25 ($36) per hour, with advance booking of at least 2 days.

HORSEBACK RIDING Saddle up at the **Drumgooland House Equestrian Centre,** 29 Dunnanew Rd., Seaforde, Downpatrick, County Down (© **028/ 4481-1956;** www.activityholidaysireland.com), which offers 1- to 4-hour treks, beach rides, and lessons. Full equestrian holidays also available.

ACCOMMODATIONS YOU CAN AFFORD

For two fine guesthouses outside the city, see "Out from Belfast," below.

Ashberry Cottage *(Value)* "Cozy" is the word for Hilary and Sam Mitchell's modern bungalow, and you'll be completely spoiled from the moment they greet you with a welcome tray of tea and goodies. Not only do they both know the Belfast area well, but Hilary works for the Northern Ireland Tourist Board and is well qualified to help you plan your travels throughout the province. Guest rooms are attractive and very comfortable. Sam is the morning cook, and his breakfasts are legendary. Evening meals also draw raves from guests. Sam will meet you at the airport or railway station with advance notice. The house is entirely nonsmoking.

19 Rosepark Central, Belfast. © 028/9028-6300. 3 units, 1 with bathroom. £40 ($58) double. Rates include full breakfast. No credit cards. Free parking. Take A20 to Rosepark, which is the second turn on the right past the Stormont Hotel. *In room:* TV, tea/coffeemaker

Ash-Rowan Guesthouse On a quiet, tree-lined street in a residential neighborhood, this four-story Victorian house sits between Lisburn and Malone Roads near Queen's University. Proprietors Evelyn and Hazlett have outfitted it with country-style furnishings, family heirlooms, and antiques, along with bouquets of fresh flowers from the garden. The mood here is relaxed and old-style, with morning papers and late breakfasts. The rates include a choice of 12 traditional breakfasts, including the Ulster fry scrambled eggs smoked salmon, kippers, or several vegetarian options like flambéed mushrooms. The location is ideal, just a short stroll into the city center. *Note:* Local interest in the house has been on the rise since the Hazletts determined last year that this was the home of Thomas Andrews, a designer of the Titanic, who went down with the ship on her maiden voyage.

12 Windsor Ave., Belfast. © 028/9066-1758. Fax 028/9066-3227. 5 units. ashrowan@hotmail.com. £72–£89 ($105–$130) double. Rates include full breakfast. MC, V. *In room:* TV.

Helga Lodge There's lots of character in this redbrick, Victorian-style town house, conveniently located in the Queen's University area. It's only a short walk to the city center, and the Botanic Gardens are also quite near. Bedrooms vary in size, but all are comfortably furnished.

7 Cromwell Rd., Belfast BT7 1JW. © 028/9032-4820. Fax 028/9032-0653. 31 units, 6 with bathroom (shower only). £40–£60 ($58–$87) double. Rates include full breakfast. MC, V. *In room:* TV, TEL.

Liserin Guesthouse Set on a quiet street shaded by lime trees, Liserin is about a 15-minute walk into the city center. There's also good bus service at the end of the block. The brick Victorian-style town house dates from 1892, and original woodwork, high ceilings, and spacious rooms add to its charm. The hostess, Mrs. Ina Smith, takes a personal interest in guests, serving evening tea and, upon request, a simple evening meal at a modest price. Guest rooms have sinks and are well furnished; those in the back catch more sun than the ones in front, but all are light and cheerful.

17 Eglantine Ave., Belfast BT9 6DW. © 028/9066-0769. 6 units. £44 ($64) double. Reduction for children. Rates include full breakfast. No credit cards. *In room:* TV, tea/coffeemaker.

GREAT DEALS ON DINING

Bewley's CAFE   Bewley's has been a Dublin fixture for a century and a half, and in recent years it has opened branches in leading cities around Ireland. This Belfast branch is in the same traditional Irish cafe style, and offers all the well-known special blends of roasted coffees, blended teas, home-cooked pastries, and a wide variety of salad plates and hot lunch selections.

Donegall Arcade, Belfast BT1. © 028/9023-4955. Fax 028/9023-5449. Lunch £6 ($8.70). MC, V. Mon–Fri 8am–5:30pm; Sat 8:30am–5:30pm.

Bittles ⭐ TRADITIONAL IRISH   John Bittle is a great believer in the Irish dishes he grew up with, and this is one place you'll find a really good Irish stew, as well as *champ,* an old Irish recipe not often encountered in restaurants. The menu is also likely to include plaice in garlic butter; a pasta dish; filled rolls and sandwiches; at least one vegetarian selection; and steak, ham, and chicken dishes, all served with potatoes and a fresh vegetable. John's cream of leek soup is terrific.

70 Upper Church Lane, Belfast BT1. © 028/9031-1088. £2–£7 ($2.90–$10). MC, V. Mon–Fri 11:30am–2pm.

La Belle Epoque FRENCH   This brasserie-style spot is housed in a double shop front in a brick building. The menu offers a creative mixture of fruit- and vegetable-based sauces. It includes dishes such as chicken with almond crust and mushroom sauce, veal in creamy artichoke sauce, filet of turbot with salmon trout mousse, and panfried salmon with broccoli and ginger sauce. All dishes are unusual and delicious, and vegetarian options are always available.

61 Dublin Rd., Belfast BT2. © 028/9032-3244. Reservations suggested. Fixed-price lunches £6.25–£10.95 ($9.10–$16); fixed-price dinner £15 ($22); dinner main courses £8.50–£12 ($12–$17). AE, DC, MC, V. Tues–Fri noon–11pm; Sat 6–11pm.

Nick's Warehouse ⭐ (Value) INTERNATIONAL   In an old warehouse between St. Anne's Cathedral and the tourist office, this extremely popular restaurant and wine bar dishes up terrific, hearty meals for a pittance. There's a wine bar setting downstairs and a classy dining room upstairs, with brick walls

---

(**Tips** **Pub Grub**

You'll find good local pub food for about £6 ($8.70) from noon to 3pm (or later) at the following: **Crown Liquor Saloon,** 46 Great Victoria St., BT2 (© 028/9024-9476); **Robinson's,** 38 Great Victoria St., BT2 (© 028/9024-7447); **Beaten Docket,** 48 Great Victoria St., BT2 (© 028/9024-2986); **The Front Page,** 106 Donegall St., BT1 (© 028/9032-4924); **Rumpoles,** 81 Chichester St., BT1 (© 028/9023-2840); **White's Tavern,** 2-4 Winecellar Entry, High Street, Belfast, County Antrim, BT1 (© 028/9024-3080); and on the outskirts of town, **The King's Head,** 829 Lisburn Rd., BT7, Balmoral, opposite King's Hall (© 028/9066-0455).

> **⌐ _Tips_ A Stop Before You Shop**
>
> Before you begin shopping, take time to visit the **Craftworks Gallery,** Bedford House, Bedford Street (✆ **028/9024-4465**), a display center and shop for the work of individual craftspeople from all over Northern Ireland. The gallery can also supply you with a free copy of the brochure "Crafts in Northern Ireland," detailing local crafts and where to find them. It's just behind Belfast City Hall.

---

and an open kitchen. Salads might include summer chicken and melon with yogurt-and-chive dressing and marinated herring with dill sauce. Stars on the main menu are lamb with red-currant sauce, filet of salmon with sorrel sauce, and sirloin steak with paprika and sour-cream sauce. Vegetarians will go for the delicious nut roast. Between meal hours, this is a good place to drop in for a glass of wine and a nibble of cheesecake.

35 Hill St. ✆ **028/9043-9690.** www.nickswarehouse.co.uk. Reservations suggested. Lunch in wine bar £3–£6 ($4.35–$8.70); lunch in restaurant £12–£20 ($17–$29); dinner main courses £10–£30 ($15–$44). AE, DC, MC, V. Mon–Fri noon–2:30pm; Tues–Sat 6–9:30pm (drinks until midnight).

SHOPPING

Shops in Belfast city center are generally open Monday through Saturday from 9am to 5:30pm, with many shops remaining open until 8 or 9pm on Thursday. Belfast's leading department stores are **Anderson & McAuley** and **Marks & Spencer,** both on Donegall Place, and **Debenham's** in the Castle Court Shopping Centre on Royal Avenue. The **Castlecourt Shopping Centre** on Royal Avenue is the main downtown multistory shopping mall, with dozens of boutiques and shops.

Smyth's Irish Linens   If you want to stock up on fine Irish linen damask tablecloths, napkins, and handkerchiefs, head for this shop in the heart of the city's prime shopping thoroughfare. It also stocks other traditional gift items and souvenirs and offers a VAT-free export program. 65 Royal Ave. ✆ **028/9024-2232.**

The Steensons   This is the main showroom of Bill and Christina Steenson, two of the most celebrated goldsmiths in Ireland. On display and for sale is the widest collection anywhere of the Steensons' own unique gold and silver jewelry, as well as work by a select number of top designers from afar. Bedford St., Belfast (behind Belfast City Hall). ✆ **028/9024-8269.**

Tom Caldwell Gallery   Come here for a selection of paintings, sculptures, and ceramics by living artists, as well as handcrafted furnishings, rugs, and cast-iron candelabras. 40 Bradbury Place. ✆ **028/9032-3226.**

BELFAST AFTER DARK
THE PUB SCENE

Pub hours are generally Monday to Saturday from 11:30am to 11pm, and Sunday from 12:30 to 2:30pm and from 7 to 10pm. Children are not permitted on licensed premises.

Crown Liquor Saloon _Finds_   Dating from 1826 and situated opposite the Europa Hotel and the Grand Opera House, this gaslit pub has what many architecture buffs consider to be the finest example of Victorian Gothic decor found anywhere. Owned by the National Trust and run by Bass Ireland, the pub boasts stained glass windows, which lend a marvelous baroque-cathedral feel when the sun is out. Step inside and see the tin ceiling, a tile floor, etched and smoked glass, a beveled mirror with floral and wildlife decorations, scalloped lamps, and a long bar with inlaid colored glass and marble trim. Of special note is the array of 10 snugs (small rooms) on the right, each guarded by a mythological beast with an armor shield. Inside each room are all the accoutrements any good Victorian could hope for: gunmetal plates for striking matches, little windows to peep discreetly out of, and even an antique system of bells to summon service. Great Victoria St. ℂ 028/9024-9476. www.belfasttelegraph.co.uk/crown.

Kelly's Cellars Recognized as Belfast's oldest tavern in continuous use, this pub dates back to 1720 and has had a storied history, including being a headquarters for leaders in the 1798 Insurrection. It's also been a favorite haunt for actors and novelists. The decor is rich in vaulted ceilings, paned windows, old barrels, whitewashed arches, and wooden snugs, and also such memorabilia as old ledgers, coins, china, prints, maps, and international soccer caps. There's often traditional music on tap in the evenings. Bank St. (just off Royal Avenue), Belfast. ℂ 028/9032-4835.

Pat's Bar For a taste of Belfast's harbor atmosphere, join the sailors, dockers, and local businesspeople at this pub at the gates of Prince's Dock. The decor includes an antique hand-carved beech bar, pinewood furnishings, red-tile floor, black-and-white photos of the pub's earliest days, and an interesting collection of memorabilia given to the bar's owner by sailors passing through the port—clogs, swords, tom-toms and maracas, a telescope, and a bayonet. There's traditional Irish music on Wednesday nights. Prince's Dock St. ℂ 028/9074-4524.

White's Tavern Tucked in a historic cobblestoned trading lane between High and Rosemary streets, this old tavern was established in 1630 as a wine-and-spirit shop. It's full of old barrels and hoists, ornate snugs, brick arches, large copper measures, framed newspaper clippings of the 200-year-old vintage, quill pens, and other memorabilia. It's a good pub for conversation and browsing and features jazz and traditional music as well as quiz nights, darts, and theme nights. Winecellar Entry, off High St. ℂ 028/9024-3080.

THE PERFORMING ARTS

For up-to-date listings of shows and concerts, there are several sources. *That's Entertainment* is free and widely available at tourist offices or pubs. *Artslink,* published monthly, is also free and useful. *The Buzz* is neither free nor particularly useful, as it comes out only every 2 months. Then, of course, there's always the *Belfast Daily Telegraph.* If you have your laptop with you, you'll find just about everything on **www.entertainment.ireland.ie**, keyword: **belfast**.

The latest, and largest, venue to appear on the Belfast arts scene is the **Belfast Waterfront Hall,** Oxford Street, Laganside (ℂ **028/9033-4400**).

The other leading concert and performance halls in Belfast are the **Grand Opera House,** Great Victoria Street (ℂ **028/9024-1919;** www.gohbelfast.com), which presents a wide variety of entertainment; **Ulster Hall,** Bedford Street (ℂ **028/9032-3900**), which stages major concerts from rock to large-scale choral and symphonic works by the Ulster Orchestra and Northern Ireland Symphony Orchestra; and **Kings Hall Exhibition and Conference Centre,** Balmoral (ℂ **028/9066-5225;** www.kingshall.co.uk), for superstar concerts and other musical events, as well as everything from sheep sales to brides' fairs.

Theaters include the **Belfast Civic Arts Theatre,** 41 Botanic Ave. (© **028/ 9031-6900**), for popular shows, musicals, and comedies; the **Lyric Theatre,** Ridgeway Street (© **028/9038-1081;** www.lyrictheatre.co.uk), for new plays by Irish and international playwrights; and the **Group Theatre,** Bedford Street (© **028/9032-9685**) for performances by local drama societies.

For stand-up comedy, the Belfast epicenter is upstairs in the **Empire Music Hall,** 42 Botanic (© **028/9032-8110**), home every Tuesday night at 9pm to *The Empire Laughs Back.* If you'd rather sit down than stand up, best to get there at least an hour early. Other occasional comedy venues include **The Old Museum Arts Centre,** College Square North (© **028/9023-5053;** www. oldmuseumartscentre.org).

Tickets, which cost £7 to £30 ($9.94–$43) for most events, can be purchased in advance from the **Virgin Ticket Shop,** Castle Court, Belfast (© **028/ 9032-3744**) or online at **www.ticketmaster.ie.** (You can always arrange to have tickets purchased online delivered to your hotel.)

3 Out from Belfast

The following are some of the best sights and excursions outside of Belfast. For places to stay and dine outside the city, see "Where to Stay & Dine near Belfast."

TWO MUSEUMS

Ulster Folk & Transport Museum ★★ (Kids)   This 176-acre museum, bringing together many parts of Ulster's past, is one of the North's most popular attractions—and deservedly so.

Sixty acres are devoted to a unique outdoor folk museum featuring a collection of 19th-century buildings, all saved from the bulldozer's path and moved intact from their original sites in various parts of Northern Ireland. You can walk among centuries-old farmhouses, mills, and churches; climb to the terraces of houses; and peruse rural schools, a forge, a bank, a print shop, and a small conical hut where a watchman would sit with his musket guarding the linen laid out on the green to bleach in the sun. Actors in period dress re-enact tasks of daily life—cooking over an open hearth, plowing the fields with horses, thatching roofs, and practicing traditional Ulster crafts such as textile making, spinning, quilting, lace making, printing, spade making, and shoemaking.

The **transport museum's** collection ranges from donkey carts to De Loreans, and includes an exhibit on the Belfast-built *Titanic.* The exhibit on Irish railways is considered one of the top 10 of its kind in Europe. The "Car in Society" exhibit is also excellent.

153 Bangor Rd., Cultra, Holywood, Co. Down. © **028/9042-8428,** or 028/9042-1444 for 24-hr. information. www.nidex.com/uftm. Day ticket to both museums £4 ($5.80) adults; £2.50 ($3.65) seniors, students, and children; £9 ($13) family. Apr–June Mon–Fri 9:30am–5pm, Sat 10:30am–6pm; July–Aug Mon–Sat 10:30am–6pm, Sun noon–6pm; Sept Mon–Fri 9:30am–5pm, Sat 10:30am–6pm, Sun noon–6pm; Oct–Mar Mon–Fri 9:30am–4pm, Sat–Sun 12:30–4:30pm. 7 miles (11km) NE of Belfast on A2.

Irish Linen Centre and Lisburn Museum   The focus of this new museum is the linen industry, long synonymous with Northern Ireland. Through the re-creation of factory scenes and multimedia presentations, visitors can trace the history of Irish linen production, from its earliest days in the 17th century to the high-tech industry of today. You'll have the opportunity to see linen in all stages of production, and to watch skilled weavers at work on restored 19th-century looms in the center's weaving workshop. There's also a cafe and a research library. *Note:* If you're seriously into linen, you can book a place in an **Irish Linen Tour** by calling the Banbridge Gateway Tourist Information Centre at *(f)* **028/4062-3322.** From May through September, there are tours every Wednesday and Saturday.

Market Sq., Lisburn, Co. Antrim. *(f)* **028/9266-3377.** paul.allison@lisburn.gov.uk. Free admission. Mon–Sat 9:30am–5pm.

CARRICKFERGUS
12 miles (19km) NE of Belfast

It's said that Carrickfergus, County Antrim, was a thriving town when Belfast was a sandbank. In 1180, John de Courcy, a Norman, built a massive keep here—the first real Irish castle—to guard the approach to Belfast Lough.

GETTING THERE   **Northern Ireland Railways** (*(f)* **028/9089-9411**) offers frequent daily service from Belfast Central Station. **Ulsterbus** (*(f)* **028/ 9033-3000**) also provides daily service from Belfast. If you're travelling by car, take A5 north from Belfast.

VISITOR INFORMATION   Stop into the **Carrickfergus Tourist Information Office,** Heritage Plaza, Antrim Street, Carrickfergus, County Antrim (*(f)* **028/9336-6455**). It's open April through June Monday to Friday 9am to 5pm, Saturday 10am to 6pm; July though August Monday to Friday 9am to 6pm, Saturday 10am to 6pm and Sunday noon to 6pm; and October through May Monday to Friday from 9am to 5pm.

SEEING THE SIGHTS

Andrew Jackson Centre   This simple one-story cottage with earthen floor and open fireplace was the ancestral home of Andrew Jackson, seventh president of the United States. His parents left here and emigrated to the United States in 1765. The house now contains a display on the life and career of Andrew Jackson and Ulster's connections with America. On weekends in July and August, there are craft demonstrations reflecting rural folklife, such as sampler making, basketweaving, griddle making, patchwork quilting, and lacemaking.

Boneybefore, Carrickfergus, Co. Antrim. *(f)* **028/9336-6455.** www.carrickfergus.org. Admission £1.75 ($2) adults, 60p (90¢) seniors and children, £3 ($4.35) family. June–Sept Mon–Fri 10am–1pm and 2–6pm; Sat–Sun 2–6pm; Apr–May and Oct reduced hours.

Carrickfergus Castle (★)   This remarkably well-preserved and formidable castle, along with Ireland's oldest Norman keep, strikes a menacing pose here at the strategic entrance to Belfast Lough. Guides, audiovisual presentation, and exhibits help visitors imagine the castle's turbulent past. In the summer months, medieval banquets, a medieval fair, and a crafts market are held here, adding a touch of play and pageantry. Gifts and refreshments are also available.

Marine Highway, Antrim St., Carrickfergus. *(f)* **028/9335-1273.** Admission £2.70 ($3.95) adults, £1.35 ($2.00) seniors and children, £7.30 ($11) family. Apr–Sept Mon–Sat 10am–6pm, Sun 2–6pm; Oct–Mar Mon–Sat 10am–4pm, Sun 2–4pm.

Knight Ride *(Kids)*   The Knight Ride is an action-packed monorail theme ride spanning 8 centuries of the story of Carrickfergus, from sailing ships to haunted houses to historic invasions. This is a good way to fill the imaginations of the whole family with pictures of the past before you explore Carrickfergus Castle. Reduced-rate tickets for admission to both the castle and the ride are £4.85 ($8) adults, £2.40 ($3.95) seniors and children, and £13.50 ($22.30) family.

The Heritage Plaza, Antrim St., Carrickfergus. © 028/9336-6455. www.carrickfergus.org. Admission £2.70 ($3.95) adults, £1.35 ($2.00) seniors and children, £7.30 ($11) family. Apr–Sept Mon–Sat 10am–6pm, Sun noon–6pm; Oct–Mar Mon–Sat 10am–5pm, Sun noon–5pm.

ARDS PENINSULA
10 miles (16km) E of Belfast

The Ards Peninsula, which curls around the western shore of Strangford Lough, is at 18 miles (29km) long one of the largest inland sea inlets in the British Isles. A place of great natural beauty, the peninsula boasts a wonderful bird sanctuary and wildlife reserve, and its shores are home to multifarious species of marine life. Two roads traverse the peninsula: A20 (the Lough road) and A2 (the coast road). Of the two, the **Lough road** is the more scenic. There are two National Trust properties in this area, one on the Ards Peninsula and the other just across the lough at Portaferry.

SEEING THE SIGHTS

Castle Espie *Kids*   This marvelous center, owned and managed by the Wildlife and Wetlands Trust, is home to a virtual U.N. of geese, ducks, and swans, many of which are extraordinarily rare. Many are so accustomed to visitors that they will eat grain from your hand. Children will have the disarming experience of meeting Hooper swans eye-to-eye. Guided trails are specially designed for children and families, and the center sponsors a host of activities and events throughout the year. The reserve is also, in the words of center manager James Orr, a "honeypot" for serious bird-watchers in search of waterfowl. Up to 3,000 pale-bellied brent can be seen in early winter. The shores of Strangford Lough rank among the top bird sites in the world, and are of extraordinary beauty even when your bird of choice is hiding. The center's book and gift shop is enticing for naturalists of all ages, and the restaurant serves deliciously diverting lunches and home-baked sweets. Every day during the summer there's a guided tour, departing at 2:30pm.

78 Ballydrain Rd., Comber, Co. Down. © 028/9187-4146. Fax 028/9187-3857. www.wwt.org.uk. Admission £3.50 ($5.10) adults, £2.75 ($4.00) students and seniors, £2.25 ($3.30) children, £9.25 ($13) family. Mar–Oct Mon–Sat 10:30am–5pm, Sun 11:30am–6pm; Nov–Feb Mon–Sat 11:30am–4pm, Sun 11:30am–5pm. 13 miles (21km) southeast of Belfast, signposted from the A22 Comber-Killyleagh-Downpatrick road.

Castle Ward   Situated 1½ miles (2.5km) west of Strangford village, this National Trust house dates from 1760 and is half classical and half Gothic in architectural style. It sits on a 700-acre country estate of formal gardens, woodlands, lakelands, and seashore. A restored 1830s corn mill and a Victorian-style laundry are on the grounds, and the theater in the stable yard is a venue for operatic performances in summer.

Strangford, Co. Down. © 028/4488-1204. www.nationaltrust.org.uk. House £2.60 ($4.30) adults, £1.30 ($2.15) children, £6.50 ($10.75) family; estate £1.75 ($2.90) per car off-season, £3.50 ($5.80) per car high season. House Apr, Sept and Oct Sat–Sun 1–6pm; May–Aug Mon–Wed and Fri–Sun 1–6pm; estate year-round dawn–dusk. 1½ miles (2.5km) west of Strangford village.

The Giant's Ring   This massive prehistoric earthwork, 600 feet (183m) in diameter, has more or less at its center a megalithic chamber with a single capstone. It was doubtlessly a significant focus of local cults as long as 5,000 years ago. Today, this 7-acre ritual enclosure is a place of wonder for the few and neglect for the many.

Ballynahatty, Co. Down. Open site. 5 miles (5km) southwest of Belfast center, west off A24; or 1 mile (1.5km) south of Shaw's Bridge, off B23.

Tips **A Short Cut**

At the southern tip of Strangford Lough, there is a continuous car ferry service connecting Portaferry with Strangford on the mainland side (📞 **028/4488-1637**). It runs every half hour, weekdays from 7:45am to 10:45pm, Saturdays 8:15am to 11:15pm, and Sundays 9:45am to 10:45pm. No reservations are needed. A one-way trip takes 5 minutes and costs £4.20 ($6.10) for a car and driver and 85p ($1.25) for each additional adult passenger, and 45p (65¢) for each child.

Grey Abbey   The impressive ruins of Grey Abbey enjoy a beautifully land-scaped setting, perfect for both reflection and a tasteful picnic. It was founded in 1193 for the Cistercians and contained one of the earliest Gothic churches in Ireland. True to Cistercian simplicity, there was and is very little embellishment here, but the Cistercians, like the Shakers, knew well that restraint is no imped-iment to beauty. All the same, amid the bare ruined choirs, there is a fragmented stone effigy of a knight in armor, possibly a likeness of John de Courcy, husband of the abbey's founder, Affrica of Cumbria. There's also a small visitor center.

Greyabbey, Co. Down. Admission £1 ($1.45) adults, 50p (75¢) children. Apr–Sept Tues–Sat 10am–7pm; Sun 2–7pm. On the east side of Greyabbey, 2 miles (3km) southeast of Mount Stewart.

Legananny Dolmen ⭐   This renowned, impressive granite dolmen on the southern slope of Slieve Croob looks, in the words of archaeologist Peter Harbi-son, like "a coffin on stilts." This is one of the most photographed dolmens in Ireland, but you have to see it up close to admire it fully. The massive capstone seems almost weightlessly poised on its three supporting uprights.

Slieve Croob, Co. Down. Open site. A24 from Belfast to Ballynahinch and B7 to Dromara. From there, it's best to ask directions.

Mount Stewart House ⭐⭐   Once the home of Lord Castlereagh, this 18th-century house sits on the eastern shore of Strangford Lough. It has one of the greatest gardens in the care of the National Trust, with an unrivaled collection of rare and unusual plants. The interior of the house is noteworthy for its art works, including *Hambletonian* by George Stubbs, one of the finest paintings in Ireland, and family portraits by Batoni, Mengs, and Lazlo. The Temple of the Winds, a banqueting house built in 1785, is also on the estate. In 1999, Mount Stewart was one of 32 sites in the United Kingdom nominated as a potential World Heritage Site. Final selection would place it in the company of such sites as the Taj Mahal and the Great Wall of China.

Newtownards (on the A20 road), Co. Down. 📞 **028/4278-8387.** www.kingdomsofdown.com. House, gar-den, and temple £3.50 ($5.10) adults, £1.75 ($2.55) children under 5, £8.75 ($13) for children 6 and older. House Apr and Oct Sat–Sun 1–6pm, May–Sept Mon and Wed–Sun 1–6pm; garden Mar Sun 2pm–5pm, Apr–Sept daily 11am–6pm, Oct Sat–Sun 11am–6pm; temple Apr–Oct Sat and Sun 2–5pm. On the east shore of Strangford Lough, southeast of Newtownards, 15 miles (24km) southeast of Belfast. Bus: 9, 9A, or 10 from Laganside Bus Centre (except Sun).

OUTDOOR PURSUITS

BICYCLING   Cycles by the day or week, as well as delivery in the North Down/Ards area, are available from **Gary Harkness Cycle Hire,** 53 Frances St., Newtownards (📞 **028/9181-1311**) for £10 ($15) per day.

DIVING   The nearby loughs and offshore waters are a diver's dream—remarkably clear and unlittered with wrecks. To charter a diving expedition in Strangford Lough, contact **Des Rogers** (✆ **028/4272-8297**). **Norsemaid Sea Enterprises,** 152 Portaferry Rd., Newtownards, County Down (✆ **028/ 9181-2081**), caters 4- to 10-day diving parties along the Northern Irish Coast, in Belfast Lough and Strangford Lough, amid the St. Kilda Isles, and along the coast of Scotland. A wide range of diving courses are offered by one of Europe's finest training centers, **DV Diving,** 138 Mountstewart Rd., Newtownards, County Down (✆ **028/9146-4671;** www.dvdiving.co.uk).

FISHING   For info, tackle, and bait, try the **Village Tackle Shop,** 55a Newtownbreda Rd., Belfast (✆ **028/9049-1916**), or **H.W. Kelly,** 54 Market St., Downpatrick, County Down (✆ **028/4461-2193**). Sea-fishing trips from Portaferry into the waters of Strangford Lough and along the County Down coast are organized by Peter Wright, **Norsemaid Sea Enterprises,** 152 Portaferry Rd., Newtownards, County Down (✆ **028/9181-2081**). Reservations are required. This company also offers diving charters, day cruises, hill walking, and wildlife cruises. To outfit yourself and fish for rainbow trout year-round, bring your lucky fishing hat to **Ballygrangee Fly Fishery,** Mountstewart Rd., Carrowdore, County Down (✆ **028/4278-8883**).

GOLF   There are several well-established courses a short drive from Belfast in north County Down. They include the **Bangor Golf Club,** Broadway, Bangor (✆ **028/9127-0922**), with greens fees of £20 ($29) weekdays and £25 ($36) weekends; **Downpatrick Golf Club,** 43 Saul Rd., Downpatrick (✆ **028/ 4461-5947**) with greens fees of £15 ($22) weekdays and £20 ($29) weekends; and the **Scrabo Golf Club,** 233 Scrabo Rd., Newtownards (✆ **028/ 9181-2355;** www.scrabo.golf.club.com) with greens fees of £15 ($22) weekdays and £20 ($29) weekends.

SAILING   RYA sailing lessons as well as yacht charter are available from Down Yachts, 37 Bayview Rd., Killinchy, County Down (✆ **028/9754-2210**).

DOWNPATRICK
23 miles (37km) SE of Belfast

Downpatrick, one of the North's oldest cities, is closely identified with **St. Patrick.** Legend tells us that when Patrick came to Ireland in 432 to begin his missionary work, strong winds blew his boat into this area. He had meant to sail up the coast to County Antrim, where as a young slave he had tended flocks on Slemish Mountain. Instead, he settled here and converted the local chieftain Dichu and his followers to Christianity. Over the next 30 years, Patrick roamed to many other places in Ireland carrying out his work, but he came back here to die. He is said to be buried in the graveyard of **Downpatrick Cathedral.** A large stone marks the spot.

GETTING THERE   Ulsterbus (✆ **028/9033-3000**) provides frequently scheduled daily service from Belfast to Downpatrick. If you're traveling by car, take A7 south from Belfast.

VISITOR INFORMATION   For information in the Down District, stop into the **Downpatrick Tourist Information Centre,** 74 Market St., Downpatrick, County Down (✆ **028/4461-2233**), open September through June Monday to Saturday from 9:30am to 5pm; July through August Monday to Saturday 9:30am to 7pm and Sunday 2 to 6pm. A "St. Patrick's Country" coach tour is offered according to demand and can be booked through this office.

SEEING THE SIGHTS

Down Cathedral   As its name suggests, Downpatrick was once a *dún* or fort, as early as the Bronze Age. Eventually, here on the Hill of Down, ancient fortifications gave way to a line of churches, which have superseded each other for 1,800 years, like a stack of Russian matryoshkas. Today's cathedral represents an 18th to 19th-century reconstruction of its 13th- and 16th-century predecessors. Just south of the cathedral stands a relatively recent monolith inscribed with the name *Patric* and roughly marking, by some accounts, the grave of the saint, who is said to have died at Saul, 2 miles (3km) to the northeast. The tradition identifying this site as Patrick's grave seems to go back no further than the 12th century, when John de Courcy reputedly transferred the bones of Saints Bridgit and Columbanus here to lie beside those of St. Patrick.

The Mall, Downpatrick, Co. Down. ℭ **028/4461-4922.** www.cathedral.down.anglican.org. Mon–Sat 9am–5pm; Sun 2–5pm.

Inch Abbey   Inch Abbey occupied a strategic site on an island in the Quoile Marshes, within sight of the Mound of Down and of Downpatrick Cathedral. It was founded in the 1180s by John de Courcy as an act of atonement for destroying the nearby abbey of Erenagh. Today, the ruins of this Cistercian abbey are aging gracefully.

Open site. Admission to abbey 75p ($1.10) adults, 40p (60¢) children. Abbey Apr–Sept Tues–Sat 10am–7pm, Sun 2–4pm; Oct–Mar Sat 10am–4pm, Sun 2–4pm.

St. Patrick Heritage Centre/Down County Museum   Next to the cathedral and sharing an extensive 18th-century jail complex, the St. Patrick Centre and the County Museum provide some intriguing glimpses into the rich history of this area. You'll also be introduced to some of the county's more notorious figures, from St. Patrick to a handful of prisoners sent off to Australia in the 19th century.

The Mall (next to the cathedral), Downpatrick, Co. Down. ℭ **028/4461-9000.** www.saintpatrickcentre.com. Free admission except for some special events. June–Aug Mon–Sat 9:30am–7pm, Sun 10am–6pm; Sept–May daily 10am–5pm.

LOUGH NEAGH
10 miles (16km) W of Belfast

Lough Neagh, at 153 square miles, is the largest lake in the British Isles. Often called an inland sea, the lough is 20 miles (32km) long and 10 miles (16km) wide, with a 65-mile (105-km) shore. It's said that Lough Neagh was created by the mighty, Fionn MacCumhail (anglicized to Finn MacCool) when he flung a sod into the sea to create the Isle of Man. But before you think about taking a dip, consider this: The lake's claim to fame is its eels. Yep, the waters are positively infested with the slimy things. Hundreds of tons of eels are taken from Lough Neagh and exported each year, mainly to Germany and Holland. This extraction has been going on since the Bronze Age, and shows no sign of letting up. The age-old method involves the use of a "long line," baited with up to 100 hooks. Given that there are often as many as 200 boats trailing a few of these lines each on the lake each night (the best time to go fishing for eels), it's less surprising that the nightly catch can be up to 10 tons of eels.

If you're not entirely creeped out, there are **boat trips** on Lough Neagh, departing regularly from the nearby **Kinnego Marina** (ℭ **028/3832-7573,** mobile), signposted from the main road. They last about 45 minutes and cost £4 ($5.68) for adults, £2 ($2.84) for children.

SEEING THE SIGHTS

Lough Neagh Discovery Centre   Midway between Belfast and Armagh city, this center is on the southern shore of Lough Neagh at Oxford Island, a 270-acre nature reserve with a range of habitats such as reed beds, woodlands, and wildflower meadows. The center provides an excellent introduction to all that the lough has to offer, with historical and geographic exhibits, an interactive lab explaining the ecosystems of the lough, walking trails, bird-watching observation points, and picnic areas. The center even rents binoculars so you can get a close look at everything in sight.

Oxford Island, Lurgan, Co. Armagh. (✆ 028/3832-2205. www.craigavon.gov.uk/discovery.htm. Admission to center £1.50 ($2.20) adults, £1.20 ($1.75) seniors, £1 ($1.45) children, £4 ($5.80) family. Apr–Sept daily 10am–7pm; Oct–Mar Wed–Sun 10am–5pm. Signposted on M1, at junction 10 near Lurgan.

ARMAGH
40 miles (64km) SW of Belfast

One of Ireland's most historic cities, Armagh takes its name from the Irish *Ard Macha,* or Macha's Height. The legendary pagan queen Macha is said to have built a fortress here in the middle of the first millennium B.C. Most of Armagh's history, however, focuses on the 5th century, when St. Patrick chose this place as a base from which to spread Christianity; he called it "my sweet hill" and built a stone church here. Ever since, Armagh has been considered the ecclesiastical capital of Ireland. Today there are two St. Patrick's cathedrals, Catholic and Anglican, seats of the primates of both denominations.

Many of the public buildings and the Georgian town houses along the Mall in Armagh are the work of Francis Johnston, a local architect who also left his mark on Georgian Dublin. Buildings here, as well as doorsteps and pavements, are made of warm-colored pink, yellow, and red local limestone that makes the city glow even on a dull day.

GETTING THERE   **Ulsterbus** (✆ **028/9033-3000**) provides hourly coach service to Armagh from Belfast. **Bus Eireann** (✆ **01/836-6111**) offers daily service from Dublin. If you're driving, Armagh is easily reached from Belfast on A3. From Derry, take A5 south. From Dublin, take N1 north to Newry and then follow A28 to Armagh.

VISITOR INFORMATION   Stop into the **Armagh Tourist Information Office,** the Old Bank Building, 40 English St., Armagh (✆ **028/3752-1800**). It's open from June through September Monday to Friday from 9am to 5:30pm, Saturday 9am to 5pm and Sunday 2 to 5pm; September through May, it's open Monday to Friday from 9am to 5pm. For a host of tourist information on County Armagh, take a look at **www.armagh-visit.com**.

SEEING THE SIGHTS

Armagh Astronomy Centre and Planetarium *(Kids)*   On your way up College Hill from the Mall, you'll pass the 200-year-old Armagh Observatory, still in service but closed to the public. Farther up the hill stands the Astronomy Centre and Planetarium complex, whose Astropark, Hall of Astronomy, and Eartharium Gallery offer an engaging array of exhibits and shows, with lots of hands-on learning for the whole family. *Note:* The planetarium itself is closed for the foreseeable future, but there is a show in the miniature inflatable planetarium at 3pm.

College Hill, Armagh. (✆ 028/3752-3689. www.armagh-planetarium.co.uk. Admission £1 ($1.25) adults, 50p (75¢) children. Mon–Fri 2–4:45pm.

Fun Fact The Big Apple

Armagh is not only the spiritual capital of Ireland; it's also known for its apple trees, earning the region the title "the Orchard of Ireland."

Armagh County Museum   Housed in what appears to be a miniature Greek temple, this is the oldest county museum in Ireland. Its rather extensive collection, documenting local life across the millennia, ranges from prehistoric ax heads to wedding dresses. In addition to natural history specimens and folklore items, the museum has an extensive art collection, which includes works by George Russell and John Luke. There is also a rotating exhibition. The museum's maps, photographs, and research library can also be consulted.

The Mall East, Armagh. ✆ **028/3752-3070.** acm@nics.gov.uk. Free admission. Mon–Fri 10am–5pm; Sat 10am–1pm and 2–5pm.

Palace Stables Heritage Centre   This living-history center, housed in a restored Georgian stable block, takes visitors back to a day in the life of the Irish primate's palace in the year 1776. The palace, icehouse, and primate's chapel are accessible only by guided tour, included in the admission price. There's also a garden, a children's playroom and adventure area, a craft shop, and the Stables Restaurant.

Palace Demesne, Armagh. ✆ **028/3752-9629.** www.armagh-visit.com. Admission £3.50 ($5.10) adults, £2.75 ($4.00) seniors, £2 ($2.90) children, £9.50 ($14) family. May–Aug Mon–Sat 10am–5:30pm, Sun 1–6pm; Sept–Apr Mon–Sat 10am–5pm, Sun 2–5pm. 10-min. walk from town, off Friary Rd.

St. Patrick's Trian Visitor Complex *(Kids)*   This modern visitor complex, housed in the old Second Presbyterian Church in the heart of town, provides an informative and engaging introduction to Armagh, the "motherhouse" of Irish Christianity. Its dramatic presentations, including the *Armagh Story* and *The Land of Lilliput* (complete with a giant Gulliver beset by Lilliputians), are entertaining for the whole family. This is a good first stop to get your bearings in local history and culture. There's a craft courtyard and a cafe, as well as a visitor genealogical service, in case you think you may have local roots.

40 English St., Armagh. ✆ **028/3752-1801.** www.armagh-visit.com. Admission (includes entrance to 3 multimedia exhibitions) £3.75 ($5.45) adults, £2.75 ($4.00) students and seniors, £2 ($2.90) children, £9.50 ($14) family. Mon–Sat 10am–5pm; Sun 2–5pm. Off Friary Rd., 10-min. walk from town.

WHERE TO STAY & DINE NEAR BELFAST

Greenlea Farm   A comfortable, thoroughly modernized old farmhouse, Greenlea looks out from its hilltop to the Ards Peninsula and across to the coast of Scotland and the Isle of Man. The warm, friendly hostess, Mrs. Evelyn McIvor, teaches crafts and enjoys sharing her considerable knowledge of the area with guests. The lounge and dining room have picture windows that frame the spectacular view, and the dining room holds lovely antique pieces, with lots of silver and crystal. Mrs. McIvor has one large family room with bunk beds for two children and a double for parents, as well as accommodations for singles and doubles. Greenlea Farm is about 23 miles (37km) southeast of Belfast on A2, at the top of the Ards Peninsula.

48 Dunover Rd., Ballywalter, Co. Down. ✆ **028/4275-8218.** www.visitcoastofdown.com/greenleafarm. 5 units, none with bathroom. £38 ($55) double. 50% reduction for children under 12 (under 5 free). 10% reduction for seniors. Rates include full breakfast. Dinner £10 ($15). No credit cards. Off A2, ½ mile north of Ballywalter, the first farm on the left on the Dunover road. *In room:* TEL, tea/coffeemaker.

Down Arts Centre Café CAFETERIA   You won't have any difficulty finding this place. Look for the clock tower atop a Victorian redbrick building in the very center of Downpatrick, and enter below. Its soups, salads, sandwiches, and pastries provide a satisfying snack or lunch break on your day's outing from Belfast.

Irish St., Downpatrick, Co. Down. ℂ 028/4461-5283. All items £2–£6 ($2.90–$8.70). Mon–Sat 9am–4pm.

Primrose Bar PUB GRUB   The Primrose—an erstwhile blacksmith shop— is known locally for its steak casseroles, open-faced prawn sandwiches, and fresh-baked wheaten bread. Other offerings include chicken dishes, pizza, and a variety of salads. There's always a nice fire blazing, and local opinion concurs that "the craic is always good." The adjacent Primrose Pop-In tearoom serves up good quiches and pies Monday to Saturday 9am to 4:30pm.

30 Main St., Ballynahinch, Co. Down. ℂ 028/9756-3177. Reservations not required. Dinner main courses £4.95–£12 ($7.65–$19.80). AE, MC, V. Lunch daily 12–2:30pm; dinner Sun–Tues from 6:45pm, Wed–Sat from 7:45pm.

4 The Causeway Coast & the Glens of Antrim

66 miles (106km) from Larne to Portstewart on the coastal A2. From Belfast to Larne is 25 miles (40km)

Steeped in myth and legend, pounded by its own history, and graced with true grandeur, the **Causeway Coast** is one of the most dramatic coastlines in Ireland. The coast takes in marine seascapes and chalky cliffs, and includes the National Trust village of Cushendun with pretty Cornish-style cottages as well as a string of beach resorts popular with Irish and English vacationers, such as Portrush, Portstewart, and Portballintrae. This coastal drive also meanders under bridges and arches, passing bays, sandy beaches, harbors, and huge rock formations. Furthermore, two of Ireland's foremost attractions are here: the **Giant's Causeway** and **Old Bushmills Distillery.**

Heralded in story and song, the **Glens of Antrim** consist of nine green valleys, stretching from Belfast to the north. All of these glens have individual names, each based on a local tale or legend. Although the meanings are not known for certain, the popular translations are as follows: Glenarm (glen of the army), Glencloy (glen of the hedges), Glenariff (ploughman's glen), Glenballyeamon (Edwardstown glen), Glenaan (glen of the rush lights), Glencorp (glen of the slaughter), Glendun (brown glen), Glenshesk (sedgy glen), and Glentaisie (Taisie's glen).

The people who live in the Glens of Antrim are descendants of both the ancient Irish and their cousins, the Hebridean Scots, so this area is one of the last places in Northern Ireland where Gaelic was spoken. To this day, the glen people are known to be great storytellers.

GETTING THERE   Ulsterbus (ℂ **028/9033-3000**) offers frequent buses from Portrush to the Giant's Causeway. In the summer, open-topped tourist buses also run from Portrush to the Causeway. If you're driving, follow A2 up the coast from Belfast to the Causeway. From Derry, take A2 east.

Moments **Don't Miss It**

Each August, the seaside town of Ballycastle plays host to one of Ireland's oldest traditional gatherings, the **Oul' Lammas Fair.** For information, contact Diane McCooke, Ballycastle TIC, 7 Mary St., Ballycastle BT54 6QH (ℂ **028/2076-2024**).

VISITOR INFORMATION   The principal **tourist information centers** in North Antrim are at the following locations: Narrow Gauge Road, Larne (© **028/2826-0008**); Sheskburn House, 7 Mary St., Ballycastle, County Antrim (© **028/2076-2024**); 44 Causeway Rd., Bushmills, County Antrim (© **028/2073-1855**); and Dunluce Centre, Sandhill Drive, Portrush, County Antrim (© **028/7082-3333**). All but the Dunluce Centre are open year-round, with hours varying according to the seasons. Summer hours, at the minimum, are Monday through Friday 10am to 5pm, Saturday 10am to 4pm, and Sunday 2 to 6pm.

SEEING THE SIGHTS

Carrick-A-Rede Rope Bridge ⭐ *Moments*

Five miles (8km) west of Ballycastle off the A2 road, this open rope bridge spans a chasm 60 feet (18m) wide and 80 feet (24m) above the sea between the mainland and a small island. Local fishermen put up the bridge each spring to allow access to the island's salmon fishery, but visitors can use it for a thrilling walk and the chance to play Indiana Jones (or Daniel Dravot, but that might not be as much fun—remember *The Man Who Would be King?*). If you are acrophobic, stay clear; if you don't know whether you are, this is not the place to find out. *Note:* The 12-mile (19km) coastal cliff path from the Giant's Causeway to the rope bridge is always open and is well worth the exhaustion.

Larrybane, Co. Antrim. © **028/2173-1159**. www.nationaltrust.org.uk. Free admission. Parking £3 ($4.35) per car. Bridge up from spring to mid-Sept with same hours as center and tearoom: May Sat–Sun 1–5pm; June–Aug daily noon–6pm. 5 miles (8km) west of Ballycastle, off A2.

Dunluce Castle ⭐⭐

This site was once the main fort of the Irish MacDonnells, chiefs of Antrim. It's the largest and most sophisticated castle in the North, consisting of a series of fortifications built on rocky outcrops extending into the sea. In 1639, part of the castle fell into the sea, taking some of the servants with it. The ruins of the castle incorporates two of the original Norman towers dating from 1305, and was the power base of the north coast for 400 years. The visitor center shows an audiovisual presentation with background on the site.

87 Dunluce Rd., Bushmills, Co. Antrim. © **028/2073-1938**. Admission £1.50 ($2.20) adults, 75p ($1.10) seniors and children under 16. Apr–May Mon–Sat 10am–6pm, Sun 2–6pm; Sept Mon–Sat 10am–7pm, Sun 2–7pm; July–Aug Mon–Sat 10am–7pm, Sun 11am–7pm; Oct–Mar Tues–Sat 10am–4pm, Sun 2–4pm. Last admission 30 min. before closing. 3 miles (5km) east of Portrush off the A2.

Dunluce Centre *Kids*

This family-oriented entertainment complex provides a variety of indoor activities. It offers a multimedia show, *Myths & Legends,* that illustrates the folklore of the Antrim coast, as well as "Turbo Tours," a thrill ride that simulates a space ride, and "Earthquest," an interactive display on the wonders of nature. There's also a viewing tower with panoramic views of the coast and a Victorian-style arcade of shops, and a restaurant with a children's play area. The facility was under construction in the fall of 2001, with two theaters and several new rides planned to open in the spring of 2002.

10 Sandhill Dr., Portrush. © **028/7082-4444**. www.causewaycoastandglens.com. All 4 attractions £5 ($7.25) per person, £16 ($23) family. Apr–May and Sept Sat–Sun noon–5pm; June daily noon–5pm; July–Aug daily 10am–7pm.

Giant's Causeway Visitors Centre ⭐

A World Heritage Site, this natural rock formation is often called the eighth wonder of the world. It consists of roughly 40,000 tightly packed basalt columns that extend for 3 miles (5km) along the coast. The tops of the columns form stepping stones that lead from the cliff foot and disappear under the sea. They're mostly hexagonal, and some are as tall as 40 feet (12m). Scientists estimate that they were formed 60 or 70 million years ago by volcanic eruptions and cooling lava. The ancients, on the other hand, believed the rock formation to be the work of giants. Another legend has it that Finn MacCool, the Ulster warrior and commander of the king of Ulster's armies, built the causeway as a highway over the sea to bring his girlfriend from the Isle of Hebrides. (And you thought sending a limo was cool.)

To reach the causeway, follow the walk from the parking area past amphitheaters of stone columns and formations with fanciful names like Honeycomb, Wishing Well, Giant's Granny, King and his Nobles, and Lover's Leap, and up a wooden staircase to Benbane Head and back along the cliff top. *Note:* In the spring of 2000, the new Giant's Causeway Visitors Centre tragically burned to the ground. There is currently a well-outfitted temporary center in place, and a new, permanent center is expected to open in the spring of 2003.

44 Causeway Rd., Bushmills, Co. Antrim. © **028/2073-1855**. Causeway free; audiovisual and exhibition £1 ($1.45) adults, 50p (75¢) children, £2.50 ($3.65) family. Parking £3 ($4.35) per car. July–Aug daily 10am–5:30pm; June and Sept daily 10am–5pm; Oct–May daily 10am–4:30pm.

Old Bushmills Distillery ⊛
This is not only the oldest distillery in Ireland, but the oldest in the world. Its license to distill spirits dates from 1608 but historical references go back to 1276. Visitors are welcome to tour the facility and watch the whole whiskey-making process, starting with fresh water from the adjacent River Bush and continuing through distilling, fermenting, and bottling. At the end of the tour, you can sample the wares in the Poststill Bar, where there are fascinating exhibits on the long history of the distillery. Twenty-five–minute tours depart regularly April to October; November to March, there are tours at 10:30am, 11:30am, noon, 1:30pm, 2:30pm, and 3:30pm. The Bushmills coffee shop serves tea, coffee, homemade snacks, and lunches.

Main St., Bushmills, Co. Antrim. © **028/2073-1521**. www.bushmills.com. Admission £3.95 ($5.75) adults, £3.50 ($5.10) students and seniors, £1.95 ($2.85) children, £11 ($16) family. Apr–Oct Mon–Sat 9:30am–5:30pm, Sun noon–5:30pm (last tour 4pm); Nov–Mar Mon–Fri tours at 10:30am, 11:30am, 1:30pm, 2:30pm, 3:30pm.

Rathlin Island Reserve
For peace and solitude, plan a trip to this boomerang-shaped island, lying 6 miles (9.5km) off the coast north of Ballycastle and 14 miles (23km) south of Scotland. It's almost 4 miles (6.5km) long, yet less than a mile wide at any point, and is almost completely treeless, with a rugged coast of 200-foot-high cliffs, a small beach, and a native population of 100. Don't worry, there's also a pub, a restaurant, and a guesthouse, in case you get stranded. This is a great bird-watching center, especially in spring and early to mid-summer.

Boats to the island leave daily from Ballycastle pier; crossing time is 50 minutes. Once you're there, a minibus (summer only) will take you from Church Bay to the West Light Platform where the Kebble Nature Reserve is located. The round-trip excursion fare (ferry only) is £8.20 ($12) for adults and £4.10 ($5.95) for children under 16. Due to unpredictable weather and possible schedule changes, it's safest to confirm departures by phoning in advance at © **028/2076-9299**.

Rathlin Island, off the coast of Ballycastle, Co. Antrim. © **028/2076-3948**. Free admission. Seabird viewing facility open Apr–Aug.

OUTDOOR PURSUITS

Ardclinis Outdoor Adventure, High Street, Cushendall, County Antrim (ℂ/fax **028/2177-1340;** Ardclinis@aol.com), offers a range of year-round outdoor programs and courses for ages eight and older, in everything from rock climbing and biking to windsurfing and rafting. Half-day, full-day, and week-long activities are offered, as well as 5- to 6-night scenic walking and cycling tours. You can show up and hope for a place, but it's far better to book your activities at least several weeks ahead. The center will also arrange for local B&B or hostel accommodation.

FISHING The best time to fish in the North Antrim Glens is July through October, both for salmon and for sea trout. The rivers of choice are the Margy, Glenshesk, Carey, and Dun. The **Marine Hotel,** 1 North St., Ballycastle (ℂ **028/2076-2222**) in Ballycastle offers an array of services to the game angler. For locally arranged game fishing, contact **Gillaroo Angles,** 7 Cooleen Park, Jordanstown, Newtownabbey, County Antrim (ℂ **028/9086-2419**). For info, tackle, and bait, try **Red Bay Boats,** Coast Road, Cushendall (ℂ **028/ 2177-1331**).

GOING SKY HIGH If you've got to have the bird's-eye view, you may want to contact the **Wild Geese Parachute Club** (ℂ **028/2955-8609**); or the **Ulster Gliding Club** (ℂ **028/7775-0301**), weekends only. While you're at it up there, keep your eyes peeled for a familiar sight, a monk from Dublin who every month or so drives north to hang-glide off the Causeway cliffs. Locals call him "Flyer Tuck." You can also book a spectacular helicopter ride over the North Antrim Coast by calling **The Helicopter Centre,** Newtownards Airfield (ℂ **028/9182-0028;** www.helicoptercentre.co.uk).

GOLF North Antrim boasts several notable courses in the short coastal stretch from Ballycastle to Portstewart: the **Ballycastle Golf Club,** Cushendall Road, Ballycastle (ℂ **028/2076-2536**); and the **Royal Portrush Golf Club** (with three links courses, including the Dunluce Course, ranked no. 3 in the U.K.), Bushmills Road, Portrush (ℂ **028/7082-2311**). Then, just over the border in County Londonderry, there are two more courses to be reckoned with: the **Portstewart Golf Club** (with three links courses), 117 Strand Rd., Portstewart (ℂ **028/7083-2015;** reservations@portstewartgc.co.uk); and the **Castlerock Golf Club** (with two links courses), 65 Circular Rd., Castlerock (ℂ **028/ 7084-8314**). As some days and times are better than others for visitors, it's advisable to ring in advance for times and fees, which range from £15 to £40 ($22–$58) for 18 holes, depending on course and day of the week.

HORSEBACK RIDING **Watertop Farm Family Activity Centre,** 188 Cushendall Rd., Ballycastle (ℂ **028/2076-2576**), offers pony trekking and other outdoor family activities, daily July to August and weekends in June and early September. In the Portrush area, contact **Maddybenny Riding Centre** (ℂ **028/7082-3394;** www.maddybenny.freeserve.co.uk).

SAILING The **Cushendall Sailing and Boating Club** offers dinghy sailing lessons to beginners for roughly £85 ($116) per week during July and August. Contact James Farrell (ℂ **028/2177-1272;** www.csbc.co.uk).

SCUBA DIVING For organized dives off Rathlin Island, contact **Tommy Cecil** (ℂ **028/2076-3915**).

WALKING   The Ulster Way, 560 miles (902km) of marked trail in all, follows the North Antrim Coast from Glenarm to Portstewart, and the **Moyle Way** offers a spectacular detour from Ballycastle south to Glenariff. Maps and accommodation listings for both ways are found in the free NITB booklet *The Ulster Way: Accommodation for Walkers;* or pick up a copy of *Walking the Ulster Way,* by Alan Warner (Belfast: Appletree Press, 1989). The NITB also offers *An Information Guide to Walking,* full of useful information for avid pedestrians.

Last but far from least is the newly upgraded (at the cost of $500,000) **Causeway Coast Path,** stretching nonstop from Bushfoot Strand, near Bushmills, in the west to Ballintoy Harbour in the east. Short of sprouting wings, this is surely the way to take in the full splendor of the North Antrim coast.

ACCOMMODATIONS YOU CAN AFFORD

Atlantis   Margaret and Norman Torrens are the gracious hosts at this Victorian-style town house, which sits just off the seafront in the eastern part of Portrush, overlooking recreation grounds and a children's adventure park. It has a large residents' lounge and a visitor's kitchen for light snacks. Five of the attractive rooms are family size. Some rooms on higher floors have terrific sea views.

10 Ramore Ave., Portrush BT56 8BB, Co. Antrim. ©/fax **028/7082-4583.** 13 units, 2 with bathroom (shower only). £32–£40 ($46–$58) double. Reduction for children and seniors. Rates include full breakfast. No credit cards. **Amenities:** Lounge; kitchen. *In room:* TV, tea/coffeemaker.

Camus House ★★   Camus House has won numerous country-house awards and gained a widespread reputation for hospitality. It's hard to say which is the more attractive, this 1685 country home overlooking the River Bann or its owner, vivacious Mrs. Josephine King (known to all and sundry as "Joey"), who welcomes guests with tea and scones in a cozy sitting room in front of a field-stone fireplace. The room's warmth is enhanced by lots of wood and the 125 handmade horse brasses that line the walls. Bedrooms are beautifully furnished and have sinks, spacious closets, and lamps placed strategically to give good light for reading. One family room sleeps four, one has three single beds, and one has a double bed as well as a single. In the sunny dining room, guests can enjoy a hearty Ulster breakfast fry of eggs and ham or bacon and wheaten bread accompanied by fresh fruit and juices. Joey will direct her guests to the best fishing spots on the river.

27 Curragh Rd., Coleraine BT51 3RY, Co. Derry. © **028/7034-2982.** 3 units, 1 with bathroom (shower only). £25 ($41) single; £45 ($65) double. Rates include full breakfast. No credit cards. 3 miles (5km) south of Coleraine via A54. *In room:* TV, tea/coffeemaker.

Cushendall Youth Hostel ★ *Value*   Renovated only a few years ago, this superior hostel has been in service for 30 years; clearly, practice makes perfect. It is quite attractive and close to immaculate. The dining and guest rooms are all nonsmoking. A comfortable TV and reading lounge, complete with open fireplace, is also available. The commodious kitchen offers far more than most hostels, both in facilities (including ovens and microwave) and in spotlessness. On an old farm half a mile outside the village center, the hostel is accessible by bus and is near the Ulster Way. A locked bike shed ensures safe storage for cyclists.

42 Layde Rd., Cushendall. © **028/2177-1344.** Fax 028/2177-2042. Sleeps 44–54. Dormitory and family rooms £10 ($15) per person 18 and over; £8.50 ($12) per person under 18. MC, V. Open Mar–Dec 22 7:30–10:30am and 5–11:30pm. Signposted from Cushendall center, ½ mile (1km) away. **Amenities:** Lounge; full kitchen; microwave.

Killeague Lodge Mrs. Margaret Moore is the gracious hostess at this 1873 home on a 130-acre dairy farm. The comfortable guest rooms are nicely furnished. Mrs. Moore can arrange horseback riding instruction in the riding arena on the farm, as well as fishing on the river that runs through the premises.

Blackhill, Coleraine BT51 3SG, Co. Derry. ©/fax **028/7086-8229**. www.nifcha.com. 2 units, both with bathroom (shower only). £45 ($65) double. Reductions for children and seniors. Rates include full breakfast. No credit cards. 5 miles (8km) from Coleraine on A29. **Amenities:** Nonsmoking house. *In room:* TV, tea/coffeemaker.

The Meadows The Meadows offers exceptional convenience, comfort, and value. This newly constructed guesthouse provides spacious, well-designed accommodation in a lovely coastal setting, across from the local boat club and a 10-minute walk from the center of Cushendall. The front-room views of the sea and, on a clear day, of Scotland are quite splendid. All rooms are nonsmoking and are simply spotless. A spacious lounge is reserved for guests, and the breakfast room is particularly inviting. In addition, if you wish, Anne Carey, your host, will gladly arrange for you to eat at the private boat club across the road.

81 Coast Rd., Cushendall. © **028/2177-2020**. Fax 028/2177-1641. 6 units. £40 ($58) double. Family rates negotiable. Rates include full Irish breakfast. No credit cards. *In room:* TV, tea/coffeemaker.

Sanda Perched high at the mouth of Glenariff, the Queen of the Glens, this guesthouse affords truly spectacular views. The two guest rooms are modest and immaculate. The beds are very firm, and a pleasant lounge, complete with TV and a stack of intriguing books about the area, is available to guests. Host Donnell O'Loan is quite knowledgeable and articulate about the area—its ancient sites, as well as its current attractions. The property offers nonsmoking rooms.

29 Kilmore Rd., Glenariff, Co. Antrim. © **028/2177-1785**. sanda@antrim.net. 3 units, 2 with bathroom (shower only). £36 ($52) double depending on season. Family rates negotiable. Rates include full breakfast. No credit cards. Free parking. **Amenities:** Lounge.

The Villa Farmhouse 🞯 Mrs. Catharine Scally's Tudor farmhouse is within easy reach of the Glens of Antrim, and has an inviting, old-fashioned air, with stained-glass windows and antiques. The rooms are very comfortably furnished, and offer beautiful views overlooking Cushendun. The entire house is nonsmoking. It's signposted from the Coast Drive.

185 Torr Rd., Cushendun BT44 0PU, Co. Antrim. ©/fax **028/2176-1252**. 3 units. £40 ($58) double. Reduction for children. Rates include full breakfast. No credit cards. *In room:* TV, tea/coffeemaker.

SELF-CATERING

Tully Cottage ★★★ (Value) This is one of the loveliest self-catering cottages available for the money. Although it has two bedrooms and is just large enough to accommodate 4 people quite comfortably, Tully is the perfect love nest or honeymoon nook. It is both elevated and secluded, affording spectacular views of Glenarm Glen and the North Channel down to the Mull of Galloway, plus total privacy. The old farm cottage has been lovingly restored and tastefully appointed to offer equal charm and comfort. The beds are firm, the tub is extralong, the traditional fireplace is up to the task, and the kitchen is well-equipped. This is a perfect base for exploring the stunning North Antrim coast or for curling up. Horse riding, day boats, trekking, and rock climbing can be arranged in advance; and if you like, bicycles can be waiting for you at the cottage.

Glenarm, Co. Antrim. © **028/9024-1100**. Fax 028/9024-1198. Self-catering cottage, 2 bedrooms. 483€ ($437) per week (less in low season). MC, V. **Amenities:** TV, TEL, full kitchen, fridge, oven/stove, microwave, washing machine.

GREAT DEALS ON DINING

See also M. McBrides, under "The Pub Scene," below.

Courtyard Coffee House CAFE   This is a good, inexpensive lunch stop as you set out on the County Antrim coastal drive. It's located across from the seafront on the northern end of town, just north of the town hall and library. The self-service menu features light lunches such as soup, sandwiches, salad plates, quiche, lasagna, and pastries. You can eat in the light, bright indoor room or outside in the inner courtyard.

38 Scotch Quarter, Carrickfergus, Co. Antrim. © 028/9335-1881. Light meals £7 ($10). No credit cards. Mon–Sat 10am–4:40pm; Sun 2–5:30pm.

Hillcrest Country House IRISH   This restaurant is surrounded by lovely gardens and offers fine views of the coast, which looks particularly lovely at sunset. The menu emphasizes local ingredients and creative sauces. Some dishes you might find include: salmon baked with cucumbers, mushrooms, and fennel sauce; grilled venison with game mousse laced with Black Bush Irish whiskey; roast North Antrim duck with sage and onion stuffing and peach brandy; and noisettes of lamb with rosemary and garlic sauce.

306 Whitepark Rd. (opposite the entrance to Giant's Causeway), Giant's Causeway, Co. Antrim. © 028/2073-1577. Reservations required. Main courses £8–£16 ($12–$23). MC, V. Mon–Thurs noon–2:30pm and 4:15–9pm; Fri–Sun noon–2:30pm and 4–9:30pm.

Ramore INTERNATIONAL   This restaurant stands on the east end of the harbor, overlooking boats and the sea. It's known for its international menu choices, such as chicken breast with fresh asparagus and vinaigrette of pine nuts, sun-dried tomatoes, Parmesan, and truffle oil; duck on a bed of shredded cabbage; and pork filled with Parma ham and Emmental cheese. Also on the menu are paella, Thai chicken, tempura prawns, fish of the day, rack of lamb, and steaks.

Ramore St., The Harbour, Portrush. © 028/7082-4313. Reservations required. Main courses £11–£15 ($16–$22). MC, V. Wine bar Mon–Sat noon–2pm and 5:30–9pm; restaurant Tues–Sat 6:30–10:30pm.

Sweeney's Wine Bar IRISH   This is a popular, informal spot on the coast, with a conservatory-style extension and outdoor seating in good weather. The menu offers good pub grub—burgers, pasta, seafood plates (prawns, scampi, cod, and whitefish), steak and kidney pie, and stir-fry vegetables.

6b Seaport Ave., Portballintrae. © 028/2073-2405. Reservations recommended for dinner. Main courses £5–£10 ($7.25–$15). No credit cards. Mon–Sat 12:30–10pm; Sun 12:30–2:30pm and 7–9pm.

Victoriana Restaurant *Kids* CAFETERIA   In the Dunluce Center, this Victorian-theme bilevel restaurant is a handy place to stop for refreshment when touring the Antrim coast. The menu includes sandwiches, omelets, salads, pastas, and steaks, as well as sausage, beans, and "Ulster fry" (a cheese-and-onion pie).

Dunluce Ave. (in the new Dunluce Center), Portrush. © 028/7082-4444. Reservations not accepted. Main courses £2–£5 ($2.90–$7.25). No credit cards. Apr–June and Sept daily noon–5pm; July–Aug daily 10am–8pm; Oct weekends noon–5pm.

THE PUB SCENE

Harbour Bar   George McAlpin's place is reputed to serve the best Guinness in the North. It's a particularly good place for a before- or after-dinner libation, and sits on the wharf overlooking the harbor. You'll find mostly locals in the plain, old-style bar. It's all so very Irish. The Wharf, Portrush. © 028/7082-5047.

J. McCollam   Known to locals as Johnny Joe's, J. McCollam has been for nearly a century the hottest scene in Cushendall for traditional music and Antrim atmosphere. You have to be willing to wedge yourself in, but you're not likely to have any regrets. Mill St., Cushendall. ℭ **028/2177-1992.**

M. McBrides   Opened in 1840, Mary McBride's was the smallest pub or bar in Europe until, quite recently, it burst its seams and expanded to include the Riverside Bistro, open for light lunches and dinners (12:30–7pm), and the Waterside Restaurant, specializing in seafood and serving a wide menu of dinners (7:30–9:30pm), with main courses ranging from £6.50 to £17 ($9.45–$25). The old Guinness record–holding pub is still intact, so squeeze in and partake of the legend for yourself. Live traditional music tends to break out in the pub's conservatory on weekend evenings. 2 Main St., Cushendun Village. ℭ **028/2176-1511.**

5 The Mourne Mountains

30 miles (48km) SW of Belfast (Belfast–Newcastle)

South and west from Downpatrick lie the rolling foothills of the Mournes, the highest mountains in Northern Ireland. A dozen of their nearly 50 summits rise above 2,000 feet (610m); the tallest is the barren peak of **Slieve Donard** at 2,796 feet (852m), whose breathtaking vista includes the full length of Strangford Lough, Lough Neagh, the Isle of Man, and, on a crystalline day, the west coasts of Wales and Scotland. The recommended ascent of Slieve Donard is from Donard Park on the south side of Newcastle.

C.S. Lewis compared the Mournes to "earth-covered potatoes." All but two of these purple peaks are soft and rounded. They're also remote and veined by very few roads, making them a rambler's dream. You're on the right track here if you're looking for barren, windswept moors. The ancestral home of the Brontës is in the Mournes, and in ruin. But all is not desolate here. There are also forest parks, sandy beaches, lush gardens, and, of course, pubs.

If you're tired of all that walking and climbing and sighing at the wuthering splendor of it all, head to **Newcastle,** a lively, popular seaside resort, with a good beach and one of the finest golf courses in Ireland. Several other coastal towns strung along A2—**Kilkeel, Rostrevor, and Warrenpoint**—have their own charms to offer. But here the mountains are the thing, and naturally you can't have cliffs and the sea without birds and castles and the odd dolmen.

GETTING THERE   If you're driving up from Dublin, turn east off the Dublin-Belfast road at Newry and take A2, tracing the north shore of Carlingford Lough, between the mountains and the sea. It's a drive you won't soon forget.

VISITOR INFORMATION   For information in the Down District, stop into the **Downpatrick Tourist Information Centre,** 74 Market St., Downpatrick, County Down (ℭ **028/4461-2233**), open year-round Monday through Saturday 9:30am to 5pm, with extended summer hours.

There's also the **Newcastle Tourist Information Centre,** 10–14 Central Promenade, Newcastle, County Down (ℭ **028/4372-2222;** fax 028/4372-2400), open year-round: July and August, Monday through Saturday from 9:30am to 7pm and Sunday from 1 to 7pm; September to June, Monday through Saturday from 10am to 5pm and Sunday from 2 to 6pm. (A coach tour of the Mournes is offered according to demand and can be booked here.)

In addition, there is the **Mourne Countryside Centre,** 91 Central Promenade, Newcastle, County Down (ℭ **028/4372-4059**), open June through

October, Monday through Friday 9am to 5pm, with plenty of information and maps for hikers in the Mournes. The center also sponsors guided mountain walks, free of charge, every Monday and Saturday.

SEEING THE SIGHTS

Annalong Cornmill   The restored early-19th-century corn mill that overlooks the small fishing harbor of Annalong is still in operating condition. It's powered by a waterwheel and a 1920s, 20-horsepower engine. The mill complex contains a kiln for drying the grain, as well as several millstones and an array of related machinery. This is not a site for thrillseekers, but it does have a certain interest for anyone wanting to imagine life long before the automatic bread machine. In fact, the guided tour by James Trainor is so spirited and informative that a visit here becomes quite interesting.

Annalong, Co. Down. ☎ **028/3026-8877**. Admission £1.30 ($1.90) adult, 65p (95¢) children, £2.65 ($3.85) family. Feb–Nov Tues–Sat 11am–5pm. 7½ miles (12km) south of Newcastle.

Castlewellan Forest Park ⭐   Surrounding a fine trout lake and watched over by a magnificent private castle, this splendid forest park just begs for picnics and outdoor outings. Woodland walks, a lakeside sculpture trail, formal walled gardens, and even excellent trout (brown and rainbow) fishing await you here. The real draw is the National Arboretum, begun in 1740 and now grown to 10 times its original size. The largest of its three greenhouses features aquatic plants and a collection of free-flying tropical birds. The town of Castlewellan, elegantly laid out around two squares, is also well worth a stroll.

The Grange, Castlewellan Forest Park, Castlewellan. ☎ **028/4377-8664**. john.watson@dardni.gov.uk. Free admission. Parking £3.80 ($5.50) per car; pedestrians £2 ($2.90). Open daily 10am–dusk. 4 miles (6.5km) northwest of Newcastle on A50.

Drumena Cashel (Stone Fort)   The walls of this irregularly shaped ancient stone-ring fort—a farmstead, dating from the early Christian period—were partially rebuilt in 1925–26 and measure 9 to 12 feet (2.5–3.5m) thick. The *souterrain* (underground stone tunnel) is T-shaped and was likely used in ancient times for cold storage. In the extreme, it hopefully provided some protection from Viking raiders. There were once, it seems, tens of thousands of such fortifications in Ireland, and this is one of the better-preserved examples in this region.

Open site. 2 miles (3km) southwest of Castlewellan, off A25.

Dundrum Castle   This was once the mightiest of the Norman castles strung along the Down coast and still commands the imagination, if nothing else. The oldest portions of these striking and quite extensive ruins date from the late 12th century, while the most recent are from the 17th century. The hilltop setting is quite lovely, and the views from the keep's parapet are especially grand.

Dundrum, Co. Down. ☎ **028/9054-3037**. Admission 75p ($1.10) adults, 45p (65¢) children. Apr–Sept Tues–Sat 10am–1pm and 1:30–7pm, Sun 2–7pm; Oct–Mar Sat 10am–4pm, Sun 2–4pm. 4 miles (6km) east of Newcastle, off A2.

Murlough Nature Reserve   Sand dunes, heathland, and forest, surrounded by estuary and sea, make for a lovely outing on a clear bright day, but you'll want to bring a windbreaker. Binoculars, too, because this is a prime habitat for a host of waders and sea birds. Bring a picnic, and you may find your dessert on the dunes, which are strewn with wild strawberries in the summertime.

On main Dundrum-Newcastle Rd. (A2), southeast of Dundrum. Open site. ☎ **028/4375-1467**. Free admission. Parking May to mid-Sept £3 ($4.35) per car.

Nautilus Centre   Opened in the spring of 1998, this multipurpose center is an ideal place to begin your exploration of Kilkeel, Northern Ireland's premier fishing port. The Nautilus Heritage Centre features a compact exhibition with an interactive multimedia display, introducing visitors to the mission and development of Northern Ireland's modern fishing fleet. You'll also find, in the center's Harbour Store, fresh fish on ice, fishing gear and tackle, and a selection of gifts and souvenirs.

Rooney Rd., Kilkeel Harbour, Kilkeel. © **028/4176-5555.** Free admission. Easter–Sept Mon–Sat 10am–9pm, Sun noon–6pm; Oct–Easter Mon–Sat 10am–6pm, Sun noon–6pm.

Silent Valley Mountain Park *Kids*   More than 90 years ago, the 22-mile (36km) drystone Mourne Wall was built to enclose Silent Valley, which was dammed to create the Silent Valley Reservoir, to this day the major source of water for County Down. As the 22-mile **Mourne Wall trek**—threading together 15 of the range's main peaks—is more than most vacationers want to take on, a fine alternative is the more modest walk from the fishing port of Kilkeel to the Silent Valley and Lough Shannagh. An even less strenuous alternative is to drive to the Silent Valley Information Centre and take the shuttle bus to the top of nearby Ben Crom. The bus runs daily in July and August, weekends only in May, June, and September, and costs £1.50 ($2.20) round-trip, 60p (85¢) for children. There is also a restaurant, gift shop, children's playscape, and picnic area.

Silent Valley, Co. Down. © **028/9074-1166.** Admission £3 ($4.95) per car. Information Centre Apr–Oct daily 10am–6pm. 4 miles (6km) north of Kilkeel on Head Rd.

Tollymore Forest Park   Tollymore House is no more. What remains is a delightful 1,200-acre wildlife and forest park, laid out in the 18th century by James Hamilton, an earl with an eye. The park offers a number of walks along the Shimna River, noted for its salmon, or up into the north slopes of the Mournes. The forest is a nature preserve inhabited by a host of local wildlife, including badgers, foxes, otters, and pine martens. Don't miss the trees for the forest—there are some exotic species here, including magnificent Himalayan cedars and a 100-foot-tall sequoia in the arboretum. For more strenuous activities, there's the **Tollymore Mountain Centre** (see below).

Tullybrannigan Rd., Newcastle. © **028/4372-2428.** Free admission. Parking £3.50 ($5.10) per car; pedestrians £2 ($2.90). Daily 9am–dusk. Just off B180, 2 miles (3km) northwest of Newcastle.

OUTDOOR PURSUITS

FISHING   The best time to fish for both trout and salmon is from August to October. Some quite sizeable sea trout can be seen on the Whitewater River in the Mournes, and not all of them get away. The **Burrendale Hotel** in Newcastle (© **028/4372-2599**) and the **Kilmorey Arms Hotel** in Kilkeel (© **028/ 4176-2220**) offer special holiday breaks for game anglers and can help see to your angling needs. For further information, as well as tackle, bait, and outfitting needs, try **Four Seasons,** 47 Main St., Newcastle (© **028/4372-5078**).

GOING SKY HIGH   You can book a 1-hour, guaranteed-to-render-you-speechless helicopter ride over the Mountains of Mourne by calling **The Helicopter Centre,** Newtownards Airfield (© **028/9182-0028;** www. helicoptercentre.co.uk). There are scheduled flights on weekends, or you can charter a helicopter during the week (seats four passengers). The cost per person for a half-hour flight on the weekend is £59 ($86), while a one-hour charter is £450 ($653).

GOLF   Royal County Down ✪, Newcastle, County Down (© **028/ 4372-3314**), is nestled in huge sand dunes with the Mountains of Mourne in the background. This 18-hole, par-71 championship course was created in 1889. Greens fees are £80 ($116) on weekdays and £90 ($131) on weekends. For a fraction of the cost, the **Kilkeel Golf Club,** Mourne Park, Ballyardle, Kilkeel (© **028/4176-2296**), is a beautiful parkland course on the historic Kilmorey Estate. The best days for visitors are weekdays except for Tuesday, and the greens fees are £16 ($23) weekdays and £18 ($26) weekends.

HORSEBACK RIDING   The **Mount Pleasant Trekking and Horse Riding Centre** (© **028/4377-8651**) offers group trekking tours into Castlewellan Forest Park for £8 ($12) an hour. For riding in the Tollymore Forest Park or on local trails, contact the **Mourne Trail Riding Centre,** 96 Castlewellan Rd., Newcastle (© **028/4372-4351;** www.mournetrailridingcentre.com), which has quality horses for experienced riders and also offers beach rides for the highly skilled. Trail riding in the Mournes is also offered by the **Drumgooland House Equestrian Centre,** 29 Dunnanew Rd., Seaforde, Downpatrick, County Down (© **028/4481-1956**), including 1½-hour treks around Tollymore and Castlewellan Forest Parks for £20 ($29). Full equestrian holidays also available.

OUTDOOR ACTIVITY CENTER   The **Tollymore Mountain Centre** (© **028/4372-2158;** www.tollymoremc.com), located on the grounds of Tollymore Forest Park (see "Seeing the Sights," above), but with its own entrance, offers courses on rock climbing, hill walking, orienteering, and canoeing.

SHOPPING

The Celtic Crafts Gallery   You'll find an impressive array of Celtic design crafts here, as well as original gold and silver jewelry by Mary Doran. In addition, there's a pleasant cafe and, as a bonus, panoramic views of the Mourne Mountains. Open April to September, Monday to Saturday 10am to 5pm and Sunday 2 to 5pm; October to March, Tuesday to Saturday 10am to 5pm. 45 Dromara Rd., Dundrum. © **028/4375-1327.**

The Mourne Grange Craft Shop and Tea Room   This gift shop is a browser's paradise, full to the brim with unique quality handcrafted goods from pottery and silk scarves to toys for young and old. There's also a fine selection of books of local interest and beyond. The cheerful, nonsmoking tearoom serves an array of freshly baked pastries to complement a cup of coffee or pot of tea. The proceeds of this shop help support the Rudolf Steiner–inspired Kilkeel Camphill Community for children and adults with special needs. The shop's hours are Monday and Wednesday through Saturday 10am to 12:30pm and 2 to 5:30pm, and Sunday 2 to 5:30pm. The tearoom closes a half hour before the shop. Camphill Village Community, 169 Newry Rd., Kilkeel. © **028/4176-0103.**

ACCOMMODATIONS YOU CAN AFFORD

Grasmere   Mrs. McCormick presides over this pleasant, well-kept modern bungalow in a residential area on the edge of Newcastle, off the Bryansford–Newcastle road (B180), with views of the Mournes. Grasmere is only a 10-minute walk from the beach, and there are a golf course and some forest walks nearby. The two double rooms both have views of the Mournes. *Note:* With only three rooms, this B&B can feel more intimate than some travelers might want, but for those on a budget, it offers a comfortable, clean, relaxed place to stay. 16 Marguerite Park, Bryansford Rd., Newcastle. © **028/4372-6801.** 2 units. £40 ($58) double. Rates include full breakfast. No credit cards. Private parking. Closed Christmas. *In room:* TV, tea/coffeemaker.

Slieve Croob Inn ★★★ *(Value* This small, family resort offers what is perhaps the best value for money in the Mournes. The setting—a patchwork of drumlin pastureland just shy of the Mournes's peaks—is exceptional. The panoramic views of Slieve Croob, Newcastle Bay, and the Isle of Man are breathtaking. This is a rambler's fantasy, with 5 miles (8km) of trails on Slieve Croob and a plethora of lazy mountain laneways to explore. The spotless inn is tastefully designed and outfitted in a homey, mountain-lodge style. The color palette of blues, yellows, and dark greens, with simple pine furniture, is consistent throughout. In addition to standard doubles, there is a fabulous three-bedroom family apartment with its own outer door. The Branny Bar is open daily with a bistro menu and traditional music every Saturday night. An 18-hole golf course is in the works, and could appear within the next few years.

There are also 10 one- to three-bedroom self-catering cottages—appealingly rustic in decor, yet fitted with all the conveniences of modern life.

Seeconnell Centre, 119 Clanvaraghan Rd., Castlewellan. ② **028/4377-1412.** Fax 028/4377-1162. www.slievecroob.mcmail.com. 7 units, all with bathroom; 10 1- to 3-bedroom self-catering cottages. Inn £60 ($99) double; cottages £170–£350 ($280.50–$577.50) per week depending on cottage and season. V. Sign-posted 1 mile (1.5km) out of Castlewellan on the A25 Castlewellan-Clough Rd. **Amenities:** Restaurant (International), bar; 18-hole golf course; laundry facilities; horseback riding; currency exchange. *In room:* TV, TEL, tea/coffeemaker, trouser press.

SELF-CATERING

Hannas Close Situated on a low bluff over a lovely shallow stream, facing the spectacular Mountains of Mourne, this born-again *clachan* is so quiet that there's little to wake you other than birdsong. In the refurbishment of the cottages, every effort was made to re-create the past while attending to contemporary codes and standards of comfort. The cottages, which sleep from two to seven, have everything you'll need, including clothes washers, microwaves, and central heating. Additionally, all have an open fireplace or a wood stove. They are ideal for families or young couples, although the steep steps and rustic character of the cottages may not be to everyone's liking. A small museum in the Close can help you imagine the former life of the rural mountainside world you'll enter here.

Mourne Country Cottages, Hanna's Close, Kilkeel. ②/fax **028/4176-5999** or ② 028/9024-1100. www.travel-ireland.com/hennas. 7 cottages (sleep 2, 3, 4, and 6 persons). 350€–490€ ($317–$444) per week depending on the cottage. V. Free parking. **Amenities:** TV; kitchen; fridge; oven/stove; microwave; washing machine.

GREAT DEALS ON DINING

Most of the dining in the Mournes, with or without frills, gourmet or generic, happens in hotels, guesthouses, and pubs; so, when your stomach growls, be sure to extend your culinary search to the accommodations listed above and the pubs in the following section.

The Fisherman SEAFOOD Locals consider this seafood joint to be the best in town, because of its fresh fish and friendly service. Luscious seasonal lobster stuffed with prawns competes for attention with mixed seafood Creole, and grilled haddock with bacon and fine herbs. Diners preferring fare from terra firma will do well to try the lamb cooked in red wine sauce with a julienne of carrots and mange tout, or tarragon chicken. The Fisherman is on the main street, opposite the BP station.

68 Greencastle St., Kilkeel. ② **028/4176-2130.** Reservations recommended. Dinner main courses £7–£17 ($10–$25). MC, V. Tues–Sun noon–2:30pm and 5:30–9:30pm.

THE PUB SCENE

Jacob Halls   If there's a chill in the air, you'll leave it behind in Jacob Halls, with its three massive fires blazing at the least pretense. This well-worn pub is a hub of hospitality for all ages—all over 18, that is. The decor is a matter of dark wood and red brick, and walls lined with vintage local photographs. There's live music of some sort every night from Wednesday through Sunday, and pub grub from lunch on. Greencastle St., Kilkeel. ✆ 028/4176-4751.

Old Harbour Inn   You won't find a more quaint "wee" harbor on the Down Coast than Annalong, and the Old Harbour Inn, as its name suggests, is poised right on the dock. Picnic tables sit out front for the perfect dockside happy hour. Otherwise, there's an inviting lounge and full restaurant serving lunch, high tea, dinner, and bar snacks. A live band of some sort, often of the Irish country-and-western persuasion, shows up every Saturday, and there's an unpredictable disco now and then. 6 Harbour Dr., Annalong Harbour, Annalong. ✆ 028/4376-8678.

The Percy French   The Percy French has stood watch over the gates of the Slieve Donard Hotel for a century. It's named after the famed Irish composer who died in 1920, leaving behind these words as an epitaph:

> *Remember me is all I ask—and yet*
> *If remembrance proves a task—forget.*

Forgetting is not a real option, however, so long as this fine old faux-Tudor pub pours the perfect pint and serves delicious fare. Under the same beamed roof there's both the lounge and a full-service restaurant, with a traditional Irish menu. Live traditional music is on tap Saturdays, and a disco breaks out every Friday. The bar is open Monday through Saturday from 11:30am to 11:30pm, and Sunday from noon to 10pm. The restaurant's hours are Monday through Saturday from 12:30 to 2:30pm and 5:30 to 10pm, and Sunday from noon to 2pm and 5:30 to 9:30pm. Downs Rd., Newcastle. ✆ 028/4372-3175.

6 Derry City

Derry is 73 miles (118km) NW of Belfast, 39 miles (63km) SW of Portrush, 70 miles (113km) NW of Armagh, 61 miles (98km) NE of Enniskillen, 144 miles (232km) NW of Dublin, and 220 miles (354km) NE of Shannon

Derry is the second-largest city of Northern Ireland (pop. 110,000) and the unofficial capital of the northwestern region of the province. Set on a hill on the banks of the Foyle estuary, Derry has often come under siege, because it is strategically close to the open sea. At the time of the Plantation of Ulster in the 17th century, the City of London sent master builders and money to rebuild the ruined medieval town, and hence its name became Londonderry, an appellation which today is still preferred by many of its inhabitants.

The city's great **17th-century walls,** about a mile in circumference and 18 feet (5.5m) thick, are a legacy of the Plantation era. Although they were the focus of sieges in 1641, 1649, and 1689, the walls have withstood the many tests of time and are unbroken. They make Derry one of the finest examples of a walled city in Europe. The rest of the city's architecture is largely Georgian, with brick-fronted town houses and imposing public buildings. Basement-level pubs and shops are common.

For longer than anyone wants to remember, Derry has been immersed in **"The Troubles."** It was here in the 1960s and 1970s that the North's civil rights movement was both born and baptized in blood. The victims of Bloody Sunday rank high in the martyrology of this movement, which almost tore Derry apart.

(*Fun Fact* **Where the Pipes Are Blowing**

About 12 miles (19km) east of Derry city is another Georgian enclave, the town of **Limavady** in the Roe Valley. It was here that Jane Ross wrote down the tune of a lovely air that she heard, played by a fiddler as he passed through town. It was to become the famous "Londonderry Air," otherwise known as "Danny Boy."

By 1980, nearly a third of the inner city was in ruins. That was then, this is now. In the years since, Derry rebuilt some of its walls and dismantled others, and became increasingly engaged in the struggle to build a new North. Today, Derry is one of the most vital and appealing centers of culture and commerce in Northern Ireland and destined to become a major tourist mecca once word gets out.

Another secret about Derry is how close it is to many of the major sights of Ireland's northwest corner. To cite a few highlights, the Inishowen Peninsula, the Giant's Causeway and the North Antrim Coast, the Northwest Passage and the Sperrins, and Glenveagh National Park in Donegal are all within an hour's drive of Derry. The bottom line is that Derry is an ideal base of operations from which to explore one of Ireland's most unspoiled and dazzling regions.

GETTING THERE **By Bus** The fastest bus between Belfast and Derry, the *Maiden City Flyer,* operated by **Ulsterbus** (✆ **028/9033-3000** in Belfast; **028/7126-2261** in Derry; www.translink.co.uk), is about twice as fast as the train and takes a little over an hour and a half. **Ulsterbus** also has service from Portrush and Portstewart. From the Republic, **Bus Eireann** offers three buses a day from Galway's **Bus Eireann Travel Centre,** Ceannt Station, Galway (✆ **091/562000;** www.buseireann.ie), via Sligo and Donegal; and **Lough Swilly Bus Service** (✆ **028/7126-2017** or 074/22853 in Donegal; www.sjp. clara.net/nibus/lswilly.htm) has service to Derry from a number of towns in County Donegal, including Dunfanaghy and Letterkenny.

By Train **Northern Ireland Railways** (✆ **888/BRITRAIL** or 028/ 9089-9411; www.nirailways.co.uk) operate frequent trains from Belfast and Portrush, which arrive at the **Northern Ireland Railways Station** (✆ **028/ 7134-2228**), on the east side of the Foyle River. A free Linkline bus brings passengers from the train station to the city center.

By Air Service to **City of Derry Airport** (✆ **028/7181-0784;** www. derrynet.com/airport/) is provided by **British Airways** (✆ **0345/222111;** www.british-airways.com) from Glasgow and Manchester, and by **Ryanair** (✆ **0541/569569** in Britain; www.ryanair.com) from London Stansted. The no. 43 Limavady bus stops at the airport. A taxi for the 8-mile (13km) journey to the city center costs about £9 ($13). If you're landing in either of the Belfast airports, without a connection to Derry, the **Airporter** coach can take you straight to Derry. Call ✆ **028/7126-9996** for information and reservations.

GETTING AROUND **Ulsterbus,** Foyle Street Depot, Derry (✆ **028/ 7126-2261;** www.translink.co.uk), operates local bus service to the suburbs. There is no bus service within the walls of the small, easily walkable city. There is also no bus service to certain nationalist areas outside the walls. Those areas are served by the black London-style taxis known in Derry and Belfast as "people's taxis," which will not go to most areas of interest to tourists. Use any of the other taxis available throughout the city, which are plentiful and offer reasonable rates.

Derry City

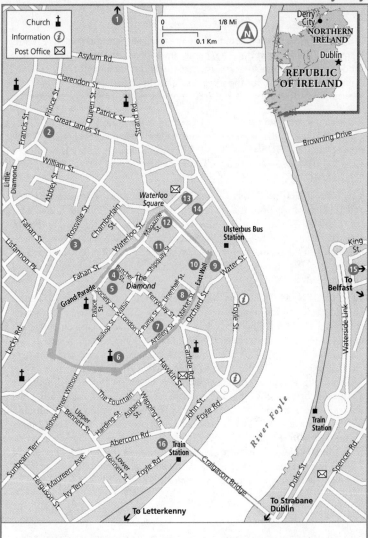

Amelia Earhart Centre **1**

Bloody Sunday Monument **3**

Cathedral of St. Colomb **6**

Derry Craft Village **11**

The Fifth Province **5**

Foyle Valley Railway Centre **16**

Genealogy Centre **4**

Guild Hall **14**

Harbour Museum **13**

Millennium Forum **10**

Orchard Gallery/Cinema **9**

Playhouse **7**

The Rialto **8**

St. Eugene's Cathedral **2**

Tower Museum **12**

Workhouse Museum **15**

Value A Note on Prices

Derry prices for both accommodations and dining are exceptionally reasonable. The fact that Derry has barely any expensive hotels or restaurants does not mean that it lacks first-class lodging or dining. The city offers more for less and is, for the foreseeable future, a real bargain.

There are **taxi stands** at the **Ulsterbus,** Foyle Street Depot (✆ 028/7126-2262), and at the **Northern Ireland Railways Station,** Duke Street, Waterside, Derry (✆ 028/7134-2228). To call a cab, contact **City Radio Cabs** (✆ 028/7126-4466), **Foyle Taxis** (✆ 028/7126-3905), or **Tower Taxis** (✆ 028/7137-1944).

VISITOR INFORMATION The **Derry Visitor and Convention Bureau and Tourist Information Centre** is at 44 Foyle St., Derry (✆ **028/7126-7284;** fax 028/7137-7992; www.derryvisitor.com). It's open November to Easter, Monday through Friday 9am to 5pm; Easter through May and October, Monday through Friday 9am to 5pm and Saturday 10am to 5pm; July through September, Monday through Friday 9am to 7pm, Saturday 10am to 6pm, and Sunday 10am to 5pm.

CITY ORIENTATION The focal point of Derry is the **Diamond,** a square in the center of the city, set just west of the banks of the Foyle River. Four streets radiate out from the Diamond: Bishop, Ferryquay, Shipquay, and Butcher. Each of these streets extends for several blocks and ends at a walled gateway of the same name (Bishop's Gate, Ferryquay Gate, Shipquay Gate, and Butcher's Gate). The gates are all connected by a massive wall that rings the inner city.

Two bridges connect the east and west banks of the River Foyle: the **Craigavon Bridge,** built in 1933 and one of the few examples of a double-decker bridge in the British Isles; and the **Foyle Bridge,** Ireland's longest bridge, which was opened in 1984 and provides a dual-lane carriageway about 2 miles (3km) north of the Craigavon Bridge. West of the river are two major areas: the walled **inner city** and, farther west, an area known as the **Bogside.** East of the Foyle is the area usually referred to as **Waterside,** where most of the fine hotels and many of the city's restaurants are located.

 FAST FACTS: Derry

Banks City-center banks include the **Bank of Ireland** (✆ **028/7126-2211**) on Shipquay Street, and the **Ulster Bank** (✆ **028/7126-1882**) at Waterloo Place. Both are open weekdays 9:30am to 4:30pm, except for 10am opening on Wednesday. The **Northern Bank** (✆ **028/7126-5333**) at Shipquay Place has Saturday hours from 9:30am to 12:30pm. A bureau de change is available at the Tourist Information Centre (see "Visitor Information," above), and at **Thomas Cook Travel** (✆ **028/7137-4174**) in the Quayside Centre.

Car Rental Local offices include **Avis Car Hire** (✆ **028/7181-1708;** www.avis.co.uk) at the City of Derry Airport.

Emergencies Dial ✆ **999** for fire, police, and ambulance.

Gay & Lesbian Resources Foyle Friend, 32 Great James Street (© **028/ 7126-3120;** www.iol.ie/~nwgay) operates a drop in center and coffee bar; check the website for other information and services. Call the **Foyle LGB Line** (© **028/7136-0420),** Thursday 7:30 to 10pm, or drop in at 37 Clarendon St., Thursday 8 to 10pm.

Hospital The best choice is the **Altnagevin Hospital,** Glenshane Road (© **028/7134-5171).**

Laundry For the new lease on life that fresh laundry brings, seek out **Dud 'n' Suds,** 141 Strand Rd. (© **028/7126-6006),** or **Foyle Dry Cleaning/ Launderette,** 147 Spencer Rd. (© **028/7131-1897).**

Library The Derry **Central Library** is at 35 Foyle St. in the city center (© **028/7127-2300).**

Publications & Radio Stations Derry has two local papers, each of which has a current "What's On" section: the *Derry Journal* and the *Londonderry Sentinel.* Additionally, the Derry Visitors and Convention Bureau publishes a free quarterly publication called *What's On?* The local Derry radio stations are Q102 (FM 102.9) and **Radio Foyle** (FM 93.1).

Police The main RUC or police station is on Strand Road (© **028/ 7136-7337).**

Post Office The main Post Office, at 3 Custom House St. (© **028/ 7136-2563),** is open Monday 8:30am to 5:30pm, Tuesday through Friday 9am to 5:30pm, and Saturday 9am to 12:30pm.

Shoe Repair For reliable, on-the-spot emergency repairs, head to **Walkrite,** 6 Great James St. (© **028/7126-9225).**

SEEING THE SIGHTS

In past years **Ulsterbus** has operated a bus tour of the Derry sights during July and August, but this service was temporarily discontinued in 2001. Call the **Tourist Information Centre** (© **028/7126-7284)** to see if this tour is on when you visit.

July through August, the Derry Visitors and Convention Bureau sponsors **Inner City Walking Tours,** Monday through Friday, departing at 11:15am and 3:15am from the Tourist Information Centre, 44 Foyle St. The price is £4 ($5.80) adults, £3 ($4.35) seniors and children. Between September and June the tours depart once a day, Monday through Friday at 2:30pm. You can also find a complete list of walking tours at the visitor center.

McNamara Walking Tours (© **028/7134-5335;** 0788-996-3858 mobile) offers an informative, entertaining walking tour of the city June to September,

---

Finds **The View from Above**

In Waterside, east of the River Foyle, is a small grassy viewing point called the "Top of the Hill" where you can enjoy spectacular eagle's-eye views of the city and its splendid environs. You'll never find your own way there, so take a taxi and bring your map. Short of a helicopter tour, this is the best way to get your initial bearings.

daily at 10am, noon, 2pm, and 4pm. The cost is £3.50 ($4.97) adults, £1.50 ($2.13) seniors and children.

Another fine option is the "Essential Walking Tour of Historic Derry," offered by **Northern Tours** (© **028/7128-9051**). It leaves from the Tourist Information Centre, May to September, daily at 10:30am and 2:30pm. The cost is £3 ($4.26) adults, free for children.

THE MAJOR ATTRACTIONS

Cathedral of St. Columb ✪ Located within the city walls near the Bishop's Gate, this Church of Ireland cathedral, built between 1628 and 1633, is a fine example of the Planters Gothic style of architecture. It was the first cathedral in the British Isles to be built after the Reformation. Several sections were added afterward, including the impressive spire and stained-glass windows that depict scenes from the great siege of 1688–89. In the chapterhouse, there's a display of city relics, including the four original keys to the city gates, and an audiovisual presentation that provides background on the history of the building and the city.

London St., Derry, Co. Derry. © **028/7126-7313**. www.stcolumbscathderal.org. Free admission to cathedral; chapter house £1.50 ($2.20). Apr–Oct Mon–Sat 9am–5pm; Nov–Mar Mon–Sat 9am–1pm and 2–4pm.

St. Eugene's Cathedral This Gothic-Revival-style church is Derry's Catholic cathedral, nestled in the heart of the Bogside district just beyond the city walls. The foundation stone was laid in 1851, but it took until 1873 for the work to be completed. The spire was added in 1902. The cathedral is built of local sandstone and is known for its stained-glass windows depicting the Crucifixion, by Meyer of Munich.

Fransic St. Free admission. Mon–Sat 7am–9pm; Sun 7am–6:30pm.

Tower Museum ✪ The award-winning Tower Museum, a must for all visitors to Derry, is just inside the city walls next to Shipquay Gate and was just expanded to include a new Spanish Armada museum. It's housed in O'Doherty Tower, a medieval-style fort, and presents the history of the city, from its geological formation to the present day. Visitors are invited to walk through time, their imaginations provoked along the way by a series of exhibits and audiovisual presentations. The Tower's collection of historical artifacts includes items salvaged from the Spanish Armada, which was ravaged by storms off the Irish coast in 1588.

Union Hall Place, Derry, Co. Derry. © **028/7137-2411**. www.derrynet/tower. Admission £4.20 ($6.10) adults, £1.60 ($2.35) children, £8.50 ($12) family. July–Aug Tues–Sat 10am–5pm, Sun 2–5pm; Sept–June Tues–Sat 10am–5pm.

Fun Fact **The City of Angels**

Derry derives its name from the Irish words *Doire Calgach,* meaning "the oak grove of Calgach." Calgach was a warrior who set up a camp here in pre-Christian times. The name survived until the 10th century, when the place became known as *Doire Colmcille* in honor of St. Columba, who founded his first monastery in Derry in A.D. 546. He is supposed to have written, "The angels of God sang in the glades of Derry and every leaf held its angel." Over the years, the name was anglicized to Derrie, or simply Derry.

OTHER ATTRACTIONS

The Fifth Province   This ambitious multimedia experience was many years in the making. Drawing from remote legends of a fifth Irish province at the navel of ancient Ireland, the idea here is to imagine and experience a once and future Ireland untroubled and unified. This multistage high-tech tour through time—past, present, and future—is designed to be absorbing for adults and children alike.

Calgach Centre, 4–22 Butcher St. (℃) **028/7137-3177**. Admission £3 ($4.35) adults, £1 ($1.45) seniors and children, £6 ($8.70) family. Mon–Fri 9:30am–4pm; extended summer hours.

Foyle Valley Railway Centre *Kids*   Just outside the city walls near the Craigavon Bridge, where four railway lines once crossed paths, this center focuses on the local history of letting off steam. Besides viewing exhibits and retired trains, you can take a 20-minute narrow-gauge trip through the Foyle Riverside Park.

Foyle Rd. (℃) **028/7126-5234**. Free admission. Train rides £2.50 ($3.65) adults, £1.25 ($1.85) seniors and children, £7 ($10) family. June–Aug daily 10am–8pm; Sept–May call ahead for hours.

Guildhall   Just outside the city walls, between Shipquay Gate and the River Foyle, this Tudor Gothic–style building looks much like its counterpart in London. The site's original structure was built in 1890, but it was rebuilt after a fire in 1908 and after a series of bombings in 1972. The hall is distinguished by its huge four-faced clock and by its stained-glass windows, made by Ulster craftsmen, that illustrate almost every episode of note in the city's history. The hall is used as a civic and cultural center for concerts, plays, and exhibitions.

Guildhall Sq., Derry, Co. Derry. (℃) **028/7137-7335**. Free guided tours available July–Aug and other months by advance arrangement. Mon–Fri 9am–5pm.

Harbour Museum   The full-size replica of St. Columba's curragh, which occupies most of the floor space of the ground-floor exhibition room, makes immediately clear the maritime focus of this small eclectic collection. It will take you only a few minutes to browse through the seemingly random yet often fascinating items on display. The building itself deserves attention as well.

Harbour Sq. (℃) **028/7137-7331**. Free admission. Mon–Fri 10am–1pm and 2–5pm. If the door is closed, just ring the bell.

Orchard Gallery   The Orchard Gallery, founded in 1978, is Derry's prime venue for contemporary visual art. Mounting 20 or more exhibitions and events each year, the gallery fosters and displays the work of a wide range of contemporary local, Irish, and international artists. Central to the gallery's mission, as well, is its innovative, multifaceted Education and Community Outreach Scheme. The art that originates here is meant to provoke a generously creative and collaborative response from the wider community, especially Derry's youth. Sharing the same building with the Orchard Gallery is the Orchard Cinema, where you're likely to find the latest international films.

Orchard St. (℃) **028/7126-9675**. Free admission. Tues–Sat 10am–6pm.

The Workhouse Museum and Library   This splendid, compact museum on the Waterside, only minutes from Derry Centre, opened in May 1998 and is still being developed. It occupies what was the central building—the inmates' dorms and the master's quarters—of a 19th-century workhouse complex. The story told here is both grim and moving. Ostensibly built to employ and maintain the poor, the workhouse was little more than a concentration camp. A visit ensures that you will leave feeling deliriously fortunate.

Fun Fact **A Poetic Persona**

Born and educated in Derry, the celebrated contemporary poet Seamus Heaney (b. 1938) has been called Ireland's Robert Frost and, perhaps more appropriately, a latter-day Yeats. Heaney's poems about his homeland in the North of Ireland appear in his collections *North* (1975), *Field Work* (1979), *Station Island* (1984), and *Seeing Things* (1991). In 1995, he was awarded the Nobel Prize for Literature, the fourth Irishman to be so honored.

The museum also presents intriguing multimedia exhibitions focused on two moments in Derry's history: the Great Famine, when between 1845 and 1849 roughly 12,000 people a year left Ireland forever from the port of Derry; and the Battle of the Atlantic, when Derry played a major role in the defeat of the Kriegsmarine. The German U-boat fleet surrendered at Derry in May 1945.

23 Glendermott Rd., Waterside. © 028/7131-8328. Free admission. Sept–June Mon–Thurs and Sat 10am–4:30pm; July–Aug Mon–Sat 10am–4:30pm.

OUTSIDE DERRY CITY

Amelia Earhart Centre   This cottage commemorates Amelia Earhart's landing here in 1932, as the first woman to fly the Atlantic solo. The grounds encompass the Ballyarnett Community Farm and Wildlife Centre, with a range of farmyard animals and wildlife.

Ballyarnett, Co. Derry. © 028/7135-4040. Free admission. Cottage Mon–Fri 10am–4pm; farm and sanctuary daily 10am–dusk. 3 miles (5km) north of Derry, off A2.

OUTDOOR PURSUITS

BICYCLING   Whether you want to rent a bike and do your own exploring or sign up for a cycling tour of the area, **Happy Days Cycle Hire,** 245 Lone Moor Rd., Derry (© **028/7128-7128;** www.happydays.ie) offers excellent service. Rental of mountain or touring bikes costs £9 ($13) a day and £35 ($51) a week.

FISHING   The Foyle System of rivers makes this a promising area for snagging brown and sea trout (from April to early July and September) and a variety of salmon (March through September). In addition, there is a stocked lake at Glenowen. Call **Glenowen Fisheries Co-operative** (© **028/7137-1544**) for bookings. You can outfit yourself and get useful information at **Rod and Line,** 1 Clarendon St., Derry (© **028/7126-2877**). For a game-fishing rod license, contact the **Foyle Fisheries Commission,** 8 Victoria Rd., Derry (© **028/7134-2100**).

GOLF   Derry has two 18-hole parkland courses: the **City of Derry Golf Club,** 49 Victoria Rd., Prehen (© **028/7134-6369**), with greens fees of £20 ($29) weekdays and £25 ($36) weekends; and the **Foyle International Golf Centre,** 12 Alder Rd., Derry (© **028/7135-2222;** fax: 028/7135-3967) with greens fees of £12 ($17) weekdays and £15 ($22) weekends. The best days for visitors at the City of Derry Golf Club are Monday through Friday, while any day of the week should be fine at the Foyle Golf Centre. It's always best, however, to phone ahead.

HORSEBACK RIDING   **Ardmore Stables,** 8 Rushall Rd., Ardmore (© **028/7134-5187**), offers lessons, trail rides, and pony trekking. Across the border, only 4 miles (6.5km) from Derry in County Donegal, **Lenamore**

Stables, Muff, Inishowen (© 077/84022; lenamorestable@eircom.net), also offers lessons and trekking, and has its own guest accommodations for all-out equestrian holidays.

LEISURE CENTERS The city leisure centers offering the fullest range of sports activities are **Templemore Sports Complex,** Buncrana Road (© 028/7126-5521), and the **Lisnagelvin Leisure Centre,** Richill Park (© 028/7134-7695). Guests are welcome at both and pay £8 ($12) for the use of the pool, tennis courts, gym, and so on.

WALKING In Derry, walking the **city walls** is a must. Just outside the city, off the main Derry–Belfast road, you'll come across **Ness Woods,** where there are scenic walks and nature trails, as well as the North's highest waterfall.

ACCOMMODATIONS YOU CAN AFFORD

Clarence House Mrs. Eleonora Slevin offers singles, doubles, twin rooms, and family rooms in this well-kept brick guesthouse. Rooms are quite comfortable, and the house and its hostess have become favorites of BBC and RTE television crews, who return again and again. The washing and ironing facilities are a bonus. Babysitting can be arranged, and there are restaurants within easy walking distance.

15 Northland Rd., Derry BT48 7HY, Co. Derry. ©/fax 028/7126-5342. 10 units, 8 with bathroom (7 with shower only). £50 ($73) double. Reduction for children. Rates include full breakfast. V. *In room:* TV, TEL, tea/coffeemaker.

The Saddlers House and the Merchant's House 𝕽𝕽 *(Finds* Peter and Joan Pyne have beautifully restored these two 19th-century town houses. The Saddlers House is cozy Victorian, while the more elegant Merchant's House is late Georgian and has been revived with such care as to win a Civic Trusts Ireland conservation award. It's now among the very last of Derry's Georgian-style houses still in service as residences. These two noteworthy houses are located several blocks from each other and are only minutes away by foot from Derry center. They offer comfort, convenience, character, and charm at excellent rates. Both properties offer nonsmoking rooms.

Saddlers House, 36 Great James St., Derry; Merchant's House, 16 Queen St., Derry. © 028/7126-9691 or 028/7126-4223. Fax 028/7126-6913. 7 units. £25 ($37.50) single; £45 ($67.50) double. Reduction for children and seniors. Rates include full breakfast. No credit cards. **Amenities:** Sitting room; currency exchange. *In room:* TV, tea/coffeemaker.

GREAT DEALS ON DINING

Austin & Co., Ltd. COFFEE SHOP One of the least expensive eateries in the city, Austins serves decent food for good prices. Dishes include chicken and ham pie with garlic potatoes, bacon or vegetable quiche with tossed salad, lasagna, fish, burgers, and a salad bar. The restaurant is on the top floor and offers good views of the city. Evening hours sometimes vary.

The Diamond and Ferryquay St. © 028/7126-1817. Lunch £3–£6 ($4.35–$8.70); average dinner £6 ($9.90). MC, V. Mon–Sat 9am–5:30pm (Fri usually to 7pm).

Badger's 𝕽 PUB GRUB This comfortable corner pub restaurant is just the place to enjoy a simple, satisfying dinner before the theater, or to settle into after your day's adventures for a drink and a chat. Tastefully decorated and graced with stained glass and wood paneling, the two levels have a Victorian feel but were designed with a more modern appreciation of light and openness. It's a

Value **Pub Grub**

Within the walls of the old city, **The Linenhall** 😊, 3 Market St. (© **028/ 7137-1665**), is a warm, convivial setting that's very popular with local businesspeople, who come for excellent pub lunches priced from £5 to £8 ($7.25 to $12). The menu includes some vegetarian dishes. Hours are Monday to Thursday and Sunday from noon to 2:30pm; Friday and Saturday from noon to 7pm.

Other good spots with similar prices are: **The Metro Pub and Wine Bar,** 3 Bank Place (© **028/7126-7401**), open for lunch daily from noon to 3pm; and **Monico Bar,** 4 Custom House St. (© **028/7126-3121**), open for lunch Monday to Saturday noon to 2:30pm.

popular meeting spot for locals who come for the friendly service and such well-prepared favorites as savory steak, vegetable and Guinness casserole with a crisp puff-pastry lid, or the flavorful hot sandwiches known as "damper melts."

16–18 Orchard St. © 028/7136-0763. No reservations. Dinner £8–£12 ($12–$17). MC, V. Mon noon–3pm; Tues–Thurs noon–7pm; Fri–Sat noon–9:30pm.

La Sosta 😊😊 ITALIAN   An evening at La Sosta begins with surprise and ends with contentment. The surprise is just that there is such a fine Italian restaurant inconspicuously tucked away on a quiet side street in Derry. Each dish is simple in conception, composed so that you can taste and enjoy each ingredient. Absent are the complicated, concealing sauces; everything here is on the surface, but this surface is varied, compelling, and always delicious. Characteristic is the memorable ravioli stuffed with spinach and ricotta with asparagus, french beans, chives, and ginger. The wine list is good, and the house wine is a particularly flavorful complement to the meal. Pure contentment is the only way to describe the selection of desserts.

45A Carlisle Rd., Derry, Co. Derry. © 028/7137-4817. Reservations recommended. Main courses £8–£15 ($12–$22). AE, MC, V. Tues–Sat 6–10:30pm.

Piemonte Pizzeria   If you're craving the thin, crispy crust and zesty toppings of a well made pizza, then come to Piemonte, where 8-inch pizzas are served at reasonable prices. Toppings include salami and cheese or more startling options like "Pizza Yellow Pages," a mixture of cheese, tomato, tuna, and banana. Less commendable are the pasta choices—portions are generous, but the bland sauce of a vegetarian cannelloni seemed to serve double duty as a tomato and basil soup. Stick to the pizza and you should leave the dark, slightly smoky interior of Piemonte well satisfied.

2 Clarendon St., Derry, Co. Derry. © 028/7126-6828. Dinner main courses £5–£7 ($7.25–$12). V. Daily 5pm–midnight.

WORTH A SPLURGE

Ardmore Room Restaurant 😊😊 CONTINENTAL   Lunch in this pretty dining room draws many business types, who can relax in what was once a billiard room overlooking gardens while enjoying a superb meal. In the evening, there's a soft, romantic ambience. Among the outstanding specialties are monkfish accompanied by vegetables with ginger and balsamic vinaigrette, and brill poached in champagne with dill butter sauce. There's an extensive international wine list, as well as an extraordinary selection of home-baked specialty breads.

Beech Hill Country House Hotel, 32 Ardmore Rd. © 028/7134-9279. www.beech-hill.com. Reservations strongly recommended. Lunch £16 ($23); dinner £22–£30 ($32–44). MC, V. Daily 12:30–2:30pm and 6:30–9:30pm.

SHOPPING

The city center of Derry offers some fine shopping, including two modern multistory malls: the Richmond Centre, within the city walls, facing the Diamond at the corner of Shipquay and Ferryquay Streets; and the new **Foyleside Shopping Centre,** just outside the walls. In general, shops are open Monday through Saturday from 9am to 5:30pm. Shops in the two large shopping centers, however, are open later on Thursday and Friday, until 9pm.

Austin & Co., Ltd. This is the city's landmark three-story Victorian-style department store, specializing in fashions, perfumes, china, crystal, and linens. In fact, this is Ireland's oldest department store, established in 1839. The coffee shop on the third floor looks out on a panorama of the city (see "Great Deals on Dining," above). The Diamond. © 028/7126-1817.

Bookworm Bookshop. This shop specializes in books on Irish history, politics, poetry, art, and fiction, as well as maps, guides, and postcards. It's situated at the corner of London Street. 18–20 Bishop St. © 028/7128-2727.

Derry Craft Village This unique shopping complex is located in the heart of the city near the Tower, with entrances on Shipquay and Magazine streets. The 16th- to 19th-century architecture reflects Old Derry, and houses retail shops, workshops, residential units, and a thatched-cottage pub. Shipquay St. © 028/7126-0329.

The McGilloway Gallery Ken McGilloway presents the work of contemporary Irish painters in his small gallery within the old city. The quality of the rotating exhibitions is particularly fine. Ken McGilloway has organized touring exhibitions of Irish painters, which have traveled throughout Ireland and to America. 6 Shipquay St. © 028/7136-6011.

MTM If you've left home without your favorite music or you're looking for something more local on the Irish traditional scene, come to this store. This is also where you can book tickets for major concerts and plays. Richmond Centre. © 028/7137-1970.

DERRY AFTER DARK

One thing to keep in mind as you're sketching out your after-dark plans is that Derry is one of Ireland's most youthful cities—roughly 40% of its population is under 30 years of age. This fact, coupled with an 18-year-old drinking age, means that the night scene is driven mostly by the young, and that there are few, if any, gray hairs to be seen in the hottest spots. The truth is that on weekends, after one or two in the morning when the clubs empty, the city center can become a rather loud and volatile area until the night's revelers have gone home and tucked themselves in.

THE PUB SCENE

Pubs here rarely resemble the small cozy nooks you often find in the Republic. Instead, they tend to be rather grand by comparison and a bit theatrical, more like stage sets than parlors. In addition, Derry pubs are known for their music and communal quiz evenings, when teams compete against each other in a free-range Irish form of Trivial Pursuit. There are even pub debating contests, during which you'll hear Irish eloquence at its well-lubricated best.

Along **Waterloo Street,** just outside the city walls, are a handful of Derry's most traditional and popular pubs, known for their live music and simply as the place to be. **The Dungloe, the Gweedore,** and **Peador O'Donnells** are three of these well-established hot spots. Walk from one end of Waterloo to the other, which will take you all of 2 minutes, and you'll likely find the bar for you.

In addition to Sandinos Cafe Bar (see below), gay and lesbian travelers might want to check out **Ascension,** at 64 Strand Rd. It's open until 1am most days and has free disco on Tuesdays and Thursdays and karaoke on Sundays.

The Clarendon   This inviting bar offers more quiet and calm than most of Derry's bars. It's a congenial pub for those who have broken 30 and are somewhere beyond the sonic boom. You can have a conversation here as well as a drink. Sundays and Tuesdays are quiz nights, when you can display whatever wisdom might have come with your years. 48 Strand Rd. ✆ **028/7126-3705.**

River Inn/Glue Pot   These two adjoining bars make up the oldest pub in Derry. The downstairs River Inn inhabits cellars opened to the thirsty public in 1684—if you've already kissed the Blarney Stone, why not kiss these revered walls? The upstairs Glue Pot is a more modern cocktail bar, not as appealing as the cellars, but a good deal more appealing than its name. Shipquay St. ✆ **028/7137-1965.**

Sandinos Cafe Bar   In 1999, the *Irish Times* named this tiny place one of the 100 top pubs in Ireland. It's certainly one of Derry's trendiest bars, where many of the city's gays and lesbians and literary folks prefer to settle in for the evening. Its "South of the Border" theme refers to the States' Mexican border, not to the North's border on the Republic. There are blues on Friday, jazz on Saturday, and an open mike for local poets every Sunday. In this intriguing shoebox of a bar, 30 is a quorum, so come early to secure a place for the evening. Water St. ✆ **028/7130-9297.**

THE CLUB SCENE

Provided you're under 230 and have no plans to be a piano tuner, there are several places where you'll want to be seen if not heard. Two multi-entertainment complexes stand out. First, there's **Squires Night Club,** 33 Shipquay St. (✆ **028/7126-6017**), behind the Townsman bar. Once you pay the cover charge, usually £2 to £5 ($2.85–$7.10), you can make your way up to the **VIP** or farther back to the 1,200-capacity voxbox. Second, there's **Earth** (possibly recognizable as such), 122–124 Strand Rd. (✆ **028/7130-9372**), where your club choices are **Café Roc** and **Coles Bar. The Strand,** 35–38 Strand Rd. (✆ **028/7126-0494**), features a classy bar serving mostly pub grub, and downstairs, an open venue for live bands. On weekend nights, in the bar, the tables are moved aside and the Strand morphs into a nightclub for the 20-plus crowd.

The night scene in Derry, like anywhere else, is a movable feast, so be sure to check the current *What's On?* listings.

PERFORMING ARTS

Derry has long been associated with the arts, especially theater, poetry, and music. While its financial resources have been modest, its commitment remains inventive and tenacious.

The **Millennium Forum** (© **028/7126-4426;** www.millenniumforum. co.uk), which opened in September of 2001, is a massive theater complex that is now the city's principal venue for opera, theater, ballet, musicals, and pantomime. Tickets run 5€ to 50€ ($4.35–$44), although most events cost between 8.25€ and 17€ ($7.25–$15). The Forum is located inside the walled city, just to the left after entering through the Shipquay Gate.

Other principal venues for concerts, plays, and poetry readings are the **Guild Hall,** Shipquay Place (© **028/7136-5151**); the **Foyle Arts Centre,** Lawrence Hill (© **028/7126-6657**); the **Playhouse,** 5–7 Artillery St. (© **028/ 7126-8027**); and the **Rialto,** 5 Market St. (© **028/7126-0516**). Ticket prices for most performances range from £12 to £15 ($17–$22).

7 The Sperrin Mountains

40 miles (64km) E to W along the Londonderry-Tyrone border

The Sperrin Mountains slowly rise up out of County Tyrone, southeast of Derry, reaching their highest point at Sawel, from which you can see as far as the Foyle Estuary and across the Northern Ireland countryside to Lough Neagh and the Mournes. This is splendid wide-open walking country that golden plover, red grouse, and thousands upon thousands of sheep call home.

In the Sperrins, you won't be likely to find the tallest, oldest, deepest, or most famous of anything in Ireland. Even the highest peak in the range—Sawel at 2,204 feet (672m)—is an easy climb. This is Ireland in a minor key, largely unsung and unspoiled. You'll find mostly wildflowers here, rather than formal gardens; cottages rather than castles. All the same, gold has been found in these mountains. Poetry, too. Seamus Heaney grew up on the edge of the Sperrins and found words to suit their subtle splendor.

Chances are you'll spend your time here exploring the dark russet blanket bogs and purple heathland, the gorse-covered hillsides, and the lovely forest parks, whether on foot, cycle, or horseback. For the more acquisitive, there are salmon and trout to be hooked on the Foyle System from Strabane to Omagh, as well as game to shoot on the moors. There are also a handful of first-rate historical museums and sites for the whole family. And, as minor destinations for a morning walk or an afternoon drive, there's no shortage of standing stones (about a thousand have been counted), high crosses, dolmens, and hill forts—more reminders that every last bit of bog on this island has its own slew of stories.

GETTING THERE   Ulsterbus (© **028/9033-3000**) provides regular coach service to Cookstown from Belfast and Derry. By car, take M1 from Belfast. From Derry, A5 and A6 are both good routes.

VISITOR INFORMATION   There are four nationally networked tourist information centers in County Tyrone. The **Cookstown Centre** at 48 Molesworth St., Cookstown (© **028/8676-6727**), is open July and August, Monday through Saturday 9am to 5pm and 2 to 4pm Sunday; the rest of the year the hours remain the same with the exception of Sunday, when the office is closed. The **Kilmaddy Centre** on Ballgawley Road (off A4), Dungannon (© **028/8776-7259**), is open year-round from Monday to Thursday, 9am to 5pm, with Friday and weekend hours in the spring and summer. The **Omagh Centre** at 1 Market St., Omagh (© **028/8224-7831**), is open Easter through September, Monday through Saturday, 9am to 5pm; and October through Easter, Monday through Friday, 9am to 5pm. The **Strabane Centre** on

Abercorn Square, Strabane (© **028/7188-3735**), is open from April to October, Monday through Friday 9:30am to 5pm, with Saturday hours during the summer months.

SEEING THE SIGHTS

Grant Ancestral Home   This farm cottage was the home of the ancestors of Ulysses S. Grant, 18th president of the United States. Grant's maternal great-grandfather, John Simpson, was born here and emigrated to Pennsylvania in 1738 at the age of 22. The cottage has two rooms with mud floors and has been restored and furnished with period pieces, including a settle bed and dresser. The site includes a visitor center with an audiovisual presentation, a tearoom, and various exhibits, including a collection of typical 18th-century agricultural implements.

Dergina, Ballygawley, Co. Tyrone. © **028/7188-3735**. Admission £1.50 ($2.20) adults, 75p ($1.10) seniors and children. Apr–Sept Mon–Sat noon–5pm, Sun 2–6pm. 20 miles (32km) southeast of Omagh off A4.

Sperrin Heritage Centre   Here, in the heart of the Sperrins, is *the* place to get the local bearings and background. A range of computerized presentations and other exhibits introduce the history, culture, geology, and wildlife of the region. This is a gold-mining area, and for a small additional fee (65p/92¢ adults, 35p/50¢ children) you'll get a chance to try your hand at panning for gold. A cafeteria, craft shop, and nature trail share the grounds.

274 Glenelly Rd., Cranagh, Co. Tyrone. © **028/8164-8142**. Admission £2.15 ($3.15) adults, £1.25 ($1.85) seniors and children, £6.70 ($9.75) family. Apr–Oct Mon–Fri 11am–5:30pm, Sat 11:30am–6pm, Sun 2–6pm. East of Plumbridge off B47.

Tyrone Crystal ⭐   With a 200-year-old tradition, this crystal factory is one of Ireland's oldest and best known. Visitors are welcome to tour the operation and see glass being blown and crafted, carved, and engraved by hand. A 25-minute audiovisual presentation tells the story of the development of Tyrone Crystal, a showroom displays the finished products, and a very good cafe adds sustenance.

Oaks Rd., Killybrackey, Dungannon, Co. Tyrone. © **028/8772-5335**. Admission £2 ($2.90) adults, seniors and children under 12 free. Hours vary; call ahead to confirm. Tours every 30 min. 2 miles (3km) east of the town.

Ulster-American Folk Park ⭐⭐   This outdoor museum presents the story of emigration from this part of rural Ireland to America in the 18th and 19th centuries. There are reconstructions of the thatched cottages the emigrants left behind, and prototypes of the log cabins that became their homes on the American frontiers. The park developed around the homestead where Thomas Mellon was born in 1813. He went to Pittsburgh and prospered to the point where his son Andrew became one of the world's richest men. Walk-through exhibits include a forge, weaver's cottage, smokehouse, schoolhouse, post office, Sperrin Mountain famine cabin, and full-scale replica of an emigrant ship in a dockside area that features original buildings from the ports of Derry, Belfast, and Newry. A self-guided tour of all the exhibits, which are staffed by interpreters in period costume, takes about 2 hours. Musical events that tie in with the Ulster-American theme, such as a bluegrass music festival in September, are hosted on the site each year.

Mellon Rd., Castletown, Camphill, Omagh, Co. Tyrone. © **028/8224-3292**. www.folkpark.com. Admission £4 ($5.80) adults, £2.50 ($3.65) seniors and children 5–16, £10 ($15) family. Oct–Easter Mon–Fri 10:30am–5pm, Sun 11am–5pm; Easter–Sept Mon–Sat 11am–6pm, Sun 11:30am–6:30pm. 3 miles (5km) north of Omagh on A5.

Moments   **A Walk in the Sperrins**

If you can spare half a day for this special part of Northern Ireland, take B47 from Draperstown and drive 10 miles (16km) west to the village of Sperrin, leave the car by the pub, and walk north along the road into the hills toward the peak of Sawel. After 2 miles (3km), leave the road and make for the summit (about an hour's walk), with its views of Lough Neagh, the Foyle estuary, and the Mournes. Continue west on the ridge to Dart Mountain, about half an hour away, then turn south for the 45-minute walk to the village of Cranagh, where the Sperrin Heritage Centre is located. Another 45 minutes will bring you back to your car.

Wilson Ancestral Home   This small thatched, whitewashed cottage on the slopes of the Sperrin Mountains was the home of Judge James Wilson, grandfather of Woodrow Wilson, 28th president of the United States. James Wilson left the house in 1807 at the age of 20. It contains some of the family's original furniture, including a tiny out-shot bed (sleeping nook) in the kitchen close to the fire, larger curtained beds, and a portrait of the president's grandfather over the fireplace. Wilsons still occupy the modern farmhouse next door. *Note:* Opening hours are subject to change; phone in advance.

Off Plumbridge Rd., Dergalt, Strabane, Co. Tyrone. ✆ 028/8224-3292. www.strabanedc.org.uk. Admission £1 ($1.45) adults, 50p (75¢) children. Apr–Sept Tues–Sun 2–5pm. Opening hours subject to change; it's best to phone in advance of visit.

ACCOMMODATIONS YOU CAN AFFORD

The Grange 🌟 *Kids*   There's loads of character in this charming little cottage near the Ballygawley roundabout and the Folk Park. It dates to 1720, but has been thoroughly modernized. Mrs. Lyttle is the hostess, and her rooms (two doubles and one single) are done up nicely with sturdy farmhouse furniture and homey bedspreads. Mrs. Lyttle welcomes small children.

15 Grange Rd., Ballygawley. ✆ 028/8556-8053. 3 units. £19 ($28) single; £36 ($52) double. Reduction for children. Rates include full breakfast. No credit cards. Free parking. Closed Dec–Mar. **Amenities:** Laundry facilities; sitting room. *In room:* TV.

Greenmount Lodge *Kids*   This large, first-rate guesthouse is set on a 150-acre farm. All the bedrooms were refurbished a few years back and are nicely appointed; four are family units. Mrs. Frances Reid, the friendly hostess, is a superb cook; both breakfasts and evening meals are a home-style delight.

58 Greenmount Rd., Gortaclare, Omagh BT79 0YE, Co. Tyrone. ✆ 028/8284-1325. Fax 028/8284-0019. greenmountlodge@linone.net. 8 units. £42 ($61) double. Reduction for children. Rates include full breakfast. Dinner £13 ($19). MC, V. Free parking. 8 miles (13km) southeast of Omagh on A5. *In room:* TV, TEL, tea/coffeemaker.

SELF-CATERING

Sperrin Clachan   This restored *clachan,* or family cottage compound, sits beside the Sperrin Heritage Centre in the beautiful Glenelly Valley. It makes an ideal base for exploring the natural riches and cultural legacy of the Sperrin region, as well as the city of Derry, only 25 miles (40km) to the north. Each cottage has everything you'll need to set up house, including central heating, a fully equipped kitchen, and an open fireplace. There are four cottages in all; each sleeps two, three, four, or five. In addition to these, Rural Cottage Holidays offers a wide array of other traditional cottages in the region, including the award-winning, four-star Glenelly Cottages.

Glenelly Valley, Cranagh, Co. Tyrone. ⁑ Rural Cottage Holidays Ltd., St. Anne's Court, 59 North St., Belfast BT1 1NB. © **028/9024-1100.** Fax 028/9024-1198. 4 cottages (sleep 2, 3, 4, and 5 people). £190–£290 ($276–$421) per week depending on cottage and season. **Amenities:** TV, full kitchen, fridge, oven/stove, microwave, dishwasher, washing machine.

GREAT DEALS ON DINING

Mellon Country Inn ⭐ INTERNATIONAL   Located 1¼ miles (2km) north of the Ulster-American Folk Park, this old-world country inn combines an Irish theme with a connection to the Mellons of Pennsylvania. One of the dining rooms, the Pennsylvania Room, has log-cabin-style decor. The menu includes simple fare—burgers, soup, salads, and ploughman's platters—as well as elegant dishes such as lobster Newburg, beef Stroganoff, coquilles St.-Jacques, and sole bonne femme. The house specialty is Tyrone black steak, a locally bred hormone-free beef. Food is available all day on a hot and cold buffet, and you can also order a late breakfast or afternoon tea.

134 Beltany Rd., Omagh, Co. Tyrone. © **028/8166-1244.** Reservations not required. Dinner main courses £7–£18 ($10–$26). AE, DC, MC, V. Daily 10:30am–10pm.

8 Enniskillen & the Fermanagh Lakelands

Enniskillen is 83 miles (134km) SW of Belfast, 61 miles (98km) SW of Derry, 52 miles (84km) W of Armagh, 27 miles (44km) SW of Omagh, 108 miles (174km) NW of Dublin, and 168 miles (271km) NE of Shannon

Tucked in the extreme southwest corner of Northern Ireland, County Fermanagh is a premier resort area dominated by **Lough Erne,** a long lake dotted with 154 islands and rimmed by countless alcoves and inlets. It has 50 miles (81km) of cruising waters—the least congested in Europe—ranging from a shallow channel in some places to a 5-mile (8km) width in others. The total signposted driving circuit around the lake is 65 miles (105km).

The hub of this lakeland paradise, wedged between the upper and lower branches of Lough Erne, is **Enniskillen,** a delightful resort town that was the medieval seat of the Maguire clan and a major crossroads between Ulster and Connaught. Both Oscar Wilde and Samuel Beckett were once students here at the royal school.

At the northern tip of the lake is **Belleek,** sitting right on the border with the Republic of Ireland, and known the world over for delicate bone chinaware. At the southern end of the lake is County Cavan and another slice of border with the Irish Republic. The surrounding countryside holds diverse attractions, from stately homes at **Florence Court** and **Castle Coole** to the unique **Marble Arch Caves.** In the waters lie myriad islands, Devenish and Boa being two of the most interesting.

In medieval times, a chain of island monasteries stretched across the waters of Lough Erne, establishing it as a haven for contemplatives. Making certain allowances for less lofty minds, the Fermanagh Lakelands remain a great place to get away from it all and to gaze, in a phrase from Hopkins, at the "pied beauty" of it all.

GETTING AROUND   The best way to get around Enniskillen and the surrounding lakelands of Lough Erne is by car or bicycle. The total signposted driving circuit around the lake is 65 miles (105km).

GETTING THERE   **Ulsterbus** (© 028/9033-3000) provides regular coach service to Enniskillen from Belfast. **Bus Eireann** (© 01/836-6111) offers daily service from Dublin and Sligo.

By car, take M1 from Belfast or A5 from Derry.

VISITOR INFORMATION   Contact the **Fermanagh Tourist Information Centre,** Wellington Road, Enniskillen, County Fermanagh (© 028/6632-3110), open year-round Monday through Friday from 9am to 5pm, with extended hours Easter through September. For an introduction to the Fermanagh Lakelands on the Web, take a look at **www.fermanagh-online.com**.

SEEING THE SIGHTS

Belleek Pottery   With the possible exception of Waterford crystal, Belleek china is the product most readily identified throughout the world as a symbol of the finest Irish craftsmanship. Established in 1857, this pottery enterprise produces distinctive and delicate porcelain china made into tableware, vases, ornaments, and other pieces. The visitor center has a museum showing the china from its earliest days to the present. Tours are conducted weekdays every 20 minutes, with the last tour at 3:30pm. The coffee shop serves tea, coffee, snacks, and a hot lunch.

Belleek, Co. Fermanagh. © 028/6865-8501. www.belleek.ie. Free admission; tours £2.50 ($3.65) adults and children over 12, £1.50 ($2.20) seniors. Apr–June and Sept Mon–Fri 9am–6pm, Sat 10am–6pm, Sun 2–6pm; July–Aug Mon–Fri 9am–6pm, Sat 10am–6pm, Sun 11am–6pm; Oct Mon–Fri 9am–5:30pm, Sat 10am–5:30pm, Sun 2–6pm; Nov–Mar Mon–Fri 9am–5:30pm. Tours begin weekdays every 30 min. Last tour Fri 3:30pm.

Castle Coole   On the east bank of Lower Lough Erne, this quintessential neo-classical mansion was designed by James Wyatt for the earl of Belmore and completed in 1796. Its rooms include a lavish state bedroom hung with crimson silk, said to have been prepared for George IV. Other features include a Chinese-style sitting room, magnificent woodwork, fireplaces, and furniture dating to the 1830s. A nearly 1,500-acre woodland estate surrounds the house. A classical music series runs from May to October at the castle; tickets cost between £10 and £15 ($15–$22).

Belfast-Enniskillen road (A4), Enniskillen, Co. Fermanagh. © 028/6632-2690. House £3 ($4.35) adults, £1.30 ($1.90) children, £8 ($12) family; grounds £2 ($2.90) car. Apr and Sept Sat–Sun and bank holidays 1–6pm; May–Aug Fri–Wed 1–6pm. On the east bank of Lower Lough Erne, about 1½ miles (2.5km) southeast of Enniskillen.

Devenish Island ★★   This is the most extensive of the ancient Christian sites in Lough Erne. In the 6th century, St. Molaise founded a monastic community here, to which the Augustinian Abbey of St. Mary was added in the 12th century. In other words, this is hallowed ground; hallowed all the more by the legend that the prophet Jeremiah is buried somewhere nearby—if you can figure that one out. The intact 12th-century round tower was erected with Vikings in mind. The island is a marvelous mélange of remnants and ruins, providing a glimpse into the lake's mystical past. While you're in the spirit, be sure to explore Boa and White Islands, with their extraordinary carved stone figures, and bring your camera (see "Island Hopping," below).

Open site except for tower and museum. © 028/6862-1588. Admission 75p ($1.10). Ferry from Trory Point (4 miles/6.5km from Enniskillen on A32) Apr–Sept daily at 10am, 1pm, 3pm and 5pm. Round-trip fare £2.25 ($3.30) adults, £1.20 ($1.75) seniors and children. 1½ mile downstream from Enniskillen.

Enniskillen Castle   Dating from the 15th century, this magnificent stone fortress sits overlooking Lough Erne on the western edge of town. It incorporates three museums in one: the medieval castle, with its unique twin-turreted Watergate tower, once the seat of the Maguires, chieftains of Fermanagh; the county museum, with exhibits on the area's history, wildlife, and landscape; and the museum of the famous Royal Inniskilling Fusiliers, with a collection of uniforms, weapons, and medals dating from the 17th century. Other exhibits include life-size figurines and 3-D models of old-time castle life.

Castle Barracks, Enniskillen, Co. Fermanagh. ✆ **028/6632-5000.** castle@fermanagh.gov.uk. Admission £2 ($2.90) adults, £1.50 ($2.20) students and seniors, £1 ($1.45) children, £5 ($7.25) family. Oct–Apr Mon 2–5pm, Tues–Fri 10am–5pm; May–June and Sept Mon 2–5pm, Tues–Fri 10am–5pm, Sat 2–5pm; July–Aug Tues–Fri 10am–5pm, Sat–Mon 2–5pm.

Florence Court   One of the most beautifully situated houses in Northern Ireland, this 18th-century Palladian mansion is set among dramatic hills, 8 miles (13km) southwest of Upper Lough Erne and Enniskillen. Originally the seat of the earls of Enniskillen, its interior is rich in rococo plasterwork and antique Irish furniture, while its exterior has a fine walled garden, an icehouse, and a water wheel–driven sawmill. The forest park offers a number of trails, one leading to the top of Mount Cuilcagh (nearly 2,200 ft.), and the Marble Arch Caves are nearby (see below). There's also a tearoom.

Florence Court, Co. Fermanagh. ✆ **028/6634-8249.** ufcest@smtp.ntrust.org.uk. House £3 ($5) adults, £1.50 ($2.50) children, £8 ($2.50) family; grounds £2 ($2.90) per car. Apr–May and Sept Sat–Sun and bank holidays 1–6pm; June–Aug Wed–Mon 1–6pm. Located off A32.

Marble Arch Caves 🌟 *Kids*   Located west of Upper Lough Erne and 12 miles (19km) from Enniskillen near the Florence Court estate, these caves are among the finest in Europe for exploring underground rivers, winding passages, and hidden chambers. Electrically powered boat tours take visitors underground, and knowledgeable guides explain the origins of the amazing stalactites and stalagmites. Tours last 75 minutes and leave at 15-minute intervals. The caves are occasionally closed after heavy rains, so phone ahead before making the trip.

Marlbank, Florence Court (near the Florence Court estate), Co. Fermanagh. ✆ **028/6634-8855.** Admission £6 ($8.70) adults, £4 ($5.80) students and seniors, £3 ($4.35) children under 18, £14 ($20) family. Reservations recommended. Late Mar to June and Sept, daily 10am–4:30pm (last tour at 4:30pm); July–Aug daily 10am–5pm (last tour at 5pm). Off A32, west of Upper Lough Erne and 12 miles (19km) from Enniskillen.

OUTDOOR PURSUITS
ON OR AROUND LOUGH ERNE
BICYCLING   Several of the watersports and activity centers in the area also rent bicycles, such as **Erne Tours** and **Lakeland Canoe Center** (see "Watersports," below). Bicycles are also available from **Corralea Activity Centre,** Belcoo (✆ **028/6638-6668**); **Out & Out Activities,** 501 Rosscor, Belleek (✆ **028/6865-8105**); and **Marble Arch Cycle Hire,** 69 Marlbank Rd., Florencecourt (✆ **028/6634-8320**). Daily bike rental runs £7 to £10 ($9.94–$14). For cycle tours with **Kingfisher Cycle Trail,** contact Pat Collum at the Tourist Information Centre, Wellington Road, Enniskillen (✆ **028/ 6632-0121;** www.cycleireland.com).

BIRD-WATCHING   These lakelands are prime bird-watching territory. You'll find whooper swans, great-crested grebes, golden plovers, curlews, corncrakes, kingfishers, herons, merlins, peregrines, kestrels, and sparrow hawks, just to mention a few. On Upper Lough Erne, the primary habitats are the reed swamps, flooded drumlins, and fen; on the lower lake, the habitats of choice are the less-visited islands and the hay meadows. Two important bird-watching preserves are at the **Crom Estate** and the **Castlecaldwell Forest and Islands.**

BOATING   If you want to spend a week or more afloat, this is one of the places to do it. Lough Erne is an explorer's dream, and you can take that dream all the way to the Atlantic if you want. The price range for 2/4-berth to 8-berth fully equipped cruisers runs from £500 to £1,200 ($725–$1,740) per week including VAT, depending on the season and the size of the boat. The many local cruiser-hire companies include **Belleek Charter Cruising,** Belleek (© **028/6865-8027;** fax 028/6865-8793; www.angelfire.com/co/belleekcruising); and **Erne Marine,** Bellanaleck (© **028/6634-8267;** fax 028/6634-8866; www.ernemarine.com).

FISHING   The Fermanagh Lakes are an angler's heaven. If you can't catch a fish here, you must have been one in a past life. The best time for salmon is from February to mid-June, and for trout, either mid-March through June or mid-August until late September. As for the coarse fishing, there are about a dozen species awaiting your line in the area's lakes and rivers. If you've left time for advance planning and consultation, contact the Fisheries Conservancy Board, 1 Mahon Rd., Portadown BT62 3EE (© **028/3833-4666**). For on-the-spot info, tackle, and bait, try **Home, Field, & Stream,** 33 Scotch St., Enniskillen (© **028/6632-2114**). For locally arranged game fishing, call or drop in on **Melvin Angling,** Garrison, County Fermanagh (© **028/6865-8194**). All necessary permits and licenses can be had at the **Fermanagh Tourist Information Centre** (see "Visitor Information," above).

GOLF   There are two 18-hole courses in the Lakelands, both in Enniskillen: the **Enniskillen Golf Club,** in the Castle Coole estate (© **028/6632-5250**), with greens fees of £15 ($22) on weekdays and £18 ($26) on weekends; and, 3½ miles (5.5km) north of Enniskillen, the **Castle Hume Golf Club,** Castle Hume (© **028/6632-7077;** fax 028/6632-7076; www.castlehumegolf.com), with greens fees of £15 ($22) on weekdays and £20 ($29) on weekends.

HORSEBACK RIDING   The **Ulster Lakeland Equestrian Centre,** Necarne Castle, Irvinestown (© **028/6862-1919**), is an international equestrian center offering full equestrian holidays. Pony trekking and riding lessons are available from **Drumhoney Stables,** Lisnarick (© **028/6862-1892**); and from **Lakeview Riding Centre,** Leggs, Belleek (© **028/6865-8163**).

ISLAND HOPPING   Independent boatmen offer ferry crossings to some of the many islands in Lough Erne. From April to September, a ferry runs to Devenish Island from Trory Point, 4 miles (6.5km) from Enniskillen on A32. From April through August, a ferry runs to White Island, departing from Castle Archdale Marina, (© **028/6862-1333** or mobile 0836/787123), 10 miles

---

⌒Tips Arts & Crafts

If you'd rather sketch a trout than snag it, you might want to contact the **Ardess Craft Centre,** near Kesh (© **028/6863-1267**). It offers a range of courses, from drawing and painting to stone walling and weaving from May to September. Room and board is an available option. For a complete guide to crafts in the Fermanagh region, go to **www.fermanaghcraft.com.**

(16km) from Enniskillen on the Kesh road. Departures April through June are on Sunday only, every hour on the hour from 11am to 6pm with the exception of 1pm. July and August the ferry runs daily, with the same sailing times. The round-trip fare is £3 ($4.35) for adults and £2 ($2.90) for children. Be sure to visit Devenish, Boa, and White Islands. Bridges connect Boa Island to the shore.

MOTORBOATS   On Lower Lough Erne, north of town, motorboats can be rented from **Manor House Marine,** Killadeas (© **028/6862-8100;** www. manormarine.com). Charges average £40 ($58) for a half day or £60 ($87) for a full day.

SIGHTSEEING CRUISES   Erne Tours Ltd., Enniskillen (© **028/ 6632-2882**), operates cruises on Lower Lough Erne on board the MV *Kestrel,* a 63-seat cruiser, departing from the Round 'O' Jetty, Brook Park, Enniskillen. Trips, including a stop at Devenish Island, last just under 2 hours. There are three sailings daily in July and August, and reduced sailings in May, June, and September. Cruises on Upper Lough Erne are operated by the **Share Holiday Village,** Smith's Strand, Lisnaskea (© **028/6772-2122;** www.sharevillage.org). These 1½-hour trips are conducted on board the *Inishcruiser,* a 57-passenger ship. Sailings are scheduled in Easter through September on Sunday at 2:30pm (July and Aug Thurs–Sun at 2:30pm). The fare is £7 ($10) for adults, and £6 ($8.70) for seniors and children under 18. Share Centre also offers other watersports activities and self-catering chalets.

WALKING   The southwestern branch of the **Ulster Way** follows the western shores of Lough Erne, between the lake and the border. The area is full of great walks. One excellent 7-mile, (11km), 3- to 7-hr. hike is from a starting point near Florence Court and the Marble Arch Caves to the summit of **Mount Cuilagh** (2,188 ft.). A trail map is included in the Northern Ireland Tourist Board's *Information Guide to Walking.*

WATERSPORTS   The **Lakeland Canoe Center,** Castle Island, Enniskillen (© **028/6632-4250**), is a watersports center based on an island west of downtown. It offers a full day of canoeing and other sports, including archery, cycling, dinghy sailing, and windsurfing, from £12 ($17) per person per day. Camping and simple accommodations are also available. The **Share Holiday Village,** Smith's Strand, Lisnaskea (© **028/6672-2122;** www.sharevillage.org), offers a range of watersports: sailing, canoeing, windsurfing, and banana-skiing. Other watersports centers include the **Boa Island Activity Centre,** Tudor Farm, Kesh (© **028/6863-1943;** www.tudorfarm.com); and the **Drumrush Watersports Centre,** Kesh (© **028/6863-1578;** www.drumrush.co.uk).

ACCOMMODATIONS YOU CAN AFFORD

Belmore Court Motel *Value*   If you're just looking for a bed on which to crash, this newish three-story motel offers a variety of accommodations, from single rooms to family rooms, at rock bottom prices. It's the same motel principle as in the US: bland decor, no amenities, but rates that you really can't beat. Most rooms have kitchenettes, and about a third of the units have two bedrooms or a suite set-up of bedroom and sitting room. Guest rooms are non-descript but inoffensive, done up with pastel colors, standard furnishings in light woods, floral fabrics, down comforters, and writing desks. The motel is on the east edge of town, within walking distance of all the major sights and shops.

Temp Rd., Enniskillen, Co. Fermanagh. © 028/6632-6633. Fax 028/6632-6362. www.motel.co.uk. 30 units. £40 ($60) double, £42 ($66) double with minikitchen. Continental breakfast £3 ($4.26). AE, MC, V. Free parking. *In room:* TV, mini kitchen or tea/coffeemaker.

WORTH A SPLURGE

Castle Leslie 🐾🐾🐾 *(Finds)*   What do W. B. Yeats, Winston Churchill, and Mick Jagger have in common? They've all loved Castle Leslie, a quintessential Victorian retreat just across the border in County Monaghan. A stay here is one of Ireland's unique surprises, an experience well worth whatever detour it takes. The 1,000-acre estate, with its three lakes (famous for pike) and ancient hardwood forests, casts a relaxing spell, and the great house—27,000 square feet of history—is as comfortable as an old slipper. Sammy Leslie, together with her remarkable family and staff, provide the quintessential Victorian retreat.

This is also a place of astounding treasures—the bridle worn by Wellington's horse Copenhagen at Waterloo, Wordsworth's harp, the Bechstein grand on which Wagner composed *Tristan and Isolde,* and Winston Churchill's baby clothes, to mention only a few. The greatest treasures are the stories you will take away with you. Each unique, anecdote-rich guestroom has its own special feature—a clawfoot tub in an alcove near the bed, a spectacular view in a bay window, or perhaps a beefy four-poster bed. (The hotel's website has photos of each room, so you can book your favorite in advance). The meals here (see below) alone are worth the drive. Be advised that the Castle is most suitable for adults—no bookings are taken for those under 18 years of age. Multiple-night specials are available on and off-season.

Glaslough, Co. Monaghan. ✆ **047/88109.** Fax 047/88256. www.castle-leslie.ie. 14 units. 184€–248€ ($167–$224) double. Includes full Irish breakfast. MC, V. Free parking. Drive through the center of Glaslough to castle gates. **Amenities:** Restaurant (Continental); tennis courts; drawing room. *In room:* TV, hair dryer.

SELF-CATERING

Shannon-Erne Luxury Cottages   These comfortable traditional cottages, located on the banks of the Shannon-Erne Waterway, are ideal for couples or families wanting to take full advantage of the splendid fishing, walking, boating, bird-watching, and exploring offered by the Lakelands. What's more, taking to the waterways could not be more convenient, as a small fleet of day cruisers is moored just beyond the cottages' front yard. You'll find everything you need to set up house here, including clothes washers. All cottages have an open fire as well as central heating.

Teemore, Co. Fermanagh. c/o Shannon-Erne Cottages and Cruisers, Teemore Business Comples, Teemore, Enniskillen, BT92 9BL. ✆ **028/6774-8893.** Fax 028/6774-8493. www.shannon-erne.co.uk. 6 cottages (sleep 3, 4, 5, and 6 people). £275–£350 ($399–$508) per week depending on cottage and season. **Amenities:** TV; kitchen; washer/dryer.

GREAT DEALS ON DINING

Saddlers   IRISH/PUB GRUB   An equestrian atmosphere prevails at this restaurant over the Horse Show Bar. Barbecued pork ribs, steaks, surf-and-turf, burgers, and mixed grills are the hearty choices, along with local seafoods, salads, pizzas, pastas, and a house special of sirloin Sandeman with bacon, shallots, peppercorns, and port-wine sauce.

66 Belmore St., Enniskillen. ✆ **028/6632-6223.** Reservations not necessary. Lunch main courses £5–£7 ($7.25–$10); dinner main courses £8–£14 ($12–$20). MC, V. Daily noon–4pm and 5:30–11pm.

WORTH A SPLURGE

Castle Leslie 🐾🐾🐾 CONTINENTAL   Dinner at Castle Leslie offers all the relaxed graciousness—and drama—of a prewar dinner party. The dining rooms in the great house look out on one of the estate's lovely lakes and on ancient hardwood forests. The view alone is a perfect appetizer. Sammy Leslie, trained at a fine Swiss culinary school, is largely responsible for the wizardry in the kitchen. The excellent cuisine is classic and French-influenced, with a well-chosen wine list. The menu changes to embrace what is freshest and most enticing to the chef; imagine starting with roast goat's-cheese salad with beetroot and hazelnuts, proceeding to honey roast quail, filet of salmon, or grilled filet of beef with Madeira sauce, and finishing with white chocolate crème brûlée. For more about the Castle, see "Accommodations You Can Afford," above.

Glaslough, Co. Monaghan. ⓒ **047/88109.** Fax 047/88256. Reservations required. Fixed-price dinner 44€ ($40); a la carte menu available. MC, V. Daily 7–9:30pm. Drive through center of Glaslough to castle gates.

ENNISKILLEN AFTER DARK

The best pub in the area is **Blakes of the Hollow** ⚔, 6 Church St., Enniskillen (ⓒ **028/6632-2143**). Opened in 1887, the pub has been in the Blake family ever since, retaining its original Victorian decor and ambience, with a long marble-topped mahogany bar and pinewood alcoves.

Plan an evening at the **Ardhowen Theatre,** Dublin Road, Enniskillen (ⓒ **028/6632-5440;** ardhowen.theatre@fermanagh.gov.uk), also known as the "Theatre by the Lakes," because of its enviable position overlooking Upper Lough Erne. This 300-seat lakeside theater presents a varied program of concerts, drama, cabarets, jazz, gospel, blues, and other types of modern music. Tickets run from £5 to £12 ($7.25–$17) for most performances; curtain time is usually 8pm.

Appendix:
Ireland In Depth

One of the first things the visitor in Ireland will notice is that the past lies all around the country, copious and stony, ensuring that every stage in Ireland's turbulent history stays vividly in mind. Far from being silent remnants of a dead age, ruins in this country speak volumes about how this landscape and this people have become what they are. Because, you see, the Irish don't abandon their monuments; they adapt them and rebuild them to meet the needs of the present. This is one of the most remarkable qualities of Ireland, a magical quality—the way the past lives on in the present.

But it's not an unambiguously *good* quality. Ireland often seems not so much inhabited as haunted by its past. For example, the worst rioting of the past decade in Northern Ireland broke out in 1996 around the Orange Day Parade, an event commemorating the 17th-century Battle of the Boyne, which solidified Protestant domination in Ireland and which to this day stirs Irish passions. During the War for Independence, when the homes of many of the Anglo-Irish gentry were destroyed, it was a family's record with its tenants that often decided its fate—families who had offered relief to tenants during the Great Famine, or who were otherwise known as benevolent landlords, were often spared the general devastation. Almost every inhabitant of Ireland's rural west can point out to you the local famine graveyard. These mass graves, in which more than a million of Ireland's people were put to rest, are usually unmarked, but their obscurity tells no less potent a tale. When the fields themselves speak so eloquently of past tragedies, it's not surprising that the historical memory of the Irish people is so remarkably acute.

Nonetheless, balanced against this Ireland of the memory, there's another side of the country that's entirely forward-looking, an Ireland that's moving into the 21st century without looking back. In the cities, there's a new prosperity and a new way of life that have little in common with the rural west. This is a young Ireland—almost half the country's population is under 25—to whom the problems of the past are simply not as pressing as the challenges of the present. Overall, the historical animosities that have fueled the conflict in Northern Ireland are on the wane, and many in the Republic are as baffled and frustrated as the rest of the world by the continuing climate of violence there. Joyce's Stephen Dedalus comments in *Ulysses* that "history is a nightmare from which I am trying to awake," and now it seems that much of the Irish population is succeeding in doing just that.

This is an exciting time to be visiting Ireland. It's easy to get caught up in the youthful energy of Galway or the vivacity of Dublin. A carnival atmosphere reigns during the major festivals, which follow each other in close succession throughout the year. And the kitchens of Ireland have never been so full of talent and creativity as they are now. Wherever you travel in Ireland, take some time to observe the landscape—the stories it contains speak of what Ireland and the Irish have been through, and what they're carrying with them into the future.

1 The Lay of the Land

Ireland covers roughly 32,600 square miles, making it about the same size as Maine or South Carolina. This island nation is 300 miles (483km) at its longest and 190 miles (306km) at its widest. Now, 300 miles may not be a daunting day's drive in Canada, Australia, or the United States, but as you'll soon discover, Irish miles have a pace of their own. Divided highways are limited to small belt-ways around Dublin, Cork, and Galway; the rest of the country's highways are narrow and pass through the center of every town. In the countryside, be pre-pared to share the road with all manner of farm machinery as well as herds of cows and sheep.

Ireland's coastline is so indented by jagged peninsulas that from any inland point the sea is never more than 70 miles (113km) distant. That glorious coastline measures more than 3,000 miles (4,800km) and encircles 9,000 miles (14,500km) of meandering rivers—the 230-mile (370km) Shannon is the longest—and some 800 lakes, the largest of which is Lough Neagh (153 sq. miles/246 km^2).

The island's **topography** has been compared to a saucer or a bowl: The inte-rior is flat, undramatic limestone plain (with some gentle hills), while the sur-rounding coastline is remarkably rugged and mountainous. The island's highest mountains—Macgillycuddy's Reeks, Mount Brandon, the Mweelrea Moun-tains, and Achill's peaks—are all at its very edge, where land meets sea, and its great sea cliffs, including Donegal's Slieve League, are among the highest in Europe.

Although it's at the same high latitude as Newfoundland, Ireland's **climate** is saved from frigid extremes by the warm waters of the Gulf Stream. You can even see palm trees in many places in the country, and in parts of the southwest, warmth and abundant rain conspire to support lush subtropical vegetation. The marine winds that buffet the west coast year-round create an environment that's too harsh for most plant life, though it's these same conditions that allow many alpine species to flourish here, at elevations much lower than normal.

These days, there aren't many **forests** to be found in Ireland, and most that are here have been planted. Back in Neolithic times, the countryside was clad in oak, ash, and rowan forests, some tiny remnants of which can still be found in isolated pockets around the country. Ireland's earliest inhabitants began to clear the central limestone plain for cultivation or grazing, and in Elizabethan times whole forests were felled and shipped to England. Since the beginning of this century, reforestation efforts have concentrated on large plantings of conifers and other evergreens, many in the national forests and in other wooded areas open to the public.

2 Ireland Today

What is easy for any visitor to miss or to underestimate about Ireland is the depth of the change occurring today, and its pace. The Ireland of today, which may present such a traditional face to the tourist, is increasingly defined and determined by its youth, whose sheer numbers and unconventional ways are cre-ating a generation gap of seismic proportions. For one thing, they aren't marry-ing and they aren't having children with anything approximating the regularity of their parents. In 1993, the Irish birth rate fell, for the first time in recorded history, below the minimum population-replacement rate of 2.1 children per woman of child-bearing age, and it continues to fall even further.

Ireland has long been a land of profound conflicts, and never more so than at present. To mention one, the terms *Irish* and *Roman Catholic* are assumed by many to be synonymous. The truth is that they have never meant the same thing, nor made lasting peace with each other. The Roman Catholicism preached by Patrick was transformed as fast as it was embraced by the Celts of Ireland. The Vatican, like the British royalty, found the Irish to be unruly and bent on taking their own road, regardless. For all their faith and devotion, Irish Catholics have never finally decided whether to trust or mistrust their hierarchy, appointed from Rome. Recent public scandals in the Church, followed not by candor but by cover-up, have only served to widen ancient misgivings. The 1996 referendum to permit legal divorce, as well as the decriminalizing of homosexuality and the passing of the abortion information law—all measures urged and supported by Ireland's first female president, Mary Robinson—point to an Ireland where the iron grip of Rome is being pried away a finger at a time.

But while Ireland today is increasingly prosperous, European, and committed to pluralistic human values, it is at the same time determined to preserve its rich legacy and distinct character. Though Irish-speaking and -reading citizens represent a small minority of the population, Irish-language writers, especially poets, continue to create new work, and Irish-language television and radio programs are common.

3 History 101

THE FIRST SETTLERS At the end of its last ice age, around the year 8000 B.C., Ireland warmed up to agreeable, even attractive, temperatures. Thus, with some degree of confidence, we can place the date for the first human habitation of the island somewhere between the late 8000s and the early 6000s B.C. Regardless of where in that span the date actually fell, Ireland seems to have been among the last lands in Europe to have felt the human footprint.

Ireland's first colonizers, Mesolithic Homo sapiens, walked, waded, or floated—depending on the status of the early land bridges—across the narrow strait from Britain in search of flint and, of course, food. They found both and stayed on, more or less uneventfully (from our perspective, at least), for a good 4,000 to 5,000 years. Their contribution to the future of Ireland may seem minimal, but most beginnings are. And they did, after all, begin the gene pool.

THE NEOLITHIC AGE The next momentous prehistoric event was the

Dateline

- 8000 B.C. Earliest human immigration to Ireland.
- 3500 B.C. Farmers and megalithic builders reach Ireland.
- 2000 B.C. First metalworkers come to Ireland.
- 700 B.C. Celtic settlement of Ireland begins.
- A.D. 432 Traditional date for Patrick's return to Ireland.
- 500–800 Ireland's monastic "Golden Age."
- 795 First Viking invasion.
- 841 The Norse build a sea fort on the River Liffey.
- 853 Danes take possession of the Norse settlement.
- 988 Dublin officially recognized as an Irish city.
- 1014 Battle of Clontarf. Brian Boru defeats the Danes.
- 1167–69 Norman invasion of Ireland.
- 1171 Henry II visits Ireland and claims feudal lordship.
- 1204 Dublin Castle becomes base of British power.
- 1297 First parliamentary sessions in Dublin.

continues

arrival of Neolithic farmers and herders, sometime around 3500 B.C. The Neolithic "revolution" was the first of many to come to Ireland a bit late, at least 5,000 years after its inception in the ancient Near East. The domestication of the human species—settled life, agriculture, animal husbandry—brought with it radically increased population, enhanced skills, stability, and all the implications of leisure. Unlike Ireland's Mesolithic hunters, who barely left a trace, this second wave of colonizers began at once to transform the island. They came with stone axes, which could fell a good-sized elm in less than an hour. The hardwood forests of Ireland, slashed and burned 1 hour at a time, began to recede to make room for tilled fields and pastureland. Villages sprung up, like those discovered and reconstructed at Lough Gur, County Limerick. Larger, more permanent homes, planked with split oak, appeared roughly at this time.

Far more startling, however, is the appearance of massive megalithic monuments—court cairns, dolmens, passage tombs, and wedge tombs—only a small percentage of which have been excavated. All the same, over 1,000 megalithic monuments have been unearthed in Ireland, mumbling symphonically about beliefs, cults, and aspirations as profound as any we might imagine. A visit to Newgrange and Knowth in the Boyne Valley and to Carrowmore in County Sligo (once possibly the largest megalithic cemetery in western Europe until the grave-robbers arrived in the last century) will both dazzle and deepen anyone's understanding of the human past. They certainly did this for the later Celtic inhabitants of the island, who wondered and told stories about the tremendous stones and mounds raised by what they assumed must have been giants. The Celts called their predecessors the people of the *sí*, who eventually

- 1534–52 Henry VIII begins suppression of Catholic Church in Ireland.
- 1541 Henry VIII proclaims himself king of Ireland.
- 1558–1603 Reign of Elizabeth I. Elizabeth conducts several Irish wars, initiates the "plantation" of Munster, divides Ireland in counties, and in 1591 founds Trinity College, Dublin.
- 1601 Mountjoy defeats combined Spanish and Irish forces at Kinsale.
- 1603 The Articles of Confederation introduced and the "plantation" of Ulster begins.
- 1607 The flight of the Irish earls marks the demise of the old Gaelic order.
- 1641 Irish Catholic revolt in Ulster led by Sir Phelim O'Neill ends in defeat.
- 1649 Oliver Cromwell invades and begins the reconquest of Ireland.
- 1690 The forces of James II, a Catholic, are defeated at the Battle of the Boyne, assuring British control of Ireland.
- 1691 Patrick Sarsfield surrenders Limerick. He and some 14,000 Irish troops, the "Wild Geese," flee to the Continent.
- 1704 Enactment of first Penal Laws. Apartheid comes to Ireland.
- 1778 The Penal Laws are progressively repealed.
- 1782 The Irish Parliament is granted independence.
- 1791 Wolfe Tone founds the Society of the United Irishmen.
- 1796–97 Wolfe Tone launches an invasion from France, fails, is taken captive, and commits suicide.
- 1798 "The Year of the French." A French invasion force is defeated at Killala Bay. General Humbert surrenders to Cornwallis.
- 1800 The Irish Parliament is induced to dissolve itself.
- 1803 In Dublin, Robert Emmet leads a rising of less than 100 men and is hung.
- 1829 Daniel O'Connell secures passage of Catholic Emancipation Act.
- 1841 Daniel O'Connell is named lord mayor of Dublin.

continues

became the *Tuatha Dí Danann,* and then the faeries, the once great and now little people, living a quite magical life mostly underground in the thousands of *raths,* or earthenwork structures, coursing through the island like giant moleworks.

In the ensuing millennia of the prehistoric period, these first farmers were followed by others, skilled in prospecting and metallurgy. Bronze implements and ornaments, and some jewelry wrought in gold, were now added to the pots and woven fabrics already being produced on the island. A still later wave of farmers and craftsmen moved their settlements from the edges of lakes to the center, where they constructed artificial islands surrounded by palisades. An example of these curious creations, called *crannógs,* has been reconstructed at the Craggaunowen Project, County Clare. A visit there—as well as to Lough Gur in County Limerick and to the Irish National Heritage Park at Ferrycarrig, County Wexford—would reward anyone interested in learning more about life in prehistoric Ireland. While the bronze-age Irish, like the stone-age Irish who preceded them, left no written records behind, they did bequeath to their dead and so to us works of exquisite beauty, examples of which may be seen in the National Museum in Dublin.

THE CELTS Irish history, before the modern period, may be sketched in terms of four invasions: those of the Celts, the Vikings, the Normans, and the English. Each left their indelible imprint on the landscape and the psyche of the island.

But of all of Ireland's uninvited guests, the Celts, cousins of the *Celtae* who sacked Rome and the *Keltoi* who did the same to Delphi, made the greatest impact. They came in waves, the first as early as perhaps the 6th century B.C. and continuing until the end of the millennium. In time, they

- 1845–48 The Great Famine. Two million Irish either die or emigrate.
- 1848 The revolt of the Young Irelanders ends in failure.
- 1858 The Irish Republican Brotherhood, a secret society known as the Fenians, is founded in New York.
- 1867 A Fenian uprising is easily crushed.
- 1879 Michael Davitt founds the National Land League to support the claims of tenant farmers.
- 1879–82 The "land war" forces the enactment of reform. The tenant system unravels and land returns to those who work it.
- 1884 Gaelic Athletic Association is formed to preserve native sports.
- 1886 and 1894 Bills for Home Rule are defeated in Parliament.
- 1893 The Gaelic League is founded to revive the Irish language.
- 1904 Establishment of the Abbey Theatre.
- 1905–08 Founding of Sinn Féin ("we ourselves"), with close links to the Irish Republican Brotherhood.
- 1912 Third Home Rule bill passes in the House of Commons and is defeated by the House of Lords.
- 1913 Founding of the Irish Citizen's Army.
- 1916 Patrick Pearse and James Connolly lead an armed uprising on Easter Monday to proclaim the Irish Republic. Defeat is followed by the execution of 15 leaders of the revolt.
- 1918 Sinn Féin wins a landslide election victory against the Irish Parliamentary Party.
- 1919 Sinn Féin, led by Eamon de Valera, constitutes itself as the first Irish Dáil and declares independence.
- 1919–21 The Irish War of Independence. Michael Collins commands the Irish forces.
- 1921 Anglo-Irish Treaty. Ireland is partitioned. Twenty-six counties form the Free State. William Cosgrave becomes the first president. His party, Cumann na nGaedheal, later becomes Fine Gael.
- 1922 The Free State adopts its first constitution.

continues

controlled the island and absorbed into their culture everyone they found there. They brought iron weapons, war chariots, codes of combat and honor, cults and contests, poetic and artistic genius, music and mania, all of which took root and flourished in Irish soil as if they were native plants. The Celts, however, were dismally disorganized in comparison with the kingdoms and empires of Europe. They divided the island among themselves into as many as 150 tribes, or *tuatha*, grouped under alliances with allegiance to one of five provincial kings. The provinces of Munster, Leinster, Ulster, and Connacht date from this period. The tribes fought among themselves, fiercely, over cattle (their currency and standard of wealth), land, and women. None of their chiefs ever achieved lasting high kingship of the island, though not for lack of trying. One of the most impressive monuments from the time of the warring Celtic chiefs is the stone fortress of Dun Aengus on the Aran Islands.

THE COMING OF CHRISTIANITY The Celtic powers neither warmly welcomed nor violently resisted the Christians who, beginning in the 5th century A.D., came ashore and walked the island with a new message. Although threatened to the core, the Celtic kings and bards settled for a bloodless rivalry and made no Christian martyrs.

Not the first but eventually the most famous of these Christian newcomers was Patrick, a young Roman citizen torn from his British homeland in a Celtic raid and brought to Ireland as a slave. In time, he escaped slavery but not Ireland, to which he felt himself called. Ordained a priest and consecrated a bishop, Patrick made his own raid on Ireland and took its people by storm. He abhorred slavery, which he had known firsthand, and he managed to preach it off the island.

■ **1922–23** The Irish civil war, between the government of the Free State and those who opposed the treaty. Michael Collins is assassinated.

■ **1932** Eamon de Valera leads Fianna Fáil to victory and becomes head of government.

■ **1932–38** Economic war with Britain brings great hardship.

■ **1937** Ireland's 26 counties adopt a new constitution, abandoning membership in British Commonwealth.

■ **1938** Douglas Hyde inaugurated as Ireland's first president.

■ **1939** Dublin is bombed by Germany at start of World War II, but Ireland remains neutral.

■ **1948** The Republic of Ireland Act. Ireland severs its last constitutional links with Britain.

■ **1955** Ireland is admitted into the United Nations.

■ **1959** Eamon de Valera becomes president of Ireland

■ **1963** U.S. President John F. Kennedy visits Dublin.

■ **1969** Violence breaks out in Northern Ireland. British troops are called in.

■ **1972** In Derry, a peaceful rally turns into "Bloody Sunday." The Northern Irish Parliament is dissolved and the North is ruled directly from Britain.

■ **1973** Ireland joins the European Community.

■ **1986** Ireland signs the Anglo-Irish Agreement.

■ **1990** Ireland elects Mary Robinson to be its first woman president.

■ **1992** Ireland approves the European Union.

■ **1993** The Joint Declaration on Northern Ireland establishes the principles and framework for a peaceful, democratic resolution of issues regarding the political status of the North.

■ **1994** The IRA announces a cease-fire, and the Protestant paramilitaries follow suit. Peace talks begin.

■ **1995** Ireland approves the European Union. The British and Irish governments issue "A New Framework for Agreement," and U.S. President Clinton makes a historic visit to Ireland, speaking to large crowds in the Republic, as well as Belfast and Derry.

continues

Within 30 years, the Christian church, like a young forest, was well rooted in Ireland and spreading in every direction. By the time of Patrick's death, around A.D. 461, the Roman Empire was in near collapse while Ireland was on the brink of its golden age.

The full truth of Ireland's conversion to Christianity, however, was that it was mutual. The church of Patrick was, like the man who brought it, Roman, something Ireland never was and never would be. Roman Catholicism didn't take in Ireland. Instead, it went native and became uniquely Celtic. Patrick's eminent successors—Columcille, Bridgit, and Columbanus—were Irish in a way that Patrick could never be and so was their church. Although orthodox on most points of doctrine, the Irish church was Celtic in structure, tribal and unruly by Roman standards. To Ireland, an island without towns or cities, the Roman system of dioceses and archdioceses was beside the point. Instead, the Irish built monasteries with extended monastic families, each more or less autonomous and regional.

- 1996 The IRA resumes its campaign of violence as the peace collapses.
- 1997 The IRA declares a new cease-fire, and, on October 7, Sinn Féin enters inclusive all-party peace talks designed to bring about a comprehensive settlement in the North.
- 1998 All-party peace talks conclude with the Good Friday Agreement, affirmed by all participating parties and strongly supported in referendums held on the same day in the Republic and in the North. The North elects its new assembly. Violence continues to erupt across the region.
- 1999 The implementation of the Good Friday Agreement is blocked by the Unionist demand—"in the spirit" but contrary to the letter of the Good Friday Agreement—that IRA arms decommissioning precede the appointment of a new Northern Ireland executive. The peace process stalls and threatens to unravel.

IRELAND OF THE SAINTED MISSIONARIES Ireland flourished for several centuries as a land of saints and scholars. Its monasteries were centers of learning and culture—some of the few left in post-Roman Europe—where literacy itself was effectively kept alive through the voluminous and imaginative work of scholars and scribes. Moreover, some of these monasteries—Bridgit's own, for instance—were models of sexual equality, populated by both men and women and sometimes presided over by a woman, a high abbess, who was likely to have a handful of bishops under her jurisdiction.

Not only were monks and scholars drawn to Ireland in great numbers, but they were sent out in great numbers as well, to Britain and the Continent, bearing with them all the otherwise forgotten knowledge of Europe. As historian Thomas Cahill wrote in his *How the Irish Saved Civilization,* "Wherever they went the Irish brought with them their books, many unseen in Europe for centuries and tied to their waists as signs of triumph, just as Irish heroes had once tied to their waists their enemies' heads." The influence of these monks cannot be underestimated. They went everywhere and they worked with a fervor, so much so that more than half the biblical commentaries written between 650 and 850 were penned by Irishmen.

The prime legacy of these monks lies in knowledge perpetuated, but like their megalithic ancestors, they too left some enduring monuments to their profound spirituality. With any imagination, visits to the early monastic sites of Glendalough in County Wicklow, Clonmacnois in County Offaly, and Skellig Michael off the Kerry coast, together with a stop at Trinity College Dublin to see the Book of Kells, will help bring to life Ireland's lost age of splendor.

THE VIKING INVASIONS The reign of the monastic city-states of early medieval Ireland died no natural death. After several centuries of dazzling peace, the sea brought new invaders, this time the Vikings, seagoing warriors from Scandinavia who, in assaulting Ireland's monasteries, went straight for the jugular of Irish civilization. Regardless of their Celtic blood, the monks were not warriors, and the round towers to which they retreated were neither high enough nor strong enough to protect them and their treasures from the Scandinavian pirates, who knew a soft touch when they saw one and just kept coming, from around the year 800 into the 900s. The Vikings knew how to pillage and they knew how to plunder, but, thankfully, they didn't know how to read, and so didn't much bother with the books they came across, allowing the monks some means besides their memories of preserving their knowledge and of passing their history down to us.

The Vikings did more than hit and run. They settled as well, securing every major harbor on Ireland's east coast with a fortified town. These were the first towns in Ireland: Dublin, Cork, Waterford, and the river city of Limerick. Eventually, the Irish, disinclined to unite, did so anyway. This led to decisive defeats of the Vikings by the armies of Brian Boru in 999 and 1014. When the Vikings left, however, they left their towns behind, forever altering the Irish way of life. The legacy of the Vikings in Ireland is complex, and a visit to Dublin's Wood Quay and the city walls of Waterford may put those interested on the scent.

With the Vikings gone, Ireland enjoyed something of a renaissance in the 11th and 12th centuries. Meanwhile, its towns grew, its regional kings made their bids for high kingship, and its church came under concerted pressure to conform with the Vatican. But prosperity only made Ireland riper for its next invasion. It was an Irish king who opened the door to the predator. Diarmait Mac Murchada, king of Leinster, whose ambition was to be ruler of all of Ireland, decided he needed outside help and called on a Welsh Norman, Richard de Clare, better known as Strongbow. Strongbow and his army, in turn, acted on behalf of Henry II of England, who had taken the pious and political precaution of securing a papal blessing for the invasion of Catholic Ireland. The accommodating Pope was Adrian IV, who must have envisioned not only a more papal Ireland but also a more British one—after all, he was the first and only Briton ever to ascend to the papacy.

THE NORMAN INVASION In successive expeditions from 1167 to 1169, the Normans crossed the Irish sea with crushing force. When you see the massive Norman fortifications at Trim, you'll realize the clout the Normans brought with them. Two years later, in 1171, Henry II of England made a royal visit to what was now one of his domains. Across the next century, the Norman invaders settled in, consolidated their power, developed Irish towns and cities, and grew terribly fond of the island, becoming as Irish as the Irish themselves.

In 1314, Scotland's Robert the Bruce defeated the English at Bannockburn and set out to fulfill his dream of a united Celtic kingdom. He installed his brother Edward on the Irish throne, but the constant state of war took a heavy toll and within 2 years famine and economic disorder had eroded any public support Edward might have enjoyed. By the time he was defeated and killed at Dundalk in 1317, few were prepared to mourn him. Over the next 2 centuries, attempts to rid Ireland of its Norman overlords were laudable but fell short. Independent Gaelic lords in the north and west continued to maintain their territories, and by the close of the 15th century, English control of the island was effectively limited to the Pale, a walled and fortified cordon around what might have been called "greater Dublin." The Normans themselves became more and more Irish and less and less English in their loyalties.

ENGLISH POWER & THE FLIGHT OF THE EARLS   In the 16th century, under the Tudors, the brutal reconquest of Ireland was set in motion. In mid-century, Henry VIII proclaimed himself king of Ireland, something his predecessors had never done, but it wasn't until late in the century that the claim was backed up by force, now under the banner of Elizabeth I, Henry's daughter, who declared that all Gaelic lords in Ireland must surrender their lands to her, with the altruistic pronouncement that she would immediately regrant them, a proposition that was met with no great joy, to say the least. The Irish, under Ulster's Hugh O'Neill and Red Hugh O'Donnell, struck out, defeating the earl of Essex, whom Elizabeth had personally sent to subdue them. In 1600, a massive force commanded by Lord Mountjoy landed and set about subduing the country, and by 1603 O'Neill was left with few allies and no option but surrender, which he did on March 23, the day before Elizabeth died. Had he waited, who knows how history would have differed. As it was, O'Neill had his lands returned, but constant harassment by the English prompted him, along with many of Ireland's other Gaelic lords, to sail for the continent on September 14, 1607, abandoning their lands and their aspirations.

THE COMING OF CROMWELL   By the 1640s, Ireland was effectively an English plantation. Family estates had been seized and foreign (Scottish) labor brought in to work them. The persecution of Catholics, begun with Henry VIII's split from Rome, barred them from practicing their faith. Resentment led in 1641 to uprisings in Ulster and Leinster, and by early 1642 most of Ireland was again controlled by the Irish, but any hope of extending their victories was destroyed by internal disunion and by the eventual decision to support the Royalist side in the English civil war. In 1648, English king Charles I was beheaded, and the following year the Royalist forces in Ireland were defeated at Rathmines. The stage was set for disaster.

In 1649, Oliver Cromwell arrived in Dublin as commander in chief and lord lieutenant of Ireland, and set about destroying all opposition. One of the most brutal and effective butchers any empire has ever enlisted, Cromwell simply devastated Ireland, which still bears the scars of his savagery today. His campaign lasted only 7 months, but his brutal and bloodthirsty methods broke the back of all resistance. In his siege of the town of Drogheda alone, 3,552 Irish were killed while Cromwell lost only 64 men. After subduing all but Galway and Waterford, Cromwell left Ireland and its administration in the care of his lieutenants and returned to England, but his stamp would linger for centuries, and the memory of it still burns.

After the massacres, anyone suspected of resisting the English forces could leave the country, give up his lands and resettle in Connacht or County Clare, or die. With this expropriation, the English gained control over most of the country's arable land and cemented English power.

After the restoration of the British monarchy in 1660, and especially after the succession to the throne of the Catholic King James II in 1685, Irish Catholics began to sense hope in the air. By 1688, Protestant power in the country was seriously diminished, but the seizure of the English throne by William of Orange in November of that year reversed the trend. James fled to France to regroup, then sailed to Ireland to launch his counterattack. He struck first at

Derry, to which he laid siege for 15 weeks before being defeated by William's forces at the Battle of the Boyne, a battle that effectively ended James's cause and the last Irish hope of freedom. Soon after, the Treaty of Limerick sealed the defeat, and many Irish patriots sailed for America.

THE PENAL LAWS   After the defeat of James, the boot of English power sat heavier than ever on Ireland's neck. Protestant lords were granted total political power and control of the land, and laws were enacted to effectively impoverish the Catholic population. Catholics could not purchase land; Catholic landhold-ings were split up unless the family that held them converted; Catholic schools and priests were banned; Catholics were barred from professions or commissions in the army and were forced to pay a tax to the Anglican church. The laws had an unintended consequence, though: As happens whenever unjust laws are inflicted on a people, they institutionalized civil disobedience and inspired cre-ative sedition.

Meanwhile, the new British lords and landlords of Ireland settled in, sank their own roots, planted crops, made laws, and sowed their own seed. Inevitably, over time, the "Angles" became the Anglo-Irish. Hyphenated or not, they were Irish, and their loyalties were increasingly unpredictable. Colonialism only works effectively for one generation, after all—the very next generation is native to the new country, not the old. As this process played out in Ireland, history settled into one of its periodic states of inactivity, and little of note transpired—prosperity remained on the Protestant side of the fence, and deprivation on the Catholic side. The penal laws continued to be in effect for a century, with the first of them being relaxed in 1770 and the bulk of them being repealed with England's 1783 acknowledgment of the Irish Parliament's right, along with the king, to determine the laws by which Ireland should be governed.

WOLFE TONE, THE UNITED IRISHMEN & THE 1798 REBELLION
England's difficulty is Ireland's opportunity, or so the saying goes, so when war broke out between the British and French in the 1790s, the United Irishmen—a nonviolent society formed to lobby for admission of Catholic and landless Irishmen to the Irish Parliament—went underground to try to persuade the French to intervene on Ireland's behalf against the British. Their emissary in this venture was a Dublin lawyer named Wolfe Tone. In 1796, Tone sailed with French invasion forces bound for Ireland, but was turned back by storms.

Come 1798, Ireland was embroiled in insurrection. Wexford and Ulster teetered, with the United Irishmen proving to have united not enough of their countrymen to mount a credible, sustainable campaign. The nadir of the rebel-lion came when Wolfe Tone, having raised another French invasion force, sailed into Lough Swilley in Donegal and was promptly captured by the British. At his trial, wearing a French uniform, Tone requested that he be shot. When the request was refused, he slit his own throat. The rebellion was over. In the space of 3 weeks more than 30,000 Irish had been killed. In the aftermath of "The Year of the French," as it came to be known, the British induced the Irish Par-liament to dissolve itself, and Ireland reverted to strict British rule.

DANIEL O'CONNELL   In 1828, a Catholic lawyer named Daniel O'Con-nell, who had earlier formed the Catholic Association to represent the interests of tenant farmers, was elected to the British Parliament to represent Ireland. Public opinion was so solidly behind him that he was able to persuade the duke of Wellington, Britain's prime minister at the time, that the only way to avoid an Irish civil war was to force the Catholic Emancipation Act through Parliament. Once this was secured, O'Connell accepted the position as Ireland's MP (member of Parliament). For 12 years he served in this post, winning concessions and fighting against unpopular leftovers of the Penal Laws. In 1841, he left Parliament and was elected lord mayor of Dublin, and from here began his push for repeal of the Irish/British union imposed after the 1798 rebellion. Toward this end, he organized enormous meetings that often reached the hundreds of thousands, but succeeded in provoking an unresponsive conservative government to such an extent that it eventually arrested O'Connell on charges of seditious conspiracy. The charges were dropped, but the incident—coupled with dissension among the Irish, criticism by a group known as the Young Irelanders, and distress from the incipient famine—led to the breaking of his power base. "The Liberator," as he had been known, faded, his health failed, and he eventually died on a trip to Rome. The Young Irelanders, led by "Meagher of the Sword," went on to stage a pathetic revolt in 1848, which was easily put down by the English authorities.

THE GREAT FAMINE   As the efforts of Ireland's hoped-for liberators failed, the Irish were faced with something they could barely imagine: a worse state of affairs.

In the years from 1845 to 1850, a blight struck Ireland's potato crop. The majority of land actually owned by the Irish was harsh and difficult, unsuitable for most farming, and for this reason the Irish had come to depend on the potato, one of the hardiest of crops, as the staple of their diet. When the blight struck, they were left with nothing to keep body and soul together.

Whether the famine was an act of God, the British, or bad farming practices on the part of the Irish peasantry remains unresolved, but the fact stands that it claimed 1½ million Irish lives and dispatched another million to the sea, most pointed toward the United States. Those who remained faced only continued hardship, and in the years ahead, emigration reached flood level. Within a century, the population of Ireland was less than half of what it had been in 1841.

THE STRUGGLE FOR HOME RULE   Fewer Irish did not mean more manageable Irish, however. On multiple fronts, violent and nonviolent, the Irish people kept up the pressure on Britain, and some partial concessions were won, but few were satisfied. The return of selected stolen goods appears generous only to thieves. What the Irish wanted back was Ireland, intact—land, religion, language, and law. In the 1870s and 1880s, Ireland's member of Parliament, Charles Stewart Parnell, was able to unite various factions of Irish nationalists, including the Fenian Brotherhood in America and the Land League, to fight for home rule. In a tumultuous decade of legislation, he came close, but revelations about his long affair with Kitty O'Shea, wife of a former follower, brought about his downfall, and brought an end to the legislative quest for home rule.

THE EASTER REBELLION & THE WAR OF INDEPENDENCE   Coming close may count for something in horseshoes or high tuba notes, but not in revolution, and near-misses on the negotiated front opened the way to violence. The 1912 defeat of the third Home Rule Bill in the House of Lords, after it had passed in the House of Commons, was followed in 1913 by the founding of the Irish Citizens Army and the Irish Volunteers. Revolution was imminent. The motive had been there for centuries, the ability was in development, and the opportunity was around the corner. In 1916, the Irish would celebrate Easter, the feast of the Resurrection, in unique fashion.

The Great Hunger

One of the most influential events in Irish history was the Great Famine, a tragedy whose impact on the people and the landscape of Ireland is still visible 150 years later.

The potato was introduced to Ireland around 1590. A good source of nutrition, and capable of being raised in abundance on the poorest of land, the potato soon became the principal food of rural farm laborers. There were several failures of the potato crop in the 18th century, and some had expressed concern at the dangers of a whole populace relying so completely on a single crop for their sustenance. Still, it seems that no one was prepared for the severity of the blight that destroyed the potato crop throughout Ireland every year between 1845 and 1850. The figures on the resulting famine are numbing: During these 6 years, Ireland lost 2½ million people, one quarter of its population. Of these, it's estimated that 1½ million died and 1 million emigrated.

Although Ireland has undergone radical transformations in the past 150 years, the story of the Famine is still there to be read in the landscape. In the early 19th century, Ireland had Europe's highest population density, with up to 700 people per square mile in the rural farming areas; today, that figure is down to 140 per square mile. Traces of this pre-Famine population can be seen in the many ruined cottages you'll find in even the most remote and mountainous areas. Another sign of these subsistence farms is "lazy beds,"—fields used to plant potatoes—that can be seen creeping up the sides of hills and mountains throughout the country.

During the Famine, some of the more benevolent landlords created relief projects for their tenants—constructing garden buildings, enlarging estate walls, or building follies, fantastic structures that still inhabit the Irish countryside. The British government provided sporadic funding for public works projects, mostly roads and bridges. More relief came in the form of workhouses, a particularly brutal institution that was used only as a last resort, often as a place to die. Upon entry, families were separated, individuals gave up all property rights, and all were subjected to hard labor in return for two meals a day. More than 100 of these workhouses were built, many on a standard plan, and you can recognize them by their bilateral symmetry—like Irish school buildings, they were designed for the separation of the sexes.

The most poignant and ubiquitous monuments to the Famine are the mass graves that can be found in most towns of the west. Often in the form of an undeveloped field, perhaps dotted with small hillocks, the Famine graveyards are like many of the most powerful testaments to the tragedies of Irish history: inconspicuous and unheralded, yet copiously eloquent in their silence for all who take the trouble to seek them out.

On Easter Monday, the Irish tricolor flag was raised over the General Post Office in the heart of Dublin. Inside were 1,500 fighters, led by the Gaelic League's Patrick Pearse and Socialist leader James Connolly. From here, Pearse read the newly written Proclamation of the Irish Republic, and his men fought off the British for 6 days before being captured. Pearse, Connolly, and 12 other leaders were imprisoned, secretly tried, and speedily executed.

In looking back over Irish history for those turning points that cumulatively led to the violence of 1916, the War of Independence, and the Irish Civil War, William Butler Yeats wrote of four bells that tolled for Ireland, one at each of its irreversibly decisive moments: the Flight of the Earls, the Battle of the Boyne, the spread of French revolutionary ideas under the United Irishmen, and the fall of Parnell. However it is that we trace the path to violence, the 1916 rising, compounded by the savage stupidity of the British response, all but guaranteed that Ireland's future would be decided by the gun. Like the religious faith they had strained for centuries to preserve, the Irish faith in revolution was seeded and nourished by the blood of martyrs—martyrs the British had been fools enough to provide.

The last straw for the British was the landslide victory of Sinn Féin in the general election of 1918 and that party's subsequent proclamation of the first Dáil, or independent Parliament. The declaration of independence issued 2 years earlier from the General Post Office now seemed a good deal more real. When the British attempted to smash the new Parliament, the result was the War of Independence, in which the Irish forces, led by Michael Collins, eventually forced the British to the negotiating table.

The Anglo-Irish Treaty of 1921 gave independence to only 26 of 32 Irish counties. The fate of the remaining six counties in Ulster was yet to be decided; in the meantime, they would remain within the United Kingdom. Some of the Irish, weary of war, accepted compromise as close enough to victory and embraced the Irish Free State. Others, led by Eamon de Valera, shouted betrayal and declared the Free State their latest enemy. The ensuing civil war claimed many casualties, including Michael Collins and Cathal Brugha, two of the revolution's shining heroes.

Victory, if civil wars can be said to have winners, went to de Valera and those who opposed the treaty. They did not overturn it, though, and their successors have yet to. Instead, they reformed the government and led the new Free State of Ireland out of the ravages of war and into the rigors of peace. In passing the Republic of Ireland Act in 1948, the Free State severed its last constitutional ties to Britain. Only 25 years later, the Republic of Ireland joined the European Community, pursuing its ties to Europe, where the Irish people had for centuries looked for friendship and support.

Impressions

There are no overall certitudes in Ireland any more. There's a lot of diversity of thinking, a lot of uncertainty, a lot of trying to assimilate to other cultures. It's a time when we need to take stock, to look into our hearts and find a sense of Irishness, to find a pride in ourselves that will make us sure of what we are.

—Mary Robinson (b. 1944)

The story still has no proper ending. The "troubles" spawned by the partitioning of Ireland in 1921 live on, a wound so far refusing to be healed. There remain two Irelands—fewer than there have been in the past and yet, for some, still one too many.

4 Some Movers & Shapers of Ireland's 20th Century

Samuel Beckett (1906–89)   Playwright and novelist; one of four Irish winners of the Nobel Prize for Literature (1969). His most-performed drama, *Waiting for Godot* (1952), remains one of the definitive plays of the 20th century.

Brendan Behan (1923–64)   Playwright, travel writer, journalist, IRA activist, and raconteur. His works include *Borstal Boy* (1958), *The Quare Fellow* (1954), and *The Hostage* (1958).

Michael Collins (1890–1922)   Member of the supreme council of the Irish Republican Brotherhood and commander-in-chief of the IRA during the war for independence. Brought the British to the negotiating table and accepted the division of Ireland. Was assassinated on August 22, 1922, 5 days before he would have turned 31. In 1996, his story, with Liam Neeson in the title role, was put on film by director Neil Jordan.

James Connolly (1868–1913)   Founded the Irish Socialist Republican Party. Emigrated to America, where he was active in the launching of the IWW (Industrial Workers of the World). Back in Ireland, Connolly was appointed commandant-general of the Dublin forces in the 1916 uprising and led the assault on the General Post Office. Wounded and unable to stand for his own execution, he was strapped to a chair when brought before the Kilmainham firing squad.

Eamon de Valera (1882–1975)   Born in New York and raised in Ireland, de Valera commanded the Boland's Mills garrison in the 1916 Easter Rising. After fiercely opposing the Anglo-Irish Treaty and serving with the IRA in the Irish civil war, de Valera formed Fianna Fáil and went on to become the first president of the Irish Parliament and the first prime minister. From 1959 to 1973, he served as president of the Republic.

Oliver St. John Gogarty (1878–1957)   Poet, wit, surgeon, senator, and athlete, Gogarty served as a model for the Buck Mulligan character in his friend James Joyce's *Ulysses.*

James Joyce (1882–1941)   Born in Dublin, Joyce left the city at age 22 and spent most of his life abroad. Even so, he used Dublin as the setting for all of his writings, including his masterwork, *Ulysses* (1922). Joyce's other works include *Portrait of the Artist as a Young Man* (1916), *Dubliners* (1914), and *Finnegans Wake* (1938).

James "Big Jim" Larkin (1876–1947)   Founded the Irish Transport and General Workers' Union and the Irish Workers' League; became a Dublin city counselor, and served in the Dáil from 1937 to 1938 and again from 1943 to 1944.

Sean O'Casey (1880–1964)   Born into poverty as John Casey in Dublin, this Abbey Theatre playwright based three of his greatest works on his early life in Dublin tenements—*The Shadow of a Gunman* (1923), *Juno and the Paycock* (1924), and *The Plough and the Stars* (1926).

Patrick Pearse (1879–1916)   Educator, poet, and commander-in-chief of the Irish Republican Brotherhood and the Irish Volunteers. He led the 1916 Easter Rising, proclaimed the birth of the Irish Republic, and accepted unconditional surrender 5 days later. He was executed by firing squad in Kilmainham Jail.

George Bernard Shaw (1856–1950)   Author of *Man and Superman* (1903), *Major Barbara* (1905), *Pygmalion* (1912), *Candida* (1903), and *St. Joan* (1923), Shaw won the Nobel Prize for Literature in 1926. His birthplace, at 33 Synge St., is a museum in his honor.

John Millington Synge (1871–1909)   Playwright best remembered for works that reflect rural life in western Ireland, including *The Shadow of the Glen* (1903), *Riders to the Sea* (1904), and *Playboy of the Western World* (1907).

Jack Butler Yeats (1871–1957)   Painter and brother of William Butler Yeats. Studied art in London and illustrated books before establishing a reputation as a painter in oils.

William Butler Yeats (1865–1939)   Poet, dramatist, founding member of the Abbey Theatre. His poems and plays, which deal with mystic and Celtic legendary themes, won him a Nobel Prize for Literature in 1923. Yeats served in the Irish Senate but rejected a knighthood in 1915. He is buried in Sligo.

5 The Irish Language

The lilting, complex, and rhythmical Irish language is rich in words and phrases that defy translation. From personal experience, I can tell you that this is one of the hardest languages on the face of the earth to get your tongue around, and one of the most rewarding when you master even a few words.

One of Western Europe's four original languages, Irish falls into the Gaelic branch of the Celtic tongue (it's called "Irish" to distinguish it from other forms of Gaelic). It's related to Welsh, Breton, and ancient Gaulish, and is very similar to the Gaelic of Scotland. Irish is the oldest written vernacular in Europe. Until the middle of the 19th century, it was the common spoken language in Ireland. Its decline, however, was rapid. By the beginning of the 20th century, it was largely confined to isolated areas in the south, west, and northwest. Academics such as Douglas Hyde (who eventually became the Republic's first president) and others of like mind founded the Gaelic League and managed to keep the language alive through the dark years before independence. When independence was finally won, Irish became the country's official language; today, all state and semi-state agencies generally require a working knowledge of Irish for employment. It's been taught in all schools since 1922; takes first place on street signs, city and town name signs, and in governmental titles; and has a radio station and TV station on which you'll hear no English at all, thank you.

Today, although the vast majority of Irish use English as their first tongue, there are some 40,000 Irish speakers who use English only occasionally. Most live in isolated, closely knit rural communities in what is called the *Gaeltacht,* the Irish-speaking region that falls mostly in Donegal, Dingle, and Connemara.

6 Myths, Legends & Folklore

Storytelling, still a gift of the Irish, was once a way of life throughout rural Ireland. The great Celtic tribes had bards, poets adept at singing the praises of each chieftain, often reciting from memory tales of his lineage for generations on end.

Malachy Kearns on the Pulse of Irish Music

Listen to any recording of Irish music and you'll hear the unmistakable racing, rolling rhythm of the bodhran, Ireland's traditional drum. With the worldwide success of the Riverdance show and the growing popularity of Irish music, this simple yet remarkable instrument is getting ever greater exposure.

The bodhran—pronounced *bow*-rawn, from an Irish word that means "deaf" or "haunting"—is a one-sided drum that usually measures 18 inches in diameter and 4 inches in depth, and is one of a family of frame-style (as opposed to barrel- or cone-shaped) drums whose branches can be found in cultures all over the world, from Native Americans and peoples in China, Russia, Lapland, the Basque country, Mongolia, and all the Islamic countries to the kid flailing a tambourine in your local rock band. Art from long before the Roman empire depicts musicians playing this type of drum, and its playing style has developed according to the needs of different cultures. In Ireland, it's played with a single short stick (known as a "beater" or "tipper"). One hand presses behind the skin to alter the timbre and pitch, while the tipper hand hits the skin with a circular style that requires great wrist flexibility and gives the playing power and subtlety.

Quite possibly, the Irish bodhran originated as a skin tray used to carry freshly cut turf from the bog to be used as fuel. From here, it evolved into a farm implement used for winnowing (separating chaff from grain) through the simple mechanism of punching holes in the skin. Keep the skin intact, though, and you have an instrument whose sound—a hauntingly dry yet resonant, nimble yet deep and grounding sound—is deeply rooted in the hearts of Irish people and connects at gut level to the life center within us all.

Later, every village had its resident *seanachai,* a storyteller who presided over long evenings around the hearth, telling and retelling tales of larger-than-life heroes, gods, and goddesses. Some of the stories they told have been preserved in written form, and continue to influence the imaginations of the Irish today. Many in this century have drawn on the popularity and continuing cultural relevance of the ancient heroes in naming political parties, public houses, and even household pets.

Some of the oldest legends tell of the coming of the Celts. Other stories speak of the brave deeds of Conaire Mor, king of Ireland in the 2nd century B.C. The hero widely known as Finn MacCool was born as Fionn MacCumhail in a blaze of glorified chivalry and courage as gigantic as the fictitious man himself. His faithful Fianna warrior band (after which the political party Fianna Fail is named) matched their leader in feats of bravery and daring.

There were tales of the Knights of the Red Branch in the north and of the Ulster hero Cuchulainn. Queen Maeve, who ruled Connaught, and the tragic Deirdre of the Sorrows were chief among the heroines who figured in song and

On St. Stephen's Day (December 26), groups of people with blackened faces and outlandish costumes enact the "Wren Hunt," parading a captured wren from house to house while playing music—especially the bodhran—and singing a ceremonial song. The bodhran is also featured in Mummers plays and harvest festivals, and nowadays Irish football supporters take their bodhrans to international matches—the secret weapon of the ancient Gael!

Recordings with beautiful bodhran playing include Christy Moore's "Live at the Point," Johnny "Ringo" McDonagh and Arcady's "Many Happy Returns," Tommy Hayes's "An Ras," and The Chieftains' "Chieftains Live!"

A tip for buying a good bodhran: There are many cheap imported split-calfskin bodhrans of very poor quality floating around out there. A good-quality, tough, 3-year-old goatskin is the most important feature. Goatskin has unique stretch properties and holds its tension well for a lifetime if not abused. Quality goatskin also has a deep, haunting sound that's very freeing to play, creating a "bounceback" effect. It's best if the skin is glued as well as tacked on the frame, especially for bodhrans going to hot climates.

—Malachy Kearns
*Malachy Kearns (also known as "Malachy Bodhran")
is the world's premier bodhran maker, and has crafted
instruments for the Chieftains, Christy Moore, and
the Riverdance ensemble, among others.
He can be seen hard at work every day at
Roundstone Musical Instruments in Connemara.
(See listing in chapter 12.)*

story. Every schoolchild in Ireland can tell you of the poor, tragic Children of Lir, who were turned into swans by a jealous stepmother and forced to wander the lakes and rivers of Ireland "until a noblewoman from the south would marry a nobleman from the north," for which event they had to wait 900 years to end their feathery exile. To this day, swans are a protected species in Ireland.

Then there are the "otherworld" tales. One tells of the mystical Tuatha Dí Danann (people of the goddess Dana) who, in defeat at the hands of the Milesians, struck a bargain to divide Ireland between them: the Milesians were to reside above ground, and the Dí Danann below in *lios* (earthen hill forts), in cairns (stone mounds), or even under hawthorn bushes. As Christianity gained a stronger foothold, the story of the Tuatha Dí Danann began to pale. Gradually they evolved into fairies (the people of the Sidhe), and ultimately degenerated into the leprechauns.

The best way to experience the tradition of storytelling in Ireland is to attend one of the many storytellers' festivals held throughout the country (see "Ireland Calendar of Events" in chapter 2, "Planning an Affordable Trip to Ireland").

7 Irish Music

Music in Ireland is ever present, spontaneous by nature, and hard to pin down. Traditional (or "trad") music has roots deep in Ireland's Celtic prehistory and is most often heard at ad hoc pub sessions. The trouble is that at many pubs you're as likely to hear country-western tunes as you are the traditional fare. In music, as in all things, Ireland is full of surprises. If traditional tunes aren't on tap, though, you're almost sure to find your fill of folk music, which is alive and well and is a continuing source of inspiration to today's rock musicians, not only in Ireland but around the world.

The **traditional music** of Ireland is an improvisational form based on set melodies and rhythms. For much of its history, traditional music was primarily music for dancing, and the names of the different musical forms—the reel, the jig, and the polka—reflect this. These days, traditional dance forms aren't widely known, though, and it's rare to find a spontaneous dance session. Comparatively rare, too, is formal instruction in this music: Many musicians are self-taught, and the best training, as with any traditional form, is said to be listening and watching accomplished players at work. The standard venue for this music is the pub session, where musicians who may never have played together before join in. Because the only reimbursement is usually a few free drinks, trad remains an art practiced primarily by amateurs—hence the atmosphere of friendly informality that typifies most sessions, and the rarity of scheduled gatherings.

You should be aware that not everything that's billed as traditional music is really traditional. The **ballad** style in particular is something that's often put on for tourists. Singalongs of "When Irish Eyes Are Smiling" and other Irish-American hits can be a lot of fun, but don't confuse these songs with the music steeped in the experiences of the Irish living in Ireland.

Aside from the standard pub venues, the national traditional music board, *Comhaltas Ceoltóirí Eireann,* sponsors scheduled traditional music gatherings (called *fleadhs*) in towns throughout the country—check with the tourist board for the latest schedule of events. Irish music is also featured at festivals, hotel cabarets, summer shows, and venues dedicated to traditional entertainment, such as the National Folk Theatre of Ireland in Tralee, An Taibhdhearc in Galway, the Bru Boru Center at Cashel, Culturlann na hÉireann near Dublin, Cois na hAbhna in Ennis, and the Shannon Traditional Evening at the Bunratty Folk Park.

In the **folk music** field, Christy Moore is the most popular musician in Ireland today, and his songs have become part of the basic repertoire. In Ireland's version of the **country-western** tradition, Donegal native Daniel O'Donnell is a fabulously successful singer and has slews of devoted fans among the country's middle-aged and older listeners. In the world of **rock,** U2 seems to be the only arena-rock band left, while many of Ireland's most successful exports have created hybrids of Celtic music and rock: The Pogues are a standout in this realm, and Van Morrison, Chris de Burgh, Clannad, and Enya each have their own take on the meeting of old and new. Dublin has been the springboard for many a great band, so when you're in the city, keep your eyes and ears open for the latest new sensation. Who knows, you could be one of the first to discover a band that the rest of the world won't be raving about for another year or two.

8 Irish Food & Drink: It's Not Just Boiled Potatoes Anymore

IRISH CUISINE TODAY

Old, oft-repeated, and widely disseminated tales of boiled meats, unrecognizable vegetables, and the mysterious and horrible white sauce have led most visitors to arrive in Ireland with low expectations for the food. The Irish aren't entirely to blame for their bad reputation—after all, they were subjugated for centuries by the British, who have their own culinary insecurity complex to deal with. Until recently, the only two things you were assured of at all Irish restaurants were huge portions and, well, huge portions.

These days, though, there's been something of a culinary renaissance in Ireland. It was bound to happen, with more of the population traveling regularly to the Continent and expanding their culinary horizons, but few would have predicted that it would come with such a vengeance. A new standard has been set by a few pioneering minimalist chefs who emphasize letting the best local ingredients speak for themselves, eschewing heavy sauces and elaborate presentation. The primary identifying feature of this new Irish cuisine is imagination—whether it's a traditional Irish dish, a continental standard, or a concoction never before seen, the approach is fresh and inventive.

There's no doubt that the ingredients available to Irish chefs have long been outstanding—it was only a matter of figuring out what to do with them. Irish dairy products are rightfully celebrated worldwide; the vegetables are outstanding; and Irish beef, lamb, and pork are among the best you'll find anywhere. **Seafood,** though, is often the best choice in this island nation. I've never had smoked salmon as good as the best Irish restaurants serve—thin slices that are perfectly smooth and supple, complemented by the pungency of capers, shallots, and perhaps a horseradish cream. Among the milder fish, monkfish is served in many delicious guises, as is hake and plaice. Some regional specialties you shouldn't miss include Dublin Bay prawns, Galway oysters, and Wexford mussels. A host of chippers (fish-and-chip shops) serve inexpensive portions of cod, shark, or even salmon.

The herds of cows and sheep you'll see everywhere in the countryside provide fabulous milk and cream, which is put to ravishing use in the many local **cheeses** you're sure to discover as you travel through the country. They're best if you can get them directly from the source, where you may find varieties that haven't yet hit the big market, or raw milk cheeses made for local consumption only. Good restaurants often take great pride in their cheese boards, which usually highlight the best of the nation and the local region. As you're traveling, keep an eye out for Cashel Blue and Cooleeney Cheese from County Tipperary, Gubbeen and Ardrahan Cheese from County Cork, and Croghan Cheese from County Wexford.

There are a few **traditional Irish dishes** you should try at least once. Bacon and cabbage is a common dish, the ancestor of the more strictly Irish-American corned beef and cabbage. Irish stew, traditionally made with lamb, is standard

---

Tips When's Dinner?

Pubs and restaurants in Ireland are usually open for lunch from noon to 2:30pm or so, and dinner is generally served from 6 or 7pm until 10 or 11pm.

Irish Baking on Your Own

When you return, you'll miss this: A warm mug of tea slipped into your chilly fingers and a plate full of freshly baked bread and scones that chase all traces of dampness away after a long walk on misty hills. Jytte Storm of Ballinatona Farm is an expert at these simple restorative foods, so comforting that you'll want to take them home with you.

Very Easy Wheat Scones
    ½ cup oat flakes
    1½ cups white flour
    3 teaspoons baking powder
    1 tablespoon sugar
    3 tablespoons butter
    1 cup milk

- Rub butter and flour together.
- Add remaining ingredients and mix until sticky.
- Divide into 3 rounds and make circles 4 inches in diameter.
- Mark with cross, bake at 400°F for 15 minutes.

Irish Pan Bread
    2 cups white flour
    2 tablespoons butter
    1 teaspoon soda
    1 teaspoon salt
    1 teaspoon sugar
    1 to 1¼ cups buttermilk

- Rub butter into flour.
- Add soda, salt, sugar, buttermilk.
- Mix until sticky and make into round ball.
- Divide into 4 portions; don't knead too much.
- Heat frying pan and cook 10 to 15 minutes.
- Cut open and eat with butter.

pub grub fare, and is often quite good. *Boxty* is a filled pancake, and *champ* a dish made of mashed potatoes and onions. Several traditional dishes, all an acquired taste, are based on seaweed—but if you see *carrigeen* on the menu, be sure to give it a try.

Soda bread is one of the delights of Irish cooking, at its best a rich, nutty concoction that's delicious with any meal or a great staple for a picnic. Most restaurants and many B&Bs bake their own, but be sure to request it at B&Bs the night before, because many otherwise serve an insipid white bread called "American pan" as the default choice. You'll encounter many varieties of soda bread as you travel through the country, and one of the best souvenirs you can bring home is a recipe for your favorite kind, if the baker is willing to reveal his or her secret.

The **full Irish breakfast** that you'll receive at most B&Bs fails to rise beyond the usual sausage and rasher (bacon) fry, but the quantities are usually more than adequate to keep you going until a late lunch or early dinner.

When you're choosing a restaurant, it's always a good idea to steer clear of places with a big a la carte menu, a sure sign that dishes aren't being prepared fresh each day. It's also best to find a restaurant where the menu changes often, indicating that the chef is taking advantage of the produce that happens to be best at the moment. As a rule, you should avoid Chinese and Indian restaurants in small towns; in the cities, though, especially Dublin, they can be very good indeed.

TALL TALES OF WHISKIES & ALES: IRISH DRINK

Order a pint in an Irish pub without calling out your preference and what you'll get is **Guinness,** a black, yeasty ale with a thick, foamy head that—if your barman's worth his salt and knows how to pull a pint—will last right down to the last drop. Brewed in Dublin since Arthur Guinness first established the drink in 1759, it depends for full effect on being trucked fresh from the original brewery at St. James's Gate straight to the nation's pubs. Even then, the quality of the pint you'll be served depends on the artfulness of its server—it requires a deftness of hand, a sure command of timing, and a little bit of magic to pour the perfect pint. Once you've sipped a few, you'll begin to appreciate the difference. The question of who pulls the best pint in Dublin, Killarney, Cork, and elsewhere is a perpetually debated subject, but one thing's for sure: If your pint arrives just seconds after you order it, you may be very sure that *your* bartender is not in the running. There's a subtle, delicate art to drawing the stout, so be prepared to wait. The Guinness Company also produces a light lager beer called Harp and a nonalcoholic beer known as Kaliber. Other Irish beers include Smithwicks, brewed in Kilkenny, and Beamish and Murphys, produced in Cork.

Many are surprised to learn that monks invented **whiskey** back in the 6th century, intending it for medicinal purposes. The Bushmills plant in County Antrim was granted the first license to distill Irish whiskey back in the year 1609. It's still in operation today. "Black Bush" is the affectionate name for 12-year-old Bushmills. Other favorite brands are Jameson and Paddy. All are wonderful, whether served on the rocks or neat, without ice. On a cold or rainy day, nothing quite beats a hot whiskey (sugar, whiskey, hot water, lemon, and cloves)—unless, that is, it's the ever-popular **Irish coffee.** And because I knew you'd want to know, here are instructions for making it at home:

1. Fill a large, stemmed glass with hot water, then empty when glass is warm.
2. Pour in one full jigger of Irish whiskey and add at least one teaspoon sugar (the more sugar, the more the cream rises to the top).
3. Add hot black coffee (the hotter, the better) to about an inch from the top and stir.
4. Top it off with lightly whipped cream (there's an art to doing that—pour the cream over the back of a spoon and try to just float it off over the sides into the glass).

As for the tea you'll be served in Ireland, well, it's downright habit-forming, and you'll probably want to stock up on your favorite blends before departing for home. A good source is Bewley's, the venerable Dublin cafe with branches throughout the country.

9 Irish Pubs

Before cellular phones, the Internet, and CNN—hell, before majority literacy—the pub was the place to go to catch up with friends, debate the latest (or oldest) scandal, and hear the news of the day. It was a place where opinions got formed, politics got made, and revolutions got hatched. It was a place where drink might loosen your tongue and an unwise comment might give a fellow patron cause to loosen your teeth. It was, all in all, the human condition with a smoke-stained ceiling and sawdust on the floor.

Though Ireland in general might be riding the cutting edge straight into the 21st century, its pubs, like pubs everywhere, God love 'em, retain much of their traditional role. You're still likely to hear spirited debate, hot politics, and friendly bickering, though I can't guarantee you'll catch any sedition or violence. Such is the price we pay for political and economic stability.

What I can almost guarantee you'll hear, at least if you pop your head into enough pubs, is **traditional music.** Some places bring in leading musical groups, while others regularly give performing space to local musicians, and these latter are particularly appealing. Like most ancient forms of traditional music, the Irish version employs instruments that (unamplified, at least) won't split your eardrums at first bray, and the musicians will be as likely to set themselves up around a table as take to a stage—two big pluses if you're looking for a really authentic and intimate musical experience.

Each pub has its own gratifyingly different personality. In cities like Dublin and Belfast, you can have a jar in an ornate Victorian-style drinking establishment; a glitzed-up chrome-and-mirrors abyss; a smooth-worn old-time pub full of mahogany, brass, and etched glass; an elegant hotel bar that's got up so fancy it counts as a pub in name only; or a bare-bones joint that depends on its colorful regulars for personality. Out in the country, a pub might well be one half of a grocery or hardware store; a traditional-style pub that's been dispensing drink and hospitality since the days of coaching inns; a cozy appendage to a guesthouse or small hotel; or a large barnlike room with linoleum on the floor and a TV behind the bar.

There are still pubs around that have little blocked-off private rooms called "snugs" and lovely old etched-glass partitions along the bar to afford a bit of privacy. In some pubs, the dartboard stays busy; in others, there's almost always a card game in progress; some keep the fireplace glowing. Most will have a main bar and an attached "lounge," which once was the only place you'd ever catch a female in what was otherwise exclusively a man's domain. Nowadays, the lounges are filled with couples of all ages, as well as singles.

Index

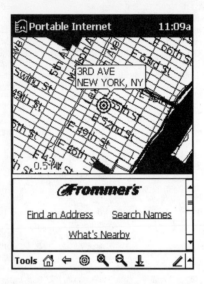

FROMMER'S® MEMORABLE WALKS

Chicago	New York	San Francisco
London	Paris	

FROMMER'S® GREAT OUTDOOR GUIDES

Arizona & New Mexico	Northern California	Vermont & New Hampshire
New England	Southern New England	

SUZY GERSHMAN'S BORN TO SHOP GUIDES

Born to Shop: France	Born to Shop: Italy	Born to Shop: New York
Born to Shop: Hong Kong,	Born to Shop: London	Born to Shop: Paris
Shanghai & Beijing		

FROMMER'S® IRREVERENT GUIDES

Amsterdam	Los Angeles	San Francisco
Boston	Manhattan	Seattle & Portland
Chicago	New Orleans	Vancouver
Las Vegas	Paris	Walt Disney World
London	Rome	Washington, D.C.

FROMMER'S® BEST-LOVED DRIVING TOURS

Britain	Germany	New England
California	Ireland	Scotland
Florida	Italy	Spain
France		

HANGING OUT™ GUIDES

Hanging Out in England	Hanging Out in France	Hanging Out in Italy
Hanging Out in Europe	Hanging Out in Ireland	Hanging Out in Spain

THE UNOFFICIAL GUIDES®

Bed & Breakfasts and Country	Florida with Kids	New Orleans
Inns in:	Golf Vacations in the	New York City
California	Eastern U.S.	Paris
New England	The Great Smoky &	San Francisco
Northwest	Blue Ridge Mountains	Skiing in the West
Rockies	Hawaii	Southeast with Kids
Southeast	Inside Disney	Walt Disney World
Beyond Disney	Las Vegas	Walt Disney World for
Branson, Missouri	London	Grown-ups
California with Kids	Mid-Atlantic with Kids	Walt Disney World for Kids
Chicago	Mini Las Vegas	Washington, D.C.
Cruises	Mini-Mickey	World's Best Diving Vacations
Disneyland	New England & New York	
	with Kids	

SPECIAL-INTEREST TITLES

Frommer's Adventure Guide to Australia & New Zealand	Frommer's Exploring America by RV
	Frommer's Gay & Lesbian Europe
Frommer's Adventure Guide to Central America	Frommer's The Moon
Frommer's Adventure Guide to India & Pakistan	Frommer's New York City with Kids
Frommer's Adventure Guide to South America	Frommer's Road Atlas Britain
Frommer's Adventure Guide to Southeast Asia	Frommer's Road Atlas Europe
Frommer's Adventure Guide to Southern Africa	Frommer's Washington, D.C., with Kids
Frommer's Britain's Best Bed & Breakfasts and Country Inns	Frommer's What the Airlines Never Tell You
	Israel Past & Present
Frommer's France's Best Bed & Breakfasts and Country Inns	The New York Times' Guide to Unforgettable Weekends
Frommer's Italy's Best Bed & Breakfasts and Country Inns	Places Rated Almanac
	Retirement Places Rated
Frommer's Caribbean Hideaways	